ABA·LSAC
OFFICIAL GUIDE TO
ABA-APPROVED LAW SCHOOLS™

Produced by the Law School Admission Council and the American Bar Association

2008 EDITION

Editors

Wendy Margolis, Director of Communications, LSAC

Bonnie Gordon, Editor and Producer, LSAC

David Rosenlieb, Data Specialist, ABA

The Law School Admission Council (LSAC) is a nonprofit corporation whose members are more than 200 law schools in the United States and Canada. It was founded in 1947 to coordinate, facilitate, and enhance the law school admission process. The organization also provides programs and services related to legal education. All law schools approved by the American Bar Association (ABA) are LSAC members. Canadian law schools recognized by a provincial or territorial law society or government agency are also included in the voting membership of the Council.

The services provided by LSAC include the Law School Admission Test (LSAT); the Law School Data Assembly Service (LSDAS), including the LSAC Letter of Recommendation Service, LSDAS Electronic Applications, and the JD Credential Assembly Service (JD CAS); LLM Credential Assembly Service; the Candidate Referral Service (CRS); software, including ADMIT-M admission office software; and various publications and LSAT preparation tools. The LSAT, LSDAS, and CRS are provided to assist law schools in serving and evaluating applicants. LSAC does not engage in assessing an applicant's chances for admission to any law school; all admission decisions are made by individual law schools.

LSAT, *The Official LSAT PrepTest*, ADMIT-M, *The Official LSAT SuperPrep*, and LSAC are registered marks of the Law School Admission Council, Inc. Law School Forums is a service mark of the Law School Admission Council, Inc. *10 Actual, Official LSAT PrepTests; 10 More Actual, Official LSAT PrepTests; The Next 10 Actual, Official LSAT PrepTests; The New Whole Law School Package; ABA-LSAC Official Guide to ABA-Approved Law Schools; ItemWise;* LSDAS; LLM Credential Assembly Service; JD CAS; ACES; ADMIT-LLM; and LSACnet are trademarks of Law School Admission Council, Inc.

© 2007 by Law School Admission Council, Inc.

Library of Congress Catalog Number:

ISBN-13: 978-0-9760245-9-0
ISBN-10: 0-9760245-9-4

ISSN: 1534-3502

Law School Admission Council fees, policies, and procedures relating to, but not limited to, test registration, test administration, test score reporting, misconduct and irregularities, and other matters may change without notice at any time. Up-to-date Law School Admission Council policies and procedures are available at *www.LSAC.org,* or you may contact our candidate service representatives.

Descriptive information about the law schools in this work, including such information and data published in electronic form, is provided by the individual law schools. Neither the ABA nor LSAC assumes any responsibility for inaccuracies or for changes in such information that may occur after publication. Questions regarding the accuracy or currency of any such descriptive information should be addressed to the specific law school.

Table of Contents

Introduction

The *Official Guide to ABA-Approved Law Schools* is a joint effort of the Law School Admission Council (LSAC) and the American Bar Association's Section of Legal Education and Admissions to the Bar (ABA).

The Law School Admission Council is a nonprofit corporation that was founded in 1947 to coordinate, facilitate, and enhance the law school admission process. LSAC provides numerous programs and services related to legal education. All law schools approved by the American Bar Association are LSAC members. Canadian law schools recognized by a provincial or territorial law society or government agency are also included in the voting membership of LSAC.

The American Bar Association is the national organization of the legal profession. The Council of the Section of Legal Education and Admissions to the Bar of the ABA is identified by the US Department of Education as the "nationally recognized accrediting agency for professional schools of law." As of February 2007, a total of 195 institutions are approved by the American Bar Association.

The information contained in this book is collected separately by the ABA and LSAC from the 194 ABA-approved law schools that are also members of the Law School Admission Council. One ABA-approved law school, the US Army Judge Advocate General's School, is a specialized law school that is not a member of the Law School Admission Council (see page 31). The two organizations agreed to combine this wealth of information to provide a comprehensive resource for data and descriptions about ABA-approved law schools.

Although no book or website can substitute for direct contact with admission offices, professors, students, alumni, and prelaw advisors, this guide can inform the process of deciding whether, and where, to attend law school. This guide is designed to provide prospective law school applicants with basic information in a simple format that will facilitate comparisons among schools. In addition to statistics on all ABA-approved law schools, this book contains information intended to help individuals prepare for the rigors and costs associated with attending law school.

The ABA collects quantitative data as part of the accreditation process using questionnaires completed annually during the fall academic semester. Standard 509 of the *Standards: Rules of Procedure for Approval of Law Schools*, as adopted by the ABA House of Delegates in August 1996, states: "A law school shall publish basic consumer information. The information shall be published in a fair and accurate manner reflective of actual practice."

The data collected in the ABA annual questionnaire and published in this guide satisfy a law school's obligation to provide basic consumer information under Standard 509. The data are certified as fair and accurate by the dean of the law school.

The Law School Admission Council collects admission profile data and school descriptions each fall as a service to its member schools and to prospective law school applicants. The information provided by the law schools to LSAC in no way affects the ABA accreditation process and is not meant to satisfy a law school's publication requirements under Standard 509.

Neither LSAC nor ABA condones, approves, or sanctions use of the data contained in this book to rank law schools. Both organizations disapprove of any and all rankings. The deans of 178 law schools have published the following statement regarding rankings:

> The idea that all law schools can be measured by the same yardstick ignores the qualities that make you and law schools unique, and is unworthy of being an important influence on the choice you are about to make. As the deans of schools that range across the spectrum of several rating systems, we strongly urge you to minimize the influence of rankings on your own judgment. In choosing the best school for you, we urge you to get information about all the schools in which you might have some interest. … Law schools may all have met the same standards of quality to become accredited, but they are quite different from each other. The unique characteristics of each law school will inform you why one school may be best for you and another school best for someone else. We want you to make the best choice for you.

The information contained in this edition of the *ABA/LSAC Official Guide to ABA-Approved Law Schools* was collected in fall 2006. Some of the information, including ABA-accreditation status, may change; check the website of the ABA Section of Legal Education and Admissions to the Bar— *www.abanet.org/legaled*—for updates. Neither the ABA nor LSAC conducts an audit to verify the accuracy of the information submitted by the respective institutions.

Chapter 1: Being a Lawyer

■ Lawyers and Their Skills

Law practice is so diverse that it is not possible to describe the so-called typical lawyer. Each lawyer works with different clients and different legal problems. Ordinarily, certain basic legal skills are required of all lawyers. They must know:

- how to analyze legal issues in light of the existing state of the law, the direction in which the law is headed, and relevant policy considerations;

- how to synthesize material in light of the fact that many issues are multifaceted and require the combination of diverse elements into a coherent whole;

- how to advocate the views of groups and individuals within the context of the legal system;

- how to give intelligent counsel on the law's requirements;

- how to write and speak clearly; and

- how to negotiate effectively.

Reading and Listening

Lawyers must be able to take in a great deal of information, often on topics about which they are unfamiliar. The ability to digest information from lengthy, dense texts is essential. Equally important is the ability to listen to clients and understand their unique issues and concerns.

Analyzing

Lawyers must be able to determine the fundamental elements of problems. They spend much time discerning the nature and significance of the many issues in a particular problem. In every issue, the lawyer must study the relationship between each element in order to arrive at an answer, result, or solution.

Synthesizing

Lawyers must learn that because of the complexities of many issues and the number of laws either directly or tangentially relevant, they must be able to pull together in a meaningful, focused, cogent manner often large amounts of material.

Advocating

As an advocate, the lawyer's role is to represent his or her client's particular point of view and interests as vigorously as possible. The American judicial system assumes that equitable solutions will emerge from the clash of opposing interests. The success of this adversarial system of American law depends upon the talents and training of the lawyers who work as advocates within it. Lawyers must be able to use their advocacy skills to marshal evidence and present arguments as to why a particular outcome is desirable.

Counseling

Lawyers also spend a good deal of their time giving clients legal advice. Few ventures in the modern world can be undertaken without some understanding of the law. Through their knowledge of what the law involves, lawyers advise clients about partnerships, decisions, actions, and many other subjects. In many cases, the lawyer's role as a counselor serves as much to prevent litigation as to support it.

Writing and Speaking

Whether in the courtroom or the law office, lawyers must be effective communicators. If lawyers could not translate thoughts and opinions into clear and precise English, it would be difficult for the law to serve society. After all, the law is embodied in words, and many of the disputes that give birth to laws begin with language—its meaning, use, and interpretation. Litigation leads to written judicial opinions; congressional enactments are recorded as printed statutes; and even economic transactions must be expressed as formal, written contracts.

Negotiating

One of the lawyer's primary roles is reconciling divergent interests and opinions. When the parties to a proposed transaction disagree, the lawyer, acting as a facilitator, may be able to help them negotiate to a common ground. Although the client's interests are a lawyer's first priority, often those interests are served best after compromise and conciliation have paved the way to an equitable settlement. Because lawyers are trained to see the implications of alternative courses of action, they are often able to break an impasse.

■ Fields of Law

Lawyers are central figures in the life of a democratic country. They may deal with major courtroom cases or minor traffic disputes, complex corporate mergers or straightforward real estate transactions. Lawyers may work for giant industries, small businesses, government agencies, international organizations, public interest groups, legal aid offices, and universities—or they may work for themselves. They represent both the impoverished and the wealthy, the helpless and the powerful. Lawyers may work solo, in a small group, or in a large law firm.

About 72.9 percent of American lawyers are in private practice, most in small, one-person offices and some in large firms. Roughly 8.2 percent of the profession work for government agencies, 9.5 percent work for private industries and associations as salaried lawyers or as managers, 1.1 percent work for legal aid or as public defenders, and 1 percent are in legal education. (About 4.6 percent are retired or inactive.) Many lawyers develop expertise in a particular field of law. Large law firms that provide a full range of legal services tend to employ more specialists. The solo practitioner, who must handle a variety of problems alone, may have greater opportunity to work in several areas. Of course, there are lawyers in large firms who maintain general practices, and lawyers in one-person offices who concentrate on a particular legal issue. Both specialized and general practice can be rewarding. One offers the satisfaction of mastering a particular legal discipline, and the other the challenge of exploring new fields. Following are brief descriptions of selected areas of specialization, though there are many areas of the law that can rightly fall into more than one category.

Corporate and Securities Law

The corporate lawyer helps clients conduct their business affairs in a manner that is efficient and consistent with the law. The responsibilities of a corporate lawyer can range from preparing the initial articles of incorporation and bylaws for a new enterprise to handling a corporate reorganization under the provisions of federal bankruptcy law. Examples of other areas of corporate law practice include (but are not limited to) contract, intellectual property, legislative compliance, and liability matters.

Securities law is an extremely complex area that almost always requires the services of a specialist. Lawyers who acquire this specialty are involved with the formation, organization, and financing of corporations through securities such as stock, as well as mergers, acquisitions, and corporate takeovers.

Criminal Law

Criminal defense lawyers represent clients accused of crimes. Their public counterparts are the prosecutors and district attorneys who represent the interests of the state in the prosecution of those accused of crimes. Both types of criminal lawyers deal with fundamental issues of the law and personal liberty. They defend many of the basic rights considered crucial to the preservation of a free and just society.

Environmental and Natural Resources Law

Environmental law was born out of widespread public and professional concern about the fate of our natural resources. Lawyers in this field may tackle legal and regulatory issues relating to air and water quality, hazardous waste practice, natural gas transportation, oil and gas exploration and development, electric power licensing, water rights, toxic torts, public land use, marine resources, and energy trade regulation. They may work directly for governmental agencies that address environmental problems or represent corporations, public interest groups, and entities concerned about protecting the environment.

Family and Juvenile Law

Family, or domestic relations, law is concerned with relationships between individuals in the context of the family. Many lawyers who practice this kind of law are members of small law firms or are solo practitioners. They specialize in solving problems that arise among family members and in creating or dissolving personal relationships through such means as adoption or divorce.

Health Law

The practice of health law encompasses many different disciplines. Lawyers in this field can be in the private bar or at government agencies. Health lawyers can represent hospitals, physician groups, health maintenance organizations (HMOs), or individual doctors, among many others. Government health lawyers can investigate fraud, deal with Medicare policy and compliance, or can oversee public health policy. Many health lawyers are engaged in the business of health care, spending significant time in mergers and acquisitions, tax law, employee benefits, and risk management issues. The impact of technology on health care has been great with health lawyers helping to guide their clients through intellectual property, biomedicine, and telemedicine issues. Other health lawyers specialize in bioethics and clinical ethics representing universities and other research academic centers.

Intellectual Property Law

Intellectual property law is concerned with the protection of inventors' rights in their discoveries, authors' rights in their creations, and businesses' rights in their identifying marks. Often, an intellectual property lawyer will specialize in a particular area of the law. For example, for those attorneys with a technical background, patent law is a way to combine one's scientific and legal background into one practice. A copyright attorney counsels authors, composers, and artists on the scope of their rights in their creations, and even personal identities, negotiates contracts, and litigates to enforce these rights. In recent years, copyright law has also focused on technological advances, particularly developments in electronic publishing. Additionally, in today's global economy, intellectual property issues are at the forefront of international trade negotiations.

International Law

International law has grown significantly as a field of practice, reflecting the increasing interdependence of nations and economies. Public international law provides a limited range of job opportunities, particularly with national governments or international institutions or with public interest bodies. Immigration and refugee law also assumes increasing importance as more people move more frequently across national boundaries for business, tourism, or permanent resettlement. Private international law may offer more extensive employment opportunities, either through law firms or for corporations, banks, or telecommunications firms. Fluency in another language or familiarity with another culture can be a decided advantage for law school graduates who seek to practice in the international arena.

Tax Law

In the past 50 years, the importance and complexity of federal, state, and local taxes have necessitated a specialty in this field of law. It is one area of the law where change is constant. The federal Internal Revenue Code and its associated regulations are now several thousand pages in length. New statutes, court decisions, and administrative rulings are issued frequently, and the tax lawyer must be alert to these changes. Economic planning usually includes attention to taxes, and the tax lawyer often assists clients in understanding and minimizing their tax liabilities.

Civil Rights

Many lawyers entered law school wishing ultimately to work in the field of civil rights—the area of law that is concerned with the balance of governmental power and individual liberties. Although the number of full-time jobs in this field is relatively small, many lawyers whose principal practices are in other fields are able to work in this area by taking cases on a pro bono basis. Full-time civil rights attorneys often work for nonprofit, public interest law firms, or as part of a larger firm with a diverse practice.

Chapter 2: Becoming a Lawyer

A legal education is both challenging and rewarding. You will develop your analytical, synthesizing, creative, and logical thinking skills, and you will strengthen your reading and debating abilities. A legal education is necessary to become a lawyer in the United States, but it is also excellent preparation for many other careers, both because of the framework for organizing knowledge it provides and the analytical approach it brings to problems. Many teachers, business people, and writers first obtained a legal education before pursuing careers other than law.

■ Preparing for Law School

Statement on Prelaw Preparation

Prepared by the Pre-Law Committee of the ABA Section of Legal Education and Admissions to the Bar

No Single Path

There is no single path that will prepare you for a legal education. Students who are successful in law school, and who become accomplished professionals, come from many walks of life and educational backgrounds. Some law students enter law school directly from their undergraduate studies without having had any postbaccalaureate work experience. Others begin their legal education significantly later in life, and they bring to their law school education the insights and perspectives gained from those life experiences. Legal education welcomes and values diversity, and you will benefit from the exchange of ideas and different points of view that your colleagues will bring to the classroom.

Undergraduate Education

The ABA does not recommend any undergraduate majors or group of courses to prepare for a legal education. Students are admitted to law school from almost every academic discipline. You may choose to major in subjects that are considered to be traditional preparation for law school, such as history, English, philosophy, political science, economics, or business, or you may focus your undergraduate studies in areas as diverse as art, music, science, mathematics, computer science, engineering, nursing, or education. Whatever major you select, you are encouraged to pursue an area of study that interests and challenges you, while taking advantage of opportunities to develop your research and writing skills. Taking a broad range of difficult courses from demanding instructors is excellent preparation for legal education.

A sound legal education will build upon and further refine the skills, values, and knowledge that you already possess. The student who comes to law school lacking a broad range of basic skills and knowledge will face a difficult challenge.

Prelaw Advisor

Undergraduate institutions often assign a person to act as an advisor to current and former students who are interested in pursuing a legal education. That individual can help you with researching and identifying law schools to which you may want to apply. If you are still attending undergraduate school, your prelaw advisor can be helpful in selecting courses that can help you achieve your goal.

Core Skills and Values

There are important skills and values, and significant bodies of knowledge that you can acquire prior to law school and that will provide a sound foundation for a legal education. These include analytic and problem-solving skills, critical reading abilities, writing skills, oral communication and listening abilities, general research skills, task organization and management skills, and the values of serving faithfully the interests of others while also promoting justice. If you wish to prepare adequately for a legal education, and for a career in law or for other professional service that involves the use of lawyering skills, you should seek educational, extracurricular and life experiences that will assist you in developing those attributes. Some brief comments about each of the listed skills and values follow.

Analytic/Problem-solving Skills

You should seek courses and other experiences that will engage you in critical thinking about important issues, challenge your beliefs, and improve your tolerance for uncertainty. Your legal education will demand that you structure and evaluate arguments for and against propositions that are susceptible to reasoned debate. Good legal education will teach you to "think like a lawyer," but the analytic and problem-solving skills required of lawyers are not fundamentally different from those employed by other professionals. Your law school experience will develop and refine those crucial skills, but you must enter law school with a reasonably well-developed set of analytic and problem-solving abilities.

Critical Reading Abilities

Preparation for legal education should include substantial experience at close reading and critical analysis of complex textual material, for much of what you will do as a law student and lawyer involves careful reading and comprehension of judicial opinions, statues, documents, and other written materials. As with the other skills discussed in this Statement, you can develop your critical reading ability in a wide range of experiences, including the close reading of complex material in literature, political, or economic theory, philosophy, or history. The particular nature of the materials examined is not crucial; what is important is that law school should not be the first time that you are rigorously engaged in the enterprise of carefully reading and understanding, and critically analyzing, complex written material of substantial length.

Writing Skills

As you seek to prepare for a legal education, you should develop a high degree of skill at written communication. Language is the most important tool of a lawyer, and lawyers must learn to express themselves clearly and concisely.

Legal education will provide you with good training in writing, and particularly in the specific techniques and forms of written expression that are common in the law. Fundamental writing skills, however, *must* be acquired and refined before you enter law school. You should seek as many experiences as possible that will require rigorous and analytical writing, including preparing original pieces of substantial length and revising written work in response to constructive criticism.

Oral Communication and Listening Abilities

The ability to speak clearly and persuasively is another skill that is essential to your success in law school and the practice of law. You must also have excellent listening skills if you are to understand your clients and others with whom you will interact daily. As with writing skills, legal education provides excellent opportunities for refining oral communication skills, and particularly for practicing the forms and techniques of oral expression that are most common in the practice of law. Before coming to law school, however, you should seek to develop your basic speaking and listening skills, such as by engaging in debate, making formal presentations in class, or speaking before groups in school, the community, or the workplace.

General Research Skills

Although there are many research sources and techniques that are specific to the law, you do not have to have developed any familiarity with these specific skills or materials before entering law school. However, it would be to your advantage to come to law school having had the experience of undertaking a project that requires significant library research and the analysis of large amounts of information obtained from that research. The ability to use a personal computer is also necessary for law students, both for word processing and for computerized legal research.

Task Organization and Management Skills

To study and practice law, you are going to need to be able to organize large amounts of information, identify objectives, and create a structure for applying that information in an efficient way in order to achieve desired results. Many law school courses, for example, are graded primarily on the basis of one examination at the end of the course, and many projects in the practice of law require the compilation of large amounts of information from a wide variety of sources. You are going to need to be able to prepare and assimilate large amounts of information in an effective and efficient manner. Some of the requisite experience can be obtained through undertaking school projects that require substantial research and writing, or through the preparation of major reports for an employer, a school, or a civic organization.

The Values of Serving Others and Promoting Justice

Each member of the legal profession should be dedicated both to the objectives of serving others honestly, competently, and responsibly, and to the goals of improving fairness and the quality of justice in the legal system. If you are thinking of entering the legal profession, you should seek some significant experience, before coming to law school, in which you may devote substantial effort toward assisting others. Participation in public service projects or similar efforts at achieving objectives established for common purposes can be particularly helpful.

General Knowledge

In addition to the fundamental skills and values listed above, there are some basic areas of knowledge that are helpful to a legal education and to the development of a competent lawyer. Some of the types of knowledge that would maximize your ability to benefit from a legal education include:

- A **broad understanding of history**, including the various factors (social, political, economic, and cultural) that have influenced the development of our society in the United States.

- A **fundamental understanding of political thought** and of the contemporary American political system.

- Some **basic mathematical and financial skills**, such as an understanding of basic precalculus mathematics and an ability to analyze financial data.

- A **basic understanding of human behavior** and social interaction.

- An **understanding of diverse cultures** within and beyond the United States, of international institutions and issues, of world events, and of the increasing interdependence of the nations and communities within our world.

Conclusion

The skills, values, and knowledge discussed in this Statement may be acquired in a wide variety of ways. You may take undergraduate, graduate, or even high school courses that can assist you in acquiring much of this information. You may also gain much of this background through self-learning by reading, in the workplace, or through various other life experiences. Moreover, it is not essential that you come to law school having fully developed all of the skills, values, and knowledge suggested in this Statement. Some of that foundation can be acquired during the initial years of law school. However, if you begin law school having already acquired many of the skills, values, and knowledge listed in this Statement, you will have a significant advantage and will be well prepared to benefit fully from a challenging legal education.

*These core skill and value areas are drawn, in substantial part, from the Statement of Skills and Values contained in the 1992 Report of the American Bar Association Task Force on Law Schools and the Profession, *Legal Education and Professional Development—An Educational Continuum*.

■ Other Resources

For a selected list of books, audiocassettes, and video programs pertaining to legal education and the legal profession, see Resources for the Prelaw Candidate, Appendix D, or go to Law School Resources/Resources for the Prelaw Candidate on LSAC's website, *www.LSAC.org*. Also included in the list are biographies and books on jurisprudence and legal issues.

■ The Juris Doctor Degree

ABA-approved law schools generally require three years of full-time study to earn the Juris Doctor (JD) degree. Most schools with part-time programs require four years of part-time study to earn the JD degree. Most law schools share a common approach to training lawyers. However, they differ in the emphasis they give to certain subjects and teaching methods, such as opportunities for independent study, legal internships, participation in clinical programs, and involvement with governmental affairs.

Law school can be an intense, competitive environment. Students have little time for other interests, especially during the first year of law school. The ABA requires that no full-time student hold an outside job for more than 20 hours a week. Most schools encourage their students to become totally immersed in reading, discussing, and thinking about the law.

The First Year

The newness of the first year of law school is exciting for many and anxiety-provoking for almost all. Professors expect you to be prepared in class, but in most courses, grades will be determined primarily from examinations administered at the end of the semester or, at some schools, the end of the year. The professor may give little feedback until the final examination.

The Case Method Approach

The "case method" is what first-year law students are likely to find least familiar. By focusing on the underlying principles that shape the law's approach to different situations, you will learn to distinguish among subtly different legal results and to identify the critical factors that determine a particular outcome. Once these distinctions are mastered, you should be able to apply this knowledge to new situations.

The case method involves the detailed examination of a number of related judicial opinions that describe an area of law. You will also learn to apply the same critical analysis to legislative materials and scholarly articles. The role of the law professor is to provoke and stimulate. For a particular case, he or she may ask questions designed to explore the facts presented, to determine the legal principles applied in reaching a decision, and to analyze the method of reasoning used. In this way, the professor encourages you to relate the case to others and to distinguish it from those with similar but inapplicable precedents. In order to encourage you to learn to defend your reasoning, the professor may adopt a position contrary to the holding of the case.

Because this process places much of the burden of learning on the student, classroom discussions can be exciting. They are also demanding. However uninformed, unprepared, or puzzled you may be, you will be expected to participate in these discussions.

The Ability to Think

The case method reflects the general belief that the primary purpose of law school is not to teach substantive law but to teach you to think like a lawyer. Teachers of law are less concerned about rules and technicalities than are their counterparts in many other disciplines. Although the memorization of specifics may be useful to you, the ability to be analytical and literate is considerably more important than the power of total recall. One reason for this approach to legal education is that in our common-law tradition, the law is constantly evolving and changing; thus, specific rules may quickly lose their relevance.

Law is more an art than a science. The reality lawyers seek in analyzing a case is not always well-defined. Legal study, therefore, requires an attentive mind and a tolerance for ambiguity. Because many people believe incorrectly that the study of law involves the memorization of rules in books and principles dictated by learned professors, law schools often attract those people who especially value structure, authority, and order. The study of law does not involve this kind of certainty, however; complex legal questions do not have simple legal solutions.

The Curriculum

As a first-year law student, you will follow a designated course of study that may cover many of the following subjects:

- **Civil procedure**—the process of adjudication in the United States; i.e., jurisdiction and standing to sue, motions and pleadings, pretrial procedure, the structure of a lawsuit, and appellate review of trial results.

- **Constitutional law**—the legislative powers of the federal and state governments, and questions of civil liberties and constitutional history, including detailed study of the Bill of Rights and constitutional freedoms.

- **Contracts**—the nature of enforceable promises and rules for determining appropriate remedies in case of nonperformance.

- **Criminal law and criminal procedure**—bases of criminal responsibility, the rules and policies for enforcing sanctions against individuals accused of committing offenses against the public order and well-being, and the rights guaranteed to those charged with criminal violations.

- **Legal method**—students' introduction to the organization of the American legal system and its processes.

- **Legal writing**—research and writing component of most first-year programs; requires students to research and write memoranda dealing with various legal problems.

- **Property law**—concepts, uses, and historical developments in the treatment of land, buildings, natural resources, and personal objects.

- **Torts**—private wrongs, such as acts of negligence, assault, and defamation, that violate obligations of the law.

In addition to attending classes, you may be required to participate in a moot court exercise in which you take responsibility for arguing a hypothetical court case.

After the first year, you will probably have the opportunity to select from a broad range of courses. Generally, you will take courses in administrative law, civil litigation, commercial law, corporations, evidence, family law, professional responsibility, taxation, and wills and trusts before completing your degree. These universal courses are basic to legal education. Every law school supplements this basic curriculum with additional courses, such as international law, environmental law, conflict of laws, labor law, criminal procedure, and jurisprudence.

Opportunities to Practice What Is Learned

Legal education is primarily academic, in that students devote most of their time to mastering general concepts and principles that shape the law. Most schools offer a variety of professional skills courses as well. Through clinical programs, law schools offer students direct experience in legal practice. These programs allow second- and third-year students to render counseling, undertake legislative drafting, participate in court trials and appeals, and do other legal work for academic credit. Schools differ in the range and variety of practical education they offer, but the benefits of integrating this experience with theoretical study are well established.

Extracurricular Activities

Student organizations greatly supplement classroom learning. Typically, these organizations are dedicated to advancing the interests of particular groups of law students, such as black, women, or Hispanic students; or to promoting greater understanding of specific legal fields, such as environmental or international law; or to providing opportunities for involvement in professional, social, and sports activities.

A unique feature of American law schools is that law students manage and edit most of the legal profession's principal scholarly journals. Membership on the editorial staffs of these journals is considered a mark of academic distinction. Selection is ordinarily based on outstanding academic performance, writing ability, or both, as discussed on page 19 of this book.

■ Admission to the Bar

The Bar Examination*

In order to obtain a license to practice law, almost all law school graduates must apply for bar admission through a state board of bar examiners. Most often this board is an agency of the highest state court in the jurisdiction, but occasionally the board is connected more closely to the state's bar association. The criteria for eligibility to take the bar examination or to otherwise qualify for bar admission are set by each state.

Licensing involves a demonstration of worthiness in two distinct areas. The first is competence. For initial licensure, competence is ordinarily established by a showing that the applicant holds an acceptable educational credential (with rare exception, a JD degree) from a law school that meets educational standards, and by achieving a passing score on the bar examination.

The most common testing configuration consists of a two-day bar examination, one day of which is devoted to the Multistate Bar Examination, a standardized 200-item test covering six areas (Constitutional Law, Contracts, Criminal Law, Evidence, Real Property, and Torts). The second day of testing is typically comprised of locally crafted essays from a broader range of subject matters; however, in a growing number of states, nationally developed tests, such as the Multistate Essay Examination and the Multistate Performance Test, are used to round out the test.

In addition, almost all jurisdictions require that the applicant present an acceptable score on the Multistate Professional Responsibility Examination, which is separately administered three times each year.

The second area of inquiry by bar examiners involves the character and fitness of applicants for a law license. In this regard, bar examiners seek background information concerning each applicant that is relevant to the appropriateness of granting a professional credential. Because law is a public profession, and because the degree of harm a lawyer lacking the necessary character or fitness can inflict is substantial, decisions about who should be admitted to practice law are made carefully by bar examining boards.

Boards of bar examiners in most jurisdictions expect to hear from prospective candidates during the final year of law school. Bar examinations are ordinarily offered at the end of February and July, with considerably more applicants taking the summer test because it falls after graduation from law school.

Some boards offer or require law student registration at an earlier point in law school. This preliminary processing, where available, permits the board to review character and fitness issues in advance.

As state-specific information is so important (and so variable) in the lawyer-licensing process, law students should contact the board of bar examiners in the jurisdiction(s) in which they are most likely to practice law.

*This section was written by Erica Moeser, President of the National Conference of Bar Examiners (NCBE).

General Information

Lawyers may practice only in the state or states where they are members of the bar in good standing. However, many states will admit a lawyer to its bar if the lawyer has been admitted to the bar of another state and has practiced law actively for a certain number of years. This is known as "motion admission." Courts often grant temporary bar admission to out-of-state lawyers for the duration of a specific case.

Many states have student practice rules that, in conjunction with students' academic programs, admit advanced law students who are under the close supervision of an admitted lawyer. A few states require law students to register with the board of bar examiners before graduation or, in some cases, soon after they are enrolled in law school, if they intend to practice in those states. So, if you're planning to attend law school, you should check the bar admission requirements for those states in which you may wish to practice after graduation.

Federal courts set their own standards for admission. It is a common requirement for federal district court admission that the lawyer be admitted to the bar in the state in which the federal district is located or, for the applicant to have one good state court admission.

Some state bar associations inquire about the law school admission records of those seeking admission to the bar. You should keep and maintain complete copies of all law school application records throughout the admission cycle and your law school career.

All states accept graduation from an ABA-approved law school as meeting the state's education requirement for eligibility to sit for the bar examination. A number of states have special rules that accept other forms of legal education as sufficient. A good source of information regarding bar admission requirements is the latest edition of the *NCBE/ABA's Comprehensive Guide to Bar Admission Requirements*, which is available online at *www.abanet.org/legaled*. It should also be available in any law school library or can be ordered through the ABA Service Center at 1.800.285.2221. If you would like additional information relating to bar admissions about a specific state, please contact the appropriate authority in that state. Also, you may want to visit the websites for NCBE (*www.ncbex.org*), the ABA (*www.abanet.org/legaled*), and LSAC (*www.LSAC.org*).

Distance Education

Educating a student for a Juris Doctor degree is a professional education of a most distinct variety. During a law school education, a student is expected to participate in a learning community to develop skills and knowledge that will advance the legal system, society, and the student's career. This law school experience involves interaction with faculty and fellow students outside the classroom as well as in class. Students also learn from each other by inquiry and challenge, review, and study groups.

ABA-approved law schools may not offer a JD degree program that is online or done through correspondence study. ABA-approved law schools may grant credit hours for distance education courses, but no more than 4-credit hours in any term, and no more than 12-credit hours toward the JD degree. Students should be aware that studying law by correspondence or other distance education programs would limit the ability to sit for the bar in many states.

Bar Associations

Bar associations are membership organizations designed to raise the standards of the legal profession and to encourage professional unity. Each state has its own bar association. There are also a variety of national, state, local, and special-interest bar associations. Many bar associations sponsor programs intended to broaden the availability of legal services and to familiarize the public with the legal profession. They also conduct extensive continuing legal education programs to help members update their skills and their knowledge of the law.

The American Bar Association (ABA) is the largest national organization of attorneys in the United States with 413,108 members. The ABA sponsors a number of programs dealing with legal education, law reform, judicial selection, and professional responsibility. The ABA also publishes the "Model Rules of Professional Conduct," a set of regulations governing ethical standards in the practice of law. Attorneys who violate such standards are subject to censure, suspension, or disbarment by the state bar admitting authorities.

Additionally, there are local and national chapters of bar associations for lawyers from minority groups. Among them are the National Bar Association, National Hispanic Bar Association, National Asian and Pacific American Bar Association, and the Native American Bar Association. For more information on events sponsored by these organizations, go to *www.LSAC.org* or contact the LSAC Office of Minority Affairs at *mile@LSAC.org*.

Chapter 3: The Law School Admission Process

■ How Law Schools Determine Whom to Admit

It is very difficult to predict with certainty which individuals will perform well in law school, so admission committees seek the most qualified from the pool of applicants. In order to be fair, schools rely heavily upon selection criteria that bear on expected performance in law school and can be applied objectively to all candidates. Law schools consider a variety of factors in admitting their students, and no single qualification will independently guarantee acceptance or rejection. The two factors that all candidates present, prior academic performance and the LSAT score, are fundamental to the admission process.

The most difficult admission decisions are those regarding candidates who are neither so well qualified nor so deficient as to present a clear-cut case for acceptance or denial. These applicants constitute the majority of the applicant pool at many law schools.

Criteria That May Be Considered by Law School Admission Committees

- Undergraduate grade-point average
- LSAT score
- Undergraduate course of study
- Graduate work, if any
- College attended
- Improvement in grades and grade distribution
- College curricular and extracurricular activities
- Ethnic/racial background
- Individual character and personality
- Letters of recommendation
- Writing skills
- Personal statement or essay
- Work experience or other postundergraduate experiences
- Community activities
- Motivation to study and reasons for deciding to study law
- State of residency
- Obstacles that have been overcome
- Past accomplishments and leadership
- Anything else that stands out in an application

■ The Law School Admission Test (LSAT)

All American Bar Association (ABA)-approved law schools and many non-ABA-approved law schools require applicants to take the LSAT as part of the admission process.

The test consists of five 35-minute sections of multiple-choice questions, in three different item types. Four of the five sections contribute to the test taker's score. The unscored section, commonly referred to as the variable section, typically is used to pretest new test questions or to preequate new test forms. The placement of this section in the LSAT will vary. A 35-minute writing sample is administered at the end of the test. LSAC does not score the writing sample. Copies of the writing sample are sent to all law schools to which you apply.

The score scale for the LSAT is 120 to 180. Some schools place greater weight than others on the LSAT; most law schools do evaluate your full range of credentials.

What the Test Measures

The LSAT is designed to measure skills that are considered essential for success in law school: the reading and comprehension of complex texts with accuracy and insight; the organization and management of information and the ability to draw reasonable inferences from it; the ability to think critically; and the analysis and evaluation of the reasoning and arguments of others.

The three multiple-choice question types in the LSAT are:

Reading Comprehension Questions
These questions measure your ability to read, with understanding and insight, examples of lengthy and complex materials similar to those commonly encountered in law school work. The reading comprehension items consist of reading selections of approximately 450 words, each followed by five to eight questions that test reading and reasoning abilities.

Analytical Reasoning Questions
These questions are designed to measure your ability to understand a structure of relationships and to draw logical conclusions about that structure. You are asked to make deductions from a set of statements, rules, or conditions that describe relationships among entities such as persons, places, things, or events. They simulate the kinds of detailed analyses of relationships that a law student must perform in solving legal problems.

Logical Reasoning Questions
These questions are designed to evaluate your ability to understand, analyze, criticize, and complete a variety of arguments. Each logical reasoning question requires you to read and comprehend a short passage, then answer one or two questions about it. The questions test a variety of abilities involved in reasoning logically and thinking critically.

Important Note Regarding Two Changes to the LSAT

Beginning with the June 2007 LSAT administration, LSAC is introducing a new variant of reading comprehension, called comparative reading, as one of the four sets in the LSAT reading comprehension section. In general, comparative reading questions are similar to traditional reading comprehension questions, except that comparative reading questions are based on two shorter passages instead of one longer passage. The two passages together are of roughly the same length as one reading comprehension passage. A few of the questions that follow a comparative reading passage pair might concern only one of the two passages, but most questions will be about both passages and how they relate to each other.

Also beginning with the June 2007 LSAT, test takers will no longer be randomly assigned one of two different kinds of writing prompt—decision or argument—for the writing sample. All test takers will be assigned a decision prompt. The writing sample will continue to be unscored. For more information, see the current edition of the *LSAT & LSDAS Information Book* or go to the LSAT information at *www.LSAC.org*.

Your Score as a Predictor of Law School Performance

The LSAT, like any admission test, is not a perfect predictor of law school performance. The predictive power of an admission test is limited by many factors, such as the complexity of the skills the test is designed to measure and the unmeasurable factors that can affect students' performances, such as motivation, physical and mental health, or work and family responsibilities. In spite of these factors, the LSAT compares very favorably with admission tests used in other graduate and professional fields of study. (For additional information about the predictive value of LSAT scores, refer to the current edition of the *LSAT & LSDAS Information Book*.)

Test Preparation

Most law school applicants familiarize themselves with test directions and question types, practice on sample tests, and study the information available on test-taking techniques and strategies. Although it is difficult to say when examinees are sufficiently prepared, very few people achieve their full potential without some preparation.

You should be so familiar with the instructions and question types that nothing you see on the test can delay or distract you from thinking about how to answer a question. At a minimum, you should review the descriptions of the question types in the *LSAT & LSDAS Information Book* and on LSAC's website and simulate the day of the test by taking a practice test that includes a writing sample under actual time constraints. Taking a practice test under timed conditions helps you to estimate the amount of time you can afford to spend on each question in a section and to determine the question types for which you may need additional practice.

LSAC publishes a variety of materials to help you prepare for the LSAT. See the ad toward the back of this book, or visit LSAC's website—*www.LSAC.org*.

Academic Record

Undergraduate performance is generally an important indicator of how someone is likely to perform in law school. Hence, many law schools look closely at college grades when considering individual applications.

Course selection also can make a difference in admission evaluations. Applicants who have taken difficult or advanced courses in their undergraduate study often are evaluated in a more favorable light than students who have concentrated on easier or less advanced subjects.

Many law schools consider undergraduate-performance trends along with a student's numerical average. Thus, they may discount a slow start in a student's undergraduate career if he or she performs exceptionally well in the later school years. Similarly, admission committees may see an undergraduate's strong start followed by a mediocre finish as an indication of less potential to do well in law school. Candidates are advised to comment on irregular grade trends in their applications.

Grade Conversion Table

LSDAS Conversion	Grades as Reported on Transcripts				
4.0 Scale	A to F	1 to 5	100–0*	Four Passing Grades	Three Passing Grades
4.33	A+	1+	98–100	Highest Passing Grade (4.0)	Highest Passing Grade (4.0)
4.00	A	1	93–97		
3.67	A–	1–	90–92		
3.50	AB				
3.33	B+	2+	87–89	Second Highest Passing Grade (3.0)	Middle Passing Grade (3.0)
3.00	B	2	83–86		
2.67	B–	2–	80–82		
2.50	BC				
2.33	C+	3+	77–79	Third Highest Passing Grade (2.0)	Lowest Passing Grade (2.0)
2.00	C	3	73–76		
1.67	C–	3–	70–72		
1.50	CD				
1.33	D+	4+	67–69	Lowest Passing Grade (1.0)	
1.00	D	4	63–66		
0.67	D–	4–	60–62		
0.50	DE or DF				
0.00	E and F	5	Below 60	Failure (0.0)	Failure (0.0)

*In some instances, a school's numeric grading scale might be converted differently than shown here.

■ Additional Admission Decision Factors

Law schools consider more than academic records and LSAT scores when evaluating applicants. Some of the most important factors are discussed below.

Letters of Recommendation

The most effective letters of recommendation are those from professors who have known you well enough to write with candor, detail, and objectivity about your academic and personal achievements and potential. Work supervisors also can write in support of your application. Letters that compare you to your academic peers are often considered the most useful. Most schools do not consider general, unreservedly praiseworthy letters helpful. Some schools do not require letters at all, and may not read letters of recommendation if they receive them.

Work Experience

Law schools want diverse, interesting classes, representative of a variety of backgrounds. A candidate who applies to law school several years after completing his or her undergraduate education, and who has demonstrated an ability to succeed in a nonacademic environment, is sometimes more motivated than one who continues his or her education without a break. In fact, only about 40 percent of law students enter directly from college.

Your Personal Essay

Each candidate to law school has something of interest to present. Maybe you've had some experience, some training, or some dream that sets you apart from others. Law schools want to recruit men and women who are qualified for reasons beyond grades and scores. The essay or personal statement in your application is the place to tell the committee about yourself.

In general, your evaluation of actual experiences and past accomplishments has more value to the committee than speculation about future accomplishments. Also, if you have overcome a serious obstacle in your life to get where you are today, by all means let the admission committee know about it. Any noteworthy personal experience or accomplishment may be an appropriate subject for your essay; however, be sure to do more than just state it. Describe your experience briefly but concretely, and why it had value to you, whether it is a job, your family, a significant accomplishment, or your upbringing. You are simultaneously trying to add information and create structure. Be brief, be factual, be comprehensive, and be organized. You are a storyteller here. You want a living person—you—to emerge. The statement is your opportunity to become vivid and alive to the reader, and it is an opportunity to demonstrate your ability to write and present a prose sample in a professional manner.

Graduate or Professional Study

Prior success or failure in other graduate or professional school work, including other law schools, may also be a factor in the admission committee's decision. In any case, you are required to report such work to any law school to which you apply.

Minority Applicants

Ethnic diversity is essential to the study of law, and greatly benefits the law class, the law school, and the legal profession. All law schools actively seek students who are members of minority groups and strongly encourage minority applicants. (See chapter 6 for further details on minority recruitment and enrollment.)

International Applicants

Students from other countries are enrolled at US law schools, most frequently in graduate programs (usually called LLM programs) that are designed to meet the needs of people who already hold a recognized law degree from another country but want to learn about the legal system of the United States.

Procedures and requirements for foreign applicants for the JD or LLM programs vary from school to school. You should contact the individual schools that interest you to learn about each school's particular requirements. Most schools will ask applicants for whom English is not their native language to take a standardized test such as the Test of English as a Foreign Language (TOEFL) or the Test of Written English (TWE). Each school sets its own standard for required minimal scores on the tests.

Many schools require foreign-educated applicants to use either LSAC's credential assembly service or another evaluation service to authenticate and evaluate a student's grades and degrees for US admission committees. The student is responsible for the cost of this service, and some law schools will require you to use a specific service.

For candidates applying to JD or post-JD programs (LLM, SJD, and other similar degrees), the LSAC offers a credential assembly service that collects, authenticates, and distributes all transcripts and TOEFL scores to each law school where the applicant submits an application. Most law schools subscribe to this service, but candidates should check with individual schools before registering. Detailed information about the service is available at *http://LLM.LSAC.org*.

Foreign students must also demonstrate the ability to pay for schooling in this country in order to apply for a student visa (F-1 form). You may be asked to complete a certification of finances form from the law school; if the school is satisfied that the student can pay, it will issue a form (I-20) to submit to the Immigration and Naturalization Service (INS) as part of your application for a student visa. Because of the time required to process entry visas, international applicants are encouraged to apply for admission as early in the process as possible.

Foreign students may be eligible for institutional grants and loans, but are ineligible for federal loans, and (in most schools) are required to have a US cosigner for private loans. Contact the financial aid office at the schools to which you are applying for more details.

Interviews

In general, interviews are not a part of the law school admission process. You are encouraged to visit law schools to gather information, and often an appointment with admission personnel will be a part of the visit. The purpose of your conversation with the admission staff usually will be informational rather than evaluative and will not become a part of your admission file. An occasional school will grant an interview, and some may even request it, but, in general, you should not count on an interview as a means to state your case for admission; this is best done in the personal statement.

■ Assessing Yourself Realistically

When selecting law schools to which you will apply, the general philosophy is that you should have a threefold plan: dream a little, be realistic, and be safe. Most applicants have no trouble selecting dream schools—those that are almost, but not quite, beyond their grasp—or safe schools—those for which admission is virtually certain. A common strategic error made by applicants is failure to evaluate realistically their chances for admission to a particular law school. The admission data and law school admission profile grids in this book are helpful sources, along with the information at *www.LSAC.org*, because the data are provided by the law schools directly to the ABA and LSAC.

Use the Admission Profile Grids in This Book

Check your qualifications against the admission profiles of the law schools that interest you. Most schools publish a grid that indicates the number of applicants with LSAT scores and GPAs like yours who were admitted in the most recent admission year. This gives you a general sense of your competitiveness at that school. These charts will help you determine which schools are your dream schools, your realistic schools, and your safe schools. If your profile meets or exceeds that of a school, it is likely that that school will be as interested in admitting you as you are in being admitted. Other statistics are contained in the school's ABA data, so that material should be read with care as well. A few words of caution: First, law schools consider many other factors beyond the LSAT score and GPA, as described in the previous section ("Additional Admission Decision Factors"), and the grids and data about these credentials only give you part of the story. Second, you should make your final decision about where you will apply only after obtaining additional qualitative information from each school. Third, the data in the grids are from a previous application year and may not reflect fluctuations in applicant volume that affect admission decisions.

Research Specific Law Schools That Interest You

Other sources of information include:

- **The school's admission office.** This is a good source for general information about the school and your chances for admission. Do not hesitate to request admission counseling. Be sure to obtain current catalogs and visit the websites for each law school you are considering.

- **Your college or university prelaw advisor.** LSAC provides the name of a prelaw advisor at your degree-granting institution. Your prelaw advisor can often provide you with reliable information about which law schools fit your personal profile. He or she may also be able to tell you which law schools have accepted students from your school in the past and provide you with an overview of the admitted students' credentials. This will help you to determine how law schools have treated applicants from your school in the recent past.

- **Law School Forums.** The Law School Forums, organized by the Law School Admission Council, are excellent opportunities to talk with law school representatives from around the country in one central, urban location—usually a hotel exhibit hall. Recent forums have been held in Atlanta, Boston, Chicago, Dallas, Houston, Los Angeles, New York City, San Francisco Bay Area, and Washington, DC. In 2006, 176 ABA-approved law schools participated in the forums, and 11,000 people registered as attendees. Because the costs of traveling to a number of law schools can be expensive, many prospective law students find the forums to be the most productive means of gathering information and making school contacts. Forum admission is free; for dates and locations of 2007 Law School Forums, see the ad toward the back of this book, or visit LSAC's website —*www.LSAC.org*. Forum preregistration is also available on the LSAC website.

- **School representatives and alumni.** Take advantage of opportunities to talk with law school representatives and alumni. When you talk with alumni, remember that law schools sometimes change fairly quickly. Try to talk to a recent graduate or to one who is active in alumni affairs and therefore knowledgeable about the school as it is today.

- **School visits.** Law schools encourage you to visit. You can learn a surprising amount about a school from talks with students and faculty members. Many law schools have formal programs in which a currently enrolled student will take you on a tour of the campus and answer your questions. Such a firsthand experience can be quite valuable in assessing how you would fit into the school.

- **The Internet.** The websites of LSAC—*www.LSAC.org*— and the ABA—*www.abanet.org/legaled*—provide links to the websites of ABA-approved law schools.

Keep Your Options Open

Flexibility is a key word in the law school admission process. Keep your options open. Even during the early stages of the admission process, you should continually reevaluate your prospects and prepare alternative plans. For example, don't set your sights on only one law school and one plan of action. You could severely limit your potential and your chance to practice law.

Chapter 4: Applying to Law School

■ Working with LSAC: Registering for the LSAT and the LSDAS

The Law School Admission Council (LSAC) administers the LSAT and serves as a liaison for much of the communication between you and the law schools. The LSDAS centralizes and standardizes undergraduate academic records to simplify the law school admission process. The LSDAS prepares a report for each law school to which you apply. The LSDAS registration fee includes law school report preparation, letter of recommendation and transcript processing, and access to electronic applications for all ABA-approved law schools.

Comprehensive information about the LSAT and LSDAS can be found at the LSAC website, *www.LSAC.org*. The quickest and easiest way to register for both the LSAT and the LSDAS is online. If you need to obtain a paper registration form, call 215.968.1001.

Planning Ahead for Law School Deadlines

Most law schools have a variety of application requirements and deadlines that you must meet to be considered for admission. If you are applying to a number of schools, the various deadlines and requirements can be confusing. It probably will be helpful if you set up a detailed calendar that will remind you of when and what you must do to complete your applications.

In registering for the LSAT, be sure to give yourself enough time to select a convenient testing location and prepare for the test. You also should determine whether each law school in which you are interested will accept scores from the February LSAT administration, which is the last test date in each admission cycle.

Below is a chart listing all scheduled test administrations, including alternate dates for Saturday Sabbath observers, along with corresponding deadlines and fees.

■ Basic LSAT Date and Deadline Information (2007–2008)

All scheduled administrations of the LSAT, both for regular test takers and test takers who are Saturday Sabbath observers, are listed below along with corresponding regular registration deadlines. Dates shown represent receipt deadlines for mail, telephone, and online registration. The basic fee for the LSAT is $123 (published test centers only). For complete information on deadlines and fees for late registrations and nonpublished test centers (domestic and foreign), partial refunds, and early score reporting, please refer to LSAC's website at *www.LSAC.org*. You can also find information in the current *LSAT & LSDAS Information Book*, or call LSAC at 215.968.1001.

Test Dates				
■ Regular	Monday, June 11, 2007	Saturday, Sept. 29, 2007	Saturday, Dec. 1, 2007	Saturday, Feb. 2, 2008 Nondisclosed*
■ Saturday Sabbath Observers		Monday, Oct. 1, 2007 Nondisclosed*	Monday, Dec. 3, 2007 Nondisclosed*	Monday, Feb. 4, 2008 Nondisclosed*
■ Score by E-mail	July 2, 2007	Oct. 22, 2007	Jan. 2, 2008	Feb. 25, 2008
■ Score Report mailed (approx.)	July 9, 2007	Oct. 29, 2007	Jan. 7, 2008	Feb. 29, 2008
Regular Registration Deadline (online, mail, and telephone)				
■ United States, Canada, and the Caribbean	May 8, 2007	Aug. 28, 2007	Oct. 30, 2007	Jan. 2, 2008
■ Outside of the United States, Canada, and the Caribbean	May 4, 2007	Aug. 24, 2007	Oct. 26, 2007	Not available. February test is not administered outside of the US, Canada, and the Caribbean.

*Persons who take a nondisclosed test receive only their scores. They do not receive their test questions, answer key, or individual responses.

■ The Law School Data Assembly Service (LSDAS)

The LSDAS centralizes and standardizes undergraduate academic records to simplify the law school admission process (for US law schools only). Nearly all American Bar Association-approved law schools (and some non-ABA-approved schools) require that applicants use the Law School Data Assembly Service. Canadian law schools do not participate in the LSDAS and do not require its use.

The LSDAS prepares a report for each law school to which you apply. There is a registration fee for the LSDAS, as well as a fee for each law school report (go to *www.LSAC.org* for current fees). Your LSDAS registration includes law school report preparation, letter of recommendation and transcript processing, and access to electronic applications for all ABA-approved law schools.

The law school report contains information that the schools use, along with your application, personal essay, letters of recommendation, and other criteria, to make their admission decisions. Information contained in the report includes

- an undergraduate academic summary;

- copies of all undergraduate, graduate, and law/professional school transcripts;

- LSAT scores and writing sample copies; and

- copies of letters of recommendation processed by LSAC.

Canadian law schools receive an LSAT Law School Report containing scores and writing sample copies.

Fee Waivers

Fee waivers are available for the LSAT, LSDAS, and *Official LSAT SuperPrep*. For US citizens, US nationals, or permanent resident aliens of the United States with an Alien Registration Receipt Card (I-151 or I-551), fee waivers can be authorized by LSAC or ABA-approved law schools, which are listed on our website and in the *Information Book*. Canadian citizens must submit their fee waiver request to a Canadian LSAC-member law school even if they plan to apply for admission to a US law school. Fee waivers cannot be granted by financial aid offices of undergraduate institutions, non-ABA-approved law schools, prelaw advisors, or any other individual or organization. Go to *www.LSAC.org* or any ABA-approved law school admission office for additional information about fee waivers.

■ The Admission Process

Law school applicants can expect that the admission process will be competitive. Nationally, there are more applicants than spaces available in first-year classes, and this means that, at some law schools, there will be considerable competition for seats. However, it is probably true that, if you assess your credentials accurately, your likelihood of admission to an ABA-accredited law school is strong.

The Importance of Complete Files

Remember that law schools require complete files before making their decisions. A law school will consider your file complete when it has received your application form, LSDAS Law School Report (or LSAT Law School Report if the law school does not require the LSDAS), letters of recommendation (if required), any requirements unique to the particular school, and application fee.

Rolling Admission

Many law schools operate what is known as a rolling admission process: The school evaluates applications and informs candidates of admission decisions on a continuous basis over several months, usually beginning in late fall and extending to midsummer for waiting-list admissions.

Even if you have not yet taken the LSAT, it might be helpful to submit your application early so that your LSDAS file can be sent to law schools as soon as your test score is available. The earlier you apply, the more places the school is likely to have available. Most schools try to make comparable decisions throughout the admission season, even those that practice rolling admission. Still, it is disadvantageous to be one of the last applicants to complete a file. Furthermore, the more decisions you receive from law schools early in the process, the better able you will be to make your own decisions, such as whether to apply to more law schools or whether to accept a particular school's offer.

Applying to More Than One School

The average applicant applies to 6 law schools. You should be sure to place your applications at schools representing a range of admission standards. Even if you have top qualifications, you should apply to at least one safety school where you are almost certain of being admitted. This is your insurance policy.

If you apply to a safety school in November, and are accepted in January or February, you may be disappointed but not panicked if you are later denied admission by your top choices.

The Preliminary Review of an Application

Applicants whose qualifications more than fulfill the school's admission standards are usually accepted by an admission committee during the first round of decisions. Candidates whose credentials fall below the school's standards are usually denied admission.

Most applications are not decided upon immediately. They are usually reviewed by a committee that bases its admission decision on many facets of each application (see "How Law Schools Determine Whom to Admit," page 9).

The length of time it takes the committee to review an application varies; consult the individual law schools to which you apply.

Waiting Lists

If you have strong qualifications, but you do not quite meet the competition of those currently being admitted at a particular law school, you may be placed on a waiting list for possible admission at a later date. The law school will send you a letter notifying you of its final decision as early as April or as late as July.

Many schools rank students who are on the waiting list. Some law schools will tell you your rank. If a law school doesn't rank its waiting list, you might ask the admission office how many students have been placed on the waiting list.

Seat Deposits

Many law schools use seat deposits to help keep track of their new classes. For example, a typical fee is $200, which is credited to your first-term tuition if you actually register at the school; if you don't register, the deposit may be forfeited or partially returned. A school may require a larger deposit around July 1, which is also credited to tuition. If you decline the offer of admission after you've paid your deposit, a portion of the money may be refunded, depending on the date you actually decline the offer. At some schools, you may not be refunded any of the deposit.

The official position of the Law School Admission Council is:

Except under early decision plans, no law school should require an enrollment commitment of any kind, binding or non-binding, to an offer of admission or scholarship prior to April 1. Admitted applicants who have submitted a timely financial aid application should not be required to commit to enroll by having to make a nonrefundable financial commitment until notified of financial aid awards that are within the control of the law school.

Multiple Deposit Notification

Each year, LSAC provides participating law schools with periodic reports detailing the number of applicants who have submitted seat deposits or commitments at other participating schools, along with identification of those other schools. Beginning June 15, 2008, those reports will also include the names and LSAC account numbers for all candidates who have deposits/commitments at multiple participating schools.

Ethical Conduct in Applying for Law School

The practice of law is an honorable, noble calling. Lawyers play an important role in society by serving both their clients' needs and the public good. Your submission of an application for admission to law school is your first step in the process of becoming a lawyer. Now is the time, as you take this first, important step, to dedicate yourself to a personal standard for your conduct that consists of the highest levels of honesty and ethical behavior.

The legal profession requires its members to behave ethically in the practice of law at all times, in order to protect the interests of clients and the public. You must understand that those who aspire to join the legal profession will be held to the same high standards for truth, full disclosure, and accuracy that are applied to those who practice law. The legal profession has set standards for ethical conduct by lawyers through the adoption of the Model Rules of Professional Conduct and the Code of Professional Responsibility by the American Bar Association (ABA). Similarly, law schools have set standards for ethical conduct by law school applicants through the Law School Admission Council (LSAC). These standards are known as the *LSAC Rules Governing Misconduct and Irregularities in the Admission Process*. Just as lawyers are required to study, understand, and comply with the ABA's ethical standards, law school applicants are expected to read, understand, and comply with LSAC's ethical standards.

If you fail to comply with LSAC's ethical standards, you may be barred from admission to law school. If you fail to disclose required information on your law school application, or if you engage in misconduct during the admission process that is discovered after you enroll in law school or start to practice law, you may face more serious sanctions. Take the time, right now, to read LSAC's statement on misconduct and irregularities in the admission process presented below.

Misconduct and Irregularities in the Admission Process

The Law School Admission Council has established procedures for dealing with instances of possible candidate misconduct or irregularities on the LSAT or in the law school admission process. Misconduct or irregularity in the admission process is a serious offense with serious consequences. Intent is not an element of a finding of misconduct or irregularity. Misconduct or irregularity is defined as the submission, as part of the law school admission process, including, but not limited to, regular, transfer, and visiting applications, of any information that is false, inconsistent, or misleading, or the omission of information that may result in a false or misleading conclusion, or the violation of any regulation governing the law school admission process, including any violation of LSAT test center regulations.

Examples of misconduct and irregularities include, but are not limited to, submission of an altered or a nonauthentic transcript; submission of an application containing false, inconsistent, or misleading information; submission of an altered, nonauthentic, or unauthorized letter of recommendation; falsification of records; impersonation of another in taking the LSAT; switching of LSAT answer sheets with another; taking the LSAT for purposes other than applying to law school; copying on, or other forms of cheating on, the LSAT; obtaining advance access to test materials; theft of test materials; working, marking, erasing, reading, or turning pages on sections of the LSAT during unauthorized times; bringing prohibited items into the test room; submission of false, inconsistent, or misleading information to the Law School Data Assembly Service (LSDAS); submission of false, inconsistent, or misleading statements or omission of information requested online or on forms as part of the LSAT and/or LSDAS registration process or on individual law school application forms; falsification of transcript information, school attendance, honors, awards, or employment; or providing false, inconsistent, or misleading information in the financial aid/scholarship application process. A charge of misconduct or irregularity may be made prior to a candidate's admission to law school, after matriculation at a law school, or after admission to practice.

When alleged misconduct or irregularity brings into question the validity of LSAC data about a candidate, the school may be notified of possible data error, and transmission of LSAT scores and LSDAS reports will be withheld until the matter has been resolved by the Law School Admission Council's Misconduct and Irregularities in the Admission Process Subcommittee. The Council will investigate all instances of alleged misconduct or irregularities in the admission process in accordance with the *LSAC Rules Governing Misconduct and Irregularities in the Admission Process*. A subcommittee representative will determine whether misconduct or an irregularity has occurred. If the subcommittee representative determines that a preponderance of the evidence shows misconduct or irregularity, then a report of the determination is sent to all law schools to which the individual has applied, subsequently applies, or has matriculated. Notation that a misconduct or irregularity report is on file is also included on LSAT & LSDAS Law School Reports. Such reports are retained indefinitely. In appropriate cases, state and national bar authorities and other affected persons and institutions may also receive notification. Individual law schools and bar authorities determine what action, if any, they will take in response to a finding of misconduct or irregularity. Such action may include the closing of an admission file, revocation of an offer of admission, dismissal from law school through a school's internal disciplinary channels, or disbarment. Thus, a finding of misconduct or irregularity is a very serious matter. More information regarding misconduct and irregularity procedures may be obtained by writing to: Law School Admission Council Misconduct and Irregularities in the Admission Process Subcommittee, 662 Penn Street, Box 40, Newtown, PA 18940-0040.

Chapter 5: Choosing a Law School

For some people, the choice of which law school to attend is an easy one. Applicants tend to select the schools they perceive to be the most prestigious or those which offer a program of particular interest, or the greatest amount of financial support. Some need to stay in a particular area perhaps because of family or job obligations, and will choose nearby schools with part-time programs.

However, the majority of applicants will have to weigh a variety of personal and academic factors to come up with a list of potential schools. Once you have a list, and more than one acceptance letter, you will have to choose a school. Applicants should consider carefully the offerings of each law school before making a decision. The quality of a law school is certainly a major consideration; however, estimations of quality are very subjective. Factors such as the campus atmosphere, the school's devotion to teaching and learning, and the applicant's enthusiasm for the school also are very important. Remember that the law school is going to be your home for three years. Adjusting to law school and the general attitudes of a professional school is difficult enough without the additional hardship of culture shock. Don't choose a law school in a large city if you can't bear crowds, noise, and a fast pace. And, if you've lived your entire life in an urban environment, can you face the change you will experience in a small town? You also may want to ask yourself if you are already set in an unshakable lifestyle or if you are eager for a new environment.

■ Ranking Law Schools

Law Schools and Reputation

Many people will tell you to apply to the schools that take students in your GPA and LSAT ranges, and then enroll in the best one that accepts you. However, law school quality can be assessed in a number of ways.

There is a hierarchy of law schools based on reputation, job placement success, strength of faculty, and the prestige of the parent institution (if there is one). In fact, a study done at one university suggests that undergraduate students perceive schools not only in terms of a hierarchy but also in terms of hierarchical clusters. In other words, certain schools are grouped together in terms of equivalent quality and prestige. Also, there are books or magazine articles that assign law schools purported numerical quality rankings.

However, according to the ABA:

> No rating of law schools beyond the simple statement of their accreditation status is attempted or advocated by the official organizations in legal education. Qualities that make one kind of school good for one student may not be as important to another. The American Bar Association and its Section of Legal Education and Admissions to the Bar have issued disclaimers of any law school rating system. Prospective law students should consider a variety of factors in making their choice among schools.[1]

Since there is no official ranking authority, you should be cautious in using such rankings. The factors that make up a law school's reputation—strength of curriculum, faculty, career services, ability of students, quality of library facilities, and the like—don't lend themselves to quantification. Even if the rankings were more or less accurate, the school's reputation is only one factor among many for you to consider.

What's in a Name?

While going to a "name" school may mean that you will have an easier time finding your first job, it doesn't necessarily mean that you will get a better legal education than if you go to a lesser-known law school. Some schools that were at their peaks years ago are still riding on the wave of that earlier reputation. Others have greatly improved their programs and have recruited talented faculty but have not yet made a name for themselves.

Once admitted, applicants should consider a variety of factors, such as the contacts you may acquire at a school in the area where you hope to practice, the size of the school, and cost. The substantive differences between schools should be your focus when making this important choice rather than the school's reputed ranking.

The Parent University

About 90 percent of ABA-approved law schools are part of a larger university, and there may be some advantages to attending a law school that is part of a university. Such law schools may have more options for joint-degree programs or for taking a nonlaw school course or two. They also may have more academic and social activities, campus theater groups, sports teams, and everything else that comes with university life. Perhaps most important, the university can act as a support system for the law school by providing a wealth of facilities, including student housing and support for career services.

National, Regional, and Local Schools

A national school will generally have an applicant population and a student body that draws almost indistinguishably from the nation as a whole and will have many international students as well. A regional school is likely to have a population that is primarily from the geographic region of its location, though many regional schools have students from all over the country; a number of regional schools draw heavily from a particular geographical area, yet graduates may find jobs all over the country. Generally speaking, a local school is drawing primarily on applicants who either come from or want to practice in the proximate area in which the school is located. Many local law schools have excellent reputations and compete with the national schools in faculty competence, in research-supporting activities, and in resources generally. Check the school's catalog or talk with the admission and placement staff to get a clear breakdown on where their students come from and where they are finding jobs.

[1] The American Bar Association Standards for Approval of Law Schools, General Information of the Council for the Section of Legal Education and Admissions to the Bar, Number 5, "Rating of Law Schools," p. 135, American Bar Association, Chicago, IL, 2001.

■ Evaluating Law Schools

The best advice on how to select a law school is to choose the school that is best for you. The law schools invest substantial time and effort in evaluating prospective students, and applicants should evaluate law schools with equivalent care. The following are some features to keep in mind as you systematically evaluate law schools. (Costs and other financial criteria are not included below; they are discussed in chapter 9.)

Each listing in this book provides school-specific information in the following categories as well.

Enrollment/Student Body

The academic qualifications of the student body are important to consider. It's a good idea to select a law school where you will be challenged by your classmates. Use the applicant profile grids in this book to check the LSAT scores and GPAs for the previous year's entering class. Try to select a school where your averages will not be significantly different from those of your fellow law students. Because of the important role of student participation in law school classes, your legal education might not be as rewarding as it could be if you are not challenged by your classmates.

You might also inquire about the diversity of the student body. Are a majority of the students the same age, race, sex, and so on? Remember, differences among students will expose you to various points of view; this will be an important aspect of your law school education.

Find out how many students are in a typical class. Much of the learning in law school depends on the quality of class discussion. Small classes provide essential interaction; large classes (and the Socratic method) provide diversity, challenge, and a good mix of reactions, opinions, and criticism.

It is also important to find out the total number of students enrolled at the school. Not surprisingly, the larger law schools tend to offer a larger selection of courses. Of course, more doesn't always mean better, and no one student has time to take all the courses offered at a large school. However, if you think you want to sample a wide range of courses, you are apt to have more opportunity to do so at a law school with a large faculty.

Part of the law school learning experience takes place after class with fellow students and with members of the faculty. Check to see whether faculty and students are on campus for a substantial part of the day.

Larger schools may also offer more extracurricular programs, greater student services, and a larger library. However, faculties and administrators at smaller schools may be able to give students more attention, and students at smaller schools may experience greater camaraderie. The size of a school is a personal consideration. Some students thrive in large schools; others prefer a smaller student community. Ask yourself which kind of student you are.

Faculty

You will undoubtedly want to assess the faculties of the law schools you are considering. School catalogs and websites will give you some idea of the backgrounds of the full-time faculty—what specialties they have, what they have published,

and their public service activities. If the catalog tells you only where degrees were earned, ask for more information. You may also want to check the latest edition of the Association of American Law Schools' *Directory of Law Teachers*, which is available at law school libraries. It may help you to know that some members of the faculty have interests similar to your own.

Is the faculty relatively diverse with respect to race, ethnic background, gender, degrees in other fields, and breadth of experience? A faculty with diverse backgrounds will have various points of view and experiences. This diversity will enrich your legal education, broaden your own point of view, and help prepare you for the variety of clients you will work with after law school.

How many full-time professors teach how many students—that is, what is the faculty/student ratio?

Although some of the most prestigious law schools are famous for their large sections in the introductory courses, they also provide smaller classes, clinics, simulations, and seminars in advanced subjects. According to the *ABA Standards: Rules of Procedure for Approval of Law Schools*, it is not favorable to have a full-time faculty to full-time student ratio of 30 to 1 or more.

Are some of the teachers recognized as authorities in their respective fields through their writings and professional activities? Law school catalogs and websites vary widely regarding information about faculty. Some merely list each faculty member's name along with schools attended and degrees earned. Others may provide details about publications, professional activities, and noteworthy achievements, particularly when an individual is an authority in his or her field.

Are there visiting professors, distinguished lecturers and visitors, symposiums and the like at the schools you are considering? Law school lectureship programs are a good means of presenting the knowledge and views of academics outside of the particular law school you attend.

The Library and Other Physical Facilities

Chances are you will spend more time in the library than anywhere else, so take stock of the library before you enroll. There are several factors to consider when assessing a law school library: the quality of its holdings, cataloging methods, access to electronic databases, participation in library networks for information retrieval, staff, facilities, and the hours the library is available to students.

Whether it has 250,000 volumes or 2.5 million volumes tells you little about the actual usefulness of the library. It may have an unfathomable number of volumes, but many of them may be outdated, irrelevant, or not readily available to students. All ABA-approved law schools must maintain a library that has the research materials considered essential for the study of law. Beyond that, find out if the school has any special collections, subscribes to computerized legal research services, or participates in interlibrary loan networks. Also, find out how many copies of essential materials are available, particularly for large classes.

Find out about the quality of the library's professional staff. Is there an adequate number of reference librarians for the number of students and faculty being served? Is the staff helpful?

Be sure the library has an adequate number of comfortable seats with at least enough carrels to accommodate a reasonable number of students at any given time. Either in the library or elsewhere in the law building, there should be suitable space for group study and other forms of collaborative work.

Because you will need to spend much of your time in the library, make sure its hours will accommodate just about any schedule you might have. While it is not necessary for a library to be open around the clock, it should be open before classes begin each day and remain open well into the night with a professional library staff on hand to assist students.

Access to technology should not only be available in the library, but throughout the law building, so that students can use computers to retrieve information outside the actual library space.

Curriculum

The range and quality of academic programs is one of the most important factors to consider when choosing a law school.

Almost all law schools follow the traditional first-year core curriculum of civil procedure, criminal law, contracts, legal research and writing, torts, and property (see chapter 2). Do not assume that all law schools have programs that suit your personal needs and special interests. If you don't have any specific interests in mind—and many beginning students don't—try to make sure the school offers a wide range of electives so that you will have many options. A thorough grounding in basic legal theory will enable you to apply the principles learned to any area of law to which they pertain.

In fact, you shouldn't overemphasize your search for specialties; most law students are not specialists when they graduate, nor do they need to be. Generally speaking, new lawyers begin to find their specialties only in the second to fifth years of their careers. A well-rounded legal education is the best preparation for almost any career path you take. The schools' catalogs and the descriptions in this book will tell you a good deal about academic programs. You may also wish to ask school representatives questions such as: Does the school offer a variety of courses, or is it especially strong in certain areas; what sizes are the classes; are seminars and small-group classroom experiences available; and are there ample opportunities for developing writing, researching, and drafting skills?

Beyond the content of law school courses, other academic program considerations may be of interest to you as a prospective law student.

Special Programs and Academic Activities

Joint-degree Programs
Joint-degree programs allow you to pursue law school and graduate degrees simultaneously. Almost every combination is available at some institutions. Among the more popular degrees are the JD/MBA and the JD/MA in such areas as economics or political science. For details, check the individual school listings in this book or check the law school's recruitment materials.

Master of Laws (LLM) Programs and Special-degree Programs
Many law schools offer advanced degrees that allow students to take graduate-level law courses. The LLM degree is quite common and usually is tailored to individual interests. Some schools offer master of laws degrees with particular concentrations, such as a master of laws in taxation and master of comparative law. Students may enroll in LLM programs only after having received the JD degree.

A few schools also offer very specific, special-degree programs. Some of these specialties include a Doctorate in Civil Law, Doctor of Juridical Science, and Doctor of Jurisprudence and Social Policy. Finding out what types of advanced degrees a law school offers may help you determine the emphases of the school. (See appendix B for a listing of post-JD programs.)

Part-time and Evening Programs
Part-time programs may be offered either in the evening or the day. For the past 10 years, approximately 17 percent of law students have been enrolled in part-time programs. The conventional wisdom is that if you are financially able to attend law school full-time, you ought to do so.

Part-time programs generally take four years to complete instead of three years. If you wish to enroll in such a program, you may be limiting your choice of law schools somewhat, since less than half of the law schools offer part-time programs.

Clinical Programs and Moot Court Competitions
Many law schools offer students authentic experiences as lawyers by involving them with clients and providing opportunities to rehearse trial and appellate advocacy in trial team and moot court competitions. It is important that students become adept at using interviewing, counseling, research, advocacy, and negotiation skills.

The best clinical programs involve students in actual legal situations, simulations of such situations, or a combination of both, either at the school itself or in the community. Clinical programs at some schools offer a team-teaching approach; practical, professional skills are taught along with traditional classroom theory. In this manner, faculty can advise and work closely with students.

Student Journals
Most law schools have a law review—a journal of scholarly articles and commentaries on the law—and other student-edited scholarly journals. Writing for the journals of a school can be important to both your legal education and your career in law. Thus, evaluating the journals at a particular law school may be worthwhile when trying to choose the right school to attend.

Traditionally, student journal editors are chosen on the basis of academic standing, but writing ability, regardless of class rank, may also be a criterion. Today, a growing number of schools select journal editors by holding a competition in which students submit a previously assigned writing sample to the current editorial board. If you are on a journal, employers may assume you are either one of the brightest in your class, or an outstanding writer—or both.

If possible, check the journals of the schools you are considering. The character of the journal may be a reflection of the character of the institution that supports it.

Order of the Coif
Many law schools have a chapter of the Order of the Coif, a national honor society for outstanding students. Students are

elected to Coif on the basis of scholarship and character. Check to see if the schools you are considering include such a chapter.

Academic Support Programs

Programs for students who need or who are expected to need assistance with legal analysis and writing are offered by most law schools. Students are invited to participate in these programs on the basis of either their entering credentials or their actual law school performance. This assistance may be offered in the summer prior to beginning law school, during the academic year, or both. The aim of academic support programs is to ensure that students have an equal opportunity to compete in law school. For further information about academic assistance programs, consult the admission office at the law school.

Student Organizations

You can also tell something about a law school's intellectual resources and its students by the number and range of student associations and organizations sponsored on campus. Many schools have chapters of the American Bar Association-Law Student Division; a student bar association; associations for minority groups, such as the Asian, Black, Hispanic, and Native American law student associations; and associations based on religious affiliations. Some, but not all, schools sponsor an environmental law society, a gay and lesbian law student society, a legal assistance society, a postconviction assistance project, an ACLU group, a federalist society, a volunteer income-tax assistance program, a law student spouses' club, an international law society, a law and technology society, or a client-counseling society. Determine which associations are important to you and check individual law school catalogs to see which law schools offer what you need.

Career Services and Employment

One of the tests of a good law school is the effort the institution makes to help its students and graduates understand their career options and find satisfying employment. Planning a career in law requires students to integrate their legal education and personal goals in the context of the employment marketplace. Some students begin law school with a clear idea of how they expect to use their legal education (although they may change their minds along the way). Others are uncertain, or see a number of tempting possibilities. The career services office, faculty, and alumni of the school are valuable resources in the process of understanding and selecting among the many opportunities available to lawyers.

The first role of the career services office is to educate students about career opportunities in all sectors, including government and public service, law firms of all sizes and specialties, corporations, and so forth. To accomplish such a task, a law school may arrange panel presentations, meetings with practicing lawyers in different fields, and a library of career information materials. Career services professionals also collect and distribute vital information and resources; teach students job-search strategies, such as effective interviewing skills and employment research; and discuss students' individual interests, options, and presentation.

In performing all of these tasks, the career services office becomes a major marketing and outreach program for its law school and a valuable resource for both law students and graduates as they chart their career paths. One of the most visible career services provided by many law schools is the opportunity to interview with employers on campus for summer and full-time jobs. Ideally, the recruiters should represent a broad range of legal options (small and large firms, government agencies, public interest groups, corporate law departments) and sufficient geographic diversity to meet your needs. Be aware that the number of recruiters at the law school does not necessarily reflect the range of options open to students.

In most schools, only a small percentage of the class gets jobs through on-campus interviewing. Therefore, it is important to investigate the additional support provided by the career services staff and the experiences of the school's students and graduates in finding jobs.

Career services offices are concerned about all students, not just those at the top of the class rankings. Most spend a great deal of time and effort working with students individually and marketing the school to potential employers in order to increase students' options. Here are some questions you may want to ask about a school's career services:

- What programs does the school offer to introduce students to career options? Do they seem interesting, relevant, and timely?

- Are the career-counseling professionals accessible, respected, well-qualified, and supportive?

- Are the school's faculty and graduates involved in educating students about their career options?

- What types of employers, and how many, recruit on campus each year? What are the average number of interviews and offers per student? What percentage of students obtain jobs through the on-campus interviewing process?

- What positions have graduates taken in recent years? What jobs do students take during the summers? In what locales do students and graduates work? Are these employment profiles changing?

- What are the average or median salaries for the school's graduates?

- What percentage of students have accepted positions by graduation; within six months of graduation?

- Does the school offer career counseling and information for its graduates?

■ Transferring to Another Law School

After starting law school, some law students seek to transfer to another law school. This occurs frequently enough to warrant advice and information. There are many reasons that law students seek to transfer, including financial reasons, job relocation of a spouse or partner, or to be closer to family. Occasionally law students will seek a transfer to another law school that they perceive as having a higher status or ranking.

There are several factors that should be taken into account when considering a decision to transfer to another law school and, frequently, a student contemplating transfer should obtain relevant information concerning the consequences of a transfer. First, many of the strongest and most sustaining relationships between lawyers occur during their first year of law school and these relationships last throughout the law student's career. Students often comment on the loss of community and close friendships they made in their first year when they transfer to another law school. Second, students transferring to another law school are often not eligible for scholarships at the new law school. This factor may be significant for students who are considering forgoing a scholarship award at their home law school to transfer to a supposedly "higher ranked" law school. Third, many law school law reviews, journals, and moot court programs do not permit transfer students to be considered for

membership on the law review and moot court teams until after a year at the new law school. This may preclude transferring law students from being considered for law review at all or for selection for the editorial board of the law review, or for selection to a moot court team. Fourth, in many schools, course selection for the fall will already have been completed by the time the student's transfer application is accepted. As a result, there may be limited access to courses that are desired or perhaps needed as prerequisites for later advanced offerings. Fifth, many law schools do not include the transferring law student's grades earned at the prior law school in the class ranking, and some do not permit transfer students to be eligible for GPA-based graduation honors such as Order of the Coif.

The decision whether to transfer schools or remain at the law school of original matriculation is a difficult one. Some law students have no or little choice but to transfer law schools for personal or hardship reasons. Other law students considering a transfer do so to "game" the law school ranking phenomenon. This may be a dangerous gamble because of the negative aspects of law school transfers. Any law student considering transferring should gather as much information as possible concerning the ramifications of the transfer.

Chapter 6: Opportunities in Law for Minority Men and Women

■ A Career in Law for Minority Group Members

The legal profession is cognizant of the minority exclusion and underrepresentation that has historically pervaded American society. The legal system, which greatly values and benefits from multicultural perspectives, acknowledges the importance of diverse legal representation. A law career provides a singular opportunity to effect change both on an individual level—by representing the interests of a client—and on a global level—by setting policy or establishing a precedent in the governmental or business arenas.

Although minority participation in law school and the legal profession has increased over the last three decades, more can and is being done to attract minority men and women to the profession. Outreach efforts by the legal system can and do counteract the shortage of minority lawyers. So does the realization on the part of minority men and women that law can be a rewarding and fulfilling career.

Acquiring a Legal Education

Individual law schools and legal organizations have worked hard to assure continued progress toward alleviating the historic shortage of minority lawyers. For example, the Law School Admission Council established a Minority Affairs Committee, which thus far has spent in excess of $3 million on projects designed to increase the number of minority men and women who attend law schools. The American Bar Association adopted a law school standard calling for specific commitments to provide full opportunities for members of minority groups. The Association of American Law Schools also requires that member schools provide full opportunities in legal education for minorities and has programs to increase the number of minority faculty.

A legal education can provide you with considerable opportunity. You will have spent approximately three years thinking critically, reading broadly, and debating forcefully, and these skills are worthwhile in most everything you do.

Admission to Law School

Admission to law school is competitive—sometimes very competitive. However, getting into law school may be less difficult than you expect. Because there are many law schools and varied admission requirements, it is advisable for you to do sufficient research and be selective. Read and reread the information in this book and study law school catalogs.

Get advice from as many people as you can, including a prelaw advisor, an academic counselor, a minority affairs advisor, and a practicing lawyer.

Let the law schools you have selected know that you are interested. Often a school will have a specific program, a minority organization, designated personnel, or a law student to provide assistance for minority applicants.

Don't be intimidated by the law school admission process. The schools take all aspects of candidates' applications into account when they evaluate them. Personal and educational background are considered, as are undergraduate records, LSAT scores, and letters of recommendation. It is to your advantage to include information on your racial or ethnic identity (even if not requested on the application); such information helps to present a complete picture of you. Similarly, interesting life experiences and past employment experiences also count.

For information on the number and percentages of specific minority students and specific minority faculty at ABA-approved law schools, consult the individual school data pages and "Key Facts for Minority Law School Applicants" on the following pages.

Once You Are in Law School

Once you are in law school, you will encounter a difficult but manageable academic program. Very often minority student groups will advise, assist, and support newcomers. Most minority students perform successfully in law school; they are also able to make effective use of their law degrees, whether practicing law or following other career avenues.

	Total # students (Full-time and Part-time)	Number and Percentage of Minority Students													Total Full-time Faculty, Fall	Total Full-time Faculty, Spring	Number and Percentage of Minority Faculty					
		American Indian/Alaskan Native		Asian/Pacific Islander		Black/African American		Mexican American		Puerto Rican		Hispanic		Total # and % Minority Students				Total # and % Full-time Minority Faculty, Fall		Total # and % Full-time Minority Faculty, Spring		Total # Part-time Minority Faculty, Fall	Total # Part-time Minority Faculty, Spring
	#	#	%	#	%	#	%	#	%	#	%	#	%	#	%	#	#	#	%	#	%	#	#
Alabama																							
Alabama	484	4	0.8	10	2.1	36	7.4	0	0.0	0	0.0	7	1.4	57	11.8	37	37	4	10.3	4	10.3	0	0
Faulkner	274	3	1.1	3	1.1	20	7.3	0	0.0	0	0.0	2	0.7	28	10.2	16	17	3	16.7	3	15.8	0	0
Samford	498	4	0.8	6	1.2	42	8.4	1	0.2	0	0.0	6	1.2	59	11.8	22	24	1	4.3	2	8.0	3	1
Arizona																							
Arizona	463	21	4.5	42	9.1	14	3.0	13	2.8	2	0.4	39	8.4	131	28.3	30	33	6	18.8	6	17.1	2	2
Arizona State	629	28	4.5	26	4.1	21	3.3	37	5.9	2	0.3	53	8.4	167	26.6	51	57	9	17.0	8	13.6	1	1
Arkansas																							
Arkansas	428	8	1.9	16	3.7	77	18.0	2	0.5	1	0.2	6	1.4	110	25.7	24	26	3	12.5	4	15.4	0	0
Arkansas-Little Rock	444	4	0.9	5	1.1	48	10.8	4	0.9	0	0.0	6	1.4	67	15.1	22	22	6	24.0	6	24.0	1	5
California																							
California-Berkeley	879	8	0.9	148	16.8	36	4.1	40	4.6	0	0.0	32	3.6	264	30.0	58	64	8	10.8	10	12.5	2	5
California-Davis	582	2	0.3	133	22.9	9	1.5	33	5.7	1	0.2	14	2.4	192	33.0	36	35	15	40.5	12	33.3	4	3
California-Hastings	1242	4	0.3	299	24.1	31	2.5	35	2.8	5	0.4	41	3.3	415	33.4	57	53	15	23.1	14	23.0	15	6
California-Los Angeles	1019	17	1.7	186	18.3	36	3.5	60	5.9	1	0.1	21	2.1	321	31.5	62	70	13	17.6	12	14.6	2	1
California Western	835	10	1.2	106	12.7	25	3.0	59	7.1	2	0.2	31	3.7	233	27.9	37	37	8	21.6	8	21.6	2	0
Chapman	566	5	0.9	95	16.8	5	0.9	25	4.4	0	0.0	15	2.7	145	25.6	26	26	4	15.4	2	7.7	2	5
Golden Gate	759	4	0.5	120	15.8	20	2.6	15	2.0	2	0.3	22	2.9	183	24.1	30	32	6	18.2	8	22.9	2	14
La Verne	265	1	0.4	31	11.7	16	6.0	41	15.5	0	0.0	0	0.0	89	33.6	15	15	3	18.8	3	18.8	1	0
Loyola Marymount	1297	7	0.5	317	24.4	55	4.2	68	5.2	4	0.3	54	4.2	505	38.9	65	61	12	18.2	11	17.7	20	8
Pacific, McGeorge	1001	8	0.8	120	12.0	32	3.2	42	4.2	1	0.1	24	2.4	227	22.7	50	58	9	15.8	9	14.1	2	3
Pepperdine	639	3	0.5	52	8.1	25	3.9	17	2.7	0	0.0	15	2.3	112	17.5	31	30	6	18.8	4	12.9	1	1
San Diego	1035	11	1.1	159	15.4	32	3.1	54	5.2	7	0.7	39	3.8	302	29.2	49	57	6	10.9	7	11.1	8	7
San Francisco	702	4	0.6	139	19.8	38	5.4	36	5.1	3	0.4	32	4.6	252	35.9	32	32	10	30.3	9	27.3	13	13
Santa Clara	932	4	0.4	243	26.1	46	4.9	0	0.0	0	0.0	85	9.1	378	40.6	35	35	10	19.6	10	19.6	4	3
Southern California	605	2	0.3	118	19.5	52	8.6	50	8.3	2	0.3	14	2.3	238	39.3	41	36	5	11.9	5	13.5	15	15
Southwestern	964	7	0.7	175	18.2	50	5.2	68	7.1	5	0.5	38	3.9	343	35.6	46	45	9	18.4	9	19.1	15	3
Stanford	534	6	1.1	66	12.4	37	6.9	52	9.7	4	0.7	3	0.6	168	31.5	52	51	13	18.6	11	15.7	0	4
Thomas Jefferson	770	4	0.5	56	7.3	36	4.7	33	4.3	8	1.0	21	2.7	158	20.5	38	38	7	17.5	7	17.5	3	1

	Total # Students (Full-time and Part-time)	American Indian/Alaskan Native		Asian/Pacific Islander		Black/African American		Mexican American		Puerto Rican		Hispanic		Total # and % Minority Students		Total Full-time Faculty, Fall	Total Full-time Faculty, Spring	Total # and % Full-time Minority Faculty, Fall		Total # and % Full-time Minority Faculty, Spring		Total # Part-time Minority Faculty, Fall	Total # Part-time Minority Faculty, Spring
	#	#	%	#	%	#	%	#	%	#	%	#	%	#	%	#	#	#	%	#	%	#	#
Western State	449	5	1.1	82	18.3	18	4.0	23	5.1	1	0.2	26	5.8	155	34.5	15	15	5	29.4	5	29.4	3	4
Whittier	673	4	0.6	125	18.6	19	2.8	42	6.2	0	0.0	27	4.0	217	32.2	30	29	1	3.1	1	3.2	6	4
Colorado																							
Colorado	511	15	2.9	43	8.4	20	3.9	15	2.9	1	0.2	24	4.7	118	23.1	30	31	6	18.8	6	18.2	2	2
Denver	1129	39	3.5	56	5.0	54	4.8	0	0.0	0	0.0	63	5.6	212	18.8	53	51	11	19.0	11	19.6	4	4
Connecticut																							
Connecticut	648	4	0.6	25	3.9	38	5.9	3	0.5	20	3.1	24	3.7	114	17.6	43	41	7	14.3	4	8.5	2	1
Quinnipiac	464	3	0.6	24	5.2	11	2.4	0	0.0	0	0.0	13	2.8	51	11.0	28	27	4	12.5	3	9.7	0	2
Yale	579	1	0.2	80	13.8	44	7.6	10	1.7	3	0.5	33	5.7	171	29.5	71	63	7	9.1	9	13.0	1	8
Delaware																							
Widener	985	3	0.3	71	7.2	58	5.9	0	0.0	0	0.0	22	2.2	154	15.6	46	45	3	6.4	3	6.5	3	8
District of Columbia																							
American	1483	15	1.0	172	11.6	122	8.2	37	2.5	14	0.9	143	9.6	503	33.9	82	77	17	20.5	11	14.1	15	16
Catholic	906	3	0.3	68	7.5	44	4.9	3	0.3	6	0.7	37	4.1	161	17.8	46	45	8	17.0	8	17.8	6	7
District of Columbia	235	2	0.9	12	5.1	71	30.2	5	2.1	0	0.0	13	5.5	103	43.8	18	16	9	47.4	9	50.0	11	7
George Washington	1693	8	0.5	166	9.8	146	8.6	0	0.0	0	0.0	118	7.0	438	25.9	90	81	13	13.5	13	14.9	17	19
Georgetown	1978	5	0.3	179	9.0	189	9.6	18	0.9	10	0.5	77	3.9	478	24.2	110	98	13	11.7	13	13.1	5	9
Howard	430	3	0.7	25	5.8	322	74.9	0	0.0	0	0.0	11	2.6	361	84.0	21	18	22	75.9	16	69.6	14	17
Florida																							
Barry	563	4	0.7	24	4.3	29	5.2	3	0.5	0	0.0	51	9.1	111	19.7	25	23	6	23.1	6	24.0	3	1
Florida A&M	541	6	1.1	18	3.3	255	47.1	0	0.0	12	2.2	80	14.8	371	68.6	21	21	20	76.9	20	76.9	10	6
Florida Coastal	1278	15	1.2	53	4.1	95	7.4	4	0.3	8	0.6	58	4.5	233	18.2	46	42	10	21.7	7	16.7	2	2
Florida	1364	3	0.2	68	5.0	80	5.9	0	0.0	0	0.0	128	9.4	279	20.5	61	63	9	13.2	8	11.4	1	1
Florida International	382	2	0.5	9	2.4	37	9.7	1	0.1	0	0.0	158	41.4	206	53.9	18	14	10	45.5	8	44.4	1	4
Florida State	765	6	0.8	33	4.3	43	5.6	0	0.0	12	1.6	48	6.3	143	18.7	44	46	3	6.8	5	10.9	1	2
Miami	1208	3	0.2	51	4.2	84	7.0	0	0.0	0	0.0	142	11.8	280	23.2	51	53	9	16.4	6	10.5	18	25
Nova Southeastern	927	3	0.3	25	2.7	42	4.5	4	0.4	13	1.4	139	15.0	226	24.4	47	54	13	23.2	14	21.5	6	8
St. Thomas	665	1	0.2	31	4.7	60	9.0	7	1.1	9	1.4	165	24.8	273	41.1	31	32	5	14.7	6	17.6	9	15
Stetson	1033	6	0.6	27	2.6	60	5.8	4	0.4	16	1.5	88	8.5	201	19.5	46	44	6	12.8	6	12.2	4	4

Number and Percentage of Minority Students

	Total # students (Full-time and Part-time)	American Indian/Alaskan Native		Asian/Pacific Islander		Black/African American		Mexican American		Puerto Rican		Hispanic		Total # and % Minority Students		Total Full-time Faculty, Fall	Total Full-time Faculty, Spring	Total # and % Full-time Minority Faculty, Fall		Total # and % Full-time Minority Faculty, Spring		Total # Part-time Minority Faculty, Fall	Total # Part-time Minority Faculty, Spring
	#	#	%	#	%	#	%	#	%	#	%	#	%	#	%	#	#	#	%	#	%	#	#
Georgia																							
Emory	674	0	0.0	72	10.7	62	9.2	0	0.0	0	0.0	43	6.4	177	26.3	45	44	6	11.5	6	11.8	0	1
Georgia	670	2	0.3	21	3.1	94	14.0	0	0.0	0	0.0	14	2.1	131	19.6	37	35	6	12.8	3	7.0	1	1
Georgia State	663	3	0.5	33	5.0	73	11.0	0	0.0	0	0.0	19	2.9	128	19.3	36	36	6	14.3	6	14.3	3	5
John Marshall-Atlanta	358	2	0.6	11	3.1	52	14.5	0	0.0	0	0.0	19	5.3	84	23.5	18	17	4	22.2	4	23.5	1	3
Mercer	446	2	0.4	12	2.7	49	11.0	1	0.2	2	0.4	7	1.6	73	16.4	28	28	2	7.1	2	7.1	1	0
Hawai'i																							
Hawai'i	308	7	2.3	187	60.7	6	1.9	4	1.3	2	0.6	4	1.3	210	68.2	19	19	5	25.0	5	25.0	6	15
Idaho																							
Idaho	314	5	1.6	20	6.4	4	1.3	7	2.2	0	0.0	6	1.9	42	13.4	18	16	1	4.8	0	0.0	0	0
Illinois																							
Chicago	600	4	0.7	77	12.8	43	7.2	17	2.8	6	1.0	32	5.3	179	29.8	53	52	6	8.8	7	10.4	1	5
Chicago-Kent	1041	2	0.2	93	8.9	61	5.9	25	2.4	3	0.3	33	3.2	217	20.8	64	62	6	9.1	5	7.7	6	7
DePaul	1070	4	0.4	59	5.5	78	7.3	15	1.4	4	0.4	85	7.9	245	22.9	49	55	7	13.7	10	17.5	1	4
Illinois	626	3	0.5	106	16.9	39	6.2	0	0.0	0	0.0	51	8.1	199	31.8	39	42	5	10.9	6	11.8	3	3
John Marshall	1414	9	0.6	96	6.8	60	4.2	28	2.0	5	0.4	29	2.1	227	16.1	56	53	6	10.7	7	13.2	13	13
Loyola-Chicago	859	2	0.2	62	7.2	39	4.5	17	2.0	1	0.1	16	1.9	137	15.9	41	40	6	14.0	7	16.7	5	5
Northern Illinois	313	1	0.3	16	5.1	27	8.6	4	1.3	2	0.6	17	5.4	67	21.4	16	15	6	28.6	6	30.0	1	0
Northwestern	768	5	0.7	133	17.3	64	8.3	9	1.2	9	1.2	46	6.0	266	34.6	65	56	12	12.0	11	12.1	2	4
Southern Illinois	355	1	0.3	11	3.1	13	3.7	1	0.3	2	0.6	2	0.6	30	8.5	26	23	2	6.9	1	3.8	0	0
Indiana																							
Indiana-Bloomington	649	2	0.3	36	5.5	43	6.6	27	4.2	0	0.0	0	0.0	108	16.6	47	42	5	10.6	4	9.5	0	0
Indiana-Indianapolis	938	1	0.1	19	2.0	54	5.8	8	0.9	4	0.4	14	1.5	100	10.7	41	41	4	9.5	4	9.5	1	1
Notre Dame	571	9	1.6	42	7.4	28	4.9	10	1.8	3	0.5	36	6.3	128	22.4	36	36	6	15.8	6	15.8	2	1
Valparaiso	513	1	0.2	11	2.1	24	4.7	8	1.6	1	0.2	15	2.9	60	11.7	25	25	2	7.7	2	7.7	0	1
Iowa																							
Drake	439	3	0.7	8	1.8	21	4.8	3	0.7	0	0.0	9	2.1	44	10.0	24	25	3	12.0	3	12.0	1	3
Iowa	644	6	0.9	45	7.0	28	4.3	32	5.0	0	0.0	0	0.0	111	17.2	43	39	5	10.6	6	14.0	0	0

Number and Percentage of Minority Students / Number and Percentage of Minority Faculty

School	Total # students (Full-time and Part-time)	American Indian/Alaskan Native #	%	Asian/Pacific Islander #	%	Black/African American #	%	Mexican American #	%	Puerto Rican #	%	Hispanic #	%	Total # and % Minority Students #	%	Total Full-time Faculty, Fall #	Total Full-time Faculty, Spring #	Total # and % Full-time Minority Faculty, Fall #	%	Total # and % Full-time Minority Faculty, Spring #	%	Total # Part-time Minority Faculty, Fall #	Total # Part-time Minority Faculty, Spring #
Kansas																							
Kansas	482	13	2.7	27	5.6	9	1.9	0	0.0	0	0.0	24	5.0	73	15.1	34	32	6	16.2	5	14.3	0	0
Washburn	449	8	1.8	15	3.3	19	4.2	5	1.1	2	0.4	12	2.7	61	13.6	27	26	6	20.7	4	13.8	0	1
Kentucky																							
Kentucky	425	0	0.0	6	1.4	23	5.4	0	0.0	0	0.0	4	0.9	33	7.8	23	21	3	13.0	3	14.3	0	0
Brandeis	398	3	0.8	3	0.8	12	3.0	0	0.0	0	0.0	5	1.3	23	5.8	22	20	2	8.0	3	12.5	2	2
Northern Kentucky	516	3	0.6	5	1.0	19	3.7	0	0.0	0	0.0	13	2.5	40	7.8	25	25	3	11.5	3	11.5	2	0
Louisiana																							
Louisiana State	578	2	0.3	6	1.0	42	7.3	0	0.0	0	0.0	7	1.2	57	9.9	28	34	4	11.1	4	9.3	2	3
Loyola-New Orleans	796	7	0.9	35	4.4	98	12.3	7	0.9	2	0.3	47	5.9	196	24.6	34	30	11	26.2	8	21.1	1	2
Southern	480	0	0.0	5	1.0	267	55.6	0	0.0	0	0.0	4	0.8	276	57.5	29	29	18	62.1	18	62.1	12	12
Tulane	769	1	0.1	39	5.1	51	6.6	5	0.7	6	0.8	21	2.7	123	16.0	47	41	6	10.3	6	11.5	0	1
Maine																							
Maine	262	0	0.0	7	2.7	3	1.1	0	0.0	1	0.4	0	0.0	11	4.2	13	13	0	0.0	0	0.0	0	1
Maryland																							
Baltimore	1032	5	0.5	50	4.8	106	10.3	0	0.0	0	0.0	20	1.9	181	17.5	40	39	9	20.5	9	20.9	12	12
Maryland	826	4	0.5	81	9.8	123	14.9	1	0.1	0	0.0	53	6.4	262	31.7	55	52	12	21.4	9	17.3	7	7
Massachusetts																							
Boston College	781	1	0.1	94	12.0	40	5.1	19	2.4	6	0.8	27	3.5	187	23.9	50	44	8	15.4	8	16.3	4	5
Boston	836	2	0.2	111	13.3	33	3.9	6	0.7	3	0.4	19	2.3	174	20.8	55	59	5	9.1	8	13.3	2	5
Harvard	1719	14	0.8	203	11.8	190	11.1	29	1.7	13	0.8	77	4.5	526	30.6	127	150	19	12.1	20	11.4	1	2
New England	1100	2	0.2	71	6.5	20	1.8	5	0.5	7	0.6	22	2.0	127	11.5	36	36	4	11.1	4	11.1	4	4
Northeastern	626	6	1.0	71	11.3	38	6.1	0	0.0	0	0.0	54	8.6	169	27.0	28	32	7	25.0	8	25.0	5	1
Suffolk	1644	8	0.5	105	6.4	47	2.9	0	0.0	0	0.0	51	3.1	211	12.8	68	66	11	14.3	10	13.9	3	4
Western New England	553	0	0.0	13	2.4	17	3.1	0	0.0	0	0.0	21	3.8	51	9.2	29	24	3	8.8	1	3.4	1	0
Michigan																							
Ave Maria	381	4	1.0	28	7.3	6	1.6	8	2.1	1	0.3	15	3.9	62	16.3	19	19	2	8.0	4	16.0	0	0
Detroit Mercy	729	1	0.1	23	3.2	45	6.2	0	0.0	0	0.0	9	1.2	78	10.7	31	27	3	9.7	2	7.4	2	2
Michigan	1130	27	2.4	144	12.7	79	7.0	0	0.0	0	0.0	64	5.7	314	27.8	67	60	8	10.7	6	8.8	1	4

Number and Percentage of Minority Students | Number and Percentage of Minority Faculty

	Total # students (Full-time and Part-time)	American Indian/Alaskan Native		Asian/Pacific Islander		Black/African American		Mexican American		Puerto Rican		Hispanic		Total # and % Minority Students		Total Full-time Faculty, Fall	Total Full-time Faculty, Spring	Total # and % Full-time Minority Faculty, Fall		Total # and % Full-time Minority Faculty, Spring		Total # Part-time Minority Faculty, Fall	Total # Part-time Minority Faculty, Spring
	#	#	%	#	%	#	%	#	%	#	%	#	%	#	%	#	#	#	%	#	%	#	#
Michigan State	937	13	1.4	37	3.9	47	5.0	0	0.0	0	0.0	24	2.6	121	12.9	39	39	6	14.6	6	14.6	1	1
Thomas M. Cooley	3606	14	0.4	219	6.1	389	10.8	53	1.5	18	0.5	112	3.1	805	22.3	87	82	11	12.5	11	13.3	10	10
Wayne State	670	5	0.7	31	4.6	66	9.9	4	0.6	0	0.0	21	3.1	127	19.0	39	39	6	13.0	6	13.0	0	1
Minnesota																							
Hamline	716	4	0.6	36	5.0	22	3.1	0	0.0	0	0.0	29	4.1	91	12.7	33	30	5	14.3	4	12.9	2	5
Minnesota	801	7	0.9	72	9.0	18	2.2	0	0.0	0	0.0	34	4.2	131	16.4	57	62	5	8.3	7	10.6	5	3
St. Thomas-Minneapolis	443	4	0.9	24	5.4	19	4.3	5	1.1	1	0.2	11	2.5	64	14.4	24	24	5	18.5	5	18.5	4	4
William Mitchell	1103	5	0.5	57	5.2	33	3.0	7	0.6	2	0.2	17	1.5	121	11.0	38	38	6	15.4	6	15.4	54	43
Mississippi																							
Mississippi	505	3	0.6	8	1.6	49	9.7	0	0.0	0	0.0	3	0.6	63	12.5	30	30	5	13.5	5	13.5	0	0
Mississippi College	528	1	0.2	2	0.4	34	6.4	0	0.0	1	0.2	4	0.8	42	8.0	18	18	2	11.1	2	11.1	3	0
Missouri																							
Missouri-Columbia	451	9	2.0	20	4.4	24	5.3	0	0.0	0	0.0	12	2.7	65	14.4	23	23	0	0.0	2	8.7	1	1
Missouri-Kansas City	489	4	0.8	14	2.9	16	3.3	1	0.2	0	0.0	11	2.2	46	9.4	30	23	4	12.5	3	9.7	0	0
St. Louis	945	5	0.5	32	3.4	46	4.9	0	0.0	0	0.0	17	1.8	100	10.6	40	40	4	8.5	4	8.5	0	0
Washington University	800	6	0.8	64	8.0	43	5.4	3	0.4	1	0.1	7	0.9	124	15.5	56	54	5	8.9	5	9.3	8	4
Montana																							
Montana	242	20	8.3	5	2.1	1	0.4	0	0.0	1	0.4	0	0.0	27	11.2	15	15	3	16.7	3	16.7	0	0
Nebraska																							
Creighton	468	3	0.6	15	3.2	10	2.1	13	2.8	2	0.4	3	0.6	46	9.8	26	26	4	14.3	4	14.3	1	1
Nebraska	399	4	1.0	10	2.5	19	4.8	15	3.8	0	0.0	4	1.0	52	13.0	26	27	2	7.7	2	7.4	0	0
Nevada																							
Nevada	471	6	1.3	57	12.1	22	4.7	24	5.1	5	1.1	13	2.8	127	27.0	21	23	7	23.3	7	21.2	1	1
New Hampshire																							
Franklin Pierce	427	1	0.2	37	8.7	17	4.0	0	0.0	1	0.2	15	3.5	71	16.6	22	23	3	12.0	2	8.0	0	0
New Jersey																							
Rutgers-Camden	766	1	0.1	65	8.5	41	5.4	9	1.2	10	1.3	37	4.8	163	21.3	50	50	4	7.1	4	7.1	4	6
Rutgers-Newark	815	2	0.2	102	12.5	120	14.7	9	1.1	30	3.7	49	6.0	312	38.3	37	42	11	28.2	11	25.0	4	4
Seton Hall	1093	2	0.2	93	8.5	37	3.4	4	0.4	13	1.2	35	3.2	184	16.8	53	54	10	18.5	9	16.4	10	9

	Total # students (Full-time and Part-time) #	American Indian/Alaskan Native #	%	Asian/Pacific Islander #	%	Black/African American #	%	Mexican American #	%	Puerto Rican #	%	Hispanic #	%	Total # and % Minority Students #	%	Total Full-time Faculty, Fall #	Total Full-time Faculty, Spring #	Total # and % Full-time Minority Faculty, Fall #	%	Total # and % Full-time Minority Faculty, Spring #	%	Total # Part-time Minority Faculty, Fall #	Total # Part-time Minority Faculty, Spring #
New Mexico																							
New Mexico	343	40	11.7	9	2.6	12	3.5	94	27.4	0	0.0	0	0.0	155	45.2	25	32	12	38.7	15	39.5	2	4
New York																							
Albany	717	0	0.0	57	7.9	32	4.5	3	0.4	9	1.3	18	2.5	119	16.6	47	47	8	16.7	8	16.7	3	4
Brooklyn	1494	2	0.1	221	14.8	88	5.9	12	0.8	18	1.2	53	3.5	394	26.4	60	48	5	8.1	3	5.9	6	5
Buffalo	731	3	0.4	57	7.8	45	6.2	1	0.1	3	0.4	25	3.4	134	18.3	48	46	5	9.3	6	11.5	4	10
Cardozo	1036	3	0.3	109	10.5	39	3.8	15	1.4	10	1.0	39	3.8	215	20.8	50	50	3	5.9	3	5.9	3	3
CUNY	421	1	0.2	66	15.7	30	7.1	0	0.0	2	0.5	32	7.6	131	31.1	27	27	12	41.4	11	37.9	7	4
Columbia	1233	11	0.9	174	14.1	95	7.7	43	3.5	14	1.1	23	1.9	360	29.2	107	92	16	14.5	16	16.3	7	10
Cornell	561	6	1.1	69	12.3	36	6.4	9	1.6	10	1.8	10	1.8	140	25.0	48	44	4	8.3	2	4.5	0	1
Fordham	1512	11	0.7	163	10.8	76	5.0	6	0.4	12	0.8	113	7.5	381	25.2	78	75	12	15.4	12	16.0	17	17
Hofstra	1129	2	0.2	96	8.5	88	7.8	0	0.0	0	0.0	63	5.6	249	22.1	43	46	4	8.9	5	10.6	0	6
New York Law	1511	3	0.2	140	9.3	88	5.8	17	1.1	17	1.1	81	5.4	346	22.9	55	52	7	11.5	7	12.1	8	7
New York	1442	0	0.0	153	10.6	124	8.6	8	0.6	6	0.4	54	3.7	345	23.9	117	104	19	14.1	19	15.3	4	7
Pace	755	1	0.1	69	9.1	21	2.8	2	0.3	6	0.8	31	4.1	130	17.2	35	35	3	7.7	4	10.5	2	2
St. John's	921	2	0.2	89	9.7	54	5.9	5	0.5	8	0.9	52	5.6	210	22.8	46	46	10	20.4	8	17.4	2	2
Syracuse	689	9	1.3	70	10.2	32	4.6	0	0.0	0	0.0	27	3.9	138	20.0	37	40	8	15.1	8	14.0	3	5
Touro	732	4	0.5	59	8.1	76	10.4	0	0.0	0	0.0	28	3.8	167	22.8	33	30	4	11.4	3	9.4	2	2
North Carolina																							
Campbell	342	5	1.5	7	2.0	7	2.0	0	0.0	0	0.0	6	1.8	25	7.3	15	16	1	5.6	0	0.0	0	1
Duke	630	2	0.3	60	9.5	64	10.2	2	0.3	1	0.2	20	3.2	149	23.7	42	45	5	10.0	4	7.5	3	3
North Carolina	712	14	2.0	45	6.3	51	7.2	5	0.7	0	0.0	35	4.9	150	21.1	28	31	3	10.0	5	15.6	1	9
North Carolina Central	537	5	0.9	18	3.4	242	45.1	1	0.2	3	0.6	8	1.5	277	51.6	18	18	12	60.0	11	57.9	7	9
Wake Forest	464	0	0.0	18	3.9	27	5.8	0	0.0	0	0.0	18	3.9	63	13.6	38	39	6	15.4	3	7.5	0	0
North Dakota																							
North Dakota	236	6	2.5	9	3.8	2	0.8	0	0.0	0	0.0	7	3.0	24	10.2	10	8	0	0.0	2	22.2	0	0
Ohio																							
Akron	526	0	0.0	21	4.0	36	6.8	0	0.0	0	0.0	11	2.1	68	12.9	27	28	3	11.1	3	10.7	1	0
Capital	695	1	0.1	14	2.0	49	7.1	0	0.0	0	0.0	11	1.6	75	10.8	32	32	4	11.8	4	11.4	2	4

School	Total # students (Full-time and Part-time)	American Indian/Alaskan Native #	%	Asian/Pacific Islander #	%	Black/African American #	%	Mexican American #	%	Puerto Rican #	%	Hispanic #	%	Total # and % Minority Students #	%	Total Full-time Faculty, Fall #	Total Full-time Faculty, Spring #	Total # and % Full-time Minority Faculty, Fall #	%	Total # and % Full-time Minority Faculty, Spring #	%	Total # Part-time Minority Faculty, Fall #	Total # Part-time Minority Faculty, Spring #
Case Western	673	2	0.3	73	10.8	29	4.3	0	0.0	0	0.0	9	1.3	113	16.8	38	44	4	8.3	4	7.4	12	12
Cincinnati	376	3	0.8	23	6.1	26	6.9	0	0.0	3	0.8	11	2.9	66	17.6	32	28	5	15.6	5	17.9	0	2
Cleveland State	702	3	0.4	26	3.7	54	7.7	0	0.0	0	0.0	18	2.6	101	14.4	38	37	2	5.1	1	2.6	0	0
Dayton	458	4	0.9	12	2.6	22	4.8	5	1.1	4	0.9	8	1.7	55	12.0	28	23	2	7.1	3	13.0	2	1
Ohio Northern	311	1	0.3	8	2.6	19	6.1	0	0.0	0	0.0	3	1.0	31	10.0	21	20	2	9.5	2	10.0	0	0
Ohio State	688	6	0.9	66	9.6	57	8.3	11	1.6	2	0.3	18	2.6	160	23.3	44	39	6	13.0	6	15.0	2	3
Toledo	524	2	0.4	10	1.9	14	2.7	0	0.0	0	0.0	13	2.5	39	7.4	29	27	2	6.9	3	10.3	0	0
Oklahoma																							
Oklahoma	501	52	10.4	22	4.4	28	5.6	19	3.8	0	0.0	1	0.2	122	24.4	36	37	6	16.2	5	12.8	0	0
Oklahoma City	605	41	6.8	21	3.5	17	2.8	28	4.6	0	0.0	0	0.0	107	17.7	25	23	4	13.8	5	17.9	1	3
Tulsa	540	24	4.4	6	1.1	17	3.1	10	1.9	0	0.0	0	0.0	57	10.6	37	37	5	13.5	5	13.5	1	1
Oregon																							
Lewis & Clark	719	10	1.4	69	9.6	16	2.2	15	2.1	3	0.4	20	2.8	133	18.5	40	34	5	9.8	3	6.5	0	1
Oregon	536	7	1.3	42	7.8	20	3.7	14	2.6	0	0.0	16	3.0	99	18.5	22	19	4	16.0	6	27.3	2	0
Willamette	424	7	1.7	18	4.2	3	0.7	6	1.4	0	0.0	2	0.5	36	8.5	25	26	3	9.7	4	12.1	0	1
Pennsylvania																							
Duquesne	652	2	0.3	10	1.5	24	3.7	0	0.0	0	0.0	6	0.9	42	6.4	28	26	2	7.1	2	7.4	0	0
Penn State	608	1	0.2	42	6.9	59	9.7	0	0.0	12	2.0	24	3.9	138	22.7	45	36	4	8.3	4	10.8	5	0
Pennsylvania	762	5	0.7	110	14.4	61	8.0	9	1.2	8	1.0	38	5.0	231	30.3	53	52	5	8.9	6	11.1	4	7
Pittsburgh	731	1	0.1	40	5.5	43	5.9	3	0.4	3	0.4	8	1.1	98	13.4	44	38	8	17.4	4	10.3	2	2
Temple	1004	6	0.6	108	10.8	81	8.1	8	0.8	9	0.9	24	2.4	236	23.5	54	51	13	24.1	13	25.5	12	17
Villanova	729	3	0.4	55	7.5	39	5.3	0	0.0	0	0.0	29	4.0	126	17.3	35	35	5	11.4	4	8.5	4	3
Widener	449	1	0.2	17	3.8	7	1.6	0	0.0	0	0.0	8	1.8	33	7.3	21	20	1	3.8	1	4.0	1	1
Puerto Rico																							
Inter American	833	0	0.0	0	0.0	0	0.0	0	0.0	833	100.0	0	0.0	833	100.0	25	25	27	100.0	27	100.0	42	43
Pontifical Catholic	509	0	0.0	0	0.0	0	0.0	1	0.2	507	99.6	1	0.2	509	100.0	24	24	24	100.0	24	100.0	14	18
Puerto Rico	702	0	0.0	0	0.0	0	0.0	0	0.0	692	98.6	0	0.0	692	98.6	40	37	38	90.5	36	87.8	28	24
Rhode Island																							
Roger Williams	593	2	0.3	27	4.6	19	3.2	2	0.3	3	0.5	16	2.7	69	11.6	24	22	4	13.3	3	11.1	1	0

	Total # of Students (Full-time and Part-time)	American Indian/Alaskan Native		Asian/Pacific Islander		Black/African American		Mexican American		Puerto Rican		Hispanic		Total # and % Minority Students		Total Full-time Faculty, Fall	Total Full-time Faculty, Spring	Total # and % Full-time Minority Faculty, Fall		Total # and % Full-time Minority Faculty, Spring		Total # Part-time Minority Faculty, Fall	Total # Part-time Minority Faculty, Spring
	#	#	%	#	%	#	%	#	%	#	%	#	%	#	%	#	#	#	%	#	%	#	#
South Carolina																							
Charleston	427	3	0.7	6	1.4	23	5.4	0	0.0	0	0.0	1	0.2	33	7.7	18	20	2	9.5	2	8.3	1	0
South Carolina	707	2	0.3	12	1.7	47	6.6	0	0.0	0	0.0	15	2.1	76	10.7	35	33	4	11.1	2	6.1	1	2
South Dakota																							
South Dakota	235	4	1.7	1	0.4	1	0.4	0	0.0	1	0.4	3	1.3	10	4.3	11	11	1	7.1	1	7.1	0	0
Tennessee																							
Memphis	408	2	0.5	6	1.5	63	15.4	0	0.0	0	0.0	3	0.7	74	18.1	18	21	1	5.6	3	14.3	3	3
Tennessee	449	2	0.4	3	0.7	61	13.6	0	0.0	0	0.0	5	1.1	71	15.8	35	34	9	23.1	7	19.4	0	0
Vanderbilt	631	5	0.8	41	6.5	51	8.1	0	0.0	0	0.0	18	2.9	115	18.2	36	34	8	21.1	6	16.7	6	6
Texas																							
Baylor	401	1	0.2	22	5.5	5	1.2	14	3.5	0	0.0	9	2.2	51	12.7	20	21	1	5.0	1	4.8	1	1
Houston	1007	9	0.9	123	12.2	43	4.3	39	3.9	0	0.0	53	5.3	267	26.5	50	48	8	13.1	7	11.9	6	5
St. Mary's	742	12	1.6	34	4.6	16	2.2	98	13.2	4	0.5	61	8.2	225	30.3	29	27	8	21.6	7	18.9	7	6
SMU Dedman	882	8	0.9	85	9.6	38	4.3	12	1.4	1	0.1	55	6.2	199	22.6	46	44	8	16.0	8	16.7	0	0
South Texas	1237	10	0.8	122	9.9	44	3.6	48	3.9	4	0.3	51	4.1	279	22.6	44	42	5	10.9	3	7.0	8	4
Texas	1313	8	0.6	73	5.6	77	5.9	196	14.9	0	0.0	62	4.7	416	31.7	72	82	7	9.5	9	10.7	6	7
Texas Southern	658	6	0.9	43	6.5	327	49.7	148	22.5	0	0.0	21	3.2	545	82.8	35	35	30	81.1	32	82.1	7	18
Texas Tech	702	5	0.7	30	4.3	28	4.0	71	10.1	3	0.4	0	0.0	137	19.5	39	38	7	17.9	6	15.4	3	2
Texas Wesleyan	660	10	1.5	38	5.8	29	4.4	0	0.0	0	0.0	51	7.7	128	19.4	27	28	3	11.1	4	14.3	2	3
Utah																							
Brigham Young	462	10	2.2	34	7.4	8	1.7	8	1.7	1	0.2	23	5.0	84	18.2	17	20	2	11.8	3	15.0	1	1
Utah	391	2	0.5	21	5.4	2	0.5	2	0.5	1	0.3	12	3.1	40	10.2	27	29	5	17.9	5	16.7	1	0
Vermont																							
Vermont	552	8	1.4	15	2.7	39	7.1	1	0.2	1	0.2	15	2.7	79	14.3	40	36	5	11.4	4	10.3	0	1
Virginia																							
Appalachian	369	1	0.3	4	1.1	5	1.4	0	0.0	2	0.5	9	2.4	21	5.7	14	14	3	20.0	3	20.0	0	0
George Mason	751	2	0.3	53	7.1	28	3.7	0	0.0	0	0.0	39	5.2	122	16.2	35	29	5	13.9	4	13.8	4	4
Liberty	155	3	1.9	3	1.9	9	5.8	0	0.0	0	0.0	2	1.3	17	11.0	13	13	1	7.7	1	7.7	0	0

	Total # students (Full-time and Part-time)	American Indian/Alaskan Native		Asian/Pacific Islander		Black/African American		Mexican American		Puerto Rican		Hispanic		Total # and % Minority Students		Total Full-time Faculty, Fall	Total Full-time Faculty, Spring	Total # and % Full-time Minority Faculty, Fall		Total # and % Full-time Minority Faculty, Spring		Total # Part-time Minority Faculty, Fall	Total # Part-time Minority Faculty, Spring
	#	#	%	#	%	#	%	#	%	#	%	#	%	#	%	#	#	#	%	#	%	#	#
Regent	491	3	0.6	18	3.7	25	5.1	0	0.0	0	0.0	13	2.6	59	12.0	22	22	6	23.0	6	23.0	1	0
Richmond	507	1	0.2	13	2.6	35	6.9	0	0.0	0	0.0	1	0.2	50	9.9	28	23	4	12.5	4	15.4	2	1
Virginia	1146	8	0.7	72	6.3	98	8.6	0	0.0	0	0.0	21	1.8	199	17.4	70	66	7	10.0	5	7.6	0	2
Washington and Lee	390	7	1.8	31	7.9	18	4.6	2	0.5	0	0.0	4	1.0	62	15.9	33	37	4	12.1	6	15.8	0	1
William & Mary	607	2	0.3	29	4.8	60	9.9	0	0.0	0	0.0	6	1.0	97	16.0	35	35	3	7.9	3	7.9	2	1
Washington																							
Gonzaga	557	11	2.0	30	5.4	1	0.2	0	0.0	0	0.0	11	2.0	53	9.5	28	30	3	10.3	3	9.7	0	1
Seattle	1090	16	1.5	142	13.0	47	4.3	32	2.9	9	0.8	19	1.7	265	24.3	53	54	15	26.8	12	21.8	4	5
Washington	544	10	1.8	64	11.8	11	2.0	6	1.1	1	0.2	15	2.8	107	19.7	43	40	8	15.7	7	14.6	5	12
West Virginia																							
West Virginia	476	1	0.2	10	2.1	34	7.1	1	0.2	0	0.0	3	0.6	49	10.3	26	26	4	15.4	4	15.4	0	0
Wisconsin																							
Marquette	689	5	0.7	19	2.8	15	2.2	5	0.7	1	0.1	18	2.6	63	9.1	33	33	3	9.1	3	9.1	1	3
Wisconsin	865	24	2.8	59	6.8	68	7.9	42	4.9	11	1.3	21	2.4	225	26.0	54	50	12	21.1	7	13.5	5	3
Wyoming																							
Wyoming	231	1	0.4	5	2.2	3	1.3	9	3.9	0	0.0	0	0.0	18	7.8	16	15	4	23.5	4	23.5	0	0

Number and Percentage of Minority Students

Number and Percentage of Minority Faculty

Chapter 7: ABA's Role in the Accreditation Process

The ABA Role in General

Law schools approved by the American Bar Association (ABA) provide a legal education that meets a minimum set of standards as promulgated by the ABA. Every jurisdiction in the United States has determined that graduates of ABA-approved law schools are able to sit for the bar in their respective jurisdictions. The role that the ABA plays as the national accrediting body has enabled accreditation to become unified and national in scope rather than fragmented, with the potential for inconsistency, among the 50 states, the District of Columbia, the Commonwealth of Puerto Rico, and other territories.

Since its inception in 1878, the American Bar Association has been concerned with improving the quality of legal education. Following numerous studies of the educational programs available in the late 1880s and early 1900s, it was determined that a national process must be developed for ensuring the quality of the education of the prospective lawyer. Consequently, in 1921, the ABA adopted a statement for minimum standards of legal education and instituted a policy of publishing a list of law schools that complied with those standards.

As of February 2007, a total of 195 institutions are approved by the American Bar Association: 194 confer the first degree in law (the JD degree); the other ABA-approved school is the US Army Judge Advocate General's School, which offers an officer's resident graduate course, a specialist program beyond the first degree in law. One of the 195 ABA-approved law schools (Widener) also has a branch campus. Seven law schools are provisionally approved: Charleston School of Law; Faulkner University, Thomas Goode Jones School of Law; Florida A&M University College of Law; John Marshall Law School (Atlanta); University of La Verne College of Law; Liberty University School of Law; and Western State University College of Law.

With an increase in the number of approved law schools, total JD enrollment in approved schools has gone from 98,042 students in 1972 to 141,031 in the fall of 2006. In that same period, enrollment of women increased from 11,878 to 66,085 and minority enrollment increased from 6,730 to 30,557.

The Council, the Standards, and the Accreditation Committee

The Council of the ABA Section of Legal Education and Admissions to the Bar is the US Department of Education recognized accrediting agency for programs that lead to the first professional degree in law. The law school approval process established by the Council is designed to provide a careful and comprehensive evaluation of a law school and its compliance with the *ABA Standards: Rules of Procedure for Approval of Law Schools*. A current copy of the Standards is available on the Section's website at *www.abanet.org/legaled*. Those Standards are reviewed frequently to ensure that they focus on matters that are central to quality legal education. The Council, which ultimately adopts the Standards, has established an extensive process to seek comment on the Standards and possible revisions to the Standards by law school deans, law faculty, university presidents, leaders of the bar and judiciary, and others interested in legal education.

Decisions concerning the approval of a law school and its compliance with the Standards are ultimately made by the Council of the Section of Legal Education and Admissions to the Bar. The Council is comprised of 21 voting members, no more than 10 of whom may be law school deans or faculty members. Other members of the Council include judges, practicing attorneys, one law student, and at least three "public" members who are neither lawyers nor employees of a law school. The Accreditation Committee, which exercises oversight of schools that have been approved by the Council and makes recommendations to the Council concerning a school's application for approval, is similarly constituted.

The Council and the Accreditation Committee are assisted by the 11-person full-time staff of the Office of the Consultant on Legal Education and Admissions to the Bar. Dean John A. Sebert has served as Consultant since September 2000.

Provisional Approval

A law school may not apply for provisional approval by the ABA until it has been in operation for one year. Schools considering applying for provisional approval are strongly encouraged to contact the Office of the Consultant as early as possible, and well before the year in which the school applies for provisional approval. The Consultant or other senior members of the Consultant Office staff meet with representatives of schools seeking provisional approval and provide them with extensive information about the *Standards: Rules of Procedure for Approval of Law Schools* and the accreditation process.

A school must apply for provisional approval after classes have begun in the fall term and before October 15, so that a full site evaluation can be properly scheduled for late in the fall or early in the spring term. The school is required to develop an extensive self-study, which describes the school in detail, contains a critical evaluation of the school's strengths and weaknesses, establishes goals for the school's future progress, and identifies the means of achieving those goals. The school also completes a Site Evaluation Questionnaire that provides much of the information that a site evaluation team needs to ascertain the basic facts concerning the school and its operation.

The Office of the Consultant appoints a site evaluation team of six or seven persons to undertake a site evaluation of the school. The team chairperson is always an experienced site evaluator and often—but not always—a present or former law school dean. The team usually consists of one or two academic law school faculty members, a law librarian, one faculty member with an expertise in professional skills instruction (clinic, simulation skills, or legal writing), one judge or practitioner, and one university administrator who is not a member of a law faculty.

The site evaluation team carefully reviews the materials the school has provided and visits the school for a three-day period, often from Sunday afternoon through Wednesday morning. During that visit the team meets with the dean and other leaders of the faculty and law school administration, with the president and other university administrators (or, in the case of a free-standing law school, with the leadership of the board of trustees), and tries to have one member of the team meet individually with every member of the faculty. The team also visits as many classes as it can during its visit in order to make judgments concerning the quality of instruction, holds an open meeting with students, and meets with student leaders. In addition, the team meets with alumni and members of the bar and judiciary who are familiar with the school.

At the end of the visit (usually on Wednesday morning), the team meets with the dean and the president (or board chair) to provide an oral report of the team's findings. Shortly after leaving the school, the team drafts and finalizes an extensive written site evaluation report. The report covers all aspects of the school's operation, including faculty and administration, the academic program, the student body and their success on the bar examination and in placement, student services, library and information resources, financial resources, and physical facilities and technological capacities.

The site evaluation team does not make judgments or reach conclusions as to whether the school complies with the Standards. Those judgments are made by the Accreditation Committee and, ultimately, the Council. The role of the site evaluation team is to provide a factual report that accurately and completely describes the situation of the school and that provides a comprehensive basis for the judgments that must be made by the Accreditation Committee and the Council.

The site evaluation report is sent to the Office of the Consultant. Then the report is sent to the school, which is given the opportunity to provide written corrections of any factual errors and other comment on the site report. Then the report is sent to the Accreditation Committee, which holds a hearing at which representatives of the school applying for provisional approval appear. After the hearing, the Accreditation Committee makes its recommendation concerning provisional approval to the Council.

A school that applies for provisional approval must establish that it "is in substantial compliance with each of the Standards and presents a reliable plan for bringing the school into full compliance with the Standards within three years after receiving provisional approval." The burden is on the school to establish that it fulfills these requirements. If the Accreditation Committee concludes that a school is in substantial compliance with the Standards and that the school has a reliable plan for coming into compliance, the Committee will recommend that the Council grant provisional approval. If the Committee concludes either that the school is not in substantial compliance or does not have a reliable plan to come into full compliance in three years, it will recommend against provisional approval.

When a school seeks provisional approval, the final decision on the school's application is made by the Council. The Accreditation Committee's findings of fact are binding on the Council unless those findings are not supported by substantial evidence in the record, but the Accreditation Committee's conclusions and recommendations are not binding on the Council.

If the decision of the Council is to grant provisional approval, that decision is transmitted to the House of Delegates for its concurrence or for nonconcurrence and referral back to the Council. If the decision of the Council is to deny provisional approval, the school has the right to appeal to the House of Delegates and ask the House to refer the matter back to the Council. If the House concurs with a Council decision to grant provisional approval, the school immediately becomes provisionally approved. If the House refers the matter back to the Council, the application process continues with the Accreditation Committee and the Council again reviewing the school to determine whether it meets the standards for provisional

approval. In the event of a referral back by the House, the Council's decision after the second referral back is final.

A school that is provisionally approved is entitled to all the rights of a fully approved law school. Similarly, graduates of provisionally approved law schools are entitled to the same recognition that is accorded graduates of fully approved schools.

Obtaining Full Approval

Once a school has obtained provisional approval, it remains in provisional status for at least three years. Unless extraordinary circumstances justify an extension, a school may not remain in provisional status for more than five years. In order to be granted full approval, a school must demonstrate that it is in full compliance with each of the standards; substantial compliance does not suffice. Again, the burden is upon the school to establish full compliance.

During a school's provisional status, the progress of the school is closely monitored. It is visited by a site evaluation team once each year. After each such site visit, a site evaluation report is submitted to the school and the Accreditation Committee. The Committee reviews the site report and the school's response and sends the school a letter that indicates any areas where the Committee concludes the school does not yet fully comply with the Standards.

In the year in which a school is considered for full approval, the process is identical to that undertaken in connection with an application for provisional approval. Decisions on full approval are made only by the Council, in reviewing the findings, conclusions, and recommendations of the Accreditation Committee. The role of the House of Delegates in reviewing Council decisions on full approval is identical to the House's role concerning decisions on provisional approval.

Oversight of Fully Approved Schools

After a school is granted full approval, it undergoes a full site evaluation in the third year after full approval, and then a full sabbatical site evaluation every seven years. The site evaluation process and the review of the site report by the Accreditation Committee is very similar to that described in connection with a school's application for provisional approval.

The Accreditation Committee's actions upon review of a site report on a fully approved school are likely to take one of three forms. If the Committee concludes that the school fully complies with all the standards, it writes the school with that conclusion and indicates that the school remains on the list of approved schools. In the remainder of the cases, the Committee will conclude either that the school does not appear to comply with one or more of the standards, or that the Committee lacks sufficient information to determine whether or not the school complies. In either case the Committee's action letter will indicate with specificity the standard or standards with which the school does not comply, or as to which the Committee lacks sufficient information to determine compliance, and will ask the school by a specified time to provide the information necessary to enable the Committee to determine compliance or to indicate what steps the school has taken to bring itself into compliance.

Chapter 8: Pro Bono Legal Services

Written by the ABA Standing Committee on Pro Bono and Public Service

When society confers the privilege to practice law on an individual, he or she accepts the responsibility to promote justice and to make justice equally accessible to all people. Thus, all lawyers should aspire to render some legal services without fee or expectation of fee for the good of the public (*pro bono publico*). Prospective students should be mindful of this responsibility when considering law as a career. When choosing a law school, they should evaluate whether a particular school will supply the necessary foundation for achieving their goals relating to pro bono. Many schools offer service opportunities through structured pro bono programs. *ABA Standards: Rules of Procedure for Approval of Law Schools* encourages schools to provide opportunities for students to participate in pro bono activities.

The Need for Pro Bono Service

The responsibility to perform pro bono services sets the legal profession apart from other societal roles. Pro bono opportunities offered by law schools teach students that for the economically disadvantaged, the inability to obtain legal services for basic needs can have dire consequences. Students learn firsthand that for many people, pro bono legal assistance is vital to maintaining minimum levels of basic needs, such as government benefits, income, shelter, utilities, child support, and physical protection. The special skills they develop during law school can significantly benefit the underprivileged. Both law students and lawyers should place greater emphasis on their ethical responsibility to provide pro bono services, in order to bridge the rapidly growing gap between the legal needs of those who cannot afford legal services and the resources available to meet those needs.

Pro Bono Opportunities in Law School

Some law schools offer pro bono opportunities, either through established, structured programs or unsupervised, unstructured programs. Typically, the opportunities cover a wide range of areas, such as family law, children's issues, consumer fraud, AIDS-related problems, housing, immigration, taxation, environmental law, criminal defense, elder law, and death penalty appeals. Pro bono legal service is currently mandatory in approximately 30 law schools. These schools may require a specific number of hours of pro bono legal service as a condition of graduation (e.g., 20–75 hours), or they may require a combination of pro bono legal service, clinical work, and community-based volunteer work. Law schools with voluntary rather than mandatory pro bono service policies encourage students to assist lawyers and legal aid organizations by offering incentives, such as awards at graduation or special notations on law school transcripts, or by making pro bono an important part of a school's culture.

Benefits of Pro Bono Programs in Law School

Pro bono programs help students develop professionalism and an understanding of a lawyer's responsibility to the community. Participation facilitates student involvement in the community and increases the availability of legal services to needy populations. Students also benefit by increasing their knowledge and marketability, gaining practical experience, developing skills, enhancing their reputations, and exploring alternative career opportunities.

Support for Pro Bono and Public Service in Law School

Other organizations also support pro bono and public service in law school, including The Public Service Law Network Worldwide (PSLawNet, formerly Pro Bono Students America/PBSA), the National Association for Public Interest Law (NAPIL), and the Association of American Law Schools (AALS).

Chapter 9: Financing Your Legal Education

■ The Cost of a Legal Education

Legal education is an investment. It can be an expensive one. The cost of a three-year law school education could exceed $150,000. Tuition alone can range from a few thousand dollars to more than $35,000 a year. When calculating the total cost of attending law school, you also have to include the cost of housing, food, books, transportation, and personal expenses. Law schools will determine the student expense budget for you. Today, approximately 80 percent of law school students rely on education loans as their largest source of financial aid for law school. Loans from governmental and private sources at low and moderate interest rates may be available to qualified students.

Financial Aid: A Student's Responsibility

The first step in applying for financial aid for law school is to complete the Free Application for Federal Student Aid (FAFSA), available online at *fafsa.ed.gov*, from your college or university financial aid office, or from the law school to which you are applying. This is a free form and you need not pay to file it. The FAFSA is a need analysis tool developed by the US Government, Department of Education. It asks for information about your income, assets, and other financial resources. The information you provide on the financial aid form will be used to compute how much you (and your spouse) should contribute toward your legal education. Most schools require copies of your actual tax return to verify financial information, so be sure to keep a photocopy for your files; some schools also require students to fill out a supplemental form to be considered for institutional aid. Once the analysis is completed, the financial aid officer at the school can determine what types of aid you will need—such as scholarships, grants, loans, or work-study—to pay your law school expenses.

A brochure published by the Law School Admission Council, *Financial Aid for Law School: A Preliminary Guide*, is available at most law school financial aid offices and at *www.LSAC.org*. For complete and individualized information on financing your law school education, contact the financial aid office at the individual law school(s) to which you apply.

Determining How You Will Pay

There are three basic types of financial aid:

- **Scholarships, Grants, and Fellowships**—Depending on the school's policies, these types of awards—which do not have to be repaid—are given according to need and/or merit. Their availability is quite limited, and they are usually awarded by the law schools themselves. The law schools' admissions and financial aid offices can give you more information.

- **Federal Work-Study**—Federal Work-Study is a program that provides funding for students to work part time during the school year and full time during the summer months. Students sometimes work on campus in a variety of settings or in off-campus nonprofit agencies. Additional information is available from any law school financial aid office. Not all law schools participate in the Federal Work-Study Program.

- **Loans**—Education loans may be awarded directly by the school or through other private agencies. The largest student loan programs are funded or guaranteed by the federal government. Some are awarded on a need basis, while others are not need-based. Federal student loans are usually offered at interest rates lower than consumer loans, and the repayment of principal and interest usually begins after the end of your educational program. Private education loans are offered at market rates. Private loans are approved on the basis of your credit.

Debt Management

An education loan is a serious financial obligation that must be repaid. Dealing with this long-term financial obligation can be made easier through the implementation of sound debt management practices—both while you are in law school and following your graduation.

Credit History

Lenders will analyze your credit report before they approve the loan. Most offer prequalification services on the Internet or by phone. If you have a poor credit history, you may be denied a loan. If there is a mistake on your credit report—and there are often mistakes—you will want adequate time to correct the error. It would be wise to clear up errors or other discrepancies before you apply for a private loan.

You may want to obtain a copy of your credit report so that you can track and clear up any problems. You can order a copy by calling 1.877.322.8228 or go to *www.annualcreditreport.com*. You may also mail a request to Annual Credit Report Request Service, Box 105281, Atlanta, GA 30348-5281.

Living on the Student Expense Budget

While loans may be available to students with good credit histories, the question of how much to borrow is often asked. The maxim, "Live like a student now or you will live like a student later" is a good one to remember. Although students may borrow up to the limit of the school-determined student expense budget, loans do have to be paid back. Consider tracking your current spending habits and comparing them to the budgets at schools of your choice. Look into having a roommate. Learn to cook; food expenses are often budget-busters. For example, $5 a day for lunch totals $25 weekly, $100 monthly, and so on. If you have to borrow to pay for lunch, the real cost is in the neighborhood of $8 a day. Bring a lunch rather than buying one. While law school may be an excellent long-term investment, paying loans in the short term can be a real burden. Remember, not all lawyers will earn the highest reported salaries.

If possible, you should pay off any outstanding consumer debt before entering law school. Student expense budgets do not allow the use of federal education loan funds to pay for prior consumer debt. Entering law school with no credit card debt will make living on your budget easier. Most federal and private education loans allow you to defer payment while you attend law school at least half time. Interest on subsidized loans does not accrue, while unsubsidized and private loans accrue interest while you are in law school. Be sure to inform your prior lenders that you have returned to school.

Loan Default or Delinquency

These two terms are often confused: neither is good. Delinquency occurs when you have begun repayment on a loan or other obligation and have missed one or more payment dates; default generally occurs when a delinquency goes beyond 150–180 days.

Delinquencies appear on credit records and may hinder you from qualifying for an education loan that requires a credit check. Defaults are even more serious and are likely to prevent you from receiving federal financial aid as well as disqualifying you for most other education loans. If you are in a default status, you must take steps to change your status if you wish to apply for a federally guaranteed loan for law school. Contact the servicer of your loan(s) for more information on this subject.

Planning Ahead: Repayment of Your Loan

Your income after law school is an important factor in determining what constitutes manageable payments on your education loans. Although it may be difficult to predict what kind of job you will get (or want) after law school, or exactly what level of salary you will receive, it is important that you make some assessment of your goals for the purpose of sound debt management. In addition to assessing expected income, you must also create a realistic picture of how much you can afford to pay back on a monthly basis while maintaining the lifestyle that you desire. You may have to adjust your thinking about how quickly you can pay your loans back, or how much money you can afford to borrow, or just how extravagantly you expect to live in the years following your graduation from law school.

Your education loan debts represent a serious financial commitment which must be repaid. A default on any loan engenders serious consequences, including possible legal action against you by the lender and/or the government.

Law school graduate debt of $90,000 amounts to almost $1,100 a month on a 10-year repayment plan*. Most lenders offer graduated and income-sensitive repayment plans that lower monthly payment amounts but increase the number of years of repayment. Federal Loan Consolidation allows students to repay their Federal Stafford Loans and William D. Ford Federal Direct Loans on an extended repayment schedule, lasting up to 30 years. Many lenders have good websites with loan repayment and budget calculators.

Strategies for Graduates Seeking Public Interest Careers

Students who seek to work in public service or the public interest sector of the profession face special challenges in financing their legal educations. Salaries for such jobs are comparatively low. Students graduating from law school with the average amount of indebtedness may find that the average entry-level public service or public interest salary ($40,000 for 2005 graduates) will not provide the resources needed to repay their law school loans and cover their basic living expenses.

Students can employ a number of strategies to make it easier (or possible) to pursue a career in the public service or interest sectors. First, students can borrow less during law school (e.g., attend a lower tuition institution; follow some of the debt management strategies mentioned in this chapter). Students may also take advantage of programs developed at some law schools to relieve the debt burden for those interested in public interest careers, including fellowships, scholarships, and loan repayment assistance programs (LRAPs). LRAPs provide financial assistance to law school graduates working in the public interest sector, government, or other lower-paying legal fields. In most cases, this aid is given to graduates in the form of a forgivable loan to help them repay their annual educational debt. Upon completion of the required service obligation, schools will forgive or cancel these loans for program participants.

The number of law schools sponsoring LRAPs is limited: as of December 2006, approximately 106 law schools sponsored such programs. The funding for these programs is limited, so that most schools are unable to provide assistance to all applicants.

LRAPs are also administered by state bar foundations, public interest legal employers, and federal and state governments to assist law graduates in pursuing and remaining in public interest jobs. The federal government offers some options to assist graduates seeking legal careers in public service, including the income contingent repayment option (ICR) of the William D. Ford Federal Direct Loan Program. The income-contingent repayment option is available to all borrowers with federal direct loans and borrowers who consolidate their federally guaranteed loans into Federal Direct Consolidation Loans. Congress created ICR to enable graduates who have high educational debt to take lower-paying community service or public service jobs. The ICR limits annual loan repayment obligations to an affordable percentage of a borrower's income. Any remaining debt is forgiven after 25 years of payments under the ICR plan.

For more information about loan repayment assistance programs or ICR, visit *www.abalegalservices.org/lrap* or *www.equaljusticeworks.org*.

*All figures and calculations are based on current interest rates, loan terms, and fees, and are subject to change.

Chapter 10: Finding a Job

■ Employment Prospects

Because the number of practicing lawyers in the United States continues to increase, it may become more difficult for recent graduates to find jobs in some fields and in certain parts of the country. Opportunities will vary from locality to locality and among legal disciplines. Future lawyers may have to devote considerable time and energy to secure a first job that they consider acceptable. Competition for certain positions will continue to be intense, while opportunities in other fields may expand.

Future demand for people with legal training is almost impossible to predict. Demand for legal services is substantially influenced by the state of the economy. Rising caseloads in the nation's courts and continuing federal and state regulations suggest that the need for lawyers is growing. Whether this expanding need will match or fall short of the parallel growth in the number of practicing lawyers is a question no one can answer with certainty. Lawyers with outstanding academic credentials will continue to obtain desirable positions.

The legal profession itself may adapt to changing job markets by encouraging the entry of lawyers into relatively new fields of law, such as environmental law, intellectual property law, immigration law, and other fields. In addition, certain parts of the country are underrepresented by lawyers.

Career Satisfaction

A job search strategy requires careful self-assessment in much the same way as a school search strategy does. A legal career should meet the interests, abilities, capacities, and priorities of the individual lawyer. Career satisfaction is a result of doing what you like to do, and being continually challenged by it. It is up to you to determine what skills you are comfortable using, and to discern which skills are required in the specialties or types of practice you are considering.

Gathering Information

Take advantage of any programs and workshops offered by the career services office at your law school. (See page 19 for more on the role of the career services office.) Place your name on file in the office, and be sure to maintain contact with the staff even after you leave school. NALP—The Association for Legal Career Professionals™ is an important source of information (see page 867 for details). Both employers and students are guided in the employment process by NALP's Principles and Standards for Law Placement and Recruitment Activities. These guidelines are promulgated to ensure that students have an adequate opportunity to make decisions about offers of employment without undue pressure and that employers will receive responses from students in a timely manner. Copies of the Principles and Standards are available through each law school or by contacting NALP.

This chapter includes a number of charts and graphs compiled by NALP that provide current information relating to employment of law school graduates.

■ Graduates Acquire Jobs at Various Times

The search for a full-time job is a process that is dictated not only by the effort and commitment of the candidate but also by the unique recruiting practices of various types of employers. Large firms tend to be more structured and predictable than smaller firms.

Summer Clerkship May Lead to First-year Associate Offer

Some law firms (typically the large firms which can predict their needs well in advance) interview on campus in the fall to hire students for the following summer. If a student's performance is acceptable and the hiring needs of the firm have remained consistent with the size of the summer class, the student may receive an offer for a full-time job following graduation. Students receiving such offers make a decision on whether to accept such an offer during the fall of their third year of law school. Some government agencies (typically the Department of Justice and other large agencies) have honors programs which work in a similar manner, although few of those agencies actually conduct on-campus interviews.

Employers Hire in Spring from Third-year Class

Smaller private practice employers and a significant number of public interest and government agencies interview and hire third-year law students during the spring of the student's third year. This timetable enables them to predict more accurately their hiring needs and offers both employers and students an additional semester of law school for hiring/career decisions.

Judicial Clerkships Are a Source of Postgraduation Employment

Jobs as clerks for judges at the local, state, or federal level provide postgraduate employment for about 10.6 percent of law graduates. These job offers typically encompass one or two years and provide invaluable experience in the court system. Judicial clerks balance the advantages of the clerkship experience with the delay of entering full-time practice.

■ Graduates Choose Jobs According to Interests

Members of each graduating class acquire full- and part-time jobs with an array of public and private, legal and nonlegal organizations. Although most graduates obtain jobs as attorneys, not all do. One kind of nonattorney job is a "JD preferred" position, requiring a Juris Doctor and substantial use of legal skills and training. Examples of jobs for which a JD is preferred (and may even be required) include corporate contracts administrator, alternative dispute resolution specialist, government regulatory analyst, FBI special agents, jobs with legal publishers, and jobs in law school career services offices. Other professional but nonlegal jobs do not require a Juris Doctor and may or may not make specific use of legal skills and background. Law graduates have in the past obtained legal, nonlegal, and full- and part-time jobs from the following general types of employers:

- **Private Practice**—includes all positions within a law firm, including solo practitioner, associate, law clerk, paralegal, and administrative or support staff.

- **Public Interest**—includes positions funded by the Legal Services Corporation and others providing civil, legal, and indigent services. Also includes public defenders as well as positions with unions, nonprofit advocacy groups, and cause-related organizations.

- **Government**—includes all levels and branches of government, including prosecutor positions, positions with the military, and all other agencies, such as the Small Business Administration, state or local transit authorities, congressional committees, law enforcement, and social services.

- **Judicial Clerkship**—a one- or two-year appointment clerking for a judge on the federal, state, or local level.

- **Business and Industry**—includes positions in accounting firms; insurance companies; banking and financial institutions; corporations, companies, and organizations of all sizes, such as private hospitals, retail establishments, and consulting and public relations firms; political campaigns; and trade associations.

- **Academic**—includes work as a law professor, law librarian, administrator, or faculty member in higher education or other academic settings, including elementary and secondary schools.

- **Nonlegal Careers for Lawyers**—Law-trained individuals pursue a wide variety of careers, and the skills discussed in the first section of this chapter provide excellent training for law school graduates who pursue directions outside the practice of law itself. Lawyers work in the media; as teachers of college, graduate school, and law school; and in law enforcement, public relations, foreign service, politics, and administration.

■ *Jobs & JD's*—Research From NALP

The charts, tables, and copy in this section were adapted with permission from *Jobs & JD's: Employment and Salaries of New Law Graduates, Class of 2005* (NALP). Almost 92 percent of all 2005 graduates from ABA-accredited law schools reported employment status, and salary information was reported for 67 percent of those employed full time.

■ Types of Employment

Class of 2005[†]
(as of February 15, 2006)

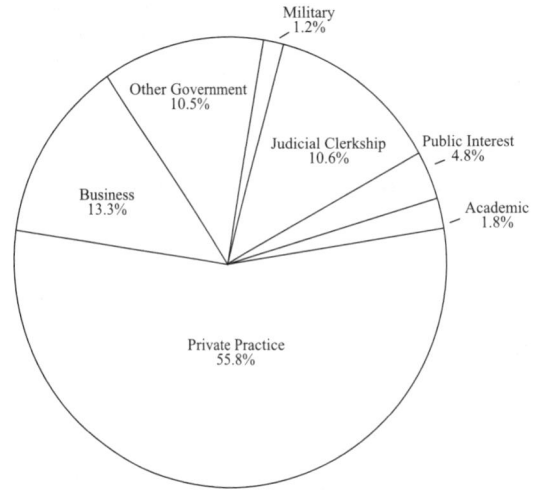

[†]Based on 35,112 graduates.
Note: The category for unknown employer type, representing 2.1% of jobs, is not shown.

■ Salary as an Employment Factor

The national median salary for the class of 2005 was $60,000, up almost $5,000 over that for the class of 2004. The median has more than doubled since 1985, when a national median was first compiled, with much of that increase occurring since the mid-nineties.

The highest-paying jobs were the exception rather than the rule: Although salaries of more than $75,000 accounted for 36 percent of the salaries reported, salaries of $55,000 or less were more common, accounting for just under half of the salaries. This is in spite of the fact that since 1996 the share of salaries of more than $70,000 has increased, from 15 percent to 40 percent, while the proportion of salaries which were $40,000 or less has decreased from 53 percent to 17 percent.

The vast majority of graduates—89.6 percent of those for whom employment status was known—were employed as of February 15, 2006. In the last eight years, the employment market for new law school graduates has remained relatively strong and remarkably stable, standing close to or above an 89 percent employment rate.

Median Starting Salaries

	Private Practice	Business	Government
Atlanta	$100,000	$63,500	$48,500
Boston	$125,000	$68,000	$38,500
Chicago	$125,000	$65,500	$44,000
Houston	$110,000	$62,000	$50,000
Los Angeles	$125,000	$68,500	$55,000
New York City	$125,000	$79,000	$50,000
Philadelphia	$110,000	$56,000	$45,000
San Diego	$70,200	$65,000	$55,053
San Francisco	$125,000	$65,000	$57,000
Washington, DC	$125,000	$60,000	$54,636

Note: Figures reflect full-time jobs only.

Note: The median is the midpoint in a ranking of salaries reported. However, because so many reported salaries are identical and especially cluster at round dollar amounts, such as $50,000, the median should generally be interpreted as the point at which half the salaries are at or above that figure and half are at or below it.

Differences in Salary Medians by Job and Employer Type

	Bar Passage Required	JD Preferred	Other Professional
All Types	$60,000	$55,000	$60,000
Academic	$45,000	$45,000	$45,325
Business	$60,000	$60,000	$65,600
Private Practice	$85,000	$50,000	$40,000
Government	$46,000	$47,000	$55,000
Public Interest	$40,000	$43,000	$40,000

Note: Figures reflect full-time jobs only.

■ Geography as an Employment Factor

Geographic considerations provide yet another perspective on the placement of new law graduates.

Jobs by City

The 20 cities reporting the largest number of jobs accounted for 43 percent of all jobs with a known location. Of these 20 cities listed in the table at right, 12 correspond to the 20 largest cities in terms of population. The three largest cities in the country—New York, Los Angeles, and Chicago—continue to be major employment centers for new law graduates.

Eight of the 20 cities providing the most jobs, however, are not among the largest cities in the country. Some of these, such as Cleveland and Pittsburgh, are older industrial cities that have been eclipsed in population by the rapidly growing cities of the south and west. Even though Washington, DC, does not rank as one of the 20 largest cities in terms of population, its importance in the legal job market is unlikely to diminish. Not surprisingly, New York City accounts for by far the largest number of jobs with location reported, just over 9 percent of the total.

Jobs by State

States vary widely in the number of jobs each provides, again reflecting the distribution of the total population. However, the top 10 states in terms of total reported jobs taken by law graduates have remained the same over the past six years, with New York and California consistently ranked first and second.

Number of Jobs by Region*—Full- and Part-time Jobs
Number of Jobs = 33,969

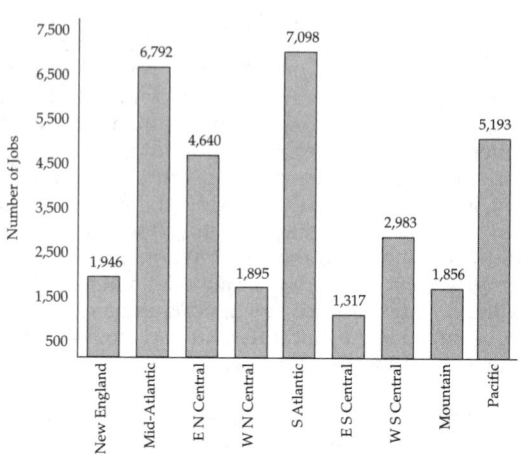

Note: Jobs in foreign locations—249 jobs—are not shown.
*See page 39 for US Census Bureau Regions.

Cities with the Largest Number of Jobs Reported

City	Number of Jobs
New York	3,165
Washington, DC	1,844
Chicago	1,505
Los Angeles	1,025
Houston	773
Boston	737
San Francisco	581
Philadelphia	568
Atlanta	516
San Diego	464
Dallas	451
Minneapolis/St. Paul	412
Miami	389
Seattle	383
Columbus	300
Cleveland	289
Pittsburgh	288
Indianapolis	264
Phoenix	255
Sacramento	250

Place of Work Versus Place of School

Nationally, about 77 percent of jobs were accepted by graduates who had attended law school in the same region. Comparing the location of graduates' law school training with the location of their first job provides an understanding of the extent to which each geographic market attracts and absorbs graduates from within that market. The data collected here (see page 39) do not allow for various factors (such as the perceived attractiveness of each market and individual preferences) to be isolated. Nonetheless, the data can provide insights into geographic variations in the employment market for new law graduates and two components of that market—the supply of new graduates and the demand for new graduates. The accompanying table shows that regions with the highest percentage of jobs going to regional graduates are also the regions where the total supply of graduates exceeded the number of jobs taken by the largest margin. This finding suggests that there is a correlation between a region's supply of graduates and the extent to which employers hired from that supply.

States in Which the Largest Number of Jobs Were Taken—2000–2005

Rank	2000	2001	2002	2003	2004	2005
1	New York	New York	New York	New York	New York	New York
2	California	California	California	California	California	California
3	Texas	Texas	Texas	Texas	Illinois	Texas
4	Washington, DC	Washington, DC	Washington, DC	Illinois	Texas	Illinois
5	Illinois	Illinois	Illinois	Florida	Washington, DC	Florida
6	Florida	Florida	Florida	Washington, DC	Florida	Washington, DC
7	Pennsylvania	Pennsylvania	Pennsylvania	Pennsylvania	Pennsylvania	Pennsylvania
8	Ohio	Ohio	Ohio	Ohio	Ohio	Ohio
9	Massachusetts	Massachusetts	Massachusetts	Massachusetts	Massachusetts	Massachusetts
10	New Jersey	New Jersey	New Jersey	New Jersey	New Jersey	New Jersey

Jobs and Graduates by Region

	New England	Mid-Atlantic	East North Central	West North Central	South Atlantic	East South Central	West South Central	Mountain	Pacific	Total
Graduates with Known Employment Status	3,220	6,705	6,280	2,500	8,071	1,557	3,462	1,543	5,831	39,169
Graduates with Known Job Location[†]	2,815	5,737	5,499	2,230	7,116	1,419	2,915	1,361	4,877	33,969
Jobs Reported in Region	1,946	6,792	4,640	1,895	7,098	1,317	2,983	1,856	5,193	33,720
Graduates Staying in Region	1,541	4,828	3,944	1,630	5,228	1,003	2,534	1,117	4,128	25,953
Percentage of Jobs to Region Graduates	79.2	71.1	85.0	86.0	73.7	76.2	84.9	60.2	79.5	77.0
Percentage of Graduates Staying in Region	54.7	84.2	71.7	73.1	73.5	70.7	86.9	82.1	84.6	77.0
Ratio of Graduates to Jobs	1.65	0.99	1.35	1.32	1.14	1.18	1.16	0.83	1.12	1.16

[†]Includes foreign locations.

US Census Bureau Regions

Region	States Included
New England	CT, ME, MA, NH, RI, VT
Mid-Atlantic	NJ, NY, PA
East North Central	IL, IN, MI, OH, WI
West North Central	IA, KS, MN, MO, NE, ND, SD
South Atlantic	DE, DC, FL, GA, MD, NC, SC, VA, WV
East South Central	AL, KY, MS, TN
West South Central	AR, LA, OK, TX
Mountain	AZ, CO, ID, MT, NV, NM, UT, WY
Pacific	AK, CA, HI, OR, WA

Career Placement and Bar Passage Chart

| | Career Placement | | | | | | | | | | | | | | Bar Passage* | | |
| | Employment Status | | | | | Type of Employment | | | | | | Location | | | | | |
	% Employment Status Known	% Employed	% Pursuing Graduate Degree	% Unemployed - Seeking	% Unemployed - Not Seeking	% in Law Firms	% in Business & Industry	% in Government	% in Public Interest	% in Judicial Clerkships	% in Academia	% Employed in State	% Employed in Foreign Nations	# States where employed	State where most take exam	% Pass rate for first-time test takers	% State's overall pass rate for first-time test takers
Alabama																	
Alabama	100.0	93.6	2.1	1.6	2.7	58.3	11.4	12.6	8.0	8.6	1.1	70.3	0.0	18	AL	97	79
Faulkner	100.0	95.9	2.0	2.0	0.0	76.6	6.4	6.4	0.0	4.3	4.3	97.9	0.0	2	AL	87	79
Samford	98.3	91.2	4.7	2.4	1.8	67.7	12.9	9.0	1.3	7.1	0.0	65.2	0.0	11	AL	91	79
Arizona																	
Arizona	99.3	95.4	0.7	3.3	0.0	46.9	4.8	26.9	2.8	17.2	1.4	75.9	0.0	12	AZ	82	71
Arizona State	98.8	93.9	1.2	0.6	4.2	61.3	5.8	14.8	6.5	9.0	2.6	83.9	0.0	13	AZ	65	71
Arkansas																	
Arkansas	100.0	75.9	9.3	5.6	2.5	57.7	17.1	17.9	3.3	1.6	2.4	74.0	0.0	10	AR	75	75
Arkansas-Little Rock	96.4	79.2	4.7	1.9	0.9	56.0	11.9	16.7	3.6	9.5	2.4	81.0	0.0	10	AR	65	75
California																	
California-Berkeley	99.3	93.8	1.7	1.0	3.4	69.1	1.8	1.5	13.2	14.0	0.4	72.1	1.1	24	CA	87	62
California-Davis	97.7	87.8	0.6	1.7	7.0	62.9	7.9	9.3	8.6	7.9	3.3	89.4	1.3	12	CA	72	62
California-Hastings	98.3	90.4	0.7	2.2	6.6	64.8	9.8	11.4	4.9	6.8	1.6	85.4	0.0	23	CA	84	62
California-Los Angeles	100.0	93.7	0.7	0.3	5.3	68.0	8.5	6.3	5.3	9.9	1.4	84.9	1.1	19	CA	88	62
California Western	90.5	84.7	2.2	1.9	2.6	63.0	16.2	10.6	4.9	3.8	1.5	70.6	0.4	23	CA	61	62
Chapman	94.6	86.2	5.7	0.8	1.6	50.0	28.3	8.5	4.7	3.8	1.9	91.5	0.9	5	CA	57	62
Golden Gate	100.0	63.6	3.3	6.5	1.6	50.4	23.9	8.5	6.0	4.3	2.6	76.9	0.0	6	CA	43	62
La Verne	43.2	75.0	0.0	12.5	6.2	66.7	25.0	8.3	0.0	0.0	0.0	100.0	0.0	0	CA	27	62
Loyola Marymount	100.0	95.1	0.3	1.0	1.0	61.8	20.4	7.8	5.4	2.7	0.5	92.5	0.0	9	CA	73	62
Pacific, McGeorge	100.0	91.8	2.1	2.1	1.8	54.1	12.9	14.5	5.3	4.6	7.9	89.4	0.0	12	CA	65	62
Pepperdine	99.1	81.7	3.1	1.8	13.4	61.2	18.6	8.2	1.6	7.1	1.1	71.0	0.0	25	CA	74	62
San Diego	91.3	83.0	6.4	3.2	2.8	60.7	16.2	13.7	3.8	2.6	0.4	79.9	0.9	19	CA	80	62
San Francisco	95.9	97.4	1.1	1.1	0.5	64.7	11.4	7.1	8.7	1.6	1.6	92.9	1.6	5	CA	73	62
Santa Clara	99.0	85.9	1.7	3.4	9.1	62.1	15.6	13.3	3.9	1.2	1.6	81.2	2.3	13	CA	66	62
Southern California	99.0	92.9	1.0	1.0	5.1	64.1	12.5	6.5	4.9	9.8	1.6	87.5	0.0	12	CA	81	62
Southwestern	94.4	89.1	0.0	2.5	4.6	59.8	19.7	9.4	2.8	1.6	1.6	89.0	0.0	13	CA	68	62
Stanford	100.0	98.1	0.0	1.2	0.0	64.8	3.8	1.3	3.8	25.8	0.6	45.3	1.9	25	CA	87	62
Thomas Jefferson	85.2	83.2	3.6	4.1	1.5	45.4	25.8	12.9	9.8	3.7	1.8	63.2	1.8	24	CA	41	62
Western State	83.0	91.0	1.3	3.8	3.8	66.2	9.9	12.7	4.2	2.8	4.2	97.2	0.0	4	CA	27	62
Whittier	96.5	91.0	1.8	1.4	2.7	48.0	35.6	6.9	5.0	1.0	3.5	84.2	0.5	15	CA	39	62
Colorado																	
Colorado	99.4	97.0	0.6	0.0	2.4	49.1	11.3	20.1	1.3	17.0	0.6	79.2	0.0	23	CO	89	76
Denver	99.2	90.9	4.4	0.6	4.1	45.3	15.2	17.3	4.6	8.2	2.1	72.6	1.8	31	CO	70	76
Connecticut																	
Connecticut	98.1	95.8	0.5	1.4	1.9	56.2	13.3	8.9	2.0	17.7	2.0	67.0	0.0	21	CT	90	82
Quinnipiac	97.6	91.5	3.5	1.5	1.5	38.3	21.9	14.2	2.2	7.7	10.4	68.9	0.0	15	CT	81	82
Yale	99.5	97.0	2.5	0.0	0.5	36.6	2.6	2.6	5.7	51.0	1.5	5.7	3.1	24	NY	94	74
Delaware																	
Widener	91.1	82.1	3.3	6.2	1.6	40.9	24.2	13.1	2.0	17.5	0.8	23.0	0.0	12	PA	71	78
District of Columbia																	
American	100.0	91.2	4.0	1.1	2.7	42.3	18.2	12.8	8.1	17.4	1.2	44.7	1.2	31	MD	80	74
Catholic	99.0	88.4	1.7	3.1	2.7	35.7	17.1	27.9	4.3	13.2	1.2	46.9	0.0	23	MD	72	74

| | Career Placement | | | | | | | | | | | | | | Bar Passage* | | |
| | Employment Status | | | | | Type of Employment | | | | | | Location | | | | | |
	% Employment Status Known	% Employed	% Pursuing Graduate Degree	% Unemployed - Seeking	% Unemployed - Not Seeking	% in Law Firms	% in Business & Industry	% in Government	% in Public Interest	% in Judicial Clerkships	% in Academia	% Employed in State	% Employed in Foreign Nations	# States where employed	State where most take exam	% Pass rate for first-time test takers	% State's overall pass rate for first-time test takers
District of Columbia	94.3	82.0	2.0	2.0	14.0	51.2	19.5	7.3	12.2	4.9	4.9	39.0	0.0	12	MD	50	74
George Washington	99.4	97.3	1.4	0.6	0.0	52.3	10.0	15.7	3.0	10.0	0.8	35.6	1.1	32	NY	88	74
Georgetown	98.6	94.0	1.9	0.6	3.6	66.0	5.1	7.7	4.3	14.5	0.0	35.5	2.5	35	NY	93	74
Howard	99.0	96.0	1.5	1.5	0.0	43.0	13.0	18.7	6.7	14.5	2.6	29.5	0.0	22	NY	68	74
Florida																	
Barry	92.8	87.8	0.0	2.2	1.1	57.0	22.8	10.1	6.3	0.0	3.8	77.2	2.5	14	FL	60	71
Florida A&M	90.9	100.0	0.0	0.0	0.0	46.0	22.0	24.0	8.0	0.0	0.0	94.0	0.0	4	FL	54	71
Florida Coastal	98.1	89.9	1.9	1.9	0.6	50.0	16.2	17.6	12.7	2.1	0.7	75.4	0.0	19	FL	80	71
Florida	100.0	87.3	5.3	0.5	4.5	57.8	9.1	19.5	7.6	5.5	0.3	82.7	0.6	12	FL	83	71
Florida International	96.1	83.7	4.1	0.0	4.1	68.3	4.9	9.8	14.6	2.4	0.0	90.2	0.0	4	FL	78	71
Florida State	99.6	95.6	1.1	0.4	2.9	50.6	6.5	25.3	8.0	2.7	3.4	80.8	1.1	20	FL	79	71
Miami	94.5	92.6	3.2	0.5	1.3	64.5	10.8	9.9	9.9	4.0	0.0	72.2	0.0	21	FL	78	71
Nova Southeastern	97.1	80.8	3.7	2.2	1.8	61.2	16.0	10.0	6.4	3.2	2.3	85.8	0.0	11	FL	64	71
St. Thomas	100.0	67.3	6.7	4.2	1.2	64.0	9.9	13.5	8.1	2.7	1.8	95.5	0.0	5	FL	53	71
Stetson	99.2	93.2	2.1	2.6	1.3	58.4	9.1	19.6	5.5	5.9	0.9	90.9	0.0	12	FL	77	71
Georgia																	
Emory	100.0	93.5	1.6	2.0	2.8	64.9	8.7	10.0	2.6	11.3	0.9	43.3	0.0	23	GA	96	84
Georgia	99.0	95.8	2.1	0.0	1.0	63.6	5.4	9.2	4.3	14.7	2.7	76.1	0.5	14	GA	91	84
Georgia State	98.4	92.0	2.1	1.1	4.8	70.3	9.9	14.0	4.1	0.6	1.2	90.7	0.0	12	GA	92	84
John Marshall-Atlanta	93.9	93.5	2.2	2.2	2.2	48.8	23.3	18.6	4.7	4.7	0.0	97.7	0.0	2	GA	52	84
Mercer	100.0	93.9	3.4	2.7	0.0	62.6	11.5	7.9	7.2	10.1	0.7	80.6	0.0	13	GA	90	84
Hawai'i																	
Hawai'i	95.0	88.5	1.0	3.1	6.2	41.2	12.9	10.6	4.7	28.2	1.2	82.4	1.2	10	HI	87	79
Idaho																	
Idaho	100.0	86.6	3.1	3.1	3.1	34.5	9.5	22.6	8.3	21.4	2.4	56.0	2.4	14	ID	80	81
Illinois																	
Chicago	100.0	94.6	0.5	1.5	3.4	71.5	2.6	2.6	1.0	20.7	1.6	31.6	1.0	26	IL	96	85
Chicago-Kent	97.3	86.8	2.2	2.5	6.6	62.8	18.4	11.2	2.9	3.2	1.1	82.7	1.1	20	IL	87	85
DePaul	97.7	93.7	0.7	2.3	1.7	55.3	18.0	11.3	7.7	2.1	1.4	89.4	0.0	17	IL	84	85
Illinois	100.0	90.9	3.5	2.2	2.2	62.7	14.4	9.6	3.8	6.7	2.4	66.0	1.0	20	IL	90	85
John Marshall	96.6	84.3	4.4	4.1	3.3	62.5	18.2	13.0	1.3	2.0	2.9	84.4	0.0	20	IL	77	85
Loyola-Chicago	99.3	90.7	1.8	2.5	3.2	58.4	14.5	16.1	3.5	5.9	1.6	82.0	0.0	19	IL	89	85
Northern Illinois	96.0	93.7	0.0	1.1	0.0	49.4	18.0	19.1	9.0	0.0	4.5	88.8	0.0	9	IL	84	85
Northwestern	100.0	96.2	1.1	0.0	2.3	71.4	8.6	3.5	2.7	13.7	0.0	44.3	1.2	28	IL	95	85
Southern Illinois	98.3	79.8	1.7	8.4	0.0	64.2	7.4	20.0	1.1	2.1	4.2	62.1	0.0	13	IL	90	85
Indiana																	
Indiana-Bloomington	99.0	90.3	2.4	2.4	1.9	58.8	11.2	13.9	2.7	7.5	3.7	39.6	0.0	26	IN	88	82
Indiana-Indianapolis	100.0	94.8	0.4	2.8	0.0	52.9	16.8	19.7	3.4	3.4	0.8	90.3	0.0	14	IN	77	82
Notre Dame	98.5	93.9	1.5	3.6	0.5	61.6	8.6	11.4	2.2	15.1	1.1	7.6	1.1	33	IL	93	85
Valparaiso	99.5	86.2	1.1	6.3	0.5	56.4	14.1	16.0	3.7	6.7	1.2	47.9	0.0	20	IN	88	82
Iowa																	
Drake	100.0	90.2	2.3	1.5	6.1	55.5	17.6	11.8	4.2	8.4	2.5	67.2	0.0	24	IA	79	85
Iowa	99.2	89.6	3.8	0.8	5.8	57.5	14.2	9.0	5.6	9.4	2.1	30.5	0.9	29	IA	91	85
Kansas																	
Kansas	97.8	94.4	1.1	3.4	1.1	49.1	14.8	15.4	8.3	8.3	3.6	49.7	1.2	20	KS	83	82
Washburn	98.2	89.4	4.3	1.9	1.9	52.8	19.4	15.3	5.6	4.2	2.8	52.8	0.0	19	KS	78	82

| | Career Placement | | | | | | | | | | | | | | | Bar Passage* | |
| | Employment Status | | | | | Type of Employment | | | | | | Location | | | | | |
	% Employment Status Known	% Employed	% Pursuing Graduate Degree	% Unemployed - Seeking	% Unemployed - Not Seeking	% in Law Firms	% in Business & Industry	% in Government	% in Public Interest	% in Judicial Clerkships	% in Academia	% Employed in State	% Employed in Foreign Nations	# States where employed	State where most take exam	% Pass rate for first-time test takers	% State's overall pass rate for first-time test takers
Kentucky																	
Kentucky	100.0	93.4	2.2	0.7	2.2	59.1	7.9	6.3	5.5	18.9	2.4	70.1	0.8	19	KY	88	77
Brandeis	99.1	92.0	0.0	1.8	3.6	60.2	9.7	11.7	9.7	6.8	1.9	76.7	0.0	13	KY	86	77
Northern Kentucky	97.0	87.7	1.5	4.6	0.8	51.8	21.1	8.8	9.6	6.1	2.6	46.5	0.0	8	KY	78	77
Louisiana																	
Louisiana State	94.3	86.7	6.1	6.1	1.1	58.6	11.5	7.6	0.0	19.7	1.3	83.4	1.3	13	LA	84	70
Loyola-New Orleans	100.0	91.3	4.2	0.0	4.5	61.0	12.0	14.9	2.9	8.3	0.8	66.4	0.8	23	LA	78	70
Southern	95.7	73.9	3.6	19.8	2.7	52.4	7.3	20.7	8.5	9.8	1.2	79.3	0.0	10	LA	38	70
Tulane	98.5	91.3	3.3	3.0	2.4	59.0	10.8	12.1	4.3	5.9	0.3	25.6	0.7	33	LA	81	70
Maine																	
Maine	96.9	88.2	5.4	2.2	0.0	47.6	19.5	9.8	11.0	12.2	0.0	70.7	0.0	11	ME	83	80
Maryland																	
Baltimore	80.3	90.5	1.3	5.6	1.3	36.2	15.2	19.0	2.4	25.2	1.0	81.0	0.0	11	MD	65	74
Maryland	99.6	90.6	4.5	1.3	3.6	39.1	9.4	13.9	5.0	27.2	4.0	68.8	0.0	17	MD	80	74
Massachusetts																	
Boston College	100.0	96.9	1.2	0.8	0.4	62.0	10.4	9.2	3.6	13.2	1.2	42.4	1.6	28	MA	90	82
Boston	99.3	94.4	4.2	0.0	1.1	64.7	5.6	11.2	3.7	8.9	5.9	43.5	1.9	26	MA	94	82
Harvard	100.0	95.6	2.5	0.0	1.8	63.6	5.1	2.3	2.8	25.2	0.9	12.1	2.3	40	NY	95	74
New England	94.3	72.7	2.7	7.4	1.0	46.8	14.4	18.1	1.9	6.9	2.8	60.6	0.5	16	MA	73	82
Northeastern	98.4	91.1	0.0	2.6	3.7	45.1	15.6	9.8	16.2	12.7	0.6	75.7	1.2	21	MA	94	82
Suffolk	98.6	87.1	2.3	6.5	1.3	46.0	20.6	17.0	4.1	9.4	1.4	77.9	0.2	25	MA	80	82
Western New England	86.9	85.6	2.2	6.5	0.7	38.7	26.9	22.7	3.4	4.2	2.5	38.7	1.7	16	CT	66	82
Michigan																	
Ave Maria	98.6	88.2	0.0	7.4	2.9	51.7	15.0	11.7	6.7	11.7	3.3	43.3	1.7	23	MI	89	74
Detroit Mercy	99.2	89.2	0.0	4.2	1.7	68.2	13.1	12.1	1.9	1.9	2.8	75.7	17.8	5	MI	69	74
Michigan	100.0	93.4	2.5	0.3	3.9	71.5	1.8	3.3	8.9	13.1	1.2	13.6	2.7	31	NY	97	74
Michigan State	93.3	85.7	4.8	4.1	0.3	48.4	15.5	14.3	5.2	7.5	2.8	63.1	2.0	25	MI	78	74
Thomas M. Cooley	68.0	81.6	3.2	9.4	0.6	49.5	16.8	14.7	5.4	9.7	1.8	44.4	1.1	30	MI	71	74
Wayne State	77.3	71.2	0.0	28.8	0.0	71.8	11.5	7.6	0.8	6.1	0.8	93.1	0.0	7	MI	80	74
Minnesota																	
Hamline	92.9	88.0	2.2	2.7	1.6	44.1	30.4	9.3	5.6	8.7	1.9	77.6	0.0	17	MN	82	89
Minnesota	99.2	96.1	1.5	0.4	1.5	52.2	12.4	8.8	4.8	18.9	2.8	59.4	1.6	27	MN	99	89
St. Thomas-Minneapolis	100.0	93.2	1.1	3.4	0.0	32.9	24.4	7.3	12.2	23.2	0.0	87.8	0.0	9	MN	85	89
William Mitchell	98.1	90.5	0.7	2.9	2.0	46.2	27.1	5.8	5.4	12.6	1.1	90.3	0.0	17	MN	85	89
Mississippi																	
Mississippi	96.0	91.6	1.6	4.2	1.0	60.0	7.4	13.1	3.4	16.0	0.0	63.4	1.1	18	MS	92	87
Mississippi College	99.3	91.3	2.2	2.9	0.0	63.5	7.9	7.9	2.4	17.5	0.8	76.2	0.0	11	MS	82	87
Missouri																	
Missouri-Columbia	98.6	91.9	5.1	1.5	1.5	58.4	8.0	10.4	6.4	12.0	2.4	87.2	0.0	12	MO	90	89
Missouri-Kansas City	100.0	96.1	0.0	0.6	0.0	66.2	7.4	4.1	5.4	13.5	2.7	73.6	0.7	8	MO	86	89
St. Louis	100.0	91.8	2.0	1.2	0.4	67.9	14.3	8.9	3.6	2.2	2.7	71.4	0.4	18	MO	87	89
Washington University	99.6	96.5	2.2	0.4	0.9	69.7	6.0	10.1	3.2	7.8	0.0	36.2	0.9	33	MO	91	89
Montana																	
Montana	96.2	92.1	3.9	1.3	2.6	50.0	4.3	18.6	2.9	24.3	0.0	71.4	0.0	12	MT	92	91

| | Career Placement | | | | | | | | | | | | | | Bar Passage* | | |
| | Employment Status | | | | | Type of Employment | | | | | | Location | | | | | |
	% Employment Status Known	% Employed	% Pursuing Graduate Degree	% Unemployed - Seeking	% Unemployed - Not Seeking	% in Law Firms	% in Business & Industry	% in Government	% in Public Interest	% in Judicial Clerkships	% in Academia	% Employed in State	% Employed in Foreign Nations	# States where employed	State where most take exam	% Pass rate for first-time test takers	% State's overall pass rate for first-time test takers
Nebraska																	
Creighton	100.0	93.5	2.0	2.6	2.0	52.4	23.1	12.6	2.8	7.0	2.1	58.7	0.0	22	NE	75	86
Nebraska	96.4	92.5	2.2	2.2	0.7	51.6	17.7	13.7	8.9	5.6	2.4	59.7	0.8	24	NE	89	86
Nevada																	
Nevada	92.2	87.4	2.5	2.5	3.4	47.1	16.3	11.5	7.7	17.3	0.0	90.4	0.0	8	NV	69	65
New Hampshire																	
Franklin Pierce	100.0	86.8	0.9	2.8	3.8	48.9	22.8	8.7	4.3	5.4	7.6	32.6	2.2	26	NH	61	60
New Jersey																	
Rutgers-Camden	95.0	91.1	2.4	6.1	0.4	36.9	8.9	6.2	0.9	40.0	0.9	35.1	0.0	12	NJ	81	77
Rutgers-Newark	96.6	93.3	0.4	2.7	3.1	41.4	12.4	10.5	3.8	27.6	3.3	68.6	0.0	11	NJ	77	77
Seton Hall	96.9	96.3	0.2	1.0	1.0	38.9	11.1	5.7	1.8	38.9	0.3	68.4	0.8	18	NJ	84	77
New Mexico																	
New Mexico	100.0	91.9	1.0	2.0	2.0	44.0	5.5	24.2	4.4	15.4	3.3	80.2	0.0	10	NM	96	90
New York																	
Albany	100.0	95.9	0.4	0.0	0.4	44.0	24.4	19.7	4.3	5.1	2.6	83.8	0.0	16	NY	78	74
Brooklyn	99.2	92.2	1.0	1.0	5.7	55.5	16.8	14.2	3.5	7.3	0.7	90.7	0.7	17	NY	84	74
Buffalo	98.3	87.3	4.6	1.7	5.5	63.8	10.6	12.6	4.3	6.8	1.4	82.1	1.9	15	NY	77	74
Cardozo	98.9	92.3	1.6	0.8	5.2	60.1	17.9	11.6	4.2	4.2	2.1	83.0	0.3	14	NY	84	74
CUNY	88.6	80.6	2.4	7.3	4.8	27.0	13.0	17.0	26.0	8.0	3.0	75.0	0.0	13	NY	61	74
Columbia	100.0	99.0	0.0	0.7	0.2	78.3	1.0	2.3	4.3	14.1	0.0	61.1	3.5	24	NY	91	74
Cornell	100.0	97.1	1.0	1.9	0.0	70.1	3.9	3.9	2.9	12.7	2.5	53.9	1.0	22	NY	94	74
Fordham	99.6	95.0	2.5	0.4	1.5	77.1	3.1	5.9	1.1	4.6	1.1	60.2	0.7	16	NY	87	74
Hofstra	97.0	85.4	5.9	1.2	4.3	64.1	15.6	12.0	1.8	4.0	0.4	83.3	0.0	13	NY	69	74
New York Law	93.0	92.3	1.0	4.3	2.4	50.5	17.3	9.6	3.0	6.6	0.6	70.1	0.0	18	NY	73	74
New York	100.0	95.6	1.6	0.7	2.2	76.3	0.7	3.7	6.7	12.3	0.0	67.5	0.9	28	NY	93	74
Pace	94.4	91.4	1.8	1.4	4.5	49.3	23.4	11.9	5.5	4.0	5.0	60.2	1.5	8	NY	72	74
St. John's	99.7	88.1	2.0	3.1	6.8	51.0	21.2	18.5	1.9	3.9	3.1	91.1	0.0	15	NY	89	74
Syracuse	98.0	90.8	1.2	1.2	4.8	42.9	19.0	15.9	4.9	12.8	3.5	43.8	2.7	32	NY	69	74
Touro	76.2	86.1	1.4	6.2	0.7	54.8	21.0	12.1	4.8	3.2	4.0	91.9	0.0	7	NY	66	74
North Carolina																	
Campbell	100.0	92.2	0.9	0.9	0.0	78.3	1.9	7.5	2.8	9.4	0.0	91.5	0.0	6	NC	88	71
Duke	100.0	98.1	1.4	0.0	0.5	66.5	5.7	6.1	1.4	17.9	1.9	10.8	1.9	34	NY	94	74
North Carolina	97.8	85.2	4.5	0.9	2.2	58.9	7.4	12.6	5.8	13.2	2.1	56.8	1.1	24	NC	83	71
North Carolina Central	90.7	89.8	4.1	0.0	1.0	58.0	18.2	9.1	10.2	4.5	0.0	86.4	0.0	11	NC	81	71
Wake Forest	98.0	95.3	2.0	1.3	0.0	64.8	7.7	8.5	4.9	12.7	0.7	43.0	0.0	27	NC	93	71
North Dakota																	
North Dakota	96.9	87.1	3.2	1.6	3.2	42.6	5.6	11.1	13.0	25.9	1.9	50.0	0.0	11	ND	94	90
Ohio																	
Akron	98.4	93.5	1.1	3.8	0.5	53.2	24.3	13.9	4.6	2.9	0.6	86.1	0.0	14	OH	79	81
Capital	85.5	84.6	1.0	2.5	1.5	40.6	22.4	22.9	8.8	3.5	1.8	90.6	0.0	11	OH	79	81
Case Western	98.2	96.7	1.9	0.5	0.9	53.6	17.9	14.0	6.3	3.4	3.4	52.2	1.4	27	OH	85	81
Cincinnati	95.9	90.7	3.4	0.8	5.1	48.6	9.3	11.2	11.2	15.0	1.9	61.7	1.9	17	OH	88	81
Cleveland State	98.5	91.1	1.0	1.6	2.1	53.1	21.7	16.6	4.0	1.7	2.9	81.7	1.1	18	OH	71	81
Dayton	96.3	85.4	1.9	6.4	0.0	56.7	19.4	12.7	6.0	3.7	0.7	53.7	0.0	21	OH	80	81
Ohio Northern	94.0	80.8	5.1	1.3	0.0	46.0	9.5	20.6	0.0	7.9	0.0	33.3	0.0	18	OH	84	81
Ohio State	99.1	95.6	2.7	0.4	1.3	49.3	12.1	21.4	6.5	5.1	5.6	68.4	0.0	21	OH	90	81
Toledo	98.0	95.9	1.4	1.4	0.7	48.9	15.8	20.1	2.9	2.2	2.9	62.6	0.7	18	OH	78	81

| | Career Placement | | | | | | | | | | | | | | Bar Passage* | | |
| | Employment Status | | | | | Type of Employment | | | | | | Location | | | | | |
	% Employment Status Known	% Employed	% Pursuing Graduate Degree	% Unemployed - Seeking	% Unemployed - Not Seeking	% in Law Firms	% in Business & Industry	% in Government	% in Public Interest	% in Judicial Clerkships	% in Academia	% Employed in State	% Employed in Foreign Nations	# States where employed	State where most take exam	% Pass rate for first-time test takers	% State's overall pass rate for first-time test takers
Oklahoma																	
Oklahoma	99.4	91.9	2.3	0.0	1.7	67.7	7.6	19.0	2.5	2.5	0.6	70.3	0.6	19	OK	97	90
Oklahoma City	95.5	83.9	1.8	8.3	2.4	50.4	24.8	18.4	0.7	4.3	0.7	68.1	0.0	19	OK	82	90
Tulsa	98.2	78.5	6.7	9.2	0.0	66.4	17.2	10.2	2.3	1.6	2.3	73.4	0.8	17	OK	91	90
Oregon																	
Lewis & Clark	96.0	92.5	0.9	2.3	3.3	48.0	15.2	12.6	12.1	10.1	2.0	64.6	0.5	29	OR	80	76
Oregon	98.2	91.0	2.4	2.4	0.0	42.4	15.2	15.2	7.3	17.2	2.6	55.6	0.0	22	OR	80	76
Willamette	96.9	78.0	2.4	7.9	2.4	59.6	10.1	12.1	4.0	11.1	2.0	61.6	1.0	15	OR	73	76
Pennsylvania																	
Duquesne	87.3	93.0	1.2	4.1	0.6	47.5	19.4	10.0	3.7	8.7	1.2	84.4	0.0	7	PA	68	78
Penn State	97.1	89.2	3.0	2.6	2.2	43.7	12.6	14.1	3.4	17.0	1.9	57.3	0.5	21	PA	80	78
Pennsylvania	100.0	97.5	1.0	0.6	0.6	79.4	2.0	3.3	2.0	12.4	1.0	18.0	1.0	25	NY	95	74
Pittsburgh	99.6	90.3	3.5	0.8	3.9	56.7	20.6	4.7	3.4	11.6	1.7	73.4	0.9	18	PA	83	78
Temple	99.1	91.8	1.3	3.5	3.5	46.6	16.4	11.0	7.5	13.0	2.7	71.6	0.3	18	PA	85	78
Villanova	100.0	91.2	3.6	3.2	2.0	59.0	13.5	8.7	0.9	16.2	0.9	66.4	0.0	15	PA	83	78
Widener	98.0	86.3	4.1	4.1	2.7	41.3	20.6	21.4	4.0	8.7	2.4	80.2	0.0	10	PA	58	78
Puerto Rico																	
Inter American	94.5	90.8	3.4	1.5	0.0	44.4	23.0	25.1	0.0	6.4	1.1	99.5	0.0	0	PR	49	46
Pontifical Catholic	81.7	50.4	4.0	34.4	0.0	36.5	4.8	12.7	0.0	3.2	0.0	98.4	0.0	0	PR	36	46
Puerto Rico	39.9	80.3	1.4	15.5	2.8	50.9	17.5	12.3	0.0	15.8	3.5	0.0	0.0	1	PR	66	46
Rhode Island																	
Roger Williams	89.0	79.5	6.2	6.8	0.7	34.5	26.7	16.4	5.2	17.2	0.0	48.3	0.0	21	RI	60	71
South Carolina																	
Charleston	0.0	0.0	0.0	0.0	0.0	0.0	0.0	0.0	0.0	0.0	0.0	0.0	0.0	0	SC		82
South Carolina	97.5	90.8	3.4	2.9	2.1	52.8	8.8	12.5	3.7	21.8	0.5	82.4	0.5	13	SC	88	82
South Dakota																	
South Dakota	100.0	69.9	2.4	25.3	0.0	44.8	8.6	12.1	3.4	25.9	1.7	62.1	0.0	8	SD	85	84
Tennessee																	
Memphis	100.0	95.1	1.2	1.2	0.6	59.7	2.6	18.8	1.3	7.8	0.6	91.6	0.0	11	TN	91	80
Tennessee	97.8	88.7	3.0	3.0	4.5	56.8	9.3	17.8	4.2	11.9	0.0	76.3	0.0	15	TN	89	80
Vanderbilt	100.0	91.5	4.0	1.0	3.5	76.5	6.0	4.4	1.1	10.9	0.5	26.2	0.0	31	TN	88	80
Texas																	
Baylor	100.0	92.8	2.6	2.6	2.0	68.1	6.4	13.5	1.4	8.5	1.4	87.9	0.7	14	TX	95	80
Houston	98.2	93.2	0.5	1.6	2.4	63.4	18.0	10.7	1.1	3.9	1.4	88.2	0.6	18	TX	84	80
St. Mary's	91.2	91.7	3.7	1.4	2.3	57.0	9.5	18.0	4.5	7.0	1.5	91.5	0.5	10	TX	73	80
SMU Dedman	99.6	93.6	1.5	1.1	3.0	64.1	10.1	16.1	2.0	5.6	2.0	87.1	0.0	15	TX	88	80
South Texas	94.3	80.0	2.6	4.9	1.2	68.1	12.0	12.3	0.7	2.5	0.7	92.8	0.0	10	TX	77	80
Texas	99.8	93.4	0.9	0.9	1.3	64.3	8.0	9.2	3.5	10.4	1.0	74.1	0.8	31	TX	90	80
Texas Southern	93.7	70.3	3.4	4.1	0.0	69.2	13.5	6.7	6.7	1.0	1.0	77.9	1.0	14	TX	63	80
Texas Tech	97.0	97.8	0.0	2.2	0.0	88.3	0.0	6.3	2.3	2.7	0.0	96.4	0.0	4	TX	89	80
Texas Wesleyan	90.1	90.2	0.0	5.5	0.0	44.9	17.7	21.1	2.7	1.4	0.7	86.4	0.7	10	TX	83	80
Utah																	
Brigham Young	100.0	92.9	1.9	1.3	3.2	62.5	5.6	11.8	2.8	16.0	1.4	45.1	0.7	25	UT	93	90
Utah	97.9	92.0	0.0	2.2	2.2	57.9	11.1	14.3	1.6	11.9	1.6	73.0	0.0	17	UT	90	90
Vermont																	
Vermont	100.0	80.4	10.1	1.8	7.7	34.8	25.9	14.1	9.6	12.6	1.5	22.2	1.5	38	VT	66	75

| | Career Placement | | | | | | | | | | | | | | Bar Passage* | | |
| | Employment Status | | | | | Type of Employment | | | | | | Location | | | | | |
	% Employment Status Known	% Employed	% Pursuing Graduate Degree	% Unemployed - Seeking	% Unemployed - Not Seeking	% in Law Firms	% in Business & Industry	% in Government	% in Public Interest	% in Judicial Clerkships	% in Academia	% Employed in State	% Employed in Foreign Nations	# States where employed	State where most take exam	% Pass rate for first-time test takers	% State's overall pass rate for first-time test takers
Virginia																	
Appalachian	65.1	93.0	1.4	2.8	0.0	59.1	12.1	10.6	3.0	10.6	3.0	25.8	0.0	14	TN	71	80
George Mason	100.0	94.9	1.3	0.4	3.4	45.0	17.1	18.9	2.3	11.7	5.0	43.2	1.4	25	VA	77	74
Liberty	0.0	0.0	0.0	0.0	0.0	0.0	0.0	0.0	0.0	0.0	0.0	0.0	0.0	0	VA		74
Regent	96.8	82.7	1.3	6.0	8.0	34.7	21.8	22.6	8.9	4.8	7.3	58.9	0.0	20	VA	68	74
Richmond	100.0	88.5	2.4	3.0	6.1	61.6	5.5	12.3	1.4	18.5	0.7	79.5	0.0	17	VA	85	74
Virginia	98.9	96.3	1.4	0.0	2.3	73.6	1.5	5.0	2.9	16.1	0.0	11.7	2.3	33	NY	96	74
Washington and Lee	93.7	89.5	3.0	1.5	0.0	52.9	8.4	11.8	2.5	20.2	0.8	26.9	0.0	27	VA	93	74
William & Mary	98.9	90.1	2.2	1.7	3.9	46.6	8.0	19.6	5.5	19.6	0.6	35.6	1.2	27	VA	89	74
Washington																	
Gonzaga	100.0	86.1	5.0	2.0	4.0	43.9	24.3	15.0	4.6	8.1	1.7	78.6	0.6	15	WA	71	75
Seattle	100.0	96.6	2.0	0.0	0.6	44.9	28.0	12.2	8.6	5.1	1.2	86.0	0.9	16	WA	78	75
Washington	100.0	90.2	4.3	0.6	4.9	39.5	10.9	16.3	10.9	16.3	4.8	72.1	0.0	15	WA	84	75
West Virginia																	
West Virginia	97.8	92.6	2.2	3.7	0.0	59.5	8.7	4.8	1.6	20.6	0.8	69.8	0.0	15	WV	72	68
Wisconsin																	
Marquette	98.5	94.8	0.0	4.1	0.0	55.4	19.6	9.2	7.1	7.1	1.6	77.7	1.1	17	WI	N/A	77
Wisconsin	99.2	95.9	2.1	0.4	0.4	55.8	6.9	16.9	8.2	7.4	3.0	55.4	1.3	21	WI	N/A	77
Wyoming																	
Wyoming	96.2	82.7	4.0	8.0	5.3	45.2	11.3	11.3	6.5	25.8	0.0	51.6	0.0	14	WY	74	80

*Bar Passage data are for the Summer 2005 and Winter 2006 exams.

New England

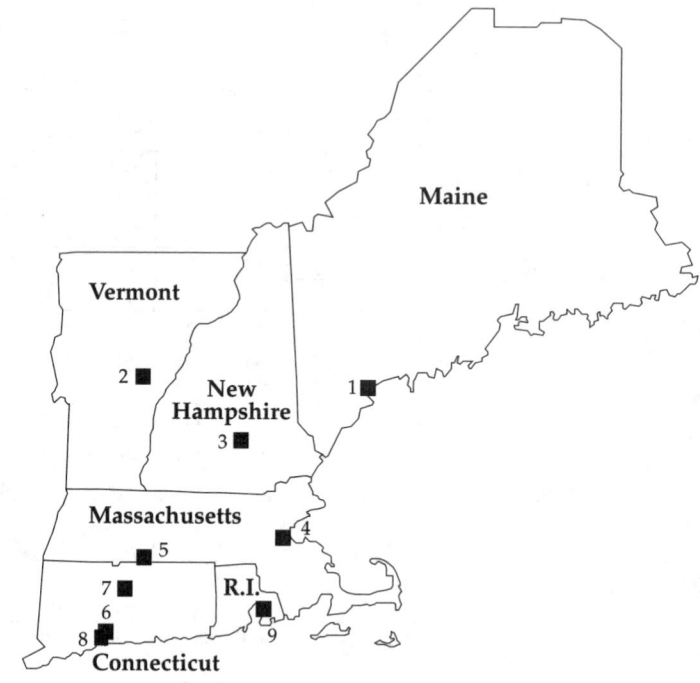

Maine
1. **Portland—Population: 64,249**
    Maine—Enrollment: 259/3

Vermont
2. **South Royalton—Population: 750**
    Vermont—Enrollment: 552/0

New Hampshire
3. **Concord—Population: 40,687**
    Franklin Pierce—Enrollment: 423/4

Massachusetts
4. **Boston—Population: 589,141**
    Boston College—Enrollment: 780/1
    Boston University—Enrollment: 821/15
    Harvard (Cambridge, MA)—Enrollment: 1,719/0
    New England—Enrollment: 719/381
    Northeastern—Enrollment: 626/0
    Suffolk—Enrollment: 1,032/612
5. **Springfield—Population: 152,082**
    Western New England—Enrollment: 384/169

Connecticut
6. **Hamden—Population: 53,200**
    Quinnipiac—Enrollment: 300/164
7. **Hartford—Population: 121,578**
    Connecticut—Enrollment: 464/184
8. **New Haven—Population: 123,626**
    Yale—Enrollment: 576/3

Rhode Island
9. **Bristol—Population: 22,469***
    Roger Williams—Enrollment: 533/60

"Enrollment" represents the numbers of total full-time/total part-time students unless otherwise indicated.

*Population information is derived from the US Bureau of the Census, Population Division, Washington, DC. Data are accurate as of the 2000 Census. City populations reflect the number of people residing in the city proper, not the metropolitan area which would include outlying suburbs as well. Donald P. Racheter, previously director of the prelaw program at Central College and now president of the Public Interest Institute in Iowa, also contributed data for these regional maps.

Northeast

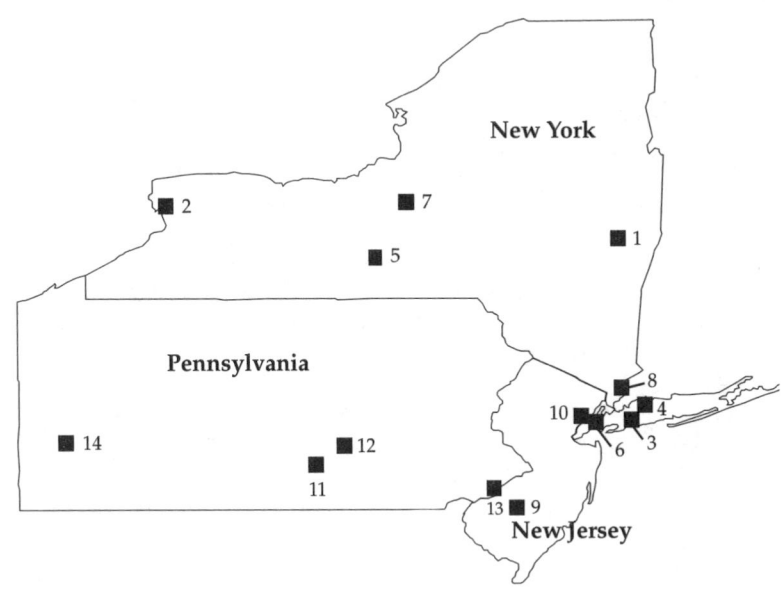

New York

1. **Albany—Population: 95,658**
   Albany—Enrollment: 680/37
2. **Buffalo—Population: 292,648**
   Buffalo—Enrollment: 728/3
3. **Hempstead—Population: 56,554**
   Hofstra—Enrollment: 890/239
4. **Huntington—Population: 18,403**
   Touro—Enrollment: 501/231
5. **Ithaca—Population: 29,287**
   Cornell—Enrollment: 561/0
6. **New York City—Population: 8,008,278**
   Brooklyn—Enrollment: 1,152/342
   Cardozo, Yeshiva University—Enrollment: 952/84
   CUNY—Enrollment: 417/4
   Columbia—Enrollment: 1,230/3
   Fordham—Enrollment: 1,186/326
   New York Law School—Enrollment: 1,150/361
   New York University—Enrollment: 1,442/0
   St. John's (Jamaica, NY)—Enrollment: 724/197
7. **Syracuse—Population: 147,306**
   Syracuse—Enrollment: 683/6
8. **White Plains—Population: 53,077**
   Pace—Enrollment: 499/256

New Jersey

9. **Camden—Population: 79,904**
   Rutgers–Camden—Enrollment: 556/210
10. **Newark—Population: 273,546**
    Rutgers–Newark—Enrollment: 561/254
    Seton Hall—Enrollment: 727/366

Pennsylvania

11. **Carlisle—Population: 17,970**
    Penn State, Dickinson—Enrollment: 540/68
12. **Harrisburg—Population: 48,950**
    Widener—Enrollment: 296/153
13. **Philadelphia—Population: 1,517,550**
    Pennsylvania—Enrollment: 762/0
    Temple—Enrollment: 775/229
    Villanova (Villanova, PA)—Enrollment: 720/9
14. **Pittsburgh—Population: 334,563**
    Duquesne—Enrollment: 465/187
    Pittsburgh—Enrollment: 731/0

Midsouth

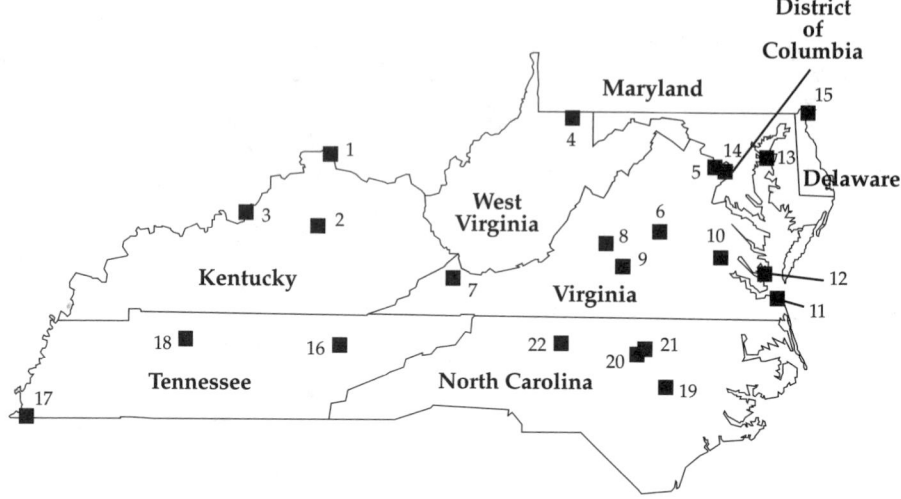

Kentucky
1. **Highland Heights—Population: 6,554**
    Northern Kentucky—Enrollment: 282/234
2. **Lexington—Population: 260,512**
    Kentucky—Enrollment: 425/0
3. **Louisville—Population: 530,000**
    Louis D. Brandeis—Enrollment: 303/95

West Virginia
4. **Morgantown—Population: 26,809**
    West Virginia—Enrollment: 474/2

Virginia
5. **Arlington—Population: 189,453**
    George Mason—Enrollment: 466/285
6. **Charlottesville—Population: 45,049**
    Virginia—Enrollment: 1,146/0
7. **Grundy—Population: 1,105**
    Appalachian—Enrollment: 369/0
8. **Lexington—Population: 6,867**
    Washington and Lee—Enrollment: 390/0
9. **Lynchburg—Population: 65,269**
    Liberty—Enrollment: 155/0
10. **Richmond—Population: 197,790**
    Richmond—Enrollment: 500/7
11. **Virginia Beach—Population: 425,257**
    Regent—Enrollment: 460/31
12. **Williamsburg—Population: 11,998**
    William & Mary—Enrollment: 607/0

Maryland
13. **Baltimore—Population: 651,154**
    Baltimore—Enrollment: 726/306
    Maryland—Enrollment: 673/153

District of Columbia
14. **Washington, DC—Population: 572,059**
    American—Enrollment: 1,216/267
    Catholic—Enrollment: 604/302
    District of Columbia—Enrollment: 235/0
    George Washington—Enrollment: 1,428/265
    Georgetown—Enrollment: 1,592/386
    Howard—Enrollment: 430/0

Delaware
15. **Wilmington—Population: 72,664**
    Widener—Enrollment: 602/383

Tennessee
16. **Knoxville—Population: 173,890**
    Tennessee—Enrollment: 449/0
17. **Memphis—Population: 650,100**
    Memphis—Enrollment: 379/29
18. **Nashville—Population: 545,524**
    Vanderbilt—Enrollment: 630/1

North Carolina
19. **Buies Creek—Population: 2,215**
    Campbell—Enrollment: 342/0
20. **Chapel Hill—Population: 48,715**
    North Carolina—Enrollment: 712/0
21. **Durham—Population: 187,035**
    Duke—Enrollment: 578/52
    North Carolina Central—Enrollment: 426/111
22. **Winston-Salem—Population: 185,776**
    Wake Forest—Enrollment: 454/10

Southeast

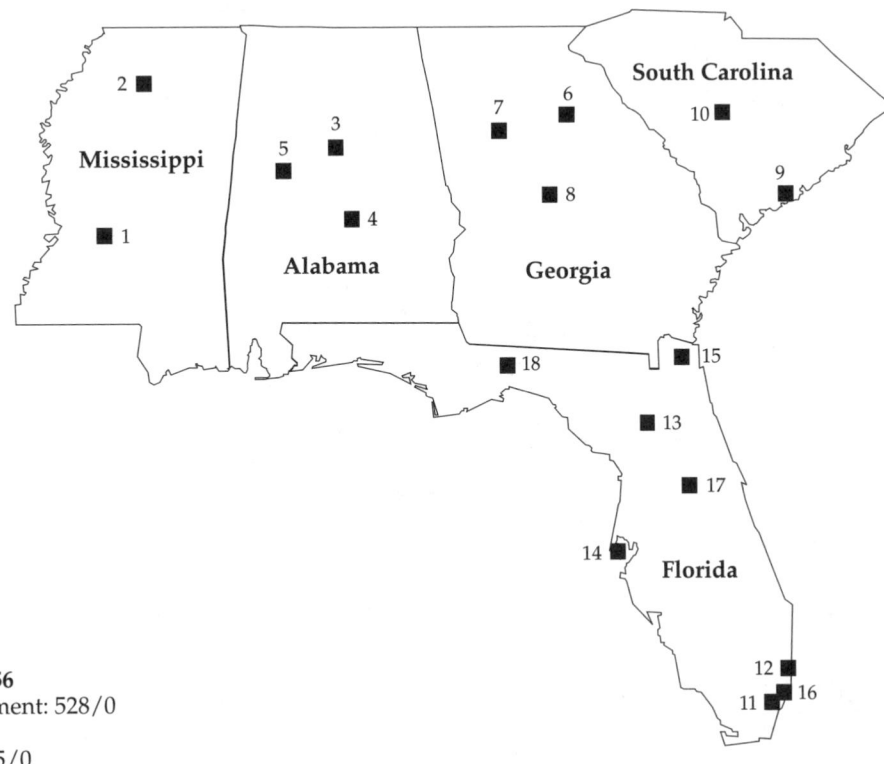

Mississippi
1. **Jackson—Population: 184,256**
   Mississippi College—Enrollment: 528/0
2. **Oxford—Population: 11,756**
   Mississippi—Enrollment: 505/0

Alabama
3. **Birmingham—Population: 242,820**
   Samford—Enrollment: 498/0
4. **Montgomery—Population: 201,568**
   Faulkner—Enrollment: 182/92
5. **Tuscaloosa—Population: 77,906**
   Alabama—Enrollment: 479/5

Georgia
6. **Athens—Population: 100,266**
   Georgia—Enrollment: 670/0
7. **Atlanta—Population: 416,474**
   Emory—Enrollment: 674/0
   Georgia State—Enrollment: 453/210
   John Marshall, Atlanta—Enrollment: 214/144
8. **Macon—Population: 97,255**
   Mercer—Enrollment: 446/0

South Carolina
9. **Charleston—Population: 96,650**
   Charleston—Enrollment: 240/187
10. **Columbia—Population: 116,278**
    South Carolina—Enrollment: 706/1

Florida
11. **Coral Gables—Population: 42,249**
    Miami—Enrollment: 1,163/45
12. **Ft. Lauderdale—Population: 152,397**
    Nova Southeastern—Enrollment: 745/182

13. **Gainesville—Population: 95,447**
    Florida—Enrollment: 1,364/0
14. **Gulfport—Population: 12,527**
    Stetson—Enrollment: 806/227
15. **Jacksonville—Population: 735,617**
    Florida Coastal—Enrollment: 1,066/212
16. **Miami—Population: 362,470**
    Florida International—Enrollment: 237/145
    St. Thomas—Enrollment: 665/0
17. **Orlando—Population: 185,951**
    Barry—Enrollment: 407/156
    Florida A&M—336/205
18. **Tallahassee—Population: 150,624**
    Florida State—Enrollment: 765/0

Puerto Rico
19. **Ponce—Population: 186,475**
    Pontifical Catholic—Enrollment: 351/158
20. **San Juan—Population: 434,374**
    Inter American—Enrollment: 622/211
    Puerto Rico—Enrollment: 521/181

South Central

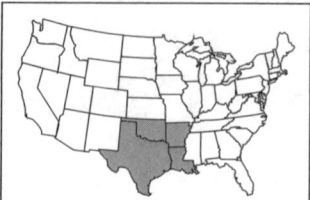

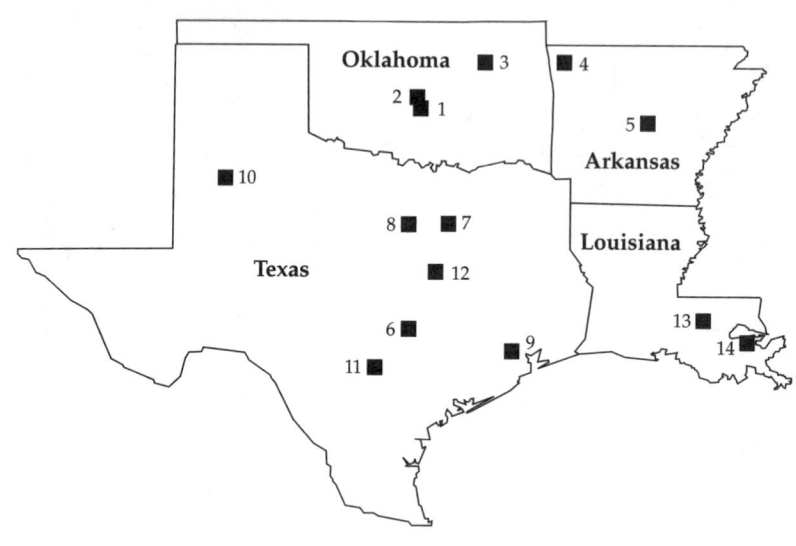

Oklahoma

1. **Norman—Population: 95,694**
   Oklahoma—Enrollment: 501/0
2. **Oklahoma City—Population: 506,132**
   Oklahoma City—Enrollment: 500/105
3. **Tulsa—Population: 393,049**
   Tulsa—Enrollment: 460/80

Arkansas

4. **Fayetteville—Population: 58,047**
   Arkansas–Fayetteville—Enrollment: 428/0
5. **Little Rock—Population: 183,133**
   Arkansas–Little Rock—Enrollment: 283/161

Texas

6. **Austin—Population: 656,562**
   Texas—Enrollment: 1,313/0
7. **Dallas—Population: 1,188,580**
   SMU Dedman—Enrollment: 554/328
8. **Fort Worth—Population: 534,694**
   Texas Wesleyan—Enrollment: 422/238
9. **Houston—Population: 1,953,631**
   Houston—Enrollment: 815/192
   South Texas—Enrollment: 913/324
   Texas Southern—Enrollment: 658/0

10. **Lubbock—Population: 199,564**
    Texas Tech—Enrollment: 702/0
11. **San Antonio—Population: 1,144,646**
    St. Mary's—Enrollment: 742/0
12. **Waco—Population: 113,726**
    Baylor—Enrollment: 401/0

Louisiana

13. **Baton Rouge—Population: 227,818**
    Louisiana State—Enrollment: 566/12
    Southern—Enrollment: 394/86
14. **New Orleans—Population: 484,674**
    Loyola–New Orleans—Enrollment: 653/143
    Tulane—Enrollment: 768/1

Mountain West

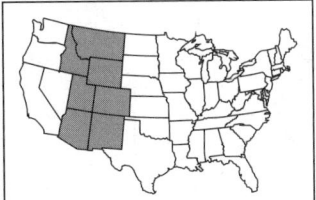

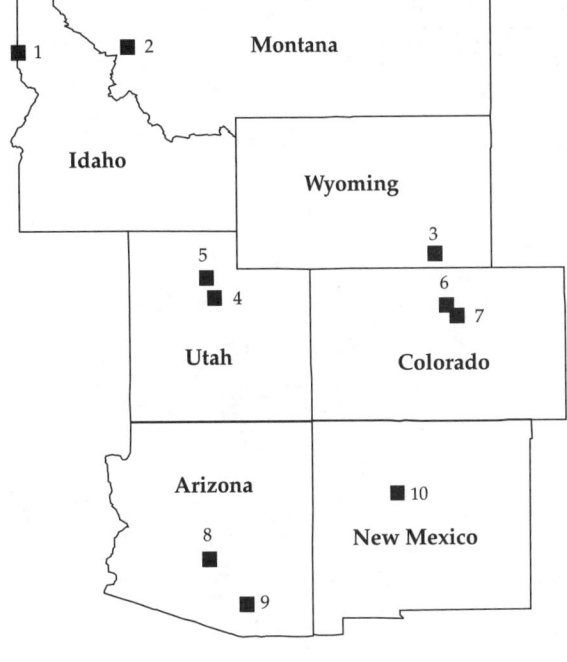

Idaho
1. **Moscow—Population: 21,291**
   Idaho—Enrollment: 313/1

Montana
2. **Missoula—Population: 57,053**
   Montana—Enrollment: 242/0

Wyoming
3. **Laramie—Population: 27,204**
   Wyoming—Enrollment: 231/0

Utah
4. **Provo—Population: 105,166**
   Brigham Young—Enrollment: 460/2
5. **Salt Lake City—Population: 181,743**
   Utah—Enrollment: 391/0

Colorado
6. **Boulder—Population: 94,673**
   Colorado—Enrollment: 511/0
7. **Denver—Population: 554,636**
   Denver—Enrollment: 827/302

Arizona
8. **Tempe—Population: 158,625**
   Arizona State—Enrollment: 629/0
9. **Tucson—Population: 486,699**
   Arizona—Enrollment: 463/0

New Mexico
10. **Albuquerque—Population: 448,607**
    New Mexico—Enrollment: 343/0

Far West

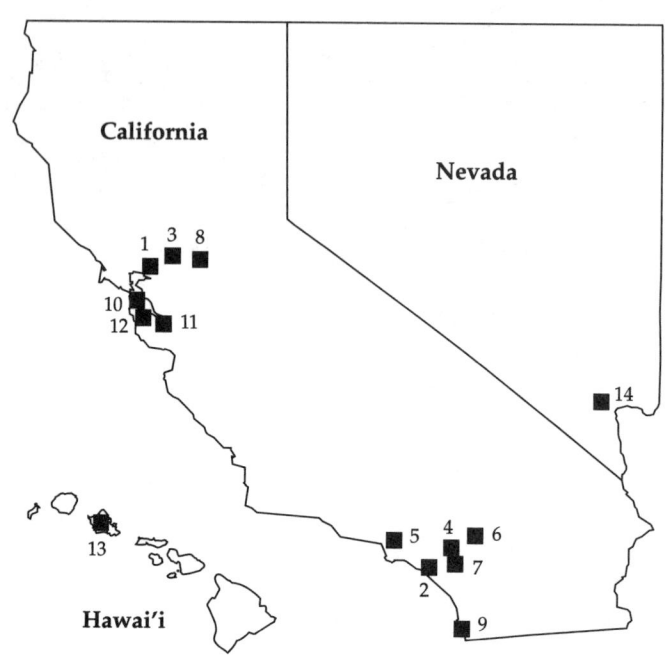

California

1. **Berkeley—Population: 102,743**
   California–Berkeley—Enrollment: 879/0
2. **Costa Mesa—Population: 108,724**
   Whittier—Enrollment: 449/224
3. **Davis—Population: 60,308**
   California–Davis—Enrollment: 582/0
4. **Fullerton—Population: 126,003**
   Western State—Enrollment: 308/141
5. **Los Angeles—Population: 3,694,820**
   California–Los Angeles—Enrollment: 1,019/0
   Loyola Marymount—Enrollment: 994/303
   Pepperdine—Enrollment: 639/0
   Southern California—Enrollment: 605/0
   Southwestern—Enrollment: 676/288
6. **Ontario—Population: 158,007**
   La Verne—Enrollment: 172/93
7. **Orange—Population: 128,821**
   Chapman—Enrollment: 516/50
8. **Sacramento—Population: 407,018**
   Pacific, McGeorge—Enrollment: 605/396

9. **San Diego—Population: 1,223,400**
   California Western—Enrollment: 748/87
   San Diego—Enrollment: 738/297
   Thomas Jefferson—Enrollment: 580/190
10. **San Francisco—Population: 776,733**
    California–Hastings—Enrollment: 1,240/2
    Golden Gate—Enrollment: 602/157
    San Francisco—Enrollment: 562/140
11. **Santa Clara—Population: 102,361**
    Santa Clara—Enrollment: 743/189
12. **Stanford—Population: 13,315**
    Stanford—Enrollment: 534/0

Hawai'i

13. **Honolulu—Population: 371,657**
    Hawai'i—Enrollment: 308/0

Nevada

14. **Las Vegas—Population: 478,434**
    Nevada–Las Vegas—Enrollment: 338/133

Northwest

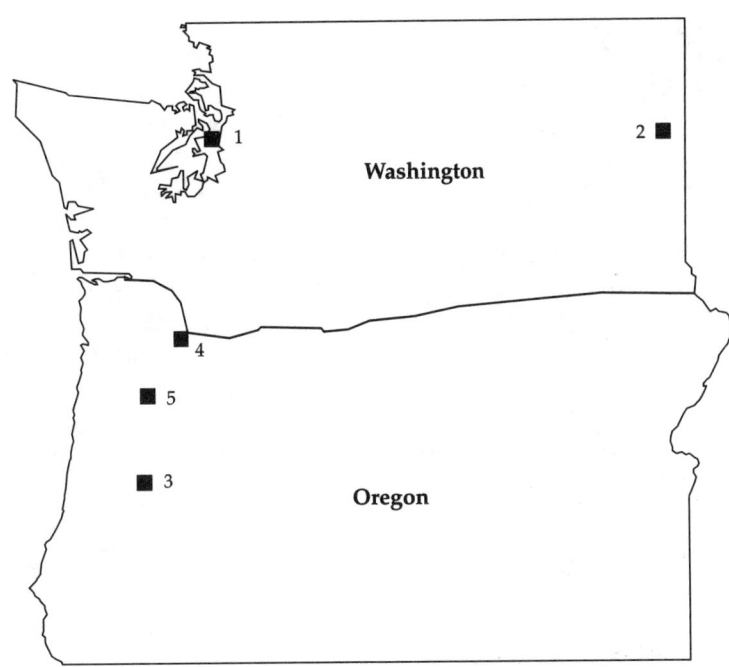

Washington

Oregon

Washington
1. **Seattle—Population: 563,374**
   Seattle—Enrollment: 863/227
   Washington—Enrollment: 544/0
2. **Spokane—Population: 195,629**
   Gonzaga—Enrollment: 535/22

Oregon
3. **Eugene—Population: 137,893**
   Oregon—Enrollment: 536/0
4. **Portland—Population: 529,121**
   Lewis & Clark—Enrollment: 537/182
5. **Salem—Population: 136,924**
   Willamette—Enrollment: 422/2

Midwest

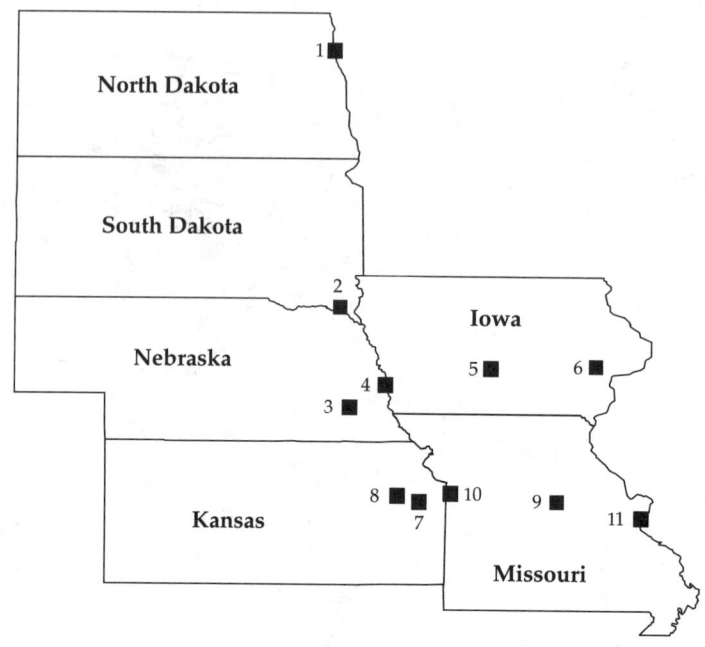

North Dakota
1. **Grand Forks—Population: 49,321**
   North Dakota—Enrollment: 236/0

South Dakota
2. **Vermillion—Population: 9,765**
   South Dakota—Enrollment: 231/4

Nebraska
3. **Lincoln—Population: 225,581**
   Nebraska—Enrollment: 396/3
4. **Omaha—Population: 390,007**
   Creighton—Enrollment: 452/16

Iowa
5. **Des Moines—Population: 198,682**
   Drake—Enrollment: 429/10
6. **Iowa City—Population: 62,220**
   Iowa—Enrollment: 644/0

Kansas
7. **Lawrence—Population: 80,098**
   Kansas—Enrollment: 482/0
8. **Topeka—Population: 122,377**
   Washburn—Enrollment: 449/0

Missouri
9. **Columbia—Population: 84,531**
   Missouri–Columbia—Enrollment: 446/5
10. **Kansas City—Population: 441,545**
    Missouri–Kansas City—Enrollment: 478/11
11. **St. Louis—Population: 348,189**
    St. Louis—Enrollment: 712/233
    Washington University—Enrollment: 788/12

Great Lakes

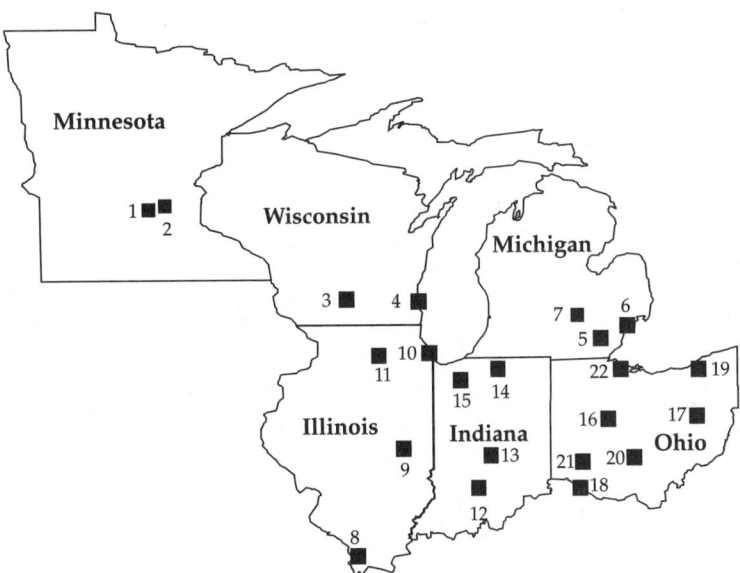

Minnesota
1. **Minneapolis—Population: 382,618**
   Minnesota—Enrollment: 801/0
   St. Thomas—Enrollment: 443/0
2. **St. Paul—Population: 287,151**
   Hamline—Enrollment: 498/218
   William Mitchell—Enrollment: 738/365

Wisconsin
3. **Madison—Population: 208,054**
   Wisconsin—Enrollment: 817/48
4. **Milwaukee—Population: 596,974**
   Marquette—Enrollment: 499/190

Michigan
5. **Ann Arbor—Population: 114,024**
   Ave Maria—Enrollment: 380/1
   Michigan—Enrollment: 1,130/0
6. **Detroit—Population: 951,270**
   Detroit, Mercy—Enrollment: 552/177
   Wayne State—Enrollment: 553/117
7. **Lansing—Population: 119,128**
   Michigan State—Enrollment: 730/207
   Thomas M. Cooley—Enrollment: 560/3,046

Illinois
8. **Carbondale—Population: 20,681**
   Southern Illinois—Enrollment: 353/2
9. **Champaign—Population: 67,518**
   Illinois—Enrollment: 626/0
10. **Chicago—Population: 2,896,016**
    Chicago—Enrollment: 600/0
    Chicago-Kent—Enrollment: 776/265
    DePaul—Enrollment: 725/345
    John Marshall—Enrollment: 1,073/341
    Loyola–Chicago—Enrollment: 607/252
    Northwestern—Enrollment: 768/0
11. **DeKalb—Population: 39,018**
    Northern Illinois—Enrollment: 297/16

Indiana
12. **Bloomington—Population: 69,291**
    Indiana–Bloomington—Enrollment: 648/1
13. **Indianapolis—Population: 781,870**
    Indiana–Indianapolis—Enrollment: 656/282
14. **South Bend—Population: 107,789**
    Notre Dame—Enrollment: 570/1
15. **Valparaiso—Population: 27,428**
    Valparaiso—Enrollment: 462/51

Ohio
16. **Ada—Population: 5,582**
    Ohio Northern—Enrollment: 311/0
17. **Akron—Population: 217,074**
    Akron—Enrollment: 306/220
18. **Cincinnati—Population: 331,285**
    Cincinnati—Enrollment: 376/0
19. **Cleveland—Population: 478,403**
    Case Western Reserve—Enrollment: 670/3
    Cleveland State—Enrollment: 486/216
20. **Columbus—Population: 711,470**
    Capital—Enrollment: 470/225
    Ohio State—Enrollment: 688/0
21. **Dayton—Population: 166,179**
    Dayton—Enrollment: 458/0
22. **Toledo—Population: 313,619**
    Toledo—Enrollment: 344/180

Admission Data

Admission Fall 2006

	App. Fee ($)	Full-time									Part-time									Total							
		75% GPA	Median GPA	25% GPA	75% LSAT	Median LSAT	25% LSAT	# of Applicants	# of Offers	# of Matriculants	75% GPA	Median GPA	25% GPA	75% LSAT	Median LSAT	25% LSAT	# of Applicants	# of Offers	# of Matriculants	75% GPA	Median GPA	25% GPA	75% LSAT	Median LSAT	25% LSAT	Total # of Offers	Total # of Matriculants
Alabama																												
Alabama	35	3.83	3.56	3.29	165	163	159	1,105	354	166	3.39	3.31	3.01	156	154	150	0	0	5	3.80	3.56	3.20	165	162	159	354	171
Faulkner	25	3.35	2.97	2.72	152	149	147	250	155	84	3.51	2.97	2.62	154	150	147	66	29	22	3.35	2.97	2.70	152	149	147	184	106
Samford	50	3.59	3.28	2.96	159	156	154	1,267	458	167	0.00	0.00	0.00	0	0	0	0	0	0	3.59	3.28	2.96	159	156	154	458	167
Arizona																												
Arizona	50	3.77	3.55	3.27	164	162	158	2,482	660	153	0.00	0.00	0.00	0	0	0	0	0	0	3.77	3.55	3.27	164	162	158	660	153
Arizona State	50	3.78	3.54	3.31	162	158	155	2,944	617	165	0.00	0.00	0.00	0	0	0	0	0	0	3.78	3.54	3.31	162	158	155	617	165
Arkansas																												
Arkansas	0	3.71	3.48	3.09	159	155	151	1,334	386	159	0.00	0.00	0.00	0	0	0	0	0	0	3.71	3.48	3.09	159	155	151	386	159
Arkansas-Little Rock	0	3.60	3.28	2.98	157	154	150	1,149	203	93	3.55	3.23	2.88	155	149	147	173	64	41	3.57	3.26	2.98	157	153	149	267	134
California																												
California-Berkeley	75	3.89	3.79	3.65	169	166	163	7,159	791	266	0.00	0.00	0.00	0	0	0	0	0	0	3.89	3.79	3.65	169	166	163	791	266
California-Davis	75	3.73	3.55	3.35	164	162	160	3,493	981	188	0.00	0.00	0.00	0	0	0	0	0	0	3.73	3.55	3.35	164	162	160	981	188
California-Hastings	75	3.74	3.59	3.41	164	162	159	5,526	1,479	421	0.00	0.00	0.00	0	0	0	0	0	0	3.74	3.59	3.41	164	162	159	1,479	421
California-Los Angeles	75	3.80	3.64	3.44	169	166	162	5,834	1,105	336	0.00	0.00	0.00	0	0	0	0	0	0	3.80	3.64	3.44	169	166	162	1,105	336
California Western	45	3.49	3.30	3.07	156	153	151	2,902	1,349	354	3.62	3.43	3.04	157	153	150	198	69	20	3.49	3.30	3.07	156	153	151	1,418	374
Chapman	60	3.52	3.19	2.90	159	158	155	2,309	684	173	3.37	3.23	3.00	154	150	149	0	121	43	3.47	3.19	2.90	159	156	155	805	216
Golden Gate	60	3.45	3.24	3.01	156	153	151	2,818	1,287	219	3.21	2.93	2.72	153	151	150	292	117	45	3.43	3.21	2.94	156	153	151	1,404	264
La Verne	60	3.31	3.05	2.82	150	148	147	510	218	68	3.41	3.10	2.66	149	148	146	211	75	36	3.33	3.05	2.80	150	148	147	293	104
Loyola Marymount	65	3.58	3.41	3.15	163	161	159	4,013	1,248	352	3.58	3.41	3.21	161	159	156	524	129	71	3.58	3.41	3.16	163	160	159	1,377	423
Pacific, McGeorge	50	3.59	3.42	3.15	160	158	155	3,033	1,006	216	3.33	3.10	2.89	156	154	151	375	162	93	3.55	3.32	3.01	159	156	154	1,168	309
Pepperdine	50	3.72	3.54	3.34	163	160	156	3,134	917	213	0.00	0.00	0.00	0	0	0	0	0	0	3.72	3.54	3.34	163	160	156	917	213
San Diego	50	3.56	3.33	3.06	164	161	159	4,436	1,322	252	3.46	3.24	3.00	159	158	156	457	196	90	3.54	3.31	3.04	163	160	158	1,518	342
San Francisco	60	3.55	3.32	3.08	161	159	157	3,090	1,031	178	3.49	3.03	2.79	159	158	155	378	93	57	3.54	3.28	3.00	161	159	156	1,124	235
Santa Clara	75	3.57	3.34	3.12	161	158	156	3,313	1,392	243	3.46	3.25	2.98	161	158	156	326	106	58	3.55	3.32	3.09	161	158	156	1,498	301
Southern California	70	3.75	3.63	3.47	167	166	165	5,670	1,084	217	0.00	0.00	0.00	0	0	0	0	0	0	3.75	3.63	3.47	167	166	165	1,084	217
Southwestern	50	3.59	3.39	3.12	157	155	153	3,011	922	245	3.33	3.13	2.90	156	153	151	544	165	103	3.55	3.29	3.04	157	155	152	1,087	348
Stanford	70	3.96	3.87	3.87	172	170	167	4,567	398	171	0.00	0.00	0.00	0	0	0	0	0	0	3.96	3.87	3.77	172	170	167	398	171
Thomas Jefferson	35	3.29	2.96	2.74	154	151	149	3,032	1,432	254	3.41	3.15	2.80	154	151	148	253	107	40	3.29	2.99	2.75	154	151	149	1,539	294
Western State	50	3.43	3.17	2.87	154	151	149	1,356	574	127	3.47	3.11	2.75	153	150	149	357	105	52	3.44	3.13	2.83	154	151	149	679	179
Whittier	50	3.34	3.15	2.91	155	153	151	2,201	911	175	3.08	2.60	2.38	155	152	151	367	83	31	3.33	3.12	2.82	155	153	151	994	206
Colorado																												
Colorado	65	3.75	3.56	3.37	165	163	159	2,517	661	172	0.00	0.00	0.00	0	0	0	0	0	0	3.75	3.56	3.37	165	163	159	661	172
Denver	60	3.63	3.40	3.11	160	158	155	3,205	824	259	3.61	3.25	2.89	159	154	149	391	144	77	3.62	3.37	3.07	160	157	154	968	336

	Application Fee ($)	Full-time									Part-time									Total							
		75% GPA	Median GPA	25% GPA	75% LSAT	Median LSAT	25% LSAT	# of Applicants	# of Offers	# of Matriculants	75% GPA	Median GPA	25% GPA	75% LSAT	Median LSAT	25% LSAT	# of Applicants	# of Offers	# of Matriculants	75% GPA	Median GPA	25% GPA	75% LSAT	Median LSAT	25% LSAT	Total # of Offers	Total # of Matriculants
Connecticut																												
Connecticut	30	3.66	3.47	3.27	163	161	159	1,814	274	139	3.67	3.41	3.19	159	156	153	784	122	70	3.66	3.45	3.24	162	160	156	396	209
Quinnipiac	40	3.66	3.36	3.00	160	158	157	2,486	648	61	3.39	3.19	2.96	155	154	152	379	163	66	3.54	3.22	2.97	158	156	154	811	127
Yale	70	3.97	3.91	3.83	176	173	170	3,677	249	189	0.00	0.00	0.00	0	0	0	0	0	0	3.97	3.91	3.83	176	173	170	249	189
Delaware																												
Widener	60	3.48	3.12	2.85	155	153	151	1,940	863	216	3.25	2.93	2.60	154	151	150	531	260	121	3.39	3.08	2.78	155	152	150	1,123	337
District of Columbia																												
American	65	3.60	3.42	3.15	163	162	158	7,601	1,877	379	3.50	3.28	3.00	161	160	157	1,063	209	90	3.59	3.38	3.13	163	161	158	2,086	469
Catholic	65	3.55	3.32	3.11	160	158	156	2,679	876	169	3.46	3.26	3.04	158	155	153	722	230	116	3.52	3.31	3.07	159	157	155	1,106	285
District of Columbia	35	3.30	3.10	2.80	153	151	149	1,344	276	95	0.00	0.00	0.00	0	0	0	0	0	0	3.30	3.10	2.80	153	151	149	276	95
George Washington	80	3.81	3.62	3.45	166	165	163	N/A	N/A	426	3.66	3.47	3.28	164	162	161	N/A	N/A	124	3.78	3.59	3.40	166	165	162	2,325	550
Georgetown	75	3.82	3.71	3.47	171	169	167	10,336	2,219	457	3.77	3.54	3.32	167	165	162	901	181	130	3.81	3.70	3.45	171	168	166	2,400	587
Howard	60	3.50	3.20	2.95	154	151	148	2,217	502	139	0.00	0.00	0.00	0	0	0	0	0	0	3.50	3.20	2.95	154	151	148	502	139
Florida																												
Barry	50	3.38	3.16	2.85	151	149	147	2,027	990	173	3.30	3.10	2.70	154	149	148	153	84	26	3.40	3.10	2.80	151	149	148	1,074	199
Florida A&M	20	3.40	3.08	2.78	147	143	141	781	406	167	3.39	2.97	2.60	147	143	138	160	125	80	3.39	3.03	2.75	147	143	140	531	247
Florida Coastal	50	3.49	3.22	2.89	154	151	149	4,940	2,365	622	3.51	3.05	2.83	153	150	148	0	0	16	3.49	3.21	2.89	154	151	149	2,365	638
Florida	30	3.83	3.66	3.42	161	159	155	2,535	1,044	447	0.00	0.00	0.00	0	0	0	0	0	0	3.83	3.66	3.42	161	159	155	1,044	447
Florida International	20	3.63	3.31	2.99	156	155	153	1,481	320	104	3.50	3.27	2.86	155	152	150	375	103	55	3.59	3.30	2.93	156	154	151	423	159
Florida State	30	3.74	3.46	3.26	161	159	158	3,313	806	196	0.00	0.00	0.00	0	0	0	0	0	0	3.74	3.46	3.26	161	159	158	806	196
Miami	60	3.66	3.47	3.25	160	158	156	4,688	2,330	416	3.40	2.81	2.48	162	158	155	89	10	4	3.66	3.47	3.25	160	158	156	2,340	420
Nova Southeastern	50	3.47	3.19	2.94	153	151	149	2,456	844	268	3.36	3.09	2.82	152	150	148	365	109	47	3.46	3.19	2.91	153	151	148	953	315
St. Thomas	45	3.38	3.04	2.70	152	150	147	2,765	1,166	235	0.00	0.00	0.00	0	0	0	0	0	0	3.38	3.04	2.70	152	150	147	1,166	235
Stetson	55	3.62	3.44	3.19	157	155	152	2,684	768	274	3.46	3.18	3.01	155	153	150	498	161	81	3.60	3.38	3.13	157	154	152	929	355
Georgia																												
Emory	70	3.69	3.50	3.30	166	164	162	3,591	1,042	207	0.00	0.00	0.00	0	0	0	0	0	0	3.69	3.50	3.30	166	164	162	1,042	207
Georgia	30	3.85	3.62	3.39	164	163	156	2,449	554	232	0.00	0.00	0.00	0	0	0	0	0	0	3.85	3.62	3.39	164	163	156	554	232
Georgia State	50	3.61	3.33	3.00	161	159	158	2,485	431	149	3.54	3.31	3.09	161	159	157	213	176	64	3.54	3.33	3.03	161	159	157	607	213
John Marshall-Atlanta	50	3.24	3.01	2.70	153	150	149	907	356	89	3.33	3.02	2.53	153	151	149	337	117	69	3.30	3.02	2.64	153	151	149	473	158
Mercer	50	3.67	3.45	3.03	158	156	153	1,290	457	176	0.00	0.00	0.00	0	0	0	0	0	0	3.67	3.45	3.03	158	156	153	457	176
Hawai'i																												
Hawai'i	60	3.72	3.50	3.15	161	158	155	1,116	215	91	0.00	0.00	0.00	0	0	0	0	0	0	3.72	3.50	3.15	161	158	155	215	91
Idaho																												
Idaho	50	3.68	3.44	3.13	157	155	151	782	301	105	0.00	0.00	0.00	0	0	0	0	0	0	3.68	3.44	3.13	157	155	151	301	105
Illinois																												
Chicago	75	3.77	3.67	3.51	172	171	169	4,818	766	192	0.00	0.00	0.00	0	0	0	0	0	0	3.77	3.67	3.51	172	171	169	766	192
Chicago-Kent	60	3.77	3.57	3.30	164	161	158	3,034	887	215	3.53	3.33	3.11	159	158	156	783	220	92	3.74	3.49	3.18	163	159	157	1,107	307

	Application Fee ($)	Full-time									Part-time									Total							
		75% GPA	Median GPA	25% GPA	75% LSAT	Median LSAT	25% LSAT	# of Applicants	# of Offers	# of Matriculants	75% GPA	Median GPA	25% GPA	75% LSAT	Median LSAT	25% LSAT	# of Applicants	# of Offers	# of Matriculants	75% GPA	Median GPA	25% GPA	75% LSAT	Median LSAT	25% LSAT	Total # of Offers	Total # of Matriculants
DePaul	60	3.59	3.34	3.02	161	160	157	4,297	1,367	249	3.55	3.34	3.09	157	156	153	644	277	86	3.58	3.34	3.02	161	159	154	1,644	335
Illinois	50	3.71	3.50	3.15	167	166	160	3,221	742	186	0.00	0.00	0.00	0	0	0	0	0	0	3.71	3.50	3.15	167	166	160	742	186
John Marshall	60	3.42	3.14	2.81	156	154	153	3,105	1,198	363	3.41	3.10	2.77	156	153	151	626	198	110	3.42	3.12	2.80	156	154	152	1,396	473
Loyola-Chicago	50	3.66	3.49	3.21	164	162	160	3,858	773	191	3.52	3.22	2.94	158	155	153	607	206	104	3.63	3.41	3.12	163	161	156	979	295
Northern Illinois	50	3.68	3.38	3.04	157	155	150	1,236	369	106	3.63	3.41	3.36	161	158	153	31	10	5	3.66	3.38	3.06	157	155	150	379	111
Northwestern	80	3.80	3.70	3.40	172	170	166	5,015	869	233	0.00	0.00	0.00	0	0	0	0	0	0	3.80	3.70	3.40	172	170	166	869	233
Southern Illinois	50	3.70	3.50	3.00	156	153	149	709	330	123	0.00	0.00	0.00	0	0	0	0	0	0	3.70	3.50	3.00	156	153	149	330	123
Indiana																											
Indiana-Bloomington	35	3.78	3.57	3.24	164	163	157	2,717	1,056	211	0.00	0.00	0.00	0	0	0	1	1	0	3.78	3.57	3.24	164	163	157	1,057	211
Indiana-Indianapolis	50	3.75	3.50	3.25	159	157	154	1,500	456	195	3.58	3.40	3.05	157	155	151	360	134	93	3.71	3.46	3.20	159	156	153	590	288
Notre Dame	55	3.69	3.50	3.28	167	166	164	3,502	853	198	0.00	0.00	0.00	0	0	0	0	0	0	3.69	3.50	3.28	167	166	164	853	198
Valparaiso	50	3.59	3.33	3.12	153	151	150	2,583	769	174	3.50	3.14	2.74	148	147	144	153	59	26	3.57	3.31	3.09	153	151	150	828	200
Iowa																											
Drake	50	3.64	3.41	3.15	157	155	154	1,103	503	140	0.00	0.00	0.00	0	0	0	35	2	1	3.64	3.41	3.15	157	155	154	505	141
Iowa	60	3.83	3.62	3.40	163	161	158	1,809	602	210	0.00	0.00	0.00	0	0	0	0	0	0	3.83	3.62	3.40	163	161	158	602	210
Kansas																											
Kansas	50	3.77	3.48	3.23	161	158	155	1,082	347	160	0.00	0.00	0.00	0	0	0	0	0	0	3.77	3.48	3.23	161	158	155	347	160
Washburn	40	3.71	3.37	3.04	157	154	152	1,049	447	158	0.00	0.00	0.00	0	0	0	0	0	0	3.71	3.37	3.04	157	154	152	447	158
Kentucky																											
Kentucky	50	3.85	3.64	3.37	162	159	155	1,255	384	138	0.00	0.00	0.00	0	0	0	0	0	0	3.85	3.64	3.37	162	159	155	384	138
Brandeis	50	3.74	3.48	3.17	160	158	155	1,065	348	102	3.61	3.39	2.98	158	156	152	179	60	40	3.69	3.43	3.13	159	157	155	408	142
Northern Kentucky	40	3.59	3.35	3.16	157	155	154	913	264	87	3.54	3.24	2.96	155	152	150	204	81	59	3.58	3.32	3.08	156	154	152	345	146
Louisiana																											
Louisiana State	25	3.78	3.49	3.16	159	156	154	1,353	475	204	0.00	0.00	0.00	0	0	0	0	0	0	3.78	3.49	3.16	159	156	154	475	204
Loyola-New Orleans	40	3.59	3.30	3.04	155	152	150	1,267	768	223	3.39	3.21	2.84	155	151	148	120	80	37	3.54	3.29	3.01	155	152	150	848	260
Southern	25	3.42	2.99	2.60	149	147	144	798	243	126	3.19	2.89	2.41	149	146	143	196	69	54	3.34	3.15	2.55	149	147	143	312	180
Tulane	60	3.70	3.57	3.35	163	161	159	2,445	818	274	0.00	0.00	0.00	0	0	0	0	0	0	3.70	3.57	3.35	163	161	159	818	274
Maine																											
Maine	50	3.65	3.34	3.14	158	155	153	760	325	101	0.00	0.00	0.00	0	0	0	0	0	0	3.65	3.34	3.14	158	155	153	325	101
Maryland																											
Baltimore	60	3.52	3.24	2.93	156	153	151	2,310	985	287	3.24	2.98	2.73	155	153	151	570	171	95	3.49	3.15	2.87	156	153	151	1,156	382
Maryland	65	3.77	3.61	3.40	165	162	160	3,790	627	207	3.67	3.66	3.29	160	157	153	541	61	56	3.76	3.60	3.38	164	161	159	688	263
Massachusetts																											
Boston College	75	3.76	3.58	3.41	166	164	162	6,321	1,224	254	0.00	0.00	0.00	0	0	0	0	0	0	3.76	3.58	3.41	166	164	162	1,224	254
Boston	75	3.83	3.68	3.52	166	165	163	6,211	1,627	269	0.00	0.00	0.00	0	0	0	0	0	0	3.83	3.68	3.52	166	165	163	1,627	269
Harvard	75	3.95	3.86	3.72	175	172	169	6,630	834	558	0.00	0.00	0.00	0	0	0	0	0	0	3.95	3.86	3.72	175	172	169	834	558
New England	65	3.47	3.27	3.05	154	152	150	2,762	1,356	270	3.40	3.22	2.97	152	150	148	738	335	123	3.45	3.25	3.04	154	151	150	1,691	393

Admission Fall 2006

	Application Fee ($)	Full-time									Part-time									Total							
		75% GPA	Median GPA	25% GPA	75% LSAT	Median LSAT	25% LSAT	# of Applicants	# of Offers	# of Matriculants	75% GPA	Median GPA	25% GPA	75% LSAT	Median LSAT	25% LSAT	# of Applicants	# of Offers	# of Matriculants	75% GPA	Median GPA	25% GPA	75% LSAT	Median LSAT	25% LSAT	Total # of Offers	Total # of Matriculants
Northeastern	75	3.65	3.40	3.17	162	161	156	3,355	988	218	0.00	0.00	0.00	0	0	0	0	0	0	3.65	3.40	3.17	162	161	156	988	218
Suffolk	60	3.53	3.28	3.01	159	156	154	2,429	1,136	331	3.49	3.15	2.88	157	154	152	611	333	199	3.51	3.24	2.96	158	155	153	1,469	530
Western New England	50	3.39	3.09	2.66	157	154	151	1,606	822	147	3.29	3.03	2.70	151	150	149	254	97	54	3.37	3.08	2.67	155	152	150	919	201
Michigan																											
Ave Maria	50	3.60	3.32	3.02	158	153	150	941	497	131	0.00	0.00	0.00	0	0	0	0	0	0	3.60	3.32	3.02	158	153	150	497	131
Detroit Mercy	50	3.43	3.21	3.01	152	150	148	1,734	726	203	3.39	3.00	2.63	152	149	145	202	99	60	3.43	3.20	2.93	152	150	148	825	263
Michigan	60	3.80	3.67	3.53	170	168	166	5,664	1,165	369	0.00	0.00	0.00	0	0	0	0	0	0	3.80	3.67	3.53	170	168	166	1,165	369
Michigan State	60	3.67	3.40	3.05	160	157	155	2,489	1,001	188	3.52	3.32	3.07	154	152	149	254	139	79	3.61	3.37	3.06	159	155	153	1,140	267
Thomas M. Cooley	0	3.37	3.05	2.79	152	148	146	4,958	3,304	342	3.30	3.05	2.71	149	146	143	760	498	1,349	3.32	3.05	2.73	149	146	144	3,802	1,691
Wayne State	50	3.69	3.51	3.29	160	156	154	1,079	465	187	3.65	3.40	3.24	159	155	152	137	42	27	3.68	3.48	3.24	159	156	153	507	214
Minnesota																											
Hamline	50	3.66	3.43	3.24	159	155	152	1,283	556	172	3.51	3.23	3.01	153	150	147	227	160	78	3.61	3.36	3.13	158	154	150	716	250
Minnesota	70	3.74	3.53	3.25	167	165	163	3,147	757	257	0.00	0.00	0.00	0	0	0	0	0	0	3.74	3.53	3.25	167	165	163	757	257
St. Thomas-Minneapolis	50	3.71	3.42	2.91	159	156	153	1,135	517	155	0.00	0.00	0.00	0	0	0	0	0	0	3.71	3.42	2.91	159	156	153	517	155
William Mitchell	50	3.66	3.43	3.15	158	155	152	1,323	631	237	3.47	3.19	2.87	157	151	147	435	186	115	3.60	3.35	3.03	158	154	150	817	352
Mississippi																											
Mississippi	40	3.76	3.53	3.25	158	155	152	1,550	489	175	0.00	0.00	0.00	0	0	0	0	0	0	3.76	3.53	3.25	158	155	152	489	175
Mississippi College	50	3.54	3.32	3.00	152	150	147	1,122	507	195	0.00	0.00	0.00	0	0	0	0	0	0	3.54	3.32	3.00	152	150	147	507	195
Missouri																											
Missouri-Columbia	50	3.72	3.49	3.24	160	158	156	875	381	152	0.00	0.00	0.00	0	0	0	0	0	0	3.72	3.49	3.24	160	158	156	381	152
Missouri-Kansas City	50	3.75	3.49	3.25	156	154	152	1,141	423	161	3.22	2.94	2.90	163	154	153	29	7	5	3.74	3.47	3.22	156	154	152	430	166
St. Louis	50	3.75	3.56	3.29	159	157	155	2,007	910	244	3.67	3.45	3.20	154	152	151	501	158	96	3.72	3.52	3.27	159	156	153	1,068	340
Washington University	70	3.70	3.60	3.20	167	166	162	3,325	933	241	0.00	0.00	0.00	0	0	0	0	0	0	3.70	3.60	3.20	167	166	162	933	241
Montana																											
Montana	60	3.71	3.44	3.23	156	153	150	479	174	83	0.00	0.00	0.00	0	0	0	0	0	0	3.71	3.44	3.23	156	153	150	174	83
Nebraska																											
Creighton	45	3.67	3.41	3.15	157	155	153	1,277	513	155	3.59	3.34	3.12	159	149	146	57	16	6	3.66	3.40	3.15	157	155	153	529	161
Nebraska	25	3.84	3.64	3.27	160	156	154	877	366	144	0.00	0.00	0.00	0	0	0	0	0	0	3.84	3.64	3.27	160	156	154	366	144
Nevada																											
Nevada	50	3.71	3.54	3.31	161	158	156	1,892	291	110	3.65	3.42	3.15	158	155	151	314	67	46	3.67	3.50	3.27	160	158	155	358	156
New Hampshire																											
Franklin Pierce	55	3.50	3.30	3.00	155	152	149	1,455	718	160	0.00	0.00	0.00	0	0	0	0	0	0	3.50	3.30	3.00	155	152	149	718	160
New Jersey																											
Rutgers-Camden	60	3.65	3.40	3.09	162	162	160	2,152	562	106	3.64	3.40	3.02	160	157	154	N/A	N/A	113	3.64	3.40	3.04	162	160	156	562	219
Rutgers-Newark	60	3.57	3.34	3.10	162	159	154	3,010	702	182	3.57	3.34	2.98	159	157	155	661	123	69	3.57	3.34	3.04	161	158	154	825	251
Seton Hall	65	3.66	3.40	3.17	163	160	158	2,400	714	192	3.48	3.25	2.98	156	154	151	605	376	167	3.58	3.33	3.08	160	157	154	1,090	359

	Application Fee ($)	Full-time									Part-time									Total							
		75% GPA	Median GPA	25% GPA	75% LSAT	Median LSAT	25% LSAT	# of Applicants	# of Offers	# of Matriculants	75% GPA	Median GPA	25% GPA	75% LSAT	Median LSAT	25% LSAT	# of Applicants	# of Offers	# of Matriculants	75% GPA	Median GPA	25% GPA	75% LSAT	Median LSAT	25% LSAT	Total # of Offers	Total # of Matriculants
New Mexico																												
New Mexico	50	3.72	3.40	3.03	158	155	152	1,405	248	115	0.00	0.00	0.00	0	0	0	0	0	0	3.72	3.40	3.03	158	155	152	248	115
New York																												
Albany	60	3.51	3.21	2.86	158	154	152	2,009	836	249	0.00	0.00	0.00	0	0	0	0	0	0	3.51	3.21	2.86	158	154	152	836	249
Brooklyn	65	3.62	3.43	3.22	164	163	162	4,229	1,141	303	3.54	3.36	3.08	160	159	158	774	290	190	3.59	3.39	3.15	163	161	159	1,431	493
Buffalo	50	3.67	3.44	3.22	158	156	153	1,508	565	248	0.00	0.00	0.00	0	0	0	0	0	0	3.67	3.44	3.22	158	156	153	565	248
Cardozo	65	3.72	3.55	3.23	166	163	161	4,411	1,226	268	3.71	3.55	3.27	161	159	157	374	143	83	3.72	3.55	3.25	165	161	159	1,369	351
CUNY	50	3.57	3.29	3.00	156	153	150	2,457	561	144	0.00	0.00	0.00	0	0	0	0	0	0	3.57	3.29	3.00	156	153	150	561	144
Columbia	70	3.82	3.70	3.51	174	172	169	7,768	1,144	384	0.00	0.00	0.00	0	0	0	0	0	0	3.82	3.70	3.51	174	172	169	1,144	384
Cornell	70	3.81	3.67	3.53	168	167	166	4,172	941	188	0.00	0.00	0.00	0	0	0	0	0	0	3.81	3.67	3.53	168	167	166	941	188
Fordham	65	3.74	3.63	3.41	167	165	163	5,724	1,373	312	3.66	3.43	3.20	163	161	160	1,060	262	160	3.71	3.58	3.30	166	163	161	1,635	472
Hofstra	60	3.65	3.51	3.23	159	157	153	4,126	1,865	311	3.47	3.20	2.92	155	153	150	684	223	102	3.63	3.45	3.13	158	155	152	2,088	413
New York Law	60	3.54	3.33	3.00	157	155	152	4,660	2,119	424	3.42	3.16	2.91	156	153	151	897	304	125	3.51	3.27	2.98	156	155	152	2,423	549
New York	85	3.89	3.75	3.58	172	171	168	7,571	1,597	448	0.00	0.00	0.00	0	0	0	0	0	0	3.89	3.75	3.58	172	171	168	1,597	448
Pace	65	3.58	3.35	3.16	157	155	153	2,467	909	196	3.53	3.26	3.01	154	153	151	468	182	77	3.56	3.33	3.13	156	154	152	1,091	273
St. John's	60	3.72	3.53	3.28	162	160	157	2,843	1,000	215	3.51	3.35	3.18	156	155	152	834	294	92	3.68	3.48	3.24	161	158	155	1,294	307
Syracuse	70	3.56	3.37	3.15	157	155	153	2,768	1,047	258	3.29	3.24	3.19	152	151	147	30	5	4	3.55	3.35	3.15	157	155	153	1,052	262
Touro	60	3.41	3.34	2.86	153	151	150	1,903	758	197	3.37	3.09	2.77	152	151	150	500	165	68	3.40	3.10	2.83	153	151	150	923	265
North Carolina																												
Campbell	50	3.54	3.19	3.04	157	155	152	1,032	272	122	0.00	0.00	0.00	0	0	0	0	0	0	3.54	3.19	3.04	157	155	152	272	122
Duke	70	3.85	3.78	3.66	169	168	165	4,340	1,011	205	0.00	0.00	0.00	0	0	0	0	0	0	3.85	3.78	3.66	169	168	165	1,011	205
North Carolina	70	3.77	3.57	3.39	164	162	158	3,581	543	229	0.00	0.00	0.00	0	0	0	0	0	0	3.77	3.57	3.39	164	162	158	543	229
North Carolina Central	40	3.49	3.20	2.91	152	148	144	1,752	437	190	3.57	3.29	3.21	158	153	150	687	97	37	3.49	3.22	2.93	153	148	144	534	227
Wake Forest	60	3.71	3.44	3.19	165	163	161	2,142	642	152	0.00	0.00	0.00	0	0	0	0	0	0	3.71	3.44	3.19	165	163	161	642	152
North Dakota																												
North Dakota	35	3.73	3.34	3.10	155	151	149	632	191	77	0.00	0.00	0.00	0	0	0	0	0	0	3.73	3.34	3.10	155	151	149	191	77
Ohio																												
Akron	0	3.63	3.30	3.07	159	158	154	1,858	512	119	3.58	3.35	3.12	156	152	151	372	122	67	3.61	3.32	3.09	159	156	151	634	186
Capital	40	3.54	3.28	2.99	155	153	151	1,279	549	181	3.38	3.11	2.82	156	153	151	237	122	67	3.51	3.23	2.94	156	153	151	671	248
Case Western	40	3.61	3.36	3.07	161	159	157	2,653	756	228	0.00	0.00	0.00	0	0	0	0	0	0	3.61	3.36	3.07	161	159	157	756	228
Cincinnati	35	3.80	3.60	3.31	161	160	157	1,183	407	113	0.00	0.00	0.00	0	0	0	0	0	0	3.80	3.60	3.31	161	160	157	407	113
Cleveland State	40	3.63	3.38	3.00	158	155	152	1,393	474	155	3.57	3.18	2.92	156	153	151	295	125	72	3.62	3.29	2.95	157	154	152	599	227
Dayton	0	3.49	3.22	2.89	155	152	150	2,400	926	181	0.00	0.00	0.00	0	0	0	0	0	0	3.49	3.22	2.89	155	152	150	926	181
Ohio Northern	40	3.65	3.35	3.09	155	152	150	1,424	472	120	0.00	0.00	0.00	0	0	0	0	0	0	3.65	3.35	3.09	155	152	150	472	120
Ohio State	60	3.79	3.61	3.36	163	161	158	2,289	653	232	0.00	0.00	0.00	0	0	0	0	0	0	3.79	3.61	3.36	163	161	158	653	232
Toledo	40	3.82	3.68	3.02	160	158	155	937	201	74	3.51	3.24	2.94	155	153	151	279	139	116	3.69	3.39	2.97	157	155	153	340	190

	Application Fee ($)	Full-time									Part-time									Total							
		75% GPA	Median GPA	25% GPA	75% LSAT	Median LSAT	25% LSAT	# of Applicants	# of Offers	# of Matriculants	75% GPA	Median GPA	25% GPA	75% LSAT	Median LSAT	25% LSAT	# of Applicants	# of Offers	# of Matriculants	75% GPA	Median GPA	25% GPA	75% LSAT	Median LSAT	25% LSAT	Total # of Offers	Total # of Matriculants
Oklahoma																												
Oklahoma	50	3.76	3.57	3.36	160	157	154	1,055	341	164	0.00	0.00	0.00	0	0	0	0	0	0	3.76	3.57	3.36	160	157	154	341	164
Oklahoma City	50	3.47	3.21	2.97	153	150	148	1,245	589	177	3.32	3.10	2.90	155	151	149	106	50	25	3.47	3.20	2.95	153	150	149	639	202
Tulsa	30	3.55	3.24	2.93	154	152	150	1,401	588	179	3.66	3.05	2.91	157	152	150	54	24	18	3.53	3.22	2.93	154	152	150	612	197
Oregon																												
Lewis & Clark	50	3.63	3.41	3.10	165	161	159	2,067	822	186	3.49	3.22	2.92	162	158	155	174	77	39	3.61	3.40	3.06	164	161	158	899	225
Oregon	50	3.63	3.40	3.08	161	159	157	2,015	807	178	0.00	0.00	0.00	0	0	0	0	0	0	3.63	3.40	3.08	161	159	157	807	178
Willamette	50	3.54	3.23	2.99	160	157	155	1,329	501	159	0.00	0.00	0.00	0	0	0	0	0	0	3.54	3.23	2.99	160	157	155	501	159
Pennsylvania																												
Duquesne	60	3.61	3.40	3.18	156	153	152	894	465	195	3.61	3.31	3.06	153	151	150	232	137	93	3.61	3.35	3.12	154	153	151	602	288
Penn State	60	3.59	3.24	2.85	159	158	157	3,350	959	181	3.78	3.62	3.30	156	153	150	0	83	56	3.68	3.31	2.91	159	157	154	1,042	237
Pennsylvania	75	3.84	3.72	3.47	171	170	167	5,649	879	249	0.00	0.00	0.00	0	0	0	0	0	0	3.84	3.72	3.47	171	170	167	879	249
Pittsburgh	55	3.63	3.40	3.11	161	159	158	2,369	736	243	0.00	0.00	0.00	0	0	0	0	0	0	3.63	3.40	3.11	161	159	158	736	243
Temple	60	3.60	3.39	3.23	163	161	159	4,310	1,605	240	3.55	3.31	3.01	160	158	157	338	114	60	3.60	3.38	3.18	163	161	158	1,719	300
Villanova	75	3.62	3.44	3.27	163	162	160	2,834	1,022	248	0.00	0.00	0.00	0	0	0	0	0	0	3.62	3.44	3.27	163	162	160	1,022	248
Widener	60	3.53	3.21	2.97	153	151	150	827	363	126	3.32	3.01	2.79	154	150	149	209	100	47	3.50	3.18	2.86	153	151	149	463	173
Puerto Rico																												
Inter American	63	3.75	3.23	3.29	140	139	137	539	214	125	3.37	3.25	3.01	149	137	140	448	181	120	3.56	3.24	3.15	145	138	139	395	245
Pontifical Catholic	75	3.57	3.22	2.76	139	136	134	356	146	109	3.55	3.23	2.93	139	136	133	161	72	60	3.57	3.21	2.95	139	136	133	218	169
Puerto Rico	20	3.79	3.61	3.39	148	144	141	341	145	131	3.76	3.48	3.14	148	145	141	220	70	66	3.78	3.56	3.32	148	144	141	215	197
Rhode Island																												
Roger Williams	60	3.46	3.21	2.97	156	152	151	1,640	838	204	0.00	0.00	0.00	0	0	0	0	0	0	3.46	3.21	2.97	156	152	151	838	204
South Carolina																												
Charleston	50	3.51	3.21	2.96	157	155	153	653	228	130	3.43	3.08	2.81	153	150	148	206	83	66	3.49	3.19	2.93	156	154	152	311	196
South Carolina	60	3.69	3.43	3.19	161	159	156	1,609	535	220	0.00	0.00	0.00	0	0	0	0	0	0	3.69	3.43	3.19	161	159	156	535	220
South Dakota																												
South Dakota	35	3.72	3.48	3.06	155	152	151	445	164	71	0.00	0.00	0.00	0	0	0	3	2	1	3.72	3.49	3.07	155	152	151	166	72
Tennessee																												
Memphis	25	3.73	3.39	3.08	158	155	153	1,061	276	130	3.50	3.22	2.87	148	145	141	52	14	14	3.70	3.36	3.06	158	155	153	290	144
Tennessee	15	3.78	3.58	3.37	161	159	155	1,390	384	151	0.00	0.00	0.00	0	0	0	0	0	0	3.78	3.58	3.37	161	159	155	384	151
Vanderbilt	50	3.88	3.70	3.49	167	166	164	3,640	921	190	0.00	0.00	0.00	0	0	0	0	0	0	3.88	3.70	3.49	167	166	164	921	190
Texas																												
Baylor	40	3.88	0.00	3.41	162	0	158	4,299	1,061	160	0.00	0.00	0.00	0	0	0	0	0	0	3.88	3.66	3.41	162	160	158	1,061	160
Houston	70	3.74	3.53	3.27	162	160	157	3,032	886	246	3.62	3.32	3.00	161	159	154	354	93	72	3.72	3.49	3.20	162	160	156	979	318
St. Mary's	55	3.39	3.11	2.76	156	154	151	1,902	764	257	0.00	0.00	0.00	0	0	0	0	0	0	3.39	3.11	2.76	156	154	151	764	257
SMU Dedman	60	3.83	3.70	3.33	164	163	158	2,066	455	180	3.67	3.46	3.01	160	157	151	542	175	113	3.80	3.54	3.23	163	161	154	630	293
South Texas	50	3.40	3.25	2.98	156	153	151	2,256	971	344	3.50	3.13	2.82	154	151	149	377	174	110	3.46	3.20	2.95	156	153	150	1,145	454

	Application Fee ($)	Full-time									Part-time									Total							
		75% GPA	Median GPA	25% GPA	75% LSAT	Median LSAT	25% LSAT	# of Applicants	# of Offers	# of Matriculants	75% GPA	Median GPA	25% GPA	75% LSAT	Median LSAT	25% LSAT	# of Applicants	# of Offers	# of Matriculants	75% GPA	Median GPA	25% GPA	75% LSAT	Median LSAT	25% LSAT	Total # of Offers	Total # of Matriculants
Texas	70	3.80	3.60	3.33	168	166	162	4,999	1,085	433	0.00	0.00	0.00	0	0	0	0	0	0	3.80	3.60	3.33	168	166	162	1,085	433
Texas Southern	55	3.19	2.91	2.65	150	147	145	2,429	692	252	0.00	0.00	0.00	0	0	0	0	0	0	3.19	2.91	2.65	150	147	145	692	252
Texas Tech	50	3.76	3.61	3.41	157	155	151	1,790	585	226	0.00	0.00	0.00	0	0	0	0	0	0	3.76	3.61	3.41	157	155	151	585	226
Texas Wesleyan	55	3.45	3.17	2.94	157	155	153	1,585	600	139	3.31	3.07	2.75	154	151	150	442	215	103	3.40	3.15	2.84	156	154	151	815	242
Utah																											
Brigham Young	50	3.80	3.63	3.40	166	164	161	917	260	145	0.00	0.00	0.00	0	0	0	0	0	0	3.80	3.63	3.40	166	164	161	260	145
Utah	60	3.81	3.58	3.36	162	160	157	1,130	360	122	0.00	0.00	0.00	0	0	0	0	0	0	3.81	3.58	3.36	162	160	157	360	122
Vermont																											
Vermont	60	3.51	3.27	2.97	157	154	149	1,119	632	202	0.00	0.00	0.00	0	0	0	0	0	0	3.51	3.27	2.97	157	154	149	632	202
Virginia																											
Appalachian	60	3.32	2.97	2.59	152	149	147	1,714	718	163	0.00	0.00	0.00	0	0	0	0	0	0	3.32	2.97	2.59	152	149	147	718	163
George Mason	35	3.78	3.60	3.10	166	164	160	5,024	1,004	178	3.77	3.50	2.99	164	161	157	1,511	112	66	3.78	3.57	3.06	165	163	159	1,116	244
Liberty	50	3.57	3.35	2.74	153	150	148	203	102	70	0.00	0.00	0.00	0	0	0	0	0	0	3.57	3.35	2.74	153	150	148	102	70
Regent	40	3.61	3.38	3.00	156	153	151	537	297	156	2.93	2.59	2.54	155	154	151	23	9	5	3.61	3.36	3.00	156	153	151	306	161
Richmond	35	3.58	3.36	3.07	162	161	159	1,873	626	158	0.00	0.00	0.00	0	0	0	0	0	0	3.58	3.36	3.07	162	161	159	626	158
Virginia	70	3.82	3.68	3.49	171	169	167	4,869	1,225	375	0.00	0.00	0.00	0	0	0	0	0	0	3.82	3.68	3.49	171	169	167	1,225	375
Washington and Lee	50	3.73	3.61	3.28	167	166	162	2,764	867	126	0.00	0.00	0.00	0	0	0	0	0	0	3.73	3.61	3.28	167	166	162	867	126
William & Mary	50	3.84	3.64	3.33	166	165	162	4,209	1,014	204	0.00	0.00	0.00	0	0	0	0	0	0	3.84	3.64	3.33	166	165	162	1,014	204
Washington																											
Gonzaga	50	3.57	3.32	3.02	157	155	153	1,599	606	206	0.00	0.00	0.00	0	0	0	0	0	0	3.57	3.32	3.02	157	155	153	606	206
Seattle	50	3.64	3.40	3.20	160	158	155	2,880	834	289	3.58	3.20	2.91	161	156	153	271	94	63	3.63	3.38	3.19	160	157	155	928	352
Washington	50	3.84	3.69	3.50	166	162	159	2,545	537	179	0.00	0.00	0.00	0	0	0	0	0	0	3.84	3.69	3.50	166	162	159	537	179
West Virginia																											
West Virginia	50	3.72	3.51	3.16	155	153	149	903	354	166	0.00	0.00	0.00	0	0	0	0	0	0	3.72	3.51	3.16	155	153	149	354	166
Wisconsin																											
Marquette	50	3.68	3.47	3.25	159	157	155	1,712	705	177	3.47	3.24	3.00	158	154	152	196	57	45	3.68	3.46	3.17	159	157	155	762	222
Wisconsin	45	3.72	3.53	3.23	163	161	156	3,005	774	278	0.00	0.00	0.00	0	0	0	0	0	5	3.72	3.53	3.23	163	161	156	774	283
Wyoming																											
Wyoming	50	3.61	3.42	3.13	154	151	150	809	212	85	0.00	0.00	0.00	0	0	0	0	0	0	3.61	3.42	3.13	154	151	150	212	85

Students, Faculty, Tuition

| | Admission Fall 2006 | | | | | | | | | | | | | | |
| | Student Body | | | | | Faculty | | | Tuition ($) | | | | Other | |
	# Full-time	# Part-time	% Men	% Women	% Minorities	# Full-time and Other	% Men	% Women	Student/Faculty Ratio	Resident, Full-time	Nonresident, Full-time	Resident, Part-time	Nonresident, Part-time	Official Guide Page #	Grid included •
Alabama															
Alabama	479	5	64.0	36.0	11.8	39	61.5	38.5	11.3	9,736	19,902	0	0	78	•
Faulkner	182	92	59.5	40.5	10.2	18	72.2	27.8	11.1	15,000	15,000	9,000	9,000	270	•
Samford	498	0	57.8	42.2	11.8	23	78.3	21.7	18.1	26,190	26,190	15,426	15,426	638	•
Arizona															
Arizona	463	0	50.8	49.2	28.3	32	71.9	28.1	12.1	16,201	25,991	0	0	94	•
Arizona State	629	0	54.7	45.3	26.6	53	71.7	28.3	9.7	13,278	23,864	0	0	98	•
Arkansas															
Arkansas	428	0	56.1	43.9	25.7	24	66.7	33.3	14.2	9,713	19,486	0	0	102	
Arkansas-Little Rock	283	161	51.1	48.9	15.1	25	44.0	56.0	14.7	9,817	19,747	6,867	13,487	106	•
California															
California-Berkeley	879	0	41.4	58.6	30.0	74	59.5	40.5	12.0	25,476	37,721	0	0	146	
California-Davis	582	0	44.8	55.2	33.0	37	56.8	43.2	14.0	24,358	36,603	0	0	150	•
California-Hastings	1240	2	46.8	53.2	33.4	65	66.2	33.8	18.9	22,190	33,415	0	0	154	•
California-Los Angeles	1019	0	53.2	46.8	31.5	74	68.9	31.1	12.6	25,457	36,381	0	0	158	•
California Western	748	87	48.5	51.5	27.9	37	62.2	37.8	18.3	32,380	32,380	22,900	22,900	162	•
Chapman	516	50	53.7	46.3	25.6	26	57.7	42.3	17.5	32,834	32,834	22,604	22,604	186	•
Golden Gate	602	157	43.2	56.8	24.1	33	57.6	42.4	19.9	31,140	31,140	21,870	21,870	322	•
La Verne	172	93	57.0	43.0	33.6	16	43.8	56.2	12.3	30,810	30,810	23,360	23,360	394	
Loyola Marymount	994	303	53.0	47.0	38.9	66	60.6	39.4	15.6	33,793	33,793	22,676	22,676	414	•
Pacific, McGeorge	605	396	54.5	45.5	22.7	57	54.4	45.6	13.4	32,905	32,905	21,901	21,901	566	•
Pepperdine	639	0	49.5	50.5	17.5	32	78.1	21.9	17.8	33,590	33,590	0	0	578	•
San Diego	738	297	55.3	44.7	29.2	55	69.1	30.9	14.3	35,896	35,896	25,516	25,516	642	•
San Francisco	562	140	49.1	50.9	35.9	33	69.7	30.3	17.3	32,190	0	23,045	0	646	•
Santa Clara	743	189	50.1	49.9	40.6	51	51.0	49.0	20.3	33,600	33,600	23,520	23,520	650	•
Southern California	605	0	51.9	48.1	39.3	42	71.4	28.6	13.1	40,262	40,262	0	0	678	•
Southwestern	676	288	47.8	52.2	35.6	49	63.3	36.7	15.8	31,700	31,700	19,100	19,100	690	•
Stanford	534	0	56.6	43.4	31.5	70	54.3	45.7	8.6	37,836	0	0	0	694	
Thomas Jefferson	580	190	55.8	44.2	20.5	40	47.5	52.5	15.2	30,250	30,250	19,050	19,050	738	
Western State	308	141	47.7	52.3	34.5	17	58.8	41.2	22.5	27,503	27,503	18,603	18,603	814	•
Whittier	449	224	49.6	50.4	32.2	32	56.3	43.8	16.9	30,870	30,870	20,620	20,620	818	•
Colorado															
Colorado	511	0	49.3	50.7	23.1	32	53.1	46.9	13.7	16,738	30,814	0	0	214	•
Denver	827	302	52.8	47.2	18.8	58	56.9	43.1	16.4	30,554	30,554	20,394	20,394	238	•

| | Admission Fall 2006 | | | | | | | | | | | | | |
| | Student Body | | | | | Faculty | | | Tuition ($) | | | | Other | |
	# Full-time	# Part-time	% Men	% Women	% Minorities	# Full-time and Other	% Men	% Women	Student/Faculty Ratio	Resident, Full-time	Nonresident, Full-time	Resident, Part-time	Nonresident, Part-time	Official Guide Page #	Grid included •
Connecticut															
Connecticut	464	184	52.2	47.8	17.6	49	59.2	40.8	11.5	17,284	35,692	12,086	24,926	222	•
Quinnipiac	300	164	49.6	50.4	11.0	32	62.5	37.5	13.1	33,840	33,840	23,840	23,840	594	•
Yale	576	3	51.5	48.5	29.5	77	76.6	23.4	7.3	40,900	40,900	0	0	848	•
Delaware															
Widener	602	383	56.5	43.5	15.6	47	55.3	44.7	15.9	29,430	29,430	22,050	22,050	822	•
District of Columbia															
American	1216	267	44.8	55.2	33.9	83	56.6	43.4	14.0	35,104	35,104	24,596	24,596	86	
Catholic	604	302	52.2	47.8	17.8	47	53.2	46.8	14.9	32,555	32,555	24,820	24,820	182	•
District of Columbia	235	0	38.7	61.3	43.8	19	52.6	47.4	11.1	7,880	15,230	0	0	250	
George Washington	1428	265	56.5	43.5	25.9	96	62.5	37.5	15.3	36,310	36,310	25,540	25,540	306	•
Georgetown	1592	386	56.5	43.5	24.2	111	70.3	29.7	14.5	37,220	37,220	27,300	27,300	310	
Howard	430	0	39.1	60.9	84.0	29	69.0	31.0	19.1	18,870	0	0	0	350	•
Florida															
Barry	407	156	51.0	49.0	19.7	26	57.7	42.3	16.6	27,560	27,560	20,776	20,776	118	•
Florida A&M	336	205	42.0	58.0	68.6	26	38.5	61.5	15.9	7,567	26,828	6,344	22,394	274	•
Florida Coastal	1066	212	53.4	46.6	18.2	46	39.1	60.9	20.3	27,088	27,088	21,910	21,910	278	•
Florida	1364	0	53.4	46.6	20.5	68	52.9	47.1	17.6	9,861	29,227	0	0	282	•
Florida International	237	145	54.2	45.8	53.9	22	59.1	40.9	15.7	8,801	23,061	6,011	15,671	286	
Florida State	765	0	60.1	39.9	18.7	44	61.4	38.6	13.8	9,837	29,849	0	0	290	•
Miami	1163	45	56.5	43.5	23.2	55	69.1	30.9	18.2	32,820	32,820	24,316	24,316	446	•
Nova Southeastern	745	182	49.5	50.5	24.4	56	44.6	55.4	13.9	27,550	27,550	20,788	20,788	538	•
St. Thomas	665	0	55.0	45.0	41.1	34	52.9	47.1	18.8	26,580	26,580	0	0	634	•
Stetson	806	227	46.9	53.1	19.5	47	59.6	40.4	17.0	27,860	27,860	19,300	19,300	698	•
Georgia															
Emory	674	0	52.1	47.9	26.3	52	61.5	38.5	12.6	36,746	36,746	0	0	266	•
Georgia	670	0	50.9	49.1	19.6	47	70.2	29.8	15.7	10,614	28,490	0	0	314	•
Georgia State	453	210	52.5	47.5	19.3	42	52.4	47.6	13.7	7,366	23,284	6,848	21,434	318	•
John Marshall-Atlanta	214	144	52.5	47.5	23.5	18	22.2	77.8	12.4	26,580	26,580	21,294	21,294	382	•
Mercer	446	0	57.4	42.6	16.4	28	71.4	28.6	11.7	30,146	30,146	0	0	442	•
Hawai'i															
Hawai'i	308	0	56.5	43.5	68.2	20	60.0	40.0	10.7	13,032	22,776	0	0	338	•
Idaho															
Idaho	313	1	57.6	42.0	13.4	21	71.4	28.6	14.9	9,540	19,140	0	0	354	•
Illinois															
Chicago	600	0	55.3	44.7	29.8	68	77.9	22.1	9.4	37,945	0	0	0	194	
Chicago-Kent	776	265	53.4	46.6	20.8	66	66.7	33.3	12.3	31,434	31,434	22,980	22,980	198	•

| | Admission Fall 2006 | | | | | | | | | | | | | | |
| | Student Body | | | | | Faculty | | | | Tuition ($) | | | | Other | |
	# Full-time	# Part-time	% Men	% Women	% Minorities	# Full-time and Other	% Men	% Women	Student/Faculty Ratio	Resident, Full-time	Nonresident, Full-time	Resident, Part-time	Nonresident, Part-time	Official Guide Page #	Grid included •
DePaul	725	345	50.7	49.3	22.9	51	58.8	41.2	16.1	30,670	30,670	19,960	19,960	242	•
Illinois	626	0	62.5	37.5	31.8	46	63.0	37.0	12.9	20,512	31,718	0	0	358	
John Marshall	1073	341	59.2	40.8	16.1	56	66.1	33.9	19.8	29,080	29,080	20,800	20,800	378	•
Loyola-Chicago	607	252	48.7	51.3	15.9	43	65.1	34.9	15.5	32,030	32,030	24,100	24,100	418	•
Northern Illinois	297	16	49.5	50.5	21.4	21	52.4	47.6	16.9	11,938	21,490	0	0	522	•
Northwestern	768	0	53.9	46.1	34.6	100	47.0	53.0	10.6	40,680	40,680	0	0	530	
Southern Illinois	353	2	58.9	41.1	8.5	29	51.7	48.3	12.2	10,861	28,621	0	0	682	•
Indiana															
Indiana-Bloomington	648	1	59.2	40.8	16.6	47	70.2	29.8	12.3	15,784	30,311	0	0	362	•
Indiana-Indianapolis	656	282	51.8	48.2	10.7	42	54.8	45.2	18.0	13,962	29,457	9,640	20,136	366	•
Notre Dame	570	1	63.0	37.0	22.4	38	63.2	36.8	13.7	34,120	34,120	0	0	534	
Valparaiso	462	51	55.2	44.8	11.7	26	57.7	42.3	16.5	28,940	28,940	18,088	18,088	762	
Iowa															
Drake	429	10	52.6	47.4	10.0	25	64.0	36.0	14.7	26,206	26,206	0	0	254	•
Iowa	644	0	52.6	47.4	17.2	47	66.0	34.0	12.8	14,542	29,986	0	0	374	
Kansas															
Kansas	482	0	60.6	39.4	15.1	37	59.5	40.5	11.9	10,399	19,232	0	0	386	•
Washburn	449	0	59.5	40.5	13.6	29	62.1	37.9	14.0	12,698	20,846	0	0	786	•
Kentucky															
Kentucky	425	0	56.5	43.5	7.8	23	60.9	39.1	16.3	12,842	23,272	0	0	390	
Brandeis	303	95	57.3	42.7	5.8	25	64.0	36.0	14.3	11,510	23,654	9,620	19,740	406	•
Northern Kentucky	282	234	55.2	44.8	7.8	26	69.2	30.8	15.1	11,112	24,240	8,334	18,180	526	•
Louisiana															
Louisiana State	566	12	50.5	49.5	9.9	36	66.7	33.3	16.2	12,124	21,220	0	0	410	•
Loyola-New Orleans	653	143	46.9	53.1	24.6	42	61.9	38.1	18.3	28,856	28,856	19,466	19,466	422	
Southern	394	86	45.6	54.4	57.5	29	55.2	44.8	12.8	6,610	11,210	5,496	10,096	686	
Tulane	768	1	56.0	44.0	16.0	58	65.5	34.5	15.3	34,696	34,696	0	0	750	•
Maine															
Maine	259	3	46.6	53.4	4.2	16	50.0	50.0	16.5	17,215	26,905	0	0	426	•
Maryland															
Baltimore	726	306	46.5	53.5	17.5	44	56.8	43.2	9.8	19,235	31,151	15,462	23,962	114	
Maryland	673	153	41.8	58.2	31.7	56	51.8	48.2	11.8	19,105	30,384	14,460	22,919	434	•
Massachusetts															
Boston College	780	1	54.8	45.2	23.9	52	57.7	42.3	14.0	34,846	34,846	0	0	126	•
Boston	821	15	47.7	52.3	20.8	55	70.9	29.1	12.2	35,398	35,398	0	0	130	
Harvard	1719	0	54.6	45.4	30.6	157	65.0	35.0	10.5	38,490	38,490	0	0	334	
New England	719	381	46.5	53.5	11.5	36	61.1	38.9	22.3	25,865	25,865	19,415	19,415	490	•

| | Admission Fall 2006 | | | | | | | | | | | | | |
| | Student Body | | | | | Faculty | | | Tuition ($) | | | | Other | |
	# Full-time	# Part-time	% Men	% Women	% Minorities	# Full-time and Other	% Men	% Women	Student/Faculty Ratio	Resident, Full-time	Nonresident, Full-time	Resident, Part-time	Nonresident, Part-time	Official Guide Page #	Grid included
Northeastern	626	0	41.2	58.8	27.0	28	46.4	53.6	17.3	34,737	34,737	0	0	518	•
Suffolk	1032	612	51.0	49.0	12.8	77	66.2	33.8	17.8	33,874	33,874	25,406	25,406	702	•
Western New England	384	169	55.2	44.8	9.2	34	47.1	52.9	15.7	30,522	30,522	22,566	22,566	810	•
Michigan															
Ave Maria	380	1	66.7	33.3	16.3	25	52.0	48.0	16.1	30,765	30,765	0	0	110	
Detroit Mercy	552	177	53.4	46.6	10.7	31	61.3	38.7	18.4	26,960	26,960	19,792	19,792	246	•
Michigan	1130	0	55.1	44.9	27.8	75	70.7	29.3	14.5	35,502	38,502	0	0	450	
Michigan State	730	207	55.6	44.4	12.9	41	61.0	39.0	19.5	28,182	28,182	21,434	21,434	454	•
Thomas M. Cooley	560	3046	52.6	47.4	22.3	88	59.1	40.9	23.7	24,260	24,260	17,340	17,340	734	•
Wayne State	553	117	52.1	47.9	19.0	46	58.7	41.3	18.8	17,358	32,231	10,046	18,545	802	•
Minnesota															
Hamline	498	218	48.5	51.5	12.7	35	57.1	42.9	16.6	27,096	27,096	19,528	19,528	330	•
Minnesota	801	0	57.2	42.8	16.4	60	66.7	33.3	11.1	21,984	31,484	0	0	458	•
St. Thomas-Minneapolis	443	0	51.7	48.3	14.4	27	51.9	48.1	17.5	27,200	0	0	0	630	•
William Mitchell	738	365	46.8	53.2	11.0	39	56.4	43.6	24.4	27,530	27,530	19,938	19,938	836	•
Mississippi															
Mississippi	505	0	54.9	45.1	12.5	37	67.6	32.4	14.4	8,300	16,180	0	0	462	•
Mississippi College	528	0	59.7	40.3	8.0	18	66.7	33.3	23.2	20,140	20,140	0	0	466	•
Missouri															
Missouri-Columbia	446	5	62.5	37.5	14.4	23	56.5	43.5	15.9	14,752	28,175	0	0	470	•
Missouri-Kansas City	478	11	57.9	42.1	9.4	32	65.6	34.4	14.4	13,183	25,234	9,486	18,094	474	•
St. Louis	712	233	51.2	48.8	10.6	47	57.4	42.6	17.4	30,190	30,190	21,995	21,995	622	•
Washington University	788	12	58.0	42.0	15.5	56	51.8	48.2	11.5	36,380	36,380	0	0	798	•
Montana															
Montana	242	0	50.4	49.6	11.2	18	72.2	27.8	13.4	9,978	20,354	0	0	478	•
Nebraska															
Creighton	452	16	56.8	43.2	9.8	28	71.4	28.6	14.7	24,828	24,828	14,486	14,486	230	•
Nebraska	396	3	52.1	47.9	13.0	26	73.1	26.9	12.4	9,213	21,580	0	0	482	•
Nevada															
Nevada	338	133	51.6	48.4	27.0	30	53.3	46.7	15.6	9,568	18,468	8,252	15,860	486	
New Hampshire															
Franklin Pierce	423	4	62.1	37.9	16.6	25	64.0	36.0	15.8	29,050	29,050	0	0	298	
New Jersey															
Rutgers-Camden	556	210	59.8	40.2	21.3	56	57.1	42.9	14.5	19,867	28,220	15,851	22,904	610	•
Rutgers-Newark	561	254	58.3	41.7	38.3	39	59.0	41.0	15.4	19,623	27,976	12,691	18,337	614	•
Seton Hall	727	366	55.8	44.2	16.8	54	66.7	33.3	15.2	35,400	35,400	26,054	26,054	658	•

	Student Body				Faculty				Tuition ($)				Other	
	# Full-time	# Part-time	% Men	% Women	% Minorities	# Full-time and Other	% Men	% Women	Student/Faculty Ratio	Resident, Full-time	Nonresident, Full-time	Resident, Part-time	Nonresident, Part-time	*Official Guide* Page #	Grid included •
New Mexico															
New Mexico	343	0	50.1	49.9	45.2	31	51.6	48.4	10.0	9,566	23,213	0	0	494	•
New York															
Albany	680	37	53.1	46.9	16.6	48	54.2	45.8	15.8	35,079	35,079	26,342	26,342	82	
Brooklyn	1152	342	50.9	49.1	26.4	62	54.8	45.2	17.8	37,525	37,525	28,233	28,233	138	
Buffalo	728	3	51.2	48.8	18.3	54	50.0	50.0	13.1	13,532	19,632	0	0	142	•
Cardozo	952	84	50.6	49.4	20.8	51	66.7	33.3	17.8	37,270	37,270	37,270	37,270	174	•
CUNY	417	4	34.2	65.8	31.1	29	48.3	51.7	12.8	10,562	16,462	0	0	206	•
Columbia	1230	3	56.7	43.3	29.2	110	69.1	30.9	10.3	41,226	41,226	0	0	218	
Cornell	561	0	51.5	48.5	25.0	48	70.8	29.2	10.0	40,648	40,648	0	0	226	
Fordham	1186	326	54.1	45.9	25.2	78	61.5	38.5	15.0	37,220	37,220	27,976	27,976	294	•
Hofstra	890	239	53.0	47.0	22.1	45	66.7	33.3	18.7	35,260	35,260	35,260	35,260	342	
New York Law	1150	361	46.9	53.1	22.9	61	63.9	36.1	20.9	40,478	40,478	31,124	31,124	498	•
New York	1442	0	53.7	46.3	23.9	135	65.2	34.8	10.7	40,385	40,385	0	0	502	
Pace	499	256	42.8	57.2	17.2	39	61.5	38.5	15.3	35,904	35,904	26,758	26,758	562	•
St. John's	724	197	51.6	48.4	22.8	49	59.2	40.8	15.7	32,700	32,700	24,525	24,525	618	•
Syracuse	683	6	55.7	44.3	20.0	53	50.9	49.1	15.5	35,790	35,790	30,909	30,909	706	•
Touro	501	231	54.6	45.4	22.8	35	60.0	40.0	17.1	32,300	32,300	24,300	24,300	746	
North Carolina															
Campbell	342	0	52.0	48.0	7.3	18	88.9	11.1	18.1	24,941	24,941	0	0	166	•
Duke	578	52	56.7	43.3	23.7	50	72.0	28.0	12.0	38,739	38,739	0	0	258	•
North Carolina	712	0	52.4	47.6	21.1	30	66.7	33.3	20.1	12,947	25,365	0	0	506	•
North Carolina Central	426	111	42.3	57.7	51.6	20	50.0	50.0	21.8	4,625	16,485	4,625	16,485	510	
Wake Forest	454	10	58.4	41.6	13.6	39	59.0	41.0	10.5	29,500	0	0	0	782	•
North Dakota															
North Dakota	236	0	53.8	46.2	10.2	12	58.3	41.7	21.2	8,386	18,038	0	0	514	•
Ohio															
Akron	306	220	57.2	42.8	12.9	27	70.4	29.6	13.2	16,388	25,980	10,447	16,522	74	•
Capital	470	225	56.0	44.0	10.8	34	55.9	44.1	15.7	26,680	26,680	16,560	16,560	170	•
Case Western	670	3	59.0	41.0	16.8	48	70.8	29.2	13.8	33,384	33,384	0	0	178	•
Cincinnati	376	0	51.1	48.9	17.6	32	50.0	50.0	10.7	18,032	32,152	0	0	202	•
Cleveland State	486	216	52.6	47.4	14.4	39	59.0	41.0	13.6	14,982	20,525	11,525	15,789	210	•
Dayton	458	0	57.0	43.0	12.0	28	60.7	39.3	14.9	31,644	31,644	0	0	234	•
Ohio Northern	311	0	53.1	46.9	10.0	21	66.7	33.3	12.6	25,050	25,050	0	0	542	•
Ohio State	688	0	57.3	42.7	23.3	46	65.2	34.8	14.1	17,551	31,969	0	0	546	•
Toledo	344	180	59.7	40.3	7.4	29	55.2	44.8	14.1	14,839	25,082	11,750	19,860	742	•

| | Admission Fall 2006 | | | | | | | | | | | | | |
| | Student Body | | | | | Faculty | | | Tuition ($) | | | | Other | |
	# Full-time	# Part-time	% Men	% Women	% Minorities	# Full-time and Other	% Men	% Women	Student/Faculty Ratio	Resident, Full-time	Nonresident, Full-time	Resident, Part-time	Nonresident, Part-time	Official Guide Page #	Grid included ●
Oklahoma															
Oklahoma	501	0	55.3	44.7	24.4	37	56.8	43.2	11.8	13,564	23,493	0	0	550	●
Oklahoma City	500	105	59.0	41.0	17.7	29	65.5	34.5	19.9	27,161	27,161	18,416	18,416	554	●
Tulsa	460	80	65.6	34.4	10.6	37	51.4	48.6	14.8	25,331	25,331	17,755	17,755	754	●
Oregon															
Lewis & Clark	537	182	53.3	46.7	18.5	51	54.9	45.1	14.6	27,670	27,670	20,752	20,752	398	●
Oregon	536	0	56.9	43.1	18.5	25	56.0	44.0	21.3	18,690	23,262	0	0	558	●
Willamette	422	2	58.3	41.7	8.5	31	64.5	35.5	13.8	26,410	0	0	0	828	
Pennsylvania															
Duquesne	465	187	54.0	46.0	6.4	28	75.0	21.4	16.9	25,785	25,785	19,968	19,968	262	
Penn State	540	68	53.6	46.4	22.7	48	58.3	41.7	11.9	28,054	28,054	24,604	24,604	570	●
Pennsylvania	762	0	53.7	46.3	30.3	56	71.4	28.6	12.1	39,330	39,330	0	0	574	
Pittsburgh	731	0	58.1	41.9	13.4	46	63.0	37.0	14.2	21,408	29,706	0	0	582	●
Temple	775	229	53.3	46.7	23.5	54	61.1	38.9	14.6	14,902	25,552	12,028	20,548	710	●
Villanova	720	9	51.7	48.3	17.3	44	54.5	45.5	17.5	29,340	29,340	0	0	774	
Widener	296	153	55.7	44.3	7.3	26	53.8	46.2	16.1	29,430	29,430	22,050	22,050	824	●
Puerto Rico															
Inter American	622	211	45.0	55.0	100.0	27	55.6	44.4	28.5	12,891	12,891	9,611	9,611	370	
Pontifical Catholic	351	158	48.5	51.5	100.0	24	75.0	25.0	16.3	13,141	0	9,419	0	586	
Puerto Rico	521	181	45.6	54.4	98.6	42	57.1	42.9	13.9	3,858	5,413	2,958	7,159	590	●
Rhode Island															
Roger Williams	533	60	51.8	48.2	11.6	30	56.7	43.3	20.5	29,670	29,670	22,629	22,629	606	●
South Carolina															
Charleston	240	187	80.6	19.4	7.7	21	76.2	23.8	19.1	28,680	28,680	19,476	19,476	190	●
South Carolina	706	1	57.1	42.9	10.7	36	75.0	25.0	17.5	16,156	32,048	0	0	666	●
South Dakota															
South Dakota	231	4	57.9	42.1	4.3	14	71.4	28.6	18.1	8,326	16,609	4,163	8,304	670	●
Tennessee															
Memphis	379	29	55.9	44.1	18.1	18	77.8	22.2	16.5	10,596	28,946	9,974	26,684	438	●
Tennessee	449	0	49.7	50.3	15.8	39	53.8	30.8	10.9	9,934	25,290	0	0	714	●
Vanderbilt	630	1	54.4	45.6	18.2	38	65.8	34.2	15.0	36,322	36,322	0	0	766	
Texas															
Baylor	401	0	56.6	43.4	12.7	20	80.0	20.0	16.8	31,246	31,246	0	0	122	●
Houston	815	192	57.5	42.5	26.5	61	62.3	37.7	15.9	15,922	22,372	8,348	10,928	346	●
St. Mary's	742	0	57.7	42.3	30.3	37	70.3	29.7	21.9	22,040	22,040	0	0	626	●
SMU Dedman	554	328	53.7	46.3	22.6	50	64.0	36.0	14.5	32,844	32,844	24,633	24,633	662	●
South Texas	913	324	55.7	44.3	22.6	46	60.9	39.1	21.8	22,440	22,440	15,160	15,160	674	●

| | Admission Fall 2006 | | | | | | | | | | | | | | |
| | Student Body | | | | | Faculty | | | | Tuition ($) | | | | Other | |
	# Full-time	# Part-time	% Men	% Women	% Minorities	# Full-time and Other	% Men	% Women	Student/Faculty Ratio	Resident, Full-time	Nonresident, Full-time	Resident, Part-time	Nonresident, Part-time	Official Guide Page #	Grid included •
Texas	1313	0	59.6	40.4	31.7	74	62.2	37.8	14.0	18,208	31,648	0	0	718	•
Texas Southern	658	0	47.6	52.4	82.8	37	43.2	56.8	15.6	11,228	14,978	0	0	722	•
Texas Tech	702	0	55.3	44.7	19.5	39	64.1	35.9	15.3	12,615	19,720	0	0	726	•
Texas Wesleyan	422	238	49.7	50.3	19.4	27	70.4	29.6	17.0	21,660	21,660	15,630	15,630	730	•
Utah															
Brigham Young	460	2	64.1	35.9	18.2	17	88.2	11.8	20.9	8,200	16,400	0	0	134	•
Utah	391	0	62.1	37.9	10.2	28	64.3	35.7	11.6	11,758	25,116	0	0	758	•
Vermont															
Vermont	552	0	47.8	52.2	14.3	44	63.6	36.4	12.8	29,955	29,955	0	0	770	•
Virginia															
Appalachian	369	0	69.1	30.9	5.7	15	60.0	40.0	21.6	22,775	22,775	0	0	90	•
George Mason	466	285	61.9	38.1	16.2	36	77.8	22.2	16.1	15,274	26,502	12,001	20,823	302	•
Liberty	155	0	61.9	38.1	11.0	13	76.9	23.1	8.1	24,085	24,085	0	0	402	
Regent	460	31	49.3	50.7	12.0	26	73.1	26.9	20.3	25,616	25,616	19,056	19,056	598	•
Richmond	500	7	53.8	46.2	9.9	32	68.8	31.3	16.0	28,390	28,390	0	0	602	•
Virginia	1146	0	60.6	39.4	17.4	70	72.9	27.1	13.9	30,700	35,700	0	0	778	
Washington and Lee	390	0	59.2	40.8	15.9	33	69.7	30.3	9.8	31,300	31,300	0	0	794	•
William & Mary	607	0	53.4	46.6	16.0	38	71.1	28.9	15.6	16,600	26,800	0	0	832	•
Washington															
Gonzaga	535	22	55.7	44.3	9.5	29	58.6	41.4	15.9	27,978	27,978	16,812	16,812	326	•
Seattle	863	227	47.2	52.8	24.3	56	55.4	44.6	15.6	27,826	27,826	18,552	18,552	654	•
Washington	544	0	43.2	56.8	19.7	51	58.8	41.2	10.8	16,255	23,878	0	0	790	•
West Virginia															
West Virginia	474	2	55.3	44.7	10.3	26	69.2	30.8	15.1	9,342	21,710	0	0	806	•
Wisconsin															
Marquette	499	190	57.3	42.7	9.1	33	54.5	45.5	16.1	27,750	27,750	16,650	16,650	430	•
Wisconsin	817	48	52.0	48.0	26.0	57	59.6	40.4	12.9	12,653	30,816	1,058	2,572	840	
Wyoming															
Wyoming	231	0	55.4	44.6	7.8	17	70.6	29.4	12.2	7,635	16,155	0	0	844	•

Chapter 13: ABA-Approved Law Schools

This chapter is designed to provide consumers with basic information in a simple format that will facilitate the consideration of ABA-approved law schools. Please note that applicants should not use this information as the sole source regarding application and admission. Rather, this book should supplement other avenues of evaluating respective schools, including making direct contact with admission officers, professors, students, alumni, or prelaw advisors.

The following section includes four pages of text and numerical data from 194 ABA-approved law schools that confer the first degree in law (the JD degree). The two pages of numerical data about each school were compiled from questionnaires completed during the fall 2006 academic semester and submitted by ABA-approved law schools to the ABA's Consultant on Legal Education as part of the accreditation process. The completed questionnaires provided to the Consultant's Office are certified by the dean of each law school. Each certification is submitted to the Consultant's Office as an assurance that the information provided accurately reflects prevailing conditions at the law school for which the certification is given. The Consultant's Office, however, does not directly audit the information submitted by the respective institutions on an annual basis.

The information contained in this book is only a small portion of what is collected in the questionnaire for accreditation purposes. Each page is divided into different segments as discussed below. In addition, many of the same data are displayed on the charts in the next section to facilitate side-by-side comparisons.

In addition to the two pages of numerical data, each law school provides two pages of descriptive text to LSAC. LSAC edits these text pages for style and formatting, but does not verify the descriptive information provided by the schools. As part of this two-page spread, most schools provide admission profile grids that illustrate admission prospects based on a combination of LSAT score and GPA. The data in these grids are based on 2005–2006 academic year admission decisions as reported by the schools to LSAC. The grids are intended to be indicative of the admission profile of last year's entering law school classes; they should not be interpreted as predictors of the likelihood of admission for any applicant.

LSAC collects admission profile data and school descriptions each fall as a service to its member schools and to prospective law school applicants. The information provided by the law schools to LSAC in no way affects the ABA accreditation process.

■ School Name

The law schools are arranged in alphabetical order by each institution's primary name. Please note that some schools are known by more than one name. A law school that has completed at least one full year of successful operation may apply for provisional approval. A law school is granted provisional approval when it establishes that it substantially complies with *Standards: Rules of Procedure for Approval of Law Schools* and gives assurances that it will be in full compliance with all of the Standards within three years after receiving provisional approval. It is the ABA's view that students at provisionally approved law schools and persons who graduate while a school is provisionally approved are entitled to the same recognition as students and graduates of fully approved law schools. Schools listed in this publication with *Provisional* to the right of their name were provisionally approved as of February 2007.

The Basics

The Basics section contains a variety of general information, sorted into the categories listed below.

Type of school: All ABA-approved law schools are either public or private. *Public* means that the school receives money from the state in which the school is located. *Private* indicates the school is not operated by the state.

Term: Indicates whether the school operates on a semester, quarter, or trimester system.

Application deadline: Not all schools have specific deadlines for admission applications. If the item was left blank in the questionnaire completed by the school, it generally means that the school considers applications on a continual basis until the class is filled.

Application fee: Fee charged by most law schools for processing an application for admission.

Financial aid deadline: Indicates the deadline for the school's financial aid form. (The school deadline may not be the same as federal and state deadlines.) If the item was left blank in the questionnaire completed by the school, it generally means that the school considers financial aid applications on a continuing basis.

Can first year start other than fall? Indicates whether the school has an entering class other than in the fall term.

Student to faculty ratio: Indicates the number of students relative to the number of instructors for the calendar year. The ratio is calculated by comparing faculty full-time equivalency (FTE) to FTE of JD enrollment. A general definition of faculty FTE is as follows: total full-time faculty plus additional instructional resources. Additional instructional resources include administrators who teach, as well as part-time faculty. Teaching administrators and part-time faculty are included in the faculty FTE at differing weighted factors ranging from .2 to .7. FTE of JD enrollment is calculated as follows: full-time JD enrollment plus two-thirds of part-time JD enrollment less enrollment in semester-abroad programs. For a detailed definition of the ABA's student/faculty ratio, please consult the ABA's *Standards: Rules of Procedure for Approval of Law Schools* at *www.abanet.org/legaled*.

Student housing: Indicates whether there is housing restricted to law students and whether there is graduate housing for which law students are eligible.

Faculty and Administrators

This section of the two-page spread contains detailed information on the number, gender, and race of the teachers at the school for both semesters. It should be noted that some schools may have lower part-time numbers in the fall semester because at their school most of the part-time instruction occurs in the spring semester. The five categories of faculty are mutually exclusive. Teachers on leave or sabbatical are not included in the full-time faculty count for the term they are on leave. The *Full-time* row indicates tenured or tenure-track faculty. *Other Full-time* indicates nontenured professional skills instructors and nontenured legal writing instructors. *Deans, librarians, & others who teach* are law school administrators who teach at least halftime. Administrators who neither teach nor hold faculty rank are not included in these numbers. Administrators who teach are typically at the school and available to students during the entire year. For this reason, they are counted in fall and spring regardless of their teaching load. *Part-time* during the fall semester includes adjuncts, permanent part time, faculty from another unit, part-time professional skills, and emeritus part time. The *Total* row combines figures from the *Full-time* row through the *Part-time* row.

JD Enrollment and Ethnicity

This section represents the JD enrollment by ethnic category, gender, first-year student, and full-time/part-time status. Students are classified for purposes of enrollment statistics on the basis of whether they are carrying a full load in the division in which they are enrolled. Minority group enrollment is the total enrollment of students who classify themselves as African American; American Indian or Alaskan Native; Asian or Pacific Islander; Mexican American; Puerto Rican; or other Hispanic American. Although Puerto Rican law students enrolled in the three approved law schools in Puerto Rico are not classified as minority students in the "Survey of Minority Group Students Enrolled in JD Programs in Approved Law Schools," they are counted as minorities in all other areas. Nonresident alien students (foreign nationals) and students whose ethnicity is unknown or unspecified are not included as minority students.

JD Degrees Awarded: This indicates the total number of JD degrees awarded during the 2005–2006 academic year.

Curriculum

All information in this category is based on the 12-month period beginning at the close of the prior academic year (e.g., June 2005 through May 2006). In courses where there was enrollment by both full-time and part-time students, schools were asked to classify each of those courses as full-time or part-time based on time of day and relative enrollment of full-time and part-time students. Some schools that have a part-time program experienced difficulty providing curriculum information which distinguished between full-time and part-time. In those cases, the part-time column contains zeros. A *small section* means a section of a substantive law course, which may include a legal writing component; small section does not mean a legal writing section standing alone. The *number of classroom course titles beyond the first-year curriculum* refers only to classroom courses offered the previous year, not to clinical or field placement possibilities. If a

title is offered in both the full-time program and part-time program, the school could count it once in each column. *Seminars* are defined as courses requiring a written work product and having an enrollment limited to no more than 25. A *simulation course* is one in which a substantial portion of the instruction is accomplished through the use of role-playing or drafting exercises (for example, trial advocacy, corporate planning and drafting, negotiations, and estate planning and drafting). *Faculty-supervised clinical courses* are those courses or placements with other agencies in which full-time faculty have primary professional responsibility for all cases on which students are working. *Field placements* refer to those cases in which someone other than full-time faculty has primary responsibility to the client; these placements are frequently called externships or internships. Schools were also asked not to double count a single course by classifying it both as full-time and part-time. *Number involved in law journals* and *number involved in interschool competitions* reflect those students beyond the first year who participated in those activities during the previous year regardless of whether they received credit.

Transfers

This section refers to the number of students who transferred in and transferred out of the law school in the 2005–2006 academic year.

Tuition and Fees

- *Full-time*: Represents the full-time tuition (plus annual fees) for the academic year for a typical first-year student.

- *Part-time*: Represents the part-time tuition (plus annual fees) for the academic year for a typical first-year student. Please note that some schools elected to report part-time tuition on a "per credit hour" basis.

Living Expenses

This represents the 2006–2007 academic year total living expenses (room, board, etc.) and book expenses for full-time, single, resident students "Living on campus," "Living off campus," and "Living at home." Tuition and fee charges are not included. The figures are used in analyzing law student budgets for loan purposes. Many schools use the same budget amount for all three categories.

GPA and LSAT Scores

This section of the two-page spread contains statistics on the 2006 entering class. All persons in this particular category, regardless of whether they were admitted through any special admission program rather than through the normal admission process, were included. The admission year was calculated from October 1, 2005 through September 30, 2006. Schools that admit in the spring and/or summer were to include those students in the totals. Figures on matriculants include all students who attended at least one class during the first week of the term in which they were admitted. For a small number of schools, applications and admitted applicants are not identified by the school as full-time or part-time. Therefore, "N/A" appears under the full-time and part-time columns, and the total application and admission offers are entered under the total column.

Percentiles of GPA and LSAT: The GPA and LSAT scores represent the 75th percentile, 25th percentile, and the median scores of the entering class. For example, one quarter (25 percent) of the first-year class has credentials that are *below* the number given for the 25th percentile. Three quarters (75 percent) of the first-year class have credentials that are below the number given for the 75th percentile. One half (50 percent) of the first-year class has credentials that are *below* the number given for the median. For example, if a school reports a 25th percentile/median/75th percentile GPA —3.01/3.25/3.47, then 25 percent of this first-year class had a GPA of *less than* 3.01, 50 percent of this class had a GPA of *less than* 3.25, and 75 percent of this class had a GPA of *less than* 3.47. The same principle holds for the 25th percentile/median/75th percentile LSAT score.

Grants and Scholarships (from prior year)

This indicates the number and percentage of students receiving internal grants or scholarships from law school or university sources. External grants such as state grants are not included. The percentages for full time and part time are based on the total number of full-time and part-time JD students, respectively. The total column percentage is based on total JD enrollment. Zeros are reported in those areas where a school did not provide data. The data represent information from the previous academic year.

Informational and Library Resources

This section of the two-page spread contains basic information about the law library. In addition, it contains brief information about the physical size of the school and the number of computers available.

- *Number of volumes and volume equivalents*: A "volume" refers to a physical unit of any printed, typewritten, mimeographed, or processed work contained in one binding or portfolio, which is cataloged, classified, or otherwise made ready for use, and was held by the law school at the end of the 2004–2005 fiscal year. "Volume equivalents" is also the number held at the end of the 2004–2005 fiscal year. Volume equivalents are computed as follows: Microfiche, six fiche = 1 volume. Microfilm, 1 roll = 5 volumes.

- *Titles:* Each item for which a separate shelf bibliographic unit record has been made.

- *Active serial subscriptions:* Subscriptions for which pieces/parts/updates have been received on a regular or irregular basis.

- *Study seating capacity inside the library:* Number of study seats available for library users.

- *Number of full-time professional librarians:* Number of full-time library employees, including librarians who teach or hold faculty rank.

- *Hours per week library is open:* Number of hours per week that professional staff are on duty in the library.

- *Wired connections available to students:* Number of open, wired, network connections available to students or, if the library has a wireless network, the number of simultaneous users accommodated within.

- *Networked computers available for use by students*: Number of workstations in law school or library computer labs, plus workstations in the library for users that are not in computer labs.

- *Simultaneous wireless users*: Number of simultaneous users accommodated within.

- *Require computer:* Indicates whether the school requires students entering the law school to have a computer.

JD Attrition (from prior year)

Attrition percentages were based on fall 2005 enrollment. *Academic* attrition, for this purpose, refers to those students not continuing their legal studies between October 1, 2005, and October 1, 2006. *Other* attrition may include transfers and students who leave for other reasons.

Employment (9 months after graduation)

This section represents statistics on the employment status of the 2005 graduating class nine months after graduation. The employment percentages are based on the graduates whose employment status was "known." Hence, for the schools reporting a large percentage of graduates for whom the employment status is unknown, the percentage reported may not be a very accurate reflection of the actual percentage of the class as a whole. *Type of employment* and geographic location percentages are based on the number of students employed.

Bar Passage Rates

This section refers to numbers and percentages of 2005 graduates who took the summer 2005 and the February 2006 examinations. The states' overall pass rates for first-time takers were obtained by an independent survey of each state bar authority with the assistance of the National Conference of Bar Examiners. Bar examination passage rates vary considerably from state to state, and for first-time and repeat test takers. For this book, schools reported data for the jurisdiction(s) in which they had the largest number of first-time takers; overall, that accounted for approximately 75 percent of all graduates in 2006. Reporting the second highest jurisdiction was optional. Wisconsin allows graduates of the University of Wisconsin Law School and Marquette University Law School to exercise the "diploma privilege" and be admitted to the bar without taking the examination.

■ Applicant Profiles

Applicant profiles are provided by some schools to give candidates information about the number of applicants and admitted applicants in each cell. For various reasons, the total number of applicants and admitted applicants do not equal the official totals that appear on the ABA data pages in this book.

The purpose of the applicant profiles is to provide information about the LSAT/GPA credentials of applicants and admitted applicants to the schools that provide the profiles. You will note that some schools provide alternatives to the grid format for their profile or no profile at all.

The University of Akron School of Law

302 Buchtel Common
Akron, OH 44325-2901
Phone: 800.4.AKRON.U or 330.972.7331; Fax: 330.258.2343
E-mail: lawadmissions@uakron.edu; Website: www.uakron.edu/law

ABA Approved Since 1961

The Basics

Type of school	Public
Term	Semester
Application deadline	3/1
Application fee	$0
Financial aid deadline	4/1
Can first year start other than fall?	No
Student to faculty ratio	13.2 to 1
Does the university offer: housing restricted to law students?	No
graduate housing for which law students are eligible?	Yes

Faculty and Administrators

	Total Fall	Total Spr	Men Fall	Men Spr	Women Fall	Women Spr	Minorities Fall	Minorities Spr
Full-time	27	28	19	19	8	9	3	3
Other Full-time	0	0	0	0	0	0	0	0
Deans, librarians, & others who teach	3	3	1	1	2	2	0	0
Part-time	25	20	18	10	7	10	1	0
Total	**55**	**51**	**38**	**30**	**17**	**21**	**4**	**3**

Curriculum

	Full-time	Part-time
Typical first-year section size	56	65
Is there typically a "small section" of the first-year class, other than Legal Writing, taught by full-time faculty	No	Yes
If yes, typical size offered last year		31
# of classroom course titles beyond first-year curriculum		130
# of upper division courses, excluding seminars with an enrollment: Under 25		95
25–49		22
50–74		10
75–99		0
100+		2
# of seminars		20
# of seminar positions available		439
# of seminar positions filled	118	49
# of positions available in simulation courses		700
# of simulation positions filled	290	152
# of positions available in faculty supervised clinical courses		224
# of faculty supervised clinical positions filled	17	5
# involved in field placements	42	7
# involved in law journals	37	14
# involved in interschool competitions	47	2
# of credit hours required to graduate		88

JD Enrollment and Ethnicity

	Men #	Men %	Women #	Women %	Full-time #	Full-time %	Part-time #	Part-time %	1st-year #	1st-year %	Total #	Total %	JD Degs. Awd.
African Amer.	10	3.3	26	11.6	25	8.2	11	5.0	20	10.0	36	6.8	8
Amer. Indian	0	0.0	0	0.0	0	0.0	0	0.0	0	0.0	0	0.0	0
Asian Amer.	11	3.7	10	4.4	11	3.6	10	4.5	10	5.0	21	4.0	2
Mex. Amer.	0	0.0	0	0.0	0	0.0	0	0.0	0	0.0	0	0.0	0
Puerto Rican	0	0.0	0	0.0	0	0.0	0	0.0	0	0.0	0	0.0	0
Hispanic	7	2.3	4	1.8	8	2.6	3	1.4	6	3.0	11	2.1	0
Total Minority	28	9.3	40	17.8	44	14.4	24	10.9	36	17.9	68	12.9	10
For. Nation.	0	0.0	2	0.9	2	0.7	0	0.0	1	0.5	2	0.4	0
Caucasian	236	78.4	163	72.4	217	70.9	182	82.7	143	71.1	399	75.9	117
Unknown	37	12.3	20	8.9	43	14.1	14	6.4	23	11.4	57	10.8	13
Total	301	57.2	225	42.8	306	58.2	220	41.8	201	38.2	526		140

Transfers

Transfers in	1
Transfers out	7

Tuition and Fees

	Resident	Nonresident
Full-time	$16,388	$25,980
Part-time	$10,447	$16,522

Living Expenses

Estimated living expenses for singles

Living on campus	Living off campus	Living at home
$14,196	$14,196	$14,196

The University of Akron School of Law

*ABA
Approved
Since
1961*

GPA and LSAT Scores

	Total	Full-time	Part-time
# of apps	2,230	1,858	372
# of offers	634	512	122
# of matrics	186	119	67
75% GPA	3.61	3.63	3.58
Median GPA	3.32	3.30	3.35
25% GPA	3.09	3.07	3.12
75% LSAT	159	159	156
Median LSAT	156	158	152
25% LSAT	151	154	151

Grants and Scholarships (from prior year)

	Total		Full-time		Part-time	
	#	%	#	%	#	%
Total # of students	525		309		216	
Total # receiving grants	182	34.7	152	49.2	30	13.9
Less than 1/2 tuition	53	10.1	41	13.3	12	5.6
Half to full tuition	29	5.5	18	5.8	11	5.1
Full tuition	46	8.8	46	14.9	0	0.0
More than full tuition	54	10.3	47	15.2	7	3.2
Median grant amount			$11,910		$5,000	

Informational and Library Resources

# of volumes and volume equivalents	290,582
# of titles	64,847
# of active serial subscriptions	3,312
Study seating capacity inside the library	295
# of full-time professional librarians	6
Hours per week library is open	95
# of open, wired connections available to students	16
# of networked computers available for use by students	46
# of simultaneous wireless users	1,380
Require computer?	No

JD Attrition (from prior year)

	Academic	Other	Total	
	#	#	#	%
1st year	15	15	30	15.8
2nd year	4	2	6	3.7
3rd year	1	0	1	0.7
4th year	0	0	0	0.0

Employment (9 months after graduation)

	Total	Percentage
Employment status known	185	98.4
Employment status unknown	3	1.6
Employed	173	93.5
Pursuing graduate degrees	2	1.1
Unemployed seeking employment	7	3.8
Unemployed not seeking employment	1	0.5
Unemployed and studying for the bar	2	1.1

Type of Employment

# employed in law firms	92	53.2
# employed in business and industry	42	24.3
# employed in government	24	13.9
# employed in public interest	8	4.6
# employed as judicial clerks	5	2.9
# employed in academia	1	0.6

Geographic Location

# employed in state	149	86.1
# employed in foreign countries	0	0.0
# of states where employed		14

Bar Passage Rates

Jurisdiction		Ohio	
Exam	Sum 05	Win 06	Total
# from school taking bar for the first time	139	30	169
School's pass rate for all first-time takers	83%	63%	79%
State's pass rate for all first-time takers	81%	76%	81%

The University of Akron School of Law

Admissions Office, 302 Buchtel Common
Akron, OH 44325-2901
Phone: 800.4.AKRON.U or 330.972.7331; Fax: 330.258.2343
E-mail: lawadmissions@uakron.edu; Website: www.uakron.edu/law

■ Introduction

Located just 45 minutes south of Cleveland, the University of Akron (UA) is one of the 50 largest universities in the country. UA is a comprehensive research and teaching university with degree programs ranging from the associate to the doctoral level. Founded in 1870, UA has celebrated more than 130 years of academic excellence while forging ahead to meet the complex needs of today's students.

The Akron School of Law was founded in 1921 and merged with UA in 1959. More than 6,000 students have graduated from the law school. Akron Law alumni practice throughout the US and abroad.

More than 150 Akron Law alumni have been or currently are judges. Akron alumni have been judges in 10 states and the District of Columbia, as well as in the federal court system.

■ Admission

In order to be considered for admission, the applicant must submit the application form and personal statement. The $35 fee is waived for online applications. The applicant must also take the LSAT and register for the LSDAS before the file may be sent to the Admission Committee. An applicant may apply during his/her final year of undergraduate studies. The bachelor's degree must be conferred prior to law school matriculation. Decisions are made on a rolling basis as soon as the files are complete. Priority deadline: March 1. For more details on admission, please see our website at *www.uakron.edu/law.*

Students enrolled in an ABA-accredited law school may apply for transfer or transient status. A law student who has completed neither more nor less than one year (approx. 30 semester credit hours) and is in good academic standing may apply for transfer. A law student who has the dean's permission to visit for one or two semesters may apply for transient status. Consult *www.uakron.edu/law* for details.

■ Tuition/Fees and Financial Aid (annual)

First-year students are considered for full or partial scholarships. No application is required. Most of the fall 2006 entering day class received scholarship assistance. Merit- and need-based loans are available. File FAFSA early.

■ Physical Facilities

The law building includes a 1987 addition to the library and a 1993 addition to the original structure. The university's $200 million New Landscape for Learning campus improvement program includes a new Student Union, Student Recreation and Wellness Center, Student Affairs Building, academic buildings, and parking decks. Approximately 30 acres of new green space were added to campus to create a more park-like setting. The law school is within one block of the Akron Municipal Court, the Court of Common Pleas, and the Ninth District Court of Appeals. The Federal Court is a few blocks from campus. While the law school is in the downtown Akron area, the campus is a green one bordered by grassy areas, decorative plantings, and fountains.

■ Intellectual Property Center

Patent, trademark, trade secret, copyright, and cyber law are among the many topics covered in the Intellectual Property Law program. Staffed by three full-time faculty, supplemented by four full-time and additional part-time faculty with special expertise, Akron's IP program is one of the most extensive in the nation, ranking fifth for intellectual property curricular offerings. Twenty-two IP courses are offered either every year or every other year, and more than six additional courses are planned.

In addition, Akron offers the only **LLM degree in IP** in Ohio and is one of only 17 such programs in the nation. This full-time or part-time graduate program provides law graduates with an opportunity to begin or continue a specialization in IP.

■ Curriculum/Special Programs

The first-year curriculum is traditional in content, using traditional and innovative interactive pedagogies. The upper-class curriculum is varied between basic courses and specialty courses, and also focuses on interactive learning pedagogies and development of crucial lawyering skills. All law students are eligible to participate in the programs offered and the services provided by the office of Academic Success. The director of academic success programs counsels students on study techniques, learning styles, time management, and other topics related to academic success. A comprehensive writing program designed to enhance students' skills in research, exposition, drafting, and argumentation is an integral part of the curriculum.

Four Juris Doctor (JD) Tracks: Litigation, business, taxation, and general. Other specialty areas include criminal, intellectual property, international, and labor and employment.

Five Joint Degrees: JD/Master in Business Administration, JD/Master of Science and Management in Human Resources, JD/Master in Taxation, JD/Master in Public Administration, and JD/Master in Applied Politics.

Two Certificate Programs: Intellectual Property and Litigation.

LLM Graduate Law Degree: Intellectual Property.

■ Competition Teams

Students have many opportunities to sharpen litigation skills by participating in regional and national mock trial, moot court, and negotiation competitions. Our litigation teams have had almost unparalleled success in competitions throughout the US and Europe. Every year that the National Institute of Trial Advocacy (NITA) ranks law school trial programs based on three-year averages of their performance in the three major national tournaments, Akron has been in the top 16 trial programs 16 times in the last 18 years. Akron tied for second in the nation in 2005–2006. In 2004, Akron won two national championships and has been second in national tournaments six times.

■ Legal Clinic

Students represent clients in court, at trial, and on appeal. A variety of opportunities for clinical training are offered.

Programs offered include Appellate Review; Clinical Seminar; Criminal, Judicial, and Public External Placement clinics; Prisoner Legal Assistance Clinic; Street Law; New Business Legal Clinic; Civil Litigation Clinic; Trial Litigation Clinic; and pro bono opportunities.

■ Student Activities and Leadership

Our more than 20 law student organizations include the *Akron Law Review*, Black Law Students Association, Environmental Law Society, Gay/Straight Law Alliance, Intellectual Property and Technology Law Association, International Law Society, Law Association for Women, Akron Public Interest Law Society, Student Bar Association, and more. Elections for leadership positions are held each year for day and evening students.

■ Library

UA's campus is wireless. The law library contains 290,000+ volumes. Students have access to 45.5 million library items, 10 million unique titles that may be delivered through OhioLink, 3.8 million library items through UA libraries catalog, and many full-text resources including 6,000 journals, 7.5 million articles, and 19,000 e-books. Students receive free e-mail and free Web access and can create free Web pages through UA. Law students receive free access to LexisNexis and Westlaw.

■ Career Planning and Placement

The Career Planning and Placement Office (CPPO) director counsels law students on résumé writing, job searches, interview skills, and preparation for entrance into the legal profession. On-campus interviews, minority clerkship program, attorney-student mentor program, employment-related seminars, and career fairs are offered. Akron's extensive law alumni database enables the CPPO to assist students with networking opportunities nationwide. This office assists in the placement of students in law-related positions during summer sessions and upper-division years. Graduates receive placement assistance, on request, throughout their careers. Akron's reputation for excellence in legal education and a subsequent high bar passage facilitates competitive placements for students and graduates in all areas of practice.

■ Visiting Akron Law

Several programs are offered throughout the year for prospective and admitted students to interact with law students, alumni, faculty, and administration at the School of Law. In addition, guests are welcome to schedule an appointment to visit a class, take a tour, or meet with an admission representative. Prospective students may join the e-mail and US mail database by registering *www.uakron.edu/law*. And for those unable to visit Akron Law, our representatives can also be met on the recruitment road each fall. Consult our website for our national recruitment schedule.

Applicant Profile

The University of Akron School of Law

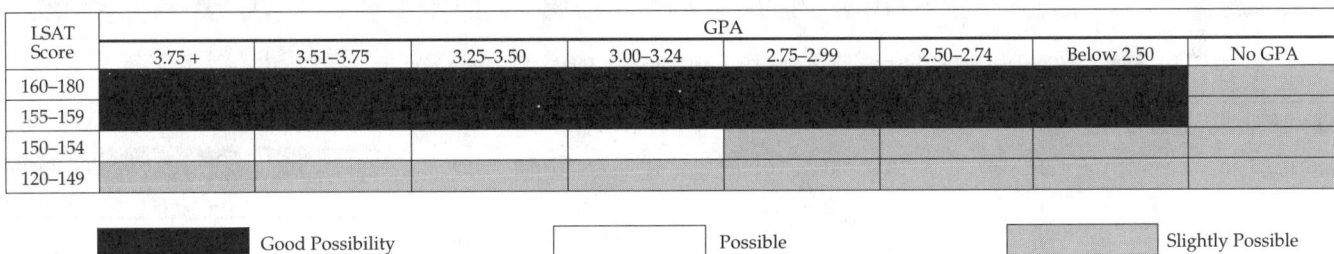

LSAT Score	GPA							
	3.75 +	3.51–3.75	3.25–3.50	3.00–3.24	2.75–2.99	2.50–2.74	Below 2.50	No GPA
160–180								
155–159								
150–154								
120–149								

■ Good Possibility   □ Possible   ▨ Slightly Possible

The University of Alabama School of Law

Box 870382
Tuscaloosa, AL 35487
Phone: 205.348.5440; Fax: 205.348.5439
E-mail: admissions@law.ua.edu; Website: www.law.ua.edu

ABA
Approved
Since
1926

The Basics

Type of school	Public
Term	Semester
Application deadline	3/1
Application fee	$35
Financial aid deadline	
Can first year start other than fall?	No
Student to faculty ratio	11.3 to 1
Does the university offer:	
housing restricted to law students?	No
graduate housing for which law students are eligible?	No

Faculty and Administrations

	Total		Men		Women		Minorities	
	Fall	Spr	Fall	Spr	Fall	Spr	Fall	Spr
Full-time	37	37	24	24	13	13	4	4
Other Full-time	2	2	0	0	2	2	0	0
Deans, librarians, & others who teach	4	4	4	4	0	0	0	0
Part-time	30	37	27	34	3	3	0	0
Total	73	80	55	62	18	18	4	4

Curriculum

	Full-time	Part-time
Typical first-year section size	52	0
Is there typically a "small section" of the first-year class, other than Legal Writing, taught by full-time faculty	No	No
If yes, typical size offered last year		
# of classroom course titles beyond first-year curriculum	114	
# of upper division courses, excluding seminars with an enrollment: Under 25	94	
25–49	39	
50–74	10	
75–99	2	
100+	2	
# of seminars	14	
# of seminar positions available	168	
# of seminar positions filled	141	0
# of positions available in simulation courses	272	
# of simulation positions filled	226	0
# of positions available in faculty supervised clinical courses	90	
# of faculty supervised clinical positions filled	87	0
# involved in field placements	76	0
# involved in law journals	128	0
# involved in interschool competitions	74	0
# of credit hours required to graduate	90	

JD Enrollment and Ethnicity

	Men #	Men %	Women #	Women %	Full-time #	Full-time %	Part-time #	Part-time %	1st-year #	1st-year %	Total #	Total %	JD Degs. Awd.
African Amer.	16	5.2	20	11.5	35	7.3	1	20.0	11	6.5	36	7.4	10
Amer. Indian	4	1.3	0	0.0	4	0.8	0	0.0	2	1.2	4	0.8	2
Asian Amer.	7	2.3	3	1.7	10	2.1	0	0.0	6	3.6	10	2.1	1
Mex. Amer.	0	0.0	0	0.0	0	0.0	0	0.0	0	0.0	0	0.0	2
Puerto Rican	0	0.0	0	0.0	0	0.0	0	0.0	0	0.0	0	0.0	0
Hispanic	3	1.0	4	2.3	7	1.5	0	0.0	4	2.4	7	1.4	0
Total Minority	30	9.7	27	15.5	56	11.7	1	20.0	23	13.6	57	11.8	15
For. Nation.	0	0.0	1	0.6	1	0.2	0	0.0	1	0.6	1	0.2	0
Caucasian	280	90.3	146	83.9	422	88.1	4	80.0	145	85.8	426	88.0	158
Unknown	0	0.0	0	0.0	0	0.0	0	0.0	0	0.0	0	0.0	0
Total	310	64.0	174	36.0	479	99.0	5	1.0	169	34.9	484		173

Transfers

Transfers in	9
Transfers out	2

Tuition and Fees

	Resident	Nonresident
Full-time	$9,736	$19,902
Part-time	$0	$0

Living Expenses

Estimated living expenses for singles

Living on campus	Living off campus	Living at home
$14,464	$14,464	$14,464

The University of Alabama School of Law

ABA Approved Since 1926

GPA and LSAT Scores

	Total	Full-time	Part-time
# of apps	1,105	1,105	0
# of offers	354	354	0
# of matrics	171	166	5
75% GPA	3.80	3.83	3.39
Median GPA	3.56	3.56	3.31
25% GPA	3.20	3.29	3.01
75% LSAT	165	165	156
Median LSAT	162	163	154
25% LSAT	159	159	150

Grants and Scholarships (from prior year)

	Total		Full-time		Part-time	
	#	%	#	%	#	%
Total # of students	482		482		0	
Total # receiving grants	184	38.2	184	38.2	0	0.0
Less than 1/2 tuition	49	10.2	49	10.2	0	0.0
Half to full tuition	45	9.3	45	9.3	0	0.0
Full tuition	58	12.0	58	12.0	0	0.0
More than full tuition	32	6.6	32	6.6	0	0.0
Median grant amount			$8,660		$0	

Informational and Library Resources

# of volumes and volume equivalents	593,705
# of titles	140,431
# of active serial subscriptions	3,393
Study seating capacity inside the library	512
# of full-time professional librarians	8
Hours per week library is open	110
# of open, wired connections available to students	38
# of networked computers available for use by students	14
# of simultaneous wireless users	325
Require computer?	No

JD Attrition (from prior year)

	Academic	Other	Total	
	#	#	#	%
1st year	0	9	9	5.8
2nd year	0	0	0	0.0
3rd year	0	0	0	0.0
4th year	0	0	0	0.0

Employment (9 months after graduation)

	Total	Percentage
Employment status known	187	100.0
Employment status unknown	0	0.0
Employed	175	93.6
Pursuing graduate degrees	4	2.1
Unemployed seeking employment	3	1.6
Unemployed not seeking employment	5	2.7
Unemployed and studying for the bar	0	0.0

Type of Employment

# employed in law firms	102	58.3
# employed in business and industry	20	11.4
# employed in government	22	12.6
# employed in public interest	14	8.0
# employed as judicial clerks	15	8.6
# employed in academia	2	1.1

Geographic Location

# employed in state	123	70.3
# employed in foreign countries	0	0.0
# of states where employed		18

Bar Passage Rates

Jurisdiction	Alabama			Georgia		
Exam	Sum 05	Win 06	Total	Sum 05	Win 06	Total
# from school taking bar for the first time	134	12	146	15	2	17
School's pass rate for all first-time takers	99%	75%	97%	80%	100%	82%
State's pass rate for all first-time takers	84%	68%	79%	86%	79%	84%

The University of Alabama School of Law

Box 870382
Tuscaloosa, AL 35487
Phone: 205.348.5440; Fax: 205.348.5439
E-mail: admissions@law.ua.edu; Website: www.law.ua.edu

■ Introduction

The University of Alabama School of Law, the only public law school in Alabama, offers students a nationally recognized, progressive legal education. The law school has served as the training ground for state and national leaders in the legal profession, business, and government. Law students are provided with an abundance of cultural, academic, and athletic opportunities through the university. The curriculum is traditional but diverse. The law school is student-centered; faculty and administration are accessible to students. Although the faculty's first priority is teaching, the professors are actively engaged in scholarly research and writing. Alabama is accredited by the ABA and the AALS.

■ Library and Physical Facilities

The law school building, which sits on 23 acres of the University of Alabama's campus in Tuscaloosa, was designed by Edward Durell Stone, who was the architect for the Museum of Modern Art in New York, the US Embassy in New Delhi, and the Kennedy Center for the Performing Arts, to name a few. Construction on a new wing and renovations to the existing building are complete. The wing includes new classrooms, the clinical offices, a cafeteria, a career services suite, meeting rooms, and a 24-hour computer lab. The Bounds Law Library provides users with a substantial research collection of Anglo-American and international legal materials. The library includes student study carrels, the Hugo Black Study, the Howell Heflin Conference Room, and the Payne Special Collections Room. The school is on a wireless network.

■ Special and Summer Programs

Clinical programs enable law students to gain valuable practical experience in interviewing clients, preparing cases, and participating in courtroom presentations. During the second and third years, students can choose to participate in the Elder Law, Domestic Violence, Civil, Community Development, Capital Defense, or public defender clinics.

The externship program offers students practical experience while receiving credit. Externships are available during the summers and the second and third academic years. The law school's Public Interest Institute awards grants to encourage students to participate in the area of public interest and honors students who perform public interest work. The institute also has a full-time director to assist students.

The joint JD/MBA program offers select students an opportunity to earn both an MBA and JD. Students may select from programs designed for them to earn both degrees within three or four years. The graduate program for international students provides international lawyers an opportunity to earn an LLM degree. The law school also offers a part-time LLM in Taxation Program for JD degree holders.

The law school's two summer programs at the University of Fribourg in Fribourg, Switzerland, and the Australian National University in Canberra, the capital of Australia, provide a unique international experience. Students may earn four to five credit hours in the Switzerland program and five credit hours in the Australian program. Both programs include a course surveying the host country's national law and a comparative doctrinal course. Summer school is open to students who have completed the first year.

■ Admission

A student must obtain a bachelor's degree at an accredited institution before enrolling, but may apply during his or her senior year. Applicants must take the LSAT, preferably in June or October in the year preceding enrollment, and register for LSDAS. Transcripts must show all schools attended. Application materials are available in the summer each year and accepted as early as August. March 1 is the application deadline. Applications are processed on a rolling basis; thus, applicants are encouraged to submit competitive applications early. The two most significant factors for admission are the undergraduate GPA and LSAT score. However, the law school believes that the law school experience is enriched by a diverse group of students. The Admissions Committee also considers other factors, such as honors, activities, unique work or service experience, difficulty of undergraduate courses, writing ability, trends in academic performance, leadership roles, travel experience, exceptional talents, career achievements, graduate school performance, and history of overcoming adversity. Written letters of recommendation are not required, but are encouraged. The law school recommends that letters be submitted to the LSDAS. Students are admitted only for the fall semester and only for full-time study.

■ Student Activities

A broad range of student activities adds to the students' law school experience. Student organizations represent diverse interests. These include the Student Bar Association, Black Law Students Association, Public Interest Law Association, Civil Rights Law Students Association, Dorbin Association (women's support group), Law Students for Choice, Gay Straight Alliance, Environmental Law Society, International Law Society, Just Democracy, Labor and Employment Law Society, Law Democrats, Law Republicans, Business Law Society, Criminal Law Association, Defense Lawyers Association, Future Trial Lawyers Association, Christian Legal Society, Sports and Entertainment Law Society, and Latin American Law Association.

The School of Law also offers numerous writing opportunities. The *Alabama Law Review*, a nationally recognized law journal, is edited by students and devotes substantial space to national and state issues. The *Journal of the Legal Profession* and the *Law and Psychology Review* are also student-edited law journals.

Moot court and trial advocacy teams have enjoyed exceptional success over the years. The law school sponsors teams in several moot court, specialty, and trial advocacy competitions. The moot court and trial advocacy teams have won many team and individual awards in both regional and national competitions.

■ Expenses and Financial Aid

The majority of students enrolled in the School of Law finance their legal education through loans, savings, earnings, or contributions from their families. Applicants are considered automatically for first-year scholarships, which are typically based on factors such as GPA and LSAT performance, and may be based on other factors such as economic need. As part of the scholarship program, outstanding nonresident students may receive a nonresident tuition waiver. Scholarships sometimes are renewable during the second and third years—depending upon funding, the student's need, and whether the recipient maintains stated levels of academic achievement. Following acceptance by the law school, each admitted student who applies for federal aid through the Free Application for Federal Student Aid (FAFSA) receives a financial aid packet from the university's Financial Aid Office. Information on loans can be obtained by contacting Student Financial Aid, the University of Alabama, Box 870162, Tuscaloosa, AL 35487-0162. Phone: 205.348.6756; *www.financialaid.ua.edu*. Applicants should complete the FAFSA form as soon after January 1 as possible, and may apply online at *www.fafsa.ed.gov*.

■ Career Services

The Career Services Office assists students in their efforts to find employment. The office provides individual career counseling, group presentations, speaker programs, and library and database resources. Seminars are presented on résumé writing, interviewing techniques, job-search techniques, judicial clerkships, and nontraditional legal jobs, to name a few. Extensive on-campus interviewing occurs. The law school also participates in job fairs in Atlanta, New York City, Chicago, and Washington, DC. The employment rate within nine months of graduation was 98 percent for the Class of 2005.

■ Housing

The University of Alabama maintains residence halls and units for students; however, most law students live off campus. The cost of living in Tuscaloosa for a single law student ranges from approximately $500 to $1,100 per month. For information on university housing, students must contact the Office of Residential Life, the University of Alabama, Box 870399, Tuscaloosa, AL 35487-0399. Phone: 205.348.6676 or e-mail: *reslife@sa.ua.edu*.

Applicant Profile

The University of Alabama School of Law
This grid includes only applicants who earned 120–180 LSAT scores under standard administrations.

LSAT Score	GPA								
	3.75 +	3.50–3.74	3.25–3.49	3.00–3.24	2.75–2.99	2.50–2.74	2.25–2.49	2.00–2.24	Below 2.00
175–180									
170–174									
165–169									
160–164									
155–159									
150–154									
145–149									
140–144									
135–139									
130–134									
125–129									
120–124									

Good Possibility   Possible   Unlikely

Albany Law School of Union University

80 New Scotland Avenue
Albany, NY 12208
Phone: 518.445.2326; Fax: 518.445.2369
E-mail: admissions@albanylaw.edu; Website: www.albanylaw.edu

ABA Approved Since 1930

The Basics

Type of school	Private
Term	Semester
Application deadline	3/15
Application fee	$60
Financial aid deadline	
Can first year start other than fall?	No
Student to faculty ratio	15.8 to 1
Does the university offer:	
housing restricted to law students?	No
graduate housing for which law students are eligible?	No

Faculty and Administrators

	Total		Men		Women		Minorities	
	Fall	Spr	Fall	Spr	Fall	Spr	Fall	Spr
Full-time	47	47	26	26	21	21	8	8
Other Full-time	1	1	0	0	1	1	0	0
Deans, librarians, & others who teach	9	9	5	5	4	4	0	0
Part-time	35	35	26	26	9	9	3	4
Total	92	92	57	57	35	35	11	12

Curriculum

	Full-time	Part-time
Typical first-year section size	63	0
Is there typically a "small section" of the first-year class, other than Legal Writing, taught by full-time faculty	Yes	No
If yes, typical size offered last year	42	
# of classroom course titles beyond first-year curriculum	113	

# of upper division courses, excluding seminars with an enrollment:		
Under 25	62	
25–49	26	
50–74	13	
75–99	4	
100+	11	

	Full-time	Part-time
# of seminars	40	
# of seminar positions available	760	
# of seminar positions filled	475	0
# of positions available in simulation courses	221	
# of simulation positions filled	199	0
# of positions available in faculty supervised clinical courses	95	
# of faculty supervised clinical positions filled	95	0
# involved in field placements	208	0
# involved in law journals	214	0
# involved in interschool competitions	36	0
# of credit hours required to graduate	87	

JD Enrollment and Ethnicity

	Men		Women		Full-time		Part-time		1st-year		Total		JD Degs. Awd.
	#	%	#	%	#	%	#	%	#	%	#	%	
African Amer.	8	2.1	24	7.1	28	4.1	4	10.8	12	4.8	32	4.5	12
Amer. Indian	0	0.0	0	0.0	0	0.0	0	0.0	0	0.0	0	0.0	0
Asian Amer.	21	5.5	36	10.7	57	8.4	0	0.0	23	9.3	57	7.9	10
Mex. Amer.	2	0.5	1	0.3	3	0.4	0	0.0	0	0.0	3	0.4	1
Puerto Rican	2	0.5	7	2.1	9	1.3	0	0.0	1	0.4	9	1.3	2
Hispanic	9	2.4	9	2.7	18	2.6	0	0.0	6	2.4	18	2.5	6
Total Minority	42	11.0	77	22.9	115	16.9	4	10.8	42	16.9	119	16.6	31
For. Nation.	7	1.8	3	0.9	9	1.3	1	2.7	5	2.0	10	1.4	7
Caucasian	326	85.6	246	73.2	540	79.4	32	86.5	191	77.0	572	79.8	211
Unknown	6	1.6	10	3.0	16	2.4	0	0.0	10	4.0	16	2.2	2
Total	381	53.1	336	46.9	680	94.8	37	5.2	248	34.6	717		251

Transfers

Transfers in	5
Transfers out	9

Tuition and Fees

	Resident	Nonresident
Full-time	$35,079	$35,079
Part-time	$26,342	$26,342

Living Expenses

Estimated living expenses for singles

Living on campus	Living off campus	Living at home
N/A	$15,855	$8,048

Albany Law School of Union University

*ABA
Approved
Since
1930*

GPA and LSAT Scores

	Total	Full-time	Part-time
# of apps	2,009	2,009	0
# of offers	836	836	0
# of matrics	249	249	0
75% GPA	3.51	3.51	0.00
Median GPA	3.21	3.21	0.00
25% GPA	2.86	2.86	0.00
75% LSAT	158	158	0
Median LSAT	154	154	0
25% LSAT	152	152	0

Grants and Scholarships (from prior year)

	Total		Full-time		Part-time	
	#	%	#	%	#	%
Total # of students	739		702		37	
Total # receiving grants	251	34.0	231	32.9	20	54.1
Less than 1/2 tuition	110	14.9	98	14.0	12	32.4
Half to full tuition	135	18.3	129	18.4	6	16.2
Full tuition	6	0.8	4	0.6	2	5.4
More than full tuition	0	0.0	0	0.0	0	0.0
Median grant amount			$16,000		$8,400	

Informational and Library Resources

# of volumes and volume equivalents	672,153
# of titles	190,761
# of active serial subscriptions	3,015
Study seating capacity inside the library	472
# of full-time professional librarians	8
Hours per week library is open	104
# of open, wired connections available to students	866
# of networked computers available for use by students	121
# of simultaneous wireless users	99,999
Require computer?	No

JD Attrition (from prior year)

	Academic	Other	Total	
	#	#	#	%
1st year	12	2	14	5.6
2nd year	0	14	14	6.4
3rd year	1	0	1	0.4
4th year	0	0	0	0.0

Employment (9 months after graduation)

	Total	Percentage
Employment status known	244	100.0
Employment status unknown	0	0.0
Employed	234	95.9
Pursuing graduate degrees	1	0.4
Unemployed seeking employment	0	0.0
Unemployed not seeking employment	1	0.4
Unemployed and studying for the bar	8	3.3

Type of Employment

	Total	Percentage
# employed in law firms	103	44.0
# employed in business and industry	57	24.4
# employed in government	46	19.7
# employed in public interest	10	4.3
# employed as judicial clerks	12	5.1
# employed in academia	6	2.6

Geographic Location

	Total	Percentage
# employed in state	196	83.8
# employed in foreign countries	0	0.0
# of states where employed	16	

Bar Passage Rates

Jurisdiction	New York		
Exam	Sum 05	Win 06	Total
# from school taking bar for the first time	218	9	227
School's pass rate for all first-time takers	78%	56%	78%
State's pass rate for all first-time takers	76%	61%	74%

Albany Law School of Union University

80 New Scotland Avenue
Albany, NY 12208
Phone: 518.445.2326; Fax: 518.445.2369
E-mail: admissions@albanylaw.edu; Website: www.albanylaw.edu

■ Introduction

The only law school in the capital of New York State, Albany Law School is the oldest private, independent law school in North America. Our location, in the center of state government, provides unprecedented opportunities for internships, field placements, clinical experience, and career opportunities upon graduation. Our world-class faculty is dedicated and accessible. Students have access to New York's highest court, federal courts, and the state legislature, as well as to a thriving tech-based economy. The employment rate for our graduates is well above the national average for law schools for the past 25 years.

■ The Academic Experience

From your first day at Albany Law School you will be challenged by a rigorous academic curriculum. You will get a firm foundation in fundamental areas of law plus opportunities to shape your learning to fit your professional interests.

As a first-year student, you begin to acquire the skills that will become the foundation of your legal career. As part of our innovative Introduction to Lawyering course, you will represent a plaintiff or defendant in a simulated case where you conduct legal research, draft motions and memoranda, and participate in client interviews and negotiations. The class culminates with each student presenting an oral argument before some of the state's most notable attorneys.

As a second- and third-year student, you can focus your studies in one of 15 concentrations to complement coursework. Opportunities include six clinical projects and more than 140 field placement internships in the Albany region, many of them in state and federal government positions as well as in law firms and high-tech companies. Students also participate in real-world work through the Government Law Center, the Science and Technology Law Center, and study-abroad programs. Some students choose to pursue a joint-degree program with an area graduate school, earning a JD while working toward a four-year master's degree.

■ Real-life Experience

Our groundbreaking legal centers and award-winning clinical programs provide the valuable hands-on experience that employers find highly desirable. You work alongside committed clinical faculty and practicing attorneys to assist low-income clients with real legal issues relating to health law, HIV/AIDS, disabilities, domestic violence, disputes with the Internal Revenue Service, and financial investments. You will also work with prosecutors, judges, and experienced attorneys through our field placement program.

Because of our unique location, you interact with the leaders in New York state government—countless Albany Law alumni—and visionaries building New York's high-technology base through the programs at the Government Law Center and the Science and Technology Law Center.

In the Government Law Center you conduct research, contribute to publications, and participate in conferences and special projects that promote the study of the issues facing government, public policy, and public service.

You can provide legal services to start-up ventures and early-stage technology companies in the Tech Valley, New York City, and throughout New York by working and studying with attorneys at the Science and Technology Law Center.

■ Your Career

From your first week at school, our Career Center helps you develop a career plan and supports you throughout your job search. Professional career counselors help you define career goals, craft resumes and cover letters, prepare you for interviews, and compare employment offers.

The Career Center is a state-of-the-art facility with multiple interview rooms set aside for professionals to conduct on-campus interviews. These rooms are equipped with all the amenities of a law office and are extremely popular with employers. Our job search software, which works like a private *Monster.com*, is exclusive to Albany Law students and alumni. Some 4,000 employers currently post jobs on the private system.

Job fairs, information sessions, workshops, and panel discussions on a variety of employment related topics occur almost daily. The Career Center hosts more than 1,200 interviews each year and conducts off-campus interview programs in metropolitan areas, including New York City and Boston, specifically for Albany Law School students. Our alumni are avid supporters of these efforts and participate enthusiastically in center activities.

Our graduates find jobs in law firms, government agencies, public interest organizations, and business and industry throughout the country. Nearly 30 percent of Albany Law School graduates work in the New York City metropolitan area, with large groups of alumni in Boston, Washington, DC, and business centers along the eastern seaboard as far as Florida.

The employment rate for the Class of 2004 was nearly 95 percent—above the national average of 88 percent, and consistently above national rates for over 20 years.

■ Our Community

The Albany Law School community of approximately 650 students, 55 full-time faculty, and 54 part-time faculty is intimate, respectful, and supportive. We welcome students and faculty with diverse backgrounds and talents, and provide an outstanding environment for the pursuit of scholarship, teaching and public service.

The small size of our student body fosters an environment that encourages camaraderie and frequent contacts between students and faculty.

Nearly 12 percent of our students graduated five or more years before entering law school and had careers in other professions prior to beginning their legal studies. Fifty percent of our students are women, 48 percent are from outside New York state, and 20 percent are members of a minority group.

■ Student Life

You have dozens of opportunities to participate in student organizations and activities around specific academic, professional, social, cultural, or athletic interests.

Three student-edited journals, the *Albany Law Review*, the *Albany Law Journal of Science and Technology*, and the *Albany Law Environmental Outlook* offer cocurricular research and writing opportunities.

Our nationally recognized Moot Court Program enables you to develop skills in trial advocacy, appellate advocacy, client counseling, and negotiating while competing in both intramural and interscholastic competitions.

The Capital Region is home to 16 colleges and universities and boasts museums, galleries, restaurants, shops, theaters, nightclubs for every taste, venues that host professional sporting events, and performing arts centers that attract national acts. The Adirondack, Berkshire, and Catskill mountains offer skiing, camping, hiking, and water sports, as well at the Saratoga Race Course for thoroughbred and harness racing. Metropolitan centers in New York City, Boston, and Montreal are all within an easy drive, and major carriers operate out of the Albany International Airport.

■ Our Campus

Albany Law School's facilities embrace our 154-year history, while supporting a twenty-first century legal education. The open design of the 53,000-square-foot Schaffer Law Library— a federal depository library—provides an inviting environment with seating for hundreds of students. Book and microfilm collections number more than half a million volumes, and the library supplements its collection with online databases and legal research systems, including LexisNexis and Westlaw. The library also houses technological devices for the hearing and visually impaired.

The main building of Albany Law School is known as the 1928 Building, acknowledging its year of construction.

The building has been recently renovated and houses contemporary lecture halls, seminar-style classrooms, a modern, paperless moot courtroom, and "smart" classrooms with wireless Internet access and advanced audio, video, computing, and conferencing systems.

A 45,000-square-foot building built in 2000 houses the Albany Law School clinic, law centers, and administrative offices, as well as several classrooms, including a high-tech distance learning classroom.

■ Admission and Financial Aid

Albany Law School has committed nearly $4 million in scholarship assistance. Approximately 35 percent of first-year students receive awards that average $20,000 for each year of study.

When evaluating each individual application, the Admissions Committee takes a holistic approach, reviewing LSAT score, undergraduate grade-point average, strength of the undergraduate program, rigor of the undergraduate curriculum, and life experience. The committee seeks to enroll a student body that enriches the educational experience of all of its members. Albany Law School also seeks to provide future members of the bar who reflect the diversity and sensibilities of our society.

Approximately 90 percent of our students qualify for financial aid, via federal, state, and private loans, or for part-time employment to assist in meeting educational expenses.

We encourage you to visit Albany Law School—meet our faculty, speak with our students, and tour our beautiful facilities. We look forward to meeting you.

Applicant Profile

Albany Law School attracts talented, diverse students from a spectrum of backgrounds. Life experience, professional and volunteer engagements, as well as cultural and political richness enhance our learning community. Applicants come from the highest ranks of their prior graduate and undergraduate institutions. LSAT scores and prior academic performance are important in assisting our faculty admissions committee in offering seats to applicants. Those indicators are, however, not the sole factors weighed when admissions decisions are made. Interested applicants are encouraged to explore how their individual characteristics might be enhanced by an Albany Law School education.

American University, Washington College of Law

4801 Massachusetts Avenue NW, Suite 507
Washington, DC 20016
Phone: 202.274.4101; Fax: 202.274.4107
E-mail: wcladmit@wcl.american.edu; Website: www.wcl.american.edu

*ABA
Approved
Since
1940*

The Basics

Type of school	Private
Term	Semester
Application deadline	3/1
Application fee	$65
Financial aid deadline	3/1
Can first year start other than fall?	No
Student to faculty ratio	14.0 to 1
Does the university offer:	
housing restricted to law students?	No
graduate housing for which law students are eligible?	Yes

Faculty and Administrators

	Total Fall	Total Spr	Men Fall	Men Spr	Women Fall	Women Spr	Minorities Fall	Minorities Spr
Full-time	82	77	46	44	36	33	17	11
Other Full-time	1	1	1	1	0	0	0	0
Deans, librarians, & others who teach	10	10	4	4	6	6	2	2
Part-time	127	142	77	94	50	48	15	16
Total	220	230	128	143	92	87	34	29

Curriculum

	Full-time	Part-time
Typical first-year section size	92	99
Is there typically a "small section" of the first-year class, other than Legal Writing, taught by full-time faculty	Yes	Yes
If yes, typical size offered last year	45	53
# of classroom course titles beyond first-year curriculum	305	
# of upper division courses, excluding seminars with an enrollment: Under 25	135	
25–49	50	
50–74	14	
75–99	20	
100+	0	
# of seminars	146	
# of seminar positions available	2,365	
# of seminar positions filled	1,537	372
# of positions available in simulation courses	468	
# of simulation positions filled	317	92
# of positions available in faculty supervised clinical courses	240	
# of faculty supervised clinical positions filled	197	26
# involved in field placements	180	12
# involved in law journals	276	25
# involved in interschool competitions	52	1
# of credit hours required to graduate	86	

JD Enrollment and Ethnicity

	Men #	Men %	Women #	Women %	Full-time #	Full-time %	Part-time #	Part-time %	1st-year #	1st-year %	Total #	Total %	JD Degs. Awd.
African Amer.	35	5.3	87	10.6	90	7.4	32	12.0	49	10.5	122	8.2	39
Amer. Indian	4	0.6	11	1.3	12	1.0	3	1.1	6	1.3	15	1.0	1
Asian Amer.	68	10.2	104	12.7	143	11.8	29	10.9	44	9.4	172	11.6	49
Mex. Amer.	13	2.0	24	2.9	35	2.9	2	0.7	13	2.8	37	2.5	9
Puerto Rican	6	0.9	8	1.0	12	1.0	2	0.7	7	1.5	14	0.9	3
Hispanic	52	7.8	91	11.1	122	10.0	21	7.9	54	11.6	143	9.6	30
Total Minority	178	26.8	325	39.7	414	34.0	89	33.3	173	37.0	503	33.9	131
For. Nation.	6	0.9	5	0.6	11	0.9	0	0.0	0	0.0	11	0.7	3
Caucasian	461	69.3	485	59.3	771	63.4	175	65.5	293	62.7	946	63.8	265
Unknown	20	3.0	3	0.4	20	1.6	3	1.1	1	0.2	23	1.6	5
Total	665	44.8	818	55.2	1216	82.0	267	18.0	467	31.5	1483		404

Transfers

Transfers in	65
Transfers out	50

Tuition and Fees

	Resident	Nonresident
Full-time	$35,104	$35,104
Part-time	$24,596	$24,596

Living Expenses

Estimated living expenses for singles

Living on campus	Living off campus	Living at home
$18,026	$18,026	$18,026

American University, Washington College of Law

*ABA
Approved
Since
1940*

GPA and LSAT Scores

	Total	Full-time	Part-time
# of apps	8,664	7,601	1,063
# of offers	2,086	1,877	209
# of matrics	469	379	90
75% GPA	3.59	3.60	3.50
Median GPA	3.38	3.42	3.28
25% GPA	3.13	3.15	3.00
75% LSAT	163	163	161
Median LSAT	161	162	160
25% LSAT	158	158	157

Grants and Scholarships (from prior year)

	Total		Full-time		Part-time	
	#	%	#	%	#	%
Total # of students	1,404		1,128		276	
Total # receiving grants	315	22.4	310	27.5	5	1.8
Less than 1/2 tuition	234	16.7	229	20.3	5	1.8
Half to full tuition	6	0.4	6	0.5	0	0.0
Full tuition	21	1.5	21	1.9	0	0.0
More than full tuition	13	0.9	13	1.2	0	0.0
Median grant amount			$11,000		$2,700	

Informational and Library Resources

# of volumes and volume equivalents	585,600
# of titles	243,746
# of active serial subscriptions	6,761
Study seating capacity inside the library	675
# of full-time professional librarians	8
Hours per week library is open	119
# of open, wired connections available to students	1,664
# of networked computers available for use by students	178
# of simultaneous wireless users	1,440
Require computer?	No

JD Attrition (from prior year)

	Academic	Other	Total	
	#	#	#	%
1st year	0	52	52	11.2
2nd year	0	0	0	0.0
3rd year	0	0	0	0.0
4th year	0	0	0	0.0

Employment (9 months after graduation)

	Total	Percentage
Employment status known	555	100.0
Employment status unknown	0	0.0
Employed	506	91.2
Pursuing graduate degrees	22	4.0
Unemployed seeking employment	6	1.1
Unemployed not seeking employment	15	2.7
Unemployed and studying for the bar	6	1.1
Type of Employment		
# employed in law firms	214	42.3
# employed in business and industry	92	18.2
# employed in government	65	12.8
# employed in public interest	41	8.1
# employed as judicial clerks	88	17.4
# employed in academia	6	1.2
Geographic Location		
# employed in state	226	44.7
# employed in foreign countries	6	1.2
# of states where employed		31

Bar Passage Rates

Jurisdiction	Maryland		
Exam	Sum 05	Win 06	Total
# from school taking bar for the first time	133	14	147
School's pass rate for all first-time takers	80%	79%	80%
State's pass rate for all first-time takers	76%	66%	74%

American University, Washington College of Law

4801 Massachusetts Avenue NW, Suite 507
Washington, DC 20016
Phone: 202.274.4101; Fax: 202.274.4107
E-mail: wcladmit@wcl.american.edu; Website: www.wcl.american.edu

■ Introduction

American University Washington College of Law (WCL) offers an opportunity for the study of law in the center of the nation's legal institutions. The law school is minutes from downtown Washington, but at the same time offers the facilities and ambiance of a campus environment in one of the city's most beautiful residential neighborhoods. Founded in 1896 by two women, the law school is national in character. WCL offers renowned programs in experiential learning (clinics and externships), international law, law and government, intellectual property, business, environmental law, health law, and gender. It is committed to the development of the intellectual abilities, professional values, and practical skills required to prepare lawyers to practice in an increasingly complex and transnational world. The school is noted for the accessibility of faculty and administration to its students.

■ Library and Physical Facilities

The two-story library is the heart of the complex and seats over 600 students. The entire law school and law library facility has wireless access, and most of the law library seating has wired access as well. The library has over 550,000 volumes and access to a number of databases including LexisNexis, Westlaw, HeinOnline, Making of Modern Law, and AccessUN. There are a number of research stations, and network printing is available to the community as well. The library collection includes European Community and US Government depositories and the Baxter Collection in International Law. Students also have access to the university's library, the Library of Congress, specialized agency libraries, and other area law libraries to which the school is electronically linked.

■ Curriculum

The law school offers full- and part-time programs leading to the JD degree, which is awarded after satisfactory completion of 86 credit hours, 34 of which are prescribed. All degree candidates must also fulfill an upper-level writing requirement. While a modified version of the Socratic method is the dominant form of teaching in the first year, faculty increasingly employ such methodologies as role-playing, simulations, and small group collaborative exercises. The goal is to develop the skills of critical analysis, provide perspectives on the law and lawyering, and deepen understanding of fundamental legal principles. In the Legal Rhetoric program, basic legal research and writing skills are taught to groups of students by full-time faculty (23 students per section) and practicing attorneys (12 students per section). In the second and third years, students elect a course of study drawing from advanced courses, seminars, independent research, externships, and clinical programs. Students are exposed to a variety of teaching approaches by the law school's distinguished full-time tenured and tenure-track faculty and its many adjunct professors.

■ Special Programs

While many of the advanced courses are taught in a traditional classroom setting, a variety of other innovative teaching modes are available to enhance research skills and provide professional training.

- **Clinical Program**—The Washington College of Law enjoys a national reputation for clinical education. Second- and third-year students may participate in the Civil Practice Clinic for both full- and part-time students, the Community and Economic Development Law Clinic, the Disability Rights Law Clinic, the International Human Rights Law Clinic, and the Intellectual Property Law Clinic; third-year students may also develop their lawyering abilities in the Criminal Justice Clinic, the DC Law Students in Court Clinic, the Domestic Violence Clinic, and the Tax Clinic. The Women and the Law program also includes a clinical component in which students represent indigent women in family law cases in the District of Columbia courts. This program is designed to integrate women's legal studies into the overall curriculum and to heighten awareness about legal issues affecting women.

- **Dual-degree Programs**—American University offers three domestic dual-degree programs for students seeking to enhance their law degree with additional graduate coursework. Complementing the law school's nationally recognized curriculum in international law, the university offers a combined JD/MA in International Affairs with the School of International Service. The JD/MBA with the Kogod School of Business prepares students to meet the demanding aspects of business-oriented practice. The JD/MS in Justice, Law, and Society with the School of Public Affairs offers a thorough understanding of how law intersects with theories of justice and justice systems in our society. In addition to our domestic dual-degree programs, the Washington College of Law offers three international dual-degree programs with law schools in Ottawa, Canada; Paris, France; and Madrid, Spain. These programs provide students more opportunities to practice law in the international arena.

- **The Externship Program**—The program places upper-level students in many governmental, nonprofit, and public interest entities throughout the DC metropolitan area. More than 300 students participate in an externship each year.

- **Graduate Study**—Graduate study is available leading to either an LLM or SJD degree in International Legal Studies or Law and Government.

- **Summer Programs**—The law school offers three intensive summer programs in the areas of international arbitration, human rights, and environmental law.

- **Study Abroad**—Students have the opportunity to study law for a semester in more than 18 different countries or during the summer in Turkey, Chile, and Europe (London, Paris, and Geneva).

■ Admission

Applicants to the law school are admitted based on the strength of their entire academic and related record. The Committee on Admissions gives primary emphasis to the undergraduate record, LSAT scores, and other major accomplishments and achievements, whether academic, work-related, or extracurricular. The benefits the school derives from racial, ethnic, cultural, and geographical diversity among its students are considered in admission decisions. Members of disadvantaged and minority groups are encouraged to apply. Admission to the law school is highly competitive and operates on a modified rolling admission basis, so early application is strongly encouraged.

■ Student Activities

The law school has four journals and several publications edited and published by students selected on the basis of scholarship and creative research. These include the *American University Law Review*, the *International Law Review*, the *Administrative Law Review*, the *Journal of Gender, Social Policy and the Law*, the *Human Rights Brief*, the *Business Law Brief*, *Sustainable Development Law and Policy*, and the *Modern American*. The Moot Court Board sponsors intraschool competitions for first-year and upper-level students and selects representatives for a number of interschool competitions, including the National Moot Court Competition. There are more than 40 active student organizations, including the Asian-Pacific American Law Students Association, Black Law Students Association, Latino/a Law Students Association, South Asian Law Students Association, Lambda Law Society, Equal Justice Foundation, Federalist Society, International Law Society, Intellectual Property Society, National Security and Law Society, Law and Government Society, and Women's Law Association.

■ Career Services

Staffed by seven full-time counselors, the Office of Career and Professional Development provides individual assistance to students on career counseling and the techniques of job searching. The office arranges for both on- and off-campus recruitment for summer and permanent legal positions, and participates in a variety of hiring consortia, including the Boston Lawyers Group, the New Hampshire Job Fair, the Delaware Minority Job Fair, regional Black Law Students Association fairs, and the ABA Business Law Section Career Forum. In addition, the office coordinates regional interview programs in New York, Boston, Atlanta, and Southern California.

Applicant Profile

The Committee on Admissions considers a number of factors when evaluating a candidate for admission; therefore we elected not to include a grid based on undergraduate GPA and LSAT scores. Many applicants have similar scores, but each applicant has a unique background of academic, cultural, and professional experiences and achievements. The committee weighs all of these factors when determining a candidate's suitability for admission.

Appalachian School of Law

Post Office Box 2825, 1169 Edgewater Drive
Grundy, VA 24614
Phone: 800.895.7411 (toll free) or 276.935.4349; Fax: 276.935.8496
E-mail: studentservices@asl.edu; Website: www.asl.edu

ABA Approved Since 2001

The Basics

Type of school	Private
Term	Semester
Application deadline	6/1
Application fee	$60
Financial aid deadline	5/15
Can first year start other than fall?	No
Student to faculty ratio	21.6 to 1
Does the university offer:	
housing restricted to law students?	No
graduate housing for which law students are eligible?	No

Faculty and Administrators

	Total		Men		Women		Minorities	
	Fall	Spr	Fall	Spr	Fall	Spr	Fall	Spr
Full-time	14	14	9	9	5	5	3	3
Other Full-time	1	1	0	0	1	1	0	0
Deans, librarians, & others who teach	4	4	3	3	1	1	1	1
Part-time	2	3	2	2	0	1	0	0
Total	**21**	**22**	**14**	**14**	**7**	**8**	**4**	**4**

Curriculum

	Full-time	Part-time
Typical first-year section size	138	0
Is there typically a "small section" of the first-year class, other than Legal Writing, taught by full-time faculty	Yes	No
If yes, typical size offered last year	72	
# of classroom course titles beyond first-year curriculum		38
# of upper division courses, excluding seminars with an enrollment: Under 25		19
25–49		4
50–74		2
75–99		2
100+		10
# of seminars		6
# of seminar positions available		150
# of seminar positions filled	100	0
# of positions available in simulation courses		579
# of simulation positions filled	450	0
# of positions available in faculty supervised clinical courses		0
# of faculty supervised clinical positions filled	0	0
# involved in field placements	135	0
# involved in law journals	27	0
# involved in interschool competitions	25	0
# of credit hours required to graduate		90

JD Enrollment and Ethnicity

	Men #	Men %	Women #	Women %	Full-time #	Full-time %	Part-time #	Part-time %	1st-year #	1st-year %	Total #	Total %	JD Degs. Awd.
African Amer.	3	1.2	2	1.8	5	1.4	0	0.0	1	0.6	5	1.4	3
Amer. Indian	1	0.4	0	0.0	1	0.3	0	0.0	1	0.6	1	0.3	0
Asian Amer.	2	0.8	2	1.8	4	1.1	0	0.0	2	1.2	4	1.1	7
Mex. Amer.	0	0.0	0	0.0	0	0.0	0	0.0	0	0.0	0	0.0	0
Puerto Rican	2	0.8	0	0.0	2	0.5	0	0.0	2	1.2	2	0.5	0
Hispanic	7	2.7	2	1.8	9	2.4	0	0.0	5	3.1	9	2.4	1
Total Minority	15	5.9	6	5.3	21	5.7	0	0.0	11	6.8	21	5.7	11
For. Nation.	0	0.0	0	0.0	0	0.0	0	0.0	0	0.0	0	0.0	0
Caucasian	197	77.3	97	85.1	294	79.7	0	0.0	110	68.3	294	79.7	103
Unknown	43	16.9	11	9.6	54	14.6	0	0.0	40	24.8	54	14.6	0
Total	255	69.1	114	30.9	369	100.0	0	0.0	161	43.6	369		114

Transfers

Transfers in	2
Transfers out	20

Tuition and Fees

	Resident	Nonresident
Full-time	$22,775	$22,775
Part-time	$0	$0

Living Expenses

Estimated living expenses for singles

Living on campus	Living off campus	Living at home
N/A	$14,795	N/A

Appalachian School of Law

*ABA
Approved
Since
2001*

GPA and LSAT Scores

	Total	Full-time	Part-time
# of apps	1,714	1,714	0
# of offers	718	718	0
# of matrics	163	163	0
75% GPA	3.32	3.32	0.00
Median GPA	2.97	2.97	0.00
25% GPA	2.59	2.59	0.00
75% LSAT	152	152	0
Median LSAT	149	149	0
25% LSAT	147	147	0

Grants and Scholarships (from prior year)

	Total		Full-time		Part-time	
	#	%	#	%	#	%
Total # of students	364		364		0	
Total # receiving grants	87	23.9	86	23.6	1	0.0
Less than 1/2 tuition	30	8.2	30	8.2	0	0.0
Half to full tuition	42	11.5	41	11.3	1	0.0
Full tuition	15	4.1	15	4.1	0	0.0
More than full tuition	0	0.0	0	0.0	0	0.0
Median grant amount			$9,950		$0	

Informational and Library Resources

# of volumes and volume equivalents	202,544
# of titles	125,063
# of active serial subscriptions	3,498
Study seating capacity inside the library	232
# of full-time professional librarians	6
Hours per week library is open	88
# of open, wired connections available to students	580
# of networked computers available for use by students	29
# of simultaneous wireless users	240
Require computer?	No

JD Attrition (from prior year)

	Academic	Other	Total	
	#	#	#	%
1st year	12	2	14	9.8
2nd year	0	24	24	22.0
3rd year	0	4	4	3.6
4th year	0	0	0	0.0

Employment (9 months after graduation)

	Total	Percentage
Employment status known	71	65.1
Employment status unknown	38	34.9
Employed	66	93.0
Pursuing graduate degrees	1	1.4
Unemployed seeking employment	2	2.8
Unemployed not seeking employment	0	0.0
Unemployed and studying for the bar	2	2.8

Type of Employment

# employed in law firms	39	59.1
# employed in business and industry	8	12.1
# employed in government	7	10.6
# employed in public interest	2	3.0
# employed as judicial clerks	7	10.6
# employed in academia	2	3.0

Geographic Location

# employed in state	17	25.8
# employed in foreign countries	0	0.0
# of states where employed		14

Bar Passage Rates

Jurisdiction	Tennessee		
Exam	Sum 05	Win 06	Total
# from school taking bar for the first time	19	5	24
School's pass rate for all first-time takers	68%	80%	71%
State's pass rate for all first-time takers	81%	76%	80%

Appalachian School of Law

Post Office Box 2825, 1169 Edgewater Drive
Grundy, VA 24614
Phone: 800.895.7411 (toll free) or 276.935.4349; Fax: 276.935.8496
E-mail: studentservices@asl.edu; Website: www.asl.edu

■ Introduction

The Appalachian School of Law (ASL) opened its doors in 1997 and is fully approved by the ABA. ASL's location, nestled in the mountains of southwestern Virginia, provides a peaceful and scenic setting for the study of law. The small size assures an individualized education and creates the opportunity for students to make their own contributions to building a young institution. ASL's commitment to community service is a special and important feature that reinforces and gives context to the academic program.

The following statement of purpose was written by representatives of the students, faculty, staff, and administration of ASL: *The Appalachian School of Law exists to provide opportunity for people from Appalachia and beyond to realize their dreams of practicing law and bettering their communities. We attract a qualified, diverse, and dedicated student body, many of whom will remain in the region after graduation and serve as legal counselors, advocates, judges, mediators, community leaders, and public officials. We offer a nationally recruited, diverse, and well-qualified faculty; a rigorous program for the professional preparation of lawyers; and a comprehensive law library. The program emphasizes professional responsibility, dispute resolution, and practice skills. The ASL community is an exciting, student-centered environment that emphasizes honesty, integrity, fairness, and respect for others. We also emphasize community service and staff and faculty development. At the same time, we are a full participant in our community, serving as a resource for the people, the bar, and other institutions of the region.*

■ Curriculum

The curriculum at ASL is structured to give students the skills and knowledge to succeed. Students receive intensive instruction in legal research, writing, analysis, and other skills essential to the practice of law through ASL's Legal Process program and required upper-level skills courses. During the summer between the first and second years, each student will serve an externship with a judge, prosecutor, or other government lawyer, or legal services organization. Recent placements have included externships in the chambers of justices of the supreme courts in North Carolina, Tennessee, and Virginia, and with the United States Department of Justice and Environmental Protection Agency. The second-year curriculum provides required courses in the subject areas that law students are typically expected to master and lawyers are universally expected to understand. The third-year curriculum will provide additional required courses in critical subject areas mixed with skill courses in a wide array of subjects. Alternative dispute resolution and professional responsibility are infused throughout the curriculum.

ASL also offers an Academic Success program, designed to assist students with the development and refinement of the skills necessary to make a successful transition to the study of law.

■ Community Service

ASL's vision is to educate community leaders. We emphasize community service as a central aspect of professional responsibility and provide a variety of service opportunities to our students. To demonstrate the commitment of the legal profession to public service, as well as to enhance the program of legal education at ASL, students at ASL are required to complete 25 hours of community service each semester in a project of their choosing.

Although students are able to structure their community service to meet their own individual preferences and schedules, ASL assists students in making time for these projects by scheduling one afternoon each week that students may devote to community service projects. Projects sponsored by ASL in recent years include a conflict resolution program taught by our students in public elementary schools; a county mapping project in which our students engage in property research and mapping; work with Buchanan Neighbors United, a group that provides housing repairs to improve substandard housing; a community recycling project; and a gender-bias study of the Virginia state court system. Students also are invited to develop alternative projects to satisfy their service obligations.

■ Faculty

ASL's expanding faculty currently consists of approximately 20 full-time professors and a talented group of adjunct professors drawn from the region's bench and bar. The full-time faculty offers an unusual depth of private and governmental practice experience, as well as experience teaching at other law schools. The ranks of the faculty include former law clerks to federal and state court judges, government officials, and partners in small and large private law firms. In addition to being dedicated classroom professors, the ASL faculty also has published a variety of scholarly works in areas ranging from constitutional law to legal ethics to business and commercial matters.

■ Students and Student Organizations

ASL enjoys the support and enthusiasm of a dedicated student body. The entering class usually numbers around 145. Students come to Grundy not only from the immediate region but from across the country.

The student body elects a Student Bar Association. Students may participate in numerous student organizations, in the *Appalachian Journal of Law*, and on moot court, trial advocacy, and alternate dispute resolution competition teams. ASL has a Family Resource Network for the spouses, partners, and families of law students. ASL also has a speaker series that brings a number of distinguished speakers to campus.

■ Facilities

ASL is housed in three buildings on a 3.5-acre campus located near the town center of Grundy. The classroom and office building was extensively renovated for the law school in 1997 into a state-of-the-art law school facility and has won an award from the American Institute of Architects. The classroom building is constructed around an open quadrangle that serves as an informal gathering place for the ASL community. The library was extensively renovated during 1998. The building provides a modern, well-organized, and technologically advanced library. A third building houses student organizations and a coffee shop.

Students have access to the Internet through connections to the ASL network that are available in most of ASL's classrooms and at all tables and carrels in the library. ASL also has wireless Internet access.

■ Admission and Financial Aid

ASL accepts for admission those students who will benefit from a challenging curriculum in a caring environment. Admission decisions are not based on a single criterion, but rather each item will be considered in relation to the applicant's total qualifications. Besides the usual undergraduate transcripts and LSAT score, other considerations include an applicant's graduate work, character, work history, professional promise, personal commitment, recommendations, life experience, and other nonacademic achievements. Students can apply online at ASL's website. We are happy to discuss our admission process and criteria with potential applicants at any time.

ASL also offers a Pre-Admission Summer Opportunity (PASO) program for students who may have the potential to succeed as law students and lawyers, but whose skills and talents may not be reflected fully by the traditional measures of the LSAT and undergraduate performance. PASO provides participants an opportunity to experience law school coursework and gives an opportunity for the faculty to evaluate the students' performance to assess their ability to succeed in law school. Participants who fail to demonstrate potential to successfully complete ASL's three-year legal education program will not be offered admission. In most years, between 20 and 40 percent of PASO participants are offered admission to the fall entering class.

While most students will depend on federal student loans to finance a legal education, ASL does offer both merit- and need-based scholarships. Merit-based scholarships are based on entering LSAT and GPA credentials; the application for admission serves as the application for a merit scholarship.

Applicant Profile

Appalachian School of Law

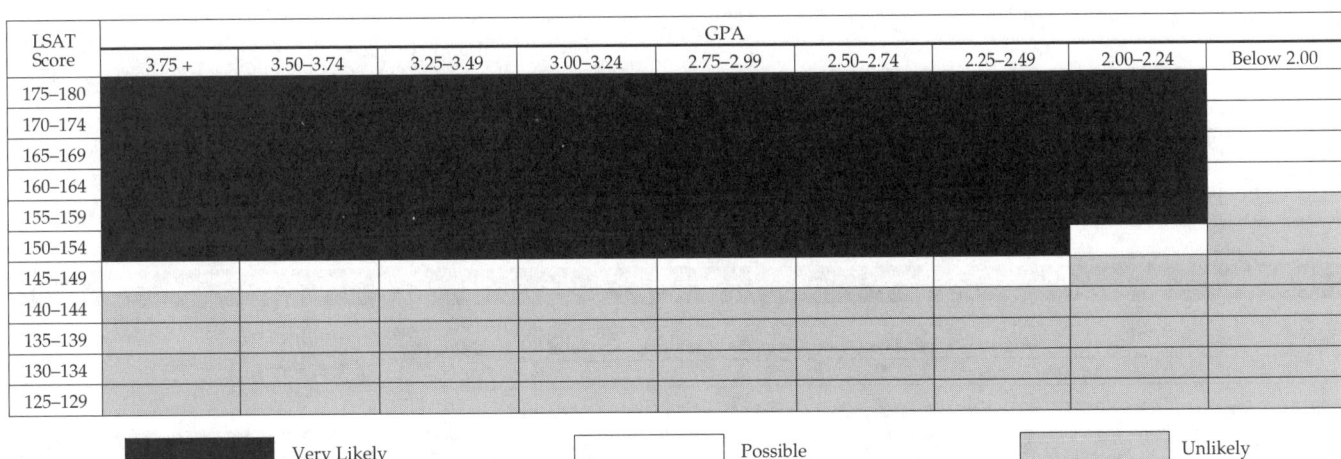

LSAT Score	GPA								
	3.75 +	3.50–3.74	3.25–3.49	3.00–3.24	2.75–2.99	2.50–2.74	2.25–2.49	2.00–2.24	Below 2.00
175–180									
170–174									
165–169									
160–164									
155–159									
150–154									
145–149									
140–144									
135–139									
130–134									
125–129									

■ Very Likely □ Possible ▨ Unlikely

This grid represents data for 100 percent of the applicant pool for fall 2006 admission. It does not reflect the possibility of invitation to participate in the Preadmission Summer Opportunity Program. This chart is to be used as a general guide only. Nonnumerical factors are strongly considered for all applicants.

The University of Arizona James E. Rogers College of Law

PO Box 210176, 1201 E. Speedway
Tucson, AZ 85721-0176
Phone: 520.621.3477; 520.621.9949; Fax: 520.621.9140
E-mail: admissions@law.arizona.edu; Website: www.law.arizona.edu

ABA
Approved
Since
1930

The Basics

Type of school	Public
Term	Semester
Application deadline	11/15 2/15
Application fee	$50
Financial aid deadline	3/1
Can first year start other than fall?	No
Student to faculty ratio	12.1 to 1
Does the university offer:	
housing restricted to law students?	No
graduate housing for which law students are eligible?	Yes

Faculty and Administrators

	Total		Men		Women		Minorities	
	Fall	Spr	Fall	Spr	Fall	Spr	Fall	Spr
Full-time	30	33	22	23	8	10	6	6
Other Full-time	2	2	1	1	1	1	0	0
Deans, librarians, & others who teach	8	7	2	2	6	5	1	1
Part-time	31	41	21	26	10	15	2	2
Total	**71**	**83**	**46**	**52**	**25**	**31**	**9**	**9**

Curriculum

	Full-time	Part-time
Typical first-year section size	77	0
Is there typically a "small section" of the first-year class, other than Legal Writing, taught by full-time faculty	Yes	No
If yes, typical size offered last year	26	
# of classroom course titles beyond first-year curriculum		120
# of upper division courses, excluding seminars with an enrollment: Under 25		93
25–49		21
50–74		7
75–99		2
100+		2
# of seminars		33
# of seminar positions available		524
# of seminar positions filled	374	0
# of positions available in simulation courses		307
# of simulation positions filled	183	0
# of positions available in faculty supervised clinical courses		36
# of faculty supervised clinical positions filled	36	0
# involved in field placements	43	0
# involved in law journals	105	0
# involved in interschool competitions	32	0
# of credit hours required to graduate		85

JD Enrollment and Ethnicity

	Men		Women		Full-time		Part-time		1st-year		Total		JD Degs. Awd.
	#	%	#	%	#	%	#	%	#	%	#	%	
African Amer.	4	1.7	10	4.4	14	3.0	0	0.0	4	2.6	14	3.0	7
Amer. Indian	8	3.4	13	5.7	21	4.5	0	0.0	7	4.6	21	4.5	10
Asian Amer.	17	7.2	25	11.0	42	9.1	0	0.0	13	8.5	42	9.1	17
Mex. Amer.	6	2.6	7	3.1	13	2.8	0	0.0	1	0.7	13	2.8	9
Puerto Rican	0	0.0	2	0.9	2	0.4	0	0.0	0	0.0	2	0.4	0
Hispanic	17	7.2	22	9.6	39	8.4	0	0.0	19	12.4	39	8.4	6
Total Minority	52	22.1	79	34.6	131	28.3	0	0.0	44	28.8	131	28.3	49
For. Nation.	0	0.0	1	0.4	1	0.2	0	0.0	0	0.0	1	0.2	3
Caucasian	172	73.2	139	61.0	311	67.2	0	0.0	109	71.2	311	67.2	94
Unknown	11	4.7	9	3.9	20	4.3	0	0.0	0	0.0	20	4.3	0
Total	235	50.8	228	49.2	463	100.0	0	0.0	153	33.0	463		146

Transfers

Transfers in	8
Transfers out	8

Tuition and Fees

	Resident	Nonresident
Full-time	$16,201	$25,991
Part-time	$0	$0

Living Expenses

Estimated living expenses for singles

Living on campus	Living off campus	Living at home
N/A	$17,706	$9,746

The University of Arizona James E. Rogers College of Law

ABA
Approved
Since
1930

GPA and LSAT Scores

	Total	Full-time	Part-time
# of apps	2,482	2,482	0
# of offers	660	660	0
# of matrics	153	153	0
75% GPA	3.77	3.77	0.00
Median GPA	3.55	3.55	0.00
25% GPA	3.27	3.27	0.00
75% LSAT	164	164	0
Median LSAT	162	162	0
25% LSAT	158	158	0

Grants and Scholarships (from prior year)

	Total		Full-time		Part-time	
	#	%	#	%	#	%
Total # of students	456		456		0	
Total # receiving grants	387	84.9	387	84.9	0	0.0
Less than 1/2 tuition	250	54.8	250	54.8	0	0.0
Half to full tuition	71	15.6	71	15.6	0	0.0
Full tuition	18	3.9	18	3.9	0	0.0
More than full tuition	48	10.5	48	10.5	0	0.0
Median grant amount			$6,000		$0	

Informational and Library Resources

# of volumes and volume equivalents	426,452
# of titles	94,442
# of active serial subscriptions	4,444
Study seating capacity inside the library	368
# of full-time professional librarians	10
Hours per week library is open	99
# of open, wired connections available to students	90
# of networked computers available for use by students	72
# of simultaneous wireless users	1,000
Require computer?	No

JD Attrition (from prior year)

	Academic	Other	Total	
	#	#	#	%
1st year	0	0	0	0.0
2nd year	0	10	10	6.5
3rd year	0	1	1	0.7
4th year	0	0	0	0.0

Employment (9 months after graduation)

	Total	Percentage
Employment status known	152	99.3
Employment status unknown	1	0.7
Employed	145	95.4
Pursuing graduate degrees	1	0.7
Unemployed seeking employment	5	3.3
Unemployed not seeking employment	0	0.0
Unemployed and studying for the bar	1	0.7

Type of Employment

# employed in law firms	68	46.9
# employed in business and industry	7	4.8
# employed in government	39	26.9
# employed in public interest	4	2.8
# employed as judicial clerks	25	17.2
# employed in academia	2	1.4

Geographic Location

# employed in state	110	75.9
# employed in foreign countries	0	0.0
# of states where employed		12

Bar Passage Rates

Jurisdiction	Arizona		
Exam	Sum 05	Win 06	Total
# from school taking bar for the first time	114	13	127
School's pass rate for all first-time takers	85%	54%	82%
State's pass rate for all first-time takers	71%	71%	71%

The University of Arizona James E. Rogers College of Law

PO Box 210176, 1201 E. Speedway

Tucson, AZ 85721-0176

Phone: 520.621.3477; 520.621.9949; Fax: 520.621.9140

E-mail: admissions@law.arizona.edu; Website: www.law.arizona.edu

■ Introduction

Founded in 1915, the University of Arizona Rogers College of Law is the oldest law school in Arizona and has a rich and distinguished history. The college is an integral part of the University of Arizona, one of the nation's leading research institutions and most spirited campuses. The College of Law has a national reputation for providing its students with an exceptional education in a collegial and intellectually challenging atmosphere. The college is located in Tucson, a vibrant, environmentally unique and culturally rich city of almost one million that is home to an active legal and judicial community. The college is approved by the ABA, has been a member of the AALS since 1931, and has a chapter of the Order of the Coif. Over 40 percent of the faculty are members of the American Law Institute.

■ The College

Four core values—justice, professional integrity, public leadership, and community service—are the foundation of the college's culture. The environment of the college is further shaped by several key components. First, its size enables students and faculty to learn in a congenial atmosphere. A school of about 480 students (460 JD students and 20 LLM students), 36 full-time faculty, and many visiting scholars and lecturers provide an environment for intellectual and personal growth and genuine community. Arizona offers a favorable faculty-to-student ratio (1 to 12) that enables full-time faculty to teach first-year classes in sections as small as 25 students. Second, the college has an outstanding, diverse faculty who are gifted teachers and nationally recognized scholars in a broad range of legal specialties. Third, the college is a leader in promoting the interdisciplinary study of law and society by collaborating with world-class departments at the University of Arizona and by supporting 10 dual-degree programs. Fourth, the college's tuition structure and generous financial aid program enable students to pursue legal education without assuming an overwhelming debt burden. Fifth, the college attracts students of intelligence, energy, and commitment. The JD student body of 460 represents over 160 different undergraduate and graduate schools, many nationalities, diverse ethnic and cultural groups, and unique work, volunteer, and personal achievements. Finally, the college nurtures an ethic of public service and community involvement through volunteer activities for students, faculty, and staff organized by the College Community Service Board and various student organizations and aimed at improving the lives of members of the Tucson community.

■ Library and Physical Facilities

The Rogers College of Law occupies a modern building that is fully wheelchair accessible. The Rountree Hall clinical facility is adjacent to the law school. Both buildings are part of the 350-acre campus of the University of Arizona, located in central Tucson. The law library is one of the foremost legal research facilities in the Southwest. In addition to a strong Anglo American collection, the library has nationally recognized collections in Mexican, Latin American, and water law. Students also have access to the resources of the Arizona Health Sciences Library and university libraries, with collections exceeding 11 million volumes. The law library is a fully networked, technologically sophisticated facility that is constantly evolving to meet research needs.

■ Curriculum

The college has committed substantial faculty resources to the first-year curriculum and the development of research and writing skills. Each first-year student meets in a section of 25 students in one of the first-semester courses and shares all other classes with that group of students. Students enroll in a three-unit Legal Analysis, Writing, and Research class of 13 in the second semester. Students must also complete a special writing seminar during the second or third year.

After completing the first-year requirements, students have considerable flexibility in determining second- and third-year coursework. The college offers a rich variety of courses taught by nationally recognized faculty and provides opportunities to pursue a general curriculum or to focus studies in specialized areas of concentration.

In 2004, the college's nationally recognized Trial Advocacy Program won the Emil Gumpert Award from the American College of Trial Lawyers, awarded annually to the best trial advocacy program in the US. The college also has numerous clinical opportunities that combine classroom instruction and field placements in child advocacy, domestic violence, immigration, indigenous peoples' law and criminal defense and prosecution, and the judicial clerking program. The Arizona Supreme Court convenes annually at the college and hears arguments on cases under review. The college awards academic credit for congressional and executive agency internships in Washington, DC; a state legislative internship; an Arizona Governor's Office internship; a university attorney internship; and internship programs with the Navajo, Pascua Yaqui, and Tohono O'Odham tribal governments.

The JD degree is normally completed in six semesters of full-time study; a total of 85 units and a cumulative grade-point average of 2.0 are required to graduate.

■ Dual-degree, LLM, and SJD Programs

The College of Law joins with other colleges at the University of Arizona to offer interdisciplinary study and dual-degree programs in the following areas: JD/PhD programs in Philosophy, Psychology, and Economics; JD/MA programs in Economics, American Indian Studies, Latin American Studies, and Women's Studies; a JD/MBA; a JD/MPA; and a JD/MMF in Management/Finance. Law students with a 2.75 GPA or better may take six units of coursework in another department and transfer that work to the College of Law for elective credit. The college offers two one-year LLM programs in International Trade Law and in Indigenous Peoples Law and Policy and a Doctor of Juridical Science (SJD) program.

■ Admission

Admission to the College of Law is very selective; the college is dedicated to assessing all candidate files in a qualitative, holistic manner. In making decisions, all information submitted by applicants is considered, with significant focus on the strength of the candidate's undergraduate academic record, LSAT score, personal statement, résumé, and letters of recommendation. Additional factors include the nature and rigor of undergraduate experience; graduate education; work and travel experience; unique talents, interests, or accomplishments; extracurricular activities; substantial community or public service; distinctive ethnic or cultural background; or other circumstances that have influenced the candidate's life or given him/her direction. The college is committed to enrolling students who bring diverse perspectives and encourages applications from minority, disadvantaged, and disabled candidates and candidates who bring varied life experiences to the educational process. The deadline for applications is February 15. To complete a timely application, applicants must take the LSAT no later than the February of the year of expected enrollment.

■ Tuition and Financial Aid

The tuition structure and generous financial aid program of the University of Arizona afford students the opportunity to pursue a legal education of outstanding quality with less debt burden than is typical of other fine law schools. Tuition and fees for JD students for the 2006–2007 year was $16,200 for Arizona residents and $25,991 for nonresidents. The College of Law awarded over $3 million in merit- and need-based scholarships to JD students in 2005–2006.

■ Student Activities

The College of Law is a cohesive community of faculty, students, and staff dedicated to pursuing excellence. The student body is self-governing through the Student Bar Association and there are over 25 law student organizations that are an important part of institutional and student life. Students also participate in school governance by serving as voting members of student-faculty committees. The *Arizona Law Review* and the *Arizona Journal of International and Comparative Law* are well-known, student operated and edited scholarly journals on current legal problems. The students in the moot court and trial advocacy programs excel in national and state appellate advocacy competitions. College-sponsored community service projects are an important element in cultivating collaboration among students, faculty, and staff.

■ Career Services

The Career and Professional Development Office is staffed by two outstanding professionals who are both attorneys who have practiced law. They have earned national recognition for the high caliber of innovative programming and guidance that they offer law students and graduates in assisting them to sort out the many options a law degree creates. The Career Office provides individual counseling, many options to meet a broad range of employers from a wide variety of practice and business settings, over 40 seminars annually on diverse topics, from résumé writing and effective interviewing to judicial clerkships and international law opportunities. The Career Office has developed five outstanding publications for use in the job search process, an outstanding Summer Public Service Internships Program, and the Sonoran Desert Public Service Career Fair, which is the largest law school-sponsored public sector career fair in the nation. Arizona's law students and graduates work throughout the US and internationally. Typically, 60–70 percent of graduates take the Arizona bar exam and 30–40 percent take the bar exams of about 20 other states. Arizona graduates perform very well on the various bar exams—over 90 percent pass a bar on the first attempt—and are very successful in the job market, with 94–95 percent of graduates employed in a law job within six months of graduation.

Applicant Profile

The University of Arizona James E. Rogers College of Law
This grid includes only applicants with 120–180 LSAT scores earned under standard administrations.

LSAT Score	3.75 +		3.50–3.74		3.25–3.49		3.00–3.24		2.75–2.99		2.50–2.74		2.25–2.49		2.00–2.24		Below 2.00		No GPA		Total	
	Apps	Adm	Apps	Adm	Apps	Adm	Apps	Adm	Apps	Adm	Apps	Adm	Apps	Adm	Apps	Adm	Apps	Adm	Apps	Adm	Apps	Adm
175–180	2	2	1	1	2	1	0	0	0	0	1	1	0	0	0	0	0	0	0	0	6	5
170–174	17	16	13	11	9	7	2	2	4	2	1	0	1	1	0	0	0	0	0	0	47	39
165–169	83	74	90	82	24	22	23	13	14	4	10	2	4	1	1	0	0	0	1	1	250	199
160–164	116	79	154	88	141	60	69	20	35	9	12	3	11	0	2	0	1	0	4	1	545	260
155–159	132	28	188	28	205	20	101	6	56	4	20	3	7	0	2	0	0	0	5	0	716	89
150–154	64	6	96	8	113	8	86	4	43	3	19	1	6	0	7	0	0	0	4	0	438	30
145–149	21	0	54	4	53	0	59	0	31	0	18	0	9	0	6	0	0	0	3	0	254	4
140–144	14	0	19	0	25	0	36	0	17	0	17	0	9	0	4	0	0	0	0	0	141	0
135–139	2	0	8	0	11	0	9	0	8	0	4	0	3	0	2	0	0	0	1	0	48	0
130–134	0	0	1	0	0	0	2	0	3	0	4	0	2	0	1	0	0	0	2	0	15	0
125–129	0	0	0	0	0	0	0	0	1	0	0	0	0	0	0	0	1	0	0	0	2	0
120–124	0	0	0	0	0	0	0	0	0	0	0	0	0	0	0	0	0	0	0	0	0	0
Total	451	205	624	222	583	118	387	45	212	22	106	10	52	2	25	0	2	0	20	2	2462	626

Apps = Number of Applicants   Adm = Number Admitted   Reflects 99% of the total applicant pool.

Arizona State University—Sandra Day O'Connor College of Law

Armstrong Hall, 1100 S. McAllister Avenue, PO Box 877906
Tempe, AZ 85287-7906
Phone: 480.965.1474; Fax: 480.727.7930
E-mail: law.admissions@asu.edu; Website: www.law.asu.edu

ABA Approved Since 1969

The Basics

Type of school	Public
Term	Semester
Application deadline	11/1 2/1
Application fee	$50
Financial aid deadline	3/1
Can first year start other than fall?	No
Student to faculty ratio	9.7 to 1
Does the university offer:	
housing restricted to law students?	No
graduate housing for which law students are eligible?	No

Faculty and Administrators

	Total		Men		Women		Minorities	
	Fall	Spr	Fall	Spr	Fall	Spr	Fall	Spr
Full-time	51	57	36	42	15	15	8	7
Other Full-time	2	2	2	2	0	0	1	1
Deans, librarians, & others who teach	7	5	3	2	4	3	0	0
Part-time	32	35	25	30	7	5	1	1
Total	92	99	66	76	26	23	10	9

Curriculum

		Full-time	Part-time
Typical first-year section size		80	0
Is there typically a "small section" of the first-year class, other than Legal Writing, taught by full-time faculty		Yes	No
If yes, typical size offered last year		35	
# of classroom course titles beyond first-year curriculum		139	
# of upper division courses, excluding seminars with an enrollment:	Under 25	97	
	25–49	30	
	50–74	6	
	75–99	3	
	100+	2	
# of seminars		37	
# of seminar positions available		481	
# of seminar positions filled	358		0
# of positions available in simulation courses		283	
# of simulation positions filled	269		0
# of positions available in faculty supervised clinical courses		100	
# of faculty supervised clinical positions filled	86		0
# involved in field placements	122		0
# involved in law journals	84		0
# involved in interschool competitions	30		0
# of credit hours required to graduate		88	

JD Enrollment and Ethnicity

	Men		Women		Full-time		Part-time		1st-year		Total		JD Degs. Awd.
	#	%	#	%	#	%	#	%	#	%	#	%	
African Amer.	5	1.5	16	5.6	21	3.3	0	0.0	7	4.2	21	3.3	6
Amer. Indian	13	3.8	15	5.3	28	4.5	0	0.0	9	5.4	28	4.5	8
Asian Amer.	12	3.5	14	4.9	26	4.1	0	0.0	7	4.2	26	4.1	10
Mex. Amer.	13	3.8	24	8.4	37	5.9	0	0.0	8	4.8	37	5.9	7
Puerto Rican	1	0.3	1	0.4	2	0.3	0	0.0	0	0.0	2	0.3	0
Hispanic	27	7.8	26	9.1	53	8.4	0	0.0	14	8.4	53	8.4	16
Total Minority	71	20.6	96	33.7	167	26.6	0	0.0	45	27.1	167	26.6	47
For. Nation.	7	2.0	4	1.4	11	1.7	0	0.0	1	0.6	11	1.7	2
Caucasian	232	67.4	157	55.1	389	61.8	0	0.0	101	60.8	389	61.8	132
Unknown	34	9.9	28	9.8	62	9.9	0	0.0	19	11.4	62	9.9	2
Total	344	54.7	285	45.3	629	100.0	0	0.0	166	26.4	629		183

Transfers

Transfers in	9
Transfers out	10

Tuition and Fees

	Resident	Nonresident
Full-time	$13,278	$23,864
Part-time	$0	$0

Living Expenses

Estimated living expenses for singles

Living on campus	Living off campus	Living at home
$14,594	$14,594	$14,594

Arizona State University—Sandra Day O'Connor College of Law

ABA
Approved
Since
1969

GPA and LSAT Scores

	Total	Full-time	Part-time
# of apps	2,944	2,944	0
# of offers	617	617	0
# of matrics	165	165	0
75% GPA	3.78	3.78	0.00
Median GPA	3.54	3.54	0.00
25% GPA	3.31	3.31	0.00
75% LSAT	162	162	0
Median LSAT	158	158	0
25% LSAT	155	155	0

Grants and Scholarships (from prior year)

	Total		Full-time		Part-time	
	#	%	#	%	#	%
Total # of students	650		650		0	
Total # receiving grants	317	48.8	317	48.8	0	0.0
Less than 1/2 tuition	213	32.8	213	32.8	0	0.0
Half to full tuition	46	7.1	46	7.1	0	0.0
Full tuition	20	3.1	20	3.1	0	0.0
More than full tuition	38	5.8	38	5.8	0	0.0
Median grant amount			$4,000		$0	

Informational and Library Resources

# of volumes and volume equivalents	414,319
# of titles	119,047
# of active serial subscriptions	3,978
Study seating capacity inside the library	527
# of full-time professional librarians	8
Hours per week library is open	111
# of open, wired connections available to students	195
# of networked computers available for use by students	84
# of simultaneous wireless users	2,000
Require computer?	No

JD Attrition (from prior year)

	Academic	Other	Total	
	#	#	#	%
1st year	14	2	16	6.3
2nd year	1	11	12	6.0
3rd year	0	0	0	0.0
4th year	0	0	0	0.0

Employment (9 months after graduation)

	Total	Percentage
Employment status known	165	98.8
Employment status unknown	2	1.2
Employed	155	93.9
Pursuing graduate degrees	2	1.2
Unemployed seeking employment	1	0.6
Unemployed not seeking employment	7	4.2
Unemployed and studying for the bar	0	0.0

Type of Employment

# employed in law firms	95	61.3
# employed in business and industry	9	5.8
# employed in government	23	14.8
# employed in public interest	10	6.5
# employed as judicial clerks	14	9.0
# employed in academia	4	2.6

Geographic Location

# employed in state	130	83.9
# employed in foreign countries	0	0.0
# of states where employed		13

Bar Passage Rates

Jurisdiction	Arizona		
Exam	Sum 05	Win 06	Total
# from school taking bar for the first time	121	32	153
School's pass rate for all first-time takers	67%	56%	65%
State's pass rate for all first-time takers	71%	71%	71%

Arizona State University—Sandra Day O'Connor College of Law

Armstrong Hall, 1100 S. McAllister Avenue, PO Box 877906
Tempe, AZ 85287-7906
Phone: 480.965.1474; Fax: 480.727.7930
E-mail: law.admissions@asu.edu; Website: www.law.asu.edu

■ Introduction

Founded in 1967, the Arizona State University College of Law (now ASU's Sandra Day O'Connor College of Law) combines the best traditions of American legal education with innovative programs supported by strong community partnerships. Our vision includes excellence in all we do, while reaching out to all parts of the university and the community, striving for inclusion, and having a meaningful impact on contemporary problems through teaching, research, and collaborative problem-solving. Students are attracted by the quality of the legal education, commitment to innovative teaching and scholarship, reasonable tuition, breadth and depth of the curriculum, and low student/faculty ratio. A busy calendar of distinguished scholars, jurists, and public officials enriches the student experience and fosters a strong sense of community. Committed to excellence, the college has an outstanding faculty, many opportunities for interdisciplinary learning, extensive pro bono opportunities, an exceptional legal writing program, and clinics of significant variety. Our students benefit greatly from the fact that Phoenix is the largest metropolitan area in the country to have only one ABA-accredited law school.

■ Admission

Every application receives full review and consideration by the Admissions Committee prior to a decision. Among the factors influencing the admission decision are undergraduate and previous graduate education, LSAT performance, quality and grading patterns of undergraduate institutions, demonstrated commitment to public service, work experience, leadership experience, extracurricular or community activities, history of overcoming economic or other disadvantages, personal experiences with discrimination, overcoming disability, geographic diversity, diversity of experience and background, maturity, ability to communicate, foreign language proficiency, honors and awards, service in the armed forces, publications, and exceptional personal talents. Students from minority groups are encouraged to apply. Students from diverse cultural, ethnic, and racial backgrounds enrich the College of Law community and ultimately further efforts to diversify the bench and bar.

■ Curriculum

The College of Law offers one of the best student/teacher ratios in the country and a wide variety of courses. Because we have a large, nationally acclaimed faculty with high standards in both teaching and research, we have unusual depth in our course offerings. More than 65 percent of the classes in the second and third year have fewer than 20 students. As part of a large, premier research institution, the opportunities for interdisciplinary work are extensive. Joint degrees are offered with the MBA program, the PhD in Psychology, the PhD in Justice Studies, and the Mayo Clinic's MD. Further, the college takes full advantage of its unique location in Phoenix by offering over 150 externship opportunities.

■ Clinical Programs

The Clinical Program is one of the most comprehensive in the nation with seven clinics in wide-ranging areas. We offer the Criminal Practice Clinic, Public Defender Clinic, Civil Justice Clinic, and Mediation Clinic. Additionally, the Technology Ventures Clinic brings law students together with students from other colleges on campus to assist an agency of the university in commercializing inventions from the ASU intellectual property portfolio. The Indian Legal Clinic trains students for practice in state, federal, and tribal courts, and offers practical experience in the application of fundamental principles of Indian law to issues affecting Native American communities. Second- and third-year law students can also work with indigent clients in immigration proceedings and delve into immigration policy projects in the Immigration Clinic.

■ Library and Physical Facilities

The College of Law is composed of Armstrong Hall and the John J. Ross-William C. Blakley Law Library and is set on the eastern edge of the university's beautiful, 700-acre, Tempe campus. Armstrong Hall's classrooms are fully accessible to students with disabilities. The Willard H. Pedrick Great Hall serves not only as a courtroom for annual visits from the Ninth Circuit Court of Appeals, the Arizona Supreme Court, the Navajo Supreme Court, and the Arizona Court of Appeals, but also as a location for campus events. The Ryan C. Harris Courtroom is a state-of-the-art facility specially designed for trial advocacy classes. Armstrong Hall also houses a legal clinic; the Center for the Study of Law, Science, and Technology; the Indian Legal Program; the Committee on Law and Philosophy; the ABA *Jurimetrics* journal; as well as the Cohen Student Center and Sidebar Café. The Ross-Blakley Law Library is a stunningly beautiful work of architecture with lots of windows to allow natural light in. It has three computer labs, a well-staffed help desk, and numerous study rooms for groups or individuals. LexisNexis and Westlaw training are held in the library. Both Armstrong Hall and the Ross-Blakley Law Library are fully equipped with a wireless network.

■ Center for the Study of Law, Science, and Technology

Founded in 1984, the Center for the Study of Law, Science, and Technology is the oldest, largest, and most comprehensive law and science center in the country. It offers certificate programs in Intellectual Property, Health Care Law, Environmental Law, and Biotechnology Law. Every year 10 students in each class are named Center Scholars and participate in special activities designed for those with special interests in law and science. Center faculty and students edit and copublish, along with the American Bar Association, the prestigious, peer-refereed *Jurimetrics: The Journal of Law, Science, and Technology*, the oldest and most widely circulated journal in the field of law and science.

■ Indian Legal Program

The Indian Legal Program enjoys a position of national preeminence. This preeminence is due to the large Native American student population, the Indian Law Certificate program, the Indian law curriculum, well-placed alumni, scholarly conferences, and the Indian Legal Clinic. An extraordinary faculty and long-term partnerships with tribal governments contribute to the strength and reputation of the College of Law in this critical area.

■ Committee on Law and Philosophy

Composed of law faculty and liberal arts and sciences faculty, the committee creates and maintains an active intellectual community specializing in criminal law theory, punishment, forgiveness, constitutional interpretation, human rights theory, law and literature, law and religion, and political obligation. The committee sponsors and hosts conferences, lectures, courses, and seminars.

■ Student Activities

To prepare proactive, socially conscious attorneys and leaders, we enhance the traditional classroom experience with extracurricular and cocurricular activities. We have approximately 50 active student groups, from the ASU Bar Association and 30 professional affiliations to 20 pro bono groups—and we grow and change with the interests of our students. On average, at least 70 percent of our students participate in pro bono work of some kind, with about one-third of the student body graduating with Pro Bono Distinction. Students are active in ASU student governance and in our communities with community service. Our students are competitive in moot court competitions, both regionally and internationally. Two formal law journals, the *Arizona State Law Journal* and *Jurimetrics*, allow additional professional opportunities for students.

■ Career Services

Our graduates have proven success in the legal employment market and hold prominent positions and leadership roles throughout the international, national, and Arizona legal communities in business, politics, government, the judiciary, and private firms. A broad range of employers interview our students on campus, at regional interview programs sponsored by the Career Services Office, and at job fairs. The Career Services professional staff serves students in all phases of their professional development and job search, and acts as a bridge between the students' academic and professional careers by offering extensive programming and individual career counseling.

■ LLM Programs

The groundbreaking Master of Laws in Biotechnology and Genomics is the first degree of its kind in the nation, which explains the overwhelming attention it received from applicants and the national media following announcement of its inception. It provides students with in-depth study of the scientific and policy aspects of genomics. Through classroom instruction and guided independent study, Master of Laws (LLM) candidates explore the laws that enable and constrain the development, control, and application of biotechnology and genomics, including areas such as public health law, agricultural law and policy, and intellectual property. Because of the strength of our Indian Legal Program, the LLM in Tribal Policy, Law, and Government was also established. It allows lawyers interested in teaching or practice related to Native American issues to further their career goals.

Applicant Profile

Arizona State University—Sandra Day O'Connor College of Law
This grid includes only applicants with 120–180 LSAT scores earned under standard administrations.

LSAT Score	3.75 +		3.50–3.74		3.25–3.49		3.00–3.24		2.75–2.99		2.50–2.74		2.25–2.49		2.00–2.24		Below 2.00		No GPA		Total	
	Apps	Adm	Apps	Adm	Apps	Adm	Apps	Adm	Apps	Adm	Apps	Adm	Apps	Adm	Apps	Adm	Apps	Adm	Apps	Adm	Apps	Adm
175–180	1	1	2	2	0	0	0	0	0	0	0	0	0	0	0	0	0	0	0	0	3	3
170–174	6	6	6	6	5	5	1	1	1	1	2	0	0	0	0	0	1	0	0	0	22	19
165–169	27	26	19	19	14	14	11	9	14	7	11	1	2	0	3	0	0	0	0	0	101	76
160–164	66	66	88	73	103	62	82	25	32	4	24	2	11	1	7	0	0	0	5	0	418	233
155–159	136	76	202	52	229	41	153	15	73	4	43	2	10	1	4	0	1	0	3	0	854	191
150–154	86	16	156	13	191	7	170	11	88	7	47	2	19	3	5	0	0	0	4	1	766	60
145–149	24	5	77	8	95	8	83	3	57	0	35	0	20	0	11	0	3	0	4	0	409	24
140–144	16	3	26	1	42	1	60	0	27	0	24	0	9	0	13	0	1	0	3	0	221	5
135–139	3	0	9	0	18	0	13	0	15	0	11	0	8	0	5	0	1	0	5	0	88	0
130–134	1	0	0	0	0	0	3	0	7	0	5	0	2	0	3	0	1	0	1	0	23	0
125–129	0	0	0	0	0	0	1	0	4	0	2	0	1	0	0	0	0	0	0	0	8	0
120–124	0	0	0	0	0	0	0	0	0	0	0	0	0	0	0	0	0	0	0	0	0	0
Total	366	199	585	174	697	138	577	64	318	23	204	7	82	5	51	0	8	0	25	1	2913	611

Apps = Number of Applicants
Adm = Number Admitted
Reflects 99% of the total applicant pool.

University of Arkansas School of Law

Robert A. Leflar Law Center
Fayetteville, AR 72701
Phone: 479.575.3102; Fax: 479.575.3937
E-mail: ualawad@uark.edu; Website: http://law.uark.edu

ABA
Approved
Since
1928

The Basics

Type of school	Public
Term	Semester
Application deadline	4/1
Application fee	$0
Financial aid deadline	
Can first year start other than fall?	No
Student to faculty ratio	14.2 to 1
Does the university offer:	
housing restricted to law students?	No
graduate housing for which law students are eligible?	Yes

Faculty and Administrators

	Total		Men		Women		Minorities	
	Fall	Spr	Fall	Spr	Fall	Spr	Fall	Spr
Full-time	24	26	16	15	8	11	3	4
Other Full-time	0	0	0	0	0	0	0	0
Deans, librarians, & others who teach	9	8	4	5	5	3	2	0
Part-time	13	12	11	11	2	1	0	0
Total	**46**	**46**	**31**	**31**	**15**	**15**	**5**	**4**

Curriculum

	Full-time	Part-time
Typical first-year section size	75	0
Is there typically a "small section" of the first-year class, other than Legal Writing, taught by full-time faculty	No	No
If yes, typical size offered last year		
# of classroom course titles beyond first-year curriculum		59

# of upper division courses, excluding seminars with an enrollment:		
Under 25		74
25–49		13
50–74		8
75–99		0
100+		4

# of seminars		11
# of seminar positions available		165
# of seminar positions filled	148	0
# of positions available in simulation courses		266
# of simulation positions filled	199	0
# of positions available in faculty supervised clinical courses		104
# of faculty supervised clinical positions filled	67	0
# involved in field placements	40	0
# involved in law journals	64	0
# involved in interschool competitions	37	0
# of credit hours required to graduate		90

JD Enrollment and Ethnicity

	Men		Women		Full-time		Part-time		1st-year		Total		JD Degs. Awd.
	#	%	#	%	#	%	#	%	#	%	#	%	
African Amer.	24	10.0	53	28.2	77	18.0	0	0.0	28	18.5	77	18.0	19
Amer. Indian	5	2.1	3	1.6	8	1.9	0	0.0	2	1.3	8	1.9	4
Asian Amer.	6	2.5	10	5.3	16	3.7	0	0.0	5	3.3	16	3.7	1
Mex. Amer.	2	0.8	0	0.0	2	0.5	0	0.0	2	1.3	2	0.5	0
Puerto Rican	0	0.0	1	0.5	1	0.2	0	0.0	1	0.7	1	0.2	0
Hispanic	5	2.1	1	0.5	6	1.4	0	0.0	2	1.3	6	1.4	2
Total Minority	42	17.5	68	36.2	110	25.7	0	0.0	40	26.5	110	25.7	26
For. Nation.	0	0.0	1	0.5	1	0.2	0	0.0	1	0.7	1	0.2	2
Caucasian	196	81.7	119	63.3	315	73.6	0	0.0	109	72.2	315	73.6	118
Unknown	2	0.8	0	0.0	2	0.5	0	0.0	1	0.7	2	0.5	0
Total	240	56.1	188	43.9	428	100.0	0	0.0	151	35.3	428		146

Transfers

Transfers in	0
Transfers out	2

Tuition and Fees

	Resident	Nonresident
Full-time	$9,713	$19,486
Part-time	$0	$0

Living Expenses

Estimated living expenses for singles

Living on campus	Living off campus	Living at home
$14,492	$14,492	$14,492

University of Arkansas School of Law

ABA
Approved
Since
1928

GPA and LSAT Scores

	Total	Full-time	Part-time
# of apps	1,334	1,334	0
# of offers	386	386	0
# of matrics	159	159	0
75% GPA	3.71	3.71	0.00
Median GPA	3.48	3.48	0.00
25% GPA	3.09	3.09	0.00
75% LSAT	159	159	0
Median LSAT	155	155	0
25% LSAT	151	151	0

Grants and Scholarships (from prior year)

	Total #	Total %	Full-time #	Full-time %	Part-time #	Part-time %
Total # of students	440		440		0	
Total # receiving grants	172	39.1	172	39.1	0	0.0
Less than 1/2 tuition	114	25.9	114	25.9	0	0.0
Half to full tuition	49	11.1	49	11.1	0	0.0
Full tuition	0	0.0	0	0.0	0	0.0
More than full tuition	9	2.0	9	2.0	0	0.0
Median grant amount			$6,000		$0	

Informational and Library Resources

# of volumes and volume equivalents	314,945
# of titles	189,830
# of active serial subscriptions	3,645
Study seating capacity inside the library	315
# of full-time professional librarians	7
Hours per week library is open	105
# of open, wired connections available to students	18
# of networked computers available for use by students	61
# of simultaneous wireless users	500
Require computer?	No

JD Attrition (from prior year)

	Academic #	Other #	Total #	Total %
1st year	3	6	9	6.4
2nd year	0	0	0	0.0
3rd year	0	0	0	0.0
4th year	0	0	0	0.0

Employment (9 months after graduation)

	Total	Percentage
Employment status known	162	100.0
Employment status unknown	0	0.0
Employed	123	75.9
Pursuing graduate degrees	15	9.3
Unemployed seeking employment	9	5.6
Unemployed not seeking employment	4	2.5
Unemployed and studying for the bar	11	6.8

Type of Employment

# employed in law firms	71	57.7
# employed in business and industry	21	17.1
# employed in government	22	17.9
# employed in public interest	4	3.3
# employed as judicial clerks	2	1.6
# employed in academia	3	2.4

Geographic Location

# employed in state	91	74.0
# employed in foreign countries	0	0.0
# of states where employed		10

Bar Passage Rates

Jurisdiction	Arkansas			Tennessee		
Exam	Sum 05	Win 06	Total	Sum 05	Win 06	Total
# from school taking bar for the first time	102	15	117	8	1	9
School's pass rate for all first-time takers	77%	60%	75%	100%	0%	89%
State's pass rate for all first-time takers	77%	71%	75%	81%	76%	80%

University of Arkansas School of Law

Robert A. Leflar Law Center
Fayetteville, AR 72701
Phone: 479.575.3102; Fax: 479.575.3937
E-mail: ualawad@uark.edu; Website: http://law.uark.edu

■ Introduction

The University of Arkansas School of Law is located on the main university campus at Fayetteville, a city of approximately 62,000 in northwest Arkansas. The School of Law was established in 1924 and has continuously sought to provide high-quality legal education in a university community. In 1926, the School of Law was approved by the ABA, and, in 1927, the school became a member of the AALS.

■ Enrollment/Student Body

Although approximately 75–80 percent of the students are Arkansas residents, others are from every part of the United States. Since the school has no undergraduate course prerequisites, the academic backgrounds and nonacademic experiences of students are varied.

■ Library and Physical Facilities

The law library has over 314,000 volumes and volume equivalents. Students are trained in the techniques of computer-assisted legal research as well as in the traditional research methods. The law library is a federal and state depository for government documents.

■ Curriculum

The primary function of the University of Arkansas School of Law is to prepare lawyers who will render the highest quality of professional service to their clients, who are interested in and capable of furthering legal process and reform, and who are prepared to fill the vital role of the lawyer as a community leader. The school offers a full-time, three-year program leading to the JD degree. The degree is conferred upon satisfactory completion of 90 semester hours, including 42 hours of required courses. The first-year curriculum is required. A broad selection of elective second- and third-year courses is available. Students who have completed the first year of law school may earn up to 12 semester hours of credit in summer school, and graduation can be accelerated one semester by summer coursework.

The School of Law offers a joint JD/MBA program with the College of Business Administration. If a student is accepted into both programs, a maximum of six hours of approved upper-level elective law courses may be used on duplicative credit toward the MBA degree, and a maximum of six hours of approved graduate courses in business administration may be used as duplicative credit toward the JD degree.

The Department of Political Science, the graduate school, and the School of Law cooperate in offering a dual-degree program that allows a student to pursue the MPA and the JD degrees concurrently. Students must be admitted to the MPA program, the School of Law, and the dual-degree program.

The School of Law and the Department of Political Science provide a dual JD/MA in International Law and Politics. This program's students must be admitted both to the School of Law and the Graduate School, Department of Political Science. The Graduate Program in Agriculture Law provides opportunities for advanced study, creative research, and specialized professional training in this rapidly developing area of law. The program is designed to prepare a small number of carefully selected attorneys as specialists in the legal problems of agriculture production, distribution, and marketing.

Applicants for admission as candidates for the Master of Laws (LLM) in Agricultural Law must have earned a JD or LLB degree from a fully accredited law school in the United States. Graduates from a law school in another country may be admitted upon the approval of the Agricultural Law Programs Committee.

■ Admission

First-year students are admitted in the fall and only for full-time study. Prior to enrolling in the School of Law, applicants must have completed all requirements for an undergraduate degree from an accredited four-year college. Admission is based on the applicant's LSAT score and undergraduate GPA. In a small percentage of cases, additional criteria such as age; gender, cultural, ethnic, and racial background; geographic origin; socioeconomic background and status; undergraduate major; graduate studies; career objectives; and nonacademic, work, and other life experiences are considered by a faculty admission committee. Preference is given to Arkansas residents; for the current status of this preference, contact the school. A nonrefundable tuition deposit is required of all admitted candidates.

The law school's application deadline is April 1 of the year in which admission is sought. Applicants must take the LSAT no later than February. Applications completed after April 1 will be considered only on a space-available basis.

■ Housing

Housing for single students is available in campus dormitories; apartments are also available for married students, and students with dependants. For more information about housing, please contact the Housing Office, University of Arkansas, Fayetteville, AR 72701, 479.575.3951. Information is also available at *http://housing.uark.edu*. A variety of private off-campus housing options are available in Fayetteville and surrounding communities, within easy commuting distance of the law school. For more information, please visit *http://offcampushousing.uark.edu/*.

■ Student Activities

The *Arkansas Law Review* is a legal periodical published quarterly by the students of the School of Law in cooperation with the Arkansas Bar Association. Candidates for the *Law Review* are selected on the basis of scholarship and writing ability. The *Journal of Food Law and Policy* is a legal periodical published twice a year by students of the School of Law. Candidates for the journal are selected from the second- and third-year law classes by the editorial board on the basis of scholarship and writing ability.

Students in their second and third years are encouraged to compete in an intramural moot court competition, and Arkansas students participate in national moot court competitions. The University of Arkansas School of Law also participates in the ABA Law Student Division Client Counseling Competition. The law school operates a legal aid clinic providing counseling and representation for university students and indigent persons seeking legal assistance. An Arkansas Supreme Court Rule permits senior law students, upon certification and under supervision, to appear in court on a no-fee basis.

The Student Bar Association sponsors a variety of academic and social activities. All students are also eligible for membership in the Law Student Division of the Arkansas Bar Association. Three of the largest national legal fraternities, Delta Theta Phi, Phi Alpha Delta, and Phi Delta Phi, maintain active chapters at the school. The Women's Law Student Association was organized to provide an opportunity for women to discuss and work with common professional interests and problems. Members of the Arkansas Chapter of Black Law Students Association work as a collective body to inform black students of the availability and advantages of a legal education, to promote the academic success of black law students at Arkansas, and to increase the awareness and commitment of the legal profession to the black community. Other organizations include the Christian Legal Society, Lambda, the Federalist Society, the Asian Pacific American Law Student Association, and Equal Justice Works.

■ Expenses and Financial Aid

Students are expected to make sufficient financial arrangements for the first year of study without the necessity of seeking employment. All law students are required to be full-time students. All financial aid in the form of Perkins Loans (formerly NDSL), higher education loans, and work-study grants is processed by the University of Arkansas Office of Student Financial Aid, University of Arkansas, Fayetteville, AR 72701. Merit scholarships are awarded to some entering students. Applications for a limited number of other scholarships are distributed following fall registration in August.

■ Career Planning and Placement

The law school maintains an Office of Career Planning and Placement with a full-time, highly qualified director and staff to assist and advise students and graduates. Services offered by the office include on-campus interviews for permanent and summer employment; individual career counseling sessions; workshops and handbooks regarding résumé preparation, interviewing skills and techniques, and job searches; panels of lawyers who present programs on a variety of topics; a job bulletin; and a comprehensive placement library. The office also maintains employment and bar passage statistics.

Applicant Profile Not Available

University of Arkansas at Little Rock, William H. Bowen School of Law

1201 McMath Avenue
Little Rock, AR 72202-5142
Phone: 501.324.9903; Fax: 501.324.9909
E-mail: lawadm@ualr.edu; Website: www.law.ualr.edu

ABA
Approved
Since
1969

The Basics

Type of school	Public
Term	Semester
Application deadline	4/15
Application fee	$0
Financial aid deadline	3/1
Can first year start other than fall?	No
Student to faculty ratio	14.7 to 1
Does the university offer:	
housing restricted to law students?	No
graduate housing for which law students are eligible?	No

Faculty and Administrators

	Total Fall	Total Spr	Men Fall	Men Spr	Women Fall	Women Spr	Minorities Fall	Minorities Spr
Full-time	22	22	11	10	11	12	5	6
Other Full-time	3	3	0	1	3	2	1	0
Deans, librarians, & others who teach	6	7	2	3	4	4	0	0
Part-time	28	32	15	23	12	9	1	5
Total	**59**	**64**	**28**	**37**	**30**	**27**	**7**	**11**

Curriculum

		Full-time	Part-time
Typical first-year section size		90	48
Is there typically a "small section" of the first-year class, other than Legal Writing, taught by full-time faculty		No	No
If yes, typical size offered last year			
# of classroom course titles beyond first-year curriculum		124	
# of upper division courses, excluding seminars with an enrollment:	Under 25	102	
	25–49	31	
	50–74	5	
	75–99	6	
	100+	0	
# of seminars		12	
# of seminar positions available		189	
# of seminar positions filled		73	84
# of positions available in simulation courses		523	
# of simulation positions filled		302	138
# of positions available in faculty supervised clinical courses		61	
# of faculty supervised clinical positions filled	53	0	
# involved in field placements	23	1	
# involved in law journals	66	17	
# involved in interschool competitions	17	21	
# of credit hours required to graduate		90	

JD Enrollment and Ethnicity

	Men #	Men %	Women #	Women %	Full-time #	Full-time %	Part-time #	Part-time %	1st-year #	1st-year %	Total #	Total %	JD Degs. Awd.
African Amer.	17	7.5	31	14.3	26	9.2	22	13.7	16	11.9	48	10.8	4
Amer. Indian	2	0.9	2	0.9	4	1.4	0	0.0	2	1.5	4	0.9	3
Asian Amer.	2	0.9	3	1.4	3	1.1	2	1.2	2	1.5	5	1.1	1
Mex. Amer.	3	1.3	1	0.5	4	1.4	0	0.0	3	2.2	4	0.9	0
Puerto Rican	0	0.0	0	0.0	0	0.0	0	0.0	0	0.0	0	0.0	0
Hispanic	4	1.8	2	0.9	5	1.8	1	0.6	2	1.5	6	1.4	2
Total Minority	28	12.3	39	18.0	42	14.8	25	15.5	25	18.5	67	15.1	10
For. Nation.	2	0.9	1	0.5	2	0.7	1	0.6	3	2.2	3	0.7	0
Caucasian	197	86.8	177	81.6	239	84.5	135	83.9	107	79.3	374	84.2	139
Unknown	0	0.0	0	0.0	0	0.0	0	0.0	0	0.0	0	0.0	0
Total	227	51.1	217	48.9	283	63.7	161	36.3	135	30.4	444		149

Transfers

Transfers in	5
Transfers out	1

Tuition and Fees

	Resident	Nonresident
Full-time	$9,817	$19,747
Part-time	$6,867	$13,487

Living Expenses

Estimated living expenses for singles

Living on campus	Living off campus	Living at home
N/A	$10,376	$10,376

University of Arkansas at Little Rock, William H. Bowen School of Law

*ABA
Approved
Since
1969*

GPA and LSAT Scores

	Total	Full-time	Part-time
# of apps	1,322	1,149	173
# of offers	267	203	64
# of matrics	134	93	41
75% GPA	3.57	3.60	3.55
Median GPA	3.26	3.28	3.23
25% GPA	2.98	2.98	2.88
75% LSAT	157	157	155
Median LSAT	153	154	149
25% LSAT	149	150	147

Grants and Scholarships (from prior year)

	Total		Full-time		Part-time	
	#	%	#	%	#	%
Total # of students	472		312		160	
Total # receiving grants	128	27.1	107	34.3	21	13.1
Less than 1/2 tuition	71	15.0	57	18.3	14	8.8
Half to full tuition	29	6.1	24	7.7	5	3.1
Full tuition	20	4.2	18	5.8	2	1.3
More than full tuition	8	1.7	8	2.6	0	0.0
Median grant amount			$4,000		$2,000	

Informational and Library Resources

# of volumes and volume equivalents	294,908
# of titles	93,053
# of active serial subscriptions	3,614
Study seating capacity inside the library	365
# of full-time professional librarians	7
Hours per week library is open	98
# of open, wired connections available to students	1
# of networked computers available for use by students	60
# of simultaneous wireless users	300
Require computer?	No

JD Attrition (from prior year)

	Academic	Other	Total	
	#	#	#	%
1st year	1	16	17	12.3
2nd year	12	2	14	8.9
3rd year	0	0	0	0.0
4th year	0	0	0	0.0

Employment (9 months after graduation)

	Total	Percentage
Employment status known	106	96.4
Employment status unknown	4	3.6
Employed	84	79.2
Pursuing graduate degrees	5	4.7
Unemployed seeking employment	2	1.9
Unemployed not seeking employment	1	0.9
Unemployed and studying for the bar	14	13.2
Type of Employment		
# employed in law firms	47	56.0
# employed in business and industry	10	11.9
# employed in government	14	16.7
# employed in public interest	3	3.6
# employed as judicial clerks	8	9.5
# employed in academia	2	2.4
Geographic Location		
# employed in state	68	81.0
# employed in foreign countries	0	0.0
# of states where employed		10

Bar Passage Rates

Jurisdiction	Arkansas		
Exam	Sum 05	Win 06	Total
# from school taking bar for the first time	118	35	153
School's pass rate for all first-time takers	64%	69%	65%
State's pass rate for all first-time takers	77%	71%	75%

University of Arkansas at Little Rock, William H. Bowen School of Law

1201 McMath Avenue
Little Rock, AR 72202-5142
Phone: 501.324.9903; Fax: 501.324.9909
E-mail: lawadm@ualr.edu; Website: www.law.ualr.edu

■ About the UALR Bowen School of Law

The William H. Bowen School of Law is located in the heart of Little Rock, within a five-minute drive of state and federal courts, as well as some of Arkansas's largest law firms and corporations. Established in 1975, the law school is fully accredited by the ABA and is a member of the AALS. In addition to being the seat of state government, Little Rock is Arkansas's legal, business, and financial center. The city's vibrant legal community affords students and alumni many professional opportunities.

■ Admission

The School of Law seeks to enroll approximately 140 students each year. The law school takes a "holistic" approach to admissions, as the Admissions Committee assesses a wide array of applicant factors. The law school values inclusion and is committed to enrolling students of diverse ethnicities and backgrounds. The application deadline is April 15, though candidates are strongly encouraged to apply by early January. First-year students are admitted for the fall semester only.

The School of Law hosts prospective students on its campus throughout the year. In addition to attending scheduled events, prospective students may contact the Admissions Office to coordinate individual tours, class visits, and meetings with faculty members and current students.

■ Juris Doctor Curriculum

The Juris Doctor (JD) curriculum seeks to provide students with strong foundations in the traditional areas of law, while providing a diverse selection of electives. To receive the JD, students must complete 90 credit hours with a cumulative GPA of 2.0 (on a 4.0 scale) or better. Courses are prescribed during the first year of full-time study (or the first two years of part time). After that, most of the curriculum is elective, allowing students to explore their interests in a wide array of areas. Course descriptions and further information about the Bowen curriculum can be found at *www.law.ualr.edu/coursedescriptions.html*.

■ Concurrent Degrees

The law school allows students to pursue law degrees while concurrently pursuing master's degrees in business (JD/MBA), public administration (JD/MPA), public health (JD/MPH), or public service (JD/MPS). A concurrent degree in law and medicine is also offered (JD/MD). In order to be eligible for one of the concurrent degree programs, students must be offered admission into both the law school and the school offering the other desired degree.

■ Enrollment Divisions

The School of Law offers both full-time and part-time divisions. Full-time study generally takes three years to complete. Part-time study is generally completed in four years. In both divisions, study may be accelerated by attending summer school.

The full-time division is principally targeted at students who wish to fully engross themselves in the study of law. Most courses in the division are scheduled during the day, though night courses are available as well. The environment for full-time students is one of a traditional "academy," where students spend significant portions of their days on campus engaging in various curricular and extracurricular activities.

Bowen is one of the few law schools in the country that is statutorily mandated to offer a part-time division. The division attracts many successful professionals, including state legislators, business executives, and lobbyists.

■ Faculty

The faculty is made up of an outstanding group of scholars, practitioners, and teachers. Full-time professors teach virtually all required courses in both the full-time and part-time divisions. Experienced adjunct professors teach upper-level courses in their areas of specialty. The quality and accessibility of professors are often cited by Bowen students as "favorite things" about the school.

■ Academic Support

The School of Law provides a comprehensive academic support program. This support begins prior to the first class during the weeklong orientation program. Once classes begin, the principles taught in orientation are reinforced through a series of relevant workshops and seminars. The assistant dean for academic support also provides advising services to all students, helping them develop study plans, choose courses, and prepare for exams. Finally, Bowen helps ease the transition from law student to lawyer by offering an in-house bar exam prep course.

■ Clinical Programs

The School of Law has three legal clinics that help students bridge the gap between theory learned in the classroom and practice. Through their clinic work, students practice law under the supervision of a faculty member, while at the same time helping to fill unmet legal needs in the community.

Litigation Clinic: Students represent clients involved in many types of cases within the broad areas of juvenile delinquency and family law. Clinic students learn substantive law, while enhancing skills in conducting client interviews, drafting pleadings, negotiating, developing trial strategy, and preparing trial presentations. Qualified students receive special licenses to practice law in Arkansas.

Mediation Clinic: Students gain valuable experience in the rapidly expanding area of alternative dispute resolution. After extensive training, clinic students act as mediators in disputes relating to child abuse and neglect, juvenile delinquency, custody and visitation, special education, and small claims.

Tax Clinic: Students represent taxpayers involved in disputes with the IRS. Clinic students gain litigation and negotiation experience, while acquiring significant knowledge of tax law.

■ Externships

The Public Service Externship provides students with another opportunity to gain hands-on experience and make significant professional contacts. Externships consist of field placements in

University of Arkansas at Little Rock, William H. Bowen School of Law

government agencies, nonprofit legal services organizations, judiciary offices, and the Arkansas Legislature. Externship students earn academic credit for their participation.

■ Facilities and Library

The School of Law is housed in a historic building originally constructed in the 1930s to house the state's medical school. The spacious facility contains over 150,000 square feet and is ADA compliant. Several lounges and balconies provide students ample space for relaxing and, of course, studying.

The six-story structure underwent a complete renovation in 1992 to create modern classrooms and courtrooms. Another renovation was completed more recently to update administrative offices and to install "smart" technology in the classrooms and courtrooms and wireless Internet throughout the building. One of the most significant technological enhancements is the Lecture Capture system that allows professors to record lectures (video and audio) and make them available to students via the Web.

Wrapped around a four-story atrium, the library seats over 300 and houses two computer labs. The library is open seven days a week, and librarians are available on weekdays and Saturdays.

■ Cost and Financial Aid

Bowen is one of fewer than 30 law schools with yearly resident tuition below $10,000—an amazing value given the high cost of education. In addition, most nonresident students at Bowen earn scholarships that lower their tuition to the resident rate. Thus, the vast majority of Bowen students pay tuition of less than $10,000 per year. The law school participates in the Federal Stafford Loan Program, the Federal Graduate PLUS Loan Program, and the Federal Work-study Program, as well as major private loan programs.

■ Scholarships

The Bowen School of Law automatically considers all admitted applicants for three scholarships:

Bowen scholarships cover full tuition and fees for up to 90 credit hours. Recipients have exceptional academic credentials, strong LSAT scores, and demonstrated leadership qualities.

Merit scholarships may be awarded in an amount up to $5,000 for up to 90 credit hours. These scholarships are awarded based on an array of factors, including academic achievement, LSAT scores, diversity, and quality of application materials. Personal statements are critical to the selection of merit scholarship recipients.

Nonresident scholarships are awarded in an amount that allows recipients to pay the resident tuition rate during their first year of study. All nonresident students are eligible for these scholarships.

■ Student Life

The relatively small student body at Bowen lends itself to a supportive and engaging community. On the curricular side, the *UALR Law Review* and the Moot Court Board are highly sought after activities. Extracurricular organizations include: American Bar Association, Arkansas Bar Association, Arkansas Association of Women Lawyers, ACLU, Black Law Students Association, Christian Legal Society, Criminal Law Society, Environmental Law Society, Federalist Society, Foundation for International Legal Affairs, Hispanic Law Students Association, International Law Society, Part-time Students Association, Student Animal Defense Fund, Student Bar Association, Young Democrats, and Young Republicans. For students in need of athletic recreation, the Student Bar Association sponsors softball, kickball, and flag football teams, as well as golf tournaments.

Applicant Profile

University of Arkansas at Little Rock, William H. Bowen School of Law
This grid includes only applicants who earned 120–180 LSAT scores under standard administrations.

LSAT Score	3.75 +		3.50–3.74		3.25–3.49		3.00–3.24		2.75–2.99		2.50–2.74		2.25–2.49		2.00–2.24		Below 2.00		No GPA		Total	
	Apps	Adm	Apps	Adm	Apps	Adm	Apps	Adm	Apps	Adm	Apps	Adm	Apps	Adm	Apps	Adm	Apps	Adm	Apps	Adm	Apps	Adm
175–180	1	1	0	0	0	0	0	0	0	0	0	0	0	0	0	0	0	0	0	0	1	1
170–174	2	2	0	0	1	1	1	0	0	0	1	1	0	0	0	0	0	0	0	0	5	4
165–169	3	2	3	2	3	3	6	4	0	0	2	2	0	0	0	0	0	0	0	0	17	13
160–164	10	7	7	5	5	1	11	6	5	2	3	2	0	0	2	0	0	0	0	0	43	23
155–159	17	13	17	9	26	13	24	9	28	15	12	3	8	2	7	4	0	0	5	1	144	69
150–154	34	13	56	18	74	14	70	15	47	8	34	4	15	4	8	2	3	0	3	0	344	78
145–149	32	8	57	13	72	15	57	9	45	6	35	4	24	1	5	2	1	0	0	0	328	58
140–144	11	1	29	3	37	1	45	3	48	2	25	2	14	0	10	0	5	0	8	1	232	13
135–139	3	0	10	1	14	0	14	0	23	0	18	0	13	0	4	0	0	0	6	0	105	1
130–134	1	0	1	0	3	0	11	0	5	0	9	0	7	0	3	0	0	0	4	0	44	0
125–129	1	0	0	0	3	0	2	0	0	0	2	0	1	0	2	0	2	0	1	0	14	0
120–124	0	0	0	0	0	0	0	0	0	0	0	0	1	0	0	0	0	0	0	0	1	0
Total	115	47	180	51	238	48	241	46	201	33	141	18	83	7	41	8	11	0	27	2	1278	260

Apps = Number of Applicants   Adm = Number Admitted   Reflects 97% of the total applicant pool.

Ave Maria School of Law

3475 Plymouth Road
Ann Arbor, MI 48105
Phone: 734.827.8063; Fax: 734.622.0123
E-mail: info@avemarialaw.edu; Website: www.avemarialaw.edu

ABA
Approved
Since
2002

The Basics

Type of school	Private
Term	Semester
Application deadline	6/10
Application fee	$50
Financial aid deadline	6/1
Can first year start other than fall?	No
Student to faculty ratio	16.1 to 1
Does the university offer:	
housing restricted to law students?	No
graduate housing for which law students are eligible?	No

Faculty and Administrators

	Total		Men		Women		Minorities	
	Fall	Spr	Fall	Spr	Fall	Spr	Fall	Spr
Full-time	19	19	13	14	6	5	1	3
Other Full-time	6	6	0	0	6	6	1	1
Deans, librarians, & others who teach	4	4	3	4	1	0	1	0
Part-time	8	13	6	12	2	1	0	0
Total	37	42	22	30	15	12	3	4

Curriculum

	Full-time	Part-time
Typical first-year section size	65	0
Is there typically a "small section" of the first-year class, other than Legal Writing, taught by full-time faculty	No	No
If yes, typical size offered last year		
# of classroom course titles beyond first-year curriculum	66	
# of upper division courses, excluding seminars with an enrollment: Under 25	45	
25–49	27	
50–74	3	
75–99	0	
100+	0	
# of seminars	9	
# of seminar positions available	153	
# of seminar positions filled	121	0
# of positions available in simulation courses	109	
# of simulation positions filled	77	0
# of positions available in faculty supervised clinical courses	38	
# of faculty supervised clinical positions filled	38	0
# involved in field placements	63	0
# involved in law journals	46	0
# involved in interschool competitions	20	0
# of credit hours required to graduate	90	

JD Enrollment and Ethnicity

	Men		Women		Full-time		Part-time		1st-year		Total		JD Degs. Awd.
	#	%	#	%	#	%	#	%	#	%	#	%	
African Amer.	2	0.8	4	3.1	6	1.6	0	0.0	1	0.8	6	1.6	1
Amer. Indian	3	1.2	1	0.8	4	1.1	0	0.0	1	0.8	4	1.0	1
Asian Amer.	16	6.3	12	9.4	28	7.4	0	0.0	9	6.9	28	7.3	2
Mex. Amer.	8	3.1	0	0.0	8	2.1	0	0.0	3	2.3	8	2.1	0
Puerto Rican	0	0.0	1	0.8	1	0.3	0	0.0	0	0.0	1	0.3	0
Hispanic	11	4.3	4	3.1	15	3.9	0	0.0	5	3.8	15	3.9	2
Total Minority	40	15.7	22	17.3	62	16.3	0	0.0	19	14.6	62	16.3	6
For. Nation.	7	2.8	1	0.8	8	2.1	0	0.0	0	0.0	8	2.1	2
Caucasian	207	81.5	104	81.9	310	81.6	1	100.0	111	85.4	311	81.6	80
Unknown	0	0.0	0	0.0	0	0.0	0	0.0	0	0.0	0	0.0	0
Total	254	66.7	127	33.3	380	99.7	1	0.3	130	34.1	381		88

Transfers

Transfers in	0
Transfers out	12

Tuition and Fees

	Resident	Nonresident
Full-time	$30,765	$30,765
Part-time	$0	$0

Living Expenses

Estimated living expenses for singles

Living on campus	Living off campus	Living at home
N/A	$19,274	N/A

Ave Maria School of Law

ABA Approved Since 2002

GPA and LSAT Scores

	Total	Full-time	Part-time
# of apps	941	941	0
# of offers	497	497	0
# of matrics	131	131	0
75% GPA	3.60	3.60	0.00
Median GPA	3.32	3.32	0.00
25% GPA	3.02	3.02	0.00
75% LSAT	158	158	0
Median LSAT	153	153	0
25% LSAT	150	150	0

Grants and Scholarships (from prior year)

	Total		Full-time		Part-time	
	#	%	#	%	#	%
Total # of students	360		360		0	
Total # receiving grants	220	61.1	220	61.1	0	0.0
Less than 1/2 tuition	64	17.8	64	17.8	0	0.0
Half to full tuition	61	16.9	61	16.9	0	0.0
Full tuition	89	24.7	89	24.7	0	0.0
More than full tuition	6	1.7	6	1.7	0	0.0
Median grant amount			$19,312		$0	

Informational and Library Resources

# of volumes and volume equivalents	462,720
# of titles	179,174
# of active serial subscriptions	4,474
Study seating capacity inside the library	285
# of full-time professional librarians	5
Hours per week library is open	105
# of open, wired connections available to students	569
# of networked computers available for use by students	66
# of simultaneous wireless users	0
Require computer?	No

JD Attrition (from prior year)

	Academic	Other	Total	
	#	#	#	%
1st year	3	4	7	4.8
2nd year	0	16	16	12.8
3rd year	0	1	1	1.1
4th year	0	0	0	0.0

Employment (9 months after graduation)

	Total	Percentage
Employment status known	68	98.6
Employment status unknown	1	1.4
Employed	60	88.2
Pursuing graduate degrees	0	0.0
Unemployed seeking employment	5	7.4
Unemployed not seeking employment	2	2.9
Unemployed and studying for the bar	1	1.5
Type of Employment		
# employed in law firms	31	51.7
# employed in business and industry	9	15.0
# employed in government	7	11.7
# employed in public interest	4	6.7
# employed as judicial clerks	7	11.7
# employed in academia	2	3.3
Geographic Location		
# employed in state	26	43.3
# employed in foreign countries	1	1.7
# of states where employed		23

Bar Passage Rates

Jurisdiction	Michigan			New York		
Exam	Sum 05	Win 06	Total	Sum 05	Win 06	Total
# from school taking bar for the first time	25	3	28	4	0	4
School's pass rate for all first-time takers	88%	100%	89%	100%		100%
State's pass rate for all first-time takers	78%	65%	74%	76%	61%	74%

Ave Maria School of Law

3475 Plymouth Road
Ann Arbor, MI 48105
Phone: 734.827.8063; Fax: 734.622.0123
E-mail: info@avemarialaw.edu; Website: www.avemarialaw.edu

■ Introduction

Ave Maria School of Law offers students a distinctive legal education that focuses on professional excellence, the moral foundations of the law, and the harmony of faith and reason. As a national Catholic law school, Ave Maria is committed to producing highly competent graduates who are able to reflect critically on the law, the principles that undergird it, and their role within the legal system.

The student body of Ave Maria School of Law is drawn from 47 states and several other nations. With a student-faculty ratio of approximately 14 to 1, students benefit from ready access to experienced faculty members who have served as attorneys in private practice and governmental service, and as judicial clerks. The faculty prepares students to practice at the highest level and to succeed on bar exams throughout the country. Graduates from the 2003–2005 classes achieved an overall bar-pass rate of 88 percent in 33 states. The quality of Ave Maria's academic program also is recognized by judges across the country who have hired graduates as judicial clerks—with 34 clerkships secured by members of the 2003–2006 graduating classes.

Ave Maria encourages applications from students of all faiths who seek a distinctive legal education enriched by the Catholic faith and the Catholic intellectual tradition.

■ Enrollment/Student Body

While many of Ave Maria's 380 students come to the School of Law directly from their undergraduate institutions, others have earned postgraduate degrees and have work experience in fields including business, medicine, engineering, military, and education. More than 200 different undergraduate colleges are represented at the School of Law, including Boston College, Christendom College, Cornell University, Franciscan University, Notre Dame, Princeton, the University of Michigan, the University of Pennsylvania, and many other fine schools.

■ Faculty

At the core of the Ave Maria School of Law education is the faculty who teach and mentor students. Faculty members bring to the classroom experiences as attorneys in private practice, judicial clerks, and teachers and administrators at other law schools. In hiring faculty, the law school administration has sought individuals who will be able to translate the mission of the School of Law in the classroom, in their scholarship, and in their service. Ave Maria faculty members actively contribute to the profession through their legal research, writing, and involvement in professional and civic organizations. Our faculty includes 21 full-time professors and Judge Robert H. Bork. Professional skills courses are taught by six legal writing lecturers and two clinicians. Select upper-level courses are taught by adjunct faculty members drawn from area law firms, corporations, and the judiciary.

■ Library/Physical Facilities

The Ave Maria Law Library is the intellectual heart of the law school, offering students and faculty access to a rich and varied collection of materials and online resources in an environment that is conducive to study and research. The library's collection is both broad and deep. The collection is composed of book, electronic, and microform formats and is especially strong in US Supreme Court materials and natural law, canon law, legal history, and legal ethics. Contemporary titles in political science, economics, history, and philosophy augment the collection. The library provides a comfortable, inviting, and technologically advanced environment for study and research. All study spaces, including carrels, table- and soft-seating, and a suite of group-study rooms, have data and electrical outlets for accessing online resources. The library's student-friendly environment allows food and beverages to be enjoyed everywhere in the library except the computer labs.

■ Curriculum

Ave Maria School of Law awards the Juris Doctor degree after three years (90 credits) of full-time residential study. The required curriculum ensures that all students develop those skills that are fundamental to the effective practice of law—analysis, reasoning, problem solving, research, writing, oral advocacy, and others. Through elective courses, students have the opportunity to focus on specific subject areas of interest, such as commercial law, employment law, international law, and intellectual property law. A central tenet of the educational philosophy at Ave Maria is that law and morality are inherently intertwined. Ave Maria School of Law affirms Catholic legal education's traditional emphasis on the natural law written on the heart of every human being.

■ Admission

Ave Maria enrolls talented individuals from diverse backgrounds who seek a rigorous and distinctive legal education. To this end, Ave Maria evaluates applicants from a whole-person perspective and considers many factors, including work experience, activities, background, obstacles overcome, accomplishments, undergraduate and graduate school records, Law School Admission Test (LSAT) scores, letters of reference, and the applicant's personal statement. Ave Maria recognizes that a diverse student body, drawn from throughout the United States and internationally, enriches the educational atmosphere.

■ Student Activities

By providing opportunities for interaction among students, faculty, and the legal community, Ave Maria ensures a vibrant, professional atmosphere and a constructive law school experience. A five-day Orientation Program, a Distinguished Speaker Series, conferences, and the Ave Maria Mentor Program, together with a challenging and comprehensive curriculum, provide Ave Maria students with an exceptional law school experience. A multitude of student organizations offer students the opportunity to pursue their specific areas of interest and augment their law school education.

■ Career Services/Placement

Ave Maria School of Law graduates accept employment with an array of employers in all regions of the country, including national and regional law firms, such as Sidley Austin; Butzel Long; Shook, Hardy & Bacon; and Holland & Hart. Other graduates have been successful in obtaining employment with state and federal governmental agencies, including the US Departments of Justice and Defense. A number of Ave Maria graduates choose to begin their legal careers with public interest law organizations such as the Thomas More Law Center, the Spanish Catholic Center, and the Bioethics Defense Fund.

The Career Services Office uses a proactive and individualized approach to assist students during each stage of the career-search process—exploration, counseling, strategizing, résumé and cover letter preparation, interviewing, and consideration of employment offers. The full-time staff of three, two of whom are attorneys, is dedicated to expanding employment opportunities for students through the cultivation of relationships with legal employers throughout the region and the nation.

■ Expenses/Financial Aid

Ave Maria offers a generous scholarship program that annually provides more than 40 full- and three-quarter tuition scholarships to members of the entering class. Additionally, the School of Law annually awards as many as 15 scholarships to entering students who have a record of service and leadership in select areas. Ave Maria School of Law is among a select group of professional schools that has adopted a "tuition pledge," whereby tuition does not increase for the student's second or third years of law school. This tuition pledge ensures that students are in a better position to create a three-year financial plan for law school. Tuition for members of the fall 2006 entering class is $30,345.

■ Housing

Ave Maria's 11-acre campus is within walking distance of apartments, condominiums, and single-family homes. The law school Admissions Office staff provides assistance to students during their search for housing and, if applicable, roommates.

Applicant Profile

Believing that the undergraduate record and the LSAT results are only two of many important facets of an applicant's qualifications for admission to the profession, the Admissions Committee at Ave Maria School of Law has chosen not to provide a data grid. Prospective applicants who wish to obtain greater information regarding admission standards are welcome to contact a member of the Admissions Office staff at 734.827.8063.

University of Baltimore School of Law

1420 North Charles Street
Baltimore, MD 21201
Phone: 410.837.4459; Fax: 410.837.4450
E-mail: lwadmiss@ubalt.edu; Website: law.ubalt.edu

ABA Approved Since 1972

The Basics

Type of school	Public
Term	Semester
Application deadline	4/1
Application fee	$60
Financial aid deadline	3/1
Can first year start other than fall?	No
Student to faculty ratio	9.8 to 1
Does the university offer:	
housing restricted to law students?	No
graduate housing for which law students are eligible?	No

Faculty and Administrators

	Total		Men		Women		Minorities	
	Fall	Spr	Fall	Spr	Fall	Spr	Fall	Spr
Full-time	40	39	24	23	16	16	8	8
Other Full-time	4	4	1	1	3	3	1	1
Deans, librarians, & others who teach	15	15	8	8	7	7	3	3
Part-time	89	87	63	59	26	28	12	12
Total	**148**	**145**	**96**	**91**	**52**	**54**	**24**	**24**

Curriculum

	Full-time	Part-time
Typical first-year section size	77	82
Is there typically a "small section" of the first-year class, other than Legal Writing, taught by full-time faculty	No	No
If yes, typical size offered last year		
# of classroom course titles beyond first-year curriculum	126	
# of upper division courses, excluding seminars with an enrollment: Under 25	173	
25–49	29	
50–74	19	
75–99	12	
100+	3	
# of seminars	32	
# of seminar positions available	650	
# of seminar positions filled	314	86
# of positions available in simulation courses	1,030	
# of simulation positions filled	571	165
# of positions available in faculty supervised clinical courses	111	
# of faculty supervised clinical positions filled	72	4
# involved in field placements	114	15
# involved in law journals	256	37
# involved in interschool competitions	47	7
# of credit hours required to graduate	90	

JD Enrollment and Ethnicity

	Men #	Men %	Women #	Women %	Full-time #	Full-time %	Part-time #	Part-time %	1st-year #	1st-year %	Total #	Total %	JD Degs. Awd.
African Amer.	29	6.0	77	13.9	49	6.7	57	18.6	28	7.3	106	10.3	41
Amer. Indian	2	0.4	3	0.5	1	0.1	4	1.3	3	0.8	5	0.5	3
Asian Amer.	24	5.0	26	4.7	37	5.1	13	4.2	19	4.9	50	4.8	13
Mex. Amer.	0	0.0	0	0.0	0	0.0	0	0.0	0	0.0	0	0.0	0
Puerto Rican	0	0.0	0	0.0	0	0.0	0	0.0	0	0.0	0	0.0	0
Hispanic	11	2.3	9	1.6	12	1.7	8	2.6	6	1.6	20	1.9	7
Total Minority	66	13.8	115	20.8	99	13.6	82	26.8	56	14.6	181	17.5	64
For. Nation.	2	0.4	5	0.9	4	0.6	3	1.0	3	0.8	7	0.7	2
Caucasian	330	68.8	351	63.6	498	68.6	183	59.8	256	66.7	681	66.0	190
Unknown	82	17.1	81	14.7	125	17.2	38	12.4	69	18.0	163	15.8	20
Total	480	46.5	552	53.5	726	70.3	306	29.7	384	37.2	1032		276

Transfers

Transfers in	12
Transfers out	22

Tuition and Fees

	Resident	Nonresident
Full-time	$19,235	$31,151
Part-time	$15,462	$23,962

Living Expenses

Estimated living expenses for singles

Living on campus	Living off campus	Living at home
N/A	$15,394	N/A

University of Baltimore School of Law

*ABA
Approved
Since
1972*

GPA and LSAT Scores

	Total	Full-time	Part-time
# of apps	2,880	2,310	570
# of offers	1,156	985	171
# of matrics	382	287	95
75% GPA	3.49	3.52	3.24
Median GPA	3.15	3.24	2.98
25% GPA	2.87	2.93	2.73
75% LSAT	156	156	155
Median LSAT	153	153	153
25% LSAT	151	151	151

Grants and Scholarships (from prior year)

	Total		Full-time		Part-time	
	#	%	#	%	#	%
Total # of students	986		674		312	
Total # receiving grants	93	9.4	73	10.8	20	6.4
Less than 1/2 tuition	66	6.7	51	7.6	15	4.8
Half to full tuition	2	0.2	2	0.3	0	0.0
Full tuition	0	0.0	0	0.0	0	0.0
More than full tuition	25	2.5	20	3.0	5	1.6
Median grant amount			$3,000		$3,000	

Informational and Library Resources

# of volumes and volume equivalents	359,262
# of titles	34,249
# of active serial subscriptions	3,345
Study seating capacity inside the library	345
# of full-time professional librarians	11
Hours per week library is open	110
# of open, wired connections available to students	348
# of networked computers available for use by students	36
# of simultaneous wireless users	700
Require computer?	No

JD Attrition (from prior year)

	Academic	Other	Total	
	#	#	#	%
1st year	6	42	48	14.5
2nd year	2	30	32	9.4
3rd year	0	7	7	2.7
4th year	0	0	0	0.0

Employment (9 months after graduation)

	Total	Percentage
Employment status known	232	80.3
Employment status unknown	57	19.7
Employed	210	90.5
Pursuing graduate degrees	3	1.3
Unemployed seeking employment	13	5.6
Unemployed not seeking employment	3	1.3
Unemployed and studying for the bar	3	1.3
Type of Employment		
# employed in law firms	76	36.2
# employed in business and industry	32	15.2
# employed in government	40	19.0
# employed in public interest	5	2.4
# employed as judicial clerks	53	25.2
# employed in academia	2	1.0
Geographic Location		
# employed in state	170	81.0
# employed in foreign countries	0	0.0
# of states where employed	11	

Bar Passage Rates

Jurisdiction	Maryland		
Exam	Sum 05	Win 06	Total
# from school taking bar for the first time	255	41	296
School's pass rate for all first-time takers	66%	59%	65%
State's pass rate for all first-time takers	76%	66%	74%

University of Baltimore School of Law

1420 North Charles Street
Baltimore, MD 21201
Phone: 410.837.4459; Fax: 410.837.4450
E-mail: lwadmiss@ubalt.edu; Website: law.ubalt.edu

■ Introduction

Founded in 1925, the University of Baltimore is one of 13 institutions in the university system of Maryland. The School of Law has a distinguished history of offering high-quality legal education in a vibrant urban environment that provides a wide range of opportunities for students to put their legal knowledge into practice. In both day and evening divisions, the school offers a comprehensive curriculum that gives students core substantive and procedural classes, as well as excellent training in legal skills. A broad selection of elective courses completes the curriculum. The school's midtown location puts it only 18 blocks from Baltimore's Inner Harbor, Oriole Park at Camden Yards, and the Baltimore Ravens' M&T Bank Stadium. Also nearby are state and federal courts, large law firms, and government offices. The School of Law is accredited by the American Bar Association and is a member of the Association of American Law Schools.

■ Library and Physical Facilities

The library's permanent collection contains approximately 317,000 books and bound volume equivalents. The collection includes the published reports of federal and state courts, statutes, administrative materials, and secondary materials such as treatises, legal encyclopedias, digests, citators, form books, looseleaf services, and law reviews. The library staff believes that technology should not be considered separate from the study and practice of law. To that end, professional reference librarians are available to students seven days a week. Legal research courses teach students how to use the computer-assisted legal systems, as well as how to access the library's many Web-based resources. The library's two computer labs are open to law students during library hours and provide access to word processing, LexisNexis, Westlaw, the Internet, online catalogs, and other resources.

■ Joint Degrees

The School of Law offers six joint degrees: JD with MBA, MPA, MS in Criminal Justice, MS in Negotiations and Conflict Management, LLM in Taxation, and the PhD in Policy Science.

■ Special Programs

Areas of Concentration—The School of Law has an innovative curriculum that allows students to develop an area of study focused on one or more areas of the law, while still providing them with the basic first-year curriculum and many electives. Students may take courses in one of 14 areas of concentration: Business Law, Criminal Practice, Electronic Commerce, Environmental Law, Estate Planning, Family Law, General Practice, Intellectual Property, International and Comparative Law, Litigation and Advocacy, Public and Governmental Service, Real Estate Practice, Tax Law, and Theories of the Law.

The Center for Families, Children, and the Courts—focuses on reforming state courts into more appropriate forums for the resolutions of family legal crises.

The Center for International and Comparative Law—promotes the study and understanding of international and comparative law and the political and economic institutions that support the international legal order. The center places special emphasis on environmental law, human rights, intellectual property, and international business transactions.

The Stephen L. Snyder Center for Litigation Skills—supports and enhances the acclaimed litigation skills training of the School of Law through a variety of programs and activities, including lectures by prominent lawyers and judges, special conferences, and litigation research.

Clinical, Advocacy, and Internship Programs—Professional development is fostered through clinics in which students represent individuals and organizations in litigation and transactional matters. Clinics include the **Appellate Practice Clinic**, which enables students to brief and argue a case in the Maryland Court of Special Appeals; the **Civil Advocacy Clinic**, which focuses on such issues as consumer protection, public benefits cases, and landlord-tenant disputes; the **Community Development Clinic**, which represents nonprofit community organizations in a variety of housing, economic, social, and cultural development areas; the **Criminal Practice Clinic**, in which students handle misdemeanor and felony matters in the district and circuit courts; the **Disability Law Clinic**, which provides representation to patients in involuntary commitment hearings; the **Family Law Clinic**, where students represent low-income clients seeking child custody, support, divorce, and protection from domestic violence; the **Family Mediation Clinic**, which permits students to co-mediate family law disputes and engage in projects designed to improve the practice of family mediation; and the **Tax Law Clinic**, which enables students to represent low-income clients before the Internal Revenue Service and the US Tax Court. **Internship Programs** give students experience clerking for academic credit in the public and private sector, including positions in the executive, legislative, and judicial branches of state and local governments.

Law Reviews, Journals, and Other Periodicals give students an opportunity to hone their skills in research, analysis, and writing. The *University of Baltimore Law Review, Journal of Environmental Law,* and *Intellectual Property Law Journal* offer in-depth analysis of issues of current concern to practitioners and judges alike. The *Law Forum* specializes in articles that trace developing trends in the law.

■ Admission

The School of Law has established an admission policy designed to obtain a diverse and well-qualified student body. In evaluating applicant files, the Admission Committee considers not only the cumulative undergraduate grade-point average and the LSAT score, but also nontraditional factors that may be relevant in determining an applicant's ability to succeed in law school. Applicants are encouraged to discuss fully in a personal statement any such factors they wish the committee to consider in evaluating their application.

■ Expenses and Financial Aid

The university's Financial Aid Office administers federal, state, and institutional loan programs. First-year and transfer applicants are advised to apply for financial aid well in advance of the March 1 deadline. Law scholarships are awarded by the School of Law on the basis of the same traditional and nontraditional factors considered for admission. Financial need is not required for scholarships, although it is a factor.

■ Career Services

Six months after graduation, 94 percent of the class of 2005 was employed. (Note: The percentage is the total number employed of those seeking employment.) The Center for Professional Development is dedicated to assisting law students in articulating, developing, and attaining their professional goals. The Center for Professional Development provides career counseling, offers a broad array of programs and workshops, maintains an extensive resource library, and is online with both LexisNexis and Westlaw.

Applicant Profile

University of Baltimore School of Law
This grid includes only applicants who earned 120–180 LSAT scores under standard administrations.

LSAT Score	3.75 +		3.50–3.74		3.25–3.49		3.00–3.24		2.75–2.99		2.50–2.74		2.25–2.49		2.00–2.24		Below 2.00		No GPA		Total	
	Apps	Adm	Apps	Adm	Apps	Adm	Apps	Adm	Apps	Adm	Apps	Adm	Apps	Adm	Apps	Adm	Apps	Adm	Apps	Adm	Apps	Adm
175–180	0	0	0	0	0	0	0	0	0	0	0	0	0	0	0	0	0	0	0	0	0	0
170–174	0	0	0	0	0	0	0	0	0	0	0	0	0	0	0	0	0	0	0	0	0	0
165–169	5	0	5	1	8	3	4	1	2	1	2	0	3	1	0	0	0	0	0	0	29	7
160–164	16	6	20	7	24	4	22	7	20	5	11	3	7	1	2	0	1	0	2	0	125	33
155–159	44	14	78	26	93	29	86	32	66	24	35	11	15	11	9	3	0	0	4	0	430	150
150–154	60	19	132	43	155	49	164	52	172	64	78	26	28	10	11	3	6	0	6	1	812	267
145–149	36	7	108	10	161	14	166	13	123	14	75	4	42	2	13	0	2	0	5	1	731	65
140–144	17	0	38	0	84	0	99	2	85	3	66	1	42	0	16	0	4	0	7	0	458	6
135–139	1	0	16	0	20	0	32	1	35	0	30	0	22	0	8	0	6	0	11	0	181	1
130–134	2	1	4	0	8	0	11	0	16	0	11	0	14	0	6	0	2	0	4	0	78	1
125–129	0	0	0	0	0	0	0	0	0	0	3	0	2	0	3	0	0	0	2	0	10	0
120–124	0	0	0	0	0	0	0	0	0	0	1	0	0	0	0	0	0	0	2	0	3	0
Total	181	47	401	87	553	99	584	108	519	111	312	45	175	25	68	6	21	0	43	2	2857	530

Apps = Number of Applicants
Adm = Number Admitted
Reflects 98% of the total applicant pool.

Barry University Dwayne O. Andreas School of Law

6441 East Colonial Drive
Orlando, FL 32807
Phone: 321.206.5600; Fax: 321.206.5654
E-mail: lawinfo@mail.barry.edu; Website: www.barry.edu/law

ABA
Approved
Since
2002

The Basics

Type of school	Private
Term	Semester
Application deadline	4/1
Application fee	$50
Financial aid deadline	4/15
Can first year start other than fall?	No
Student to faculty ratio	16.6 to 1
Does the university offer:	
housing restricted to law students?	No
graduate housing for which law students are eligible?	No

Faculty and Administrators

	Total		Men		Women		Minorities	
	Fall	Spr	Fall	Spr	Fall	Spr	Fall	Spr
Full-time	25	23	15	14	10	9	6	6
Other Full-time	1	2	0	1	1	1	0	0
Deans, librarians, & others who teach	5	5	4	4	1	1	1	1
Part-time	18	15	15	11	3	4	3	1
Total	49	45	34	30	15	15	10	8

Curriculum

	Full-time	Part-time
Typical first-year section size	80	47
Is there typically a "small section" of the first-year class, other than Legal Writing, taught by full-time faculty	No	No
If yes, typical size offered last year		
# of classroom course titles beyond first-year curriculum	88	
# of upper division courses, excluding seminars with an enrollment: Under 25	76	
25–49	21	
50–74	14	
75–99	3	
100+	1	
# of seminars	5	
# of seminar positions available	100	
# of seminar positions filled	56	13
# of positions available in simulation courses	325	
# of simulation positions filled	190	91
# of positions available in faculty supervised clinical courses	0	
# of faculty supervised clinical positions filled	17	9
# involved in field placements	71	15
# involved in law journals	35	9
# involved in interschool competitions	41	10
# of credit hours required to graduate	90	

JD Enrollment and Ethnicity

	Men		Women		Full-time		Part-time		1st-year		Total		JD Degs. Awd.
	#	%	#	%	#	%	#	%	#	%	#	%	
African Amer.	13	4.5	16	5.8	16	3.9	13	8.3	6	3.0	29	5.2	6
Amer. Indian	1	0.3	3	1.1	3	0.7	1	0.6	0	0.0	4	0.7	0
Asian Amer.	9	3.1	15	5.4	18	4.4	6	3.8	5	2.5	24	4.3	4
Mex. Amer.	0	0.0	3	1.1	0	0.0	3	1.9	0	0.0	3	0.5	0
Puerto Rican	0	0.0	0	0.0	0	0.0	0	0.0	0	0.0	0	0.0	0
Hispanic	31	10.8	20	7.2	36	8.8	15	9.6	17	8.4	51	9.1	13
Total Minority	54	18.8	57	20.7	73	17.9	38	24.4	28	13.9	111	19.7	23
For. Nation.	1	0.3	0	0.0	1	0.2	0	0.0	1	0.5	1	0.2	0
Caucasian	203	70.7	175	63.4	282	69.3	96	61.5	142	70.3	378	67.1	94
Unknown	29	10.1	44	15.9	51	12.5	22	14.1	31	15.3	73	13.0	11
Total	287	51.0	276	49.0	407	72.3	156	27.7	202	35.9	563		128

Transfers

Transfers in	4
Transfers out	17

Tuition and Fees

	Resident	Nonresident
Full-time	$27,560	$27,560
Part-time	$20,776	$20,776

Living Expenses

Estimated living expenses for singles

Living on campus	Living off campus	Living at home
N/A	$18,100	$18,100

Barry University Dwayne O. Andreas School of Law

ABA
Approved
Since
2002

GPA and LSAT Scores

	Total	Full-time	Part-time
# of apps	2,180	2,027	153
# of offers	1,074	990	84
# of matrics	199	173	26
75% GPA	3.40	3.38	3.30
Median GPA	3.10	3.16	3.10
25% GPA	2.80	2.85	2.70
75% LSAT	151	151	154
Median LSAT	149	149	149
25% LSAT	148	147	148

Grants and Scholarships (from prior year)

	Total		Full-time		Part-time	
	#	%	#	%	#	%
Total # of students	537		351		186	
Total # receiving grants	449	83.6	328	93.4	121	65.1
Less than 1/2 tuition	390	72.6	288	82.1	102	54.8
Half to full tuition	57	10.6	39	11.1	18	9.7
Full tuition	2	0.4	1	0.3	1	0.5
More than full tuition	0	0.0	0	0.0	0	0.0
Median grant amount			$5,000		$4,000	

Informational and Library Resources

# of volumes and volume equivalents	267,586
# of titles	113,339
# of active serial subscriptions	1,782
Study seating capacity inside the library	338
# of full-time professional librarians	10
Hours per week library is open	100
# of open, wired connections available to students	0
# of networked computers available for use by students	47
# of simultaneous wireless users	512
Require computer?	Yes

JD Attrition (from prior year)

	Academic	Other	Total	
	#	#	#	%
1st year	15	43	58	27.6
2nd year	5	1	6	3.4
3rd year	0	5	5	4.9
4th year	0	0	0	0.0

Employment (9 months after graduation)

	Total	Percentage
Employment status known	90	92.8
Employment status unknown	7	7.2
Employed	79	87.8
Pursuing graduate degrees	0	0.0
Unemployed seeking employment	2	2.2
Unemployed not seeking employment	1	1.1
Unemployed and studying for the bar	8	8.9
Type of Employment		
# employed in law firms	45	57.0
# employed in business and industry	18	22.8
# employed in government	8	10.1
# employed in public interest	5	6.3
# employed as judicial clerks	0	0.0
# employed in academia	3	3.8
Geographic Location		
# employed in state	61	77.2
# employed in foreign countries	2	2.5
# of states where employed	14	

Bar Passage Rates

Jurisdiction	Florida			Maryland		
Exam	Sum 05	Win 06	Total	Sum 05	Win 06	Total
# from school taking bar for the first time	55	22	77	0	2	2
School's pass rate for all first-time takers	58%	64%	60%		50%	50%
State's pass rate for all first-time takers	71%	73%	71%	76%	66%	74%

Barry University Dwayne O. Andreas School of Law

6441 East Colonial Drive
Orlando, FL 32807
Phone: 321.206.5600; Fax: 321.206.5654
E-mail: lawinfo@mail.barry.edu; Website: www.barry.edu/law

■ A Growing Presence in Higher Education

Founded in early 1993, the University of Orlando School of Law admitted its first class in 1995. In March of 1999, the School of Law became a part of Barry University, a Catholic international university located in Miami Shores, Florida. The affiliation is an extremely positive one, since both administrations have the same focus—to offer quality academics grounded in a strong ethical foundation with the goal of preparing qualified, competent practicing attorneys.

The School of Law is situated on a beautiful 20-acre campus in East Orlando, about 15 minutes from downtown. The School of Law facilities include a two-story, 20,000-square-foot Law Center building; a 9,000-square-foot Administration and Moot Court building; a 9,000-square-foot classroom and faculty office building; and a 36,000-square-foot law library.

The Barry Law mission guides everything the law school does, from awarding and maintaining scholarships to arranging mentors, to providing career service guidance and bar prep programs. The School of Law is proud of the quality education provided, with an emphasis on social justice and a spiritual dimension all within a caring environment. Candidates who choose to study at Barry Law will enjoy the benefits of a mission-centered university where students get the attention they need to succeed.

■ The Perfect Venue for Your Legal Education

Central Florida is one of the fastest growing areas in the country. A host of attractions bring millions of visitors to central Florida each year. Just an hour away are Kennedy Space Center and the beaches of the Atlantic.

Orlando is a major commercial center; many national corporations have headquarters in the city. The area is fast becoming a television and motion picture production center.

Central Florida provides a wealth of first-hand exposure to the practice of corporate and entertainment law, as well as juvenile and criminal law. The Advisory Board is composed of many prominent central Florida attorneys, judges, government officials, and others in the community. Their community affiliations enhance the networking and career opportunities available to Barry's students.

Central Florida enjoys a year-round subtropical climate and offers a wide range of cultural and recreational activities. Accommodations in the immediate area include fully furnished or unfurnished apartments as well as a wide range of single-family dwellings. Orlando has a large number of hotels and executive lodges that offer reduced rates on a weekly or monthly basis.

Orlando is the ideal venue to pursue your legal education.

■ Mission and Goals of the School of Law

Barry University School of Law seeks to offer a quality legal education in a caring environment that will enable its graduates to apply the skills and knowledge they have acquired to their own personal development, and to the good of society, through the competent and ethical practice of law. The School of Law seeks to provide a learning environment that challenges students to accept intellectual, personal, ethical,
spiritual, and social responsibilities. The school commits itself to assuring a religious dimension in an atmosphere of religious freedom and to providing community service.

■ An Overview

The School of Law teaches students to become responsible lawyers, trained to assume an active role in the legal community. Students are trained to act in strict accord with the highest ethical standards and to exercise their professional skills competently, with sensitivity to the needs and concerns of their clients.

The School of Law offers a three-year daytime program structured for full-time students. The School of Law also offers a four-year extended studies program in the evening to accommodate working adults or anyone who is unable to pursue full-time study.

Students at the School of Law have many opportunities to experience the "law-in-action" concept, both in the classroom and through practical application. Small classes foster a collegial student/professor relationship and enable the School of Law to provide legal education at its best.

Through the in-house Children and Families Clinic, Barry students gain solid practical experience working on actual cases involving disadvantaged children in need of legal services. Barry Law also offers a wealth of externship opportunities that allow students to further develop their skills as emerging attorneys while working in various venues. Externship placement currently includes opportunities in the following areas: civil government, civil poverty, judicial, mediation, public defender, and state attorney.

■ Juris Doctor

The School of Law offers the Juris Doctor (JD) degree. All students in the program must complete 90 semester hours of study in areas that are essential to the understanding and practice of law. Students in the fall entering class must complete required courses in subjects that provide a common core of understanding in the law. Students may choose from a wide variety of electives to meet the remaining requirements necessary for graduation.

■ Scholarship Program

The School of Law proudly offers a merit-based scholarship program. Generally, between 80 and 90 percent of the entering class receive a Barry Law scholarship between $1,000 and $21,000. Admitted candidates are automatically considered for scholarships and do not need to complete any additional forms. If a scholarship is offered to a candidate, notice will be sent within three to four weeks of the official acceptance letter.

Barry Law also offers a Scholarship Reward Program to second- and third-year students. Students who rank in the top 10 percent and hold at least a 3.2 grade-point average after the first and second year of law school are offered a 75 percent scholarship. What great motivation to rank in the top 10 percent, among other obvious reasons!

■ Program Objective

The School of Law combines traditional and innovative teaching methods to provide a dynamic, professional program. The JD curriculum is designed to develop students' analytical ability, communication skills, and understanding of the codes of professional responsibility and ethics that are central to the practice of law. The faculty utilizes a variety of teaching methods, including simulations and role-playing. Seminars and advanced courses provide close interaction with faculty.

Barry Law emphasizes research and writing proficiency from the first day of class. Armed with a strong foundation in research and writing, Barry Law students gain an advantage in the legal marketplace.

■ Graduation Requirements

To be eligible to receive the degree of JD, a student must (1) complete 90 academic credits of instruction with a cumulative grade-point average of 2.0 or above; (2) earn a cumulative grade-point average of 1.8 for all required courses and a passing grade in each of the required courses; (3) successfully complete the writing requirement; (4) complete a minimum of 60 out of 90 academic credits in residence at Barry University School of Law; (5) successfully complete the pro bono requirement; (6) satisfy all financial obligations to Barry University; and (7) be approved by the faculty for graduation.

Applicant Profile

Barry University Dwayne O. Andreas School of Law

LSAT Score	GPA								
	3.75 +	3.50–3.74	3.25–3.49	3.00–3.24	2.75–2.99	2.50–2.74	2.25–2.49	2.00–2.24	Below 2.00
175–180									
170–174									
165–169									
160–164									
155–159									
150–154									
145–149									
140–144									
Below 140									

Good Possibility   Possible   Unlikely

Baylor University School of Law

1114 South University Parks Drive, One Bear Place #97288
Waco, TX 76798-7288
Phone: 800.BAYLOR.U, 254.710.1911; Fax: 254.710.2316
E-mail: Heather_Creed@baylor.edu; Website: law.baylor.edu

ABA Approved Since 1931

The Basics

Type of school	Private
Term	Quarter
Application deadline	11/1 2/1 3/1
Application fee	$40
Financial aid deadline	2/15 11/1 2/1
Can first year start other than fall?	Yes
Student to faculty ratio	16.8 to 1
Does the university offer:	
housing restricted to law students?	No
graduate housing for which law students are eligible?	Yes

Faculty and Administrators

	Total Fall	Total Spr	Men Fall	Men Spr	Women Fall	Women Spr	Minorities Fall	Minorities Spr
Full-time	20	21	16	18	4	3	1	1
Other Full-time	0	0	0	0	0	0	0	0
Deans, librarians, & others who teach	5	5	3	3	2	2	0	0
Part-time	8	16	7	13	1	3	1	1
Total	**33**	**42**	**26**	**34**	**7**	**8**	**2**	**2**

Curriculum

	Full-time	Part-time
Typical first-year section size	59	0
Is there typically a "small section" of the first-year class, other than Legal Writing, taught by full-time faculty	Yes	No
If yes, typical size offered last year	54	
# of classroom course titles beyond first-year curriculum	79	
# of upper division courses, excluding seminars with an enrollment: Under 25	66	
25–49	35	
50–74	17	
75–99	6	
100+	0	
# of seminars	5	
# of seminar positions available	92	
# of seminar positions filled	92	0
# of positions available in simulation courses	1,071	
# of simulation positions filled	1,071	0
# of positions available in faculty supervised clinical courses	7	
# of faculty supervised clinical positions filled	7	0
# involved in field placements	93	0
# involved in law journals	68	0
# involved in interschool competitions	49	0
# of credit hours required to graduate	126	

JD Enrollment and Ethnicity

	Men #	Men %	Women #	Women %	Full-time #	Full-time %	Part-time #	Part-time %	1st-year #	1st-year %	Total #	Total %	JD Degs. Awd.
African Amer.	1	0.4	4	2.3	5	1.2	0	0.0	2	1.3	5	1.2	1
Amer. Indian	1	0.4	0	0.0	1	0.2	0	0.0	0	0.0	1	0.2	3
Asian Amer.	11	4.8	11	6.3	22	5.5	0	0.0	9	5.7	22	5.5	6
Mex. Amer.	8	3.5	6	3.4	14	3.5	0	0.0	3	1.9	14	3.5	5
Puerto Rican	0	0.0	0	0.0	0	0.0	0	0.0	0	0.0	0	0.0	0
Hispanic	6	2.6	3	1.7	9	2.2	0	0.0	2	1.3	9	2.2	1
Total Minority	27	11.9	24	13.8	51	12.7	0	0.0	16	10.2	51	12.7	16
For. Nation.	0	0.0	3	1.7	3	0.7	0	0.0	2	1.3	3	0.7	0
Caucasian	200	88.1	147	84.5	347	86.5	0	0.0	139	88.5	347	86.5	136
Unknown	0	0.0	0	0.0	0	0.0	0	0.0	0	0.0	0	0.0	0
Total	227	56.6	174	43.4	401	100.0	0	0.0	157	39.2	401		152

Transfers

Transfers in	1
Transfers out	6

Tuition and Fees

	Resident	Nonresident
Full-time	$31,246	$31,246
Part-time	$0	$0

Living Expenses

Estimated living expenses for singles		
Living on campus	Living off campus	Living at home
$14,638	$16,831	$7,198

Baylor University School of Law

ABA Approved Since 1931

GPA and LSAT Scores

	Fall	Spring	Summer	Total
# of apps	2,450	1,357	492	4,299
# of offers	771	157	133	1,061
# of matrics	70	60	30	160
75% GPA	3.94	3.81	3.71	3.88
Median GPA	3.75	3.63	3.59	3.66
25% GPA	3.42	3.41	3.27	3.41
75% LSAT	163	161	161	162
Median LSAT	162	159	159	160
25% LSAT	160	157	156	158

Grants and Scholarships (from prior year)

	Total		Full-time		Part-time	
	#	%	#	%	#	%
Total # of students	435		435		0	
Total # receiving grants	300	69.0	300	69.0	0	0.0
Less than 1/2 tuition	165	37.9	165	37.9	0	0.0
Half to full tuition	73	16.8	73	16.8	0	0.0
Full tuition	46	10.6	46	10.6	0	0.0
More than full tuition	16	3.7	16	3.7	0	0.0
Median grant amount			$8,033		$0	

Informational and Library Resources

# of volumes and volume equivalents	229,391
# of titles	28,584
# of active serial subscriptions	2,203
Study seating capacity inside the library	279
# of full-time professional librarians	7
Hours per week library is open	108
# of open, wired connections available to students	733
# of networked computers available for use by students	44
# of simultaneous wireless users	1,700
Require computer?	No

JD Attrition (from prior year)

	Academic	Other	Total	
	#	#	#	%
1st year	0	22	22	12.1
2nd year	2	5	7	5.4
3rd year	0	0	0	0.0
4th year	0	0	0	0.0

Employment (9 months after graduation)

	Total	Percentage
Employment status known	152	100.0
Employment status unknown	0	0.0
Employed	141	92.8
Pursuing graduate degrees	4	2.6
Unemployed seeking employment	4	2.6
Unemployed not seeking employment	3	2.0
Unemployed and studying for the bar	0	0.0

Type of Employment

# employed in law firms	96	68.1
# employed in business and industry	9	6.4
# employed in government	19	13.5
# employed in public interest	2	1.4
# employed as judicial clerks	12	8.5
# employed in academia	2	1.4

Geographic Location

# employed in state	124	87.9
# employed in foreign countries	1	0.7
# of states where employed	14	

Bar Passage Rates

Jurisdiction	Texas		
Exam	Sum 05	Win 06	Total
# from school taking bar for the first time	77	64	141
School's pass rate for all first-time takers	94%	97%	95%
State's pass rate for all first-time takers	81%	77%	80%

Baylor University School of Law

1114 South University Parks Drive, One Bear Place #97288
Waco, TX 76798-7288
Phone: 800.BAYLOR.U, 254.710.1911; Fax: 254.710.2316
E-mail: Heather_Creed@baylor.edu; Website: law.baylor.edu

■ Introduction

Baylor University School of Law is a private, ABA-approved law school and is a member of the Association of American Law Schools. Formally organized in 1857, Baylor law school is the oldest law school in Texas and is located on the campus of Baylor University in Waco, Texas. Waco is located in central Texas, has a population of over 220,000, and offers a diverse and rich array of cultural and recreational opportunities, as well as very moderate living costs.

Baylor law school stands at the forefront of practice-oriented law schools nationally. Baylor is singularly clear about its mission—to equip students upon graduation to practice law effectively and ethically. That is the key difference. Students are trained and mentored in all facets of law, including theoretical analysis, practical application, legal writing, advocacy, professional responsibility, and negotiation and counseling skills.

■ Enrollment/Student Body

Baylor law school is small by choice, with entering classes of approximately 70 students in the spring, 30 in the summer, and 70 in the fall. Baylor law school has a target student population of 400. We keep our program small because, at Baylor, we are interested in producing quality, not quantity.

Baylor is committed to enrolling a diverse student body. In 2005, the entering classes included 14 percent minority students. Baylor law students come from 30 states and hold degrees from more than 130 colleges and universities. Also, a small enrollment fosters productive relationships.

■ Faculty

Baylor law school is first a teaching school and one of the few law schools in the nation in which the granting of tenure is primarily based upon a professor's teaching effectiveness. Faculty members hold degrees from law schools and universities throughout the nation and include former law clerks for various appellate courts throughout the nation.

Faculty members are experts in their areas and have substantial practical experience. They produce a significant amount of legal scholarship, which results in their demand as speakers at legal institutes and civic functions. One of the distinctive features of the faculty is that professors maintain unrestricted hours for student consultation. Every professor is available for lending advice and guidance in all academic, professional, and other matters of concern to students.

■ Facilities and Technology

The home of Baylor law school, the award-winning Sheila and Walter Umphrey Law Center, was dedicated in 2002. At every stage of the design of the Law Center, the most important goal was to put teaching first. The building houses every facility a modern law school requires: classrooms that are unsurpassed as teaching facilities; an advocacy suite, including state-of-the-art courtrooms that provide the optimum environment for advocacy training—Baylor's centerpiece of excellence; a large, two-story appellate advocacy courtroom/classroom; a library with comfortable study and seating space in several impressive reading rooms overlooking the Brazos River; and faculty offices that support the faculty mentoring, which is the hallmark of our program.

Technology permeates the Law Center, including data and electric ports at virtually every seat in the building, along with a concurrent wireless network. Classrooms are equipped with cutting-edge technology, including audio, video, and Internet access. The automatic cameras in the courtrooms can be aimed at a desired location in the room through use of joystick controllers mounted in the console tabletops. The law school uses a sophisticated course-management system that allows the faculty to post assignments, syllabi, and course announcements, and provides discussion boards.

■ Trial Advocacy Program

Procedure is the tool of the trial lawyer, and the bedrock of Baylor's nationally ranked advocacy program is Practice Court—an ultraintensive study of civil procedure. In addition to the science of procedure, students will learn the art of trial advocacy in a rigorous and tough six-month program of skills training during the third year of law school. Students try lawsuits from beginning to end. This course prepares students to be competent, responsible, and ethical lawyers.

Baylor has a long record of successfully competing at the national and regional levels in both moot court and mock trial interscholastic competitions. In 2005, Baylor's mock trial team became the mock trial national champions by winning the prestigious annual mock trial advocacy competition sponsored by the Association of Trial Lawyers of America.

■ Curriculum and Special Programs

The required curriculum is structured to provide a logical progression for legal study from fundamental legal doctrine in first-year courses to increasingly more sophisticated and complex second- and third-year courses. The challenging curriculum, along with the opportunity to perform specialized lawyering tasks under the direct supervision of accomplished lawyers, prepares students for the rigors of any type of modern legal practice. Additionally, students have the opportunity to complete a more concentrated course of study and training in six areas of interest: general civil litigation, business litigation, business transactions, criminal practice, estate planning, and administrative practice.

There are three joint degrees: JD/MBA, JD/MTax, and JD/MPPA.

■ Admission

The law school has three entering classes—spring (February), summer (May), and fall (August) with completely separate application processes. Each class has far more applications than seats available; however, admission to the spring or summer classes is slightly less competitive than admission to the fall class.

The Admission Committee considers each application in its entirety and considers many factors beyond test scores and undergraduate GPA. Such factors include employment experience, demonstrated leadership potential, cocurricular and extracurricular activities, ethnicity, academic performance trends, undergraduate major, caliber of undergraduate school, life experience, circumstances of particular disadvantage, and any other relevant information submitted by the applicant. Any factors the applicant would like for the Admission Committee to take into consideration should be addressed in a personal statement.

■ Scholarships and Financial Aid

Numerous academic-merit scholarships are awarded to entering students based upon their UGPA and LSAT score. Additionally, special scholarships are awarded to persons with evidence of academic achievement despite significant disadvantage. The law school also participates in nationally recognized financial aid programs. Texas residents are eligible for the Texas Tuition Equalization Grant.

■ Student Life

Students will find a stimulating variety of enjoyable student activities and organizations that will enhance their legal education. Students can compete interscholastically with Baylor's nationally recognized mock trial and moot court teams. Students can hone their writing and legal scholarship abilities by being a member of the *Baylor Law Review*, which is a legal periodical published quarterly by the students under the supervision of faculty. Baylor law school also offers a wide

array of "special interest" student organizations focused on particular areas of law.

■ Career Services and Bar Passage

The Career Services Office is committed year-round to providing students with the support and resources they need in pursuing their chosen career paths. Shortly after graduation, 97 percent of our 2005 graduates were employed or enrolled in graduate degree programs. Baylor graduates are placed throughout the nation in private practice in large and small firms, government agencies, judicial clerkships, public interest organizations, and public and private corporations.

The director of the Career Services Office is a lawyer and a graduate of Baylor law school. The director provides extensive one-on-one training on job-search techniques, interview skills, job strategies, and résumé and cover letter writing techniques. The office also coordinates an extensive on-campus interview program, and posts over 1,200 job listings from law firms, government agencies, corporations, and public interest groups.

Our record of success on the Texas bar exam is unsurpassed by any other Texas law school. In July 2006, 97.87 percent of Baylor graduates passed the Texas bar exam the first time. The average bar passage rate for the July bar exam in Texas was 86 percent. Graduates taking other state bar exams have been exceptionally successful as well.

Applicant Profile

Baylor University School of Law
This grid includes only the fall 2006 entering class and includes applicants who earned 120–180 LSAT scores under standard administrations.

LSAT Score	3.75 +		3.50–3.74		3.25–3.49		3.00–3.24		2.75–2.99		2.50–2.74		2.25–2.49		2.00–2.24		Below 2.00		No GPA		Total	
	Apps	Adm	Apps	Adm	Apps	Adm	Apps	Adm	Apps	Adm	Apps	Adm	Apps	Adm	Apps	Adm	Apps	Adm	Apps	Adm	Apps	Adm
175–180	1	1	1	1	0	0	0	0	0	0	0	0	0	0	0	0	0	0	0	0	2	2
170–174	21	21	11	11	16	16	0	0	1	1	1	0	1	1	1	1	0	0	0	0	52	51
165–169	71	70	58	57	50	48	10	10	4	3	4	1	1	1	0	0	0	0	0	0	198	190
160–164	182	176	190	133	137	90	44	28	17	2	4	2	5	0	0	0	1	0	4	2	584	433
155–159	269	64	223	14	170	10	61	0	28	0	13	0	6	0	2	0	0	0	2	0	774	88
150–154	51	2	78	1	104	0	60	1	31	0	22	0	11	0	4	0	0	0	2	0	363	4
145–149	22	0	38	0	38	0	53	0	20	0	21	0	12	0	5	0	0	0	2	0	211	0
140–144	14	0	20	0	32	0	34	0	24	0	16	0	8	0	2	0	0	0	2	0	150	0
135–139	0	0	4	0	12	0	19	0	10	0	8	0	3	0	3	0	0	0	2	0	61	0
130–134	2	0	1	0	0	0	4	0	4	0	6	0	3	0	1	0	0	0	0	0	21	0
125–129	0	0	0	0	0	0	2	0	0	0	2	0	1	0	0	0	1	0	1	0	7	0
120–124	0	0	0	0	0	0	0	0	0	0	0	0	0	0	0	0	0	0	0	0	0	0
Total	633	334	624	217	559	164	287	39	139	6	97	3	51	2	18	1	2	0	13	2	2423	768

Apps = Number of Applicants
Adm = Number Admitted
Reflects 99% of the total fall applicant pool.

Boston College Law School

885 Centre Street
Newton, MA 02459
Phone: 617.552.4351; Fax: 617.552.2917
E-mail: bclawadm@bc.edu; Website: www.bc.edu/law

ABA
Approved
Since
1932

The Basics

Type of school	Private
Term	Semester
Application deadline	3/1
Application fee	$75
Financial aid deadline	3/15
Can first year start other than fall?	No
Student to faculty ratio	14.0 to 1
Does the university offer:	
housing restricted to law students?	Yes
graduate housing for which law students are eligible?	Yes

Faculty and Administrators

	Total		Men		Women		Minorities	
	Fall	Spr	Fall	Spr	Fall	Spr	Fall	Spr
Full-time	50	44	30	26	20	18	8	8
Other Full-time	2	5	0	0	2	5	0	0
Deans, librarians, & others who teach	13	12	3	3	10	9	1	1
Part-time	35	44	25	32	10	12	4	5
Total	100	105	58	61	42	44	13	14

Curriculum

	Full-time	Part-time
Typical first-year section size	86	0
Is there typically a "small section" of the first-year class, other than Legal Writing, taught by full-time faculty	Yes	No
If yes, typical size offered last year	35	

# of classroom course titles beyond first-year curriculum		146
# of upper division courses, excluding seminars with an enrollment:	Under 25	40
	25–49	29
	50–74	12
	75–99	11
	100+	0
# of seminars		49
# of seminar positions available		929

	Full-time	Part-time
# of seminar positions filled	576	0
# of positions available in simulation courses	537	
# of simulation positions filled	419	0
# of positions available in faculty supervised clinical courses	158	
# of faculty supervised clinical positions filled	156	0
# involved in field placements	69	0
# involved in law journals	154	0
# involved in interschool competitions	37	0
# of credit hours required to graduate	85	

JD Enrollment and Ethnicity

	Men		Women		Full-time		Part-time		1st-year		Total		JD Degs. Awd.
	#	%	#	%	#	%	#	%	#	%	#	%	
African Amer.	15	3.5	25	7.1	40	5.1	0	0.0	13	5.1	40	5.1	12
Amer. Indian	0	0.0	1	0.3	1	0.1	0	0.0	1	0.4	1	0.1	0
Asian Amer.	44	10.3	50	14.2	94	12.1	0	0.0	30	11.8	94	12.0	23
Mex. Amer.	13	3.0	6	1.7	19	2.4	0	0.0	5	2.0	19	2.4	1
Puerto Rican	4	0.9	2	0.6	6	0.8	0	0.0	4	1.6	6	0.8	0
Hispanic	13	3.0	14	4.0	27	3.5	0	0.0	9	3.5	27	3.5	6
Total Minority	89	20.8	98	27.8	187	24.0	0	0.0	62	24.4	187	23.9	42
For. Nation.	10	2.3	5	1.4	15	1.9	0	0.0	7	2.8	15	1.9	6
Caucasian	275	64.3	215	60.9	489	62.7	1	100.0	159	62.6	490	62.7	203
Unknown	54	12.6	35	9.9	89	11.4	0	0.0	26	10.2	89	11.4	37
Total	428	54.8	353	45.2	780	99.9	1	0.1	254	32.5	781		288

Transfers

Transfers in	17
Transfers out	6

Tuition and Fees

	Resident	Nonresident
Full-time	$34,846	$34,846
Part-time	$0	$0

Living Expenses

Estimated living expenses for singles

Living on campus	Living off campus	Living at home
N/A	$16,715	$16,715

Boston College Law School

ABA
Approved
Since
1932

GPA and LSAT Scores

	Total	Full-time	Part-time
# of apps	6,321	6,321	0
# of offers	1,224	1,224	0
# of matrics	254	254	0
75% GPA	3.76	3.76	0.00
Median GPA	3.58	3.58	0.00
25% GPA	3.41	3.41	0.00
75% LSAT	166	166	0
Median LSAT	164	164	0
25% LSAT	162	162	0

Grants and Scholarships (from prior year)

	Total		Full-time		Part-time	
	#	%	#	%	#	%
Total # of students	809		807		2	
Total # receiving grants	448	55.4	448	55.5	0	0.0
Less than 1/2 tuition	351	43.4	351	43.5	0	0.0
Half to full tuition	97	12.0	97	12.0	0	0.0
Full tuition	0	0.0	0	0.0	0	0.0
More than full tuition	0	0.0	0	0.0	0	0.0
Median grant amount			$11,000		$0	

Informational and Library Resources

# of volumes and volume equivalents	459,004
# of titles	97,710
# of active serial subscriptions	3,121
Study seating capacity inside the library	653
# of full-time professional librarians	13
Hours per week library is open	105
# of open, wired connections available to students	1,226
# of networked computers available for use by students	146
# of simultaneous wireless users	1,950
Require computer?	No

JD Attrition (from prior year)

	Academic	Other	Total	
	#	#	#	%
1st year	0	7	7	2.5
2nd year	0	0	0	0.0
3rd year	0	0	0	0.0
4th year	0	0	0	0.0

Employment (9 months after graduation)

	Total	Percentage
Employment status known	258	100.0
Employment status unknown	0	0.0
Employed	250	96.9
Pursuing graduate degrees	3	1.2
Unemployed seeking employment	2	0.8
Unemployed not seeking employment	1	0.4
Unemployed and studying for the bar	2	0.8

Type of Employment

# employed in law firms	155	62.0
# employed in business and industry	26	10.4
# employed in government	23	9.2
# employed in public interest	9	3.6
# employed as judicial clerks	33	13.2
# employed in academia	3	1.2

Geographic Location

# employed in state	106	42.4
# employed in foreign countries	4	1.6
# of states where employed		28

Bar Passage Rates

Jurisdiction	Massachusetts		
Exam	Sum 05	Win 06	Total
# from school taking bar for the first time	141	14	155
School's pass rate for all first-time takers	91%	79%	90%
State's pass rate for all first-time takers	84%	75%	82%

Boston College Law School

Office of Admissions, 885 Centre Street
Newton, MA 02459
Phone: 617.552.4351; Fax: 617.552.2917
E-mail: bclawadm@bc.edu; Website: www.bc.edu/law

■ Introduction

Since its founding in 1929, Boston College Law School has earned a national reputation for educational excellence and the highest standards of professionalism while fostering a unique spirit of community among its students, faculty, and staff. The diverse curriculum is designed to help students develop the skills and knowledge needed to adapt successfully to changes in society and the legal profession. Boston College Law School is located on an attractive 40-acre campus in Newton, Massachusetts, just minutes from downtown Boston. It is fully accredited and has a chapter of Order of the Coif, the prestigious national law school honorary society.

■ Library and Physical Facilities

Stretched over 40 acres of rolling hills and gently sloping lawns, the BC Law campus is an intriguing mix of old-style elegance and new-world innovation, a testament to the power of technology, engineering, and design. Students can connect to the network anywhere. Data ports are available from every library carrel and every classroom seat, and wireless technology is also available anywhere in the library and in every classroom. The library encourages individual or group study, with its desk and lounge areas, computer centers, audiovisual resource rooms, and private study rooms. Each Computer Center is fully equipped for searching LexisNexis and Westlaw databases; legal periodical literature; official publications of Massachusetts, the United States, and United Nations; and other legal indices. With its soaring atrium entry and light-filled spaces, the East Wing includes five classrooms, 15 faculty offices, administrative offices for a Career Services Center and a Career Resources Library, two conference rooms, a student lounge, and the John J. and Mary Daly Curtin Public Interest Center—a suite of offices for student groups working on public service projects. The East Wing's brick exterior complements the law library and the Stuart House administration building, as well as the Barat House alumni and development building. The three buildings form an attractive interior courtyard for outdoor use by the law school community.

All academic, administrative, library, and service facilities are accessible to physically challenged persons.

■ Curriculum

The faculty of Boston College Law School strongly believes in the importance of a general legal education designed to enable graduates to adapt to the changing demands of law practice. Areas of particular focus include international law, constitutional law, business law, dispute resolution, environmental law, family law, tax law, intellectual property law, and clinical programs.

In the first year, all students take traditional courses, including Civil Procedure, Constitutional Law, Contracts, Property Law, Criminal Law, and Torts, as well as Legal Reasoning, Research and Writing, and an innovative skills course titled Introduction to Lawyering and Professional Responsibility. More than 100 courses offered in the second and third years are elective.

■ Externships

The **Semester in Practice** program offers individually designed placement with judges, government agencies, public interest organizations, and law firms in the greater Boston area. The **Attorney General Program** provides an intensive full-year clinical experience in the Government Bureau of the Massachusetts Office of the Attorney General. The **International Criminal Tribunals** (ICT) offer a unique opportunity to work on-site at the criminal tribunal established by the UN Security Council in The Hague, the Netherlands. The **London Program** has both academic and experiential components. The program provides students with a critical insight into comparative legal institutions with special emphasis on international regulatory process, whether in environmental or securities regulation, antitrust, intellectual property, or human rights.

■ Clinical Programs

The Law School is committed to making clinical experiences available to all students who desire them. At the **Boston College Legal Assistance Bureau** (LAB), students assume responsibility for representation of indigent clients through the **Civil Litigation**, **Homelessness**, and **Women and the Law** clinics.

Students in the **Criminal Justice Clinic** prosecute or defend criminal cases in state court. The **Judge and Community Courts** class examines the interaction between the local court and the community it serves. The **Judicial Process** course includes clinical placement with a specific Superior Court justice. In **Juvenile Rights Advocacy**, students advocate for troubled youth and work toward juvenile justice policy reform. In the **Immigration Law Clinic**, students advise clients and work on administrative and appellate litigation under the supervision of practicing attorneys.

■ Student Activities

Selected students may participate in the following writing programs: *Boston College Law Review, Boston College Environmental Affairs Law Review, Boston College International and Comparative Law Review, Boston College Third World Law Journal,* and the *Uniform Commercial Code Reporter-Digest.*

Boston College Law School supports several annual moot court competitions that help students develop writing, courtroom-advocacy, and client-counseling skills. Over the years, Boston College has performed extremely well in regional and national competitions, which are judged by faculty, state and federal judges, and practicing attorneys.

■ Admission

The Law School has no minimum cutoff either for GPA or LSAT. Academic achievement and LSAT scores are extremely significant, but work and professional experience, college extracurricular activities, the quality of recommendations, and the personal statement also play an important role in decision making.

In evaluating the undergraduate record, class rank as well as courses taken are considered. If the LSAT has been taken more than once, all scores are considered in the review process.

■ Minorities and Affirmative Action

Boston College Law School strongly encourages applications from qualified minority, disabled, or other students who have been socially, economically, or culturally disadvantaged. Each applicant is evaluated in an effort to ensure that all relevant credentials are favorably considered. The Law School has been very successful both in admitting minority and special students and in retaining them to graduation. Both academic support and minority student mentor programs are available.

■ Expenses and Financial Aid

The Financial Aid Office administers the Law School's scholarship and grant programs, federal and private loan programs, and the Federal Work-Study Program. Scholarship funds are awarded on the basis of both need and merit. Approximately 85 percent of the students currently enrolled are awarded financial aid and approximately 50 percent of these students receive scholarship and grant assistance as part of their financial aid awards.

Each year, several entering students are awarded Public Service Scholarships because of their demonstrated commitment to public service law. The Law School also offers a Loan Repayment Assistance program for graduates who pursue careers in legal services, government, and not-for-profit corporations.

■ Housing

The Boston College Graduate Housing Office is a valuable resource in securing housing. That office offers a limited number of apartments to first-year law students. These apartments are one mile from the Chestnut Hill campus and within a block of public transportation. In addition, the Boston College Off-Campus Housing Office provides information about neighborhoods, lists of local rental agencies, maps of local areas, and public transportation information. The office also maintains housing listings that include renting rooms in private homes, apartments, and house rentals. For more information, please visit the Office of Residential Life website at *www.bc.edu/reslife*.

■ Career Services

The Office of Career Services is dedicated to helping students make the transition from law student to employed professional. The range of opportunities for graduates spans virtually the entire spectrum of legal practice. Each year more than 1,000 prospective employers solicit applications from Boston College law students. During the 2005 recruitment season, approximately 425 law firms, government agencies, corporations, and public interest organizations from 23 states interviewed Boston College students as part of on- and off-campus recruiting programs. More than 10,900 alumni are presently practicing in 50 states and 19 foreign countries.

Applicant Profile

Boston College Law School
This grid includes only applicants who earned 120–180 LSAT scores under standard administrations.

LSAT Score	3.75 +		3.50–3.74		3.25–3.49		3.00–3.24		2.75–2.99		Below 2.75		No GPA		Total	
	Apps	Adm	Apps	Adm	Apps	Adm	Apps	Adm	Apps	Adm	Apps	Adm	Apps	Adm	Apps	Adm
175–180	7	6	11	8	8	8	7	2	1	1	0	0	0	0	34	25
170–174	54	46	83	60	52	31	27	6	20	4	10	3	1	1	247	151
165–169	229	174	317	210	242	106	124	39	63	8	24	2	7	3	1006	542
160–164	486	190	670	161	499	50	210	17	87	2	50	1	19	4	2021	425
150–159	418	27	689	25	617	23	320	8	176	4	95	1	22	0	2337	88
140–149	50	2	105	0	133	4	117	3	80	0	84	0	20	0	589	9
Below 140	1	0	8	0	8	0	17	0	13	0	22	0	8	0	77	0
Total	1245	445	1883	464	1559	222	822	75	440	19	285	7	77	8	6311	1240

Apps = Number of Applicants
Adm = Number Admitted
Reflects 99% of the total applicant pool.

Boston University School of Law

765 Commonwealth Avenue
Boston, MA 02215
Phone: 617.353.3100; Fax: 617.353.0578
E-mail: bulawadm@bu.edu; Website: www.bu.edu/law

ABA Approved Since 1925

The Basics

Type of school	Private
Term	Semester
Application deadline	3/1
Application fee	$75
Financial aid deadline	3/1
Can first year start other than fall?	No
Student to faculty ratio	12.2 to 1
Does the university offer:	
housing restricted to law students?	No
graduate housing for which law students are eligible?	Yes

Curriculum

		Full-time	Part-time
Typical first-year section size		98	0
Is there typically a "small section" of the first-year class, other than Legal Writing, taught by full-time faculty		Yes	No
If yes, typical size offered last year		49	
# of classroom course titles beyond first-year curriculum		165	
# of upper division courses, excluding seminars with an enrollment:	Under 25	79	
	25–49	34	
	50–74	22	
	75–99	7	
	100+	4	
# of seminars		60	
# of seminar positions available		1,066	
# of seminar positions filled		811	0
# of positions available in simulation courses		338	
# of simulation positions filled		310	0
# of positions available in faculty supervised clinical courses		180	
# of faculty supervised clinical positions filled	158		0
# involved in field placements		54	0
# involved in law journals		342	0
# involved in interschool competitions		28	0
# of credit hours required to graduate		84	

Faculty and Administrators

	Total		Men		Women		Minorities	
	Fall	Spr	Fall	Spr	Fall	Spr	Fall	Spr
Full-time	55	59	39	43	16	16	5	7
Other Full-time	0	1	0	1	0	0	0	1
Deans, librarians, & others who teach	3	3	2	2	1	1	0	0
Part-time	47	45	39	34	8	11	2	5
Total	**105**	**108**	**80**	**80**	**25**	**28**	**7**	**13**

JD Enrollment and Ethnicity

	Men		Women		Full-time		Part-time		1st-year		Total		JD Degs. Awd.
	#	%	#	%	#	%	#	%	#	%	#	%	
African Amer.	11	2.8	22	5.0	31	3.8	2	13.3	10	3.7	33	3.9	6
Amer. Indian	1	0.3	1	0.2	2	0.2	0	0.0	2	0.7	2	0.2	2
Asian Amer.	50	12.5	61	14.0	108	13.2	3	20.0	26	9.7	111	13.3	35
Mex. Amer.	3	0.8	3	0.7	6	0.7	0	0.0	4	1.5	6	0.7	2
Puerto Rican	0	0.0	3	0.7	3	0.4	0	0.0	1	0.4	3	0.4	2
Hispanic	10	2.5	9	2.1	18	2.2	1	6.7	6	2.2	19	2.3	10
Total Minority	75	18.8	99	22.7	168	20.5	6	40.0	49	18.2	174	20.8	57
For. Nation.	8	2.0	18	4.1	26	3.2	0	0.0	7	2.6	26	3.1	8
Caucasian	316	79.2	320	73.2	627	76.4	9	60.0	213	79.2	636	76.1	203
Unknown	0	0.0	0	0.0	0	0.0	0	0.0	0	0.0	0	0.0	0
Total	399	47.7	437	52.3	821	98.2	15	1.8	269	32.2	836		268

Transfers

Transfers in	6
Transfers out	13

Tuition and Fees

	Resident	Nonresident
Full-time	$35,398	$35,398
Part-time	$0	$0

Living Expenses

Estimated living expenses for singles

Living on campus	Living off campus	Living at home
$16,402	$16,402	$10,268

Boston University School of Law

ABA Approved Since 1925

GPA and LSAT Scores

	Total	Full-time	Part-time
# of apps	6,211	6,211	0
# of offers	1,627	1,627	0
# of matrics	269	269	0
75% GPA	3.83	3.83	0.00
Median GPA	3.68	3.68	0.00
25% GPA	3.52	3.52	0.00
75% LSAT	166	166	0
Median LSAT	165	165	0
25% LSAT	163	163	0

Grants and Scholarships (from prior year)

	Total		Full-time		Part-time	
	#	%	#	%	#	%
Total # of students	856		831		25	
Total # receiving grants	441	51.5	441	53.1	0	0.0
Less than 1/2 tuition	246	28.7	246	29.6	0	0.0
Half to full tuition	172	20.1	172	20.7	0	0.0
Full tuition	1	0.1	1	0.1	0	0.0
More than full tuition	22	2.6	22	2.6	0	0.0
Median grant amount			$15,000		$0	

Informational and Library Resources

# of volumes and volume equivalents	639,507
# of titles	238,435
# of active serial subscriptions	4,740
Study seating capacity inside the library	646
# of full-time professional librarians	13
Hours per week library is open	102
# of open, wired connections available to students	25
# of networked computers available for use by students	110
# of simultaneous wireless users	500
Require computer?	No

JD Attrition (from prior year)

	Academic	Other	Total	
	#	#	#	%
1st year	1	17	18	6.1
2nd year	0	3	3	1.0
3rd year	0	0	0	0.0
4th year	0	0	0	0.0

Employment (9 months after graduation)

	Total	Percentage
Employment status known	285	99.3
Employment status unknown	2	0.7
Employed	269	94.4
Pursuing graduate degrees	12	4.2
Unemployed seeking employment	0	0.0
Unemployed not seeking employment	3	1.1
Unemployed and studying for the bar	1	0.4

Type of Employment

	Total	Percentage
# employed in law firms	174	64.7
# employed in business and industry	15	5.6
# employed in government	30	11.2
# employed in public interest	10	3.7
# employed as judicial clerks	24	8.9
# employed in academia	16	5.9

Geographic Location

	Total	Percentage
# employed in state	117	43.5
# employed in foreign countries	5	1.9
# of states where employed	26	

Bar Passage Rates

Jurisdiction	Massachusetts			New York		
Exam	Sum 05	Win 06	Total	Sum 05	Win 06	Total
# from school taking bar for the first time	137	6	143	97	5	102
School's pass rate for all first-time takers	93%	100%	94%	94%	80%	93%
State's pass rate for all first-time takers	84%	75%	82%	76%	61%	74%

Boston University School of Law

765 Commonwealth Avenue

Boston, MA 02215

Phone: 617.353.3100; Fax: 617.353.0578

E-mail: bulawadm@bu.edu; Website: www.bu.edu/law

■ Introduction

Boston University School of Law offers one of the finest legal educations in the nation, attracting students from all over the country and abroad. A pioneer in American legal education, the school was founded in 1872 on the principles that legal education should be open to all men and women of ability without regard to background or beliefs, and that it should balance theory and analysis with practical training. Today, the school's innovative curriculum combines theoretical courses, clinical training, and specialized offerings—including concentrations, dual degrees, and semesters abroad. The full-time faculty of distinguished scholars and teachers ranks among the most productive of the nation's law schools. The students represent a range of educational backgrounds, ethnicities, races, age groups, and employment histories— evidence of the school's "open-door" admission policy, a firm part of its tradition for over 130 years.

The city of Boston is a great place to study the law and launch a career. BU Law's location presents students with enormous opportunities. They can gain invaluable experience while in school, whether or not they intend to stay in Boston, through myriad job and internship opportunities, which flow from Boston's unique status as a major business, financial, and legal center. Boston is home to many high-tech, start-up companies and is also a leading center in health care. In addition, Boston, as the state capital, is an active government center at both the federal and state levels, making it a laboratory for clinics, pro bono volunteering, and externships.

■ Faculty

At BU Law, our faculty members make the difference—to our students, as teachers; to the law, as scholars; and to the local and global community, as advocates. They are among the nation's leading scholars, lecturers, and teachers. BU Law faculty members come from a range of backgrounds— including six US Supreme Court clerks and numerous federal court of appeals clerks—and from several schools of legal thought, such as law and economics and feminist legal theory. They have authored authoritative texts in several key fields, such as securitization, labor and employment, federal courts, contracts, and administrative law, among others. They are not only the leading scholars in their fields, but they excel inside the classroom as well. Impassioned advocates who frequently lend their expertise to pro bono causes—locally, nationally, and internationally—they bring these experiences back to the school, to share inside and outside the classroom.

■ Curriculum

Not only does BU Law offer an exceptionally strong teaching faculty, but it also offers one of the widest ranges of academic opportunities available at any American law school. At BU Law, students can explore virtually any area of law from among the school's 150 classes and seminars. They can concentrate and focus their studies in any of five important fields—international law, health law, intellectual property law, business organizations and finance law, or litigation and dispute resolution—and thus design a curriculum around courses that prepare them for exciting work in specific areas of interest.

Students can also expand beyond law by pursuing any of nine dual-degree programs, combining law study with graduate coursework in a program that leads to a JD and a master's degree. Those dual degrees are JD/MA in International Relations, JD/MS in Mass Communications, JD/MBA, JD/MBA in Health Care Management, JD/MA in Historic Preservation, JD/MA in Philosophy, and JD/MPH in Public Health. Students interested in tax or banking can earn a combined JD/master of laws (LLM) degree in these fields on an accelerated seven-semester basis.

Students at BU Law can also immerse themselves in a foreign legal culture for a semester, studying international and comparative law in one of BU Law's 11 semester-long study-abroad programs. Programs offered in 2007–2008 are at Oxford University (United Kingdom); Université Panthéon-Assas Paris II (France); Université Jean Moulin, Lyon 3 (France); Universidad Pontificia Comillas de Madrid (Spain); Leiden University (the Netherlands); Bucerius Law School, Hamburg (Germany); the University of Florence (Italy); the University of Hong Kong (China); the University of Buenos Aires (Argentina); Tel Aviv University (Israel); or Tsinghua Law School (China).

For hands-on practical training, BU Law has long been recognized for having some of the finest clinical offerings in the country. The clinical faculty is among the most experienced in American legal clinical education. Students can gain valuable experience through one of these clinics: Civil Litigation, Criminal Law, Legal Externship, Judicial Internship, and the Legislation Clinic.

■ Career Development

The BU Law Career Development Office is committed to helping each law student see all the possibilities that a BU degree affords them. The office offers a comprehensive program of services to students and alumni—from personal counseling to instructional workshops and events, to print and online resources and tools. First-year students benefit from the expertise of a diverse range of career advisors in the office and can participate in numerous workshops to hone job search skills. Alumni assist students through the Career Assistance Program and the Mock Interview Program.

BU Law offers an extensive on- and off-campus recruiting program. Each year, more than 570 law firms, government agencies, public interest organizations, and corporations from all regions of the United States recruit BU Law students at specialty job fairs. Over 180 employers from 23 states come to campus to interview students; about 200 more meet our law students through eight regional job fairs; and many more advertise positions through the Career Development Office. Starting salaries of BU Law graduates entering the private sector are among the highest in the nation ($125,000, median private sector). The geographic reach of BU Law graduates is extremely broad, with 38 percent located in the New England region—an obvious stronghold—and the other 62 percent spread throughout the South, West, and Mid-Atlantic region.

■ Financial Aid

Boston University School of Law is committed to making a legal education affordable for its students. Through scholarship awards, federal and private loans, and work-study awards, the School of Law provides funding for over 85 percent of its enrolled JD students.

A significant pool of scholarship funds is awarded every year based on both financial need and academic merit. Because Boston University School of Law's scholarship resources are among the largest of all law schools, we are able to assist more than 50 percent of our enrolled students with some form of scholarship aid.

A small number of applicants who demonstrate outstanding academic achievement are recognized through the Dean's Scholar Program, which offers awards covering full tuition and fees. These awards are based solely on merit and do not require an application separate from the application for admission. The School of Law is also committed to upholding the diversity of its student body. It offers several scholarship programs intended to achieve this goal. Students applying through the regular financial aid application process will be considered for all types of aid available.

The Office of Financial Aid encourages all applicants to observe the March 1 financial aid application deadline, to follow the directions for application carefully, and to check with the financial aid office to ensure the completeness of their financial aid files.

Applicant Profile

Boston University School of Law
This grid includes only applicants who earned 120–180 LSAT scores under standard administrations.

LSAT Score	3.75 +		3.50–3.74		3.25–3.49		3.00–3.24		2.75–2.99		2.50–2.74		2.25–2.49		2.00–2.24		Below 2.00		No GPA		Total	
	Apps	Adm	Apps	Adm	Apps	Adm	Apps	Adm	Apps	Adm	Apps	Adm	Apps	Adm	Apps	Adm	Apps	Adm	Apps	Adm	Apps	Adm
175–180	14	14	18	17	14	13	6	2	3	0	0	0	1	0	0	0	0	0	0	0	56	46
170–174	92	84	94	85	87	48	37	5	21	2	5	1	2	0	1	0	0	0	1	0	340	225
165–169	352	332	413	373	271	131	149	16	51	0	16	0	6	0	0	0	0	0	12	12	1270	864
160–164	497	263	654	126	482	21	178	7	62	1	30	0	7	0	2	0	2	0	23	3	1937	421
155–159	236	12	399	17	302	18	150	7	55	2	19	0	8	0	3	0	0	0	15	0	1187	56
150–154	102	4	153	7	187	9	92	0	76	0	23	0	7	0	1	0	0	0	14	0	655	20
145–149	35	0	48	0	75	1	52	1	47	0	26	0	9	0	3	0	0	0	11	0	306	2
140–144	13	0	27	0	39	0	28	0	26	0	13	0	6	0	2	0	2	0	7	0	163	0
135–139	1	0	2	0	10	0	13	0	11	0	7	0	1	0	3	0	1	0	2	0	51	0
130–134	0	0	1	0	1	0	4	0	3	0	2	0	2	0	1	0	0	0	0	0	14	0
125–129	0	0	0	0	0	0	1	0	1	0	0	0	0	0	2	0	0	0	1	0	5	0
120–124	0	0	0	0	0	0	0	0	1	0	0	0	0	0	0	0	0	0	0	0	1	0
Total	1342	709	1809	625	1468	241	710	38	357	5	141	1	49	0	18	0	5	0	86	15	5985	1634

Apps = Number of Applicants
Adm = Number Admitted
Reflects 99% of the total applicant pool.

Brigham Young University—J. Reuben Clark Law School

340 JRCB, Box 28000
Provo, UT 84602-8000
Phone: 801.422.4277; Fax: 801.422.0389
E-mail: admissions@lawgate.byu.edu; Website: www.law.byu.edu

ABA
Approved
Since
1974

The Basics

Type of school	Private
Term	Semester
Application deadline	3/1
Application fee	$50
Financial aid deadline	7/1
Can first year start other than fall?	No
Student to faculty ratio	20.9 to 1
Does the university offer:	
housing restricted to law students?	No
graduate housing for which law students are eligible?	No

Curriculum

	Full-time	Part-time
Typical first-year section size	100	0
Is there typically a "small section" of the first-year class, other than Legal Writing, taught by full-time faculty	Yes	No
If yes, typical size offered last year	50	
# of classroom course titles beyond first-year curriculum	100	

# of upper division courses, excluding seminars with an enrollment:		
	Under 25	29
	25–49	16
	50–74	12
	75–99	4
	100+	2

# of seminars		37
# of seminar positions available		829
# of seminar positions filled	498	0
# of positions available in simulation courses	559	
# of simulation positions filled	466	0
# of positions available in faculty supervised clinical courses	184	
# of faculty supervised clinical positions filled	144	0
# involved in field placements	249	0
# involved in law journals	222	0
# involved in interschool competitions	45	0
# of credit hours required to graduate		90

Faculty and Administrators

	Total		Men		Women		Minorities	
	Fall	Spr	Fall	Spr	Fall	Spr	Fall	Spr
Full-time	17	20	15	17	2	3	2	3
Other Full-time	0	0	0	0	0	0	0	0
Deans, librarians, & others who teach	17	18	12	13	5	5	0	0
Part-time	31	28	20	18	11	10	1	1
Total	**65**	**66**	**47**	**48**	**18**	**18**	**3**	**4**

JD Enrollment and Ethnicity

	Men		Women		Full-time		Part-time		1st-year		Total		JD Degs. Awd.
	#	%	#	%	#	%	#	%	#	%	#	%	
African Amer.	6	2.0	2	1.2	8	1.7	0	0.0	2	1.4	8	1.7	0
Amer. Indian	3	1.0	7	4.2	10	2.2	0	0.0	3	2.1	10	2.2	2
Asian Amer.	24	8.1	10	6.0	34	7.4	0	0.0	13	9.0	34	7.4	15
Mex. Amer.	6	2.0	2	1.2	8	1.7	0	0.0	1	0.7	8	1.7	2
Puerto Rican	1	0.3	0	0.0	1	0.2	0	0.0	1	0.7	1	0.2	0
Hispanic	15	5.1	8	4.8	23	5.0	0	0.0	9	6.3	23	5.0	8
Total Minority	55	18.6	29	17.5	84	18.3	0	0.0	29	20.1	84	18.2	27
For. Nation.	0	0.0	4	2.4	4	0.9	0	0.0	0	0.0	4	0.9	2
Caucasian	236	79.7	133	80.1	367	79.8	2	100.0	110	76.4	369	79.9	129
Unknown	5	1.7	0	0.0	5	1.1	0	0.0	5	3.5	5	1.1	0
Total	296	64.1	166	35.9	460	99.6	2	0.4	144	31.2	462		158

Transfers

Transfers in	7
Transfers out	2

Tuition and Fees

	Resident	Nonresident
Full-time	$8,200	$16,400
Part-time	$0	$0

Living Expenses

Estimated living expenses for singles

Living on campus	Living off campus	Living at home
$11,076	$11,076	$5,260

Brigham Young University—J. Reuben Clark Law School

*ABA
Approved
Since
1974*

GPA and LSAT Scores

	Total	Full-time	Part-time
# of apps	917	917	0
# of offers	260	260	0
# of matrics	145	145	0
75% GPA	3.80	3.80	0.00
Median GPA	3.63	3.63	0.00
25% GPA	3.40	3.40	0.00
75% LSAT	166	166	0
Median LSAT	164	164	0
25% LSAT	161	161	0

Grants and Scholarships (from prior year)

	Total		Full-time		Part-time	
	#	%	#	%	#	%
Total # of students	472		472		0	
Total # receiving grants	208	44.1	208	44.1	0	0.0
Less than 1/2 tuition	158	33.5	158	33.5	0	0.0
Half to full tuition	35	7.4	35	7.4	0	0.0
Full tuition	13	2.8	13	2.8	0	0.0
More than full tuition	2	0.4	2	0.4	0	0.0
Median grant amount			$1,750		$0	

Informational and Library Resources

# of volumes and volume equivalents	492,101
# of titles	173,955
# of active serial subscriptions	3,991
Study seating capacity inside the library	879
# of full-time professional librarians	12
Hours per week library is open	105
# of open, wired connections available to students	603
# of networked computers available for use by students	45
# of simultaneous wireless users	1,000
Require computer?	Yes

JD Attrition (from prior year)

	Academic	Other	Total	
	#	#	#	%
1st year	0	6	6	3.9
2nd year	0	0	0	0.0
3rd year	0	0	0	0.0
4th year	0	0	0	0.0

Employment (9 months after graduation)

	Total	Percentage
Employment status known	155	100.0
Employment status unknown	0	0.0
Employed	144	92.9
Pursuing graduate degrees	3	1.9
Unemployed seeking employment	2	1.3
Unemployed not seeking employment	5	3.2
Unemployed and studying for the bar	1	0.6

Type of Employment

# employed in law firms	90	62.5
# employed in business and industry	8	5.6
# employed in government	17	11.8
# employed in public interest	4	2.8
# employed as judicial clerks	23	16.0
# employed in academia	2	1.4

Geographic Location

# employed in state	65	45.1
# employed in foreign countries	1	0.7
# of states where employed		25

Bar Passage Rates

Jurisdiction	Utah			California		
Exam	Sum 05	Win 06	Total	Sum 05	Win 06	Total
# from school taking bar for the first time	77	11	88	17	3	20
School's pass rate for all first-time takers	94%	91%	93%	94%	100%	95%
State's pass rate for all first-time takers	90%	92%	90%	64%	54%	62%

Brigham Young University—J. Reuben Clark Law School

340 JRCB, Box 28000
Provo, UT 84602-8000
Phone: 801.422.4277; Fax: 801.422.0389
E-mail: admissions@lawgate.byu.edu; Website: www.law.byu.edu

■ Introduction

Since its founding just over 30 years ago, the J. Reuben Clark Law School at Brigham Young University has been distinguished by the strength of its program and the accomplishments of its graduates. The Law School has produced 12 US Supreme Court Clerkships and has an enviable placement record throughout the United States in all branches of the legal profession. The Law School's relatively small entering class of 150 lends itself to individualized instruction, while the university, with its 30,000 students, provides all the athletic, cultural, and social opportunities that a student may expect from a larger school. The Law School is fully accredited by the American Bar Association, is a member of the Association of American Law Schools, and has a chapter of the Order of the Coif.

■ Library and Physical Facilities

The Howard W. Hunter Law Library is one of the most technologically advanced law libraries in the world. It houses 475 individual study carrels with full Internet and LAN computer connectivity (hardwired and wireless). Thus each student in his or her private study space has access to electronic resources that include Westlaw, LexisNexis, and the growing Hunter Law Library Electronic Reserve, including archives of past examinations. The Ashton Legal Research Training Lab provides state-of-the-art facilities for advanced legal research and related computer training. In convenient locations, printers, copy machines, and scanners are available for students on all library floors. The law library also contains 18 group-study rooms (three of which are family-support rooms to assist parents who need to view closed-circuit broadcasts of classes) and spacious casual seating in open areas. Office and research space along with a conference room for the Law School's four scholarly journals, two advocacy programs, and the Student Bar Association are also conveniently located in the library. Specialized rooms are dedicated to video viewing, interactive video, microforms, and television hookups. The Rex E. Lee Reading Room and the Quiet Reading Room provide ample space for special seminars and receptions. The library houses a collection of over 470,000 volumes or volume equivalents. Via interlibrary loan, students have access to many more titles found in the catalogs and collections of over 167 other worldwide institutions that, like the Hunter Library, subscribe to the Research Libraries Information Network (RLIN).

■ Faculty and Curriculum

The combination of the small entering class size and our internationally renowned faculty creates unique opportunities for learning. Together they seek to meet the challenge of making a difference worldwide as they engage in joint research, publishing, and advocacy. The objective of the Law School's curriculum is to maximize the students' mastery of legal reasoning and legal methods while teaching a core of the basic substantive rules of the law. Over 60 courses and 40 seminars are offered each year by a faculty of 32 full-time members and 29 adjunct faculty members. In addition, the Law School provides opportunities for students to develop practical skills through international and US externships with private law firms, corporations, and agencies, as well as public defenders, legal services, city and county attorneys, judges, attorneys general, and guardians ad litem. Students receive one credit for every 50 hours of work.

■ The Rex E. Lee Advocacy Program

Lawyers must not only know the law. They must also synthesize complex information, analyze and formulate strategy, predict outcomes, and present information persuasively. The Rex E. Lee Advocacy Program administers a two-semester required course for first-year law students in the essential skills of legal writing, research, analysis, and oral advocacy. Students receive individualized attention during one-on-one conferences with instructors and teaching assistants and in small classes. The Legal Writing Center provides additional instruction and assistance to students through individual writing conferences and online resources. In the Advocacy Program, students learn and practice the critical skills that bring success in both law school and the profession.

■ International Center for Law and Religion Studies

The BYU International Center for Law and Religion Studies promotes freedom of religion by studying and disseminating information on the laws, principles, and institutions affecting the interaction of state and religion throughout the world. The center works with scholars, government leaders, nongovernment groups, and religious organizations from a variety of countries and faith traditions, playing an important role in promoting religious liberty and the accompanying relationships between governments and religious organizations.

■ World Family Policy Center

The World Family Policy Center participates in major United Nations events and sponsors important international conferences on family policy. The center seeks to provide balanced, solidly researched, pro-family education to member states and institutions within the United Nations system.

■ The Schooley Mediation Program

The Schooley Mediation Program trains interested law students to become certified mediators. The program includes actual client experiences in juvenile victim-offender cases, small claims court programs, domestic cases, landlord-tenant disputes, and others.

■ The Externship Program

The Law School offers a five-week academic externship program as a capstone experience for students at the completion of their first year. This program places first-year students with judges, outstanding law firms, corporations, public interest groups, and governmental organizations throughout the world. During the summer of 2006, 173 students externed with 129 employers, earning an average of four units of law school credit.

Thirty-two placements were international. Many of the domestic externships involved international aspects as well.

■ The Academic Success Program

The Academic Success Program (ASP) is designed to help students adjust to and meet the rigorous demands of a legal education. The ASP offers legal skills workshops with personal feedback, weekly tutorial sessions in each first-year course, individual tutoring, and one-on-one legal writing instruction to all students upon request and by dean's referral.

■ Cocurricular Programs

The objective of the cocurricular program at the Law School is to make a law review-quality experience available to larger numbers of students. Comparable standards of excellence in research, writing, and editing are offered in six programs: the *Brigham Young University Law Review*, the Board of Advocates Moot Court, Trial Advocacy, the *BYU Journal of Public Law*, the *Brigham Young University Education and Law Journal*, and *International Law and Management Review*.

■ Career Services

The Career Services Office (CSO) is available to all students and graduates seeking employment. The CSO offers two legal career-planning courses featuring skills training and presentations by practicing attorneys who participate as guest lecturers. It also publishes a *Professional Development Handbook, Job Hunt Book*, and *Judicial Clerkship Handbook* and maintains a webpage with links for both students and employers. About 98 percent of the graduates who are seeking work accept employment within nine months after graduation, and graduates are placed in all 50 states and a number of foreign countries. The CSO brings firms to campus every year for on-campus interviews and has interviewing events and job fairs in DC, New York, Southern California, and Nevada.

Applicant Profile

Brigham Young University—J. Reuben Clark Law School
This grid includes only applicants who earned 120–180 LSAT scores under standard administrations.

LSAT Score	3.75 +		3.50–3.74		3.25–3.49		3.00–3.24		2.75–2.99		2.50–2.74		2.25–2.49		2.00–2.24		Below 2.00		No GPA		Total	
	Apps	Adm	Apps	Adm	Apps	Adm	Apps	Adm	Apps	Adm	Apps	Adm	Apps	Adm	Apps	Adm	Apps	Adm	Apps	Adm	Apps	Adm
175–180	9	9	1	0	1	0	1	0	0	0	0	0	0	0	0	0	0	0	0	0	12	9
170–174	25	23	9	8	7	7	3	3	4	4	1	0	0	0	0	0	0	0	0	0	49	45
165–169	38	35	43	38	16	13	13	7	4	1	1	0	0	0	0	0	0	0	0	0	115	94
160–164	67	40	67	26	46	8	23	4	5	2	5	0	2	1	0	0	0	0	1	0	216	81
155–159	56	6	68	5	47	4	34	1	13	1	5	0	0	0	0	0	0	0	4	0	227	17
150–154	29	1	41	3	32	5	27	2	12	0	6	0	1	0	2	0	0	0	4	0	154	11
145–149	11	0	15	1	19	0	15	1	9	0	5	0	2	0	1	0	0	0	2	0	79	2
140–144	3	0	2	0	6	0	12	0	5	0	3	0	4	0	0	0	0	0	2	0	37	0
135–139	0	0	1	0	4	0	1	0	1	0	1	0	1	0	3	1	0	0	3	0	15	1
130–134	0	0	1	0	2	0	0	0	2	0	1	0	1	0	0	0	0	0	3	0	10	0
125–129	0	0	0	0	0	0	0	0	0	0	0	0	0	0	0	0	0	0	0	0	0	0
120–124	0	0	0	0	0	0	0	0	0	0	0	0	0	0	0	0	0	0	0	0	0	0
Total	238	114	248	81	180	37	129	18	55	8	28	0	11	1	6	1	0	0	19	0	914	260

Apps = Number of Applicants
Adm = Number Admitted
Reflects 99% of the total applicant pool.

Brooklyn Law School

250 Joralemon Street
Brooklyn, NY 11201-9846
Phone: 718.780.7906; Fax: 718.780.0395
E-mail: admitq@brooklaw.edu; Website: www.brooklaw.edu

ABA Approved Since 1937

The Basics

Type of school	Private
Term	Semester
Application deadline	
Application fee	$65
Financial aid deadline	4/30
Can first year start other than fall?	No
Student to faculty ratio	17.8 to 1
Does the university offer:	
housing restricted to law students?	Yes
graduate housing for which law students are eligible?	No

Faculty and Administrators

	Total		Men		Women		Minorities	
	Fall	Spr	Fall	Spr	Fall	Spr	Fall	Spr
Full-time	60	48	32	27	28	21	5	3
Other Full-time	2	3	2	3	0	0	0	0
Deans, librarians, & others who teach	8	8	3	3	5	5	1	1
Part-time	70	91	51	64	19	26	6	5
Total	140	150	88	97	52	52	12	9

Curriculum

	Full-time	Part-time
Typical first-year section size	51	39
Is there typically a "small section" of the first-year class, other than Legal Writing, taught by full-time faculty	Yes	No
If yes, typical size offered last year	40	
# of classroom course titles beyond first-year curriculum	166	
# of upper division courses, excluding seminars with an enrollment: Under 25	153	
25–49	52	
50–74	30	
75–99	9	
100+	18	
# of seminars	58	
# of seminar positions available	1,042	
# of seminar positions filled	871	44
# of positions available in simulation courses	1,052	
# of simulation positions filled	758	185
# of positions available in faculty supervised clinical courses	266	
# of faculty supervised clinical positions filled	251	12
# involved in field placements	447	20
# involved in law journals	187	17
# involved in interschool competitions	75	9
# of credit hours required to graduate	86	

JD Enrollment and Ethnicity

	Men #	Men %	Women #	Women %	Full-time #	Full-time %	Part-time #	Part-time %	1st-year #	1st-year %	Total #	Total %	JD Degs. Awd.
African Amer.	29	3.8	59	8.0	44	3.8	44	12.9	36	7.3	88	5.9	18
Amer. Indian	1	0.1	1	0.1	2	0.2	0	0.0	1	0.2	2	0.1	0
Asian Amer.	90	11.8	131	17.8	189	16.4	32	9.4	69	14.0	221	14.8	63
Mex. Amer.	5	0.7	7	1.0	12	1.0	0	0.0	6	1.2	12	0.8	3
Puerto Rican	12	1.6	6	0.8	14	1.2	4	1.2	7	1.4	18	1.2	6
Hispanic	21	2.8	32	4.4	37	3.2	16	4.7	20	4.1	53	3.5	13
Total Minority	158	20.8	236	32.2	298	25.9	96	28.1	139	28.2	394	26.4	103
For. Nation.	2	0.3	6	0.8	7	0.6	1	0.3	2	0.4	8	0.5	6
Caucasian	592	77.9	482	65.7	836	72.6	238	69.6	336	68.2	1074	71.9	351
Unknown	8	1.1	10	1.4	11	1.0	7	2.0	16	3.2	18	1.2	0
Total	760	50.9	734	49.1	1152	77.1	342	22.9	493	33.0	1494		460

Transfers

Transfers in	19
Transfers out	29

Tuition and Fees

	Resident	Nonresident
Full-time	$37,525	$37,525
Part-time	$28,233	$28,233

Living Expenses

Estimated living expenses for singles

Living on campus	Living off campus	Living at home
$19,094	$19,094	$7,094

Brooklyn Law School

ABA
Approved
Since
1937

GPA and LSAT Scores

	Total	Full-time	Part-time
# of apps	5,003	4,229	774
# of offers	1,431	1,141	290
# of matrics	493	303	190
75% GPA	3.59	3.62	3.54
Median GPA	3.39	3.43	3.36
25% GPA	3.15	3.22	3.08
75% LSAT	163	164	160
Median LSAT	161	163	159
25% LSAT	159	162	158

Grants and Scholarships (from prior year)

	Total		Full-time		Part-time	
	#	%	#	%	#	%
Total # of students	1,490		1,134		356	
Total # receiving grants	864	58.0	779	68.7	85	23.9
Less than 1/2 tuition	745	50.0	668	58.9	77	21.6
Half to full tuition	115	7.7	107	9.4	8	2.2
Full tuition	4	0.3	4	0.4	0	0.0
More than full tuition	0	0.0	0	0.0	0	0.0
Median grant amount			$15,037		$10,360	

Informational and Library Resources

# of volumes and volume equivalents	553,072
# of titles	167,144
# of active serial subscriptions	2,404
Study seating capacity inside the library	665
# of full-time professional librarians	9
Hours per week library is open	108
# of open, wired connections available to students	1,984
# of networked computers available for use by students	138
# of simultaneous wireless users	1,000
Require computer?	No

JD Attrition (from prior year)

	Academic	Other	Total	
	#	#	#	%
1st year	1	42	43	8.7
2nd year	1	2	3	0.6
3rd year	0	0	0	0.0
4th year	0	0	0	0.0

Employment (9 months after graduation)

	Total	Percentage
Employment status known	490	99.2
Employment status unknown	4	0.8
Employed	452	92.2
Pursuing graduate degrees	5	1.0
Unemployed seeking employment	5	1.0
Unemployed not seeking employment	28	5.7
Unemployed and studying for the bar	0	0.0
Type of Employment		
# employed in law firms	251	55.5
# employed in business and industry	76	16.8
# employed in government	64	14.2
# employed in public interest	16	3.5
# employed as judicial clerks	33	7.3
# employed in academia	3	0.7
Geographic Location		
# employed in state	410	90.7
# employed in foreign countries	3	0.7
# of states where employed	17	

Bar Passage Rates

Jurisdiction	New York		
Exam	Sum 05	Win 06	Total
# from school taking bar for the first time	446	17	463
School's pass rate for all first-time takers	84%	82%	84%
State's pass rate for all first-time takers	76%	61%	74%

Brooklyn Law School

250 Joralemon Street
Brooklyn, NY 11201-9846
Phone: 718.780.7906; Fax: 718.780.0395
E-mail: admitq@brooklaw.edu; Website: www.brooklaw.edu

■ The Law Campus

Situated at the junction of the Brooklyn Heights Historic
District, the Brooklyn Civic Center, and downtown Brooklyn,
our school boasts a location unrivaled for its legal, cultural, and
historical character. Students share their environs with federal
and state judges, government officials, and lawyers in private
practice, many of them alumni. Within a few-block radius are
the US District Court; US Bankruptcy Court; US Attorney's
Office; the New York State Supreme Court, Appellate Division;
Family Court; the Brooklyn District Attorney; the Kings
County Surrogate's Court; the New York City Civil and
Criminal Courts; The Legal Aid Society; and numerous law
firms. These are our laboratories, a backdrop for learning few
schools can replicate.

■ Renaissance Brooklyn

Multibillion-dollar construction projects have recast downtown
Brooklyn as the city's third business hub, after Wall Street
and midtown Manhattan. Here, moreover, is Brooklyn's most
charming neighborhood, Brooklyn Heights. Overlooking
New York Harbor and lower Manhattan, the Heights is where
you will find much of our campus. Brooklyn Heights is the
first New York City neighborhood designated as a historic
district. Many of its original townhouses, brownstone
mansions, carriage houses, churches, and public buildings
survive, some registered as national historic landmarks. Many
of our students and faculty live here in residence halls or in
private apartments and homes. Nearby neighborhoods—
Carroll Gardens, Cobble Hill, and Park Slope—also offer
convenient, affordable housing.

■ Manhattan at Our Doorstep

Minutes away is the financial, legal, business, and cultural
crossroads of the world: Manhattan. Proximity to Wall Street
gives students easy access to school-year externships and
summer jobs with major law firms and financial institutions.
Students enjoy a great campus in a dynamic urban
environment, softened by a small-neighborhood feel.
This is New York City on a human scale—Manhattan without
the hassle.

■ Building for Your Future

In recent years, Brooklyn Law School (BLS) has undertaken
$132 million in capital improvements to serve its needs
well into the twenty-first century. Ten residences—including
our largest, the 21-story high-rise, Feil Hall—allow us to
guarantee housing to all first-year students, engendering a
strong sense of campus community. A 78,000-square-foot
library, one of the largest and most modern in the city, includes
more than 544,000 volumes, 5 computer labs, 26 group-study
rooms, and seating for nearly 700. We also provide about 90
computer workstations and over 2,400 other student-accessible
network connections throughout our academic and residential
buildings, as well as over 2,000 wi-fi connections.

■ Our Faculty: Diverse, Brilliant, and User-friendly

Our 66 full-time faculty members comprise one of the largest
faculties in New York. They are joined by nearly 130 adjuncts,
including many distinguished judges, practitioners, and
corporate counsel. They are extraordinarily talented and, above
all, superb teachers. Shaping public policy and making law in
the community at large, they are also prolific authors. They are
recognized nationally and globally for their scholarship in
such areas as Commercial and Bankruptcy Law, Corporate and
Securities Law, Evidence, Health Care, Information Privacy
and Internet Law, Intellectual Property, International Business
Law, Human Rights, and Women's Rights. BLS offers a
congenial community. Its learning environment, while rigorous
and challenging, remains supportive and nurturing. A
desirable student-faculty ratio facilitates this dynamic. Faculty
members are accessible to students in a way that few faculties
are. There is a strong correlation between the priority we assign
to teaching and mentoring and the fact that in the past three
years, our average passing rate of over 84 percent was more
than 7 percent ahead of the state-wide rate for first-time takers
of the New York State Bar examination.

■ Our Students: The Best and the Brightest

The fall 2006 entering class included students from 32 states
and DC and 12 foreign countries, who earned degrees from
nearly 160 universities and colleges, including many of the
nation's most prestigious. Seventy-three percent completed
undergraduate work at least one year before enrolling here.
Sixty-four percent had LSAT scores in the top 10 percent
nationwide. Minorities represented 28.4 percent of that class;
about half of the students were women.

■ Our Alumni: Accomplished and Accessible

One of our great strengths is the size, stature, and loyalty of our
more than 18,000 graduates in 49 states and DC, 2 US territories,
and 23 foreign countries—among the largest alumni families of
any law school.

■ The Career Center

Our Career Center is staffed by seven attorney-counselors and
an attorney dedicated to job development/employer relations.
Job listings are readily available to students and graduates via
the Internet. In the most recently reported year, 98 percent of
our students were employed nine months after graduation,
placing us among the top law schools nationwide. For current
salary information, see *www.brooklaw.edu/career/empstats/*.

■ First-year Program of Study

Day students take one core course in a seminar section of about
40 students, allowing for significant individualized skills training.
Our goal is to help students cultivate the ability to think clearly,
analyze problems thoroughly and carefully, and recognize that
no "legal" issue exists in a social, philosophical, economic, or
political vacuum. Students participate in a Legal Writing
Program structured to fully develop their writing abilities. An

Academic Success Program, combining an early-start summer course with a series of support workshops, helps students reach their potential. This contributes to our exceptionally high retention rate between the first and second year.

■ Upper-class Program of Study: The Art and Craft of Lawyering

Our upper-class curriculum bridges the gap between law school and law practice, making law school something students enjoy, not merely endure. Students create individualized programs, choosing from among 240 electives in 19 concentrations and areas of interest. Some 75 percent of full-time and 60 percent of all students participate in one or more of our 21 clinics, including more than 150 enrolled this year in one of our in-house clinics and over 400 students participating in externships in legal departments and judicial chambers, experiencing the law in real time. Simulation courses enroll over 925 students annually.

■ Beyond the Core Curriculum

We are consistently recognized as among the country's top law schools in supporting public interest law. Our **Edward V. Sparer Public Interest Law Fellowship Program** has placed nearly 375 students in a wide array of summer internships at leading public interest organizations nationwide and abroad. Our **International Business Law Fellowship Program** is a rewarding educational experience for those pursuing careers in that field. We sponsor four student-edited journals: the *Brooklyn Law Review*, the *Journal of Law and Policy*, the *Brooklyn Journal of International Law*, and the *Brooklyn Journal of Corporate, Financial, and Commercial Law*. **Barry L. Zaretsky Fellowships** are awarded to students based on demonstrated academic achievement and commitment to bankruptcy and/or commercial law. Our **Moot Court Program**, one of the nation's finest, garnered 60 top honors—including 17 national championships—in recent competitions. Our **Center for the Study of Law, Language, and Cognition** explores how developments in the cognitive sciences—including neuroscience, psychology, and linguistics—have dramatic implications for the theory and practice of law. A **Center for Health, Science, and Public Policy** engages students in the legal issues and public policy concerns confronting health care organizations. A **joint-degree option** allows students to earn master's degrees in business administration, city and regional planning, urban planning, political science, or library and information science. Finally, we offer **study-abroad programs** in China, Germany, and Italy.

Applicant Profile

Admission to Brooklyn Law School is based on an appraisal of each applicant's character, academic achievements, aptitude for the study of law, life experience, and other indications of professional promise.

BLS does not offer an LSAT/GPA admission profile, for numbers alone cannot provide a comprehensive assessment of a candidate's potential for law school success. While matrices may be helpful to some, too often they needlessly discourage others—those with profiles slightly below our published numerical benchmarks who may still be competitive for admission here. Moreover, such profiles tend to reduce the selection process to a two-dimensional matrix, one which fails to portray accurately our admission practices.

To be sure, candidates with high test scores and commensurate grades are more likely to gain admission than those with lower grades and scores. Nevertheless, no combination of grades and scores guarantees admission.

Nonquantifiable factors also significantly influence our decisions. A partial list includes the quality of schools attended, the strength of the program of study, grade trends, the content of faculty letters of evaluation, the cogency of the candidate's writing, campus leadership, significant service to the community, the nature and quality of any work experience or foreign study/travel, awards and honors, and military service. We have a century-long tradition of offering opportunities to members of underrepresented groups.

University at Buffalo Law School, The State University of New York (SUNY)

309 John Lord O'Brian Hall
Buffalo, NY 14260
Phone: 716.645.2907; Fax: 716.645.6676
E-mail: law-admissions@buffalo.edu; Website: www.law.buffalo.edu

ABA
Approved
Since
1936

The Basics

Type of school	Public
Term	Semester
Application deadline	3/15
Application fee	$50
Financial aid deadline	3/1
Can first year start other than fall?	No
Student to faculty ratio	13.1 to 1
Does the university offer:	
housing restricted to law students?	Yes
graduate housing for which law students are eligible?	Yes

Faculty and Administrators

	Total		Men		Women		Minorities	
	Fall	Spr	Fall	Spr	Fall	Spr	Fall	Spr
Full-time	48	46	26	23	22	23	5	6
Other Full-time	6	6	1	1	5	5	0	0
Deans, librarians, & others who teach	5	5	2	2	3	3	0	0
Part-time	47	86	35	56	12	30	4	10
Total	106	143	64	82	42	61	9	16

Curriculum

	Full-time	Part-time
Typical first-year section size	80	0
Is there typically a "small section" of the first-year class, other than Legal Writing, taught by full-time faculty	No	No
If yes, typical size offered last year		
# of classroom course titles beyond first-year curriculum	226	
# of upper division courses, excluding seminars with an enrollment: Under 25	129	
25–49	52	
50–74	14	
75–99	5	
100+	2	
# of seminars	43	
# of seminar positions available	636	
# of seminar positions filled	455	0
# of positions available in simulation courses	961	
# of simulation positions filled	779	0
# of positions available in faculty supervised clinical courses	131	
# of faculty supervised clinical positions filled	131	0
# involved in field placements	75	0
# involved in law journals	326	0
# involved in interschool competitions	162	0
# of credit hours required to graduate	90	

JD Enrollment and Ethnicity

	Men		Women		Full-time		Part-time		1st-year		Total		JD Degs. Awd.
	#	%	#	%	#	%	#	%	#	%	#	%	
African Amer.	17	4.5	28	7.8	45	6.2	0	0.0	16	6.6	45	6.2	11
Amer. Indian	2	0.5	1	0.3	2	0.3	1	33.3	0	0.0	3	0.4	1
Asian Amer.	29	7.8	28	7.8	57	7.8	0	0.0	19	7.8	57	7.8	14
Mex. Amer.	0	0.0	1	0.3	1	0.1	0	0.0	1	0.4	1	0.1	0
Puerto Rican	2	0.5	1	0.3	3	0.4	0	0.0	3	1.2	3	0.4	2
Hispanic	13	3.5	12	3.4	25	3.4	0	0.0	8	3.3	25	3.4	6
Total Minority	63	16.8	71	19.9	133	18.3	1	33.3	47	19.3	134	18.3	34
For. Nation.	0	0.0	0	0.0	0	0.0	0	0.0	0	0.0	0	0.0	0
Caucasian	271	72.5	257	72.0	526	72.3	2	66.7	180	73.8	528	72.2	170
Unknown	40	10.7	29	8.1	69	9.5	0	0.0	17	7.0	69	9.4	32
Total	374	51.2	357	48.8	728	99.6	3	0.4	244	33.4	731		236

Transfers

Transfers in	15
Transfers out	20

Tuition and Fees

	Resident	Nonresident
Full-time	$13,532	$19,632
Part-time	$0	$0

Living Expenses

Estimated living expenses for singles

Living on campus	Living off campus	Living at home
$14,444	$14,444	$14,444

University at Buffalo Law School, The State University of New York (SUNY)

ABA
Approved
Since
1936

GPA and LSAT Scores

	Total	Full-time	Part-time
# of apps	1,508	1,508	0
# of offers	565	565	0
# of matrics	248	248	0
75% GPA	3.67	3.67	0.00
Median GPA	3.44	3.44	0.00
25% GPA	3.22	3.22	0.00
75% LSAT	158	158	0
Median LSAT	156	156	0
25% LSAT	153	153	0

Grants and Scholarships (from prior year)

	Total #	Total %	Full-time #	Full-time %	Part-time #	Part-time %
Total # of students	731		731		0	
Total # receiving grants	508	69.5	508	69.5	0	0.0
Less than 1/2 tuition	439	60.1	439	60.1	0	0.0
Half to full tuition	0	0.0	0	0.0	0	0.0
Full tuition	64	8.8	64	8.8	0	0.0
More than full tuition	5	0.7	5	0.7	0	0.0
Median grant amount			$1,250		$0	

Informational and Library Resources

# of volumes and volume equivalents	578,943
# of titles	111,134
# of active serial subscriptions	6,597
Study seating capacity inside the library	510
# of full-time professional librarians	11
Hours per week library is open	102
# of open, wired connections available to students	70
# of networked computers available for use by students	123
# of simultaneous wireless users	520
Require computer?	No

JD Attrition (from prior year)

	Academic #	Other #	Total #	Total %
1st year	1	1	2	0.8
2nd year	0	22	22	9.1
3rd year	1	0	1	0.4
4th year	0	0	0	0.0

Employment (9 months after graduation)

	Total	Percentage
Employment status known	237	98.3
Employment status unknown	4	1.7
Employed	207	87.3
Pursuing graduate degrees	11	4.6
Unemployed seeking employment	4	1.7
Unemployed not seeking employment	13	5.5
Unemployed and studying for the bar	2	0.8

Type of Employment

# employed in law firms	132	63.8
# employed in business and industry	22	10.6
# employed in government	26	12.6
# employed in public interest	9	4.3
# employed as judicial clerks	14	6.8
# employed in academia	3	1.4

Geographic Location

# employed in state	170	82.1
# employed in foreign countries	4	1.9
# of states where employed	15	

Bar Passage Rates

Jurisdiction	New York			Pennsylvania		
Exam	Sum 05	Win 06	Total	Sum 05	Win 06	Total
# from school taking bar for the first time	197	17	214	4	2	6
School's pass rate for all first-time takers	79%	53%	77%	100%	100%	100%
State's pass rate for all first-time takers	76%	61%	74%	79%	75%	78%

University at Buffalo Law School, The State University of New York (SUNY)

309 John Lord O'Brian Hall
Buffalo, NY 14260
Phone: 716.645.2907; Fax: 716.645.6676
E-mail: law-admissions@buffalo.edu; Website: www.law.buffalo.edu

■ Introduction

Long recognized as one of the leading public law schools in the Northeast, the University at Buffalo Law School, New York State's only public law school, continues to provide students with cutting-edge legal tools to formulate their legal education. This education allows students to gain the practical skills necessary in today's ever-changing legal community.

Located in Amherst, New York—a suburb of Buffalo—the Law School has a small-school feel with all the advantages of a large university, including access to other professional and graduate departments, Division I sports, a fine arts center, Slee Concert Hall, and numerous other academic, social, and cultural opportunities. The city of Buffalo offers great skiing, great sailing, major-league sports, a first-rate orchestra, many professional theaters, a lively club scene, and access to Canada, all within minutes of the Law School. You can live comfortably, not to mention affordably, in Buffalo, the second largest city in New York.

■ Library and Physical Facilities

The Law School is housed in John Lord O'Brian Hall, a seven-story building recently renovated to include a state-of-the-art courtroom that provides students with an opportunity to watch judges and lawyers in action. Other new facilities include classrooms, apartments, and an elegant student lounge. The library is the core of the Law School, occupying six of the seven floors.

The law library follows the Law School's commitment to providing students with exceptional research and writing skills by assigning librarians to each research and writing instructor. This enables first-year law students to gain one-on-one instruction in various research methods.

■ Curriculum

The Law School provides a comprehensive curriculum while affording students a broad range of curricular options, practical coursework, and special programs. The Buffalo curriculum emphasizes the study of law in its social context, and a large number of interdisciplinary courses and programs support this emphasis. A strong clinical education program is closely tied to the core curriculum and enhances the optional concentrations. Current concentration subjects include Family Law, Finance Transactions, Affordable Housing and Community Development Law, Environmental Law, Civil Litigation, Criminal Law, Health Law, International Law, Labor and Employment Law, and Technology and Intellectual Property.

Instruction is offered in two semesters from early September to May, including a January bridge term, and a summer session from mid-May to mid-July. Six full-time semesters or five full-time semesters plus two summer sessions are required for graduation.

In addition to standard first-year subjects, the first year includes a course in legal profession and ethics. These courses afford an introduction to the social and economic context of the legal system and to legal institutions and processes.

Beyond the first year, students are required to complete 60 semester credit hours of work, including at least one seminar. The upper-division program is wholly elective. Second- and third-year students may choose from a full spectrum of survey and advanced courses covering the main fields of public and private law; a very rich selection of seminars and small group courses in special or emerging areas of law study and research; and clinics and simulations devoted to professional skills training.

The Law School also offers an LLM degree in Criminal Law and a General LLM for international and domestic students. For international students, there are special courses designed to introduce them to American law and to prepare them for the New York State Bar Exam. All students benefit from our small group personalized approach and flexible curriculum that allows students to design their own concentration.

■ Special Programs

Clinical Program—The Law School is committed to programs that emphasize interdisciplinary study and applications of law. The clinical program is distinguished in that the skills training is coordinated with substantive law courses to give students theoretical understanding of practical issues. Students serve clients and conduct research and fieldwork in areas such as economic development, affordable housing, family violence, criminal law, elder law, environmental and development law, and securities law.

Centers and Program—The Law School's centers and program provide multiple perspectives on the law. The Baldy Center for Law and Social Policy serves as a focal point for interdisciplinary research and teaching. The Buffalo Human Rights Center maintains cooperative links worldwide with human rights organizations, think tanks, and governmental agencies. The Edwin F. Jaeckle Center for State and Local Government supports a balanced academic program of theoretical study of democratic processes and the education of lawyers for public service. The Center for the Study of Business Transactions, a joint venture of the Law School and UB School of Management, sponsors a variety of courses, research opportunities, and distinguished speakers. Because of the Buffalo Criminal Law Center, UB Law is a national leader in criminal law scholarship. Finally, the UB Law Program for Excellence in Family Law integrates teaching, research, policy, and practice to provide students with the skills and experience needed to practice family law.

Dual-degree Programs—The school also has an extensive dual-degree program, which permits students to earn credit toward a master's or PhD degree and the JD. In recent years, the most active dual-degree programs have been with political science, management, philosophy, public health, legal information and management, and analysis, social work, sociology, and economics. Two additional dual-degree programs were added recently, allowing students to pursue pharmacy and urban planning degree programs. Special programs can also be arranged with other departments.

Bridge Term—Second- and third-year students can enroll in up to three one-credit bridge courses taught by experienced lawyers and judges, giving students a window into current issues in practice.

University at Buffalo/Levin Institute—A unique educational collaboration provides University at Buffalo law, management, and JD/MBA students with an introduction to

New York City's international financial markets and a gateway to its highly competitive financial-sector job market. Each year, approximately 20 students are selected to participate in the program.

■ Admission

The Law School admits first-year students only in the fall semester; transfer and visiting students in both fall and spring. Application priority deadline: March 15. LSAT and LSDAS are required.

Because quantitative factors—GPA and LSAT—may not accurately reflect a student's potential for law school success, the Admissions Committee pays close attention to the qualitative factors presented in an application. These factors include, but are not limited to, academic achievement, personal statements, character traits, writing ability, recommendations, and work experience. If an application reveals that the applicant has been educationally, socially, economically, or otherwise disadvantaged, the Admissions Committee will review the application for signs of achievement that should lead to success in law school.

■ Student Activities

There are ample extracurricular activities for students to get involved in. The Student Bar Association, an elected representative body, oversees all law school student organizations. The Moot Court Board sponsors mock appellate practice competitions, *The Opinion* is the student newspaper, the *Buffalo Law Review* is a professional journal edited by students, and there are specialty journals in environmental law, affordable housing and community development law, intellectual property, criminal law, human rights law, and social policy concerning women.

■ Expenses and Financial Aid

UB is able to offer a state-subsidized tuition to New York residents and a reasonable out-of-state tuition charge. In-state tuition—$12,170; out-of-state—$18,270. Estimated additional expenses—$12,000–$13,000.

This results in overall educational expenses that are less than half the cost of many law schools. Dean's tuition waivers are available to students demonstrating high academic achievement, and state aid is offered on a need basis to qualified students. Additional alumni-sponsored scholarships are offered to second- and third-year students.

■ Career Services

The Law School's Career Services Office (CSO) should become every law student's first point of reference as he or she begins a job search. In addition to providing job search and résumé services for third-year and LLM students, the CSO also aids first- and second-year students in conducting their summer job searches.

Over the last several years, the placement rate of eligible graduates who have been employed in legal work or enrolled in an advanced-degree program within nine months of graduation has been 98 percent. While Buffalo and New York City continue to employ the greatest number of our graduates, several northeastern states, including Washington, DC; southern states (Florida, Georgia, North Carolina); western states (California, Arizona); and midwestern states are presenting an increase in opportunities for our graduates. For more information about career services, contact the office: telephone 716.645.2056; fax 716.645.7336; e-mail *law-careers@buffalo.edu*.

Applicant Profile

University at Buffalo Law School, The State University of New York (SUNY)
This grid includes only applicants who earned 120–180 LSAT scores under standard administrations.

LSAT Score	3.75 +		3.50–3.74		3.25–3.49		3.00–3.24		2.75–2.99		2.50–2.74		2.25–2.49		2.00–2.24		Below 2.00		No GPA		Total	
	Apps	Adm	Apps	Adm	Apps	Adm	Apps	Adm	Apps	Adm	Apps	Adm	Apps	Adm	Apps	Adm	Apps	Adm	Apps	Adm	Apps	Adm
175–180	0	0	0	0	0	0	0	0	0	0	0	0	0	0	0	0	0	0	0	0	0	0
170–174	2	1	0	0	2	2	3	2	1	1	0	0	0	0	0	0	0	0	0	0	8	6
165–169	7	7	11	10	10	9	5	3	3	3	2	1	2	0	0	0	0	0	0	0	40	33
160–164	34	32	30	28	33	32	20	13	17	5	11	3	4	0	2	0	0	0	1	0	152	113
155–159	52	48	86	80	103	80	69	38	27	11	27	6	7	0	5	0	2	0	4	4	382	267
150–154	51	22	124	47	109	28	99	22	46	4	32	2	13	2	8	1	2	0	3	2	487	130
145–149	18	2	50	7	68	7	42	4	32	0	27	3	12	1	4	1	0	0	5	0	258	25
140–144	6	0	8	1	25	0	17	0	14	0	14	0	9	0	5	0	1	0	4	0	103	1
135–139	3	0	4	0	7	0	8	0	7	0	3	0	3	0	0	0	0	0	2	0	37	0
130–134	0	0	1	0	0	0	3	0	2	0	4	0	2	0	2	0	0	0	2	0	16	0
125–129	0	0	0	0	0	0	0	0	0	0	2	0	0	0	1	0	0	0	0	0	3	0
120–124	0	0	0	0	0	0	0	0	0	0	0	0	0	0	0	0	0	0	1	0	1	0
Total	173	112	314	173	357	158	266	82	149	24	122	15	52	3	27	2	5	0	22	6	1487	575

Apps = Number of Applicants   Adm = Number Admitted   Reflects 99% of the total applicant pool.

University of California, Berkeley School of Law (Boalt Hall)

5 Boalt Hall
Berkeley, CA 94720-7200
Phone: 510.642.2274
E-mail: admissions@law.berkeley.edu; Website: www.law.berkeley.edu

ABA Approved Since 1923

The Basics

Type of school	Public
Term	Semester
Application deadline	2/1 6/15
Application fee	$75
Financial aid deadline	3/2
Can first year start other than fall?	No
Student to faculty ratio	12.0 to 1
Does the university offer:	
housing restricted to law students?	No
graduate housing for which law students are eligible?	No

Faculty and Administrators

	Total		Men		Women		Minorities	
	Fall	Spr	Fall	Spr	Fall	Spr	Fall	Spr
Full-time	58	64	38	41	20	23	6	8
Other Full-time	16	16	6	6	10	10	2	2
Deans, librarians, & others who teach	15	15	7	7	8	8	2	2
Part-time	44	69	33	50	11	19	2	5
Total	**133**	**164**	**84**	**104**	**49**	**60**	**12**	**17**

Curriculum

	Full-time	Part-time
Typical first-year section size	95	0
Is there typically a "small section" of the first-year class, other than Legal Writing, taught by full-time faculty	Yes	No
If yes, typical size offered last year	30	
# of classroom course titles beyond first-year curriculum	229	

# of upper division courses, excluding seminars with an enrollment:		
Under 25	146	
25–49	38	
50–74	14	
75–99	6	
100+	8	

	Full-time	Part-time
# of seminars	41	
# of seminar positions available	896	
# of seminar positions filled	480	0
# of positions available in simulation courses	309	
# of simulation positions filled	242	0
# of positions available in faculty supervised clinical courses	144	
# of faculty supervised clinical positions filled	142	0
# involved in field placements	98	0
# involved in law journals	256	0
# involved in interschool competitions	41	0
# of credit hours required to graduate	85	

JD Enrollment and Ethnicity

	Men #	Men %	Women #	Women %	Full-time #	Full-time %	Part-time #	Part-time %	1st-year #	1st-year %	Total #	Total %	JD Degs. Awd.
African Amer.	9	2.5	27	5.2	36	4.1	0	0.0	13	4.9	36	4.1	16
Amer. Indian	2	0.5	6	1.2	8	0.9	0	0.0	1	0.4	8	0.9	3
Asian Amer.	57	15.7	91	17.7	148	16.8	0	0.0	54	20.1	148	16.8	61
Mex. Amer.	13	3.6	27	5.2	40	4.6	0	0.0	10	3.7	40	4.6	24
Puerto Rican	0	0.0	0	0.0	0	0.0	0	0.0	0	0.0	0	0.0	0
Hispanic	16	4.4	16	3.1	32	3.6	0	0.0	12	4.5	32	3.6	13
Total Minority	97	26.6	167	32.4	264	30.0	0	0.0	90	33.6	264	30.0	117
For. Nation.	0	0.0	0	0.0	0	0.0	0	0.0	0	0.0	0	0.0	0
Caucasian	186	51.1	248	48.2	434	49.4	0	0.0	134	50.0	434	49.4	117
Unknown	81	22.3	100	19.4	181	20.6	0	0.0	44	16.4	181	20.6	66
Total	364	41.4	515	58.6	879	100.0	0	0.0	268	30.5	879		300

Transfers

Transfers in	37
Transfers out	17

Tuition and Fees

	Resident	Nonresident
Full-time	$25,476	$37,721
Part-time	$0	$0

Living Expenses

Estimated living expenses for singles		
Living on campus	Living off campus	Living at home
$20,851	$20,851	$20,851

University of California, Berkeley School of Law (Boalt Hall)

ABA
Approved
Since
1923

GPA and LSAT Scores

	Total	Full-time	Part-time
# of apps	7,159	7,159	0
# of offers	791	791	0
# of matrics	266	266	0
75% GPA	3.89	3.89	0.00
Median GPA	3.79	3.79	0.00
25% GPA	3.65	3.65	0.00
75% LSAT	169	169	0
Median LSAT	166	166	0
25% LSAT	163	163	0

Grants and Scholarships (from prior year)

	Total		Full-time		Part-time	
	#	%	#	%	#	%
Total # of students	874		874		0	
Total # receiving grants	621	71.1	621	71.1	0	0.0
Less than 1/2 tuition	507	58.0	507	58.0	0	0.0
Half to full tuition	92	10.5	92	10.5	0	0.0
Full tuition	6	0.7	6	0.7	0	0.0
More than full tuition	16	1.8	16	1.8	0	0.0
Median grant amount			$8,300		$0	

Informational and Library Resources

# of volumes and volume equivalents	863,568
# of titles	279,200
# of active serial subscriptions	7,801
Study seating capacity inside the library	381
# of full-time professional librarians	17
Hours per week library is open	100
# of open, wired connections available to students	109
# of networked computers available for use by students	112
# of simultaneous wireless users	1,200
Require computer?	No

JD Attrition (from prior year)

	Academic	Other	Total	
	#	#	#	%
1st year	0	3	3	1.1
2nd year	0	6	6	1.9
3rd year	0	21	21	7.0
4th year	0	0	0	0.0

Employment (9 months after graduation)

	Total	Percentage
Employment status known	290	99.3
Employment status unknown	2	0.7
Employed	272	93.8
Pursuing graduate degrees	5	1.7
Unemployed seeking employment	3	1.0
Unemployed not seeking employment	10	3.4
Unemployed and studying for the bar	0	0.0

Type of Employment

# employed in law firms	188	69.1
# employed in business and industry	5	1.8
# employed in government	4	1.5
# employed in public interest	36	13.2
# employed as judicial clerks	38	14.0
# employed in academia	1	0.4

Geographic Location

# employed in state	196	72.1
# employed in foreign countries	3	1.1
# of states where employed		24

Bar Passage Rates

Jurisdiction	California		
Exam	Sum 05	Win 06	Total
# from school taking bar for the first time	228	10	238
School's pass rate for all first-time takers	87%	80%	87%
State's pass rate for all first-time takers	64%	54%	62%

University of California, Berkeley School of Law (Boalt Hall)

5 Boalt Hall
Berkeley, CA 94720-7200
Phone: 510.642.2274
E-mail: admissions@law.berkeley.edu; Website: www.law.berkeley.edu

■ Introduction

Learning law at Boalt Hall means joining a stimulating intellectual community that is part of a tradition of academic excellence, professional leadership, and public service. Boalt's location in the San Francisco Bay Area, with influences from Silicon Valley and the Pacific Rim, provides an unparalleled opportunity to study at one of the world's leading institutions of legal education and research. Boalt's academic program includes specialized study in business, law, and economics; environmental law; law and technology; international and comparative legal studies; and social justice and public interest. The curriculum is complemented by research centers and clinical programs that provide real client work. Boalt offers a broad three-year curriculum leading to the JD degree and postgraduate programs leading to LLM and JSD degrees. The interdisciplinary Jurisprudence and Social Policy (JSP) program leads to MA and PhD degrees. Boalt is a member of AALS and is ABA approved.

■ Location

UC Berkeley is a beautiful 1,232-acre campus bordered by wooded rolling hills. Berkeley is known for its intellectual, social, and political engagement. With its global population, rich diversity of arts, and sense of political adventure, Berkeley reflects and affects the rest of the country. Yet, it is an intimate city of friendly neighborhoods, renowned restaurants, coffeehouses, bookstores, parks, and open spaces. Across the bay lies San Francisco, home to internationally recognized museums, the opera, ballet, symphony, and restaurants. The mild climate makes outdoor activities possible year-round.

■ Students

Boalt seeks a student body with a broad set of interests, backgrounds, life experiences, and perspectives. The intellectual excellence, varied interests, and backgrounds of the students are among Boalt's great strengths. Students received undergraduate degrees from more than 100 universities, about half at schools outside California.

■ Faculty

Boalt's faculty members are internationally recognized experts in the law, from law and technology to youth violence and juvenile justice to environmental law. They include recipients of Fulbright and Guggenheim fellowships and a MacArthur "genius" grant, as well as authors of casebooks used worldwide. Lecturers are drawn from prominent law firms and institutions.

■ Library and Physical Facilities

The law library contains more than 850,000 volumes and is one of the finest law collections in the world. Its holdings include the Robbins Religious and Civil Law Collection of titles in ecclesiastical, civil, comparative, and international law, and extensive collections of foreign, comparative, human rights, and environmental law. The law library is also a depository for United States, United Nations, and European Union documents and is linked to the UC system's holdings of more than seven million volumes.

The law library provides online databases, three computer labs with Internet access, four spacious reading rooms, and a photocopying service. Multimedia capabilities are available. Wireless access is available throughout the law school complex and much of the Berkeley campus.

Boalt is composed of three adjoining buildings (and two courtyards) with classrooms, seminar rooms, auditoriums, the law library, a lounge, a reception room, a café, dining and study areas, and offices.

■ Housing

The campus Housing Office offers apartments, rental listings, residence halls, and student family apartments. International House accommodates students from the United States and abroad.

■ Admission

Requirements: Bachelor's degree, LSAT, and LSDAS; application fee: $75; deadline: February 1 (early application strongly preferred).

Applicants' LSAT scores and undergraduate grade-point averages (GPAs) are important criteria to evaluate academic ability. Applicants may use the mean LSAT percentile and undergraduate GPAs of the previous year's admitted applicant pool as a guide for assessing their chances of admission. Because Boalt takes other factors into account in making admission decisions, higher or lower scores and grades neither ensure nor preclude admission.

■ Student Activities

Students edit and publish 11 legal periodicals: *Asian American Law Journal; Berkeley Business Law Journal; Berkeley Journal of African American Law and Policy; Boalt Journal of Criminal Law; Berkeley Journal of Employment and Labor Law; Berkeley Journal of Gender, Law, and Justice; Berkeley Journal of International Law; Berkeley La Raza Law Journal; Berkeley Technology Law Journal; California Law Review;* and *Ecology Law Quarterly.*

More than 50 student groups focus on a variety of interests, including animal law, disability law, sports and entertainment law, and workers' rights.

■ JD Curriculum

Boalt's broad and innovative curriculum is one of the most dynamic among law schools. Opportunities for study in specific areas of the law connect you to Boalt's renowned faculty members. The first-year curriculum includes Civil Procedure, Contracts, Criminal Law, Legal Research and Writing, Property, Torts, Written and Oral Advocacy, and two elective courses. The flexible second- and third-year curriculum offers a variety of legal topics and course styles, including seminars, individual and group research projects, clinical work, and judicial externships. Students may work on clinical projects providing direct legal services to clients or work with lawyers on large cases or legal matters. The Center for Clinical Education, Boalt's in-house clinical facility, offers the Death Penalty Clinic, the International Human Rights Law Clinic, and the Samuelson Law, Technology, and Public Policy Clinic. The East Bay Community Law Center is the community-based component of the program. Other clinical opportunities include the Domestic Violence Practicum and field placements.

■ Centers and Institutes

Boalt Hall's centers and institutes act as incubators for cutting-edge legal research, where students collaborate with leading scholars and practitioners working on complex issues. Projects are often centered on specific cases or legislation, and can have broad influence on law and policy in such areas as business, philosophy, public policy, sociology, and technology. The centers also sponsor conferences, roundtables, and other presentations on pertinent issues. Boalt's centers push the frontiers of legal scholarship and make Boalt one of the most exciting places in the world to study law. They include:

- Berkeley Center for Criminal Justice
- Berkeley Center for Law, Business, and the Economy
- Berkeley Center for Law and Technology
- California Center for Environmental Law and Policy
- Center for Clinical Education
- Center for the Study of Law and Society
- Chief Justice Earl Warren Institute on Race, Ethnicity, and Diversity
- Institute for Legal Research
- Thelton E. Henderson Center for Social Justice
- Kadish Center for Morality, Law, and Public Affairs
- Robert D. Burch Center for Tax Policy and Public Finance

■ Financial Aid

Requirements: Boalt Hall Financial Aid Application (optional); FAFSA need analysis form; deadline for priority consideration: March 2.

The law school seeks to provide need-based financial aid sufficient to permit any admitted student to attend. A majority of the students at Boalt Hall receive some form of financial aid.

The financial aid awarded by UC Berkeley's Financial Aid Office is need-based and includes mostly federal student loans. The financial aid awarded by Boalt Hall includes federal student loans and other campus-based awards such as work study. Additionally, the law school administers a variety of grants and scholarships based on financial need and/or need and academic merit.

■ Career Development

The Office of Career Development is a resource for students, alumni, and prospective employers. It operates one of the largest on-campus recruitment programs in the country, provides opportunities for legal employment, and maintains an online job database of positions available throughout the nation. The staff conducts career counseling, résumé workshops, and programs on traditional and nontraditional law careers in the private and public sectors.

Applicant Profile Not Available

University of California, Davis School of Law (King Hall)

400 Mrak Hall Drive
Davis, CA 95616-5201
Phone: 530.752.6477
E-mail: lawadmissions@ucdavis.edu; Website: www.law.ucdavis.edu

ABA Approved Since 1968

The Basics

Type of school	Public
Term	Semester
Application deadline	2/1
Application fee	$75
Financial aid deadline	3/2
Can first year start other than fall?	No
Student to faculty ratio	14.0 to 1
Does the university offer:	
housing restricted to law students?	No
graduate housing for which law students are eligible?	No

Faculty and Administrators

	Total		Men		Women		Minorities	
	Fall	Spr	Fall	Spr	Fall	Spr	Fall	Spr
Full-time	36	35	20	20	16	15	15	12
Other Full-time	1	1	1	1	0	0	0	0
Deans, librarians, & others who teach	4	5	2	3	2	2	1	1
Part-time	16	22	11	18	5	4	4	3
Total	57	63	34	42	23	21	20	16

Curriculum

	Full-time	Part-time
Typical first-year section size	65	0
Is there typically a "small section" of the first-year class, other than Legal Writing, taught by full-time faculty	Yes	No
If yes, typical size offered last year	32	
# of classroom course titles beyond first-year curriculum		83
# of upper division courses, excluding seminars with an enrollment: Under 25		33
25–49		27
50–74		9
75–99		6
100+		4
# of seminars		18
# of seminar positions available		305
# of seminar positions filled	193	0
# of positions available in simulation courses		496
# of simulation positions filled	389	0
# of positions available in faculty supervised clinical courses		113
# of faculty supervised clinical positions filled	98	0
# involved in field placements	97	0
# involved in law journals	201	0
# involved in interschool competitions	111	0
# of credit hours required to graduate		88

JD Enrollment and Ethnicity

	Men		Women		Full-time		Part-time		1st-year		Total		JD Degs. Awd.
	#	%	#	%	#	%	#	%	#	%	#	%	
African Amer.	5	1.9	4	1.2	9	1.5	0	0.0	3	1.6	9	1.5	4
Amer. Indian	0	0.0	2	0.6	2	0.3	0	0.0	0	0.0	2	0.3	2
Asian Amer.	53	20.3	80	24.9	133	22.9	0	0.0	41	21.8	133	22.9	46
Mex. Amer.	15	5.7	18	5.6	33	5.7	0	0.0	7	3.7	33	5.7	20
Puerto Rican	0	0.0	1	0.3	1	0.2	0	0.0	0	0.0	1	0.2	0
Hispanic	6	2.3	8	2.5	14	2.4	0	0.0	3	1.6	14	2.4	7
Total Minority	79	30.3	113	35.2	192	33.0	0	0.0	54	28.7	192	33.0	79
For. Nation.	4	1.5	2	0.6	6	1.0	0	0.0	4	2.1	6	1.0	3
Caucasian	136	52.1	156	48.6	292	50.2	0	0.0	100	53.2	292	50.2	86
Unknown	42	16.1	50	15.6	92	15.8	0	0.0	30	16.0	92	15.8	21
Total	261	44.8	321	55.2	582	100.0	0	0.0	188	32.3	582		189

Transfers

Transfers in	14
Transfers out	11

Tuition and Fees

	Resident	Nonresident
Full-time	$24,358	$36,603
Part-time	$0	$0

Living Expenses

Estimated living expenses for singles

Living on campus	Living off campus	Living at home
N/A	$14,787	N/A

University of California, Davis School of Law (King Hall)

ABA
Approved
Since
1968

GPA and LSAT Scores

	Total	Full-time	Part-time
# of apps	3,493	3,493	0
# of offers	981	981	0
# of matrics	188	188	0
75% GPA	3.73	3.73	0.00
Median GPA	3.55	3.55	0.00
25% GPA	3.35	3.35	0.00
75% LSAT	164	164	0
Median LSAT	162	162	0
25% LSAT	160	160	0

Grants and Scholarships (from prior year)

	Total		Full-time		Part-time	
	#	%	#	%	#	%
Total # of students	571		571		0	
Total # receiving grants	437	76.5	437	76.5	0	0.0
Less than 1/2 tuition	427	74.8	427	74.8	0	0.0
Half to full tuition	5	0.9	5	0.9	0	0.0
Full tuition	1	0.2	1	0.2	0	0.0
More than full tuition	4	0.7	4	0.7	0	0.0
Median grant amount			$8,700		$0	

Informational and Library Resources

# of volumes and volume equivalents	441,848
# of titles	97,833
# of active serial subscriptions	4,126
Study seating capacity inside the library	311
# of full-time professional librarians	7
Hours per week library is open	78
# of open, wired connections available to students	0
# of networked computers available for use by students	89
# of simultaneous wireless users	600
Require computer?	No

JD Attrition (from prior year)

	Academic	Other	Total	
	#	#	#	%
1st year	0	18	18	9.3
2nd year	0	1	1	0.5
3rd year	0	0	0	0.0
4th year	0	0	0	0.0

Employment (9 months after graduation)

	Total	Percentage
Employment status known	172	97.7
Employment status unknown	4	2.3
Employed	151	87.8
Pursuing graduate degrees	1	0.6
Unemployed seeking employment	3	1.7
Unemployed not seeking employment	12	7.0
Unemployed and studying for the bar	5	2.9

Type of Employment

	Total	Percentage
# employed in law firms	95	62.9
# employed in business and industry	12	7.9
# employed in government	14	9.3
# employed in public interest	13	8.6
# employed as judicial clerks	12	7.9
# employed in academia	5	3.3

Geographic Location

	Total	Percentage
# employed in state	135	89.4
# employed in foreign countries	2	1.3
# of states where employed	12	

Bar Passage Rates

Jurisdiction	California		
Exam	Sum 05	Win 06	Total
# from school taking bar for the first time	160	9	169
School's pass rate for all first-time takers	74%	44%	72%
State's pass rate for all first-time takers	64%	54%	62%

University of California, Davis School of Law (King Hall)

Admissions Office, 400 Mrak Hall Drive
Davis, CA 95616-5201
Phone: 530.752.6477
E-mail: lawadmissions@ucdavis.edu; Website: www.law.ucdavis.edu

■ Introduction

The School of Law at the University of California, Davis, was founded in 1965. It is accredited by the American Bar Association and is a member of the Association of American Law Schools. The law school building, King Hall, was named for Dr. Martin Luther King Jr. in recognition of his efforts to bring social and political justice to disadvantaged peoples. The school has a chapter of the Order of the Coif, the national honor society. A statue of Dr. King is located in the law school lobby.

The Davis campus is 20 minutes from Sacramento and a little over an hour from San Francisco, within easy reach of the major recreational areas of Lake Tahoe. The campus occupies 3,600 acres within the college town of Davis, where the law school is well-known for its commitment to community among students and faculty as well as its cutting-edge scholarship, teaching, and service.

The close proximity to the state capitol and the Bay Area provide the opportunity for a well-rounded educational experience. The campus offers a full range of graduate and professional programs.

■ Library and Physical Facilities

Faculty offices, classrooms, and the law library are housed in King Hall on the Davis campus. It has a moot courtroom, a pretrial-skills laboratory, a large computer lab, study carrels, student journal offices, lounges, infant care co-op, and offices for student organizations, all easily accessible to disabled students. Every law student is given a key to the building allowing 24-hour access.

First-year students are assigned to carrels where books can be charged. Students have access to many online databases via the library and California Digital Library. The library is a federal and California document depository.

Classrooms have state-of-the-art audiovisual and multimedia equipment. Wireless Internet access is available throughout the building.

The law school's clinical programs are housed in law offices a short distance from King Hall.

■ Curriculum

The law school offers a three-year, full-time program in law leading to the Juris Doctor degree and a postgraduate program leading to an LLM. At King Hall, a faculty with a national reputation for excellent scholarship and teaching is combined with an outstanding and diverse student body. The faculty's scholarship is renowned in many different fields, including Constitutional Law; Environmental Law; Civil Rights; Critical Race Theory; Trusts, Wills, and Estate Planning; Property; Contracts; Evidence; Criminal Law and Procedure; Civil Procedure; Federal Courts; Complex Litigation; Latinos and the Law; and Immigration Law and Policy. Ordinarily each first-year section has less than 70 students. Each student is taught at least one of the required first-year courses in small sections of 25–35 students. The first year begins with a weeklong introductory course and includes courses in legal research and writing. Upper-division courses may be selected within broad areas of concentration such as criminal justice, business and taxation,

civil litigation, estate planning and taxation, labor and employment law, environmental law, human rights and social justice law, immigration law, intellectual property, international law, and public law. Students may also combine JD studies with another graduate or professional program such as an MBA degree.

■ Special Programs

King Hall is renowned for its excellent clinical programs. Students have the opportunity to work under the supervision of practicing lawyers in many different substantive areas. Students also participate in judicial externships in trial and appellate courts.

The law school has four of its own clinics: Immigration, Civil Rights, Prison Law, and Family Protection. The Immigration Law Clinic, in which students have as a resource one of the best immigration law faculty in the United States, allows students to assist immigrants facing deportation. Students prepare clients and their cases for hearings.

King Hall has an integrated civil rights curriculum, including a substantive course in civil rights law and clinics representing clients in federal civil rights cases. Students participating in the Civil Rights Clinic are certified to appear in federal court, where they represent people who might otherwise have no counsel, and gain firsthand experience in constitutional litigation.

The Family Protection Clinic is based in a small town and represents low income people, including many Spanish speakers needing family law and domestic violence assistance.

First-year students engage in oral argument as a part of the required legal research and writing course. This provides basic preparation for participation in the formal Moot Court Program, which emphasizes appellate advocacy. Skills courses cover the major elements of both litigation and nonlitigation practice. These include pretrial skills (interviewing, counseling, and document drafting); negotiation, mediation, and alternative dispute resolution; and trial practice.

Students in the Public Interest Law Program receive a certificate based on required coursework, practical experience, and community service. A Public Service Graduation ceremony is the culmination of this program. Students in the Environmental Law Program receive a certificate for completion of an environmental curriculum. King Hall students participate in a Pro Bono Program designed to help address the unmet legal service needs of disadvantaged persons and nonprofit organizations while inculcating the professional responsibility of lawyers to perform public service.

■ Admission

The Admission Committee seeks students of diverse backgrounds and interests. The entire application is carefully reviewed with consideration given to many factors, including undergraduate grades, LSAT score, economic and other disadvantages, advanced studies, work experience, extracurricular and community activities, maturity, and commitment to the study of law. Residency is not a factor in the admission process. An open house for prospective applicants takes place in October, and information sessions are held November through January. Guided tours can be arranged.

University of California, Davis School of Law (King Hall)

Student Life

King Hall is renowned for its wonderful sense of community. The student body is small compared to that of most law schools, which lessens competition among a highly qualified student cohort. Students work extraordinarily well with each other, faculty, administrators, and staff. Cooperation and collegiality are the hallmarks of student life at King Hall.

Faculty and administrators have an open-door policy for students. Student/faculty relations are excellent. Alumni of the School of Law look back fondly on their law school years.

An academic support program is available to students in the first-year class. Students run five journals: the *UC Davis Law Review* and specialized journals in international law, environmental law, juvenile justice law, and business law.

Students sit on the student-faculty Educational Policy, Faculty Appointments, and Admission Committees. There are about 30 active student organizations encompassing a wide variety of interests. The La Raza Law Students Association's Lorenzo Patiño Banquet honoring a Latino alumnus and the King Hall Legal Foundation auction to raise funds for public interest are two of many student-sponsored events that highlight each academic year. The extremely positive attitude of King Hall students was noted and commented upon in our most recent ABA inspection report.

Expenses and Financial Aid

The School of Law Financial Aid Office, located in King Hall, is available for the exclusive use of law students and is available for counseling and advice. All financial aid services, from entrance through graduation, are administered at the law school. The law school Financial Aid Office administers all nationally recognized aid programs, such as Federal Perkins Loans and Federal Work-Study, and participates in the Federal Direct Loan Program. Over 70 percent of King Hall students receive need-based grants as part of their financial aid award. Each year, two entering students are selected to receive the prestigious MLK scholarship based on demonstrated commitment to public interest. University student loan and grant funds are available for child care.

Housing

A wide variety of reasonably priced housing is available in the local community. The university maintains on-campus apartments for students and student families.

Career Services

The office successfully and enthusiastically assists students in securing rewarding summer and post-JD positions. Close to 150 employers visit the school to interview students, and advertise many positions through the office. Career Services presents speakers and training workshops geared to student needs and to the hiring cycles of various segments of the legal and law-related job markets. Students also have access to many professional opportunities through job fairs, online nationwide listings, and other sources. Virtually all students are employed nine months after graduation.

Applicant Profile

University of California, Davis School of Law (King Hall)
This grid includes only applicants who earned 120–180 LSAT scores under standard administrations.

LSAT Score	3.75 +		3.50–3.74		3.25–3.49		3.00–3.24		2.75–2.99		2.50–2.74		2.25–2.49		2.00–2.24		Below 2.00		No GPA		Total	
	Apps	Adm	Apps	Adm	Apps	Adm	Apps	Adm	Apps	Adm	Apps	Adm	Apps	Adm	Apps	Adm	Apps	Adm	Apps	Adm	Apps	Adm
175–180	5	4	0	0	2	2	1	1	1	0	0	0	0	0	0	0	0	0	0	0	9	7
170–174	23	21	24	24	18	14	8	4	8	1	3	1	2	0	1	0	0	0	0	0	87	65
165–169	76	74	137	119	103	80	80	31	25	3	16	2	5	2	1	0	0	0	0	0	443	311
160–164	165	155	315	198	253	86	125	14	48	3	24	0	14	0	5	0	0	0	13	6	962	462
155–159	182	60	284	35	271	20	142	4	73	0	33	0	6	0	2	0	0	0	7	0	1000	119
150–154	74	4	131	2	161	4	101	4	68	0	17	0	10	0	3	0	0	0	4	0	569	14
145–149	22	0	62	0	74	0	50	0	40	0	16	0	3	0	1	0	1	0	6	0	275	0
140–144	12	0	13	0	27	0	42	0	25	0	13	0	4	0	2	0	1	0	1	0	140	0
135–139	1	0	4	0	6	0	10	0	8	0	6	0	1	0	0	0	0	0	1	0	37	0
130–134	1	0	1	0	1	0	3	0	4	0	1	0	1	0	1	0	1	0	0	0	14	0
125–129	0	0	2	0	0	0	0	0	0	0	0	0	0	0	2	0	0	0	0	0	4	0
120–124	0	0	0	0	0	0	0	0	0	0	0	0	0	0	0	0	0	0	0	0	0	0
Total	561	318	973	378	916	206	562	58	300	7	129	3	46	2	18	0	3	0	32	6	3540	978

Apps = Number of Applicants
Adm = Number Admitted
Reflects 99% of the total applicant pool.

University of California, Hastings College of the Law

200 McAllister Street
San Francisco, CA 94102
Phone: 415.565.4623; Fax: 415.581.8946
E-mail: admiss@uchastings.edu; Website: www.uchastings.edu

ABA Approved Since 1939

The Basics

Type of school	Public
Term	Semester
Application deadline	3/1
Application fee	$75
Financial aid deadline	3/1
Can first year start other than fall?	No
Student to faculty ratio	18.9 to 1
Does the university offer:	
housing restricted to law students?	Yes
graduate housing for which law students are eligible?	Yes

Faculty and Administrators

	Total		Men		Women		Minorities	
	Fall	Spr	Fall	Spr	Fall	Spr	Fall	Spr
Full-time	57	53	38	34	19	19	14	13
Other Full-time	8	8	5	5	3	3	1	1
Deans, librarians, & others who teach	7	7	2	2	5	5	1	1
Part-time	99	85	58	53	40	32	15	6
Total	171	153	103	94	67	59	31	21

Curriculum

	Full-time	Part-time
Typical first-year section size	85	0
Is there typically a "small section" of the first-year class, other than Legal Writing, taught by full-time faculty	No	No
If yes, typical size offered last year		
# of classroom course titles beyond first-year curriculum	150	

# of upper division courses, excluding seminars with an enrollment:		
Under 25	116	
25–49	36	
50–74	16	
75–99	19	
100+	9	

# of seminars	56	
# of seminar positions available	1,052	
# of seminar positions filled	762	0
# of positions available in simulation courses	1,132	
# of simulation positions filled	964	0
# of positions available in faculty supervised clinical courses	202	
# of faculty supervised clinical positions filled	169	0
# involved in field placements	127	0
# involved in law journals	410	0
# involved in interschool competitions	306	0
# of credit hours required to graduate	86	

JD Enrollment and Ethnicity

	Men		Women		Full-time		Part-time		1st-year		Total		JD Degs. Awd.
	#	%	#	%	#	%	#	%	#	%	#	%	
African Amer.	8	1.4	23	3.5	31	2.5	0	0.0	12	2.8	31	2.5	11
Amer. Indian	1	0.2	3	0.5	4	0.3	0	0.0	1	0.2	4	0.3	1
Asian Amer.	126	21.7	173	26.2	299	24.1	0	0.0	93	22.0	299	24.1	98
Mex. Amer.	17	2.9	18	2.7	35	2.8	0	0.0	5	1.2	35	2.8	13
Puerto Rican	1	0.2	4	0.6	5	0.4	0	0.0	1	0.2	5	0.4	1
Hispanic	14	2.4	27	4.1	41	3.3	0	0.0	19	4.5	41	3.3	18
Total Minority	167	28.7	248	37.5	415	33.5	0	0.0	131	31.0	415	33.4	142
For. Nation.	4	0.7	11	1.7	15	1.2	0	0.0	7	1.7	15	1.2	3
Caucasian	273	47.0	272	41.1	544	43.9	1	50.0	170	40.2	545	43.9	187
Unknown	137	23.6	130	19.7	266	21.5	1	50.0	115	27.2	267	21.5	77
Total	581	46.8	661	53.2	1240	99.8	2	0.2	423	34.1	1242		409

Transfers

Transfers in	16
Transfers out	17

Tuition and Fees

	Resident	Nonresident
Full-time	$22,190	$33,415
Part-time	$0	$0

Living Expenses

Estimated living expenses for singles

Living on campus	Living off campus	Living at home
$19,341	$19,341	$19,341

University of California, Hastings College of the Law

ABA
Approved
Since
1939

GPA and LSAT Scores

	Total	Full-time	Part-time
# of apps	5,526	5,526	0
# of offers	1,479	1,479	0
# of matrics	421	421	0
75% GPA	3.74	3.74	0.00
Median GPA	3.59	3.59	0.00
25% GPA	3.41	3.41	0.00
75% LSAT	164	164	0
Median LSAT	162	162	0
25% LSAT	159	159	0

Grants and Scholarships (from prior year)

	Total		Full-time		Part-time	
	#	%	#	%	#	%
Total # of students	1,255		1,251		4	
Total # receiving grants	920	73.3	920	73.5	0	0.0
Less than 1/2 tuition	913	72.7	913	73.0	0	0.0
Half to full tuition	7	0.6	7	0.6	0	0.0
Full tuition	0	0.0	0	0.0	0	0.0
More than full tuition	0	0.0	0	0.0	0	0.0
Median grant amount			$5,500		$0	

Informational and Library Resources

# of volumes and volume equivalents	708,079
# of titles	215,745
# of active serial subscriptions	7,851
Study seating capacity inside the library	720
# of full-time professional librarians	11
Hours per week library is open	102
# of open, wired connections available to students	702
# of networked computers available for use by students	151
# of simultaneous wireless users	1,460
Require computer?	No

JD Attrition (from prior year)

	Academic	Other	Total	
	#	#	#	%
1st year	4	17	21	4.9
2nd year	1	21	22	5.1
3rd year	0	1	1	0.3
4th year	0	0	0	0.0

Employment (9 months after graduation)

	Total	Percentage
Employment status known	408	98.3
Employment status unknown	7	1.7
Employed	369	90.4
Pursuing graduate degrees	3	0.7
Unemployed seeking employment	9	2.2
Unemployed not seeking employment	27	6.6
Unemployed and studying for the bar	0	0.0
Type of Employment		
# employed in law firms	239	64.8
# employed in business and industry	36	9.8
# employed in government	42	11.4
# employed in public interest	18	4.9
# employed as judicial clerks	25	6.8
# employed in academia	6	1.6
Geographic Location		
# employed in state	315	85.4
# employed in foreign countries	0	0.0
# of states where employed	23	

Bar Passage Rates

Jurisdiction	California		
Exam	Sum 05	Win 06	Total
# from school taking bar for the first time	362	16	378
School's pass rate for all first-time takers	84%	81%	84%
State's pass rate for all first-time takers	64%	54%	62%

University of California, Hastings College of the Law

200 McAllister Street
San Francisco, CA 94102
Phone: 415.565.4623; Fax: 415.581.8946
E-mail: admiss@uchastings.edu; Website: www.uchastings.edu

■ Introduction

UC Hastings College of the Law offers a superb legal education in San Francisco, one of the world's great cities. Hastings was the first public law school in California, founded in 1878 as the law department of the University of California. The faculty at Hastings is composed of exceptional teachers who are also nationally known scholars. They are accessible to students and encourage a collaborative learning environment. Hastings has produced more judges than any other law school in the state, and its graduates can be found practicing law throughout California and the nation, in every kind of setting. Hastings graduates also have a significant presence in business and government.

The law school is situated in the heart of the city, near City Hall, state and federal courts, the arts district, the financial district, and the downtown shopping area. This central location provides access for students to pursue internships and externships with judges, city and state agencies, and nearby nonprofit research and advocacy groups. The location also provides unparalleled opportunities for recreation: theater, music, restaurants, professional and amateur sports; and a world-class transportation system.

■ Library, Technology, and Housing

Hastings is an urban campus with three buildings, all having wireless Internet access. The classroom building was renovated in 2000, and renovation of the library/administration building will be completed by the fall of 2007. The new library is designed to be both comfortable and functional, with small-group study rooms, both open areas and individual carrels, and access to traditional and online research tools. McAllister Tower is a splendid, remodeled art-deco building with 250 apartments, many with stunning views of the city. The building also features a comfortable lounge and a gym, including a basketball court often frequented by local attorneys and judges as well as Hastings students.

■ Curriculum

The UC Hastings curriculum offers a broad spectrum of basic and specialized courses. The law school's curricular strengths mirror the strengths of San Francisco. Students can focus on international human rights and business law, public interest law, intellectual property law, business and tax law, or litigation and its alternatives. San Francisco is a global city that draws on experts from Silicon Valley and the greater Bay Area to enrich course offerings.

■ Special Programs

- **Concentrations**: Students may earn a certificate of concentration in any of the following areas: Civil Litigation, Criminal Law, Family Law, International Law, Public Interest Law, or Tax Law.
- **Clinics and Judicial Externships**: Hastings provides an exciting and diverse array of opportunities for students to gain practical experience. Under clinical faculty supervision, students represent real clients in in-house and out-placement clinics specializing in community development, environmental law, labor and employment, housing and disability rights, law reform, international human rights, immigrants' rights, and legislation. In these clinics, students learn a variety of lawyering techniques, including counseling and planning, litigation, alternative dispute resolution, and legislation. Simulation courses teach trial and appellate advocacy, negotiation, mediation, contract drafting, problem solving, and professional ethics. More than 100 students a year spend a semester serving as externs in the state and federal courts, including the California Supreme Court.
- **International Programs**: Hastings offers an exceptionally strong curriculum focusing on international human rights, as well as international business and trade law. In addition, students may participate in the work of the Center for Gender and Refugee Studies, the Immigrants' Rights Clinic, and the Hastings-to-Haiti program. Hastings also offers study-abroad programs in Argentina, Australia, China, Denmark, England, Germany, Hungary, Italy, and the Netherlands and supports students who wish to study abroad in other locations.
- **Joint-degree Programs**: Hastings students may participate in a joint-degree program with any accredited graduate program. Hastings students have simultaneously earned degrees in public policy, public health, and business administration, among others.
- **Legal Education Opportunity Program (LEOP)**: LEOP recognizes that the traditional academic criteria used to determine admissions might not be the best indicators of academic potential for students from nontraditional backgrounds. LEOP admits students who have had to overcome significant obstacles and assists them to excel academically.
- **Centers and Institutes**: Students have opportunities to work in the law school's highly acclaimed research and advocacy centers: the Center for Gender and Refugee Studies, the Center for Negotiation and Dispute Resolution, the Center for State and Local Government Law, the Center for WorkLife Law, and the Public Law Research Institute.
- **LLM Program**: Graduates of non-US law schools may earn a master of laws degree in US Legal Studies.

■ Cocurricular and Student Activities

The strength and diversity of the Hastings student body are reflected in more than 60 student organizations that sponsor intellectual, social, and political events. Hastings publishes eight student-edited law reviews. The *Hastings Law Journal* is a general-interest publication. In addition, seven specialty law reviews focus on a variety of issues, including business law, constitutional law, communication and entertainment law, international and comparative law, environmental law, and the law relating to race or gender. Students may also join the college's award-winning moot court, negotiation, client counseling, and trial practice teams, which compete in state, national, and international competitions. Students also engage in a variety of legal and nonlegal community service activities in and around the Hastings neighborhood.

■ Financial Aid

Approximately 80 percent of UC Hastings students receive need-based and merit-based financial assistance from college-administered sources. Scholarships and grants recognize and encourage the achievement, service, and professional promise of students. Students who pursue qualifying public interest and government sector employment may receive loan repayment assistance after graduation through the Public Interest Career Assistance Program (PICAP).

■ Career Services

UC Hastings offers one of the most comprehensive law career services offices in the West. The office assists students and alumni in clarifying their goals, acquiring job search strategies, and honing interviewing techniques. It provides access to full-time, part-time, and summer job listings. Every year, more than 200 employers visit the campus to interview students for both summer associate positions and permanent postgraduation employment. Several hundred additional employers from throughout the nation participate in the recruit-by-mail program.

Applicant Profile

University of California, Hastings College of the Law
This grid includes only applicants who earned 120–180 LSAT scores under standard administrations.

LSAT Score	3.75 +		3.50–3.74		3.25–3.49		3.00–3.24		2.75–2.99		2.50–2.74		2.25–2.49		2.00–2.24		Below 2.00		No GPA		Total	
	Apps	Adm	Apps	Adm	Apps	Adm	Apps	Adm	Apps	Adm	Apps	Adm	Apps	Adm	Apps	Adm	Apps	Adm	Apps	Adm	Apps	Adm
175–180	10	9	7	7	4	4	2	2	6	4	1	0	0	0	0	0	0	0	0	0	30	26
170–174	35	34	48	44	43	33	20	14	16	4	7	1	2	0	1	0	0	0	0	0	172	130
165–169	133	126	239	206	168	139	111	39	59	0	19	2	7	0	1	0	0	0	2	2	739	514
160–164	249	229	454	293	356	80	202	9	75	2	42	0	19	1	7	0	0	0	18	6	1422	620
155–159	256	58	410	45	400	11	214	6	120	2	50	1	10	0	5	0	2	0	16	1	1483	124
150–154	78	4	182	10	243	11	181	2	102	2	30	1	18	0	5	0	2	0	8	0	849	30
145–149	26	1	87	6	100	4	91	5	78	0	33	0	12	0	6	0	0	0	9	0	442	16
140–144	14	1	16	0	48	2	52	1	40	0	26	0	16	0	5	0	1	0	8	0	226	4
135–139	0	0	6	0	14	0	14	0	14	0	13	0	4	0	1	0	0	0	4	0	70	0
130–134	1	0	1	0	1	0	9	0	5	0	4	0	1	0	5	0	1	0	2	0	30	0
125–129	0	0	0	0	0	0	1	0	0	0	2	0	0	0	0	0	0	0	1	0	4	0
120–124	0	0	0	0	0	0	0	0	0	0	1	0	0	0	0	0	0	0	0	0	1	0
Total	802	462	1450	611	1377	284	897	78	515	14	228	5	89	1	36	0	6	0	68	9	5468	1464

Apps = Number of Applicants
Adm = Number Admitted
Reflects 99% of the total applicant pool.

University of California at Los Angeles (UCLA) School of Law

71 Dodd Hall, Box 951445
Los Angeles, CA 90095-1445
Phone: 310.825.2080
E-mail: admissions@law.ucla.edu; Website: www.law.ucla.edu

*ABA
Approved
Since
1950*

The Basics

Type of school	Public
Term	Semester
Application deadline	2/1
Application fee	$75
Financial aid deadline	3/1
Can first year start other than fall?	No
Student to faculty ratio	12.6 to 1
Does the university offer:	
housing restricted to law students?	No
graduate housing for which law students are eligible?	Yes

Faculty and Administrators

	Total		Men		Women		Minorities	
	Fall	Spr	Fall	Spr	Fall	Spr	Fall	Spr
Full-time	62	70	45	53	17	17	9	8
Other Full-time	12	12	6	6	6	6	4	4
Deans, librarians, & others who teach	9	11	3	4	6	7	1	2
Part-time	18	19	13	10	5	9	2	1
Total	101	112	67	73	34	39	16	15

Curriculum

	Full-time	Part-time
Typical first-year section size	80	0
Is there typically a "small section" of the first-year class, other than Legal Writing, taught by full-time faculty	Yes	No
If yes, typical size offered last year	34	
# of classroom course titles beyond first-year curriculum	152	
# of upper division courses, excluding seminars with an enrollment: Under 25	82	
25–49	26	
50–74	13	
75–99	11	
100+	5	
# of seminars	36	
# of seminar positions available	639	
# of seminar positions filled	558	0
# of positions available in simulation courses	84	
# of simulation positions filled	84	0
# of positions available in faculty supervised clinical courses	342	
# of faculty supervised clinical positions filled	303	0
# involved in field placements	42	0
# involved in law journals	461	0
# involved in interschool competitions	21	0
# of credit hours required to graduate	87	

JD Enrollment and Ethnicity

	Men		Women		Full-time		Part-time		1st-year		Total		JD Degs. Awd.
	#	%	#	%	#	%	#	%	#	%	#	%	
African Amer.	16	3.0	20	4.2	36	3.5	0	0.0	14	4.2	36	3.5	17
Amer. Indian	10	1.8	7	1.5	17	1.7	0	0.0	5	1.5	17	1.7	5
Asian Amer.	78	14.4	108	22.6	186	18.3	0	0.0	74	22.0	186	18.3	37
Mex. Amer.	28	5.2	32	6.7	60	5.9	0	0.0	18	5.4	60	5.9	23
Puerto Rican	1	0.2	0	0.0	1	0.1	0	0.0	1	0.3	1	0.1	0
Hispanic	10	1.8	11	2.3	21	2.1	0	0.0	12	3.6	21	2.1	1
Total Minority	143	26.4	178	37.3	321	31.5	0	0.0	124	36.9	321	31.5	83
For. Nation.	6	1.1	4	0.8	10	1.0	0	0.0	3	0.9	10	1.0	4
Caucasian	236	43.5	184	38.6	420	41.2	0	0.0	130	38.7	420	41.2	155
Unknown	157	29.0	111	23.3	268	26.3	0	0.0	79	23.5	268	26.3	73
Total	542	53.2	477	46.8	1019	100.0	0	0.0	336	33.0	1019		315

Transfers

Transfers in	38
Transfers out	3

Tuition and Fees

	Resident	Nonresident
Full-time	$25,457	$36,381
Part-time	$0	$0

Living Expenses

Estimated living expenses for singles

Living on campus	Living off campus	Living at home
N/A	$20,084	$11,646

University of California at Los Angeles (UCLA) School of Law

*ABA
Approved
Since
1950*

GPA and LSAT Scores

	Total	Full-time	Part-time
# of apps	5,834	5,834	0
# of offers	1,105	1,105	0
# of matrics	336	336	0
75% GPA	3.80	3.80	0.00
Median GPA	3.64	3.64	0.00
25% GPA	3.44	3.44	0.00
75% LSAT	169	169	0
Median LSAT	166	166	0
25% LSAT	162	162	0

Grants and Scholarships (from prior year)

	Total		Full-time		Part-time	
	#	%	#	%	#	%
Total # of students	970		970		0	
Total # receiving grants	591	60.9	591	60.9	0	0.0
Less than 1/2 tuition	401	41.3	401	41.3	0	0.0
Half to full tuition	153	15.8	153	15.8	0	0.0
Full tuition	5	0.5	5	0.5	0	0.0
More than full tuition	32	3.3	32	3.3	0	0.0
Median grant amount			$10,364		$0	

Informational and Library Resources

# of volumes and volume equivalents	631,575
# of titles	235,470
# of active serial subscriptions	8,545
Study seating capacity inside the library	774
# of full-time professional librarians	17
Hours per week library is open	97
# of open, wired connections available to students	1,610
# of networked computers available for use by students	171
# of simultaneous wireless users	1,500
Require computer?	No

JD Attrition (from prior year)

	Academic	Other	Total	
	#	#	#	%
1st year	0	9	9	2.8
2nd year	0	0	0	0.0
3rd year	0	0	0	0.0
4th year	0	0	0	0.0

Employment (9 months after graduation)

	Total	Percentage
Employment status known	303	100.0
Employment status unknown	0	0.0
Employed	284	93.7
Pursuing graduate degrees	2	0.7
Unemployed seeking employment	1	0.3
Unemployed not seeking employment	16	5.3
Unemployed and studying for the bar	0	0.0
Type of Employment		
# employed in law firms	193	68.0
# employed in business and industry	24	8.5
# employed in government	18	6.3
# employed in public interest	15	5.3
# employed as judicial clerks	28	9.9
# employed in academia	4	1.4
Geographic Location		
# employed in state	241	84.9
# employed in foreign countries	3	1.1
# of states where employed	19	

Bar Passage Rates

Jurisdiction	California		
Exam	Sum 05	Win 06	Total
# from school taking bar for the first time	266	13	279
School's pass rate for all first-time takers	89%	69%	88%
State's pass rate for all first-time takers	64%	54%	62%

University of California at Los Angeles (UCLA) School of Law

Law Admissions Office, 71 Dodd Hall, Box 951445
Los Angeles, CA 90095-1445
Phone: 310.825.2080
E-mail: admissions@law.ucla.edu; Website: www.law.ucla.edu

■ Introduction

The School of Law is set on the beautiful UCLA campus, located in the foothills of the Santa Monica Mountains. Our location provides ready access to the exciting city of Los Angeles while at the same time offering students a refuge from urban life.

■ Library

The renovated and expanded law library gives UCLA law students a spacious, electronically equipped facility for quiet study and reflection. The UCLA library system is among the top 10 research libraries in the US.

■ Admission

All applicants must have a baccalaureate degree from an accredited university or college of approved standing and must take the LSAT no later than the February administration. Students are admitted for the fall semester only.

Admission is based primarily on proven outstanding academic and intellectual ability measured largely by the LSAT and the quality of undergraduate education as determined by not only the GPA, but also by such factors as the breadth, depth, and rigor of the undergraduate educational program. The Admissions Committee may also consider whether economic, physical, or other hardships and challenges have been overcome. Distinctive programmatic contributions, community or public service, letters of recommendation, work experience, career achievement, language ability, and career goals (with particular attention paid to the likelihood of the applicant representing underrepresented communities) are also factors taken into consideration.

UCLA accepts transfer applications into the second-year class from students with excellent first-year credentials from an ABA-accredited law school. Transfer applications are available online in May and due in early July.

■ Residency

Applicants admitted to the law school as nonresident students (for tuition purposes) are eligible to be considered for resident classification if certain eligibility requirements are met. Most nonresident law students achieve residency status during the second year of law school.

■ Financial Aid

Three types of financial aid are available to students attending UCLA School of Law:

1. Grants and scholarships—Aid that does not have to be repaid; may be used to pay living expenses (includes Need Access grant, scholarships, and fellowships).

2. Federal Work-study—Earned aid. Job opportunities for students wishing to reduce loan indebtedness (includes teaching assistantships and summer work-study).

3. Educational loans—Aid that does have to be repaid (includes federal, private, and bar loans).

The FAFSA must be filed by March 2. The Summary of Financial Resources should be submitted with the law school application, both of which are due on or before February 1.

■ Curriculum

The law school offers a three-year, full-time course of study leading to a Juris Doctor degree. Evening, summer, or part-time programs are not offered. UCLA differs from many other institutions in that it invests major resources in its first-year Lawyering Skills Program. This program combines the beginning of skills training, such as client interviewing and counseling, with traditional legal research and writing.

As a requirement for graduation, each student must complete a Substantial Analytic Writing (SAW) project during the second or third year of law school.

The Clinical Education Program provides extensive and rigorous practical training through simulated and actual client contact. Examples of UCLA's 26 diverse clinical courses offered are the Environmental Law Clinic, Trial Advocacy, Doing Business in China, Sports Law, and Interviewing, Counseling, and Negotiation.

In addition to the JD degree, we offer a one-year Master of Laws (LLM) Program for domestic and foreign students seeking a year of advanced legal studies. Specializations are available in Business Law, Entertainment and Media Law and Policy, International and Comparative Law, and four business-related fields: Bankruptcy, Business Law, Securities Regulation, and Tax. Students may also design their own specializations in a range of fields.

The Doctor of Juridical Science (SJD) is a highly selective degree program designed for those pursuing careers as teachers and scholars of law. Applicants must hold a JD degree or foreign equivalent and an LLM degree (or be enrolled in a program leading to an LLM degree).

■ Special Programs

The Public Interest Law and Policy Program marks a distinct break with the way schools have traditionally trained lawyers for public interest careers. This program, which has a limited enrollment of 25 students, builds on the array of public interest oriented courses, programs, and activities. Participants take a special section of Lawyering Skills and participate in a first-year workshop, advanced seminars, and extracurricular programs.

The Program in Business Law and Policy offers second- and third-year law students a unique program that integrates corporate law, commercial law, and tax law.

The Critical Race Studies Concentration is available to second- and third-year students. This specialization is appropriate for law students who seek advanced study in areas such as race and the law, critical race theory, civil rights, public policy, and other legal practice areas that are likely to involve working with racial minority clients and communities or working to combat inequalities.

The Williams Institute is the nation's first think tank dedicated to the field of sexual orientation law and public policy. The project supports legal scholarship, legal research, policy analysis, and education regarding sexual orientation discrimination and other legal issues that affect lesbian and gay people.

The Entertainment and Media Law and Policy Program provides second- and third-year students with a solid grounding in the law, custom, theory, and policy attendant to the practice of law in the motion picture, television, music, and other industries involved in creative and artistic matters.

The law school also has full-time, semester-long Judicial and Agency Externship Programs. Nonprofit and government agency placements are primarily in Los Angeles, New York, San Francisco, and Washington, DC; judicial externships are with federal judges in Los Angeles.

■ Academic Support

UCLA School of Law is a recognized leader in academic support, providing assistance to students both before matriculation and throughout their law school careers.

■ Joint Degrees

UCLA School of Law offers preapproved programs that lead to a joint Juris Doctor and master's degrees in Afro-American Studies, American Indian Studies, Business Administration, Public Health, Public Policy, Social Welfare, and Urban Planning. In addition to the formal concurrent degree programs listed above, students may design an individually tailored joint-degree program drawing from multiple disciplines in UCLA's vast curriculum.

■ Student Activities

Students edit and publish the *UCLA Law Review, Asian Pacific American Law Journal, Chicano/Latino Law Review, National Black Law Journal, Pacific Basin Law Journal, Entertainment Law Review, Journal of Environmental Law and Policy, Journal of Islamic and Near Eastern Law, Journal of Law and Technology, Dukeminier Awards: Best Sexual Orientation Law Review Articles, Women's Law Journal, Indigenous Peoples' Journal of Law, Culture and Resistance,* and the *Journal of International Law and Foreign Affairs.* Diverse student interests are represented in nearly 40 student

organizations. The Moot Court Honors Program is open to all second-year students and offers a large and effective program of mock appellate advocacy. In addition, there is a very active Student Bar Association.

■ Housing

Many housing options are open to UCLA School of Law students. There are university-owned apartments for single graduate students, single students who are parents, and married students with or without children. Also available for rent are privately owned apartments.

■ Career Services

The Office of Career Services coordinates on-campus interviews and other career fairs with approximately 400 interviewers from law firms, corporations, government agencies, and public interest organizations who visit the school annually.

The office provides private counseling sessions to students and alumni. It also sponsors educational programs and receptions, including an alumni-mentor program, a mock-interview program, a government reception and information fair, a small/midsize law firm reception, a public interest career day, and a law firm diversity reception.

In the Class of 2005, there was a 99.6 percent employment rate nine months after graduation. The average median starting salary was $115,000 ($125,000 for those entering the private sector).

In addition, UCLA Law graduates sitting for the July 2005 bar examination for the first time earned the highest bar passage rate in California with 89 percent passing.

Applicant Profile

University of California at Los Angeles (UCLA) School of Law
This grid includes only applicants who earned 120–180 LSAT scores under standard administrations.

LSAT Score	3.75 + Apps	Adm	3.50–3.74 Apps	Adm	3.25–3.49 Apps	Adm	3.00–3.24 Apps	Adm	2.75–2.99 Apps	Adm	2.50–2.74 Apps	Adm	2.25–2.49 Apps	Adm	2.00–2.24 Apps	Adm	Below 2.00 Apps	Adm	No GPA Apps	Adm	Total Apps	Adm
175–180	30	29	15	15	15	13	6	5	6	1	3	0	1	0	0	0	0	0	1	1	77	64
170–174	140	138	157	151	91	51	26	7	14	0	5	0	2	0	1	0	0	0	1	0	437	347
165–169	371	267	495	201	248	36	145	15	33	1	24	2	7	0	2	0	0	0	11	0	1336	522
160–164	411	35	542	31	342	17	140	4	50	0	29	0	8	0	3	0	1	0	23	1	1549	88
155–159	241	21	349	10	291	12	147	2	61	0	37	0	2	0	3	0	0	0	15	1	1146	46
150–154	83	6	155	13	176	9	102	4	63	0	26	0	15	0	1	0	0	0	9	0	630	32
145–149	29	0	65	0	83	0	75	1	41	0	19	0	9	0	4	0	0	0	8	0	333	1
140–144	10	0	23	0	42	0	46	0	40	0	20	0	5	0	4	0	2	0	7	0	199	0
135–139	2	0	5	0	13	0	10	0	9	0	8	0	3	0	2	0	0	0	1	0	53	0
130–134	0	0	1	0	1	0	3	0	6	0	2	0	0	0	2	0	1	0	0	0	16	0
125–129	0	0	0	0	0	0	0	0	1	0	1	0	0	0	1	0	0	0	0	0	3	0
120–124	0	0	0	0	0	0	0	0	0	0	0	0	1	0	0	0	0	0	1	0	2	0
Total	1317	496	1807	421	1302	138	700	38	324	2	174	2	53	0	23	0	4	0	77	3	5781	1100

Apps = Number of Applicants
Adm = Number Admitted
Reflects 99% of the total applicant pool.

California Western School of Law

225 Cedar Street
San Diego, CA 92101
Phone: 800.255.4252, ext. 1401; Bulletin requests: 619.525.7083; Fax: 619.615.1401
E-mail: admissions@cwsl.edu; Website: www.californiawestern.edu

ABA
Approved
Since
1962

The Basics

Type of school	Private
Term	Semester
Application deadline	4/1 11/1
Application fee	$45
Financial aid deadline	3/16 10/15
Can first year start other than fall?	Yes
Student to faculty ratio	18.3 to 1
Does the university offer:	
housing restricted to law students?	No
graduate housing for which law students are eligible?	No

Faculty and Administrators

	Total		Men		Women		Minorities	
	Fall	Spr	Fall	Spr	Fall	Spr	Fall	Spr
Full-time	37	37	23	23	14	14	8	8
Other Full-time	0	0	0	0	0	0	0	0
Deans, librarians, & others who teach	11	11	4	4	7	7	1	1
Part-time	30	27	14	15	16	12	2	0
Total	**78**	**75**	**41**	**42**	**37**	**33**	**11**	**9**

Curriculum

	Full-time	Part-time
Typical first-year section size	100	0
Is there typically a "small section" of the first-year class, other than Legal Writing, taught by full-time faculty	No	No
If yes, typical size offered last year		
# of classroom course titles beyond first-year curriculum	112	
# of upper division courses, excluding seminars with an enrollment: Under 25	114	
25–49	34	
50–74	13	
75–99	11	
100+	5	
# of seminars	24	
# of seminar positions available	519	
# of seminar positions filled	342	39
# of positions available in simulation courses	1,690	
# of simulation positions filled	1,395	122
# of positions available in faculty supervised clinical courses	134	
# of faculty supervised clinical positions filled	73	10
# involved in field placements	161	17
# involved in law journals	54	3
# involved in interschool competitions	34	4
# of credit hours required to graduate	89	

JD Enrollment and Ethnicity

	Men		Women		Full-time		Part-time		1st-year		Total		JD Degs. Awd.
	#	%	#	%	#	%	#	%	#	%	#	%	
African Amer.	9	2.2	16	3.7	16	2.1	9	10.3	9	2.8	25	3.0	8
Amer. Indian	4	1.0	6	1.4	8	1.1	2	2.3	3	0.9	10	1.2	6
Asian Amer.	50	12.3	56	13.0	102	13.6	4	4.6	43	13.1	106	12.7	30
Mex. Amer.	23	5.7	36	8.4	49	6.6	10	11.5	21	6.4	59	7.1	17
Puerto Rican	1	0.2	1	0.2	2	0.3	0	0.0	1	0.3	2	0.2	1
Hispanic	16	4.0	15	3.5	27	3.6	4	4.6	11	3.4	31	3.7	4
Total Minority	103	25.4	130	30.2	204	27.3	29	33.3	88	26.9	233	27.9	66
For. Nation.	5	1.2	3	0.7	8	1.1	0	0.0	2	0.6	8	1.0	4
Caucasian	231	57.0	247	57.4	434	58.0	44	50.6	193	59.0	478	57.2	198
Unknown	66	16.3	50	11.6	102	13.6	14	16.1	44	13.5	116	13.9	26
Total	405	48.5	430	51.5	748	89.6	87	10.4	327	39.2	835		294

Transfers

Transfers in	5
Transfers out	22

Tuition and Fees

	Resident	Nonresident
Full-time	$32,380	$32,380
Part-time	$22,900	$22,900

Living Expenses

Estimated living expenses for singles

Living on campus	Living off campus	Living at home
N/A	$19,796	$12,786

California Western School of Law

ABA
Approved
Since
1962

GPA and LSAT Scores

	Total	Full-time	Part-time
# of apps	3,100	2,902	198
# of offers	1,418	1,349	69
# of matrics	374	354	20
75% GPA	3.49	3.49	3.62
Median GPA	3.30	3.30	3.43
25% GPA	3.07	3.07	3.04
75% LSAT	156	156	157
Median LSAT	153	153	153
25% LSAT	151	151	150

Grants and Scholarships (from prior year)

	Total		Full-time		Part-time	
	#	%	#	%	#	%
Total # of students	855		745		110	
Total # receiving grants	269	31.5	228	30.6	41	37.3
Less than 1/2 tuition	112	13.1	92	12.3	20	18.2
Half to full tuition	80	9.4	65	8.7	15	13.6
Full tuition	60	7.0	57	7.7	3	2.7
More than full tuition	17	2.0	14	1.9	3	2.7
Median grant amount			$15,250		$10,375	

Informational and Library Resources

# of volumes and volume equivalents	328,714
# of titles	142,420
# of active serial subscriptions	4,079
Study seating capacity inside the library	626
# of full-time professional librarians	9
Hours per week library is open	110
# of open, wired connections available to students	515
# of networked computers available for use by students	83
# of simultaneous wireless users	400
Require computer?	No

JD Attrition (from prior year)

	Academic	Other	Total	
	#	#	#	%
1st year	43	29	72	23.6
2nd year	2	6	8	2.9
3rd year	2	0	2	0.7
4th year	0	0	0	0.0

Employment (9 months after graduation)

	Total	Percentage
Employment status known	313	90.5
Employment status unknown	33	9.5
Employed	265	84.7
Pursuing graduate degrees	7	2.2
Unemployed seeking employment	6	1.9
Unemployed not seeking employment	8	2.6
Unemployed and studying for the bar	27	8.6
Type of Employment		
# employed in law firms	167	63.0
# employed in business and industry	43	16.2
# employed in government	28	10.6
# employed in public interest	13	4.9
# employed as judicial clerks	10	3.8
# employed in academia	4	1.5
Geographic Location		
# employed in state	187	70.6
# employed in foreign countries	1	0.4
# of states where employed	23	

Bar Passage Rates

Jurisdiction	California			Arizona		
Exam	Sum 05	Win 06	Total	Sum 05	Win 06	Total
# from school taking bar for the first time	175	70	245	16	13	29
School's pass rate for all first-time takers	58%	69%	61%	94%	69%	83%
State's pass rate for all first-time takers	64%	54%	62%	71%	71%	71%

California Western School of Law

225 Cedar Street
San Diego, CA 92101
Phone: 800.255.4252, ext. 1401; Bulletin requests: 619.525.7083; Fax: 619.615.1401
E-mail: admissions@cwsl.edu; Website: www.californiawestern.edu

■ Introduction

Chartered in 1924, California Western School of Law is an independent, not-for-profit institution accredited by the ABA (1962) and is a member of the AALS (1967). The downtown San Diego law school complements the traditional curriculum with innovative programs that advance a student's educational experience and capacity to enter the legal profession with superior training.

■ Library and Physical Facilities

The award winning, four-story, 50,000-square-foot law library was dedicated September 11, 2000. The law library is wired with high-speed digital lines for fast network communications. There are 250 data ports for laptop computers in the building. Recently completed extensive renovation of the historic classroom building provides a 74-seat lecture hall, office space for 30 on-campus student organizations, a 1,840-square-foot student lounge, individual study rooms, and a computer lab. Students enjoy additional access to the student network and Internet via campus-wide wireless technology.

■ Curriculum

The trimester academic calendar allows students to study law year-round to complete their legal education in two years. California Western offers a part-time day program. The curriculum offers a broad and diverse selection that includes such contemporary fields as entertainment and sports law, alternative dispute resolution, and environmental law.

Areas of concentration, with curriculum requirements for upper-level students, provide an overview of international law; labor and employment law; child, family, and elder law; criminal prosecution and defense; creative problem-solving; intellectual property, telecommunications, and technology-regulations law; and health law.

■ Dual-degree Program

Students interested in business, social work, history, or political science can apply to the dual-degree program, which permits students to study two disciplines concurrently at California Western and San Diego State University (JD/MBA and JD/MSW) or the University of California, San Diego (JD/PhD in political science or history).

■ University of California, San Diego Affiliation

California Western and the University of California, San Diego, have an Agreement of Association that will provide broad interdisciplinary opportunities for the faculty and students of both institutions. Plans include provisions for new academic programs, joint research efforts, sharing of facilities and involvement of faculty and board members in each other's academic bodies, and community outreach programs. Planned programs in law and medicine draw on the expertise of both institutions.

■ Study-abroad

Students have the opportunity to study abroad and intern at British legal offices. Law in London is a summer program that provides students with a chance to study English and European Union Law and Practice. The program is offered in conjunction with the College of Law of England and Wales—Europe's largest provider of legal training. Students may also participate in the Free Trade Academy program for four weeks during the summer. This program offers an experience in the laws concerning NAFTA and future hemispheric trade. The program coursework utilizes lectures, site visits, and workshops in San Diego, California; and Tijuana and Baja California, Mexico. Students may also spend a summer abroad studying international law in Galway, Ireland; in Prague, Czech Republic; or at the University of Malta. Semester abroad opportunities are available at Victoria University of Wellington in New Zealand, the University of Aarhus in Denmark, and at Leiden University School of Law in the Netherlands.

■ Special Programs

The McGill Center for Creative Problem Solving is a training institute at California Western that provides the community with collaborative approaches to communication, conflict resolution, and problem solving.

Through the California Innocence Project, which is part of the Institute for Criminal Defense Advocacy, law students work alongside practicing criminal defense lawyers to seek the release of wrongfully convicted prisoners. Law students assist in the investigation, write briefs, and advocate for the release of clients. The school also offers an LLM program for foreign law graduates and an LLM in trial advocacy.

■ Clinical Internship Program

California Western's Clinical Internship Program provides opportunities for students to gain practical lawyering experience in law offices, agencies, and courts. Nearly 80 percent of California Western students participate in this popular program. Students have the opportunity to intern in almost any area of law. Some out-of-town internships are available for situations where a similar experience is not available in San Diego. Students have arranged internships at the United Nations, Paramount Studios, the Federal Communications Commission, and abroad, such as in Brazil, Poland, Singapore, Jamaica, and Liechtenstein.

■ Student Activities

The *Law Review* and the *International Law Journal* publish articles by experts in particular fields of work and study as well as by California Western students. Students edit and manage the publications under supervision from faculty advisors. Nearly 30 student organizations reflect a broad range of interests and diversity. Students also participate in advocacy and trial competitions.

California Western School of Law

■ Career Services

Career Services offers individualized, professional advice to students about their personal career goals and tailors strategies to assist students in reaching those goals. The department coordinates the on-campus recruitment program, practice area panel discussions, a national alumni mentor network, the Pro Bono Honors Program, and access to technological resources for career development.

■ Alumni

More than 6,000 California Western alumni work in large firms, domestic and foreign governments, large corporations, private practice, the judiciary, and academia. The law school's Alumni Admissions Recruiter program matches alumni with prospective students in the areas in which they reside. The Admissions Office can provide prospective students with a list of alumni in their area who are available to talk with them.

■ Diversity

California Western's belief is that a richly diversified student body enhances the academic and interpersonal experiences of the law school. Half of the student body is female and approximately one-third is of an ethnic minority. California Western does not discriminate on the basis of race, color, creed, religion, sex, national origin, disability, sexual orientation, or veteran status.

■ Admission

Admission decisions are made on a rolling basis. Applicants are admitted based on an evaluation of the LSAT score, undergraduate academic record, personal statement, letters of recommendation, and other criteria, including work experience, campus and community activities, life/personal experiences, and evidence of leadership promise. Students are admitted to California Western both in August and January. Bachelor's degree and registration with LSDAS are required. Application deadlines: Fall—April 1; Spring—November 1.

■ Financial Aid and Scholarships

More than 85 percent of California Western's students are assisted with their legal education by financial aid programs. Need-based financial aid includes loans and work study. Numerous scholarships are awarded based on academic criteria and LSAT scores. Scholarships include the prestigious Kennedy Scholarship, which, among other benefits, provides full tuition for three years. Other merit-based full and partial scholarships are awarded to incoming students, including diversity, career transition, and creative problem-solving scholarships. Academic achievement scholarships are available to continuing students. Scholarships are awarded by the Admissions Office using your admission application.

Applicant Profile

California Western School of Law

LSAT Score	3.75 + Apps	3.75 + Adm	3.50–3.74 Apps	3.50–3.74 Adm	3.25–3.49 Apps	3.25–3.49 Adm	3.00–3.24 Apps	3.00–3.24 Adm	2.75–2.99 Apps	2.75–2.99 Adm	2.50–2.74 Apps	2.50–2.74 Adm	Below 2.50 Apps	Below 2.50 Adm	No GPA Apps	No GPA Adm	Total Apps	Total Adm
170–180	1	1	0	0	0	0	0	0	0	0	0	0	0	0	0	0	1	1
165–169	7	7	9	8	2	2	7	7	4	4	6	6	2	2	0	0	37	36
160–164	11	11	13	12	22	21	16	15	19	19	18	16	15	14	2	1	116	109
155–159	39	37	67	66	108	104	110	105	86	72	44	34	19	8	3	0	476	426
150–154	52	52	123	120	229	204	207	154	165	60	79	12	53	5	4	4	912	611
145–149	30	19	111	40	154	23	171	15	131	1	73	1	48	1	4	1	722	101
140–144	12	0	33	1	72	0	88	1	71	1	43	0	38	0	4	0	361	3
Below 140	2	0	6	0	12	0	29	0	20	0	28	0	24	0	7	0	128	0
Total	154	127	362	247	599	354	628	297	496	157	291	69	199	30	24	6	2753	1287

Apps = Number of Applicants
Adm = Number Admitted
Applicants with 120–180 LSAT scores earned under standard administrations
Miscellaneous applicants with no LSAT (i.e., MCL/LLM program) and nonstandard administration (not in grid)

Campbell University, Norman Adrian Wiggins School of Law

PO Box 158, 113 Main Street
Buies Creek, NC 27506
Phone: 800.334.4111, ext. 1754; Fax: 910.893.1780
E-mail: admissions@law.campbell.edu; Website: www.law.campbell.edu

The Basics

Type of school	Private
Term	Semester
Application deadline	3/31
Application fee	$50
Financial aid deadline	3/15
Can first year start other than fall?	No
Student to faculty ratio	18.1 to 1
Does the university offer:	
housing restricted to law students?	No
graduate housing for which law students are eligible?	Yes

Faculty and Administrators

	Total		Men		Women		Minorities	
	Fall	Spr	Fall	Spr	Fall	Spr	Fall	Spr
Full-time	15	16	14	14	1	2	1	0
Other Full-time	3	2	2	2	1	0	0	0
Deans, librarians, & others who teach	5	5	2	3	3	2	0	0
Part-time	7	10	6	9	1	1	0	1
Total	30	33	24	28	6	5	1	1

Curriculum

	Full-time	Part-time
Typical first-year section size	80	0
Is there typically a "small section" of the first-year class, other than Legal Writing, taught by full-time faculty	Yes	No
If yes, typical size offered last year	40	
# of classroom course titles beyond first-year curriculum	70	
# of upper division courses, excluding seminars with an enrollment: Under 25	31	
25–49	15	
50–74	8	
75–99	8	
100+	1	
# of seminars	13	
# of seminar positions available	351	
# of seminar positions filled	236	0
# of positions available in simulation courses	113	
# of simulation positions filled	113	0
# of positions available in faculty supervised clinical courses	12	
# of faculty supervised clinical positions filled	8	0
# involved in field placements	45	0
# involved in law journals	46	0
# involved in interschool competitions	48	0
# of credit hours required to graduate	90	

JD Enrollment and Ethnicity

	Men		Women		Full-time		Part-time		1st-year		Total		JD Degs. Awd.
	#	%	#	%	#	%	#	%	#	%	#	%	
African Amer.	1	0.6	6	3.7	7	2.0	0	0.0	1	0.8	7	2.0	1
Amer. Indian	2	1.1	3	1.8	5	1.5	0	0.0	0	0.0	5	1.5	0
Asian Amer.	3	1.7	4	2.4	7	2.0	0	0.0	1	0.8	7	2.0	1
Mex. Amer.	0	0.0	0	0.0	0	0.0	0	0.0	0	0.0	0	0.0	0
Puerto Rican	0	0.0	0	0.0	0	0.0	0	0.0	0	0.0	0	0.0	0
Hispanic	3	1.7	3	1.8	6	1.8	0	0.0	2	1.6	6	1.8	3
Total Minority	9	5.1	16	9.8	25	7.3	0	0.0	4	3.2	25	7.3	5
For. Nation.	0	0.0	0	0.0	0	0.0	0	0.0	0	0.0	0	0.0	0
Caucasian	169	94.9	147	89.6	316	92.4	0	0.0	120	96.0	316	92.4	91
Unknown	0	0.0	1	0.6	1	0.3	0	0.0	1	0.8	1	0.3	3
Total	178	52.0	164	48.0	342	100.0	0	0.0	125	36.5	342		99

Transfers

Transfers in	2
Transfers out	1

Tuition and Fees

	Resident	Nonresident
Full-time	$24,941	$24,941
Part-time	$0	$0

Living Expenses

Estimated living expenses for singles

Living on campus	Living off campus	Living at home
$10,749	$13,063	N/A

Campbell University, Norman Adrian Wiggins School of Law

*ABA
Approved
Since
1979*

GPA and LSAT Scores

	Total	Full-time	Part-time
# of apps	1,032	1,032	0
# of offers	272	272	0
# of matrics	122	122	0
75% GPA	3.54	3.54	0.00
Median GPA	3.19	3.19	0.00
25% GPA	3.04	3.04	0.00
75% LSAT	157	157	0
Median LSAT	155	155	0
25% LSAT	152	152	0

Grants and Scholarships (from prior year)

	Total		Full-time		Part-time	
	#	%	#	%	#	%
Total # of students	340		340		0	
Total # receiving grants	166	48.8	166	48.8	0	0.0
Less than 1/2 tuition	147	43.2	147	43.2	0	0.0
Half to full tuition	16	4.7	16	4.7	0	0.0
Full tuition	3	0.9	3	0.9	0	0.0
More than full tuition	0	0.0	0	0.0	0	0.0
Median grant amount			$5,000		$0	

Informational and Library Resources

# of volumes and volume equivalents	184,112
# of titles	24,474
# of active serial subscriptions	2,665
Study seating capacity inside the library	429
# of full-time professional librarians	9
Hours per week library is open	98
# of open, wired connections available to students	165
# of networked computers available for use by students	58
# of simultaneous wireless users	350
Require computer?	No

JD Attrition (from prior year)

	Academic	Other	Total	
	#	#	#	%
1st year	11	0	11	9.2
2nd year	7	1	8	6.7
3rd year	0	0	0	0.0
4th year	0	0	0	0.0

Employment (9 months after graduation)

	Total	Percentage
Employment status known	115	100.0
Employment status unknown	0	0.0
Employed	106	92.2
Pursuing graduate degrees	1	0.9
Unemployed seeking employment	1	0.9
Unemployed not seeking employment	0	0.0
Unemployed and studying for the bar	7	6.1

Type of Employment

# employed in law firms	83	78.3
# employed in business and industry	2	1.9
# employed in government	8	7.5
# employed in public interest	3	2.8
# employed as judicial clerks	10	9.4
# employed in academia	0	0.0

Geographic Location

# employed in state	97	91.5
# employed in foreign countries	0	0.0
# of states where employed	6	

Bar Passage Rates

Jurisdiction	North Carolina		
Exam	Sum 05	Win 06	Total
# from school taking bar for the first time	98	4	102
School's pass rate for all first-time takers	90%	50%	88%
State's pass rate for all first-time takers	72%	69%	71%

Campbell University, Norman Adrian Wiggins School of Law

PO Box 158, 113 Main Street
Buies Creek, NC 27506
Phone: 800.334.4111, ext. 1754; Fax: 910.893.1780
E-mail: admissions@law.campbell.edu; Website: www.law.campbell.edu

■ Introduction

Campbell University School of Law is a private law school that is fully accredited by the American Bar Association and is located on the campus of Campbell University, the second largest Baptist university in the country, in Buies Creek, North Carolina.

Campbell Law School is a highly demanding, purposely small, intensely personal community of faculty and students whose aim, guided by transcendent values, is to develop lawyers who possess moral conviction, social compassion, and professional competence and who view the practice of law as a calling to serve others and to create a more just society.

Buies Creek is a small university village that offers very moderate living costs. In addition to its close proximity to Raleigh, the state capital, the law school is within commuting distance of the Research Triangle Park, the Raleigh-Durham International Airport, and Fayetteville, North Carolina. The law school is located a few hours from legendary beaches in one direction and the scenic Blue Ridge Mountains in the other.

■ Enrollment

Campbell Law School purposely limits enrollment to an entering class of approximately 120 students each fall. Students come from 17 different states and hold degrees from 99 colleges and universities. The School of Law is committed to enrolling a diverse student body.

■ Faculty

Campbell Law School's faculty is a community of scholars who make teaching their priority and are readily accessible to students. They are mentors, coaches, and professional role models for the students. All faculty members have open-door office policies and consult regularly with students one-on-one. Our professors are deeply committed to the search for knowledge through meaningful legal scholarship, but never at the expense of their devotion to the academic success and professional development of each student.

■ Facilities and Technology

Housed in Wiggins Hall and Kivett Hall, Campbell Law School contains the law library, classrooms, and courtrooms, featuring the latest in electronic instructional equipment, faculty and administrative offices, a student commons and lounge area, and offices for various student organizations.

The library contains individual study carrels, reading tables, casual seating, conference rooms, and computer labs that provide students with a variety of study and research options. A wireless network is available throughout the entire law school.

■ Curriculum

The curriculum is rigorous and designed to produce competent attorneys ready to practice in any state.

Combining the theoretical with the practical, a majority of the total hours of study consists of required courses, providing our students extensive knowledge and exceptional professional skills. For the past 15 years, Campbell Law School graduates have had the highest average overall bar passage rate among North Carolina law schools. On the July 2006 North Carolina bar exam, Campbell graduates achieved a 97 percent success rate, the highest among North Carolina law schools. Campbell graduates who took the July 2006 bar exam in other states enjoyed a 100 percent passage rate.

■ Special Programs

The Juvenile Justice Project provides students the opportunity to mediate disputes involving criminal juvenile offenders. Instead of prosecuting the juvenile in the traditional court system, this project allows the juvenile and his or her victim to meet together in a mediation setting, affording the juvenile the ability to acknowledge his or her crime and express remorse. Our students play a critical role in preventing the juvenile from becoming a repeat offender by giving the juvenile the opportunity to take responsibility for and become accountable to the victim for his or her actions.

Prisoner Assistance and Legal Services (PALS) provides our students with the opportunity to serve older prisoners by addressing the unique problems of aging in prison. Our students offer legal and nonlegal assistance to prisoners incarcerated in North Carolina. Students work under the direction and supervision of attorneys at North Carolina Prison Legal Services.

Externship Programs—Students may receive up to two hours of academic credit through externship placements with numerous opportunities, including offices of state and federal prosecutors, appellate courts, and the state legislature, among others.

Korean Cooperative Summer Program is a cooperative program with Handong International Law School, which allows Campbell students to receive academic credit by attending summer school in South Korea.

Trial Advocacy Program—In a national survey of law schools, Campbell Law School's trial advocacy program has been called one of the most rigorous in the nation. Every second-year student is required to plan and participate in a mock trial. Graduates are exceptionally well-prepared to advocate for their clients, whether in the boardroom or the courtroom.

Joint-degree Programs—Campbell Law School offers joint Juris Doctor/Master of Business Administration degrees and has pioneered the joint Juris Doctor/Master of Trust Investment Management degrees, the only program of its kind in the country.

■ Student Publications and Organizations

Campbell Law School's size allows its students outstanding opportunities to participate in cocurricular activities, including: contributing to the *Campbell Law Observer*, a legal newspaper distributed to lawyers in North Carolina; serving as editors and staff members of the *Campbell Law Review*; and participating in regional and national trial and moot court advocacy competitions.

Every student is a member of the Student Bar Association. Students are also active in a variety of other organizations, including the ABA Law Student Division, the Black Law Students Association, the Christian Legal Society, Women in

Law, and two law fraternities. Campbell Law School is the official international headquarters for the Delta Theta Phi Law Fraternity.

A Christian Perspective on Law and Justice

Campbell Law School encourages students to examine the relationship between spiritual and legal issues, to explore the theological foundations for law, to think differently about justice and the legal system, and to consider how we can help achieve a more just and merciful society.

While the Campbell Law School embraces an intellectual perspective rooted in Christian tradition, it is committed to free and open discussion of ideas and students are under no obligation to embrace any particular way of thinking.

Admission

Campbell Law School's Admissions Committee considers each application individually. Factors considered include the applicant's GPA; LSAT score; work experience; participation and leadership in cocurricular, civic, or volunteer activities; character; work ethic; and maturity.

Summer Performance-based Admission Program

Select students who are not offered regular admission in the fall class may be invited to participate in the Summer Performance-based Admission Program. Each summer, between 50 and 75 applicants are admitted to this program and attend a seven-week session. Admission to the fall class is offered to those students who perform satisfactorily in both courses. Historically, 20–30 percent of the applicants gain admission to the fall class.

Expenses and Financial Aid

The cost of living in Buies Creek is low by national standards. Approximately 35 percent of students receive scholarship assistance. Approximately 95 percent of students receive financial aid.

Housing and Recreational Facilities

Private housing and apartments are available in Buies Creek and surrounding towns. Law students are welcome to enjoy the recreational facilities available to the university community, including Keith Hills Country Club, home of two of North Carolina's best golf courses; Nisbet Tennis Center; Carter Gymnasium, the center for basketball, weight training, and volleyball; Johnson Memorial Natatorium, offering year-round indoor swimming; the university track facility; and concerts, movies, and theatrical productions on the university campus. A 109,000-square-foot convocation center housing a 3,000-seat basketball arena and a 5,000-square-foot fitness center is anticipated for completion in the fall of 2008.

Career Services

The Career Services Office provides individualized attention to students seeking summer and permanent positions. A large number of employers interview students on campus each year or request that résumés be forwarded by the Career Services Office. Campbell graduates historically have enjoyed a placement rate that exceeds 91 percent nine months after graduation. Graduates practice in large and small firms, government agencies, and corporations across the nation and in numerous foreign countries.

Applicant Profile

Campbell University, Norman Adrian Wiggins School of Law
This grid includes only applicants who earned 120–180 LSAT scores under standard administrations.

LSAT Score	GPA 3.75 +		3.50–3.74		3.25–3.49		3.00–3.24		2.75–2.99		2.50–2.74		2.25–2.49		2.00–2.24		Below 2.00		No GPA		Total	
	Apps	Adm	Apps	Adm	Apps	Adm	Apps	Adm	Apps	Adm	Apps	Adm	Apps	Adm	Apps	Adm	Apps	Adm	Apps	Adm	Apps	Adm
175–180	0	0	0	0	0	0	0	0	0	0	0	0	0	0	0	0	0	0	0	0	0	0
170–174	0	0	0	0	0	0	0	0	0	0	0	0	0	0	0	0	0	0	0	0	0	0
165–169	2	1	2	2	0	0	0	0	3	1	1	1	0	0	0	0	0	0	0	0	8	5
160–164	5	3	8	5	9	6	13	9	8	5	5	3	3	1	2	1	0	0	0	0	53	33
155–159	23	18	32	17	34	25	45	38	18	9	11	6	6	2	3	0	0	0	1	1	173	116
150–154	26	15	53	23	66	28	58	21	44	12	20	3	11	0	6	0	1	0	2	2	287	104
145–149	19	3	37	4	40	4	53	6	41	3	26	3	16	1	10	0	0	0	0	0	242	24
140–144	10	1	16	0	24	0	25	1	38	0	24	0	13	0	7	0	1	0	2	0	160	2
135–139	4	0	6	0	8	0	13	0	18	0	8	0	9	0	4	0	1	0	2	0	73	0
130–134	1	0	2	0	0	0	4	0	3	0	0	0	1	0	1	0	1	0	0	0	13	0
125–129	0	0	1	0	0	0	1	0	0	0	0	0	0	0	0	0	0	0	1	0	3	0
120–124	0	0	0	0	0	0	0	0	0	0	0	0	0	0	0	0	0	0	0	0	0	0
Total	90	41	157	51	181	63	212	75	173	30	95	16	59	4	33	1	4	0	8	3	1012	284

Apps = Number of Applicants   Adm = Number Admitted   Reflects 99% of the fall applicant pool.

Note: The admissions in the grid above include individuals who gain admission through the summer PBAP program.

Capital University Law School

303 E. Broad Street
Columbus, OH 43215-3200
Phone: 614.236.6310; Fax: 614.236.6972
E-mail: admissions@law.capital.edu; Website: www.law.capital.edu

ABA Approved Since 1950

The Basics

Type of school	Private
Term	Semester
Application deadline	5/1
Application fee	$40
Financial aid deadline	4/1
Can first year start other than fall?	No
Student to faculty ratio	15.7 to 1
Does the university offer:	
housing restricted to law students?	No
graduate housing for which law students are eligible?	No

Faculty and Administrators

	Total		Men		Women		Minorities	
	Fall	Spr	Fall	Spr	Fall	Spr	Fall	Spr
Full-time	32	32	19	17	13	15	3	3
Other Full-time	2	3	0	0	2	3	1	1
Deans, librarians, & others who teach	7	7	5	5	2	2	2	2
Part-time	38	38	32	34	6	4	2	4
Total	**79**	**80**	**56**	**56**	**23**	**24**	**8**	**10**

Curriculum

	Full-time	Part-time
Typical first-year section size	78	76
Is there typically a "small section" of the first-year class, other than Legal Writing, taught by full-time faculty	Yes	Yes
If yes, typical size offered last year	37	38
# of classroom course titles beyond first-year curriculum		145
# of upper division courses, excluding seminars with an enrollment: Under 25		114
25–49		36
50–74		12
75–99		12
100+		0
# of seminars		11
# of seminar positions available		165
# of seminar positions filled	94	48
# of positions available in simulation courses	754	
# of simulation positions filled	424	163
# of positions available in faculty supervised clinical courses		64
# of faculty supervised clinical positions filled	42	16
# involved in field placements	102	29
# involved in law journals	30	15
# involved in interschool competitions	19	4
# of credit hours required to graduate		89

Transfers

Transfers in	3
Transfers out	10

JD Enrollment and Ethnicity

	Men		Women		Full-time		Part-time		1st-year		Total		JD Degs. Awd.
	#	%	#	%	#	%	#	%	#	%	#	%	
African Amer.	22	5.7	27	8.8	37	7.9	12	5.3	26	10.7	49	7.1	15
Amer. Indian	1	0.3	0	0.0	1	0.2	0	0.0	0	0.0	1	0.1	0
Asian Amer.	9	2.3	5	1.6	6	1.3	8	3.6	4	1.6	14	2.0	4
Mex. Amer.	0	0.0	0	0.0	0	0.0	0	0.0	0	0.0	0	0.0	0
Puerto Rican	0	0.0	0	0.0	0	0.0	0	0.0	0	0.0	0	0.0	0
Hispanic	4	1.0	7	2.3	10	2.1	1	0.4	4	1.6	11	1.6	2
Total Minority	36	9.3	39	12.7	54	11.5	21	9.3	34	14.0	75	10.8	21
For. Nation.	1	0.3	1	0.3	1	0.2	1	0.4	0	0.0	2	0.3	2
Caucasian	307	78.9	239	78.1	365	77.7	181	80.4	185	76.1	546	78.6	171
Unknown	45	11.6	27	8.8	50	10.6	22	9.8	26	10.7	72	10.4	7
Total	389	56.0	306	44.0	470	67.6	225	32.4	243	35.0	695		201

Tuition and Fees

	Resident	Nonresident
Full-time	$26,680	$26,680
Part-time	$16,560	$16,560

Living Expenses

Estimated living expenses for singles

Living on campus	Living off campus	Living at home
$10,580	$10,580	$10,580

Capital University Law School

*ABA
Approved
Since
1950*

GPA and LSAT Scores

	Total	Full-time	Part-time
# of apps	1,516	1,279	237
# of offers	671	549	122
# of matrics	248	181	67
75% GPA	3.51	3.54	3.38
Median GPA	3.23	3.28	3.11
25% GPA	2.94	2.99	2.82
75% LSAT	156	155	156
Median LSAT	153	153	153
25% LSAT	151	151	151

Grants and Scholarships (from prior year)

	Total		Full-time		Part-time	
	#	%	#	%	#	%
Total # of students	730		457		273	
Total # receiving grants	386	52.9	296	64.8	90	33.0
Less than 1/2 tuition	309	42.3	226	49.5	83	30.4
Half to full tuition	77	10.5	70	15.3	7	2.6
Full tuition	0	0.0	0	0.0	0	0.0
More than full tuition	0	0.0	0	0.0	0	0.0
Median grant amount			$10,000		$3,000	

Informational and Library Resources

# of volumes and volume equivalents	271,447
# of titles	49,785
# of active serial subscriptions	2,568
Study seating capacity inside the library	460
# of full-time professional librarians	6
Hours per week library is open	92
# of open, wired connections available to students	692
# of networked computers available for use by students	72
# of simultaneous wireless users	275
Require computer?	No

JD Attrition (from prior year)

	Academic	Other	Total	
	#	#	#	%
1st year	15	43	58	22.8
2nd year	3	11	14	6.4
3rd year	1	3	4	2.2
4th year	0	0	0	0.0

Employment (9 months after graduation)

	Total	Percentage
Employment status known	201	85.5
Employment status unknown	34	14.5
Employed	170	84.6
Pursuing graduate degrees	2	1.0
Unemployed seeking employment	5	2.5
Unemployed not seeking employment	3	1.5
Unemployed and studying for the bar	21	10.4
Type of Employment		
# employed in law firms	69	40.6
# employed in business and industry	38	22.4
# employed in government	39	22.9
# employed in public interest	15	8.8
# employed as judicial clerks	6	3.5
# employed in academia	3	1.8
Geographic Location		
# employed in state	154	90.6
# employed in foreign countries	0	0.0
# of states where employed		11

Bar Passage Rates

Jurisdiction		Ohio	
Exam	Sum 05	Win 06	Total
# from school taking bar for the first time	181	31	212
School's pass rate for all first-time takers	79%	81%	79%
State's pass rate for all first-time takers	81%	76%	81%

Capital University Law School

303 E. Broad Street
Columbus, OH 43215-3200
Phone: 614.236.6310; Fax: 614.236.6972
E-mail: admissions@law.capital.edu; Website: www.law.capital.edu

■ Introduction

Capital University Law School, located in downtown Columbus, is in the heart of Ohio's legal community. Columbus is home to the Ohio Supreme Court, the state legislature, and numerous state agencies, including the Ohio Attorney General's Office. In addition, a federal district court, the Ohio Court of Appeals, and various trial courts are within a short walk of the Law School. Our location provides a wealth of learning opportunities through clinical and externship programs, and our facility affords Capital University law students a state-of-the-art law school that is second to none.

For more than a century, Capital University Law School has produced some of the region's finest lawyers, judges, and business professionals. We invite you to take a closer look at the factors that distinguish this law school: an excellent teaching faculty, an ideal location, high placement rates, innovative institutes and programs, distinguished alumni, and reasonable tuition.

■ Curriculum

The school's primary mission is to provide both day- and evening-division students with an excellent educational experience that combines competency-based legal education with a commitment to service and leadership. Capital combines a theoretical education with a program that emphasizes the skills and values necessary to practice in the twenty-first century and combines the best of a traditional legal education with innovative programs. Our professors are accomplished scholars whose first and foremost duty is teaching. For further details and specific course offerings, visit our website at *www.law.capital.edu*.

■ Multicultural Affairs

Capital University Law School takes pride in its history of providing a legal education for groups who historically have been excluded from or underrepresented in law schools. Capital University Law School is committed to racial and cultural diversity and beyond. The Law School supports and embraces diversity in all of its varying forms. The Law School actively recruits students who are African American, Asian, Hispanic, Native American, and students who identify as gay, lesbian, bisexual, or transgender.

Students come to Capital with diverse educational, cultural, social, and professional backgrounds. Capital University Law School embraces and values the varied perspectives that our students bring to the school. These multiple perspectives allow students to share their varied life experiences in the classroom and help to enrich the experience of everyone in the Law School.

Capital has many programs and benefits that support and aid in the retention of students of color—the presence of minority faculty, a director of multicultural affairs, availability of financial aid, academic as well as nonacademic support, and participation in the Columbus Bar Association Minority Clerkship Program are some of the things available to our students. In addition to the services at the Law School, the Columbus community also presents a diverse and supportive community for our law students to explore.

■ Special Programs

Diversity of opportunity is a trademark of Capital University Law. Capital offers certificate programs to students who wish to develop their skills and knowledge in an area of particular interest.

Capital's **Governmental Affairs** concentration allows students to participate in externships with local, state, and federal courts and governmental agencies, and to conduct extensive research in the area of governmental affairs.

The **Labor and Employment Law** concentration is designed for law students who have an interest in studying laws and regulations governing the workplace.

The **Small Business Entities and Publicly Held Companies** concentrations give interested students an opportunity to focus part of their legal education on exploring the many legal issues and policies affecting business entities.

The **Dispute Resolution** concentration prepares students to understand the full spectrum of settlement processes. Capital's concentration in **Environmental Law** prepares students for employment in the field of environmental law and policy.

The **Children and Family Law** concentration provides students an in-depth understanding of the legal rights and obligations of parents, children, and family units. Innovative programs give students an opportunity to explore various specialties within the legal profession, to improve their skills, and to provide a valuable service to the community.

The Center for Dispute Resolution is a multifaceted resource for the teaching, development, and implementation of various dispute resolution methods.

The National Center for Adoption Law and Policy at Capital, the first resource of its kind in the nation, creates programs and promotes activities focusing on all aspects of family law dealing with adoption. Adoption Law Fellowships are available to outstanding incoming first-year Capital University Law School students who are interested in pursuing a career in child welfare or adoption law upon graduation. Fellows are offered an extraordinary array of benefits in exchange for a commitment to spend at least the first two years of their careers working in this area of law.

The Tobacco Public Policy Center at Capital University Law School is a new legal resource center for the Ohio tobacco control community and for government entities trying to reduce smoking and tobacco use in their communities. The center is funded by a generous grant from the Ohio Tobacco Prevention Foundation.

The Family Advocacy Clinic provides students with the opportunity to represent victims of domestic violence in court.

Capital offers the following joint-degree programs: **JD/Master of Sports Administration**, **JD/Master of Business Administration**, **JD/Master of Science in Nursing**, **JD/LLM in Taxation**, **JD/LLM in Business**, and **JD/Master of Theological Studies**. Participation in these dual-degree programs allows students to earn both degrees in less time than pursuing them separately.

■ Admission

The Law School seeks applicants who rank in the upper-half of their undergraduate class and achieve an LSAT score above the

60th percentile. Other factors used in evaluation include the competitiveness and difficulty of the candidate's undergraduate school and course of study, letters of recommendation, graduate coursework, employment history, writing ability, leadership experience, and general background.

■ Student Activities

Extra- and cocurricular activities range from over 30 student groups and at least 10 competition teams to the *Capital University Law Review*. Clubs are educational, professional, and social while encouraging the legal community's collaboration and engagement. Student organizations at Capital Law School offer many opportunities for leadership development, networking, and interaction with professionals in various specialties.

The Law School supports associations for African American, Hispanic, Asian, Jewish, Christian, women, and gay, lesbian, bisexual, and transgender students in order to bring together individuals with similar backgrounds and interests. Additionally, there are organizations for those considering pursuing specific areas of practice such as sports and entertainment law, intellectual property, and public interest.

The *Capital University Law Review* provides the legal community with scholarly analysis of contemporary legal issues. Students may expand their writing and editing skills through membership on the *Law Review* and our student newspaper, *Res Ipsa Loquitur*. Those wishing to hone their skills

and test them in competition will want to investigate Capital's highly successful moot court teams. Students may participate in national competitions, such as the Philip C. Jessup International Law and the Frederick Douglass Moot Court competitions. Teams are also selected in the areas of environmental law, sports law, labor law, and tax.

■ Career Services

Capital Law's Career Services Office provides counseling and information so individuals can explore legal career options. It also serves as a resource to help students assess their skills and plan a productive job-search strategy. The office is responsible for developing an on-campus interview program that last year brought over 60 firms, companies, and organizations from different geographical locations to campus to interview for internships, clerkships, and full-time positions. Capital graduates have had great success seeking employment after graduation. More than 97 percent of the 2005 graduating class was employed within nine months of graduation.

Capital Law School graduates are employed in a variety of different fields of law. Private practice is the largest of these areas, with approximately 42 percent of the graduating class entering this field. Many Capital graduates also enter the corporate sector (22 percent) or government work (23 percent). Other fields that graduates have entered are judicial clerkships, public interest, and academia.

Applicant Profile

Capital University Law School

LSAT Score	GPA								
	3.75 +	3.50–3.74	3.25–3.49	3.00–3.24	2.75–2.99	2.50–2.74	2.25–2.49	2.00–2.24	Below 2.00
175–180									
170–174									
165–169									
160–164									
155–159									
150–154									
145–149									
140–144									
135–139									
130–134									
125–129									
120–124									

■ Very Likely □ Possible ▨ Unlikely

Benjamin N. Cardozo School of Law, Yeshiva University

55 Fifth Avenue
New York, NY 10003
Phone: 212.790.0274; Fax: 212.790.0482
E-mail: lawinfo@yu.edu; Website: www.cardozo.yu.edu/

*ABA
Approved
Since
1978*

The Basics

Type of school	Private
Term	Semester
Application deadline	4/1 12/1
Application fee	$65
Financial aid deadline	4/15 12/1
Can first year start other than fall?	Yes
Student to faculty ratio	17.8 to 1
Does the university offer:	
housing restricted to law students?	Yes
graduate housing for which law students are eligible?	No

Faculty and Administrators

	Total		Men		Women		Minorities	
	Fall	Spr	Fall	Spr	Fall	Spr	Fall	Spr
Full-time	50	50	33	33	17	17	3	3
Other Full-time	1	1	1	1	0	0	0	0
Deans, librarians, & others who teach	4	4	2	2	2	2	0	0
Part-time	64	75	49	55	15	20	3	3
Total	**119**	**130**	**85**	**91**	**34**	**39**	**6**	**6**

Curriculum

	Full-time	Part-time
Typical first-year section size	48	0
Is there typically a "small section" of the first-year class, other than Legal Writing, taught by full-time faculty	No	No
If yes, typical size offered last year		
# of classroom course titles beyond first-year curriculum	130	

# of upper division courses, excluding seminars with an enrollment:		
Under 25	21	
25–49	44	
50–74	18	
75–99	10	
100+	16	

	Full-time	Part-time
# of seminars	41	
# of seminar positions available	778	
# of seminar positions filled	592	0
# of positions available in simulation courses	479	
# of simulation positions filled	404	0
# of positions available in faculty supervised clinical courses	110	
# of faculty supervised clinical positions filled	102	0
# involved in field placements	187	0
# involved in law journals	254	0
# involved in interschool competitions	65	0
# of credit hours required to graduate	84	

JD Enrollment and Ethnicity

	Men		Women		Full-time		Part-time		1st-year		Total		JD Degs. Awd.
	#	%	#	%	#	%	#	%	#	%	#	%	
African Amer.	13	2.5	26	5.1	37	3.9	2	2.4	14	4.2	39	3.8	12
Amer. Indian	0	0.0	3	0.6	3	0.3	0	0.0	1	0.3	3	0.3	1
Asian Amer.	49	9.4	60	11.7	102	10.7	7	8.3	34	10.2	109	10.5	31
Mex. Amer.	8	1.5	7	1.4	15	1.6	0	0.0	1	0.3	15	1.4	1
Puerto Rican	4	0.8	6	1.2	8	0.8	2	2.4	5	1.5	10	1.0	6
Hispanic	22	4.2	17	3.3	38	4.0	1	1.2	11	3.3	39	3.8	21
Total Minority	96	18.3	119	23.2	203	21.3	12	14.3	66	19.9	215	20.8	72
For. Nation.	12	2.3	15	2.9	25	2.6	2	2.4	11	3.3	27	2.6	7
Caucasian	416	79.4	378	73.8	724	76.1	70	83.3	255	76.8	794	76.6	283
Unknown	0	0.0	0	0.0	0	0.0	0	0.0	0	0.0	0	0.0	0
Total	524	50.6	512	49.4	952	91.9	84	8.1	332	32.0	1036		362

Transfers

Transfers in	45
Transfers out	16

Tuition and Fees

	Resident	Nonresident
Full-time	$37,270	$37,270
Part-time	$37,270	$37,270

Living Expenses

Estimated living expenses for singles

Living on campus	Living off campus	Living at home
$23,700	$23,700	$9,150

Benjamin N. Cardozo School of Law, Yeshiva University

ABA Approved Since 1978

GPA and LSAT Scores

	Total	Full-time	Part-time
# of apps	4,785	4,411	374
# of offers	1,369	1,226	143
# of matrics	351	268	83
75% GPA	3.72	3.72	3.71
Median GPA	3.55	3.55	3.55
25% GPA	3.25	3.23	3.27
75% LSAT	165	166	161
Median LSAT	161	163	159
25% LSAT	159	161	157

Grants and Scholarships (from prior year)

	Total #	Total %	Full-time #	Full-time %	Part-time #	Part-time %
Total # of students	1,046		931		115	
Total # receiving grants	660	63.1	646	69.4	14	12.2
Less than 1/2 tuition	459	43.9	447	48.0	12	10.4
Half to full tuition	178	17.0	176	18.9	2	1.7
Full tuition	16	1.5	16	1.7	0	0.0
More than full tuition	7	0.7	7	0.8	0	0.0
Median grant amount			$10,000		$4,000	

Informational and Library Resources

# of volumes and volume equivalents	530,698
# of titles	98,751
# of active serial subscriptions	6,407
Study seating capacity inside the library	483
# of full-time professional librarians	8
Hours per week library is open	88
# of open, wired connections available to students	104
# of networked computers available for use by students	140
# of simultaneous wireless users	683
Require computer?	No

JD Attrition (from prior year)

	Academic #	Other #	Total #	Total %
1st year	2	28	30	9.2
2nd year	0	3	3	0.8
3rd year	0	0	0	0.0
4th year	0	0	0	0.0

Employment (9 months after graduation)

	Total	Percentage
Employment status known	364	98.9
Employment status unknown	4	1.1
Employed	336	92.3
Pursuing graduate degrees	6	1.6
Unemployed seeking employment	3	0.8
Unemployed not seeking employment	19	5.2
Unemployed and studying for the bar	0	0.0

Type of Employment

# employed in law firms	202	60.1
# employed in business and industry	60	17.9
# employed in government	39	11.6
# employed in public interest	14	4.2
# employed as judicial clerks	14	4.2
# employed in academia	7	2.1

Geographic Location

# employed in state	279	83.0
# employed in foreign countries	1	0.3
# of states where employed	14	

Bar Passage Rates

Jurisdiction	New York		
Exam	Sum 05	Win 06	Total
# from school taking bar for the first time	292	23	315
School's pass rate for all first-time takers	86%	70%	84%
State's pass rate for all first-time takers	76%	61%	74%

Benjamin N. Cardozo School of Law, Yeshiva University

55 Fifth Avenue
New York, NY 10003
Phone: 212.790.0274; Fax: 212.790.0482
E-mail: lawinfo@yu.edu; Website: www.cardozo.yu.edu/

■ Introduction

Benjamin N. Cardozo School of Law offers students a stimulating and supportive educational experience. Its curriculum combines practical training in basic skills and legal doctrine, sophisticated study of recent developments in legal theory, and interdisciplinary approaches to the study of law. Courses provide depth and breadth in all the standard subjects of legal study, as well as many more specialized ones, including intellectual property law and alternative dispute resolution. Extensive clinical and externship opportunities allow students to gain practical lawyering experience while performing important community service. A Cardozo education emphasizes ethics and the pursuit of intellectual excellence.

■ Faculty

Professors at Cardozo are vibrant, intellectually curious, accessible to students, and committed to the twin goals of teaching and scholarship. They are an interdisciplinary faculty, curious and serious about how the law relates to other expressions of the human spirit such as philosophy, literature, economics, politics, and history. More than half hold advanced degrees in addition to a law degree; about a dozen hold PhDs as well. The faculty is prolific, writing on both visionary and practical subjects; many of their publications are required reading in law schools across the nation.

■ A Campus in New York City

Cardozo is in an elegant residential neighborhood in the heart of Greenwich Village. It is easily accessible to all points in New York City, including the courts, Wall Street, Midtown, and the art and music centers on the East and West Sides of Manhattan. The law school recently completed a $50 million renovation and expansion of its facilities, including a new moot courtroom, additional library space, the center for student life, a new lobby, student offices, faculty offices, and state-of-the-art classrooms and seminar rooms.

The Cardozo residence hall is located on a residential, tree-lined street just one block south of the main building. A limited number of studio and one-bedroom apartments—all of which are air-conditioned, fully furnished, and equipped with kitchens—are available for incoming students.

■ Career Services

Cardozo students benefit from a career services office staffed by professional counselors, all of whom have JD degrees, that offers individual assistance with interviewing techniques, résumé writing, and job search strategies as well as panels and other opportunities for learning about a variety of legal careers. An impressive 98.3 percent of those reporting from the class of 2005 were employed within several months of graduation. Sixty percent of these graduates went into private practice at an average starting salary of $94,142; the average overall starting salary was $82,334.

■ Curriculum

Cardozo offers a rich curriculum that has been especially recognized for its offerings in Intellectual Property Law (students may receive both the JD and Master of Laws (LLM) degrees in seven semesters), Alternative Dispute Resolution, Criminal Law, Corporate Law, and International Law. Upper-level courses are elective except for a course in Professional Responsibility, completion of Advanced Legal Research, an upper-level writing requirement, and fulfillment of minimal distribution requirements.

Cardozo offers LLM degrees in Intellectual Property Law, Comparative Legal Thought, and in General Studies. A joint-degree program between Cardozo and the Wurzweiler School of Social Work allows students to earn the JD and MSW in four years of study.

■ Students/Student Activities

The student body at Cardozo is a diverse and impressive group. A typical entering class includes graduates from well more than 130 colleges, and from over 35 states and several foreign countries. Roughly 20 percent of the class are members of minority groups and 15–20 percent are returning to school after spending at least five years in the working world.

More than half of the second- and third-year students participate on one of six student-edited journals or in the Moot Court Honor Society. Scholarly journals include the *Cardozo Law Review, Cardozo Arts and Entertainment Law Journal, Cardozo Journal of International and Comparative Law, Cardozo Journal of Law and Gender, Cardozo Journal of Conflict Resolution,* and *Cardozo Public Law, Policy, and Ethics Journal.*

■ Clinical Opportunities/Special Programs

Cardozo has a commitment to a particular style of education that seeks to blend theory and practice; to expose students to the abstractions, intellectual and ethical conundrums, and overarching theories of the American legal system and to the concrete skills and values they need to be first-rate attorneys. A wealth of clinical programs combine professional work experience with academic supervision, yielding students uniquely qualified to apply what they have studied. Nearly 400 students each year take advantage of one of these opportunities to represent real clients, under the supervision of expert attorneys, gaining invaluable skills while performing important community service representing the poor, the elderly, and the indigent.

In the **Holocaust Claims Restitution Practicum**, students pursue claims made by Holocaust survivors and their heirs; students in the **Criminal Defense Clinic** represent defendants in the Manhattan Criminal Court; in the **Innocence Project**, students represent prisoners whose innocence may be proved through DNA testing; in the **Prosecutor Practicum**, students work in the Manhattan District Attorney's Office; the **Bet Tzedek Legal Services Clinic** provides legal assistance to the elderly and disabled; the **Mediation Clinic** provides training in alternative dispute resolution; the **Human Rights and Genocide Clinic** provides students with the opportunity to design and implement creative solutions to improve the lives of victims of human rights abuses throughout the world; and

Cardozo's simulation-based **Intensive Trial Advocacy Program** sharpens students' trial skills. Other clinics include the **Family Court Clinic**, **Tax Clinic**, **Criminal Appeals Clinic**, **Immigration Law Clinic**, and **Securities Arbitration Clinic**.

Externships offer students the opportunity to work in a legal position, thereby developing important skills and gaining significant real-world experience. Through externships and internships, students can obtain credit for substantive legal work under the direct supervision of an attorney or judge at the work site. The **Intellectual Property Law Program** combines a specialized curriculum with related externships in this burgeoning area of practice; the **Alexander Judicial Fellows Program** places outstanding third-year students in clerkships with prominent federal judges; the **Labor and Employment Law Externship** places students in law firms, government agencies, and unions; and the **New York City Law Department Externship** places students in the Appeals Division of the New York City Law Department (Corporation Counsel).

Cardozo's **Center for Public Service** emphasizes the law school's commitment to serving the greater public good and helping students find meaningful ways to engage in public service. In 2006, through the **Public Service Summer Stipend Program**, 114 students received $3,500 stipends while working in government agencies, judicial chambers, and with such underrepresented groups as the elderly, the homeless, recent immigrants, and juveniles. A **Public Service Scholars Program** awards scholarships to students who demonstrate an interest in public service through their application for admission. The **Loan Repayment Assistance Program (LRAP)** benefits graduates who choose to pursue careers in public interest/public service law by assisting with some of the burden of large educational debts.

Intellectual life at Cardozo extends beyond the classroom. The school sponsors numerous conferences, panels, and symposia that provoke dialogue and critical thought on wide-ranging topics such as constitutional law, communications law and policy, human rights, corporate governance, and legal ethics.

■ Admission/Alternative Entry/Financial Aid

Students may enter Cardozo in September, January, or May. Those entering in January and May complete six semesters of law school in two and one-half years. This can be particularly appealing to midyear graduates, juniors in college who wish to jumpstart their graduate education, and returning students.

Both need- and merit-based scholarships are available. Approximately 60 percent of the students receive scholarship aid. Instructions on applying for aid can be found at *www.cardozo.yu.edu/admissions/tuition.asp*.

Applicant Profile

Benjamin N. Cardozo School of Law, Yeshiva University
This grid includes only applicants who earned 120–180 LSAT scores under standard administrations.

LSAT Score	3.75 +		3.50–3.74		3.25–3.49		3.00–3.24		2.75–2.99		2.50–2.74		2.25–2.49		2.00–2.24		Below 2.00		No GPA		Total	
	Apps	Adm	Apps	Adm	Apps	Adm	Apps	Adm	Apps	Adm	Apps	Adm	Apps	Adm	Apps	Adm	Apps	Adm	Apps	Adm	Apps	Adm
175–180	3	3	5	3	4	3	2	2	2	0	2	1	0	0	0	0	0	0	0	0	18	12
170–174	32	32	21	20	24	19	14	12	15	11	6	5	3	2	0	0	0	0	0	0	115	101
165–169	107	101	144	132	107	91	96	79	39	24	20	6	3	2	0	0	1	0	3	2	520	437
160–164	199	156	280	169	241	78	160	38	60	11	23	7	11	0	3	1	1	0	10	4	988	464
155–159	149	40	262	33	254	16	155	14	79	7	25	2	14	0	3	1	1	0	9	2	951	115
150–154	57	4	123	13	146	8	111	8	69	2	41	1	12	0	6	0	2	0	6	0	573	36
145–149	22	0	56	3	84	1	75	0	53	0	18	0	17	0	5	0	0	0	13	0	343	4
140–144	15	0	20	0	35	0	47	0	32	0	23	0	15	0	4	0	4	0	6	0	201	0
135–139	1	0	5	0	12	0	11	0	13	0	11	0	3	0	1	0	3	0	2	0	62	0
130–134	1	0	3	0	4	0	9	0	6	0	9	0	3	0	2	0	1	0	2	0	40	0
125–129	0	0	1	0	0	0	1	0	2	0	4	0	1	0	0	0	1	0	0	0	10	0
120–124	0	0	0	0	0	0	0	0	0	0	0	0	0	0	0	0	0	0	1	0	1	0
Total	586	336	920	373	911	216	681	153	370	55	182	22	82	4	24	2	14	0	52	8	3822	1169

Apps = Number of Applicants
Adm = Number Admitted
Reflects 99% of the fall applicant pool.

Case Western Reserve University School of Law

11075 East Boulevard
Cleveland, OH 44122
Phone: 216.368.3600, 800.756.0036; Fax: 216.368.1042
E-mail: lawadmissions@case.edu, lawmoney@case.edu; Website: www.law.case.edu

ABA
Approved
Since
1923

The Basics

Type of school	Private
Term	Semester
Application deadline	11/15 2/1 4/1
Application fee	$40
Financial aid deadline	5/1
Can first year start other than fall?	No
Student to faculty ratio	13.8 to 1
Does the university offer:	
housing restricted to law students?	No
graduate housing for which law students are eligible?	No

Faculty and Administrators

	Total Fall	Total Spr	Men Fall	Men Spr	Women Fall	Women Spr	Minorities Fall	Minorities Spr
Full-time	38	44	29	33	9	11	4	4
Other Full-time	10	10	5	5	5	5	0	0
Deans, librarians, & others who teach	2	2	1	1	1	1	0	0
Part-time	66	102	48	63	18	39	12	12
Total	116	158	83	102	33	56	16	16

Curriculum

	Full-time	Part-time
Typical first-year section size	76	0
Is there typically a "small section" of the first-year class, other than Legal Writing, taught by full-time faculty	No	No
If yes, typical size offered last year		
# of classroom course titles beyond first-year curriculum	169	
# of upper division courses, excluding seminars with an enrollment: Under 25	136	
25–49	42	
50–74	12	
75–99	8	
100+	2	
# of seminars	17	
# of seminar positions available	227	
# of seminar positions filled	204	0
# of positions available in simulation courses	427	
# of simulation positions filled	409	0
# of positions available in faculty supervised clinical courses	60	
# of faculty supervised clinical positions filled	60	0
# involved in field placements	70	0
# involved in law journals	85	0
# involved in interschool competitions	35	0
# of credit hours required to graduate	88	

JD Enrollment and Ethnicity

	Men #	Men %	Women #	Women %	Full-time #	Full-time %	Part-time #	Part-time %	1st-year #	1st-year %	Total #	Total %	JD Degs. Awd.
African Amer.	14	3.5	15	5.4	29	4.3	0	0.0	12	5.2	29	4.3	6
Amer. Indian	2	0.5	0	0.0	2	0.3	0	0.0	0	0.0	2	0.3	0
Asian Amer.	38	9.6	35	12.7	72	10.7	1	33.3	28	12.2	73	10.8	26
Mex. Amer.	0	0.0	0	0.0	0	0.0	0	0.0	0	0.0	0	0.0	1
Puerto Rican	0	0.0	0	0.0	0	0.0	0	0.0	0	0.0	0	0.0	0
Hispanic	5	1.3	4	1.4	9	1.3	0	0.0	0	0.0	9	1.3	1
Total Minority	59	14.9	54	19.6	112	16.7	1	33.3	40	17.4	113	16.8	34
For. Nation.	3	0.8	4	1.4	7	1.0	0	0.0	1	0.4	7	1.0	4
Caucasian	314	79.1	203	73.6	515	76.9	2	66.7	164	71.3	517	76.8	203
Unknown	21	5.3	15	5.4	36	5.4	0	0.0	25	10.9	36	5.3	0
Total	397	59.0	276	41.0	670	99.6	3	0.4	230	34.2	673		241

Transfers

Transfers in	29
Transfers out	21

Tuition and Fees

	Resident	Nonresident
Full-time	$33,384	$33,384
Part-time	$0	$0

Living Expenses

Estimated living expenses for singles

Living on campus	Living off campus	Living at home
$16,240	$16,240	$11,503

Case Western Reserve University School of Law

ABA
Approved
Since
1923

GPA and LSAT Scores

	Total	Full-time	Part-time
# of apps	2,653	2,653	0
# of offers	756	756	0
# of matrics	228	228	0
75% GPA	3.61	3.61	0.00
Median GPA	3.36	3.36	0.00
25% GPA	3.07	3.07	0.00
75% LSAT	161	161	0
Median LSAT	159	159	0
25% LSAT	157	157	0

Grants and Scholarships (from prior year)

	Total		Full-time		Part-time	
	#	%	#	%	#	%
Total # of students	692		667		25	
Total # receiving grants	334	48.3	334	50.1	0	0.0
Less than 1/2 tuition	271	39.2	271	40.6	0	0.0
Half to full tuition	61	8.8	61	9.1	0	0.0
Full tuition	2	0.3	2	0.3	0	0.0
More than full tuition	0	0.0	0	0.0	0	0.0
Median grant amount			$11,000		$0	

Informational and Library Resources

# of volumes and volume equivalents	406,227
# of titles	108,781
# of active serial subscriptions	5,249
Study seating capacity inside the library	346
# of full-time professional librarians	12
Hours per week library is open	108
# of open, wired connections available to students	100
# of networked computers available for use by students	91
# of simultaneous wireless users	750
Require computer?	No

JD Attrition (from prior year)

	Academic	Other	Total	
	#	#	#	%
1st year	0	0	0	0.0
2nd year	2	24	26	11.6
3rd year	0	1	1	0.4
4th year	0	0	0	0.0

Employment (9 months after graduation)

	Total	Percentage
Employment status known	214	98.2
Employment status unknown	4	1.8
Employed	207	96.7
Pursuing graduate degrees	4	1.9
Unemployed seeking employment	1	0.5
Unemployed not seeking employment	2	0.9
Unemployed and studying for the bar	0	0.0

Type of Employment

# employed in law firms	111	53.6
# employed in business and industry	37	17.9
# employed in government	29	14.0
# employed in public interest	13	6.3
# employed as judicial clerks	7	3.4
# employed in academia	7	3.4

Geographic Location

# employed in state	108	52.2
# employed in foreign countries	3	1.4
# of states where employed		27

Bar Passage Rates

Jurisdiction	Ohio		
Exam	Sum 05	Win 06	Total
# from school taking bar for the first time	106	8	114
School's pass rate for all first-time takers	85%	88%	85%
State's pass rate for all first-time takers	81%	76%	81%

Case Western Reserve University School of Law

11075 East Boulevard
Cleveland, OH 44122
Phone: 216.368.3600, 800.756.0036; Fax: 216.368.1042
E-mail: lawadmissions@case.edu, lawmoney@case.edu; Website: www.law.case.edu

■ Welcome

Case School of Law has responded to the growing complexities of the ever-changing legal, social, and economic environments by implementing major curricular reforms. The result is an innovative program that provides our students with an enhanced classical legal education, a phenomenal array of hands-on learning (over 400 spaces in skills courses alone), opportunities for in-depth study in key fields, extensive coursework in emerging and leading-edge areas of the law (169 upper-level courses, 82 percent of which have fewer than 50 students), an understanding of the context in which legal matters and disputes take place, knowledge of other disciplines that can be used to solve legal problems, and unique methods of instruction.

■ The Curriculum and Concentrations

Shape the Law; Serve the World: We guide our students to become lawyers who help clients achieve their strategic goals by serving as their partners and counselors, and who take leadership roles in their communities and address key societal issues. The centerpiece of our curriculum is the four-semester Case*Arc* program, which coordinates experientially based instruction in fundamental lawyering skills with traditional classroom methods for teaching legal analysis.

Capstone Service Opportunities: We offer a capstone service opportunity for every student: our six labs, seven clinics, and three externship programs offer students the opportunity, not only to study the law in practice, but also to contribute to its development. Just a few examples: represent burgeoning art entrepreneurs by drafting intellectual property strategies in our **Intellectual Property Entrepreneurship Clinic**; submit a memorandum for prosecutors in the Iraqi Special Tribunal in Baghdad, the International Criminal Court in The Hague, the Special Court for Sierra Leone, the International Criminal Tribunal for Rwanda, or the International Criminal Tribunal for the Former Yugoslavia through our **War Crimes Research Lab**; provide assessments of the military commissions at Guantanamo Bay in our **Counterterrorism Lab**; do research for the International Monetary Fund and the World Bank in our **Global Corporate Governance Lab**; or conduct an examination of a medical expert in a social security disability claim in the **Health Law Clinic**.

Optional Concentration Program: Our Concentration Program offers in-depth learning in an area of interest and of value to employers seeking increased contributions from new lawyers. Options: Law and Technology, Law and the Arts, Criminal Law, Business Organizations, Litigation, Health Law, International Law, Individual Rights and Social Reform, and Public and Regulatory Institutions.

Dual-degree Programs: Law, Management, Bioethics, Social Work, Biochemistry, Medicine, Nonprofit Management, Public Health, and Legal History.

■ Centers of Excellence

The Academic Centers provide rich opportunities that stimulate learning, networking, and career development, and include first-year electives, special seminars and symposia, clinical opportunities, internships, and work-abroad opportunities.

- Law-Medicine Center
- Frederick K. Cox International Law Center
- Milton A. Kramer Law Clinic Center
- Center for Business Law and Regulation
- Center for the Interdisciplinary Study of Conflict and Dispute Resolution
- Institute for Global Security Law and Policy
- Center for Professional Ethics

■ Work and Study Abroad

Our students have far-ranging opportunities to work abroad and to receive generous stipends that support their international internships. Each year, we fund over 20 international law-related summer internships and postgraduate fellowships for work abroad or in the US with an international organization, a governmental agency, or nonprofit agency. Just a sampling of recent placements:

- United Nations Development Programme, Hanoi, Vietnam
- Amnesty International, Washington, DC
- Chang Tsi and Partners, Beijing, People's Republic of China
- Government of Dominica, Ministry of Legal Affairs, Dominica West Indies
- International Bar Association, London, UK
- War Crimes Research Office, Iraq; Special Tribunal for the trials of Saddam Hussein
- International Trade Centre, Geneva, Switzerland
- Special Court for Sierra Leone, Prosecutor's Office, Sierra Leone
- Supreme Court of the Philippines
- Médicins Sans Frontières, Rangoon, Burma

■ The University and Cleveland

Case stands among the nation's foremost independent research institutions. It is 14th among private universities in federal research and development awards. The law school is located on the university's campus in the heart of University Circle—the world's greatest concentration of cultural and educational institutions.

As the nation's 14th largest metropolitan area, Cleveland is among the nation's premier legal, corporate, and health care centers, providing students with a wealth of local job opportunities, externships, and affordable nearby housing; a recent student survey indicated that the average per person monthly rent for a single was $671 and $392 for shared accommodations.

■ Commitment to Career Success

The Career Services Office (CSO) has implemented an ambitious program that delivers to our students real job opportunities with leading employers coast-to-coast. Our aggressive approach to employer development has resulted in great job success for our graduates: 98.6 percent employment rate for our class of 2004 (national average: 91.4 percent); median salary for class of 2004: $65,000 (national median: $55,000); 56 percent of students obtained employment through a CSO-sponsored program (national figure: 40 percent); over 43 percent of our graduates took positions out-of-state (national figure: 32.8 percent placement outside of the law school's state). Over 400 employers participate in our fall recruitment programs, which include on-campus interviews as well as interview programs in New York, Chicago, Los Angeles, Boston, and Washington, DC.

■ Student Activities and Leadership

There are over 45 student organizations, reflecting the wide range of interest of our students, including the largest school-based Big Brothers/Big Sisters program in the country. Our student organizations not only allow students the opportunity to explore legal interests with peers, they also provide a valuable proving ground for leadership skill development. Our student organization leaders have also taken leadership roles in their groups' national and regional organizations, including the Black Law Students Association, the American Law Students' Association's Law Students Division, the National Security and Law Society, the National Lawyers Guild, and the Asian Pacific American Law Students' Association, just to name a few. Our scholarly journals are the *Case Western Reserve Law Review,* the *Journal of International Law,* and *Health Matrix: Journal of Law-Medicine.*

■ Admission and Financial Aid

The Admission Process—Our admission process is selective. Each applicant receives full-file review. The Early Decision

program application deadline is November 15; applicants are notified by December 20. The regular admission process begins in December and concludes by May 15, at which time a summer wait list is established. The application fee for candidates who apply electronically is waived.

Financial Aid and Scholarships—We provide scholarship support to approximately one-third of each entering class: Academic Scholarships ($5,000 to $32,000), Leadership Grants, Law-Medicine Scholarships, Law-Medicine Fellowships (combination of scholarship aid and summer research position with faculty), and Grotius International Law and de Vattel International Human Rights Scholarships.

Loan Repayment Assistance Program—We provide financial assistance for selected graduates who use their legal training to provide services that are in the public interest.

■ Visiting the Case School of Law

We welcome visits by prospective students. Just check our website for the schedule for the visitation day or daily Taste of Case individual visit that is most convenient for you or to take our "Virtual Tour." Feel free to join in one of our three online message boards that are accessible via our website: Admissions, Financial Aid, and Student Services.

Applicant Profile

Case Western Reserve University School of Law
This grid includes only applicants who earned 120–180 LSAT scores.

LSAT Score	GPA						
	3.75 +	3.50–3.74	3.25–3.49	3.00–3.24	2.75–2.99	2.50–2.74	Below 2.50
165–180							
163–164							
161–162							
159–160							
157–158							
154–156							
150–153							
Below 150							

	Good Possibility		Possibility		Slight Possibility

The Catholic University of America, Columbus School of Law

Cardinal Station
Washington, DC 20064
Phone: 202.319.5151; Fax: 202.319.6285
E-mail: admissions@law.edu; Website: www.law.edu

The Basics

Type of school	Private
Term	Semester
Application deadline	3/1
Application fee	$65
Financial aid deadline	4/15 6/1 8/1
Can first year start other than fall?	No
Student to faculty ratio	14.9 to 1
Does the university offer:	
housing restricted to law students?	No
graduate housing for which law students are eligible?	No

Faculty and Administrators

	Total		Men		Women		Minorities	
	Fall	Spr	Fall	Spr	Fall	Spr	Fall	Spr
Full-time	46	45	24	24	22	21	8	8
Other Full-time	1	0	1	0	0	0	0	0
Deans, librarians, & others who teach	3	2	1	1	2	1	1	1
Part-time	55	63	44	47	11	16	6	7
Total	**105**	**110**	**70**	**72**	**35**	**38**	**15**	**16**

Curriculum

		Full-time	Part-time
Typical first-year section size		80	80
Is there typically a "small section" of the first-year class, other than Legal Writing, taught by full-time faculty		Yes	Yes
If yes, typical size offered last year		40	42
# of classroom course titles beyond first-year curriculum		126	
# of upper division courses, excluding seminars with an enrollment:	Under 25	121	
	25–49	35	
	50–74	18	
	75–99	5	
	100+	0	
# of seminars		42	
# of seminar positions available		745	
# of seminar positions filled		364	182
# of positions available in simulation courses		217	
# of simulation positions filled		121	61
# of positions available in faculty supervised clinical courses		135	
# of faculty supervised clinical positions filled		57	17
# involved in field placements		130	65
# involved in law journals		110	54
# involved in interschool competitions		24	11
# of credit hours required to graduate		84	

JD Enrollment and Ethnicity

	Men		Women		Full-time		Part-time		1st-year		Total		JD Degs. Awd.
	#	%	#	%	#	%	#	%	#	%	#	%	
African Amer.	16	3.4	28	6.5	22	3.6	22	7.3	16	5.7	44	4.9	8
Amer. Indian	2	0.4	1	0.2	2	0.3	1	0.3	1	0.4	3	0.3	1
Asian Amer.	26	5.5	42	9.7	49	8.1	19	6.3	19	6.7	68	7.5	23
Mex. Amer.	2	0.4	1	0.2	2	0.3	1	0.3	1	0.4	3	0.3	11
Puerto Rican	5	1.1	1	0.2	2	0.3	4	1.3	0	0.0	6	0.7	2
Hispanic	18	3.8	19	4.4	27	4.5	10	3.3	9	3.2	37	4.1	1
Total Minority	69	14.6	92	21.2	104	17.2	57	18.9	46	16.3	161	17.8	46
For. Nation.	2	0.4	2	0.5	2	0.3	2	0.7	1	0.4	4	0.4	0
Caucasian	301	63.6	256	59.1	375	62.1	182	60.3	175	61.8	557	61.5	169
Unknown	101	21.4	83	19.2	123	20.4	61	20.2	61	21.6	184	20.3	64
Total	473	52.2	433	47.8	604	66.7	302	33.3	283	31.2	906		279

Transfers

Transfers in	9
Transfers out	26

Tuition and Fees

	Resident	Nonresident
Full-time	$32,555	$32,555
Part-time	$24,820	$24,820

Living Expenses

Estimated living expenses for singles

Living on campus	Living off campus	Living at home
$21,340	$21,340	$21,340

The Catholic University of America, Columbus School of Law

ABA
Approved
Since
1925

GPA and LSAT Scores

	Total	Full-time	Part-time
# of apps	3,401	2,679	722
# of offers	1,106	876	230
# of matrics	285	169	116
75% GPA	3.52	3.55	3.46
Median GPA	3.31	3.32	3.26
25% GPA	3.07	3.11	3.04
75% LSAT	159	160	158
Median LSAT	157	158	155
25% LSAT	155	156	153

Grants and Scholarships (from prior year)

	Total #	Total %	Full-time #	Full-time %	Part-time #	Part-time %
Total # of students	949		688		261	
Total # receiving grants	266	28.0	222	32.3	44	16.9
Less than 1/2 tuition	224	23.6	181	26.3	43	16.5
Half to full tuition	42	4.4	41	6.0	1	0.4
Full tuition	0	0.0	0	0.0	0	0.0
More than full tuition	0	0.0	0	0.0	0	0.0
Median grant amount			$10,000		$6,000	

Informational and Library Resources

# of volumes and volume equivalents	413,985
# of titles	131,079
# of active serial subscriptions	5,058
Study seating capacity inside the library	502
# of full-time professional librarians	10
Hours per week library is open	115
# of open, wired connections available to students	368
# of networked computers available for use by students	125
# of simultaneous wireless users	902
Require computer?	No

JD Attrition (from prior year)

	Academic #	Other #	Total #	Total %
1st year	3	47	50	15.3
2nd year	0	4	4	1.5
3rd year	0	0	0	0.0
4th year	1	0	1	1.7

Employment (9 months after graduation)

	Total	Percentage
Employment status known	292	99.0
Employment status unknown	3	1.0
Employed	258	88.4
Pursuing graduate degrees	5	1.7
Unemployed seeking employment	9	3.1
Unemployed not seeking employment	8	2.7
Unemployed and studying for the bar	12	4.1
Type of Employment		
# employed in law firms	92	35.7
# employed in business and industry	44	17.1
# employed in government	72	27.9
# employed in public interest	11	4.3
# employed as judicial clerks	34	13.2
# employed in academia	3	1.2
Geographic Location		
# employed in state	121	46.9
# employed in foreign countries	0	0.0
# of states where employed	23	

Bar Passage Rates

Jurisdiction	Maryland		
Exam	Sum 05	Win 06	Total
# from school taking bar for the first time	130	8	138
School's pass rate for all first-time takers	72%	63%	72%
State's pass rate for all first-time takers	76%	66%	74%

The Catholic University of America, Columbus School of Law

Cardinal Station
Washington, DC 20064
Phone: 202.319.5151; Fax: 202.319.6285
E-mail: admissions@law.edu; Website: www.law.edu

■ Introduction

Founded in 1897, The Catholic University of America, Columbus School of Law is located on the 193-acre campus of the university. Students and faculty have easy access to nearly limitless legal resources: the Supreme Court, Congress, the United States and District of Columbia courts, and other federal, executive, and administrative agencies and branches of government. For a campus so close to a center of world power, it is peaceful, pleasant, and scenic, offering a sense of neighborhood and community. Classes are small and personal.

The law school is proud of its vibrant intellectual tradition and extends it to exploring new intersections of issues of law and morality. Students are trained and encouraged to use their hearts and minds, in concert with their skills, to practice effectively in the complex world of the twenty-first century. The school welcomes students of all religious, racial, and ethnic backgrounds to a program that is renowned for its consistently high number of graduates entering public and community service. The Columbus School of Law has been a member of the AALS since 1921 and approved by the ABA since 1925.

■ Enrollment/Student Body

Total enrollment is typically more than 900 students, making the School of Law the 33rd largest law school in the US. Law students come from nearly every state and a dozen foreign countries. More than 25 percent of the school's enrollment is part time, making its evening program one of the most flexible and accommodating available anywhere. First-year classes typically have 32–70 students. Upper-class courses range from 10 to 70 students. Faculty members keep posted office hours and are accessible for informal sessions, making for a more personal education.

■ Faculty

The 55-member full-time faculty brings a wealth of experience and expertise to the classroom. The majority have practiced in the private sector. Adjunct faculty members are primarily active legal practitioners and complement the "real-world" flavor of course offerings. Classroom instruction is supplemented by many distinguished guest speakers, such as federal appellate judges, justices of the US Supreme Court, and leading academicians and theologians from around the world.

■ Library and Physical Facilities

The Library of Congress and specialized law collections throughout the city complement the law school's legal collections of over 400,000 titles. The law school facility, completed in 1994, houses all components of the law school. Law students have full access to other campus facilities, including a 40-acre athletic complex.

■ Curriculum

The prescribed first-year curriculum and method of teaching are designed to develop the analytical skills that characterize the able lawyer and to give the student familiarity with the major substantive areas of law. It is also designed as an introduction to jurisprudence and the Catholic intellectual tradition as it relates to the larger questions of social justice. While lawyers traditionally have been heavily involved with the commercial interests of private or corporate clients, law is becoming increasingly responsive to problems that affect the public interest. The CUA law school curriculum is designed to provide students with the basic knowledge to become effective lawyers in a changing legal environment.

■ Special Programs

CUA Law's institutes and special programs offer certification of a student's developed expertise in his or her chosen legal specialty. Each program provides invaluable externship opportunities, offering for-credit placements available nowhere else but in Washington, DC.

The Institute for Communications Law Studies offers unique specialized training in communications law, ranging from First Amendment law to FCC practices and procedures. Students are trained to think critically about the broader impact that mass media has upon society and human behavior.

The Comparative and International Law Institute provides superb background training to students who intend to specialize in international law. The institute offers a six-week summer-abroad program at the Jagiellonian University in Krakow, Poland.

The Law and Public Policy Program is designed for students who desire to make a difference through legislative change. The program combines classroom study in legislative and administrative processes with externships in government agencies and advocacy organizations that affect national public policy.

The Corporate and Securities Law Program integrates a broad concentration of securities and corporate law courses with a required externship program. Adjunct instructors and program faculty bring vast knowledge to the classroom, as many have practiced with the Securities and Exchange Commission (SEC), the National Association of Securities Dealers (NASD), and private firms.

The Interdisciplinary Program on Law and Religion was created to provide a forum for study, research, and public discussion of the questions that arise from the nexus of law and religion. These include many of society's most challenging issues, such as bioethics, international human rights, and marriage law.

■ Clinical Programs

Columbus Community Legal Services recently observed its 35th year of assisting the underserved population of the nation's capital. The law school offers eight clinical programs, including five that emphasize client representation, case planning, and trial and administrative advocacy. Nine simulation courses are also offered that closely approximate real-life lawyering through simulated courtroom, mediation, and arbitration exercises. The two other clinical offerings are the SEC Observer Program and the Legal Externship Program.

The Catholic University of America, Columbus School of Law

■ Admission

While considerable weight is given to an applicant's grade-point average and LSAT score, admission decisions are also influenced by such factors as leadership potential, class rank, substantial involvement in volunteer community service activities, potential for contributing to diversity, and relevant work experience. Close attention is also paid to a candidate's personal statement and reasons for wanting to study at CUA.

■ Student Activities

The *Catholic University Law Re*view, the *Journal of Contemporary Health Law and Policy*, and *CommLaw Conspectus: Journal of Communications Law and Policy* are scholarly law journals staffed and published by outstanding students. The Moot Court Board, in addition to facilitating at least eight intraschool competitions each year, also hosts two major contests at CUA: the National Telecommunications Competition and the Sutherland Cup. There are over 30 voluntary student organizations at the Columbus School of Law, encompassing a broad range of professional interests, ethnic and racial affiliations, political and religious perspectives, and recreational activities.

■ Financial Aid

Following the offer of admission, all prospective students are automatically evaluated for merit-based scholarships.

Approximately 25–30 percent of each year's entering class has been awarded a scholarship. Given the significant financial investment of a law degree, the Office of Financial Aid is committed to providing all students with timely information and guidance.

■ Career Services

The Office of Legal Career Services actively supports students and graduates in their search for employment by providing counseling as well as workshops, panel discussions, and access to a national alumni network. A comprehensive on-campus interviewing program is conducted annually. The school's small size makes it possible for all students to secure guidance with individualized career strategy and planning.

■ Housing

The Washington, DC, metropolitan area boasts many off-campus housing opportunities for prospective law students. Each summer, the Office of Admissions assists incoming students with the housing search by coordinating a roommate name exchange, a housing workshop, and an online housing forum. The law school is convenient to public transportation, including Washington's Metrorail system.

Applicant Profile

The Catholic University of America, Columbus School of Law
This grid includes only applicants who earned 120–180 LSAT scores under standard administrations.

LSAT Score	3.75 +		3.50–3.74		3.25–3.49		3.00–3.24		2.75–2.99		2.50–2.74		2.25–2.49		2.00–2.24		Below 2.00		No GPA		Total	
	Apps	Adm	Apps	Adm	Apps	Adm	Apps	Adm	Apps	Adm	Apps	Adm	Apps	Adm	Apps	Adm	Apps	Adm	Apps	Adm	Apps	Adm
175–180	0	0	0	0	0	0	0	0	2	2	0	0	0	0	0	0	0	0	0	0	2	2
170–174	2	1	0	0	1	1	2	2	1	1	0	0	0	0	0	0	0	0	0	0	6	5
165–169	15	12	13	13	17	15	19	18	11	7	10	4	1	0	0	0	0	0	0	0	86	69
160–164	44	42	66	63	85	82	67	59	58	38	29	11	18	4	2	0	0	0	4	2	373	301
155–159	112	85	242	175	323	176	209	91	114	26	48	5	25	4	10	1	0	0	8	2	1091	565
150–154	91	15	203	28	256	38	213	20	150	11	54	2	22	1	9	0	4	0	12	4	1014	119
145–149	34	1	95	6	105	10	130	8	74	3	59	2	23	1	8	0	1	0	9	0	538	31
140–144	17	1	34	0	51	0	57	2	48	0	40	0	17	0	10	0	0	0	6	0	280	3
135–139	3	0	5	0	17	0	16	0	23	0	10	0	9	0	5	0	3	0	3	0	94	0
130–134	1	0	4	0	2	0	4	0	7	0	8	0	6	0	4	0	0	0	2	0	38	0
125–129	0	0	0	0	0	0	0	0	0	0	1	0	1	0	1	0	1	0	2	0	6	0
120–124	0	0	0	0	0	0	0	0	0	0	1	0	0	0	0	0	0	0	0	0	1	0
Total	319	157	662	285	857	322	717	200	488	88	260	24	122	10	49	1	9	0	46	8	3529	1095

Apps = Number of Applicants
Adm = Number Admitted
Reflects 99% of the total applicant pool.

This grid should be used only as a general guide, as many nonnumerical factors are considered in admission decisions.

Chapman University School of Law

One University Drive
Orange, CA 92866
Phone: 877.CHAPLAW or 714.628.2500; Fax: 714.628.2501
E-mail: lawadm@chapman.edu; Website: www.chapman.edu/law

ABA
Approved
Since
1998

The Basics

Type of school	Private
Term	Semester
Application deadline	6/1
Application fee	$60
Financial aid deadline	3/2
Can first year start other than fall?	No
Student to faculty ratio	17.5 to 1
Does the university offer:	
housing restricted to law students?	No
graduate housing for which law students are eligible?	No

Faculty and Administrators

	Total Fall	Total Spr	Men Fall	Men Spr	Women Fall	Women Spr	Minorities Fall	Minorities Spr
Full-time	26	26	15	16	11	10	4	2
Other Full-time	0	0	0	0	0	0	0	0
Deans, librarians, & others who teach	7	5	4	3	3	2	0	0
Part-time	31	34	27	27	4	7	2	5
Total	**64**	**65**	**46**	**46**	**18**	**19**	**6**	**7**

Curriculum

	Full-time	Part-time
Typical first-year section size	65	65
Is there typically a "small section" of the first-year class, other than Legal Writing, taught by full-time faculty	No	No
If yes, typical size offered last year		
# of classroom course titles beyond first-year curriculum	84	
# of upper division courses, excluding seminars with an enrollment: Under 25	58	
25–49	23	
50–74	12	
75–99	8	
100+	0	
# of seminars	9	
# of seminar positions available	158	
# of seminar positions filled	140	0
# of positions available in simulation courses	246	
# of simulation positions filled	222	12
# of positions available in faculty supervised clinical courses	70	
# of faculty supervised clinical positions filled	54	0
# involved in field placements	97	0
# involved in law journals	96	0
# involved in interschool competitions	48	0
# of credit hours required to graduate	88	

JD Enrollment and Ethnicity

	Men #	Men %	Women #	Women %	Full-time #	Full-time %	Part-time #	Part-time %	1st-year #	1st-year %	Total #	Total %	JD Degs. Awd.
African Amer.	3	1.0	2	0.8	2	0.4	3	6.0	3	1.4	5	0.9	2
Amer. Indian	2	0.7	3	1.1	5	1.0	0	0.0	2	0.9	5	0.9	2
Asian Amer.	40	13.2	55	21.0	86	16.7	9	18.0	33	15.6	95	16.8	34
Mex. Amer.	16	5.3	9	3.4	23	4.5	2	4.0	11	5.2	25	4.4	7
Puerto Rican	0	0.0	0	0.0	0	0.0	0	0.0	0	0.0	0	0.0	0
Hispanic	11	3.6	4	1.5	12	2.3	3	6.0	7	3.3	15	2.7	5
Total Minority	72	23.7	73	27.9	128	24.8	17	34.0	56	26.5	145	25.6	50
For. Nation.	1	0.3	1	0.4	2	0.4	0	0.0	2	0.9	2	0.4	1
Caucasian	166	54.6	145	55.3	291	56.4	20	40.0	113	53.6	311	54.9	91
Unknown	65	21.4	43	16.4	95	18.4	13	26.0	40	19.0	108	19.1	38
Total	304	53.7	262	46.3	516	91.2	50	8.8	211	37.3	566		180

Transfers

Transfers in	7
Transfers out	8

Tuition and Fees

	Resident	Nonresident
Full-time	$32,834	$32,834
Part-time	$22,604	$22,604

Living Expenses

Estimated living expenses for singles

Living on campus	Living off campus	Living at home
$20,532	$20,532	$11,532

Chapman University School of Law

ABA Approved Since 1998

GPA and LSAT Scores

	Total	Full-time	Part-time
# of apps	2,309	2,309	0
# of offers	805	684	121
# of matrics	216	173	43
75% GPA	3.47	3.52	3.37
Median GPA	3.19	3.19	3.23
25% GPA	2.90	2.90	3.00
75% LSAT	159	159	154
Median LSAT	156	158	150
25% LSAT	155	156	149

Grants and Scholarships (from prior year)

	Total #	Total %	Full-time #	Full-time %	Part-time #	Part-time %
Total # of students	556		515		41	
Total # receiving grants	185	33.3	179	34.8	6	14.6
Less than 1/2 tuition	153	27.5	147	28.5	6	14.6
Half to full tuition	7	1.3	7	1.4	0	0.0
Full tuition	25	4.5	25	4.9	0	0.0
More than full tuition	0	0.0	0	0.0	0	0.0
Median grant amount			$14,350		$3,950	

Informational and Library Resources

# of volumes and volume equivalents	284,257
# of titles	163,869
# of active serial subscriptions	3,111
Study seating capacity inside the library	322
# of full-time professional librarians	10
Hours per week library is open	100
# of open, wired connections available to students	488
# of networked computers available for use by students	45
# of simultaneous wireless users	500
Require computer?	No

JD Attrition (from prior year)

	Academic #	Other #	Total #	Total %
1st year	6	3	9	4.6
2nd year	2	8	10	5.3
3rd year	0	1	1	0.6
4th year	1	0	1	4.5

Employment (9 months after graduation)

	Total	Percentage
Employment status known	123	94.6
Employment status unknown	7	5.4
Employed	106	86.2
Pursuing graduate degrees	7	5.7
Unemployed seeking employment	1	0.8
Unemployed not seeking employment	2	1.6
Unemployed and studying for the bar	7	5.7

Type of Employment

	Total	Percentage
# employed in law firms	53	50.0
# employed in business and industry	30	28.3
# employed in government	9	8.5
# employed in public interest	5	4.7
# employed as judicial clerks	4	3.8
# employed in academia	2	1.9

Geographic Location

	Total	Percentage
# employed in state	97	91.5
# employed in foreign countries	1	0.9
# of states where employed	5	

Bar Passage Rates

Jurisdiction	California		
Exam	Sum 05	Win 06	Total
# from school taking bar for the first time	111	14	125
School's pass rate for all first-time takers	59%	36%	57%
State's pass rate for all first-time takers	64%	54%	62%

Chapman University School of Law

One University Drive
Orange, CA 92866
Phone: 877.CHAPLAW or 714.628.2500; Fax: 714.628.2501
E-mail: lawadm@chapman.edu; Website: www.chapman.edu/law

■ Introduction

Chapman University School of Law is located in the historic Old Towne district of Orange, California, and shares the campus with the university, a 144-year-old institution. The law school, established in 1995, received full approval by the ABA in 2002. AALS accreditation was received in January 2006.

In 11 short years, the law school has rapidly gained a national reputation for its high quality of faculty, students, and facilities. Offering a curriculum strong in business and corporate law, the law school also has focus areas in taxation, environmental/real estate/land use, and advocacy and dispute resolution; a joint JD/MBA degree; and an LLM degree in taxation. We also offer clinical opportunities in the areas of elder law, constitutional law, and the 9th Circuit Appellate Clinic. Our students have obtained rewarding externship and internship opportunities. The law school's successes have been aided by its location in vibrant and dynamic Orange County.

Affiliation with a well-established university allows for cross-disciplinary engagement, joint degrees, and a lively and engaging intellectual environment beyond the classroom. Chapman University offers an impressive selection of artistic and cultural opportunities for its students.

■ Enrollment/Student Body

Chapman Law has committed itself to building a small, talented, and diverse student body. Total student enrollment in 2006–2007 was 550 law students.

The 2006 entering class consisted of 197 law students. The students were divided into three small first-year sections. The Legal Research and Writing course has approximately 12 to 15 students in each of the 15 sections. Currently, about 18 percent of the entering class comes from outside California; that number is expected to increase over the next few years as Chapman's reputation reaches a more national audience. The minority enrollment hovers around 26 percent.

Competition for seats is keen. Approximately, 34 percent of applicants in the 2006 applicant pool were admitted.

■ Faculty

Chapman has assembled an impressive law faculty (including three former US Supreme Court clerks) who are excellent teachers, accomplished scholars, and outstanding mentors. Chapman Law's environment is conducive to learning. Students have access to the faculty and frequent opportunities to engage them in both formal and informal settings. Our student to faculty ratio remains 16:1.

■ Library and Physical Facilities

The stately and beautiful Donald P. Kennedy Hall opened in 1999, with state-of-the-art learning facilities in its classrooms, law library, and trial and appellate courtrooms.

Library holdings now exceed 282,000 volumes and volume equivalents, and the collection is expected to continue its rapid growth. The collection is fully accessible to students both in hard copy and through the computer network.

Library carrels and desktops are generous in number, and many are wired for Internet access. Several private study rooms are available for student use and extended research.

Two state-of-the-art courtrooms provide computers, cameras, and electronic blackboards for trial advocacy exercises, competitions, and formal hearings by visiting courts.

Student relaxation lounges, locker areas, and office spaces are located throughout the building.

■ Special Programs/Clinics/Externships

The law school offers the JD/MBA program, affording students the opportunity to earn the equivalent of two accredited professional degrees in four instead of the typical five years. Chapman's George L. Argyros School of Business and Economics is AACSB accredited.

About 10 percent of the students choose to focus their electives in one of three certificate areas: taxation, environmental/real estate/land use, or advocacy and dispute resolution. The Tax Program affords students the opportunity to represent claimants against the IRS in the US Tax Court Clinic. The Center for Land Resources allows students to network with practicing professionals. In the Externship Program, students receive placements in the offices of appellate justices, trial judges, district attorneys, and public defenders, where they gain hands-on experience and academic credit.

Clinic offerings include those in elder law, constitutional litigation, tax law, and appellate practice. Nearly all clinics allow students additional opportunities to represent actual clients in an array of legal settings.

The law school's Academic Achievement Program assists students in the mastery of the skills necessary to become successful law students and productive attorneys. The program includes individualized counseling and instruction, as well as group workshops and peer tutoring.

■ Admission

The School of Law seeks to admit stellar students who are passionately interested in a legal education that will challenge them to grow intellectually, ethically, and professionally. The law school seeks a diverse student body that will make a meaningful contribution to the legal profession. Many variables enter into the decision-making process. The applicant's entire file is considered, and each application is individually reviewed. The Admission Committee reviews the traditional numbers—your academic record and LSAT—but also considers additional indicators of potential success in law school. Such indicators include the nature and rigor of the undergraduate discipline, an upward trend in academic performance, coursework, writing ability, employment history, graduate-level courses taken and degrees earned, scholarly achievement, community and volunteer service, research projects, demonstrated leadership ability, fluency in foreign languages, and personal background, including a history of overcoming adversity, and unusual contributions or other maturing experiences.

Electronic applications are preferred. Two letters of recommendation are required; these should be submitted directly to the LSAC. A personal statement and résumé are also required, and they should be submitted with your application.

Applying early is encouraged as the entering class is filled on a rolling basis, and scholarship funds may be exhausted early in the admission cycle.

There is a priority consideration deadline of April 1, 2007, for merit-based scholarships. The application deadline for the fall 2007 entering class is June 1, 2007.

■ Student Curricular and Cocurricular Activities

The law school offers many activities that enrich the academic program and provide important training in leadership. Two journals offer valuable experience in research, writing, and editing. The Student Bar Association administers a full range of programs. Other organizations include, but are not limited to, the Minority Law Students Association, Asian Pacific American Law Student Association, the Public Interest Law Foundation, the Federalist Society, and the student-run Honor Council.

Externships allow students to earn academic credit while working in a variety of government agencies, judges' chambers, and public interest organizations, developing the practical skills and confidence they will need after graduation.

Chapman offers a range of advocacy experiences, including participation in mock trial, moot court, client counseling, international law, and negotiation competitions. Chapman teams have won regional competitions and have performed competitively in national and international tournaments. The Moot Court Board and the Mock Trial Board administer their programs and provide excellent practical training.

■ Scholarships and Financial Aid

Chapman Law offers a generous merit- and need-based scholarship program. For the 2006 entering class, more than 60 percent of new students received scholarships. After the first year, law students are eligible to renew their merit scholarships provided they maintain a GPA of 3.0 or above in their classes after the first-year grades are posted. For 2006, over $3.5 million in scholarship funds were distributed among a student body of approximately 550. This included merit- and need-based scholarships.

Chapman also offers a full range of loan programs to complement students' financial needs, including Stafford loans, Perkins loans, and private loans. All students receiving scholarship funds and/or loans should plan to file the FAFSA and a preliminary financial aid application. International students are eligible for merit scholarships.

■ Career Services

Chapman University School of Law provides students and alumni with comprehensive career services and resources that aid law students in selecting their career direction and reaching their goals. The Career Services and Professional Development Office facilitates interviews for our students with legal employers during our On-Campus Interviewing Program in both the fall and spring. The Career Services Office also provides students the opportunity to meet with prominent members of the legal community through frequent panels, a highly successful Attorney Mentor Program, and an extensive Mock Interview Program.

Career Services helps to match students' educational and experiential skills with both traditional and nontraditional employment opportunities. In keeping with the Chapman mission of personalized education, the Career Services Office staff meets personally, and often, with individual students to review résumés and cover letters; to aid in self-assessment and goal orientation; to discuss specific opportunities unique to the student's needs; and to provide training, support, and encouragement in all aspects of exploring career options.

Applicant Profile

Chapman University School of Law

LSAT Score	GPA								
	3.75 +	3.50–3.74	3.25–3.49	3.00–3.24	2.75–2.99	2.50–2.74	2.25–2.49	2.00–2.24	Below 2.00
175–180									
170–174									
165–169									
160–164									
155–159									
150–154									
145–149									
140–144									
135–139									
130–134									
125–129									
120–124									

Very Likely   Likely   Possible   Unlikely

Charleston School of Law

81 Mary Street, PO Box 535
Charleston, SC 29402
Phone: 843.329.1000, ext. 2143; Fax: 843.329.0491
Website: www.charlestonlaw.org

The Basics

Type of school	Private
Term	Semester
Application deadline	3/15
Application fee	$50
Financial aid deadline	4/1
Can first year start other than fall?	No
Student to faculty ratio	19.1 to 1
Does the university offer:	
housing restricted to law students?	No
graduate housing for which law students are eligible?	No

Faculty and Administrators

	Total		Men		Women		Minorities	
	Fall	Spr	Fall	Spr	Fall	Spr	Fall	Spr
Full-time	18	20	13	14	5	6	2	2
Other Full-time	3	4	3	4	0	0	0	0
Deans, librarians, & others who teach	3	3	2	2	1	1	0	0
Part-time	19	14	15	12	4	2	1	0
Total	**43**	**41**	**33**	**32**	**10**	**9**	**3**	**2**

Curriculum

	Full-time	Part-time
Typical first-year section size	65	62
Is there typically a "small section" of the first-year class, other than Legal Writing, taught by full-time faculty	Yes	No
If yes, typical size offered last year	30	
# of classroom course titles beyond first-year curriculum		36
# of upper division courses, excluding seminars with an enrollment: Under 25		26
25–49		15
50–74		17
75–99		3
100+		0
# of seminars		8
# of seminar positions available		200
# of seminar positions filled	71	30
# of positions available in simulation courses		210
# of simulation positions filled	98	43
# of positions available in faculty supervised clinical courses		120
# of faculty supervised clinical positions filled	0	0
# involved in field placements	45	35
# involved in law journals	33	5
# involved in interschool competitions	18	12
# of credit hours required to graduate		88

JD Enrollment and Ethnicity

	Men		Women		Full-time		Part-time		1st-year		Total		JD Degs. Awd.
	#	%	#	%	#	%	#	%	#	%	#	%	
African Amer.	7	2.0	16	19.3	10	4.2	13	7.0	10	5.1	23	5.4	0
Amer. Indian	2	0.6	1	1.2	2	0.8	1	0.5	3	1.5	3	0.7	0
Asian Amer.	5	1.5	1	1.2	5	2.1	1	0.5	0	0.0	6	1.4	0
Mex. Amer.	0	0.0	0	0.0	0	0.0	0	0.0	0	0.0	0	0.0	0
Puerto Rican	0	0.0	0	0.0	0	0.0	0	0.0	0	0.0	0	0.0	0
Hispanic	1	0.3	0	0.0	1	0.4	0	0.0	0	0.0	1	0.2	0
Total Minority	15	4.4	18	21.7	18	7.5	15	8.0	13	6.6	33	7.7	0
For. Nation.	0	0.0	0	0.0	0	0.0	0	0.0	0	0.0	0	0.0	0
Caucasian	298	86.6	62	74.7	202	84.2	158	84.5	118	60.2	360	84.3	0
Unknown	31	9.0	3	3.6	20	8.3	14	7.5	10	5.1	34	8.0	0
Total	344	80.6	83	19.4	240	56.2	187	43.8	196	45.9	427		

Transfers

Transfers in	3
Transfers out	0

Tuition and Fees

	Resident	Nonresident
Full-time	$28,680	$28,680
Part-time	$19,476	$19,476

Living Expenses

Estimated living expenses for singles

Living on campus	Living off campus	Living at home
N/A	$12,600	$10,000

*ABA
Approved
Since
2006*

GPA and LSAT Scores

	Total	Full-time	Part-time
# of apps	859	653	206
# of offers	311	228	83
# of matrics	196	130	66
75% GPA	3.49	3.51	3.43
Median GPA	3.19	3.21	3.08
25% GPA	2.93	2.96	2.81
75% LSAT	156	157	153
Median LSAT	154	155	150
25% LSAT	152	153	148

Grants and Scholarships (from prior year)

	Total		Full-time		Part-time	
	#	%	#	%	#	%
Total # of students	402		275		127	
Total # receiving grants	180	44.8	163	59.3	17	13.4
Less than 1/2 tuition	164	40.8	147	53.5	17	13.4
Half to full tuition	16	4.0	16	5.8	0	0.0
Full tuition	0	0.0	0	0.0	0	0.0
More than full tuition	0	0.0	0	0.0	0	0.0
Median grant amount			$7,000		$5,000	

Informational and Library Resources

# of volumes and volume equivalents	22,827
# of titles	138,844
# of active serial subscriptions	809
Study seating capacity inside the library	220
# of full-time professional librarians	5
Hours per week library is open	103
# of open, wired connections available to students	0
# of networked computers available for use by students	0
# of simultaneous wireless users	700
Require computer?	Yes

JD Attrition (from prior year)

	Academic	Other	Total	
	#	#	#	%
1st year	0	0	0	0.0
2nd year	5	0	5	2.5
3rd year	4	0	4	0.0
4th year	0	0	0	0.0

Employment (9 months after graduation)

	Total	Percentage
Employment status known	0	0.0
Employment status unknown	0	0.0
Employed	0	0.0
Pursuing graduate degrees	0	0.0
Unemployed seeking employment	0	0.0
Unemployed not seeking employment	0	0.0
Unemployed and studying for the bar	0	0.0

Type of Employment

	Total	Percentage
# employed in law firms	0	0.0
# employed in business and industry	0	0.0
# employed in government	0	0.0
# employed in public interest	0	0.0
# employed as judicial clerks	0	0.0
# employed in academia	0	0.0

Geographic Location

	Total	Percentage
# employed in state	0	0.0
# employed in foreign countries	0	0.0
# of states where employed	0	

Bar Passage Rates

Jurisdiction	South Carolina		
Exam	Sum 05	Win 06	Total
# from school taking bar for the first time	0	0	0
School's pass rate for all first-time takers			
State's pass rate for all first-time takers	85%	76%	82%

Charleston School of Law

81 Mary Street, PO Box 535
Charleston, SC 29402
Phone: 843.329.1000, ext. 2143; Fax: 843.329.0491
Website: www.charlestonlaw.org

■ Introduction

The Charleston School of Law (CSOL) offers students the unique opportunity to study the time-honored practice of law amid the beauty and grace of one of the South's oldest and most prestigious cities, Charleston, South Carolina. Founded in 2003, CSOL is a freestanding school. The School of Law received provisional approval from the ABA in December 2006, and graduates are qualified to seek admission to the bar in all 50 states and the District of Columbia.

Located in beautiful downtown Charleston, South Carolina, the school is conveniently situated near the historic "four corners of the law" as well as the thriving legal community and the federal and county courthouses. The open intellectual environment at CSOL complements the progressive nature of the city of Charleston. With its diverse economy, rich cultural heritage, thriving tourist industry, and natural amenities, the city—home to one of the nation's busiest ports—is a hub of activity. Charleston is attractive, fun, and consistently named one of the best places in the country to live, work, and learn. The city is home to other institutions of higher education, including the Medical University of South Carolina, The Citadel, and the College of Charleston. The 580,000-person metropolitan area is served by a strong program of cultural activities. Spoleto Festival USA, an internationally renowned arts festival of opera, dance, music, and theater, draws more than 85,000 people to the city each summer. Visitors and residents delight in Charleston's nationally recognized restaurants, vibrant nightlife, walks along the historic Battery, tours of historic homes, boating, sailing, golf, and beachcombing on nearby Sullivan's Island, Isle of Palms, Folly Beach, or Kiawah Island.

■ Library

The Sol Blatt Jr. Law Library, located in a historic 1857 railroad building, provides the feel of Charleston while housing a state-of-the-art wireless network that provides access to the ever-growing digital collection of the library. In just three years the library has built a digital collection that includes over 260,000 electronic titles.

Students have access on campus or through the Internet from anywhere in the world to full-text materials such as e-books, e-journals, and legal research databases on law and other law-related and interdisciplinary subjects. In addition to the basic legal research databases Lexis and Westlaw, the library offers digital collections of books and journals from Thomson Gale, NetLibrary, ebrary, Greenwood Press, LexisNexis Matthew Bender, Law Library Microform Consortium, HeinOnline, and JSTOR. Through the library's online catalog students gain access to services such as BNA, RIA, LexisNexis Congressional, and several indices. The print collection provides students with access to materials that support classroom studies.

The library is working to offer seamless searching of all electronic resources while providing students with group-study space. The purchase and implementation of a self-checkout system provides a nonmediated circulation system to both students and faculty.

■ Admission

CSOL requires applicants to have earned a bachelor's degree from an accredited institution prior to enrolling in the school. CSOL offers both a full- and part-time program of study leading to the Juris Doctor degree. Beginning students are accepted for the fall semester only. All applicants are required to take the LSAT and register with LSDAS. Applicants should submit a completed application, a personal statement, a dean's certification from all colleges attended for 12 or more credit hours, and two letters of recommendation, plus pay a $50 application fee. The deadline for applying to the full-time program is applications postmarked on or before March 1 and on or before April 1 for those applying for the part-time program.

Consideration is given to many factors; however, the two most important factors in reviewing an application are the cumulative undergraduate GPA and the LSAT. If an applicant has multiple LSAT scores, the high score will be considered. A score is valid for three years. Other factors taken into consideration are graduate work, military or significant work experience, letters of recommendation, the personal statement, and community service.

■ Expenses and Financial Aid

Tuition for the 2006–2007 academic year was as follows: full time—$27,970, part time—$20,980; fees—$1,000; estimated living expenses—$14,000. The school offers both need- and merit-based scholarships. Applicants wanting to be considered for merit scholarships must have a complete file on or before February 1. Merit-based scholarship decisions are made in early March. Need-based scholarship applications must be postmarked no later than June 1. Beginning in fall 2007, students should be eligible for federal student loans and will be required to complete the FAFSA.

■ Curriculum

Students at CSOL study law as a profession with an emphasis on excellence in the classroom. The low faculty/student ratio is a testament to the student-centered focus. Small class size promotes individual inquiry in a collegial learning atmosphere. The goals of CSOL include teaching the practice of law as a profession with the chief aim of providing public service; and instituting and coordinating legal outreach programs to the South Carolina and American Bars; local, state, and federal governments; and the general populations.

Courses in torts, property, contracts, civil procedure, and legal writing and research comprise the first-year curriculum. Required upper-level courses include business associations, commercial law, constitutional law, criminal law, criminal procedure, domestic relations, equity, evidence, insurance, trust and estates, and professional responsibility, as well as an advanced writing requirement and a skills course.

All students are required to perform a minimum of 30 hours of public service prior to graduation and to participate in a professionalism program during each of the three years of law school.

■ Special Programs

The school offers a dynamic externship program that provides students the opportunity to get practical work experience in legal business environments while earning course credit. Students have the opportunity to work under the direct supervision of members of the judiciary and attorneys in private practice, as well as in the public sector or in public interest jobs. In 2006, more than 80 organizations including county public defenders' offices, state agencies, state and federal courts, and nonprofit agencies in South Carolina and beyond offered more than 120 externship opportunities to students.

Courses in admiralty and maritime law are available to students enrolled in the school. The Charleston Maritime Law Institute was founded by students and publishes the *Maritime Law Bulletin* (MALABU).

■ Housing

The school does not offer on-campus housing. Charleston offers many options for off-campus living. Whether a student opts to live in the downtown historic district, at one of the nearby beaches, or in one of the many convenient neighborhoods and communities, carriage houses, apartments, or rental houses are available. The office of admission works with incoming and continuing students to find housing in the Charleston area.

■ Student Activities

Students have the opportunity to work on the publication of two law reviews. A student board publishes the *Charleston Law Review* on a quarterly basis. Students also have the chance to work with federal magistrate judges to publish the printed edition of the *Federal Courts Law Review*.

Moot court opportunities are also available to students enrolled in the school. In its first-ever national competition in 2006, a team of students from CSOL won the grand prize in the National Constitutional Law Moot Court Competition.

The school has more than 23 student organizations, including, but not limited to, the Student Bar Association, the Black Law Student Association, International Law Society, Environmental Law Society, Real Estate Society, Student Trial Lawyers Association, and Women in Law.

■ Career Services

The Career Services Office provides a wide range of career development services for CSOL students and creates opportunities to connect students with employers in an efficient and supportive manner. The office serves as a liaison between students and legal employers. The staff provides individual career counseling, programming on career-related issues, and individualized résumé-writing assistance. They also coordinate the on-campus interview program and résumé-forwarding services, as well as the school's participation in national and regional career fairs. In addition, the staff is responsible for the maintenance of a dynamic database of employers and an online career resource center.

The office is available to assist students in finding part-time employment while enrolled in law school, summer employment, and full-time permanent employment upon graduation. The Charleston area provides myriad opportunities for part-time employment while students are enrolled in their second and third years of law school.

CSOL prepares students for careers in all areas of legal practice. Regardless of a student's path after graduation, CSOL strives to instill in students the value of public service. All students must complete 30 hours of pro bono legal service under the supervision of an attorney licensed in South Carolina before they graduate. The Career Services Office develops and supports pro bono opportunities in the legal community and provides guidance to students in their selection of pro bono work.

Applicant Profile

Charleston School of Law

LSAT Score	GPA								
	3.75 +	3.50–3.74	3.25–3.49	3.00–3.24	2.75–2.99	2.50–2.74	2.25–2.49	2.00–2.24	Below 2.00
175–180									
170–174									
165–169									
160–164									
155–159									
150–154									
145–149									
140–144									
135–139									
130–134									
125–129									
120–124									

Good Possibility Possible Unlikely

The University of Chicago Law School

1111 E. 60th Street
Chicago, IL 60637
Phone: 773.702.9494; Fax: 773.834.0942
E-mail: admissions@law.uchicago.edu; Website: www.law.uchicago.edu

*ABA
Approved
Since
1923*

The Basics

Type of school	Private
Term	Quarter
Application deadline	2/1
Application fee	$75
Financial aid deadline	3/1
Can first year start other than fall?	No
Student to faculty ratio	9.4 to 1
Does the university offer:	
housing restricted to law students?	No
graduate housing for which law students are eligible?	Yes

Faculty and Administrators

	Total		Men		Women		Minorities	
	Fall	Spr	Fall	Spr	Fall	Spr	Fall	Spr
Full-time	53	52	44	43	9	9	3	4
Other Full-time	15	15	9	9	6	6	3	3
Deans, librarians, & others who teach	2	2	1	1	1	1	0	0
Part-time	15	58	13	48	2	10	1	5
Total	85	127	67	101	18	26	7	12

Curriculum

	Full-time	Part-time
Typical first-year section size	96	0
Is there typically a "small section" of the first-year class, other than Legal Writing, taught by full-time faculty	No	No
If yes, typical size offered last year		
# of classroom course titles beyond first-year curriculum	156	

# of upper division courses, excluding seminars with an enrollment:	Under 25	30
	25–49	34
	50–74	19
	75–99	13
	100+	4

# of seminars	82	
# of seminar positions available	1,543	
# of seminar positions filled	1,271	0
# of positions available in simulation courses	140	
# of simulation positions filled	121	0
# of positions available in faculty supervised clinical courses	124	
# of faculty supervised clinical positions filled	124	0
# involved in field placements	12	0
# involved in law journals	130	0
# involved in interschool competitions	0	0
# of credit hours required to graduate	105	

JD Enrollment and Ethnicity

	Men		Women		Full-time		Part-time		1st-year		Total		JD Degs. Awd.
	#	%	#	%	#	%	#	%	#	%	#	%	
African Amer.	20	6.0	23	8.6	43	7.2	0	0.0	12	6.3	43	7.2	15
Amer. Indian	1	0.3	3	1.1	4	0.7	0	0.0	3	1.6	4	0.7	1
Asian Amer.	33	9.9	44	16.4	77	12.8	0	0.0	26	13.5	77	12.8	27
Mex. Amer.	7	2.1	10	3.7	17	2.8	0	0.0	5	2.6	17	2.8	6
Puerto Rican	4	1.2	2	0.7	6	1.0	0	0.0	1	0.5	6	1.0	3
Hispanic	15	4.5	17	6.3	32	5.3	0	0.0	10	5.2	32	5.3	13
Total Minority	80	24.1	99	36.9	179	29.8	0	0.0	57	29.7	179	29.8	65
For. Nation.	2	0.6	3	1.1	5	0.8	0	0.0	2	1.0	5	0.8	1
Caucasian	209	63.0	133	49.6	342	57.0	0	0.0	111	57.8	342	57.0	111
Unknown	41	12.3	33	12.3	74	12.3	0	0.0	22	11.5	74	12.3	15
Total	332	55.3	268	44.7	600	100.0	0	0.0	192	32.0	600		192

Transfers

Transfers in	18
Transfers out	2

Tuition and Fees

	Resident	Nonresident
Full-time	$37,945	$0
Part-time	$0	$0

Living Expenses

Estimated living expenses for singles

Living on campus	Living off campus	Living at home
$21,333	$21,333	$21,333

The University of Chicago Law School

*ABA
Approved
Since
1923*

GPA and LSAT Scores

	Total	Full-time	Part-time
# of apps	4,818	4,818	0
# of offers	766	766	0
# of matrics	192	192	0
75% GPA	3.77	3.77	0.00
Median GPA	3.67	3.67	0.00
25% GPA	3.51	3.51	0.00
75% LSAT	172	172	0
Median LSAT	171	171	0
25% LSAT	169	169	0

Grants and Scholarships (from prior year)

	Total		Full-time		Part-time	
	#	%	#	%	#	%
Total # of students	589		589		0	
Total # receiving grants	300	50.9	300	50.9	0	0.0
Less than 1/2 tuition	244	41.4	244	41.4	0	0.0
Half to full tuition	56	9.5	56	9.5	0	0.0
Full tuition	0	0.0	0	0.0	0	0.0
More than full tuition	0	0.0	0	0.0	0	0.0
Median grant amount			$9,950		$0	

Informational and Library Resources

# of volumes and volume equivalents	656,531
# of titles	264,796
# of active serial subscriptions	8,424
Study seating capacity inside the library	450
# of full-time professional librarians	9
Hours per week library is open	90
# of open, wired connections available to students	1,036
# of networked computers available for use by students	26
# of simultaneous wireless users	500
Require computer?	Yes

JD Attrition (from prior year)

	Academic	Other	Total	
	#	#	#	%
1st year	0	2	2	1.0
2nd year	0	2	2	1.0
3rd year	0	4	4	2.1
4th year	0	0	0	0.0

Employment (9 months after graduation)

	Total	Percentage
Employment status known	204	100.0
Employment status unknown	0	0.0
Employed	193	94.6
Pursuing graduate degrees	1	0.5
Unemployed seeking employment	3	1.5
Unemployed not seeking employment	7	3.4
Unemployed and studying for the bar	0	0.0
Type of Employment		
# employed in law firms	138	71.5
# employed in business and industry	5	2.6
# employed in government	5	2.6
# employed in public interest	2	1.0
# employed as judicial clerks	40	20.7
# employed in academia	3	1.6
Geographic Location		
# employed in state	61	31.6
# employed in foreign countries	2	1.0
# of states where employed	26	

Bar Passage Rates

Jurisdiction	Illinois			New York		
Exam	Sum 05	Win 06	Total	Sum 05	Win 06	Total
# from school taking bar for the first time	77	13	90	80	6	86
School's pass rate for all first-time takers	97%	85%	96%	88%	100%	88%
State's pass rate for all first-time takers	86%	83%	85%	76%	61%	74%

The University of Chicago Law School

Admissions Office, 1111 E. 60th Street
Chicago, IL 60637
Phone: 773.702.9494; Fax: 773.834.0942
E-mail: admissions@law.uchicago.edu; Website: www.law.uchicago.edu

■ Introduction

Chicago graduates lead and innovate in government, public causes, academia, and business, as well as law. For this reason, Chicago aims not to certify lawyers, but to train well-rounded, critical, and socially conscious thinkers and doers. Three cornerstones provide the foundation for Chicago's educational mission: the marketplace of ideas, participatory learning, and interdisciplinary inquiry.

■ Enrollment/Student Body

Our students' chief passion is intellectual rigor. They have shown this passion through their academic success, and they exhibit signs of great professional promise. About 5,000 applicants seek approximately 190–195 seats in each incoming class. Chicago students come from more than 100 undergraduate institutions with degrees in nearly every discipline, and one in ten have graduate degrees. Many of our students have also had interesting and successful careers before law school.

■ Faculty

What distinguishes Chicago faculty is their devotion to both teaching and scholarship. This might seem a contradiction at first, but at Chicago, teaching and scholarship complement each other. Chicago professors blaze trails in legal thought, and their revolutionary ideas infuse classroom discussion with immediacy and excitement. Our professors write the books, draft the statutes, and decide the cases that students read at law schools across America. During the 2006–2007 academic year, our faculty will teach more than 170 courses and seminars at the Law School.

■ Curriculum

As a first-year student, you will take a core sequence covering five principal areas of the law: contracts, torts, property, criminal law, and civil procedure; a required interdisciplinary course called Elements of the Law; an elective; and a year-long course on research and writing. This curriculum familiarizes you with the basic principles of Anglo-American law, cultivates legal reasoning, develops writing ability, and introduces students to interdisciplinary approaches to the law.

In the second and third years, you can choose courses from the full range of Chicago's more than 170 classes. Generally, classes are small; more than 60 percent have fewer than 25 students in them. Additionally, in an average year, about one-third of the second- and third-year students take classes in other divisions of the university.

■ Special Programs

The Law School encourages interdisciplinary work. All students may take 12 hours of coursework anywhere in the university. Students may also apply for three formal joint-degree programs either at the same time they apply to the Law School or in their first year. They may also work with Law School and university staff to arrange concurrent degrees. Formal joint-degree

programs are with the Graduate School of Business (MBA, PhD), the Harris School of Public Policy (MPP), and the Committee on International Relations (MA).

The Law School is home to a wide variety of research programs. These programs provide excellent outlets for both the theoretical and empirical work of both faculty and students. In addition, these programs host conferences, publish working papers, and support journals. Centers currently at the Law School include the Center on Civil Justice, the Center for Comparative Constitutionalism, the Center for Studies in Criminal Justice, and the John M. Olin Program in Law and Economics.

The Law School is committed to making big contributions to topics of national interest—health care, animal rights, and immigration policy just to name a few. The Chicago Policy Initiatives encourage faculty members and students to work together, think hard about important social problems, and propose solutions. Current projects include the Chicago Judges Project, Chicago Project on Animal Treatment, and Chicago Project on Foster Care.

■ Clinical Opportunities

Housed in the Arthur Kane Center, our clinics involve more than 100 students each year in representing clients with real-world problems. The Mandel Legal Aid Clinic handles matters involving appellate advocacy, criminal and juvenile justice, employment discrimination, civil rights, housing, immigration, and mental health. The Institute for Justice Clinic on Entrepreneurship assists aspiring entry-level entrepreneurs from low- and moderate-income neighborhoods. The Law School also partners with outside agencies to provide additional clinical opportunities to our students.

■ Student Activities

About 40 percent of upper-class students serve on one of the three student-edited journals, the newest of which is *The Chicago Journal of International Law*. The Hinton Moot Court Board conducts a program in appellate advocacy for upper-class students, and first-year students participate in a moot court as part of the writing and research program. More than 40 student organizations provide opportunities for the exploration of legal specialties, affiliation with like-minded students, or networking within identity groups.

■ Career Services

Our career services office assists students with permanent and summer employment. Four professional career advisors counsel students in one-on-one planning sessions. Programs on types of practices and nontraditional careers are organized throughout the year for students. Graduates of the Class of 2006 took jobs in these areas: 72 percent joined law firms, 21 percent are clerking for judges, 5 percent are in government/public service, and 2 percent are in business. The top four destinations for our graduates are Chicago, Los Angeles, New York, and Washington, DC.

■ Location

Hyde Park provides Chicago students with the best of all possible worlds: a campus with a college-town atmosphere just a few miles from the downtown of a vibrant city. Hyde Park is a dynamic community with parks, museums, and multiple bookstores. The Law School is located at the southern end of campus, facing an expansive "front lawn" known as the Midway Plaisance. Surrounding the Law School are a tree-lined, diverse residential neighborhood, a sandy Lake Michigan beach, and two sprawling parks. The campus itself is a Gothic masterpiece where limestone buildings, built around tree-shaded quadrangles, sport gargoyles, ivy, and turrets. The Law School's modern building promotes interaction among faculty and students, while the recently remodeled classroom wing enhances the learning experience.

■ Housing

A graduate residence hall, located two blocks from the Law School, is available to law students. Most rooms are singles with private baths. In addition, the university has plenty of single and married student neighborhood housing available. Many students choose to rent housing from private landlords. Buses run frequently throughout the surrounding neighborhood, providing transportation to and from residences and the Law School. Public transportation is easily accessible to other neighborhoods in Chicago.

■ Admission

Each year we seek to create a community from among the best and brightest law school applicants. We want students who are intellectually curious, lively, collegial, and rigorous in their academic approach. We want students who will take their legal education seriously but not take themselves too seriously. And because we are preparing students to enter a multifaceted profession, we want multidimensional students with a wide range of talents, backgrounds, experiences, and accomplishments. We do not use indices, formulas, or cutoffs.

■ Financial Aid

Your Chicago legal education is an investment in your future. Because many students will not have sufficient personal resources to make this investment, Chicago provides generous financial aid. Approximately 50 percent of the students receive scholarships and most of these are supplemented if the student engages in public interest work during the summer after second year. The Law School also guarantees funding for students who work in public interest positions during their first year summer. After graduation, the Law School provides financial assistance to graduates who enter careers in public interest legal work through our generous Hormel Public Interest Program.

Applicant Profile

We seek to create a community from among the best, the brightest, and the most interesting law school applicants. We do not believe that the LSAT and GPA alone provide us with sufficient information to evaluate an applicant's likely contributions to our community; therefore, we do not use any formulas, indices, or numerical cutoffs. We do not provide an applicant profile here because it would be bast solely on the LSAT and GPA.

Chicago-Kent College of Law, Illinois Institute of Technology

565 West Adams Street
Chicago, IL 60661
Phone: 312.906.5020; Fax: 312.906.5274
E-mail: admit@kentlaw.edu; Website: www.kentlaw.edu

ABA
Approved
Since
1936

The Basics

Type of school	Private
Term	Semester
Application deadline	3/1
Application fee	$60
Financial aid deadline	
Can first year start other than fall?	No
Student to faculty ratio	12.3 to 1
Does the university offer:	
housing restricted to law students?	No
graduate housing for which law students are eligible?	Yes

Faculty and Administrators

	Total		Men		Women		Minorities	
	Fall	Spr	Fall	Spr	Fall	Spr	Fall	Spr
Full-time	64	62	43	40	21	21	6	5
Other Full-time	2	3	1	2	1	1	0	0
Deans, librarians, & others who teach	4	4	2	2	2	2	1	1
Part-time	81	87	59	64	22	23	6	7
Total	151	156	105	108	46	47	13	13

Curriculum

	Full-time	Part-time
Typical first-year section size	56	51
Is there typically a "small section" of the first-year class, other than Legal Writing, taught by full-time faculty	No	No
If yes, typical size offered last year		
# of classroom course titles beyond first-year curriculum	131	

# of upper division courses, excluding seminars with an enrollment:		
Under 25	203	
25–49	45	
50–74	14	
75–99	13	
100+	5	

# of seminars	34	
# of seminar positions available	465	
# of seminar positions filled	269	63
# of positions available in simulation courses	606	
# of simulation positions filled	209	291
# of positions available in faculty supervised clinical courses	246	
# of faculty supervised clinical positions filled	224	9
# involved in field placements	130	15
# involved in law journals	56	9
# involved in interschool competitions	65	5
# of credit hours required to graduate	87	

JD Enrollment and Ethnicity

	Men		Women		Full-time		Part-time		1st-year		Total		JD Degs. Awd.
	#	%	#	%	#	%	#	%	#	%	#	%	
African Amer.	29	5.2	32	6.6	41	5.3	20	7.5	23	7.5	61	5.9	15
Amer. Indian	0	0.0	2	0.4	1	0.1	1	0.4	0	0.0	2	0.2	3
Asian Amer.	51	9.2	42	8.7	68	8.8	25	9.4	23	7.5	93	8.9	32
Mex. Amer.	15	2.7	10	2.1	18	2.3	7	2.6	9	2.9	25	2.4	3
Puerto Rican	2	0.4	1	0.2	2	0.3	1	0.4	0	0.0	3	0.3	1
Hispanic	17	3.1	16	3.3	24	3.1	9	3.4	11	3.6	33	3.2	7
Total Minority	114	20.5	103	21.2	154	19.8	63	23.8	66	21.4	217	20.8	61
For. Nation.	6	1.1	6	1.2	10	1.3	2	0.8	4	1.3	12	1.2	5
Caucasian	399	71.8	340	70.1	554	71.4	185	69.8	216	70.1	739	71.0	192
Unknown	37	6.7	36	7.4	58	7.5	15	5.7	22	7.1	73	7.0	24
Total	556	53.4	485	46.6	776	74.5	265	25.5	308	29.6	1041		282

Transfers

Transfers in	30
Transfers out	17

Tuition and Fees

	Resident	Nonresident
Full-time	$31,434	$31,434
Part-time	$22,980	$22,980

Living Expenses

Estimated living expenses for singles

Living on campus	Living off campus	Living at home
$16,814	$19,700	$11,150

Chicago-Kent College of Law, Illinois Institute of Technology

ABA
Approved
Since
1936

GPA and LSAT Scores

	Total	Full-time	Part-time
# of apps	3,817	3,034	783
# of offers	1,107	887	220
# of matrics	307	215	92
75% GPA	3.74	3.77	3.53
Median GPA	3.49	3.57	3.33
25% GPA	3.18	3.30	3.11
75% LSAT	163	164	159
Median LSAT	159	161	158
25% LSAT	157	158	156

Grants and Scholarships (from prior year)

	Total		Full-time		Part-time	
	#	%	#	%	#	%
Total # of students	1,049		800		249	
Total # receiving grants	549	52.3	427	53.4	122	49.0
Less than 1/2 tuition	342	32.6	233	29.1	109	43.8
Half to full tuition	116	11.1	104	13.0	12	4.8
Full tuition	72	6.9	71	8.9	1	0.4
More than full tuition	19	1.8	19	2.4	0	0.0
Median grant amount			$10,000		$4,000	

Informational and Library Resources

# of volumes and volume equivalents	548,780
# of titles	176,702
# of active serial subscriptions	2,279
Study seating capacity inside the library	470
# of full-time professional librarians	11
Hours per week library is open	96
# of open, wired connections available to students	1,800
# of networked computers available for use by students	99
# of simultaneous wireless users	600
Require computer?	Yes

JD Attrition (from prior year)

	Academic	Other	Total	
	#	#	#	%
1st year	6	28	34	10.2
2nd year	4	6	10	2.7
3rd year	0	1	1	0.3
4th year	0	0	0	0.0

Employment (9 months after graduation)

	Total	Percentage
Employment status known	319	97.3
Employment status unknown	9	2.7
Employed	277	86.8
Pursuing graduate degrees	7	2.2
Unemployed seeking employment	8	2.5
Unemployed not seeking employment	21	6.6
Unemployed and studying for the bar	6	1.9

Type of Employment

	Total	Percentage
# employed in law firms	174	62.8
# employed in business and industry	51	18.4
# employed in government	31	11.2
# employed in public interest	8	2.9
# employed as judicial clerks	9	3.2
# employed in academia	3	1.1

Geographic Location

	Total	Percentage
# employed in state	229	82.7
# employed in foreign countries	3	1.1
# of states where employed		20

Bar Passage Rates

Jurisdiction		Illinois	
Exam	Sum 05	Win 06	Total
# from school taking bar for the first time	257	32	289
School's pass rate for all first-time takers	87%	84%	87%
State's pass rate for all first-time takers	86%	83%	85%

Chicago-Kent College of Law, Illinois Institute of Technology

Office of Admissions, 565 West Adams Street
Chicago, IL 60661
Phone: 312.906.5020; Fax: 312.906.5274
E-mail: admit@kentlaw.edu; Website: www.kentlaw.edu

■ Introduction

Chicago-Kent College of Law, Illinois Institute of Technology, is a national leader in legal education, recognized for the strength of its faculty and for its innovative approaches to traditional legal education. The second oldest law school in Illinois, Chicago-Kent was founded in 1888 by two judges who believed that legal education should be available to working men and women. In 1895, Chicago-Kent graduated its first female and minority students. Today, Chicago-Kent students come from 42 states and several foreign countries and from more than 260 colleges and universities.

Drawing on its distinctive affiliation with Illinois Institute of Technology, Chicago-Kent is at the vanguard of exploring new frontiers in the law raised by biotechnology, cyberspace, environmental regulation, intellectual property, international criminal law enforcement, and much more. Chicago-Kent is located in downtown Chicago, the heart of the city's commercial and legal communities. The law school is fully accredited by the ABA and the AALS, and is a member of the Order of the Coif.

■ Faculty

The foundation for academic excellence at Chicago-Kent is derived from its faculty, which engages in broad-ranging legal scholarship and research. Chicago-Kent's faculty is among the nation's most productive law faculties based on the number of scholarly books and articles that its members have published in leading academic presses, law reviews, and journals. As advisors frequently approached for their expertise, faculty members help shape policy and thinking on a variety of issues, and make it a point to involve students in their particular areas of influence.

■ Library and Physical Facilities

Chicago-Kent's modern, 10-story building features a 3-story atrium, 5-level library, technologically advanced courtroom, auditorium, computer labs, student lounges, and cafeteria. Chicago-Kent's library is one of the largest law school libraries in the country. The collection includes the Library of International Relations, one of the most comprehensive international law collections, and a wealth of material on environmental and energy law, intellectual property law, international trade law, and labor law.

The law school houses a sophisticated computer network with more than 1,900 network connections located throughout the building and library, and at each seat in the majority of classrooms. Wireless service is available in the courtroom, front lobby, cafeteria, student lounge, and select classrooms.

Affordable housing is available in nearby urban and suburban neighborhoods. On-campus housing is available on the university's main campus, approximately five miles south of the law school. A free shuttle runs between the two campuses. The law school is close to all public transportation downtown.

■ Curriculum

Both full-time and part-time programs are available. Full-time students usually complete the JD degree in three years.

Part-time students usually finish in four years. Students may apply to transfer between divisions after completing the required courses in the division in which they originally enrolled. First-year class sizes range from 30 to 90 students.

Degrees available include JD, JD/MBA, JD/MPA, JD/MPH, JD/LLM in Taxation, JD/LLM in Financial Services Law, JD/LLM in Family Law, JD/MS in Financial Markets and Trading, JD/MS in Environmental Management, LLM in Taxation, LLM in Financial Services Law, LLM in Family Law, LLM in International Intellectual Property Law, and LLM in International and Comparative Law.

■ Special Programs

Legal Research and Writing—Chicago-Kent's acclaimed legal research and writing program is one of the most comprehensive in the nation. The three-year, five-course curriculum teaches students to analyze a wide range of legal problems and to write about them persuasively.

Clinical Education—The Law Offices of Chicago-Kent, one of the largest in-house clinical education programs in the country, offers 10 clinical programs and externships with government agencies and federal judges.

Trial Skills/Litigation and Alternative Dispute Resolution—The law school offers a two-semester sequence in trial advocacy and an intensive course taught by veteran judges and experienced practitioners. Students in the Litigation and Alternative Dispute Resolution program receive training in case analysis as well as exposure to the theoretical and ethical foundations of the law to develop their skills in using litigation and alternative methods to resolve disputes.

Environmental and Energy Law—The program's interdisciplinary approach to the problems of environmental regulation and natural resources allocation prepares students for practice through a series of courses in law, economic and public policy analysis, and in the scientific aspects of environmental problems.

Intellectual Property Law—The program focuses on issues relating to patent, trademark, copyright, trade secrets, and unfair competition, both in the US and abroad.

International and Comparative Law—The program encompasses study in international business and trade, international and comparative law, and international human rights. The Library of International Relations, an official depository for documents of the United Nations and the European Union, is one of the largest public research collections of this material in the Midwest.

Labor and Employment Law—The program provides students with theoretical and practical training in the law governing the workplace.

Public Interest Law—The program provides students with a background in public interest law and policy, in addition to individualized curriculum and career planning. The law school also supports a number of public interest resources and activities, including the Center for Access to Justice and Technology, which aims to make justice more accessible to the public through the use of the Internet; and the Public Interest Resource Center, a student-run initiative dedicated to finding internships and volunteer opportunities for those pursuing the public interest.

Institutes and Centers

Chicago-Kent is home to six institutes and centers with missions that range from conducting scholarly and practical research on legal and social issues to providing topical programming to developing public interest services. These are the Center for Access to Justice and Technology; the Global Law and Policy Initiative; the Institute on Biotechnology and the Human Future; the Institute for Law and the Humanities; the Institute for Law and the Workplace; and the Institute for Science, Law, and Technology. Through these initiatives, many of which involve cross-disciplinary projects, students learn to appreciate and adapt to major social and global influences that can change the legal profession and its practice.

Admission

Admission is highly selective. Each application is individually reviewed and decisions are based on a range of factors, including quantitative and qualitative criteria. Although the GPA and LSAT are important criteria, consideration also is given to nonnumerical factors such as the nature and rigor of the undergraduate curriculum, writing ability, graduate work and professional experience, extracurricular activities, diversity, and the personal statement. The admission requirements for the full- and part-time divisions are the same. Entering classes begin only in the fall. The law school is committed to attracting and retaining students from a variety of racial, ethnic, economic, geographic, and educational backgrounds.

Student Activities

Student editors and staff, in association with a faculty editor, publish the *Chicago-Kent Law Review* in symposium format. Moot Court and Trial Advocacy teams successfully compete in local, regional, and national competitions each year providing numerous opportunities to develop litigation expertise. Diverse student interests are represented in a wide variety of social, political, and professional student groups.

Scholarship Support

Substantial scholarship assistance is offered to entering and continuing students based on factors that include merit, financial need, and contribution to the law school community. The Honors Scholars Program provides renewable scholarships of full-tuition and living expenses, research assistantships, and special seminars to a select group of students who demonstrate exceptional academic and leadership ability.

Career Services

The Office of Career Services, with six full-time staff, offers individual counseling on résumé writing, interview techniques, and job-search strategies and sponsors both on- and off-campus interview programs. Typically, 97 percent of recent graduates find professional employment within nine months of graduation.

Applicant Profile

Chicago-Kent College of Law, Illinois Institute of Technology

LSAT Score	3.75 +		3.50–3.74		3.25–3.49		3.00–3.24		2.75–2.99		2.50–2.74		2.25–2.49		2.00–2.24		Below 2.00		No GPA		Total	
	Apps	Adm	Apps	Adm	Apps	Adm	Apps	Adm	Apps	Adm	Apps	Adm	Apps	Adm	Apps	Adm	Apps	Adm	Apps	Adm	Apps	Adm
170–180	23	14	16	13	7	7	5	4	6	5	3	1	3	1	0	0	0	0	1	1	64	46
165–169	62	30	91	51	44	41	40	36	27	23	7	2	6	5	1	0	1	0	4	2	283	190
160–164	92	82	134	119	126	110	103	70	50	33	35	11	12	1	4	0	0	0	5	5	561	431
155–159	152	110	212	95	272	81	215	42	115	15	57	2	21	1	6	0	1	0	22	4	1073	350
150–154	90	21	168	21	197	15	181	8	112	6	52	1	17	0	11	0	1	0	10	0	839	72
Below 150	51	0	100	4	161	4	172	3	125	1	101	0	57	0	27	0	6	0	33	1	833	13
Total	470	257	721	303	807	258	716	163	435	83	255	17	116	8	49	0	9	0	75	13	3653	1102

Apps = Number of Applicants
Adm = Number Admitted
Reflects 99% of the total applicant pool.

This grid represents admission data for applicants to both the full- and part-time programs. The information in this grid is to be used only as an approximate gauge of the likelihood of admission and not as a guarantee. Individual accomplishments and other nonnumerical factors are also of importance to the Admissions Committee.

University of Cincinnati College of Law

PO Box 210040
Cincinnati, OH 45221-0040
Phone: 513.556.6805; Fax: 513.556.2391
E-mail: admissions@law.uc.edu; Website: www.law.uc.edu

ABA
Approved
Since
1923

The Basics

Type of school	Public
Term	Semester
Application deadline	3/1
Application fee	$35
Financial aid deadline	3/1
Can first year start other than fall?	No
Student to faculty ratio	10.7 to 1
Does the university offer:	
housing restricted to law students?	No
graduate housing for which law students are eligible?	Yes

Faculty and Administrators

	Total		Men		Women		Minorities	
	Fall	Spr	Fall	Spr	Fall	Spr	Fall	Spr
Full-time	32	28	16	12	16	16	5	5
Other Full-time	0	0	0	0	0	0	0	0
Deans, librarians, & others who teach	4	4	2	2	2	2	0	0
Part-time	23	35	20	28	3	7	0	2
Total	**59**	**67**	**38**	**42**	**21**	**25**	**5**	**7**

Curriculum

	Full-time	Part-time
Typical first-year section size	48	0
Is there typically a "small section" of the first-year class, other than Legal Writing, taught by full-time faculty	Yes	No
If yes, typical size offered last year	19	
# of classroom course titles beyond first-year curriculum		111
# of upper division courses, excluding seminars with an enrollment: Under 25		47
25–49		12
50–74		6
75–99		4
100+		1
# of seminars		27
# of seminar positions available		407
# of seminar positions filled	320	0
# of positions available in simulation courses		248
# of simulation positions filled	208	0
# of positions available in faculty supervised clinical courses		37
# of faculty supervised clinical positions filled	37	0
# involved in field placements	112	0
# involved in law journals	137	0
# involved in interschool competitions	34	0
# of credit hours required to graduate		90

JD Enrollment and Ethnicity

	Men		Women		Full-time		Part-time		1st-year		Total		JD Degs. Awd.
	#	%	#	%	#	%	#	%	#	%	#	%	
African Amer.	10	5.2	16	8.7	26	6.9	0	0.0	9	8.0	26	6.9	12
Amer. Indian	1	0.5	2	1.1	3	0.8	0	0.0	0	0.0	3	0.8	1
Asian Amer.	10	5.2	13	7.1	23	6.1	0	0.0	10	8.8	23	6.1	7
Mex. Amer.	0	0.0	0	0.0	0	0.0	0	0.0	0	0.0	0	0.0	0
Puerto Rican	1	0.5	2	1.1	3	0.8	0	0.0	0	0.0	3	0.8	0
Hispanic	2	1.0	9	4.9	11	2.9	0	0.0	4	3.5	11	2.9	1
Total Minority	24	12.5	42	22.8	66	17.6	0	0.0	23	20.4	66	17.6	21
For. Nation.	1	0.5	0	0.0	1	0.3	0	0.0	0	0.0	1	0.3	0
Caucasian	167	87.0	142	77.2	309	82.2	0	0.0	90	79.6	309	82.2	102
Unknown	0	0.0	0	0.0	0	0.0	0	0.0	0	0.0	0	0.0	0
Total	192	51.1	184	48.9	376	100.0	0	0.0	113	30.1	376		123

Transfers

Transfers in	8
Transfers out	12

Tuition and Fees

	Resident	Nonresident
Full-time	$18,032	$32,152
Part-time	$0	$0

Living Expenses

Estimated living expenses for singles

Living on campus	Living off campus	Living at home
$14,495	$14,495	$14,495

University of Cincinnati College of Law

ABA
Approved
Since
1923

GPA and LSAT Scores

	Total	Full-time	Part-time
# of apps	1,183	1,183	0
# of offers	407	407	0
# of matrics	113	113	0
75% GPA	3.80	3.80	0.00
Median GPA	3.60	3.60	0.00
25% GPA	3.31	3.31	0.00
75% LSAT	161	161	0
Median LSAT	160	160	0
25% LSAT	157	157	0

Grants and Scholarships (from prior year)

	Total		Full-time		Part-time	
	#	%	#	%	#	%
Total # of students	397		397		0	
Total # receiving grants	240	60.5	240	60.5	0	0.0
Less than 1/2 tuition	188	47.4	188	47.4	0	0.0
Half to full tuition	38	9.6	38	9.6	0	0.0
Full tuition	14	3.5	14	3.5	0	0.0
More than full tuition	0	0.0	0	0.0	0	0.0
Median grant amount			$6,000		$0	

Informational and Library Resources

# of volumes and volume equivalents	427,181
# of titles	200,053
# of active serial subscriptions	8,387
Study seating capacity inside the library	333
# of full-time professional librarians	13
Hours per week library is open	95
# of open, wired connections available to students	6
# of networked computers available for use by students	70
# of simultaneous wireless users	320
Require computer?	No

JD Attrition (from prior year)

	Academic	Other	Total	
	#	#	#	%
1st year	0	12	12	9.2
2nd year	0	1	1	0.7
3rd year	0	0	0	0.0
4th year	0	0	0	0.0

Employment (9 months after graduation)

	Total	Percentage
Employment status known	118	95.9
Employment status unknown	5	4.1
Employed	107	90.7
Pursuing graduate degrees	4	3.4
Unemployed seeking employment	1	0.8
Unemployed not seeking employment	6	5.1
Unemployed and studying for the bar	0	0.0
Type of Employment		
# employed in law firms	52	48.6
# employed in business and industry	10	9.3
# employed in government	12	11.2
# employed in public interest	12	11.2
# employed as judicial clerks	16	15.0
# employed in academia	2	1.9
Geographic Location		
# employed in state	66	61.7
# employed in foreign countries	2	1.9
# of states where employed		17

Bar Passage Rates

Jurisdiction		Ohio		
Exam	Sum 05	Win 06	Total	
# from school taking bar for the first time	80	8	88	
School's pass rate for all first-time takers	88%	88%	88%	
State's pass rate for all first-time takers	81%	76%	81%	

University of Cincinnati College of Law

PO Box 210040, Office of Admission and Financial Aid
Cincinnati, OH 45221-0040
Phone: 513.556.6805; Fax: 513.556.2391
E-mail: admissions@law.uc.edu; Website: www.law.uc.edu

■ Introduction

The College of Law has a rich heritage and proud traditions. Throughout its 175-year history, graduates have been leaders of the bench and bar, served in senior governmental positions, been active in the public service community, and succeeded in business, academia, and countless other fields. With a vision to be the premier small, urban, public law school in America, the college is focused on being nationally recognized for its excellence, relevance, and impact. The size of the school allows for small classes and a high degree of personal interaction with faculty and other students. The law school is located on UC's recently renovated main campus in Clifton, approximately 10 minutes north of the city's central business district. This provides easy access to state, county, and federal courts, including the US Court of Appeals for the Sixth Circuit. A charter member of the AALS, UC was one of the first law schools to have a chapter of the Order of the Coif and to be approved by the ABA.

■ Student Body

The 385 students in the College of Law, no more than 135 per class, come from an amazingly wide variety of backgrounds, experiences, and perspectives. The student body is also talented academically, as the 75th/25th LSAT and UGPA percentiles for fall 2006 are 161/157 and 3.80/3.31. The applicant pool and offers of admission were evenly divided between resident and nonresident applicants, although a typical first-year class has a resident population of about 65 percent. The College of Law is committed to enrolling a diverse class, as 20 percent of our students are from minority backgrounds, about one-half are female, and 33 percent enroll from states other than Ohio. The average age of the entering class is 24; however, 18 percent of the class are 27 or older.

■ Faculty

The college employs a full-time faculty of 26 who pride themselves on their teaching, scholarship, and accessibility to students. As the core of the academic program, faculty members bring areas of expertise into the classroom that add depth, perspective, and professionalism to the law students' studies. The student-to-faculty ratio of under 10.7:1 provides ample opportunities for individual discussions with faculty or in-depth research in areas of interest.

■ Library and Physical Facilities

The Robert S. Marx Law Library has a seasoned staff that is able to assist students with research and technical questions. Two computer labs and a wireless network throughout the law building enable students to maximize online research capabilities, and our skilled IT staff members are readily available to assist law students. The law library, which can seat the entire law student body at one time, manages collections carefully to support faculty and student research and the college curriculum.

■ Curriculum

First-year students are divided into six individual sections, creating an unusual advantage of very small first-year sections (typically no larger than 23). The small section modules allow for further inquiry beyond the typical first-year curriculum. First-year students take two courses in small sections with opportunities to study with all members of their class over the entire year. The upper level is well balanced between theory and skills-related courses. Institutes and research centers exist in the areas of International Human Rights, Law and Justice/Ohio Innocence Project, Corporate Law, Center for Practice in Negotiation and Problem Solving (Dispute Resolution), and Law and Psychiatry. The college also offers joint programs with Women's Studies, Business, Community Planning, Political Science, and Social Work. The law school also has an appellate law clinic with the Sixth Circuit Court of Appeals as well as a domestic relations clinic housed downtown at the Cincinnati Legal Aid offices.

■ Special Programs

The College of Law recognizes that a lawyer needs both a firm grasp of subject matter and expertise in professional skills. The college has therefore developed an extensive legal research and writing program that not only encompasses the first year, but upper-level courses as well. The Center for Professional Development provides students with extern experiences, which are opportunities to work with practicing attorneys and public clinics. The Rosenthal Institute for Justice has also been recently endowed to ensure popular programs like the Ohio Innocence Project are available to students now and in the future. Each institute and research center offers a fellowship program, research opportunities, and in-depth study in their respective areas. The college was the first to offer a joint degree in law and women's studies and has the oldest endowed international human rights program at an American law school, the Urban Morgan Institute for Human Rights.

■ Admission Standards

Admission to the college is based upon a selective review of each applicant's file by the Admissions Committee. Although the Admissions Committee relies on the grade-point average and LSAT score to determine the applicant's academic potential, other nonquantitative factors believed to be relevant to success in law school are considered; that is, the quality of the applicant's education, participation in community service, employment experience, graduate work, and letters of recommendation. The educational philosophy of the college reflects a belief that a quality legal education is enhanced through having a heterogeneous student body. The committee, therefore, also considers race, cultural background, unusual personal circumstances, and age. Admission decisions are made on a rolling basis. The College of Law has also instituted a binding early decision program. Students interested in applying through the Early Decision Program must have a completed application on file by December 1. The college is committed to enrolling a diverse and engaging class each year.

Student Activities

The College of Law offers numerous opportunities for students to sharpen their legal writing, advocacy, and leadership skills. The *University of Cincinnati Law Review* was founded in 1927 and was the first law review published by an Ohio law school. The Urban Morgan Institute for Human Rights edits the *Human Rights Quarterly*, the leading international human rights journal in the world. The *Immigration and Nationality Law Review* is an annual publication of papers on the subjects of immigration and citizenship. The *Freedom Center Journal*, a collaboration between the law school and the National Underground Railroad Freedom Center, offers opportunities to publish scholarly works about cutting-edge issues of today, informed by the legacy of historic struggles for freedom. The College of Law also offers a well-respected Moot Court Program with teams participating in many national competitions. The college hosts the Rendigs National Products Liability Moot Court Competition each April. The college supports 29 student organizations and honor societies that assist students in developing leadership skills while building professional and social networks.

Expenses and Financial Aid

For the 2006–2007 academic year, resident and nonresident tuition and fees figures are $18,032 and $32,152, respectively.

Nonresidents can reclassify as state residents by becoming independent and self-sustaining for their first year in law school. Cincinnati is a cosmopolitan yet affordable Midwestern city with living expenses estimated at $14,687 for the nine-month academic year. Scholarships are awarded to approximately 50–60 percent of the student body in order to attract an academically talented and diverse student body. The FAFSA should be filed by March 1 as a priority deadline in order to qualify for student loan packages by spring. A large percentage of second- and third-year students work with law firms, companies, and agencies in the Greater Cincinnati area in order to offset living expenses or student loan debt.

Placement

The College of Law maintains an active Center for Professional Development with a staff of three attorneys, creating one of the best staff-to-law student ratios in the country. Each year, we promote hundreds of full-time, summer, and part-time job opportunities for our students' consideration. For our class of 2005, 97 percent of those in the job market were either employed or enrolled in a full-time degree program within nine months of graduation. For those accepting employment with law firms (49.1 percent) the median salary was $95,000, with a maximum of $142,500. Graduates are employed throughout the United States and abroad.

Applicant Profile

University of Cincinnati College of Law
This grid includes only applicants who earned 120–180 LSAT scores under standard administrations.

LSAT Score	3.75 +		3.50–3.74		3.25–3.49		3.00–3.24		2.75–2.99		2.50–2.74		2.25–2.49		2.00–2.24		Below 2.00		No GPA		Total	
	Apps	Adm	Apps	Adm	Apps	Adm	Apps	Adm	Apps	Adm	Apps	Adm	Apps	Adm	Apps	Adm	Apps	Adm	Apps	Adm	Apps	Adm
175–180	0	0	0	0	0	0	0	0	0	0	0	0	0	0	0	0	0	0	0	0	0	0
170–174	0	0	2	2	2	2	0	0	0	0	0	0	0	0	0	0	0	0	0	0	4	4
165–169	19	19	8	8	14	14	5	5	3	3	2	2	1	1	1	0	0	0	0	0	53	52
160–164	42	39	53	52	36	34	29	27	10	9	11	9	4	3	2	1	0	0	0	0	187	174
155–159	69	57	70	31	78	16	61	6	28	2	17	2	7	1	3	1	1	0	4	1	338	117
150–154	59	23	77	12	59	9	50	2	32	2	18	0	11	0	3	0	1	0	3	0	313	48
145–149	17	1	34	1	39	3	35	3	22	0	14	0	4	0	2	0	0	0	1	0	168	8
140–144	6	0	8	1	14	0	16	0	13	0	7	0	6	0	2	0	0	0	4	0	76	1
135–139	0	0	2	0	2	0	6	0	7	0	2	0	1	0	4	0	0	0	3	0	27	0
130–134	1	0	0	0	1	0	0	0	3	0	4	0	2	0	0	0	1	0	0	0	12	0
125–129	0	0	0	0	0	0	1	0	1	0	0	0	1	0	0	0	1	0	1	0	5	0
120–124	0	0	0	0	0	0	0	0	0	0	0	0	0	0	0	0	0	0	0	0	0	0
Total	213	139	254	107	245	78	203	43	119	16	75	13	37	5	17	2	4	0	16	1	1183	404

Apps = Number of Applicants
Adm = Number Admitted
Reflects 99% of the total applicant pool.

City University of New York School of Law

65-21 Main Street
Flushing, NY 11367
Phone: 718.340.4210; Fax: 718.340.4435
E-mail: admissions@mail.law.cuny.edu; Website: www.law.cuny.edu

ABA Approved Since 1985

The Basics

Type of school	Public
Term	Semester
Application deadline	3/15
Application fee	$50
Financial aid deadline	5/1
Can first year start other than fall?	No
Student to faculty ratio	12.8 to 1
Does the university offer:	
housing restricted to law students?	No
graduate housing for which law students are eligible?	No

Curriculum

	Full-time	Part-time
Typical first-year section size	80	0
Is there typically a "small section" of the first-year class, other than Legal Writing, taught by full-time faculty	Yes	No
If yes, typical size offered last year	20	
# of classroom course titles beyond first-year curriculum		65
# of upper division courses, excluding seminars with an enrollment: Under 25		30
25–49		10
50–74		6
75–99		1
100+		1
# of seminars		16
# of seminar positions available		320
# of seminar positions filled	333	0
# of positions available in simulation courses		320
# of simulation positions filled	333	0
# of positions available in faculty supervised clinical courses		166
# of faculty supervised clinical positions filled	145	0
# involved in field placements	44	0
# involved in law journals	41	0
# involved in interschool competitions	43	0
# of credit hours required to graduate		91

Faculty and Administrators

	Total		Men		Women		Minorities	
	Fall	Spr	Fall	Spr	Fall	Spr	Fall	Spr
Full-time	27	27	13	12	14	15	11	10
Other Full-time	2	2	1	1	1	1	1	1
Deans, librarians, & others who teach	9	10	3	3	6	7	3	3
Part-time	16	9	6	4	10	5	7	4
Total	54	48	23	20	31	28	22	18

Transfers

Transfers in	4
Transfers out	10

JD Enrollment and Ethnicity

	Men		Women		Full-time		Part-time		1st-year		Total		JD Degs. Awd.
	#	%	#	%	#	%	#	%	#	%	#	%	
African Amer.	10	6.9	20	7.2	29	7.0	1	25.0	10	6.7	30	7.1	15
Amer. Indian	1	0.7	0	0.0	1	0.2	0	0.0	1	0.7	1	0.2	1
Asian Amer.	21	14.6	45	16.2	66	15.8	0	0.0	21	14.0	66	15.7	10
Mex. Amer.	0	0.0	0	0.0	0	0.0	0	0.0	0	0.0	0	0.0	0
Puerto Rican	1	0.7	1	0.4	2	0.5	0	0.0	0	0.0	2	0.5	1
Hispanic	8	5.6	24	8.7	31	7.4	1	25.0	7	4.7	32	7.6	16
Total Minority	41	28.5	90	32.5	129	30.9	2	50.0	39	26.0	131	31.1	43
For. Nation.	7	4.9	10	3.6	17	4.1	0	0.0	4	2.7	17	4.0	3
Caucasian	86	59.7	146	52.7	230	55.2	2	50.0	89	59.3	232	55.1	74
Unknown	10	6.9	31	11.2	41	9.8	0	0.0	17	11.3	41	9.7	8
Total	144	34.2	277	65.8	417	99.0	4	1.0	150	35.6	421		128

Tuition and Fees

	Resident	Nonresident
Full-time	$10,562	$16,462
Part-time	$0	$0

Living Expenses

Estimated living expenses for singles

Living on campus	Living off campus	Living at home
N/A	$12,916	$5,905

City University of New York School of Law

*ABA
Approved
Since
1985*

GPA and LSAT Scores

	Total	Full-time	Part-time
# of apps	2,457	2,457	0
# of offers	561	561	0
# of matrics	144	144	0
75% GPA	3.57	3.57	0.00
Median GPA	3.29	3.29	0.00
25% GPA	3.00	3.00	0.00
75% LSAT	156	156	0
Median LSAT	153	153	0
25% LSAT	150	150	0

Grants and Scholarships (from prior year)

	Total #	Total %	Full-time #	Full-time %	Part-time #	Part-time %
Total # of students	437		436		1	
Total # receiving grants	166	38.0	166	38.1	0	0.0
Less than 1/2 tuition	134	30.7	134	30.7	0	0.0
Half to full tuition	7	1.6	7	1.6	0	0.0
Full tuition	25	5.7	25	5.7	0	0.0
More than full tuition	0	0.0	0	0.0	0	0.0
Median grant amount			$1,787		$0	

Informational and Library Resources

# of volumes and volume equivalents	281,035
# of titles	35,986
# of active serial subscriptions	3,117
Study seating capacity inside the library	267
# of full-time professional librarians	9
Hours per week library is open	61
# of open, wired connections available to students	62
# of networked computers available for use by students	99
# of simultaneous wireless users	300
Require computer?	No

JD Attrition (from prior year)

	Academic #	Other #	Total #	Total %
1st year	21	5	26	14.6
2nd year	2	10	12	9.5
3rd year	0	0	0	0.0
4th year	0	0	0	0.0

Employment (9 months after graduation)

	Total	Percentage
Employment status known	124	88.6
Employment status unknown	16	11.4
Employed	100	80.6
Pursuing graduate degrees	3	2.4
Unemployed seeking employment	9	7.3
Unemployed not seeking employment	6	4.8
Unemployed and studying for the bar	6	4.8

Type of Employment

	Total	Percentage
# employed in law firms	27	27.0
# employed in business and industry	13	13.0
# employed in government	17	17.0
# employed in public interest	26	26.0
# employed as judicial clerks	8	8.0
# employed in academia	3	3.0

Geographic Location

	Total	Percentage
# employed in state	75	75.0
# employed in foreign countries	0	0.0
# of states where employed	13	

Bar Passage Rates

Jurisdiction	New York		
Exam	Sum 05	Win 06	Total
# from school taking bar for the first time	109	13	122
School's pass rate for all first-time takers	62%	54%	61%
State's pass rate for all first-time takers	76%	61%	74%

City University of New York School of Law

65-21 Main Street
Flushing, NY 11367
Phone: 718.340.4210; Fax: 718.340.4435
E-mail: admissions@mail.law.cuny.edu; Website: www.law.cuny.edu

■ Mission

Following its motto of "Law in the Service of Human Needs," the mission of the City University of New York (CUNY) School of Law is to train excellent public interest lawyers through a curriculum that integrates doctrine, legal theory, clinical education, and professional responsibility.

■ Academic Program

Our innovative educational program, leading to the Juris Doctor (JD) degree, honors students' aspirations toward a legal career built on a commitment to justice, fairness, and equality. The law school's commitment to professional education and training reflecting these values pervades the core doctrinal classes and comes to life in our program of experiential learning, which is comprehensively integrated throughout the course of study. All first-year students take a required two-semester Lawyering Seminar where they focus on the fundamental skills of legal analysis and legal writing and engage in simulations requiring a wide range of lawyering tasks: They draft documents, interview and counsel clients, engage in negotiations, and make arguments before trial and appellate courts. Faculty guidance, supervision, and feedback permeate the process. In the second year, each student elects a four-credit Lawyering Seminar focused on developing more advanced lawyering skills in a subject matter area of his or her choice, including trial practice, mediation, labor, and appellate advocacy. The law school's Workfare Advocacy Project, which is a second-year lawyering seminar, received the New York State Bar Association's 2002 President's Pro Bono Service Award. Excellent and comprehensive academic support is provided by the Irene Diamond Professional Skills Center.

■ Clinical Programs

Each third-year student devotes 12 to 16 credits to participation in CUNY's nationally recognized clinical program, either in a concentration of Equality or Health Law or in one of the following clinics: Battered Women's Rights, Defender, Immigrant and Refugee Rights, International Women's Human Rights, Elder Law, and Mediation. The clinics are organized under the umbrella of Main Street Legal Services, Inc., an in-house law firm that provides information, counseling, or representation to more than 1,000 clients yearly, as well as prepares students for a seamless transition into practice. Students' work in clinics often has enormous impact; for example, students and faculty in the International Women's Human Rights Clinic drafted an amicus brief to the International Criminal Tribunal for Rwanda that was instrumental in the tribunal's decision, for the first time in international law, to include systematic rape as a crime of genocide.

■ Diversity

The diversity of the City of New York is reflected in our dynamic student body and faculty. Women constitute 66 percent of the student body; minorities, 31 percent. Faculty percentages are similar: 58 percent are women and 37 percent are people of color. The concern for diversity is also threaded through the curriculum; for example, a required course for all first-year students is Liberty, Equality, and Due Process, which examines issues of racial and gender equality and sexual orientation in the context of legal and historical analysis.

■ Student Life

Despite the relatively small size of the law school, numerous student organizations thrive on campus. Students also have a major role in the law school's governance, recognizing and preparing them for their future as professionals and community leaders. One exemplary student program is the Mississippi Project, which, since 1992, has sent a delegation of law students to Mississippi over midyear break to work with lawyers in civil rights organizations across the state. CUNY students work and learn together in an exceptionally collaborative, noncompetitive atmosphere and interact on a first-name basis with the faculty. The student experience is further enriched by New York City's cultural offerings and by the exceptional resources of the third-largest university system in the country, CUNY.

■ Faculty

Most of the faculty have themselves been public interest practitioners, with experience in a wide area of issues, including employment discrimination, immigration, racial justice, environmental law, women's rights, labor, and international law. They have worked in China, Haiti, South Africa, Mongolia, Costa Rica, the Middle East, Russia, Papua New Guinea, Australia, Central America, the Philippines, and many other countries. Their prestigious awards include Fulbright, Ford, MacArthur, Revson, Rockefeller, National Endowment for the Humanities fellowships; and their scholarship reflects their interest in, among other areas, international human rights and access to justice for underserved communities.

■ Career Opportunities

CUNY law graduates are employed in the full range of public interest jobs—legal services and public defender organizations, government agencies, international human rights organizations, not-for-profits, and the judiciary. Approximately 85 percent of alumni/ae secure positions within eight months of graduation. Historically, 60–65 percent of graduates enter the public interest/public service profession each year, while 25–30 percent are employed at private firms from large to small and solo community-based practices. CUNY law graduates are consistently awarded judicial clerkships and prestigious public interest postgraduate fellowships that include the Equal Justice Works, Skadden, Soros, Echoing Green, New Voices, Independence Foundation, and the Georgetown University Law Center Fellowships. Although the vast majority are employed in the mid-Atlantic states, CUNY graduates can be found throughout the United States and abroad where they are engaged in international human rights work.

■ Child Care

The law school offers an on-site Children's Center, which provides high-quality, reasonably priced all-day care for children of students from 2.3 to 6 years of age. The center enables parents to pursue their education while fulfilling their responsibility to their children.

■ Special Opportunities

The law school offers a number of unique programs and initiatives that enrich the experience of students and provide continuing support for graduates. The Haywood Burns Chair in Civil Rights is a visiting faculty position, which allows distinguished faculty, practitioners, and jurists—this year, Professor Anthony Farley from Boston College Law School— to share their experience and knowledge of civil and human rights. The Community Legal Resource Network provides resources and supports graduates working in solo or small-firm practices in underserved communities. Students in CUNY Immigrant Initiatives expand their knowledge of issues facing immigrant communities and provide direct service in a variety of areas. A new curricular initiative, the Worker, Employment, Labor Program, is designed to develop legal skills in representing workers in diverse settings. Finally, the law school is part of a rich university, the City University of New York, and law students may take some interdisciplinary graduate courses with the approval of the academic dean.

■ Nontraditional Students

The law school's student profile includes many individuals returning to school after careers, and many who possess advanced degrees. The average age of the student body is 28; some students enter directly from undergraduate school while others are older, making the law school a comfortable environment.

■ Affordable Tuition

CUNY offers an excellent legal education at substantially less than half the cost of most private law schools.

Applicant Profile

City University of New York School of Law
This grid includes only applicants who earned 120–180 LSAT scores under standard administrations.

LSAT Score	3.75 +		3.50–3.74		3.25–3.49		3.00–3.24		2.75–2.99		2.50–2.74		2.25–2.49		2.00–2.24		Below 2.00		No GPA		Total	
	Apps	Adm	Apps	Adm	Apps	Adm	Apps	Adm	Apps	Adm	Apps	Adm	Apps	Adm	Apps	Adm	Apps	Adm	Apps	Adm	Apps	Adm
175–180	0	0	0	0	0	0	0	0	0	0	1	0	0	0	0	0	0	0	0	0	1	0
170–174	0	0	0	0	1	1	0	0	1	0	0	0	0	0	0	0	0	0	1	1	3	2
165–169	4	2	9	9	0	0	5	3	1	1	1	0	0	0	2	0	0	0	0	0	22	15
160–164	18	13	18	16	10	7	20	15	10	5	10	3	3	0	4	1	2	1	1	1	96	62
155–159	29	22	53	38	65	48	51	28	45	12	27	11	12	2	8	1	1	1	6	6	297	169
150–154	34	21	91	57	116	51	124	47	90	21	73	14	28	1	10	3	2	0	8	4	576	219
145–149	41	12	107	23	144	20	164	23	121	5	78	3	51	3	15	0	5	0	12	0	738	89
140–144	19	0	55	1	92	0	95	0	104	0	62	0	44	0	14	0	4	0	15	0	504	1
135–139	4	0	16	0	29	0	25	0	35	0	28	0	29	0	15	0	4	0	9	0	194	0
130–134	2	0	4	0	7	0	8	0	14	0	12	0	11	0	5	0	1	0	4	0	68	0
125–129	0	0	0	0	0	0	2	0	4	0	3	0	1	0	3	0	3	0	2	0	18	0
120–124	0	0	0	0	0	0	0	0	0	0	0	0	0	0	0	0	0	0	0	0	0	0
Total	151	70	353	144	464	127	494	116	425	44	295	31	179	6	76	5	22	2	58	12	2517	557

Apps = Number of Applicants
Adm = Number Admitted
Reflects 99% of the total applicant pool.

Cleveland State University—Cleveland-Marshall College of Law

2121 Euclid Avenue — LB 138
Cleveland, OH 44115-2214
Phone: 216.687.2304, 866.687.2304; Fax: 216.687.6881
E-mail: admissions@law.csuohio.edu; Website: www.law.csuohio.edu

ABA Approved Since 1957

The Basics

Type of school	Public
Term	Semester
Application deadline	5/1
Application fee	$40
Financial aid deadline	5/1
Can first year start other than fall?	No
Student to faculty ratio	13.6 to 1
Does the university offer:	
housing restricted to law students?	No
graduate housing for which law students are eligible?	Yes

Faculty and Administrators

	Total		Men		Women		Minorities	
	Fall	Spr	Fall	Spr	Fall	Spr	Fall	Spr
Full-time	38	37	23	25	15	12	2	1
Other Full-time	1	1	0	0	1	1	0	0
Deans, librarians, & others who teach	5	5	3	4	2	1	1	2
Part-time	27	28	21	22	6	6	0	0
Total	**71**	**71**	**47**	**51**	**24**	**20**	**3**	**3**

Curriculum

	Full-time	Part-time
Typical first-year section size	59	48
Is there typically a "small section" of the first-year class, other than Legal Writing, taught by full-time faculty	No	No
If yes, typical size offered last year		
# of classroom course titles beyond first-year curriculum	92	

# of upper division courses, excluding seminars with an enrollment:		
	Under 25	103
	25–49	45
	50–74	14
	75–99	0
	100+	0

	Full-time	Part-time
# of seminars	8	
# of seminar positions available	120	
# of seminar positions filled	70	28
# of positions available in simulation courses	186	
# of simulation positions filled	96	50
# of positions available in faculty supervised clinical courses	120	
# of faculty supervised clinical positions filled	64	21
# involved in field placements	45	4
# involved in law journals	87	34
# involved in interschool competitions	20	4
# of credit hours required to graduate	90	

JD Enrollment and Ethnicity

	Men		Women		Full-time		Part-time		1st-year		Total		JD Degs. Awd.
	#	%	#	%	#	%	#	%	#	%	#	%	
African Amer.	20	5.4	34	10.2	34	7.0	20	9.3	17	7.7	54	7.7	10
Amer. Indian	3	0.8	0	0.0	3	0.6	0	0.0	1	0.5	3	0.4	0
Asian Amer.	10	2.7	16	4.8	18	3.7	8	3.7	8	3.6	26	3.7	7
Mex. Amer.	0	0.0	0	0.0	0	0.0	0	0.0	0	0.0	0	0.0	0
Puerto Rican	0	0.0	0	0.0	0	0.0	0	0.0	0	0.0	0	0.0	0
Hispanic	13	3.5	5	1.5	10	2.1	8	3.7	6	2.7	18	2.6	6
Total Minority	46	12.5	55	16.5	65	13.4	36	16.7	32	14.5	101	14.4	23
For. Nation.	2	0.5	4	1.2	5	1.0	1	0.5	1	0.5	6	0.9	1
Caucasian	314	85.1	265	79.6	403	82.9	176	81.5	188	85.1	579	82.5	187
Unknown	7	1.9	9	2.7	13	2.7	3	1.4	1	0.5	16	2.3	6
Total	369	52.6	333	47.4	486	69.2	216	30.8	221	31.5	702		217

Transfers

Transfers in	4
Transfers out	9

Tuition and Fees

	Resident	Nonresident
Full-time	$14,982	$20,525
Part-time	$11,525	$15,789

Living Expenses

Estimated living expenses for singles

Living on campus	Living off campus	Living at home
$16,262	$16,262	$16,262

Cleveland State University—Cle

*ABA
Approved
Since
1957*

GPA and LSAT Scores

	Total	Full-time	Part-time
# of apps	1,688	1,393	295
# of offers	599	474	125
# of matrics	227	155	72
75% GPA	3.62	3.63	3.57
Median GPA	3.29	3.38	3.18
25% GPA	2.95	3.00	2.92
75% LSAT	157	158	156
Median LSAT	154	155	153
25% LSAT	152	152	151

Grants and Scholarships (from prior year)

	Total		Full-time		Part-time	
	#	%	#	%	#	%
Total # of students	724		463		261	
Total # receiving grants	213	29.4	181	39.1	32	12.3
Less than 1/2 tuition	124	17.1	96	20.7	28	10.7
Half to full tuition	44	6.1	40	8.6	4	1.5
Full tuition	40	5.5	40	8.6	0	0.0
More than full tuition	5	0.7	5	1.1	0	0.0
Median grant amount			$4,000		$2,000	

Informational and Library Resources

# of volumes and volume equivalents	525,268
# of titles	154,362
# of active serial subscriptions	3,120
Study seating capacity inside the library	487
# of full-time professional librarians	8
Hours per week library is open	94
# of open, wired connections available to students	148
# of networked computers available for use by students	121
# of simultaneous wireless users	1,000
Require computer?	No

JD Attrition (

1st year	
2nd year	
3rd year	
4th year	

Employment (9 months after graduation)

	Total	Percentage
Employment status known	192	98.5
Employment status unknown	3	1.5
Employed	175	91.1
Pursuing graduate degrees	2	1.0
Unemployed seeking employment	3	1.6
Unemployed not seeking employment	4	2.1
Unemployed and studying for the bar	8	4.2

Type of Employment

# employed in law firms	93	53.1
# employed in business and industry	38	21.7
# employed in government	29	16.6
# employed in public interest	7	4.0
# employed as judicial clerks	3	1.7
# employed in academia	5	2.9

Geographic Location

# employed in state	143	81.7
# employed in foreign countries	2	1.1
# of states where employed		18

Bar Passage Rates

Jurisdiction	Ohio		
Exam	Sum 05	Win 06	Total
# from school taking bar for the first time	117	31	148
School's pass rate for all first-time takers	72%	68%	71%
State's pass rate for all first-time takers	81%	76%	81%

...ty—Cleveland-Marshall College of Law

...d Avenue — LB 138

...2304; Fax: 216.687.6881
...suohio.edu; Website: www.law.csuohio.edu

...897, Cleveland-Marshall College of Law was the ...ool in Ohio to admit women and one of the first to ...norities. Becoming part of Cleveland State University ..., the law school has maintained its long-standing ...tation for educating some of the region's outstanding ...aders of the bench and bar, heads of law firms and corporations, and distinguished public servants. The College of Law continues to enhance its national reputation and influence with its law lecture series and visiting scholars program, through outreach efforts with its National Advisory Council and through the law school's recruiting activities. The college receives applications from prospective students from over 450 different colleges and universities. Tuition for Ohio residents is among the lowest in the state and tuition for non-Ohio residents is the lowest in the state.

The college offers a full-time day, a part-time day, and a part-time evening program. After completing the program selected for the first year of law school, a student may switch programs according to his or her scheduling needs. The student body is diverse in many ways. Approximately half of the students are female, roughly 15 to 20 percent of each entering class is likely to be over the age of 30, and many students have had careers in other fields or earned advanced degrees before beginning the study of law. The college's pro bono, extracurricular, and cocurricular activities help to round out the richness of experience gained by studying law at Cleveland-Marshall.

■ Location

The College of Law is located on the university's urban campus in downtown Cleveland on Lake Erie. Students at Cleveland-Marshall enjoy all that the city has to offer, including the Cleveland Museum of Art; Severance Hall, home of the world-renowned Cleveland Orchestra; the Museum of Contemporary Art; the Botanical Garden; Playhouse Square; the House of Blues; and major professional sports teams. On the North Coast Harbor sit the Great Lakes Science Center and the Rock and Roll Hall of Fame and Museum. The law school is in close proximity to the federal, state, and county courthouses. Cleveland is also headquarters for many large corporations and law firms.

■ Library and Technology

The College of Law library is one of the 15 largest academic law libraries in the country, with 85,000 net square feet, housing more than 500,000 volumes. At Cleveland-Marshall, students have access to online research services, a computer lab, group study rooms, a bibliographic instruction room, and a media center. Students study in the four-story, light-filled atrium where there are over 200 student carrels with built-in power and network ports for portable computers. Cutting-edge technology is used in classrooms and our moot courtroom, and a state-of-the-art wireless network allows use of personal computers throughout the campus. Cleveland-Marshall has been recognized for its use and support of technology by *The National Jurist* magazine and the American Association of Law Libraries.

■ The Curriculum

The urban setting of the college brings challenging legal experiences to students. Clinical programs and externships include (1) the employment law, urban development law, fair housing, and environmental law clinics that offer students academic credit for serving clients in a variety of areas; (2) the Judicial Externship Program in which students work with state appellate and federal court judges; (3) the Public Interest Externship Program designed to offer experiences in office settings such as the county prosecutor and public defender, the bankruptcy trustee, the Office of Immigration and Customs Enforcement, and the US Attorney (civil and criminal); and (4) the Independent Externship Program where students may propose a placement in a public service office. By completing core and elective courses in their chosen areas, students may undertake a concentration in five areas: business law, civil litigation and dispute resolution, criminal law, employment and labor law, and tax law.

■ Joint-degree Programs and Graduate Program

Five joint-degree programs are offered: the JD/MPA (Master of Public Administration); the JD/MUPDD (Master of Urban Planning, Design, and Development); the JD/MBA (Master of Business Administration); the JD/MAES (Master of Arts in Environmental Studies); and the JD/MSES (Master of Science in Environmental Science). The law school also offers a graduate LLM degree.

■ Pro Bono Program

The Pro Bono Program at Cleveland-Marshall offers a variety of community service opportunities. Some of these experiences include building homes with Habitat for Humanity and planting gardens in the city of Cleveland. Popular placements include teaching practical law in public high schools, assisting with the legal needs of women recently released from incarceration, or addressing the concerns of the poor by delivering legal assistance in cooperation with local attorneys and community agencies.

■ Admission

Applicants are admitted by the dean upon the recommendation of an admission committee composed of faculty, professional staff, and students. Criteria for admission are identical for the full-time and part-time programs. Each applicant must have received a bachelor's degree from an accredited college or university by the time law classes begin. Undergraduate academic performance and LSAT scores are generally the most reliable measures for predicting success in law school. However, an applicant's personal statement, letters of recommendation, and overall strength of the file are factors also strongly considered in the admission process.

■ The Legal Career Opportunities Program

The Legal Career Opportunities Program (LCOP) is a special admission program for applicants who have encountered adversity in their lives that negatively affected their traditional academic indicators (i.e., LSAT score or undergraduate grades), but whose employment history or life experiences may indicate stronger candidacy for success in law school than traditional indicators. In most cases, applicants to this program have academic indicators that are generally a bit lower than those of regularly admitted applicants. The LCOP is not a provisional program. Being admitted through the program is acceptance to law school. Students admitted through the program are required to enroll in a course during the summer prior to the beginning of their first year.

■ Career Services

Cleveland, the largest legal market between New York City and Chicago, is home to more than 300 law firms. The location of the college enables students to access these firms for law clerk positions easily. Likewise, the federal and state courts nearby provide an external classroom for judicial externships.

The Office of Career Planning (OCP) invites many practicing attorneys to participate in programs and presentations. Many times these attorneys are alumni in the area, but often they are from firms desiring to help students professionally. The OCP staff offers over 20 programs per year providing a base of knowledge about legal and professional careers. The programs range from interview techniques and judicial clerkship seminars to practice-specific areas such as intellectual property, employment law, and health care law. The OCP posts over 1,500 permanent and law clerk jobs per year. Counseling and career guidance is provided by experienced staff members with JDs and counseling experience.

Programs and materials are easily accessible for both full- and part-time students. Handbooks and pamphlets are available to students in hard copy and many are also on the Web. State-of-the-art Web-based recruitment programs provide students with access 24-7.

■ Housing and Student Life

The majority of Cleveland-Marshall students live in convenient and affordable housing throughout the city and surrounding suburbs. There is new on-campus housing and meal plans are offered through the university. On-campus housing information is available from the Cleveland State University Department of Residence Life at 216.687.5196 or online at *www.csuohio.edu/reslife/*. The law school's Office of Admissions provides admitted students with information to assist with locating housing off campus.

The university's brand-new $29 million recreation center connects to the Physical Education Building, which houses Woodling Gym and Busbey Natatorium—providing direct access to the university's Olympic-size swimming pool. The state-of-the-art facility has basketball, racquetball, and squash courts; weight training and fitness areas; an indoor jogging track; locker rooms; multipurpose rooms; and a parking facility.

■ Scholarships, Financial Aid, and Loan Repayment Assistance

Applicants are considered for scholarships when their files are reviewed. There is no separate application process. Scholarships range from $2,000 a year to full tuition. Our financial aid program utilizes combinations of scholarships, fellowships, work-study employment, and loans. Additionally, the College of Law has a loan repayment assistance program (LRAP) to help support students choosing to work in public service jobs upon graduation. Each student may receive $3,000 for three years.

Applicant Profile

Cleveland State University—Cleveland-Marshall College of Law

LSAT Score	GPA									
	3.75 +	3.50–3.74	3.25–3.49	3.00–3.24	2.75–2.99	2.50–2.74	2.25–2.49	2.00–2.24	Below 2.00	No GPA
175–180										
170–174										
165–169										
160–164										
155–159										
150–154										
145–149										
140–144										
135–139										
130–134										
125–129										
120–124										

Very Likely   Likely   Possible   Unlikely

University of Colorado School of Law

UCB 403
Boulder, CO 80309-0403
Phone: 303.492.7203; Fax: 303.492.2542
E-mail: lawadmin@colorado.edu; Website: www.colorado.edu/law

*ABA
Approved
Since
1923*

The Basics

Type of school	Public
Term	Semester
Application deadline	3/1
Application fee	$65
Financial aid deadline	4/1
Can first year start other than fall?	No
Student to faculty ratio	13.7 to 1
Does the university offer:	
housing restricted to law students?	No
graduate housing for which law students are eligible?	Yes

Faculty and Administrators

	Total		Men		Women		Minorities	
	Fall	Spr	Fall	Spr	Fall	Spr	Fall	Spr
Full-time	30	31	17	19	13	12	6	6
Other Full-time	2	2	0	0	2	2	0	0
Deans, librarians, & others who teach	13	12	9	8	4	4	3	3
Part-time	22	19	15	15	7	4	2	2
Total	**67**	**64**	**41**	**42**	**26**	**22**	**11**	**11**

Curriculum

	Full-time	Part-time
Typical first-year section size	83	0
Is there typically a "small section" of the first-year class, other than Legal Writing, taught by full-time faculty	Yes	No
If yes, typical size offered last year	41	
# of classroom course titles beyond first-year curriculum		91
# of upper division courses, excluding seminars with an enrollment: Under 25		56
25–49		38
50–74		9
75–99		3
100+		1
# of seminars		19
# of seminar positions available		228
# of seminar positions filled	210	0
# of positions available in simulation courses	366	
# of simulation positions filled	351	0
# of positions available in faculty supervised clinical courses	126	
# of faculty supervised clinical positions filled	110	0
# involved in field placements	195	0
# involved in law journals	153	0
# involved in interschool competitions	66	0
# of credit hours required to graduate		89

JD Enrollment and Ethnicity

	Men		Women		Full-time		Part-time		1st-year		Total		JD Degs. Awd.
	#	%	#	%	#	%	#	%	#	%	#	%	
African Amer.	10	4.0	10	3.9	20	3.9	0	0.0	9	5.2	20	3.9	5
Amer. Indian	5	2.0	10	3.9	15	2.9	0	0.0	5	2.9	15	2.9	3
Asian Amer.	16	6.3	27	10.4	43	8.4	0	0.0	12	7.0	43	8.4	11
Mex. Amer.	9	3.6	6	2.3	15	2.9	0	0.0	7	4.1	15	2.9	7
Puerto Rican	1	0.4	0	0.0	1	0.2	0	0.0	0	0.0	1	0.2	1
Hispanic	11	4.4	13	5.0	24	4.7	0	0.0	9	5.2	24	4.7	1
Total Minority	52	20.6	66	25.5	118	23.1	0	0.0	42	24.4	118	23.1	28
For. Nation.	3	1.2	1	0.4	4	0.8	0	0.0	3	1.7	4	0.8	1
Caucasian	197	78.2	192	74.1	389	76.1	0	0.0	127	73.8	389	76.1	137
Unknown	0	0.0	0	0.0	0	0.0	0	0.0	0	0.0	0	0.0	0
Total	252	49.3	259	50.7	511	100.0	0	0.0	172	33.7	511		166

Transfers

Transfers in	15
Transfers out	2

Tuition and Fees

	Resident	Nonresident
Full-time	$16,738	$30,814
Part-time	$0	$0

Living Expenses

Estimated living expenses for singles		
Living on campus	Living off campus	Living at home
$12,814	$12,069	$8,524

University of Colorado School of Law

ABA
Approved
Since
1923

GPA and LSAT Scores

	Total	Full-time	Part-time
# of apps	2,517	2,517	0
# of offers	661	661	0
# of matrics	172	172	0
75% GPA	3.75	3.75	0.00
Median GPA	3.56	3.56	0.00
25% GPA	3.37	3.37	0.00
75% LSAT	165	165	0
Median LSAT	163	163	0
25% LSAT	159	159	0

Grants and Scholarships (from prior year)

	Total		Full-time		Part-time	
	#	%	#	%	#	%
Total # of students	495		491		4	
Total # receiving grants	372	75.2	372	75.8	0	0.0
Less than 1/2 tuition	318	64.2	318	64.8	0	0.0
Half to full tuition	51	10.3	51	10.4	0	0.0
Full tuition	0	0.0	0	0.0	0	0.0
More than full tuition	3	0.6	3	0.6	0	0.0
Median grant amount			$3,450		$0	

Informational and Library Resources

# of volumes and volume equivalents	543,535
# of titles	174,411
# of active serial subscriptions	4,117
Study seating capacity inside the library	340
# of full-time professional librarians	10
Hours per week library is open	108
# of open, wired connections available to students	70
# of networked computers available for use by students	77
# of simultaneous wireless users	400
Require computer?	No

JD Attrition (from prior year)

	Academic	Other	Total	
	#	#	#	%
1st year	0	4	4	2.4
2nd year	0	2	2	1.2
3rd year	0	0	0	0.0
4th year	0	0	0	0.0

Employment (9 months after graduation)

	Total	Percentage
Employment status known	164	99.4
Employment status unknown	1	0.6
Employed	159	97.0
Pursuing graduate degrees	1	0.6
Unemployed seeking employment	0	0.0
Unemployed not seeking employment	4	2.4
Unemployed and studying for the bar	0	0.0
Type of Employment		
# employed in law firms	78	49.1
# employed in business and industry	18	11.3
# employed in government	32	20.1
# employed in public interest	2	1.3
# employed as judicial clerks	27	17.0
# employed in academia	1	0.6
Geographic Location		
# employed in state	126	79.2
# employed in foreign countries	0	0.0
# of states where employed		23

Bar Passage Rates

Jurisdiction	Colorado		
Exam	Sum 05	Win 06	Total
# from school taking bar for the first time	128	14	142
School's pass rate for all first-time takers	91%	71%	89%
State's pass rate for all first-time takers	78%	70%	76%

University of Colorado School of Law

Office of Admissions, UCB 403
Boulder, CO 80309-0403
Phone: 303.492.7203; Fax: 303.492.2542
E-mail: lawadmin@colorado.edu; Website: www.colorado.edu/law

■ Introduction

The School of Law, established in 1892, is located on the Boulder campus of the University of Colorado and lies at the foot of the Rocky Mountains. High admission standards, a relatively small student body, and a favorable faculty-to-student ratio assure a stimulating and challenging academic environment that encourages class participation and interaction with faculty. The school is a charter member of the AALS and is ABA approved.

■ Faculty

The faculty members have a demonstrated record of excellence in teaching, research, and public service. They include some of the nation's leading scholars on constitutional law, criminal law, dispute resolution, environmental law, evidence, family law, health law, international law, labor and employment, natural resources, securities, tax, and telecommunications law.

■ Physical Facilities and Library

The law school is now housed in the new 180,000-square-foot Wolf Law Building, located on the southern edge of the CU Boulder campus. The Wolf Law Building features state-of-the-art classrooms, two high-tech courtrooms, 50 percent more space for law journal offices and law clinics, and the largest resource collection and most technologically advanced law library in the 12-state Rocky Mountain region. Colorado Law is also striving to make the Wolf Law Building the first LEED Gold-certified public law school building in the country under the exacting standards of the US Green Building Council's Leadership in Energy and Environmental Design certification program.

The William A. Wise Law Library, the largest law library in the state, serves the students, staff, and faculty of Colorado Law as well as the bench and bar of the state. The library holds over half a million volumes or equivalents and provides access to thousands of electronic journals and databases. Law students also have access to the resources of other university and college libraries in Colorado through a statewide delivery system.

Comfortable seating, lounge areas, and ample study space make the library an inviting space where students meet to work on projects or study. Students can connect laptops to the school's wireless network or use one of the 65 computers available in the library to perform online legal research. Librarians provide reference service, research instruction, and personal assistance with student research.

■ Special Programs

The Natural Resources Law Center has three major areas of activity: research and publication, legal education, and the distinguished visitors and fellows program. The National Wildlife Federation's Natural Resources Litigation Clinic involves students in complex environmental litigation, much of which reaches the state supreme court or federal appellate court level.

The Legal Aid and Defender Program allows students to represent low-income clients in civil and criminal cases in Colorado courts under supervision of full-time faculty who are experienced trial attorneys. The American Indian Law Clinic provides students with the opportunity to work with Native Americans on their unique legal problems.

The Juvenile and Family Law Program (JFLP) provides students with opportunities to acquire specialized knowledge in the field, fosters collaboration between students, academics, and practitioners, and engages in interdisciplinary study and practice. JFLP runs many programs, including a juvenile law clinic where students represent child clients, various externships in the field, and symposia on hot topics.

The Appellate Advocacy Clinic alternates annually between attorneys from the public defender's office and the attorney general's office. Each student, under direct supervision of an instructor, is responsible for completing an appellate brief and attending the oral argument in the Colorado Supreme Court or the Colorado Court of Appeals.

The Wrongful Convictions Clinic allows students to work with attorneys representing Colorado inmates whose traditional appellate remedies have been exhausted. Students focus on legal and factual issues commonly arising in wrongful conviction cases.

The Byron R. White Center for the Study of American Constitutional Law furthers the study, teaching, and publication of constitutional law. The White Center hosts the annual Ira C. Rothgerber Constitutional Law Conference, which exposes students to analysis and debate of contemporary constitutional issues.

The Entrepreneurial Law Center's mission is to connect the law school, faculty, and students with the flourishing Colorado entrepreneurial community. It is a hub of high-tech start-ups and emerging growth companies, conducting educational, research, and service activities on legal matters relevant to entrepreneurs, venture capitalists, and the lawyers who serve them. The center also conducts a clinic.

The Silicon Flatirons Telecommunications Program's mission is to create an environment for analyzing the dynamic changes in the telecommunications marketplace and regulatory environment. The program supports the academic community by fostering relationships between students and telecommunications professionals through its mentor and internship opportunities.

■ Curriculum

The first semester runs from late August to mid-December, and the second semester runs from mid-January to mid-May. Three summer sessions from three to five weeks each begin in May for students enrolled at any accredited law school. With a limited number of additional hours, a certificate in tax or environmental policy is attainable. The first-year curriculum is required of all students. During the second and third years, students may emphasize such areas of the law as natural resources, environment, crime, business, constitution, taxation, public interest, American Indians, litigation, intellectual property, and jurisprudence. Established joint-degree programs are the JD/MBA, JD/MPA, JD/MST, JD/MSES, and JD/PhD in Environmental Studies.

University of Colorado School of Law

■ Admission

A bachelor's degree from an institution that is accredited by an agency recognized by the Department of Education is required. The application deadline is March 1. The LSAT and registration with the LSDAS are required. Offers of admission are based on GPA and LSAT score, but these scores are considered in the context of the entire application. Substantial weight is accorded to special qualities such as motivation, undergraduate program, diversity, unusual employment or other experience, leadership, and perseverance in overcoming personal handicaps or disadvantages. The school seeks to increase ethnic, cultural, and other diversity of its student body. The earliest admission letters go out in December, and the class is filled in May or June. Admission thereafter is from a wait list.

Several transfer and visiting students are admitted each year. Admission criteria for these students include law school performance.

■ Financial Aid

Privately funded scholarships are available. Scholarships are based on merit, financial need, and diversity. State grants, available to eligible resident students, are awarded on the basis of need. Nonresident students qualify for lower resident tuition rates by maintaining domicile in Colorado for 12 consecutive months. Students may not be employed during their first year, but limited outside employment is compatible with second- and third-year schedules. Students applying for financial aid must file the FAFSA as soon as possible after January 1.

■ Student Activities

Over 20 student organizations invite participation in projects, programs, and social activities. The *University of Colorado Law Review, Journal on Telecommunications and High Technology Law,* and *Colorado Journal of International Environmental Law and Policy* are professional journals edited entirely by students. Students also participate in a number of moot court competitions and have won regional, national, and international recognition in these events.

■ Housing

For information about the university's family housing, call 303.492.6384, and, for off-campus housing, call 303.492.7053. Call 303.492.8491 about dormitories.

■ Career Development

Career Development staff provide individual counseling to students and alumni on job-search strategies and career options, including legal employers and alternative career paths. The office solicits employers nationwide to interview on campus and to hire students through off-campus programs as well. The office also sponsors and coordinates numerous information sessions and career development programs throughout the academic year. The office helped develop the Colorado Pledge to Diversity 1L Summer Clerkship Program and also participates in other diversity hiring programs.

Applicant Profile

University of Colorado School of Law
This grid includes only applicants who earned 120–180 LSAT scores under standard administrations.

LSAT Score	3.75 +		3.50–3.74		3.25–3.49		3.00–3.24		2.75–2.99		2.50–2.74		2.25–2.49		2.00–2.24		Below 2.00		No GPA		Total	
	Apps	Adm	Apps	Adm	Apps	Adm	Apps	Adm	Apps	Adm	Apps	Adm	Apps	Adm	Apps	Adm	Apps	Adm	Apps	Adm	Apps	Adm
175–180	4	4	1	1	2	2	0	0	0	0	0	0	0	0	0	0	0	0	0	0	7	7
170–174	17	17	18	18	5	4	6	4	5	2	2	1	1	0	1	0	0	0	2	1	57	47
165–169	46	45	65	63	60	50	41	23	23	6	9	0	2	1	0	0	0	0	3	3	246	188
160–164	135	112	190	122	171	54	84	15	52	4	20	2	8	0	1	0	0	0	3	3	743	65
155–159	140	22	232	18	182	13	115	9	47	1	13	0	10	0	1	0	0	0	3	2	664	312
150–154	70	6	118	15	131	12	99	2	49	3	21	2	10	0	5	0	1	1	3	1	507	42
145–149	27	0	42	2	37	0	36	0	21	0	20	0	13	0	0	0	1	0	4	0	201	2
140–144	8	0	9	0	14	0	23	0	10	0	13	0	9	0	3	0	1	0	0	0	90	0
135–139	1	0	1	0	1	0	4	0	5	0	4	0	3	0	1	0	0	0	1	0	21	0
130–134	0	0	0	0	0	0	1	0	5	0	3	0	0	0	0	0	1	0	2	0	12	0
125–129	0	0	0	0	0	0	0	0	0	0	0	0	0	0	0	0	0	0	0	0	0	0
120–124	0	0	0	0	0	0	0	0	0	0	0	0	0	0	0	0	0	0	0	0	0	0
Total	448	206	676	239	603	135	409	53	217	16	105	5	56	1	12	0	4	1	18	7	2548	663

Apps = Number of Applicants
Adm = Number Admitted
Reflects 99% of the total applicant pool.

Columbia University School of Law

435 West 116th Street
New York, NY 10027
Phone: 212.854.2670; Fax: 212.854.1109
E-mail: admissions@law.columbia.edu; Website: www.law.columbia.edu

The Basics

Type of school	Private
Term	Semester
Application deadline	2/15
Application fee	$70
Financial aid deadline	3/1
Can first year start other than fall?	No
Student to faculty ratio	10.3 to 1
Does the university offer:	
housing restricted to law students?	Yes
graduate housing for which law students are eligible?	Yes

Faculty and Administrators

	Total		Men		Women		Minorities	
	Fall	Spr	Fall	Spr	Fall	Spr	Fall	Spr
Full-time	107	92	73	60	34	32	14	12
Other Full-time	3	6	3	5	0	1	2	4
Deans, librarians, & others who teach	6	6	4	4	2	2	0	0
Part-time	82	93	56	71	26	22	7	10
Total	**198**	**197**	**136**	**140**	**62**	**57**	**23**	**26**

Curriculum

	Full-time	Part-time
Typical first-year section size	120	0
Is there typically a "small section" of the first-year class, other than Legal Writing, taught by full-time faculty	Yes	No
If yes, typical size offered last year	27	
# of classroom course titles beyond first-year curriculum	210	
# of upper division courses, excluding seminars with an enrollment: Under 25	63	
25–49	17	
50–74	23	
75–99	15	
100+	18	
# of seminars	130	
# of seminar positions available	2,286	
# of seminar positions filled	1,815	0
# of positions available in simulation courses	405	
# of simulation positions filled	374	0
# of positions available in faculty supervised clinical courses	217	
# of faculty supervised clinical positions filled	217	0
# involved in field placements	97	0
# involved in law journals	584	0
# involved in interschool competitions	60	0
# of credit hours required to graduate	83	

JD Enrollment and Ethnicity

	Men		Women		Full-time		Part-time		1st-year		Total		JD Degs. Awd.
	#	%	#	%	#	%	#	%	#	%	#	%	
African Amer.	36	5.2	59	11.0	95	7.7	0	0.0	31	8.1	95	7.7	45
Amer. Indian	4	0.6	7	1.3	11	0.9	0	0.0	3	0.8	11	0.9	0
Asian Amer.	91	13.0	83	15.5	173	14.1	1	33.3	51	13.3	174	14.1	66
Mex. Amer.	26	3.7	17	3.2	43	3.5	0	0.0	14	3.7	43	3.5	9
Puerto Rican	6	0.9	8	1.5	14	1.1	0	0.0	5	1.3	14	1.1	7
Hispanic	13	1.9	10	1.9	23	1.9	0	0.0	10	2.6	23	1.9	7
Total Minority	176	25.2	184	34.5	359	29.2	1	33.3	114	29.8	360	29.2	134
For. Nation.	57	8.2	57	10.7	113	9.2	1	33.3	21	5.5	114	9.2	58
Caucasian	454	64.9	286	53.6	739	60.1	1	33.3	239	62.4	740	60.0	279
Unknown	12	1.7	7	1.3	19	1.5	0	0.0	9	2.3	19	1.5	2
Total	699	56.7	534	43.3	1230	99.8	3	0.2	383	31.1	1233		473

Transfers

Transfers in	40
Transfers out	1

Tuition and Fees

	Resident	Nonresident
Full-time	$41,226	$41,226
Part-time	$0	$0

Living Expenses

Estimated living expenses for singles

Living on campus	Living off campus	Living at home
$18,800	$18,800	$4,945

Columbia University School of Law

ABA
Approved
Since
1923

GPA and LSAT Scores

	Total	Full-time	Part-time
# of apps	7,768	7,768	0
# of offers	1,144	1,144	0
# of matrics	384	384	0
75% GPA	3.82	3.82	0.00
Median GPA	3.70	3.70	0.00
25% GPA	3.51	3.51	0.00
75% LSAT	174	174	0
Median LSAT	172	172	0
25% LSAT	169	169	0

Grants and Scholarships (from prior year)

	Total		Full-time		Part-time	
	#	%	#	%	#	%
Total # of students	1,242		1,242		0	
Total # receiving grants	572	46.1	572	46.1	0	0.0
Less than 1/2 tuition	436	35.1	436	35.1	0	0.0
Half to full tuition	101	8.1	101	8.1	0	0.0
Full tuition	35	2.8	35	2.8	0	0.0
More than full tuition	0	0.0	0	0.0	0	0.0
Median grant amount			$10,000		$0	

Informational and Library Resources

# of volumes and volume equivalents	1,111,775
# of titles	423,485
# of active serial subscriptions	6,843
Study seating capacity inside the library	370
# of full-time professional librarians	20
Hours per week library is open	102
# of open, wired connections available to students	3,132
# of networked computers available for use by students	116
# of simultaneous wireless users	2,944
Require computer?	Yes

JD Attrition (from prior year)

	Academic	Other	Total	
	#	#	#	%
1st year	0	1	1	0.3
2nd year	0	2	2	0.5
3rd year	1	0	1	0.2
4th year	0	0	0	0.0

Employment (9 months after graduation)

	Total	Percentage
Employment status known	400	100.0
Employment status unknown	0	0.0
Employed	396	99.0
Pursuing graduate degrees	0	0.0
Unemployed seeking employment	3	0.7
Unemployed not seeking employment	1	0.2
Unemployed and studying for the bar	0	0.0

Type of Employment

	Total	Percentage
# employed in law firms	310	78.3
# employed in business and industry	4	1.0
# employed in government	9	2.3
# employed in public interest	17	4.3
# employed as judicial clerks	56	14.1
# employed in academia	0	0.0

Geographic Location

	Total	Percentage
# employed in state	242	61.1
# employed in foreign countries	14	3.5
# of states where employed	24	

Bar Passage Rates

Jurisdiction	New York		
Exam	Sum 05	Win 06	Total
# from school taking bar for the first time	285	23	308
School's pass rate for all first-time takers	90%	100%	91%
State's pass rate for all first-time takers	76%	61%	74%

Columbia University School of Law

435 West 116th Street
New York, NY 10027
Phone: 212.854.2670; Fax: 212.854.1109
E-mail: admissions@law.columbia.edu; Website: www.law.columbia.edu

■ Introduction

Columbia law school is distinguished, perhaps uniquely among leading US law schools, as an international center of legal education that stimulates its students to consider the full dimensions of the possibility of the law—as an intellectual pursuit, as a career, and as an instrument of human progress. The character of academic and social life at Columbia is fiercely democratic, dynamic, creative, and innovative. The law school is especially committed to educating students of differing perspectives, from diverse backgrounds, and with varied life experiences.

Professional prospects for Columbia Law graduates are quite extraordinary. Our graduates proceed to productive careers in every conceivable arena of practice, business, and advocacy. While Columbia-trained attorneys are especially well-regarded for their work in corporate law and finance, an unusually high number also serve as state and federal judges, prosecutors, civil rights and human rights advocates, legal scholars, public defenders, entrepreneurs, business executives, elected government officials, and national and international leaders. Many Columbia Law alumni/ae contribute significantly to the shaping of US culture at large. Currently our graduates serve in leadership roles across the fields of art, music, film, publishing, science, professional athletics, philanthropy, and higher education.

With an exceptionally talented student body and faculty and a strong tradition of encouraging students with specialized interests to develop those interests in depth, Columbia law school provides a legal education that gives our students a singular capacity for imagination, originality, and high responsibility in their professional lives.

■ JD Student Body Profile

Columbia continues to place among the handful of the most highly selective JD programs in our nation—as evaluated by the principal criteria used to measure admissions selectivity (application volume, acceptance rates, LSAT scores, and academic performance). Indeed, in recent years, the demand for a Columbia legal education has never been greater, and the academic credentials of our entering classes are stronger than ever. Columbia's JD student body is further distinguished by standing as one of the most culturally diverse among America's leading law schools. Men and women choosing to study law at Columbia hail from the small towns, farms, and suburbs of the West, Midwest, and South; the industrial corridors and ivy halls of the Northeast; the inner cities of every major US metropolis; and the international centers of Europe, Asia, Africa, and Latin America.

Each entering class reflects the broad range of economic, ethnic, and cultural backgrounds found in the United States. And from around the world, we welcome students who will enrich learning at Columbia and thereafter advance the developing legal cultures of their homelands.

With one of the largest percentages of international students in its JD program of any leading law school; with one of the very highest percentages of students of color; with its students hailing from 48 states, roughly 35 foreign countries, and more than 210 different colleges and universities; with 11 percent of its JD students having earned at least one graduate or

professional degree before studying law, Columbia's student body abounds with a diversity of life experiences, cultural backgrounds, and intellectual perspectives.

■ The Law School Campus

Columbia law school's main building, Jerome Greene Hall, has undergone significant expansion and improvements devoted primarily to our students, including library renovations and the creation of a student commons that includes a student lounge and café. New seminar rooms and state-of-the-art multimedia classrooms have also been designed to provide students with full Internet and other legal research access. Across the street from Greene Hall is William C. Warren Hall, home to the *Columbia Law Review,* Morningside Heights Legal Services (a law school clinic serving our community), and the Center for Public Interest Law.

William and June Warren Hall, opened in 1999, includes amphitheater-style classrooms equipped with modern teaching resources, a center for the law school's international programs, and conference facilities. It is also home to the Offices of Admissions, Financial Aid, Registration Services, Student Services, Graduate Legal Studies, and International Programs.

The renovation and expansion of the law school's facilities have greatly enhanced the quality of life and learning at Columbia. Students have a superb learning environment that is conducive to community building and social and intellectual engagement, and reflects the changing nature of legal education in the twenty-first century.

■ Library Resources and Research Facilities

Columbia's library is one of the largest and most comprehensive law collections in the world. It is especially rich in US law and legal history, international law, comparative law, Roman law, and the legal literature of the major European countries, China, and Japan. Access to the Internet and electronic documents provide additional resources, with materials from Germany, South Africa, and a wide range of international organizations. In addition, the many libraries of the university, containing more than seven million volumes, are available to law students.

The law library's online catalog provides complete access to the library's collection, acts as an index to the major legal serials, and provides access to the online catalogs of other major law school libraries. Columbia provides its law students with some of the most sophisticated technologies of any law school in the nation.

■ Curriculum

The foundation of the JD program consists of Legal Methods (a three-week introductory course), Legal Practice Workshop (a two-semester course that provides intensive training in legal research, writing, and analysis), Contracts, Torts, Constitutional Law, Civil Procedure, Property, Criminal Law, and one elective focusing on the law's engagement with public policy, the intellectual and historical foundations of the rule of law, or law's transnational and comparative expression. Recent elective offerings have included Critical Legal Thought; Law and Contemporary Society; Law and Economics; Law and Social Science; Lawyering Across Multiple Legal Orders; Legislation; Principles of Intellectual Property; Regulation: Decentralization and Globalization; Terror and Consent; the Regulatory and Administrative State; the Rule of Law: Perspectives on Legal Thought; and Law, Culture, and Notions of Justice.

Columbia has a special commitment to clinical education, which places the student in the role of a lawyer doing a lawyer's actual work under intensive faculty supervision. Some examples of clinical opportunities are Lawyering in the Digital Age, Law and the Arts, Nonprofit Organizations, Prisoners and Families, Child Advocacy, Mediation, Environmental Law, Human Rights, and a newly launched clinic in Sexuality and Gender Law. Unique to Columbia is a summer program which places more than 150 students in civil and human rights internships in law firms and organizations throughout this country and around the world. Especially distinguished are Columbia's offerings in international, foreign, and comparative law; constitutional law and theory; corporate and securities law; intellectual property; critical race theory; human rights; and public interest law.

■ Research Centers and Special Programs

Research centers and special programs include the Kernochan Center for Law, Media, and the Arts; Julius Silver Program in Law, Science, and Technology; Center for Law and Philosophy; Center for Law and Economic Studies; Center for the Study of Law and Culture; Center for Public Interest Law; Program on Careers in Law and Teaching; Human Rights Institute; Parker School of Foreign and Comparative Law; Center for Chinese Legal Studies; Center for Japanese Legal Studies; Center for Korean Legal Studies; European Legal Studies Center; and programs in alternative dispute resolution and in law and history.

■ Admission

All first-year students enter in mid-August. Candidates applying for regular admission should apply after September 1 of the year preceding their desired matriculation, but before February 15, the application deadline. Early Decision candidates must complete their applications by November 15 and are notified in December. All other applications are generally reviewed in the order in which they are completed, and decisions are made and sent out on a rolling basis.

Applicant Profile

Columbia has chosen not to provide prospective students with an admission selectivity profile based on LSAT scores and undergraduate GPA, because we believe it does not accurately portray our selection process. Ours is a comprehensive, multivariate evaluation of academic performance and professional promise. Columbia evaluates every application individually—while carefully considering the candidate's background, interests, accomplishments, and goals. We are proud that Columbia is among the handful of the most highly selective law schools in the country, as measured by LSAT and UGPA statistics and other selectivity measures. But we wish to emphasize, by not reducing our selection process to a two-dimensional grid, that the recognized excellence of our student body and distinction of our alumni/ae are rooted not only in their intellectual power and outstanding academic records, but also in their personal strengths, professional skills, and diverse backgrounds.

University of Connecticut School of Law

45 Elizabeth Street
Hartford, CT 06105
Phone: 860.570.5100; Fax: 860.570.5153
E-mail: admit@law.uconn.edu; Website: www.law.uconn.edu

ABA
Approved
Since
1933

The Basics

Type of school	Public
Term	Semester
Application deadline	3/1
Application fee	$30
Financial aid deadline	3/1
Can first year start other than fall?	No
Student to faculty ratio	11.5 to 1
Does the university offer:	
housing restricted to law students?	No
graduate housing for which law students are eligible?	No

Faculty and Administrators

	Total		Men		Women		Minorities	
	Fall	Spr	Fall	Spr	Fall	Spr	Fall	Spr
Full-time	43	41	28	28	15	13	6	3
Other Full-time	6	6	1	1	5	5	1	1
Deans, librarians, & others who teach	4	4	2	2	2	2	0	0
Part-time	23	38	18	31	5	7	2	1
Total	**76**	**89**	**49**	**62**	**27**	**27**	**9**	**5**

Curriculum

	Full-time	Part-time
Typical first-year section size	62	73
Is there typically a "small section" of the first-year class, other than Legal Writing, taught by full-time faculty	Yes	Yes
If yes, typical size offered last year	22	37
# of classroom course titles beyond first-year curriculum		131

# of upper division courses, excluding seminars with an enrollment:		
	Under 25	92
	25–49	33
	50–74	15
	75–99	0
	100+	0

# of seminars		46
# of seminar positions available		907
# of seminar positions filled	612	118
# of positions available in simulation courses	593	
# of simulation positions filled	389	174
# of positions available in faculty supervised clinical courses	180	
# of faculty supervised clinical positions filled	156	14
# involved in field placements	92	40
# involved in law journals	172	7
# involved in interschool competitions	27	0
# of credit hours required to graduate		86

JD Enrollment and Ethnicity

	Men		Women		Full-time		Part-time		1st-year		Total		JD Degs. Awd.
	#	%	#	%	#	%	#	%	#	%	#	%	
African Amer.	11	3.3	27	8.7	29	6.3	9	4.9	14	6.6	38	5.9	15
Amer. Indian	4	1.2	0	0.0	2	0.4	2	1.1	1	0.5	4	0.6	0
Asian Amer.	10	3.0	15	4.8	17	3.7	8	4.3	8	3.8	25	3.9	20
Mex. Amer.	2	0.6	1	0.3	3	0.6	0	0.0	1	0.5	3	0.5	3
Puerto Rican	8	2.4	12	3.9	16	3.4	4	2.2	6	2.8	20	3.1	6
Hispanic	10	3.0	14	4.5	16	3.4	8	4.3	6	2.8	24	3.7	15
Total Minority	45	13.3	69	22.3	83	17.9	31	16.8	36	16.9	114	17.6	59
For. Nation.	2	0.6	4	1.3	3	0.6	3	1.6	2	0.9	6	0.9	2
Caucasian	255	75.4	188	60.6	322	69.4	121	65.8	150	70.4	443	68.4	175
Unknown	36	10.7	49	15.8	56	12.1	29	15.8	25	11.7	85	13.1	2
Total	338	52.2	310	47.8	464	71.6	184	28.4	213	32.9	648		238

Transfers

Transfers in	13
Transfers out	7

Tuition and Fees

	Resident	Nonresident
Full-time	$17,284	$35,692
Part-time	$12,086	$24,926

Living Expenses

Estimated living expenses for singles

Living on campus	Living off campus	Living at home
N/A	$15,800	$7,800

University of Connecticut School of Law

ABA
Approved
Since
1933

GPA and LSAT Scores

	Total	Full-time	Part-time
# of apps	2,598	1,814	784
# of offers	396	274	122
# of matrics	209	139	70
75% GPA	3.66	3.66	3.67
Median GPA	3.45	3.47	3.41
25% GPA	3.24	3.27	3.19
75% LSAT	162	163	159
Median LSAT	160	161	156
25% LSAT	156	159	153

Grants and Scholarships (from prior year)

	Total		Full-time		Part-time	
	#	%	#	%	#	%
Total # of students	671		497		174	
Total # receiving grants	416	62.0	387	77.9	29	16.7
Less than 1/2 tuition	183	27.3	155	31.2	28	16.1
Half to full tuition	213	31.7	212	42.7	1	0.6
Full tuition	0	0.0	0	0.0	0	0.0
More than full tuition	20	3.0	20	4.0	0	0.0
Median grant amount			$8,000		$2,950	

Informational and Library Resources

# of volumes and volume equivalents	536,025
# of titles	156,357
# of active serial subscriptions	4,940
Study seating capacity inside the library	759
# of full-time professional librarians	15
Hours per week library is open	87
# of open, wired connections available to students	783
# of networked computers available for use by students	115
# of simultaneous wireless users	490
Require computer?	No

JD Attrition (from prior year)

	Academic	Other	Total	
	#	#	#	%
1st year	0	9	9	4.5
2nd year	0	4	4	2.0
3rd year	0	2	2	0.9
4th year	0	0	0	0.0

Employment (9 months after graduation)

	Total	Percentage
Employment status known	212	98.1
Employment status unknown	4	1.9
Employed	203	95.8
Pursuing graduate degrees	1	0.5
Unemployed seeking employment	3	1.4
Unemployed not seeking employment	4	1.9
Unemployed and studying for the bar	1	0.5
Type of Employment		
# employed in law firms	114	56.2
# employed in business and industry	27	13.3
# employed in government	18	8.9
# employed in public interest	4	2.0
# employed as judicial clerks	36	17.7
# employed in academia	4	2.0
Geographic Location		
# employed in state	136	67.0
# employed in foreign countries	0	0.0
# of states where employed		21

Bar Passage Rates

Jurisdiction	Connecticut		
Exam	Sum 05	Win 06	Total
# from school taking bar for the first time	132	20	152
School's pass rate for all first-time takers	90%	90%	90%
State's pass rate for all first-time takers	81%	83%	82%

University of Connecticut School of Law

45 Elizabeth Street
Hartford, CT 06105
Phone: 860.570.5100; Fax: 860.570.5153
E-mail: admit@law.uconn.edu; Website: www.law.uconn.edu

The information on these pages was provided by the law school.

■ Introduction

As a result of several decades of sustained intellectual growth, the University of Connecticut School of Law has emerged as one of the leading public law schools in the United States. Because of Connecticut's extraordinary ratio of full-time students to full-time faculty, 40 percent of the first-year curriculum is offered in seminar format and 70 percent of the advanced courses have 24 or fewer students. An outstanding and accessible faculty, an intensive first-year skills program, a rich and varied curriculum, including dozens of legal clinics, four student-edited journals, student organizations active across the spectrum of legal and social concerns, a regular flow of visiting lecturers, and a committed body of graduates throughout the country combine to make the University of Connecticut a law school of exceptional strength.

■ Library and Physical Facilities

The campus, listed on the National Register of Historic Sites, is arguably the most beautiful in the United States. The library, completed in 1996, is one of the largest legal research and technology centers in the world, with more than 500,000 volumes housed in the 120,000-square-foot facility.

With its immediate neighbors—the Hartford Seminary, the Hartford College for Women, the Connecticut Historical Society, and the Connecticut Attorney General's Office—the school is part of an academic enclave in a turn-of-the-century residential neighborhood.

■ Dual-degree Programs

The law school offers several interdisciplinary programs: JD/LLM in Insurance Law, JD/Master of Business Administration, JD/Master of Library Science (with Southern Connecticut State University), JD/Master of Public Administration, JD/Master of Public Health, and JD/Master of Social Work.

■ International Study Programs

The economic and political realities of globalization place new demands on the graduates of the law school. International law occupies an increasingly prominent place in the curriculum, reinforced by the student-edited *Connecticut Journal of International Law*. The law school has formal and informal study-abroad programs with universities in Aix-Marseille, Berlin, Dublin, Exeter, Leiden, London, Mannheim, San Juan, Sienna, and Tilburg. These relationships bring a wealth of international visitors to the school. Legal scholars have visited and lectured from Albania, Bosnia, Bulgaria, China, France, Germany, Great Britain, Hungary, Israel, Japan, Korea, Latvia, the Netherlands, Poland, Russia, South Africa, Taiwan, and Ukraine.

The LLM in United States Legal Studies for graduates of foreign law schools provides further opportunity for our students to learn from and study with peers trained in different legal systems.

■ Special Programs

Connecticut was a pioneer in clinical legal education, and our clinics continue to be a distinguishing strength of the school. If you are interested in the way law intersects with other disciplines or with such varied topics as critical identity theory, intellectual property, or European Community law, you will find courses and specialists to meet your needs. Offerings in environmental law are supplemented by a semester exchange program with the Environmental Law Center at Vermont Law School.

The **Center for Children's Advocacy, Inc.**, a nonprofit corporation housed at the law school, works on behalf of the legal rights of underprivileged children. The **Connecticut Urban Legal Initiative, Inc.**, another nonprofit corporation housed at the law school, involves law students and the bar in identifying neighborhood problems that typify urban blight and devising strategies to address them. The **Insurance Law Center** offers a specialized insurance curriculum with its LLM program, innovative research initiatives on the role of insurance in law and society, conferences and workshops, and the student-edited *Connecticut Insurance Law Journal*.

The **Intellectual Property Certificate Program**, for students with a special interest in IP law, exposes participants to a broad curriculum of courses, from classes on patent, trademark, and copyright law to specialized seminars, including those in art law, cyberlaw, and European Union IP law. The **Tax Certificate Program** affords an opportunity to participate in a supervised writing project, externship, or clinic in the area of tax law. Participants in the Certificate Program may begin their tax studies in Federal Income Taxation in their first year and continue the study of taxation in a variety of courses during the last four semesters of law school. A new **Human Rights Certificate Program** offers students the opportunity to work with world-renowned experts at the law school and the College of Liberal Arts and Sciences in a demanding and varied interdisciplinary study of global affairs and social justice. The law school has also created a new **Law and Public Policy Certificate Program**, a flexible program in which students may enroll in a diverse collection of courses with faculty at the law school and within the University of Connecticut's Department of Public Policy.

■ Student Activities

Selected students may participate in four student-edited journals: the *Connecticut Law Review*, the *Connecticut Journal of International Law*, the *Connecticut Insurance Law Journal*, and the *Connecticut Public Interest Law Journal*.

The **Connecticut Moot Court Board** provides students with the opportunity to practice oral advocacy in intramural and interscholastic competitions. Participants have placed extremely well in regional, national, and international competitions.

The **Student Bar Association** is the representative student government of the school. It manages an annual budget consisting of funds derived from the student activities fee and university tuition to support the various student organizations and to generally enhance the quality of student life. Under the governance of the Student Bar, a large number of student-run organizations, reflecting the diversity of our students, have active chapters on campus.

■ Career Services

Connecticut operates a comprehensive career services office for the benefit of students and alumni/ae. The school offers a large and geographically diverse on-campus interviewing program (*www.law.uconn.edu/careersvcs/employer-list.htm*), extensive individual and group counseling, a resource library, job listings, mentor programs, employment information sessions, newsletters, and job bulletins. The school also participates in several off-site job fairs.

Within six months of graduation, 95.8 percent of the class of 2005 were employed, including 17.7 percent in judicial clerkships.

■ Services for Students With Disabilities

The Assistant to the Dean for Student Services at the School of Law works with students with disabilities in the development and implementation of reasonable accommodations to allow access to both its physical facilities and its educational and extracurricular programs. Dr. Jane Thierfeld Brown serves in this capacity.

Students with disabilities who are considering applying or who have been admitted to the School of Law are invited to tour the campus. Students may contact the dean's office for discussion of accommodations.

Applicant Profile

University of Connecticut School of Law

LSAT Score	GPA																											
	3.75 +		3.50–3.74		3.25–3.49		3.00–3.24		2.75–2.99		2.50–2.74		2.25–2.49		2.00–2.24		Below 2.00		No GPA		Total	
	Apps	Adm	Apps	Adm	Apps	Adm	Apps	Adm	Apps	Adm	Apps	Adm	Apps	Adm	Apps	Adm	Apps	Adm	Apps	Adm	Apps	Adm
175–180	0	0	0	0	1	1	1	0	0	0	0	0	0	0	0	0	0	0	1	0	3	1
170–174	5	2	8	1	9	1	5	0	1	0	1	1	1	0	0	0	0	0	0	0	30	5
165–169	18	9	27	6	33	7	19	4	15	1	5	0	1	0	0	0	0	0	1	0	119	27
160–164	65	25	113	46	128	41	85	26	30	5	14	0	7	1	2	0	1	0	7	1	452	145
155–159	73	23	139	34	182	35	88	13	40	5	22	0	9	0	2	0	1	0	5	2	561	112
150–154	41	8	80	9	107	9	93	6	52	4	29	2	9	0	3	0	0	0	7	3	421	41
145–149	23	4	44	6	62	3	64	3	40	3	22	0	8	0	4	0	0	0	7	0	274	19
140–144	8	2	24	0	25	2	35	0	30	0	27	0	7	0	3	0	0	0	3	0	162	4
135–139	3	0	4	0	5	0	11	0	14	0	4	0	8	0	4	0	1	0	2	0	56	0
130–134	0	0	3	0	1	0	5	0	2	0	4	0	4	0	3	0	0	0	1	0	23	0
125–129	0	0	0	0	0	0	0	0	0	0	0	0	1	0	0	0	0	0	0	0	1	0
120–124	0	0	0	0	0	0	0	0	0	0	0	0	0	0	0	0	0	0	0	0	0	0
Total	236	73	442	102	553	99	406	52	224	18	128	3	55	1	21	0	3	0	34	6	2102	354

Apps = Number of Applicants
Adm = Number Admitted

This grid includes only full-time applicants with LSAT scores earned under standard administrations (99% of all full-time applicants).

Cornell Law School

Myron Taylor Hall
Ithaca, NY 14853-4901
Phone: 607.255.5141
E-mail: lawadmit@lawschool.cornell.edu; Website: www.lawschool.cornell.edu

ABA
Approved
Since
1923

The Basics

Type of school	Private
Term	Semester
Application deadline	2/1
Application fee	$70
Financial aid deadline	3/15
Can first year start other than fall?	No
Student to faculty ratio	10.0 to 1
Does the university offer:	
housing restricted to law students?	Yes
graduate housing for which law students are eligible?	Yes

Faculty and Administrators

	Total		Men		Women		Minorities	
	Fall	Spr	Fall	Spr	Fall	Spr	Fall	Spr
Full-time	48	44	34	32	14	12	4	2
Other Full-time	0	0	0	0	0	0	0	0
Deans, librarians, & others who teach	12	10	7	6	5	4	1	1
Part-time	23	32	17	23	6	9	0	1
Total	**83**	**86**	**58**	**61**	**25**	**25**	**5**	**4**

Curriculum

	Full-time	Part-time
Typical first-year section size	96	0
Is there typically a "small section" of the first-year class, other than Legal Writing, taught by full-time faculty	Yes	No
If yes, typical size offered last year	32	
# of classroom course titles beyond first-year curriculum	116	

# of upper division courses, excluding seminars with an enrollment:		
	Under 25	59
	25–49	24
	50–74	8
	75–99	6
	100+	3

# of seminars	43	
# of seminar positions available	688	
# of seminar positions filled	516	0
# of positions available in simulation courses	319	
# of simulation positions filled	273	0
# of positions available in faculty supervised clinical courses	163	
# of faculty supervised clinical positions filled	150	0
# involved in field placements	55	0
# involved in law journals	268	0
# involved in interschool competitions	240	0
# of credit hours required to graduate	84	

JD Enrollment and Ethnicity

	Men #	Men %	Women #	Women %	Full-time #	Full-time %	Part-time #	Part-time %	1st-year #	1st-year %	Total #	Total %	JD Degs. Awd.
African Amer.	14	4.8	22	8.1	36	6.4	0	0.0	10	5.3	36	6.4	16
Amer. Indian	4	1.4	2	0.7	6	1.1	0	0.0	3	1.6	6	1.1	1
Asian Amer.	32	11.1	37	13.6	69	12.3	0	0.0	17	9.1	69	12.3	30
Mex. Amer.	3	1.0	6	2.2	9	1.6	0	0.0	2	1.1	9	1.6	4
Puerto Rican	4	1.4	6	2.2	10	1.8	0	0.0	4	2.1	10	1.8	1
Hispanic	3	1.0	7	2.6	10	1.8	0	0.0	4	2.1	10	1.8	3
Total Minority	60	20.8	80	29.4	140	25.0	0	0.0	40	21.4	140	25.0	55
For. Nation.	16	5.5	26	9.6	42	7.5	0	0.0	9	4.8	42	7.5	9
Caucasian	213	73.7	166	61.0	379	67.6	0	0.0	138	73.8	379	67.6	128
Unknown	0	0.0	0	0.0	0	0.0	0	0.0	0	0.0	0	0.0	0
Total	289	51.5	272	48.5	561	100.0	0	0.0	187	33.3	561		192

Transfers

Transfers in	18
Transfers out	12

Tuition and Fees

	Resident	Nonresident
Full-time	$40,648	$40,648
Part-time	$0	$0

Living Expenses

Estimated living expenses for singles

Living on campus	Living off campus	Living at home
$17,200	$17,200	$17,200

Cornell Law School

ABA
Approved
Since
1923

GPA and LSAT Scores

	Total	Full-time	Part-time
# of apps	4,172	4,172	0
# of offers	941	941	0
# of matrics	188	188	0
75% GPA	3.81	3.81	0.00
Median GPA	3.67	3.67	0.00
25% GPA	3.53	3.53	0.00
75% LSAT	168	168	0
Median LSAT	167	167	0
25% LSAT	166	166	0

Grants and Scholarships (from prior year)

	Total		Full-time		Part-time	
	#	%	#	%	#	%
Total # of students	581		580		1	
Total # receiving grants	242	41.7	242	41.7	0	0.0
Less than 1/2 tuition	171	29.4	171	29.5	0	0.0
Half to full tuition	71	12.2	71	12.2	0	0.0
Full tuition	0	0.0	0	0.0	0	0.0
More than full tuition	0	0.0	0	0.0	0	0.0
Median grant amount			$13,000		$0	

Informational and Library Resources

# of volumes and volume equivalents	721,439
# of titles	216,264
# of active serial subscriptions	6,680
Study seating capacity inside the library	430
# of full-time professional librarians	10
Hours per week library is open	168
# of open, wired connections available to students	32
# of networked computers available for use by students	74
# of simultaneous wireless users	510
Require computer?	No

JD Attrition (from prior year)

	Academic	Other	Total	
	#	#	#	%
1st year	0	15	15	7.9
2nd year	0	4	4	2.1
3rd year	0	1	1	0.5
4th year	0	0	0	0.0

Employment (9 months after graduation)

	Total	Percentage
Employment status known	210	100.0
Employment status unknown	0	0.0
Employed	204	97.1
Pursuing graduate degrees	2	1.0
Unemployed seeking employment	4	1.9
Unemployed not seeking employment	0	0.0
Unemployed and studying for the bar	0	0.0

Type of Employment

	Total	Percentage
# employed in law firms	143	70.1
# employed in business and industry	8	3.9
# employed in government	8	3.9
# employed in public interest	6	2.9
# employed as judicial clerks	26	12.7
# employed in academia	5	2.5

Geographic Location

	Total	Percentage
# employed in state	110	53.9
# employed in foreign countries	2	1.0
# of states where employed	22	

Bar Passage Rates

Jurisdiction	New York		
Exam	Sum 05	Win 06	Total
# from school taking bar for the first time	151	7	158
School's pass rate for all first-time takers	95%	86%	94%
State's pass rate for all first-time takers	76%	61%	74%

Cornell Law School

Myron Taylor Hall
Ithaca, NY 14853-4901
Phone: 607.255.5141
E-mail: lawadmit@lawschool.cornell.edu; Website: www.lawschool.cornell.edu

■ Lawyers in the Best Sense

When Cornell University's founding president, Andrew Dickson White, began to lay plans for a law department at Cornell University, he wrote that he wanted to educate "not swarms of hastily prepared pettifoggers, but a fair number of well-trained, large-minded, morally based *lawyers in the best sense . . .*" He hoped graduates of the school would become "a blessing to the country, at the bar, on the bench, and in various public bodies." More than a century since President White's vision, this ideal still holds true. A small, top-tier law school located in beautiful surroundings, Cornell draws on, and contributes to, the resources of a great university, consistently producing well-rounded lawyers and accomplished practitioners cut from a different cloth. Cornell is a national center of learning located in Ithaca, New York, the heart of the Finger Lakes region of New York State. The Law School's small classes, broad curriculum, and distinguished faculty, combined with the advantages of being part of one of the world's leading research universities, make it ideal for those who value both depth and breadth in their legal studies. Students find Ithaca to be a safe and nonstressful, yet culturally rich, environment in which to pursue legal studies.

■ Enrollment/Student Body

Sixty percent of Cornell's entering students have taken one or more years between completion of their undergraduate degree and enrollment in law school. Selective admission standards, combined with an emphasis on applicants' unique records and achievements, ensure that the student body is made up of people with wide-ranging interests, skills, concerns, and backgrounds.

■ Faculty

Cornell's faculty are known not only as prolific scholars but also as great teachers. Tenured and tenure-track faculty teach and produce scholarship in their area of law; clinical faculty run client-focused and simulation courses centered around legal aid and several specialty clinics; and a large number of visitors, associated faculty from other university divisions, and adjunct faculty teach at the school each year. Many of the latter group are legal scholars and professors from other countries who teach in the law school's significant international program.

■ Library, Physical Facilities, and Computing

The Law School is located in the renovated and expanded Myron Taylor Hall, at the heart of the scenic 740-acre Cornell University campus. Hughes Hall, the Law School dormitory, is adjacent to the main Law School building and contains single rooms for about 48 students and a dining facility.

Cornell is one of the nation's leaders in the development and support of electronic legal research. It combines outstanding collections with professional expertise and access to worldwide electronic information sources, for Anglo-American, as well as foreign and international law. Students have access to the full array of Internet services. The Law School's multiple-node network, wireless network, and computer terminals are available to students for word processing, legal research, statistical analysis, and database management. Students also

have access to the many satellite computer clusters and mainframe facilities located on the university campus.

■ Curriculum/Clinical Studies

Cornell offers a national law curriculum leading to the JD degree. First-year students take a group of required courses and an intensive lawyering course stressing a variety of legal research, writing, and advocacy techniques. After the first year, students may choose from a wide range of elective courses, including many seminars and problem courses.

The Cornell Legal Aid Clinic, offering legal services to individuals financially unable to employ an attorney, provides students with the chance to engage in the supervised practice of law under the direction of experienced attorneys. Clinical faculty also conduct a variety of other specialized clinics and skills courses within the regular curriculum. Students can select from a bevy of clinical courses, such as the Public Interest Clinic (three different levels), the Asylum and Convention Against Torture Appellate Clinic, Capital Punishment Clinic: Post-Conviction Litigation Clinic, Criminal Defense Trial Clinic, International Human Rights Clinic, Labor Law Clinic, Prosecution Trial Clinic, Water Law Clinic, and US Attorney's Office Clinic.

■ Joint Degrees

Being part of a world-renowned university, and the interdisciplinary environment it provides, is of great benefit. Cornell Law School and Cornell University offer many opportunities for combined degree programs, including the JD/MBA (Business degree from the Johnson School of Graduate Management); JD/MPA (Public Affairs degree from the Cornell Institute of Public Affairs); JD/MILR (Labor Relations degree from the School of Industrial and Labor Relations); JD/MRP (Regional Planning degree from the College of Architecture, Art, and Planning); and a JD/MA or PhD in a variety of fields (Master or PhD degree from the Graduate School). Law students can also take as many as 12 credits outside of the law school for law school credit.

■ International Legal Studies

The Berger International Legal Studies Program is one of the country's oldest and most distinguished programs in international legal education. Cornell's comprehensive program features a unique JD specialization opportunity; a three-year JD/LLM degree in International and Comparative Law; a four-year JD/Master en Droit (French law degree) program; a four-year JD/MLLP (German law degree) program; a three-year JD/DESS in Global Business Law; a Paris summer institute with the University of Paris I (Panthéon-Sorbonne); a Suzhou, China Summer Law Institute in partnership with Kenneth Wang School of Law, Soochow University, Suzhou, China and Bucerius Law School, Hamburg, Germany; a comprehensive speaker series; Mori, Hamada & Matsumoto (Tokyo law firm) Faculty Exchange; a large number of visiting foreign professors and scholars; a weekly luncheon discussion series; and a leading journal of international and comparative law edited by students. Students have the option to spend one semester abroad at a partner law school (we have agreements with 13 partner schools in 10 different countries) or to design an individual "term away" at a foreign law facility with which Cornell is not partnered.

In addition, the Clarke Center for International and Comparative Legal Studies brings scholars, students, philosophers, and experts to support the study of law in Asia and the Middle East.

■ Programs and Projects

Cornell Law School is the home for several unique programs and projects of interest to students. These programs and projects include the following: Cornell Death Penalty Project (clinics and symposia related to capital punishment); Clarke Scholars Program (visiting scholars); *Journal of Empirical Legal Studies* (only legal journal dedicated exclusively to empirical legal scholarship); Clarke Program in East Asian Law and Culture (broad interdisciplinary and humanistic focus on the study of law in East Asia); Legal Information Institute (world's leading investigator of new ways to do electronic legal research); Keck Focus on Legal Ethics Program (practitioners-in-residence, visiting fellows, colloquia, and an online ethics library); and Empirical Studies Project (empirical study of court cases).

■ Student Activities

Student-edited law journals include the *Cornell Law Review* (published continuously since 1916), the *Cornell International Law Journal* (established in 1967), and the *Cornell Journal of Law and Public Policy*. Student organizations and activities include American Constitution Society; Amicus; Asian Pacific American Law Students Association; Black Law Students Association; Briggs Society of International Law; Business Law Society; Christian Legal Society; Cornell Advocates for Human Rights; Cornell Bioethics and Law Society; Cornell Sports and Entertainment Law Consortium; Cornell European Law Student Association; Cornell Law Student Association; Cornell Law Democrats; Law, Economics, and Business Society; Cornell

Law Republicans; Cornell Law School Cocounsel; Discourses; the *Tower*; Environmental Law Society; Federalist Society; Intellectual Property Student Organization; J. Reuben Clark Law Society; Jewish Law Student Association; *Juris Diction*; LAMBDA; Latino American Law Students Association; LLM Association; Moot Court Board; National Lawyers Guild; Native American Law Students Association; Phi Alpha Delta; Phi Delta Phi; Public Interest Law Union; the Society of Law and the Arts; South Asian Law Students Association; Students for Marriage Equality; the Veteran's Society; and the Women's Law Coalition.

■ Expenses and Financial Aid

Cornell offers an institutional-based financial aid program. About 50 percent of students receive scholarship aid (with need-based awards averaging more than $13,000 per year), with a higher percentage receiving government-backed loans. Minority or economically disadvantaged students are eligible for enhanced scholarship awards.

Our Public Interest Low Income Protection Plan, one of the most generous of such programs, assists those choosing qualifying public interest law jobs through the use of a moderated loan repayment plan and loan forgiveness.

■ Career Services

Cornell's students continue to be among the most recruited in the country. Every fall, hundreds of employers from across the country visit the Law School and conduct employment interviews. Employers also participate in law school-sponsored job fairs in locations such as Boston, Chicago, Dallas, Los Angeles, New York, San Francisco, Miami, Atlanta, and Washington, DC. A professionally staffed Career Services Office provides employment counseling to students and serves as a liaison to legal employers, both public and private. In addition, Cornell has a full-time professional staff member (Dean for Public Service) dedicated to public interest job opportunities and counseling.

Applicant Profile

Admission to Cornell Law is very competitive. Members of the most recent entering class had an aggregate 3.67 undergraduate grade-point average and median LSAT scores that placed them in the 96th percentile nationwide (167). But Cornell Law does not evaluate candidates by the numbers alone. The admission committee carefully considers such nonquantifiable factors as extracurricular and community activities, life experience and work background, and recommendations. Cornell Law

subscribes to the university's 130-year tradition of affirmative action, and members of traditionally underrepresented minority groups are encouraged to mention their status where they think it is relevant. The decision to offer admission ultimately rests on whether the committee is convinced that the applicant will be an energetic, productive, and successful member of the Cornell Law community and eventually, the legal profession.

Creighton University School of Law

2500 California Plaza
Omaha, NE 68178
Phone: 402.280.2872; Fax: 402.280.5564
E-mail: lawadmit@creighton.edu; Website: law.creighton.edu

ABA
Approved
Since
1924

The Basics

Type of school	Private
Term	Semester
Application deadline	5/1
Application fee	$45
Financial aid deadline	7/1
Can first year start other than fall?	No
Student to faculty ratio	14.7 to 1
Does the university offer:	
housing restricted to law students?	No
graduate housing for which law students are eligible?	Yes

Faculty and Administrators

	Total		Men		Women		Minorities	
	Fall	Spr	Fall	Spr	Fall	Spr	Fall	Spr
Full-time	26	26	18	17	8	9	4	4
Other Full-time	2	2	2	2	0	0	0	0
Deans, librarians, & others who teach	7	6	6	5	1	1	0	0
Part-time	22	23	13	16	7	5	1	1
Total	**57**	**57**	**39**	**40**	**16**	**15**	**5**	**5**

Curriculum

	Full-time	Part-time
Typical first-year section size	78	0
Is there typically a "small section" of the first-year class, other than Legal Writing, taught by full-time faculty	No	No
If yes, typical size offered last year		
# of classroom course titles beyond first-year curriculum		79
# of upper division courses, excluding seminars with an enrollment: Under 25		87
25–49		27
50–74		10
75–99		3
100+		2
# of seminars		4
# of seminar positions available		90
# of seminar positions filled	68	0
# of positions available in simulation courses		446
# of simulation positions filled	383	0
# of positions available in faculty supervised clinical courses		28
# of faculty supervised clinical positions filled	23	0
# involved in field placements	10	0
# involved in law journals	51	0
# involved in interschool competitions	168	0
# of credit hours required to graduate		94

JD Enrollment and Ethnicity

	Men		Women		Full-time		Part-time		1st-year		Total		JD Degs. Awd.
	#	%	#	%	#	%	#	%	#	%	#	%	
African Amer.	4	1.5	6	3.0	10	2.2	0	0.0	2	1.2	10	2.1	2
Amer. Indian	1	0.4	2	1.0	3	0.7	0	0.0	0	0.0	3	0.6	1
Asian Amer.	5	1.9	10	5.0	15	3.3	0	0.0	3	1.8	15	3.2	3
Mex. Amer.	9	3.4	4	2.0	12	2.7	1	6.3	2	1.2	13	2.8	3
Puerto Rican	1	0.4	1	0.5	2	0.4	0	0.0	1	0.6	2	0.4	0
Hispanic	2	0.8	1	0.5	2	0.4	1	6.3	2	1.2	3	0.6	2
Total Minority	22	8.3	24	11.9	44	9.7	2	12.5	10	6.1	46	9.8	11
For. Nation.	0	0.0	1	0.5	1	0.2	0	0.0	0	0.0	1	0.2	0
Caucasian	244	91.7	177	87.6	407	90.0	14	87.5	154	93.9	421	90.0	138
Unknown	0	0.0	0	0.0	0	0.0	0	0.0	0	0.0	0	0.0	0
Total	266	56.8	202	43.2	452	96.6	16	3.4	164	35.0	468		149

Transfers

Transfers in	3
Transfers out	7

Tuition and Fees

	Resident	Nonresident
Full-time	$24,828	$24,828
Part-time	$14,486	$14,486

Living Expenses

Estimated living expenses for singles

Living on campus	Living off campus	Living at home
$16,530	$16,530	$16,530

Creighton University School of Law

*ABA
Approved
Since
1924*

GPA and LSAT Scores

	Total	Full-time	Part-time
# of apps	1,334	1,277	57
# of offers	529	513	16
# of matrics	161	155	6
75% GPA	3.66	3.67	3.59
Median GPA	3.40	3.41	3.34
25% GPA	3.15	3.15	3.12
75% LSAT	157	157	159
Median LSAT	155	155	149
25% LSAT	153	153	146

Grants and Scholarships (from prior year)

	Total #	Total %	Full-time #	Full-time %	Part-time #	Part-time %
Total # of students	469		451		18	
Total # receiving grants	192	40.9	190	42.1	2	11.1
Less than 1/2 tuition	124	26.4	122	27.1	2	11.1
Half to full tuition	48	10.2	48	10.6	0	0.0
Full tuition	19	4.1	19	4.2	0	0.0
More than full tuition	1	0.2	1	0.2	0	0.0
Median grant amount			$7,000		$4,000	

Informational and Library Resources

# of volumes and volume equivalents	361,823
# of titles	135,186
# of active serial subscriptions	4,662
Study seating capacity inside the library	363
# of full-time professional librarians	8
Hours per week library is open	104
# of open, wired connections available to students	160
# of networked computers available for use by students	51
# of simultaneous wireless users	360
Require computer?	No

JD Attrition (from prior year)

	Academic #	Other #	Total #	Total %
1st year	6	12	18	10.8
2nd year	0	0	0	0.0
3rd year	0	0	0	0.0
4th year	0	0	0	0.0

Employment (9 months after graduation)

	Total	Percentage
Employment status known	153	100.0
Employment status unknown	0	0.0
Employed	143	93.5
Pursuing graduate degrees	3	2.0
Unemployed seeking employment	4	2.6
Unemployed not seeking employment	3	2.0
Unemployed and studying for the bar	0	0.0

Type of Employment

	Total	Percentage
# employed in law firms	75	52.4
# employed in business and industry	33	23.1
# employed in government	18	12.6
# employed in public interest	4	2.8
# employed as judicial clerks	10	7.0
# employed in academia	3	2.1

Geographic Location

	Total	Percentage
# employed in state	84	58.7
# employed in foreign countries	0	0.0
# of states where employed	22	

Bar Passage Rates

Jurisdiction		Nebraska			Iowa	
Exam	Sum 05	Win 06	Total	Sum 05	Win 06	Total
# from school taking bar for the first time	66	3	69	19	2	21
School's pass rate for all first-time takers	77%	33%	75%	84%	100%	86%
State's pass rate for all first-time takers	88%	62%	86%	86%	81%	85%

Creighton University School of Law

2500 California Plaza
Omaha, NE 68178
Phone: 402.280.2872; Fax: 402.280.5564
E-mail: lawadmit@creighton.edu; Website: law.creighton.edu

■ The School of Law

The School of Law, established in 1904, has been a member of the AALS since 1907 and approved by the ABA for more than 80 years. Alumni from the law school are practicing in all 50 states and in more than 13 foreign countries. The law school's current enrollment is 473. Students come from 34 states and 160 undergraduate institutions.

■ Introduction

Creighton University, a privately endowed and supported Jesuit university, was founded in 1878. Creighton is the most diverse educational institution of its size in the nation. In addition to the School of Law, Creighton has a School of Medicine, School of Dentistry, School of Pharmacy and Health Professions, School of Nursing, School of Business Administration, College of Arts and Sciences, and a Graduate School, making it the center of professional education in the Midwest. The university is located just blocks from downtown Omaha, a metropolitan area with a population of approximately 800,000. Known as the River City, Omaha is the heart of the Midlands and the largest metroplex between Chicago and Denver.

■ Faculty

The faculty is composed of 27 full-time professors and a group of part-time specialists chosen from the bench and bar. Creighton's full-time faculty members have earned reputations as outstanding classroom teachers. In addition, faculty scholarship brings to the classroom insights gained through the publication of leading texts and thought-provoking articles. A distinguished adjunct faculty of judges and practicing attorneys teach courses in specialty areas. Faculty offices surround the Law School Commons making them easily accessible to students. Faculty members maintain an open-door policy that encourages students to drop-in to discuss the latest case, current events, or the newest restaurant in town.

■ Library and Physical Facilities

The School of Law is entirely contained in the Ahmanson Law Center built in 1974. The Klutznik Law Library/McGrath North Legal Research Center houses one of the Midwest's finest legal collections. Students have access to a wealth of applications and research material through the network. The law school also has full range and wireless coverage throughout the building.

■ Areas of Concentration

Students may earn a certificate indicating that they focused their studies in a particular area of concentration. Areas of concentration are (a) Business, Taxation, and Commercial Transactions; (b) Criminal Law and Procedure; (c) International and Comparative Law; and (d) Trial Practice. The curriculum prepares students for the practice of law in any state.

■ Combined-degree Programs

Creighton's School of Law, College of Business Administration, and Graduate School offer a JD/MBA and JD/MS in Information Technology Management, JD/MS in Negotiation and Dispute Resolution, and JD/MA in International Relations. The Graduate School also offers a Certificate in Health Services Administration in connection with the JD degree.

■ Clinics and Internships

The Milton R. Abrahams Legal Clinic provides third-year students with the opportunity to learn the lawyering process in a way that is not provided in most law school courses. Clinic students represent low-income clients on a variety of civil matters that vary in complexity. Student case work is reviewed in individual case meetings with the supervisor on a weekly basis.

The Community Economic Development (CED) Clinic provides students with an opportunity to work on a broad range of transactional and business law issues affecting community development. Students in the CED Clinic represent a client base of nonprofit and community-based organizations that serve low-income communities across the state of Nebraska and small business owners.

Students may also participate in a broad variety of internships with city, county, and federal legal offices in the Omaha area.

■ Werner Institute for Negotiation and Dispute Resolution

The Werner Institute, the most richly endowed program of its kind in the country, is an emerging national leader in the field of conflict resolution with an interdisciplinary curriculum leading to graduate certificates and master's degrees in the field. The Institute places a strong emphasis on a systems approach in conflict resolution as well as a focus on preparation of leaders in the field with specialized applications in areas of greatest need such as conflict within and among organizations, among businesses, in health care, and in communities.

■ Student Activities

The Student Bar Association (SBA) is the student government of the law school. The purposes of the organization are to make law students aware of the obligations and opportunities existing for lawyers through SBA activities, promote a consciousness of professional responsibility, and provide a forum for student activities. The *Creighton Law Review*, edited and managed by students, is a scholarly legal journal that is circulated nationally and internationally. The school has over 27 different active student organizations.

■ Financial Aid and Scholarships

Creighton University School of Law offers two types of financial aid: merit-based scholarships and government loans. Students seeking financial aid and scholarships must complete the Free Application for Federal Student Aid (FAFSA). The loan program consists of the Federal Stafford Loan program and the Grad PLUS Loan program. All first-year scholarships have merit requirements, including, but not limited to, LSAT score and undergraduate grade-point average. Admitted applicants with an LSAT score and undergraduate grade-point average above Creighton's medians for the previous year will receive strong consideration for scholarship assistance. In 2006, over one-third of all students received scholarship assistance with an average award of over $9,300. Applicants who qualify for a Dean's Academic Scholarship will be notified at the time of acceptance.

■ Frances M. Ryan Diversity Scholarship Program

The School of Law actively recruits minority students and has a substantial diversity scholarship program. Applicants who wish to be considered for a Ryan Diversity Scholarship must make note of it on their admission application.

■ Career and Professional Development Office

The Career and Professional Development Office provides a full array of services to Creighton Law students, including individual career counseling, a law alumni network stretching from coast-to-coast, on-campus and off-campus (Denver and Kansas City) interviews, and a dynamic website that allows students to explore thousands of career opportunities throughout the world. Creighton's 2005 graduating class had a 97.4 percent employment rate nine months after graduation. Graduates of 2005 are working in the areas of academics, business, government, private practice, public interest, and as judicial clerks in 24 states.

Applicant Profile

Creighton University School of Law
This grid includes only applicants who earned 120–180 LSAT scores under standard administration.

LSAT Score	3.75 +		3.50–3.74		3.25–3.49		3.00–3.24		2.75–2.99		2.50–2.74		2.25–2.49		2.00–2.24		Below 2.00		No GPA		Total	
	Apps	Adm	Apps	Adm	Apps	Adm	Apps	Adm	Apps	Adm	Apps	Adm	Apps	Adm	Apps	Adm	Apps	Adm	Apps	Adm	Apps	Adm
175–180	1	1	0	0	0	0	0	0	0	0	0	0	0	0	0	0	0	0	0	0	1	1
170–174	2	2	0	0	0	0	0	0	0	0	0	0	0	0	0	0	0	0	0	0	2	2
165–169	7	7	0	0	2	2	4	4	2	2	1	1	0	0	1	1	0	0	0	0	17	17
160–164	13	13	11	11	13	13	8	8	5	5	4	4	5	4	3	1	0	0	0	0	62	59
155–159	38	38	41	40	55	50	43	39	30	22	11	3	6	3	2	1	0	0	2	1	228	197
150–154	63	57	90	57	117	57	103	27	56	10	30	0	9	3	4	0	0	0	1	1	473	212
145–149	38	14	69	15	82	3	63	2	46	2	17	0	12	0	4	0	1	0	1	0	333	36
140–144	9	0	19	1	26	1	39	0	23	0	16	0	10	0	3	0	1	0	2	0	148	2
135–139	5	0	5	0	5	0	11	0	8	0	6	0	4	0	2	0	1	0	2	0	49	0
130–134	1	0	0	0	1	0	3	0	2	0	2	0	1	0	2	0	0	0	0	0	12	0
125–129	0	0	0	0	0	0	0	0	0	0	0	0	0	0	0	0	0	0	0	0	0	0
120–124	0	0	0	0	0	0	0	0	0	0	0	0	0	0	0	0	0	0	0	0	0	0
Total	177	132	235	124	301	126	274	80	172	41	87	8	47	10	21	3	3	0	8	2	1325	526

Apps = Number of Applicants
Adm = Number Admitted
Reflects 99% of the total applicant pool.

University of Dayton School of Law

300 College Park, 112 Keller Hall
Dayton, OH 45469-2760
Phone: 937.229.3555; Fax: 937.229.4194
E-mail: lawinfo@notes.udayton.edu; Website: http://law.udayton.edu

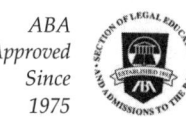

ABA
Approved
Since
1975

The Basics

Type of school	Private
Term	Semester
Application deadline	3/1 5/1
Application fee	$0
Financial aid deadline	3/1 5/1
Can first year start other than fall?	Yes
Student to faculty ratio	14.9 to 1
Does the university offer:	
housing restricted to law students?	Yes
graduate housing for which law students are eligible?	Yes

Faculty and Administrators

	Total		Men		Women		Minorities	
	Fall	Spr	Fall	Spr	Fall	Spr	Fall	Spr
Full-time	28	23	17	14	11	8	2	3
Other Full-time	0	0	0	0	0	0	0	0
Deans, librarians, & others who teach	3	3	1	1	2	2	0	0
Part-time	23	23	13	16	10	7	2	1
Total	54	49	31	31	23	17	4	4

Curriculum

	Full-time	Part-time
Typical first-year section size	80	0
Is there typically a "small section" of the first-year class, other than Legal Writing, taught by full-time faculty	Yes	No
If yes, typical size offered last year	35	
# of classroom course titles beyond first-year curriculum		79

# of upper division courses, excluding seminars with an enrollment:	Under 25	74
	25–49	16
	50–74	10
	75–99	15
	100+	2

# of seminars		9
# of seminar positions available		188
# of seminar positions filled	135	0
# of positions available in simulation courses		459
# of simulation positions filled	385	0
# of positions available in faculty supervised clinical courses		74
# of faculty supervised clinical positions filled	42	0
# involved in field placements	35	0
# involved in law journals	50	0
# involved in interschool competitions	38	0
# of credit hours required to graduate		90

JD Enrollment and Ethnicity

	Men		Women		Full-time		Part-time		1st-year		Total		JD Degs. Awd.
	#	%	#	%	#	%	#	%	#	%	#	%	
African Amer.	8	3.1	14	7.1	22	4.8	0	0.0	11	6.0	22	4.8	5
Amer. Indian	2	0.8	2	1.0	4	0.9	0	0.0	1	0.5	4	0.9	1
Asian Amer.	6	2.3	6	3.0	12	2.6	0	0.0	2	1.1	12	2.6	13
Mex. Amer.	5	1.9	0	0.0	5	1.1	0	0.0	2	1.1	5	1.1	1
Puerto Rican	3	1.1	1	0.5	4	0.9	0	0.0	3	1.6	4	0.9	0
Hispanic	4	1.5	4	2.0	8	1.7	0	0.0	1	0.5	8	1.7	2
Total Minority	28	10.7	27	13.7	55	12.0	0	0.0	20	10.9	55	12.0	22
For. Nation.	1	0.4	1	0.5	2	0.4	0	0.0	0	0.0	2	0.4	0
Caucasian	232	88.9	169	85.8	401	87.6	0	0.0	163	89.1	401	87.6	142
Unknown	0	0.0	0	0.0	0	0.0	0	0.0	0	0.0	0	0.0	0
Total	261	57.0	197	43.0	458	100.0	0	0.0	183	40.0	458		164

Transfers

Transfers in	1
Transfers out	15

Tuition and Fees

	Resident	Nonresident
Full-time	$31,644	$31,644
Part-time	$0	$0

Living Expenses

Estimated living expenses for singles

Living on campus	Living off campus	Living at home
$11,111	$11,111	$5,775

ABA
Approved
Since
1975

GPA and LSAT Scores

	Total	Full-time	Part-time
# of apps	2,400	2,400	0
# of offers	926	926	0
# of matrics	181	181	0
75% GPA	3.49	3.49	0.00
Median GPA	3.22	3.22	0.00
25% GPA	2.89	2.89	0.00
75% LSAT	155	155	0
Median LSAT	152	152	0
25% LSAT	150	150	0

Grants and Scholarships (from prior year)

	Total		Full-time		Part-time	
	#	%	#	%	#	%
Total # of students	469		468		1	
Total # receiving grants	245	52.2	245	52.4	0	0.0
Less than 1/2 tuition	230	49.0	230	49.1	0	0.0
Half to full tuition	15	3.2	15	3.2	0	0.0
Full tuition	0	0.0	0	0.0	0	0.0
More than full tuition	0	0.0	0	0.0	0	0.0
Median grant amount			$10,000		$0	

Informational and Library Resources

# of volumes and volume equivalents	312,785
# of titles	42,172
# of active serial subscriptions	4,856
Study seating capacity inside the library	483
# of full-time professional librarians	5
Hours per week library is open	102
# of open, wired connections available to students	0
# of networked computers available for use by students	50
# of simultaneous wireless users	1,500
Require computer?	No

JD Attrition

1st year	
2nd year	
3rd year	
4th year	

University of Dayton School
300 College Park, 112 Keller Hall
Dayton, OH 45469-2760
Phone: 937.229.3555; Fax: 937.229
E-mail: lawinfo@notes.udayton

■ **Introduction and**

The mission of the
intellectually c
and women
procedur
gradua
high

Employment (9 months after graduation)

	Total	Percentage
Employment status known	157	96.3
Employment status unknown	6	3.7
Employed	134	85.4
Pursuing graduate degrees	3	1.9
Unemployed seeking employment	10	6.4
Unemployed not seeking employment	0	0.0
Unemployed and studying for the bar	10	6.4
Type of Employment		
# employed in law firms	76	56.7
# employed in business and industry	26	19.4
# employed in government	17	12.7
# employed in public interest	8	6.0
# employed as judicial clerks	5	3.7
# employed in academia	1	0.7
Geographic Location		
# employed in state	72	53.7
# employed in foreign countries	0	0.0
# of states where employed	21	

Bar Passage Rates

Jurisdiction	Ohio		
Exam	Sum 05	Win 06	Total
# from school taking bar for the first time	79	8	87
School's pass rate for all first-time takers	81%	75%	80%
State's pass rate for all first-time takers	81%	76%	81%

The information on these pages was provided by the law school.

▨ of Law

.4194
.edu; Website: http://law.udayton.edu

▨ Mission

▨ School of Law is to enroll a diverse group of ▨rious, self-disciplined, and well-motivated men ▨ and to educate them in the substantive and ▨ principles of public and private law. We seek to ▨te highly qualified attorneys who will uphold the ▨st professional standards and recognize that service to ▨ers is the chief measure of professional competence.

We are a full-time JD program, providing a distinguished tradition of concern for the individual student in a supportive and professional environment. Our curriculum gives students a foundation in traditional courses but also helps them develop their skills with innovative programs such as our Legal Skills courses, our curricular tracks in Advocacy and Dispute Resolution, Personal and Transactional Law, and Intellectual Property, Cyberlaw and Creativity. Our diverse student body of 450 promotes ample opportunity for one-on-one interaction with faculty, staff, and fellow students, creating an atmosphere of collegiality and active involvement in a myriad of law school organizations. The University of Dayton School of Law is accredited by the ABA and is a member of the AALS.

▪ Keller Hall and the University of Dayton

Joseph E. Keller Hall is a 122,500-square-foot complex featuring a dramatic atrium, a variety of classroom space, and a spacious law library with technology integrated throughout the building. Ready access is provided by 1,400 data and power outlets and wireless capability to the law school network from virtually any location in the law building. Every seat in the 270,000 volume **Zimmerman Law Library** has a data and power outlet and contains a computer training center where students learn to conduct online and computer-based research. Group study rooms allow students to meet in groups of up to 25.

Founded in 1850, the **University of Dayton** enrolls more than 10,000 undergraduate and graduate students in a campus setting. Located minutes from the city's center, the campus contains a physical activities center and provides student services, on-campus housing, child care, meal plans, and banking. On-campus housing is available for half of the entering law students within three blocks of the law school.

▪ The Dayton Community

With a population of approximately 950,000, Dayton and the Miami Valley offer the many amenities of larger urban areas while retaining its scenic, lush, and open green spaces. As the birthplace of the Wright Brothers, the city offers a variety of flight-related museums and events, as well as a variety of other cultural and recreational activities. Housing is varied and affordable, as are shopping, restaurants, and entertainment districts. Many state and local parks are available for biking, swimming, hiking, and boating. If students want to explore beyond Dayton, they can reach Cincinnati or Columbus in a 50–75 minute drive, or the quaint towns of Yellow Springs, Waynesville, or Lebanon within a 30 minute drive from campus.

▪ Curriculum and Programs

Five- or Six-semester Study Options—Studies may be completed in either five semesters (accelerated) or six semesters (traditional). Either option allows students at least one summer off, during which students can participate in valuable clerkship opportunities.

Fall or Summer Start Options—Our calendar is designed so that students may choose between a fall or summer start. The five-semester study option combined with the summer start option allows the JD to be earned in only 24 calendar months.

Curricular Tracks—The three different curricular tracks — Advocacy and Dispute Resolution, Personal and Transactional Law, and Intellectual Property, Cyberlaw and Creativity— provide in-depth knowledge of a particular area of law.

Capstone Courses—To bring closure to each track, these courses take the knowledge gained from your track courses and apply it to real-world experience.

Intrasession Courses—These one-week courses are taught during the middle week of each semester and are offered in a variety of topics.

Externships—These semester-long positions of legal work under the supervision of a licensed attorney allow firsthand experience in a legal career.

▪ Faculty

With backgrounds that span a spectrum of legal endeavors, many of our faculty members are known nationally for their expertise and scholarship. As prominent scholars and leaders, our professors transfer their expertise to students both inside and outside of the classroom. Students consistently praise our faculty, not only for their outstanding teaching skills, but also for their constant involvement in, concern for, and support of students' lives. They are also interesting individuals with diverse backgrounds and a variety of experiences.

▪ Student Life

Collegiality, support, and a positive atmosphere distinguish our student body, which benefits from the diversity of classmates in race, age, gender, and background. Students may participate in organizations that help develop writing, research, and oral advocacy skills; those which speak to their mutual professional interests; or those that provide support of a student's personal and biographical background and interests. Our Student Bar Association is made up of officers and representatives from each class who oversee all student organizations and is the voice of student governance at the law school.

▪ Career Services and Bar Passage

Our Career Services Dean and his staff are committed to providing comprehensive career planning and placement services to assist students with identifying and securing positions commensurate with each individual's interests and career goals. Over half of our students are employed in private practice and about one-third find positions in business, industry, the government, or the military. Our graduates are employed in most states and several countries. They take an active interest in the life of the law school, participating in panel discussions, mentor programs, and alumni events, as well as contributing their time and resources to various scholarship and fundraising activities.

Our graduates have been consistently successful in bar passage and attribute this success to our curriculum as well as to our excellent **Road to Bar Passage Program**. This program involves students from their first year of law school right through to the exam. A series of workshops inform students about bar examinations and how to prepare for them, as well as details about the exam atmosphere and scoring. The program also includes many, many opportunities to practice sample bar exam questions, including not only essays, but also multiple choice questions and the new practice tests. Thanks to our curriculum and Road to Bar Passage Program, our graduates have been highly successful passing the Ohio and other states' bar examinations.

■ Admission

The Admissions Committee looks for a well-rounded and diverse group of students. Undergraduate GPA and LSAT score are highly considered, but commitment, motivation, leadership, and a breadth and depth of experiences are also a large part of the applicant review. Decisions are made on a

rolling basis, beginning November 1 and continuing through late spring.

■ Financial Aid

One-third to one-half of the entering class receives **scholarships**. The majority of our scholarships are merit-based, with the goal of diversifying the class also taken into consideration. Renewal of merit scholarships is dependent upon academic performance at the end of the preceding two semesters.

Federal loans up to $20,500 are also available to our students. Private alternative loans may also be used to cover the cost of a legal education, should scholarships and federal loans not do so. Federal and private loans are available pending a student's citizenship status and credit rating.

■ Prospective Students

Prospective students are encouraged to contact the School of Law Office of Admissions to schedule informational visits or obtain assistance with questions or concerns. The office holds open houses during the year, and staff participate in many events off-campus so that students may easily acquire more information. Office hours are 8:30 AM to 4:30 PM, Monday through Friday.

Applicant Profile

University of Dayton School of Law
This grid includes all full-time applicants who earned LSAT scores on the 120–180 scale under standard test administrations and whose submission files were complete and reviewed by the faculty admission committee.

LSAT Score	3.75 +		3.50–3.74		3.25–3.49		3.00–3.24		2.75–2.99		2.50–2.74		2.25–2.49		2.00–2.24		Below 2.00		No GPA		Total	
	Apps	Adm	Apps	Adm	Apps	Adm	Apps	Adm	Apps	Adm	Apps	Adm	Apps	Adm	Apps	Adm	Apps	Adm	Apps	Adm	Apps	Adm
175–180	0	0	0	0	0	0	0	0	0	0	0	0	0	0	0	0	0	0	0	0	0	0
170–174	0	0	1	1	1	1	0	0	0	0	0	0	0	0	0	0	0	0	0	0	2	2
165–169	2	2	1	1	2	2	2	2	1	1	3	3	4	4	0	0	0	0	0	0	15	15
160–164	6	4	9	9	6	6	9	9	8	7	7	6	5	4	3	1	0	0	0	0	53	46
155–159	20	19	32	31	56	55	49	48	33	32	27	25	14	8	6	3	0	0	3	2	240	223
150–154	43	40	102	87	137	102	127	82	123	60	63	23	30	2	11	2	3	1	2	0	641	399
145–149	39	13	98	21	139	23	118	18	90	10	57	6	34	2	11	0	1	0	4	0	591	93
140–144	14	1	39	5	46	7	72	8	57	3	45	1	20	0	12	0	3	0	4	0	312	25
135–139	1	0	14	2	17	0	25	0	24	1	17	1	16	0	3	0	2	0	2	0	121	4
130–134	1	0	1	0	1	0	8	0	9	0	7	0	4	0	2	0	0	0	2	0	35	0
125–129	0	0	0	0	0	0	2	0	1	0	1	0	1	0	0	0	1	0	0	0	6	0
120–124	0	0	0	0	0	0	0	0	0	0	0	0	0	0	0	0	0	0	0	0	0	0
Total	126	79	297	157	405	196	412	167	346	114	227	65	128	20	48	6	10	1	17	2	2016	807

The information on this grid should be used as a general guide only. The University of Dayton School of Law Admissions Committee reviews all aspects of the application, including the undergraduate record, letters of recommendation, personal statement and optional diversity statement, work and extracurricular activities, and the breadth and depth of an applicant's personal background and experiences. All of these factors are fully considered before a final decision is made.

University of Denver Sturm College of Law

2255 E. Evans Avenue
Denver, CO 80208
Phone: 303.871.6135; Fax: 303.871.6992
E-mail: admissions@law.du.edu; Website: www.law.du.edu

ABA
Approved
Since
1923

The Basics

Type of school	Private
Term	Semester
Application deadline	
Application fee	$60
Financial aid deadline	
Can first year start other than fall?	No
Student to faculty ratio	16.3 to 1
Does the university offer:	
housing restricted to law students?	No
graduate housing for which law students are eligible?	Yes

Faculty and Administrators

	Total		Men		Women		Minorities	
	Fall	Spr	Fall	Spr	Fall	Spr	Fall	Spr
Full-time	53	51	29	26	24	25	10	8
Other Full-time	5	5	4	3	1	2	1	3
Deans, librarians, & others who teach	10	9	4	4	6	5	3	3
Part-time	49	55	42	45	7	10	4	4
Total	117	120	79	78	38	42	18	18

Curriculum

	Full-time	Part-time
Typical first-year section size	90	91
Is there typically a "small section" of the first-year class, other than Legal Writing, taught by full-time faculty	Yes	No
If yes, typical size offered last year	45	

# of classroom course titles beyond first-year curriculum		137
# of upper division courses, excluding seminars with an enrollment:	Under 25	175
	25–49	48
	50–74	20
	75–99	18
	100+	0
# of seminars		20
# of seminar positions available		296
# of seminar positions filled	180	33
# of positions available in simulation courses		506
# of simulation positions filled	258	140
# of positions available in faculty supervised clinical courses		184
# of faculty supervised clinical positions filled	184	0
# involved in field placements	210	70
# involved in law journals	247	0
# involved in interschool competitions	30	0
# of credit hours required to graduate		90

JD Enrollment and Ethnicity

	Men		Women		Full-time		Part-time		1st-year		Total		JD Degs. Awd.
	#	%	#	%	#	%	#	%	#	%	#	%	
African Amer.	25	4.2	29	5.4	31	3.7	23	7.6	15	4.5	54	4.8	15
Amer. Indian	23	3.9	16	3.0	30	3.6	9	3.0	12	3.6	39	3.5	20
Asian Amer.	27	4.5	29	5.4	44	5.3	12	4.0	19	5.7	56	5.0	20
Mex. Amer.	0	0.0	0	0.0	0	0.0	0	0.0	0	0.0	0	0.0	0
Puerto Rican	0	0.0	0	0.0	0	0.0	0	0.0	0	0.0	0	0.0	0
Hispanic	29	4.9	34	6.4	43	5.2	20	6.6	18	5.4	63	5.6	14
Total Minority	104	17.4	108	20.3	148	17.9	64	21.2	64	19.0	212	18.8	69
For. Nation.	0	0.0	0	0.0	0	0.0	0	0.0	0	0.0	0	0.0	0
Caucasian	341	57.2	299	56.1	631	76.3	9	3.0	191	56.8	640	56.7	291
Unknown	151	25.3	126	23.6	48	5.8	229	75.8	81	24.1	277	24.5	7
Total	596	52.8	533	47.2	827	73.3	302	26.7	336	29.8	1129		367

Transfers

Transfers in	21
Transfers out	12

Tuition and Fees

	Resident	Nonresident
Full-time	$30,554	$30,554
Part-time	$20,394	$20,394

Living Expenses

Estimated living expenses for singles

Living on campus	Living off campus	Living at home
$13,898	$13,898	$13,898

ABA
Approved
Since
1923

University o

University of Denver St

2255 E. Evans Avenue
Denver, CO 80208
Phone: 303.871.6135; Fax:
E-mail: admissions@law

■ **Introduction**

The Sturm
facility i
the fir
Co

GPA and LSAT Scores

	Total	Full-time	Part-time
# of apps	3,596	3,205	391
# of offers	968	824	144
# of matrics	336	259	77
75% GPA	3.62	3.63	3.61
Median GPA	3.37	3.40	3.25
25% GPA	3.07	3.11	2.89
75% LSAT	160	160	159
Median LSAT	157	158	154
25% LSAT	154	155	149

JD Attrition (fro

	A
1st year	
2nd year	
3rd year	
4th year	

Grants and Scholarships (from prior year)

	Total		Full-time		Part-time	
	#	%	#	%	#	%
Total # of students	1,242		814		428	
Total # receiving grants	376	30.3	333	40.9	43	10.0
Less than 1/2 tuition	285	22.9	254	31.2	31	7.2
Half to full tuition	75	6.0	65	8.0	10	2.3
Full tuition	16	1.3	14	1.7	2	0.5
More than full tuition	0	0.0	0	0.0	0	0.0
Median grant amount			$10,000		$6,000	

Informational and Library Resources

# of volumes and volume equivalents	380,167
# of titles	177,894
# of active serial subscriptions	6,217
Study seating capacity inside the library	333
# of full-time professional librarians	14
Hours per week library is open	84
# of open, wired connections available to students	1,535
# of networked computers available for use by students	77
# of simultaneous wireless users	650
Require computer?	Yes

Employment (9 months after graduation)

	Total	Percentage
Employment status known	362	99.2
Employment status unknown	3	0.8
Employed	329	90.9
Pursuing graduate degrees	16	4.4
Unemployed seeking employment	2	0.6
Unemployed not seeking employment	15	4.1
Unemployed and studying for the bar	0	0.0
Type of Employment		
# employed in law firms	149	45.3
# employed in business and industry	50	15.2
# employed in government	57	17.3
# employed in public interest	15	4.6
# employed as judicial clerks	27	8.2
# employed in academia	7	2.1
Geographic Location		
# employed in state	239	72.6
# employed in foreign countries	6	1.8
# of states where employed		31

Bar Passage Rates

Jurisdiction	Colorado		
Exam	Sum 05	Win 06	Total
# from school taking bar for the first time	229	65	294
School's pass rate for all first-time takers	72%	65%	70%
State's pass rate for all first-time takers	78%	70%	76%

urm College of Law

03.871.6992
.du.edu; Website: www.law.du.edu

College of Law relocated to a new, state-of-the-art
August 2003. The 210,000-square-foot structure is
st in the nation to conform to the US Green Building
ncil's Leadership in Energy and Environmental Design
rtification system. Downtown Denver—where the state
legislature, courthouses, regional federal agencies, state
agencies, and law firms are found—is 15 minutes away on the
light-rail. The Rocky Mountains are 15 miles from the campus.

■ Curriculum

Lawyering Process Course—The first-year curriculum
includes an innovative Lawyering Process course, which offers
students, in small group settings, instruction in the essential
tools of lawyering. Students learn by assuming the role of
lawyers representing clients in realistic fact situations.

■ Special Programs

Drawing upon its location in one of the nation's natural resource
and energy capitals, the University of Denver Sturm College of
Law offers a rich program in environmental and natural
resources law. Extensive course offerings are supplemented with
abundant opportunities for independent research and
internships in the local energy, environment, and natural
resources community.

The International Legal Studies program is designed for
students interested in international comparative law, international
organizations, or transnational business. Students in the
program may work on the *Denver Journal of International Law
and Policy* as staff members and editors. The International Law
Society sponsors a rich schedule of outside speakers and an
annual conference with invited guests from many organizations.

The Business and Commercial Law program not only trains
students to work with business entities, but also prepares them
for the specific needs of the corporate and business attorney.
The program culminates in specialized seminars in business
and commercial law. Corporate internships, highly prized
one-semester assignments with large local corporations, are a
valuable supplement to the coursework.

Courses in the regular curriculum are supplemented by the
practical experience gained through legal work in the Student
Law Office or through internships or externships. The capstone
of the clinical program is the Student Law Office (Civil
Representation Clinic, Criminal Representation Clinic,
Mediation/Arbitration Clinic, Low-Income Taxpayer
Representation Clinic, Civil Rights and Disability Clinic, and
Child Advocacy Clinic), where students represent needy clients
at all levels of the dispute resolution process. If the case reaches
the litigation phase, the student handles all aspects of pretrial,
trial preparation, and the trial itself under faculty supervision.
Focusing on one-to-one teaching and student responsibility, the
program offers a rare opportunity to acquire lawyering skills.

The University of Denver has a number of unique programs.
Lawyering in Spanish is one of the few programs in the United
States offering substantive law and skills courses in Spanish.
The Sports and Entertainment Law program includes a
comprehensive cluster of classes designed to prepare students

to practice in those areas. The Law and Technology program
looks at the interrelationship between law and technology in
the areas of litigation, privacy, and intellectual property.

■ Admission

All applications should be submitted online and reach the
Sturm College of Law between November and February to
receive maximum consideration for admission the following
August. Students may begin law study only in August.
Applicants must take the LSAT and register for the LSDAS.
LSAT scores and records of academic performances are
individually evaluated in the admission process. Of equal
importance, however, are the applicant's work experience,
significant personal accomplishments, interests, goals, and
reasons for seeking admission to law school.

■ Student Activities

The University of Denver Sturm College of Law Moot Court
program is designed to promote the necessary development
of students' oral and written skills. DU's law students have
the opportunity to participate in six different moot court
competitions. Working with members of the faculty, the
student-run Moot Court Board operates DU's moot court
program. Based upon their performance in national trial
competition and the Association of Trial Lawyers of America
National Student Trial Advocacy Competition, the trial
advocacy team has been among the 16 law school teams invited
to participate in the National Institute for Trial Advocacy
Tournament of Champions.

Five scholarly journals are edited at the Sturm College of
Law, allowing students to participate in scholarly research in
varied fields. Academic credit is awarded for work on the
*Denver University Law Review, Denver Journal of International Law
and Policy, Sports and Entertainment Law Journal, Transportation
Law Journal*, and the *Water Law Review*.

A wide range of student organizations contribute to the
vibrant environment of the Sturm College of Law. Among
those groups are the Animal Legal Defense Fund, Asian Pacific
American Law Students' Association, the Black Law Students'
Association, the Business Law Society, the Christian Legal
Society, the Federalist Society, International Law Society,
Intellectual Property Law Society, Natural Resources and
Environmental Law Society, Jewish Law Students Association,
Latino Law Students Association, Native American Law
Students' Association, Phi Alpha Delta, Phi Delta Phi, Public
Interest Law Group, and Sports and Entertainment Law Society.

■ Expenses and Financial Aid

All admitted students are considered for scholarships. No
additional application is required, except for the Chancellor's
Scholarship. Scholarships offered to entering first-year
students may be renewed each year based on satisfactory
academic performance.

The Chancellor's Scholarship Program provides 12
full-tuition scholarships to entering first-year students who
demonstrate a commitment to a career in public interest law.
The annual scholarships are renewed for successive years

based on satisfactory academic performance and full participation in all the activities of the program.

Additional one-year scholarships may be offered to continuing students based on law school performance.

Students may also apply for federal and private student loans, up to the cost of attendance.

■ Housing

Residence halls are available on campus. Both traditional dorm-style living and unfurnished apartments are available.

■ Career Services

The law school maintains a Career Development Center staffed by six professionals who aid students and alumni in securing employment. The Career Development Center offers direct referral to part-time, full-time, summer, and career positions; arrangement of on-campus interviews each fall for second-and third-year students with law firms, governmental agencies, and corporations; and extensive career counseling.

Applicant Profile

University of Denver Sturm College of Law
This grid includes only applicants who earned 120–180 LSAT scores under standard administrations.

LSAT Score	3.75 +		3.50–3.74		3.25–3.49		3.00–3.24		2.75–2.99		2.50–2.74		2.25–2.49		2.00–2.24		Below 2.00		No GPA		Total	
	Apps	Adm	Apps	Adm	Apps	Adm	Apps	Adm	Apps	Adm	Apps	Adm	Apps	Adm	Apps	Adm	Apps	Adm	Apps	Adm	Apps	Adm
175–180	1	1	0	0	0	0	0	0	0	0	1	1	0	0	0	0	0	0	0	0	2	2
170–174	2	2	3	3	2	2	1	1	0	0	0	0	0	0	0	0	0	0	0	0	8	8
165–169	9	9	9	9	16	15	20	12	16	7	10	4	2	2	2	0	0	0	0	0	84	58
160–164	57	49	72	63	85	71	59	48	56	37	33	17	15	4	8	3	0	0	4	1	389	293
155–159	118	64	203	107	256	112	222	53	128	24	64	9	31	2	3	0	1	0	7	1	1033	372
150–154	94	20	205	31	245	25	253	37	174	20	70	4	28	2	7	0	1	0	13	4	1090	143
145–149	42	3	70	9	117	10	128	13	96	10	50	6	41	2	9	0	3	0	7	1	563	54
140–144	19	4	31	3	34	3	68	4	49	5	37	2	19	0	6	1	4	0	8	0	275	22
135–139	3	0	8	0	12	0	8	1	17	1	12	0	9	0	2	0	1	0	10	0	82	2
130–134	1	0	1	0	1	0	4	0	3	0	3	1	0	0	1	0	0	0	1	0	15	1
125–129	0	0	0	0	0	0	0	0	1	0	2	1	2	0	0	0	0	0	3	0	8	1
120–124	0	0	0	0	0	0	0	0	0	0	0	0	0	0	0	0	0	0	0	0	0	0
Total	346	152	602	225	768	238	763	169	540	104	282	45	147	12	38	4	10	0	53	7	3549	956

Apps = Number of Applicants
Adm = Number Admitted
Reflects 99% of the total applicant pool.

DePaul University College of Law

25 East Jackson Boulevard
Chicago, IL 60604-2219
Phone: 312.362.6831 or 800.428.7453; Fax: 312.362.5280
E-mail: lawinfo@depaul.edu; Website: www.law.depaul.edu

ABA Approved Since 1925

The Basics

Type of school	Private
Term	Semester
Application deadline	3/1
Application fee	$60
Financial aid deadline	3/1
Can first year start other than fall?	No
Student to faculty ratio	16.1 to 1
Does the university offer:	
housing restricted to law students?	No
graduate housing for which law students are eligible?	Yes

Faculty and Administrators

	Total Fall	Total Spr	Men Fall	Men Spr	Women Fall	Women Spr	Minorities Fall	Minorities Spr
Full-time	49	55	30	31	19	24	7	10
Other Full-time	2	2	0	0	2	2	0	0
Deans, librarians, & others who teach	4	4	4	4	0	0	0	0
Part-time	56	47	36	29	20	18	1	4
Total	111	108	70	64	41	44	8	14

Curriculum

	Full-time	Part-time
Typical first-year section size	83	82
Is there typically a "small section" of the first-year class, other than Legal Writing, taught by full-time faculty	No	No
If yes, typical size offered last year		
# of classroom course titles beyond first-year curriculum	175	
# of upper division courses, excluding seminars with an enrollment: Under 25	103	
25–49	37	
50–74	17	
75–99	22	
100+	0	
# of seminars	23	
# of seminar positions available	460	
# of seminar positions filled	314	89
# of positions available in simulation courses	526	
# of simulation positions filled	39	338
# of positions available in faculty supervised clinical courses	105	
# of faculty supervised clinical positions filled	94	0
# involved in field placements	152	0
# involved in law journals	77	3
# involved in interschool competitions	33	0
# of credit hours required to graduate	86	

JD Enrollment and Ethnicity

	Men #	Men %	Women #	Women %	Full-time #	Full-time %	Part-time #	Part-time %	1st-year #	1st-year %	Total #	Total %	JD Degs. Awd.
African Amer.	23	4.2	55	10.4	60	8.3	18	5.2	35	10.4	78	7.3	19
Amer. Indian	2	0.4	2	0.4	4	0.6	0	0.0	2	0.6	4	0.4	1
Asian Amer.	29	5.4	30	5.7	38	5.2	21	6.1	12	3.6	59	5.5	35
Mex. Amer.	3	0.6	12	2.3	13	1.8	2	0.6	15	4.5	15	1.4	0
Puerto Rican	1	0.2	3	0.6	4	0.6	0	0.0	4	1.2	4	0.4	0
Hispanic	49	9.0	36	6.8	66	9.1	19	5.5	28	8.4	85	7.9	15
Total Minority	107	19.7	138	26.1	185	25.5	60	17.4	96	28.7	245	22.9	70
For. Nation.	1	0.2	7	1.3	8	1.1	0	0.0	8	2.4	8	0.7	0
Caucasian	420	77.5	365	69.1	523	72.1	262	75.9	209	62.4	785	73.4	308
Unknown	14	2.6	18	3.4	9	1.2	23	6.7	22	6.6	32	3.0	0
Total	542	50.7	528	49.3	725	67.8	345	32.2	335	31.3	1070		378

Transfers

Transfers in	21
Transfers out	7

Tuition and Fees

	Resident	Nonresident
Full-time	$30,670	$30,670
Part-time	$19,960	$19,960

Living Expenses

Estimated living expenses for singles

Living on campus	Living off campus	Living at home
$21,184	$21,184	$21,184

ABA
Approved
Since
1925

GPA and LSAT Scores

	Total	Full-time	Part-time
# of apps	4,941	4,297	644
# of offers	1,644	1,367	277
# of matrics	335	249	86
75% GPA	3.58	3.59	3.55
Median GPA	3.34	3.34	3.34
25% GPA	3.02	3.02	3.09
75% LSAT	161	161	157
Median LSAT	159	160	156
25% LSAT	154	157	153

Grants and Scholarships (from prior year)

	Total		Full-time		Part-time	
	#	%	#	%	#	%
Total # of students	1,158		804		354	
Total # receiving grants	505	43.6	450	56.0	55	15.5
Less than 1/2 tuition	418	36.1	374	46.5	44	12.4
Half to full tuition	83	7.2	76	9.5	7	2.0
Full tuition	0	0.0	0	0.0	0	0.0
More than full tuition	4	0.3	0	0.0	4	1.1
Median grant amount			$12,000		$4,000	

Informational and Library Resources

# of volumes and volume equivalents	385,557
# of titles	77,748
# of active serial subscriptions	5,101
Study seating capacity inside the library	465
# of full-time professional librarians	8
Hours per week library is open	94
# of open, wired connections available to students	120
# of networked computers available for use by students	260
# of simultaneous wireless users	800
Require computer?	No

JD Attri

1st year
2nd yea
3rd year
4th year

Employ

DePaul University College
25 East Jackson Boulevard
Chicago, IL 60604-2219
Phone: 312.362.6831 or 800.428.74
E-mail: lawinfo@depaul.edu; W

■ Introduction

DePaul University
and enjoys the a
strong reputa
its dedicate
its genui
Loca
com
w

	Total	Percentage
Employment status known	303	97.7
Employment status unknown	7	2.3
Employed	284	93.7
Pursuing graduate degrees	2	0.7
Unemployed seeking employment	7	2.3
Unemployed not seeking employment	5	1.7
Unemployed and studying for the bar	5	1.7

Type of Employment

	Total	Percentage
# employed in law firms	157	55.3
# employed in business and industry	51	18.0
# employed in government	32	11.3
# employed in public interest	22	7.7
# employed as judicial clerks	6	2.1
# employed in academia	4	1.4

Geographic Location

	Total	Percentage
# employed in state	254	89.4
# employed in foreign countries	0	0.0
# of states where employed	17	

Bar Passage Rates

Jurisdiction	Illinois			Wisconsin		
Exam	Sum 05	Win 06	Total	Sum 05	Win 06	Total
# from school taking bar for the first time	229	47	276	3	6	9
School's pass rate for all first-time takers	84%	81%	84%	100%	83%	89%
State's pass rate for all first-time takers	86%	83%	85%	79%	74%	77%

of Law

3; Fax: 312.362.5280
ebsite: www.law.depaul.edu

is the largest private university in Illinois
dvantages of its vibrant urban setting. Its
ion for academic excellence is distinguished by
faculty, unrivaled professional skills training, and
e sense of community.
ted in the heart of Chicago's business and legal
munities, the College of Law affords extensive contact
th Chicago's legal community. It is within walking distance
of the state and federal courts, government offices, and many
law firms. DePaul law alumni include the mayor of Chicago,
numerous state and federal judges, and managing partners
of Chicago law firms. The college offers full-time, part-time,
and summer programs. DePaul is fully accredited by the ABA,
and is a member of AALS and Order of the Coif.

■ Students

Founded in 1898 by Vincentian Fathers as a school for children
of immigrants, DePaul University students represent a rich
diversity in age, ethnicity, education, and career experiences.
Because of the broad diversity of backgrounds and experiences
of its law students, there is a connectedness within the
institution that creates a genuine sense of community.
Approximately 50 percent of full-time students in the entering
class of 2006 were women, while 31 percent were minorities.
Almost 60 percent of the 2006 entering full-time class were
from out of state. The average age of full-time students is 24,
while the average age of part-time students is 25.

■ Faculty

DePaul faculty members, including many who have earned
advanced degrees, are recognized scholars who represent a
variety of professional backgrounds and interests. Consistent
with the university's Vincentian mission of service to the
community, faculty members work tirelessly in service to the
legal profession and to the community, and they have achieved
national recognition in teaching, research, scholarly activities,
and professional service. The faculty is extremely accessible,
approachable, and deeply committed to its students.

■ Library, Research Centers, and Institutes

The three-story law library offers extensive resources for study
and research. Its staff includes 8 professional librarians and
11 full-time support staff.
  The College of Law also maintains 10 research centers
and institutes:
- Health Law Institute;
- International Aviation Law Institute;
- International Human Rights Law Institute;
- Schiller, DuCanto and Fleck Family Law Center;
- Center for Intellectual Property Law and
  Information Technology;
- Center for Justice in Capital Cases;
- Center for Law and Science;

- Center for the Study of Race and Bioethics;
- Center for Public Interest Law; and
- Center for Dispute Resolution

■ Special Programs

Academic Support Program: DePaul is committed to ensuring
that all students have the tools they need to attain academic
success. Toward that end, DePaul has one of the premier
academic support programs in the nation.
  Legal Clinic: Students gain valuable hands-on experience
in six clinical concentrations: Asylum/Immigration, Civil
Rights, Criminal Appeals, Death Penalty, Family Law, and
Technology/Intellectual Property.
  Field Placement Program: Providing students with academic
credit through supervised field work, externships are offered
by federal and state judges, various municipal agencies, and
a number of not-for-profit organizations.
  Mediation Program: Students learn essential client
counseling skills by working with mediators on cases referred
by the County Domestic Relations Courts.
  Skills Competitions: As a leader in the field of professional
skills, DePaul has enjoyed considerable success in skills
competitions. DePaul student teams regularly place among
the top in both regional and national moot court competitions.
  Certificate Programs: DePaul offers 10 comprehensive
certificate programs, including Criminal Law, Family Law,
Health Law, International and Comparative Law, Public Interest
Law, Taxation, and four in Intellectual Property Law (General,
Arts and Museum, Information Technology, and Patents).
  **University College Dublin (UCD) Student Exchange
Program**: DePaul and UCD have a student exchange program
in which second-year students undertake legal studies abroad
during their spring semester.
  Asian Legal Studies Institute: Students receive academic
credit for summer courses taken at Beijing Foreign Studies
University in China. Students focus on legal principles and
planning related to international transactions in the
Asia-Pacific region. Lectures are presented by professors
from DePaul and major Chinese law schools.
  Joint-degree and Master of Laws (LLM) Programs: DePaul
offers five joint-degree and three master of laws programs:
- JD/MBA in coordination with DePaul's nationally
  recognized Kellstadt Graduate School of Business.
- JD/MS in Public Service Management promotes effective
  management of government and nonprofit organizations.
- JD/MA in International Studies offers concentrations in
  International Political Economy and Global Culture and
  complements DePaul's strong international law offerings.
- JD/MA and JD/MS in Computer Science explore the
  intersections of law, computer science, telecommunications,
  and information systems.
- DePaul's Master of Laws (LLM) programs include Health
  Law, Intellectual Property Law, and Taxation.
  Special First-year Legal Writing Sections: Students may
apply for a seat in one of three special sections of Legal
Analysis, Research, and Communication, focusing on health
law, intellectual property law, and public interest law.

■ Housing

Located in Chicago's Loop just two blocks south of the law school, the University Center of Chicago (UCC) is a new residence hall offering furnished apartments and suites. Amenities include a rooftop garden, multimedia rooms, a fitness center, food court, laundry facilities, shops on the lower level, 24-hour security, and keycard access to the building and elevators.

■ Admission

DePaul adheres to a policy of nondiscrimination and encourages applications from traditionally underrepresented minority groups. Admission decisions are based on a variety of factors, and each file is reviewed thoroughly. Undergraduate GPA and LSAT scores are significant admission criteria. For the 2006–2007 academic year, 4,297 candidates applied for admission to the full-time division, while 644 applied to the part-time division. Admitted students are automatically considered for available merit-based scholarships.

■ Career Services

Alumni, faculty, and students contribute to an active and aggressive career services network. The teaching and publishing reputations of the faculty, as well as the largest alumni bench and bar network in the Chicago area, complement three full-time DePaul law career services officers.

Applicant Profile

DePaul University College of Law
This grid includes only applicants with 120–180 LSAT scores earned under standard administrations.

LSAT Score	3.75 +		3.50–3.74		3.25–3.49		3.00–3.24		2.75–2.99		2.50–2.74		2.25–2.49		2.00–2.24		Below 2.00		No GPA		Total	
	Apps	Adm	Apps	Adm	Apps	Adm	Apps	Adm	Apps	Adm	Apps	Adm	Apps	Adm	Apps	Adm	Apps	Adm	Apps	Adm	Apps	Adm
175–180	0	0	1	1	2	2	0	0	1	1	0	0	0	0	0	0	0	0	1	1	5	5
170–174	5	5	4	4	6	6	2	2	4	3	5	4	2	0	0	0	2	0	2	2	28	24
165–169	29	29	42	42	43	43	39	39	24	21	15	11	9	6	1	1	0	0	7	6	206	194
160–164	130	128	186	182	170	161	147	139	88	75	49	43	24	17	10	1	0	0	11	2	811	752
155–159	201	125	280	130	328	113	291	64	141	26	81	6	31	1	10	1	2	0	9	0	1376	468
150–154	116	15	239	30	300	26	281	36	163	17	66	4	33	2	15	0	0	0	9	0	1222	130
145–149	53	5	120	15	181	18	158	16	109	10	81	4	30	0	13	0	5	0	14	0	764	68
120–144	18	0	40	1	81	0	99	0	81	0	79	1	50	0	16	0	6	0	18	0	488	2
Total	552	307	912	405	1111	369	1017	296	611	153	376	73	179	26	65	3	15	0	62	11	4900	1643

Apps = Number of Applicants
Adm = Number Admitted
Reflects 99% of the total applicant pool.

The information in this grid represents admission data for applicants to both the full-time and part-time programs and should be used only as a gauge of the likelihood of admission and not as a guarantee.

University of Detroit Mercy School of Law

651 East Jefferson Avenue
Detroit, MI 48226
Phone: 313.596.0264
E-mail: udmlawao@udmercy.edu; Website: www.law.udmercy.edu

ABA
Approved
Since
1933

The Basics

Type of school	Private
Term	Semester
Application deadline	4/15
Application fee	$50
Financial aid deadline	4/1
Can first year start other than fall?	No
Student to faculty ratio	18.4 to 1
Does the university offer:	
housing restricted to law students?	No
graduate housing for which law students are eligible?	No

Faculty and Administrators

	Total		Men		Women		Minorities	
	Fall	Spr	Fall	Spr	Fall	Spr	Fall	Spr
Full-time	31	27	19	16	12	11	3	2
Other Full-time	0	0	0	0	0	0	0	0
Deans, librarians, & others who teach	6	6	4	4	2	2	0	0
Part-time	27	28	18	21	9	7	2	2
Total	64	61	41	41	23	20	5	4

Curriculum

	Full-time	Part-time
Typical first-year section size	63	44
Is there typically a "small section" of the first-year class, other than Legal Writing, taught by full-time faculty	No	No
If yes, typical size offered last year		

# of classroom course titles beyond first-year curriculum		85
# of upper division courses, excluding seminars with an enrollment:	Under 25	62
	25–49	37
	50–74	12
	75–99	2
	100+	0
# of seminars		11
# of seminar positions available		176

# of seminar positions filled	100	40
# of positions available in simulation courses	308	
# of simulation positions filled	229	79
# of positions available in faculty supervised clinical courses	78	
# of faculty supervised clinical positions filled	52	10
# involved in field placements	125	8
# involved in law journals	50	6
# involved in interschool competitions	45	6
# of credit hours required to graduate	90	

JD Enrollment and Ethnicity

	Men		Women		Full-time		Part-time		1st-year		Total		JD Degs. Awd.
	#	%	#	%	#	%	#	%	#	%	#	%	
African Amer.	10	2.6	35	10.3	17	3.1	28	15.8	26	9.9	45	6.2	7
Amer. Indian	0	0.0	1	0.3	1	0.2	0	0.0	1	0.4	1	0.1	0
Asian Amer.	11	2.8	12	3.5	18	3.3	5	2.8	11	4.2	23	3.2	2
Mex. Amer.	0	0.0	0	0.0	0	0.0	0	0.0	0	0.0	0	0.0	0
Puerto Rican	0	0.0	0	0.0	0	0.0	0	0.0	0	0.0	0	0.0	0
Hispanic	5	1.3	4	1.2	6	1.1	3	1.7	4	1.5	9	1.2	3
Total Minority	26	6.7	52	15.3	42	7.6	36	20.3	42	16.0	78	10.7	12
For. Nation.	37	9.5	43	12.6	79	14.3	1	0.6	35	13.4	80	11.0	28
Caucasian	265	68.1	203	59.7	350	63.4	118	66.7	140	53.4	468	64.2	128
Unknown	61	15.7	42	12.4	81	14.7	22	12.4	45	17.2	103	14.1	11
Total	389	53.4	340	46.6	552	75.7	177	24.3	262	35.9	729		179

Transfers

Transfers in	1
Transfers out	17

Tuition and Fees

	Resident	Nonresident
Full-time	$26,960	$26,960
Part-time	$19,792	$19,792

Living Expenses

Estimated living expenses for singles

Living on campus	Living off campus	Living at home
$14,788	$18,085	$11,120

University of Detroit Mercy School of Law

ABA Approved Since 1933

GPA and LSAT Scores

	Total	Full-time	Part-time
# of apps	1,936	1,734	202
# of offers	825	726	99
# of matrics	263	203	60
75% GPA	3.43	3.43	3.39
Median GPA	3.20	3.21	3.00
25% GPA	2.93	3.01	2.63
75% LSAT	152	152	152
Median LSAT	150	150	149
25% LSAT	148	148	145

Grants and Scholarships (from prior year)

	Total #	Total %	Full-time #	Full-time %	Part-time #	Part-time %
Total # of students	708		519		189	
Total # receiving grants	89	12.6	71	13.7	18	9.5
Less than 1/2 tuition	49	6.9	39	7.5	10	5.3
Half to full tuition	40	5.6	32	6.2	8	4.2
Full tuition	0	0.0	0	0.0	0	0.0
More than full tuition	0	0.0	0	0.0	0	0.0
Median grant amount			$11,408		$10,703	

Informational and Library Resources

# of volumes and volume equivalents	364,280
# of titles	159,972
# of active serial subscriptions	2,828
Study seating capacity inside the library	418
# of full-time professional librarians	7
Hours per week library is open	92
# of open, wired connections available to students	22
# of networked computers available for use by students	57
# of simultaneous wireless users	5,000
Require computer?	No

JD Attrition (from prior year)

	Academic #	Other #	Total #	Total %
1st year	23	36	59	21.9
2nd year	1	4	5	2.6
3rd year	0	1	1	0.5
4th year	0	0	0	0.0

Employment (9 months after graduation)

	Total	Percentage
Employment status known	120	99.2
Employment status unknown	1	0.8
Employed	107	89.2
Pursuing graduate degrees	0	0.0
Unemployed seeking employment	5	4.2
Unemployed not seeking employment	2	1.7
Unemployed and studying for the bar	6	5.0

Type of Employment

# employed in law firms	73	68.2
# employed in business and industry	14	13.1
# employed in government	13	12.1
# employed in public interest	2	1.9
# employed as judicial clerks	2	1.9
# employed in academia	3	2.8

Geographic Location

# employed in state	81	75.7
# employed in foreign countries	19	17.8
# of states where employed	5	

Bar Passage Rates

Jurisdiction	Michigan		
Exam	Sum 05	Win 06	Total
# from school taking bar for the first time	77	28	105
School's pass rate for all first-time takers	73%	57%	69%
State's pass rate for all first-time takers	78%	65%	74%

University of Detroit Mercy School of Law

Admissions Office, 651 East Jefferson Avenue
Detroit, MI 48226
Phone: 313.596.0264
E-mail: udmlawao@udmercy.edu; Website: www.law.udmercy.edu

■ Introduction

Founded in 1912, the University of Detroit Mercy (UDM) School of Law is a well-established Catholic law school in downtown Detroit sponsored by the Society of Jesus (Jesuits) and the Sisters of Mercy of the Americas. Located opposite the General Motors headquarters in the Renaissance Center, the School of Law is within walking distance of federal and state courts, downtown law firms, and Detroit's municipal centers. Windsor, Ontario, Canada, is a five-minute drive by tunnel or bridge across the Detroit River. Metropolitan Detroit not only offers renowned cultural institutions like the Detroit Institute of Art, the Detroit Symphony, and the Detroit Opera House, but also provides a distinctive setting for the study of contemporary legal issues, including urban redevelopment, corporate entity formation, immigration, international trade, and many more.

The School of Law offers a comprehensive legal education through day and evening programs that incorporate a broad array of required and elective courses. The school is approved by the ABA and is a member of the AALS.

■ Law School Campus

The School of Law campus includes faculty offices, classrooms, and common areas with wireless access, administrative and student services offices, a bookstore, a cafeteria, and student organization offices, all located within the law school complex. The school's Kresge Law Library contains comfortable individual and group study, reading, and computer areas. The library houses more than 340,000 volumes and serves as a federal depository.

■ Curriculum

The School of Law offers a three-year full-time program, four-year part-time day and evening programs, and a five-year part-time evening program, all leading to the JD degree. Required courses include Core Concepts, Contracts, Property, Torts, Civil Procedure, Applied Legal Theory and Analysis, Criminal Law, Constitutional Law, Evidence, Professional Responsibility, Taxation, the Law Firm Program (two courses), an international or comparative law elective, a clinic or externship, and a senior seminar.

The school's first-year Core Concepts course not only introduces students to statutory analysis and interpretation, but requires them to solve legal problems that cut across torts, contracts, property, and civil procedure. In UDM's Law Firm Program, students in their last year of law school work on complex transactions. As in a law firm, they work with their fellow students in different capacities to resolve the various issues that make up the core transaction. Throughout the required Law Firm Program courses, students draft documents, complete due diligence, counsel clients and receive instruction, litigate, and more.

The School of Law's legal education program offers numerous clinical opportunities: the Urban Law Clinic, the Immigration Law Clinic, mediation training and the Mediation Clinic, an Appellate Advocacy Clinic through the State Appellate Defender Office, and a wide array of externships.

With faculty supervision, students in these externships and clinical programs represent clients with a variety of legal problems, including landlord-tenant conflicts, immigration issues, elder law cases, and others. The UDM Mobile Law Office has taken many of the clinics' legal services into the community since 2003.

Required courses after the first year integrate legal writing and document drafting. Faculty explore ethical and professional responsibility issues in all upper-class courses. Students complete the 90 credits required with elective courses. The school's full-time director of academic support provides individual and group counseling specific to the study of law.

■ Special Programs

- **Joint JD/MBA**—The School of Law and the College of Business Administration collaborate to offer an integrated degree program leading to the JD and MBA degrees. Students enrolled in the joint-degree program can earn both degrees in significantly less time than would be required for degrees pursued independently. Students are first admitted to and attend law school. At the end of the first year of law school, students apply to the joint-degree program.
- **JD/LLB**—The School of Law and the University of Windsor Faculty of Law offer a unique JD/LLB program designed to educate students to understand the legal doctrines and cultures of the United States and Canada. A student completes 60 credit hours of coursework at UDM and 44 credit hours of coursework at the University of Windsor. Most required courses taken at both law schools cover US and Canadian law relevant to the subject areas. The program enables the successful student to obtain an American Bar Association-approved Juris Doctor (JD) from the University of Detroit Mercy and the Bachelor of Laws (LLB) degree from the University of Windsor.
- **Intellectual Property Law Institute**—Through a consortium with other law schools, the School of Law offers a wide variety of courses in intellectual property such as Copyright Law, Patent Law, Computer Law, Entertainment Law, and others.
- **The McElroy Chair in Law and Religion**—The school's McElroy Chair in Law and Religion hosts an annual lecture and special colloquia on issues related to law and religion. Recent speakers have included John T. Noonan Jr., Martha Minow, and many others.
- **French Scholar Program**—The School of Law participates in a professional exchange program with the University of Clermont-Ferrand. French scholars visiting the law school each spring teach a comparative law course in English while UDM scholars teach at Clermont-Ferrand.
- **Special Summer Program (SSP)**—The School of Law offers this program for applicants who do not meet the minimum standards for admission, but who show potential for the study of law. This seven-week program, beginning in late May, requires students to demonstrate ability in the study of substantive law and in legal writing and research in order to gain admission as a regular student in the fall semester.

University of Detroit Mercy School of Law

Student Organizations and Activities

The School of Law's students edit and publish the *Law Review*, a quarterly publication of scholarly articles.

A student **Moot Court Board of Advocacy** administers the School of Law's Gallagher and Professional Responsibility competitions; participates in state, regional, and national competitions in first amendment law, ethics, and other areas; and helps to administer the G. Mennen Williams mandatory moot court competition for first-year students.

The **Student Bar Association (SBA)**, affiliated with the Law Student Division of the American Bar Association, plays a significant role in student affairs. As the student government of the school, the SBA authorizes other student organizations, including the Black Law Student Alliance, the Environmental Law Society, Phi Alpha Delta, St. Thomas More Society, the Women's Law Caucus, the Arab and Chaldean Law Student Society, the Sports and Entertainment Law Society, and many others. Students also regularly publish a student newsletter, *In Brief*.

Career Services

The school's Career Services Office provides students with a wide range of opportunities through which they may explore career paths in law. The office sponsors a Preparing to Practice series for upper-class students that introduces a variety of practice areas and issues. The assistant dean for career services and the national employment counselor provide career counseling services, including résumé and cover letter review. The office administers the school's annual on-campus interview programs, maintains a job information hotline and newsletter, sponsors a mock interview program for first-year students, and hosts special events to acquaint students with practitioners.

Admission

The School of Law encourages applicants to submit an application for admission by April 15. The Admission Committee considers all elements of an application, including undergraduate grade-point average, Law School Admission Test scores, writing skills, leadership and maturity as evidenced by work and service experiences, graduate work, letters of recommendation, and the personal statement. The committee reviews applications as they become complete on a continuous basis and communicates decisions as early as possible. An applicant may accept an offer of admission by submitting the required nonrefundable deposits, which are credited toward tuition. The University of Detroit Mercy and the School of Law adhere to nondiscrimination policies.

Applicant Profile

University of Detroit Mercy School of Law
This grid includes only applicants who earned 120–180 LSAT scores under standard administrations.

LSAT Score	3.75 +		3.50–3.74		3.25–3.49		3.00–3.24		2.75–2.99		2.50–2.74		2.25–2.49		2.00–2.24		Below 2.00		No GPA		Total	
	Apps	Adm	Apps	Adm	Apps	Adm	Apps	Adm	Apps	Adm	Apps	Adm	Apps	Adm	Apps	Adm	Apps	Adm	Apps	Adm	Apps	Adm
175–180	0	0	0	0	0	0	0	0	0	0	0	0	0	0	0	0	0	0	0	0	0	0
170–174	0	0	0	0	0	0	0	0	0	0	0	0	0	0	0	0	0	0	0	0	0	0
165–169	1	1	0	0	1	1	0	0	0	0	1	1	0	0	0	0	0	0	0	0	3	3
160–164	7	6	5	4	3	3	3	3	6	4	2	1	4	2	3	1	0	0	0	0	33	24
155–159	8	7	10	8	18	15	22	20	8	4	14	12	8	5	3	1	1	0	2	1	94	73
150–154	18	17	47	42	73	61	80	72	49	37	31	24	7	1	7	1	4	1	0	0	316	256
145–149	27	23	80	63	107	84	113	75	88	42	47	9	31	5	9	1	2	0	6	1	510	303
140–144	12	4	39	13	56	15	82	9	51	7	39	5	17	2	11	2	4	0	6	0	317	57
135–139	4	0	8	0	14	1	26	2	20	0	15	0	5	0	7	0	2	0	4	0	41	0
130–134	1	0	0	0	4	0	8	0	7	0	6	0	4	0	5	0	2	0	4	0	10	0
125–129	0	0	0	0	1	0	1	0	2	0	2	0	1	0	1	0	0	0	2	0	10	0
120–124	0	0	0	0	0	0	0	0	1	0	0	0	0	0	0	0	0	0	0	0	1	0
Total	78	58	189	130	277	180	335	181	232	94	157	52	77	15	46	6	15	1	25	2	1431	719

Apps = Number of Applicants
Adm = Number Admitted
Reflects 99% of the total applicant pool.

University of the District of Columbia—David A. Clarke School of Law

4200 Connecticut Avenue NW
Washington, DC 20008
Phone: 202.274.7341; Fax: 202.274.5583
E-mail: lawadmission@udc.edu; Website: www.law.udc.edu

ABA
Approved
Since
1991

The Basics

Type of school	Public
Term	Semester
Application deadline	3/15
Application fee	$35
Financial aid deadline	3/31
Can first year start other than fall?	No
Student to faculty ratio	11.1 to 1
Does the university offer:	
housing restricted to law students?	No
graduate housing for which law students are eligible?	No

Faculty and Administrators

	Total		Men		Women		Minorities	
	Fall	Spr	Fall	Spr	Fall	Spr	Fall	Spr
Full-time	18	16	10	8	8	8	8	7
Other Full-time	1	2	0	1	1	1	1	2
Deans, librarians, & others who teach	3	2	1	0	2	2	1	0
Part-time	15	13	9	8	6	5	11	7
Total	37	33	20	17	17	16	21	16

Curriculum

	Full-time	Part-time
Typical first-year section size	81	0
Is there typically a "small section" of the first-year class, other than Legal Writing, taught by full-time faculty	Yes	No
If yes, typical size offered last year	40	
# of classroom course titles beyond first-year curriculum		41
# of upper division courses, excluding seminars with an enrollment: Under 25		32
25–49		4
50–74		8
75–99		1
100+		0
# of seminars		5
# of seminar positions available		60
# of seminar positions filled	40	0
# of positions available in simulation courses		40
# of simulation positions filled	26	0
# of positions available in faculty supervised clinical courses		135
# of faculty supervised clinical positions filled	135	0
# involved in field placements	12	0
# involved in law journals	36	0
# involved in interschool competitions	2	0
# of credit hours required to graduate		90

JD Enrollment and Ethnicity

	Men #	Men %	Women #	Women %	Full-time #	Full-time %	Part-time #	Part-time %	1st-year #	1st-year %	Total #	Total %	JD Degs. Awd.
African Amer.	31	34.1	40	27.8	71	30.2	0	0.0	28	29.2	71	30.2	28
Amer. Indian	1	1.1	1	0.7	2	0.9	0	0.0	0	0.0	2	0.9	0
Asian Amer.	0	0.0	12	8.3	12	5.1	0	0.0	4	4.2	12	5.1	5
Mex. Amer.	1	1.1	4	2.8	5	2.1	0	0.0	2	2.1	5	2.1	0
Puerto Rican	0	0.0	0	0.0	0	0.0	0	0.0	0	0.0	0	0.0	2
Hispanic	3	3.3	10	6.9	13	5.5	0	0.0	5	5.2	13	5.5	4
Total Minority	36	39.6	67	46.5	103	43.8	0	0.0	39	40.6	103	43.8	39
For. Nation.	3	3.3	8	5.6	11	4.7	0	0.0	4	4.2	11	4.7	4
Caucasian	52	57.1	69	47.9	121	51.5	0	0.0	54	56.3	121	51.5	32
Unknown	0	0.0	0	0.0	0	0.0	0	0.0	0	0.0	0	0.0	0
Total	91	38.7	144	61.3	235	100.0	0	0.0	96	40.9	235		75

Transfers

Transfers in	5
Transfers out	8

Tuition and Fees

	Resident	Nonresident
Full-time	$7,880	$15,230
Part-time	$0	$0

Living Expenses

Estimated living expenses for singles

Living on campus	Living off campus	Living at home
N/A	$25,150	$14,650

University of the District of Columbia—David A. Clarke School of Law

ABA
Approved
Since
1991

GPA and LSAT Scores

	Total	Full-time	Part-time
# of apps	1,344	1,344	0
# of offers	276	276	0
# of matrics	95	95	0
75% GPA	3.30	3.30	0.00
Median GPA	3.10	3.10	0.00
25% GPA	2.80	2.80	0.00
75% LSAT	153	153	0
Median LSAT	151	151	0
25% LSAT	149	149	0

Grants and Scholarships (from prior year)

	Total		Full-time		Part-time	
	#	%	#	%	#	%
Total # of students	232		232		0	
Total # receiving grants	183	78.9	183	78.9	0	0.0
Less than 1/2 tuition	144	62.1	144	62.1	0	0.0
Half to full tuition	30	12.9	30	12.9	0	0.0
Full tuition	9	3.5	9	3.9	0	0.0
More than full tuition	0	0.0	0	0.0	0	0.0
Median grant amount			$4,000		$0	

Informational and Library Resources

# of volumes and volume equivalents	249,621
# of titles	134,239
# of active serial subscriptions	1,645
Study seating capacity inside the library	230
# of full-time professional librarians	7
Hours per week library is open	100
# of open, wired connections available to students	0
# of networked computers available for use by students	5
# of simultaneous wireless users	1,778
Require computer?	Yes

JD Attrition (from prior year)

	Academic	Other	Total	
	#	#	#	%
1st year	8	8	16	20.0
2nd year	2	0	2	2.9
3rd year	0	0	0	0.0
4th year	0	0	0	0.0

Employment (9 months after graduation)

	Total	Percentage
Employment status known	50	94.3
Employment status unknown	3	5.7
Employed	41	82.0
Pursuing graduate degrees	1	2.0
Unemployed seeking employment	1	2.0
Unemployed not seeking employment	7	14.0
Unemployed and studying for the bar	0	0.0

Type of Employment

# employed in law firms	21	51.2
# employed in business and industry	8	19.5
# employed in government	3	7.3
# employed in public interest	5	12.2
# employed as judicial clerks	2	4.9
# employed in academia	2	4.9

Geographic Location

# employed in state	16	39.0
# employed in foreign countries	0	0.0
# of states where employed	12	

Bar Passage Rates

Jurisdiction	Maryland		
Exam	Sum 05	Win 06	Total
# from school taking bar for the first time	20	2	22
School's pass rate for all first-time takers	55%	0%	50%
State's pass rate for all first-time takers	76%	66%	74%

University of the District of Columbia—David A. Clarke School of Law

4200 Connecticut Avenue NW
Washington, DC 20008
Phone: 202.274.7341; Fax: 202.274.5583
E-mail: lawadmission@udc.edu; Website: www.law.udc.edu

■ Introduction

In 1986, the District of Columbia Council authorized the establishment of the District of Columbia School of Law. The council created a dual mission for the School of Law and charged its Board of Governors with a mandate to recruit and enroll, to the degree feasible, students from ethnic, racial, or other population groups that in the past have been underrepresented among persons admitted to the bar. It also charged the board with representing the legal needs of low-income persons, particularly those who reside in the District of Columbia.

The DC School of Law, the only publicly funded law school in Washington, DC, merged with the University of the District of Columbia (UDC) in 1996 and became the University of the District of Columbia School of Law. In April 1998, the UDC School of Law was named the UDC David A. Clarke School of Law (UDC-DCSL). The law school operates a full-time day program.

■ Library and Physical Facilities

The School of Law is located on the University of the District of Columbia's Van Ness campus in the upper northwest section of Washington, DC, a neighborhood known for its harmonious blend of residences, businesses, and embassies.

The law library is a teaching-, research-, and practice-oriented library. It contains more than 250,000 volumes and volume equivalents. The law library expands its collection on an ongoing basis, with an emphasis on reference and scholarly materials. The library's online catalog is available at *http://catalog.law.udc.edu/search.*

In 2004, the law library completed a major expansion and renovation project. The new Charles N. and Hilda H. M. Mason Law Library is a beautiful and modern facility that provides the traditional and high-tech resources required for today's study of the law. Power is available at every seat. In addition, the Internet/Portal is accessible via the law library's wireless LAN throughout the law library.

The UDC campus is conveniently located on the Metro's Red Line at the UDC/Van Ness subway stop.

■ Curriculum

Consistent with UDC School of Law's mission, the basic program is designed to provide a well-rounded theoretical and practical legal education that will enable students to be effective and ethical advocates, and to represent the legal needs of low-income residents through the school's legal clinics.

First-year students participate in a two-week orientation program that introduces them to the study of law and the School of Law community. During orientation, students take the course Law and Justice, which introduces legal, political, social, and philosophical aspects of poverty and inequality in American society. They also take the course Lawyering Process I. Students participate in the Dean's Reception and in other events planned by student organizations and the Office of Admission.

In the first year, students must complete 40 hours of community service and take a prescribed program consisting of required courses and one elective course. After the first year, students must also take courses in Evidence, Constitutional

Law I and II, Professional Responsibility, and Moot Court. Each UDC-DCSL student is required to produce significant pieces of writing each of the three years of study. The School of Law offers a limited number of summer courses and clinics, including an internship program; however, it does not allow early graduation.

While the emphasis of the school is on public interest law, the overall curriculum—clinic and classroom—provides the skills necessary to pursue any field of law.

■ Clinical Program

Students must complete two 7-credit clinics during their second and third years. The clinics offered in the 2006–2007 academic year were Housing and Consumer, HIV/AIDS, Juvenile and Special Education, Legislation, Government Accountability Project, Community Development and Small Business Law Center, and Low-Income Tax. Students may do an internship or work-study in the school's Immigration Law Center.

■ Academic Support and Summer Program

UDC-DCSL considers academic support to be an integral part of its course of study. Students in academic difficulty at the end of their first semester may apply to the enhanced program, which may involve adjusting course loads, taking a legal reasoning course, counseling, and group and individual tutoring. In addition, faculty members hold extra review sessions during the semester in required courses and provide sample examination questions with model answers.

The School of Law offers the Mason Enhancement Program for Academic Success, a four-week conditional-admission summer program, to selected entering students.

■ Internship Program

Students in the second and third year may elect to do a 4 or 10 credit internship, in which they work in federal or local government agencies; judicial, legislative, or congressional offices; or in public interest legal organizations. Students are required to attend a weekly internship seminar at the school. The School of Law emphasizes the importance of supervision, educational merit, and public service in each internship.

■ Admission

Admission is based upon academic and nonacademic achievements and professional promise. UDC-DCSL looks at the applicant's LSAT and grades in tandem with other criteria that it believes may provide a more accurate measure of a candidate's determination, commitment, and potential for success in the study of law. The Admission Committee considers all submitted application materials, such as personal statement and essays, recommendations, community service, and employment experience. Applicants are encouraged to contact the Admission Office or to visit *www.law.udc.edu* for information about visiting the School of Law, sitting in on a class, and attending one of the LAW DAY-Open House programs.

■ Financial Assistance and Scholarships

The financial aid policy provides students with financial assistance to support full-time study for three years. This is usually accomplished through a combination of scholarships, grants, and loans. These include merit- and need-based scholarships, the Federal Stafford and GradPLUS loan programs, and federal and other work-study employment. About 71 percent of UDC-DCSL students receive scholarship assistance, and 96 percent receive some form of financial aid. Detailed information about financial aid application policies and procedures is available on the School of Law's website.

■ Student Activities

The first issue of the annual *District of Columbia Law Review* was published in 1992. Active student groups include the Student Bar Association, Black Law Students Association, International Law Students Association, Voces Juridicas, OUTLAW, Women's Law Society, Sports and Entertainment Student Lawyers Association, Phi Alpha Delta, Innocence Project, and the National Lawyers Guild.

■ Career Services

The Career Services Office provides employment information, individual career counseling, and résumé assistance to the School of Law's student body and graduates. The office maintains listings of permanent job openings, fellowships, summer clerkships, and part-time opportunities. The office also coordinates potential internship sites and invites employers to conduct on-campus interviews. The office provides resources for career planning, counseling sessions to assist students in developing their career goals, résumé workshops, and other relevant seminars.

Applicant Profile

The David A. Clarke School of Law prides itself on its admission philosophy, comprehensive and competitive admission process, and student diversity. While the applicant profile grids can be helpful to students, they may also discourage some students whose numerical profiles are slightly below the school's LSAT and GPA medians, but whose life experiences, for example, may be compelling. Numbers do not always provide an accurate picture of an applicant's potential for law study or motivation to succeed. The School of Law, therefore, does not provide an applicant profile grid, but rather a brief description of its student body.

The student body is a diverse and accomplished group. The age range of students is 20 to 62 years. The average age is 28 years. People of color comprise about half of the student body. Women comprise more than half of the students. More than 30 states and over 85 undergraduate schools are represented in the student body. About 100 students are admitted each year. Smaller class sizes provide students with an ideal student-faculty ratio and a rich theoretical and practical learning environment. The LSAT mean for the fall 2006 entering class was 152, and the 25th and 75th LSAT percentiles were 149 and 154, respectively. The GPA median and mean were both about 3.00. The student body represents strong competency and contribution potential for the study of law.

Drake University Law School

2507 University Avenue
Des Moines, IA 50311-4505
Phone: 800.44.DRAKE, ext. 2782 or 515.271.2782; Fax: 515.271.1990
E-mail: lawadmit@drake.edu; Website: www.law.drake.edu

ABA Approved Since 1923

The Basics

Type of school	Private
Term	Semester
Application deadline	4/1
Application fee	$50
Financial aid deadline	3/1
Can first year start other than fall?	No
Student to faculty ratio	14.7 to 1
Does the university offer:	
housing restricted to law students?	No
graduate housing for which law students are eligible?	No

Faculty and Administrators

	Total		Men		Women		Minorities	
	Fall	Spr	Fall	Spr	Fall	Spr	Fall	Spr
Full-time	24	25	15	15	9	10	2	3
Other Full-time	1	0	1	0	0	0	1	0
Deans, librarians, & others who teach	4	4	3	3	1	1	0	0
Part-time	17	15	12	10	5	5	1	3
Total	**46**	**44**	**31**	**28**	**15**	**16**	**4**	**6**

Curriculum

	Full-time	Part-time
Typical first-year section size	72	0
Is there typically a "small section" of the first-year class, other than Legal Writing, taught by full-time faculty	No	No
If yes, typical size offered last year		
# of classroom course titles beyond first-year curriculum	170	

# of upper division courses, excluding seminars with an enrollment:		
Under 25	104	
25–49	23	
50–74	7	
75–99	9	
100+	0	

	Full-time	Part-time
# of seminars	16	
# of seminar positions available	291	
# of seminar positions filled	144	0
# of positions available in simulation courses	644	
# of simulation positions filled	429	0
# of positions available in faculty supervised clinical courses	196	
# of faculty supervised clinical positions filled	196	0
# involved in field placements	103	0
# involved in law journals	82	0
# involved in interschool competitions	49	0
# of credit hours required to graduate	90	

JD Enrollment and Ethnicity

	Men		Women		Full-time		Part-time		1st-year		Total		JD Degs. Awd.
	#	%	#	%	#	%	#	%	#	%	#	%	
African Amer.	10	4.3	11	5.3	21	4.9	0	0.0	9	6.0	21	4.8	5
Amer. Indian	1	0.4	2	1.0	3	0.7	0	0.0	1	0.7	3	0.7	0
Asian Amer.	1	0.4	7	3.4	7	1.6	1	10.0	2	1.3	8	1.8	8
Mex. Amer.	2	0.9	1	0.5	3	0.7	0	0.0	0	0.0	3	0.7	1
Puerto Rican	0	0.0	0	0.0	0	0.0	0	0.0	0	0.0	0	0.0	0
Hispanic	7	3.0	2	1.0	9	2.1	0	0.0	6	4.0	9	2.1	2
Total Minority	21	9.1	23	11.1	43	10.0	1	10.0	18	11.9	44	10.0	16
For. Nation.	1	0.4	6	2.9	7	1.6	0	0.0	6	4.0	7	1.6	2
Caucasian	193	83.5	171	82.2	355	82.8	9	90.0	111	73.5	364	82.9	140
Unknown	16	6.9	8	3.8	24	5.6	0	0.0	16	10.6	24	5.5	1
Total	231	52.6	208	47.4	429	97.7	10	2.3	151	34.4	439		159

Transfers

Transfers in	3
Transfers out	5

Tuition and Fees

	Resident	Nonresident
Full-time	$26,206	$26,206
Part-time	$0	$0

Living Expenses

Estimated living expenses for singles

Living on campus	Living off campus	Living at home
N/A	$12,150	$5,450

Drake University Law School

*ABA
Approved
Since
1923*

GPA and LSAT Scores

	Total	Full-time	Part-time
# of apps	1,138	1,103	35
# of offers	505	503	2
# of matrics	141	140	1
75% GPA	3.64	3.64	0.00
Median GPA	3.41	3.41	0.00
25% GPA	3.15	3.15	0.00
75% LSAT	157	157	0
Median LSAT	155	155	0
25% LSAT	154	154	0

Grants and Scholarships (from prior year)

	Total #	Total %	Full-time #	Full-time %	Part-time #	Part-time %
Total # of students	471		462		9	
Total # receiving grants	278	59.0	278	60.2	0	0.0
Less than 1/2 tuition	176	37.4	176	38.1	0	0.0
Half to full tuition	67	14.2	67	14.5	0	0.0
Full tuition	18	3.8	18	3.9	0	0.0
More than full tuition	17	3.6	17	3.7	0	0.0
Median grant amount			$9,000		$0	

Informational and Library Resources

# of volumes and volume equivalents	325,018
# of titles	67,870
# of active serial subscriptions	3,255
Study seating capacity inside the library	705
# of full-time professional librarians	6
Hours per week library is open	109
# of open, wired connections available to students	160
# of networked computers available for use by students	143
# of simultaneous wireless users	760
Require computer?	No

JD Attrition (from prior year)

	Academic #	Other #	Total #	Total %
1st year	6	7	13	8.3
2nd year	1	3	4	2.5
3rd year	0	0	0	0.0
4th year	0	0	0	0.0

Employment (9 months after graduation)

	Total	Percentage
Employment status known	132	100.0
Employment status unknown	0	0.0
Employed	119	90.2
Pursuing graduate degrees	3	2.3
Unemployed seeking employment	2	1.5
Unemployed not seeking employment	8	6.1
Unemployed and studying for the bar	0	0.0

Type of Employment

# employed in law firms	66	55.5
# employed in business and industry	21	17.6
# employed in government	14	11.8
# employed in public interest	5	4.2
# employed as judicial clerks	10	8.4
# employed in academia	3	2.5

Geographic Location

# employed in state	80	67.2
# employed in foreign countries	0	0.0
# of states where employed	24	

Bar Passage Rates

Jurisdiction	Iowa		
Exam	Sum 05	Win 06	Total
# from school taking bar for the first time	66	30	96
School's pass rate for all first-time takers	77%	83%	79%
State's pass rate for all first-time takers	86%	81%	85%

Drake University Law School

2507 University Avenue
Des Moines, IA 50311-4505
Phone: 800.44.DRAKE, ext. 2782 or 515.271.2782; Fax: 515.271.1990
E-mail: lawadmit@drake.edu; Website: www.law.drake.edu

■ Introduction

Drake University Law School can trace its history back to 1865, making it one of the nation's 25 oldest law schools. Accredited by the ABA, the Law School provides a personal education with a low student-to-faculty ratio. Our commitment to an education that balances theory and practice has earned the Law School a reputation for training proven practitioners.

Drake Law School is located in Iowa's capital, Des Moines, providing law students the opportunity to get hands-on experience with the executive, judicial, and legislative branches of state government, the federal courts, federal and state administrative agencies, and a wide array of law firms and businesses.

■ Legal Clinic

Drake had one of the first clinics in the country and has built on that tradition. The Neal and Bea Smith Law Center, built in 1987, houses the Drake Law School Legal Clinic. The center is a state-of-the-art law office that enables Drake students to represent real clients out of their own fully computerized offices. The center was selected as the national training and resource institute for public service attorneys. The $1.75 million addition, built in 1994, includes a technologically enhanced courtroom and training facilities. In fall 2001, the clinic added the Joan and Lyle Middleton Center for Children's Rights to its operations.

■ First-year Trial Practicum

The only program of its kind in the country, the trial practicum adds an important experiential learning dimension to the first-year curriculum. During the spring semester, first-year students observe a real trial—from jury selection to verdict—in the courtroom of the Neal and Bea Smith Law Center. Break-out discussion groups and posttrial debriefings of the attorneys, judges, and jurors poignantly illustrate how law on the books becomes law in action.

■ Centers of Excellence and Certificate Programs

Constitutional Law Center—Drake is one of only four schools selected to receive a congressional endowment for the establishment of a Constitutional Law Resource Center. The center sponsors a lecture series and annual symposia featuring nationally recognized constitutional scholars. The nationally renowned Dwight D. Opperman Lecture in Constitutional Law has been delivered by nine current and former justices of the US Supreme Court. On three occasions justices have returned for a week-long residency to teach a course to Drake law students.

In 2005 the center began offering a **Constitutional Law and Civil Rights Certificate** program. The center also conducts the Summer Institute in Constitutional Law, a program designed for first-year students interested in getting their law school careers off to an early start. During the six-week session, students enroll in three courses that examine different aspects of constitutional law combined with a writing component to help establish the critical thinking, research, writing, and study skills needed for law school success. Students beginning in the Summer Institute and taking additional summer courses may

elect to accelerate their studies and graduate in December of their third year.

Agricultural Law Center—Our internationally recognized agricultural law program addresses the important issues in American and international law and policy regarding food production. Students conduct research, publish an agricultural law journal, and write articles on a wide range of topics. Lecturers from France, the United Kingdom, Canada, Italy, and China have visited the center in recent years to share their knowledge and expertise on topics such as farmland preservation, legal issues in biotechnology, and tax planning for agricultural businesses. The center also offers a series of one-week courses for students and attorneys in the Summer Agricultural Law Institute. The center offers a **Food and Agricultural Law Certificate** program, the first of its kind at an American law school.

Center for Legislative Practice—Drake is one of a few schools in the country that offers a **Legislative Practice Certificate.** Classroom study and a wide range of internships expose students to the underpinnings of legislative and rule-making processes. Students who complete the program are uniquely prepared to work for administrative or government agencies, to research and draft legislation, to represent businesses and organizations with government interests, or to work in a variety of other public policy-making positions. Drake's close proximity to the state capital and other state and federal offices, trade associations, union headquarters, and public interest group agencies provides students with numerous opportunities to learn firsthand how these institutions operate.

Litigation and Dispute Resolution Certification—Drake Law School has achieved a well-deserved reputation for its education and training of future litigators, mediators, negotiators, and judges. Our alumni are well represented among the nation's leading trial and appellate lawyers and on both the federal and state courts. The **Litigation and Dispute Resolution Certificate** program capitalizes on the school's traditional strengths in advocacy and dispute resolution.

■ Summer in France

You can add an international element to your legal education by participating in our summer program at the University of Nantes Law School in France. Classes in comparative and international law and on-site visits to European legal institutions allow you to absorb and experience another country's legal system and be better prepared to practice law in a global society.

■ Joint-degree Programs

If you are interested in combining your legal studies with other academic disciplines, you can do so in one of several joint-degree programs that will broaden your skills and increase your career options. Students may combine their Juris Doctor degrees with the following: Master of Business Administration, Master of Public Administration, Doctor of Pharmacy, Master of Arts in Political Science (in cooperation with Iowa State University), Master of Science in Agricultural Economics (in cooperation with Iowa State University), and Master of Social Work (in cooperation with the University of Iowa).

Student Activities

Law students participate in many student organizations and cocurricular activities. The *Drake Law Review*, a student-edited journal, is published quarterly. *Drake Law Review* was recently named among the nation's most-cited legal periodicals by the courts from 1997 to 2004. Drake moot court teams consistently win regional competitions and finish strongly in national competitions. Drake's National Moot Court team won the 2001 national championship. The Student Bar Association, Legal Research Service, and honorary societies provide students with leadership, public service, and learning opportunities. Drake students have also formed a variety of organizations around their special interests, including the Drake Law Women, Black Law Students Association, Asian Pacific Law Student Association, Hispanic Law Student Association, International Law Society, Christian Legal Society, Environmental Law Society, Federalist Society, American Constitution Society, National Lawyers Guild, Intellectual Property Law Society, Agricultural Law Society, Alternative Dispute Resolution Society, and an organization for students with alternative sexual orientation.

Networking

Drake Law School alumni practice in all 50 states and several foreign countries. The Career Development Office has a comprehensive, national alumni network set up to assist students with their career plans no matter where they want to go. Attorneys who participate in the alumni career network help students learn about the job market in their state and help ensure a smooth transition for students from law school to practice. Many area alumni also participate in our Partner's Program, which pairs first-year law students with practicing attorneys.

Career Services

The Career Development Office offers career planning and counseling services, assistance with résumés and cover letter preparation, salary and geographical employment statistics, nationwide job postings, and state bar examination information. The office also arranges interviews—both on and off campus—and exchanges job listings with 90 other law schools around the country.

Applicant Profile

Drake University Law School
This grid includes only applicants who earned 120–180 LSAT scores under standard administrations.

LSAT Score	3.75 +		3.50–3.74		3.25–3.49		3.00–3.24		2.75–2.99		2.50–2.74		2.25–2.49		2.00–2.24		Below 2.00		No GPA		Total	
	Apps	Adm	Apps	Adm	Apps	Adm	Apps	Adm	Apps	Adm	Apps	Adm	Apps	Adm	Apps	Adm	Apps	Adm	Apps	Adm	Apps	Adm
175–180	0	0	0	0	0	0	0	0	0	0	1	1	0	0	0	0	0	0	0	0	1	1
170–174	2	2	0	0	0	0	0	0	0	0	0	0	0	0	0	0	0	0	0	0	2	2
165–169	8	8	5	5	1	0	5	5	3	3	0	0	0	0	0	0	0	0	0	0	22	21
160–164	24	23	16	15	7	7	6	6	6	6	4	4	1	1	2	1	0	0	0	0	66	63
155–159	35	34	45	45	44	42	48	46	20	17	9	7	7	7	4	1	0	0	1	1	213	200
150–154	50	39	77	46	91	52	82	32	35	6	22	6	12	0	5	0	1	0	2	0	377	181
145–149	23	2	40	4	67	10	52	10	28	1	24	3	14	1	4	0	0	0	1	0	253	31
140–144	7	0	13	2	20	1	26	2	24	0	14	2	6	0	1	0	2	0	2	0	115	7
135–139	3	0	2	0	7	0	9	0	8	0	3	0	3	0	1	0	1	0	2	0	39	0
130–134	1	0	0	0	2	0	4	0	1	0	3	0	1	0	1	0	0	0	0	0	13	0
125–129	0	0	0	0	0	0	0	0	0	0	2	0	0	0	2	0	0	0	0	0	4	0
120–124	0	0	0	0	0	0	0	0	0	0	0	0	0	0	0	0	0	0	0	0	0	0
Total	153	108	198	117	239	112	232	101	125	33	82	23	44	9	20	2	4	0	8	1	1105	506

Apps = Number of Applicants
Adm = Number Admitted
Reflects 99% of the total applicant pool.

Duke University School of Law

Science Drive & Towerview Road, Box 90393
Durham, NC 27708-0393
Phone: 919.613.7020; Fax: 919.613.7257
E-mail: admissions@law.duke.edu; Website: admissions.law.duke.edu

ABA Approved Since 1931

The Basics

Type of school	Private
Term	Semester
Application deadline	2/15
Application fee	$70
Financial aid deadline	3/15
Can first year start other than fall?	Yes
Student to faculty ratio	12.0 to 1
Does the university offer:	
housing restricted to law students?	No
graduate housing for which law students are eligible?	No

Faculty and Administrators

	Total		Men		Women		Minorities	
	Fall	Spr	Fall	Spr	Fall	Spr	Fall	Spr
Full-time	42	45	31	35	11	10	4	3
Other Full-time	8	8	5	5	3	3	1	1
Deans, librarians, & others who teach	11	11	4	4	7	7	2	2
Part-time	32	45	21	31	11	14	3	3
Total	**93**	**109**	**61**	**75**	**32**	**34**	**10**	**9**

Curriculum

		Full-time	Part-time
Typical first-year section size		68	0
Is there typically a "small section" of the first-year class, other than Legal Writing, taught by full-time faculty		Yes	No
If yes, typical size offered last year		32	
# of classroom course titles beyond first-year curriculum		148	
# of upper division courses, excluding seminars with an enrollment:	Under 25	45	
	25–49	34	
	50–74	17	
	75–99	4	
	100+	5	
# of seminars		52	
# of seminar positions available		787	
# of seminar positions filled		645	0
# of positions available in simulation courses		316	
# of simulation positions filled		290	0
# of positions available in faculty supervised clinical courses		103	
# of faculty supervised clinical positions filled		92	0
# involved in field placements		42	0
# involved in law journals		273	0
# involved in interschool competitions		93	0
# of credit hours required to graduate		84	

JD Enrollment and Ethnicity

	Men		Women		Full-time		Part-time		1st-year		Total		JD Degs. Awd.
	#	%	#	%	#	%	#	%	#	%	#	%	
African Amer.	26	7.3	38	13.9	60	10.4	4	7.7	20	9.8	64	10.2	22
Amer. Indian	1	0.3	1	0.4	2	0.3	0	0.0	0	0.0	2	0.3	1
Asian Amer.	30	8.4	30	11.0	59	10.2	1	1.9	14	6.8	60	9.5	18
Mex. Amer.	1	0.3	1	0.4	2	0.3	0	0.0	2	1.0	2	0.3	0
Puerto Rican	0	0.0	1	0.4	0	0.0	1	1.9	1	0.5	1	0.2	0
Hispanic	12	3.4	8	2.9	16	2.8	4	7.7	8	3.9	20	3.2	9
Total Minority	70	19.6	79	28.9	139	24.0	10	19.2	45	22.0	149	23.7	50
For. Nation.	4	1.1	2	0.7	4	0.7	2	3.8	6	2.9	6	1.0	0
Caucasian	220	61.6	166	60.8	357	61.8	29	55.8	128	62.4	386	61.3	144
Unknown	63	17.6	26	9.5	78	13.5	11	21.2	26	12.7	89	14.1	26
Total	357	56.7	273	43.3	578	91.7	52	8.3	205	32.5	630		220

Transfers

Transfers in	10
Transfers out	5

Tuition and Fees

	Resident	Nonresident
Full-time	$38,739	$38,739
Part-time	$0	$0

Living Expenses

Estimated living expenses for singles

Living on campus	Living off campus	Living at home
$16,019	$16,019	N/A

Duke University School of Law

ABA
Approved
Since
1931

GPA and LSAT Scores

	Total	Full-time	Part-time
# of apps	4,340	4,340	0
# of offers	1,011	1,011	0
# of matrics	205	205	0
75% GPA	3.85	3.85	0.00
Median GPA	3.78	3.78	0.00
25% GPA	3.66	3.66	0.00
75% LSAT	169	169	0
Median LSAT	168	168	0
25% LSAT	165	165	0

Grants and Scholarships (from prior year)

	Total		Full-time		Part-time	
	#	%	#	%	#	%
Total # of students	648		617		31	
Total # receiving grants	461	71.1	461	74.7	0	0.0
Less than 1/2 tuition	400	61.7	400	64.8	0	0.0
Half to full tuition	47	7.3	47	7.6	0	0.0
Full tuition	14	2.2	14	2.3	0	0.0
More than full tuition	0	0.0	0	0.0	0	0.0
Median grant amount			$8,000		$0	

Informational and Library Resources

# of volumes and volume equivalents	634,267
# of titles	219,065
# of active serial subscriptions	7,185
Study seating capacity inside the library	503
# of full-time professional librarians	9
Hours per week library is open	104
# of open, wired connections available to students	847
# of networked computers available for use by students	120
# of simultaneous wireless users	500
Require computer?	No

JD Attrition (from prior year)

	Academic	Other	Total	
	#	#	#	%
1st year	0	7	7	3.5
2nd year	0	6	6	2.6
3rd year	0	0	0	0.0
4th year	0	0	0	0.0

Employment (9 months after graduation)

	Total	Percentage
Employment status known	216	100.0
Employment status unknown	0	0.0
Employed	212	98.1
Pursuing graduate degrees	3	1.4
Unemployed seeking employment	0	0.0
Unemployed not seeking employment	1	0.5
Unemployed and studying for the bar	0	0.0

Type of Employment

# employed in law firms	141	66.5
# employed in business and industry	12	5.7
# employed in government	13	6.1
# employed in public interest	3	1.4
# employed as judicial clerks	38	17.9
# employed in academia	4	1.9

Geographic Location

# employed in state	23	10.8
# employed in foreign countries	4	1.9
# of states where employed		34

Bar Passage Rates

Jurisdiction	New York			North Carolina		
Exam	Sum 05	Win 06	Total	Sum 05	Win 06	Total
# from school taking bar for the first time	64	3	67	23	0	23
School's pass rate for all first-time takers	94%	100%	94%	96%		96%
State's pass rate for all first-time takers	76%	61%	74%	72%	69%	71%

Duke University School of Law

Science Drive & Towerview Road, Box 90393
Durham, NC 27708-0393
Phone: 919.613.7020; Fax: 919.613.7257
E-mail: admissions@law.duke.edu; Website: admissions.law.duke.edu

■ Introduction

Located in North Carolina's technology-focused Research Triangle area, Duke law school has established itself as one of the leading law schools in the nation. Students come to Duke Law from every state and, as alumni, are dispersed throughout the country and around the world.

One of the reasons students choose Duke Law is for its collaborative environment, where growth is encouraged not only through rigorous scholarship, but also through cooperation and support. Within this close academic community, students discover a rare level of interaction with faculty and fellow students.

Duke law school's faculty members have long-established reputations for being not only insightful and engaging in their teaching, but also accessible and responsive to students. The open-door policy practiced by faculty encourages students to ask questions, continue discussions, and seek advice on specialized interests. Faculty-student interaction extends beyond the classroom to committee work, pro bono opportunities, career counseling, and mentoring. Ultimately, students experience a nurturing environment where the focus is on training and developing the whole person in a diverse atmosphere that values different perspectives, backgrounds, and orientations.

■ Enrollment/Student Body

Duke Law admits a select group of students with diverse backgrounds who have in common a record of academic excellence. In 2006, JD students came to Duke from 38 states and 4 foreign countries. These students represented 105 different undergraduate institutions and had a wealth of different experiences. Approximately 40 percent of the students entering Duke Law in 2006 came directly from college, while the other 60 percent entered law school after gaining experience for a year or more in another profession or graduate school.

■ Faculty

Central to Duke Law's success is its faculty. Well-respected in the legal field, Duke Law professors are known for groundbreaking legal scholarship and the practice of law in both the public and private sectors in the United States and abroad. Their backgrounds are as varied as they are distinguished; they are former Fulbright Scholars, Rhodes Scholars, and Marshall Scholars. A number of faculty members have served as Supreme Court clerks, and one was the chief judge for the US Court of Military Appeals. Faculty members hold joint appointments in departments throughout the university and have obtained PhDs in a wide variety of disciplines. Several visiting professors from abroad teach at Duke Law each year, and many full-time faculty members have extensive international connections.

■ Joint Degrees

The Duke Law faculty believe that society is best served by lawyers with diverse education and training. The law school jointly sponsors numerous academic and professional programs, including 27 joint-degree programs, in conjunction with other schools or departments at Duke University. In

addition, students may pursue a three-year JD/DESS (Diplôme d'études supérieures spécialisées) in global business law in partnership with University of Paris I and Sciences Po in Paris.

The law school and the graduate school jointly sponsor programs of study in law and several other disciplines, including (at the master's level) Biomedical Engineering, Classical Studies, Cultural Anthropology, East Asian Studies, Economics, Electrical and Computer Engineering, English, Environmental Management, Environmental Science and Policy, History, Humanities, Literature, Mechanical Engineering, Philosophy, Political Science, Psychology, Public Policy Studies, Religion, Romance Studies, and Sociology. The only additional time necessary to obtain both degrees is the summer prior to the first year of school. At the doctoral level, joint programs in Philosophy and Political Science are available.

The law school offers joint professional degrees with the Fuqua School of Business, the Divinity School, the Nicholas School of the Environment, the Medical School, and the Sanford Institute of Public Policy. A special option is available to complete the JD/MBA in seven semesters rather than the usual eight. Specific information about applying to the joint professional degree programs and time requirements for these programs is available on the Duke Law website.

Duke Law students may also earn graduate certificates in Slavic, Eurasian, and East European Legal Studies; Health Care Policy; Health System Management; or Women's Studies.

■ Special Programs

- **JD/LLM in International and Comparative Law**—Duke Law has pioneered a unique joint-degree program that makes it possible for students to earn a JD and a Master of Laws in International and Comparative Law concurrently in three years. The only additional time needed to complete both degrees is the summer prior to the first year of law school and the first half of the following summer, during which students attend one of Duke's Institutes of Transnational Law, either in Switzerland or Asia.
- **International Study Abroad and Externships**—Duke law school has arrangements with 19 top foreign universities, which give all interested Duke students an opportunity to study abroad. Programs are arranged on an individual basis and are supervised by Duke and the host institution. Duke Law also offers international externship opportunities in legal internships for one semester's credit at public sector institutions that engage in international work. Duke has preapproved externships with certain agencies, but students are also encouraged to submit their own proposals if they are interested in working with other groups.
- **Legal Clinics**—Duke law school has experienced an explosion of in-house clinics, offering a variety of opportunities that is unmatched. A newly constructed clinic wing brings a number of the programs together, allowing them to function as a public interest law firm. Clinical opportunities include: AIDS Legal Project, Animal Law Clinic, Children's Education Law Clinic, Community Enterprise Clinic, Death Penalty Clinic, Environmental Law and Policy Clinic, Guantanamo Defense Clinic, Low-Income Taxpayer Clinic.
- **Centers**—Interdisciplinary collaboration at Duke is fostered by a number of centers and programs, including the Arts

Project; Center for Genome Ethics, Law, and Policy; Center for the Study of the Public Domain; Center on Law, Ethics, and National Security; Global Capital Markets Center; Nicholas Institute for Environmental Policy Solutions; and Program in Public Law.

■ Admission and Financial Aid

Admission to Duke law school is highly competitive. In addition to the academic criteria, other factors may help to distinguish some applicants. These include capacity for leadership, dedication to community service, excellence in a particular field, motivation, graduate study, work experience, extracurricular activities, and character.

Duke Law tries to achieve broad diversity in terms of general background, geography, and undergraduate institutions represented. Students are chosen not only for their potential for academic success but also because of qualities that will enhance the overall character of the class.

Admitted applicants are eligible for consideration for merit- and need-based scholarship awards. A select group of outstanding entering students are chosen each year as Mordecai Scholars and receive a full-tuition scholarship. Mordecai Scholars possess a record of extraordinary leadership and scholarly achievement prior to law school, and the personal qualities that are likely to result in community involvement and leadership.

■ Cocurricular Activities

Scholarship in the classroom is reinforced through a variety of opportunities for hands-on leadership training and professional experience. These begin soon after students arrive and continue throughout their tenure at Duke Law. Through pro bono work, legal clinics, public interest projects, moot

court, and opportunities for scholarly writing and editing on eight different legal journals, Duke prepares students for the real-world practice of law.

■ Professional Development

The award-winning Duke Blueprint provides structure to students' legal education and professional development by challenging them to engage intellectually, embody integrity, build relationships, serve the community, and become effective leaders. Integrated into every aspect of the community, the Blueprint underlines the expectation that students' experience at Duke will be transformative of the whole person, not merely a means to obtain a formal credential.

Duke Law graduates find employment in all sectors of the legal profession. Many begin their careers in law firms. Top law firms from across the country interview on campus each year, and the number of interviews available and offers made far exceeds the number of students interviewing. Others pursue judicial clerkships—20 percent of the graduating class of 2006—or work for government agencies or business enterprises. Historically, 100 percent of each class finds employment, and average salaries are among the highest in the country. In addition, graduates spread themselves broadly across the country. Top markets typically include New York, Washington, DC, California, North Carolina, and Texas.

Duke places special emphasis on support for students interested in a career in public service. Staff from both the Career Center and the Office of Pro Bono and Public Interest help students find opportunities both during and after law school. The law school provides financial support for these goals with grants to subsidize summer employment and a Loan Repayment Assistance Program for graduates who enter a life of public service.

Applicant Profile

Duke University School of Law
This grid includes only applicants who earned 120–180 LSAT scores under standard administrations.

LSAT Score	3.75 +		3.50–3.74		3.25–3.49		3.00–3.24		2.75–2.99		2.50–2.74		Below 2.50		No GPA		Total	
	Apps	Adm	Apps	Adm	Apps	Adm	Apps	Adm	Apps	Adm	Apps	Adm	Apps	Adm	Apps	Adm	Apps	Adm
170–180	275	262	225	156	102	14	41	1	24	0	3	0	4	1	1	0	675	434
165–169	560	280	491	134	211	23	74	4	34	0	10	0	4	0	14	2	1398	443
160–164	370	34	401	24	266	12	96	3	28	0	9	0	4	0	14	0	1188	73
155–159	153	7	181	12	147	14	57	1	19	0	10	0	3	0	9	0	579	34
150–154	46	2	54	3	66	1	39	0	18	0	4	0	3	0	9	0	239	6
145–149	13	0	36	0	28	0	20	0	9	0	7	0	2	0	8	0	123	0
140–144	11	0	8	0	15	0	11	0	13	0	5	0	5	0	2	0	70	0
Below 140	1	0	3	0	4	0	8	0	6	0	2	0	4	0	3	0	31	0
Total	1429	585	1399	329	839	64	346	9	151	0	50	0	29	1	60	2	4303	990

Apps = Number of Applicants
Adm = Number Admitted
Reflects 99% of the total applicant pool.

Duquesne University School of Law

201 Edward J. Hanley Hall, 900 Locust Street
Pittsburgh, PA 15282-0700
Phone: 412.396.6296; Fax: 412.396.1073
E-mail: campion@duq.edu; Website: www.law.duq.edu

ABA
Approved
Since
1960

The Basics

Type of school	Private
Term	Semester
Application deadline	4/1 5/1
Application fee	$60
Financial aid deadline	5/31
Can first year start other than fall?	No
Student to faculty ratio	16.9 to 1
Does the university offer:	
housing restricted to law students?	No
graduate housing for which law students are eligible?	No

Faculty and Administrators

	Total		Men		Women		Minorities	
	Fall	Spr	Fall	Spr	Fall	Spr	Fall	Spr
Full-time	28	26	21	19	6	7	2	2
Other Full-time	0	1	0	1	0	0	0	0
Deans, librarians, & others who teach	3	3	1	1	2	2	1	1
Part-time	26	27	21	22	5	5	0	0
Total	**57**	**57**	**43**	**43**	**13**	**14**	**3**	**3**

Curriculum

	Full-time	Part-time
Typical first-year section size	101	90
Is there typically a "small section" of the first-year class, other than Legal Writing, taught by full-time faculty	Yes	No
If yes, typical size offered last year	46	
# of classroom course titles beyond first-year curriculum		85

# of upper division courses, excluding seminars with an enrollment:		
	Under 25	80
	25–49	26
	50–74	24
	75–99	19
	100+	0

	Full-time	Part-time
# of seminars	11	
# of seminar positions available	165	
# of seminar positions filled	77	15
# of positions available in simulation courses	309	
# of simulation positions filled	131	44
# of positions available in faculty supervised clinical courses	54	
# of faculty supervised clinical positions filled	46	8
# involved in field placements	64	10
# involved in law journals	58	17
# involved in interschool competitions	30	0
# of credit hours required to graduate	86	

JD Enrollment and Ethnicity

	Men		Women		Full-time		Part-time		1st-year		Total		JD Degs. Awd.
	#	%	#	%	#	%	#	%	#	%	#	%	
African Amer.	7	2.0	17	5.7	14	3.0	10	5.3	12	4.2	24	3.7	4
Amer. Indian	1	0.3	1	0.3	1	0.2	1	0.5	2	0.7	2	0.3	0
Asian Amer.	4	1.1	6	2.0	8	1.7	2	1.1	7	2.5	10	1.5	1
Mex. Amer.	0	0.0	0	0.0	0	0.0	0	0.0	0	0.0	0	0.0	0
Puerto Rican	0	0.0	0	0.0	0	0.0	0	0.0	0	0.0	0	0.0	0
Hispanic	2	0.6	4	1.3	6	1.3	0	0.0	4	1.4	6	0.9	2
Total Minority	14	4.0	28	9.3	29	6.2	13	7.0	25	8.8	42	6.4	7
For. Nation.	0	0.0	0	0.0	0	0.0	0	0.0	0	0.0	0	0.0	0
Caucasian	337	95.7	271	90.3	435	93.5	173	92.5	258	90.5	608	93.3	153
Unknown	1	0.3	1	0.3	1	0.2	1	0.5	2	0.7	2	0.3	0
Total	352	54.0	300	46.0	465	71.3	187	28.7	285	43.7	652		160

Transfers

Transfers in	1
Transfers out	2

Tuition and Fees

	Resident	Nonresident
Full-time	$25,785	$25,785
Part-time	$19,968	$19,968

Living Expenses

Estimated living expenses for singles

Living on campus	Living off campus	Living at home
$10,792	$10,792	$3,400

Duquesne University School of Law

*ABA
Approved
Since
1960*

GPA and LSAT Scores

	Total	Full-time	Part-time
# of apps	1,126	894	232
# of offers	602	465	137
# of matrics	288	195	93
75% GPA	3.61	3.61	3.61
Median GPA	3.35	3.40	3.31
25% GPA	3.12	3.18	3.06
75% LSAT	154	156	153
Median LSAT	153	153	151
25% LSAT	151	152	150

Grants and Scholarships (from prior year)

	Total		Full-time		Part-time	
	#	%	#	%	#	%
Total # of students	565		422		143	
Total # receiving grants	123	21.8	107	25.4	16	11.2
Less than 1/2 tuition	57	10.1	46	10.9	11	7.7
Half to full tuition	15	2.7	10	2.4	5	3.5
Full tuition	51	9.0	51	12.1	0	0.0
More than full tuition	0	0.0	0	0.0	0	0.0
Median grant amount			$15,465		$4,689	

Informational and Library Resources

# of volumes and volume equivalents	297,956
# of titles	82,244
# of active serial subscriptions	4,471
Study seating capacity inside the library	411
# of full-time professional librarians	6
Hours per week library is open	102
# of open, wired connections available to students	68
# of networked computers available for use by students	86
# of simultaneous wireless users	800
Require computer?	No

JD Attrition (from prior year)

	Academic	Other	Total	
	#	#	#	%
1st year	13	0	13	6.8
2nd year	0	0	0	0.0
3rd year	0	2	2	1.2
4th year	0	0	0	0.0

Employment (9 months after graduation)

	Total	Percentage
Employment status known	172	87.3
Employment status unknown	25	12.7
Employed	160	93.0
Pursuing graduate degrees	2	1.2
Unemployed seeking employment	7	4.1
Unemployed not seeking employment	1	0.6
Unemployed and studying for the bar	2	1.2

Type of Employment

# employed in law firms	76	47.5
# employed in business and industry	31	19.4
# employed in government	16	10.0
# employed in public interest	6	3.7
# employed as judicial clerks	14	8.7
# employed in academia	2	1.2

Geographic Location

# employed in state	135	84.4
# employed in foreign countries	0	0.0
# of states where employed	7	

Bar Passage Rates

Jurisdiction	Pennsylvania		
Exam	Sum 05	Win 06	Total
# from school taking bar for the first time	172	8	180
School's pass rate for all first-time takers	68%	63%	68%
State's pass rate for all first-time takers	79%	75%	78%

Duquesne University School of Law

201 Edward J. Hanley Hall, 900 Locust Street
Pittsburgh, PA 15282-0700
Phone: 412.396.6296; Fax: 412.396.1073
E-mail: campion@duq.edu; Website: www.law.duq.edu

■ Introduction

The Duquesne University School of Law is a Catholic law
school that has been in existence since 1911 and is the only
multiple-division law school in western Pennsylvania.
Admission requirements, instruction, and the nature and scope
of the work required of students are identical for both the
full-time day division and the part-time evening and part-time
day divisions. The School of Law is approved by the ABA and
is a member of the AALS.

Situated on the attractive 43-acre Duquesne University
campus, the law school is within walking distance to the
vibrant Pittsburgh downtown legal, corporate, and
government communities.

Recognized as one of the best cities in which to practice law
and a center for corporate and legal headquarters, Pittsburgh is
a leading metropolis for high technology ventures and a
thriving arts and cultural community, with major-league
sports entertainment.

■ Library and Physical Facilities

Duquesne's proximity to the Pittsburgh region's legal center
makes the law school library a major source for legal research
and information services. The Duquesne law library has
assumed management responsibility of the Allegheny County
Law Library, resulting in one of the largest collections of legal
materials in Pennsylvania.

The law school recently completed a $12 million renovation
and expansion, adding 33,000 square feet to Hanley Hall. The
four new floors of space include a state-of-the-art moot
courtroom (giving us three); three new technology-aided
classrooms with ports and power sources at every seat; an
upgraded lounge area with a cafeteria; new faculty and
administrative offices; student locker areas; a conference room;
and a wireless computer lab.

■ Curriculum

The course of study offered at the School of Law is sufficiently
broad to prepare students for practice in all states. Three years
are required for completion of the course of study in the
day division, four years in the evening division as well as
the part-time day division. Eighty-six credits are required
for graduation.

While emphasis is placed upon skills such as legal research
and writing and trial advocacy, the required courses are
sufficiently broad to provide all students with the requisite skills
to become competent lawyers in any field of practice. A wide
selection of elective courses, seminars, and student in-house and
internal clinics allows students to focus on specialized legal
fields and explore the contemporary problems of law and society.

■ Admission

*Bachelor's degree required; Application deadlines: day, April 1;
evening, May 1; part-time day, June 1; rolling admission; LSAT,
LSDAS required.*

All candidates for admission must take the LSAT, register
for the LSDAS, and be graduates of an accredited college or

university before enrolling in the law school. Personal
interviews are not granted, but applicants are encouraged to
schedule an appointment to visit the school for an information
session or a tour of the facilities.

The admission process is selective. Most applicants apply
well in advance of the deadlines. Students are admitted only
for the fall semester.

In evaluating applications, the complete academic record is
reviewed with consideration given to the competitiveness of
the undergraduate institution, the college major, rank in class,
and the overall academic performance. The LSAT is considered
an important factor. Graduate study, extracurricular activities,
and recommendations also contribute to the committee's
assessment. Work experience is considered when an applicant
has been employed full time for a significant length of time.

■ Joint-degree Programs

The School of Law offers the following joint-degree programs:
JD/MBA, JD/MS Environmental Science and Management,
JD/MS Taxation, and JD/MDiv.

■ Clinical Opportunities

The School of Law operates five in-house live client clinics.

The **Economic and Community Development Law Clinic** is a
unique, nationally recognized clinic. Students represent nonprofit
organizations that provide a vast array of greatly needed services
to the community. Through the **Civil and Family Justice Law
Clinic**, students represent indigent individuals who would not
otherwise find assistance through the civil justice system. The
Criminal Advocacy Clinic is operated in cooperation with the
Allegheny County District Attorney's and Public Defender's
offices. Through the **Federal Low-Income Tax Practicum**,
students learn litigation skills as they represent clients in
appeals conferences, settlement negotiations, and before the US
Tax Court. The **Securities Arbitration Practicum**, created with
the support of the Securities and Exchange Commission, is
designed to enable law students to represent small investors
through the NASD Dispute Resolution process.

■ International Programs

The law school has established a summer program and faculty
exchange with the Chinese University of Political Science and
Law (CUPL). Located in Beijing, CUPL, with official ties to
China's Ministry of Justice, is the most prestigious center for
legal study in all of China. Duquesne has an outstanding
ABA-approved summer program of study on Comparative Law
and the European Union at the American College, Dublin. The
Duquesne law school has recently established an ABA-approved
program for law students in Vatican City, focusing on subjects
relating to Canon Law and Roman Law. Duquesne is the only law
school offering a program for law students within Vatican City.

■ Student Activities

The Student Bar Association maintains a liaison between
students and faculty and sponsors social and professional
activities for the student body.

Membership in the *Duquesne Law Review* is based on the demonstrated academic ability of the student as well as his or her interest in becoming active in this publication. *Juris*, the law school news magazine, is an ABA award winning publication containing articles of current interest to the entire legal community. Students also publish the *Duquesne Business Law Journal*.

■ Financial Aid

Duquesne consistently strives to ensure that the outstanding private legal education provided by the law school is within the reach of all qualified students. Merit scholarships are awarded to outstanding day-division applicants; grants-in-aid are awarded primarily on the basis of need; and state and federal government-sponsored loans are available.

■ Housing

Law students have access to an array of housing options throughout the neighborhoods of Pittsburgh and the surrounding communities. The Office of Commuter Affairs will assist law students in their search for housing by providing a list of available locations. For further information, please write to the Office of Commuter Affairs, Duquesne University, Pittsburgh, PA 15282 or call 412.396.6660.

■ Career Services

The Career Services Office staff offers assistance to students and alumni who are interested in obtaining full-time, part-time, and summer employment. The office offers a fall and spring on-campus interview program in which law firms, government agencies, corporations, and accounting firms conduct individual interviews.

The School of Law is a member of the National Association for Law Placement, the National Association for Public Interest Law Publication Network, and the Allegheny County Bar Association Minority Job Fair.

Graduates have consistently been placed at a rate at or above 90 percent within six months of graduation. The law school has nearly 5,000 alumni throughout the United States and in several foreign countries.

Applicant Profile

The law school recognizes the different strengths presented by our day division, evening division, and part-time day students and acknowledges that the diversity in the groups cannot be accurately or completely represented in a single grid of average undergraduate GPA and LSAT scores. Graduate degrees, personal and professional accomplishments, and extensive employment experience predominate in the evening, part-time, and day divisions.

These factors are considered crucial to an individual assessment of admissibility. Applications are reviewed individually, and factors such as leadership experience, community service, and other nonacademic experiences are considered. Applicants should contact the Admissions Office for specific information on the current year's class; phone: 412.396.6296. Applicants are encouraged to visit the law school.

Emory University School of Law

Gambrell Hall, 1301 Clifton Road
Atlanta, GA 30322-2770
Phone: 404.727.6802; Fax: 404.727.2477
E-mail: lawinfo@law.emory.edu; Website: www.law.emory.edu

ABA
Approved
Since
1923

The Basics

Type of school	Private
Term	Semester
Application deadline	3/1
Application fee	$70
Financial aid deadline	3/1
Can first year start other than fall?	No
Student to faculty ratio	12.6 to 1
Does the university offer:	
housing restricted to law students?	No
graduate housing for which law students are eligible?	Yes

Faculty and Administrators

	Total		Men		Women		Minorities	
	Fall	Spr	Fall	Spr	Fall	Spr	Fall	Spr
Full-time	45	44	31	30	14	14	6	6
Other Full-time	7	7	1	0	6	7	0	0
Deans, librarians, & others who teach	5	5	3	3	2	2	1	1
Part-time	26	29	22	26	4	3	0	1
Total	**83**	**85**	**57**	**59**	**26**	**26**	**7**	**8**

Curriculum

	Full-time	Part-time
Typical first-year section size	70	0
Is there typically a "small section" of the first-year class, other than Legal Writing, taught by full-time faculty	Yes	No
If yes, typical size offered last year	36	
# of classroom course titles beyond first-year curriculum	124	
# of upper division courses, excluding seminars with an enrollment: Under 25	71	
25–49	32	
50–74	17	
75–99	7	
100+	1	
# of seminars	18	
# of seminar positions available	270	
# of seminar positions filled	216	0
# of positions available in simulation courses	540	
# of simulation positions filled	510	0
# of positions available in faculty supervised clinical courses	48	
# of faculty supervised clinical positions filled	41	0
# involved in field placements	191	0
# involved in law journals	163	0
# involved in interschool competitions	95	0
# of credit hours required to graduate	90	

JD Enrollment and Ethnicity

	Men		Women		Full-time		Part-time		1st-year		Total		JD Degs. Awd.
	#	%	#	%	#	%	#	%	#	%	#	%	
African Amer.	14	4.0	48	14.9	62	9.2	0	0.0	23	11.1	62	9.2	25
Amer. Indian	0	0.0	0	0.0	0	0.0	0	0.0	0	0.0	0	0.0	0
Asian Amer.	37	10.5	35	10.8	72	10.7	0	0.0	18	8.7	72	10.7	16
Mex. Amer.	0	0.0	0	0.0	0	0.0	0	0.0	0	0.0	0	0.0	0
Puerto Rican	0	0.0	0	0.0	0	0.0	0	0.0	0	0.0	0	0.0	0
Hispanic	16	4.6	27	8.4	43	6.4	0	0.0	8	3.9	43	6.4	12
Total Minority	67	19.1	110	34.1	177	26.3	0	0.0	49	23.7	177	26.3	53
For. Nation.	8	2.3	8	2.5	16	2.4	0	0.0	6	2.9	16	2.4	5
Caucasian	271	77.2	196	60.7	467	69.3	0	0.0	148	71.5	467	69.3	162
Unknown	5	1.4	9	2.8	14	2.1	0	0.0	4	1.9	14	2.1	1
Total	351	52.1	323	47.9	674	100.0	0	0.0	207	30.7	674		221

Transfers

Transfers in	28
Transfers out	6

Tuition and Fees

	Resident	Nonresident
Full-time	$36,746	$36,746
Part-time	$0	$0

Living Expenses

Estimated living expenses for singles

Living on campus	Living off campus	Living at home
$19,268	$19,268	$19,268

Emory University School of Law

*ABA
Approved
Since
1923*

GPA and LSAT Scores

	Total	Full-time	Part-time
# of apps	3,591	3,591	0
# of offers	1,042	1,042	0
# of matrics	207	207	0
75% GPA	3.69	3.69	0.00
Median GPA	3.50	3.50	0.00
25% GPA	3.30	3.30	0.00
75% LSAT	166	166	0
Median LSAT	164	164	0
25% LSAT	162	162	0

Grants and Scholarships (from prior year)

	Total #	Total %	Full-time #	Full-time %	Part-time #	Part-time %
Total # of students	680		680		0	
Total # receiving grants	244	35.9	244	35.9	0	0.0
Less than 1/2 tuition	115	16.9	115	16.9	0	0.0
Half to full tuition	76	11.2	76	11.2	0	0.0
Full tuition	36	5.3	36	5.3	0	0.0
More than full tuition	17	2.5	17	2.5	0	0.0
Median grant amount			$17,350		$0	

Informational and Library Resources

# of volumes and volume equivalents	407,266
# of titles	141,782
# of active serial subscriptions	4,029
Study seating capacity inside the library	487
# of full-time professional librarians	8
Hours per week library is open	110
# of open, wired connections available to students	123
# of networked computers available for use by students	79
# of simultaneous wireless users	500
Require computer?	No

JD Attrition (from prior year)

	Academic #	Other #	Total #	Total %
1st year	0	4	4	1.7
2nd year	0	8	8	3.6
3rd year	0	0	0	0.0
4th year	0	0	0	0.0

Employment (9 months after graduation)

	Total	Percentage
Employment status known	247	100.0
Employment status unknown	0	0.0
Employed	231	93.5
Pursuing graduate degrees	4	1.6
Unemployed seeking employment	5	2.0
Unemployed not seeking employment	7	2.8
Unemployed and studying for the bar	0	0.0
Type of Employment		
# employed in law firms	150	64.9
# employed in business and industry	20	8.7
# employed in government	23	10.0
# employed in public interest	6	2.6
# employed as judicial clerks	26	11.3
# employed in academia	2	0.9
Geographic Location		
# employed in state	100	43.3
# employed in foreign countries	0	0.0
# of states where employed		23

Bar Passage Rates

Jurisdiction		Georgia	
Exam	Sum 05	Win 06	Total
# from school taking bar for the first time	109	12	121
School's pass rate for all first-time takers	96%	92%	96%
State's pass rate for all first-time takers	86%	79%	84%

Emory University School of Law

Gambrell Hall, 1301 Clifton Road
Atlanta, GA 30322-2770
Phone: 404.727.6802; Fax: 404.727.2477
E-mail: lawinfo@law.emory.edu; Website: www.law.emory.edu

■ Introduction

Emory's location in Atlanta, a national business and legal center, gives Emory law students the opportunity to take advanced classes from, and work with, some of the leading judges and lawyers in the United States. Atlanta also is one of America's most beautiful and most livable cities.

The law school also benefits from being located on the campus of Emory University, which was founded in 1836. Emory University School of Law is accredited by the American Bar Association, is a member of the Association of American Law Schools, and has a chapter of the Order of the Coif.

■ Library and Physical Facilities

The Emory School of Law is located in Gambrell Hall, a part of Emory's 630-acre campus in Druid Hills, six miles southeast of downtown Atlanta.

Gambrell Hall contains classrooms, faculty offices, administrative offices, student-organization offices, and a 320-seat auditorium. The law school provides wireless Internet access throughout its facilities. Gambrell Hall also houses a state-of-the-art courtroom with computer connections for judge, counsel, and jury; a document camera; DVD player; videoconferencing; and four-camera operation with feeds to remote locations.

The Hugh F. McMillan Law Library sits adjacent to Gambrell Hall and is designed for easy student access. Students are trained on LexisNexis and Westlaw terminals and learn both the techniques of computer-assisted legal research and traditional research methods. Students also may use the library's computer labs that offer Macintosh and IBM-compatible computers.

■ Curriculum

The basic program of study involves three years of full-time study leading to the JD degree. The fall semester runs from late August to mid-December; the spring semester begins in early January and ends in mid-May.

The program of courses for the first year is prescribed. The program of courses for the second and third years is primarily elective. Students can sample a broad spectrum of courses or concentrate on a particular area of law.

All first-year courses and the basic second- and third-year courses are taught by full-time faculty members. A distinguished group of judges and practicing attorneys offer specialized courses.

■ Special Programs

Emory Law School is committed to the legal profession as a service profession, to teaching the practice of law as well as the study of law, and to our premier centers of excellence. The essential role of service is reflected in our public interest curriculum and organizations. We teach the practice of law through our outstanding programs in trial techniques, intellectual property, child advocacy, and environmental law, and through expanded emphasis on transactional skills. Our centers of excellence in law and religion, world law, feminism

and legal theory, and health law are interdisciplinary, integrative, and international in approach.

Emory's Trial Techniques Program is consistently ranked among the best in the nation. Students are exposed to the challenges of conducting direct and cross-examination, developing a case theory and approach, and conducting opening and closing arguments. More than half of the students participate in Emory's field placement program, where students may earn academic credit doing things such as clerking for a federal judge, researching intellectual property issues for The Coca-Cola Company, and representing clients on behalf of Atlanta Legal Aid.

Students also may gain practical experience in intellectual property and corporate/commercial law by participating in TI:GER (Technological Innovation: Generating Economic Results), a program of technology law and business law cosponsored by Emory's School of Law and Economics Department and Georgia Tech's Dupree School of Management. Students may participate in one of Emory's own clinics: the Barton Child Law and Policy Clinic, working to promote and protect the well-being of neglected and abused children; the Barton Juvenile Defender Clinic, representing children charged with delinquent acts; the Indigent Criminal Defense Clinic, representing indigent misdemeanor defendants; and the Turner Environmental Law Clinic, offering a practical clinical education to the aspiring environmental attorney.

Emory offers a comprehensive international law program and is home to the World Law Institute. Emory Law capitalizes on the presence of other strong campus programs by combining coursework and programs to create unique and synergistic programs of study. The law school offers joint-degree programs with Emory's School of Business Administration, School of Theology, School of Public Health, and the Graduate School of Arts and Sciences.

■ Admission

The law school accepts beginning students for the fall term only. Prior to enrollment, a student must have earned a bachelor's degree from an approved institution. Applications for admission must be received by Emory no later than March 1. Early applications are encouraged. Many factors are considered in making admission decisions. Of particular importance are academic accomplishments and LSAT scores. Extracurricular activities, work experience, level of quality and difficulty of undergraduate courses, performance in graduate school, and letters of recommendation also are considered. We encourage applications from members of underrepresented groups, and such applicants should provide the Dean of Admission with specific information about their background or accomplishments that would be of particular interest. Applicants are encouraged to visit the law school. Upon acceptance, applicants are required to submit a nonrefundable $750 tuition deposit to reserve a space in the entering class.

■ Student Activities

A wide variety of organizations and activities are available to students. There are three law reviews at Emory—*Emory Law*

Journal, Emory Bankruptcy Developments Journal, and *Emory International Law Review*; more than 30 percent of the second- and third-year students are involved in law review research, writing, and editing.

Students also participate in moot court. Each first-year student prepares a brief and presents an oral argument. In addition, many second- and third-year students compete in intramural and national moot court competitions.

There are numerous special interest and social groups and a very active Student Bar Association.

■ Career Services

The law school regards career services as a matter of highest priority. A full-time career services office assists students in obtaining permanent, summer, and part-time employment. It arranges interviews with employers from many parts of the country and maintains extensive files on a wide variety of professional opportunities all over the United States. Many Emory graduates join private law firms after graduation. Others work as judicial clerks, enter government service, or work for banks, corporations, or legal aid agencies.

The majority of Emory's students stay in the Southeast. Approximately 20 percent work in the Northeast and Mid-Atlantic. Smaller percentages work in the Midwest, Southwest, and West.

The career services office provides extensive training on résumés, interview skills, and job-search techniques, as well as numerous opportunities to network with attorneys in a variety of practice areas and settings.

Applicant Profile

Emory University School of Law

LSAT Score	GPA								
	3.75 +	3.50–3.74	3.25–3.49	3.00–3.24	2.75–2.99	2.50–2.74	2.25–2.49	2.00–2.24	Below 2.00
175–180									
170–174									
165–169									
160–164									
155–159									
150–154									
145–149									
140–144									
135–139									
130–134									
125–129									
120–124									

■ Good Possibility   □ Possible   ▨ Unlikely

Note: This graph reflects admission decisions as of 6/1/06 and is to be used as a general guide to determining chances for admittance. It does not reflect actual decisions but should serve as a guideline.

Faulkner University, Thomas Goode Jones School of Law

5345 Atlanta Highway
Montgomery, AL 36109
Phone: 334.386.7210
E-mail: law@faulkner.edu; Website: www.faulkner.edu/law

Provisional

ABA Approved Since 2006

The Basics

Type of school	Private
Term	Semester
Application deadline	5/1
Application fee	$25
Financial aid deadline	6/1
Can first year start other than fall?	No
Student to faculty ratio	11.1 to 1
Does the university offer:	
housing restricted to law students?	No
graduate housing for which law students are eligible?	No

Faculty and Administrators

	Total		Men		Women		Minorities	
	Fall	Spr	Fall	Spr	Fall	Spr	Fall	Spr
Full-time	16	17	12	13	4	4	3	3
Other Full-time	2	2	1	1	1	1	0	0
Deans, librarians, & others who teach	7	7	4	3	3	4	0	0
Part-time	4	1	1	1	3	0	0	0
Total	29	27	18	18	11	9	3	3

Curriculum

	Full-time	Part-time
Typical first-year section size	60	30
Is there typically a "small section" of the first-year class, other than Legal Writing, taught by full-time faculty	No	No
If yes, typical size offered last year		
# of classroom course titles beyond first-year curriculum		48
# of upper division courses, excluding seminars with an enrollment: Under 25		43
25–49		17
50–74		2
75–99		0
100+		0
# of seminars		8
# of seminar positions available		96
# of seminar positions filled	36	40
# of positions available in simulation courses		118
# of simulation positions filled	70	22
# of positions available in faculty supervised clinical courses		50
# of faculty supervised clinical positions filled	44	3
# involved in field placements	19	8
# involved in law journals	13	5
# involved in interschool competitions	8	0
# of credit hours required to graduate		90

JD Enrollment and Ethnicity

	Men		Women		Full-time		Part-time		1st-year		Total		JD Degs. Awd.
	#	%	#	%	#	%	#	%	#	%	#	%	
African Amer.	5	3.1	15	13.5	11	6.0	9	9.8	9	8.5	20	7.3	2
Amer. Indian	2	1.2	1	0.9	3	1.6	0	0.0	2	1.9	3	1.1	1
Asian Amer.	0	0.0	3	2.7	1	0.5	2	2.2	1	0.9	3	1.1	0
Mex. Amer.	0	0.0	0	0.0	0	0.0	0	0.0	0	0.0	0	0.0	0
Puerto Rican	0	0.0	0	0.0	0	0.0	0	0.0	0	0.0	0	0.0	0
Hispanic	1	0.6	1	0.9	0	0.0	2	2.2	1	0.9	2	0.7	0
Total Minority	8	4.9	20	18.0	15	8.2	13	14.1	13	12.3	28	10.2	3
For. Nation.	0	0.0	0	0.0	0	0.0	0	0.0	0	0.0	0	0.0	0
Caucasian	154	94.5	91	82.0	166	91.2	79	85.9	92	86.8	245	89.4	51
Unknown	1	0.6	0	0.0	1	0.5	0	0.0	1	0.9	1	0.4	0
Total	163	59.5	111	40.5	182	66.4	92	33.6	106	38.7	274		54

Transfers

Transfers in	3
Transfers out	0

Tuition and Fees

	Resident	Nonresident
Full-time	$15,000	$15,000
Part-time	$9,000	$9,000

Living Expenses

Estimated living expenses for singles

Living on campus	Living off campus	Living at home
N/A	$10,800	$10,800

Faulkner University, Thomas Goode Jones School of Law

ABA
Approved
Since
2006

GPA and LSAT Scores

	Total	Full-time	Part-time
# of apps	316	250	66
# of offers	184	155	29
# of matrics	106	84	22
75% GPA	3.35	3.35	3.51
Median GPA	2.97	2.97	2.97
25% GPA	2.70	2.72	2.62
75% LSAT	152	152	154
Median LSAT	149	149	150
25% LSAT	147	147	147

Grants and Scholarships (from prior year)

	Total		Full-time		Part-time	
	#	%	#	%	#	%
Total # of students	259		141		118	
Total # receiving grants	62	23.9	39	27.7	23	19.5
Less than 1/2 tuition	26	10.0	17	12.1	9	7.6
Half to full tuition	25	9.7	15	10.6	10	8.5
Full tuition	11	4.2	7	5.0	4	3.4
More than full tuition	0	0.0	0	0.0	0	0.0
Median grant amount			$5,119		$4,095	

Informational and Library Resources

# of volumes and volume equivalents	175,746
# of titles	99,558
# of active serial subscriptions	4,566
Study seating capacity inside the library	211
# of full-time professional librarians	7
Hours per week library is open	98
# of open, wired connections available to students	205
# of networked computers available for use by students	41
# of simultaneous wireless users	240
Require computer?	No

JD Attrition (from prior year)

	Academic	Other	Total	
	#	#	#	%
1st year	13	17	30	32.3
2nd year	5	1	6	8.7
3rd year	1	1	2	3.3
4th year	0	0	0	0.0

Employment (9 months after graduation)

	Total	Percentage
Employment status known	49	100.0
Employment status unknown	0	0.0
Employed	47	95.9
Pursuing graduate degrees	1	2.0
Unemployed seeking employment	1	2.0
Unemployed not seeking employment	0	0.0
Unemployed and studying for the bar	0	0.0
Type of Employment		
# employed in law firms	36	76.6
# employed in business and industry	3	6.4
# employed in government	3	6.4
# employed in public interest	0	0.0
# employed as judicial clerks	2	4.3
# employed in academia	2	4.3
Geographic Location		
# employed in state	46	97.9
# employed in foreign countries	0	0.0
# of states where employed	2	

Bar Passage Rates

Jurisdiction	Alabama		
Exam	Sum 05	Win 06	Total
# from school taking bar for the first time	40	12	52
School's pass rate for all first-time takers	90%	75%	87%
State's pass rate for all first-time takers	84%	68%	79%

Faulkner University, Thomas Goode Jones School of Law

5345 Atlanta Highway
Montgomery, AL 36109
Phone: 334.386.7210
E-mail: law@faulkner.edu; Website: www.faulkner.edu/law

■ Introduction

Faulkner University's Thomas Goode Jones School of Law has a long and rich tradition of educating students for the practice of law in Alabama. The school was founded in 1928 by Circuit Judge Walter B. Jones and named in honor of his father, a former soldier, lawyer, and governor. In 1901, at the urging of Booker T. Washington, Thomas Goode Jones was appointed by President Theodore Roosevelt to be United States District Judge for the Northern and Middle Districts of Alabama. He authored the Alabama Code of Ethics, a document that was the first state code of ethics and the model for the American Bar Association's 1908 Canons of Professional Ethics.

The School of Law is committed to the education of outstanding lawyers. In keeping with its distinctive Christian mission, the school embraces academic excellence and emphasizes a strong commitment to integrity within a caring Christian environment that sustains and nurtures faith. Students are encouraged to dedicate their lives to the service of others.

The School of Law became part of Faulkner University in 1983. Since its inception, the school has produced over 2,000 alumni who have become practicing attorneys, judges, and other contributors to the legal profession. The American Bar Association granted provisional approval of the School of Law in June 2006.

■ Montgomery and the River Region

The School of Law is located in the capital of Alabama. Montgomery is widely known as the birthplace of the Confederacy and the civil rights movement. It is regarded as one of the nation's most historically significant cities. One can visit the First White House of the Confederacy and the steps of the state capitol building where Jefferson Davis was sworn in as president of the Confederate States of America. It was on these same steps where Dr. Martin Luther King Jr. completed the freedom march from Selma to Montgomery. Here Dr. King asked for equality for all people, regardless of race. Other historic sites include the Dexter Avenue King Memorial Baptist Church, the Civil Rights Memorial designed by Maya Lin, and the Rosa L. Parks Library and Museum.

Along with its rich history, Montgomery is known for its contribution to the arts. Its most notable contribution is the Wynton M. Blount Cultural Park, which includes the Montgomery Museum of Fine Arts, the internationally acclaimed Alabama Shakespeare Festival and the beautiful Shakespeare Gardens.

Montgomery offers a small-town atmosphere with big-city amenities that add to the quality of life enjoyed by all who reside in the capital city. It is also an excellent place to study law with the Supreme Court of Alabama, the Alabama legislature, and over 200 law firms and other organizations that employ lawyers within a short driving distance of campus.

■ Library and Physical Facilities

The George H. Jones, Jr. Law Library supports the School of Law's curriculum and the legal research requirements of its students and faculty. It provides access to legal and academic materials offered by the latest technology. Computers on both floors of the library enable free access to the Internet, word processing packages, and legal databases. A spacious computer lab facilitates computer-assisted legal instruction and research. Data ports are available throughout the library and every study room and study carrel is electronically wired and ready for laptop computers.

The School of Law is housed in a beautiful, neo-federal-style building that accommodates the George H. Jones, Jr. Law Library, the Judge Walter B. Jones Moot Court Room, and the Institute for Dispute Resolution. It includes state-of-the-art research and lecture facilities with seven classrooms and two large conference rooms. All classrooms are outfitted for laptop computers and wireless Internet is available throughout the building and library. Students have access to the student lounge for congregation and conference rooms for student organization meetings.

■ Institute for Dispute Resolution

The Alternative Dispute Resolution (ADR) Program enables law students to integrate their knowledge of conflict management principles and dispute resolution processes with professional skills. This program allows students to receive training normally available only through on-the-job experience after graduation.

Students can earn a certificate in ADR which is not a supplemental degree but an opportunity for Juris Doctor candidates to enrich their skills training while still in law school. The certificate in ADR requires completion of the following courses: Arbitration, Dispute Resolution Processes, Interviewing/Counseling & Negotiation, Mediation Clinic, and an elective skills course. All of the certificate courses contain both an academic component and a skills component.

■ Clinical Opportunities and Externships

The School of Law operates three clinical programs: the Mediation Clinic, the Family Violence Clinic, and the Elder Law Clinic. The Mediation Clinic allows students to mediate cases set for trial at Montgomery County District Court. The Family Violence Clinic provides pro bono services for clients unable to pay for representation and works in conjunction with the Legal Services Corporation of Alabama and the Family Sunshine Center. Students with limited-practice cards interview clients, provide advice, prepare pleadings, and represent clients in court proceedings. Students without limited-practice cards assist in case preparation and research. The School of Law and Legal Services Corporation of Alabama are the recipients of the Family Sunshine Center's President's Special Service Award in recognition of outstanding service and support through the Family Violence Clinic.

The School of Law established the Elder Law Clinic after receiving a grant from the federal government through the Commerce, Justice, and Science spending bill. This clinic provides pro bono services in matters of estate planning, Medicare, nursing home issues, social security, long-term care insurance, and disability planning to name a few.

The School of Law's Externship Program affords students the opportunity to supplement their classroom experience by working in a variety of legal settings. Externships include a classroom component that covers topics relating to the legal system, judicial process, and professionalism. Students develop their lawyering skills and gain real-world experience in the legal community, as they work side by side with judges and practicing attorneys, under the supervision of a full-time faculty member.

■ Public Interest Program

As part of a Christian university, the School of Law seeks not only to provide legal knowledge and practical skills necessary to produce competent and ethical members of the legal community, but also to instill in students an attitude of service. This commitment to serve those who otherwise could not afford such assistance complements the legal profession's rich tradition of service.

The Public Interest Program provides opportunities for students to begin their career of service while utilizing the practical skills obtained in their legal education. This program is voluntary and provides students with opportunities to work for nonprofit organizations, government agencies, and private attorneys or firms conducting pro bono legal work. Students are challenged to perform at least 35 hours of voluntary service during the academic year. This goal can be met in less than four and one-half hours per month. Students providing public interest service qualify for recognition, including notation of service on transcripts, a certificate of accomplishment, special recognition in the graduation program, and eligibility for the Public Interest Service Award.

■ Student Organizations

The Student Bar Association (SBA) serves the student body and every student is a member. The SBA fosters relationships with members of the legal community and sponsors social functions and fundraising events. Other student organizations at the law school include American Constitution Society, Association of Trial Lawyers of America, Black Law Students Association, Christian Legal Society, Delta Theta Phi, Federalist Society, Honor Court, Phi Alpha Delta, and Women Students Association.

The *Jones Law Review* is a scholarly legal journal published by student editors and members. Members write comments and notes on legal developments and landmark cases. They also select and edit articles submitted for publication by lawyers, judges, professors, and other scholars. Membership is considered an honor and provides students an opportunity to hone their research and writing skills.

■ Scholarships, Tuition, and Fees

The School of Law offers merit-based scholarships to qualified entering students. Admitted applicants are automatically under scholarship consideration. Awards range from 10 percent tuition forgiveness to 100 percent tuition forgiveness. Scholarships are available to students who perform well academically in law school. Leadership and need-based scholarships are also available.

The tuition rate for a full-time student in the academic year of 2007–2008 is $22,000. The tuition rate for a part-time student is $16,500.

Applicant Profile

Faulkner University, Thomas Goode Jones School of Law

LSAT Score	GPA								
	3.75 +	3.50–3.74	3.25–3.49	3.00–3.24	2.75–2.99	2.50–2.74	2.25–2.49	2.00–2.24	Below 2.00
175–180									
170–174									
165–169									
160–164									
155–159									
150–154									
145–149									
140–144									
Below 140									

■ Good Possibility   ■ Possible   □ Unlikely

Florida A&M University College of Law

201 Beggs Avenue
Orlando, FL 32801
Phone: 407.254.3268; Fax: 407.254.3213
E-mail: famulaw.admissions@famu.edu; Website: www.famu.edu/law

Provisional

ABA Approved Since 2004

The Basics

Type of school	Public
Term	Semester
Application deadline	5/1
Application fee	$20
Financial aid deadline	3/1
Can first year start other than fall?	No
Student to faculty ratio	15.9 to 1
Does the university offer:	
housing restricted to law students?	No
graduate housing for which law students are eligible?	No

Faculty and Administrators

	Total Fall	Total Spr	Men Fall	Men Spr	Women Fall	Women Spr	Minorities Fall	Minorities Spr
Full-time	21	21	9	9	12	12	16	16
Other Full-time	5	5	1	1	4	4	4	4
Deans, librarians, & others who teach	5	5	1	1	4	4	5	5
Part-time	13	10	11	8	2	2	10	6
Total	**44**	**41**	**22**	**19**	**22**	**22**	**35**	**31**

Curriculum

		Full-time	Part-time
Typical first-year section size		85	85
Is there typically a "small section" of the first-year class, other than Legal Writing, taught by full-time faculty		No	No
If yes, typical size offered last year			
# of classroom course titles beyond first-year curriculum		48	
# of upper division courses, excluding seminars with an enrollment:	Under 25	43	
	25–49	8	
	50–74	7	
	75–99	0	
	100+	0	
# of seminars		13	
# of seminar positions available		152	
# of seminar positions filled		37	22
# of positions available in simulation courses		240	
# of simulation positions filled		101	30
# of positions available in faculty supervised clinical courses		240	
# of faculty supervised clinical positions filled		101	30
# involved in field placements		37	11
# involved in law journals		42	15
# involved in interschool competitions		28	12
# of credit hours required to graduate		90	

JD Enrollment and Ethnicity

	Men #	Men %	Women #	Women %	Full-time #	Full-time %	Part-time #	Part-time %	1st-year #	1st-year %	Total #	Total %	JD Degs. Awd.
African Amer.	88	38.8	167	53.2	174	51.8	81	39.5	133	52.8	255	47.1	29
Amer. Indian	3	1.3	3	1.0	3	0.9	3	1.5	1	0.4	6	1.1	0
Asian Amer.	8	3.5	10	3.2	13	3.9	5	2.4	12	4.8	18	3.3	1
Mex. Amer.	0	0.0	0	0.0	0	0.0	0	0.0	0	0.0	0	0.0	0
Puerto Rican	8	3.5	4	1.3	8	2.4	4	2.0	12	4.8	12	2.2	0
Hispanic	38	16.7	42	13.4	38	11.3	42	20.5	34	13.5	80	14.8	12
Total Minority	145	63.9	226	72.0	236	70.2	135	65.9	192	76.2	371	68.6	42
For. Nation.	0	0.0	0	0.0	0	0.0	0	0.0	0	0.0	0	0.0	0
Caucasian	80	35.2	73	23.2	86	25.6	67	32.7	58	23.0	153	28.3	46
Unknown	2	0.9	15	4.8	14	4.2	3	1.5	2	0.8	17	3.1	0
Total	227	42.0	314	58.0	336	62.1	205	37.9	252	46.6	541		88

Transfers

Transfers in	0
Transfers out	7

Tuition and Fees

	Resident	Nonresident
Full-time	$7,567	$26,828
Part-time	$6,344	$22,394

Living Expenses

Estimated living expenses for singles

Living on campus	Living off campus	Living at home
N/A	$17,402	$7,948

*ABA
Approved
Since
2004*

GPA and LSAT Scores

	Total	Full-time	Part-time
# of apps	941	781	160
# of offers	531	406	125
# of matrics	247	167	80
75% GPA	3.39	3.40	3.39
Median GPA	3.03	3.08	2.97
25% GPA	2.75	2.78	2.60
75% LSAT	147	147	147
Median LSAT	143	143	143
25% LSAT	140	141	138

Grants and Scholarships (from prior year)

	Total		Full-time		Part-time	
	#	%	#	%	#	%
Total # of students	393		231		162	
Total # receiving grants	25	6.4	18	7.8	7	4.3
Less than 1/2 tuition	24	6.1	17	7.4	7	4.3
Half to full tuition	0	0.0	0	0.0	0	0.0
Full tuition	1	0.3	1	0.4	0	0.0
More than full tuition	0	0.0	0	0.0	0	0.0
Median grant amount			$1,000		$1,500	

Informational and Library Resources

# of volumes and volume equivalents	329,410
# of titles	35,699
# of active serial subscriptions	927
Study seating capacity inside the library	558
# of full-time professional librarians	8
Hours per week library is open	100
# of open, wired connections available to students	625
# of networked computers available for use by students	61
# of simultaneous wireless users	1,000
Require computer?	No

Florida A&M University College of Law

201 Beggs Avenue
Orlando, FL 32801
Phone: 407.254.3268; Fax: 407.254.3213
E-mail: famulaw.admissions@famu.edu; Webs

■ Introduction

Established in 1887, Florida A&
comprehensive, public, coedu
land-grant university offeri
research, and service pro
and professional level
acres located in the
Law's rich traditi
founding in 19
graduated 57
reopened
moved

Employed		
Pursuing graduate degrees	0	0.0
Unemployed seeking employment	0	0.0
Unemployed not seeking employment	0	0.0
Unemployed and studying for the bar	0	0.0

Type of Employment

# employed in law firms	23	46.0
# employed in business and industry	11	22.0
# employed in government	12	24.0
# employed in public interest	4	8.0
# employed as judicial clerks	0	0.0
# employed in academia	0	0.0

Geographic Location

# employed in state	47	94.0
# employed in foreign countries	0	0.0
# of states where employed	4	

Bar Passage Rates

Jurisdiction	Florida		
Exam	Sum 05	Win 06	Total
# from school taking bar for the first time	51	14	65
School's pass rate for all first-time takers	53%	57%	54%
State's pass rate for all first-time takers	71%	73%	71%

aw

te: www.famu.edu/law

M University (FAMU) is a
cational, and fully accredited
g a broad range of instruction,
rams at the undergraduate, graduate,
. The main campus occupies over 419
capital city of Tallahassee. The College of
n of excellence dates back to its original
9. From 1949 to 1968, the College of Law
students. In 2002, the FAMU College of Law
downtown Orlando, Florida, and in 2006,
nto its new state-of-the-art facility.

Location and Physical Facilities

Considered one of the fastest growing metropolitan areas in
Florida and the nation, the city of Orlando is a racially and
culturally diverse community, ideal for a progressive law
school. Located in downtown Orlando, the College of Law is
within walking distance of the courts, county library, government
buildings, and a wide variety of cultural, educational, and
recreational opportunities. The new, state-of-the-art, four-story,
112,000-square-foot law school building is conveniently
accessible from Interstate 4. The facility houses a law library,
classrooms, faculty and administrative offices, and an area
dealing with student affairs, including admission, financial
aid, the registrar, alumni affairs, and career planning and
placement. There is a moot courtroom, space for student
organizations and meetings, and space allocated for students
to participate in the hands-on clinical program.

Enrollment and Student Body

Since opening in the fall of 2002, the Florida A&M University
College of Law has admitted three entering classes and has a
current student enrollment of 679 students. The student body
is composed of 540 full-time day students and 139 part-time
evening students. With 60 percent women and 70 percent
minority students, the FAMU College of Law is one of the
most diverse law schools in the state of Florida. The College of
Law is committed to helping its students further develop their
talents, professional skills, and goals. To that end, we offer
cocurricular and extracurricular activities, including the
Academic Success Program and the Law in America lecture
series. These programs enhance not only the study of the law,
but students' leadership and professional abilities, and oral
and written communication skills. FAMU College of Law
students are very active within the law school and in the
Central Florida community. As students at a recently
reestablished law school, they have taken on the challenge of
establishing organizations that will serve current and future
students for years to come. The FAMU College of Law Student
Bar Association supports and governs all student activities and
organizations at the College of Law. In three short years,
students have founded: the Jesse J. McCrary Jr. Chapter of the
National Black Law Students Association; the Association of
Trial Lawyers of America; the Women's Law Caucus; the
Entertainment, Arts, and Sports Law Society; the Hispanic Law
Students; the Federalist Society; Phi Alpha Delta; and many

other student organizations. Over the next several years, the
law school will continue to support students in their efforts to
establish additional organizations and interest groups.

■ Programs of Study

The FAMU College of Law offers both a full-time day program
and a part-time evening program of study. Full-time day
program students must successfully complete six semesters
or three academic years in order to fulfill their degree
requirements. Enrollment in the day program represents a
commitment to the full-time study of law. Part-time evening
program students must successfully complete their degree
requirements in four years consisting of eight semesters and
three summers. Part-time evening classes meet Monday
through Thursday evenings from 6:00 to 10:00 PM. The
part-time evening program is designed for students who are
unable to attend school on a full-time basis and want to earn a
law degree while working full time. Courses in both programs
demand the same standards of performance by students and
are taught by full-time faculty members who are assisted by
adjunct faculty.

■ Curriculum

The law school offers a rigorous traditional curriculum of
required and elective courses that are complemented by
extensive skills training that includes an intensive three-year
writing program and a strong clinical program. The College
of Law's curriculum is designed to provide students with
both the intellectual and practical skills necessary to meet the
demands of the modern practice of law by combining
theoretical coursework with clinical and practical experiences.
Through the use of elective courses and leading practitioners as
adjunct faculty, students are introduced to emerging trends and
developments in the law.

■ Expenses and Financial Aid

Tuition rates and fees are set annually by the Florida
Legislature and the Florida A&M University Board of
Trustees and may be changed at any time without advance
notice. For the 2006–2007 academic year, tuition for law
students was $239.25 per credit hour for Florida residents
and $886 per credit hour for non-Florida residents. In addition,
Florida A&M University imposes additional fees on all
graduate and professional students. Approximately 90 percent
of law students are receiving some form of financial aid,
including federal loans, law loans, need-based stipends, and
merit-based scholarships. Need-based stipends and
merit-based scholarships are awarded to a select number
of entering full-time and part-time students who have
excelled academically and who possess other outstanding
qualifications for the study of law. All admitted students
are automatically considered for these awards. Scholarships
are not automatically renewable and may vary in the
amount awarded. The average scholarship award in
2006–2007 was $1,500.

Florida A&M University College of Law

■ Admission

Admission to the College of Law is highly competitive. The law school seeks diligent, hardworking students with a broad array of talents and experiences who demonstrate both an exceptional aptitude for the study of law and a strong history of, or commitment to, public service. Selection for admission is based on a thorough evaluation of all factors in an applicant's file. While an applicant's academic record and LSAT performance are weighted heavily in the evaluative process, the Admissions Committee considers other factors, including writing ability, as evidenced by the LSAT writing sample and the personal statement; community and public service; academic honors and awards; work experience; leadership ability; extracurricular activities; letters of recommendation; and character and motivation.

■ Applicant Profile

While an applicant's undergraduate record and LSAT score are important, they are not the sole determinants for admission to law school. No index or cut-off is used in reviewing applications. There are no combinations of grades or scores that assure admission or denial.

An applicant's transcripts are analyzed for breadth and depth of coursework, trends in grades, and rank; the competitiveness of the school and major are taken into consideration, as are special honors, awards, and activities. Other aspects of the application significantly influence the decision, such as work experience and evidence of a commitment or interest in public service.

In making its decision, the committee aims to enroll an entering class of students with the strongest combination of qualifications and the greatest potential to contribute to FAMU College of Law and to the legal profession.

Applicant Profile

Florida A&M University College of Law

This grid includes only applicants who earned 120–180 LSAT scores under standard administrations.

LSAT Score	GPA 3.75 +		3.50–3.74		3.25–3.49		3.00–3.24		2.75–2.99		2.50–2.74		2.25–2.49		2.00–2.24		Below 2.00		No GPA		Total	
	Apps	Adm	Apps	Adm	Apps	Adm	Apps	Adm	Apps	Adm	Apps	Adm	Apps	Adm	Apps	Adm	Apps	Adm	Apps	Adm	Apps	Adm
175–180	0	0	0	0	0	0	0	0	0	0	0	0	0	0	0	0	0	0	0	0	0	0
170–174	0	0	0	0	0	0	0	0	0	0	0	0	0	0	0	0	0	0	0	0	0	0
165–169	0	0	1	1	1	1	2	2	0	0	0	0	0	0	0	0	0	0	0	0	4	4
160–164	1	1	0	0	4	3	3	3	1	1	1	1	1	1	0	0	0	0	0	0	11	10
155–159	3	3	4	2	5	5	2	0	7	5	5	0	8	7	3	2	0	0	0	0	37	24
150–154	8	5	10	8	17	14	29	25	19	15	18	14	4	0	3	1	1	0	3	0	112	82
145–149	11	8	21	18	36	28	52	32	51	18	42	17	19	9	16	8	3	0	2	0	253	138
140–144	13	9	43	27	49	33	70	33	78	44	59	19	33	9	18	6	2	0	7	0	372	180
135–139	6	1	13	9	33	14	34	11	38	8	33	10	22	3	16	4	4	0	5	0	203	61
130–134	1	0	5	1	8	0	17	2	14	0	10	0	12	0	10	0	3	0	5	0	85	3
125–129	0	0	1	0	0	0	4	0	2	0	3	0	0	0	2	0	0	0	2	0	14	0
120–124	0	0	0	0	0	0	1	0	0	0	0	0	1	0	0	0	0	0	2	0	4	0
Total	43	27	98	66	153	98	214	108	210	91	171	61	100	29	68	21	13	0	25	1	1095	502

Apps = Number of Applicants
Adm = Number Admitted
Reflects 98% of the applicant pool.

Florida Coastal School of Law

8787 Baypine Road
Jacksonville, FL 32256
Phone: 904.680.7710; Toll-free: 877.210.2591; Fax: 904.680.7692
E-mail: admissions@fcsl.edu; Website: www.fcsl.edu

ABA Approved Since 2002

The Basics

Type of school	Private
Term	Semester
Application deadline	
Application fee	$50
Financial aid deadline	
Can first year start other than fall?	Yes
Student to faculty ratio	20.3 to 1
Does the university offer:	
housing restricted to law students?	No
graduate housing for which law students are eligible?	No

Faculty and Administrators

	Total Fall	Total Spr	Men Fall	Men Spr	Women Fall	Women Spr	Minorities Fall	Minorities Spr
Full-time	46	42	18	20	28	22	10	7
Other Full-time	0	0	0	0	0	0	0	0
Deans, librarians, & others who teach	12	11	4	4	8	7	2	2
Part-time	34	35	26	26	8	9	2	2
Total	**92**	**88**	**48**	**50**	**44**	**38**	**14**	**11**

Curriculum

	Full-time	Part-time
Typical first-year section size	75	75
Is there typically a "small section" of the first-year class, other than Legal Writing, taught by full-time faculty	No	No
If yes, typical size offered last year		
# of classroom course titles beyond first-year curriculum	162	
# of upper division courses, excluding seminars with an enrollment: Under 25	78	
25–49	52	
50–74	36	
75–99	5	
100+	0	
# of seminars	18	
# of seminar positions available	450	
# of seminar positions filled	221	86
# of positions available in simulation courses	590	
# of simulation positions filled	281	176
# of positions available in faculty supervised clinical courses	86	
# of faculty supervised clinical positions filled	68	7
# involved in field placements	112	12
# involved in law journals	105	14
# involved in interschool competitions	90	5
# of credit hours required to graduate	90	

JD Enrollment and Ethnicity

	Men #	Men %	Women #	Women %	Full-time #	Full-time %	Part-time #	Part-time %	1st-year #	1st-year %	Total #	Total %	JD Degs. Awd.
African Amer.	33	4.8	62	10.4	70	6.6	25	11.8	46	8.2	95	7.4	15
Amer. Indian	10	1.5	5	0.8	14	1.3	1	0.5	9	1.6	15	1.2	6
Asian Amer.	23	3.4	30	5.0	48	4.5	5	2.4	36	6.4	53	4.1	5
Mex. Amer.	2	0.3	2	0.3	4	0.4	0	0.0	4	0.7	4	0.3	0
Puerto Rican	3	0.4	5	0.8	6	0.6	2	0.9	3	0.5	8	0.6	1
Hispanic	24	3.5	34	5.7	44	4.1	14	6.6	35	6.2	58	4.5	7
Total Minority	95	13.9	138	23.2	186	17.4	47	22.2	133	23.7	233	18.2	34
For. Nation.	0	0.0	0	0.0	0	0.0	0	0.0	0	0.0	0	0.0	0
Caucasian	392	57.4	320	53.8	602	56.5	110	51.9	284	50.6	712	55.7	184
Unknown	196	28.7	137	23.0	278	26.1	55	25.9	141	25.1	333	26.1	61
Total	683	53.4	595	46.6	1066	83.4	212	16.6	561	43.9	1278		279

Transfers

Transfers in	7
Transfers out	30

Tuition and Fees

	Resident	Nonresident
Full-time	$27,088	$27,088
Part-time	$21,910	$21,910

Living Expenses

Estimated living expenses for singles

Living on campus	Living off campus	Living at home
N/A	$17,670	$17,670

Florida Coastal School of Law

*ABA
Approved
Since
2002*

GPA and LSAT Scores

	Total	Full-time	Part-time
# of apps	4,940	4,940	0
# of offers	2,365	2,365	0
# of matrics	638	622	16
75% GPA	3.49	3.49	3.51
Median GPA	3.21	3.22	3.05
25% GPA	2.89	2.89	2.83
75% LSAT	154	154	153
Median LSAT	151	151	150
25% LSAT	149	149	148

Grants and Scholarships (from prior year)

	Total		Full-time		Part-time	
	#	%	#	%	#	%
Total # of students	1,040		824		216	
Total # receiving grants	513	49.3	475	57.6	38	17.6
Less than 1/2 tuition	422	40.6	389	47.2	33	15.3
Half to full tuition	89	8.6	85	10.3	4	1.9
Full tuition	0	0.0	0	0.0	0	0.0
More than full tuition	2	0.2	1	0.1	1	0.5
Median grant amount			$5,000		$4,000	

Informational and Library Resources

# of volumes and volume equivalents	220,381
# of titles	104,402
# of active serial subscriptions	3,052
Study seating capacity inside the library	507
# of full-time professional librarians	10
Hours per week library is open	104
# of open, wired connections available to students	3,060
# of networked computers available for use by students	76
# of simultaneous wireless users	1,000
Require computer?	No

JD Attrition (from prior year)

	Academic	Other	Total	
	#	#	#	%
1st year	48	45	93	23.7
2nd year	25	5	30	8.3
3rd year	4	0	4	1.4
4th year	0	0	0	0.0

Employment (9 months after graduation)

	Total	Percentage
Employment status known	158	98.1
Employment status unknown	3	1.9
Employed	142	89.9
Pursuing graduate degrees	3	1.9
Unemployed seeking employment	3	1.9
Unemployed not seeking employment	1	0.6
Unemployed and studying for the bar	9	5.7

Type of Employment

	Total	Percentage
# employed in law firms	71	50.0
# employed in business and industry	23	16.2
# employed in government	25	17.6
# employed in public interest	18	12.7
# employed as judicial clerks	3	2.1
# employed in academia	1	0.7

Geographic Location

	Total	Percentage
# employed in state	107	75.4
# employed in foreign countries	0	0.0
# of states where employed	19	

Bar Passage Rates

Jurisdiction	Florida		
Exam	Sum 05	Win 06	Total
# from school taking bar for the first time	83	57	140
School's pass rate for all first-time takers	82%	77%	80%
State's pass rate for all first-time takers	71%	73%	71%

Florida Coastal School of Law

8787 Baypine Road
Jacksonville, FL 32256
Phone: 904.680.7710; Toll-free: 877.210.2591; Fax: 904.680.7692
E-mail: admissions@fcsl.edu; Website: www.fcsl.edu

■ Introduction

Florida Coastal School of Law (FCSL) was founded upon and is dedicated to the proposition that your future is our first and foremost priority. The student-centered ethos that defines and permeates our institution responds to the reality that today's law school graduates confront a world of unprecedented challenge and change. Professional success in the twenty-first century hinges not only upon academic achievement, but also upon accelerated development of practical skills and effective appreciation of the imperatives of technology, globalization, and multiculturalism.

Until recently, law school graduates could enter the legal profession with the luxury of growing and polishing practical skills during their early years of practice. Today's market realities, however, demand immediate productivity and performance. Knowing that traditional indicators of and grounds for academic excellence no longer accurately predict professional success, we offer a learning partnership that aims to develop the broad spectrum of competencies you must have to succeed.

At the core of our program is a course of study designed to help you effectively reach your career goals after graduation. Formal instruction is delivered by a faculty composed of individuals with records of professional achievement and a sincere interest in sharing their expertise with you. Consistent with the reality that today's law students require more attention to, support for, and facilitation of their interests, faculty responsibilities do not end with the traditional functions of classroom instruction and scholarship. Each faculty member has mentoring responsibilities that include seeking out opportunities for personal interaction and impact.

At Florida Coastal School of Law, student-centeredness is not empty rhetoric. It is at the core of our philosophy, the basis for our founding, and the predicate for our program, policies, and daily interactions.

We invite you to visit our campus and speak with any member of the law school community, particularly our students, and learn firsthand about the nature of our commitment to your future.

■ Our Students

Student-centeredness, multiculturalism as a norm, and a partnered learning experience that effectively prepares you to meet the challenges of an increasingly competitive world are the cornerstones of your educational experience here. Teaching, mentoring, networking, and getting to know you personally and professionally are responsibilities we take seriously. Multiculturalism as a norm means that diversity is not just our future, it is now. Particularly against the backdrop of modern societal and global realities, multicultural functionality cannot be a mere aspiration. Effective interaction with and appreciation of diverse experiences and lives are essential prerequisites for high achievement both personally and professionally.

■ FCSL's Learning Partnership

A learning partnership means working closely inside and outside the classroom with faculty members who are committed to sharing their expertise, experience, and networks; are eager to learn from your life experience; and aim to develop synergies on the basis of shared opportunity and mutual respect. These qualities are among those that have distinguished FCSL as a law school that takes your aspirations seriously. We believe that our supportive learning environment makes a difference in your educational experience, personal growth, and professional functioning. Our students, more than anyone, can attest to the fact that our words and promises are not empty rhetoric. We urge you not to take our representations at face value, but to call or visit us, meet with our students, and learn firsthand of their experience and enthusiasm.

■ Faculty

The faculty includes not only outstanding legal scholars, but also former judges, trial attorneys, government officials, and corporate leaders who interact with students on a daily basis and bring a practical perspective to the learning process. The vast majority of the faculty at FCSL have at least a decade of practical experience in their respective fields of expertise. We consider this an essential factor in developing well-rounded graduates capable of meeting the challenges of the twenty-first century.

■ Curriculum

The infusion curriculum is a program that brings professional responsibility, ethics, values, skills training, multiculturalism, and internationalism into all first-year and some advanced courses as a part of the pedagogical process. Through the use of role-playing, simulations, special problems, and multidiscipline presentations, students directly experience the lawyering process, observe the interaction of law with other disciplines, and acquire an appreciation for the relationship of law to the client, the court, and the community.

■ Center for Law and Sports

Florida Coastal School of Law established the Center for Law and Sports in 2005. The center offers students a comprehensive sports law curriculum in which to obtain a certificate in sports law and concentrate their legal studies on the rapidly changing and dynamic sports industry. A variety of unique and specialized course offerings are taught by three dedicated full-time sports law faculty members, as well as adjunct faculty employed in the sports industry. Students enrolled in the certificate program may also have the unique opportunity to participate in an internship with a sports organization or university athletic department. The law school also participates annually in a national sports law moot court competition.

There is a collective body of specific areas of the law (for example, antitrust law, labor law, tort law, constitutional law, intellectual property law, and contract law) that apply within the business of sports. Lawyers working in the sports industry, whether at the amateur or professional level, must be well-versed as to how different areas of the law come together and apply to various legal and business issues confronted on a daily basis. The center is dedicated to preparing students to handle these challenges, and to serving as a local and national resource for sports industry attorneys and professionals, sports law academics, and the media.

■ Closing Invitation from the Dean

Florida Coastal School of Law has been described as "the most exciting experiment in American legal education." This description reflects a growing sense of enthusiasm within legal education and the legal profession for our institution's unique attributes. Foremost among these is the proposition that students are our overarching priority.

Florida Coastal School of Law was founded upon and is defined by the premise that students are the axis upon which our school turns. This originating premise differentiates us from institutions where other priorities make faculty remote from and inaccessible, or even indifferent, to students. FCSL has its share of distinguished and prolific scholars. The entire faculty is composed, however, of persons with extensive experience in the real world of lawyering who consciously have rejected an ivory-tower existence. They have a common commitment and the know-how to provide a legal education that enables you to hit the ground running as a lawyer when you graduate.

Every law school has a mission and underlying value system that define it programmatically and culturally. Ours are rooted in the premise of student-centeredness. The result is a supportive learning environment where students are seen, heard, listened and responded to, and the administration's, faculty's, and staff's commitment to them and their future is pervasive. Student-centeredness is why FCSL is dedicated to programs and policies that will secure the institution's prominence and increase the value of your degree, maintaining an environment in which multiculturalism is a norm rather than aspiration, infusing practical skills and international perspective into its program of study, and offering a faculty of teachers and mentors who engage you in a learning partnership that graduates lawyers rather than law students.

To appreciate the difference that these student-centered qualities can make for your future, I encourage you to contact any member of our law school community. I urge you to meet with our graduates or current students, particularly those who have transferred from other law schools. You will be impressed by what they will confirm as the value of learning in an environment that is actively, sincerely, and sharply focused upon your life and aspirations. I welcome the opportunity to meet and discuss our interest in and commitment to your future.

Applicant Profile

Florida Coastal School of Law

LSAT Score	GPA								
	3.75 +	3.50–3.74	3.25–3.49	3.00–3.24	2.75–2.99	2.50–2.74	2.25–2.49	2.00–2.24	Below 2.00
175–180									
170–174									
165–169									
160–164									
155–159									
150–154									
145–149									
140–144									
135–139									
130–134									
125–129									
120–124									

■ Good Possibility ▨ Possible □ Unlikely

University of Florida, Fredric G. Levin College of Law

PO Box 117622, 141 Bruton-Geer Hall
Gainesville, FL 32611-7622
Phone: 352.273.0890, Toll-free: 877.429.1297; Fax: 352.392.4087
E-mail: admissions@law.ufl.edu; Website: www.law.ufl.edu

*ABA
Approved
Since
1925*

The Basics

Type of school	Public
Term	Semester
Application deadline	1/15
Application fee	$30
Financial aid deadline	3/15
Can first year start other than fall?	No
Student to faculty ratio	17.6 to 1
Does the university offer:	
housing restricted to law students?	No
graduate housing for which law students are eligible?	No

Faculty and Administrators

	Total		Men		Women		Minorities	
	Fall	Spr	Fall	Spr	Fall	Spr	Fall	Spr
Full-time	61	63	30	32	31	31	8	7
Other Full-time	7	7	6	6	1	1	1	1
Deans, librarians, & others who teach	9	9	6	6	3	3	0	0
Part-time	38	38	29	26	9	12	1	1
Total	115	117	71	70	44	47	10	9

Curriculum

	Full-time	Part-time
Typical first-year section size	115	0
Is there typically a "small section" of the first-year class, other than Legal Writing, taught by full-time faculty	No	No
If yes, typical size offered last year		
# of classroom course titles beyond first-year curriculum	140	

# of upper division courses, excluding seminars with an enrollment:		
	Under 25	89
	25–49	55
	50–74	32
	75–99	5
	100+	13

# of seminars	41	
# of seminar positions available	627	
# of seminar positions filled	521	0
# of positions available in simulation courses	276	
# of simulation positions filled	230	0
# of positions available in faculty supervised clinical courses	211	
# of faculty supervised clinical positions filled	193	0
# involved in field placements	199	0
# involved in law journals	296	0
# involved in interschool competitions	120	0
# of credit hours required to graduate	88	

JD Enrollment and Ethnicity

	Men		Women		Full-time		Part-time		1st-year		Total		JD Degs. Awd.
	#	%	#	%	#	%	#	%	#	%	#	%	
African Amer.	23	3.2	57	9.0	80	5.9	0	0.0	26	5.8	80	5.9	31
Amer. Indian	1	0.1	2	0.3	3	0.2	0	0.0	1	0.2	3	0.2	1
Asian Amer.	32	4.4	36	5.7	68	5.0	0	0.0	21	4.7	68	5.0	13
Mex. Amer.	0	0.0	0	0.0	0	0.0	0	0.0	0	0.0	0	0.0	0
Puerto Rican	0	0.0	0	0.0	0	0.0	0	0.0	0	0.0	0	0.0	0
Hispanic	57	7.8	71	11.2	128	9.4	0	0.0	45	10.0	128	9.4	38
Total Minority	113	15.5	166	26.1	279	20.5	0	0.0	93	20.7	279	20.5	83
For. Nation.	30	4.1	21	3.3	51	3.7	0	0.0	20	4.4	51	3.7	2
Caucasian	585	80.4	449	70.6	1034	75.8	0	0.0	337	74.9	1034	75.8	257
Unknown	0	0.0	0	0.0	0	0.0	0	0.0	0	0.0	0	0.0	28
Total	728	53.4	636	46.6	1364	100.0	0	0.0	450	33.0	1364		370

Transfers

Transfers in	0
Transfers out	2

Tuition and Fees

	Resident	Nonresident
Full-time	$9,861	$29,227
Part-time	$0	$0

Living Expenses

Estimated living expenses for singles

Living on campus	Living off campus	Living at home
$12,620	$12,730	$6,620

University of Florida, Fredric G. Levin College of Law

*ABA
Approved
Since
1925*

GPA and LSAT Scores

	Total	Full-time	Part-time
# of apps	2,535	2,535	0
# of offers	1,044	1,044	0
# of matrics	447	447	0
75% GPA	3.83	3.83	0.00
Median GPA	3.66	3.66	0.00
25% GPA	3.42	3.42	0.00
75% LSAT	161	161	0
Median LSAT	159	159	0
25% LSAT	155	155	0

Grants and Scholarships (from prior year)

	Total		Full-time		Part-time	
	#	%	#	%	#	%
Total # of students	1,156		1,156		0	
Total # receiving grants	241	20.8	241	20.8	0	0.0
Less than 1/2 tuition	197	17.0	197	17.0	0	0.0
Half to full tuition	37	3.2	37	3.2	0	0.0
Full tuition	6	0.5	6	0.5	0	0.0
More than full tuition	1	0.1	1	0.1	0	0.0
Median grant amount			$3,000		$0	

Informational and Library Resources

# of volumes and volume equivalents	628,749
# of titles	205,221
# of active serial subscriptions	8,024
Study seating capacity inside the library	765
# of full-time professional librarians	9
Hours per week library is open	94
# of open, wired connections available to students	2
# of networked computers available for use by students	14
# of simultaneous wireless users	3,000
Require computer?	Yes

JD Attrition (from prior year)

	Academic	Other	Total	
	#	#	#	%
1st year	0	2	2	0.5
2nd year	0	2	2	0.5
3rd year	0	0	0	0.0
4th year	0	0	0	0.0

Employment (9 months after graduation)

	Total	Percentage
Employment status known	377	100.0
Employment status unknown	0	0.0
Employed	329	87.3
Pursuing graduate degrees	20	5.3
Unemployed seeking employment	2	0.5
Unemployed not seeking employment	17	4.5
Unemployed and studying for the bar	9	2.4

Type of Employment

# employed in law firms	190	57.8
# employed in business and industry	30	9.1
# employed in government	64	19.5
# employed in public interest	25	7.6
# employed as judicial clerks	18	5.5
# employed in academia	1	0.3

Geographic Location

# employed in state	272	82.7
# employed in foreign countries	2	0.6
# of states where employed		12

Bar Passage Rates

Jurisdiction	Florida		
Exam	Sum 05	Win 06	Total
# from school taking bar for the first time	207	150	357
School's pass rate for all first-time takers	79%	87%	83%
State's pass rate for all first-time takers	71%	73%	71%

University of Florida, Fredric G. Levin College of Law

Assistant Dean for Admissions, PO Box 117622, 141 Bruton-Geer Hall
Gainesville, FL 32611-7622
Phone: 352.273.0890, Toll-free: 877.429.1297; Fax: 352.392.4087
E-mail: admissions@law.ufl.edu; Website: www.law.ufl.edu

■ Introduction

The University of Florida Levin College of Law is one of the nation's most comprehensive and widely respected law schools. It was founded in 1909, has been a member of the Association of American Law Schools since 1920, and was approved by the American Bar Association in 1925. It is among the nation's top 20 public and top 50 overall law schools, and efforts such as the $25 million expansion and renovation project completed in 2005 and new trial advocacy center scheduled for 2007 are steadily enhancing its already strong programs and reputation.

The college's faculty are highly accomplished scholars, educators, and practitioners whose broad knowledge base and teaching skills challenge each student to reach new heights of intellectual achievement. Many are authors of treatises, casebooks, or major books used by law schools and practitioners throughout the nation, as well as hundreds of articles in law reviews and specialty journals.

The law school also is known for graduating state and national legal, political, business, government, and educational leaders, and for nurturing a strong alumni network. UF law graduates include four ABA presidents, numerous federal and state judges, partners in major national and international law firms, members of Congress and the Cabinet, governors, and state legislators. Alumni support has built the endowment into one of the largest in the country for public law schools. This, combined with the state's financial assistance, allows the college to remain affordable while its academic quality rivals many of the best-known private colleges.

The University of Florida is one of the nation's largest and most comprehensive universities, is a member of the prestigious Association of American Universities and is recognized as one of the nation's leading research universities by the Carnegie Commission on Higher Education. The campus occupies 2,000 acres, mostly within the city of Gainesville's 118,000 population urban area in North Central Florida. The area is consistently ranked among the best places to live in America, with extensive educational, cultural, and recreational offerings.

■ Programs and Curriculum

The Levin College of Law offers students both strong fundamentals and a diverse offering of specializations and interdisciplinary options. The activities and scholarship of approximately 80 full-time faculty allow for interesting programs and curricular concentrations. More than 80 courses and 15–20 seminars are offered each semester. Students can earn a certificate in Estates and Trusts Practice, Intellectual Property Law, Environmental and Land Use Law, Family Law, or International and Comparative Law. The Levin College of Law also offers one of the most extensive joint-degree programs of any US law school. Among the more popular joint-degree tracks are Business Administration, Public Health, Accounting, and Health Administration.

Semesters begin in August and January, and the summer term begins in May. The first-year curriculum is required, as is a second-year drafting course. All students must complete a major senior-year research and writing project.

The richness and diversity of the school's faculty, student body, and course offerings also are strengthened by the presence of its top ranked Graduate Tax Program—leading to an LLM in Taxation, LLM in International Taxation, or SJD in Taxation—as well as its LLM in Comparative Law Program for foreign lawyers from countries around the globe. The college's innovative centers and institutes include the Center for Estate and Elder Law Planning, Center for Children and Families, Institute for Dispute Resolution, Center for the Study of Race and Race Relations, and Center for Governmental Responsibility.

UF is a major hub for international legal programs and has decades of experience and relationships in Latin America, Asia, and Europe. Students can gain hands-on experience in litigation, negotiation, mediation, client relations, and government service at the highest levels through a broad array of courses, study abroad opportunities, externships, pro bono work, and clinical programs.

■ Student/Extracurricular Activities

More than 40 active extracurricular organizations at the law school help students develop valuable skills and professional contacts as well as make a positive difference in the community. Students can earn credits and polish their legal skills through cocurricular organizations such as *Florida Law Review, Florida Journal of International Law, University of Florida Journal of Law and Public Policy, Journal of Technology Law and Policy,* and trophy-winning US and international moot court and trial teams.

■ Library and Facilities

Following completion in 2005 of a major expansion and renovation project, the Lawton Chiles Legal Information Center is now the largest academic law library in the Southeast and among the top 20 in the nation in terms of space. The expanded library offers comfortable study areas, reading rooms, computer training labs, multimedia workstations, and reference rooms for use by students and faculty. Two new three-story education towers feature spacious, state-of-the-art classrooms equipped to offer the latest in teaching technology, including desktop outlets for laptop use, wireless Internet access, and "smart podia."

Ground will be broken in 2007 for a new advocacy center projected to place the college at the forefront of major law schools providing students with sophisticated facilities and services. The two-and-a-half story complex will feature a fully functional trial and appellate courtroom with a 120-seat gallery and bench for seven judges, as well as offices and accommodations for distinguished scholars and visitors.

■ Career Services

Professional counselors in the college's Center for Career Services offer a wide variety of services and programs to help students plan a self-directed career search and develop marketing skills that will serve them for many years to come. Staff members help students develop legal credentials, capitalize on their diverse strengths and experiences, explore legal and nontraditional career paths, and find summer internships, externships, and clerkships as well as permanent postgraduation employment. They also help link students with alumni, practitioners, and the community. UF Law continues to host one of the South's largest on-campus recruiting programs, which brings almost 250 employers to campus each year. Other resources include workshops and seminars on practical career skills, individual career and job search counseling, networking events on and off campus, and a Web-based job bank with downloadable handouts, samples, and forms.

■ Admission

Applications for fall 2008 are due by January 15. Early completion of applications is strongly recommended (but not more than one year in advance). The LSAT and LSDAS are required, and applicants must take the LSAT prior to the application deadline (no later than December). Applicants must provide a personal statement and résumé, and up to four evaluation letters are requested. Students must have earned a bachelor's degree from an accredited college or university prior to enrolling.

The admissions staff and the faculty admissions committee base their decisions on the applicant's academic credentials, including LSAT score, UGPA, level of writing skills, breadth of studies, and on other information including but not limited to the applicant's work and other life experience, leadership experience, depth of particular interest, and any other aspect of an applicant's background suggesting a suitability for the study and practice of law.

Students may transfer in August, January, or May from ABA-approved law schools, but only applicants who have completed the required first-year full-time curriculum before enrolling at UF and who are in the upper one-third of their class will be considered. A transfer certification form from the dean is required and no more than 29 semester hours will be transferred.

The law school seeks to enroll approximately 400 (full-time only) students each fall. The college places great importance on obtaining a diverse class, and actively recruits minority students. To arrange a meeting or tour of the law school, contact the Admissions Office.

■ Expenses and Financial Aid

The 2006–2007 semester credit-hour fees were $329 for Florida residents and $975 for nonresidents. Additional expenses totaled approximately $12,830 for books, supplies, laptop computer (required), clothing, room, board, transportation, and insurance.

Merit-based and merit/need-based scholarships and grants and short- and long-term loans (FAFSA required) are available to qualified students. Merit awards are based on information collected in the application for admission. To be considered for merit/need-based scholarships and need-based grants, an applicant must have the electronic FAFSA results and the application for need-based scholarships and grants on file with the Levin College of Law by April 7, 2008. The application can be downloaded online, and also is sent out by the admissions office following acceptance.

Address inquiries to: Office of Admissions, University of Florida Levin College of Law, PO Box 117622, Gainesville, FL 32611-7622, or *admissions@law.ufl.edu*.

■ Housing

Housing is available for single students in dormitories and for families in university apartments. Plentiful off-campus housing is available. New and current UF law students may access the UF College of Law Roommate Referral System online.

Applicant Profile

University of Florida, Fredric G. Levin College of Law
This grid includes only applicants who earned 120–180 LSAT scores under standard administrations. Data reflects 99% of the fall candidate pool.

LSAT Score	3.75 +		3.50–3.74		3.25–3.49		3.00–3.24		2.75–2.99		2.50–2.74		2.25–2.49		2.00–2.24		Below 2.00		No GPA		Total	
	Apps	Adm	Apps	Adm	Apps	Adm	Apps	Adm	Apps	Adm	Apps	Adm	Apps	Adm	Apps	Adm	Apps	Adm	Apps	Adm	Apps	Adm
175–180	1	1	2	2	0	0	0	0	1	1	1	0	0	0	0	0	0	0	0	0	5	4
170–174	12	12	5	5	4	4	5	4	4	3	3	2	0	0	1	1	0	0	0	0	34	31
165–169	52	51	49	45	22	21	17	16	13	9	6	3	2	1	0	0	0	0	1	1	162	147
160–164	127	120	133	116	115	72	68	32	25	5	8	2	7	1	1	0	0	0	4	1	488	349
155–159	166	134	248	105	196	48	111	18	43	7	18	2	12	0	2	0	1	0	6	6	803	320
150–154	114	59	163	36	164	35	125	9	53	5	19	1	9	0	1	0	1	0	6	1	655	146
145–149	49	14	65	7	79	9	63	4	26	1	16	1	9	0	2	0	0	0	6	2	315	38
140–144	12	3	40	2	31	0	34	2	24	0	18	0	3	0	0	0	1	0	2	0	165	7
135–139	2	0	5	0	9	1	12	1	8	0	5	0	2	0	1	0	0	0	1	0	45	2
130–134	0	0	1	0	7	0	4	0	2	0	3	0	4	0	1	0	0	0	1	0	23	0
125–129	0	0	0	0	0	0	1	0	0	0	0	0	0	0	1	0	0	0	0	0	2	0
120–124	0	0	0	0	0	0	0	0	0	0	0	0	0	0	0	0	0	0	0	0	0	0
Total	535	394	711	318	627	190	440	86	199	31	97	11	48	2	10	1	3	0	27	11	2697	1044

Apps = Number of Applicants
Adm = Number Admitted

Florida International University College of Law

RDB 1055
Miami, FL 33186
Phone: 305.348.8006; Fax: 305.348.2965
E-mail: lawadmit@fiu.edu; Website: http://law.fiu.edu/

*ABA
Approved
Since
2004*

The Basics

Type of school	Public
Term	Semester
Application deadline	5/1
Application fee	$20
Financial aid deadline	3/1
Can first year start other than fall?	No
Student to faculty ratio	15.7 to 1
Does the university offer:	
housing restricted to law students?	Yes
graduate housing for which law students are eligible?	Yes

Faculty and Administrators

	Total		Men		Women		Minorities	
	Fall	Spr	Fall	Spr	Fall	Spr	Fall	Spr
Full-time	18	14	12	8	6	6	8	6
Other Full-time	4	4	1	1	3	3	2	2
Deans, librarians, & others who teach	7	5	5	3	2	2	4	2
Part-time	6	9	4	7	2	1	1	4
Total	**35**	**32**	**22**	**19**	**13**	**12**	**15**	**14**

Curriculum

	Full-time	Part-time
Typical first-year section size	82	56
Is there typically a "small section" of the first-year class, other than Legal Writing, taught by full-time faculty	No	No
If yes, typical size offered last year		
# of classroom course titles beyond first-year curriculum	71	
# of upper division courses, excluding seminars with an enrollment: Under 25	42	
25–49	26	
50–74	4	
75–99	0	
100+	0	
# of seminars	8	
# of seminar positions available	128	
# of seminar positions filled	71	30
# of positions available in simulation courses	120	
# of simulation positions filled	88	29
# of positions available in faculty supervised clinical courses	64	
# of faculty supervised clinical positions filled	47	11
# involved in field placements	15	3
# involved in law journals	22	7
# involved in interschool competitions	16	7
# of credit hours required to graduate	90	

JD Enrollment and Ethnicity

	Men		Women		Full-time		Part-time		1st-year		Total		JD Degs. Awd.
	#	%	#	%	#	%	#	%	#	%	#	%	
African Amer.	11	5.3	26	14.9	16	6.8	21	14.5	20	11.4	37	9.7	7
Amer. Indian	1	0.5	1	0.6	1	0.4	1	0.7	0	0.0	2	0.5	0
Asian Amer.	5	2.4	4	2.3	8	3.4	1	0.7	3	1.7	9	2.4	3
Mex. Amer.	0	0.0	0	0.0	0	0.0	0	0.0	0	0.0	0	0.0	0
Puerto Rican	0	0.0	0	0.0	0	0.0	0	0.0	0	0.0	0	0.0	0
Hispanic	83	40.1	75	42.9	95	40.1	63	43.4	75	42.6	158	41.4	32
Total Minority	100	48.3	106	60.6	120	50.6	86	59.3	98	55.7	206	53.9	42
For. Nation.	0	0.0	0	0.0	0	0.0	0	0.0	0	0.0	0	0.0	0
Caucasian	98	47.3	63	36.0	106	44.7	55	37.9	67	38.1	161	42.1	37
Unknown	9	4.3	6	3.4	11	4.6	4	2.8	11	6.3	15	3.9	6
Total	207	54.2	175	45.8	237	62.0	145	38.0	176	46.1	382		85

Transfers

Transfers in	7
Transfers out	2

Tuition and Fees

	Resident	Nonresident
Full-time	$8,801	$23,061
Part-time	$6,011	$15,671

Living Expenses

Estimated living expenses for singles

Living on campus	Living off campus	Living at home
$12,800	$14,052	$8,608

Florida

Florida International University C...

RDB 1055
Miami, FL 33186
Phone: 305.348.8006; Fax: 305.348.2965
E-mail: lawadmit@fiu.edu; Website: htt...

ABA
Approved
Since
2004

GPA and LSAT Scores

	Total	Full-time	Part-time
# of apps	1,856	1,481	375
# of offers	423	320	103
# of matrics	159	104	55
75% GPA	3.59	3.63	3.50
Median GPA	3.30	3.31	3.27
25% GPA	2.93	2.99	2.86
75% LSAT	156	156	155
Median LSAT	154	155	152
25% LSAT	151	153	150

Grants and Scholarships (from prior year)

	Total		Full-time		Part-time	
	#	%	#	%	#	%
Total # of students	332		176		156	
Total # receiving grants	115	34.6	101	57.4	14	9.0
Less than 1/2 tuition	63	19.0	53	30.1	10	6.4
Half to full tuition	48	14.5	44	25.0	4	2.6
Full tuition	1	0.3	1	0.6	0	0.0
More than full tuition	3	0.9	3	1.7	0	0.0
Median grant amount			$4,505		$2,000	

Informational and Library Resources

# of volumes and volume equivalents	198,206
# of titles	79,323
# of active serial subscriptions	1,179
Study seating capacity inside the library	322
# of full-time professional librarians	6
Hours per week library is open	110
# of open, wired connections available to students	40
# of networked computers available for use by students	46
# of simultaneous wireless users	1,850
Require computer?	No

Introduction

The Florida International...
established by an act of...
first class was admit...
College of Law w...
American Bar A...
be eligible to...
50 states a...
full app...
Flo...

Employment status known	47	96.1
Employment status unknown	2	3.9
Employed	41	83.7
Pursuing graduate degrees	2	4.1
Unemployed seeking employment	0	0.0
Unemployed not seeking employment	2	4.1
Unemployed and studying for the bar	4	8.2

Type of Employment

# employed in law firms	28	68.3
# employed in business and industry	2	4.9
# employed in government	4	9.8
# employed in public interest	6	14.6
# employed as judicial clerks	1	2.4
# employed in academia	0	0.0

Geographic Location

# employed in state	37	90.2
# employed in foreign countries	0	0.0
# of states where employed		4

Bar Passage Rates

Jurisdiction	Florida			New York		
Exam	Sum 05	Win 06	Total	Sum 05	Win 06	Total
# from school taking bar for the first time	41	22	63	1	0	1
School's pass rate for all first-time takers	73%	86%	78%	100%		100%
State's pass rate for all first-time takers	71%	73%	71%	76%	61%	74%

College of Law

http://law.fiu.edu/

University College of Law was
the Florida legislature in June 2000. Its
ed in the fall of 2002. In August 2004, the
s awarded provisional accreditation by the
ssociation, assuring that its graduates would
apply for admission to the practice of law in all
d the District of Columbia. The law school received
roval by the ABA in December 2006.

rida International University is a public research
versity which enrolls approximately 38,000 students, most
n its beautiful University Park campus where the College of
Law is located. This campus is the site of the new
state-of-the-art law building designed by nationally and
internationally renowned architect Robert A. M. Stern. The
campus enjoys nearby access to South Florida's beaches,
Everglades National Park, and the Florida Keys.

The College of Law reflects the diverse character and the
international perspective of the city of Miami. The curriculum
incorporates important developments in the globalization of
both public and private law. The academic program takes a
pervasive approach to both international and comparative law,
incorporating their perspectives into all domestic law classes.

■ Curriculum and Special Programs

The FIU College of Law's academic program, while devoted to
all the historic building block components of an excellent
American legal education, places special emphasis on
international and comparative law. The required curriculum
includes a three-hour, first-year course entitled Introduction to
International and Comparative Law. Further, all domestic law
courses include an international or comparative law
dimension. This pervasive approach to international and
comparative law encourages students to analyze legal
systemic, political, economic, social, and other cultural
differences that may contribute to different legal treatment of
comparable problems in different countries. The College of
Law offers foreign summer programs in Sevilla, Spain, and Rio
de Janeiro, Brazil.

The curriculum also emphasizes instruction in the legal
skills and values of the profession. The Legal Skills and
Values Program combines demanding traditional instruction
in legal research and writing with an introduction to other
lawyering skills, like interviewing and counseling, and issues
of professionalism.

The Clinical Program advances the law school's goals
of educating lawyers for the ethical and effective practice of
law and of promoting community service through the
representation of real clients. Presently, there are three clinics
available, the Carlos A. Costa Immigration and Human Rights
Clinic, the Community Development Clinic, and the Criminal
Law Clinic.

As a public, urban law school, the College of Law is
committed to serving the community of which it is a part by
educating future lawyers who will understand the value—to
the community and to them personally—of helping those in
need. In recognition of this important mission, students must
satisfy a community service requirement.

As the state of Florida's public research university in South
Florida, FIU offers a broad range of high quality, graduate-level
degree programs. Law students interested in interdisciplinary
study may take advantage of these curricula through one of the
following joint-degree programs: JD/Master of Business
Administration, JD/Master of International Business,
JD/Master of Latin American and Caribbean Studies,
JD/Master of Public Administration, JD/MS in Psychology,
JD/Master of Social Work, JD/MS in Criminal Justice, and
JD/Master of Science in Environmental Sciences.

■ Admission

The FIU College of Law offers both a full-time day and
part-time evening program. The review of applications is done
on a rolling basis. An LSDAS report, three letters of
recommendation, and a personal statement are required.

While a prospective student's academic record and LSAT
performance are weighted heavily in the evaluative process,
the Admissions Committee considers other factors, including
leadership ability, commitment to public service, command of
global issues, work history, military service, any history of
criminality or academic misconduct, and evidence of obstacles
that an applicant may have overcome (for example, English is
not the applicant's native language, discrimination, economic
or family hardship, and severe medical conditions, etc.). The
Admissions Committee encourages each applicant to answer
all questions with candor, detail, and, where appropriate, to
give specific examples of relevant background experiences.

Transfer students from other ABA-approved law schools
may apply if they are in good standing at their current
institutions. Visit our website at *http://law.fiu.edu/* for
additional information.

■ Financial Aid

The primary financial aid resources available to students are
loans and need- or merit-based scholarships. Students must
apply for financial aid (FAFSA) to be considered for any type
of loan or need-based scholarships. No separate application is
needed for merit-based scholarships. Eligible students will be
considered based on the information provided in their
admission application. Financial aid is granted on an annual
basis, and awards are subject to student eligibility and
availability of funds. Tuition is comparable to other Florida
state-supported law schools at $292 per credit for Florida
residents and $751 per credit for nonresidents. An additional
$16,300 (approximate) can be expected to cover room and
board, books, transportation, and personal expenses. Please
call 305.348.8006 for further information.

■ Library

The Law Library supports the law school curriculum and
research of its students and faculty. It contains approximately
200,000 volumes in book and microform format. The Law
Library also provides law students with a full range of
electronic legal information resources, including Westlaw,
LexisNexis, and an extensive array of Web-based databases.
When doing cross-discipline research, law students may use

the FIU Green Library's 1.5 million volumes and extensive electronic resources. The Law Library is staffed by seven professional librarians, three with JD degrees. In addition to a comprehensive collection of core US materials, the library is developing an extensive collection of international, comparative, and foreign law materials, with a particular focus on Latin America and the Caribbean, international trade, and the workings of international law institutions.

■ Career Planning and Placement

The Office of Career Planning and Placement is committed to providing law students with the skills and resources necessary to identify their career goals and assisting students in tailoring strategies for reaching those goals. The office facilitates both on- and off-campus recruitment for summer and permanent legal positions as well as an active internship program. Other services include individual career counseling sessions; workshops and handbooks regarding résumé preparation, interview skills and techniques, and job searches; and mock interviews with local attorneys.

■ Student Activities

Success in law school involves more than just intellectual curiosity and a sense of purpose. It involves the refining of time management skills, handling stress proactively, and forging relationships with faculty and peers. It also involves making the best possible use of available services and opportunities. Students bring a wealth of distinctive educational and professional experiences to the College of Law. However, they all share a common interest and goal: service to the law school, the local community, and the profession. Together with the support of the faculty and the administration, students have created a number of organizations and cocurricular activities reflective of this commitment. In its brief but productive history, the College of Law has established the student-edited *Law Review*; an award-winning moot court program, competing locally and nationally against teams throughout the country; and 15 student organizations, including the Student Bar Association.

Applicant Profile

The Florida International University College of Law Admissions Committee seeks to enroll a diverse group of students who have demonstrated academic and personal achievement. While a prospective student's academic record and LSAT performance are weighted heavily in the evaluative process, the Admissions Committee considers other factors, including leadership ability, commitment to public service, command of global issues, work history, military service, any history of criminality or academic misconduct, and evidence of obstacles that an applicant may have overcome (for example, English is not the applicant's native language, discrimination, economic or family hardship, severe medical condition, disability, etc.).

The Florida State University College of Law

425 West Jefferson Street
Tallahassee, FL 32306-1601
Phone: 850.644.3787; Fax: 850.644.5487
E-mail: admissions@law.fsu.edu; Website: www.law.fsu.edu

ABA
Approved
Since
1968

The Basics

Type of school	Public
Term	Semester
Application deadline	3/15
Application fee	$30
Financial aid deadline	2/15
Can first year start other than fall?	No
Student to faculty ratio	13.8 to 1
Does the university offer:	
housing restricted to law students?	No
graduate housing for which law students are eligible?	Yes

Faculty and Administrators

	Total		Men		Women		Minorities	
	Fall	Spr	Fall	Spr	Fall	Spr	Fall	Spr
Full-time	44	46	27	28	17	18	3	5
Other Full-time	0	0	0	0	0	0	0	0
Deans, librarians, & others who teach	13	12	3	3	10	9	2	2
Part-time	26	39	19	25	7	14	1	2
Total	83	97	49	56	34	41	6	9

Curriculum

		Full-time	Part-time
Typical first-year section size		92	0
Is there typically a "small section" of the first-year class, other than Legal Writing, taught by full-time faculty		No	No
If yes, typical size offered last year			
# of classroom course titles beyond first-year curriculum		110	
# of upper division courses, excluding seminars with an enrollment:	Under 25	66	
	25–49	33	
	50–74	13	
	75–99	9	
	100+	2	
# of seminars		29	
# of seminar positions available		621	
# of seminar positions filled		366	0
# of positions available in simulation courses		675	
# of simulation positions filled		580	0
# of positions available in faculty supervised clinical courses		55	
# of faculty supervised clinical positions filled	52		0
# involved in field placements	112		0
# involved in law journals	172		0
# involved in interschool competitions	60		0
# of credit hours required to graduate		88	

JD Enrollment and Ethnicity

	Men		Women		Full-time		Part-time		1st-year		Total		JD Degs. Awd.
	#	%	#	%	#	%	#	%	#	%	#	%	
African Amer.	14	3.0	29	9.5	43	5.6	0	0.0	13	6.7	43	5.6	13
Amer. Indian	5	1.1	1	0.3	6	0.8	0	0.0	0	0.0	6	0.8	2
Asian Amer.	16	3.5	17	5.6	33	4.3	0	0.0	6	3.1	33	4.3	12
Mex. Amer.	0	0.0	1	0.3	1	0.1	0	0.0	0	0.0	1	0.1	0
Puerto Rican	5	1.1	7	2.3	12	1.6	0	0.0	3	1.5	12	1.6	4
Hispanic	26	5.7	22	7.2	48	6.3	0	0.0	9	4.6	48	6.3	15
Total Minority	66	14.3	77	25.2	143	18.7	0	0.0	31	15.9	143	18.7	46
For. Nation.	5	1.1	7	2.3	12	1.6	0	0.0	4	2.1	12	1.6	3
Caucasian	375	81.5	218	71.5	593	77.5	0	0.0	151	77.4	593	77.5	195
Unknown	14	3.0	3	1.0	17	2.2	0	0.0	9	4.6	17	2.2	0
Total	460	60.1	305	39.9	765	100.0	0	0.0	195	25.5	765		244

Transfers

Transfers in	59
Transfers out	11

Tuition and Fees

	Resident	Nonresident
Full-time	$9,837	$29,849
Part-time	$0	$0

Living Expenses

Estimated living expenses for singles

Living on campus	Living off campus	Living at home
$16,500	$16,500	$16,500

The Florida State University College of Law

*ABA
Approved
Since
1968*

GPA and LSAT Scores

	Total	Full-time	Part-time
# of apps	3,313	3,313	0
# of offers	806	806	0
# of matrics	196	196	0
75% GPA	3.74	3.74	0.00
Median GPA	3.46	3.46	0.00
25% GPA	3.26	3.26	0.00
75% LSAT	161	161	0
Median LSAT	159	159	0
25% LSAT	158	158	0

Grants and Scholarships (from prior year)

	Total		Full-time		Part-time	
	#	%	#	%	#	%
Total # of students	772		772		0	
Total # receiving grants	260	33.7	260	33.7	0	0.0
Less than 1/2 tuition	226	29.3	226	29.3	0	0.0
Half to full tuition	30	3.9	30	3.9	0	0.0
Full tuition	2	0.3	2	0.3	0	0.0
More than full tuition	2	0.3	2	0.3	0	0.0
Median grant amount			$1,500		$0	

Informational and Library Resources

# of volumes and volume equivalents	510,662
# of titles	199,619
# of active serial subscriptions	3,580
Study seating capacity inside the library	410
# of full-time professional librarians	10
Hours per week library is open	168
# of open, wired connections available to students	0
# of networked computers available for use by students	48
# of simultaneous wireless users	800
Require computer?	Yes

JD Attrition (from prior year)

	Academic	Other	Total	
	#	#	#	%
1st year	1	11	12	4.4
2nd year	0	0	0	0.0
3rd year	1	0	1	0.4
4th year	0	0	0	0.0

Employment (9 months after graduation)

	Total	Percentage
Employment status known	273	99.6
Employment status unknown	1	0.4
Employed	261	95.6
Pursuing graduate degrees	3	1.1
Unemployed seeking employment	1	0.4
Unemployed not seeking employment	8	2.9
Unemployed and studying for the bar	0	0.0
Type of Employment		
# employed in law firms	132	50.6
# employed in business and industry	17	6.5
# employed in government	66	25.3
# employed in public interest	21	8.0
# employed as judicial clerks	7	2.7
# employed in academia	9	3.4
Geographic Location		
# employed in state	211	80.8
# employed in foreign countries	3	1.1
# of states where employed	20	

Bar Passage Rates

Jurisdiction	Florida		
Exam	Sum 05	Win 06	Total
# from school taking bar for the first time	184	34	218
School's pass rate for all first-time takers	77%	91%	79%
State's pass rate for all first-time takers	71%	73%	71%

The Florida State University College of Law

425 West Jefferson Street
Tallahassee, FL 32306-1601
Phone: 850.644.3787; Fax: 850.644.5487
E-mail: admissions@law.fsu.edu; Website: www.law.fsu.edu

■ Introduction

The Florida State University College of Law is widely recognized for both its commitment to teaching and its cutting-edge scholarship. The college subscribes to the idea that the best legal education is the result of a lively dialogue in an intimate learning environment. The law school's distinguished faculty is highly accessible to students and strives to provide a legal education with a personal touch.

The curriculum at the College of Law is continuously evolving to reflect the changes in the practice of law. Environmental and land use law, international law, and business law and economics are among the areas that have received increased emphasis in the curriculum in recent years. Students with an interest in these areas have opportunities to take a rich curriculum with interdisciplinary opportunities, work on student-run legal journals, and participate in extracurricular activities that help hone practical skills.

Tallahassee is also a wonderful community in which to study law. The college is situated blocks from the Florida Capitol, the First District Court of Appeal, the Florida Supreme Court, the United States District Court, and other centers for judicial and administrative activity. All branches of state government are headquartered in Florida's capital city, which is also home to local offices of top law firms from throughout Florida and the nation.

■ Enrollment/Student Body

More than 3,300 applications are received for approximately 230 places in the entering class. The current student body represents 37 states, 10 countries, and 222 undergraduate institutions. The student body is diverse and gifted, and the racial and ethnic mix represents society as a whole. The college prides itself on having a warm and collegial student body, which is also extremely competitive in state and national trial and appellate advocacy competitions.

■ Curriculum

The College of Law's three-year curriculum provides students with a foundational first-year program and a rich and varied offering of upper-level courses, seminars, clinics, and cocurricular opportunities. The curriculum is designed to prepare graduates for the basic demands of legal practice through a broad "liberal arts" approach to curricular offerings supplemented with a wide variety of specialized courses emphasizing the college's strengths in environmental and land use law and international law.

■ Special Programs

The College of Law offers seven joint-degree programs, two certificate programs, and an LLM program for foreign lawyers. The following joint degrees are available: JD/MBA, JD/MPA, JD/MSW, JD/MIS, JD/Master in International Affairs, JD/Master in Urban and Regional Planning, and JD/MS in Library Information Systems. The college offers certificate programs in Environmental, Natural Resources, and Land

Use Law; and in International Law. The certificate programs are rigorous, focused courses of study designed to prepare graduates to work in highly specialized areas of the law. The college also offers an LLM program for foreign lawyers, which provides foreign graduate students trained in law with the opportunity to develop an understanding of the American legal system and the role of law in the United States.

The college offers one of the most extensive clinical externship programs in the United States. Judicial externships are available with state trial and appellate courts, including the Florida Supreme Court and the federal courts. Externship opportunities with government agencies and commissions, the state attorney, the White House, the public defender, and legal services offices are also provided, as well as opportunities abroad with the International Bar Association in London and the International Criminal Tribunal for the former Yugoslavia. The college's Children's Advocacy Center, an in-house legal clinic, offers law students an opportunity to represent children in a variety of legal areas under the supervision of clinical faculty.

The college also sponsors a summer program at Oxford University in England. As the oldest ongoing program in Oxford sponsored by a US law school, it provides students with a unique opportunity to study comparative law and the history of the common law and its institutions in their original setting.

■ Library and Physical Facilities

The College of Law has a wireless Ethernet network that extends throughout the facilities. This provides Internet access to all wireless-capable laptops within range of the college at a speed of 11 megabits per second (over 100 times the speed of a conventional modem).

The physical facilities of the College of Law consist of B.K. Roberts Hall, opened in 1971; a separate, connected law library, opened in 1983; and the Village Green, completed in 1988.

Roberts Hall houses faculty, staff, and student offices; lounges; classrooms; seminar rooms; and a practice courtroom making extensive use of video technology. Both Roberts Hall and the law library comply with all architectural regulations facilitating use for students with disabilities.

The law library's collections are among the most significant law collections in the Southeast. Individual and group study, video viewing, microform reading, and computer use and instruction are available within the law library.

■ Student Activities

One of the most attractive aspects of the College of Law's academic climate is the wide variety of educational and professional opportunities available outside the traditional classroom. The College of Law sponsors *Law Review*, the *Journal of Land Use and Environmental Law*, the *Journal of Transnational Law and Policy*, a nationally recognized moot court and trial advocacy program, and a variety of social and professional organizations. Some of the active student organizations include American Constitution Society; Real Estate Legal Society; Public Interest Law Students; Women's Law Society; Black Law

Students Association; Christian Legal Society; Entertainment, Arts, and Sports Law Society; Federalist Society; International Law Society; Dispute Resolution Society; Environmental Law Society; Spanish American Law Students Association; Asian Law Students Association; and Law Partners, a support group for spouses and significant others of law students. Both Phi Delta Phi and Phi Alpha Delta legal honoraries maintain a chapter on campus. The College of Law was granted a chapter of the Order of the Coif in 1979. The Student Bar Association serves an active student government role and coordinates many law school-sponsored social activities, community projects, and programs.

■ Career Services

The College of Law's Placement Office takes pride in helping students acquire the tools needed to successfully launch legal careers. The office offers individualized career planning, on-campus and off-campus interview programs, job search assistance, an alumni mentorship program, and skills workshops and seminars on topics ranging from effective résumé writing to interviewing techniques.

The college's most recent placement statistics show that approximately 99 percent of its graduates reported they were either employed, seeking another graduate degree, or not seeking employment nine months after graduation. The college's graduates work in 47 states and in major markets, including Atlanta, Chicago, New York, and Washington, DC. Graduates are prominent in all Florida cities.

Applicant Profile

The Florida State University College of Law
This grid includes only applicants who earned 120–180 LSAT scores under standard administrations.

LSAT Score	3.75 +		3.50–3.74		3.25–3.49		3.00–3.24		2.75–2.99		2.50–2.74		2.25–2.49		2.00–2.24		Below 2.00		No GPA		Total	
	Apps	Adm	Apps	Adm	Apps	Adm	Apps	Adm	Apps	Adm	Apps	Adm	Apps	Adm	Apps	Adm	Apps	Adm	Apps	Adm	Apps	Adm
175–180	2	2	1	1	0	0	0	0	0	0	1	1	0	0	0	0	0	0	0	0	4	4
170–174	3	3	2	2	1	1	4	3	1	1	2	2	0	0	1	1	0	0	0	0	14	13
165–169	18	18	16	16	9	9	16	16	8	8	4	4	2	1	2	0	0	0	0	0	75	72
160–164	61	61	77	76	97	96	66	61	32	21	26	7	9	2	2	0	0	0	0	0	370	324
155–159	151	112	240	115	229	71	142	27	71	10	31	1	18	4	5	0	0	0	11	1	898	341
150–154	135	21	202	19	227	16	154	0	96	2	33	0	23	0	1	0	3	0	10	0	884	58
145–149	58	3	111	3	142	3	118	0	69	0	38	1	15	0	6	0	4	0	7	0	568	10
140–144	18	0	42	0	76	0	66	0	51	0	35	0	13	0	3	0	3	0	8	0	315	0
135–139	2	0	15	0	23	0	29	0	18	0	16	0	7	0	7	0	0	0	8	0	125	0
130–134	1	0	3	0	7	0	7	0	6	0	8	0	5	0	4	0	1	0	1	0	43	0
125–129	0	0	0	0	0	0	2	0	1	0	1	0	2	0	4	0	1	0	0	0	11	0
120–124	0	0	0	0	0	0	1	0	0	0	0	0	1	0	0	0	0	0	1	0	3	0
Total	449	220	709	232	811	196	605	107	353	42	195	16	95	7	35	1	12	0	46	1	3310	822

Apps = Number of Applicants
Adm = Number Admitted
Reflects 99% of the total applicant pool.

Fordham University School of Law

140 West 62nd Street
New York, NY 10023
Phone: 212.636.6810; Fax: 212.636.7984
E-mail: lawadmissions@law.fordham.edu; Website: law.fordham.edu

ABA
Approved
Since
1936

The Basics

Type of school	Private
Term	Semester
Application deadline	3/1
Application fee	$65
Financial aid deadline	4/1
Can first year start other than fall?	No
Student to faculty ratio	15.0 to 1
Does the university offer:	
housing restricted to law students?	Yes
graduate housing for which law students are eligible?	Yes

Faculty and Administrators

	Total		Men		Women		Minorities	
	Fall	Spr	Fall	Spr	Fall	Spr	Fall	Spr
Full-time	78	75	48	50	30	25	12	12
Other Full-time	0	0	0	0	0	0	0	0
Deans, librarians, & others who teach	14	15	9	10	5	5	1	1
Part-time	128	154	84	101	44	53	17	17
Total	220	244	141	161	79	83	30	30

Curriculum

	Full-time	Part-time
Typical first-year section size	80	80
Is there typically a "small section" of the first-year class, other than Legal Writing, taught by full-time faculty	Yes	Yes
If yes, typical size offered last year	40	40
# of classroom course titles beyond first-year curriculum	222	
# of upper division courses, excluding seminars with an enrollment: Under 25	61	
25–49	55	
50–74	17	
75–99	15	
100+	8	
# of seminars	147	
# of seminar positions available	2,960	
# of seminar positions filled	2,276	305
# of positions available in simulation courses	1,403	
# of simulation positions filled	953	141
# of positions available in faculty supervised clinical courses	283	
# of faculty supervised clinical positions filled	180	12
# involved in field placements	207	71
# involved in law journals	498	23
# involved in interschool competitions	191	31
# of credit hours required to graduate	83	

JD Enrollment and Ethnicity

	Men #	Men %	Women #	Women %	Full-time #	Full-time %	Part-time #	Part-time %	1st-year #	1st-year %	Total #	Total %	JD Degs. Awd.
African Amer.	31	3.8	45	6.5	57	4.8	19	5.8	25	5.3	76	5.0	31
Amer. Indian	6	0.7	5	0.7	9	0.8	2	0.6	3	0.6	11	0.7	1
Asian Amer.	78	9.5	85	12.2	122	10.3	41	12.6	50	10.6	163	10.8	54
Mex. Amer.	4	0.5	2	0.3	3	0.3	3	0.9	2	0.4	6	0.4	2
Puerto Rican	8	1.0	4	0.6	10	0.8	2	0.6	1	0.2	12	0.8	8
Hispanic	50	6.1	63	9.1	91	7.7	22	6.7	47	10.0	113	7.5	25
Total Minority	177	21.6	204	29.4	292	24.6	89	27.3	128	27.2	381	25.2	121
For. Nation.	0	0.0	0	0.0	0	0.0	0	0.0	0	0.0	0	0.0	0
Caucasian	499	61.0	381	54.9	698	58.9	182	55.8	264	56.2	880	58.2	287
Unknown	142	17.4	109	15.7	196	16.5	55	16.9	78	16.6	251	16.6	69
Total	818	54.1	694	45.9	1186	78.4	326	21.6	470	31.1	1512		477

Transfers

Transfers in	38
Transfers out	15

Tuition and Fees

	Resident	Nonresident
Full-time	$37,220	$37,220
Part-time	$27,976	$27,976

Living Expenses

Estimated living expenses for singles

Living on campus	Living off campus	Living at home
$21,200	$21,200	$21,200

ABA
Approved
Since
1936

GPA and LSAT Scores

	Total	Full-time	Part-time
# of apps	6,784	5,724	1,060
# of offers	1,635	1,373	262
# of matrics	472	312	160
75% GPA	3.71	3.74	3.66
Median GPA	3.58	3.63	3.43
25% GPA	3.30	3.41	3.20
75% LSAT	166	167	163
Median LSAT	163	165	161
25% LSAT	161	163	160

Grants and Scholarships (from prior year)

	Total		Full-time		Part-time	
	#	%	#	%	#	%
Total # of students	1,516		1,170		346	
Total # receiving grants	492	32.5	412	35.2	80	23.1
Less than 1/2 tuition	450	29.7	379	32.4	71	20.5
Half to full tuition	33	2.2	27	2.3	6	1.7
Full tuition	6	0.4	4	0.3	2	0.6
More than full tuition	3	0.2	2	0.2	1	0.3
Median grant amount			$7,300		$5,940	

Informational and Library Resources

# of volumes and volume equivalents	631,526
# of titles	286,880
# of active serial subscriptions	5,006
Study seating capacity inside the library	431
# of full-time professional librarians	13
Hours per week library is open	119
# of open, wired connections available to students	474
# of networked computers available for use by students	205
# of simultaneous wireless users	1,450
Require computer?	No

JD Attrition (from prior year)

	Academic	Other	Total	
	#	#	#	%
1st year	1	12	13	2.7
2nd year	0	19	19	4.0
3rd year	1	0	1	0.2
4th year	0	0	0	0.0

Employment (9 months after graduation)

	Total	Percentage
Employment status known	479	99.6
Employment status unknown	2	0.4
Employed	455	95.0
Pursuing graduate degrees	12	2.5
Unemployed seeking employment	2	0.4
Unemployed not seeking employment	7	1.5
Unemployed and studying for the bar	3	0.6

Type of Employment

	Total	Percentage
# employed in law firms	351	77.1
# employed in business and industry	14	3.1
# employed in government	27	5.9
# employed in public interest	5	1.1
# employed as judicial clerks	21	4.6
# employed in academia	5	1.1

Geographic Location

	Total	Percentage
# employed in state	274	60.2
# employed in foreign countries	3	0.7
# of states where employed	16	

Bar Passage Rates

Jurisdiction	New York		
Exam	Sum 05	Win 06	Total
# from school taking bar for the first time	428	41	469
School's pass rate for all first-time takers	88%	78%	87%
State's pass rate for all first-time takers	76%	61%	74%

Fordham University School of Law

140 West 62nd Street
New York, NY 10023
Phone: 212.636.6810; Fax: 212.636.7984
E-mail: lawadmissions@law.fordham.edu; Website: law.fordham.edu

■ Introduction

Fordham law school is an extraordinary place, where a nationally recognized faculty of scholar-teachers and a deep commitment to social justice create an atmosphere in which students feel appreciated and valued as they prepare to become part of the next generation of leaders. Over the past century, Fordham has trained attorneys who have made their mark throughout society. Today, our graduates practice in 49 states, in the District of Columbia, and in dozens of nations around the world. Among our 15,000 living alumni are partners and associates of leading law firms, CEOs of major corporations, academics, and a legion of individuals engaged in numerous areas of public service.

Fordham's central Manhattan location provides instant access to all New York City has to offer, enabling students to begin their careers at the center of the world's legal, financial, and entertainment capital. Such proximity puts students close to a broad range of professional opportunities at some of the largest law firms in the world, the busiest federal and state courts, the US and New York State Attorneys General Offices, a myriad of state and federal agencies, and Wall Street.

Also within easy reach are New York's equally famous diversions. The campus is just two blocks away from Central Park. Lincoln Center for the Performing Arts—home to the world-renowned Metropolitan Opera, New York Philharmonic, and the Julliard School of Music—is right across the street.

■ Curriculum

Fordham's faculty prides itself on being teachers as well as scholars. As teachers they recognize the importance of welcoming students, being accessible, and encouraging them. The large faculty enables Fordham to offer 200 courses that reinforce its traditional strengths in contracts, commercial law, corporate law, evidence, and international law, as well as enhance its significant scholarship in the fields of constitutional law and jurisprudence, international human rights, legal ethics, legal history, intellectual property, and clinical legal education.

Fordham also promotes the art and science of legal analysis and the cultivation of a vigorous ongoing dialogue between students and professor through the following nationally renowned academic centers.

Brendan Moore Advocacy Center fosters the teaching and study of lawyers as advocates, with special emphasis on client representation at the trial level.

Center for Corporate, Securities, and Financial Law serves as the focal point for the school's business law programs and includes roundtable discussions with business leaders, corporate law practitioners, and state and federal regulators.

Joseph R. Crowley Program in International Human Rights is one of the nation's premier academic organizations dealing with the rights of individuals throughout the world. The program's annual fact-finding human rights mission to a designated host country is unprecedented in American legal education.

Louis Stein Center for Law and Ethics promotes the integration of ethical perspectives in legal practice, legal institutions, and the development of the law generally. The center also oversees the Stein Scholars Program, a three-year program for students who demonstrate commitment to public service and who undertake specialized academic work in legal ethics.

The Feerick Center for Social Justice and Dispute Resolution brings together the major stakeholders responsible for solving our most difficult urban social issues. Uniquely combining the insights of a think tank, the urgency inherent in a mission to achieve social justice, the balance required of a mediation center, and the educational mission of a law school, the center works with all parties to frame concrete and achievable solutions to the endemic problems plaguing the urban poor. Fordham law school has institutionalized one of the largest and most creative commitments in legal education to obtain social change. The vital work of this center, and the inspiration it provides, will be fostered at home in New York and around the globe.

■ Cocurricular Activities

There are six student-edited law journals at Fordham, as well as two intramural moot court competitions.

The school also participates in interschool competitions, fielding award-winning appellate moot court teams, trial advocacy teams, and alternative dispute resolution teams.

■ Worldwide Significance

Long before "globalism" was mainstream, Fordham was devoting resources to programs that, today, are internationally known, including:

- the nation's preeminent Center on European Union Law;
- the school's Stein Center for Law and Ethics (see Curriculum section);
- an International Antitrust Law and Policy Conference, now in its 32nd year;
- an annual International Intellectual Property Law Conference;
- the Joseph R. Crowley Program in International Human Rights (see Curriculum section);
- a Belfast/Dublin summer program, which offers two weeks of study in each city with a special emphasis on international alternative dispute resolution;
- a summer program in Seoul, Korea, at Sungkyunkwan University College of Law (SKKU); taught by Fordham law school professors and by distinguished practitioners, the program offers courses in international and comparative law as well as internships at local law firms, companies, and governmental offices;
- semester study-abroad programs offered in the Netherlands, Germany, Spain, Mexico, and Canada; and
- three graduate degree programs—the LLM in International Business and Trade Law; the LLM in Banking, Corporate, and Finance Law; and the LLM in Intellectual Property and Information Technology Law—that have created a network of Fordham alumni in 70 countries.

■ Experiential Programs

Fordham's clinical program affords opportunities for students to integrate legal analysis with lawyering theory and skills by assuming lawyering roles or performing lawyering functions in problem-solving settings. With 17 full-time faculty, three part-time professors, one adjunct, and one full-time social worker, Fordham Law's clinical program—one of the largest in the nation—engages more than 300 students in live-client clinics and simulation courses in 17 practice areas, including an innovative interdisciplinary Child and Family Litigation Clinic, where students are placed on teams supervised by law, social work, and psychology faculty. Fordham also offers one of the widest ranges of externship placements in American legal education—more than 250 opportunities at nonprofit and nongovernmental organizations and in state and federal courts.

■ Career Services and Placement

Fordham offers a fully staffed career services office to assist students and alumni in planning their careers. For the past several years, between 97 and 100 percent of our graduates obtained employment within nine months of graduation. The program features:

- an on-campus interview program that brings nearly 300 potential employers to campus to conduct more than 5,000 individual student interviews;
- a searchable, proprietary, online database of job listings; and
- individualized student counseling, mock videotaped interviews with optional critiques, seminars on interviewing skills and networking, and assistance with résumé preparation, including 24-hour turnaround time for edits.

■ Public Service

Fordham believes that the development of a lifelong commitment to public service is an integral part of a legal education. Last year, Fordham law students volunteered 62,000 hours of their time to some form of pro bono work through the school's nationally recognized Public Interest Resource Center. The PIRC's 15 student-run organizations address issues

concerning the environment, housing for the poor, domestic violence, unemployment, police brutality, the death penalty, immigration, and community service. Fordham also has created a Loan Forgiveness Program as well as a Loan Repayment Assistance Program (LRAP) to assist those who pursue public service careers. Today, Fordham continues to set the standard for law schools nationwide by assisting and inspiring those students who, regardless of their ultimate career choice, are committed to the spirit of *pro bono publico*—work for the public good.

■ Living at Lincoln Center

Approximately 80 spaces are set aside for entering students in McMahon Hall, the university's Lincoln Center residence. Students live in two- or three-bedroom apartments, each of which contains private bedrooms, a living room, full kitchen, and bath. Preference is given to those students who live beyond a commutable distance from the law school. Inquiries regarding housing should be directed to the law school admission office.

■ Applicant Profile

Fordham law school's Admissions Committee—comprised of full-time faculty members and assistant deans—evaluates each complete application received. While the best available evidence suggests that LSAT scores and undergraduate GPAs should be accorded significant weight in evaluating most applicants, the Admissions Committee believes that securing the most interesting, diverse, and exciting class involves the evaluation of other qualitative factors as well. The combination of academic excellence and experiences is considered in evaluating applicants' potential contributions to the success of their Fordham and professional experiences.

Applicant Profile

Fordham University School of Law
This grid includes only applicants who earned 120–180 LSAT scores under standard administrations.

LSAT Score	GPA												
	3.75 +		3.50–3.74		3.25–3.49		3.00–3.24		Below 3.00		No GPA		Totals	
	Apps	Adm	Apps	Adm	Apps	Adm	Apps	Adm	Apps	Adm	Apps	Adm	Apps	Adm
170–180	94	88	99	90	83	59	44	20	49	7	3	2	374	264
165–169	273	242	383	315	283	133	161	49	86	12	8	3	1197	751
160–164	397	135	590	160	507	88	246	44	156	11	15	6	1917	438
155–159	254	30	432	29	408	34	231	22	196	12	15	1	1537	127
120–154	153	11	305	14	369	12	329	4	501	3	42	0	1699	44
Total	1171	506	1809	608	1650	326	1011	139	988	45	83	12	6724	1624

Apps = Number of Applicants
Adm = Number Admitted

Franklin Pierce Law Center

Two White Street
Concord, NH 03301
Phone: 603.228.9217; Fax: 603.228.1074
E-mail: admissions@piercelaw.edu; Website: www.piercelaw.edu

The Basics

Type of school	Private
Term	Semester
Application deadline	4/1
Application fee	$55
Financial aid deadline	
Can first year start other than fall?	No
Student to faculty ratio	15.8 to 1
Does the university offer:	
housing restricted to law students?	No
graduate housing for which law students are eligible?	No

Faculty and Administrators

	Total		Men		Women		Minorities	
	Fall	**Spr**	**Fall**	**Spr**	**Fall**	**Spr**	**Fall**	**Spr**
Full-time	22	23	15	17	7	6	3	2
Other Full-time	3	2	1	1	2	1	0	0
Deans, librarians, & others who teach	6	5	3	3	3	2	0	0
Part-time	27	34	18	19	9	15	0	0
Total	**58**	**64**	**37**	**40**	**21**	**24**	**3**	**2**

Curriculum

	Full-time	Part-time
Typical first-year section size	71	0
Is there typically a "small section" of the first-year class, other than Legal Writing, taught by full-time faculty	Yes	No
If yes, typical size offered last year	16	
# of classroom course titles beyond first-year curriculum	92	
# of upper division courses, excluding seminars with an enrollment: Under 25	78	
25–49	22	
50–74	10	
75–99	8	
100+	0	
# of seminars	17	
# of seminar positions available	260	
# of seminar positions filled	182	0
# of positions available in simulation courses	433	
# of simulation positions filled	390	0
# of positions available in faculty supervised clinical courses	144	
# of faculty supervised clinical positions filled	96	0
# involved in field placements	89	0
# involved in law journals	54	0
# involved in interschool competitions	44	0
# of credit hours required to graduate	84	

JD Enrollment and Ethnicity

	Men #	Men %	Women #	Women %	Full-time #	Full-time %	Part-time #	Part-time %	1st-year #	1st-year %	Total #	Total %	JD Degs. Awd.
African Amer.	5	1.9	12	7.4	17	4.0	0	0.0	6	3.7	17	4.0	3
Amer. Indian	0	0.0	1	0.6	1	0.2	0	0.0	1	0.6	1	0.2	0
Asian Amer.	23	8.7	14	8.6	37	8.7	0	0.0	13	8.1	37	8.7	23
Mex. Amer.	0	0.0	0	0.0	0	0.0	0	0.0	0	0.0	0	0.0	0
Puerto Rican	0	0.0	1	0.6	1	0.2	0	0.0	1	0.6	1	0.2	0
Hispanic	11	4.2	4	2.5	15	3.5	0	0.0	3	1.9	15	3.5	2
Total Minority	39	14.7	32	19.8	71	16.8	0	0.0	24	14.9	71	16.6	28
For. Nation.	12	4.5	5	3.1	17	4.0	0	0.0	5	3.1	17	4.0	4
Caucasian	177	66.8	112	69.1	285	67.4	4	100.0	105	65.2	289	67.7	108
Unknown	37	14.0	13	8.0	50	11.8	0	0.0	27	16.8	50	11.7	11
Total	265	62.1	162	37.9	423	99.1	4	0.9	161	37.7	427		151

Transfers

Transfers in	1
Transfers out	9

Tuition and Fees

	Resident	Nonresident
Full-time	$29,050	$29,050
Part-time	$0	$0

Living Expenses

Estimated living expenses for singles

Living on campus	Living off campus	Living at home
$14,907	$14,907	$14,907

Franklin Pierce Law Center

*ABA
Approved
Since
1974*

GPA and LSAT Scores

	Total	Full-time	Part-time
# of apps	1,455	1,455	0
# of offers	718	718	0
# of matrics	160	160	0
75% GPA	3.50	3.50	0.00
Median GPA	3.30	3.30	0.00
25% GPA	3.00	3.00	0.00
75% LSAT	155	155	0
Median LSAT	152	152	0
25% LSAT	149	149	0

Grants and Scholarships (from prior year)

	Total		Full-time		Part-time	
	#	%	#	%	#	%
Total # of students	440		437		3	
Total # receiving grants	302	68.6	301	68.9	1	33.3
Less than 1/2 tuition	292	66.4	292	66.8	0	0.0
Half to full tuition	7	1.6	7	1.6	0	0.0
Full tuition	2	0.5	1	0.2	1	33.3
More than full tuition	1	0.2	1	0.2	0	0.0
Median grant amount			$3,200		$0	

Informational and Library Resources

# of volumes and volume equivalents	285,857
# of titles	94,706
# of active serial subscriptions	4,636
Study seating capacity inside the library	243
# of full-time professional librarians	6
Hours per week library is open	105
# of open, wired connections available to students	338
# of networked computers available for use by students	58
# of simultaneous wireless users	540
Require computer?	No

JD Attrition (from prior year)

	Academic	Other	Total	
	#	#	#	%
1st year	0	28	28	19.9
2nd year	3	0	3	2.0
3rd year	0	0	0	0.0
4th year	0	0	0	0.0

Employment (9 months after graduation)

	Total	Percentage
Employment status known	106	100.0
Employment status unknown	0	0.0
Employed	92	86.8
Pursuing graduate degrees	1	0.9
Unemployed seeking employment	3	2.8
Unemployed not seeking employment	4	3.8
Unemployed and studying for the bar	6	5.7

Type of Employment

# employed in law firms	45	48.9
# employed in business and industry	21	22.8
# employed in government	8	8.7
# employed in public interest	4	4.3
# employed as judicial clerks	5	5.4
# employed in academia	7	7.6

Geographic Location

# employed in state	30	32.6
# employed in foreign countries	2	2.2
# of states where employed	26	

Bar Passage Rates

Jurisdiction	New Hampshire			Massachusetts		
Exam	Sum 05	Win 06	Total	Sum 05	Win 06	Total
# from school taking bar for the first time	36	2	38	19	2	21
School's pass rate for all first-time takers	58%	100%	61%	79%	100%	81%
State's pass rate for all first-time takers	60%	0%	60%	84%	75%	82%

Franklin Pierce Law Center

Admissions Office, Two White Street
Concord, NH 03301
Phone: 603.228.9217; Fax: 603.228.1074
E-mail: admissions@piercelaw.edu; Website: www.piercelaw.edu

■ Introduction

Franklin Pierce Law Center is known throughout the world as an innovative leader in legal education, providing its students with the skills to lead and serve, and to meet the emerging needs of a global society. Pierce Law emphasizes individually tailored legal programs and a broad range of learning settings, including lectures and seminars, real-client clinics, independent study, and externships in law firms, in courts, and in private and public agencies. In addition, we promote a community spirit of caring and compassion, with a close working relationship between students and faculty. Self-reliant students who know their own strengths and objectives thrive at Pierce Law and find the focus on personal pride and responsibility more motivating than fear or competition.

Pierce Law is one of the smallest private law schools in the United States. Each entering class numbers approximately 150 students, allowing for a 13 to 1 student-teacher ratio. Classes are small, especially after the first year. Seventy-five of the 109 elective courses enroll 35 or fewer students.

Located in New Hampshire's capital city of Concord (45,000 population), Pierce Law is ideally situated one hour from Boston, the Atlantic seacoast, the state's Lakes Region, and the White Mountains.

■ Special Programs

- **Intellectual Property**—The internationally recognized intellectual and industrial property specialization (patents, licensing, technology transfer, trade secrets, trademarks, cyberlaw, and copyrights) is supported by 12 full-time faculty members, all intellectual property lawyers. Training includes learning to advise clients regarding intellectual property protection, infringement, and technology transfer. Students with technical backgrounds may focus on patent law, many passing the patent bar prior to graduation. Other intellectual property areas do not require a technical background.
- **Commerce and Technology Law**—The business curriculum prepares students for traditional types of practice and brings new opportunities for students choosing to confront the legal issues involving electronic commerce. The business and e-commerce curriculum also integrates well with the intellectual property curriculum, particularly for students interested in business and legal innovations associated with the Internet.
- **Social Justice Institute**—This hands-on professional training program prepares students for public interest law in private practice, governmental service, social policy advocacy, and criminal practice. Clinic students provide legal assistance to clients in cases involving divorce, neglect and abuse of children, juvenile issues, social security, personal bankruptcy, consumer issues, and housing problems. In addition, students have the opportunity to assist in projects with the Institute for Health, Law, and Ethics.
- **Criminal Law**—As part of our Social Justice Institute, our criminal law curriculum offers courses, individual mentoring, clinics, and externships to prepare students for careers in prosecution or defense. Criminal Practice Clinic students represent clients charged with misdemeanor and juvenile offenses at the district court level. In the Appellate Defender Program, students prepare briefs for the New Hampshire Supreme Court in criminal cases. Externship opportunities are available in prosecutorial positions at the local, state, and federal level and in defense positions with law firms and governmental agencies.

■ International Summer Institutes in China and Ireland

- The Intellectual Property Summer Institute at Tsinghua University in Beijing offers an overview of China's patent, copyright, and trademark laws as well as an introduction to some of the major international instruments and institutions regulating international trade and intellectual property.
- The eLaw Summer Institute at University College Cork, Ireland, focuses on law and emerging policy of the Information Age.

■ Academic Opportunities

The *Webster Scholar Program* is a comprehensive, practice-based honors program focused on making law students client-ready. Second- and third-year students complete a range of courses, demonstrate their developing professional skills and judgment, and compile a portfolio of work. Students who successfully complete the program will be certified as having passed the New Hampshire bar examination, subject to passing character and fitness requirements.

The Pierce Law *Externship Program* exchanges a full-credit semester in the classroom for a real-life experience working in an active legal position. Externs work with experienced attorneys and judges while under the close supervision of a faculty member.

■ Joint-degree Programs and LLM

Pierce Law offers the JD/Master of Intellectual Property, Commerce, and Technology dual degree. Summer programs enable students to earn additional credits needed to complete joint-degree programs in three years. The Master of Laws (LLM) in Intellectual Property, Commerce, and Technology is designed for law graduates who wish to examine the legally sophisticated intellectual property issues that often arise in policymaking and teaching.

■ Student Activities

Students prepare notes and comments for *IDEA: The Intellectual Property Law Review*; *Pierce Law Review*; and *Annual Survey of New Hampshire Law*, an annual publication consisting of six articles focusing on recent New Hampshire Supreme Court opinions. Students organize and participate in a wide variety of formal organizations and informal activities and events throughout the year.

■ Career Services

The Career Services Office works with students and alumni to find the best match to meet their skills and interests in changing legal markets. The office provides extensive individual counseling and guidance; brings attorneys to campus to provide firsthand information about the practice of law; advises students of all resources through weekly publications and job boards; coordinates the efforts of faculty, staff, and student groups to provide information about opportunities to gain experience; and conducts outreach to employers. More than 75 percent of our graduates secure positions outside New Hampshire. Over 95 percent of our graduates are employed within six months after graduation.

■ Clinics

- Intellectual Property and Transaction
- Administrative Law and Advocacy
- Pierce Law Innocence Project
- Consumer and Commercial Law
- Criminal Practice
- Appellate Defender Program
- Street Law

■ Admission

While LSAT scores and grade-point average are factors that must be considered in the decision-making process, neither alone determines admission. Every application receives a thorough and thoughtful review. The candidate's personal statement, letters of recommendation, and résumé are evaluated along with the numbers. Community service, employment during college, and other nonacademic accomplishments are given weight to the extent that they reflect initiative, social responsibility, focus, and maturity.

Applicant Profile Not Available

George Mason University School of Law

3301 Fairfax Drive
Arlington, VA 22201
Phone: 703.993.8010; Fax: 703.993.8088
E-mail: aprice1@gmu.edu; Website: www.law.gmu.edu

*ABA
Approved
Since
1980*

The Basics

Type of school	Public
Term	Semester
Application deadline	4/1
Application fee	$35
Financial aid deadline	3/1
Can first year start other than fall?	No
Student to faculty ratio	16.1 to 1
Does the university offer:	
housing restricted to law students?	No
graduate housing for which law students are eligible?	No

Faculty and Administrators

	Total		Men		Women		Minorities	
	Fall	Spr	Fall	Spr	Fall	Spr	Fall	Spr
Full-time	35	29	28	26	7	3	5	4
Other Full-time	1	0	0	0	1	0	0	0
Deans, librarians, & others who teach	4	5	4	4	0	1	0	0
Part-time	75	77	57	57	18	20	4	4
Total	**115**	**111**	**89**	**87**	**26**	**24**	**9**	**8**

Curriculum

	Full-time	Part-time
Typical first-year section size	81	89
Is there typically a "small section" of the first-year class, other than Legal Writing, taught by full-time faculty	No	No
If yes, typical size offered last year		
# of classroom course titles beyond first-year curriculum		195
# of upper division courses, excluding seminars with an enrollment: Under 25		159
25–49		38
50–74		2
75–99		4
100+		4
# of seminars		33
# of seminar positions available		495
# of seminar positions filled	197	189
# of positions available in simulation courses		204
# of simulation positions filled	58	120
# of positions available in faculty supervised clinical courses		240
# of faculty supervised clinical positions filled	74	76
# involved in field placements	66	10
# involved in law journals	79	28
# involved in interschool competitions	31	3
# of credit hours required to graduate		89

JD Enrollment and Ethnicity

	Men		Women		Full-time		Part-time		1st-year		Total		JD Degs. Awd.
	#	%	#	%	#	%	#	%	#	%	#	%	
African Amer.	12	2.6	16	5.6	13	2.8	15	5.3	10	4.0	28	3.7	5
Amer. Indian	1	0.2	1	0.3	2	0.4	0	0.0	0	0.0	2	0.3	2
Asian Amer.	32	6.9	21	7.3	28	6.0	25	8.8	12	4.8	53	7.1	15
Mex. Amer.	0	0.0	0	0.0	0	0.0	0	0.0	0	0.0	0	0.0	0
Puerto Rican	0	0.0	0	0.0	0	0.0	0	0.0	0	0.0	0	0.0	0
Hispanic	26	5.6	13	4.5	24	5.2	15	5.3	11	4.4	39	5.2	4
Total Minority	71	15.3	51	17.8	67	14.4	55	19.3	33	13.3	122	16.2	26
For. Nation.	6	1.3	5	1.7	8	1.7	3	1.1	3	1.2	11	1.5	5
Caucasian	388	83.4	230	80.4	391	83.9	227	79.6	212	85.5	618	82.3	175
Unknown	0	0.0	0	0.0	0	0.0	0	0.0	0	0.0	0	0.0	0
Total	465	61.9	286	38.1	466	62.1	285	37.9	248	33.0	751		206

Transfers

Transfers in	13
Transfers out	7

Tuition and Fees

	Resident	Nonresident
Full-time	$15,274	$26,502
Part-time	$12,001	$20,823

Living Expenses

Estimated living expenses for singles

Living on campus	Living off campus	Living at home
$13,288	$20,228	$9,388

George Mason University School of Law

ABA
Approved
Since
1980

GPA and LSAT Scores

	Total	Full-time	Part-time
# of apps	6,535	5,024	1,511
# of offers	1,116	1,004	112
# of matrics	244	178	66
75% GPA	3.78	3.78	3.77
Median GPA	3.57	3.60	3.50
25% GPA	3.06	3.10	2.99
75% LSAT	165	166	164
Median LSAT	163	164	161
25% LSAT	159	160	157

Grants and Scholarships (from prior year)

	Total		Full-time		Part-time	
	#	%	#	%	#	%
Total # of students	717		414		303	
Total # receiving grants	90	12.6	79	19.1	11	3.6
Less than 1/2 tuition	63	8.8	58	14.0	5	1.7
Half to full tuition	18	2.5	15	3.6	3	1.0
Full tuition	0	0.0	0	0.0	0	0.0
More than full tuition	9	1.3	6	1.4	3	1.0
Median grant amount			$8,000		$5,000	

Informational and Library Resources

# of volumes and volume equivalents	453,812
# of titles	164,750
# of active serial subscriptions	5,634
Study seating capacity inside the library	320
# of full-time professional librarians	7
Hours per week library is open	96
# of open, wired connections available to students	888
# of networked computers available for use by students	80
# of simultaneous wireless users	800
Require computer?	No

JD Attrition (from prior year)

	Academic	Other	Total	
	#	#	#	%
1st year	5	13	18	8.3
2nd year	0	5	5	2.3
3rd year	0	0	0	0.0
4th year	0	0	0	0.0

Employment (9 months after graduation)

	Total	Percentage
Employment status known	234	100.0
Employment status unknown	0	0.0
Employed	222	94.9
Pursuing graduate degrees	3	1.3
Unemployed seeking employment	1	0.4
Unemployed not seeking employment	8	3.4
Unemployed and studying for the bar	0	0.0

Type of Employment

	Total	Percentage
# employed in law firms	100	45.0
# employed in business and industry	38	17.1
# employed in government	42	18.9
# employed in public interest	5	2.3
# employed as judicial clerks	26	11.7
# employed in academia	11	5.0

Geographic Location

	Total	Percentage
# employed in state	96	43.2
# employed in foreign countries	3	1.4
# of states where employed	25	

Bar Passage Rates

Jurisdiction	Virginia		
Exam	Sum 05	Win 06	Total
# from school taking bar for the first time	118	35	153
School's pass rate for all first-time takers	79%	71%	77%
State's pass rate for all first-time takers	76%	65%	74%

George Mason University School of Law

3301 Fairfax Drive
Arlington, VA 22201
Phone: 703.993.8010; Fax: 703.993.8088
E-mail: aprice1@gmu.edu; Website: www.law.gmu.edu

■ Introduction

George Mason University School of Law sits on the doorstep of the nation's capital. One of three public law schools in Virginia, it was established by authority of the Virginia General Assembly in 1979.

■ Enrollment/Student Body

George Mason University is an equal opportunity/affirmative action institution.

■ Library and Physical Facilities

In January 1999, the law school relocated to a new, state-of-the-art facility equipped with electrical and data connections at every classroom and library seat, and two ultramodern moot courtrooms.

The school is a member of the library network of the Consortium for Continuing Higher Education in Northern Virginia, affording access to general university and public library collections.

■ Curriculum

George Mason University offers both full- and part-time divisions. The full-time division operates during the day and takes three years to complete. Students who elect the part-time division study at night and take four years to complete the requirements for the Juris Doctor degree.

A grounding in economics and basic mathematical and financial skills is important to a sophisticated legal education and to the development of a competent attorney. To ensure that George Mason graduates have this grounding, all students take a first-year course in Economic Foundations.

George Mason law students complete a three-year legal writing program, which emphasizes the use of technology and continual practice of skills in the development of actual transactions and cases. A separate writing grade-point average further underscores the importance of good writing at George Mason.

The curriculum begins with exposure to the courses fundamental to a well-rounded legal education. Students at George Mason can also elect one of our specialty programs, thus demonstrating depth as well as breadth in their training. All specialties are offered in both the full-time and part-time divisions.

George Mason has a number of clinical program offerings: the Immigration Law Clinic, the Legal Clinic, the Public Interest Law Clinic, the Domestic Relations Legal Clinic, the Telehealth Clinic, the Law and Mental Illness Clinic, the Regulatory Law Clinic, and the Clinic for Legal Assistance to Service Members. George Mason is a leader in technology and law and is the headquarters for the Tech Center (National Center for Technology and Law), which brings together academics, high-tech industry leaders, and policymakers to debate and formulate national policy to keep pace with technological advances. George Mason is also home to the Critical Infrastructure Protection (CIP) Project, a program that fully integrates the disciplines of law, policy, and technology for enhancing the security of cyber networks and economic processes supporting the nation's critical infrastructure.

■ Special Programs

- **Corporate and Securities Law**—prepares students to work in a variety of fields related to corporate law and financial markets. By developing a thorough understanding of both law and underlying theory, students are prepared to deal with rapidly changing business and legal environments.
- **Regulatory Law**—prepares students for practice in and before the numerous agencies that regulate business and other activities. Students are taught economics, the economic analysis of law, administrative law, legislation, lobbying, and negotiation, as well as several substantive areas of regulatory law.
- **International Business**—prepares students for practice in the rapidly changing global business community and provides them with a well-rounded legal education emphasizing analytical and writing skills.
- **Litigation Law**—provides an academic program for students interested in litigation and other dispute resolution processes. This is not a clinical training program. The track courses focus on the processes of dispute resolution and lawyers' roles from an analytical perspective.
- **Intellectual Property Law**—is designed for students having a degree in engineering or one of the physical or biological sciences who intend to practice within the field of intellectual property.
- **Technology Law Program**—combines coursework in the fields of technology law, intellectual property law, and business law. The program prepares students for work in law firms that serve high-technology clients, as in-house counsel for Internet start-up companies, and as attorneys for state and federal regulatory agencies with jurisdiction over technology industries.
- **LLM Programs**—for students wishing to pursue specialized study beyond the JD, George Mason offers two LLM programs: (1) the **LLM in Law and Economics**, and (2) the **LLM in Intellectual Property Law**. Detailed information about these programs is available at *www.law.gmu.edu/academics/llm.html*.

■ Admission

Two of the primary factors considered in the admission process are performance on the LSAT and undergraduate grade-point average. Other factors that are considered include difficulty of undergraduate major, undergraduate institution attended, possession of advanced degrees, writing ability, recommendations, extracurricular activities, employment experience, demonstrated commitment to public and community service, leadership skills and experience, history of overcoming personal or professional challenges, and other academic, personal, and professional achievements.

■ Student Activities

George Mason University provides many services to enhance the law school experience and enable students to take full advantage of the university's educational and personal enrichment opportunities.

Student activities include the *George Mason Law Review*, *Civil Rights Law Journal*, *Federal Circuit Bar Journal*, and the *Journal of Law, Economics and Policy*, a newspaper, and numerous law-related organizations. Students have an unparalleled opportunity to gain experience in such varied settings as the Office of the US Attorney for both the District of Columbia and the Eastern District of Virginia, as well as federal courts and agencies, local governments, and private firms.

Diversity Student Services, Academic Support Services, Disability Support Services, and the Office of Veterans Services provide specialized assistance, as does the Counseling Center, where a staff of professionals helps students to reach personal, social, and academic goals.

Expenses and Financial Aid

George Mason University participates in the Direct Lending Program. There is no deadline for applying for financial aid, but applicants should complete the FAFSA as soon as possible in order to assure the timely award of aid.

In addition to loans available through the Direct Lending Program, George Mason students are eligible for a number of merit-based fellowships.

Career Services

The Office of Career Services aids students and alumni in finding permanent, part-time, and summer jobs by serving as a clearinghouse for information on available positions. It also advises on résumé and interview preparation and coordinates on-campus interviews. More than 150 firms, businesses, and government agencies recruit on campus each year. Graduates find employment in the legal profession throughout the country.

Applicant Profile

George Mason University School of Law
This grid includes only applicants who earned 120–180 LSAT scores under standard administrations.

LSAT Score	3.75 +		3.50–3.74		3.25–3.49		3.00–3.24		2.75–2.99		2.50–2.74		2.25–2.49		2.00–2.24		Below 2.00		No GPA		Total	
	Apps	Adm	Apps	Adm	Apps	Adm	Apps	Adm	Apps	Adm	Apps	Adm	Apps	Adm	Apps	Adm	Apps	Adm	Apps	Adm	Apps	Adm
175–180	3	3	2	2	3	3	0	0	1	1	0	0	0	0	0	0	0	0	0	0	9	9
170–174	17	16	15	15	18	17	25	21	13	11	10	5	0	0	0	0	0	0	1	1	99	86
165–169	74	69	97	90	108	103	87	76	56	44	28	13	10	4	5	1	0	0	3	2	468	402
160–164	220	207	350	101	302	53	195	29	116	12	76	14	33	3	6	0	0	0	6	1	1304	420
155–159	258	87	405	36	416	13	309	13	164	6	68	3	37	2	13	1	0	0	20	0	1690	161
150–154	125	8	213	2	248	1	199	1	167	0	72	0	33	0	11	0	8	0	15	0	1091	12
145–149	49	0	78	0	100	0	114	0	81	0	54	0	29	0	7	0	2	0	16	0	530	0
140–144	25	0	26	0	61	0	71	0	48	0	50	0	32	0	12	0	0	0	14	0	339	0
135–139	2	0	8	0	20	0	24	0	26	0	17	0	12	0	7	0	3	0	4	0	123	0
130–134	2	0	5	0	4	0	12	0	14	0	9	0	5	0	3	0	1	0	3	0	58	0
125–129	0	0	0	0	0	0	1	0	0	0	1	0	3	0	1	0	0	0	1	0	7	0
120–124	0	0	0	0	0	0	0	0	0	0	1	0	0	0	0	0	0	0	0	0	1	0
Total	775	390	1199	246	1280	190	1037	140	686	74	386	35	194	9	65	2	14	0	83	4	5719	1090

Apps = Number of Applicants
Adm = Number Admitted
Reflects 99% of the total applicant pool.

This chart is to be used as a general guide only. Every application is reviewed and evaluated in its entirety.

The George Washington University Law School

2000 H Street NW
Washington, DC 20052
Phone: 202.994.6288; Fax: 202.994.3597
E-mail: jdadmit@law.gwu.edu; Website: www.law.gwu.edu

ABA
Approved
Since
1923

The Basics

Type of school	Private
Term	Semester
Application deadline	3/1
Application fee	$80
Financial aid deadline	1/1
Can first year start other than fall?	No
Student to faculty ratio	15.3 to 1
Does the university offer:	
housing restricted to law students?	Yes
graduate housing for which law students are eligible?	Yes

Faculty and Administrators

	Total		Men		Women		Minorities	
	Fall	Spr	Fall	Spr	Fall	Spr	Fall	Spr
Full-time	90	81	56	50	34	31	12	12
Other Full-time	6	6	4	4	2	2	1	1
Deans, librarians, & others who teach	5	5	5	5	0	0	0	0
Part-time	169	187	113	125	56	62	17	19
Total	270	279	178	184	92	95	30	32

Curriculum

	Full-time	Part-time
Typical first-year section size	105	120
Is there typically a "small section" of the first-year class, other than Legal Writing, taught by full-time faculty	Yes	No
If yes, typical size offered last year	36	
# of classroom course titles beyond first-year curriculum	196	

# of upper division courses, excluding seminars with an enrollment:		
	Under 25	166
	25–49	60
	50–74	30
	75–99	12
	100+	15

# of seminars	29	
# of seminar positions available	460	
# of seminar positions filled	229	135
# of positions available in simulation courses	875	
# of simulation positions filled	278	436
# of positions available in faculty supervised clinical courses	120	
# of faculty supervised clinical positions filled	107	13
# involved in field placements	277	12
# involved in law journals	362	13
# involved in interschool competitions	199	20
# of credit hours required to graduate	84	

JD Enrollment and Ethnicity

	Men #	Men %	Women #	Women %	Full-time #	Full-time %	Part-time #	Part-time %	1st-year #	1st-year %	Total #	Total %	JD Degs. Awd.
African Amer.	56	5.9	90	12.2	128	9.0	18	6.8	45	8.1	146	8.6	44
Amer. Indian	6	0.6	2	0.3	7	0.5	1	0.4	4	0.7	8	0.5	5
Asian Amer.	77	8.1	89	12.1	128	9.0	38	14.3	55	9.9	166	9.8	57
Mex. Amer.	0	0.0	0	0.0	0	0.0	0	0.0	0	0.0	0	0.0	0
Puerto Rican	0	0.0	0	0.0	0	0.0	0	0.0	0	0.0	0	0.0	0
Hispanic	65	6.8	53	7.2	114	8.0	4	1.5	37	6.6	118	7.0	41
Total Minority	204	21.3	234	31.8	377	26.4	61	23.0	141	25.3	438	25.9	147
For. Nation.	4	0.4	6	0.8	9	0.6	1	0.4	2	0.4	10	0.6	3
Caucasian	643	67.3	442	60.0	915	64.1	170	64.2	363	65.1	1085	64.1	308
Unknown	105	11.0	55	7.5	127	8.9	33	12.5	52	9.3	160	9.5	41
Total	956	56.5	737	43.5	1428	84.3	265	15.7	558	33.0	1693		499

Transfers

Transfers in	33
Transfers out	17

Tuition and Fees

	Resident	Nonresident
Full-time	$36,310	$36,310
Part-time	$25,540	$25,540

Living Expenses

Estimated living expenses for singles

Living on campus	Living off campus	Living at home
$18,490	$18,490	$18,490

The George Washington University Law School

ABA
Approved
Since
1923

GPA and LSAT Scores

	Total	Full-time	Part-time
# of apps	9,829	8,766	1,063
# of offers	2,325	2,122	203
# of matrics	550	426	124
75% GPA	3.78	3.81	3.66
Median GPA	3.59	3.62	3.47
25% GPA	3.40	3.45	3.28
75% LSAT	166	166	164
Median LSAT	165	165	162
25% LSAT	162	163	161

Grants and Scholarships (from prior year)

	Total #	Total %	Full-time #	Full-time %	Part-time #	Part-time %
Total # of students	1,636		1,366		270	
Total # receiving grants	670	41.0	643	47.1	27	10.0
Less than 1/2 tuition	638	39.0	612	44.8	26	9.6
Half to full tuition	31	1.9	30	2.2	1	0.4
Full tuition	1	0.1	1	0.1	0	0.0
More than full tuition	0	0.0	0	0.0	0	0.0
Median grant amount			$10,000		$7,000	

Informational and Library Resources

# of volumes and volume equivalents	603,385
# of titles	140,861
# of active serial subscriptions	3,971
Study seating capacity inside the library	643
# of full-time professional librarians	20
Hours per week library is open	110
# of open, wired connections available to students	54
# of networked computers available for use by students	94
# of simultaneous wireless users	3,000
Require computer?	Yes

JD Attrition (from prior year)

	Academic #	Other #	Total #	Total %
1st year	1	19	20	3.7
2nd year	1	4	5	1.0
3rd year	2	2	4	0.7
4th year	0	0	0	0.0

Employment (9 months after graduation)

	Total	Percentage
Employment status known	485	99.4
Employment status unknown	3	0.6
Employed	472	97.3
Pursuing graduate degrees	7	1.4
Unemployed seeking employment	3	0.6
Unemployed not seeking employment	0	0.0
Unemployed and studying for the bar	3	0.6
Type of Employment		
# employed in law firms	247	52.3
# employed in business and industry	47	10.0
# employed in government	74	15.7
# employed in public interest	14	3.0
# employed as judicial clerks	47	10.0
# employed in academia	4	0.8
Geographic Location		
# employed in state	168	35.6
# employed in foreign countries	5	1.1
# of states where employed	32	

Bar Passage Rates

Jurisdiction	New York		
Exam	Sum 05	Win 06	Total
# from school taking bar for the first time	121	15	136
School's pass rate for all first-time takers	86%	100%	88%
State's pass rate for all first-time takers	76%	61%	74%

The George Washington University Law School

2000 H Street NW
Washington, DC 20052
Phone: 202.994.6288; Fax: 202.994.3597
E-mail: jdadmit@law.gwu.edu; Website: www.law.gwu.edu

■ Introduction

Established in 1865, the George Washington University Law School is the oldest law school in the District of Columbia. Its history of academic excellence, significant contributions to legal scholarship, and outstanding record of service to the community have earned GW a position of local, national, and international prominence. Its talented student body is one of the most diverse of any national law school, and its students graduate to become leaders in all areas of practice. While GW has long been recognized as a leader in fields including constitutional law, intellectual property law, international law, environmental law, government procurement, and clinical education, all of the Law School's academic programs reflect the demands of a changing profession and the global nature of society and the law.

■ Facilities and Library

The Law School complex extends along two sides of the University Yard, the largest open space on GW's urban campus. Its attractive and comfortable classrooms and three moot courtrooms incorporate technology to support a broad range of teaching methods. "Smart podiums" provide access to the Internet and local network and support videoconferencing. Cameras and microphones allow faculty to teach online in streaming video or record classes for later viewing or listening. Power outlets for notebook computers are provided at each student station in most classrooms, and there are more than 70 wireless access points throughout the facility, including in the spacious student lounge areas.

More than 500,000 volumes are at the core of the Jacob Burns Law Library's research collection. In addition, the library offers a variety of legal and law-related databases and automated indexes to enhance research capabilities. A staff of 40 full-time and numerous part-time employees administers and maintains the library during its liberal hours of operation and offers information, instruction, and other research support services.

Law students also have full access to the many amenities of the GW campus, including the Lerner Health and Wellness Center, a state-of-the-art complex featuring a wide range of fitness facilities and classes.

■ Curriculum

One of the Law School's greatest strengths is the richness and diversity of its curriculum. With more than 240 elective courses and seminars, students have an opportunity to sample a broad array of areas of the law and to tailor their programs to their interests and career aspirations. In addition to traditionally taught classes, the curriculum includes a number of simulation courses that teach skills such as drafting, trial and appellate advocacy, negotiations, and mediation, as well as over a dozen different clinical programs in which students learn skills while working directly with clients.

To teach this extensive curriculum, a dynamic and accessible full-time faculty is joined by distinguished members of the bar and bench who teach some of the more specialized courses on an adjunct basis. Excellence in teaching is highly prized at GW, a fact that is readily apparent from scores and comments on semester course evaluations.

■ Clinical Programs and Public Interest

GW's long-standing commitment to public service has culminated in a wide variety of opportunities for students to serve the community while gaining important practical experience. A nationally recognized clinical program gives students the opportunity to work with real clients—many of whom might otherwise be without representation—while at the same time honing their skills. Clinical programs include civil litigation, consumer mediation, domestic violence advocacy, federal and criminal appeal, environmental law, health rights law, immigration, international human rights, older prisoners, public justice advocacy, small business/community development, and vaccine injury.

A student-faculty public interest committee publicizes and encourages student participation in volunteer legal activities, provides career development programs, and administers the Pro Bono Program, which extends special commendation to students who engage in a certain number of pro bono hours while attending the Law School. The Law School makes public service a more feasible option for its students by providing special forms of financial assistance in the form of summer subsidies, fellowships for third-year students, and loan reimbursement assistance for recent graduates of the Law School.

The Law School takes full advantage of its location in the nation's capital through its extensive externship program, which lets students work on a broad range of issues in government agencies, nonprofit organizations, and courts.

■ Joint-degree and Study-abroad Programs

Joint degrees are offered in the areas of business, public administration, public health, public policy, international affairs, history, and women's studies.

Summer study-abroad opportunities include the GW-Oxford Program in International Human Rights Law, the GW–Munich Intellectual Property Law Program, and the GW–Augsburg (Germany) Student Exchange Program. GW is also a member of the North American Consortium on Legal Education, which allows students to study at member Canadian and Mexican law schools.

■ Student Activities

Membership is available on four publications—the *George Washington Law Review*, the *George Washington International Law Review*, the *Public Contract Law Journal* (cosponsored by the ABA section), and the *American Intellectual Property Law Quarterly Journal* (published by AIPLA and housed at GW). Three skills boards—the Moot Court Board, Mock Trial Board, and Alternative Dispute Resolution Board—provide opportunities for participation in inter- and intrascholastic competitions. In addition, approximately 40 student groups are active at the Law School, sponsoring social, educational, career, and public interest related programs. Each year, the Enrichment Program hosts a series of distinguished speakers.

Recent guests have included Supreme Court justices, legal scholars, popular authors, and leaders from government and public interest organizations.

■ Career Development

The Career Development Office provides effective career advising services to students and alumni, enabling them to engage in a meaningful job search, to compete as professionals in the employment market, and to make well-informed choices leading to long-term career satisfaction. The CDO offers a broad range of services, including individual counseling, group seminars, substantive legal practice area programs, interviewing programs, job and internship fairs, online job postings, handouts, a career resource library, an alumni career advisor network, a biweekly newsletter, and a comprehensive website.

■ Financial Assistance

The Law Financial Aid Office counsels and assists applicants and current students in applying for various sources of financial aid: federal and commercial loans at negotiated, competitive terms; need-based tuition grants; and outside scholarships. All applicants are considered for merit-based aid. An estimated 85 percent of GW Law students receive some sort of financial aid.

The Law School's Loan Reimbursement Assistance Program (LRAP) is designed to alleviate the financial burdens of GW Law graduates who pursue public interest employment. The LRAP assists qualified graduates by providing "forgivable" loans to those whose annual income—after taking into consideration their annual law school loan payments—falls below a certain target income.

Applicant Profile

The George Washington University Law School
This grid includes only applicants who earned 120–180 LSAT scores under standard administrations.

LSAT Score	3.75 +		3.50–3.74		3.25–3.49		3.00–3.24		2.75–2.99		2.50–2.74		2.25–2.49		2.00–2.24		Below 2.00		No GPA		Total	
	Apps	Adm	Apps	Adm	Apps	Adm	Apps	Adm	Apps	Adm	Apps	Adm	Apps	Adm	Apps	Adm	Apps	Adm	Apps	Adm	Apps	Adm
175–180	15	14	17	17	9	9	6	4	7	3	1	0	0	0	0	0	1	0	0	0	56	47
170–174	118	114	145	136	101	79	58	15	25	3	12	1	2	0	1	0	0	0	1	1	463	349
165–169	487	458	595	521	406	180	210	38	79	2	27	1	8	0	0	0	0	0	9	3	1821	1203
160–164	700	246	989	133	758	73	312	32	125	2	55	3	22	0	5	0	1	0	14	3	2981	492
155–159	415	31	696	43	617	46	330	18	144	0	57	0	23	0	4	0	1	0	28	1	2315	139
150–154	161	10	306	31	331	33	202	8	135	1	50	0	20	0	4	0	2	0	21	0	1232	83
145–149	48	0	93	0	106	0	109	0	70	0	30	0	16	0	10	0	0	0	14	0	496	0
140–144	22	0	33	0	53	0	51	0	37	0	28	0	12	0	9	0	0	0	7	0	252	0
135–139	1	0	4	0	12	0	21	0	17	0	9	0	5	0	2	0	0	0	9	0	80	0
130–134	1	0	4	0	2	0	5	0	8	0	5	0	6	0	1	0	1	0	3	0	36	0
125–129	0	0	0	0	0	0	0	0	1	0	1	0	0	0	1	0	0	0	0	0	3	0
120–124	0	0	0	0	0	0	0	0	1	0	0	0	0	0	0	0	0	0	1	0	2	0
Total	1968	873	2882	881	2395	420	1304	115	649	11	275	5	114	0	37	0	6	0	107	8	9737	2313

Apps = Number of Applicants
Adm = Number Admitted
Reflects 99% of the total applicant pool.

Georgetown University Law Center

600 New Jersey Avenue NW, Room 589
Washington, DC 20001
Phone: 202.662.9010; Fax: 202.662.9439
E-mail: admis@law.georgetown.edu; Website: www.law.georgetown.edu

*ABA
Approved
Since
1924*

The Basics

Type of school	Private
Term	Semester
Application deadline	2/1
Application fee	$75
Financial aid deadline	3/1
Can first year start other than fall?	No
Student to faculty ratio	14.5 to 1
Does the university offer:	
housing restricted to law students?	Yes
graduate housing for which law students are eligible?	No

Faculty and Administrators

	Total Fall	Total Spr	Men Fall	Men Spr	Women Fall	Women Spr	Minorities Fall	Minorities Spr
Full-time	110	98	77	65	33	33	13	13
Other Full-time	1	1	1	1	0	0	0	0
Deans, librarians, & others who teach	13	13	8	8	5	5	1	1
Part-time	112	140	89	108	23	32	5	9
Total	**236**	**252**	**175**	**182**	**61**	**70**	**19**	**23**

Curriculum

	Full-time	Part-time
Typical first-year section size	112	125
Is there typically a "small section" of the first-year class, other than Legal Writing, taught by full-time faculty	Yes	Yes
If yes, typical size offered last year	26	32
# of classroom course titles beyond first-year curriculum	331	
# of upper division courses, excluding seminars with an enrollment: Under 25	152	
25–49	55	
50–74	35	
75–99	16	
100+	14	
# of seminars	191	
# of seminar positions available	3,146	
# of seminar positions filled	1,424	874
# of positions available in simulation courses	1,123	
# of simulation positions filled	559	417
# of positions available in faculty supervised clinical courses	288	
# of faculty supervised clinical positions filled	281	6
# involved in field placements	36	7
# involved in law journals	709	40
# involved in interschool competitions	154	34
# of credit hours required to graduate	84	

JD Enrollment and Ethnicity

	Men #	Men %	Women #	Women %	Full-time #	Full-time %	Part-time #	Part-time %	1st-year #	1st-year %	Total #	Total %	JD Degs. Awd.
African Amer.	62	5.5	127	14.8	154	9.7	35	9.1	56	9.5	189	9.6	48
Amer. Indian	4	0.4	1	0.1	3	0.2	2	0.5	0	0.0	5	0.3	1
Asian Amer.	91	8.1	88	10.2	142	8.9	37	9.6	55	9.4	179	9.0	66
Mex. Amer.	13	1.2	5	0.6	12	0.8	6	1.6	5	0.9	18	0.9	4
Puerto Rican	5	0.4	5	0.6	7	0.4	3	0.8	3	0.5	10	0.5	0
Hispanic	40	3.6	37	4.3	61	3.8	16	4.1	28	4.8	77	3.9	19
Total Minority	215	19.2	263	30.6	379	23.8	99	25.6	147	25.0	478	24.2	138
For. Nation.	37	3.3	26	3.0	47	3.0	16	4.1	16	2.7	63	3.2	16
Caucasian	761	68.1	502	58.4	1034	64.9	229	59.3	303	51.6	1263	63.9	455
Unknown	105	9.4	69	8.0	132	8.3	42	10.9	121	20.6	174	8.8	2
Total	1118	56.5	860	43.5	1592	80.5	386	19.5	587	29.7	1978		611

Transfers

Transfers in	100
Transfers out	13

Tuition and Fees

	Resident	Nonresident
Full-time	$37,220	$37,220
Part-time	$27,300	$27,300

Living Expenses

Estimated living expenses for singles

Living on campus	Living off campus	Living at home
$19,580	$19,580	$14,495

Georgetown University Law Center

*ABA
Approved
Since
1924*

GPA and LSAT Scores

	Total	Full-time	Part-time
# of apps	11,237	10,336	901
# of offers	2,400	2,219	181
# of matrics	587	457	130
75% GPA	3.81	3.82	3.77
Median GPA	3.70	3.71	3.54
25% GPA	3.45	3.47	3.32
75% LSAT	171	171	167
Median LSAT	168	169	165
25% LSAT	166	167	162

Grants and Scholarships (from prior year)

	Total		Full-time		Part-time	
	#	%	#	%	#	%
Total # of students	1,940		1,580		360	
Total # receiving grants	485	25.0	476	30.1	9	2.5
Less than 1/2 tuition	335	17.3	326	20.6	9	2.5
Half to full tuition	117	6.0	117	7.4	0	0.0
Full tuition	33	1.7	33	2.1	0	0.0
More than full tuition	0	0.0	0	0.0	0	0.0
Median grant amount			$12,650		$7,950	

Informational and Library Resources

# of volumes and volume equivalents	1,129,462
# of titles	362,264
# of active serial subscriptions	8,883
Study seating capacity inside the library	1,169
# of full-time professional librarians	23
Hours per week library is open	107
# of open, wired connections available to students	1,278
# of networked computers available for use by students	320
# of simultaneous wireless users	5,000
Require computer?	

JD Attrition (from prior year)

	Academic	Other	Total	
	#	#	#	%
1st year	0	6	6	1.0
2nd year	1	16	17	2.6
3rd year	0	2	2	0.3
4th year	0	1	1	1.5

Employment (9 months after graduation)

	Total	Percentage
Employment status known	647	98.6
Employment status unknown	9	1.4
Employed	608	94.0
Pursuing graduate degrees	12	1.9
Unemployed seeking employment	4	0.6
Unemployed not seeking employment	23	3.6
Unemployed and studying for the bar	0	0.0
Type of Employment		
# employed in law firms	401	66.0
# employed in business and industry	31	5.1
# employed in government	47	7.7
# employed in public interest	26	4.3
# employed as judicial clerks	88	14.5
# employed in academia	0	0.0
Geographic Location		
# employed in state	216	35.5
# employed in foreign countries	15	2.5
# of states where employed	35	

Bar Passage Rates

Jurisdiction	New York			Maryland		
Exam	Sum 05	Win 06	Total	Sum 05	Win 06	Total
# from school taking bar for the first time	208	20	228	82	16	98
School's pass rate for all first-time takers	94%	80%	93%	87%	88%	87%
State's pass rate for all first-time takers	76%	61%	74%	76%	66%	74%

Georgetown University Law Center

600 New Jersey Avenue NW, Room 589
Washington, DC 20001
Phone: 202.662.9010; Fax: 202.662.9439
E-mail: admis@law.georgetown.edu; Website: www.law.georgetown.edu

■ Introduction

Georgetown University Law Center, founded in 1870, is a dynamic and diverse intellectual community in which to study law. Its curriculum includes more courses and seminars than any other law school. Its distinguished full-time faculty is the nation's largest and is augmented by the experience and perspective of outstanding members of the bench and bar. The goal is education in its fullest sense—not only mastery of law, but a sense of the philosophical, political, and ethical dimensions of law. Preeminent in the fields of constitutional, international, and tax law, as well as clinical legal education, the Georgetown faculty is also known for its expertise in civil rights, corporate law, environmental law, family law, feminist jurisprudence, health law, human rights, immigration and refugee law, intellectual property law, legal history, and securities law. The Supreme Court, the Congress of the United States, and the Library of Congress are within walking distance of the campus, forming a unique environment for creative legal thought and learning.

■ The Law Center Campus

Georgetown Law Center's campus completion project added two buildings to the Law Center campus: the Eric E. Hotung International Law Center Building and the Sport and Fitness Center. The construction project was the culmination of a goal set more than two decades ago to create a campus that would nurture students in mind, body, and spirit. The Hotung building brings all the major components of Georgetown's international programs under one roof, and includes the new John Wolff International and Comparative Law Library. The Sport and Fitness Center features a four-lane lap pool and basketball and racquetball courts, as well as a café and lounge with wireless network connectivity.

The Law Center's Edward Bennett Williams Law Library houses the third largest academic law library collection in the nation. The library also provides students access to many Web-based services to ensure they have the most advanced research support available.

Georgetown's McDonough Hall, with its lecture halls, seminar rooms, faculty offices, bookstore, student dining area, and lounges, is the academic center of the campus.

Housing for approximately 300 students is available in the Gewirz Student Center. It offers a variety of apartment styles with one, two, and three bedrooms. Apartments designed for students with disabilities are also available.

■ Curriculum

The Law Center offers day and evening programs leading to the JD degree. Entry to both programs is in the fall. First-year students choose either the A or B curriculum. Students in the A curriculum begin their studies with eight courses, including one elective course in the spring semester. The B curriculum includes courses that emphasize the sources of law in history, philosophy, political theory, and economics. It also seeks to reflect the increasingly public nature of contemporary law. A residency of six semesters is required for full-time students, eight semesters for part-time students.

The Law Center offers, by far, the largest number of elective courses among US law schools. Of the more than 275 courses offered to upperclass students, more than 150 have enrollments under 25 students.

In the spring of 2006, the Law Center launched an innovative program for first-year students, entitled, "Week One: Law in a Global Context." Involving an intensive week of study of complex problems of international and transnational law, the purpose is to deepen students' understanding of how legal problems increasingly transcend national boundaries and involve more than one legal system.

■ Joint Degrees

Georgetown has established 11 joint-degree programs: JD/Master of Public Policy; JD/Master of Science in Foreign Service; JD/Master of Arts in Arab Studies; JD/Master of Arts in German and European Studies; JD/Master of Arts in Latin American Studies; JD/Master of Arts in Eurasian, Russian, and East European Studies; JD/Master of Arts in Security Studies; JD/Master of Business Administration; JD/Master of Public Health (with Johns Hopkins School of Public Health); JD/Master or Doctorate in Philosophy; and the JD/Doctorate in Government.

■ International and Comparative Law Programs

The Law Center has many highly regarded programs dealing with different aspects of international law.

The Global Law Scholars Program provides an opportunity for a limited number of full-time JD students to prepare for a law practice involving more than one legal system. The program combines language skills with directed legal training to produce lawyers who are ready to practice in the global legal environment of the twenty-first century.

The Law Center's Institute of International Economic Law offers students the opportunity to obtain a certificate testifying to special competence in World Trade Organization (WTO) understanding. In addition, the Law Center's International Summer Internship Program offers students opportunities to work abroad in law firms, corporations, and government organizations. Georgetown also offers a summer law program in London with distinguished professors from Europe and the US, as well as the opportunity to study abroad for a semester at prestigious institutions in Europe and Latin America.

■ Clinical Programs and Public Interest Law

Georgetown Law Center, a pioneer in clinical legal education, offers an unmatched clinical program. Clinical programs are divided into two categories: (1) programs that permit students to represent clients in court or in administrative hearings and (2) programs that enable students to participate in a nontrial context in federal and local agencies, schools, and other institutions.

The Public Interest Law Scholars Program gives special encouragement, in the form of enriched educational opportunities, career counseling, financial support of up to one-third tuition, and a limited number of summer employment stipends, to eight students per class who are committed to practicing law in the public interest.

The Office of Public Interest and Community Service promotes community service projects, provides academic counseling, conducts career-related programs and workshops, and maintains public interest job listings for all students and graduates interested in pursuing public interest employment.

■ Admission

The Law Center evaluates candidates on two scales: academic or objective criteria and personal criteria. Academic information includes undergraduate records and LSAT scores. Personal factors include extracurricular activities, recommendations, work experience, and diversity of background. Georgetown does not use numerical cutoffs. Early application is encouraged since Georgetown employs a rolling admission process.

■ Student Activities

Students edit and publish 10 scholarly journals. The *Law Weekly*, the school newspaper, is printed under student direction. The Barristers Council is responsible for the many appellate advocacy, mock trial, and alternative dispute resolution programs. Students participate in the decision

processes of the Law Center through the Student Bar Association and student/faculty committees. Over 70 law student organizations support personal, social, and professional interests.

■ Financial Aid

Georgetown offers need-based, three-year financial aid grants to approximately one-third of the entering full-time class. Federal and commercial loans with preferred terms, along with on- and off-campus work-study opportunities, are available. Approximately 87 percent of Georgetown's JD students obtain financial aid.

Acknowledged as one of the nation's top programs by Equal Justice Works, Georgetown's Loan Repayment Assistance Program assists JD graduates in pursuing careers in public service.

■ Career Services

The Office of Career Services offers a wide range of career counseling and job-related programming. First-year students are assigned a section advisor who works individually with them throughout law school. The on-campus interview program is one of the largest in the country. The office also coordinates the Judicial Clerkship program.

Applicant Profile

Since the Georgetown Admissions Committee takes into consideration a number of factors in evaluating whether a candidate would be suitable for admission, we cannot provide an applicant profile based solely on GPA and LSAT scores. In

making such determinations, the committee focuses on various aspects of a candidate's background and experience which, in combination with GPA and LSAT scores, give insight into a candidate's suitability for admission.

University of Georgia School of Law

Harold Hirsch Hall, 225 Herty Drive
Athens, GA 30602-6012
Phone: 706.542.7060; Fax: 706.542.5556
E-mail: ugajd@uga.edu; Website: www.law.uga.edu

ABA
Approved
Since
1930

The Basics

Type of school	Public
Term	Semester
Application deadline	2/1
Application fee	$30
Financial aid deadline	3/1
Can first year start other than fall?	No
Student to faculty ratio	15.7 to 1
Does the university offer:	
housing restricted to law students?	No
graduate housing for which law students are eligible?	Yes

Faculty and Administrators

	Total		Men		Women		Minorities	
	Fall	Spr	Fall	Spr	Fall	Spr	Fall	Spr
Full-time	37	35	28	27	9	8	6	3
Other Full-time	10	8	5	3	5	5	0	0
Deans, librarians, & others who teach	5	5	2	2	3	3	0	0
Part-time	13	23	10	17	3	6	1	1
Total	65	71	45	49	20	22	7	4

Curriculum

	Full-time	Part-time
Typical first-year section size	76	0
Is there typically a "small section" of the first-year class, other than Legal Writing, taught by full-time faculty	No	No
If yes, typical size offered last year		

# of classroom course titles beyond first-year curriculum		126
# of upper division courses, excluding seminars with an enrollment:	Under 25	82
	25–49	32
	50–74	18
	75–99	3
	100+	9
# of seminars		22
# of seminar positions available		442
# of seminar positions filled	344	0
# of positions available in simulation courses	342	
# of simulation positions filled	312	0
# of positions available in faculty supervised clinical courses	349	
# of faculty supervised clinical positions filled	287	0
# involved in field placements	124	0
# involved in law journals	197	0
# involved in interschool competitions	360	0
# of credit hours required to graduate	88	

JD Enrollment and Ethnicity

	Men		Women		Full-time		Part-time		1st-year		Total		JD Degs. Awd.
	#	%	#	%	#	%	#	%	#	%	#	%	
African Amer.	32	9.4	62	18.8	94	14.0	0	0.0	35	15.1	94	14.0	37
Amer. Indian	1	0.3	1	0.3	2	0.3	0	0.0	1	0.4	2	0.3	1
Asian Amer.	11	3.2	10	3.0	21	3.1	0	0.0	11	4.7	21	3.1	13
Mex. Amer.	0	0.0	0	0.0	0	0.0	0	0.0	0	0.0	0	0.0	0
Puerto Rican	0	0.0	0	0.0	0	0.0	0	0.0	0	0.0	0	0.0	0
Hispanic	7	2.1	7	2.1	14	2.1	0	0.0	5	2.2	14	2.1	6
Total Minority	51	15.0	80	24.3	131	19.6	0	0.0	52	22.4	131	19.6	57
For. Nation.	1	0.3	4	1.2	5	0.7	0	0.0	4	1.7	5	0.7	0
Caucasian	233	68.3	206	62.6	439	65.5	0	0.0	135	58.2	439	65.5	188
Unknown	56	16.4	39	11.9	95	14.2	0	0.0	41	17.7	95	14.2	5
Total	341	50.9	329	49.1	670	100.0	0	0.0	232	34.6	670		250

Transfers

Transfers in	5
Transfers out	1

Tuition and Fees

	Resident	Nonresident
Full-time	$10,614	$28,490
Part-time	$0	$0

Living Expenses

Estimated living expenses for singles

Living on campus	Living off campus	Living at home
$10,248	$12,700	$7,042

University of Georgia School of Law

ABA
Approved
Since
1930

GPA and LSAT Scores

	Total	Full-time	Part-time
# of apps	2,449	2,449	0
# of offers	554	554	0
# of matrics	232	232	0
75% GPA	3.85	3.85	0.00
Median GPA	3.62	3.62	0.00
25% GPA	3.39	3.39	0.00
75% LSAT	164	164	0
Median LSAT	163	163	0
25% LSAT	156	156	0

Grants and Scholarships (from prior year)

	Total		Full-time		Part-time	
	#	%	#	%	#	%
Total # of students	694		694		0	
Total # receiving grants	227	32.7	227	32.7	0	0.0
Less than 1/2 tuition	179	25.8	179	25.8	0	0.0
Half to full tuition	34	4.9	34	4.9	0	0.0
Full tuition	11	1.6	11	1.6	0	0.0
More than full tuition	3	0.4	3	0.4	0	0.0
Median grant amount			$2,000		$0	

Informational and Library Resources

# of volumes and volume equivalents	519,569
# of titles	200,289
# of active serial subscriptions	7,151
Study seating capacity inside the library	446
# of full-time professional librarians	9
Hours per week library is open	109
# of open, wired connections available to students	0
# of networked computers available for use by students	41
# of simultaneous wireless users	600
Require computer?	No

JD Attrition (from prior year)

	Academic	Other	Total	
	#	#	#	%
1st year	2	1	3	1.4
2nd year	0	0	0	0.0
3rd year	0	2	2	0.8
4th year	0	0	0	0.0

Employment (9 months after graduation)

	Total	Percentage
Employment status known	192	99.0
Employment status unknown	2	1.0
Employed	184	95.8
Pursuing graduate degrees	4	2.1
Unemployed seeking employment	0	0.0
Unemployed not seeking employment	2	1.0
Unemployed and studying for the bar	2	1.0
Type of Employment		
# employed in law firms	117	63.6
# employed in business and industry	10	5.4
# employed in government	17	9.2
# employed in public interest	8	4.3
# employed as judicial clerks	27	14.7
# employed in academia	5	2.7
Geographic Location		
# employed in state	140	76.1
# employed in foreign countries	1	0.5
# of states where employed	14	

Bar Passage Rates

Jurisdiction	Georgia		
Exam	Sum 05	Win 06	Total
# from school taking bar for the first time	153	10	163
School's pass rate for all first-time takers	92%	90%	91%
State's pass rate for all first-time takers	86%	79%	84%

University of Georgia School of Law

Harold Hirsch Hall, 225 Herty Drive
Athens, GA 30602-6012
Phone: 706.542.7060; Fax: 706.542.5556
E-mail: ugajd@uga.edu; Website: www.law.uga.edu

■ Introduction

The University of Georgia (UGA) School of Law, founded in 1859, is on the campus of the University of Georgia in Athens, Georgia. The university provides an excellent setting for the study of law with superb libraries and outstanding academic, cultural, recreational, and social opportunities. Athens, a town of 100,000, is the commercial and legal center for northeast Georgia and is approximately one hour from downtown Atlanta. Athens also features a cultural richness ranging from antebellum homes to the latest in the alternative music scene.

The School of Law is approved by the ABA, is a member of the AALS, and has a chapter of the Order of the Coif.

■ The Student Body

The law school student body shares a strong sense of community, and the school prides itself on the collegiality among students, faculty, and staff. The entering class usually numbers in the low 200s, and the entire student body, including LLM students, averages 650 students. The law school is also a vital part of the university community, which supports a cosmopolitan mix of over 33,000 undergraduate, graduate, and professional students. Many law students take advantage of these assets by taking courses in other schools and colleges of the university and by participating in the intellectual and social life of the campus.

■ Curriculum

The law curriculum is rich and diverse. The first year of study consists of required core courses, but, after its completion, students may choose from a wealth of classes, seminars, and clinical programs to suit their interests.

Clinical program opportunities, both criminal and civil, abound. Clinical education expands upon the classroom knowledge by providing essential experiential learning. Students interested in criminal law can participate in the Prosecutorial Clinic, the Criminal Defense Clinic, or the Capital Assistance Project. Students interested in environmental law, family law, public interest law, and any of a number of other areas of study will find that the Civil Externship Clinic, Family Violence Clinic, Land Use Clinic, Mediation Practicum, Public Interest Practicum, and the Environmental Law Practicum add to their understanding and preparedness.

■ Faculty

While some law schools choose to emphasize either scholarship or teaching, the University of Georgia seeks a balance of the two, firmly believing that classroom teaching is enhanced by scholarly expertise. The college town setting fosters student-faculty interaction by increasing faculty availability and promoting a conducive atmosphere for dialogue.

The faculty includes authors of some of our country's leading legal scholarship, recipients of the university's highest honors for teaching excellence, Fulbright Scholars, and former law clerks for the US Supreme Court and appellate courts. Most bring practical experience to the classroom as well; they

have been trial and corporate attorneys, and many continue to accept pro bono cases or serve as consultants.

Faculty expertise is expanded by the addition of outstanding adjuncts, attorneys from the region's most powerful firms, international attorneys, government leaders, and prominent practitioners. In addition, the law school's Dean Rusk Center—International, Comparative, and Graduate Legal Studies annually is host to several international scholars who may teach mini-courses in their areas of interest. Recent courses include international human rights, dispute settlement in the World Trade Organization, and EC competition law.

■ Educational Enrichment Programs

University of Georgia law students have several opportunities to expand their educational horizons. First, joint programs with other schools and colleges in the university enable students to complete two degrees in less time than it would take to pursue them separately. Existing joint programs include JD/MBA (business administration), JD/MPA (public administration), JD/MHP (historic preservation), JD/MSW (social work), and JD/MEd in Sports Studies.

Students may also take graduate coursework in other schools and colleges of the university and have it count as elective credit toward the 88 semester hours required for graduation. For example, students interested in tax law might take courses in the school of accounting, and students interested in public policy might take courses in the department of political science. Finally, those who are not interested in the joint-degree programs but want more coursework than can be satisfied by elective credit may be concurrently enrolled; that is, students may pursue other advanced degrees at the same time they are fulfilling the requirements for the law degree.

■ Study Abroad

Nothing helps one to better understand the culture of another country than actually studying and living in a foreign land. At UGA, this concept is fully embraced. Currently, UGA is ninth in the nation for the number of students studying abroad. Several opportunities for legal study and work experience in other parts of the world are provided on an annual basis. They include:

Georgia Law at Oxford—This exciting 15-week program runs from January through April and is one of the few semester-long study-abroad programs offered by an American law school. Selected second- and third-year law students take 4 courses and receive 12 semester hours of credit.

International Externship Program—Established in 2001, this initiative provides students with four to eight weeks of study or work experience in a legal learning environment in a variety of countries.

Brussels Seminar on the Law and Institutions of the European Union—For more than three decades, Georgia Law has participated in this seminar, a three-week intensive course on EU law held at the Institut d'Etudes Européennes of the Université Libre de Bruxelles.

Georgia Law Summer Program in China—Partnering with Tsinghua University in Beijing and Fudan University in Shanghai, this three-week study-abroad program in China's two largest cities offers an introduction to the Chinese legal system with an emphasis on commercial and trade law.

Equal Justice Foundation Fellowships—These awards provide grants to law students who engage in public interest legal work in positions that otherwise would not be funded.

■ Library and Physical Facilities

The law library's vast collection makes it among the largest in legal education. While it has extensive holdings in international law, it focuses on being a functional library serving the needs of students. It is currently placed 2nd nationally in expenditures for electronic resources and 22nd in holdings with over 505,000 volumes. The university's main library is adjacent to the law school and is one of the largest research libraries in the nation.

The law school is headquartered in Hirsch Hall on the northern edge of the campus, the most scenic and historic section of the university. Dean Rusk Hall, adjacent to Hirsch Hall, provides additional classroom and office space. The majority of clinical settings are just a short walk away in the downtown area.

■ Career Services

The law school offers a fully staffed career services office that assists law students and graduates. Placement rates are among the highest in the nation, and a very high percentage of students work as summer associates around the country prior to beginning the second and third years of study. The career services website is a comprehensive source of information.

Alumni practice in 48 states and over 45 countries. Over 2,600 employer connections were made available in 2005–2006. Employers from all 50 states and 25 countries utilized the Legal Career Services Office to target UGA students for summer and full-time employment.

■ Advocacy Programs

At Georgia Law, many students participate in the school's acclaimed moot court and mock trial programs and appear before members of the state's and region's highest courts. Team members spend substantial time writing persuasively and learning how to make the most powerful oral presentations that will withstand intense scrutiny by the court. In the last five years, Georgia Law has captured 5 national titles, 15 regional crowns, and 4 state trophies.

Moot Court—Twice in the last 15 years, UGA has reigned supreme in the oldest and most prestigious moot court tournament in the country, the National Moot Court Competition. Georgia Law has captured the regional crown en route to the nationals four of the last five years. Additional opportunities are offered through moot court exchanges held in alternating years with Gray's Inn of London and King's Inn of Dublin.

Mock Trial—UGA won the Association of Trial Lawyers of America (ATLA) title in 1997—becoming the only law school in recent history to hold both the National Moot Court Competition and the ATLA titles in the same year. UGA has also claimed the ATLA regional crown five times.

■ Student Publications

Students at Georgia Law publish three highly regarded legal journals: the *Georgia Law Review*, the *Georgia Journal of International and Comparative Law*, and the *Journal of Intellectual Property Law*, a nationally recognized IP specialty journal. The journals, which are frequently cited by federal and state courts, textbooks, treatises and other law reviews, follow the customary format, with articles from leading scholars and practitioners comprising the bulk of the content and another section consisting of student notes.

Applicant Profile

University of Georgia School of Law
This grid includes only applicants who earned 120–180 LSAT scores under standard administrations.

LSAT Score	3.75 +		3.50–3.74		3.25–3.49		3.00–3.24		2.75–2.99		2.50–2.74		2.25–2.49		2.00–2.24		Below 2.00		No GPA		Total	
	Apps	Adm	Apps	Adm	Apps	Adm	Apps	Adm	Apps	Adm	Apps	Adm	Apps	Adm	Apps	Adm	Apps	Adm	Apps	Adm	Apps	Adm
175–180	2	2	1	1	3	2	0	0	2	1	0	0	0	0	0	0	0	0	0	0	8	6
170–174	9	8	9	9	9	8	7	6	3	1	2	1	0	0	0	0	0	0	0	0	39	33
165–169	45	45	39	36	45	42	30	26	7	4	8	3	1	0	0	0	0	0	2	0	176	156
160–164	113	64	153	58	129	48	82	24	29	3	20	1	9	1	2	0	0	0	5	1	539	199
155–159	153	38	195	17	173	11	110	5	40	2	20	0	6	0	2	0	0	0	7	0	497	53
150–154	80	19	114	12	114	15	101	6	40	1	24	0	15	0	2	0	1	0	6	1	257	24
145–149	34	8	47	4	49	9	62	1	29	0	17	0	9	1	3	0	1	0	6	0	154	0
140–144	5	0	22	0	26	0	40	0	28	0	16	0	9	0	2	0	0	0	4	0	39	0
135–139	0	0	5	0	5	0	10	0	8	0	6	0	1	0	0	0	0	0	2	0	19	0
130–134	0	0	2	0	1	0	2	0	2	0	4	0	1	0	4	0	1	0	2	0	7	0
125–129	0	0	1	0	0	0	0	0	1	0	2	0	0	0	1	0	0	0	0	0	2	0
120–124	0	0	0	0	0	0	0	0	1	0	0	0	0	0	1	0	0	0	0	0	34	2
Total	441	184	588	137	554	135	444	68	190	12	119	5	51	2	17	0	3	0	34	2	2441	545

Apps = Number of Applicants   Adm = Number Admitted   Reflects 99% of the total applicant pool.

Georgia State University College of Law

PO Box 4037
Atlanta, GA 30302-4037
Phone: 404.651.2048; Fax: 404.651.1244
E-mail: admissions@gsulaw.gsu.edu; Website: http://law.gsu.edu

ABA
Approved
Since
1984

The Basics

Type of school	Public
Term	Semester
Application deadline	3/15
Application fee	$50
Financial aid deadline	4/1
Can first year start other than fall?	No
Student to faculty ratio	13.7 to 1
Does the university offer:	
housing restricted to law students?	No
graduate housing for which law students are eligible?	No

Faculty and Administrators

	Total		Men		Women		Minorities	
	Fall	Spr	Fall	Spr	Fall	Spr	Fall	Spr
Full-time	36	36	22	24	14	12	5	5
Other Full-time	6	6	0	0	6	6	1	1
Deans, librarians, & others who teach	12	12	5	5	7	7	3	3
Part-time	13	36	8	25	5	11	3	5
Total	67	90	35	54	32	36	12	14

Curriculum

	Full-time	Part-time
Typical first-year section size	67	67
Is there typically a "small section" of the first-year class, other than Legal Writing, taught by full-time faculty	No	No
If yes, typical size offered last year		
# of classroom course titles beyond first-year curriculum		96
# of upper division courses, excluding seminars with an enrollment: Under 25		74
25–49		44
50–74		20
75–99		3
100+		0
# of seminars		26
# of seminar positions available		363
# of seminar positions filled	274	0
# of positions available in simulation courses		252
# of simulation positions filled	246	0
# of positions available in faculty supervised clinical courses		110
# of faculty supervised clinical positions filled	59	0
# involved in field placements	171	0
# involved in law journals	62	0
# involved in interschool competitions	86	0
# of credit hours required to graduate		90

JD Enrollment and Ethnicity

	Men		Women		Full-time		Part-time		1st-year		Total		JD Degs. Awd.
	#	%	#	%	#	%	#	%	#	%	#	%	
African Amer.	27	7.8	46	14.6	45	9.9	28	13.3	26	12.9	73	11.0	14
Amer. Indian	3	0.9	0	0.0	2	0.4	1	0.5	0	0.0	3	0.5	0
Asian Amer.	12	3.4	21	6.7	27	6.0	6	2.9	9	4.5	33	5.0	13
Mex. Amer.	0	0.0	0	0.0	0	0.0	0	0.0	0	0.0	0	0.0	0
Puerto Rican	0	0.0	0	0.0	0	0.0	0	0.0	0	0.0	0	0.0	0
Hispanic	10	2.9	9	2.9	12	2.6	7	3.3	7	3.5	19	2.9	4
Total Minority	52	14.9	76	24.1	86	19.0	42	20.0	42	20.9	128	19.3	31
For. Nation.	0	0.0	0	0.0	0	0.0	0	0.0	0	0.0	0	0.0	0
Caucasian	246	70.7	202	64.1	309	68.2	139	66.2	138	68.7	448	67.6	127
Unknown	50	14.4	37	11.7	58	12.8	29	13.8	22	10.9	87	13.1	23
Total	348	52.5	315	47.5	453	68.3	210	31.7	201	30.3	663		181

Transfers

Transfers in	8
Transfers out	3

Tuition and Fees

	Resident	Nonresident
Full-time	$7,366	$23,284
Part-time	$6,848	$21,434

Living Expenses

Estimated living expenses for singles

Living on campus	Living off campus	Living at home
$13,110	$13,476	$4,866

Georgia State University College of Law

*ABA
Approved
Since
1984*

GPA and LSAT Scores

	Total	Full-time	Part-time
# of apps	2,698	2,485	213
# of offers	607	431	176
# of matrics	213	149	64
75% GPA	3.54	3.61	3.54
Median GPA	3.33	3.33	3.31
25% GPA	3.03	3.00	3.09
75% LSAT	161	161	161
Median LSAT	159	159	159
25% LSAT	157	158	157

Grants and Scholarships (from prior year)

	Total		Full-time		Part-time	
	#	%	#	%	#	%
Total # of students	685		494		191	
Total # receiving grants	98	14.3	56	11.3	42	22.0
Less than 1/2 tuition	54	7.9	32	6.5	22	11.5
Half to full tuition	4	0.6	0	0.0	4	2.1
Full tuition	40	5.8	24	4.9	16	8.4
More than full tuition	0	0.0	0	0.0	0	0.0
Median grant amount			$6,022		$6,022	

Informational and Library Resources

# of volumes and volume equivalents	345,092
# of titles	66,072
# of active serial subscriptions	2,137
Study seating capacity inside the library	354
# of full-time professional librarians	9
Hours per week library is open	103
# of open, wired connections available to students	882
# of networked computers available for use by students	113
# of simultaneous wireless users	240
Require computer?	No

JD Attrition (from prior year)

	Academic	Other	Total	
	#	#	#	%
1st year	13	19	32	14.7
2nd year	0	0	0	0.0
3rd year	0	0	0	0.0
4th year	0	0	0	0.0

Employment (9 months after graduation)

	Total	Percentage
Employment status known	187	98.4
Employment status unknown	3	1.6
Employed	172	92.0
Pursuing graduate degrees	4	2.1
Unemployed seeking employment	2	1.1
Unemployed not seeking employment	9	4.8
Unemployed and studying for the bar	0	0.0

Type of Employment

# employed in law firms	121	70.3
# employed in business and industry	17	9.9
# employed in government	24	14.0
# employed in public interest	7	4.1
# employed as judicial clerks	1	0.6
# employed in academia	2	1.2

Geographic Location

# employed in state	156	90.7
# employed in foreign countries	0	0.0
# of states where employed		12

Bar Passage Rates

Jurisdiction	Georgia		
Exam	Sum 05	Win 06	Total
# from school taking bar for the first time	154	15	169
School's pass rate for all first-time takers	94%	73%	92%
State's pass rate for all first-time takers	86%	79%	84%

Georgia State University College of Law

PO Box 4037
Atlanta, GA 30302-4037
Phone: 404.651.2048; Fax: 404.651.1244
E-mail: admissions@gsulaw.gsu.edu; Website: http://law.gsu.edu

■ Introduction

Georgia State University College of Law is located in downtown Atlanta, the center for legal, financial, and governmental activities in the Southeast. This location provides easy access to federal, state, and local courts and agencies, the state capitol and legislature, corporations, major law firms in the metropolitan area, and the library and other facilities of Georgia State University.

The College of Law began operation in 1982. The College of Law is accredited by the ABA and is a member of the AALS.

■ Library and Physical Facilities

The College of Law library is designed and equipped to meet the demanding research needs of today's students, faculty members, staff, and members of the legal community. With a collection of more than 156,000 volumes, the library provides research materials in American, British, Canadian, and international law. Students find a host of computer applications available in the law library computer lab, which is staffed by computer consultants. The college dedicates state-of-the-art computer equipment for training purposes only in our computer training room. The classrooms and study carrels accommodate laptop computers.

The College of Law is one of the leading law schools in the Southeast. Located on a 25-acre campus in the heart of downtown Atlanta, the building houses a moot courtroom equipped with state-of-the-art video technology and provides activities directed toward trial and appellate advocacy. Students have access to many other campus facilities including the athletic complex, which offers a variety of individual fitness opportunities and team sports.

■ Curriculum

The college offers students the opportunity to study full or part time and provides a traditional yet innovative curriculum. It offers extensive coverage of the foundational areas of the law to first-year students while providing an array of elective opportunities in public and private law. Opportunities range from the study of legal philosophy and jurisprudence to vital skills training through courses in litigation, counseling, negotiation, legal drafting, and alternative dispute resolution.

The growth of technology in our lives is reflected in courses in Intellectual Property and Computers and the Law; in our innovative course, Law and the Internet; and in the increasing use of computer programs and online discussion groups. Opportunities exist for in-depth study in international and comparative law, environmental law, health law, tax law, employment law, commercial law, and bankruptcy.

■ Admission

The College of Law actively seeks to enroll a student body with diversity in educational, cultural, and racial backgrounds that will enrich the educational experience of the entire group.

Applicants are encouraged to visit. Please make arrangements through the Admissions Office to tour the campus; talk with students, faculty, and admission staff; or attend a class.

■ Special Programs

Joint-degree Programs—Six joint JD and master's degree programs are available with the J. Mack Robinson College of Business, the Andrew Young School of Policy Studies, the Department of Philosophy in the College of Arts and Sciences, and the College of Architecture at the Georgia Institute of Technology.

International Programs—Students have the opportunity to participate in two summer-abroad programs. These are the Transnational Comparative Dispute Resolution Program in Europe and the Summer Legal and Policy Study program in comparative and international law in Brazil.

Clinics—The Tax Clinic and the Health Law Partnership (HeLP) Clinic provide a live-client component to the college's Lawyer Skills Development Program. Both clinics give students hands-on, real-life experience in client representation and handling cases. Work in the Tax Clinic teaches case management, evidence gathering, document preparation, interviewing, counseling, and effective negotiation. The Health Law Partnership Clinic offers a community service clinic that provides students with opportunities to work on cases related to children's health and welfare, including clinics on site at two Atlanta area children's hospitals where low-income children and their families are eligible for these services aimed at eliminating socioeconomic barriers to optimum health.

Externships—Externships are designed to tie theoretical knowledge to a practical base of experience in the profession. Externships involve actual participation in rendering legal services. Students interested in the externship program should contact the Lawyer Skills Development Office.

Trial Advocacy—The College of Law offers students an extensive variety of opportunities in the area of trial advocacy. Our litigation workshop, offered each spring semester, provides second-year students with an intensive skills training experience. Working in small seminar groups, students are asked to conduct drafting and simulation exercises on all phases of the pretrial and trial process, including a full jury trial. In addition to the workshop, the college offers several advanced litigation courses in which students can further enhance their advocacy skills in civil and criminal areas.

Moot Court—Each year, students compete in several of the most challenging and prestigious moot court competitions throughout the country. The Moot Court program has achieved substantial renown and success in its 23-year history. The National Moot Court Competition, sponsored by the Association of the Bar of the City of New York, is the oldest and most recognized national competition, and the College of Law became the first law school in Georgia to place first in that competition. Teams from the college have since won numerous other competitions.

Centers—The College of Law has two centers: the Center for Law, Health, and Society and the Center for the Comparative Study of Metropolitan Growth. The Center for Law, Health, and Society promotes the integration of health law and ethics into (1) health policy and research, (2) the health sciences, (3) the provision of health services, and (4) the interdisciplinary education of law students. The Center for the Comparative Study of Metropolitan Growth produces research, teaching, and academic exchange on the range of issues relating to metropolitan growth.

■ Student Activities

The *Georgia State University Law Review* is published four times a year by students who have demonstrated outstanding writing and academic skills.

The college also boasts a nationally renowned student mock trial program in which our students compete annually in numerous mock trial competitions held at locations throughout the country. Our student teams have amassed an incredible record of success at the national, regional, and state levels. The College of Law has won three national championships, competed in four national finals, and won eight regional championships and several state championships.

The College of Law regards student organizations as an important part of a legal education experience and encourages participation in our wide variety of organizations, some traditionally found in law schools, some less common. The college recognizes 25 organizations, most of which are affiliated with national professional associations. We are proud of the accomplishments of these groups.

■ Career Services

The Career Services Office offers a broad range of services. Students may begin using the office in November of the first year of law school and may continue utilizing career planning services throughout their careers. Specific programs geared toward minority students are the Atlanta Bar Association Minority Clerkship Program and the Southeastern Minority Job Fair. Typically, over 95 percent of each graduating class accepts employment within six months of graduation.

Applicant Profile

Georgia State University College of Law
This grid includes only applicants who earned 120–180 LSAT scores under standard administrations.

LSAT Score	GPA 3.75 +		3.50–3.74		3.25–3.49		3.00–3.24		2.75–2.99		2.50–2.74		2.25–2.49		2.00–2.24		Below 2.00		No GPA		Total	
	Apps	Adm	Apps	Adm	Apps	Adm	Apps	Adm	Apps	Adm	Apps	Adm	Apps	Adm	Apps	Adm	Apps	Adm	Apps	Adm	Apps	Adm
175–180	1	1	0	0	1	1	0	0	1	1	0	0	0	0	0	0	0	0	0	0	3	3
170–174	1	1	2	2	2	2	1	1	1	1	2	1	3	1	0	0	1	0	0	0	12	9
165–169	10	10	8	8	15	13	4	4	6	5	6	4	1	1	0	0	0	0	2	1	51	45
160–164	32	32	61	59	59	54	51	46	28	18	21	11	13	4	2	0	0	0	6	5	269	225
155–159	90	63	162	83	169	70	125	37	81	21	41	7	17	2	11	1	1	0	6	5	703	289
150–154	85	10	124	12	172	10	156	8	87	8	48	2	29	1	10	0	2	0	6	1	719	52
145–149	36	0	85	0	97	0	110	2	72	0	47	0	29	0	14	1	3	0	7	0	500	3
140–144	13	0	36	0	63	1	89	0	58	0	45	0	23	0	15	0	4	0	6	0	353	1
135–139	1	0	11	0	23	0	29	0	31	0	31	0	15	0	15	0	0	0	3	0	166	0
130–134	1	0	1	0	6	0	10	0	15	0	14	0	8	0	6	0	0	0	1	0	64	0
125–129	0	0	1	0	0	0	0	0	1	0	2	0	4	0	3	0	1	0	1	0	13	0
120–124	0	0	0	0	1	0	1	0	0	0	0	0	0	0	0	0	0	0	0	0	2	0
Total	270	117	491	164	608	151	576	98	381	54	257	25	142	9	72	2	14	0	44	7	2855	627

Apps = Number of Applicants
Adm = Number Admitted
Reflects 99% of the total applicant pool.

Golden Gate University School of Law

536 Mission Street
San Francisco, CA 94105-2968
Phone: 415.442.6630 or 800.GGU.4YOU; Fax: 415.442.6631
E-mail: lawadmit@ggu.edu; Website: www.ggu.edu/law

Probation

ABA Approved Since 1956

The Basics

Type of school	Private
Term	Semester
Application deadline	4/1
Application fee	$60
Financial aid deadline	
Can first year start other than fall?	No
Student to faculty ratio	19.9 to 1
Does the university offer:	
housing restricted to law students?	No
graduate housing for which law students are eligible?	No

Faculty and Administrators

	Total		Men		Women		Minorities	
	Fall	Spr	Fall	Spr	Fall	Spr	Fall	Spr
Full-time	30	32	19	21	11	11	5	7
Other Full-time	3	3	0	0	3	3	1	1
Deans, librarians, & others who teach	9	11	4	3	5	8	1	2
Part-time	66	76	40	43	26	33	14	14
Total	**108**	**122**	**63**	**67**	**45**	**55**	**21**	**24**

Curriculum

	Full-time	Part-time
Typical first-year section size	70	53
Is there typically a "small section" of the first-year class, other than Legal Writing, taught by full-time faculty	Yes	No
If yes, typical size offered last year	36	
# of classroom course titles beyond first-year curriculum	120	
# of upper division courses, excluding seminars with an enrollment: Under 25	138	
25–49	29	
50–74	13	
75–99	10	
100+	0	
# of seminars	10	
# of seminar positions available	220	
# of seminar positions filled	87	31
# of positions available in simulation courses	393	
# of simulation positions filled	248	93
# of positions available in faculty supervised clinical courses	97	
# of faculty supervised clinical positions filled	60	0
# involved in field placements	129	32
# involved in law journals	50	4
# involved in interschool competitions	73	12
# of credit hours required to graduate	88	

JD Enrollment and Ethnicity

	Men		Women		Full-time		Part-time		1st-year		Total		JD Degs. Awd.
	#	%	#	%	#	%	#	%	#	%	#	%	
African Amer.	6	1.8	14	3.2	11	1.8	9	5.7	8	3.0	20	2.6	8
Amer. Indian	1	0.3	3	0.7	4	0.7	0	0.0	3	1.1	4	0.5	3
Asian Amer.	51	15.5	69	16.0	98	16.3	22	14.0	40	15.0	120	15.8	37
Mex. Amer.	5	1.5	10	2.3	11	1.8	4	2.5	5	1.9	15	2.0	7
Puerto Rican	0	0.0	2	0.5	1	0.2	1	0.6	1	0.4	2	0.3	0
Hispanic	11	3.4	11	2.6	13	2.2	9	5.7	8	3.0	22	2.9	10
Total Minority	74	22.6	109	25.3	138	22.9	45	28.7	65	24.3	183	24.1	65
For. Nation.	4	1.2	2	0.5	5	0.8	1	0.6	1	0.4	6	0.8	1
Caucasian	211	64.3	256	59.4	374	62.1	93	59.2	161	60.3	467	61.5	124
Unknown	39	11.9	64	14.8	85	14.1	18	11.5	40	15.0	103	13.6	40
Total	328	43.2	431	56.8	602	79.3	157	20.7	267	35.2	759		230

Transfers

Transfers in	2
Transfers out	32

Tuition and Fees

	Resident	Nonresident
Full-time	$31,140	$31,140
Part-time	$21,870	$21,870

Living Expenses

Estimated living expenses for singles

Living on campus	Living off campus	Living at home
N/A	$21,315	N/A

Golden Gate University School of Law

*ABA
Approved
Since
1956*

GPA and LSAT Scores

	Total	Full-time	Part-time
# of apps	3,110	2,818	292
# of offers	1,404	1,287	117
# of matrics	264	219	45
75% GPA	3.43	3.45	3.21
Median GPA	3.21	3.24	2.93
25% GPA	2.94	3.01	2.72
75% LSAT	156	156	153
Median LSAT	153	153	151
25% LSAT	151	151	150

Grants and Scholarships (from prior year)

	Total		Full-time		Part-time	
	#	%	#	%	#	%
Total # of students	851		669		182	
Total # receiving grants	261	30.7	223	33.3	38	20.9
Less than 1/2 tuition	206	24.2	177	26.5	29	15.9
Half to full tuition	34	4.0	29	4.3	5	2.7
Full tuition	20	2.4	16	2.4	4	2.2
More than full tuition	1	0.1	1	0.1	0	0.0
Median grant amount			$6,000		$5,410	

Informational and Library Resources

# of volumes and volume equivalents	373,373
# of titles	77,243
# of active serial subscriptions	4,925
Study seating capacity inside the library	308
# of full-time professional librarians	9
Hours per week library is open	95
# of open, wired connections available to students	526
# of networked computers available for use by students	116
# of simultaneous wireless users	600
Require computer?	No

JD Attrition (from prior year)

	Academic	Other	Total	
	#	#	#	%
1st year	60	58	118	36.9
2nd year	7	10	17	6.0
3rd year	2	0	2	0.9
4th year	0	0	0	0.0

Employment (9 months after graduation)

	Total	Percentage
Employment status known	184	100.0
Employment status unknown	0	0.0
Employed	117	63.6
Pursuing graduate degrees	6	3.3
Unemployed seeking employment	12	6.5
Unemployed not seeking employment	3	1.6
Unemployed and studying for the bar	46	25.0
Type of Employment		
# employed in law firms	59	50.4
# employed in business and industry	28	23.9
# employed in government	10	8.5
# employed in public interest	7	6.0
# employed as judicial clerks	5	4.3
# employed in academia	3	2.6
Geographic Location		
# employed in state	90	76.9
# employed in foreign countries	0	0.0
# of states where employed	6	

Bar Passage Rates

Jurisdiction	California		
Exam	Sum 05	Win 06	Total
# from school taking bar for the first time	137	46	183
School's pass rate for all first-time takers	44%	41%	43%
State's pass rate for all first-time takers	64%	54%	62%

Golden Gate University School of Law

536 Mission Street, Office of Admissions
San Francisco, CA 94105-2968
Phone: 415.442.6630 or 800.GGU.4YOU; Fax: 415.442.6631
E-mail: lawadmit@ggu.edu; Website: www.ggu.edu/law

■ Introduction

Founded in 1901, Golden Gate University School of Law is located in the heart of San Francisco's legal and financial district. The law school is noted for integrating legal theory and practical skills training. Golden Gate has a distinguished faculty who share a strong commitment to both excellence in teaching and accessibility to students. The law school is a fully ABA-accredited program and is a member in good standing with the AALS.

The curriculum at Golden Gate University School of Law is designed to lay the foundations of modern legal theory but also to foster those practical skills necessary to be a successful lawyer. For example, because writing is the lawyer's basic tool, the school trains students to master the skills to draft a wide array of legal documents.

■ Program Options

The law school offers both a full-time day and a part-time evening program. The full-time program involves three years of study and the part-time program involves four years of study. Golden Gate Law also offers an enhanced JD program under the Honors Lawyering Program and offers two formal joint-degree programs.

■ Honors Lawyering Program

As an enhancement to the standard law school curriculum, Golden Gate Law offers the Honors Lawyering Program (HLP). Honors Lawyering students spend two semesters working as apprentices in law offices. They attend two intensive summer programs in simulated law firm settings to learn substantive law and prepare themselves for their apprenticeships. In this way, the program integrates classroom theory, skills, values, and practice. Honors Lawyering students complete law school in three years, pay the same tuition, and must complete the same number of units as students in the standard curriculum.

■ Public Interest Law

At Golden Gate Law, the law curriculum and programs integrate public interest law and service to the community. Students may earn a public interest law certificate of specialization by completing 14 credits of approved elective courses, a 150-hour public interest practicum, and 25 hours of work for a campus or community organization. Students with prior commitment to public and community service may be selected to participate in the Public Interest Law Scholars Program (PISP), which provides students with scholarships and a summer employment stipend.

■ Joint Degrees and Certificates of Specialization

Students may earn the following joint degrees: JD/MBA and JD/PhD in Clinical Psychology.

Golden Gate also offers JD students the opportunity to earn specialization certificates in Business Law, Criminal Law, Environmental Law, Intellectual Property Law, International Law, Labor and Employment Law, Litigation, Public Interest Law, Real Estate Law, and Taxation. Requirements for the areas of specialization vary, but students generally complete coursework and clinical practice to earn a certificate.

■ Clinical Programs

Golden Gate University has one of the most extensive clinical programs in the country, offering students opportunities to earn academic credit while working closely with practicing attorneys.

The law school has two on-site clinics. In the Women's Employment Rights Clinic, students represent low-income women with employment-related problems. Through the Environmental Law and Justice Clinic, students assist Northern California communities in protecting their environmental interests and reducing their exposure to toxins.

In field-placement clinics, students work under the supervision of faculty, judges, and attorneys in government agencies, law offices, and judges' chambers. These off-site clinics include the Civil Practice Clinic, Criminal Litigation Clinic, Environmental Law Clinic, Family Law Clinic, Immigration and Refugee Policy Clinic, Judicial Externships, Landlord-Tenant Law Clinic, Public Interest/Government Counsel Clinic, Real Estate Clinic, and Tax-Aid Clinic.

■ Summer Programs

Students in our study-abroad programs take courses covering a number of international topics currently of interest in the legal world. The curriculum combines introductory courses on the host country's legal systems and comparative law courses. Students also benefit from learning under the guidance of faculty from Golden Gate University School of Law, from faculty and practitioners at other ABA-accredited law schools, and from faculty and practitioners in the host country. Golden Gate Law currently offers summer-abroad programs in Bangkok, Thailand, and Paris, France.

■ Graduate Programs

Golden Gate University School of Law offers five LLM programs: Environmental Law, Intellectual Property Law, International Legal Studies, Taxation, and US Legal Studies. It also offers an SJD program in International Legal Studies.

■ Law Library

The Law Library houses the largest law collection in the San Francisco financial district—more than 350,000 volumes. Its holdings include a comprehensive series of case law reporters, statutes, digests, encyclopedias, periodicals, and treatises dealing with American law; a strong tax collection; a microforms collection; and a growing body of work in environmental law, law and literature, and international law. International law holdings target selected Pacific Rim countries and English, Canadian, and Commonwealth materials. Students in the Law Library have access to the Internet and a variety of Internet-based legal databases.

Career Services and Placement

The Law Career Services (LCS) office helps students prepare for a successful legal career by providing many services throughout law school and beyond. LCS helps students to research the legal market, develop contacts, and build skills through jobs and internships. For first-year students, LCS provides an online *Job Search Guide* and workshops on writing résumés and cover letters. For upper-division students, LCS offers print and online job listings; talks by graduates about their career experiences; individual and small-group career counseling; job-search skills workshops, panels, and events highlighting the career paths of Golden Gate alumni and other attorneys; special recruitment programs; and more. Many of these services continue after graduation.

Law Reviews, Journals, and Student Organizations

Golden Gate Law publishes the *Golden Gate University Law Review*, the *Environmental Law Journal*, and the *Annual Survey of International and Comparative Law*. The law review and journals provide students with the opportunity to showcase their research, writing, and editing skills. The law school also has more than 25 student organizations ranging from groups representing minority students to groups focusing on specific areas of law. An active student government represents the law school student body on important issues facing individuals, student organizations, and the law school. Through these groups, students have many opportunities to participate in programs and attend lectures hosted by a variety of organizations and journals. These opportunities enrich the law school and learning experience, and students are strongly encouraged to participate at all levels.

Admission and Scholarships

Golden Gate University School of Law awards scholarships to both entering and continuing students. All students are reviewed for scholarships as part of the admission review process. Scholarships awarded to entering students are awarded on a three-year basis. Students maintain their full-tuition dean's scholarship or their partial-tuition faculty scholarship by earning a 3.0 required course GPA. Students not receiving a scholarship at the time they are admitted may have the opportunity to receive a scholarship at the end of their spring semester. Students who receive a 3.0 required course GPA are eligible for a merit scholarship. To maintain a merit scholarship students must continue to earn a 3.0 required course GPA.

Golden Gate Law also offers a Public Interest Scholars Program (PISP) Scholarship, an Environmental Law Scholarship, and a Diversity Scholarship. These scholarships are awarded in the amount of $5,000 per year, awarded on a three-year basis, and require a 2.5 required course GPA to maintain the scholarship. Both the PISP Scholarship and the Environmental Law Scholarship require a separate statement of interest and a list of prior commitment/activities from the student to be considered. Students interested in the Diversity Scholarship should highlight the diverse set of experiences and voice they will bring to the law school community through their application, personal statement, and optional writings.

Applicant Profile

Golden Gate University School of Law
This grid includes only applicants who earned 120–180 LSAT scores under standard administrations.

LSAT Score	3.75 +		3.50–3.74		3.25–3.49		3.00–3.24		2.75–2.99		2.50–2.74		2.25–2.49		2.00–2.24		Below 2.00		No GPA		Total	
	Apps	Adm	Apps	Adm	Apps	Adm	Apps	Adm	Apps	Adm	Apps	Adm	Apps	Adm	Apps	Adm	Apps	Adm	Apps	Adm	Apps	Adm
175–180	0	0	1	1	0	0	0	0	0	0	0	0	0	0	0	0	0	0	0	0	1	1
170–174	0	0	2	1	2	2	0	0	0	0	1	1	1	0	0	0	0	0	0	0	6	4
165–169	3	3	8	6	4	3	6	5	9	9	4	4	3	3	1	0	0	0	0	0	38	33
160–164	21	20	28	23	40	37	33	30	20	18	19	17	11	6	8	4	0	0	2	2	182	157
155–159	35	30	71	69	129	119	94	89	84	66	40	26	17	5	5	0	0	0	5	4	480	408
150–154	50	44	118	111	203	175	186	149	134	70	81	20	37	2	11	1	4	0	9	3	833	575
145–149	28	12	98	29	133	25	145	15	115	10	73	4	45	3	12	0	0	0	12	0	661	98
140–144	15	1	33	1	65	2	78	3	70	3	51	0	26	0	12	0	3	0	6	0	359	10
135–139	1	0	4	0	19	0	23	0	31	0	17	1	9	0	2	0	1	0	4	0	111	1
130–134	1	0	4	0	4	0	9	0	7	0	8	0	5	0	1	0	1	0	1	0	41	0
125–129	0	0	1	0	1	0	2	0	0	0	1	0	0	0	1	0	0	0	0	0	6	0
120–124	0	0	0	0	0	0	0	0	0	0	0	0	0	0	0	0	0	0	0	0	0	0
Total	154	110	368	241	600	363	576	291	470	176	295	73	154	19	53	5	9	0	39	9	2718	1287

Apps = Number of Applicants
Adm = Number Admitted
Reflects 99% of the total applicant pool.

This chart is a general guide only. Nonnumerical factors are strongly considered for all applicants. "No GPA" includes applicants who received their undergraduate degrees from foreign institutions and/or US institutions in which letter grades are not utilized or calculated.

Gonzaga University School of Law

PO Box 3528
Spokane, WA 99220-3528
Phone: 800.793.1710 or 509.323.5532; Fax: 509.323.3697
E-mail: admissions@lawschool.gonzaga.edu; Website: www.law.gonzaga.edu

The Basics

Type of school	Private
Term	Semester
Application deadline	4/15
Application fee	$50
Financial aid deadline	2/1
Can first year start other than fall?	Yes
Student to faculty ratio	15.9 to 1
Does the university offer:	
housing restricted to law students?	No
graduate housing for which law students are eligible?	No

Faculty and Administrators

	Total		Men		Women		Minorities	
	Fall	Spr	Fall	Spr	Fall	Spr	Fall	Spr
Full-time	28	30	16	16	12	14	3	3
Other Full-time	1	1	1	1	0	0	0	0
Deans, librarians, & others who teach	5	6	2	3	3	3	0	0
Part-time	23	34	17	25	6	9	0	1
Total	57	71	36	45	21	26	3	4

Curriculum

	Full-time	Part-time
Typical first-year section size	90	0
Is there typically a "small section" of the first-year class, other than Legal Writing, taught by full-time faculty	No	No
If yes, typical size offered last year		
# of classroom course titles beyond first-year curriculum	101	
# of upper division courses, excluding seminars with an enrollment: Under 25	50	
25–49	22	
50–74	23	
75–99	5	
100+	1	
# of seminars	8	
# of seminar positions available	169	
# of seminar positions filled	107	0
# of positions available in simulation courses	257	
# of simulation positions filled	228	0
# of positions available in faculty supervised clinical courses	110	
# of faculty supervised clinical positions filled	109	0
# involved in field placements	71	0
# involved in law journals	37	0
# involved in interschool competitions	40	0
# of credit hours required to graduate	90	

JD Enrollment and Ethnicity

	Men		Women		Full-time		Part-time		1st-year		Total		JD Degs. Awd.
	#	%	#	%	#	%	#	%	#	%	#	%	
African Amer.	0	0.0	1	0.4	0	0.0	1	4.5	0	0.0	1	0.2	1
Amer. Indian	6	1.9	5	2.0	10	1.9	1	4.5	5	2.5	11	2.0	1
Asian Amer.	16	5.2	14	5.7	29	5.4	1	4.5	10	4.9	30	5.4	15
Mex. Amer.	0	0.0	0	0.0	0	0.0	0	0.0	0	0.0	0	0.0	0
Puerto Rican	0	0.0	0	0.0	0	0.0	0	0.0	0	0.0	0	0.0	0
Hispanic	3	1.0	8	3.2	11	2.1	0	0.0	1	0.5	11	2.0	9
Total Minority	25	8.1	28	11.3	50	9.3	3	13.6	16	7.9	53	9.5	26
For. Nation.	1	0.3	0	0.0	1	0.2	0	0.0	1	0.5	1	0.2	0
Caucasian	277	89.4	211	85.4	469	87.7	19	86.4	171	84.2	488	87.6	165
Unknown	7	2.3	8	3.2	15	2.8	0	0.0	15	7.4	15	2.7	0
Total	310	55.7	247	44.3	535	96.1	22	3.9	203	36.4	557		191

Transfers

Transfers in	2
Transfers out	12

Tuition and Fees

	Resident	Nonresident
Full-time	$27,978	$27,978
Part-time	$16,812	$16,812

Living Expenses

Estimated living expenses for singles

Living on campus	Living off campus	Living at home
$13,475	$13,475	$13,475

Gonzaga University School of Law

ABA
Approved
Since
1951

GPA and LSAT Scores

	Total	Full-time	Part-time
# of apps	1,599	1,599	0
# of offers	606	606	0
# of matrics	206	206	0
75% GPA	3.57	3.57	0.00
Median GPA	3.32	3.32	0.00
25% GPA	3.02	3.02	0.00
75% LSAT	157	157	0
Median LSAT	155	155	0
25% LSAT	153	153	0

Grants and Scholarships (from prior year)

	Total		Full-time		Part-time	
	#	%	#	%	#	%
Total # of students	578		556		22	
Total # receiving grants	400	69.2	400	71.9	0	0.0
Less than 1/2 tuition	359	62.1	359	64.6	0	0.0
Half to full tuition	41	7.1	41	7.4	0	0.0
Full tuition	0	0.0	0	0.0	0	0.0
More than full tuition	0	0.0	0	0.0	0	0.0
Median grant amount			$9,000		$0	

Informational and Library Resources

# of volumes and volume equivalents	291,866
# of titles	66,102
# of active serial subscriptions	2,546
Study seating capacity inside the library	428
# of full-time professional librarians	6
Hours per week library is open	110
# of open, wired connections available to students	140
# of networked computers available for use by students	83
# of simultaneous wireless users	800
Require computer?	No

JD Attrition (from prior year)

	Academic	Other	Total	
	#	#	#	%
1st year	11	16	27	14.2
2nd year	0	5	5	2.8
3rd year	0	0	0	0.0
4th year	0	0	0	0.0

Employment (9 months after graduation)

	Total	Percentage
Employment status known	201	100.0
Employment status unknown	0	0.0
Employed	173	86.1
Pursuing graduate degrees	10	5.0
Unemployed seeking employment	4	2.0
Unemployed not seeking employment	8	4.0
Unemployed and studying for the bar	6	3.0
Type of Employment		
# employed in law firms	76	43.9
# employed in business and industry	42	24.3
# employed in government	26	15.0
# employed in public interest	8	4.6
# employed as judicial clerks	14	8.1
# employed in academia	3	1.7
Geographic Location		
# employed in state	136	78.6
# employed in foreign countries	1	0.6
# of states where employed	15	

Bar Passage Rates

Jurisdiction	Washington		
Exam	Sum 05	Win 06	Total
# from school taking bar for the first time	98	13	111
School's pass rate for all first-time takers	71%	69%	71%
State's pass rate for all first-time takers	75%	74%	75%

Gonzaga University School of Law

PO Box 3528
Spokane, WA 99220-3528
Phone: 800.793.1710 or 509.323.5532; Fax: 509.323.3697
E-mail: admissions@lawschool.gonzaga.edu; Website: www.law.gonzaga.edu

■ Introduction

Gonzaga University School of Law belongs to a long and distinguished tradition of humanistic, Catholic, and Jesuit education. Founded in 1887, Gonzaga continues to maintain the tradition of academic excellence in education that is at the heart of the mission of the 450-year-old Jesuit order. The School of Law, established in 1912, is a member of the AALS and is approved by the ABA. The campus is located in Spokane, Washington, a four-season city with the Spokane River flowing through its center. The metropolitan area of approximately 400,000 people serves as the regional hub of the Inland Northwest, a large area running from the Cascade Mountains in the west to the Rockies in the east. Canada is a mere 100 miles to the north.

Spokane is not only an economic hub for manufacturing, agriculture, and light industry, but it is also a recreational sports area abundant with lakes, mountains, and forests. In minutes you can get away from the city's robust, rapidly growing business community to the surrounding pine-covered hills.

■ Physical Facilities and Library

Rising from the banks of the beautiful Spokane River, Gonzaga University School of Law, which opened in May 2000, provides a stunning setting for research and learning. The law school offers a variety of classroom and library environments that support today's interactive teaching methods. Features throughout the building encourage students to greet each other and linger to talk and debate ideas in beautiful outdoor spaces, roof plazas and balconies, and comfortable lounges. Miles of state-of-the-art voice, data, and video cable provide the highway for audiovisual, computer, and telecommunications technology throughout the building. The mix of classrooms, rooms for simulations of various sizes, and clinical teaching spaces provides flexibility to preserve the best of traditional law teaching while introducing new methods. The Chastek Library is the largest legal research facility north of Portland and between Seattle and Minneapolis. With a collection of 294,000 volumes and microform equivalents plus electronic resources, the library provides excellent information and computing resources and services to support the instructional, research, and scholarly endeavors of the law school and university community. The library is equipped with a wireless network, has two computer labs, and laptops are made available for circulation. The staff provides reference support and personalized assistance with research and network navigation.

■ Curriculum and Faculty

There is a deliberate and delicate balance to legal education at Gonzaga. The rigorous curriculum focuses on legal analysis, problem solving, values, and ethics. Equally as important is the emphasis on practical experience to develop real-world lawyering skills. As a capstone to its innovative approach to legal education, the School of Law offers Juris Doctor degrees with special concentrations in public interest law,

environmental/natural resource law, and business law (including tax law).

The term "teaching faculty" applies in a very special way to the School of Law faculty. The Jesuit tradition demands a high degree of student-professor interaction inside and outside the classroom, and this emphasis attracts exceptional faculty. Gonzaga's focus on the individual student, a favorable student-to-faculty ratio, and the promotion of positive rather than negative competition provides an atmosphere of success in which to study.

■ Special Programs

The first year of coursework is devoted to building a strong legal foundation for upper-division study. In order to ease the transition to the rigorous demands of law school, entering students may take advantage of the support offered through orientation, academic resource programs, academic advisors, and special tutorials. Entering students also have the option of enrolling in the summer through the Early Start Program.

There are three dual-degree programs leading to the JD/MBA, the JD/MAcc, and the JD/MSW degrees, which are offered to prepare students who anticipate careers in fields that require thorough knowledge of business, accountancy, social services, and the law.

An added dimension to the legal education for many law students is the opportunity to practice law while in school through Gonzaga's Center for Law and Justice, the nationally recognized clinical law program.

■ Admission

The School of Law endeavors to attract students with ambitious minds, professional motivation, and commitment to the highest ethics and values of the legal profession and to public service. Consideration of applicants is not restricted to impersonal statistics, but includes recognition and review of the enriching qualities of applicants, reflected in their personal statement, résumé, and letters of recommendation. Gonzaga seeks to enroll an ethnically and geographically diverse student body.

■ Student Activities

Students find it easy to become involved in a broad range of activities at the School of Law. Gonzaga is a major player in moot court competition through five moot court teams. The student-run *Gonzaga Law Review* is circulated throughout the country, and *Gonzaga Journal of International Law,* the online international law journal, receives submissions from around the world. The Student Bar Association is a strong, active organization that encourages student involvement, and there is also opportunity to participate in intraschool moot court competition, legal fraternities, and other numerous organizations and activities. Gonzaga's student organizations are diverse in nature and whatever your interests or career goals, there are activities available that will enhance your knowledge and abilities, while contributing to the community.

■ Housing

The Gonzaga campus is in a residential area within close proximity to downtown Spokane. Housing is available within walking distance to the law school, and rental rates are reasonably priced compared to most large population centers.

■ Financial Aid

Law school is a career investment. For students who need financial assistance to help fund this investment, we encourage filing the FAFSA. Gonzaga also provides more than one million dollars in scholarship aid each year, and your admission application will serve as your scholarship application.

However, students who are interested in applying for the Thomas More Scholarship need to apply separately. Gonzaga awards up to five Thomas More Scholarships a year, which covers 80 percent of tuition.

■ Career Services

Gonzaga's active Career Services Office successfully assists law students and alumni in planning their careers and in seeking employment, throughout both law school and the course of their professional careers. The size of the student body allows the director the opportunity to work individually with students and alumni in their job searches across the country.

Applicant Profile

Gonzaga University School of Law
This grid includes only applicants who earned 120–180 LSAT scores under standard administrations.

LSAT Score	3.75 + Apps	3.75 + Adm	3.50–3.74 Apps	3.50–3.74 Adm	3.25–3.49 Apps	3.25–3.49 Adm	3.00–3.24 Apps	3.00–3.24 Adm	2.75–2.99 Apps	2.75–2.99 Adm	2.50–2.74 Apps	2.50–2.74 Adm	2.25–2.49 Apps	2.25–2.49 Adm	2.00–2.24 Apps	2.00–2.24 Adm	Below 2.00 Apps	Below 2.00 Adm	No GPA Apps	No GPA Adm	Total Apps	Total Adm
175–180	0	0	0	0	0	0	0	0	0	0	0	0	0	0	0	0	0	0	0	0	0	0
170–174	0	0	0	0	0	0	0	0	1	1	1	1	0	0	0	0	0	0	1	1	3	3
165–169	2	2	4	4	4	4	3	3	1	1	1	1	3	1	0	0	0	0	1	1	18	16
160–164	12	12	13	13	11	11	11	11	7	7	12	11	3	1	3	1	0	0	1	1	73	68
155–159	32	30	67	67	60	58	45	42	40	36	19	16	8	4	1	0	0	0	0	0	272	253
150–154	51	30	103	58	150	78	135	59	73	27	28	10	16	2	4	0	1	0	1	0	562	264
145–149	32	1	86	1	104	0	102	0	45	0	36	0	13	0	10	0	1	0	3	0	432	2
140–144	12	0	22	0	34	0	40	0	31	0	15	0	7	0	3	0	1	0	1	0	166	0
135–139	1	0	3	0	13	0	13	0	10	0	6	0	3	0	1	0	1	0	0	0	51	0
130–134	1	0	1	0	1	0	0	0	4	0	2	0	2	0	1	0	0	0	1	0	13	0
125–129	0	0	0	0	0	0	0	0	1	0	0	0	1	0	0	0	0	0	0	0	2	0
120–124	0	0	0	0	0	0	0	0	0	0	0	0	0	0	0	0	0	0	0	0	0	0
Total	143	75	299	143	377	151	349	115	213	72	120	39	56	8	23	1	4	0	8	2	1592	606

Apps = Number of Applicants
Adm = Number Admitted
Reflects 99% of the total applicant pool.

Hamline University School of Law

1536 Hewitt Avenue
St. Paul, MN 55104
Phone: 651.523.2461, 800.388.3688; Fax: 651.523.3064
E-mail: lawadm@hamline.edu; Website: www.hamline.edu/law

*ABA
Approved
Since
1975*

The Basics

Type of school	Private
Term	Semester
Application deadline	4/1
Application fee	$50
Financial aid deadline	4/1
Can first year start other than fall?	No
Student to faculty ratio	16.6 to 1
Does the university offer:	
housing restricted to law students?	No
graduate housing for which law students are eligible?	Yes

Faculty and Administrators

	Total		Men		Women		Minorities	
	Fall	Spr	Fall	Spr	Fall	Spr	Fall	Spr
Full-time	33	30	20	19	13	11	5	4
Other Full-time	2	1	0	0	2	1	0	0
Deans, librarians, & others who teach	7	6	2	2	5	4	0	0
Part-time	55	72	34	49	21	23	2	5
Total	97	109	56	70	41	39	7	9

Curriculum

	Full-time	Part-time
Typical first-year section size	58	44
Is there typically a "small section" of the first-year class, other than Legal Writing, taught by full-time faculty	No	No
If yes, typical size offered last year		
# of classroom course titles beyond first-year curriculum	121	
# of upper division courses, excluding seminars with an enrollment: Under 25	81	
25–49	65	
50–74	24	
75–99	0	
100+	0	
# of seminars	17	
# of seminar positions available	276	
# of seminar positions filled	191	50
# of positions available in simulation courses	1,172	
# of simulation positions filled	212	740
# of positions available in faculty supervised clinical courses	116	
# of faculty supervised clinical positions filled	81	10
# involved in field placements	65	37
# involved in law journals	83	36
# involved in interschool competitions	42	8
# of credit hours required to graduate	88	

JD Enrollment and Ethnicity

	Men		Women		Full-time		Part-time		1st-year		Total		JD Degs. Awd.
	#	%	#	%	#	%	#	%	#	%	#	%	
African Amer.	7	2.0	15	4.1	13	2.6	9	4.1	6	2.5	22	3.1	9
Amer. Indian	0	0.0	4	1.1	3	0.6	1	0.5	3	1.2	4	0.6	2
Asian Amer.	16	4.6	20	5.4	23	4.6	13	6.0	13	5.3	36	5.0	8
Mex. Amer.	0	0.0	0	0.0	0	0.0	0	0.0	0	0.0	0	0.0	0
Puerto Rican	0	0.0	0	0.0	0	0.0	0	0.0	0	0.0	0	0.0	0
Hispanic	15	4.3	14	3.8	15	3.0	14	6.4	11	4.5	29	4.1	11
Total Minority	38	11.0	53	14.4	54	10.8	37	17.0	33	13.6	91	12.7	30
For. Nation.	2	0.6	5	1.4	6	1.2	1	0.5	2	0.8	7	1.0	2
Caucasian	287	82.7	300	81.3	413	82.9	174	79.8	192	79.0	587	82.0	189
Unknown	20	5.8	11	3.0	25	5.0	6	2.8	16	6.6	31	4.3	7
Total	347	48.5	369	51.5	498	69.6	218	30.4	243	33.9	716		228

Transfers

Transfers in	5
Transfers out	7

Tuition and Fees

	Resident	Nonresident
Full-time	$27,096	$27,096
Part-time	$19,528	$19,528

Living Expenses

Estimated living expenses for singles

Living on campus	Living off campus	Living at home
$10,453	$14,043	$14,043

ABA
Approved
Since
1975

Hamline

Hamline University
1536 Hewitt Avenue
St. Paul, MN 55104
Phone: 651.523.246?
E-mail: lawadm@

GPA and LSAT Scores

	Total	Full-time	Part-time
# of apps	1,510	1,283	227
# of offers	716	556	160
# of matrics	250	172	78
75% GPA	3.61	3.66	3.51
Median GPA	3.36	3.43	3.23
25% GPA	3.13	3.24	3.01
75% LSAT	158	159	153
Median LSAT	154	155	150
25% LSAT	150	152	147

Grants and Scholarships (from prior year)

	Total		Full-time		Part-time	
	#	%	#	%	#	%
Total # of students	710		516		194	
Total # receiving grants	280	39.4	223	43.3	57	29.4
Less than 1/2 tuition	96	13.5	61	11.8	35	18.0
Half to full tuition	98	13.8	80	15.5	18	9.3
Full tuition	83	11.7	81	15.7	2	1.0
More than full tuition	3	0.4	1	0.2	2	1.0
Median grant amount			$18,934		$8,575	

Informational and Library Resources

# of volumes and volume equivalents	274,195
# of titles	135,721
# of active serial subscriptions	2,707
Study seating capacity inside the library	335
# of full-time professional librarians	10
Hours per week library is open	116
# of open, wired connections available to students	319
# of networked computers available for use by students	47
# of simultaneous wireless users	250
Require computer?	

JD Attrition (from prio

	Academ			
	#			
1st year	3			
2nd year	0			
3rd year	0	3	3	1.3
4th year	0	0	0	0.0

Employment (9 months after graduation)

	Total	Percentage
Employment status known	183	92.9
Employment status unknown	14	7.1
Employed	161	88.0
Pursuing graduate degrees	4	2.2
Unemployed seeking employment	5	2.7
Unemployed not seeking employment	3	1.6
Unemployed and studying for the bar	10	5.5
Type of Employment		
# employed in law firms	71	44.1
# employed in business and industry	49	30.4
# employed in government	15	9.3
# employed in public interest	9	5.6
# employed as judicial clerks	14	8.7
# employed in academia	3	1.9
Geographic Location		
# employed in state	125	77.6
# employed in foreign countries	0	0.0
# of states where employed	17	

Bar Passage Rates

Jurisdiction	Minnesota		
Exam	Sum 05	Win 06	Total
# from school taking bar for the first time	121	19	140
School's pass rate for all first-time takers	81%	89%	82%
State's pass rate for all first-time takers	89%	88%	89%

School of Law

800.388.3688; Fax: 651.523.3064
hamline.edu; Website: www.hamline.edu/law

Introduction

Students at Hamline University School of Law become professional and ethical lawyers who apply legal knowledge with disciplined imagination and a global perspective. Hamline fosters a community of collaborative faculty, staff, students, and alumni who make a difference to each other and society, while striving to achieve professional and educational excellence.

The school also serves as a catalyst for reframing the legal landscape through distinguished guest speakers, thought-provoking symposia, and nationally recognized centers of excellence, such as Hamline's Dispute Resolution Institute. Hamline's faculty includes nationally recognized experts in bioethics, intellectual property, international trade, corporate law, and critical race theory. Other faculty members are renowned for scholarship and academic leadership in health law, dispute resolution, commercial law, state constitutional law, and many other fields.

■ Library and Facilities

Located within a vibrant urban setting, the School of Law is situated on 55 acres of beautifully maintained wooded land as part of the Hamline University campus. The Law Library staff is readily available to provide supportive services, along with nearly 300,000 volumes and electronic databases—giving students access to the libraries of seven other colleges and universities through a consortium agreement. Hamline's Annette K. Levine courtroom provides a technologically up-to-date setting for moot court competitions and for observing actual court proceedings.

■ Rigorous and Supportive Learning Environment

Hamline's core curriculum provides the analytical grounding necessary for success. In addition to a rich three-year full-time program, Hamline offers a unique four-year weekend program that is taught by the same respected faculty members who teach in the day program. The law school also offers dual-degree and course-exchange options, which allow students to combine their legal education with a second disciplinary focus in the areas of public administration, management, nonprofit management, organizational leadership, and library and information science.

Led by the internationally heralded Dispute Resolution Institute, our rich curriculum in negotiations, arbitration, and mediation is second to none. The school launched a Health Law Institute during fall 2006, which offers extensive academic and experiential learning opportunities for students interested in pursuing careers in the health law arena.

Hamline's rigorous offerings reflect considerable depth, enabling students to concentrate their studies in a variety of substantive areas: alternative dispute resolution, corporate/commercial law, child advocacy, criminal law, government and regulatory affairs, health law, intellectual property, international law, labor and employment law, litigation and trial practice, property law, and public law and human rights.

At Hamline, professors move beyond traditional lectures to offer truly collaborative, student-centered classroom

experiences while simultaneously conducting cutting-edge scholarship. Our professors are dedicated to an open-door policy. An emphasis on seminars allows students to learn in small classes, make presentations, and create original research on topics of personal interest, ensuring that students work closely with Hamline's dedicated faculty throughout their law school experience. The Constance L. Bakken Fellowship program provides funding for collaborative research between faculty and students.

■ Experiential Learning: At Home and Abroad

Hamline students further expand their skills by competing in appellate advocacy and negotiation competitions throughout the country and around the world. Hamline's nine legal clinics give students real-world experience in the practice of health law, immigration law, small business planning, criminal law, child advocacy, education law, mediation, and trial practice. Each clinic operates as a small law office with students handling their own caseload and representing clients.

Likewise, Hamline's externship program enables students to work directly with mentor attorneys and judges, and places students in private law firms, corporations, judges' chambers, public agencies, legislative offices, and businesses. This training allows students to absorb real-world legal lessons and provides them with valuable professional legal contacts.

Hamline encourages international study for the development of a truly global perspective. Many students participate in an international exchange program with Hamline's European law school partners. Others compete in the Vienna International Commercial Arbitration Moot Court competition. Hamline provides conferences, classes, and training in London, Rome, Budapest, and Jerusalem, among other foreign locations. With international lawyers from around the world in our LLM program and our academic programs in Latin America, Europe, the Middle East, and Asia, Hamline has become one of the most international law schools in the world.

■ A Vibrant Student Community

Hamline strives to attract a vibrant and diverse student population. Students in our fall 2006 incoming class represented 28 states and 14 percent were students of color. Hamline also offers a graduate program leading to a Master of Laws (LLM) degree for lawyers holding an LLB or equivalent degree from outside the United States. Recent LLM students have hailed from India, Cameroon, Italy, and beyond. These students contribute to the cultural richness of the Hamline learning community.

Opportunities for student involvement abound at Hamline University School of Law. The *Hamline Law Review* and the *Hamline Journal of Public Law and Policy* are entirely staffed by law students. Hamline students also provide editorial assistance for the internationally respected *Journal of Law and Religion*. Hamline students can participate in more than 15 moot court teams, and with 25 active student organizations, students easily find professional, cultural, and social connections to match their interests.

■ Career Assistance

The Career Services Office (CSO) is passionate about assisting all Hamline law students in career planning and job searches. Committed and experienced counselors provide informational programs, mock interviews, one-on-one career counseling, résumé assistance, networking opportunities, and an online job bank. They also organize on-campus interviews with prospective employers and work extensively with employers to advance Hamline law students and to solicit postings and information. Students are strongly encouraged to participate in CSO programs at Hamline and to build professional networks with alumni and other legal professionals while they're earning their Juris Doctor.

■ Admission and Financial Aid

The School of Law maintains a selection process that emphasizes a rigorous but fair examination of each person as an individual, not merely as a set of credentials. In addition to the LSAT and undergraduate GPA, the admission committee gives significant weight to motivation, personal experiences, employment history, graduate education, maturity, letters of recommendation, and the ability to articulate one's interest in, and suitability for, the study of law. Hamline's admission policy is designed to enhance the academic rigor, professional dedication, social concern, and diversity of the student body, including cultural, economic, sexual orientation, racial, and ethnic composition. Hamline also provides a comprehensive financial aid program, which includes merit-based scholarships. At Hamline, 95 percent of law students qualify for need-based loans.

Applicant Profile

Hamline University School of Law
This grid includes only applicants with 120–180 LSAT scores earned under standard administrations.

LSAT Score	3.75 +		3.50–3.74		3.25–3.49		3.00–3.24		2.75–2.99		2.50–2.74		2.25–2.49		2.00–2.24		Below 2.00		No GPA		Totals	
	Apps	Adm	Apps	Adm	Apps	Adm	Apps	Adm	Apps	Adm	Apps	Adm	Apps	Adm	Apps	Adm	Apps	Adm	Apps	Adm	Apps	Adm
175–180	0	0	1	1	0	0	0	0	0	0	0	0	0	0	0	0	0	0	0	0	1	1
170–174	0	0	0	0	0	0	1	1	0	0	0	0	0	0	0	0	0	0	0	0	1	1
165–169	3	3	7	6	3	3	7	6	3	3	1	1	1	1	0	0	0	0	1	0	26	23
160–164	23	22	12	12	16	15	14	13	9	8	5	5	2	2	3	0	0	0	1	1	85	78
155–159	50	49	49	45	55	53	40	36	23	19	19	12	7	3	2	0	0	0	2	2	247	219
150–154	39	30	92	63	113	77	93	50	46	20	24	7	13	1	9	2	2	0	4	3	435	253
145–149	29	13	97	32	91	28	102	33	45	8	23	4	26	1	9	1	1	0	9	1	432	121
140–144	9	2	28	7	29	2	48	4	44	2	27	2	11	0	6	0	1	0	6	1	209	20
135–139	3	0	4	0	11	0	22	1	14	0	14	0	11	0	3	0	2	0	6	0	90	1
130–134	0	0	0	0	1	0	3	0	5	0	6	0	5	0	0	0	1	0	1	0	22	0
125–129	0	0	0	0	0	0	2	0	1	0	1	0	2	0	0	0	1	0	4	0	11	0
120–124	0	0	1	0	0	0	0	0	0	0	0	0	0	0	0	0	0	0	0	0	1	0
Total	156	119	291	166	319	178	332	144	190	60	120	31	78	8	32	3	8	0	34	8	1560	717

Apps = Number of Applicants
Adm = Number Admitted
Reflects 99% of the total applicant pool.

This chart is to be used as a general guide only. Nonnumerical factors are strongly considered for all applicants.

Harvard Law School

1515 Massachusetts Avenue, Austin Hall
Cambridge, MA 02138
Phone: 617.495.3109
E-mail: jdadmiss@law.harvard.edu; Website: www.law.harvard.edu

ABA
Approved
Since
1923

The Basics

Type of school	Private
Term	Semester
Application deadline	2/1
Application fee	$75
Financial aid deadline	3/1
Can first year start other than fall?	No
Student to faculty ratio	10.5 to 1
Does the university offer:	
housing restricted to law students?	Yes
graduate housing for which law students are eligible?	Yes

Faculty and Administrators

	Total Fall	Total Spr	Men Fall	Men Spr	Women Fall	Women Spr	Minorities Fall	Minorities Spr
Full-time	127	150	91	103	36	47	16	19
Other Full-time	30	25	11	12	19	13	3	1
Deans, librarians, & others who teach	3	3	1	1	2	2	0	0
Part-time	28	26	17	15	11	11	1	2
Total	**188**	**204**	**120**	**131**	**68**	**73**	**20**	**22**

Curriculum

	Full-time	Part-time
Typical first-year section size	80	0
Is there typically a "small section" of the first-year class, other than Legal Writing, taught by full-time faculty	No	No
If yes, typical size offered last year		
# of classroom course titles beyond first-year curriculum	267	
# of upper division courses, excluding seminars with an enrollment: Under 25	70	
25–49	40	
50–74	33	
75–99	14	
100+	27	
# of seminars	83	
# of seminar positions available	1,660	
# of seminar positions filled	956	0
# of positions available in simulation courses	294	
# of simulation positions filled	267	0
# of positions available in faculty supervised clinical courses	520	
# of faculty supervised clinical positions filled	458	0
# involved in field placements	114	0
# involved in law journals	1,200	0
# involved in interschool competitions	747	0
# of credit hours required to graduate	84	

JD Enrollment and Ethnicity

	Men #	Men %	Women #	Women %	Full-time #	Full-time %	Part-time #	Part-time %	1st-year #	1st-year %	Total #	Total %	JD Degs. Awd.
African Amer.	82	8.7	108	13.8	190	11.1	0	0.0	67	12.0	190	11.1	54
Amer. Indian	9	1.0	5	0.6	14	0.8	0	0.0	6	1.1	14	0.8	4
Asian Amer.	97	10.3	106	13.6	203	11.8	0	0.0	71	12.7	203	11.8	79
Mex. Amer.	14	1.5	15	1.9	29	1.7	0	0.0	11	2.0	29	1.7	6
Puerto Rican	7	0.7	6	0.8	13	0.8	0	0.0	5	0.9	13	0.8	4
Hispanic	43	4.6	34	4.4	77	4.5	0	0.0	27	4.8	77	4.5	11
Total Minority	252	26.8	274	35.1	526	30.6	0	0.0	187	33.6	526	30.6	158
For. Nation.	34	3.6	37	4.7	71	4.1	0	0.0	29	5.2	71	4.1	21
Caucasian	522	55.6	380	48.7	902	52.5	0	0.0	291	52.2	902	52.5	324
Unknown	131	14.0	89	11.4	220	12.8	0	0.0	50	9.0	220	12.8	79
Total	939	54.6	780	45.4	1719	100.0	0	0.0	557	32.4	1719		582

Transfers

Transfers in	34
Transfers out	0

Tuition and Fees

	Resident	Nonresident
Full-time	$38,490	$38,490
Part-time	$0	$0

Living Expenses

Estimated living expenses for singles

Living on campus	Living off campus	Living at home
$19,336	$19,336	$19,336

*ABA
Approved
Since
1923*

GPA and LSAT Scores

	Total	Full-time	Part-time
# of apps	6,630	6,630	0
# of offers	834	834	0
# of matrics	558	558	0
75% GPA	3.95	3.95	0.00
Median GPA	3.86	3.86	0.00
25% GPA	3.72	3.72	0.00
75% LSAT	175	175	0
Median LSAT	172	172	0
25% LSAT	169	169	0

Grants and Scholarships (from prior year)

	Total		Full-time		Part-time	
	#	%	#	%	#	%
Total # of students	1,712		1,712		0	
Total # receiving grants	679	39.7	679	39.7	0	0.0
Less than 1/2 tuition	421	24.6	421	24.6	0	0.0
Half to full tuition	232	13.6	232	13.6	0	0.0
Full tuition	22	1.3	22	1.3	0	0.0
More than full tuition	4	0.2	4	0.2	0	0.0
Median grant amount			$14,310		$0	

Informational and Library Resources

# of volumes and volume equivalents	2,224,088
# of titles	842,001
# of active serial subscriptions	15,499
Study seating capacity inside the library	802
# of full-time professional librarians	43
Hours per week library is open	115
# of open, wired connections available to students	4,000
# of networked computers available for use by students	207
# of simultaneous wireless users	4,500
Require computer?	No

JD Attrition (from prior year)

	Academic	Other	Total	
	#	#	#	%
1st year	0	3	3	0.5
2nd year	0	2	2	0.4
3rd year	0	2	2	0.3
4th year	0	0	0	0.0

Employment (9 months after graduation)

	Total	Percentage
Employment status known	551	100.0
Employment status unknown	0	0.0
Employed	527	95.6
Pursuing graduate degrees	14	2.5
Unemployed seeking employment	0	0.0
Unemployed not seeking employment	10	1.8
Unemployed and studying for the bar	0	0.0
Type of Employment		
# employed in law firms	335	63.6
# employed in business and industry	27	5.1
# employed in government	12	2.3
# employed in public interest	15	2.8
# employed as judicial clerks	133	25.2
# employed in academia	5	0.9
Geographic Location		
# employed in state	64	12.1
# employed in foreign countries	12	2.3
# of states where employed	40	

Bar Passage Rates

Jurisdiction	New York			Massachusetts		
Exam	Sum 05	Win 06	Total	Sum 05	Win 06	Total
# from school taking bar for the first time	196	16	212	75	7	82
School's pass rate for all first-time takers	95%	100%	95%	99%	100%	99%
State's pass rate for all first-time takers	76%	61%	74%	84%	75%	82%

Harvard Law School

1515 Massachusetts Avenue, Austin Hall
Cambridge, MA 02138
Phone: 617.495.3109
E-mail: jdadmiss@law.harvard.edu; Website: www.law.harvard.edu

■ A Legal Metropolis

Harvard Law School combines the resources of the world's premier center for legal education and research with educational settings designed to enrich individual and interactive learning. The result is a uniquely vibrant and collaborative environment. Harvard's scope generates enormous vitality—an unparalleled breadth and depth of academic options, a wide array of research programs, a diverse student body drawn from across the nation and around the world, and a global network of distinguished alumni. Within this dynamic environment, law students have broad opportunities for intellectual engagement with faculty and classmates: first-year sections have fewer than 80 students, more than 100 courses have an enrollment of 25 or fewer, and opportunities to work directly with faculty members abound. For example, all first-year students may join in intimate (10–12 students), faculty-led reading groups on topics ranging from cyberlaw to climate change to terrorism. Harvard's extensive resources and collaborative approach create unmatched opportunities to prepare for leadership in public service, private practice, the judiciary, academia, business, or government.

■ Public Service

HLS strongly promotes public service. The school guarantees funding for summer public interest work, and over 360 JD students received funds to work in 31 states and 38 countries in 2006. The Office of Public Interest Advising provides comprehensive services to students pursuing public service careers. The Low Income Protection Plan allows graduates substantial financial flexibility to pursue lower-paying employment, and a variety of fellowship programs provide additional support to graduates entering public service. Reflecting its public service commitment, HLS has a 40-hour minimum pro bono work requirement, with students actually completing an average of more than 400 hours of pro bono work during law school.

■ Faculty

The centerpiece of the HLS experience is working directly with scholars who shape the landscape of American and international law. The faculty includes leading scholars and specialists in every subject area. Beyond the classroom, students provide critical support to faculty producing cutting-edge research and influencing the development of the law and of societies around the world. The student/faculty ratio has fallen dramatically in recent years, and Harvard Law School's commitment to hire more core faculty means that this trend is likely to continue.

■ International Scope

Harvard Law School presents students with tremendous opportunities to engage in the world. With students coming from more than 70 countries to study here and with hundreds of current students going abroad each year to work, study, engage in research, or advocate for change, HLS is truly a global crossroads. Each year, the Law School offers more than 60 courses and reading groups focusing on international, foreign, or comparative law. Research centers, such as the East Asian Legal Studies Program or the Program on International Financial Systems, offer students access to visiting scholars and cutting-edge ideas through colloquia, conferences, and research opportunities. Harvard's more than 4,000 alumni living outside the US provide an unparalleled network of opportunity for potential collaboration and camaraderie for members of the community. In addition, scholars come to HLS from all over the world to make use of the incredible international collections housed in the law library.

■ Student Life

At HLS, a wide variety of extracurricular activities complement and enrich the classroom and clinical experiences. Whether exploring professional interests, serving the public, or merely socializing, students engage in an enormous range of activity on the HLS campus beyond the classroom. At present, there are more than 100 student organizations and journals at HLS. Student organizations based on social, political, service, or professional interests plan workshops, panels, concerts, networking opportunities, and conferences for almost every day of the academic year. Other activities planned by first-year social chairs, the second-year social committee, and the third-year class marshals, as well as the Dean of Students office, create a collegial and community-oriented environment on campus. Students are given a wide range of opportunities to create and implement ideas for activities and are encouraged to pursue their interests by forming new student organizations or planning one-time events.

■ Clinical Programs

HLS has one of the most extensive clinical programs in the country, with in-house clinics in Immigration, Human Rights, CyberLaw, Children's Rights, Criminal Defense, Criminal Prosecution, Family Law, Art/Entertainment Law, Death Penalty, Housing, Worker's Rights, Employment Discrimination, Consumer Law, Small Business and Nonprofit Organization, Health Care Law, Special Education, Prisoner's Rights, Environmental Law, and Mediation and Negotiation.

Clinical education at HLS helps to introduce and explore the roles and responsibilities of a lawyer. Taking a clinical course may aid students in thinking about what sort of law practice or lawyering work they most like. Mentored practice, in an educational setting, also helps students begin to understand their practice learning styles while getting a head start on learning the skills they will need when they begin their careers.

The Clinical Legal Education Program at Harvard Law School has three basic components:

- direct student responsibility for clients in a realistic practice setting;
- supervision and mentoring by an experienced practitioner; and
- companion classroom sessions in which clinical experience supports and contributes to further discussion and thought.

In 2005–2006, over 600 students participated in at least one clinic. Clinical courses get enthusiastic reviews from student participants, most of whom find them challenging and educational. Many students find that this practical lawyering produces a sense of personal accomplishment as well as professional development because in most cases, they are truly increasing access to justice for the most marginalized members of society. We also have externship placements at various government agencies, nonprofits, and small firms. Students can also design faculty-sponsored independent clinical work projects in any area they cannot find as part of the curriculum. Finally, many students take advantage of our winter term, spending three to four weeks off campus in a clinical setting and then coming back to campus and continuing the work long distance for the following semester.

■ Employment After Graduation

More than 600 employers recruit on campus at HLS each year. Upon graduation, about 65 percent of HLS graduates enter private practice, about 25 percent enter judicial clerkships, and the remainder enter public interest or government work, business and industry, academia, or other unique pursuits. Virtually every year, the number of HLS graduates clerking for the US Supreme Court surpasses the number from any other law school. In fact, approximately one-fourth of all Supreme Court clerks over the last decade graduated from HLS. After clerkships, many HLS graduates pursue careers in public interest, government, and academia.

Applicant Profile

HLS does not provide a profile chart because it would be based solely upon undergraduate GPA and LSAT scores. Admission decisions are based on many factors beyond GPA and LSAT. Each application is read thoroughly, sometimes by as many as five people, including members of the faculty admission committee. Although most admitted candidates graduated near the top of their college classes and presented LSAT scores in the top few percentiles, a significant proportion of candidates who meet these characterizations may not be offered admission. At the same time, some admitted candidates do not have as high college or LSAT standings but present combined academic and other achievements that are comparable nonetheless. Candidates with higher grades and scores tend to be admitted at higher rates than candidates with lower grades and scores, but at no point on the GPA or LSAT scales are the chances for admission to Harvard Law School zero or 100 percent.

University of Hawai'i at Mānoa—William S. Richardson School of Law

2515 Dole Street
Honolulu, HI 96822
Phone: 808.956.7966; Fax: 808.956.3813
E-mail: lawadm@hawaii.edu; Website: www.hawaii.edu/law

ABA
Approved
Since
1974

The Basics

Type of school	Public
Term	Semester
Application deadline	3/1
Application fee	$60
Financial aid deadline	3/1
Can first year start other than fall?	No
Student to faculty ratio	10.7 to 1
Does the university offer:	
housing restricted to law students?	No
graduate housing for which law students are eligible?	Yes

Faculty and Administrators

	Total		Men		Women		Minorities	
	Fall	Spr	Fall	Spr	Fall	Spr	Fall	Spr
Full-time	19	19	12	12	7	7	4	4
Other Full-time	1	1	0	0	1	1	1	1
Deans, librarians, & others who teach	7	7	2	2	5	5	4	4
Part-time	14	26	9	20	5	6	6	15
Total	**41**	**53**	**23**	**34**	**18**	**19**	**15**	**24**

Curriculum

	Full-time	Part-time
Typical first-year section size	94	0
Is there typically a "small section" of the first-year class, other than Legal Writing, taught by full-time faculty	No	No
If yes, typical size offered last year		
# of classroom course titles beyond first-year curriculum	77	

# of upper division courses, excluding seminars with an enrollment:		
Under 25	56	
25–49	13	
50–74	4	
75–99	11	
100+	3	

# of seminars	44	
# of seminar positions available	510	
# of seminar positions filled	480	0
# of positions available in simulation courses	240	
# of simulation positions filled	190	0
# of positions available in faculty supervised clinical courses	48	
# of faculty supervised clinical positions filled	43	0
# involved in field placements	134	0
# involved in law journals	60	0
# involved in interschool competitions	53	0
# of credit hours required to graduate	89	

JD Enrollment and Ethnicity

	Men		Women		Full-time		Part-time		1st-year		Total		JD Degs. Awd.
	#	%	#	%	#	%	#	%	#	%	#	%	
African Amer.	4	2.3	2	1.5	6	1.9	0	0.0	3	3.3	6	1.9	3
Amer. Indian	3	1.7	4	3.0	7	2.3	0	0.0	3	3.3	7	2.3	2
Asian Amer.	99	56.9	88	65.7	187	60.7	0	0.0	53	58.2	187	60.7	60
Mex. Amer.	1	0.6	3	2.2	4	1.3	0	0.0	0	0.0	4	1.3	1
Puerto Rican	0	0.0	2	1.5	2	0.6	0	0.0	0	0.0	2	0.6	0
Hispanic	3	1.7	1	0.7	4	1.3	0	0.0	1	1.1	4	1.3	0
Total Minority	110	63.2	100	74.6	210	68.2	0	0.0	60	65.9	210	68.2	66
For. Nation.	5	2.9	3	2.2	8	2.6	0	0.0	3	3.3	8	2.6	1
Caucasian	41	23.6	16	11.9	57	18.5	0	0.0	18	19.8	57	18.5	22
Unknown	18	10.3	15	11.2	33	10.7	0	0.0	10	11.0	33	10.7	12
Total	174	56.5	134	43.5	308	100.0	0	0.0	91	29.5	308		101

Transfers

Transfers in	0
Transfers out	2

Tuition and Fees

	Resident	Nonresident
Full-time	$13,032	$22,776
Part-time	$0	$0

Living Expenses

Estimated living expenses for singles		
Living on campus	Living off campus	Living at home
$9,934	$13,949	$5,375

University of Hawai'i at Mānoa—William S. Richardson School of Law

*ABA
Approved
Since
1974*

GPA and LSAT Scores

	Total	Full-time	Part-time
# of apps	1,116	1,116	0
# of offers	215	215	0
# of matrics	91	91	0
75% GPA	3.72	3.72	0.00
Median GPA	3.50	3.50	0.00
25% GPA	3.15	3.15	0.00
75% LSAT	161	161	0
Median LSAT	158	158	0
25% LSAT	155	155	0

Grants and Scholarships (from prior year)

	Total		Full-time		Part-time	
	#	%	#	%	#	%
Total # of students	305		305		0	
Total # receiving grants	107	35.1	107	35.1	0	0.0
Less than 1/2 tuition	58	19.0	58	19.0	0	0.0
Half to full tuition	47	15.4	47	15.4	0	0.0
Full tuition	2	0.7	2	0.7	0	0.0
More than full tuition	0	0.0	0	0.0	0	0.0
Median grant amount			$6,000		$0	

Informational and Library Resources

# of volumes and volume equivalents	351,763
# of titles	42,928
# of active serial subscriptions	4,334
Study seating capacity inside the library	429
# of full-time professional librarians	5
Hours per week library is open	94
# of open, wired connections available to students	280
# of networked computers available for use by students	61
# of simultaneous wireless users	500
Require computer?	Yes

JD Attrition (from prior year)

	Academic	Other	Total	
	#	#	#	%
1st year	0	2	2	1.9
2nd year	0	3	3	3.1
3rd year	0	0	0	0.0
4th year	0	0	0	0.0

Employment (9 months after graduation)

	Total	Percentage
Employment status known	96	95.0
Employment status unknown	5	5.0
Employed	85	88.5
Pursuing graduate degrees	1	1.0
Unemployed seeking employment	3	3.1
Unemployed not seeking employment	6	6.2
Unemployed and studying for the bar	1	1.0
Type of Employment		
# employed in law firms	35	41.2
# employed in business and industry	11	12.9
# employed in government	9	10.6
# employed in public interest	4	4.7
# employed as judicial clerks	24	28.2
# employed in academia	1	1.2
Geographic Location		
# employed in state	70	82.4
# employed in foreign countries	1	1.2
# of states where employed	10	

Bar Passage Rates

Jurisdiction	Hawaii		
Exam	Sum 05	Win 06	Total
# from school taking bar for the first time	71	7	78
School's pass rate for all first-time takers	89%	71%	87%
State's pass rate for all first-time takers	79%	N/A	79%

University of Hawai'i at Mānoa—William S. Richardson School of Law

2515 Dole Street
Honolulu, HI 96822
Phone: 808.956.7966; Fax: 808.956.3813
E-mail: lawadm@hawaii.edu; Website: www.hawaii.edu/law

■ Introduction

The William S. Richardson School of Law at the University of Hawai'i is located at the foot of beautiful Mānoa Valley; minutes from sandy beaches and lush rain forests, as well as from the economic and legal center of urban Honolulu. The School of Law offers an excellent academic program with professors committed to scholarship and research who have a national reputation for teaching excellence. The school is noted for its friendly and collegial student body, its accessible faculty, and its rich cultural and ethnic diversity.

Placement after graduation is consistently very high. The school's distinguished alumni serve as leaders in Hawai'i as well as in national and international arenas. The University of Hawai'i is recognized as a center for environmental law study and international law with an Asian and Pacific focus. The William S. Richardson School of Law is fully accredited by the American Bar Association and is a member of the American Association of Law Schools.

■ Curriculum

The JD program is a three-year program of full-time day study. Full-time registration is defined as enrollment for a minimum of 12 credits each semester. First-year students begin with a three-day orientation; the first-year curriculum is entirely prescribed. All students must complete 60 hours of pro bono law-related community service in order to graduate.

■ Library and Physical Facilities

The library contains a study carrel with wired and wireless Internet access for most students and seminar/discussion rooms for study groups. The air-conditioned classroom building features a moot courtroom with video technology for support of clinical education programs. Law students have full access to all facilities of the university, including the health, counseling, and computing centers, and extensive athletic facilities. The classroom building has wireless Internet access for students, faculty, and staff.

■ Pacific-Asian Legal Studies

Enhanced by Hawai'i's location, population, culture, and economic relationships, the law school offers a program in Pacific-Asian Legal Studies (PALS). The program has the twofold purpose of conducting new research and enriching the JD curriculum. A number of faculty have expertise in Pacific/Asian research, teaching, and law reform. Recent course offerings in PALS have included Chinese Business Law, Chinese Law and Society, Pacific Island Legal Systems, Korean Law, Philippine Law, Japanese Law and Society, and US-Japan Business Transactions. The certificate in Pacific-Asian Legal Studies allows students to focus their coursework and to earn the certificate in addition to the JD.

Selected students may do a full semester externship for academic credit with the court systems in certain Pacific Island nations or, with approval, in agencies or entities in Asia. Students may also arrange a semester of study with law faculties in Asia with prior approval.

■ Environmental/Ocean Law Programs

Students may focus their elective courses in the area of environmental law and can earn a certificate in Environmental Law along with the JD degree. Emphasis is on freshwater resources, oceans, coastal waters, and land use—all areas of special interest to Hawai'i and the Pacific.

The University of Hawai'i also has extensive programs in different types of marine research, and the law faculty is particularly interested in ocean law and policy. Law students may elect to combine their JD studies with a university certificate program in Ocean Policy. The university also offers a certificate in Resource Management.

■ Admission

Admission is determined by an applicant's academic achievement, aptitude for the study of law, and professional promise. Preference is given to residents of Hawai'i and to nonresidents with strong ties to or special interest in Hawai'i, the Asia/Pacific region, or other programs in the law school. Approximately 30 percent of the student body may be nonresidents.

Besides LSAT and undergraduate GPA and major, other factors considered include academic work beyond the bachelor's degree, work experience, writing ability, community service, diversity, overcoming hardship, and unusual accomplishments.

Applications from students wishing to transfer, or from those wishing to visit for a semester or two, are considered for both August and January admission.

■ Student Activities

Student editorial boards publish the *University of Hawai'i Law Review* and the online *Asian and Pacific Law and Policy Journal*. Students also regularly organize and participate in the moot court program, including national moot court competitions in international and environmental law. Student teams have performed very well, bringing home national and international titles and awards in the Jessup International Moot Court Competition, the Environmental Moot Court Competition, the Native American Moot Court Competition, and the Client Counseling Competition.

Many students are active in a variety of organizations within the school and the Honolulu community including, for example, Advocates for Public Interest Law (APIL); student divisions of the American Bar Association, National Lawyers Guild, and American Trial Lawyers Association; American Inns of Court; Student Bar Association; Phi Delta Phi and Delta Theta Phi International Legal Fraternities; the Pacific Islands and Pacific-Asian Legal Studies Organizations; Association of Women Law Students; and Environmental Law Society. Student affinity groups include the Filipino Law Students Association, Black Law Students Association, Hispanic Law Students Association, and the 'Ahahui 'O Hawai'i, an organization of Native Hawaiian law students.

■ Career Services

Career counseling and services assist students and alumni in obtaining part-time, summer clerk, or associate positions in both the public and private sectors. Placement emphasis is on Hawai'i and the Asia/Pacific region, and about 85 percent of our graduates remain here immediately upon graduation.

On-campus facilities are available for interviews. All large firms in Honolulu and many medium and small firms participate in the fall on-campus interview season for second- and third-year students. Our students are highly successful in obtaining much sought after judicial clerkships upon graduation. Most recent graduating classes have had a greater than 90 percent employment rate six months after graduation.

Applicant Profile

University of Hawai'i at Mānoa—William S. Richardson School of Law
This grid includes only applicants who earned 120–180 LSAT scores under standard administrations.

LSAT Score	3.75 +		3.50–3.74		3.25–3.49		3.00–3.24		2.75–2.99		2.50–2.74		2.25–2.49		2.00–2.24		Below 2.00		No GPA		Totals	
	Apps	Adm	Apps	Adm	Apps	Adm	Apps	Adm	Apps	Adm	Apps	Adm	Apps	Adm	Apps	Adm	Apps	Adm	Apps	Adm	Apps	Adm
	0	0	0	0	0	0	0	0	0	0	0	0	0	0	0	0	0	0	0	0	0	0
175–180	0	0	0	0	0	0	0	0	0	0	0	0	0	0	0	0	0	0	1	1	12	9
170–174	2	2	5	4	2	1	1	0	0	0	1	1	0	0	0	0	0	0	0	0	48	28
165–169	7	7	8	5	10	5	14	9	5	1	3	1	1	0	0	0	0	0	0	0	148	73
160–164	16	12	31	22	33	19	27	13	21	5	9	1	8	0	3	1	0	0	0	0	295	69
155–159	28	10	65	25	85	14	54	11	31	3	17	4	7	0	3	0	0	0	5	2	281	28
150–154	23	6	48	8	74	7	67	2	35	2	17	2	11	1	4	0	1	0	1	0	175	5
145–149	14	1	27	2	26	0	43	0	34	0	20	0	4	2	5	0	0	0	2	0	95	3
140–144	9	0	7	0	16	0	22	1	7	0	4	0	5	0	3	0	0	0	1	0	35	0
135–139	0	0	1	0	4	0	10	0	7	0	4	0	2	0	3	0	0	0	1	0	18	0
130–134	1	0	2	0	0	0	3	0	2	0	4	0	0	0	0	0	0	0	0	0	0	0
125–129	0	0	0	0	0	0	0	0	0	0	0	0	0	0	0	0	0	0	0	0	0	0
120–124	0	0	0	0	0	0	0	0	0	0	0	0	0	0	0	0	0	0	0	0	0	0
Total	100	38	194	66	250	46	241	36	149	13	91	9	45	3	23	1	2	0	12	3	1107	215

Apps = Number of Applicants
Adm = Number Admitted
Reflects 99% of the total applicant pool.

Hofstra University School of Law

121 Hofstra University
Hempstead, NY 11549
Phone: 516.463.5916; Fax: 516.463.6264
E-mail: lawadmissions@hofstra.edu; Website: www.law.hofstra.edu

ABA Approved Since 1971

The Basics

Type of school	Private
Term	Semester
Application deadline	4/15
Application fee	$60
Financial aid deadline	4/1
Can first year start other than fall?	No
Student to faculty ratio	18.7 to 1
Does the university offer:	
housing restricted to law students?	Yes
graduate housing for which law students are eligible?	Yes

Faculty and Administrators

	Total		Men		Women		Minorities	
	Fall	Spr	Fall	Spr	Fall	Spr	Fall	Spr
Full-time	43	46	28	30	15	16	4	5
Other Full-time	2	1	2	1	0	0	0	0
Deans, librarians, & others who teach	9	9	2	2	7	7	2	2
Part-time	23	37	23	31	0	6	0	6
Total	77	93	55	64	22	29	6	13

Curriculum

	Full-time	Part-time
Typical first-year section size	115	86
Is there typically a "small section" of the first-year class, other than Legal Writing, taught by full-time faculty	Yes	Yes
If yes, typical size offered last year	29	44
# of classroom course titles beyond first-year curriculum	153	
# of upper division courses, excluding seminars with an enrollment: Under 25	94	
25–49	41	
50–74	13	
75–99	7	
100+	13	
# of seminars	56	
# of seminar positions available	840	
# of seminar positions filled	622	58
# of positions available in simulation courses	1,000	
# of simulation positions filled	736	150
# of positions available in faculty supervised clinical courses	85	
# of faculty supervised clinical positions filled	82	3
# involved in field placements	84	27
# involved in law journals	205	0
# involved in interschool competitions	39	0
# of credit hours required to graduate	87	

JD Enrollment and Ethnicity

	Men #	Men %	Women #	Women %	Full-time #	Full-time %	Part-time #	Part-time %	1st-year #	1st-year %	Total #	Total %	JD Degs. Awd.
African Amer.	22	3.7	66	12.4	61	6.9	27	11.3	35	8.3	88	7.8	25
Amer. Indian	2	0.3	0	0.0	1	0.1	1	0.4	0	0.0	2	0.2	2
Asian Amer.	52	8.7	44	8.3	76	8.5	20	8.4	39	9.3	96	8.5	14
Mex. Amer.	0	0.0	0	0.0	0	0.0	0	0.0	0	0.0	0	0.0	0
Puerto Rican	0	0.0	0	0.0	0	0.0	0	0.0	0	0.0	0	0.0	0
Hispanic	26	4.3	37	7.0	53	6.0	10	4.2	27	6.4	63	5.6	22
Total Minority	102	17.1	147	27.7	191	21.5	58	24.3	101	24.0	249	22.1	63
For. Nation.	0	0.0	0	0.0	0	0.0	0	0.0	0	0.0	0	0.0	0
Caucasian	393	65.7	303	57.1	566	63.6	130	54.4	237	56.4	696	61.6	207
Unknown	103	17.2	81	15.3	133	14.9	51	21.3	82	19.5	184	16.3	31
Total	598	53.0	531	47.0	890	78.8	239	21.2	420	37.2	1129		301

Transfers

Transfers in	27
Transfers out	40

Tuition and Fees

	Resident	Nonresident
Full-time	$35,260	$35,260
Part-time	$35,260	$35,260

Living Expenses

Estimated living expenses for singles

Living on campus	Living off campus	Living at home
$16,196	$20,121	$8,920

Hofstra University School of Law

*ABA
Approved
Since
1971*

GPA and LSAT Scores

	Total	Full-time	Part-time
# of apps	4,810	4,126	684
# of offers	2,088	1,865	223
# of matrics	413	311	102
75% GPA	3.63	3.65	3.47
Median GPA	3.45	3.51	3.20
25% GPA	3.13	3.23	2.92
75% LSAT	158	159	155
Median LSAT	155	157	153
25% LSAT	152	153	150

Grants and Scholarships (from prior year)

	Total		Full-time		Part-time	
	#	%	#	%	#	%
Total # of students	1,038		835		203	
Total # receiving grants	466	44.9	432	51.7	34	16.7
Less than 1/2 tuition	329	31.7	301	36.0	28	13.8
Half to full tuition	87	8.4	82	9.8	5	2.5
Full tuition	43	4.1	43	5.1	0	0.0
More than full tuition	7	0.7	6	0.7	1	0.5
Median grant amount			$10,610		$6,000	

Informational and Library Resources

# of volumes and volume equivalents	558,815
# of titles	153,093
# of active serial subscriptions	5,954
Study seating capacity inside the library	588
# of full-time professional librarians	11
Hours per week library is open	99
# of open, wired connections available to students	166
# of networked computers available for use by students	115
# of simultaneous wireless users	1,050
Require computer?	No

JD Attrition (from prior year)

	Academic	Other	Total	
	#	#	#	%
1st year	0	43	43	11.2
2nd year	0	1	1	0.2
3rd year	0	0	0	0.0
4th year	0	0	0	0.0

Employment (9 months after graduation)

	Total	Percentage
Employment status known	323	97.0
Employment status unknown	10	3.0
Employed	276	85.4
Pursuing graduate degrees	19	5.9
Unemployed seeking employment	4	1.2
Unemployed not seeking employment	14	4.3
Unemployed and studying for the bar	10	3.1
Type of Employment		
# employed in law firms	177	64.1
# employed in business and industry	43	15.6
# employed in government	33	12.0
# employed in public interest	5	1.8
# employed as judicial clerks	11	4.0
# employed in academia	1	0.4
Geographic Location		
# employed in state	230	83.3
# employed in foreign countries	0	0.0
# of states where employed	13	

Bar Passage Rates

Jurisdiction	New York		
Exam	Sum 05	Win 06	Total
# from school taking bar for the first time	246	15	261
School's pass rate for all first-time takers	69%	67%	69%
State's pass rate for all first-time takers	76%	61%	74%

Hofstra University School of Law

121 Hofstra University
Hempstead, NY 11549
Phone: 516.463.5916; Fax: 516.463.6264
E-mail: lawadmissions@hofstra.edu; Website: law.hofstra.edu

■ Introduction

Hofstra University School of Law offers both full- and part-time JD programs as well as master of laws programs in Family Law, International Law, and American Legal Studies. Hofstra's curriculum teaches the craft of lawyering while preparing students for practice in any jurisdiction. We focus on imparting knowledge, developing analytical abilities, and training law students in the professional skills needed to excel. The law school offers two joint-degree programs in conjunction with the business school: a JD/MBA program and a combined JD/MS in Taxation. The law school is located on the Hofstra University campus, 20 miles outside of New York City in suburban Long Island.

■ Faculty

The Hofstra faculty consists of nationally and internationally recognized authorities in diverse fields. Faculty members have clerked for justices of the US Supreme Court, chaired major ABA and law reform committees, won awards for scholarship and leadership in legal education, and are recognized as leaders in skills training. The faculty's open-door policy creates an accessible and collegial environment.

■ International Law

Hofstra is at the forefront of international law, with an exceptional faculty whose expertise encompasses every area of the field, from international trade and business to human rights, the law of war to immigration or global environmental issues. We offer more than two dozen international law courses, in addition to an LLM program, and are one of the only US law schools to have Transnational Law as a required first-year course. We offer extensive study-abroad programs, including summer programs in Sorrento, Italy; Nice, France; and Sydney, Australia; and a winter intersession program on the Caribbean island of Curaçao. These programs often feature prominent jurists, such as the Supreme Court Justices Antonin Scalia and Ruth Bader Ginsburg. Hofstra law school is also a founding member of the European American Consortium of Legal Education (EACLE). As such, Hofstra law students can participate in a semester-long exchange program with Erasmus University, Ghent University, Helsinki University, or Warsaw University.

■ Center for Legal Advocacy

Hofstra law school offers one of the nation's most comprehensive programs for hands-on training in the skills of trial and appellate advocacy. The Center for Legal Advocacy offers programs for both law students and practicing lawyers through traditional classroom teaching, simulation-based courses, moot trial competitions, externships, clinical experiences, and workshops with accomplished practitioners and distinguished faculty. Each January, students are able to select a unique three-credit "immersion" course on trial techniques patterned on the programs offered by the National Institute for Trial Advocacy. A sequence of exercises builds

students' abilities so they are able to conduct a mock jury trial at the end of the course. Other highlights of the center include numerous trial competitions, in which Hofstra teams routinely place nationally, and the Trial Advocacy Club, which sponsors lectures on litigation techniques and strategies and hosts an intramural trial competition.

■ Child and Family Advocacy Fellowships

Hofstra has one of the most extensive family law programs in the country. Each year, in conjunction with the Center for Children, Families, and the Law, Hofstra selects up to five fellows. Fellows receive scholarship assistance and internship experience and pursue an interdisciplinary course of study that provides the knowledge and skills needed to advocate effectively for the interests of children and families.

■ Center for Children, Families, and the Law

The center is devoted to education, research, and public service focused on children and families involved in the legal system. Its interdisciplinary approach is designed to encourage law and mental health students and professionals to work together to promote effective justice in both the juvenile and family court systems.

■ Fellowship for Health Law and Policy

Through a comprehensive program and course of study, this fellowship will train lawyers in health law to represent medical providers, patients, and the health care industry, and to advance health law policy. Fellows receive scholarship assistance and externship experience.

■ LGBT Fellowships

Each year, Hofstra selects several entering students to receive fellowships based on their demonstrated commitment to advocacy on behalf of the lesbian, gay, bisexual, and transgender community. These students receive tuition assistance, gain valuable internship experience, and pursue a course of study that provides the knowledge and skills needed to advocate effectively for the interests of the LGBT community. The fellowship is open to persons of all sexual identities, not only to recognize the diversity of individuals who ally themselves with sexual equality, but also to underscore the importance of alliances between the LGBT community and the public needed to guarantee full civil rights for all.

■ Externship Programs

The Civil Externship Program provides students opportunities to learn lawyering skills through placement in a variety of employment settings. The Criminal Externship Program provides experience in criminal law-related agencies. The Judicial Externship Program places students with state and federal judges for a semester, performing research, writing memoranda, observing court proceedings, and discussing cases with their judges.

■ Clinics

The law school offers seven clinics in different areas of practice, permitting students to work in business and litigation contexts, collaborate with medical and social work experts in children's rights cases, or develop counseling and mediation skills. In the **Child Advocacy Clinic**, students represent children in abuse, neglect, custody, and order of protection cases. Students in the **Community and Economic Development Clinic** perform public service in a transactional (nonlitigation) setting and learn valuable lawyering skills, such as negotiating agreements, drafting documents, and so on. The **Criminal Justice Clinic** allows students to represent criminal defendants in pretrial conferences, witness interviewing, motion and brief writing, case investigations, and trials. Students in the **Housing Rights Clinic** handle a wide variety of housing cases for low-income clients, including defenses of eviction cases, actions against landlords challenging substandard conditions, fair housing and exclusionary zoning cases, public utility shut-off cases, and work on behalf of housing rehabilitation. In the **Mediation Clinic**, students facilitate the negotiations of parties involved in a conflict and help them make decisions about the outcome. Students counsel parties on mediation and help draft settlement agreements. In the **Securities Arbitration Clinic**, students represent investors of limited income who are unable to obtain private representation in cases against brokers

and broker-dealers accused of misconduct. The **Political Asylum (Immigration) Clinic** allows students to represent clients who are fleeing from other countries because of persecution. Students represent their clients in hearings before asylum officers, Immigration Court proceedings, and appeals to the US Court of Appeals for the Second Circuit.

■ Student Life

Hofstra students publish four journals: the *Hofstra Law Review*, the *Labor and Employment Law Journal*, the *Family Court Review*, and the *Journal of International Business and Law*. There are currently more than 30 student organizations, from OWLS (Older and Wiser Law Students) and the Black Law Students Association, to the Public Justice Foundation and the Corporate Law Society. Current students can form new organizations with the support of the Office of Student Affairs.

■ Career Services

The Office of Career Services provides a wide range of services to facilitate job placement. These include educational programming, individual counseling, mock interviews, job postings, and on-campus interviewing. OCS has a record of success, with 96 percent of our recent graduates obtaining employment within nine months of graduation.

Applicant Profile

While admission to Hofstra law school is competitive, many factors are taken into consideration during the review process. Full-time students of the most recent entering class had a median LSAT score of 157 and a median undergraduate GPA of 3.51. In evaluating an applicant, the Admissions Committee looks at the academic record and performance on the LSAT, but also considers the entire application when determining

whether or not an applicant is likely to be successful at Hofstra law school and to enhance the experience of his or her classmates. Hofstra seeks students who will thrive on the challenge of an experiential learning program that uses rigorous classroom, clinical, externship, and simulation courses to develop a deep, practical understanding of the law and its effects on people.

University of Houston Law Center

100 Law Center
Houston, TX 77204-6060
Phone: 713.743.2280; Fax: 713.743.2194
E-mail: lawadmissions@uh.edu; Website: www.law.uh.edu

ABA
Approved
Since
1950

The Basics

Type of school	Public
Term	Semester
Application deadline	11/1 2/1 2/15
Application fee	$70
Financial aid deadline	4/1
Can first year start other than fall?	Yes
Student to faculty ratio	15.9 to 1
Does the university offer:	
housing restricted to law students?	No
graduate housing for which law students are eligible?	No

Faculty and Administrators

	Total		Men		Women		Minorities	
	Fall	Spr	Fall	Spr	Fall	Spr	Fall	Spr
Full-time	50	48	35	30	15	18	7	7
Other Full-time	11	11	3	4	8	7	1	0
Deans, librarians, & others who teach	4	5	4	4	0	1	0	0
Part-time	65	65	51	49	14	16	6	5
Total	130	129	93	87	37	42	14	12

Curriculum

		Full-time	Part-time
Typical first-year section size		80	60
Is there typically a "small section" of the first-year class, other than Legal Writing, taught by full-time faculty		Yes	Yes
If yes, typical size offered last year		40	30
# of classroom course titles beyond first-year curriculum		220	
# of upper division courses, excluding seminars with an enrollment:	Under 25	151	
	25–49	47	
	50–74	22	
	75–99	17	
	100+	0	
# of seminars		21	
# of seminar positions available		316	
# of seminar positions filled		225	44
# of positions available in simulation courses		622	
# of simulation positions filled		524	72
# of positions available in faculty supervised clinical courses		185	
# of faculty supervised clinical positions filled	144		11
# involved in field placements		195	5
# involved in law journals		195	24
# involved in interschool competitions		160	15
# of credit hours required to graduate		90	

JD Enrollment and Ethnicity

	Men		Women		Full-time		Part-time		1st-year		Total		JD Degs. Awd.
	#	%	#	%	#	%	#	%	#	%	#	%	
African Amer.	14	2.4	29	6.8	36	4.4	7	3.6	18	5.8	43	4.3	8
Amer. Indian	5	0.9	4	0.9	6	0.7	3	1.6	2	0.6	9	0.9	3
Asian Amer.	68	11.7	55	12.9	97	11.9	26	13.5	43	13.7	123	12.2	43
Mex. Amer.	17	2.9	22	5.1	30	3.7	9	4.7	13	4.2	39	3.9	11
Puerto Rican	0	0.0	0	0.0	0	0.0	0	0.0	0	0.0	0	0.0	0
Hispanic	22	3.8	31	7.2	43	5.3	10	5.2	15	4.8	53	5.3	12
Total Minority	126	21.8	141	32.9	212	26.0	55	28.6	91	29.1	267	26.5	77
For. Nation.	0	0.0	0	0.0	0	0.0	0	0.0	0	0.0	0	0.0	0
Caucasian	452	78.1	283	66.1	599	73.5	136	70.8	222	70.9	735	73.0	219
Unknown	1	0.2	4	0.9	4	0.5	1	0.5	0	0.0	5	0.5	14
Total	579	57.5	428	42.5	815	80.9	192	19.1	313	31.1	1007		310

Transfers

Transfers in	14
Transfers out	4

Tuition and Fees

	Resident	Nonresident
Full-time	$15,922	$22,372
Part-time	$8,348	$10,928

*Full-time (15 hours); part-time (7 hours)

Living Expenses

Estimated living expenses for singles

Living on campus	Living off campus	Living at home
$12,120	$15,176	$9,524

*ABA
Approved
Since
1950*

GPA and LSAT Scores

	Total	Full-time	Part-time
# of apps	3,386	3,032	354
# of offers	979	886	93
# of matrics	318	246	72
75% GPA	3.72	3.74	3.62
Median GPA	3.49	3.53	3.32
25% GPA	3.20	3.27	3.00
75% LSAT	162	162	161
Median LSAT	160	160	159
25% LSAT	156	157	154

Grants and Scholarships (from prior year)

	Total		Full-time		Part-time	
	#	%	#	%	#	%
Total # of students	1,037		838		199	
Total # receiving grants	579	55.8	579	69.1	0	0.0
Less than 1/2 tuition	539	52.0	539	64.3	0	0.0
Half to full tuition	38	3.7	38	4.5	0	0.0
Full tuition	0	0.0	0	0.0	0	0.0
More than full tuition	2	0.2	2	0.2	0	0.0
Median grant amount			$1,950		$0	

Informational and Library Resources

# of volumes and volume equivalents	533,721
# of titles	88,739
# of active serial subscriptions	3,590
Study seating capacity inside the library	546
# of full-time professional librarians	12
Hours per week library is open	107
# of open, wired connections available to students	0
# of networked computers available for use by students	114
# of simultaneous wireless users	3,000
Require computer?	Yes

JD Attrition (from prior year)

	Academic	Other	Total	
	#	#	#	%
1st year	0	4	4	1.3
2nd year	0	9	9	2.9
3rd year	0	4	4	1.1
4th year	0	1	1	2.2

Employment (9 months after graduation)

	Total	Percentage
Employment status known	381	98.2
Employment status unknown	7	1.8
Employed	355	93.2
Pursuing graduate degrees	2	0.5
Unemployed seeking employment	6	1.6
Unemployed not seeking employment	9	2.4
Unemployed and studying for the bar	9	2.4

Type of Employment

	Total	Percentage
# employed in law firms	225	63.4
# employed in business and industry	64	18.0
# employed in government	38	10.7
# employed in public interest	4	1.1
# employed as judicial clerks	14	3.9
# employed in academia	5	1.4

Geographic Location

	Total	Percentage
# employed in state	313	88.2
# employed in foreign countries	2	0.6
# of states where employed	18	

Bar Passage Rates

Jurisdiction	Texas		
Exam	Sum 05	Win 06	Total
# from school taking bar for the first time	270	47	317
School's pass rate for all first-time takers	85%	79%	84%
State's pass rate for all first-time takers	81%	77%	80%

University of Houston Law Center

100 Law Center
Houston, TX 77204-6060
Phone: 713.743.2280; Fax: 713.743.2194
E-mail: lawadmissions@uh.edu; Website: www.law.uh.edu

■ Introduction

The University of Houston (UH) Law Center is located at the University of Houston, three miles south of downtown. The state-assisted UH Law Center, located in one of the nation's top 10 largest legal markets, is noted throughout the South and Southwest not only for its excellence, but also for its progressive and innovative approach to the teaching of law. The College of Law, the academic branch of the UH Law Center, is fully accredited by the American Bar Association and the American Association of Law Schools and has a chapter of the Order of the Coif, the national legal honorary scholastic society. The Law Center confers a Juris Doctor (JD) degree as a first degree in law and a Master of Laws (LLM) degree to students pursuing work beyond the JD degree.

■ Curriculum/Basic Program of Study

The first-year curriculum at the UH Law Center is prescribed. Students are also required to complete a course in professional responsibility and one major piece of legal research and writing before graduation. Emphasis is placed on legal theory and the varying approaches to the law.

■ Special Programs

The University of Houston Law Center emphasizes current legal and administrative problems confronting the region and nation, including intellectual property law, environmental law, energy law, tax law, health law, and international law. The UH Law Center is home to the Health Law and Policy Institute, a research and instruction center on interdisciplinary issues. The UH Law Center is also host to the Criminal Justice Institute, the Institute for Higher Education Law and Governance, the Institute for Intellectual Property and Information Law, and the Blakely Advocacy Institute.

■ Clinical Programs and Trial Advocacy

The UH Law Center offers a wide variety of clinical courses. Students can choose from among different areas of concentration, such as agency or judicial internships, health or environmental law, and juvenile or consumer law. The UH Law Center houses the legal aid clinic, which gives students clinic opportunities in providing legal services to the indigent in the areas of family law, bankruptcy, or immigration law.

Practice skills courses coordinated through the Blakely Advocacy Institute are an integral part of the curriculum. Students can enhance their skills in trial, negotiation, pretrial, and appellate work through hands-on courses that simulate real-life situations. Several levels of courses are offered in civil and criminal advocacy. Intramural mock trial and moot court competitions are sponsored by the Advocates, an affiliated student organization. The institute also sponsors teams for criminal and civil interscholastic moot court and mock trial competitions, with UH Law Center students earning top honors in national and international competitions.

■ Activities

Extracurricular activities give voice to the diversity of the campus. Student groups represent special interests and provide important avenues to help law students succeed. Many arrange mentoring programs and match first-year students with second- or third-year students or working professionals. Others coordinate résumé-writing workshops, guest-speaker forums, preregistration discussions of specific course offerings, or law-related charitable efforts that benefit the community.

The Student Bar Association (SBA) has input into every facet of student life at the UH Law Center. The SBA participates in the first-year orientation, organizes the annual charity Fun Run, aids in the selection of student representatives to sit on various faculty committees, and presents student attitudes and views both within and outside the UH Law Center.

Students are encouraged to become involved in one or more student organizations; to participate in the scholarly *Houston Law Review, Houston Journal of International Law, Houston Journal of Health Law and Policy, Houston Business and Tax Law Journal, Environmental and Energy Law and Policy Journal,* and the *Journal of Texas Consumer Law;* and to compete in tournaments ranging from moot court to mock trial, from mediation to negotiation.

Other student organizations include the Association of Women in Law, Black Law Students Association, Hispanic Law Students Association, Asian Law Students Association, Outlaw (GLBT Student Organization), Lex Judaica (Jewish students), Public Interest Law Organization, Health Law Organization, Intellectual Property Student Organization, Energy and Environmental Law Society, Phi Delta Phi, Phi Alpha Delta, and Evening Law Students Association.

■ Career Development

The Office of Career Development strives for a creative approach in its job-search partnership with students. The First Year Initiative exposes first-year students to a comprehensive career education series that surveys dozens of career opportunities. Students in small groups actively gather the information they need to make informed decisions on their career plans.

The Office of Career Development also presents a variety of panel discussions, receptions, and seminars with members of the Houston legal community to assist students in understanding law career options. Topics covered include duties and responsibilities of a law clerk, judicial clerkship opportunities, solo practice, and nontraditional uses of a law degree.

The office provides individual assistance in résumé preparation and interviewing techniques for all students and alumni. The annual On Campus Interview Program for second- and third-year students seeking summer clerkships and permanent positions to commence upon graduation attracts approximately 130 prospective employers to the campus.

■ Admission

The UH Law Center enrolls first-year, full-time students beginning in the fall semester, which starts in August. First-year, part-time students who will attend evening classes enroll in the summer semester, which starts in May. There are no spring admissions.

Demonstrated academic ability and strong LSAT scores are not the only criteria for admission. Consideration is also given to background, achievements, honors, extracurricular activities, service to others, unique abilities, hardships overcome, advanced degrees, employment, and leadership. The UH Law Center is also committed to diversity, and the UH System Board of Regents recognizes and endorses the benefits of diversity in the university setting. The Admissions Committee will consider the following additional factors: cultural history, ethnic origin, and race. These and other elements may be addressed in a personal statement of up to three pages, double-spaced.

Applicant Profile

University of Houston Law Center
This grid includes only applicants who earned 120–180 LSAT scores under standard administrations.

LSAT Score	GPA 3.75 +		3.50–3.74		3.25–3.49		3.00–3.24		2.75–2.99		2.50–2.74		Below 2.50		No GPA		Total	
	Apps	Adm	Apps	Adm	Apps	Adm	Apps	Adm	Apps	Adm	Apps	Adm	Apps	Adm	Apps	Adm	Apps	Adm
170–180	10	10	6	6	7	7	5	5	6	5	5	3	1	0	0	0	40	36
165–169	34	34	29	29	30	30	22	21	10	6	11	8	2	2	1	1	139	131
160–164	87	86	101	98	109	88	96	64	44	26	37	8	19	0	5	4	498	374
155–159	136	103	206	91	207	55	138	19	80	5	39	3	23	1	8	3	837	280
150–154	92	25	179	38	199	29	150	12	95	2	54	0	42	0	6	2	817	108
145–149	39	7	90	14	115	11	127	4	77	2	50	1	37	0	9	1	544	40
140–144	12	2	35	2	66	2	65	1	56	0	57	0	46	0	9	0	346	7
Below 140	2	0	12	0	27	0	30	0	34	0	41	0	30	0	10	0	186	0
Total	412	267	658	278	760	222	633	126	402	46	294	23	200	3	48	11	3407	976

Apps = Number of Applicants
Adm = Number Admitted
Reflects 99% of the total applicant pool.

Howard University School of Law

2900 Van Ness Street NW
Washington, DC 20008
Phone: 202.806.8008/8009; Fax: 202.806.8162
E-mail: admissions@law.howard.edu; Website: www.law.howard.edu

ABA
Approved
Since
1931

The Basics

Type of school	Private
Term	Semester
Application deadline	3/31
Application fee	$60
Financial aid deadline	2/15
Can first year start other than fall?	No
Student to faculty ratio	19.1 to 1
Does the university offer:	
housing restricted to law students?	No
graduate housing for which law students are eligible?	No

Faculty and Administrators

	Total		Men		Women		Minorities	
	Fall	Spr	Fall	Spr	Fall	Spr	Fall	Spr
Full-time	21	18	15	14	6	4	16	13
Other Full-time	8	5	5	3	3	2	6	3
Deans, librarians, & others who teach	8	8	1	1	7	7	8	8
Part-time	17	22	9	16	8	6	14	17
Total	**54**	**53**	**30**	**34**	**24**	**19**	**44**	**41**

Curriculum

	Full-time	Part-time
Typical first-year section size	54	0
Is there typically a "small section" of the first-year class, other than Legal Writing, taught by full-time faculty	No	No
If yes, typical size offered last year		
# of classroom course titles beyond first-year curriculum	138	

# of upper division courses, excluding seminars with an enrollment:	Under 25	37
	25–49	20
	50–74	12
	75–99	2
	100+	0

# of seminars	24	
# of seminar positions available	360	
# of seminar positions filled	319	0
# of positions available in simulation courses	226	
# of simulation positions filled	214	0
# of positions available in faculty supervised clinical courses	56	
# of faculty supervised clinical positions filled	42	0
# involved in field placements	43	0
# involved in law journals	52	0
# involved in interschool competitions	54	0
# of credit hours required to graduate	88	

JD Enrollment and Ethnicity

	Men #	Men %	Women #	Women %	Full-time #	Full-time %	Part-time #	Part-time %	1st-year #	1st-year %	Total #	Total %	JD Degs. Awd.
African Amer.	123	73.2	199	76.0	322	74.9	0	0.0	97	70.8	322	74.9	125
Amer. Indian	2	1.2	1	0.4	3	0.7	0	0.0	0	0.0	3	0.7	0
Asian Amer.	11	6.5	14	5.3	25	5.8	0	0.0	11	8.0	25	5.8	2
Mex. Amer.	0	0.0	0	0.0	0	0.0	0	0.0	0	0.0	0	0.0	0
Puerto Rican	0	0.0	0	0.0	0	0.0	0	0.0	0	0.0	0	0.0	0
Hispanic	4	2.4	7	2.7	11	2.6	0	0.0	1	0.7	11	2.6	2
Total Minority	140	83.3	221	84.4	361	84.0	0	0.0	109	79.6	361	84.0	129
For. Nation.	18	10.7	21	8.0	39	9.1	0	0.0	18	13.1	39	9.1	6
Caucasian	7	4.2	12	4.6	19	4.4	0	0.0	7	5.1	19	4.4	8
Unknown	3	1.8	8	3.1	11	2.6	0	0.0	3	2.2	11	2.6	2
Total	168	39.1	262	60.9	430	100.0	0	0.0	137	31.9	430		145

Transfers

Transfers in	1
Transfers out	1

Tuition and Fees

	Resident	Nonresident
Full-time	$18,870	$0
Part-time	$0	$0

Living Expenses

Estimated living expenses for singles

Living on campus	Living off campus	Living at home
N/A	$17,641	N/A

Howard University School of Law

*ABA
Approved
Since
1931*

GPA and LSAT Scores

	Total	Full-time	Part-time
# of apps	2,217	2,217	0
# of offers	502	502	0
# of matrics	139	139	0
75% GPA	3.50	3.50	0.00
Median GPA	3.20	3.20	0.00
25% GPA	2.95	2.95	0.00
75% LSAT	154	154	0
Median LSAT	151	151	0
25% LSAT	148	148	0

Grants and Scholarships (from prior year)

	Total		Full-time		Part-time	
	#	%	#	%	#	%
Total # of students	451		451		0	
Total # receiving grants	335	74.3	335	74.3	0	0.0
Less than 1/2 tuition	186	41.2	186	41.2	0	0.0
Half to full tuition	117	25.9	117	25.9	0	0.0
Full tuition	14	3.1	14	3.1	0	0.0
More than full tuition	18	4.0	18	4.0	0	0.0
Median grant amount			$10,000		$0	

Informational and Library Resources

# of volumes and volume equivalents	632,218
# of titles	31,878
# of active serial subscriptions	2,624
Study seating capacity inside the library	374
# of full-time professional librarians	8
Hours per week library is open	105
# of open, wired connections available to students	579
# of networked computers available for use by students	186
# of simultaneous wireless users	3,283
Require computer?	No

JD Attrition (from prior year)

	Academic	Other	Total	
	#	#	#	%
1st year	5	7	12	7.7
2nd year	1	3	4	2.6
3rd year	1	1	2	1.4
4th year	0	0	0	0.0

Employment (9 months after graduation)

	Total	Percentage
Employment status known	201	99.0
Employment status unknown	2	1.0
Employed	193	96.0
Pursuing graduate degrees	3	1.5
Unemployed seeking employment	3	1.5
Unemployed not seeking employment	0	0.0
Unemployed and studying for the bar	2	1.0
Type of Employment		
# employed in law firms	83	43.0
# employed in business and industry	25	13.0
# employed in government	36	18.7
# employed in public interest	13	6.7
# employed as judicial clerks	28	14.5
# employed in academia	5	2.6
Geographic Location		
# employed in state	57	29.5
# employed in foreign countries	0	0.0
# of states where employed	22	

Bar Passage Rates

Jurisdiction	New York		
Exam	Sum 05	Win 06	Total
# from school taking bar for the first time	40	1	41
School's pass rate for all first-time takers	70%	0%	68%
State's pass rate for all first-time takers	76%	61%	74%

Howard University School of Law

Office of Admissions, 2900 Van Ness Street NW
Washington, DC 20008
Phone: 202.806.8008/8009; Fax: 202.806.8162
E-mail: admissions@law.howard.edu; Website: www.law.howard.edu

■ Introduction

Howard University, a coeducational, private institution in Washington, DC, was chartered by the US Congress in 1867. Howard is a historically black institution that offers an educational experience of exceptional quality and value to students with high academic potential. Particular emphasis is placed on providing educational opportunities for promising African Americans and other persons of color who have been underrepresented in the legal profession, and nonminority persons with a strong interest in civil and human rights, as well as public service. The main campus of Howard is located in northwest Washington.

The School of Law opened its doors in 1869. There was a great need to train lawyers with a strong commitment to helping black Americans secure and protect their newly established rights. In those days, the law school did not have classrooms, at least not the way we know them today. The students (there were six in the first class) met at night in the homes and offices of the faculty, all of whom were part time.

In time, the law school grew. The law school has a diverse student body and faculty. The law school is located on a separate 22-acre campus, also in northwest Washington, approximately three miles from the main campus. Howard University School of Law is fully accredited by the American Bar Association and the Association of American Law Schools, and certifies its graduates for bar examination in all jurisdictions of the United States.

■ Degree Programs

The School of Law offers programs leading to the Juris Doctor (JD); Master of Laws (LLM) for foreign law graduates; and Juris Doctor/Master in Business Administration (JD/MBA) degrees.

An applicant applying to the JD program must have a baccalaureate degree from an accredited college or university before enrolling in the Howard University School of Law. Competitive numerical predictors for admission to Howard University include a Law School Admission Test (LSAT) score of 153 and above and an undergraduate grade-point average of 3.4. In addition to the LSAT score and UGPA, we consider the rigor of an applicant's undergraduate course of study, letters of recommendation (particularly from faculty members who have taught the applicant), any graduate study, employment, extracurricular activities, and other indicators of potential for success in law school and excellence in the profession.

Applicants applying to the JD/MBA program must apply and meet the independent admission requirements of both schools, including completion of the GMAT.

The LLM program offers foreign law graduates an opportunity to further their legal studies through advanced study and research. To be admitted as a candidate for the master of laws degree, applicants must be in high academic standing and must have a degree in law from an accredited foreign university or its equivalent (as determined by the faculty of law) and some experience in the judiciary, administrative establishment, bar, or law faculty.

■ Special Programs

The School of Law has a strong commitment to public service and to human and civil rights. Many programs and activities of the school reflect that fact. The school also provides an opportunity for clinical experience in civil and criminal litigation. Howard law school also offers a summer study-abroad program in comparative and international law at the University of Western Cape in South Africa. The six-week program is approved by the ABA and offers constitutional, business, and trade law courses for credit. A student-exchange program has been established with Vermont Law School and Brigham Young University. Through the exchange program, a limited number of third-year JD students may spend a semester at one of these law schools to take advantage of curricular offerings that may be of specific interest to students.

■ Curriculum

The curriculum leading to the first degree in law covers three academic years of two semesters each. During the first two years, emphasis is on the fundamental analytical concepts and skills of the law and the system by which it is administered—the functions required of a lawyer within a legal system based upon the common law. The curriculum in the third year provides diversified experience and a solid foundation of whatever specialization is desired.

■ Research Facilities

In May 2001, Howard University School of Law Library moved into its new, state-of-the-art facility. This four-story, 76,000-square-foot building provides space for a book collection of up to 215,000 volumes; seating for over 295 students (more than 70 percent of the student population), including 90 open carrels, with all locations wired for computer use; enlarged microfilm and audiovisual facilities; and distinctive rooms of wood and brick for special collections, newspaper and periodical reading, and the rare book collection.

The Law Library is both a working collection for law students and lawyers and a research institution for legal scholars. The civil rights archive contains briefs, working papers, and materials of the NAACP and other civil rights organizations. The library has a collection that emphasizes civil and political rights and literature to support study of the legal problems of the poor. Its collection has been expanded to also include considerable CD-ROM resources. The Law Library has an online catalogue system, e-mail capabilities, and Internet access.

■ Student Activities

The *Howard Law Journal* publishes legal materials for scholarly and professional interest. The national and international moot court teams, which sponsor intramural competition and participate in competitions nationwide, have won numerous honors. The Student Bar Association is the general student government organization. The *Barrister*, the student newspaper, publishes several issues a year. Other organizations represent students from diverse ethnic backgrounds, including African Americans, Latinos, Africans, Caribbean Islanders, and Asian Pacific Islanders.

■ Career Services

The Career Services office is an integral part of the law school. To assist students, the office offers workshops on job-search techniques and résumé writing and seminars on career development and practice specialties. The office also maintains an extensive resource library with online employer research systems, newsletters, and updated listings of career opportunities. Each year, the Career Services office sponsors two on-campus interview programs, and more than 450 recruiters from law firms, government agencies, and corporations visit the law school with offers of employment for promising students and graduates. Approximately 4,500 interviews are scheduled annually. Graduates receive highly competitive and prestigious judicial clerkships and work for large and small private firms; federal, state, and local government agencies; public interest organizations; and public and private corporations throughout the United States.

Applicant Profile

Howard University School of Law

LSAT Score	3.75 +		3.50–3.74		3.25–3.49		3.00–3.24		2.75–2.99		2.50–2.74		2.25–2.49		2.00–2.24		Below 2.00		No GPA		Totals	
	Apps	Adm	Apps	Adm	Apps	Adm	Apps	Adm	Apps	Adm	Apps	Adm	Apps	Adm	Apps	Adm	Apps	Adm	Apps	Adm	Apps	Adm
175–180	0	0	0	0	0	0	0	0	0	0	0	0	0	0	0	0	0	0	0	0	0	0
170–174	0	0	0	0	0	0	0	0	0	0	1	0	0	0	1	0	0	0	0	0	10	7
165–169	1	1	2	2	2	2	2	1	1	1	1	0	0	0	1	0	2	0	1	1	57	36
160–164	5	4	6	5	8	6	12	7	12	9	5	3	5	1	1	0	0	0	1	1	191	109
155–159	17	13	24	18	44	24	36	23	32	16	19	9	12	5	6	0	4	0	3	1	474	216
150–154	33	26	73	44	107	53	98	44	91	35	35	10	22	2	8	1	4	0	7	0	668	90
145–149	39	14	85	20	127	21	149	19	119	10	77	5	45	1	16	0	4	0	8	0	670	21
140–144	32	7	70	5	108	3	157	3	130	2	96	1	51	0	13	0	5	0	8	0	298	1
135–139	3	0	21	1	51	0	57	0	66	0	46	0	28	0	12	0	4	0	10	0	100	0
130–134	1	0	7	0	8	0	19	0	23	0	17	0	12	0	8	0	2	0	3	0	20	0
125–129	1	0	1	0	1	0	2	0	1	0	4	0	3	0	3	0	1	0	3	0	1	0
120–124	0	0	0	0	0	0	0	0	1	0	0	0	0	0	0	0	0	0	0	0		
Total	132	65	289	95	456	109	532	97	476	73	300	28	178	9	68	1	22	0	36	3	2489	480

Apps = Number of Applicants
Adm = Number Admitted
Reflects 99% of the total applicant pool.

University of Idaho College of Law

PO Box 442321
Moscow, ID 83844-2321
Phone: 208.885.2300; Fax: 208.885.5709
E-mail: lawadmit@uidaho.edu; Website: www.law.uidaho.edu

ABA
Approved
Since
1925

The Basics

Type of school	Public
Term	Semester
Application deadline	2/15
Application fee	$50
Financial aid deadline	2/15
Can first year start other than fall?	No
Student to faculty ratio	14.9 to 1
Does the university offer:	
housing restricted to law students?	No
graduate housing for which law students are eligible?	Yes

Faculty and Administrators

	Total		Men		Women		Minorities	
	Fall	Spr	Fall	Spr	Fall	Spr	Fall	Spr
Full-time	18	16	14	11	4	5	1	0
Other Full-time	3	3	1	1	2	2	0	0
Deans, librarians, & others who teach	5	5	4	4	1	1	0	0
Part-time	5	7	5	6	0	1	0	0
Total	31	31	24	22	7	9	1	0

Curriculum

		Full-time	Part-time
Typical first-year section size		53	0
Is there typically a "small section" of the first-year class, other than Legal Writing, taught by full-time faculty		No	No
If yes, typical size offered last year			
# of classroom course titles beyond first-year curriculum		53	
# of upper division courses, excluding seminars with an enrollment:	Under 25	48	
	25–49	4	
	50–74	5	
	75–99	5	
	100+	5	
# of seminars		15	
# of seminar positions available		315	
# of seminar positions filled	205		0
# of positions available in simulation courses		315	
# of simulation positions filled	193		0
# of positions available in faculty supervised clinical courses		178	
# of faculty supervised clinical positions filled	73		0
# involved in field placements	49		0
# involved in law journals	23		0
# involved in interschool competitions	77		0
# of credit hours required to graduate		88	

JD Enrollment and Ethnicity

	Men		Women		Full-time		Part-time		1st-year		Total		JD Degs. Awd.
	#	%	#	%	#	%	#	%	#	%	#	%	
African Amer.	2	1.1	2	1.5	4	1.3	0	0.0	0	0.0	4	1.3	0
Amer. Indian	2	1.1	3	2.3	5	1.6	0	0.0	3	2.9	5	1.6	1
Asian Amer.	10	5.5	10	7.6	20	6.4	0	0.0	7	6.7	20	6.4	2
Mex. Amer.	3	1.7	4	3.0	7	2.2	0	0.0	2	1.9	7	2.2	1
Puerto Rican	0	0.0	0	0.0	0	0.0	0	0.0	0	0.0	0	0.0	0
Hispanic	3	1.7	3	2.3	6	1.9	0	0.0	3	2.9	6	1.9	0
Total Minority	20	11.0	22	16.7	42	13.4	0	0.0	15	14.3	42	13.4	4
For. Nation.	2	1.1	1	0.8	3	1.0	0	0.0	2	1.9	3	1.0	0
Caucasian	149	82.3	101	76.5	250	79.9	1	100.0	80	76.2	250	79.6	76
Unknown	10	5.5	8	6.1	18	5.8	0	0.0	8	7.6	18	5.7	9
Total	181	57.6	132	42.0	313	99.7	1	0.3	105	33.4	314		89

Transfers

Transfers in	4
Transfers out	0

Tuition and Fees

	Resident	Nonresident
Full-time	$9,540	$19,140
Part-time	$0	$0

Living Expenses

Estimated living expenses for singles

Living on campus	Living off campus	Living at home
$13,960	$13,960	$13,960

University of Idaho College of Law

*ABA
Approved
Since
1925*

GPA and LSAT Scores

	Total	Full-time	Part-time
# of apps	782	782	0
# of offers	301	301	0
# of matrics	105	105	0
75% GPA	3.68	3.68	0.00
Median GPA	3.44	3.44	0.00
25% GPA	3.13	3.13	0.00
75% LSAT	157	157	0
Median LSAT	155	155	0
25% LSAT	151	151	0

Grants and Scholarships (from prior year)

	Total		Full-time		Part-time	
	#	%	#	%	#	%
Total # of students	297		297		0	
Total # receiving grants	125	42.1	125	42.1	0	0.0
Less than 1/2 tuition	91	30.6	91	30.6	0	0.0
Half to full tuition	16	5.4	16	5.4	0	0.0
Full tuition	14	4.7	14	4.7	0	0.0
More than full tuition	4	1.3	4	1.3	0	0.0
Median grant amount			$4,000		$0	

Informational and Library Resources

# of volumes and volume equivalents	239,902
# of titles	38,420
# of active serial subscriptions	4,871
Study seating capacity inside the library	360
# of full-time professional librarians	3
Hours per week library is open	86
# of open, wired connections available to students	308
# of networked computers available for use by students	26
# of simultaneous wireless users	920
Require computer?	No

JD Attrition (from prior year)

	Academic	Other	Total	
	#	#	#	%
1st year	0	7	7	6.7
2nd year	0	0	0	0.0
3rd year	0	0	0	0.0
4th year	0	0	0	0.0

Employment (9 months after graduation)

	Total	Percentage
Employment status known	97	100.0
Employment status unknown	0	0.0
Employed	84	86.6
Pursuing graduate degrees	3	3.1
Unemployed seeking employment	3	3.1
Unemployed not seeking employment	3	3.1
Unemployed and studying for the bar	4	4.1
Type of Employment		
# employed in law firms	29	34.5
# employed in business and industry	8	9.5
# employed in government	19	22.6
# employed in public interest	7	8.3
# employed as judicial clerks	18	21.4
# employed in academia	2	2.4
Geographic Location		
# employed in state	47	56.0
# employed in foreign countries	2	2.4
# of states where employed		14

Bar Passage Rates

Jurisdiction	Idaho			Washington		
Exam	Sum 05	Win 06	Total	Sum 05	Win 06	Total
# from school taking bar for the first time	53	6	59	14	2	16
School's pass rate for all first-time takers	81%	83%	80%	79%	50%	75%
State's pass rate for all first-time takers	81%	79%	81%	75%	74%	75%

University of Idaho College of Law

PO Box 442321
Moscow, ID 83844-2321
Phone: 208.885.2300; Fax: 208.885.5709
E-mail: lawadmit@uidaho.edu; Website: www.law.uidaho.edu

■ Introduction

Emphasizing quality over quantity, the College of Law offers a distinctive legal education founded on collegiality and a dedication to the highest ideals of a noble profession. Each student is assured individual attention. The college provides emphases in natural resources and environmental law, business law and entrepreneurship, and advocacy coupled with mediation and dispute resolution. Students may combine study in a small residential environment with an opportunity to spend a semester in Boise, Idaho, one of America's fastest-growing metropolitan areas.

The College of Law was established in 1909. It has been a member of the AALS since 1914 and has been accredited by the ABA since 1925. The College of Law is located on the main campus of the University of Idaho, about 90 miles southeast of Spokane, Washington, and about eight miles east of Pullman, Washington. The Moscow-Pullman community is the cultural center of a vast inland area of the Northwest covering parts of Idaho, Washington, and Oregon. This area is renowned for outstanding opportunities for outdoor recreation, in addition to cultural events available from two major research universities.

■ Enrollment/Student Body

Approximately 60 percent of our students are Idaho residents. Historically, our nonresident students have come from all over the United States and Canada. Although the total enrollment of the College of Law is relatively small (approximately 300), students typically represent over 70 different colleges and universities. The administration and student body welcome and actively seek diversity in the student body, with particular attention to students of color and those who have overcome socioeconomic disadvantage. Due to our highly selective admission process and positive learning environment, which includes an academic support program run by a licensed attorney, academic attrition is less than 5 percent.

■ Library and Physical Facilities

The College of Law occupies a modern building designed for, and dedicated to, its use. The law library houses a collection of over 240,000 volumes and volume-equivalents and more than 4,800 serial titles. This is combined with two computer labs, wireless Internet access throughout the building, and LexisNexis, Westlaw, Dialog, and HeinOnline services, plus the Readex database of the US Congressional Serial Set. Membership in the Western Library Network and the Inland Northwest Library Automation Network allows users to access holdings of libraries across the nation. Law students have access to the other libraries of the University of Idaho and those at Washington State University.

■ Curriculum

The College of Law focuses on professionalism, featuring small-group discussions with distinguished lawyers and judges during New Student Orientation. A distinctive, universal pro bono program engages every student in a substantial, law-related work of donated public service. After a

traditional first year of study, students in the second and third year may choose to focus on advocacy/dispute resolution, business law/entrepreneurship, or natural resources/environmental law, including an interdisciplinary Water of the West program (see Dual Degrees section). The curriculum also provides enrichments in international law, technology and the law, and ethics and civic leadership. Real-world exposure is provided through extensive clinical opportunities, a Semester in Practice program in the Boise metropolitan area, and our Extern Program. Graduates of the college enter careers throughout the nation.

■ Practical Skills

All students gain practical experience through participation in the distinctive pro bono program described in the Curriculum section. In addition, third-year students may earn their limited license to practice under the laws of Idaho and work in our live-client clinic. The live-client offerings include a general practice clinic, an appellate clinic in which students argue before federal and state appellate courts, a tribal/immigration law clinic in which students serve as public defenders in the Nez Perce Tribal Court and represent clients in federal immigration matters, a small business legal clinic, a tax clinic, a domestic violence clinic, and a victims' rights clinic. The college also sponsors a special trial advocacy course and is home to the Northwest Institute for Dispute Resolution.

Externships are also available, with students working with the Supreme Court and Court of Appeals of Idaho, the United States Court of Appeals for the Ninth Circuit, the United States District Court for the District of Idaho, the Attorney General of Idaho, the United States Attorney for the District of Idaho, various county offices, and selected nonprofit organizations. Eligible third-year students may participate in the Semester in Practice program in Boise.

■ Dual Degrees

The College of Law offers several opportunities to add to your legal education through our dual-degree programs.

A JD/MS Environmental Science degree is available in cooperation with the University of Idaho College of Graduate Studies Environmental Science Program. Students are able to earn both degrees in four rather than the usual five years. Beginning fall 2007, students will also be able to earn a joint JD/MS or JD/PhD in Water Resources and Law as part of the innovative Water of the West program.

A dual JD/Master of Accounting degree in cooperation with the University of Idaho College of Business and Economics is also available. The program allows students to earn both degrees in as few as seven semesters.

Finally, a joint JD/Master of Business Administration is offered in cooperation with Washington State University allowing students to take advantage of the resources of two of the Northwest's premier educational institutions.

■ Admission

Applications are accepted beginning in October preceding the year in which enrollment is desired. The only program offered is full-time in Moscow. Applicants must submit college transcripts and letters of recommendation through the LSDAS. We recommend late-fall application; the deadline is February 15. Applications completed after February 15 will be reviewed, but timely applications will receive priority consideration. The Admission Committee looks at each applicant holistically, including but not limited to LSAT score, academic record and background, writing ability, personal statement, work and life experiences, and recommendations.

■ Student Activities

Students belong to more than 20 active student organizations. The Student Bar Association represents student interests, both educational and social. The *Idaho Law Review*, which covers topics ranging from state and regional problems to national and international issues, and the *German Law Journal*, the only English-language journal of German and international public law, give students valuable writing and editing experience. The Board of Student Advocates and the Law Students for Appropriate Dispute Resolution coordinate intramural competitions and provide opportunities for students to participate in national competitions that build professional skills. Other groups include the Multicultural Law Caucus, Student Advocates for Hispanic/Latino Support and Awareness, the Sexual Orientation Diversity Alliance, and the Women's Law Caucus.

■ Career Development

The college has a career development office run by a licensed attorney. The office facilitates students' career planning and their search for summer and permanent employment. Legal employers come to the College of Law for on-campus interviews, and the office coordinates recruit-by-mail programs for other employers. Historically, 90–95 percent of graduates find employment within six months of graduation or go on to advanced graduate study. The college has exceptional success placing students in federal and state judicial clerkships as the first step in their careers. A majority of students find employment in Idaho, although Utah, Washington, and Oregon continue to be popular. Idaho graduates are employed throughout the US and several foreign countries.

Applicant Profile

University of Idaho College of Law
This grid includes only applicants who earned 120–180 LSAT scores under standard administrations.

LSAT Score	3.75 + Apps	Adm	3.50–3.74 Apps	Adm	3.25–3.49 Apps	Adm	3.00–3.24 Apps	Adm	2.75–2.99 Apps	Adm	2.50–2.74 Apps	Adm	2.25–2.49 Apps	Adm	2.00–2.24 Apps	Adm	Below 2.00 Apps	Adm	No GPA Apps	Adm	Total Apps	Adm
175–180	0	0	0	0	0	0	0	0	0	0	0	0	0	0	0	0	0	0	0	0	0	0
170–174	1	1	0	0	0	0	0	0	0	0	0	0	0	0	0	0	0	0	0	0	1	1
165–169	2	1	4	4	3	2	2	2	2	2	1	1	1	1	0	0	0	0	0	0	15	13
160–164	8	8	12	12	9	7	11	11	7	3	6	6	0	0	3	2	0	0	0	0	56	49
155–159	24	20	32	22	39	30	43	27	20	13	7	3	4	1	1	0	0	0	0	0	170	116
150–154	34	15	68	27	57	24	67	15	26	4	17	2	8	1	1	0	0	0	0	0	278	88
145–149	17	3	38	14	54	7	36	7	21	1	18	0	4	0	3	0	2	0	1	0	194	32
140–144	3	1	11	2	14	3	16	0	17	0	8	0	6	0	3	0	0	0	1	0	79	6
135–139	0	0	2	0	5	0	7	0	9	1	3	0	0	0	1	0	2	0	1	0	30	1
130–134	0	0	0	0	0	0	1	0	3	0	0	0	1	0	1	0	0	0	0	0	6	0
125–129	0	0	0	0	0	0	0	0	0	0	1	0	0	0	0	0	0	0	0	0	1	0
120–124	0	0	0	0	0	0	0	0	0	0	0	0	0	0	0	0	0	0	0	0	0	0
Total	89	49	167	81	181	73	183	62	105	24	61	12	24	3	13	2	4	0	3	0	830	306

Apps = Number of Applicants
Adm = Number Admitted
Reflects 99% of the total applicant pool.

University of Illinois College of Law

504 East Pennsylvania Avenue
Champaign, IL 61820
Phone: 217.244.6415
E-mail: admissions@law.uiuc.edu; Website: www.law.uiuc.edu

ABA
Approved
Since
1923

The Basics

Type of school	Public
Term	Semester
Application deadline	3/15
Application fee	$50
Financial aid deadline	3/15
Can first year start other than fall?	No
Student to faculty ratio	12.9 to 1
Does the university offer:	
housing restricted to law students?	No
graduate housing for which law students are eligible?	Yes

Faculty and Administrators

	Total		Men		Women		Minorities	
	Fall	Spr	Fall	Spr	Fall	Spr	Fall	Spr
Full-time	39	42	27	25	12	17	5	4
Other Full-time	7	9	2	5	5	4	0	2
Deans, librarians, & others who teach	8	8	5	5	3	3	0	0
Part-time	25	30	18	22	7	8	3	3
Total	**79**	**89**	**52**	**57**	**27**	**32**	**8**	**9**

Curriculum

	Full-time	Part-time
Typical first-year section size	66	0
Is there typically a "small section" of the first-year class, other than Legal Writing, taught by full-time faculty	Yes	No
If yes, typical size offered last year	31	
# of classroom course titles beyond first-year curriculum	147	
# of upper division courses, excluding seminars with an enrollment: Under 25	124	
25–49	32	
50–74	10	
75–99	10	
100+	2	
# of seminars	22	
# of seminar positions available	382	
# of seminar positions filled	241	0
# of positions available in simulation courses	841	
# of simulation positions filled	732	0
# of positions available in faculty supervised clinical courses	88	
# of faculty supervised clinical positions filled	88	0
# involved in field placements	169	0
# involved in law journals	155	0
# involved in interschool competitions	50	0
# of credit hours required to graduate	90	

JD Enrollment and Ethnicity

	Men #	Men %	Women #	Women %	Full-time #	Full-time %	Part-time #	Part-time %	1st-year #	1st-year %	Total #	Total %	JD Degs. Awd.
African Amer.	27	6.9	12	5.1	39	6.2	0	0.0	13	7.1	39	6.2	15
Amer. Indian	3	0.8	0	0.0	3	0.5	0	0.0	1	0.5	3	0.5	1
Asian Amer.	58	14.8	48	20.4	106	16.9	0	0.0	28	15.2	106	16.9	40
Mex. Amer.	0	0.0	0	0.0	0	0.0	0	0.0	0	0.0	0	0.0	0
Puerto Rican	0	0.0	0	0.0	0	0.0	0	0.0	0	0.0	0	0.0	0
Hispanic	29	7.4	22	9.4	51	8.1	0	0.0	17	9.2	51	8.1	16
Total Minority	117	29.9	82	34.9	199	31.8	0	0.0	59	32.1	199	31.8	72
For. Nation.	10	2.6	11	4.7	21	3.4	0	0.0	5	2.7	21	3.4	3
Caucasian	230	58.8	123	52.3	353	56.4	0	0.0	108	58.7	353	56.4	129
Unknown	34	8.7	19	8.1	53	8.5	0	0.0	12	6.5	53	8.5	9
Total	391	62.5	235	37.5	626	100.0	0	0.0	184	29.4	626		213

Transfers

Transfers in	41
Transfers out	9

Tuition and Fees

	Resident	Nonresident
Full-time	$20,512	$31,718
Part-time	$0	$0

Living Expenses

Estimated living expenses for singles

Living on campus	Living off campus	Living at home
$14,225	$14,225	$14,225

University of Illinois College of Law

ABA
Approved
Since
1923

GPA and LSAT Scores

	Total	Full-time	Part-time
# of apps	3,221	3,221	0
# of offers	742	742	0
# of matrics	186	186	0
75% GPA	3.71	3.71	0.00
Median GPA	3.50	3.50	0.00
25% GPA	3.15	3.15	0.00
75% LSAT	167	167	0
Median LSAT	166	166	0
25% LSAT	160	160	0

Grants and Scholarships (from prior year)

	Total #	Total %	Full-time #	Full-time %	Part-time #	Part-time %
Total # of students	640		640		0	
Total # receiving grants	365	57.0	365	57.0	0	0.0
Less than 1/2 tuition	278	43.4	278	43.4	0	0.0
Half to full tuition	30	4.7	30	4.7	0	0.0
Full tuition	57	8.9	57	8.9	0	0.0
More than full tuition	0	0.0	0	0.0	0	0.0
Median grant amount			$6,000		$0	

Informational and Library Resources

# of volumes and volume equivalents	761,652
# of titles	270,841
# of active serial subscriptions	8,788
Study seating capacity inside the library	366
# of full-time professional librarians	10
Hours per week library is open	102
# of open, wired connections available to students	802
# of networked computers available for use by students	56
# of simultaneous wireless users	1,500
Require computer?	Yes

JD Attrition (from prior year)

	Academic #	Other #	Total #	Total %
1st year	0	1	1	0.5
2nd year	0	12	12	5.2
3rd year	0	1	1	0.5
4th year	0	0	0	0.0

Employment (9 months after graduation)

	Total	Percentage
Employment status known	230	100.0
Employment status unknown	0	0.0
Employed	209	90.9
Pursuing graduate degrees	8	3.5
Unemployed seeking employment	5	2.2
Unemployed not seeking employment	5	2.2
Unemployed and studying for the bar	3	1.3

Type of Employment

# employed in law firms	131	62.7
# employed in business and industry	30	14.4
# employed in government	20	9.6
# employed in public interest	8	3.8
# employed as judicial clerks	14	6.7
# employed in academia	5	2.4

Geographic Location

# employed in state	138	66.0
# employed in foreign countries	2	1.0
# of states where employed		20

Bar Passage Rates

Jurisdiction	Illinois		
Exam	Sum 05	Win 06	Total
# from school taking bar for the first time	159	24	183
School's pass rate for all first-time takers	92%	79%	90%
State's pass rate for all first-time takers	86%	83%	85%

University of Illinois College of Law

504 East Pennsylvania Avenue
Champaign, IL 61820
Phone: 217.244.6415
E-mail: admissions@law.uiuc.edu; Website: www.law.uiuc.edu

■ Introduction

Established over a century ago, the University of Illinois College of Law fosters excellence in legal education through a close community of faculty members and students, where teaching goes hand in hand with scholarship. The resources —intellectual, cultural, and recreational—of one of the world's largest and best universities are readily available to our law students, as is the appealing ambience of a university community. The college's comparatively low tuition makes the program an outstanding value.

■ Library and Physical Facilities

A hallmark of a great university and a great law school is its library. The University Library in Urbana-Champaign is the largest public university library in the country. The Jenner Law Library holds 750,000 volumes and provides access to an equally wide array of electronic resources. In addition to US legal materials, the Jenner Law Library has extensive holdings in foreign and international law and houses a world-class collection of rare legal materials. Equally significant is Jenner's professional staff. Ten of its eleven law librarians have JDs in addition to master's degrees in library science. Law librarians teach legal research and work closely with students to support research and learning.

Directly across the street from the law school is one of the country's largest physical education buildings, with indoor and outdoor swimming pools, tennis courts, four gyms, weight and exercise equipment, archery, and ball courts of all kinds. The facility is free for students.

■ Joint-degree Programs

The College of Law administers 11 formal joint JD and master's or doctoral degree programs. The combined degrees available are JD/MBA, JD/DVM, JD/MHRIR in Human Resources and Industrial Relations, JD/MA in Urban Planning, JD/Master of Education, JD/Doctor of Education, JD/MA in Journalism, JD/MS in Chemistry, MD/MS in Natural Resources and Environmental Sciences, and JD/MCS in Computer Science.

■ Special Programs

Environmental Law—The college has an active program of environmental and planning studies. Beyond the first-year course in property, the college offers courses in environmental law, natural resources, and land-use planning.

Intellectual Property (IP)—The College of Law boasts a strong intellectual property curriculum and offers a rich array of courses taught by nationally known faculty and experienced practitioners. Students choose from a variety of offerings ranging from core patent, copyright, and trademark courses to cutting edge classes like Law and Regulation of Cyberspace, Internet and Web Law, International Copyright Principles, and International IP Transfers. Beyond its own curriculum, the College of Law's intellectual property faculty capitalizes upon the university's highly regarded academic programs in science and engineering, as well as its National Center for Supercomputing Applications, recognized as the world's

leader in computer design applications. The College of Law is currently collaborating with these premier university departments to develop joint-degree programs in the rapidly changing intellectual property arena.

Interdisciplinary Study—While the College of Law course offerings are so varied that it would take a student 12 years to sample all of them, students interested in related subjects outside the law school may receive up to 12 hours of credit for study in another discipline. This flexibility allows students to complement their legal education with advanced coursework in a highly regarded university.

International Legal Studies—Students pursuing international legal studies can choose from 15 international and comparative law courses. Faculty members have long-standing international connections, and some collaborate with international scholars and legal experts to teach these courses.

Public Interest Law and Public Policy—As one of the premier public law schools, the College of Law plays a special role in educating students to serve both the public interest and formulate public policy. The college's commitment to public interest law is demonstrated by the pro bono notation placed on diplomas of graduates who have performed at least 60 hours of unpaid legal work. In addition, students may choose from a variety of timely courses addressing public interest and policy issues.

Skills Training—The college offers four live-client clinics: Civil Litigation Clinic, International Human Rights Clinic, Transactional and Community Economic Development Clinic, and Employees Justice Clinic, as well as classes in legal drafting, business planning, advanced bankruptcy, environmental management, estate planning, and tax practice; all challenge students to solve concrete problems and draft legal documents in a variety of fields. Courses on computer applications in the law and quantitative methods in legal decision-making familiarize students with sophisticated techniques necessary in today's law practice; these include computerized methods of document preparation and information retrieval, statistical analysis, the use of computer simulations in litigation, and the calculation of damage awards.

Taxation—Illinois offers one of the strongest tax curricula in the country, with core courses that address all aspects of tax practice and advanced offerings that integrate tax problems with other fields of law.

Trial Advocacy Program—The college's Trial Advocacy Program is especially popular, enrolling about three-quarters of the third-year class. The year-long program teaches the art of courtroom litigation and concludes with students conducting a day-long mock trial.

■ Housing

College of Law students live both off campus and in graduate- or married-student campus housing. For information concerning campus housing, contact the Graduate and Family Housing Department at 217.333.5656.

In addition, the Urbana-Champaign area has ample private rental opportunities available at relatively low costs. Most current College of Law students choose to live in private, off-campus housing due to its low cost and easy access to the award-winning Urbana-Champaign mass transit system, which is free for all University of Illinois students.

■ Student Activities

The small size and tight-knit community of the College of Law allows students to directly participate in an extensive variety of activities. Students run and write for the *University of Illinois Law Review*, the *Elder Law Journal*, the *University of Illinois Journal of Law, Technology and Policy*, and the *Illinois Law Update* during their second and third years. In addition, second- and third-year students may participate in seven different moot court competitions that feature internal, external, and national contests, and several live-client legal clinics. First-year students also have many opportunities to get involved at the College of Law through the negotiation and client counseling competitions and several faculty-student committees. Finally, most students participate in at least one of the almost 35 student organizations. These organizations plan countless lectures, debates, charitable activities, sporting events, law firm visits, and social receptions, including the always anticipated annual formal ball.

■ Scholarships

The College of Law offers a number of scholarships, ranging from $1,000 to full tuition, awarded to students who show the greatest promise in the study of law. Previous academic success is a primary consideration; the committee also considers other relevant factors.

Applicant Profile

Our admission process takes into consideration many factors beyond the undergraduate GPA and the LSAT score. A statistical grid, as is typically provided here, only takes into consideration these two factors. Admission decisions at the University of Illinois College of Law are based on the Admission Committee's experienced judgment applied to individual cases. Consequently, we have chosen not to provide applicants with a grid that does not accurately portray our admission process.

Indiana University School of Law—Bloomington

211 S. Indiana Avenue, Law Building
Bloomington, IN 47405-7001
Phone: 812.855.4765; Fax: 812.855.1967
E-mail: lawadmis@indiana.edu; Website: www.law.indiana.edu

ABA
Approved
Since
1937

The Basics

Type of school	Public
Term	Semester
Application deadline	
Application fee	$35
Financial aid deadline	3/1
Can first year start other than fall?	Yes
Student to faculty ratio	12.3 to 1
Does the university offer:	
housing restricted to law students?	No
graduate housing for which law students are eligible?	Yes

Faculty and Administrators

	Total		Men		Women		Minorities	
	Fall	Spr	Fall	Spr	Fall	Spr	Fall	Spr
Full-time	47	42	33	29	14	13	5	4
Other Full-time	0	0	0	0	0	0	0	0
Deans, librarians, & others who teach	12	11	7	6	5	5	1	1
Part-time	15	26	11	19	4	7	0	0
Total	74	79	51	54	23	25	6	5

Curriculum

	Full-time	Part-time
Typical first-year section size	73	0
Is there typically a "small section" of the first-year class, other than Legal Writing, taught by full-time faculty	No	No
If yes, typical size offered last year		
# of classroom course titles beyond first-year curriculum	120	
# of upper division courses, excluding seminars with an enrollment: Under 25	96	
25–49	41	
50–74	12	
75–99	6	
100+	6	
# of seminars	15	
# of seminar positions available	258	
# of seminar positions filled	228	0
# of positions available in simulation courses	239	
# of simulation positions filled	203	0
# of positions available in faculty supervised clinical courses	71	
# of faculty supervised clinical positions filled	71	0
# involved in field placements	171	0
# involved in law journals	74	0
# involved in interschool competitions	26	0
# of credit hours required to graduate	88	

JD Enrollment and Ethnicity

	Men		Women		Full-time		Part-time		1st-year		Total		JD Degs. Awd.
	#	%	#	%	#	%	#	%	#	%	#	%	
African Amer.	20	5.2	23	8.7	43	6.6	0	0.0	17	8.1	43	6.6	14
Amer. Indian	1	0.3	1	0.4	2	0.3	0	0.0	1	0.5	2	0.3	0
Asian Amer.	19	4.9	17	6.4	36	5.6	0	0.0	11	5.3	36	5.5	14
Mex. Amer.	12	3.1	15	5.7	27	4.2	0	0.0	7	3.3	27	4.2	7
Puerto Rican	0	0.0	0	0.0	0	0.0	0	0.0	0	0.0	0	0.0	0
Hispanic	0	0.0	0	0.0	0	0.0	0	0.0	0	0.0	0	0.0	0
Total Minority	52	13.5	56	21.1	108	16.7	0	0.0	36	17.2	108	16.6	35
For. Nation.	1	0.3	0	0.0	1	0.2	0	0.0	0	0.0	1	0.2	0
Caucasian	318	82.8	200	75.5	517	79.8	1	100.0	168	80.4	518	79.8	172
Unknown	13	3.4	9	3.4	22	3.4	0	0.0	5	2.4	22	3.4	8
Total	384	59.2	265	40.8	648	99.8	1	0.2	209	32.2	649		215

Transfers

Transfers in	0
Transfers out	10

Tuition and Fees

	Resident	Nonresident
Full-time	$15,784	$30,311
Part-time	$0	$0

Living Expenses

Estimated living expenses for singles

Living on campus	Living off campus	Living at home
$12,600	$12,600	$7,200

Indiana University S

ABA
Approved
Since
1937

Indiana University S
211 S. Indiana Avenue, Law B
Bloomington, IN 47405-70
Phone: 812.855.4765:
E-mail: lawadmis@

GPA and LSAT Scores

	Total	Full-time	Part-time
# of apps	2,718	2,717	1
# of offers	1,057	1,056	1
# of matrics	211	211	0
75% GPA	3.78	3.78	0.00
Median GPA	3.57	3.57	0.00
25% GPA	3.24	3.24	0.00
75% LSAT	164	164	0
Median LSAT	163	163	0
25% LSAT	157	157	0

Grants and Scholarships (from prior year)

	Total		Full-time		Part-time	
	#	%	#	%	#	%
Total # of students	663		662		1	
Total # receiving grants	477	71.9	477	72.1	0	0.0
Less than 1/2 tuition	383	57.8	383	57.9	0	0.0
Half to full tuition	61	9.2	61	9.2	0	0.0
Full tuition	6	0.9	6	0.9	0	0.0
More than full tuition	27	4.1	27	4.1	0	0.0
Median grant amount			$7,000		$0	

Informational and Library Resources

# of volumes and volume equivalents	734,180
# of titles	246,432
# of active serial subscriptions	8,948
Study seating capacity inside the library	680
# of full-time professional librarians	11
Hours per week library is open	115
# of open, wired connections available to students	60
# of networked computers available for use by students	74
# of simultaneous wireless users	900
Require computer?	Yes

JD Attrition (from pr

	Acade			
	#			
1st year	0			
2nd year	0			
3rd year	0		2	0.9
4th year	0	0	0	0.0

Employment (9 months after graduation)

	Total	Percentage
Employment status known	207	99.0
Employment status unknown	2	1.0
Employed	187	90.3
Pursuing graduate degrees	5	2.4
Unemployed seeking employment	5	2.4
Unemployed not seeking employment	4	1.9
Unemployed and studying for the bar	6	2.9
Type of Employment		
# employed in law firms	110	58.8
# employed in business and industry	21	11.2
# employed in government	26	13.9
# employed in public interest	5	2.7
# employed as judicial clerks	14	7.5
# employed in academia	7	3.7
Geographic Location		
# employed in state	74	39.6
# employed in foreign countries	0	0.0
# of states where employed		26

Bar Passage Rates

Jurisdiction	Indiana		
Exam	Sum 05	Win 06	Total
# from school taking bar for the first time	76	9	85
School's pass rate for all first-time takers	88%	89%	88%
State's pass rate for all first-time takers	84%	77%	82%

chool of Law—Bloomington

uilding
01
ax: 812.855.1967
indiana.edu; Website: www.law.indiana.edu

ction

diana University School of Law—Bloomington provides highest quality legal education in a relaxed, collegial etting. Founded in 1842, the law school is located on the beautifully wooded campus of one of the nation's largest teaching and research universities. The presence of the university, including its world famous School of Music, offers students cultural opportunities available in few urban areas, while retaining the advantages of a small university town. With a student body of fewer than 675 students, drawn from more than 200 undergraduate schools in the United States and abroad, the law school is small enough to retain its distinctive sense of community and collegiality, while large enough to facilitate a stimulating, cosmopolitan environment. The school is a charter member of the AALS and is approved by the ABA.

■ Library and Physical Facilities

With nearly 750,000 volumes, the law library is one of the 20 largest law libraries in the US, the largest in the state of Indiana, and was recently named one of the top law school libraries in the nation by a national law school magazine. Law-trained librarians give instruction in research techniques and provide reference assistance. While continuing its commitment to a high quality print collection, the library is a national leader in computer applications in legal education. Through Internet access (from the School of Law or their homes) students can utilize systems specific to law, such as LexisNexis and Westlaw, or access the rapidly expanding array of global information sources. All students are required to possess a laptop computer and may connect with the library, the Indiana University network, and the Internet through the School of Law's wireless network, which is available throughout the law school building. Network connection is also available via Ethernet cable connections throughout the library. Students may write their examinations using their laptops, but are not required to do so.

■ Curriculum

The curriculum offers traditional courses as well as specialized courses, such as intellectual property, communications and Internet law, law and biomedical advances, immigration law, international business transactions, and environmental law. The school offers intensive training in litigation and dispute resolution. Students may participate in clinics that enable them to deal with client problems and, in some cases, represent clients in local courts, all under close faculty supervision. The law school divides first-year law students into small, informal groups of five to seven, which are mentored by second- and third-year students. These groups are supervised by faculty and provide both academic and peer support.

■ Joint-degree Programs

Formal joint-degree programs combine award of a JD degree and a master's degree in business, accounting, public affairs, environmental science, journalism, telecommunications, or library science. The duration of most joint-degree programs is

four years. However, the School of Law and the Kelley School of Business have recently established an intensive three-year JD/MBA program. Informal concurrent-degree programs with other disciplines, pursuing a JD and a master's or doctoral degree, are frequently designed to meet students' learning and career goals.

■ Opportunities to Study Abroad

The School of Law provides students with a wide variety of opportunities to study abroad. A limited number of second- and third-year students can take advantage of the unique opportunity to study in and immerse themselves in the legal education system and culture of another country. Semester-long opportunities are available through the London Law Consortium and exchange programs with Université Panthéon-Assas (Paris II) Law School; ESADE Law School in Barcelona, Spain; Bucerius Law School in Hamburg, Germany; China University of Political Science and Law in Beijing (CUPL); the Law School at the University of Hong Kong (HKU); Friedrich-Schiller University in Jena, Germany; Warsaw University in Warsaw, Poland; and the University of Auckland in Auckland, New Zealand. All classes, with the exception of those taken at Bucerius and HKU, are taught in the schools' respective native language. Finally, the law school offers all students the opportunity to participate in summer study-abroad programs hosted by the Institute on International and Comparative Law in England, France, Ireland, Italy, Russia, and Spain. All courses are taught in English.

■ Early Start Program

An early start program is offered for students who wish to begin their legal studies in the summer session. This program allows students to take one 4-credit-hour class in the summer in a small, intimate environment as they make the transition into the law school.

■ Admission

Generally, the quality and size of the applicant pool forces the Admissions Committee to rely heavily on the undergraduate grade-point average and the LSAT score. However, numerical indicators are not the only considerations used in evaluating applications. The committee considers the quality of the applicant's undergraduate institution, level and rigor of coursework, letters of recommendation (particularly those from faculty), graduate work, employment during and after college, extracurricular activities, potential for service to the profession, educational/geographic/socioeconomic diversity, and the applicant's personal statement. Applicants are encouraged to explain matters that may have adversely affected their undergraduate performance. Applicants who feel they have been disadvantaged because of economic, educational, racial, or cultural factors are urged to bring this to the attention of the Admissions Committee. Printable and online applications are available at *www.law.indiana.edu*.

Housing

The Bloomington area offers a variety of housing options for students. There are numerous apartments and houses available as off-campus rentals as well as on-campus housing. Information regarding off-campus housing options is available on the law school's website, *www.law.indiana.edu*. For information concerning on-campus housing, contact Indiana University Residential Programs and Services, *www.rps.indiana.edu*.

Student Activities

A variety of student organizations present opportunities for involvement in groups focused on specialized areas of the law and public service. Some of the most active groups include the Black Law Student Association, Women's Law Caucus, Public Interest Law Foundation, Latino Law Student Association, and the Environmental Law Society. Students may also obtain practical experience in a number of clinical opportunities, including the Community Legal Clinic, Conservation Law Clinic, Disability Law Clinic, Elder Law Clinic, Family and Children Mediation Clinic, Inmate Legal Assistance Project, Tenant Assistance Project, Public Interest Internship Program,

Federal Courts Clinic, Entrepreneurship Law Clinic, and Protective Order Project. Second- and third-year students are offered the opportunity to gain valuable writing, editing, and advocacy skills through participation in the Moot Court Competition or one of our three journals. The *Indiana Law Journal* publishes articles by legal scholars, practitioners, jurists, and IU law students. The *Federal Communications Law Journal* is the nation's oldest and largest circulation communications law journal. The *Indiana Journal of Global Legal Studies* is a multidisciplinary journal that specializes in international and comparative law articles.

Career Services

The Career Services Office actively provides career planning and employment assistance to law students and alumni. Both on- and off-campus interviews are coordinated to facilitate contact between students and employers. In recent years, more than 97 percent of graduates have secured employment within nine months of graduation. Over one half locate outside the state of Indiana. Graduates are found in all 50 states and in 31 foreign countries.

Applicant Profile

Indiana University School of Law—Bloomington
This grid includes only applicants who earned 120–180 LSAT scores under standard administrations.

LSAT Score	GPA 3.75 + Apps	Adm	3.50–3.74 Apps	Adm	3.25–3.49 Apps	Adm	3.00–3.24 Apps	Adm	2.75–2.99 Apps	Adm	2.50–2.74 Apps	Adm	Below 2.50 Apps	Adm	No GPA Apps	Adm	Total Apps	Adm
175–180	6	6	8	6	0	0	1	1	1	0	3	1	0	0	0	0	19	14
170–174	42	42	29	28	17	16	9	9	5	4	7	3	0	0	0	0	109	102
165–169	78	77	88	83	54	52	71	69	37	17	16	8	8	3	2	0	354	309
160–164	174	137	181	126	135	70	102	50	56	28	25	8	12	6	3	0	688	425
155–159	108	44	171	38	158	17	100	8	40	0	17	0	9	0	4	1	607	108
150–154	72	26	127	35	146	17	89	5	51	0	18	0	11	0	9	0	523	83
145–149	23	1	50	4	51	2	42	0	30	1	22	0	13	0	6	0	237	8
140–144	9	0	15	2	16	0	24	0	16	0	14	0	9	0	3	1	106	3
Below 140	0	0	4	0	7	0	12	0	8	0	7	0	11	0	2	0	51	0
Total	512	333	673	322	584	174	450	142	244	50	129	20	73	9	29	2	2694	1052

Apps = Number of Applicants
Adm = Number Admitted
Reflects 99% of the total applicant pool.

Indiana University School of Law—Indianapolis

530 West New York Street
Indianapolis, IN 46202-3225
Phone: 317.274.2459; Fax: 317.278.4780
E-mail: lawadmit@iupui.edu; Website: www.indylaw.indiana.edu

*ABA
Approved
Since
1944*

The Basics

Type of school	Public
Term	Semester
Application deadline	3/1
Application fee	$50
Financial aid deadline	3/1
Can first year start other than fall?	No
Student to faculty ratio	18.0 to 1
Does the university offer:	
housing restricted to law students?	No
graduate housing for which law students are eligible?	Yes

Faculty and Administrators

	Total Fall	Total Spr	Men Fall	Men Spr	Women Fall	Women Spr	Minorities Fall	Minorities Spr
Full-time	41	41	23	23	18	18	4	4
Other Full-time	1	1	0	0	1	1	0	0
Deans, librarians, & others who teach	10	10	6	6	4	4	0	0
Part-time	40	38	28	26	12	12	1	1
Total	92	90	57	55	35	35	5	5

Curriculum

	Full-time	Part-time
Typical first-year section size	96	82
Is there typically a "small section" of the first-year class, other than Legal Writing, taught by full-time faculty	No	No
If yes, typical size offered last year		
# of classroom course titles beyond first-year curriculum		128
# of upper division courses, excluding seminars with an enrollment: Under 25		82
25–49		61
50–74		18
75–99		18
100+		2
# of seminars		13
# of seminar positions available		286
# of seminar positions filled	167	75
# of positions available in simulation courses		417
# of simulation positions filled	288	85
# of positions available in faculty supervised clinical courses		82
# of faculty supervised clinical positions filled	43	19
# involved in field placements	125	14
# involved in law journals	120	26
# involved in interschool competitions	187	58
# of credit hours required to graduate		90

JD Enrollment and Ethnicity

	Men #	Men %	Women #	Women %	Full-time #	Full-time %	Part-time #	Part-time %	1st-year #	1st-year %	Total #	Total %	JD Degs. Awd.
African Amer.	15	3.1	39	8.6	36	5.5	18	6.4	21	5.6	54	5.8	18
Amer. Indian	0	0.0	1	0.2	0	0.0	1	0.4	1	0.3	1	0.1	1
Asian Amer.	10	2.1	9	2.0	13	2.0	6	2.1	5	1.3	19	2.0	6
Mex. Amer.	4	0.8	4	0.9	4	0.6	4	1.4	1	0.3	8	0.9	8
Puerto Rican	2	0.4	2	0.4	2	0.3	2	0.7	0	0.0	4	0.4	1
Hispanic	9	1.9	5	1.1	11	1.7	3	1.1	2	0.5	14	1.5	4
Total Minority	40	8.2	60	13.3	66	10.1	34	12.1	30	7.9	100	10.7	38
For. Nation.	12	2.5	10	2.2	16	2.4	6	2.1	7	1.9	22	2.3	3
Caucasian	434	89.3	382	84.5	574	87.5	242	85.8	341	90.2	816	87.0	219
Unknown	0	0.0	0	0.0	0	0.0	0	0.0	0	0.0	0	0.0	0
Total	486	51.8	452	48.2	656	69.9	282	30.1	378	40.3	938		260

Transfers

Transfers in	26
Transfers out	6

Tuition and Fees

	Resident	Nonresident
Full-time	$13,962	$29,457
Part-time	$9,640	$20,136

Living Expenses

Estimated living expenses for singles		
Living on campus	Living off campus	Living at home
$18,044	$19,524	N/A

Indiana University School of Law—Indianapolis

ABA Approved Since 1944

GPA and LSAT Scores

	Total	Full-time	Part-time
# of apps	1,860	1,500	360
# of offers	590	456	134
# of matrics	288	195	93
75% GPA	3.71	3.75	3.58
Median GPA	3.46	3.50	3.40
25% GPA	3.20	3.25	3.05
75% LSAT	159	159	157
Median LSAT	156	157	155
25% LSAT	153	154	151

Grants and Scholarships (from prior year)

	Total #	Total %	Full-time #	Full-time %	Part-time #	Part-time %
Total # of students	913		642		271	
Total # receiving grants	286	31.3	238	37.1	48	17.7
Less than 1/2 tuition	209	22.9	170	26.5	39	14.4
Half to full tuition	67	7.3	62	9.7	5	1.8
Full tuition	0	0.0	0	0.0	0	0.0
More than full tuition	10	1.1	6	0.9	4	1.5
Median grant amount			$6,000	.	$2,000	

Informational and Library Resources

# of volumes and volume equivalents	597,911
# of titles	196,872
# of active serial subscriptions	3,092
Study seating capacity inside the library	506
# of full-time professional librarians	9
Hours per week library is open	99
# of open, wired connections available to students	1,140
# of networked computers available for use by students	155
# of simultaneous wireless users	1,200
Require computer?	No

JD Attrition (from prior year)

	Academic #	Other #	Total #	Total %
1st year	3	14	17	4.7
2nd year	2	5	7	2.4
3rd year	3	0	3	1.2
4th year	0	0	0	0.0

Employment (9 months after graduation)

	Total	Percentage
Employment status known	251	100.0
Employment status unknown	0	0.0
Employed	238	94.8
Pursuing graduate degrees	1	0.4
Unemployed seeking employment	7	2.8
Unemployed not seeking employment	0	0.0
Unemployed and studying for the bar	5	2.0

Type of Employment

	Total	Percentage
# employed in law firms	126	52.9
# employed in business and industry	40	16.8
# employed in government	47	19.7
# employed in public interest	8	3.4
# employed as judicial clerks	8	3.4
# employed in academia	2	0.8

Geographic Location

	Total	Percentage
# employed in state	215	90.3
# employed in foreign countries	0	0.0
# of states where employed	14	

Bar Passage Rates

Jurisdiction	Indiana		
Exam	Sum 05	Win 06	Total
# from school taking bar for the first time	174	34	208
School's pass rate for all first-time takers	78%	76%	77%
State's pass rate for all first-time takers	84%	77%	82%

Indiana University School of Law—Indianapolis

530 West New York Street
Indianapolis, IN 46202-3225
Phone: 317.274.2459; Fax: 317.278.4780
E-mail: lawadmit@iupui.edu; Website: www.indylaw.indiana.edu

■ Introduction

Founded in 1894 as the Indiana Law School, the IU School of Law—Indianapolis has emerged as a premier educational institution, located in the dynamic heart of Indiana on the Indianapolis campus of Indiana University–Purdue University. This campus is also home to the Schools of Medicine, Dentistry, Nursing, and Social Work. The law school building, Lawrence W. Inlow Hall, is a state-of-the-art facility, enabling the faculty to employ the latest technology and teaching methods. The building houses modern classrooms, private study areas, and an unparalleled law library. The school is just minutes away from the state's courts, the legislature, and major law firms, giving students opportunities to observe the legal process in action and to participate in that process as law clerks, judicial interns, and legislative staff assistants. The school is the largest in the state of Indiana and one of the few Big Ten law schools to offer the cultural, recreational, and professional advantages of an urban educational environment.

■ Clinical Experiences

The law school offers several clinical programs. The Civil Practice Clinic allows students the opportunity to represent clients in a variety of cases, including housing, divorce, child support, consumer, and administrative matters. In the Civil Practice Disability Clinic, students represent school-age children with special needs, as well as persons who are afflicted with the HIV virus, Alzheimer's disease, and AIDS. In the Criminal Defense Clinic, students represent clients in criminal cases involving a variety of misdemeanor or class D felony charges. Students who enroll in the Criminal Defense Clinic for a second semester may work on Innocence Project cases, which involve inmates who are making claims of innocence in postconviction proceedings.

■ Internships and Special Programs

The school's research centers and programs make significant contributions to the profession, both locally and nationally. The William S. and Christine S. Hall Center for Law and Health is considered one of the top health law programs in the nation. The center serves as a preeminent information resource on health law issues for the bar, government, and health care community. Through the center, students may pursue a concentration in Law and Health and participate in the *Indiana Health Law Review*.

The Program on Law and State Government enriches the dialogue between the academic legal community and state government policymakers. The program offers internships with more than 40 government offices and also sponsors a mediation course that qualifies students to become registered civil mediators. Additionally, the program sponsors a fellowship that allows students to host an academic event and write a publishable academic paper on critical legal or regulatory issues pertinent to state government.

The Court Internship Program provides internships with federal, state, and local courts. Interns work closely with judges and law clerks, learning about the legal process by experiencing it firsthand.

The newly established Center for Intellectual Property Law and Innovation allows students to pursue in-depth study of intellectual property issues and provides an important resource to the legal community.

■ International Law Program

Because the school recognizes that international considerations touch all areas of the law from human rights to economic issues, it established the Center for International and Comparative Law. A wide variety of international courses, combined with opportunities for overseas experiences, demonstrate our commitment to a legal education with a worldview. Our program in International Human Rights Law has placed students in internships in locations from Argentina to Zimbabwe.

The study of European law takes place each summer in Strasbourg, France, at the Robert Schuman University. Strasbourg not only boasts one of France's preeminent universities, but it is also the seat of the Parliament of the European Union and the European Court of Human Rights. It is the perfect starting point for educational field trips and excursions to Paris, London, Luxembourg, and Brussels. The law school also sponsors a summer program in cooperation with the University of Zagreb School of Law in the ancient Croatian city of Dubrovnik.

Established in 1987, the Chinese Law Summer Program is hosted by Renmin (People's) University of China School of Law and introduces students to the Chinese legal and lawyering systems, its dispute resolution mechanisms, and Chinese constitutional law.

Students can also travel to Argentina and other Latin American countries to study the legal system of Latin America through the Latin America Law Program offered in cooperation with the Universidad Nacional de La Plata.

In addition to offering several courses and seminars in the area of international law, the school sponsors the *Indiana International and Comparative Law Review* and a student organization, the International Law Society. It is also home to the editorial offices of the *European Journal of Law Reform*.

■ Joint-degree Programs

The school offers six joint-degree options in cooperation with IU's School of Business, School of Public and Environmental Affairs, School of Medicine, School of Library and Information Science, and School of Liberal Arts. Available degrees are the Doctor of Jurisprudence and Master of Business Administration (JD/MBA), Master of Health Administration (JD/MHA), Master of Public Affairs (JD/MPA), Master of Public Health (JD/MPH), Master of Library Science (JD/MLS), and Master of Arts in Philosophy (JD/MPhil).

■ Special Summer Program

Summer admission is offered to a select group of applicants who can benefit from a class emphasizing writing and analytical skills. Applicants who have either an LSAT score or GPA that is outside of the median range of accepted students, persons who are returning to school after several years outside of the classroom, and students for whom English is a second language may be considered for the summer program. Summer admittees earn two credits toward their JD degrees. Continuation in the fall is not contingent upon performance in the summer program. There is no special application procedure. Applicants who are not presumptively admitted and whose files are completed by February 1 may be considered for this program.

Additionally, the school strongly supports the Indiana Conference for Legal Education Opportunity program, which provides those who are currently underrepresented in the legal profession or underrepresented in practice areas with assistance in preparing for law school through a six-week summer institute.

■ Admission

LSAT and LSDAS are required.

The law school seeks to attain a culturally rich and diverse student body. To this end, admission decisions are based on a variety of factors in addition to the LSAT score and undergraduate GPA.

Indiana University School of Law—Indianapolis offers an early decision program. Early decision candidates must have their applications completed by November 30 and will be notified of the admission committee's decision by late December.

■ Academic Support Programs

Students are offered assistance through the Dean's Tutorial Society. Supervised by a tenured faculty member, the tutorial society is staffed by academically distinguished students who offer individual tutoring as well as assistance in case briefing and exam preparation.

■ Student Activities

Students can participate in any of 30 different interest groups and organizations, ranging from the Equal Justice Works to the Law and Technology Society. The school also offers an extensive moot court program, a client counseling program, and three law reviews.

■ Office for Professional Development

The Office for Professional Development provides career counseling and job search assistance to students and alumni. Services include an on-campus interview program, a résumé review service, a mock interview program, and a variety of workshops and seminars.

Applicant Profile

Indiana University School of Law—Indianapolis
This grid includes only applicants who earned 120–180 LSAT scores under standard administrations.

LSAT Score	3.75+ Apps	3.75+ Adm	3.50–3.74 Apps	3.50–3.74 Adm	3.25–3.49 Apps	3.25–3.49 Adm	3.00–3.24 Apps	3.00–3.24 Adm	2.75–2.99 Apps	2.75–2.99 Adm	2.50–2.74 Apps	2.50–2.74 Adm	2.25–2.49 Apps	2.25–2.49 Adm	2.00–2.24 Apps	2.00–2.24 Adm	Below 2.00 Apps	Below 2.00 Adm	No GPA Apps	No GPA Adm	Total Apps	Total Adm
175–180	0	0	0	0	0	0	0	0	0	0	0	0	0	0	0	0	0	0	0	0	0	0
170–174	1	1	0	0	0	0	0	0	0	0	0	0	0	0	0	0	0	0	0	0	1	1
165–169	5	4	5	5	3	2	2	2	3	2	0	0	1	1	0	0	0	0	2	1	19	16
160–164	28	28	13	12	25	23	23	18	14	11	11	4	8	0	1	0	0	0	9	1	125	97
155–159	58	55	82	61	91	69	55	32	39	19	20	4	5	1	3	0	1	0	12	3	363	242
150–154	78	51	132	39	125	34	139	23	81	11	24	7	16	1	6	0	1	0	12	3	614	169
145–149	31	7	63	14	89	9	87	11	53	3	34	1	14	0	13	0	0	0	10	1	394	46
140–144	13	0	28	4	43	3	57	2	24	2	19	0	12	0	4	0	2	0	9	1	209	11
135–139	2	0	11	1	14	1	17	0	11	0	11	0	5	0	3	0	1	0	2	0	93	3
130–134	0	0	1	0	2	0	3	0	3	0	2	0	5	0	2	0	1	0	0	0	22	0
125–129	0	0	1	0	0	0	0	0	1	0	0	0	0	0	0	0	0	0	0	0	5	0
120–124	0	0	0	0	0	0	0	0	0	0	0	0	1	0	0	0	0	0	7	0	1	0
Total	216	146	336	136	392	141	383	88	229	48	121	16	72	3	40	0	7	0	50	7	1846	585

Apps = Number of Applicants
Adm = Number Admitted
Reflects 99% of the total applicant pool.

Inter American University School of Law

PO Box 70351
San Juan, PR 00936-8351
Phone: 787.751.1912, exts. 2011, 2012
Website: www.derecho.inter.edu

The Basics

Type of school	Private
Term	Semester
Application deadline	3/30
Application fee	$63
Financial aid deadline	10/10
Can first year start other than fall?	No
Student to faculty ratio	28.5 to 1
Does the university offer:	
housing restricted to law students?	No
graduate housing for which law students are eligible?	No

Faculty and Administrators

	Total		Men		Women		Minorities	
	Fall	Spr	Fall	Spr	Fall	Spr	Fall	Spr
Full-time	25	25	15	15	10	10	25	25
Other Full-time	2	2	0	0	2	2	2	2
Deans, librarians, & others who teach	5	5	4	4	1	1	5	5
Part-time	43	44	31	35	12	9	42	43
Total	75	76	50	54	25	22	74	75

Curriculum

	Full-time	Part-time
Typical first-year section size	12	9
Is there typically a "small section" of the first-year class, other than Legal Writing, taught by full-time faculty	No	No
If yes, typical size offered last year		
# of classroom course titles beyond first-year curriculum		57
# of upper division courses, excluding seminars with an enrollment: Under 25		36
25–49		28
50–74		26
75–99		0
100+		0
# of seminars		7
# of seminar positions available		20
# of seminar positions filled	20	20
# of positions available in simulation courses		6
# of simulation positions filled	4	2
# of positions available in faculty supervised clinical courses		10
# of faculty supervised clinical positions filled	7	3
# involved in field placements	0	0
# involved in law journals	0	0
# involved in interschool competitions	0	0
# of credit hours required to graduate		92

JD Enrollment and Ethnicity

	Men		Women		Full-time		Part-time		1st-year		Total		JD Degs. Awd.
	#	%	#	%	#	%	#	%	#	%	#	%	
African Amer.	0	0.0	0	0.0	0	0.0	0	0.0	0	0.0	0	0.0	0
Amer. Indian	0	0.0	0	0.0	0	0.0	0	0.0	0	0.0	0	0.0	0
Asian Amer.	0	0.0	0	0.0	0	0.0	0	0.0	0	0.0	0	0.0	0
Mex. Amer.	0	0.0	0	0.0	0	0.0	0	0.0	0	0.0	0	0.0	0
Puerto Rican	375	100.0	458	100.0	622	100.0	211	100.0	327	100.0	833	100.0	204
Hispanic	0	0.0	0	0.0	0	0.0	0	0.0	0	0.0	0	0.0	0
Total Minority	375	100.0	458	100.0	622	100.0	211	100.0	327	100.0	833	100.0	204
For. Nation.	0	0.0	0	0.0	0	0.0	0	0.0	0	0.0	0	0.0	0
Caucasian	0	0.0	0	0.0	0	0.0	0	0.0	0	0.0	0	0.0	0
Unknown	0	0.0	0	0.0	0	0.0	0	0.0	0	0.0	0	0.0	0
Total	375	45.0	458	55.0	622	74.7	211	25.3	327	39.3	833		204

Transfers

Transfers in	23
Transfers out	20

Tuition and Fees

	Resident	Nonresident
Full-time	$12,891	$12,891
Part-time	$9,611	$9,611

Living Expenses

Estimated living expenses for singles

Living on campus	Living off campus	Living at home
N/A	$15,223	$13,172

Inter American University School of Law

ABA Approved Since 1969

GPA and LSAT Scores

	Total	Full-time	Part-time
# of apps	987	539	448
# of offers	395	214	181
# of matrics	245	125	120
75% GPA	3.56	3.75	3.37
Median GPA	3.24	3.23	3.25
25% GPA	3.15	3.29	3.01
75% LSAT	145	140	149
Median LSAT	138	139	137
25% LSAT	139	137	140

Grants and Scholarships (from prior year)

	Total		Full-time		Part-time	
	#	%	#	%	#	%
Total # of students	806		514		292	
Total # receiving grants	89	11.0	55	10.7	34	11.6
Less than 1/2 tuition	0	0.0	0	0.0	0	0.0
Half to full tuition	7	0.9	3	0.6	4	1.4
Full tuition	72	8.9	51	9.9	21	7.2
More than full tuition	10	1.2	1	0.2	9	3.1
Median grant amount			$5,123		$4,784	

Informational and Library Resources

# of volumes and volume equivalents	196,605
# of titles	27,604
# of active serial subscriptions	154
Study seating capacity inside the library	307
# of full-time professional librarians	7
Hours per week library is open	102
# of open, wired connections available to students	14
# of networked computers available for use by students	48
# of simultaneous wireless users	200
Require computer?	No

JD Attrition (from prior year)

	Academic	Other	Total	
	#	#	#	%
1st year	7	21	28	11.3
2nd year	3	3	6	1.8
3rd year	0	0	0	0.0
4th year	0	1	1	2.4

Employment (9 months after graduation)

	Total	Percentage
Employment status known	206	94.5
Employment status unknown	12	5.5
Employed	187	90.8
Pursuing graduate degrees	7	3.4
Unemployed seeking employment	3	1.5
Unemployed not seeking employment	0	0.0
Unemployed and studying for the bar	9	4.4

Type of Employment

# employed in law firms	83	44.4
# employed in business and industry	43	23.0
# employed in government	47	25.1
# employed in public interest	0	0.0
# employed as judicial clerks	12	6.4
# employed in academia	2	1.1

Geographic Location

# employed in state	186	99.5
# employed in foreign countries	0	0.0
# of states where employed	0	

Bar Passage Rates

Jurisdiction	Puerto Rico		
Exam	Sum 05	Win 06	Total
# from school taking bar for the first time	168	21	189
School's pass rate for all first-time takers	47%	62%	49%
State's pass rate for all first-time takers	50%	33%	46%

Inter American University School of Law

PO Box 70351
San Juan, PR 00936-8351
Phone: 787.751.1912, exts. 2011, 2012
Website: www.derecho.inter.edu

Introduction

The Inter American University School of Law is one of the 11 units of the Inter American University of Puerto Rico, a private nonprofit educational corporation accredited by the Middle States Association of Colleges and Secondary Schools, the Puerto Rico Council of Higher Education, and the Commonwealth of Puerto Rico Department of Education. The School of Law is approved by the ABA and is located in San Juan, the capital city of Puerto Rico. Since its founding, the School of Law has succeeded in meeting the needs of the legal profession, in particular, and Puerto Rico's society in general.

Enrollment/Student Body

The incoming class for academic year 2006–2007 was composed of 244 students. The student body comes mainly from Puerto Rico, although applicants from the mainland are encouraged to apply.

Library and Physical Facilities

The law school has developed its library into a center of access to traditional library services as well as computerized legal-research services.

The school was relocated to a new building in 1993, which includes seven classrooms equipped with air-conditioning, accessibility for students with disabilities, state-of-the-art audiovisual equipment, seminar rooms, library, legal clinic, faculty offices, conference room, lounge, Continuing Legal Education Program office, *Law Review* offices, student organization offices, administrative offices, chapel, student center, cafeteria, bookstore, auditorium with a seating capacity of 310, parking, and more. The site has been landscaped to achieve a sense of serenity and beauty compatible with the building's functions.

In January 1990, the library signed a collaboration agreement to establish a consortium with the law school library of the Catholic University of Puerto Rico and the library of the Supreme Court of Puerto Rico, with the purpose of coordinating collection development and sharing its resources through an automated bibliographic network, interlibrary loans, and telecommunication services.

Curriculum

The JD program covers three years in the day division and four years in the evening division. Candidates must complete a minimum of 92 credit hours with a GPA of not less than 2.5 to qualify for graduation.

Inter American University School of Law offers a three-week preparation course to be taken during the summer on a compulsory basis by students admitted to the school. Students who enter law school must be willing to make a heavy commitment.

For its part, Inter American University is willing to provide the best possible professional educational experience through the careful recruitment of a first-rate faculty, the development of a progressive curriculum, and a willingness to create new and exciting programs of clinical studies and research.

Admission

Proficiency in Spanish is essential in the program. Applicants must have a minimum grade-point average of 2.5, a medical certificate for students 21 years or younger, a police department certificate of good conduct, and appear for a personal interview, if required.

Candidates are required to take the Examen de Admisión a Estudios de Posgrado (EXADEP), the Aptitude Test for Graduate Education, and the Law School Admission Test (LSAT). Students should attain a 575 minimum score on the EXADEP and a minimum score of 130 on the LSAT. Application forms and other relevant information concerning the EXADEP may be obtained from Educational Testing Service, American International Plaza, 250 Muñoz Rivera Avenue, Suite 315, Hato Rey, PR 00918.

Housing

The university does not provide housing for law students. However, the areas surrounding the School of Law contain many private houses, apartments, and condominiums for rent.

Student Activities

Student organizations include the student council, an organization that represents the student body and participates in matters of administrative policy related to students' interests. Council representatives serve on various faculty committees as well as the university senate and the board of trustees.

Other student organizations are the Law Student Division of the American Bar Association, Phi Alpha Delta legal fraternity (composed not only of law students but also of distinguished honorary members who are Supreme Court justices, federal district court judges, and prominent attorneys), the National Association of Law Students, Women Law Students Association, United Students Forging an Environmental Consciousness, Law Student Division of the Inter-American Federation of Lawyers, the Association of Trial Lawyers of America, the Hispanic National Bar Association, the Federal Bar Association, Student's Cooperative Bookstore, and the Hispanic Notarial Bar Association.

The *Inter American School of Law Review* is the official publication of the School of Law. Its members work under the supervision of an editorial board of four students chosen on the basis of merit and dedication to the *Review* and an academic advisor who is a faculty member appointed by the dean.

Clinical Programs

The Legal Aid Clinical Program of the faculty is integrated with the Community Law Office through a combined effort of the US Legal Services Corporation and Inter American University. Law students are provided with the opportunity to learn skills such as interviewing, negotiation, counseling, fact gathering and analysis, legal research and drafting, decision making about alternative strategies, and preparation for trial and field practice. They also represent clients before administrative agencies and courts with the close supervision of the program's staff attorney-professors, pursuant to rules of the Supreme Court of Puerto Rico. Students also gain practical experience by serving with Puerto Rico Legal Services, Inc.; San Juan Community Law Office, Inc.; Legal Aid Society of Puerto Rico; the district attorney's offices; and the Environmental Quality Board.

■ Career Services

The mission of the Career Placement Office is to prepare students and alumni for the legal job market by encouraging them to conduct self-assessment in an effort to focus their job search and to educate them on their legal and nonlegal options in today's competitive legal market. This is accomplished through a variety of services including, but not limited to, individual counseling, group seminars, self-assessment materials, interviewing programs, a career resource library, and the alumni network.

■ Continuing Legal Education Program

The Continuing Legal Education Program offers advanced courses and seminars concerning different fields of the law of interest to practicing lawyers as well as to the community in general.

The CLE Program enjoys a good reputation and has been able to develop a consistent course offering, primarily in the following categories: courses designed for specialists; refresher courses for experienced lawyers; courses designed to provide information in nontraditional areas or stimulated by recent legislation, decisions, or agency rulings; and courses designed to develop lawyering skills.

■ Cost and Financial Aid

As of the date this report was published, the cost per credit is $410. Once admitted, the student pays $125 to reserve a place in the class and $350 for the preparatory course that takes place in July.

There is a deferred-payment plan, and financial aid options that include the Federal Guaranteed Loan Program, Stafford, the Commonwealth Education Fund, the Students Incentive Grant Program, the Institutional College Work-Study Program, Alternative Loans for Regular Academic Program, and for Bar Study (Alternative Bar Loans). The university also has an Honor Scholarship program for law students based on academic accomplishment and financial need.

Applicant Profile Not Available

The University of Iowa College of Law

320 Melrose Avenue
Iowa City, IA 52242
Phone: 800.553.IOWA, ext. 9095; 319.335.9095; Fax: 319.335.9646
E-mail: law-admissions@uiowa.edu; Website: www.law.uiowa.edu

ABA Approved Since 1923

The Basics

Type of school	Public
Term	Semester
Application deadline	3/1
Application fee	$60
Financial aid deadline	1/1
Can first year start other than fall?	Yes
Student to faculty ratio	12.8 to 1
Does the university offer:	
housing restricted to law students?	No
graduate housing for which law students are eligible?	No

Faculty and Administrators

	Total Fall	Total Spr	Men Fall	Men Spr	Women Fall	Women Spr	Minorities Fall	Minorities Spr
Full-time	43	39	29	25	14	14	5	6
Other Full-time	4	4	2	3	2	1	0	0
Deans, librarians, & others who teach	8	6	4	3	4	3	1	0
Part-time	16	19	10	9	6	10	0	0
Total	71	68	45	40	26	28	6	6

Curriculum

	Full-time	Part-time
Typical first-year section size	75	0
Is there typically a "small section" of the first-year class, other than Legal Writing, taught by full-time faculty	Yes	No
If yes, typical size offered last year	25	
# of classroom course titles beyond first-year curriculum	73	
# of upper division courses, excluding seminars with an enrollment: Under 25	50	
25–49	34	
50–74	10	
75–99	10	
100+	0	
# of seminars	27	
# of seminar positions available	337	
# of seminar positions filled	319	0
# of positions available in simulation courses	336	
# of simulation positions filled	322	0
# of positions available in faculty supervised clinical courses	90	
# of faculty supervised clinical positions filled	57	0
# involved in field placements	36	0
# involved in law journals	176	0
# involved in interschool competitions	247	0
# of credit hours required to graduate	90	

JD Enrollment and Ethnicity

	Men #	Men %	Women #	Women %	Full-time #	Full-time %	Part-time #	Part-time %	1st-year #	1st-year %	Total #	Total %	JD Degs. Awd.
African Amer.	9	2.7	19	6.2	28	4.3	0	0.0	8	3.8	28	4.3	15
Amer. Indian	3	0.9	3	1.0	6	0.9	0	0.0	2	1.0	6	0.9	3
Asian Amer.	18	5.3	27	8.9	45	7.0	0	0.0	22	10.5	45	7.0	8
Mex. Amer.	13	3.8	19	6.2	32	5.0	0	0.0	13	6.2	32	5.0	10
Puerto Rican	0	0.0	0	0.0	0	0.0	0	0.0	0	0.0	0	0.0	0
Hispanic	0	0.0	0	0.0	0	0.0	0	0.0	0	0.0	0	0.0	0
Total Minority	43	12.7	68	22.3	111	17.2	0	0.0	45	21.4	111	17.2	36
For. Nation.	5	1.5	3	1.0	8	1.2	0	0.0	4	1.9	8	1.2	0
Caucasian	291	85.8	234	76.7	525	81.5	0	0.0	161	76.7	525	81.5	181
Unknown	0	0.0	0	0.0	0	0.0	0	0.0	0	0.0	0	0.0	1
Total	339	52.6	305	47.4	644	100.0	0	0.0	210	32.6	644		218

Transfers

Transfers in	4
Transfers out	8

Tuition and Fees

	Resident	Nonresident
Full-time	$14,542	$29,986
Part-time	$0	$0

Living Expenses

Estimated living expenses for singles

Living on campus	Living off campus	Living at home
$12,672	$12,672	$7,200

The University of Iowa College of Law

*ABA
Approved
Since
1923*

GPA and LSAT Scores

	Total	Full-time	Part-time
# of apps	1,809	1,809	0
# of offers	602	602	0
# of matrics	210	210	0
75% GPA	3.83	3.83	0.00
Median GPA	3.62	3.62	0.00
25% GPA	3.40	3.40	0.00
75% LSAT	163	163	0
Median LSAT	161	161	0
25% LSAT	158	158	0

Grants and Scholarships (from prior year)

	Total		Full-time		Part-time	
	#	%	#	%	#	%
Total # of students	656		656		0	
Total # receiving grants	259	39.5	259	39.5	0	0.0
Less than 1/2 tuition	90	13.7	90	13.7	0	0.0
Half to full tuition	22	3.4	22	3.4	0	0.0
Full tuition	142	21.6	142	21.6	0	0.0
More than full tuition	5	0.8	5	0.8	0	0.0
Median grant amount			$12,320		$0	

Informational and Library Resources

# of volumes and volume equivalents	1,179,089
# of titles	421,377
# of active serial subscriptions	10,233
Study seating capacity inside the library	679
# of full-time professional librarians	14
Hours per week library is open	106
# of open, wired connections available to students	518
# of networked computers available for use by students	97
# of simultaneous wireless users	1,500
Require computer?	No

JD Attrition (from prior year)

	Academic	Other	Total	
	#	#	#	%
1st year	0	11	11	4.9
2nd year	0	11	11	4.7
3rd year	0	0	0	0.0
4th year	0	0	0	0.0

Employment (9 months after graduation)

	Total	Percentage
Employment status known	260	99.2
Employment status unknown	2	0.8
Employed	233	89.6
Pursuing graduate degrees	10	3.8
Unemployed seeking employment	2	0.8
Unemployed not seeking employment	15	5.8
Unemployed and studying for the bar	0	0.0

Type of Employment

# employed in law firms	134	57.5
# employed in business and industry	33	14.2
# employed in government	21	9.0
# employed in public interest	13	5.6
# employed as judicial clerks	22	9.4
# employed in academia	5	2.1

Geographic Location

# employed in state	71	30.5
# employed in foreign countries	2	0.9
# of states where employed	29	

Bar Passage Rates

Jurisdiction	Iowa			Missouri		
Exam	Sum 05	Win 06	Total	Sum 05	Win 06	Total
# from school taking bar for the first time	73	8	81	11	0	11
School's pass rate for all first-time takers	90%	100%	91%	100%		100%
State's pass rate for all first-time takers	86%	81%	85%	88%	90%	89%

The University of Iowa College of Law

320 Melrose Avenue
Iowa City, IA 52242
Phone: 800.553.IOWA, ext. 9095; 319.335.9095; Fax: 319.335.9646
E-mail: law-admissions@uiowa.edu; Website: www.law.uiowa.edu

■ Introduction

The University of Iowa College of Law, founded in 1865, is the oldest law school in continuous operation west of the Mississippi River. Iowa enjoys a top national reputation, and its faculty is renowned for its outstanding scholarship and teaching.

The college is located in Iowa City, a cosmopolitan college town that is home to a dynamic teaching and research university and over 60,000 people. Students from all 50 states and roughly 100 countries attend the university. Iowa City offers a rich cultural life, Big Ten athletic events, and the world-famous Iowa Writers' Workshop.

The Boyd Law Building's central campus location on a bluff overlooking the Iowa River provides a professional enclave well suited to the college's intensive style of education and easy access to the academic, cultural, social, and recreational resources of a major research university.

■ Admission

Iowa strives to enroll a student body that reflects the academic quality and diversity expected of a leading national law school. The college's numbers-plus policy looks beyond numerical indicators and utilizes a full file review to evaluate an applicant's potential contribution to enhancing classroom discussion. Factors such as maturity, work experience, ability to overcome adversity, and cultural background are considered.

■ Curriculum

The students are the heart of our institution. A broad and wide-ranging curriculum, small classes, accessible professors, and caring administrators are not the only examples of Iowa's student-centered orientation.

Iowa's curriculum establishes a solid foundation for a lifetime of professional growth and personal development. Students take an active role in their professional training. We go the extra measure to ensure that our students have the proper resources and learning environment to maximize their individual development as professionals.

First-year students have at least one class in the fall semester with approximately 30 students and one class in the spring semester with approximately 20 students; courses taught in this small-section format allow extensive class participation and interaction with a faculty member. After completing the set of required first-year courses exploring fundamental legal concepts, students plan their own courses of study from a rich menu of mainstream, specialized, and clinical offerings. Second- and third-year courses cover the range of specialties within the legal profession, allowing students to sample liberally and follow professional interests.

At Iowa, students benefit from the serious commitment the college places on both interdisciplinary study and the study of international and comparative law. Interdisciplinary courses and research programs are actively encouraged; nearly one third of the college's faculty members offer courses or conduct research in the international and comparative law fields.

■ Legal Analysis, Writing, and Research Program

The Legal Analysis, Writing, and Research Program (LAWR) at the College of Law is a two-semester first-year course, two credits each semester, designed to equip students with effective skills in legal analysis, writing, and research.

■ Iowa Law Library

The University of Iowa College of Law Library is consistently recognized as one of the finest and largest law libraries anywhere. The library's international holdings are impressive; it includes a complete collection of United Nations documents since the UN's founding in 1945. The Law Library received significant and high praise in the 2004 *National Jurist* survey of law libraries that are located in the United States.

Additionally, wireless Internet is available throughout the library.

■ Special Programs

The first writing center in the country established specifically for a law school community, Iowa's Writing Resource Center serves as an extension of the classroom and supplements the college's Legal Analysis, Writing, and Research program. Members of the writing center's staff help law students with a broad range of writing, including class assignments, law journal articles, and résumés and cover letters. The center's staff teaches strategies for overcoming writer's block, adapting materials for various audiences, and generally improving the quality of students' writing.

The Academic Achievement Program (AAP) helps students achieve their full academic potential as they move from successful undergraduate careers to face the new challenges of law study. AAP presents a variety of programs, including a first-semester lecture series for new students. Individual study-skills counseling is also available for all students.

■ Legal Clinic

The Clinical Law Program gives students opportunities to gain experience in many different areas of substantive law, including assistive technology, consumer rights, criminal defense, disability rights, domestic violence, general civil, immigration, nonprofit organizations, and workers' rights. Externship opportunities are available with federal trial courts, the Iowa Attorney General, legal services offices, US Attorney's offices, Federal Public Defender's offices, and the Iowa City City Attorney among others. Through the representation of real clients, students are able to develop and hone a diverse complement of lawyering skills from interviewing, counseling, and drafting court papers to trial practice, appellate advocacy, legislative lobbying, and policy development.

■ International Law

Iowa offers one of the nation's strongest programs for the study of international and comparative law. More than 40 percent of the faculty regularly teach or conduct research on international and comparative law subjects. Iowa offers three study-abroad programs. Iowa is the stateside home of the London Law Consortium through which seven US law schools conduct a study-abroad program for a spring semester in London. The Iowa/Bordeaux Summer Program offers one month of intensive coursework in Arcachon, France. Students also have the opportunity to participate in an exchange program with Bucerius Law School in Germany. In addition, students may receive credit for participating in other study-abroad programs offered by ABA-approved law schools.

■ Accelerated/Summer Program

Iowa offers two starting dates for entering students: May and August. These are not separate applicant pools, and the qualifications for admission are the same. Students who elect to enter law school in August may attend summer school at any point during their academic careers.

Students entering in May complete nearly a full semester of work in the first summer term, which consists of 2 five and a-half week sessions. All students, whether they start in May or August, may "accelerate" their course of study toward the JD degree by taking summer and intersession classes. The minimum time of study is no fewer than 27 months after the student has started law study at this law school or at a law school from which transfer credit has been accepted.

■ Student Activities

American Constitution Society; Amnesty International; Asian American Law Students Association; Black Law Students Association; Christian Legal Society; Client Counseling; Environmental Law Society; Equal Justice Foundation; The Federalist Society; Intellectual Property Law Society; International Law Society; Iowa Campaign for Human Rights; *Iowa Law Review*; Iowa Law Student Animal Legal Defense Fund; Iowa Student Bar Association; J. Reuben Clark Law Society; *Journal of Corporation Law*; *Journal of Gender, Race and Justice*; *Journal of Transnational Law and Contemporary Problems*; Latino Law Student Association (formerly known as Alianza); Law Students for Choice; Moot Court; National Lawyers Guild; Native American Law Students Association; Order of the Coif; Organization for Women Law Students and Staff; The Outlaws

(formerly known as the National Lesbian and Gay Law Association); Parents/Partners Weekend; Phi Alpha Delta; *Pro Bono* Society; Stephenson Competition; Supreme Court Day; Trial Advocacy.

■ Expenses and Financial Aid

All admitted students are automatically considered for merit scholarships and fellowships based on their academic achievements. A separate application is not required. The college administers its substantial financial aid program to advance the goals of its selective admission policy. More than 90 percent of our students receive some form of financial aid. Grants, scholarships, work-study funds, and loans are awarded on a need or merit basis for the purpose of providing access to legal education for the talented and diverse students admitted to the college. A number of part-time employment opportunities are also available to second- and third-year students; nonresident students with a quarter-time research assistant position (10 hours per week) are classified as a resident for tuition purposes. Eligibility for financial aid based on need is established by completion of the FAFSA, available at *www.fafsa.ed.gov*.

■ Career Services

Each year the Career Services Office provides students with access to numerous job fairs, posts openings for over 2,500 employers interested in Iowa students, and hosts a substantial number of employers for its on-campus interview program. Over the past five years, more than 1,000 employers have visited the campus to recruit students for positions in private firms, corporations, and government as well as for judicial clerkships. In 2006, Career Services introduced its Early Interview Week, during which 72 employers interviewed our students the week before the start of the fall term. Additionally, over the past five years, between 97 and 100 percent of our students have been employed within nine months of graduation. The Career Services Office strives to work with all students throughout their law school careers to help them seek and find summer employment as well as permanent employment.

Applicant Profile Not Available

The John Marshall Law School

315 South Plymouth Court
Chicago, IL 60604
Phone: 800.537.4280; 312.987.1406; Fax: 312.427.5136
E-mail: admission@jmls.edu; Website: www.jmls.edu

*ABA
Approved
Since
1951*

The Basics

Type of school	Private
Term	Semester
Application deadline	3/1 10/15
Application fee	$60
Financial aid deadline	6/1
Can first year start other than fall?	Yes
Student to faculty ratio	19.8 to 1
Does the university offer:	
housing restricted to law students?	No
graduate housing for which law students are eligible?	No

Faculty and Administrators

	Total		Men		Women		Minorities	
	Fall	Spr	Fall	Spr	Fall	Spr	Fall	Spr
Full-time	56	53	37	36	19	17	6	7
Other Full-time	0	0	0	0	0	0	0	0
Deans, librarians, & others who teach	10	10	6	6	4	4	2	2
Part-time	121	135	87	97	34	38	13	13
Total	**187**	**198**	**130**	**139**	**57**	**59**	**21**	**22**

Curriculum

	Full-time	Part-time
Typical first-year section size	75	50
Is there typically a "small section" of the first-year class, other than Legal Writing, taught by full-time faculty	No	No
If yes, typical size offered last year		
# of classroom course titles beyond first-year curriculum	207	
# of upper division courses, excluding seminars with an enrollment: Under 25	248	
25–49	53	
50–74	33	
75–99	14	
100+	2	
# of seminars	96	
# of seminar positions available	1,920	
# of seminar positions filled	655	453
# of positions available in simulation courses	1,860	
# of simulation positions filled	691	695
# of positions available in faculty supervised clinical courses	90	
# of faculty supervised clinical positions filled	56	12
# involved in field placements	172	22
# involved in law journals	169	13
# involved in interschool competitions	103	8
# of credit hours required to graduate	90	

JD Enrollment and Ethnicity

	Men		Women		Full-time		Part-time		1st-year		Total		JD Degs. Awd.
	#	%	#	%	#	%	#	%	#	%	#	%	
African Amer.	21	2.5	39	6.8	36	3.4	24	7.0	21	4.6	60	4.2	23
Amer. Indian	6	0.7	3	0.5	9	0.8	0	0.0	3	0.7	9	0.6	2
Asian Amer.	55	6.6	41	7.1	74	6.9	22	6.5	37	8.2	96	6.8	26
Mex. Amer.	16	1.9	12	2.1	23	2.1	5	1.5	10	2.2	28	2.0	5
Puerto Rican	4	0.5	1	0.2	3	0.3	2	0.6	2	0.4	5	0.4	0
Hispanic	23	2.7	6	1.0	21	2.0	8	2.3	11	2.4	29	2.1	9
Total Minority	125	14.9	102	17.7	166	15.5	61	17.9	84	18.6	227	16.1	65
For. Nation.	8	1.0	9	1.6	13	1.2	4	1.2	4	0.9	17	1.2	9
Caucasian	664	79.3	442	76.6	841	78.4	265	77.7	340	75.2	1106	78.2	342
Unknown	40	4.8	24	4.2	53	4.9	11	3.2	24	5.3	64	4.5	15
Total	837	59.2	577	40.8	1073	75.9	341	24.1	452	32.0	1414		431

Transfers

Transfers in	13
Transfers out	39

Tuition and Fees

	Resident	Nonresident
Full-time	$29,080	$29,080
Part-time	$20,800	$20,800

Living Expenses

Estimated living expenses for singles

Living on campus	Living off campus	Living at home
$21,902	$21,902	$21,902

ABA
Approved
Since
1951

The J [...]

The John Marshall [...]
315 South Plymouth Court [...]
Chicago, IL 60604
Phone: 800.537.428[...]
E-mail: admissio[...]

■ Introd[...]

John[...]

GPA and LSAT Scores

	Total	Full-time	Part-time
# of apps	3,731	3,105	626
# of offers	1,396	1,198	198
# of matrics	473	363	110
75% GPA	3.42	3.42	3.41
Median GPA	3.12	3.14	3.10
25% GPA	2.80	2.81	2.77
75% LSAT	156	156	156
Median LSAT	154	154	153
25% LSAT	152	153	151

JD Attrition (from prior [...])

	Academi[...]			
	#			
1st year	44			
2nd year	20			
3rd year	1	6	7	1.5
4th year	0	0	0	0.0

Grants and Scholarships (from prior year)

	Total		Full-time		Part-time	
	#	%	#	%	#	%
Total # of students	1,495		1,133		362	
Total # receiving grants	525	35.1	440	38.8	85	23.5
Less than 1/2 tuition	499	33.4	420	37.1	79	21.8
Half to full tuition	9	0.6	8	0.7	1	0.3
Full tuition	3	0.2	2	0.2	1	0.3
More than full tuition	14	0.9	10	0.9	4	1.1
Median grant amount			$6,000		$3,875	

Employment (9 months after graduation)

	Total	Percentage
Employment status known	364	96.6
Employment status unknown	13	3.4
Employed	307	84.3
Pursuing graduate degrees	16	4.4
Unemployed seeking employment	15	4.1
Unemployed not seeking employment	12	3.3
Unemployed and studying for the bar	14	3.8

Type of Employment

# employed in law firms	192	62.5
# employed in business and industry	56	18.2
# employed in government	40	13.0
# employed in public interest	4	1.3
# employed as judicial clerks	6	2.0
# employed in academia	9	2.9

Geographic Location

# employed in state	259	84.4
# employed in foreign countries	0	0.0
# of states where employed		20

Informational and Library Resources

# of volumes and volume equivalents	392,150
# of titles	92,935
# of active serial subscriptions	6,047
Study seating capacity inside the library	681
# of full-time professional librarians	7
Hours per week library is open	100
# of open, wired connections available to students	12
# of networked computers available for use by students	108
# of simultaneous wireless users	2,250
Require computer?	No

Bar Passage Rates

Jurisdiction	Illinois		
Exam	Sum 05	Win 06	Total
# from school taking bar for the first time	242	137	379
School's pass rate for all first-time takers	74%	80%	77%
State's pass rate for all first-time takers	86%	83%	85%

Law School

; 312.987.1406; Fax: 312.427.5136
@jmls.edu; Website: www.jmls.edu

Introduction

Marshall is an independent law school, well-known for consistently training attorneys who are ready to step directly into integral firm, corporate, and public service roles. John Marshall graduates enter the legal profession with confidence, secure in the practical benefits gained from rigorous classes and through clinical and externship experiences.

An innovator in offering legal education to women, minorities, and students who need to work while attending law school, John Marshall remains true to the guiding ideals it has espoused for more than a century. Its legacy of opportunity includes maintaining diversity in its academic programs, student body, and faculty, and providing a harmonious blend of the theory and practice of law.

John Marshall's location in the heart of Chicago's legal, financial, and commercial districts offers students a vibrant, cosmopolitan setting for legal study. The federal courthouse is across the street, and the nation's largest circuit court—Cook County—is just a few blocks away, as are many government offices. This proximity offers enhanced learning experiences to John Marshall students.

The John Marshall Law School is also renowned for its outstanding specialty programs: Nationally recognized in both trial advocacy and intellectual property, John Marshall offers the nation's only graduate program in employee benefits and one of the first-ever programs in information technology and privacy law, and is one of two schools in the nation to offer a concentration in real estate law.

Curriculum

John Marshall has day and evening divisions, with identical instruction, course content, and scholastic requirements. Our nationally recognized legal writing faculty forms the backbone of our Lawyering Skills program. Lawyering Skills courses, which focus on writing, research, and oral argument, are an integral part of the core curriculum. These courses are taught in small groups to maximize the individual attention given to each student. A student may specialize in a certain area of the law and receive a certificate, or focus more emphatically and earn a joint degree (JD/LLM).

Clinics, Externships, and Special Programs

Practical legal experience plays a vital role in education at the John Marshall Law School. John Marshall is the only law school in the nation with a training program in fair housing law and enforcement. Other clinical programs provide valuable training for future attorneys who want to practice in areas such as intellectual property law, immigration law, employee benefits law, tax law, prosecution, defense, and municipal and state government work.

We also offer several programs that enable students to learn important lawyering skills while working as externs with various members of the bench and bar, as well as practicum opportunities in litigation and real estate law.

The John Marshall Law School offers seven Master of Laws (LLM) programs for attorneys seeking specialized education in legal issues, and for current JD students who would like the maximum concentration in particular areas of the law. As the largest advanced-degree law school in the Midwest, John Marshall offers a comprehensive curriculum in the following areas: employee benefits law, information technology and privacy law, intellectual property law, international business and trade law, real estate law, and tax law. John Marshall also offers Master of Science (MS) degrees for nonlawyers in information technology, employee benefits, tax, and real estate.

Library

The Louis L. Biro Law Library collection includes more than 380,000 volumes and 2,500 audiovisual tapes and serves as the library resource for the Chicago Bar Association, whose headquarters building is next door. The John Marshall Law School was the first law school in Chicago to teach legal research on computers. The library has more than 75 IBM-compatible computers available for student use. John Marshall has a school-wide computer network with a backbone of high-speed, digital fiber-optic cabling that allows students, faculty, and staff access to word processing software, LexisNexis, Westlaw, CALI, and the Internet. In addition, a wireless network allows laptop users anywhere in the school to connect to the Internet without being tethered by cords. Computerized research and reference resources are available to students through the law school's website, *www.jmls.edu.*

Admission

Students are admitted in August and January. Applications for August entrance may be filed between October 1 and March 1; for January entrance, between May 1 and October 15. The LSAT score is evaluated together with the cumulative grade-point average and other relevant factors, including difficulty of undergraduate program, postgraduate experience, leadership potential, business and professional background, and letters of recommendation. Applicants from minority and other disadvantaged groups will be given special consideration in cases where their overall records are competitive with other applicants. Minority representation in the class enrolled in 2005 was 25 percent. Applicants with a B average overall and an LSAT score in the 60th percentile may be presumed to be within the range for favorable consideration.

Student Activities

There are five honors programs: the *John Marshall Law Review,* the *Journal of Computer and Information Law,* the *Review of Intellectual Property Law* (an online journal), the Moot Court Honors Program, and the Trial Advocacy and Dispute Resolution Honors Program. John Marshall has a long-standing tradition of success in interscholastic competitions and sends teams to more than 30 moot court and mock trial competitions annually.

The student community at the John Marshall Law School includes more than 40 student organizations engaging in social awareness, community service, legal discussions, and social activities. Every student group at John Marshall reflects the diversity, highlights the talents, and enhances the opportunities of our total student body.

John Marshall welcomes numerous well-known visitors and scholars each year. In addition to lectures and presentations, our distinguished guests can be found meeting with individual classes or holding roundtable discussions with interested students and faculty.

■ Career Opportunities

The Career Services Office (CSO) offers personal assistance to help students assess and refine their career goals. The CSO sponsors more than 60 career-related programs each year, many featuring alumni as panelists and speakers, including a robust Alumni Mentor Program, where mentors meet with students one-on-one to provide real-world advice on practice areas, law school courses, and the day-to-day practice of law. The CSO also aggressively promotes John Marshall students to employers. John Marshall graduates are employed at 34 of Chicago's 35 largest firms. Public service is another favored career path, with graduates serving as attorneys in the courts and government. Nearly one-fifth of all Illinois judges (circuit, appellate, and state supreme court) are John Marshall alumni.

■ Correspondence

We encourage you to visit our website, *www.jmls.edu*, and to come see us in person. Visit a class and talk with our faculty and our students. Find out for yourself what it's like to learn, in an intimate classroom environment, from a top-notch faculty that consistently imparts an understanding of both the theory and the practice of law.

Visit with our personable admission and financial aid staff. Then, if you feel drawn to become a member of the John Marshall community—if the excellence and diversity we represent resonate with your desires for your own legal education—we would be pleased to receive your application.

Applicant Profile

The John Marshall Law School
This grid includes only applicants who earned 120–180 LSAT scores under standard administrations.

LSAT Score	GPA						
	3.75 +	3.50–3.74	3.25–3.49	3.00–3.24	2.75–2.99	2.50–2.74	Below 2.50
175–180							
170–174							
165–169							
160–164							
155–159							
150–154							
145–149							
140–144							
135–139							
130–134							
125–129							
120–124							

Likely   Possible   Unlikely

John Marshall Law School—Atlanta

1422 W. Peachtree Street NW
Atlanta, GA 30309
Phone: 404.872.3593; Fax: 404.873.3802
E-mail: admissions@johnmarshall.edu; Website: www.johnmarshall.edu

Provisional

ABA Approved Since 2006

The Basics

Type of school	Private
Term	Semester
Application deadline	
Application fee	$50
Financial aid deadline	
Can first year start other than fall?	No
Student to faculty ratio	12.4 to 1
Does the university offer:	
housing restricted to law students?	No
graduate housing for which law students are eligible?	No

Faculty and Administrators

	Total Fall	Total Spr	Men Fall	Men Spr	Women Fall	Women Spr	Minorities Fall	Minorities Spr
Full-time	18	17	4	5	14	12	4	4
Other Full-time	0	0	0	0	0	0	0	0
Deans, librarians, & others who teach	4	4	2	2	2	2	0	0
Part-time	12	10	7	6	5	4	1	3
Total	34	31	13	13	21	18	5	7

Curriculum

	Full-time	Part-time
Typical first-year section size	55	52
Is there typically a "small section" of the first-year class, other than Legal Writing, taught by full-time faculty	No	No
If yes, typical size offered last year		
# of classroom course titles beyond first-year curriculum	43	

# of upper division courses, excluding seminars with an enrollment:		
Under 25	51	
25–49	7	
50–74	2	
75–99	2	
100+	0	

	Full-time	Part-time
# of seminars	3	
# of seminar positions available	48	
# of seminar positions filled	23	4
# of positions available in simulation courses	180	
# of simulation positions filled	57	35
# of positions available in faculty supervised clinical courses	0	
# of faculty supervised clinical positions filled	0	0
# involved in field placements	9	0
# involved in law journals	0	0
# involved in interschool competitions	12	4
# of credit hours required to graduate	88	

JD Enrollment and Ethnicity

	Men #	Men %	Women #	Women %	Full-time #	Full-time %	Part-time #	Part-time %	1st-year #	1st-year %	Total #	Total %	JD Degs. Awd.
African Amer.	14	7.4	38	22.4	21	9.8	31	21.5	28	17.2	52	14.5	9
Amer. Indian	1	0.5	1	0.6	2	0.9	0	0.0	1	0.6	2	0.6	0
Asian Amer.	5	2.7	6	3.5	9	4.2	2	1.4	6	3.7	11	3.1	1
Mex. Amer.	0	0.0	0	0.0	0	0.0	0	0.0	0	0.0	0	0.0	0
Puerto Rican	0	0.0	0	0.0	0	0.0	0	0.0	0	0.0	0	0.0	0
Hispanic	10	5.3	9	5.3	10	4.7	9	6.3	13	8.0	19	5.3	0
Total Minority	30	16.0	54	31.8	42	19.6	42	29.2	48	29.4	84	23.5	10
For. Nation.	2	1.1	0	0.0	1	0.5	1	0.7	0	0.0	2	0.6	0
Caucasian	150	79.8	110	64.7	164	76.6	96	66.7	108	66.3	260	72.6	28
Unknown	6	3.2	6	3.5	7	3.3	5	3.5	7	4.3	12	3.4	0
Total	188	52.5	170	47.5	214	59.8	144	40.2	163	45.5	358		38

Transfers

Transfers in	5
Transfers out	3

Tuition and Fees

	Resident	Nonresident
Full-time	$26,580	$26,580
Part-time	$21,294	$21,294

Living Expenses

Estimated living expenses for singles

Living on campus	Living off campus	Living at home
N/A	$15,920	$15,920

John Marshall Law School—Atlanta

*ABA
Approved
Since
2006*

GPA and LSAT Scores

	Total	Full-time	Part-time
# of apps	1,244	907	337
# of offers	473	356	117
# of matrics	158	89	69
75% GPA	3.30	3.24	3.33
Median GPA	3.02	3.01	3.02
25% GPA	2.64	2.70	2.53
75% LSAT	153	153	153
Median LSAT	151	150	151
25% LSAT	149	149	149

Grants and Scholarships (from prior year)

	Total #	Total %	Full-time #	Full-time %	Part-time #	Part-time %
Total # of students	267		143		124	
Total # receiving grants	0	0.0	0	0.0	0	0.0
Less than 1/2 tuition	0	0.0	0	0.0	0	0.0
Half to full tuition	0	0.0	0	0.0	0	0.0
Full tuition	0	0.0	0	0.0	0	0.0
More than full tuition	0	0.0	0	0.0	0	0.0
Median grant amount			$0		$0	

Informational and Library Resources

# of volumes and volume equivalents	232,482
# of titles	121,262
# of active serial subscriptions	2,671
Study seating capacity inside the library	220
# of full-time professional librarians	5
Hours per week library is open	86
# of open, wired connections available to students	117
# of networked computers available for use by students	33
# of simultaneous wireless users	1,500
Require computer?	No

JD Attrition (from prior year)

	Academic #	Other #	Total #	Total %
1st year	5	20	25	16.3
2nd year	2	2	4	7.1
3rd year	0	0	0	0.0
4th year	0	0	0	0.0

Employment (9 months after graduation)

	Total	Percentage
Employment status known	46	93.9
Employment status unknown	3	6.1
Employed	43	93.5
Pursuing graduate degrees	1	2.2
Unemployed seeking employment	1	2.2
Unemployed not seeking employment	1	2.2
Unemployed and studying for the bar	0	0.0

Type of Employment

# employed in law firms	21	48.8
# employed in business and industry	10	23.3
# employed in government	8	18.6
# employed in public interest	2	4.7
# employed as judicial clerks	2	4.7
# employed in academia	0	0.0

Geographic Location

# employed in state	42	97.7
# employed in foreign countries	0	0.0
# of states where employed	2	

Bar Passage Rates

Jurisdiction	Georgia		
Exam	Sum 05	Win 06	Total
# from school taking bar for the first time	37	5	42
School's pass rate for all first-time takers	51%	60%	52%
State's pass rate for all first-time takers	86%	79%	84%

John Marshall Law School—Atlanta

1422 W. Peachtree Street NW
Atlanta, GA 30309
Phone: 404.872.3593; Fax: 404.873.3802
E-mail: admissions@johnmarshall.edu; Website: www.johnmarshall.edu

The Dean's Introduction

Atlanta's John Marshall Law School has been educating lawyers and leaders in Georgia since 1933 and now attracts students from around the country. We provide a rigorous, high-quality program of legal education that produces competent and ethical lawyers who are dedicated to helping people, especially in underserved communities. We intentionally instill in our students a sense of obligation to the community and to the legal profession—an obligation to pursue justice, rather than mere personal gain, and to improve society, rather than to solely advance personal ambition. Whether our graduates remain in law practice, become judges, enter politics, or succeed in business, these rich values stay with them.

The Mission

The mission of the Law School is to prepare highly competent and professional lawyers who possess a strong social conscience, continually demonstrate high ethical standards, and are committed to the improvement of the legal system and society. The school is dedicated to providing a quality educational opportunity to nontraditional or adult learners and to other significantly underserved segments of the community. We emphasize the highest standards of ethical and professional conduct. As Supreme Court Justice Thurgood Marshall once said, "There's only one kind of reputation a young lawyer gets in a hurry." Graduates of this law school are trained to do the right thing.

Atlanta Living

The Law School campus is centrally located in midtown Atlanta, the social, cultural, and economic hub of the South. It is in close proximity to Atlanta's largest law firms, as well as government offices, state and federal courts, and nonprofit legal organizations. Atlanta also boasts an extensive array of arts, music, sports, and recreational events, making it an exciting place to live.

Facilities, Library, and Modern Technology

The Law School is housed in a modern, nine-story building located on one of the major streets in Atlanta. The facilities of the school continue to undergo major renovations, adding new classrooms and new trial and appellate courtrooms.

The Law School has made the inclusion of new technologies throughout the school a priority. All students and faculty enjoy direct and unlimited access to wireless Internet, massive online legal databases, as well as new state-of-the-art technology in multiple classrooms that allows for interactive learning experiences. Students can take both midterm and final exams on their laptops and download them to the school's network.

Our library spreads over three floors, contains over 200,000 total volumes and equivalents, and provides students and faculty with access to all legal materials necessary to learn the skill of legal research.

Dedicated Faculty

The John Marshall faculty makes the difference in the student experience and is committed to students' success throughout their legal education and beyond. The faculty is dedicated to providing an intellectually rigorous academic program while instilling the highest sense of professional, ethical, and moral responsibilities that are required of members of the legal profession. All of our faculty members have extensive practical experience in their respective fields of expertise, bringing real-world experience into the classroom. Our student-faculty ratio is the lowest in Georgia and one of the best among American law schools. All first-year and required courses are taught in small classes, and professors are easily accessible to their students outside of class. Our small class sizes and low faculty-to-student ratio create a supportive environment where students can enjoy learning and express their views.

Commitment to Diversity

Because John Marshall's educational environment focuses on an interactive learning process, a diverse student body is essential to providing a broad range of perspectives in the classroom and the Law School community. The fall 2006 entering class of 158 students was made up of 50 percent women and 29 percent minorities. The student body is not only ethnically diverse, but it is varied in life experience and professional backgrounds. In the 2006 entering class, the median age of full-time students was 25, and the median age of part-time students was 31.

The Legal Program

John Marshall's rigorous program of study is designed toward the development of intellectual, analytical, and lawyering skills. From the first-year curriculum, with its predetermined set of core courses, through the third year, with courses that emphasize practical skill development, the degree program is designed to promote analytical reasoning, precision in both oral and written communication, and problem-solving skills. A broad variety of elective courses allow upper-class students to pursue their areas of interest.

Full-time and Part-time Law Study. John Marshall remains dedicated to providing access to legal education to both traditional and nontraditional students by offering both full-time and part-time law programs. Individuals who are unable to devote full time to the study of law may attend either the part-time evening or part-time day program.

The **Legal Skills and Professionalism Program** takes a holistic approach to preparing students for success during and after law school. Beginning with writing, the program teaches legal skills and professionalism. The same tools that students use to draft documents in their writing classes are employed to solve legal problems in Negotiations, Mediation, Trial Advocacy, Client Interviewing and Counseling, and other skills courses. In addition, a professionalism component is built into every course in the program, preparing students to confront and resolve real-world professionalism issues as they learn to solve legal problems and meet client goals. The Law School faculty come with diverse law practice backgrounds, including medical malpractice litigation, commercial litigation, administrative law, domestic relations practice, and corporate/transactional work.

Academic Support. Tools for academic growth and professional success are not only fostered through interactive classroom teaching, but also individually and in small groups. The director of academic support meets individually with students and also plans lectures and special programs to assist in the development of students' legal writing, studying, and exam skills. Each student is paired with a faculty advisor, who serves as a mentor through the student's entire law school career. A student mentor program is also in place to match incoming first-year students with upper-class students to provide further support and advice.

Pro Bono and Externship Programs. The director of pro bono and externships encourages students to be involved in pro bono work, both legal and nonlegal. The director also supervises students in externships throughout Atlanta, including externships for academic credit. Externship placements include the ACLU, Atlanta City Council, Atlanta Legal Aid Society, district attorneys and public defenders offices throughout the city, the Landlord/Tenant Mediation Project, the Georgia Innocence Project, the Georgia Court of Appeals, and the Southern Center for Human Rights, among others.

■ Career Development

The Office of Career Development offers individualized, professional advice to students about their personal career goals and tailors strategies to assist students in reaching those goals. In addition to providing résumé and interview workshops to facilitate job searches, John Marshall also participates in the Georgia Law School Consortium to plan job fairs and other state-wide recruiting efforts, such as judicial clerkships; placement with prosecutors, public interest agencies, and public defenders; and minority recruiting. As a member of the National Association of Law Placement, John Marshall allows its students the opportunity to attend regional hiring consortia that attract private and government recruiters throughout the Southeast.

■ Accreditation

John Marshall Law School was provisionally approved by the American Bar Association on February 14, 2005. With provisional approval, John Marshall Law School students and graduates are entitled to the same recognition given to students of fully approved law schools. The ABA accreditation process is designed to assure quality legal education among approved schools. John Marshall Law School has carefully planned to not only meet, but exceed, the standards for full approval.

■ Admission

The Admissions Committee is committed to finding a well-rounded and diverse group of students. In addition to the candidate's academic record and standardized test results, the Admissions Committee will examine with particular care those factors that indicate a high probability for success in law study. Such factors include life experiences, personal or family hardships overcome, demonstrated personal and professional achievements, ability to overcome life's obstacles, the capacity for rigorous intellectual study, the self-discipline demanded by the profession, and a commitment to be of service to the profession and society as a whole.

■ Law School Visits

The Office of Admissions makes numerous college visits and holds open houses throughout the year to provide prospective students with information and guidance about the law school admission process. Please visit our website for additional information regarding the dates and times of events. We also invite you to contact us for a personalized tour, to sit in on a class, or to meet personally with an admission professional.

Applicant Profile

John Marshall Law School—Atlanta
This grid includes only applicants who earned 120–180 LSAT scores under standard administrations.

LSAT Score	GPA								
	3.75 +	3.50–3.74	3.25–3.49	3.00–3.24	2.75–2.99	2.50–2.74	2.25–2.49	2.00–2.24	Below 2.00
155–180									
150–154									
145–149									
120–144									

Likely | Possible | Unlikely

The University of Kansas School of Law

1535 West 15th Street
Lawrence, KS 66045-7577
Phone: 866.220.3654 (toll free), 785.864.4378; Fax: 785.864.5054
E-mail: admitlaw@ku.edu; Website: www.law.ku.edu

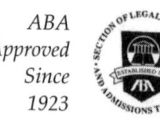

The Basics

Type of school	Public
Term	Semester
Application deadline	3/15
Application fee	$50
Financial aid deadline	3/1
Can first year start other than fall?	Yes
Student to faculty ratio	11.9 to 1
Does the university offer:	
housing restricted to law students?	No
graduate housing for which law students are eligible?	Yes

Faculty and Administrators

	Total		Men		Women		Minorities	
	Fall	Spr	Fall	Spr	Fall	Spr	Fall	Spr
Full-time	34	32	22	21	12	11	6	5
Other Full-time	3	3	0	0	3	3	0	0
Deans, librarians, & others who teach	6	6	3	4	3	2	1	1
Part-time	17	19	12	13	5	6	0	0
Total	**60**	**60**	**37**	**38**	**23**	**22**	**7**	**6**

Curriculum

	Full-time	Part-time
Typical first-year section size	52	0
Is there typically a "small section" of the first-year class, other than Legal Writing, taught by full-time faculty	Yes	No
If yes, typical size offered last year	18	
# of classroom course titles beyond first-year curriculum	92	
# of upper division courses, excluding seminars with an enrollment: Under 25	88	
25–49	30	
50–74	7	
75–99	3	
100+	3	
# of seminars	9	
# of seminar positions available	236	
# of seminar positions filled	159	0
# of positions available in simulation courses	334	
# of simulation positions filled	254	0
# of positions available in faculty supervised clinical courses	216	
# of faculty supervised clinical positions filled	172	0
# involved in field placements	109	0
# involved in law journals	79	0
# involved in interschool competitions	53	0
# of credit hours required to graduate	90	

JD Enrollment and Ethnicity

	Men #	Men %	Women #	Women %	Full-time #	Full-time %	Part-time #	Part-time %	1st-year #	1st-year %	Total #	Total %	JD Degs. Awd.
African Amer.	6	2.1	3	1.6	9	1.9	0	0.0	2	1.3	9	1.9	7
Amer. Indian	8	2.7	5	2.6	13	2.7	0	0.0	6	3.8	13	2.7	7
Asian Amer.	12	4.1	15	7.9	27	5.6	0	0.0	8	5.1	27	5.6	9
Mex. Amer.	0	0.0	0	0.0	0	0.0	0	0.0	0	0.0	0	0.0	0
Puerto Rican	0	0.0	0	0.0	0	0.0	0	0.0	0	0.0	0	0.0	0
Hispanic	13	4.5	11	5.8	24	5.0	0	0.0	7	4.5	24	5.0	13
Total Minority	39	13.4	34	17.9	73	15.1	0	0.0	23	14.6	73	15.1	36
For. Nation.	9	3.1	9	4.7	18	3.7	0	0.0	5	3.2	18	3.7	4
Caucasian	233	79.8	144	75.8	377	78.2	0	0.0	128	81.5	377	78.2	119
Unknown	11	3.8	3	1.6	14	2.9	0	0.0	1	0.6	14	2.9	14
Total	292	60.6	190	39.4	482	100.0	0	0.0	157	32.6	482		173

Transfers

Transfers in	12
Transfers out	3

Tuition and Fees

	Resident	Nonresident
Full-time	$10,399	$19,232
Part-time	$0	$0

Living Expenses

Estimated living expenses for singles

Living on campus	Living off campus	Living at home
$13,642	$13,642	$13,642

The University of Kansas School of Law

ABA
Approved
Since
1923

GPA and LSAT Scores

	Total	Full-time	Part-time
# of apps	1,082	1,082	0
# of offers	347	347	0
# of matrics	160	160	0
75% GPA	3.77	3.77	0.00
Median GPA	3.48	3.48	0.00
25% GPA	3.23	3.23	0.00
75% LSAT	161	161	0
Median LSAT	158	158	0
25% LSAT	155	155	0

Grants and Scholarships (from prior year)

	Total		Full-time		Part-time	
	#	%	#	%	#	%
Total # of students	497		497		0	
Total # receiving grants	367	73.8	367	73.8	0	0.0
Less than 1/2 tuition	299	60.2	299	60.2	0	0.0
Half to full tuition	51	10.3	51	10.3	0	0.0
Full tuition	0	0.0	0	0.0	0	0.0
More than full tuition	17	3.4	17	3.4	0	0.0
Median grant amount			$3,513		$0	

Informational and Library Resources

# of volumes and volume equivalents	426,250
# of titles	138,228
# of active serial subscriptions	6,120
Study seating capacity inside the library	381
# of full-time professional librarians	7
Hours per week library is open	102
# of open, wired connections available to students	0
# of networked computers available for use by students	56
# of simultaneous wireless users	245
Require computer?	No

JD Attrition (from prior year)

	Academic	Other	Total	
	#	#	#	%
1st year	0	7	7	4.5
2nd year	0	2	2	1.2
3rd year	0	0	0	0.0
4th year	0	0	0	0.0

Employment (9 months after graduation)

	Total	Percentage
Employment status known	179	97.8
Employment status unknown	4	2.2
Employed	169	94.4
Pursuing graduate degrees	2	1.1
Unemployed seeking employment	6	3.4
Unemployed not seeking employment	2	1.1
Unemployed and studying for the bar	0	0.0

Type of Employment

# employed in law firms	83	49.1
# employed in business and industry	25	14.8
# employed in government	26	15.4
# employed in public interest	14	8.3
# employed as judicial clerks	14	8.3
# employed in academia	6	3.6

Geographic Location

# employed in state	84	49.7
# employed in foreign countries	2	1.2
# of states where employed		20

Bar Passage Rates

Jurisdiction	Kansas			Missouri		
Exam	Sum 05	Win 06	Total	Sum 05	Win 06	Total
# from school taking bar for the first time	90	37	127	36	29	65
School's pass rate for all first-time takers	80%	92%	83%	94%	97%	95%
State's pass rate for all first-time takers	78%	90%	82%	88%	90%	89%

The University of Kansas School of Law

1535 West 15th Street
Lawrence, KS 66045-7577
Phone: 866.220.3654 (toll free), 785.864.4378; Fax: 785.864.5054
E-mail: admitlaw@ku.edu; Website: www.law.ku.edu

■ Introduction

The University of Kansas School of Law is an excellent place to begin a legal career. It has a venerable history and a commitment to educating for the future. Legal education at KU began in 1878, and the school was a charter member of the Association of American Law Schools. It has had a chapter of Order of the Coif, a national law school honor society with chapters at leading law schools throughout the country, since 1924. The law school is fully accredited by the American Bar Association.

The law school is on KU's main campus—one of the most beautiful in the country. It occupies Green Hall, named in honor of James Woods Green, first dean of the school. Green Hall is a modern, five-story building with extensive clinical facilities, spacious and attractive classrooms, seminar rooms, a formal courtroom, and common areas. The school is equipped with a state-of-the-art wireless network, allowing students to access the Internet and e-mail from anywhere in the law school.

The school's primary mission is to prepare its students to be outstanding members of the legal profession, well educated in the law, with a commitment to professional achievement and public service. The school educates students in both general principles of law and the skills needed for practice in a changing legal environment. Students develop technical competence, pride in legal craftsmanship, a sound sense of ethics and professionalism, and an appreciation for the role of law, and the practice of law in society.

■ Faculty

Law faculty care about teaching. They are committed to excellence in the classroom and to serving as mentors for law students. This is the KU law tradition. Students are encouraged to consult regularly with their teachers about their progress in the study of law as well as about career plans, job opportunities, and the professional responsibilities of lawyers. Law faculty offices are scattered throughout Green Hall, and doors are open to students.

Faculty members enrich their teaching by researching and writing about the areas of law they teach. They regularly participate in symposia, publish widely in legal journals, and enjoy national and international recognition for the quality of their work. Many have written important treatises and casebooks used at law schools around the country.

■ Learning the Law

Entering students take basic courses that provide a solid foundation for upper-level classes and for the practice of law. The lawyering course focuses on the skills and values of the profession. Taught by faculty members with extensive practice experience, the course introduces students to the tools all lawyers use and brings them to an understanding of the legal system and legal institutions, case law and statutes, legal research and writing, and advocacy. First-year students take one of their other required courses in a small section of approximately 20 students, providing an informal learning atmosphere and encouraging in-depth discussions and critical analysis.

More than 100 courses are available to upper-level students, covering a broad range of practice areas from agricultural law to the law of cyberspace. Ten clinical programs permit students, acting under faculty supervision, to develop legal skills and learn professional values in actual practice settings: Criminal Justice Clinic, Paul E. Wilson Defender Project, Elder Law Clinic, Judicial Clerkship Clinic, Legal Aid Clinic, Legislative Clinic, Media Law Clinic, Public Policy Clinic, Tribal Judicial Support Clinic, and the Externship Clinic. The large number of clinical placements available means that every student can take at least one clinic and many take more than one.

The school's setting at the heart of a major university makes possible the eight joint-degree programs open to law students. The most popular joint-degree programs are business, health policy and administration, and social welfare, but joint degrees are also available in economics, philosophy, public administration, urban planning, and indigenous nations studies. In addition, the school offers six certification programs: Elder Law; Media, Law and Policy; Tax Law; Environmental and Natural Resources Law; Tribal Lawyering; and International Trade and Finance.

■ Library

The Wheat Law Library collection, with over 400,000 volumes, is the largest law library in Kansas. Its hallmark is excellent service for students and faculty. The law library is a wireless environment that allows students, faculty, and staff access to LexisNexis, Westlaw, CALI, HeinOnline, LLMC-Digital, the Internet, and numerous university-wide interdisciplinary databases. Access is also available on desktop computers in carrels and throughout the library. The law library's award-winning website, *www.ku.edu/~kulaw/library/*, is a comprehensive gateway that provides access to virtual resources beyond the scope of the physical collection as well as in-house topical research guides. Seven professional librarians and research attorneys are eager to help with legal research ranging from the rich heritage of historical materials to cutting-edge digitized images.

■ Accelerated/Summer Program

The law school's unique summer school program is fully integrated with the curriculum of the fall and spring semesters. Students who begin law school in May and attend summer school each of the following two summers may complete degree requirements in just 27 months.

■ Student Life

Because the school seeks students with strong personal qualities in addition to high academic credentials, students learn law with classmates who have the interpersonal skills, maturity, judgment, and ambition to succeed. The law school values diversity, and students have a wide range of education and work experience, enriching classroom discussions and student life.

KU law students develop friendships that last a lifetime. They find as many opportunities for collaboration as for competition. They socialize and develop leadership skills and an appreciation for community service through membership in the many student organizations. They hone research, writing, and editing skills through work on two student-edited publications: the *Kansas Law Review* and the *Kansas Journal of Law and Public Policy*. They participate regularly and successfully in moot court, mock trial, and client counseling competitions. Study abroad is available through the London Consortium, the school's Limerick and Istanbul Programs, and other programs approved by the American Bar Association.

■ Career Services and Alumni

The school's Office of Career Services helps students define career goals and find employment that matches their interests. The office coordinates an extensive on-campus interviewing program, sponsors workshops exploring career options, and helps students develop job-seeking skills.

KU law students and graduates are highly sought after by employers throughout the state, region, and nation. Most recent graduates chose employment in private law firms, but many chose government service, including work as prosecutors, public interest work, the military, graduate study, and nontraditional careers. A considerable number of graduates accept judicial clerkships. Recent graduates have been law clerks at all levels, including the Supreme Court of the United States.

KU graduates have been highly successful in passing Kansas and Missouri bar examinations and have performed extremely well on examinations in other states. The Office of Career Services provides up-to-date information on bar requirements for all states.

The school's 6,000+ alumni live in all 50 states, the District of Columbia, Guam, and 12 foreign countries. Many participate in the law school's mentor program for first-year law students or in the Career Services Alumni Network, serving as sources of information about practice specialties and practice opportunities.

Applicant Profile

The University of Kansas School of Law
This grid includes applicants who earned 120–180 LSAT scores under standard administrations.

LSAT Score	3.75 +		3.50–3.74		3.25–3.49		3.00–3.24		2.75–2.99		2.50–2.74		2.25–2.49		2.00–2.24		Below 2.00		No GPA		Total	
	Apps	Adm	Apps	Adm	Apps	Adm	Apps	Adm	Apps	Adm	Apps	Adm	Apps	Adm	Apps	Adm	Apps	Adm	Apps	Adm	Apps	Adm
175–180	0	0	0	0	0	0	0	0	0	0	0	0	0	0	0	0	0	0	0	0	0	0
170–174	3	3	2	2	2	1	0	0	1	1	0	0	0	0	0	0	0	0	0	0	8	7
165–169	9	9	10	9	5	4	3	3	4	1	1	1	1	1	0	0	0	0	0	0	33	28
160–164	28	26	31	31	23	22	10	8	10	7	9	2	2	0	1	0	0	0	1	0	115	96
155–159	64	53	60	37	64	40	35	26	30	7	5	0	4	1	1	0	1	0	3	0	267	164
150–154	58	9	75	10	83	13	63	5	26	3	28	1	5	0	2	0	0	0	1	1	341	42
145–149	26	3	32	0	44	2	39	0	24	2	15	0	5	0	2	0	0	0	3	1	190	8
140–144	13	1	12	0	21	0	20	0	12	0	11	0	6	0	0	0	0	0	6	0	101	1
135–139	4	0	3	0	6	0	4	0	13	0	5	0	5	0	1	0	0	0	1	0	42	0
130–134	0	0	1	0	3	0	0	0	3	0	0	0	1	0	0	0	1	0	0	0	9	0
125–129	0	0	1	0	0	0	0	0	0	0	0	0	0	0	1	0	1	0	0	0	3	0
120–124	0	0	1	0	0	0	0	0	0	0	0	0	0	0	0	0	0	0	0	0	1	0
Total	205	104	228	89	251	82	174	42	123	21	74	4	29	2	8	0	2	0	16	2	1110	346

Apps = Number of Applicants
Adm = Number Admitted
Reflects 100% of the total applicant pool.

University of Kentucky College of Law

209 Law Building, South Limestone Street
Lexington, KY 40506-0048
Phone: 859.257.1678; Fax: 859.323.1061
E-mail: lawadmissions@email.uky.edu; Website: www.uky.edu/Law

The Basics

Type of school	Public
Term	Semester
Application deadline	3/1
Application fee	$50
Financial aid deadline	4/1
Can first year start other than fall?	No
Student to faculty ratio	16.3 to 1
Does the university offer:	
housing restricted to law students?	No
graduate housing for which law students are eligible?	No

Faculty and Administrators

	Total		Men		Women		Minorities	
	Fall	Spr	Fall	Spr	Fall	Spr	Fall	Spr
Full-time	23	21	14	13	9	8	3	3
Other Full-time	0	0	0	0	0	0	0	0
Deans, librarians, & others who teach	6	6	4	4	2	2	1	1
Part-time	15	20	13	15	2	3	0	0
Total	44	47	31	32	13	13	4	4

Curriculum

		Full-time	Part-time
Typical first-year section size		76	0
Is there typically a "small section" of the first-year class, other than Legal Writing, taught by full-time faculty		Yes	No
If yes, typical size offered last year		36	
# of classroom course titles beyond first-year curriculum		53	
# of upper division courses, excluding seminars with an enrollment:	Under 25	14	
	25–49	21	
	50–74	6	
	75–99	3	
	100+	5	
# of seminars		12	
# of seminar positions available		188	
# of seminar positions filled	135		0
# of positions available in simulation courses		150	
# of simulation positions filled	97		0
# of positions available in faculty supervised clinical courses		27	
# of faculty supervised clinical positions filled	27		0
# involved in field placements	44		0
# involved in law journals	53		0
# involved in interschool competitions	50		0
# of credit hours required to graduate		90	

JD Enrollment and Ethnicity

	Men		Women		Full-time		Part-time		1st-year		Total		JD Degs. Awd.
	#	%	#	%	#	%	#	%	#	%	#	%	
African Amer.	6	2.5	17	9.2	23	5.4	0	0.0	12	8.8	23	5.4	5
Amer. Indian	0	0.0	0	0.0	0	0.0	0	0.0	0	0.0	0	0.0	0
Asian Amer.	4	1.7	2	1.1	6	1.4	0	0.0	1	0.7	6	1.4	0
Mex. Amer.	0	0.0	0	0.0	0	0.0	0	0.0	0	0.0	0	0.0	0
Puerto Rican	0	0.0	0	0.0	0	0.0	0	0.0	0	0.0	0	0.0	0
Hispanic	2	0.8	2	1.1	4	0.9	0	0.0	1	0.7	4	0.9	0
Total Minority	12	5.0	21	11.4	33	7.8	0	0.0	14	10.3	33	7.8	5
For. Nation.	0	0.0	0	0.0	0	0.0	0	0.0	0	0.0	0	0.0	0
Caucasian	228	95.0	164	88.6	392	92.2	0	0.0	122	89.7	392	92.2	136
Unknown	0	0.0	0	0.0	0	0.0	0	0.0	0	0.0	0	0.0	0
Total	240	56.5	185	43.5	425	100.0	0	0.0	136	32.0	425		141

Transfers

Transfers in	0
Transfers out	5

Tuition and Fees

	Resident	Nonresident
Full-time	$12,842	$23,272
Part-time	$0	$0

Living Expenses

Estimated living expenses for singles

Living on campus	Living off campus	Living at home
$14,326	$14,326	$5,826

University of Kentucky College of Law

ABA
Approved
Since
1925

GPA and LSAT Scores

	Total	Full-time	Part-time
# of apps	1,255	1,255	0
# of offers	384	384	0
# of matrics	138	138	0
75% GPA	3.85	3.85	0.00
Median GPA	3.64	3.64	0.00
25% GPA	3.37	3.37	0.00
75% LSAT	162	162	0
Median LSAT	159	159	0
25% LSAT	155	155	0

Grants and Scholarships (from prior year)

	Total		Full-time		Part-time	
	#	%	#	%	#	%
Total # of students	453		453		0	
Total # receiving grants	222	49.0	222	49.0	0	0.0
Less than 1/2 tuition	133	29.4	133	29.4	0	0.0
Half to full tuition	68	15.0	68	15.0	0	0.0
Full tuition	8	1.8	8	1.8	0	0.0
More than full tuition	13	2.9	13	2.9	0	0.0
Median grant amount			$5,000		$0	

Informational and Library Resources

# of volumes and volume equivalents	471,169
# of titles	74,068
# of active serial subscriptions	3,908
Study seating capacity inside the library	354
# of full-time professional librarians	4
Hours per week library is open	100
# of open, wired connections available to students	76
# of networked computers available for use by students	27
# of simultaneous wireless users	250
Require computer?	No

JD Attrition (from prior year)

	Academic	Other	Total	
	#	#	#	%
1st year	3	12	15	8.7
2nd year	2	0	2	1.4
3rd year	1	0	1	0.7
4th year	0	0	0	0.0

Employment (9 months after graduation)

	Total	Percentage
Employment status known	136	100.0
Employment status unknown	0	0.0
Employed	127	93.4
Pursuing graduate degrees	3	2.2
Unemployed seeking employment	1	0.7
Unemployed not seeking employment	3	2.2
Unemployed and studying for the bar	2	1.5
Type of Employment		
# employed in law firms	75	59.1
# employed in business and industry	10	7.9
# employed in government	8	6.3
# employed in public interest	7	5.5
# employed as judicial clerks	24	18.9
# employed in academia	3	2.4
Geographic Location		
# employed in state	89	70.1
# employed in foreign countries	1	0.8
# of states where employed	19	

Bar Passage Rates

Jurisdiction	Kentucky		
Exam	Sum 05	Win 06	Total
# from school taking bar for the first time	91	13	104
School's pass rate for all first-time takers	88%	92%	88%
State's pass rate for all first-time takers	81%	67%	77%

University of Kentucky College of Law

209 Law Building, South Limestone Street
Lexington, KY 40506-0048
Phone: 859.257.1678; Fax: 859.323.1061
E-mail: lawadmissions@email.uky.edu; Website: www.uky.edu/Law

■ Introduction

The University of Kentucky College of Law is a small, state-supported law school on the main campus of the university in scenic Lexington, Kentucky, a city of approximately 250,000 in the center of the Bluegrass horse farm region. Founded in 1908, the college has been a member of the AALS since 1912 and has been accredited by the ABA since 1925. The faculty has wide experience in law practice and government service, as well as teaching and research. UK Law has a strong tradition of faculty concern about their students' progress and success. The curriculum offers broad training in the law and legal methods, drawing upon sources from all jurisdictions. Accordingly, UK Law graduates are prepared to practice in any of the 50 states.

■ Library and Physical Facilities

The college is self-contained in a contemporary building that provides all facilities for a complete program of legal education. All classrooms have been renovated with the addition of state-of-the-art teaching technology. Classrooms provide for student use of laptop computers with wired and wireless Internet access. The law library includes two large study areas and a number of study carrels that are wired for laptop access, and laptops are available for you to check out and use in the library.

■ Curriculum

UK Law offers a full-time program only, designed to be completed over three academic years or two and one-half years if you take classes during both summer sessions. The first-year program is prescribed. As an upper-level student, you can select from a full range of elective courses in both traditional and newly developing legal fields. After the first year, the only specific requirements are that you take a course in professional ethics and complete a seminar that involves substantial writing.

■ Legal Clinic

UK Law's Legal Clinic is located in its own building near the college. As a third-year student in the clinic course, you would represent low-income clients in a variety of civil legal matters. The clinic is supervised by a faculty member who was a very successful trial attorney for 10 years.

■ Externships

UK Law offers five externships for course credit in which you can obtain experience in applied research, fact gathering, interviewing, counseling, negotiation, trial advocacy, and appellate practice.

The judicial clerkship externship enables you to serve as a law clerk for a local state or federal judge. The participating judges see that you are exposed to every aspect of motion and litigation practice.

In your third year, you can be placed in the Fayette Commonwealth Attorney's Office, where you will gain criminal trial experience and participate in court proceedings under the close supervision of an attorney.

A unique program at the Federal Correctional Institute in Lexington permits you to counsel inmates in civil and criminal matters.

In the externship with the Kentucky Innocence Project, you work with the Kentucky Department of Public Advocacy on selected criminal appeals where a claim of factual innocence is made.

UK Law's new externship with the US Attorney's Office in Lexington gives students an invaluable opportunity to work on appellate briefs dealing with issues of federal law in both criminal and civil cases.

■ Joint Degrees

The **JD/MBA** joint degree can be obtained in as little time as four years. You must apply and be admitted to both UK's College of Law and its Carol Martin Gatton College of Business and Economics.

If you are interested in a career in public administration, public service, or politics, you should consider the four-year **JD/MPA** joint-degree program with UK's Martin School of Public Policy. You must apply and be admitted to both programs.

If you are interested in a career in international law, in public or private law, in international business, or in government service in the international sector, you should consider the four-year **JD/MA** dual-degree program with UK's Patterson School of Diplomacy and International Commerce. You must apply and be admitted to both programs.

■ Student Activities

There are a variety of cocurricular activities in which you may earn course credit. The *Kentucky Law Journal* is the 10th oldest American law review and is edited entirely by students, as is the *Journal of Natural Resources and Environmental Law*. The college fields several moot court teams that participate in both national and international competitions. UK Law's Trial Advocacy teams advanced to national title competitions in five of the last six years. In 2006, the Mock Trial Team for UK's Black Law Students Association placed second in the nation in the Thurgood Marshall Moot Court Competition in Washington, DC.

UK Law's Student Bar Association serves as the law student governing body and student activities board. The SBA publishes a weekly student newspaper and sponsors regular student social events and community service activities. UK's SBA was recognized by the ABA as the best SBA in the nation in 2002.

The Student Public Interest Law Foundation, through grants and fundraising, sponsors 15–20 summer internships with public interest and public service organizations selected by the students who apply. Other active student groups include the Black Law Students Association, the Women's Law Caucus, the International Law Society, the Environmental Law Society, the Equine Law Society, the Federalist Society, and the Intellectual Property Law Society.

■ Admission

Admission is considered and granted by the faculty Admissions Committee. Each file is reviewed completely and is voted on by the full committee. While your undergraduate record and LSAT score are the primary indicators of potential for success in law school, all other factors you present will be considered. You are urged to read the full description of the admission process contained in the UK Law Bulletin and to provide full information about your intellectual and nonacademic achievements. The February LSAT is the last examination accepted by the Admissions Committee for that year. Admission as a first-year student is for the fall term only.

■ Scholarships and Financial Aid

Scholarships for the first year of study are based on merit and/or contributions to diversity. The largest and most prestigious awards, the Combs Scholars and Ashland Scholars, require an application and an interview. To be considered for the diversity awards or the Kentucky Legal Education Opportunity Fellowships, you must include a brief statement about your eligibility with your admission application. For all other entering student awards, including the nonresident tuition reduction scholarships, no application is necessary. Over 60 percent of the 2006 entering class received some form of scholarship award.

UK Law students are eligible for loan assistance through the Federal Direct Student Loan Program, as well as three national private loan programs. Admitted candidates are mailed the FAFSA form and complete information on financial aid. To receive forms and information prior to admission, contact UK's Student Financial Aid Office, 128 Funkhouser Building, University of Kentucky, Lexington, KY 40506-0054.

Two new loan forgiveness programs are available: the Rural Drug Prosecution Project for UK Law graduates only, and Kentucky's new loan forgiveness program for graduates staying in the state and working in the public interest. See the UK Law Bulletin for more information.

■ Career Services

UK Law students have the benefit of a large on-campus job interview program for regional employers, as well as national placement through the college's participation in numerous off-campus interviewing conferences. The Career Services Office also uses alumni contacts to connect students with employers nationwide.

UK Law's job placement rate consistently exceeds national averages. For the 2005 graduating class, over 95 percent were employed or in advanced-degree programs within nine months after graduation. A majority of UK Law graduates choose private practice, with 15–25 percent of each graduating class selected for prestigious state and federal judicial clerkships.

Applicant Profile

University of Kentucky College of Law
Probability of admission to the University of Kentucky College of Law, based on admission decisions for the 2003 entering class.

LSAT Score	GPA								
	3.75–4.00	3.50–3.74	3.25–3.49	3.00–3.24	2.75–2.99	2.50–2.74	2.25–2.49	Below 2.25	GPA not scaled
165 & Above									
160–164									
157–159									
155–156									
153–154									
150–152									
145–149									
Below 145									

Probable   Very Competitive   Somewhat Competitive   Possible   Unlikely

University of La Verne College of Law

320 East D Street
Ontario, CA 91764
Phone: 909.460.2001; Fax: 909.460.2082
E-mail: lawadm@ulv.edu; Website: http://law.ulv.edu

Provisional

ABA
Approved
Since
2006

The Basics

Type of school	Private
Term	Semester
Application deadline	7/1 12/1
Application fee	$60
Financial aid deadline	3/2
Can first year start other than fall?	Yes
Student to faculty ratio	12.3 to 1
Does the university offer:	
housing restricted to law students?	No
graduate housing for which law students are eligible?	No

Faculty and Administrators

	Total		Men		Women		Minorities	
	Fall	Spr	Fall	Spr	Fall	Spr	Fall	Spr
Full-time	15	15	6	6	9	9	3	3
Other Full-time	1	1	1	1	0	0	0	0
Deans, librarians, & others who teach	5	5	5	5	0	0	1	1
Part-time	8	12	6	8	2	4	1	0
Total	29	33	18	20	11	13	5	4

Curriculum

	Full-time	Part-time
Typical first-year section size	60	30
Is there typically a "small section" of the first-year class, other than Legal Writing, taught by full-time faculty	No	No
If yes, typical size offered last year		
# of classroom course titles beyond first-year curriculum	41	

# of upper division courses, excluding seminars with an enrollment:	Under 25	41
	25–49	19
	50–74	3
	75–99	0
	100+	0

	Full-time	Part-time
# of seminars	5	
# of seminar positions available	75	
# of seminar positions filled	48	9
# of positions available in simulation courses	100	
# of simulation positions filled	77	23
# of positions available in faculty supervised clinical courses	20	
# of faculty supervised clinical positions filled	9	2
# involved in field placements	49	11
# involved in law journals	19	2
# involved in interschool competitions	9	3
# of credit hours required to graduate	88	

JD Enrollment and Ethnicity

	Men		Women		Full-time		Part-time		1st-year		Total		JD Degs. Awd.
	#	%	#	%	#	%	#	%	#	%	#	%	
African Amer.	5	3.3	11	9.6	7	4.1	9	9.7	4	4.0	16	6.0	6
Amer. Indian	0	0.0	1	0.9	1	0.6	0	0.0	1	1.0	1	0.4	0
Asian Amer.	13	8.6	18	15.8	22	12.8	9	9.7	13	13.0	31	11.7	9
Mex. Amer.	23	15.2	18	15.8	24	14.0	17	18.3	16	16.0	41	15.5	8
Puerto Rican	0	0.0	0	0.0	0	0.0	0	0.0	0	0.0	0	0.0	0
Hispanic	0	0.0	0	0.0	0	0.0	0	0.0	0	0.0	0	0.0	0
Total Minority	41	27.2	48	42.1	54	31.4	35	37.6	34	34.0	89	33.6	23
For. Nation.	0	0.0	0	0.0	0	0.0	0	0.0	0	0.0	0	0.0	0
Caucasian	88	58.3	54	47.4	95	55.2	47	50.5	48	48.0	142	53.6	36
Unknown	22	14.6	12	10.5	23	13.4	11	11.8	18	18.0	34	12.8	8
Total	151	57.0	114	43.0	172	64.9	93	35.1	100	37.7	265		67

Transfers

Transfers in	3
Transfers out	2

Tuition and Fees

	Resident	Nonresident
Full-time	$30,810	$30,810
Part-time	$23,360	$23,360

Living Expenses

Estimated living expenses for singles

Living on campus	Living off campus	Living at home
N/A	$16,814	N/A

University of La Verne College of Law

ABA
Approved
Since
2006

GPA and LSAT Scores

	Total	Full-time	Part-time
# of apps	721	510	211
# of offers	293	218	75
# of matrics	104	68	36
75% GPA	3.33	3.31	3.41
Median GPA	3.05	3.05	3.10
25% GPA	2.80	2.82	2.66
75% LSAT	150	150	149
Median LSAT	148	148	148
25% LSAT	147	147	146

Grants and Scholarships (from prior year)

	Total		Full-time		Part-time	
	#	%	#	%	#	%
Total # of students	256		173		83	
Total # receiving grants	191	74.6	122	70.5	69	83.1
Less than 1/2 tuition	82	32.0	48	27.7	34	41.0
Half to full tuition	84	32.8	58	33.5	26	31.3
Full tuition	24	9.4	16	9.2	8	9.6
More than full tuition	1	0.4	0	0.0	1	1.2
Median grant amount			$12,250		$9,200	

Informational and Library Resources

# of volumes and volume equivalents	297,041
# of titles	38,495
# of active serial subscriptions	2,313
Study seating capacity inside the library	293
# of full-time professional librarians	5
Hours per week library is open	94
# of open, wired connections available to students	100
# of networked computers available for use by students	35
# of simultaneous wireless users	550
Require computer?	No

JD Attrition (from prior year)

	Academic	Other	Total	
	#	#	#	%
1st year	8	8	16	17.0
2nd year	4	1	5	7.0
3rd year	2	0	2	2.5
4th year	0	0	0	0.0

Employment (9 months after graduation)

	Total	Percentage
Employment status known	16	43.2
Employment status unknown	21	56.8
Employed	12	75.0
Pursuing graduate degrees	0	0.0
Unemployed seeking employment	2	12.5
Unemployed not seeking employment	1	6.2
Unemployed and studying for the bar	1	6.2

Type of Employment

	Total	Percentage
# employed in law firms	8	66.7
# employed in business and industry	3	25.0
# employed in government	1	8.3
# employed in public interest	0	0.0
# employed as judicial clerks	0	0.0
# employed in academia	0	0.0

Geographic Location

	Total	Percentage
# employed in state	12	100.0
# employed in foreign countries	0	0.0
# of states where employed	0	

Bar Passage Rates

Jurisdiction	California		
Exam	Sum 05	Win 06	Total
# from school taking bar for the first time	25	8	33
School's pass rate for all first-time takers	32%	13%	27%
State's pass rate for all first-time takers	64%	54%	62%

University of La Verne College of Law

320 East D Street
Ontario, CA 91764
Phone: 909.460.2001; Fax: 909.460.2082
E-mail: lawadm@ulv.edu; Website: http://law.ulv.edu

■ Welcome

Just as the practice of law is more than courtrooms and conflict, law school should be more than classrooms and legal briefs. At the University of La Verne (ULV) College of Law, our small class sizes and optimal student-to-teacher ratios will allow you to thoroughly explore your interests and discover the best path to your successful legal career, a journey that will not only fulfill your dreams but help you make a positive impact in your community as well. The professionalism of our graduates is highly regarded, and we are particularly proud of more than three dozen alumni who currently serve on the bench.

You will find that ULV College of Law professors practice a true open-door policy, taking a personal interest in your success. It won't be unusual to have the same leading scholar who mentors you by day attend your softball game or student BBQ at night. In fact, in our distinctively personal environment, you're as likely to discuss the day's headlines with the dean as you are with another student, both of whom will know you by name.

We invite you to take a closer look at the uniquely rewarding experience that awaits you at ULV College of Law.

■ A Focus on Your Career Development

If you're looking for solid job prospects, the College of Law has an enviable track record: More than 88 percent of our graduates find a job within nine months of graduation. To assist you in launching an effective job search, our Career Services Office offers a number of valuable services, including:

- individualized career counseling for our students and alumni;
- career and professional development workshops, including résumé writing, interviewing techniques, and so on;
- seminars and receptions featuring potential employers, including law firms, business organizations, and government agencies;
- employment opportunity postings for our students and alumni, including internships, judicial clerkships, and professional positions;
- networking opportunities with regional firms, corporations, and bar associations;
- on-campus interview opportunities with representatives from local firms, businesses, and government agencies, including the Office of the Judge Advocate General's Corps (JAG); and
- campus and regional career fairs with other Southern California ABA-accredited law schools.

■ Location, Location, Location!

What's a law student to do when not studying case or statutory law, practicing oral arguments, or debating with some of the best minds in the legal profession? When you're conveniently located in the heart of Southern California, you can do anything you'd like. ULV College of Law is not only freeway close to Los Angeles, Orange, and San Diego counties, but also the nearby LA-Ontario International Airport. The law campus is also within a short drive of sprawling shopping centers, NASCAR action at the California Speedway, Disneyland, and Knott's Berry Farm. Moreover, Palm Springs, the California Theatre of the Performing Arts, the Riverside Philharmonic, exceptional museums and art galleries, hot air balloon festivals, and wine country tours are all less than an hour away. Law students also take advantage of the blue Pacific and its warm, sandy beaches as well as the snowcapped ski and snowboard country of the San Gabriel and San Bernardino mountains.

■ Curriculum: Rigorous Yet Practical

The rigorous academic program of the College of Law is designed to provide you with a strong foundation in legal theory, lawyering skills, and ethics—areas critical to the modern practice of law. Many of our courses will exercise and strengthen your legal research and writing skills, and all will stress the practical application of legal rules. In our Lawyering Skills Practicum (LSP) and clinical externships, you will have the opportunity to counsel clients and effectively represent varied legal positions. In short, you will enter the legal profession not only with a solid comprehension of the law, but also with a strong understanding of the industry's professional expectations and legal rules of conduct.

■ Programs of Study

The law school offers both full- and part-time programs of study as well as day and evening courses to help students pursue their goals while managing personal responsibilities.

■ Areas of Concentration

Located 40 miles east of Hollywood, ULV College of Law is the first law school in the nation to offer an academic focus in computer game law. Topics discussed in game law courses include the acquisition of game rights and ideas, intellectual property rights and licenses, end-user rights, anti-competitive practices, industry content regulation, and property rights in virtual words.

The curriculum at the College of Law is also particularly strong in advocacy, child and family law, business law, and public interest law.

■ Combined Degree Programs

ULV's College of Law and College of Business and Public Management have joined to offer combined Juris Doctor/Master of Business Administration (JD/MBA) and Juris Doctor/Master of Public Administration (JD/MPA) degree programs. Applicants must meet the admission standards of each degree program and should consult with each college for specific entrance requirements.

■ Law Faculty

At the College of Law, our full- and part-time teaching and research faculty enjoy low student-to-professor ratios, and they dedicate themselves to expanded knowledge of the law, increased skills, and enhanced personal growth for every student. Faculty members come from diverse personal, professional, and academic backgrounds, and many have significant practical experience in a variety of legal fields. ULV professors are also admired for their friendly open-door policy, allowing you to obtain additional assistance when challenging subject matter arises.

■ The Law Library

With a nationally acclaimed legal research expert as its dean, ULV College of Law boasts a particularly robust law library. The 300,000-plus print and microform collection includes federal and California statutory law, court opinions, administrative rules and regulations, all titles from California Continuing Education of the Law, major treatises on a variety of legal topics, form and practice books, and numerous legal periodicals. The Law Library also serves as a selective depository for federal and State of California government documents, including legislative materials, and includes Fundamentals of Legal Research by Dean Dunn and University of Texas's Roy Mersky, voted one of the most influential legal texts in the last century.

In addition, the Law Library has a variety of advanced electronic research methods available for your use. Most applications are accessible via the Internet on a wireless network, so you are able to conduct research from various campus access points.

■ Valuable Student Organizations

A variety of activities are available for you at the College of Law. Perhaps the most prominent is our elite law review.

Reserved for students with exceptional academic records, the *Journal of Juvenile Law* is the first law review devoted solely to issues involving legal minors. Its subscribers include the United States Supreme Court, state and local courts, individuals, and academic law libraries throughout the world.

The College of Law also offers a variety of enriching and rewarding moot court programs. Our traveling moot court teams compete and place well in national competitions involving criminal procedure, entertainment law, cybercrime, and other topics.

At ULV, you will also have the opportunity to join one or more of our student organizations. Collectively, they provide you the opportunity to engage in community service, network among your peers, participate in professional events, or just take a well-deserved break from your studies. For a list of student organizations, visit our website.

■ A Technologically Advanced Facility

ULV College of Law's 64,000-square-foot building sits on a seven-acre site in the city of Ontario. The facility, designed to give you ready access to technology, includes an up-to-date computer lab with student workstations and on-campus Internet access via a combination of hardwired and wireless connections. Classrooms are equipped with the latest in audiovisual technologies to enhance the classroom experience, and the College of Law's courtroom includes a custom-designed audio-video system used for trial and appellate exercises and instruction. A large grassy park provides shade trees, tables, and benches for students to relax.

Applicant Profile

At the University of La Verne College of Law, we strive to provide you with the personalized attention you need to achieve your individual goals and become a successful member of the legal community. This philosophy extends to our admission process, during which we will consider your unique attributes independent from those of other applicants. Selection criteria include, but are not limited to, your background, motivation for entering the legal profession, educational and professional achievements, work ethic, letters of recommendation, leadership skills, dedication to community service, and core values. By evaluating each application on a case-by-case basis, we are able to shape our incoming class with diverse personalities and a collective aptitude for success in law. If you seek a legal education tailored to your individual needs, we invite you to visit us in person or on the Web.

Lewis & Clark Law School

10015 SW Terwilliger Boulevard
Portland, OR 97219-7799
Phone: 800.303.4860 or 503.768.6613; Fax: 503.768.6793
E-mail: lawadmss@lclark.edu; Website: http://law.lclark.edu

ABA
Approved
Since
1970

The Basics

Type of school	Private
Term	Semester
Application deadline	3/1
Application fee	$50
Financial aid deadline	3/1
Can first year start other than fall?	No
Student to faculty ratio	14.6 to 1
Does the university offer:	
housing restricted to law students?	Yes
graduate housing for which law students are eligible?	No

Faculty and Administrators

	Total		Men		Women		Minorities	
	Fall	Spr	Fall	Spr	Fall	Spr	Fall	Spr
Full-time	40	34	26	22	14	12	4	2
Other Full-time	11	12	2	3	9	9	1	1
Deans, librarians, & others who teach	14	15	3	4	11	11	1	1
Part-time	33	41	20	27	13	14	0	1
Total	98	102	51	56	47	46	6	5

Curriculum

		Full-time	Part-time
Typical first-year section size		73	40
Is there typically a "small section" of the first-year class, other than Legal Writing, taught by full-time faculty		Yes	Yes
If yes, typical size offered last year		37	37
# of classroom course titles beyond first-year curriculum		162	
# of upper division courses, excluding seminars with an enrollment:	Under 25	65	
	25–49	38	
	50–74	16	
	75–99	10	
	100+	0	
# of seminars		33	
# of seminar positions available		585	
# of seminar positions filled		319	135
# of positions available in simulation courses		212	
# of simulation positions filled		114	53
# of positions available in faculty supervised clinical courses		144	
# of faculty supervised clinical positions filled		84	43
# involved in field placements		69	35
# involved in law journals		108	18
# involved in interschool competitions		97	37
# of credit hours required to graduate		86	

JD Enrollment and Ethnicity

	Men		Women		Full-time		Part-time		1st-year		Total		JD Degs. Awd.
	#	%	#	%	#	%	#	%	#	%	#	%	
African Amer.	6	1.6	10	3.0	9	1.7	7	3.8	3	1.3	16	2.2	4
Amer. Indian	5	1.3	5	1.5	5	0.9	5	2.7	2	0.9	10	1.4	5
Asian Amer.	28	7.3	41	12.2	52	9.7	17	9.3	26	11.4	69	9.6	22
Mex. Amer.	8	2.1	7	2.1	10	1.9	5	2.7	3	1.3	15	2.1	3
Puerto Rican	2	0.5	1	0.3	3	0.6	0	0.0	1	0.4	3	0.4	2
Hispanic	10	2.6	10	3.0	15	2.8	5	2.7	8	3.5	20	2.8	7
Total Minority	59	15.4	74	22.0	94	17.5	39	21.4	43	18.9	133	18.5	43
For. Nation.	4	1.0	7	2.1	8	1.5	3	1.6	3	1.3	11	1.5	5
Caucasian	281	73.4	228	67.9	385	71.7	124	68.1	158	69.3	509	70.8	186
Unknown	39	10.2	27	8.0	50	9.3	16	8.8	24	10.5	66	9.2	26
Total	383	53.3	336	46.7	537	74.7	182	25.3	228	31.7	719		260

Transfers

Transfers in	20
Transfers out	2

Tuition and Fees

	Resident	Nonresident
Full-time	$27,670	$27,670
Part-time	$20,752	$20,752

Living Expenses

Estimated living expenses for singles		
Living on campus	Living off campus	Living at home
N/A	$14,590	N/A

*ABA
Approved
Since
1970*

GPA and LSAT Scores

	Total	Full-time	Part-time
# of apps	2,241	2,067	174
# of offers	899	822	77
# of matrics	225	186	39
75% GPA	3.61	3.63	3.49
Median GPA	3.40	3.41	3.22
25% GPA	3.06	3.10	2.92
75% LSAT	164	165	162
Median LSAT	161	161	158
25% LSAT	158	159	155

Grants and Scholarships (from prior year)

	Total		Full-time		Part-time	
	#	%	#	%	#	%
Total # of students	748		549		199	
Total # receiving grants	299	40.0	251	45.7	48	24.1
Less than 1/2 tuition	250	33.4	218	39.7	32	16.1
Half to full tuition	33	4.4	20	3.6	13	6.5
Full tuition	15	2.0	13	2.4	2	1.0
More than full tuition	1	0.1	0	0.0	1	0.5
Median grant amount			$8,000		$6,750	

Informational and Library Resources

# of volumes and volume equivalents	514,855
# of titles	99,033
# of active serial subscriptions	7,114
Study seating capacity inside the library	385
# of full-time professional librarians	9
Hours per week library is open	113
# of open, wired connections available to students	961
# of networked computers available for use by students	116
# of simultaneous wireless users	650
Require computer?	No

JD Attrition (from prior year)

	Academic	Other	Total	
	#	#	#	%
1st year	1	5	6	2.6
2nd year	1	9	10	4.3
3rd year	0	0	0	0.0
4th year	0	0	0	0.0

Employment (9 months after graduation)

	Total	Percentage
Employment status known	214	96.0
Employment status unknown	9	4.0
Employed	198	92.5
Pursuing graduate degrees	2	0.9
Unemployed seeking employment	5	2.3
Unemployed not seeking employment	7	3.3
Unemployed and studying for the bar	2	0.9
Type of Employment		
# employed in law firms	95	48.0
# employed in business and industry	30	15.2
# employed in government	25	12.6
# employed in public interest	24	12.1
# employed as judicial clerks	20	10.1
# employed in academia	4	2.0
Geographic Location		
# employed in state	128	64.6
# employed in foreign countries	1	0.5
# of states where employed	29	

Bar Passage Rates

Jurisdiction	Oregon		
Exam	Sum 05	Win 06	Total
# from school taking bar for the first time	124	37	161
School's pass rate for all first-time takers	80%	78%	80%
State's pass rate for all first-time takers	76%	74%	76%

Lewis & Clark Law School

10015 SW Terwilliger Boulevard
Portland, OR 97219-7799
Phone: 800.303.4860 or 503.768.6613; Fax: 503.768.6793
E-mail: lawadmss@lclark.edu; Website: http://law.lclark.edu

■ Introduction

Lewis & Clark Law School believes in a balanced approach to legal education that assures a solid theoretical foundation along with hands-on experience in practice. The campus is one of the most beautiful in the nation. Situated next to a state park, students are only a moment away from an extensive trail system used by joggers, walkers, and bicyclists.

■ Enrollment/Student Body

The approximately 750 students attending the Law School represent a spectrum of ages, experiences, and priorities. Business executives, scientists, students of politics, musicians, and school teachers—people from many disciplines meet at the Law School in a common pursuit. The atmosphere is one of mutual support during a time of academic challenge. Students and faculty can often be found discussing questions long after class has ended.

■ Faculty

The full-time faculty were educated at the nation's most distinguished law schools. The faculty reflect a breadth of experience and interests that give depth and creative energy to their teaching. A number of faculty members have spent sabbaticals in recent years teaching in other countries; several have been Fulbright professors in such places as China, Greece, Germany, and Venezuela.

■ Library and Physical Facilities

The resources and staff of the Paul Boley Law Library, the largest law library in the state, and the second largest in the Northwest, well exceed the standards set by the Association of American Law Schools.

Our collection includes extensive materials in environmental law, federal legislative history, tax law, commercial law, intellectual property, and legal history. It is also the only academic law library in the country to be a Patent and Trademark Depository Library. Supporting our collection is a sophisticated computer infrastructure of instruction labs and local area networks.

The Law School library is an exquisite study space, with computer labs equipped with the latest technology. Wireless access is available on the entire campus.

Framed by majestic fir trees, the campus is composed of contemporary buildings with classrooms and a large state park within a moment's walk from the library. Traditional student needs and those of individuals with disabilities are met through a variety of facilities.

■ Curriculum

The Law School confers both the JD degree and a specialized LLM in Environmental and Natural Resources Law. To earn a JD, a student must take a prescribed first-year set of courses. In the upper division, students must take a seminar, Constitutional Law II, and Professionalism, and fulfill two writing requirements. Students choose between a three-year

day program and a four-year evening program. Admission criteria, faculty, academic opportunities, and graduation requirements are the same for each.

Because the Law School offers both a full-time and a part-time program, students have great flexibility in scheduling courses and in determining the pace at which they want to pursue law school. Classes are offered both during the day and in the evening. Many students transfer between divisions and use the summer school program to accelerate progress toward graduation. Regardless of the division in which a student is enrolled, students may select courses from either the day or evening schedule as they find appropriate.

■ Specific Special Programs

Certificates: By taking a group of upper-division courses approved by the faculty, and by maintaining a superior grade-point average in those courses, a student may earn a certificate showing a concentration in environmental and natural resources law, business law, tax law, intellectual property law, or criminal law.

The Law School has a nationally recognized natural resources and environmental law program. The school is also home to a strong business and commercial law program. The intellectual property law program is particularly dynamic. All the traditional areas of legal study are fully covered. Students who do not wish to pursue a certificate may choose to study another area of particular interest.

Clinical Opportunities, Externships, and Simulations: A student may create a schedule with precisely the mix of practical skills courses that fit that student's interests and needs. Students may choose among live client clinical experience, externships and internships, or simulation courses. The legal clinic located in downtown Portland offers students the opportunity to interview and counsel real clients, prepare documents, conduct trials, negotiate settlements, and prepare appeals. Other established clinics at Lewis & Clark are the small business legal clinic, an environmental law clinic, an international environmental law clinic, a low-income taxpayer clinic, an animal law clinic, a crime victim advocacy clinic, and a business law practicum. Externships place a student in full-time work for a semester or for a summer and require a substantial research paper and attendance at a special seminar. Externs are placed throughout the United States and in foreign countries. Clinical internship seminars are similar to externships but the student works only part-time, attending other classes during the semester. Clinical internship seminars include placements with in-house counsel, government agencies, law firms, and public interest, nonprofit organizations. Other courses such as moot courts, advanced advocacy, trial advocacy, criminal law seminar, estate planning seminar, corporate transactions seminar, and family mediation seminar involve extensive simulations.

■ Admission

Lewis & Clark affirmatively seeks a diverse student body. The Admission Committee makes a serious effort to consider each applicant as an individual. Factors such as college, program, length of time since the degree was obtained, experience, writing ability, and community activities are taken into consideration. Only those candidates with excellent professional promise are admitted. Academic attrition is low, averaging 2 to 4 percent.

■ Student Activities

Activities include three law reviews, *Environmental Law, Animal Law,* and *Lewis & Clark Law Review*; numerous speakers on campus; programs that bring outstanding legal scholars to campus for lectures and seminars; and many student organizations reflecting the diverse makeup of the student body.

■ Expenses and Financial Aid

Approximately 40 percent of the students at Lewis & Clark receive some scholarship support during their law school career. The school annually awards Dean's Scholarships, Natural Resources Law Scholarships, Business Law Scholarships, Tax Law Scholarships, Animal Law Scholarships,

and Public Interest Law Scholarships. In addition, loan money and work-study funds are available. There is no separate application procedure for scholarship funds. Scholarship consideration is part of the admission process. Students are reviewed on the basis of undergraduate record, LSAT score, writing ability, and activities.

Students interested in loans need to apply for financial aid as early as possible and should not wait for an admission decision to begin the financial aid application. Applicants should submit the FAFSA (Free Application for Federal Student Aid) at *www.fafsa.ed.gov*.

■ Career Services

The Career Services Office maintains and runs an extraordinary number and variety of programs. In addition to posting clerk positions for law students and running the on-campus interviews, the office maintains an extensive mentoring program, runs dozens of panels each year on various areas of practice, and counsels individual students from the first year onward.

Applicant Profile

Lewis & Clark Law School

LSAT Score	GPA																
	3.75 +		3.50–3.74		3.25–3.49		3.00–3.24		2.75–2.99		2.50–2.74		Below 2.50		No GPA		Total	
	Apps	Adm	Apps	Adm	Apps	Adm	Apps	Adm	Apps	Adm	Apps	Adm	Apps	Adm	Apps	Adm	Apps	Adm
170–180	13	13	11	11	6	6	4	4	4	4	2	2	0	0	3	3	43	43
165–169	35	35	56	54	25	25	38	38	22	19	11	10	5	5	1	0	193	186
160–164	84	75	97	91	104	90	81	71	44	37	36	25	24	13	5	5	475	407
155–159	83	43	144	58	167	48	117	23	55	11	30	4	17	0	10	5	623	192
150–154	40	6	105	8	102	9	99	8	70	4	27	3	19	2	4	0	466	40
145–149	22	2	50	8	57	4	60	5	36	4	19	0	14	0	4	0	262	23
140–144	9	3	18	1	23	2	36	0	21	0	9	0	14	1	2	0	132	7
Below 140	3	0	9	0	9	0	13	0	17	0	15	0	9	1	1	0	76	1
Total	289	177	490	231	493	184	448	149	269	79	149	44	102	22	30	13	2270	899

Apps = Number of Applicants
Adm = Number Admitted
Reflects 99% of the total applicant pool.

This chart is to be used as a guide only. Nonnumerical factors are strongly considered for all applicants.

Liberty University School of Law

1971 University Boulevard
Lynchburg, VA 24502
Phone: 434.592.5300; Fax: 434.592.5400
E-mail: law@liberty.edu; Website: www.law.liberty.edu

Provisional

ABA
Approved
Since
2006

The Basics

Type of school	Private
Term	Semester
Application deadline	6/1
Application fee	$50
Financial aid deadline	
Can first year start other than fall?	No
Student to faculty ratio	8.1 to 1
Does the university offer:	
housing restricted to law students?	No
graduate housing for which law students are eligible?	No

Faculty and Administrators

	Total		Men		Women		Minorities	
	Fall	Spr	Fall	Spr	Fall	Spr	Fall	Spr
Full-time	13	13	10	10	3	3	1	1
Other Full-time	0	0	0	0	0	0	0	0
Deans, librarians, & others who teach	4	4	2	2	2	2	0	0
Part-time	5	2	5	2	0	0	0	0
Total	22	19	17	14	5	5	1	1

Curriculum

	Full-time	Part-time
Typical first-year section size	50	0
Is there typically a "small section" of the first-year class, other than Legal Writing, taught by full-time faculty	No	No
If yes, typical size offered last year		
# of classroom course titles beyond first-year curriculum	15	

# of upper division courses, excluding seminars with an enrollment:		
Under 25	7	
25–49	0	
50–74	8	
75–99	0	
100+	0	

# of seminars	0	
# of seminar positions available	0	
# of seminar positions filled	0	0
# of positions available in simulation courses	190	
# of simulation positions filled	190	0
# of positions available in faculty supervised clinical courses	0	
# of faculty supervised clinical positions filled	0	0
# involved in field placements	0	0
# involved in law journals	13	0
# involved in interschool competitions	12	0
# of credit hours required to graduate	90	

JD Enrollment and Ethnicity

	Men		Women		Full-time		Part-time		1st-year		Total		JD Degs. Awd.
	#	%	#	%	#	%	#	%	#	%	#	%	
African Amer.	4	4.2	5	8.5	9	5.8	0	0.0	6	9.0	9	5.8	0
Amer. Indian	3	3.1	0	0.0	3	1.9	0	0.0	1	1.5	3	1.9	0
Asian Amer.	2	2.1	1	1.7	3	1.9	0	0.0	1	1.5	3	1.9	0
Mex. Amer.	0	0.0	0	0.0	0	0.0	0	0.0	0	0.0	0	0.0	0
Puerto Rican	0	0.0	0	0.0	0	0.0	0	0.0	0	0.0	0	0.0	0
Hispanic	2	2.1	0	0.0	2	1.3	0	0.0	1	1.5	2	1.3	0
Total Minority	11	11.5	6	10.2	17	11.0	0	0.0	9	13.4	17	11.0	0
For. Nation.	2	2.1	1	1.7	3	1.9	0	0.0	2	3.0	3	1.9	0
Caucasian	80	83.3	52	88.1	132	85.2	0	0.0	54	80.6	132	85.2	0
Unknown	3	3.1	0	0.0	3	1.9	0	0.0	2	3.0	3	1.9	0
Total	96	61.9	59	38.1	155	100.0	0	0.0	67	43.2	155		0

Transfers

Transfers in	2
Transfers out	0

Tuition and Fees

	Resident	Nonresident
Full-time	$24,085	$24,085
Part-time	$0	$0

Living Expenses

Estimated living expenses for singles

Living on campus	Living off campus	Living at home
$18,500	$18,500	$18,500

Liberty University School of Law

*ABA
Approved
Since
2006*

GPA and LSAT Scores

	Total	Full-time	Part-time
# of apps	203	203	0
# of offers	102	102	0
# of matrics	70	70	0
75% GPA	3.57	3.57	0.00
Median GPA	3.35	3.35	0.00
25% GPA	2.74	2.74	0.00
75% LSAT	153	153	0
Median LSAT	150	150	0
25% LSAT	148	148	0

Grants and Scholarships (from prior year)

	Total #	Total %	Full-time #	Full-time %	Part-time #	Part-time %
Total # of students	100		100		0	
Total # receiving grants	102	102.0	102	102.0	0	0.0
Less than 1/2 tuition	10	10.0	10	10.0	0	0.0
Half to full tuition	32	32.0	32	32.0	0	0.0
Full tuition	60	60.0	60	60.0	0	0.0
More than full tuition	0	0.0	0	0.0	0	0.0
Median grant amount			$22,000		$0	

Informational and Library Resources

# of volumes and volume equivalents	240,739
# of titles	199,105
# of active serial subscriptions	1,015
Study seating capacity inside the library	239
# of full-time professional librarians	5
Hours per week library is open	95
# of open, wired connections available to students	55
# of networked computers available for use by students	48
# of simultaneous wireless users	400
Require computer?	No

JD Attrition (from prior year)

	Academic #	Other #	Total #	Total %
1st year	5	8	13	27.1
2nd year	1	1	2	3.8
3rd year	0	0	0	0.0
4th year	0	0	0	0.0

Employment (9 months after graduation)

	Total	Percentage
Employment status known	0	0.0
Employment status unknown	0	0.0
Employed	0	0.0
Pursuing graduate degrees	0	0.0
Unemployed seeking employment	0	0.0
Unemployed not seeking employment	0	0.0
Unemployed and studying for the bar	0	0.0

Type of Employment

# employed in law firms	0	0.0
# employed in business and industry	0	0.0
# employed in government	0	0.0
# employed in public interest	0	0.0
# employed as judicial clerks	0	0.0
# employed in academia	0	0.0

Geographic Location

# employed in state	0	0.0
# employed in foreign countries	0	0.0
# of states where employed	0	

Bar Passage Rates

Jurisdiction	Virginia		
Exam	Sum 05	Win 06	Total
# from school taking bar for the first time	0	0	0
School's pass rate for all first-time takers			
State's pass rate for all first-time takers	76%	65%	74%

Liberty University School of Law

1971 University Boulevard
Lynchburg, VA 24502
Phone: 434.592.5300; Fax: 434.592.5400
E-mail: law@liberty.edu; Website: www.law.liberty.edu

■ Introduction

Liberty University School of Law enrolled its inaugural class in 2004. Distinctively Christian, the law school has quickly attracted national attention for achieving provisional ABA approval in 18 months, for its innovative program of legal education, and for its practice opportunities for its students. The school expects its student body to reach approximately 450 within a few years, maintaining the collegiality that students and faculty now enjoy. The law school and adjoining law library are advantageously located on one level in Liberty University's million-square-foot Campus North complex. The 330-seat ceremonial courtroom features a nine-seat bench, which replicates the US Supreme Court bench, and is designed to prepare students to argue before the nation's highest court. Two other mock trial courtrooms, all classrooms, and the law library have the latest technologies, including SMART technology and wireless connectivity throughout. The 4,900-acre campus of Liberty University rests in the eastern foothills of the Blue Ridge Mountains in Central Virginia, approximately 180 miles southwest of the nation's capital, Washington, DC.

■ Program of Legal Education

Liberty's innovative law program has three distinct but related components: foundations of law, substantive law courses, and lawyering skills. In keeping with the law school's mission "to equip future leaders in law with a superior legal education in fidelity to the Christian faith expressed through the Holy Scriptures," the foundations courses explore the thoughts and writings of those who shaped the Western legal tradition. The Christian worldview permeates the curriculum. The unrivaled, six-semester, lawyering skills program has two threads: a litigation thread and a planning thread. Each student moves a simulated case from the initial client interview to the court verdict and develops the practice skills essential to planning client affairs. While the core courses look much the same as at other law schools—same course names, same subject matter coverage, same casebooks—Liberty's distinction is in the linkage of the substantive law courses to the foundations and lawyering skills courses. Typical course integration would be learning contract law in Contracts, drafting contracts in Lawyering Skills, and discussing the origins of contracts in Foundations of Law. The law faculty is highly accessible to students throughout each day. In addition to academic advising and support from faculty, many Liberty law students take advantage of the academic support program.

■ Academic Support

The Academic Support Program begins with an intensive four-day Barristers' Orientation for entering students. During the academic year, the program staff assists law students in achieving their full academic potential, helping them with class preparation, class participation, and examination strategies. Support includes postclass reviews prior to taking law school examinations and practice-exam workshops. The program director holds voluntary workshops on case briefing, note-taking, time and stress management, outlining, exam preparation, and legal writing. All students may take advantage of one-on-one tutorials to help them assimilate course material and apply classroom knowledge to law school examinations. The Academic Support Program also provides training to assist students with bar examination preparation.

■ Clinics, Externships, and Centers

The law school places a high priority on equipping students with the skills necessary to practice law, as evidenced in its Lawyering Skills program. Its externship and clinical programs provide the next step in the continuum of classroom learning, to simulation, to live-client and other real-life practice experience. The Constitutional Litigation Clinic works in conjunction with Liberty Counsel, a nonprofit legal organization specializing in constitutional law, which has offices on the Liberty University campus. Students work on cases with a heavy constitutional law component. They experience all phases of newly filed and ongoing Liberty Counsel cases, including having direct client contact, attending attorney strategy sessions, drafting legal documents, and, where permitted by local rules, participating in hearings and trials.

The Criminal Law Externship Program is the flagship of the law school's externship offerings. It places law students as externs in county and federal prosecutors' offices under the supervision of experienced practitioners. Students are being placed in a host of field-study venues including state and US attorney's offices; local, state, and federal courts; state supreme courts; and in public interest organizations. The public service externship component gives students a wide variety of individualized experiences in public service law and pro bono legal assistance. In addition, Liberty students are obtaining summer positions ranging from the White House and the Department of Homeland Security to private law firms and corporations.

The School of Law has formed a partnership with Liberty Counsel in founding the Center for Constitutional Litigation and Policy. The center trains law students who have career plans in public interest litigation that focuses on constitutional and religious liberty advocacy. It offers externships in constitutional litigation and trains students to become policymakers and leaders in strategy and tactics.

■ Cocurricular and Student Activities

In addition to the Student Bar Association (SBA), the law school has an active law review, which produces the *Liberty University Law Review*, a highly competitive moot court program, and a new mock trial program. Student life for Liberty law students includes taking advantage of the wide range of events on the campus of Liberty University and enjoying the sociability within the law school community. Law students have access to all of the university's recreational and student-life facilities. In keeping with the school's Christian view of volunteerism, many law students volunteer their time in pro bono activities, such as the Street Law program, which is designed for young people involved in the juvenile justice system. The law school also matches students with private practitioners engaged in pro bono work and notifies students of opportunities to intern in legal aid offices, public defender offices, and prosecutorial offices.

■ Career Services

The Center for Career and Professional Development serves law students and alumni by providing a variety of tools to develop skills essential for career development, by cultivating a life-long commitment to professionalism and community service, and by promoting regional and national awareness of the law school's distinctive program of legal study. The center works cooperatively with the law school's clinical and externship programs, and internship and pro bono activities, to foster relationships with members of the bench and bar to the benefit of students and alumni.

■ Information Resources and Technologies

With many comfortable seating areas and easy access from the classrooms, Ehrhorn Law Library provides an environment conducive to research, study, and writing. To its growing collection of approximately 250,000 volumes and volume equivalents, the law library is continually adding titles that support the curriculum. The classics of the Western legal tradition and the writings of the great legal thinkers, educators, and judges of the past and present undergird the law school's mission. Along with its extensive microform archives, the law library provides access to law-related and general databases via the Internet through any Web browser. These electronic databases are available to law students on or off campus. Reliable wired and wireless access to the Internet is provided throughout the law school facility. The law school community benefits from a high level of university support for its state-of-the-art computing, instructional, informational, and audiovisual technologies.

■ Admission and Financial Aid

Many law schools have developed courses of study that give expression to a particular jurisprudential perspective, be it law and economics, legal realism, or policy-oriented jurisprudence. Liberty University School of Law has chosen to do the same, developing its curriculum and standards of conduct consistent with the Christian worldview. Its admissions process is designed to identify those who desire to receive a legal education from this perspective. The Admissions Committee gives careful attention to a full range of factors that indicate the applicant's likelihood of success in law school and the legal profession. It attempts to identify strengths and indicators of success that may not show up in test scores and to ensure that students make fully informed decisions in deciding to attend Liberty University School of Law.

Written applications and letters of recommendation are used to identify applicants with strong communication skills, levels of interest, personal traits, and life experiences that evince a calling to law and potential for success in legal education and the practice of law. The personal statement, which addresses prescribed discussion points noted in the application for admission, is of particular importance in the admission decision.

Institutional scholarships, up to full tuition, are awarded on the basis of prior academic excellence and indicators of law school success, and for demonstrated leadership and service in keeping with the law school's mission. Committed to debt management, the law school assists each student with a financial aid package to meet individual needs.

To schedule a visit, call the Office of Admissions and Financial Aid at 434.592.5300 or e-mail *law@liberty.edu*.

Applicant Profile

The law school's mission-driven, practice-oriented program of legal education has attracted applicants from across the country and from many foreign countries. The diverse student body of approximately 160 students in 2006–2007 is projected to grow to approximately 450 in the next three years. Members of the 2006–2007 student body hail from 33 states. Seventy-eight percent of the students come from outside the Commonwealth of Virginia. They represent 107 universities and 18 students have advanced degrees. They range in age from 20 to 54. The average age is 27. Eleven percent are minorities. Thirty-six percent are women. Thirty-seven percent are married. LSAT scores for the 25th percentile, median, and 75th percentile are 149, 152, and 155, respectively. The undergraduate GPAs for the 25th percentile, median, and 75th percentile are 2.90, 3.29, and 3.61, respectively.

Louis D. Brandeis School of Law at the University of Louisville

University of Louisville
Louisville, KY 40292
Phone: 502.852.6364; Fax: 502.852.8971
E-mail: lawadmissions@louisville.edu; Website: www.louisville.edu/brandeislaw/

ABA Approved Since 1931

The Basics

Type of school	Public
Term	Semester
Application deadline	3/1 5/15
Application fee	$50
Financial aid deadline	4/15
Can first year start other than fall?	No
Student to faculty ratio	14.3 to 1
Does the university offer:	
housing restricted to law students?	No
graduate housing for which law students are eligible?	Yes

Faculty and Administrators

	Total		Men		Women		Minorities	
	Fall	Spr	Fall	Spr	Fall	Spr	Fall	Spr
Full-time	22	20	15	13	7	7	2	3
Other Full-time	3	4	1	2	2	2	0	0
Deans, librarians, & others who teach	6	6	5	5	1	1	1	1
Part-time	9	15	8	14	1	1	2	2
Total	**40**	**45**	**29**	**34**	**11**	**11**	**5**	**6**

Curriculum

	Full-time	Part-time
Typical first-year section size	50	36
Is there typically a "small section" of the first-year class, other than Legal Writing, taught by full-time faculty	No	No
If yes, typical size offered last year		
# of classroom course titles beyond first-year curriculum	62	
# of upper division courses, excluding seminars with an enrollment: Under 25	31	
25–49	29	
50–74	14	
75–99	0	
100+	0	
# of seminars	15	
# of seminar positions available	270	
# of seminar positions filled	151	47
# of positions available in simulation courses	261	
# of simulation positions filled	154	29
# of positions available in faculty supervised clinical courses	0	
# of faculty supervised clinical positions filled	0	0
# involved in field placements	106	21
# involved in law journals	66	6
# involved in interschool competitions	28	4
# of credit hours required to graduate	90	

JD Enrollment and Ethnicity

	Men		Women		Full-time		Part-time		1st-year		Total		JD Degs. Awd.
	#	%	#	%	#	%	#	%	#	%	#	%	
African Amer.	7	3.1	5	2.9	10	3.3	2	2.1	4	3.0	12	3.0	3
Amer. Indian	1	0.4	2	1.2	2	0.7	1	1.1	0	0.0	3	0.8	0
Asian Amer.	1	0.4	2	1.2	1	0.3	2	2.1	0	0.0	3	0.8	6
Mex. Amer.	0	0.0	0	0.0	0	0.0	0	0.0	0	0.0	0	0.0	0
Puerto Rican	0	0.0	0	0.0	0	0.0	0	0.0	0	0.0	0	0.0	0
Hispanic	3	1.3	2	1.2	4	1.3	1	1.1	1	0.7	5	1.3	2
Total Minority	12	5.3	11	6.5	17	5.6	6	6.3	5	3.7	23	5.8	11
For. Nation.	0	0.0	0	0.0	0	0.0	0	0.0	0	0.0	0	0.0	1
Caucasian	209	91.7	156	91.8	279	92.1	86	90.5	128	94.8	365	91.7	99
Unknown	7	3.1	3	1.8	7	2.3	3	3.2	2	1.5	10	2.5	0
Total	228	57.3	170	42.7	303	76.1	95	23.9	135	33.9	398		111

Transfers

Transfers in	11
Transfers out	7

Tuition and Fees

	Resident	Nonresident
Full-time	$11,510	$23,654
Part-time	$9,620	$19,740

Living Expenses

Estimated living expenses for singles

Living on campus	Living off campus	Living at home
$15,940	$15,940	$9,508

Louis D. Brandeis School of Law at the University of Louisville

ABA
Approved
Since
1931

GPA and LSAT Scores

	Total	Full-time	Part-time
# of apps	1,244	1,065	179
# of offers	408	348	60
# of matrics	142	102	40
75% GPA	3.69	3.74	3.61
Median GPA	3.43	3.48	3.39
25% GPA	3.13	3.17	2.98
75% LSAT	159	160	158
Median LSAT	157	158	156
25% LSAT	155	155	152

Grants and Scholarships (from prior year)

	Total #	Total %	Full-time #	Full-time %	Part-time #	Part-time %
Total # of students	396		296		100	
Total # receiving grants	139	35.1	123	41.6	16	16.0
Less than 1/2 tuition	81	20.5	73	24.7	8	8.0
Half to full tuition	54	13.6	46	15.5	8	8.0
Full tuition	1	0.3	1	0.3	0	0.0
More than full tuition	3	0.8	3	1.0	0	0.0
Median grant amount			$5,000		$4,500	

Informational and Library Resources

# of volumes and volume equivalents	420,025
# of titles	76,668
# of active serial subscriptions	5,408
Study seating capacity inside the library	441
# of full-time professional librarians	5
Hours per week library is open	89
# of open, wired connections available to students	6
# of networked computers available for use by students	34
# of simultaneous wireless users	1,792
Require computer?	No

JD Attrition (from prior year)

	Academic #	Other #	Total #	Total %
1st year	17	14	31	22.5
2nd year	5	2	7	5.4
3rd year	0	0	0	0.0
4th year	0	0	0	0.0

Employment (9 months after graduation)

	Total	Percentage
Employment status known	112	99.1
Employment status unknown	1	0.9
Employed	103	92.0
Pursuing graduate degrees	0	0.0
Unemployed seeking employment	2	1.8
Unemployed not seeking employment	4	3.6
Unemployed and studying for the bar	3	2.7

Type of Employment

# employed in law firms	62	60.2
# employed in business and industry	10	9.7
# employed in government	12	11.7
# employed in public interest	10	9.7
# employed as judicial clerks	7	6.8
# employed in academia	2	1.9

Geographic Location

# employed in state	79	76.7
# employed in foreign countries	0	0.0
# of states where employed	13	

Bar Passage Rates

Jurisdiction	Kentucky		
Exam	Sum 05	Win 06	Total
# from school taking bar for the first time	89	12	101
School's pass rate for all first-time takers	87%	83%	86%
State's pass rate for all first-time takers	81%	67%	77%

Louis D. Brandeis School of Law at the University of Louisville

University of Louisville
Louisville, KY 40292
Phone: 502.852.6364; Fax: 502.852.8971
E-mail: lawadmissions@louisville.edu; Website: www.louisville.edu/brandeislaw/

■ Introduction

Founded in 1846, the Louis D. Brandeis School of Law at the University of Louisville is Kentucky's oldest law school and America's fifth oldest law school in continuous operation. Heir to the legacy of Justice Louis D. Brandeis, the school is distinguished by a rich history, national outreach, and profound dedication to public service. It is an integral part of the University of Louisville, a public institution and major research center founded in 1798. The metropolitan area, with a population of approximately one million, combines the gracious ambience of southern hospitality with cultural, aesthetic, and recreational attractions (including historic Churchill Downs, the Actors' Theatre of Louisville, the J.B. Speed Art Museum, and the Mohammed Ali Peace Center).

■ Enrollment/Student Body

The Brandeis School of Law enrolls first-year students beginning in the fall semester, which starts in August. Candidates may apply for admission to either the full-time (three-year) division or the part-time (four-year) division.

Candidates must have completed a bachelor's degree at an accredited college or university prior to enrollment. All undergraduate majors are acceptable, with courses that emphasize critical reasoning, writing, and communication skills recognized as good preparation for the study of law.

With the entering class numbering about 140 each fall, first-year class size seldom exceeds 50. Basic Legal Skills (the first-year writing course) has classes that are only half that size.

The entire student body, composed of almost as many women as men, numbers about 400, enabling every student to be a name, not just a number, and presenting students the opportunity to develop close relationships with their professors.

■ Faculty

With 30 full-time faculty members (including 10 women and 3 faculty of color) and numerous part-time or adjunct teachers, the faculty/student ratio is one of the best in the country at 1 to 14.

The faculty gives a high priority to excellence in teaching and accessibility to students. They are also a community of active scholars.

■ Library and Physical Facilities

The law school is housed in Wilson W. Wyatt Hall, a gracious colonial style building overlooking the formal entrance to the University of Louisville Belknap campus—a traditional college campus located in an urban setting. The University of Louisville also includes two other campuses: the Health Sciences Center (housing the Medical and Dental schools) and the Shelby Campus, which offers continuing education classes.

The school's law library houses a collection of more than 400,000 volumes and microform volume equivalents, carefully selected to aid student instruction and promote research. The library still receives original briefs of the US Supreme Court—

a rare distinction for a law school and a practice originated by Justice Brandeis that continues today.

State-of-the-art instructional and research technologies, two computer labs, the Allen Courtroom's contemporary litigation environment, wireless access in the library, classrooms, and common areas, and a full-time technology staff provide a wealth of services to every Brandeis School of Law student. The Brandeis School's Intranet is an internal website that serves as our community bulletin board. Students can download course syllabi, assignments, handouts, old exams, and other materials; browse job listings from the Career Services office; review the Academic Support Program's catalog of study aids; and get news, calendars, schedules, and more. Technology is becoming part of law teaching and learning as the faculty incorporate presentations and Internet resources into the classroom experience.

■ Curriculum

The law school's full-time and part-time division share the same curriculum, faculty, and academic standards. After basic courses in the first year, students take core courses in doctrinal subjects, advanced research and writing, and professional responsibility. Students also may choose from among a rich variety of specialized and interdisciplinary electives. The Brandeis School of Law conducts a Summer Enrichment Program for a limited number of newly admitted students.

A highly successful academic support program provides tutoring groups in all first-year courses and guidance in study and test-taking skills, as well as individual advising and counseling.

■ Samuel L. Greenebaum Public Service Program

Reflecting the spirit of Justice Louis D. Brandeis, the School of Law was one of America's first five law schools to adopt public service as part of the prescribed course of study. Through this public service work, students develop practical skills, serve their communities, and establish professional values.

■ Special Programs

The Brandeis School of Law offers several dual-degree programs designed to enhance the student's understanding, skills, and career opportunities in both areas of study. Each requires application and admission to both participating schools: Master of Business Administration/Juris Doctor (MBA/JD); Master of Science in Social Work/Juris Doctor (MSSW/JD); Juris Doctor/Master of Arts in Humanities (JD/MAH); Juris Doctor/Master of Divinity—at the Louisville Presbyterian Theological Seminary (JD/MDiv); Juris Doctor/Master of Arts in Political Science (JD/MAPS); and Juris Doctor/Master of Urban Planning (JD/MAUP).

The school also operates clinical externship programs in which upper-class students, with supervision, represent clients and appear in court. A third-year student may receive credit by working in the criminal arena (DA or PD), in tax (IRS), in the judicial branch (various judges), in family law (Center for Women and Families or Legal Aid Society), or in technology (University of Louisville Office of Technology Transfer).

Louis D. Brandeis School of Law at the University of Louisville

International experience is another unique opportunity. The Brandeis School offers faculty or student exchanges with law schools in France, England, Germany, Finland, Australia, and South Africa.

■ Practical Success

Participating annually in about a dozen moot court and skills competitions, the law school has won several regional and national championships.

Students are also actively involved in writing for and publishing the *Brandeis Law Journal* and the *Journal of Law and Education*. Graduates of the Brandeis School of Law consistently achieve high employment rates.

■ Admission

Applicants are urged to apply beginning **October 1** and before **March 1** of the year they intend to enter law school. However, applications received prior to **May 15** will be given consideration on a space-available basis. Both full-time and part-time first-year students must start classes in the fall semester.

For the best chance of consideration, it is recommended that the LSAT be taken no later than December. LSAT scores taken in June, prior to the first semester of enrollment, will be considered only under extraordinary circumstances.

Applicant Profile

Louis D. Brandeis School of Law at the University of Louisville
This grid includes only applicants who earned 120–180 LSAT scores under standard administrations.

LSAT Score	3.75 +		3.50–3.74		3.25–3.49		3.00–3.24		2.75–2.99		2.50–2.74		2.25–2.49		2.00–2.24		Below 2.00		No GPA		Total	
	Apps	Adm	Apps	Adm	Apps	Adm	Apps	Adm	Apps	Adm	Apps	Adm	Apps	Adm	Apps	Adm	Apps	Adm	Apps	Adm	Apps	Adm
175–180	0	0	0	0	0	0	0	0	0	0	0	0	0	0	0	0	0	0	0	0	0	0
170–174	0	0	0	0	1	1	0	0	0	0	0	0	0	0	0	0	0	0	0	0	1	1
165–169	6	6	6	6	3	2	3	2	2	2	2	0	0	0	1	1	0	0	3	1	23	19
160–164	24	22	17	16	13	13	13	12	14	12	9	7	4	2	1	0	0	0	1	1	98	85
155–159	56	53	71	58	64	45	59	34	34	11	18	7	9	2	4	0	2	0	5	0	313	211
150–154	55	20	87	26	82	10	89	8	50	6	24	1	11	0	4	0	1	0	2	1	409	71
145–149	29	0	36	3	56	2	41	3	25	1	24	0	10	0	1	0	2	0	1	0	225	10
140–144	9	1	15	0	17	0	22	0	11	0	14	0	5	0	3	1	2	0	2	0	100	2
135–139	1	0	4	0	9	0	8	0	7	0	3	0	3	0	2	0	0	0	1	0	38	0
130–134	0	0	0	0	2	0	2	0	2	0	3	0	1	0	1	0	0	0	1	0	12	0
125–129	0	0	1	0	0	0	0	0	1	0	1	0	1	0	1	0	0	0	1	0	6	0
120–124	0	0	0	0	0	0	0	0	0	0	0	0	0	0	1	0	0	0	0	0	1	0
Total	180	102	237	109	247	73	237	59	146	32	98	15	44	4	15	2	6	0	16	3	1226	399

Apps = Number of Applicants
Adm = Number Admitted
Reflects 98% of the total applicant pool.

The faculty admission committee reads all files very carefully. Beyond numerical indicators (LSAT scores and grade-point averages), the committee looks for individuals with unique attributes who will bring diversity to the entering class and good character to the legal profession. Numerical quantifiers are not automatic grounds for admission or denial.

Louisiana State University, Paul M. Hebert Law Center

202 Law Center
Baton Rouge, LA 70803
Phone: 225.578.8646; Fax: 225.578.8647
E-mail: admissions@law.lsu.edu; Website: www.law.lsu.edu

ABA Approved Since 1926

The Basics

Type of school	Public
Term	Semester
Application deadline	3/1
Application fee	$25
Financial aid deadline	4/1
Can first year start other than fall?	No
Student to faculty ratio	16.2 to 1
Does the university offer:	
housing restricted to law students?	No
graduate housing for which law students are eligible?	No

Faculty and Administrators

	Total Fall	Total Spr	Men Fall	Men Spr	Women Fall	Women Spr	Minorities Fall	Minorities Spr
Full-time	28	34	21	26	7	8	4	4
Other Full-time	8	9	3	5	5	4	0	0
Deans, librarians, & others who teach	6	6	5	5	1	1	0	0
Part-time	25	29	22	26	2	3	2	3
Total	**67**	**78**	**51**	**62**	**15**	**16**	**6**	**7**

Curriculum

	Full-time	Part-time
Typical first-year section size	68	0
Is there typically a "small section" of the first-year class, other than Legal Writing, taught by full-time faculty	Yes	No
If yes, typical size offered last year	40	
# of classroom course titles beyond first-year curriculum	81	

# of upper division courses, excluding seminars with an enrollment:		
Under 25	120	
25–49	60	
50–74	32	
75–99	17	
100+	5	

# of seminars	18	
# of seminar positions available	280	
# of seminar positions filled	246	0
# of positions available in simulation courses	631	
# of simulation positions filled	545	0
# of positions available in faculty supervised clinical courses	0	
# of faculty supervised clinical positions filled	0	0
# involved in field placements	25	0
# involved in law journals	50	0
# involved in interschool competitions	105	0
# of credit hours required to graduate	97	

JD Enrollment and Ethnicity

	Men #	Men %	Women #	Women %	Full-time #	Full-time %	Part-time #	Part-time %	1st-year #	1st-year %	Total #	Total %	JD Degs. Awd.
African Amer.	11	3.8	31	10.8	42	7.4	0	0.0	10	4.9	42	7.3	20
Amer. Indian	1	0.3	1	0.3	2	0.4	0	0.0	1	0.5	2	0.3	0
Asian Amer.	5	1.7	1	0.3	6	1.1	0	0.0	2	1.0	6	1.0	4
Mex. Amer.	0	0.0	0	0.0	0	0.0	0	0.0	0	0.0	0	0.0	0
Puerto Rican	0	0.0	0	0.0	0	0.0	0	0.0	0	0.0	0	0.0	0
Hispanic	3	1.0	4	1.4	6	1.1	1	8.3	4	2.0	7	1.2	5
Total Minority	20	6.8	37	12.9	56	9.9	1	8.3	17	8.3	57	9.9	29
For. Nation.	0	0.0	0	0.0	0	0.0	0	0.0	0	0.0	0	0.0	0
Caucasian	233	79.8	229	80.1	453	80.0	9	75.0	169	82.8	462	79.9	202
Unknown	39	13.4	20	7.0	57	10.1	2	16.7	18	8.8	59	10.2	17
Total	292	50.5	286	49.5	566	97.9	12	2.1	204	35.3	578		248

Transfers

Transfers in	2
Transfers out	0

Tuition and Fees

	Resident	Nonresident
Full-time	$12,124	$21,220
Part-time	$0	$0

Living Expenses

Estimated living expenses for singles

Living on campus	Living off campus	Living at home
$13,142	$15,026	$10,526

Louisiana State University, Paul M. Hebert Law Center

ABA
Approved
Since
1926

GPA and LSAT Scores

	Total	Full-time	Part-time
# of apps	1,353	1,353	0
# of offers	475	475	0
# of matrics	204	204	0
75% GPA	3.78	3.78	0.00
Median GPA	3.49	3.49	0.00
25% GPA	3.16	3.16	0.00
75% LSAT	159	159	0
Median LSAT	156	156	0
25% LSAT	154	154	0

Grants and Scholarships (from prior year)

	Total		Full-time		Part-time	
	#	%	#	%	#	%
Total # of students	647		630		17	
Total # receiving grants	465	71.9	465	73.8	0	0.0
Less than 1/2 tuition	345	53.3	345	54.8	0	0.0
Half to full tuition	83	12.8	83	13.2	0	0.0
Full tuition	0	0.0	0	0.0	0	0.0
More than full tuition	37	5.7	37	5.9	0	0.0
Median grant amount			$4,701		$0	

Informational and Library Resources

# of volumes and volume equivalents	844,540
# of titles	219,197
# of active serial subscriptions	11,590
Study seating capacity inside the library	478
# of full-time professional librarians	11
Hours per week library is open	101
# of open, wired connections available to students	61
# of networked computers available for use by students	57
# of simultaneous wireless users	1,250
Require computer?	No

JD Attrition (from prior year)

	Academic	Other	Total	
	#	#	#	%
1st year	15	18	33	15.7
2nd year	0	0	0	0.0
3rd year	0	0	0	0.0
4th year	0	0	0	0.0

Employment (9 months after graduation)

	Total	Percentage
Employment status known	181	94.3
Employment status unknown	11	5.7
Employed	157	86.7
Pursuing graduate degrees	11	6.1
Unemployed seeking employment	11	6.1
Unemployed not seeking employment	2	1.1
Unemployed and studying for the bar	0	0.0
Type of Employment		
# employed in law firms	92	58.6
# employed in business and industry	18	11.5
# employed in government	12	7.6
# employed in public interest	0	0.0
# employed as judicial clerks	31	19.7
# employed in academia	2	1.3
Geographic Location		
# employed in state	131	83.4
# employed in foreign countries	2	1.3
# of states where employed	13	

Bar Passage Rates

Jurisdiction	Louisiana		
Exam	Sum 05	Win 06	Total
# from school taking bar for the first time	160	10	170
School's pass rate for all first-time takers	86%	60%	84%
State's pass rate for all first-time takers	73%	48%	70%

Louisiana State University, Paul M. Hebert Law Center

202 Law Center
Baton Rouge, LA 70803
Phone: 225.578.8646; Fax: 225.578.8647
E-mail: admissions@law.lsu.edu; Website: www.law.lsu.edu

■ Introduction

The Louisiana State University (LSU) Law Center was originally established as the Louisiana State University Law School in 1906, pursuant to an authorization contained in the university charter. In 1979, the Law Center was renamed the Paul M. Hebert Law Center of Louisiana State University. The Law Center holds membership in the AALS and is on the approved list of the ABA.

■ Library and Physical Facilities

The Law Center, completed in October 1969, added extensive facilities to the original Law Center building, dedicated in 1938. This complex provides classroom areas, seminar and discussion rooms, and meeting areas as well as a courtroom. Separate offices for student research and student activities such as the *Louisiana Law Review*, Moot Court Board, and Student Bar Association are included in the facility. The law library, housed in the complex, provides one of the most complete collections of Roman and modern civil law reports and materials in the country. Library resources include reading and discussion rooms, study carrels, computer labs, and audiovisual facilities. Students also have access to other campus facilities, including the Student Health Center, residential housing, and the Sports Recreational Complex.

■ Curriculum

The LSU Law Center has established a joint JD/BCL program through which all graduates receive the JD (Juris Doctor) degree and a BCL (Bachelor of Civil Law) degree. First-year students follow a prescribed curriculum and, thereafter, students choose from a wide variety of courses to complete their degrees. An orientation program and library tour introduce the first-year class to the study of law. The Law Center's dedication to the study of both the civil and the common law prepares its graduates to practice in any state and in many foreign countries. Seven semesters of resident study are required for the degree. In addition to its full-time law faculty, the LSU Law Center invites a number of distinguished lecturers, including practicing attorneys and legal scholars, to teach courses in their areas of specialty each semester. A number of faculty members have law degrees from foreign countries.

■ Summer Session Abroad

The Law Center conducts a six-week summer program in France. All classes are conducted in English and are designed to meet the requirements of the ABA and AALS.

■ Special Programs

A wide variety of courses affords each student the opportunity to participate in the preparation and trial of mock cases, both civil and criminal, and also to develop skills in legal negotiation and counseling. LSU sponsors and encourages student participation in national trial and appellate competitions throughout the school year.

In cooperation with the Center for Continuing Professional Development, the Law Center presents seminars, institutes, and conferences for practicing lawyers.

The LSU Law Center admits candidates for the degrees of Master of Laws (LLM) and Master of Civil Law (MCL). These programs are highly selective and admit students with exceptional ability.

■ Admission

The Admissions Committee considers many factors in reaching admission decisions. While the quantitative predictors of success in law school (performance on the LSAT and the undergraduate GPA of applicants) are typically the most important factors in the admission decision, the Admissions Committee considers many other factors, such as the ability to analyze and write well, as demonstrated by the personal statement and the written portion of the LSAT; two letters of recommendation from teachers and others who can express an opinion on the applicant's aptitude for the study of law; the rigor of the undergraduate program of study and grade trends; extracurricular activities; work experience or military service; social and economic background; and other evidence of an applicant's aptitude for the study of law and likely contribution to academic and community life. A baccalaureate degree from an accredited college or university is required for admission.

Applicants are advised to take the LSAT in October, and not later than December, prior to the year in which they seek admission to the Law Center. The Law Center admits students only in the fall and only for full-time study. There are no night courses offered. Transfer applications are considered.

Louisiana State University assures equal opportunity for all qualified persons without regard to race, color, religion, sexual orientation, national origin, age, disability, marital status, or veteran's status in the admission to, participation in, or employment in the programs and activities that the university operates.

■ Joint Programs

The LSU Law Center offers the JD/BCL-MPA and the JD/BCL-MBA joint-degree programs. Admission requirements for each program are listed in the LSU Graduate School Catalog and the Law Center Catalog. Students must apply separately for each program.

■ Student Activities

The *Louisiana Law Review* was established to encourage high-quality legal scholarship in the student body, to contribute to the development of the law by scholarly criticism and analysis, and to serve the bar of Louisiana by comments and discussion of current cases and legal problems. It is edited by a board of student editors with faculty cooperation.

The Louisiana Chapter of the Order of the Coif, a national honorary law fraternity, was established in the Law Center in 1942. Election to the Order of the Coif is recognized as the highest honor a law student may receive.

Since a large number of graduates of the Law Center go directly into practice, the LSU Law Center has an extensive Trial Advocacy Program in which moot court training is offered both for trial work and in appellate argument.

All students in the Law Center are members of the Student Bar Association. This association promotes and coordinates student activities within the Law Center and serves as an instructional medium for postgraduate bar association activities.

■ Expenses and Financial Aid

The Scholarship Committee automatically considers all admitted students for scholarship support. Most scholarships range in size from $1,000 to full-tuition awards. Awards are offered to applicants who the committee believes will best contribute to the academic and social life of the Law Center.

A number of loan funds are available to help deserving students who need financial assistance to continue their education. All such funds are subject to the policies and regulations authorized by the LSU Student Loan Fund Committee. Detailed information on all loan funds may be secured by contacting the Student Loan Section, LSU Office of Financial Aid and Scholarships, 202 Himes Hall, Baton Rouge, LA 70803.

■ Career Services

The Career Services Office of the Law Center is dedicated to enhancing the personal growth and professional opportunities for LSU law students and alumni. The office offers a series of workshops and individual counseling sessions to assist students as they search for summer and permanent employment opportunities. More than 165 legal employers visit the school each year to recruit our students.

Applicant Profile

Louisiana State University, Paul M. Hebert Law Center
This grid includes only applicants who earned 120–180 LSAT scores under standard administrations.

LSAT Score	3.75 +		3.50–3.74		3.25–3.49		3.00–3.24		2.75–2.99		2.50–2.74		2.25–2.49		2.00–2.24		Below 2.00		No GPA		Total	
	Apps	Adm	Apps	Adm	Apps	Adm	Apps	Adm	Apps	Adm	Apps	Adm	Apps	Adm	Apps	Adm	Apps	Adm	Apps	Adm	Apps	Adm
175–180	0	0	0	0	0	0	0	0	1	1	0	0	0	0	0	0	0	0	0	0	1	1
170–174	3	3	2	2	3	3	1	1	1	1	0	0	1	1	0	0	0	0	0	0	11	11
165–169	8	8	5	5	4	3	2	2	2	2	5	5	0	0	0	0	0	0	0	0	26	25
160–164	19	19	18	17	14	14	17	17	12	10	10	4	2	0	2	0	0	0	1	0	297	205
155–159	39	39	63	53	75	57	59	36	32	12	22	8	4	0	2	0	0	0	1	0	461	132
150–154	63	36	84	29	119	34	98	25	49	3	24	3	20	2	3	0	0	0	1	0	461	132
145–149	23	8	56	9	66	3	56	1	34	1	21	0	17	0	3	0	0	0	3	0	279	22
140–144	8	0	19	0	32	1	31	0	25	0	12	0	5	0	3	0	1	0	2	0	138	1
135–139	0	0	3	0	3	0	11	0	8	0	8	0	7	0	2	0	1	0	0	0	43	0
130–134	0	0	1	0	0	0	2	0	2	0	4	0	2	0	0	0	0	0	1	0	12	0
125–129	0	0	0	0	0	0	0	0	0	0	2	0	0	0	0	0	0	0	0	0	2	0
120–124	0	0	0	0	0	0	0	0	0	0	0	0	1	0	0	0	0	0	0	0	1	0
Total	163	113	251	115	316	115	277	82	166	30	108	20	59	3	15	0	2	0	8	0	1365	478

Apps = Number of Applicants
Adm = Number Admitted
Reflects 99% of the total applicant pool.

Loyola Law School, Loyola Marymount University

919 Albany Street
Los Angeles, CA 90015
Phone: 213.736.1074; Fax: 213.736.6523
E-mail: admissions@lls.edu; Website: www.lls.edu

ABA Approved Since 1935

The Basics

Type of school	Private
Term	Semester
Application deadline	2/2 4/13
Application fee	$65
Financial aid deadline	3/16
Can first year start other than fall?	No
Student to faculty ratio	15.6 to 1
Does the university offer:	
housing restricted to law students?	No
graduate housing for which law students are eligible?	No

Faculty and Administrators

	Total Fall	Total Spr	Men Fall	Men Spr	Women Fall	Women Spr	Minorities Fall	Minorities Spr
Full-time	65	61	39	34	26	27	12	11
Other Full-time	1	1	1	1	0	0	0	0
Deans, librarians, & others who teach	10	12	4	5	6	7	3	4
Part-time	51	45	39	29	11	16	20	8
Total	**127**	**119**	**83**	**69**	**43**	**50**	**35**	**23**

Curriculum

	Full-time	Part-time
Typical first-year section size	83	77
Is there typically a "small section" of the first-year class, other than Legal Writing, taught by full-time faculty	No	No
If yes, typical size offered last year		

# of classroom course titles beyond first-year curriculum		148
# of upper division courses, excluding seminars with an enrollment:	Under 25	140
	25–49	44
	50–74	11
	75–99	12
	100+	9

	Full-time	Part-time
# of seminars		23
# of seminar positions available		474
# of seminar positions filled	236	33
# of positions available in simulation courses		698
# of simulation positions filled	400	195
# of positions available in faculty supervised clinical courses		180
# of faculty supervised clinical positions filled	138	24
# involved in field placements	186	42
# involved in law journals	173	35
# involved in interschool competitions	94	15
# of credit hours required to graduate		87

JD Enrollment and Ethnicity

	Men #	Men %	Women #	Women %	Full-time #	Full-time %	Part-time #	Part-time %	1st-year #	1st-year %	Total #	Total %	JD Degs. Awd.
African Amer.	22	3.2	33	5.4	44	4.4	11	3.6	20	4.8	55	4.2	14
Amer. Indian	6	0.9	1	0.2	2	0.2	5	1.7	3	0.7	7	0.5	5
Asian Amer.	156	22.7	161	26.4	249	25.1	68	22.4	106	25.2	317	24.4	102
Mex. Amer.	29	4.2	39	6.4	55	5.5	13	4.3	23	5.5	68	5.2	29
Puerto Rican	1	0.1	3	0.5	4	0.4	0	0.0	3	0.7	4	0.3	1
Hispanic	26	3.8	28	4.6	48	4.8	6	2.0	15	3.6	54	4.2	13
Total Minority	240	34.9	265	43.5	402	40.4	103	34.0	170	40.5	505	38.9	164
For. Nation.	2	0.3	1	0.2	3	0.3	0	0.0	0	0.0	3	0.2	2
Caucasian	356	51.7	266	43.7	456	45.9	166	54.8	212	50.5	622	48.0	219
Unknown	90	13.1	77	12.6	133	13.4	34	11.2	38	9.0	167	12.9	34
Total	688	53.0	609	47.0	994	76.6	303	23.4	420	32.4	1297		419

Transfers

Transfers in	35
Transfers out	13

Tuition and Fees

	Resident	Nonresident
Full-time	$33,793	$33,793
Part-time	$22,676	$22,676

Living Expenses

Estimated living expenses for singles		
Living on campus	Living off campus	Living at home
N/A	$18,272	$10,198

Loyola Law School, Loyola Marymount University

ABA
Approved
Since
1935

GPA and LSAT Scores

	Total	Full-time	Part-time
# of apps	4,537	4,013	524
# of offers	1,377	1,248	129
# of matrics	423	352	71
75% GPA	3.58	3.58	3.58
Median GPA	3.41	3.41	3.41
25% GPA	3.16	3.15	3.21
75% LSAT	163	163	161
Median LSAT	160	161	159
25% LSAT	159	159	156

Grants and Scholarships (from prior year)

	Total #	Total %	Full-time #	Full-time %	Part-time #	Part-time %
Total # of students	1,319		994		325	
Total # receiving grants	244	18.5	219	22.0	25	7.7
Less than 1/2 tuition	26	2.0	25	2.5	1	0.3
Half to full tuition	79	6.0	62	6.2	17	5.2
Full tuition	0	0.0	0	0.0	0	0.0
More than full tuition	139	10.5	132	13.3	7	2.2
Median grant amount			$31,880		$16,750	

Informational and Library Resources

# of volumes and volume equivalents	584,527
# of titles	255,071
# of active serial subscriptions	7,351
Study seating capacity inside the library	549
# of full-time professional librarians	13
Hours per week library is open	108
# of open, wired connections available to students	700
# of networked computers available for use by students	199
# of simultaneous wireless users	1,000
Require computer?	No

JD Attrition (from prior year)

	Academic #	Other #	Total #	Total %
1st year	20	29	49	12.0
2nd year	4	6	10	2.5
3rd year	1	3	4	1.0
4th year	0	0	0	0.0

Employment (9 months after graduation)

	Total	Percentage
Employment status known	391	100.0
Employment status unknown	0	0.0
Employed	372	95.1
Pursuing graduate degrees	1	0.3
Unemployed seeking employment	4	1.0
Unemployed not seeking employment	4	1.0
Unemployed and studying for the bar	10	2.6

Type of Employment

# employed in law firms	230	61.8
# employed in business and industry	76	20.4
# employed in government	29	7.8
# employed in public interest	20	5.4
# employed as judicial clerks	10	2.7
# employed in academia	2	0.5

Geographic Location

# employed in state	344	92.5
# employed in foreign countries	0	0.0
# of states where employed	9	

Bar Passage Rates

Jurisdiction	California			New York		
Exam	Sum 05	Win 06	Total	Sum 05	Win 06	Total
# from school taking bar for the first time	335	45	380	6	5	11
School's pass rate for all first-time takers	75%	62%	73%	67%	40%	55%
State's pass rate for all first-time takers	64%	54%	62%	76%	61%	74%

Loyola Law School, Loyola Marymount University

919 Albany Street
Los Angeles, CA 90015
Phone: 213.736.1074; Fax: 213.736.6523
E-mail: admissions@lls.edu; Website: www.lls.edu

■ Law School and Campus

Loyola Law School was founded in 1920 and is one of California's largest law schools. Having graduated more than 13,000 men and women, Loyola has had a profound effect on the legal profession and on American history. Known best for producing many of our nation's most exciting and influential attorneys, Loyola instills in its graduates a deep commitment to public service and ethical practice while emphasizing the philosophical, analytical, and professional skills essential to the lawyering process.

The Law School, a division of Loyola Marymount University (LMU), includes 1,350 full-time day and part-time evening students, nearly 140 full-time and adjunct faculty, and 110 administrative and technical staff. Housed on a modern, innovative campus, including eight buildings, a spacious parking facility, green lawns, and athletic courts, Loyola encompasses an entire city block in downtown Los Angeles. The campus, designed by architect Frank Gehry, is both unique and inviting.

The William M. Rains Law Library is one of the largest private law libraries in the western United States, providing extensive research capabilities with a collection of over 550,000 volumes and the latest advances in information technology.

■ Juris Doctor

The Juris Doctor prepares students to be effective lawyers and judges in any jurisdiction in the United States. Loyola recognizes that a quality education must do more than simply prepare a student to file a lawsuit or draft a contract. The program is designed to teach students to think and reason critically. The faculty strives to instill in students a respect and appreciation for the law and a desire to improve the society in which we live. The Juris Doctor is offered in both a full-time, three-year day division and a part-time, four-year evening division.

■ Master of Laws

Loyola also offers two Master of Laws (LLM) degrees—one in Taxation and another in American Law and International Legal Practice. The LLM in Taxation degree distinguishes tax specialists by its advanced legal theory, tax policy, and scholarship. Law students can take advanced tax courses for double credit—counting toward both the Juris Doctor and the Tax LLM. The Master of Laws program in American Law and International Legal Practice provides American and international law school graduates with the unique opportunity to earn an American LLM from Loyola while attending the University of Bologna, a premiere European university.

■ JD/ MBA and International JD/MBA

Loyola Law School and the Graduate Program of the College of Business Administration of Loyola Marymount University offer a dual-degree program in law and business. Graduates of the program receive the Juris Doctor degree (JD) and the Master of Business Administration (MBA). The International Master of Business Administration program may also be completed concurrently with the Law School curriculum. A Graduate Certificate in International Business will be awarded with the MBA.

The dual-degree program provides for the achievement of both degrees in four years instead of the five normally required to complete the degree programs separately. The program is only open to full-time day students. Students may receive up to 12 units of business classes toward the 87 units required to earn a JD, and may be allowed to count up to 12 units of law classes toward the 54 units required to earn an MBA.

Applicants must apply and be accepted separately to the Law School and the MBA program. Applicants must also apply and be accepted to the JD/MBA program. Applications for the MBA and JD/MBA program may be submitted in the same year as the Law School application or during the first year of Law School. Interested applicants should contact the LMU College of Business Administration to request an application for the MBA program and the Law School Admissions Office to request an application for the JD/MBA program.

■ Faculty

The faculty is composed of scholars who publish innovative theories, influencing the development and direction of the legal profession. They draft hundreds of scholarly articles and books, advise law firms and agencies on recent developments, and lecture at universities around the world. They also include seasoned attorneys with extensive and varied practice experience as Supreme Court clerks, public interest lawyers, agency chiefs, and law firm partners. But most importantly, the Loyola faculty are exceptional teachers who maintain an open-door policy to encourage free and continuous interaction with their students.

■ Curriculum

The curriculum is designed to provide the knowledge and skills that will enable students to become excellent practicing lawyers. The curriculum integrates traditional instruction in legal doctrine and theory with a special commitment to the development of legal skills.

The Law School has a wide variety of course offerings and seminars in business/corporate law, commercial law, constitutional and civil rights law, criminal law, environmental law, entertainment/sports law, intellectual property law, international law, jurisprudence, law and social policy, litigation and legal skills, personal injury law, property law, public interest law, and taxation law.

■ Innovative Programs

Loyola demonstrates its commitment to public service by requiring all students to donate 40 hours to working in the **public interest** sector. The **Public Interest Law Department** coordinates public interest activities, counsels students about law practice and fellowships, and administers the five public service programs. The **Entertainment Law Practicum** provides students with an opportunity to get hands-on experience through field placements at television networks, major movie studios, record companies, talent agencies, and entertainment law firms. **International Programs** allow upper-division students to study abroad in Costa Rica, China, and Italy. The **Center for Ethical Lawyering** is one of Loyola's greatest strengths, featuring specialized training courses and externships designed to prepare students for the courtroom. Loyola students have won numerous international and national moot court competitions in recent years.

■ Career Services

The Office of Career Services offers a wealth of services, programs, and resources to students and alumni. A large professional staff counsels and assists students and graduates in the job development process. Hundreds of national, international, and regional employers recruit from Loyola annually. Graduates are employed by the nation's most prestigious private and public legal organizations.

■ Admission/Financial Aid/Scholarships

Applications for admission are accepted on a rolling basis. Deadlines are February 2 for the day program and April 13 for the evening program. Early applicants have greater prospects for gaining admission and receiving scholarship awards. Three different types of scholarships are awarded: merit, diversity/merit, and public interest/merit. Financial aid to cover education and personal expenses is available to all qualifying applicants.

Applicant Profile

Loyola Law School, Loyola Marymount University
This grid includes only applicants who earned 120–180 LSAT scores under standard administrations.

LSAT Score	3.75 +		3.50–3.74		3.25–3.49		3.00–3.24		2.75–2.99		2.50–2.74		2.25–2.49		2.00–2.24		Below 2.00		No GPA		Total	
	Apps	Adm	Apps	Adm	Apps	Adm	Apps	Adm	Apps	Adm	Apps	Adm	Apps	Adm	Apps	Adm	Apps	Adm	Apps	Adm	Apps	Adm
175–180	2	2	1	1	2	2	0	0	2	2	1	0	0	0	0	0	0	0	0	0	8	7
170–174	11	10	10	9	9	8	7	6	7	6	4	0	0	0	1	0	0	0	0	0	49	39
165–169	63	61	81	67	64	62	65	49	32	15	18	11	8	2	2	0	0	0	10	3	333	267
160–164	131	121	236	205	197	165	141	88	83	48	40	17	17	4	5	0	0	0	10	3	860	651
155–159	171	50	333	103	363	92	237	39	135	14	68	11	16	1	8	0	1	0	7	0	1339	310
150–154	74	9	227	24	293	37	236	16	144	4	65	0	25	0	5	0	1	0	11	0	1081	90
145–149	31	0	98	1	130	1	139	1	88	0	43	0	19	0	5	0	2	0	15	0	570	3
140–144	10	0	36	0	54	0	55	0	54	0	33	0	18	0	5	0	2	0	6	0	273	0
135–139	3	0	4	0	10	0	21	0	16	0	16	0	3	0	4	0	0	0	4	0	81	0
130–134	1	0	0	0	2	0	7	0	11	0	8	0	4	0	1	0	2	0	1	0	37	0
125–129	0	0	0	0	0	0	0	0	1	0	1	0	0	0	0	0	0	0	1	0	3	0
120–124	0	0	0	0	0	0	0	0	0	0	0	0	0	0	1	0	0	0	0	0	1	0
Total	497	253	1026	410	1124	367	908	199	573	89	297	39	110	7	37	0	8	0	55	3	4635	1367

Apps = Number of Applicants
Adm = Number Admitted
Represents 99% of applicant pool.

Loyola University Chicago School of Law

25 East Pearson Street, Suite 1440
Chicago, IL 60611
Phone: 312.915.7170, 800.545.5744; Fax: 312.915.7906
E-mail: law-admissions@luc.edu; Website: www.luc.edu/law

ABA
Approved
Since
1925

The Basics

Type of school	Private
Term	Semester
Application deadline	4/1
Application fee	$50
Financial aid deadline	3/1
Can first year start other than fall?	No
Student to faculty ratio	15.5 to 1
Does the university offer:	
housing restricted to law students?	Yes
graduate housing for which law students are eligible?	Yes

Faculty and Administrators

	Total		Men		Women		Minorities	
	Fall	Spr	Fall	Spr	Fall	Spr	Fall	Spr
Full-time	41	40	26	25	15	15	6	7
Other Full-time	2	2	2	2	0	0	0	0
Deans, librarians, & others who teach	2	2	2	2	0	0	0	0
Part-time	97	86	44	50	53	36	5	5
Total	142	130	74	79	68	51	11	12

Curriculum

	Full-time	Part-time
Typical first-year section size	63	76
Is there typically a "small section" of the first-year class, other than Legal Writing, taught by full-time faculty	No	No
If yes, typical size offered last year		
# of classroom course titles beyond first-year curriculum	138	

# of upper division courses, excluding seminars with an enrollment:		
Under 25	106	
25–49	28	
50–74	19	
75–99	1	
100+	0	

	Full-time	Part-time
# of seminars	19	
# of seminar positions available	427	
# of seminar positions filled	220	93
# of positions available in simulation courses	1,338	
# of simulation positions filled	794	391
# of positions available in faculty supervised clinical courses	123	
# of faculty supervised clinical positions filled	75	37
# involved in field placements	78	33
# involved in law journals	280	121
# involved in interschool competitions	68	34
# of credit hours required to graduate	86	

JD Enrollment and Ethnicity

	Men #	Men %	Women #	Women %	Full-time #	Full-time %	Part-time #	Part-time %	1st-year #	1st-year %	Total #	Total %	JD Degs. Awd.
African Amer.	14	3.3	25	5.7	29	4.8	10	4.0	17	5.7	39	4.5	8
Amer. Indian	1	0.2	1	0.2	0	0.0	2	0.8	1	0.3	2	0.2	0
Asian Amer.	23	5.5	39	8.8	43	7.1	19	7.5	17	5.7	62	7.2	30
Mex. Amer.	11	2.6	6	1.4	14	2.3	3	1.2	9	3.0	17	2.0	5
Puerto Rican	0	0.0	1	0.2	1	0.2	0	0.0	0	0.0	1	0.1	1
Hispanic	7	1.7	9	2.0	12	2.0	4	1.6	6	2.0	16	1.9	7
Total Minority	56	13.4	81	18.4	99	16.3	38	15.1	50	16.8	137	15.9	51
For. Nation.	5	1.2	7	1.6	6	1.0	6	2.4	7	2.3	12	1.4	7
Caucasian	322	77.0	316	71.7	450	74.1	188	74.6	227	76.2	638	74.3	185
Unknown	35	8.4	37	8.4	52	8.6	20	7.9	14	4.7	72	8.4	21
Total	418	48.7	441	51.3	607	70.7	252	29.3	298	34.7	859		264

Transfers

Transfers in	11
Transfers out	11

Tuition and Fees

	Resident	Nonresident
Full-time	$32,030	$32,030
Part-time	$24,100	$24,100

Living Expenses

Estimated living expenses for singles		
Living on campus	Living off campus	Living at home
$18,940	$18,940	$18,940

Loyola University Chicago School of Law

*ABA
Approved
Since
1925*

GPA and LSAT Scores

	Total	Full-time	Part-time
# of apps	4,465	3,858	607
# of offers	979	773	206
# of matrics	295	191	104
75% GPA	3.63	3.66	3.52
Median GPA	3.41	3.49	3.22
25% GPA	3.12	3.21	2.94
75% LSAT	163	164	158
Median LSAT	161	162	155
25% LSAT	156	160	153

Grants and Scholarships (from prior year)

	Total #	Total %	Full-time #	Full-time %	Part-time #	Part-time %
Total # of students	843		602		241	
Total # receiving grants	483	57.3	393	65.3	90	37.3
Less than 1/2 tuition	426	50.5	342	56.8	84	34.9
Half to full tuition	54	6.4	48	8.0	6	2.5
Full tuition	3	0.4	3	0.5	0	0.0
More than full tuition	0	0.0	0	0.0	0	0.0
Median grant amount			$7,500		$4,000	

Informational and Library Resources

# of volumes and volume equivalents	404,136
# of titles	61,640
# of active serial subscriptions	905
Study seating capacity inside the library	456
# of full-time professional librarians	8
Hours per week library is open	101
# of open, wired connections available to students	328
# of networked computers available for use by students	64
# of simultaneous wireless users	660
Require computer?	No

JD Attrition (from prior year)

	Academic #	Other #	Total #	Total %
1st year	0	0	0	0.0
2nd year	0	13	13	4.7
3rd year	0	0	0	0.0
4th year	0	0	0	0.0

Employment (9 months after graduation)

	Total	Percentage
Employment status known	281	99.3
Employment status unknown	2	0.7
Employed	255	90.7
Pursuing graduate degrees	5	1.8
Unemployed seeking employment	7	2.5
Unemployed not seeking employment	9	3.2
Unemployed and studying for the bar	5	1.8
Type of Employment		
# employed in law firms	149	58.4
# employed in business and industry	37	14.5
# employed in government	41	16.1
# employed in public interest	9	3.5
# employed as judicial clerks	15	5.9
# employed in academia	4	1.6
Geographic Location		
# employed in state	209	82.0
# employed in foreign countries	0	0.0
# of states where employed		19

Bar Passage Rates

Jurisdiction	Illinois		
Exam	Sum 05	Win 06	Total
# from school taking bar for the first time	208	40	248
School's pass rate for all first-time takers	91%	78%	89%
State's pass rate for all first-time takers	86%	83%	85%

Loyola University Chicago School of Law

25 East Pearson Street, Suite 1440
Chicago, IL 60611
Phone: 312.915.7170, 800.545.5744; Fax: 312.915.7906
E-mail: law-admissions@luc.edu; Website: www.luc.edu/law

■ Introduction

The School of Law is located on the Water Tower campus of
the university, a few blocks north of the Chicago Loop. This
campus adjoins Michigan Avenue at the historical Water Tower,
a Chicago landmark, in approximately the center of the
renowned Magnificent Mile, a commercial center over which
the John Hancock Center towers. This location provides ready
access to the state and federal courts and to the offices of most
other institutions of federal, state, and local government, as
well as the cultural centers of Chicago. The school is a member
of the AALS and is approved by the ABA.

■ Library and Facilities

The School of Law is located at Loyola University Chicago's
downtown campus. Renamed the Loyola Law Center, the
university building at 25 East Pearson Street provides Loyola's
law students with a modern and enhanced learning environment.
The School of Law library is located on floors 3–5 of the Law
Center. More than 400,000 volumes enhance Loyola's broad-based
law curriculum and support the varied research needs of students
and faculty. Offering custom-designed furnishings and custom
carrels, the 43,900-square-foot facility creates a comfortable and
accommodating atmosphere for users. The library is open 100
hours each week, with expanded hours during examination
periods. The law library is fully staffed with professional
librarians and paraprofessionals to assist students and faculty.

Across the street from the Law Center is a new 25-story, 600-bed
residence hall. Baumhart Hall, which opened in the fall of 2006, is
one of several new and renovated facilities at Loyola's dynamic
Water Tower campus. This new structure enables graduate,
professional, and undergraduate student residents to experience
contemporary living in fully furnished apartments with
spectacular city views in the heart of the city. Amenities include a
24-hour security staff, a food court and late-night café, a
state-of-the-art fitness center with individual televisions on cardio
machines, wireless access in apartment bedrooms and public
areas, a laundry room equipped with "smart system" washers
and dryers that enable residents to monitor usage and track
laundry from their apartments, and rent includes all utilities, heat
and air-conditioning, cable, and high-speed Internet access.

■ Foreign Study Programs

Since 1983, the School of Law has offered a program of
international and comparative law courses at the Rome Center
for Liberal Arts, the university's campus in Rome, Italy. Each
summer, for approximately five weeks, law students from the
United States and elsewhere can take one or more of the courses
offered in Rome by members of the full-time Loyola law faculty.

In 1997, the law school added a program in Strasbourg,
France, at the European Court of Human Rights in the Council
of Europe, and at NATO and the Commission of the European
Union in Brussels, Belgium. Coursework is completed through
Loyola's summer program in Oxford, England.

In 1989, Loyola inaugurated its London Comparative
Advocacy Program in which students travel to London for
approximately 15 days to become immersed in the world of the
British barrister.

In spring 2003, Loyola inaugurated an immersion program
at Universidad Alberto Hurtado, a Jesuit law school in
Santiago, Chile.

■ Special Opportunities

The School of Law has dual-degree programs with the School
of Social Work's graduate program in the Department of Political
Science, and the Graduate School of Business. Automatic
acceptance is granted to the MA in Political Science for
candidates admitted to the law school. Provisional admission
to the MBA program is granted based upon LSAT score and law
school grades. The multidegree programs are structured to allow
completion after four years. Loyola offers accelerated LLM
programs in health law, child and family law, and taxation to
JD students who fulfill program requirements. Recognizing the
increasing need for specialization in legal education and
practice, the school offers specialized curricula in five key areas:
International Law and Practice, Health Law, Child and Family
Law, Advocacy, and Tax Law.

■ Clinical Legal Education

For students, faculty, and alumni, Loyola's five legal clinics
represent a valuable bridge between theory and practice,
classroom and career. Through the clinics, the School of Law
offers service to others in a way that gives them dignity while
providing students with practical legal experience. In spring
2003, the law school celebrated the 20th anniversary of its
clinical program that began with the founding of its Community
Law Center, followed in later years by the Federal Tax, Child
and Family Law, Business Law Center, and Elder Law Clinics.

■ Child and Family Law Center

The Loyola ChildLaw Center was created in 1993 to prepare
law students to represent abused and neglected children. The
center is the first of its kind at any American law school; it was
the recipient of the National Association of Counsel for Children
1996 Outstanding Legal Advocacy Award; and it draws on the
full resources of Loyola University, including the schools of
medicine, social work, and education. The program includes an
LLM degree and a master's degree program for nonlawyers.

The law school and Teach for America have entered into a
partnership. TFA corps members who are interested in using
their legal education to advocate for children's legal interests
and well-being will receive an application fee waiver and
matching AmeriCorps Awards.

Annually, eight Child and Family Law Fellows are selected
from the entering law class. One fellowship is reserved for a
TFA corps member. Each fellow receives financial support.
At the conclusion of the three-year JD program, students are
trained thoroughly to serve as skilled litigators and advocates
for children.

■ Institute for Health Law

The Beazley Institute for Health Law was created in 1984 in
recognition of the need for an academic forum to study the
field of health law and to act as a vehicle to foster dialogue

between the law and the health sciences. Through the institute, the law school offers an SJD in Health Law and Policy and an LLM in Health Law. In addition, it offers the first Master of Jurisprudence (MJ) in Health Law and Doctor of Law (DLaw) in Health Law and Policy, providing health care professionals with an intensive overview in health law. More than two dozen health law classes are offered in the law school.

■ Business Law Center

The Business Law Center was created in 1996 to further enhance Loyola's corporate law curriculum by offering more specialized and practical skills classes to its students. The center offers corporate externships for law students, sponsors continuing education programs for both corporate attorneys and employees, and includes a legal clinic for small business.

■ Institute for Consumer Antitrust Studies

The Institute for Consumer Antitrust Studies is an independent, academically based institute designed to explore the effect of antitrust and consumer law enforcement on the individual consumer and the general public. The institute was founded by a grant from the US District Court for the Northern District of Illinois and is supported by Loyola and private donors.

■ Advocacy

Loyola prepares its students for careers of leadership at the bar and on the bench. For nearly 100 years, Loyola's tradition of educating and training top litigators has produced some of the country's most accomplished and recognized trial attorneys and judges. The advocacy program comprises a second-year required course in advocacy, courses in beginning and advanced trial advocacy, numerous moot court competitions, the Corboy Fellowship Program in Trial Advocacy for mock trial competitions, and a wide variety of litigation-related courses. A certificate in advocacy is available for students who complete a menu of advocacy courses.

Symbolic of our advocacy success is our selection by the National Institute for Trial Advocacy as the site for two of its largest advocacy training programs, the Midwest Regional Trial Advocacy Program and the Midwest Regional Deposition Training Program.

■ Admission

Factors other than LSAT scores and college grades are considered. Such factors include work experience, personal goals, specialized education, and other evidence of ability to contribute invaluable insight to law classes.

■ Career Services

The Career Resources Office assists students and alumni with career planning and employment selection.

A year-round, on-campus employer interview and recruitment program provides employment opportunities.

Seminars by practicing attorneys and alumni, résumé preparation, interviewing techniques, individual counseling, and job-search strategies are just some of the many programs administered by the Career Resources Office.

The School of Law is a member of NALP.

■ Cocurricular Activities

Students are encouraged to participate in cocurricular activities. There are six student-edited publications, including the *Annals of Health Law, Children's Legal Rights Journal, Consumer Law Review, International Law Review, Loyola University Chicago Law Journal,* and *Public Interest Law Reporter.* Students compete in more than 10 moot court and mock trial national and international competitions. All students are members of the Loyola Student Bar Association, the principal instrument of student government. There are over 25 student organizations and groups devoted to legal practice, ethnic groups, or law student chapters of professional bar associations.

Applicant Profile

Loyola University Chicago School of Law
This grid includes only applicants who earned 120–180 LSAT scores under standard administrations.

LSAT Score	GPA																
	3.75 +		3.50–3.74		3.25–3.49		3.00–3.24		2.50–2.99		2.00–2.49		Below 2.00		No GPA		Total	
	Apps	Adm	Apps	Adm	Apps	Adm	Apps	Adm	Apps	Adm	Apps	Adm	Apps	Adm	Apps	Adm	Apps	Adm
165–180	34	34	46	45	48	46	38	30	37	17	9	4	1	1	1	1	214	178
160–164	130	112	211	169	185	124	143	69	101	21	20	4	0	0	3	1	793	500
155–159	206	31	316	43	346	41	259	37	154	24	31	6	2	0	9	0	1323	182
145–154	158	15	334	24	406	27	377	27	308	17	64	2	5	0	16	0	1668	112
120–144	20	1	41	0	67	0	100	0	126	0	57	0	5	0	13	1	429	2
Total	548	193	948	281	1052	238	917	163	726	79	181	16	13	1	42	3	4427	974

Apps = Number of Applicants
Adm = Number Admitted
Reflects 99% of the total applicant pool.

Loyola University New Orleans College of Law

7214 St. Charles Avenue, Box 904
New Orleans, LA 70118
Phone: 504.861.5575; Fax: 504.861.5772
E-mail: ladmit@loyno.edu; Website: law.loyno.edu

ABA
Approved
Since
1931

The Basics

Type of school	Private
Term	Semester
Application deadline	
Application fee	$40
Financial aid deadline	
Can first year start other than fall?	No
Student to faculty ratio	18.3 to 1
Does the university offer:	
housing restricted to law students?	Yes
graduate housing for which law students are eligible?	Yes

Faculty and Administrators

	Total		Men		Women		Minorities	
	Fall	Spr	Fall	Spr	Fall	Spr	Fall	Spr
Full-time	34	30	23	20	11	10	7	6
Other Full-time	8	8	3	5	5	3	4	2
Deans, librarians, & others who teach	4	4	4	4	0	0	0	0
Part-time	17	28	14	23	3	5	1	2
Total	63	70	44	52	19	18	12	10

Curriculum

	Full-time	Part-time
Typical first-year section size	80	19
Is there typically a "small section" of the first-year class, other than Legal Writing, taught by full-time faculty	No	No
If yes, typical size offered last year		
# of classroom course titles beyond first-year curriculum	76	

# of upper division courses, excluding seminars with an enrollment:		
Under 25	42	
25–49	35	
50–74	10	
75–99	5	
100+	1	

	Full-time	Part-time
# of seminars	7	
# of seminar positions available	146	
# of seminar positions filled	104	15
# of positions available in simulation courses	47	
# of simulation positions filled	35	8
# of positions available in faculty supervised clinical courses	52	
# of faculty supervised clinical positions filled	52	0
# involved in field placements	8	0
# involved in law journals	64	7
# involved in interschool competitions	18	1
# of credit hours required to graduate	90	

JD Enrollment and Ethnicity

	Men		Women		Full-time		Part-time		1st-year		Total		JD Degs. Awd.
	#	%	#	%	#	%	#	%	#	%	#	%	
African Amer.	32	8.6	66	15.6	81	12.4	17	11.9	37	12.4	98	12.3	17
Amer. Indian	3	0.8	4	0.9	5	0.8	2	1.4	3	1.0	7	0.9	2
Asian Amer.	12	3.2	23	5.4	33	5.1	2	1.4	14	4.7	35	4.4	8
Mex. Amer.	3	0.8	4	0.9	4	0.6	3	2.1	5	1.7	7	0.9	2
Puerto Rican	0	0.0	2	0.5	2	0.3	0	0.0	1	0.3	2	0.3	3
Hispanic	18	4.8	29	6.9	39	6.0	8	5.6	20	6.7	47	5.9	7
Total Minority	68	18.2	128	30.3	164	25.1	32	22.4	80	26.8	196	24.6	39
For. Nation.	3	0.8	3	0.7	6	0.9	0	0.0	2	0.7	6	0.8	0
Caucasian	267	71.6	265	62.6	428	65.5	104	72.7	195	65.2	532	66.8	146
Unknown	35	9.4	27	6.4	55	8.4	7	4.9	22	7.4	62	7.8	8
Total	373	46.9	423	53.1	653	82.0	143	18.0	299	37.6	796		193

Transfers

Transfers in	10
Transfers out	41

Tuition and Fees

	Resident	Nonresident
Full-time	$28,856	$28,856
Part-time	$19,466	$19,466

Living Expenses

Estimated living expenses for singles

Living on campus	Living off campus	Living at home
$14,366	$14,366	$8,000

Loyola University New Orleans College of Law

*ABA
Approved
Since
1931*

GPA and LSAT Scores

	Total	Full-time	Part-time
# of apps	1,387	1,267	120
# of offers	848	768	80
# of matrics	260	223	37
75% GPA	3.54	3.59	3.39
Median GPA	3.29	3.30	3.21
25% GPA	3.01	3.04	2.84
75% LSAT	155	155	155
Median LSAT	152	152	151
25% LSAT	150	150	148

Grants and Scholarships (from prior year)

	Total		Full-time		Part-time	
	#	%	#	%	#	%
Total # of students	662		567		95	
Total # receiving grants	312	47.1	277	48.9	35	36.8
Less than 1/2 tuition	180	27.2	147	25.9	33	34.7
Half to full tuition	118	17.8	116	20.5	2	2.1
Full tuition	6	0.9	6	1.1	0	0.0
More than full tuition	8	1.2	8	1.4	0	0.0
Median grant amount			$13,146		$3,000	

Informational and Library Resources

# of volumes and volume equivalents	364,642
# of titles	140,945
# of active serial subscriptions	3,813
Study seating capacity inside the library	448
# of full-time professional librarians	8
Hours per week library is open	107
# of open, wired connections available to students	61
# of networked computers available for use by students	77
# of simultaneous wireless users	0
Require computer?	No

JD Attrition (from prior year)

	Academic	Other	Total	
	#	#	#	%
1st year	1	21	22	10.2
2nd year	0	22	22	9.9
3rd year	0	3	3	1.5
4th year	0	0	0	0.0

Employment (9 months after graduation)

	Total	Percentage
Employment status known	264	100.0
Employment status unknown	0	0.0
Employed	241	91.3
Pursuing graduate degrees	11	4.2
Unemployed seeking employment	0	0.0
Unemployed not seeking employment	12	4.5
Unemployed and studying for the bar	0	0.0

Type of Employment

# employed in law firms	147	61.0
# employed in business and industry	29	12.0
# employed in government	36	14.9
# employed in public interest	7	2.9
# employed as judicial clerks	20	8.3
# employed in academia	2	0.8

Geographic Location

# employed in state	160	66.4
# employed in foreign countries	2	0.8
# of states where employed		23

Bar Passage Rates

Jurisdiction	Louisiana		
Exam	Sum 05	Win 06	Total
# from school taking bar for the first time	165	10	175
School's pass rate for all first-time takers	77%	90%	78%
State's pass rate for all first-time takers	73%	48%	70%

Loyola University New Orleans College of Law

7214 St. Charles Avenue, Box 904
New Orleans, LA 70118
Phone: 504.861.5575; Fax: 504.861.5772
E-mail: ladmit@loyno.edu; Website: law.loyno.edu

■ Introduction

Loyola University New Orleans survived Hurricane Katrina exceedingly well. The campus and its surrounding area suffered very little damage, thus allowing the school to reopen on the New Orleans campus with its spring 2006 semester as usual. Immediately following the hurricane, Loyola provided a forum for its first-year students to begin their education and for its upper-class students to stay on track for graduation by running the fall semester, including a full first-year curriculum, at the University of Houston Law Center.

Loyola New Orleans is a Catholic institution of higher learning in the Jesuit tradition. The College of Law was established in 1914, approved by the ABA in 1931, and has been a member of the AALS since 1934. The College of Law is committed to excellence in legal education in the tradition of its spiritual heritage, with the goal being wisdom, not mere technical competence. The law school welcomes all persons who strive for the truth and who are prepared to challenge all assumptions in light of this commitment.

■ Physical Facilities and Library

Loyola University has two campuses, both located approximately five miles from the historic French Quarter. The 20-acre main campus, in the heart of the uptown residential community, faces the nationally recognized Audubon Park and Zoo. The 4.2-acre Broadway campus is the home of the College of Law.

The law library's collection of 345,000 volumes and microform equivalents supports the curriculum and research needs of the students. In addition to conventional resources, the library has extensive computer facilities in place to access information outside its confines. The Online Catalog Library Center service permits the library to access a national bibliographic database of over 10 million publications. The law library houses remote-controlled viewing/listening rooms, a computerized legal research room, and two computer labs equipped with 59 personal computers on a network with access to the Internet, LexisNexis, Westlaw, e-mail, and other computer resources.

■ Curriculum and Special Programs

The curricula of Loyola New Orleans have been shaped by Louisiana's unique role as the only state in the union that has a legal system based on significant elements of both the civil law and common law traditions. The civil law was imported into Louisiana during the eighteenth century, when it was first a colony of France, and later, Spain. As a result of Louisiana's unique legal heritage, Loyola New Orleans has developed three separate curricula: two full-time divisions—civil law and common law; and one part-time civil law division. It is important to note that the JD degree offered by Loyola New Orleans will allow a student to sit for the bar in any of the 50 states, without regard for the curriculum chosen. Loyola offers a Certificate in Common Law Studies and a Certificate in Civil Law Studies for students who wish to acquire a foundation in both disciplines. Full-time students are required to be in residence for a minimum of six full semesters. The normal time frame for part-time students is eight semesters and one summer session.

Practical Lawyering Skills Program—Loyola has one of the most unique and far-reaching Professional Lawyering Skills Programs in the country. Recognizing hands-on, learn-by-doing opportunities that develop the future practitioner's skills to be as important as traditional academic studies, the curriculum incorporates specialized courses and the expertise of attorneys and judges. Currently, over 100 members of the bench and bar teach in the skills curriculum. Each student must accumulate a number of lawyering-skills points in order to graduate.

International Law Specialty—Loyola has founded summer sessions in four continents and six countries, established ties with a number of important foreign law schools, and sent its professors to teach or lecture at law schools in more than a dozen foreign countries. Courses are taught in special five-week summer-abroad sessions in Mexico and Eastern Europe (Russia, Hungary, and Austria). There are also two- and three-week sessions offered each summer in Brazil or Costa Rica. Additionally, students may obtain a Certificate in International Legal Studies.

Environmental Law Specialty—Loyola recently received a $2 million grant to establish a faculty chair for environmental law. The nationally renowned scholar in environmental law has created a Certificate in Environmental Law, which is part of the Loyola Center for Environmental Law and Land Use. The center was created to address legal issues relative to economic development, protection of the environment, and the public's role in environmental policy issues.

Other Specialties at Loyola—Loyola's other major area of specialization is Public Interest Law. Areas of significant emphasis also include Corporate, Maritime, and Tax Law.

Clinical Education—The Law Clinic is a vital component of the law school. Students chosen to participate in the senior-year program will be assigned cases, both civil and criminal, and will be expected to prepare them for trial prior to actually participating in the trial process. The areas of law practiced in the clinic are criminal (both prosecution and defense), immigration, family law, civil rights, and landlord/tenant. Additionally, two new supervising attorneys have joined the clinical faculty to address legal issues stemming from Hurricane Katrina. Upper-division students also have an opportunity to serve as judicial clerks in the federal extern program, sponsored in conjunction with the US District Court for the Eastern District of Louisiana.

Joint-degree Programs—Loyola offers three combined degrees: JD/Master of Business Administration, JD/Master of Public Administration, and JD/Master of Urban and Regional Planning. The last two programs are offered in conjunction with the University of New Orleans College of Urban and Public Affairs. Each program is reduced by nine semester hours because each program accepts nine semester hours from the other program as part of its requirements. Upon completion of the program, the student will be awarded two separate degrees.

■ Scholarly Publications and Student Activities

The *Loyola Law Review* is published by a student editorial board and includes student work and articles written by specialists from the practicing bar and academic community. Staff membership is based on scholarship and interest in legal writing.

The *Law Journal of Public Interest Law* is devoted to issues faced by the poor, children, the elderly, and all others who are unable to afford legal representation.

The *Loyola Intellectual Property and High Technology Law Annual* is a scholarly publication focusing on current legal issues in patents, copyrights, trademarks, and technology law.

The *Loyola Maritime Law Journal* provides an avenue for research and writing in the field of maritime law. Staff membership is based on scholarship.

The Moot Court Board, selected from prior years' competitions, is responsible for the Moot Court Program. Teams are entered each year in competitions. Loyola teams have an impressive winning record in a wide variety of national and international competitions.

There are a number of student organizations, including three legal fraternities. Other organizations include the Environmental Law Society, Sports and Entertainment Law Society, St. Thomas More Law Club, and the Association of Trial Lawyers of America.

■ Admission

The law school begins processing applications for admission on September 1 each year. The first decision letters are generally released in December. The admission decision is based on an initial evaluation of a combination of the LSAT score and the undergraduate cumulative grade-point average. Additionally, the undergraduate institution attended, the undergraduate major, and any grade trends will be taken into consideration. Also included in the evaluation will be letters of recommendation, résumés, and a personal statement from the applicant, all of which may present a more illuminating portrait of the applicant's skills and accomplishments. Competition for acceptance to the law school is high, thus all information provided is used to make the final admission decision.

■ Career Services

The College of Law Career Services Office offers a variety of services to both students and alumni. The office maintains and operates a career-planning center, assists students in preparing résumés, videotapes mock interviews, and conducts seminars on career planning, employment opportunities, and interviewing techniques. The office actively solicits job opportunities for summer and school-term clerkships, as well as employment options for each year's graduating class.

Applicant Profile

Loyola University New Orleans College of Law
This grid includes only applicants who earned 120–180 LSAT scores under standard administrations.

LSAT Score	GPA								
	3.75 +	3.50–3.74	3.25–3.49	3.00–3.24	2.75–2.99	2.50–2.74	2.25–2.49	2.00–2.24	Below 2.00
175–180									
170–174									
165–169									
160–164									
155–159									
150–154									
145–149									
140–144									
135–139									
130–134									
125–129									
120–124									

■ Excellent   ■ Possible   □ Unlikely

The College of Law considers many factors beyond LSAT score and GPA. This chart should be used only as a general guide.

University of Maine School of Law

246 Deering Avenue
Portland, ME 04102
Phone: 207.780.4355
E-mail: mainelaw@usm.maine.edu; Website: mainelaw.maine.edu

ABA
Approved
Since
1962

The Basics

Type of school	Public
Term	Semester
Application deadline	3/1
Application fee	$50
Financial aid deadline	2/15
Can first year start other than fall?	No
Student to faculty ratio	16.5 to 1
Does the university offer:	
housing restricted to law students?	No
graduate housing for which law students are eligible?	Yes

Curriculum

	Full-time	Part-time
Typical first-year section size	73	0
Is there typically a "small section" of the first-year class, other than Legal Writing, taught by full-time faculty	Yes	No
If yes, typical size offered last year	36	
# of classroom course titles beyond first-year curriculum		67
# of upper division courses, excluding seminars with an enrollment: Under 25		52
25–49		15
50–74		14
75–99		4
100+		0
# of seminars		15
# of seminar positions available		252
# of seminar positions filled	153	0
# of positions available in simulation courses	201	
# of simulation positions filled	150	0
# of positions available in faculty supervised clinical courses		40
# of faculty supervised clinical positions filled	40	0
# involved in field placements	21	0
# involved in law journals	46	0
# involved in interschool competitions	18	0
# of credit hours required to graduate		90

Faculty and Administrators

	Total		Men		Women		Minorities	
	Fall	Spr	Fall	Spr	Fall	Spr	Fall	Spr
Full-time	13	13	7	9	6	4	0	0
Other Full-time	3	3	1	1	2	2	0	0
Deans, librarians, & others who teach	6	5	3	2	3	3	0	0
Part-time	13	16	12	12	1	4	0	1
Total	35	37	23	24	12	13	0	1

JD Enrollment and Ethnicity

	Men		Women		Full-time		Part-time		1st-year		Total		JD Degs. Awd.
	#	%	#	%	#	%	#	%	#	%	#	%	
African Amer.	0	0.0	3	2.1	3	1.2	0	0.0	0	0.0	3	1.1	2
Amer. Indian	0	0.0	0	0.0	0	0.0	0	0.0	0	0.0	0	0.0	0
Asian Amer.	3	2.5	4	2.9	7	2.7	0	0.0	2	2.0	7	2.7	6
Mex. Amer.	0	0.0	0	0.0	0	0.0	0	0.0	0	0.0	0	0.0	0
Puerto Rican	1	0.8	0	0.0	1	0.4	0	0.0	0	0.0	1	0.4	0
Hispanic	0	0.0	0	0.0	0	0.0	0	0.0	0	0.0	0	0.0	0
Total Minority	4	3.3	7	5.0	11	4.2	0	0.0	2	2.0	11	4.2	8
For. Nation.	0	0.0	0	0.0	0	0.0	0	0.0	0	0.0	0	0.0	0
Caucasian	118	96.7	133	95.0	248	95.8	3	100.0	97	99.0	251	95.8	84
Unknown	0	0.0	0	0.0	0	0.0	0	0.0	0	0.0	0	0.0	4
Total	122	46.6	140	53.4	259	98.9	3	1.1	98	37.4	262		96

Transfers

Transfers in	4
Transfers out	1

Tuition and Fees

	Resident	Nonresident
Full-time	$17,215	$26,905
Part-time	$0	$0

Living Expenses

Estimated living expenses for singles

Living on campus	Living off campus	Living at home
$11,671	$11,671	$6,355

University of Maine School of Law

ABA
Approved
Since
1962

GPA and LSAT Scores

	Total	Full-time	Part-time
# of apps	760	760	0
# of offers	325	325	0
# of matrics	101	101	0
75% GPA	3.65	3.65	0.00
Median GPA	3.34	3.34	0.00
25% GPA	3.14	3.14	0.00
75% LSAT	158	158	0
Median LSAT	155	155	0
25% LSAT	153	153	0

Grants and Scholarships (from prior year)

	Total #	Total %	Full-time #	Full-time %	Part-time #	Part-time %
Total # of students	254		249		5	
Total # receiving grants	128	50.4	128	51.4	0	0.0
Less than 1/2 tuition	115	45.3	115	46.2	0	0.0
Half to full tuition	8	3.1	8	3.2	0	0.0
Full tuition	0	0.0	0	0.0	0	0.0
More than full tuition	5	2.0	5	2.0	0	0.0
Median grant amount			$3,300		$0	

Informational and Library Resources

# of volumes and volume equivalents	327,678
# of titles	75,297
# of active serial subscriptions	2,871
Study seating capacity inside the library	209
# of full-time professional librarians	7
Hours per week library is open	97
# of open, wired connections available to students	9
# of networked computers available for use by students	23
# of simultaneous wireless users	300
Require computer?	No

JD Attrition (from prior year)

	Academic #	Other #	Total #	Total %
1st year	0	4	4	5.6
2nd year	1	1	2	2.3
3rd year	0	0	0	0.0
4th year	0	0	0	0.0

Employment (9 months after graduation)

	Total	Percentage
Employment status known	93	96.9
Employment status unknown	3	3.1
Employed	82	88.2
Pursuing graduate degrees	5	5.4
Unemployed seeking employment	2	2.2
Unemployed not seeking employment	0	0.0
Unemployed and studying for the bar	4	4.3

Type of Employment

# employed in law firms	39	47.6
# employed in business and industry	16	19.5
# employed in government	8	9.8
# employed in public interest	9	11.0
# employed as judicial clerks	10	12.2
# employed in academia	0	0.0

Geographic Location

# employed in state	58	70.7
# employed in foreign countries	0	0.0
# of states where employed	11	

Bar Passage Rates

Jurisdiction	Maine		
Exam	Sum 05	Win 06	Total
# from school taking bar for the first time	62	9	71
School's pass rate for all first-time takers	84%	78%	83%
State's pass rate for all first-time takers	82%	75%	80%

University of Maine School of Law

246 Deering Avenue
Portland, ME 04102
Phone: 207.780.4355
E-mail: mainelaw@usm.maine.edu; Website: mainelaw.maine.edu

■ Introduction

Maine Law is a wonderful, distinctive place to study law. Students study law in a supportive and personalized environment and are prepared for success in today's global economy.

Maine Law holds a pivotal place in state and regional affairs and is a destination point for students, scholars, and civic leaders from near and far. The state's only law school, and one of the smallest in the nation, Maine Law fosters educational and scholarly excellence, professionalism, and public service through a close community of faculty members and students. Our location in the vibrant coastal city of Portland, Maine—the largest city in the state and two hours north of Boston—allows students to benefit from a multitude of hands-on training opportunities offered through clinical programs, externships, community service projects, and employment. We have a tradition of training remarkably distinguished graduates—governors, federal and state judges, prominent lawyers, and civic leaders—who remain close to the law school. We are the law school of the University of Maine System and an administrative unit of the University of Southern Maine (USM).

■ Location

The law school is located in Portland, one of the most livable cities in the US, and the largest city in Maine. It has the charm of a small town with the cultural activities of a large city. Opportunities to participate in year-round outdoor activities are abundant.

■ Faculty

Faculty members are well-regarded for their commitment to teaching and for their accessibility to students. They come from a variety of backgrounds and have extensive experience in private practice and government service. They make significant contributions to legislative, judicial, and professional bodies; community organizations; and in the courtroom. Their research spans matters of state, national, and international interest and examines topics as varied as international treaty practice, Maine tort law, coastal zone management, federal tax elections, constitutional controls over the military, intellectual property, and commercial practice.

■ Curriculum

Maine Law offers a broad-based curriculum that helps prepare students for practice in all states. The school's strengths are in business and commercial law, environmental and marine law, international law, intellectual property, clinical training, and trial advocacy. Ninety credit hours are required for graduation.

The first-year curriculum is a prescribed program of courses that allows students to develop legal analytical skills and the ability to read and understand cases and statutory material. The program provides the foundation course in legal research and writing, including a moot court experience. Most courses after the first year are elective. All students are required to complete Professional Responsibility, Constitutional Law II, and a perspective course—one that places the law in a broader philosophical, historical, or comparative context. Each student must fulfill the Independent Writing Requirement through a substantial research paper under the direction of a member of the faculty, or through membership on the *Maine Law Review* or *Ocean and Coastal Law Journal*. Maine Law's practical skills program includes courses in trial practice, negotiation, and alternative dispute resolution. The course in advanced trial advocacy has fielded award-winning teams.

■ Special Programs

Cumberland Legal Aid Clinic—Third-year students represent clients under faculty supervision in this approved legal assistance office. Students work on family law and domestic matters, criminal, consumer, housing, employment, and probate issues at both the trial and appellate levels. A Prisoner Assistance Clinic provides representation for prisoners in a variety of civil matters. All clinical courses coordinate with the state's domestic violence project.

Intellectual Property Law Clinic—Students have the rare opportunity to work with clients involved with developing new products and businesses. Under the supervision of intellectual property lawyers at the Center for Law and Innovation, students work directly with independent inventors, entrepreneurs, and research scientists engaged in technology transfer.

Externships—Students have access to numerous clinical externship opportunities, for academic credit, in many areas. Externships are available with government agencies and nonprofit organizations.

Center for Law and Innovation—The Center for Law and Innovation provides students with courses, conferences, and hands-on experiences to enhance their understanding of the role of law in the development of technological progress and innovation. In addition to offering courses in intellectual property and Internet law, the center provides summer session technology law courses that bring distinguished scholars and practitioners to the school. Externship opportunities are available with the Maine Patent Program, a unique service program established by the Maine legislature to provide education and legal assistance regarding the patent process to Maine inventors, entrepreneurs, and businesses.

Marine Law Institute (MLI), Ocean and Coastal Law Program—The MLI conducts research on laws and policies affecting ocean and coastal resources under grants and contracts from federal and state agencies and private foundations. The Ocean and Coastal Law Program also supports a student-edited journal and offers courses in coastal zone law, marine resources law, and a law of the sea seminar.

Pro Bono Program—The faculty has established a voluntary standard of 80 hours of pro bono legal service for each student during his or her three years of law school and has instituted a means of encouraging students to fulfill that standard while recognizing those who follow through with it.

Joint-degree Programs—Maine Law and the University of Southern Maine offer the following joint-degree programs: JD/MCP in Community Planning and Development; JD/MS in Health Policy and Management; JD/MA in Public Policy and Management with the Edmund S. Muskie School of Public Service; and a JD/MBA with the School of Business.

International Exchange Programs—Semester exchange programs are available with Dalhousie University Faculty of Law, University of New Brunswick Faculty of Law, National University of Ireland, Universite du Maine, and University of Buckingham.

■ Student Activities

The Student Bar Association performs the varied functions of student government and acts as an umbrella organization of other student organizations, including the American Constitution Society, Animal Legal Defense Fund, Black Law Students Association, Business Law Association, Environmental Law Society, Federalist Society, Health Law Association, International Law Society, Latino/a Law Students Association, Lesbian/Gay/Bisexual Law Caucus, Maine Association for Public Interest Law, Maine Law and Technology Association, National Lawyers Guild, Native American Law Association, Prisoner Justice Project, Sports and Entertainment Law Society, and the Women's Law Association.

The Maine Law Review and the *Ocean and Coastal Law Journal* are scholarly journals managed, edited, and published by students. Students interested in developing written and oral advocacy skills participate in Moot Court and/or the Trial Advocacy Team.

■ Career Services

The Career Services Office provides a full range of services, including counseling; career resource materials; specific summer, full-time, part-time, and work-study job listings; and extensive on-campus recruiting. The small size of the law school ensures services tailored to meet the specific needs of its students. A number of workshops, speakers, and panel discussions throughout the year assist students in learning about the diverse opportunities available to them.

■ Expenses, Financial Aid, and Housing

Maine Law offers a reasonable tuition charge to both residents and nonresidents. The 2006–2007 in-state tuition was $16,590; NEBHE (residents of MA, NH, RI, and VT) and Canadian residents, $24,900; and nonresidents, $26,280. The FAFSA priority deadline is February 15. A number of scholarships are available for entering students. Candidates for admission will automatically be considered for all scholarships for which they are eligible. Housing at USM's Portland Hall is open to law students. Portland also offers ample private apartment housing.

Applicant Profile

University of Maine School of Law
This grid includes only applicants who earned 120–180 LSAT scores under standard administrations.

LSAT Score	GPA 3.75 + Apps	Adm	3.50–3.74 Apps	Adm	3.25–3.49 Apps	Adm	3.00–3.24 Apps	Adm	2.75–2.99 Apps	Adm	2.50–2.74 Apps	Adm	2.25–2.49 Apps	Adm	2.00–2.24 Apps	Adm	Below 2.00 Apps	Adm	No GPA Apps	Adm	Total Apps	Adm
175–180	0	0	0	0	0	0	0	0	0	0	0	0	0	0	0	0	0	0	0	0	0	0
170–174	0	0	2	2	3	3	0	0	1	0	0	0	0	0	0	0	0	0	0	0	6	5
165–169	3	3	4	4	3	3	7	7	5	4	3	1	0	0	0	0	0	0	0	0	63	54
160–164	11	11	7	7	10	10	13	11	9	6	7	5	6	4	0	0	0	0	2	1	177	137
155–159	19	19	24	23	52	45	38	33	17	9	11	5	7	1	6	1	1	0	1	0	248	98
150–154	26	21	46	24	57	24	61	21	30	6	19	2	3	0	5	0	0	0	2	0	131	12
145–149	15	2	19	5	32	2	24	3	14	0	17	0	3	0	4	0	1	0	0	0	69	1
140–144	4	1	4	0	13	0	19	0	15	0	9	0	4	0	0	0	1	0	0	0	19	0
135–139	0	0	1	0	3	0	7	0	4	0	2	0	2	0	0	0	0	0	0	0	19	0
130–134	0	0	1	0	0	0	1	0	2	0	1	0	0	0	1	0	2	0	0	0	8	0
125–129	0	0	1	0	0	0	1	0	0	0	2	0	0	0	0	0	0	0	1	0	5	0
120–124	0	0	0	0	0	0	0	0	0	0	0	0	0	0	0	0	0	0	0	0	0	0
Total	78	57	109	65	173	87	171	75	97	25	71	13	25	5	16	1	5	0	6	1	751	329

Apps = Number of Applicants
Adm = Number Admitted
Reflects 99% of the total applicant pool.

This chart is to be used as a general guide only. Nonnumerical factors are strongly considered for all applicants.

Marquette University Law School

Sensenbrenner Hall, 1103 W. Wisconsin Avenue, PO Box 1881
Milwaukee, WI 53201-1881
Phone: 414.288.6767; Fax: 414.288.0676
E-mail: law.admission@marquette.edu; Website: http://law.marquette.edu

ABA Approved Since 1925

The Basics

Type of school	Private
Term	Semester
Application deadline	4/1 6/1
Application fee	$50
Financial aid deadline	3/1
Can first year start other than fall?	No
Student to faculty ratio	16.1 to 1
Does the university offer:	
housing restricted to law students?	No
graduate housing for which law students are eligible?	No

Faculty and Administrators

	Total		Men		Women		Minorities	
	Fall	Spr	Fall	Spr	Fall	Spr	Fall	Spr
Full-time	33	33	18	16	15	17	3	3
Other Full-time	0	0	0	0	0	0	0	0
Deans, librarians, & others who teach	9	8	5	4	4	4	0	0
Part-time	21	50	18	30	3	20	1	3
Total	**63**	**91**	**41**	**50**	**22**	**41**	**4**	**6**

Curriculum

	Full-time	Part-time
Typical first-year section size	90	45
Is there typically a "small section" of the first-year class, other than Legal Writing, taught by full-time faculty	Yes	Yes
If yes, typical size offered last year	44	45
# of classroom course titles beyond first-year curriculum	129	
# of upper division courses, excluding seminars with an enrollment: Under 25	83	
25–49	36	
50–74	15	
75–99	6	
100+	0	
# of seminars	21	
# of seminar positions available	315	
# of seminar positions filled	217	55
# of positions available in simulation courses	608	
# of simulation positions filled	406	101
# of positions available in faculty supervised clinical courses	67	
# of faculty supervised clinical positions filled	44	11
# involved in field placements	158	40
# involved in law journals	109	27
# involved in interschool competitions	68	17
# of credit hours required to graduate	90	

JD Enrollment and Ethnicity

	Men		Women		Full-time		Part-time		1st-year		Total		JD Degs. Awd.
	#	%	#	%	#	%	#	%	#	%	#	%	
African Amer.	6	1.5	9	3.1	12	2.4	3	1.6	5	2.3	15	2.2	8
Amer. Indian	1	0.3	4	1.4	2	0.4	3	1.6	2	0.9	5	0.7	1
Asian Amer.	13	3.3	6	2.0	13	2.6	6	3.2	6	2.7	19	2.8	5
Mex. Amer.	3	0.8	2	0.7	4	0.8	1	0.5	1	0.5	5	0.7	0
Puerto Rican	0	0.0	1	0.3	1	0.2	0	0.0	0	0.0	1	0.1	0
Hispanic	9	2.3	9	3.1	15	3.0	3	1.6	7	3.2	18	2.6	2
Total Minority	32	8.1	31	10.5	47	9.4	16	8.4	21	9.5	63	9.1	16
For. Nation.	4	1.0	1	0.3	5	1.0	0	0.0	0	0.0	5	0.7	1
Caucasian	358	90.6	262	89.1	446	89.4	174	91.6	200	90.1	620	90.0	215
Unknown	1	0.3	0	0.0	1	0.2	0	0.0	1	0.5	1	0.1	0
Total	395	57.3	294	42.7	499	72.4	190	27.6	222	32.2	689		232

Transfers

Transfers in	6
Transfers out	11

Tuition and Fees

	Resident	Nonresident
Full-time	$27,750	$27,750
Part-time	$16,650	$16,650

Living Expenses

Estimated living expenses for singles

Living on campus	Living off campus	Living at home
$16,606	$16,606	$16,606

Marquette University Law School

ABA Approved Since 1925

GPA and LSAT Scores

	Total	Full-time	Part-time
# of apps	1,908	1,712	196
# of offers	762	705	57
# of matrics	222	177	45
75% GPA	3.68	3.68	3.47
Median GPA	3.46	3.47	3.24
25% GPA	3.17	3.25	3.00
75% LSAT	159	159	158
Median LSAT	157	157	154
25% LSAT	155	155	152

Grants and Scholarships (from prior year)

	Total #	Total %	Full-time #	Full-time %	Part-time #	Part-time %
Total # of students	715		569		146	
Total # receiving grants	302	42.2	209	36.7	93	63.7
Less than 1/2 tuition	235	32.9	172	30.2	63	43.2
Half to full tuition	35	4.9	18	3.2	17	11.6
Full tuition	30	4.2	18	3.2	12	8.2
More than full tuition	2	0.3	1	0.2	1	0.7
Median grant amount			$6,000		$4,000	

Informational and Library Resources

# of volumes and volume equivalents	338,830
# of titles	159,910
# of active serial subscriptions	3,411
Study seating capacity inside the library	396
# of full-time professional librarians	9
Hours per week library is open	106
# of open, wired connections available to students	88
# of networked computers available for use by students	32
# of simultaneous wireless users	1,500
Require computer?	No

JD Attrition (from prior year)

	Academic #	Other #	Total #	Total %
1st year	1	15	16	7.1
2nd year	0	1	1	0.5
3rd year	0	0	0	0.0
4th year	0	0	0	0.0

Employment (9 months after graduation)

	Total	Percentage
Employment status known	194	98.5
Employment status unknown	3	1.5
Employed	184	94.8
Pursuing graduate degrees	0	0.0
Unemployed seeking employment	8	4.1
Unemployed not seeking employment	0	0.0
Unemployed and studying for the bar	2	1.0

Type of Employment

	Total	Percentage
# employed in law firms	102	55.4
# employed in business and industry	36	19.6
# employed in government	17	9.2
# employed in public interest	13	7.1
# employed as judicial clerks	13	7.1
# employed in academia	3	1.6

Geographic Location

	Total	Percentage
# employed in state	143	77.7
# employed in foreign countries	2	1.1
# of states where employed	17	

Bar Passage Rates

Jurisdiction	Wisconsin		
Exam	Sum 05	Win 06	Total
# from school taking bar for the first time	184	13	197
School's pass rate for all first-time takers	N/A	N/A	N/A
State's pass rate for all first-time takers	79%	74%	77%

All graduates were admitted to the Wisconsin bar via the diploma privilege.

Marquette University Law School

Office of Admissions, Sensenbrenner Hall, 1103 W. Wisconsin Avenue, PO Box 1881
Milwaukee, WI 53201-1881
Phone: 414.288.6767; Fax: 414.288.0676
E-mail: law.admission@marquette.edu; Website: http://law.marquette.edu

■ Introduction

For more than a century, Marquette University Law School has been committed to training men and women to serve the public interest by becoming highly skilled and ethical attorneys. Traditionally, the curriculum has emphasized the practical aspects of legal education. In recent years, that emphasis has expanded to include particular excellence in the areas of intellectual property, dispute resolution, sports law, labor and employment law, criminal law, children and the law, and litigation-related courses. The National Sports Law Institute, the premier sports law program in the US, is a part of the Law School. Our more than 6,700 alumni/ae serve in a broad range of legal, public, and corporate positions throughout the US.

The Law School is located on the university campus—two blocks from the state courthouse and a short walk to the federal courthouse and downtown Milwaukee. Marquette is the only law school in southeast Wisconsin. Marquette—a Catholic, Jesuit, and urban university—is the largest private university in the state. The Catholic and Jesuit nature of the school translates into a specific concern for the well-being of each individual, whether he or she is a student, a legal client, or the victim of a crime. Persons of all religious backgrounds attend Marquette, serve on our faculty, and are valued in our community. The Law School is committed to academic freedom, the broadest possible scope of inquiry, and the examination of any subject.

Milwaukee is a lively city on Lake Michigan, 90 miles north of Chicago. Wisconsin's largest city, with a metropolitan-area population of about 1.5 million, Milwaukee retains the appeal of a small town. Clean and well-run, it is known for its many ethnic festivals and the variety of cuisine.

■ Enrollment/Student Body

Within the Marquette Law School community, people know and care about one another. Our students come together from over 190 colleges and universities. They hail from more than 38 states and the District of Columbia, as well as a handful of foreign countries. Our faculty includes 37 full-time professors and prominent practicing attorneys and judges who serve as adjunct professors.

Law students at Marquette represent a broad range of backgrounds, beliefs, and life experiences. Students of color comprise about 10 percent of the student body. We respect our different traditions and believe diversity enriches the legal education we offer.

■ Library and Physical Facilities

The law school building, Sensenbrenner Hall, is an attractive, comfortable building that houses faculty and administrative offices, classrooms, and a courtroom. The law library, a four-level facility, is connected to the Law School. The law library has two computer labs and provides students access to electronic legal research tools and computer-assisted legal instruction exercises. The law library is a federal document depository and is the largest legal research facility in southeast Wisconsin. Law students have access to all Marquette University campus facilities, including the computer center. Wireless capability exists throughout Sensenbrenner Hall, including the law library.

■ Curriculum

The Law School offers full- and part-time programs leading to the JD degree. The Law School's curriculum is rooted in core courses that include consideration of the theoretical underpinnings of the law, as well as the practical application of substantive legal concepts. The curriculum is national in focus and scope and emphasizes the skills and values necessary to be a competent and ethical lawyer, as well as a contributing citizen and community leader. Our adjunct faculty includes many of the state's outstanding practitioners who supplement required and core courses by teaching a broad range of electives.

Students may earn a **JD/MBA** through the Law School and the College of Business Administration; of special note is the JD/MBA with a **sports business** concentration. Joint programs with the graduate school allow students to earn a **JD/MA** in **international affairs**, the **history of philosophy**, **social and applied philosophy**, or **political science**. The Law School offers a joint program with Marquette University's graduate program in dispute resolution that allows a student to graduate with a **JD** and a **certificate in dispute resolution**. In conjunction with the Medical College of Wisconsin, we offer the **JD/MA** in **bioethics**. Each joint-degree program requires meeting all requirements of both the Law School and the other degree-granting institution; typically, each can be completed in four years. As an alternative to a joint degree, law students may take up to six hours of coursework in a related graduate program at Marquette, such as public policy, sociology, philosophy, or history.

■ Special Programs

Our comprehensive trial-practice courses provide an exceptional opportunity for students to develop trial skills. Distinctive clinics include the Prosecutor and Defender Clinics, Judicial Internships, and numerous supervised field work opportunities.

Marquette University Law School's sports law program provides the nation's most comprehensive offering of sports law courses and student internships with sports organizations, as well as opportunities for memberships on the *Marquette Sports Law Review* and the sports law moot court team. Our broad, well-rounded curriculum is designed to provide students with both theoretical and practical education concerning legal regulation of the amateur and professional sports industries. Law students who fulfill certain requirements are eligible to earn a **sports law certificate** in addition to the **JD**. More information on the program and the certificate may be found on the Law School's website at *http://law.marquette.edu/jw/sports*.

The Law School's Restorative Justice Initiative gives law students the opportunity to work with victims of crime, offenders, and community members toward repairing the harm that crime has caused. More information on the RJI may be found on the Law School's website at *http://law.marquette.edu/jw/restorative*.

Admission and Financial Aid

Review of completed applications begins after October 1 and continues through the spring. Although the applicant's LSAT score and academic record are important considerations in the selection process, the Admissions Committee also considers qualitative factors, such as letters of recommendation, essays, work experience, extracurricular activities, and personal accomplishments and characteristics that contribute to the diversity of the school, the legal community, and the profession. Admitted applicants are required to submit nonrefundable tuition deposits in April and June. These deposits are applied to the student's fall semester tuition. Interviews are not part of the application process.

Although most students finance their education through a combination of federal and private loan programs, all applicants offered admission are automatically considered for merit scholarship awards. Additionally, the Law School has recently established a Loan Repayment Assistance Program to help graduates in government service or public interest practice repay the cost of their educational loans. More information on LRAP may be found on the Law School's website at *http://law.marquette.edu/jw/lrap*.

Diploma Privilege

Since 1933, graduates of the Law School who qualify have been admitted to the practice of law in Wisconsin without having to take the Wisconsin Bar Examination. Marquette graduates are entitled to sit for bar examinations in any American jurisdiction.

Student Activities

The Law School publishes the *Marquette Law Review*, the *Marquette Sports Law Review*, the *Marquette Intellectual Property Law Review*, and the *Marquette Elder's Advisor* (Elder Law Journal). Students may develop advocacy skills in moot court competitions. Marquette moot court teams have won regional titles and championships in national competitions. A wide variety of student organizations are active at the Law School. A listing of student groups and descriptions of their activities may be found on the Law School's website.

Career Services

The Career Planning Center processes hundreds of listings of employment opportunities, coordinates campus interviews, and provides counseling assistance to students. In recent years, approximately 95 percent of our graduates secured employment within nine months of graduation. Our on-campus interview program includes a broad range of legal employers from major cities and legal markets across the nation. The office will help students network with Marquette alumni and other potential resource persons. Our goals are to keep our placement rate high and to ensure a good fit and job satisfaction for all our graduates.

Housing

Ample, affordable housing is available throughout Milwaukee and its suburbs. Information and assistance on securing housing may be obtained from the Office of University Apartments and Off-campus Student Services; telephone: 414.288.7281, Web: *www.marquette.edu/pages/home/orl/uni*.

Applicant Profile

Marquette University Law School
This grid includes only applicants who earned 120–180 LSAT scores under standard administrations.

LSAT Score	3.75 +		3.50–3.74		3.25–3.49		3.00–3.24		2.75–2.99		2.50–2.74		2.25–2.49		2.00–2.24		Below 2.00		No GPA		Total	
	Apps	Adm	Apps	Adm	Apps	Adm	Apps	Adm	Apps	Adm	Apps	Adm	Apps	Adm	Apps	Adm	Apps	Adm	Apps	Adm	Apps	Adm
175–180	1	1	0	0	0	0	0	0	0	0	0	0	0	0	0	0	0	0	0	0	1	1
170–174	0	0	1	1	0	0	1	1	0	0	0	0	0	0	0	0	0	0	0	0	2	2
165–169	7	6	9	9	6	5	8	7	3	3	2	2	1	1	1	0	0	0	1	0	38	34
160–164	26	25	54	48	36	32	31	29	22	19	9	6	7	4	4	1	0	0	1	0	190	164
155–159	69	66	122	113	130	104	108	60	58	28	25	10	14	2	2	1	0	0	0	0	528	384
150–154	70	36	129	50	173	44	152	17	86	12	32	2	14	0	4	0	2	0	4	1	666	162
145–149	22	1	47	3	81	3	63	3	51	3	28	1	7	0	3	0	0	0	8	1	310	15
Below 145	8	0	23	0	32	0	47	0	40	0	31	0	21	0	9	0	3	0	8	0	222	0
Total	203	135	385	224	458	188	410	117	260	65	127	21	64	7	23	2	5	0	22	3	1957	762

Apps = Number of Applicants
Adm = Number Admitted
Reflects 99% of the total applicant pool.

University of Maryland School of Law

500 West Baltimore Street
Baltimore, MD 21201
Phone: 410.706.3492; Fax: 410.706.1793
E-mail: admissions@law.umaryland.edu; Website: www.law.umaryland.edu

ABA
Approved
Since
1930

The Basics

Type of school	Public
Term	Semester
Application deadline	3/1
Application fee	$65
Financial aid deadline	3/1
Can first year start other than fall?	No
Student to faculty ratio	11.8 to 1
Does the university offer:	
housing restricted to law students?	No
graduate housing for which law students are eligible?	Yes

Faculty and Administrators

	Total		Men		Women		Minorities	
	Fall	Spr	Fall	Spr	Fall	Spr	Fall	Spr
Full-time	55	52	28	29	27	23	11	9
Other Full-time	1	0	1	0	0	0	1	0
Deans, librarians, & others who teach	12	13	3	3	9	10	0	0
Part-time	64	69	45	40	19	29	7	7
Total	132	134	77	72	55	62	19	16

Curriculum

		Full-time	Part-time
Typical first-year section size		73	27
Is there typically a "small section" of the first-year class, other than Legal Writing, taught by full-time faculty		Yes	Yes
If yes, typical size offered last year		25	27
# of classroom course titles beyond first-year curriculum		152	
# of upper division courses, excluding seminars with an enrollment:	Under 25	169	
	25–49	35	
	50–74	17	
	75–99	6	
	100+	2	
# of seminars		62	
# of seminar positions available		961	
# of seminar positions filled		506	146
# of positions available in simulation courses		1,073	
# of simulation positions filled		481	359
# of positions available in faculty supervised clinical courses		424	
# of faculty supervised clinical positions filled	301		69
# involved in field placements		163	9
# involved in law journals		165	5
# involved in interschool competitions		58	4
# of credit hours required to graduate		85	

JD Enrollment and Ethnicity

	Men		Women		Full-time		Part-time		1st-year		Total		JD Degs. Awd.
	#	%	#	%	#	%	#	%	#	%	#	%	
African Amer.	34	9.9	89	18.5	90	13.4	33	21.6	33	12.6	123	14.9	24
Amer. Indian	1	0.3	3	0.6	4	0.6	0	0.0	2	0.8	4	0.5	1
Asian Amer.	24	7.0	57	11.9	70	10.4	11	7.2	25	9.5	81	9.8	34
Mex. Amer.	1	0.3	0	0.0	0	0.0	1	0.7	0	0.0	1	0.1	0
Puerto Rican	0	0.0	0	0.0	0	0.0	0	0.0	0	0.0	0	0.0	2
Hispanic	20	5.8	33	6.9	44	6.5	9	5.9	24	9.2	53	6.4	3
Total Minority	80	23.2	182	37.8	208	30.9	54	35.3	84	32.1	262	31.7	64
For. Nation.	3	0.9	7	1.5	8	1.2	2	1.3	7	2.7	10	1.2	3
Caucasian	253	73.3	284	59.0	443	65.8	94	61.4	166	63.4	537	65.0	181
Unknown	9	2.6	8	1.7	14	2.1	3	2.0	5	1.9	17	2.1	5
Total	345	41.8	481	58.2	673	81.5	153	18.5	262	31.7	826		253

Transfers

Transfers in	16
Transfers out	7

Tuition and Fees

	Resident	Nonresident
Full-time	$19,105	$30,384
Part-time	$14,460	$22,919

Living Expenses

Estimated living expenses for singles

Living on campus	Living off campus	Living at home
$20,338	$23,848	$13,693

University of Maryland School of Law

*ABA
Approved
Since
1930*

GPA and LSAT Scores

	Total	Full-time	Part-time
# of apps	4,331	3,790	541
# of offers	688	627	61
# of matrics	263	207	56
75% GPA	3.76	3.77	3.67
Median GPA	3.60	3.61	3.66
25% GPA	3.38	3.40	3.29
75% LSAT	164	165	160
Median LSAT	161	162	157
25% LSAT	159	160	153

Grants and Scholarships (from prior year)

	Total #	Total %	Full-time #	Full-time %	Part-time #	Part-time %
Total # of students	809		666		143	
Total # receiving grants	475	58.7	426	64.0	49	34.3
Less than 1/2 tuition	392	48.5	343	51.5	49	34.3
Half to full tuition	61	7.5	61	9.2	0	0.0
Full tuition	22	2.7	22	3.3	0	0.0
More than full tuition	0	0.0	0	0.0	0	0.0
Median grant amount			$6,577		$3,600	

Informational and Library Resources

# of volumes and volume equivalents	479,930
# of titles	115,848
# of active serial subscriptions	3,902
Study seating capacity inside the library	522
# of full-time professional librarians	11
Hours per week library is open	96
# of open, wired connections available to students	1,208
# of networked computers available for use by students	218
# of simultaneous wireless users	20
Require computer?	Yes

JD Attrition (from prior year)

	Academic #	Other #	Total #	Total %
1st year	1	9	10	3.9
2nd year	1	0	1	0.4
3rd year	0	1	1	0.4
4th year	0	0	0	0.0

Employment (9 months after graduation)

	Total	Percentage
Employment status known	223	99.6
Employment status unknown	1	0.4
Employed	202	90.6
Pursuing graduate degrees	10	4.5
Unemployed seeking employment	3	1.3
Unemployed not seeking employment	8	3.6
Unemployed and studying for the bar	0	0.0
Type of Employment		
# employed in law firms	79	39.1
# employed in business and industry	19	9.4
# employed in government	28	13.9
# employed in public interest	10	5.0
# employed as judicial clerks	55	27.2
# employed in academia	8	4.0
Geographic Location		
# employed in state	139	68.8
# employed in foreign countries	0	0.0
# of states where employed	17	

Bar Passage Rates

Jurisdiction	Maryland		
Exam	Sum 05	Win 06	Total
# from school taking bar for the first time	160	19	179
School's pass rate for all first-time takers	81%	74%	80%
State's pass rate for all first-time takers	76%	66%	74%

University of Maryland School of Law

500 West Baltimore Street
Baltimore, MD 21201
Phone: 410.706.3492; Fax: 410.706.1793
E-mail: admissions@law.umaryland.edu; Website: www.law.umaryland.edu

■ Community of Students, Faculty, and Alumni

Entering students quickly become part of our supportive community. We are a diverse group (age, gender, race, academic background, and prior employment), and this diversity is reflected in our students and in our faculty and deans. The faculty/student ratio of 1:11.9 provides opportunity for close working relationships in a professional yet collegial setting. Many resources are available to students to ease the transition to law school, including upper-class peer advisors, skills enhancement sessions, and one-on-one academic counseling. Students also directly benefit from a wide network of involved alumni who occupy positions of professional leadership throughout the state, region, and nation.

■ Introduction

The University of Maryland School of Law provides students with the knowledge, experience, and expertise to prepare them for professional leadership as lawyers, business executives, legislators, public policymakers, community advocates, and other agents of social, political, and economic progress. Its favorable tuition structure makes it a superb value in American legal education.

The law school is an integral part of the Baltimore-Washington-Annapolis legal-business community. Located in downtown Baltimore, just a few blocks from the Inner Harbor's tourist attractions, the school's location affords opportunities for extensive interaction with local, state, and national governments, as well as many law firms, public interest institutions, agencies, and other organizations of prominence.

Founded in 1816, the School of Law is fully accredited by the ABA and is a member of the AALS. The Juris Doctor curriculum is available in a three-year day or four-year evening program.

■ Law School Complex and Library

The School of Law and the Thurgood Marshall Law Library occupy a state-of-the-art complex supportive of the school's programs integrating classroom and experiential learning.

The Thurgood Marshall Law Library houses a collection of approximately 456,529 volumes and equivalents accessible through the online catalog. A staff of 23, including 10 librarians, provides customized reference and consulting services to faculty and students.

■ Curriculum

The required curriculum includes civil, constitutional, criminal, contract, property, and tort law, as well as a three-semester course focusing on legal skills of analysis, research, writing, and oral argument. More than 150 electives include a wide range of courses, seminars, independent studies, simulations, clinics, and externships. Each student must produce at least one substantial paper based on extensive research.

Maryland's strong academic programs in business/corporation/commercial law; criminal law; environmental law; family law/child advocacy; general practice; health law; intellectual property and technology transfer; international/comparative law; jurisprudence/legal history; labor/employment/administrative law; litigation/advocacy; legislation/politics/public policy; property/real estate/decedent's estates law; public interest law/community development; and tax law enable students to develop expertise and experience in fields of critical importance to the future.

■ Clinical Law Program

The clinical training program, among the best in the country, offers students real-life court appearances on behalf of a wide range of clients. In addition to this variety of in-house clinical student practice settings, students may gain hands-on experience in public and private nonprofit externships in the Baltimore/Washington region.

■ Dual Degrees and Interdisciplinary Study

Maryland's interdisciplinary programs, including environment, healthcare, and technology-transfer law offer students the opportunity to work with lawyers and other professionals toward the resolution of problems that transcend traditional disciplinary boundaries. Dual-degree programs include Business Administration, Community Planning, Criminal Justice, Liberal Education, Pharmacy, Policy Sciences, Public Health, Public Management, Risk and Environmental Assessment, and Social Work. Students are encouraged to enroll in as many as nine credits in related graduate-level programs.

■ Admission

Maryland's law faculty believe the quality of legal education is directly affected by the diversity of our students. The admission committee selects applicants with the greatest potential for law school studies and whose background, character, and experience contribute to the diversity we believe is important to the law school learning experience and to the future benefit of the community. Factors considered in this selection process include geographic origin; cultural and language background; racial, social, disability, or economic barriers overcome; interpersonal skills as demonstrated by extracurricular pursuits, work or service experience, leadership activities, and social experience; potential for intellectual and social growth, as demonstrated by talents, skills, maturity, and compassion; and other special circumstances and characteristics that, when combined with academic skills needed for sound legal education, hold promise as qualities that will be valuable to the school community. The personal statement and letters of recommendation are the primary means for candidates to convey this information and these characteristics to the admission and scholarship committees.

First-year students are admitted only in the fall. The School of Law uses a rolling admission process, reviewing applications in the order in which files are completed. Applicants should file applications as early as possible after September 1 of the year preceding enrollment and prior to March 1. Applicants are encouraged to complete the application early; applications completed later may be at a competitive disadvantage. Multiple LSAT scores normally are averaged. Residency may be a factor in close cases. Applicants are encouraged to visit the school, but interviews are not part of the admission process.

■ Student Activities

Maryland law students participate in a variety of activities. The law school is home to over 30 active and diverse student-run organizations.

More than half of our students participate in inter- and intrascholastic advocacy competitions. Students also have the opportunity to participate in four student-edited publications.

■ Scholarships and Need-based Financial Assistance

The School of Law offers a number of scholarships as well as a traditional need-based financial aid program. Scholarships are awarded on the basis of grades, test score(s), and other evidence of potential for unusual contributions to the academic, cocurricular, and student affairs programs. Such potential should be clearly described in the personal statement

included with the application for admission. All admitted applicants are automatically considered for law school scholarship awards. Applications for financial aid (FAFSA) should be submitted as soon after January 1 as possible.

■ Career Development

Maryland law students benefit from extensive connections to the bar, judiciary, business and industry, government, and community organizations within the state of Maryland; Washington, DC; and beyond.

The Career Development Office assists law students and graduates in developing effective job-search strategies to secure legal employment and experience. In the class of 2004, 97 percent of the 343 graduates reported employment in the following categories: 32 percent in private practice, 19 percent in judicial clerkships, 22 percent in government and other public service, 14 percent in business and industry, 5.48 percent in public interest organizations, and 7 percent in academia.

Applicant Profile

University of Maryland School of Law
This grid includes only applicants with 120–180 LSAT scores earned under standard administrations.

GPA	LSAT Score									
	149 & Below		150–154		155–159		160–164		165 & Above	
	Apps	Adm	Apps	Adm	Apps	Adm	Apps	Adm	Apps	Adm
3.75–4.00	58	3	127	15	229	66	101	71	46	40
3.50–3.74	143	10	220	17	355	58	198	133	55	38
3.25–3.49	224	4	257	14	360	28	188	94	56	30
3.00–3.24	212	7	183	13	208	13	115	28	35	22
2.99 & Below	363	3	203	6	176	5	118	13	48	18
Total	1000	27	990	65	1328	170	720	339	240	148

Apps = Number of Applicants
Adm = Number Admitted
Reflects 99% of the total applicant pool.

The University of Memphis—Cecil C. Humphreys School of Law

207 Humphreys Law School
Memphis, TN 38152-3140
Phone: 901.678.5403; Fax: 901.678.5210
E-mail: lawadmissions@mail.law.memphis.edu; Website: www.law.memphis.edu

ABA Approved Since 1965

The Basics

Type of school	Public
Term	Semester
Application deadline	3/1
Application fee	$25
Financial aid deadline	3/1
Can first year start other than fall?	No
Student to faculty ratio	16.5 to 1
Does the university offer:	
housing restricted to law students?	No
graduate housing for which law students are eligible?	Yes

Faculty and Administrators

	Total Fall	Total Spr	Men Fall	Men Spr	Women Fall	Women Spr	Minorities Fall	Minorities Spr
Full-time	18	21	14	13	4	8	1	3
Other Full-time	0	0	0	0	0	0	0	0
Deans, librarians, & others who teach	5	5	4	4	1	1	0	0
Part-time	18	24	11	13	7	11	3	3
Total	41	50	29	30	12	20	4	6

Curriculum

	Full-time	Part-time
Typical first-year section size	75	0
Is there typically a "small section" of the first-year class, other than Legal Writing, taught by full-time faculty	No	No
If yes, typical size offered last year		
# of classroom course titles beyond first-year curriculum	71	
# of upper division courses, excluding seminars with an enrollment: Under 25	50	
25–49	15	
50–74	15	
75–99	3	
100+	1	
# of seminars	11	
# of seminar positions available	132	
# of seminar positions filled	85	0
# of positions available in simulation courses	152	
# of simulation positions filled	121	0
# of positions available in faculty supervised clinical courses	72	
# of faculty supervised clinical positions filled	54	0
# involved in field placements	21	0
# involved in law journals	99	0
# involved in interschool competitions	26	0
# of credit hours required to graduate	90	

JD Enrollment and Ethnicity

	Men #	Men %	Women #	Women %	Full-time #	Full-time %	Part-time #	Part-time %	1st-year #	1st-year %	Total #	Total %	JD Degs. Awd.
African Amer.	17	7.5	46	25.6	42	11.1	21	72.4	19	13.3	63	15.4	8
Amer. Indian	0	0.0	2	1.1	2	0.5	0	0.0	2	1.4	2	0.5	0
Asian Amer.	3	1.3	3	1.7	5	1.3	1	3.4	3	2.1	6	1.5	0
Mex. Amer.	0	0.0	0	0.0	0	0.0	0	0.0	0	0.0	0	0.0	0
Puerto Rican	0	0.0	0	0.0	0	0.0	0	0.0	0	0.0	0	0.0	0
Hispanic	0	0.0	3	1.7	3	0.8	0	0.0	1	0.7	3	0.7	0
Total Minority	20	8.8	54	30.0	52	13.7	22	75.9	25	17.5	74	18.1	8
For. Nation.	0	0.0	0	0.0	0	0.0	0	0.0	0	0.0	0	0.0	0
Caucasian	208	91.2	126	70.0	327	86.3	7	24.1	118	82.5	334	81.9	117
Unknown	0	0.0	0	0.0	0	0.0	0	0.0	0	0.0	0	0.0	0
Total	228	55.9	180	44.1	379	92.9	29	7.1	143	35.0	408		125

Transfers

Transfers in	3
Transfers out	1

Tuition and Fees

	Resident	Nonresident
Full-time	$10,596	$28,946
Part-time	$9,974	$26,684

Living Expenses

Estimated living expenses for singles

Living on campus	Living off campus	Living at home
$12,772	$12,772	$8,188

The University of Memphis—Cecil C. Humphreys School of Law

ABA
Approved
Since
1965

GPA and LSAT Scores

	Total	Full-time	Part-time
# of apps	1,113	1,061	52
# of offers	290	276	14
# of matrics	144	130	14
75% GPA	3.70	3.73	3.50
Median GPA	3.36	3.39	3.22
25% GPA	3.06	3.08	2.87
75% LSAT	158	158	148
Median LSAT	155	155	145
25% LSAT	153	153	141

Grants and Scholarships (from prior year)

	Total		Full-time		Part-time	
	#	%	#	%	#	%
Total # of students	400		368		32	
Total # receiving grants	118	29.5	90	24.5	28	87.5
Less than 1/2 tuition	72	18.0	47	12.8	25	78.1
Half to full tuition	31	7.8	28	7.6	3	9.4
Full tuition	14	3.5	14	3.8	0	0.0
More than full tuition	1	0.3	1	0.3	0	0.0
Median grant amount			$3,200		$4,500	

Informational and Library Resources

# of volumes and volume equivalents	271,828
# of titles	48,291
# of active serial subscriptions	2,328
Study seating capacity inside the library	291
# of full-time professional librarians	3
Hours per week library is open	105
# of open, wired connections available to students	30
# of networked computers available for use by students	43
# of simultaneous wireless users	2,500
Require computer?	No

JD Attrition (from prior year)

	Academic	Other	Total	
	#	#	#	%
1st year	3	4	7	4.9
2nd year	2	2	4	3.3
3rd year	0	0	0	0.0
4th year	0	0	0	0.0

Employment (9 months after graduation)

	Total	Percentage
Employment status known	162	100.0
Employment status unknown	0	0.0
Employed	154	95.1
Pursuing graduate degrees	2	1.2
Unemployed seeking employment	2	1.2
Unemployed not seeking employment	1	0.6
Unemployed and studying for the bar	3	1.9

Type of Employment

	Total	Percentage
# employed in law firms	92	59.7
# employed in business and industry	4	2.6
# employed in government	29	18.8
# employed in public interest	2	1.3
# employed as judicial clerks	12	7.8
# employed in academia	1	0.6

Geographic Location

	Total	Percentage
# employed in state	141	91.6
# employed in foreign countries	0	0.0
# of states where employed		11

Bar Passage Rates

Jurisdiction	Tennessee		
Exam	Sum 05	Win 06	Total
# from school taking bar for the first time	130	18	148
School's pass rate for all first-time takers	91%	94%	91%
State's pass rate for all first-time takers	81%	76%	80%

The University of Memphis—Cecil C. Humphreys School of Law

207 Humphreys Law School
Memphis, TN 38152-3140
Phone: 901.678.5403; Fax: 901.678.5210
E-mail: lawadmissions@mail.law.memphis.edu; Website: www.law.memphis.edu

■ History of the School of Law

The Cecil C. Humphreys School of Law at the University of Memphis was founded in response to wide-spread interest in developing a full-time accredited legal preparation program to serve Memphis and West Tennessee. The Cecil C. Humphreys School of Law was founded in 1962 and accredited by the American Bar Association (ABA) in 1965. The school was named in honor of Cecil C. Humphreys, then president of Memphis State University and an educator of great distinction. Mr. Humphreys led the group that worked with the state legislature and the ABA to accredit the law school. The school is also an active member of the American Association of Legal Scholars (AALS).

Since its inception, the School of Law has graduated over 5,000 students and continues its tradition of preparing competent and ethical attorneys. Our graduates can be found throughout the United States employed in private practice, the federal and state judiciary, corporate boardrooms, government agencies, and public service organizations.

■ Memphis and the School of Law

Memphis is one of the South's largest and most beautiful and diverse cities. Memphis has one of the lowest cost-of-living rates of any major US city, and its temperate climate provides ample opportunity for year-round activities. Memphis has a rich history and an unmatched musical heritage.

The School of Law brings together unique individuals with a wide variety of cultural, geographical, employment, and academic backgrounds. Many of its students come to law school immediately after finishing their undergraduate education; however, a significant number have been in the workforce or have completed advanced degrees. The diversity within the student body enriches the classroom experience for all students and enhances the overall quality of the educational program.

The university has acquired the historic Memphis Post Office Front Street Station to serve as the future home for the Cecil C. Humphreys School of Law. Current plans call for occupancy in fall 2009. This beautiful building is situated near downtown law offices and state and federal courthouses.

■ The University of Memphis

The University of Memphis serves as a regional center for education, service, and research. It is a comprehensive urban university that enrolls over 20,000 students and is accredited by the Commission on Colleges of the Southern Association of Colleges and Schools.

The University of Memphis is linked historically, intellectually, and emotionally with its community. The university is situated in the pleasant surroundings of residential neighborhoods away from the hustle of the city.

■ Curriculum

The School of Law offers a full-time day program and a limited part-time day program. Our challenging curriculum prepares our students for the modern practice of law. The curriculum reflects a commitment to traditional legal education, and academic emphasis is placed on fundamental lawyering skills and areas of knowledge.

■ Lawyering Skills and Legal Clinics

The School of Law provides the opportunity to take advanced courses in lawyering skills. These include trial advocacy, mediation, and alternative dispute resolution. Several externships are available for students to work under the supervision of a faculty instructor in the criminal justice field. Students can also choose from one of three legal clinics operated by the School of Law: a General Litigation Clinic, an Elder Law Clinic, and a Child Advocacy Clinic. Students enrolled in the legal clinic courses work with indigent and elderly clients through the Memphis Area Legal Services and with children in delinquency and dependency proceedings.

■ Joint and Dual Programs

The School of Law and the Fogelman College of Business and Economics offer a coordinated degree program leading to both the JD and MBA degrees. The purpose of this program is to allow students to study both modern business management and law. The JD/MBA program enables the student to complete both the JD and MBA in considerably less time than would be required to complete each degree separately.

The School of Law and the Department of Political Science offer a dual degree leading to both the JD and MA degrees. Credit towards degrees in these disciplines can be earned simultaneously if admissions and curricula are carefully structured, and students can complete both degrees in less time than would normally be required.

■ Library and Information Technology

The University of Memphis law library enhances the School of Law's reputation as an information technology center for the Mid-South region, assisting students and the legal community with legal research and the efficient delivery of legal services. In addition to the law school's computer lab, our students have wireless access throughout the university campus. The Ned R. McWherter Library, the main campus library, features state-of-the-art information technology and is a regional federal depository library as well as a depository for Tennessee state publications.

■ Student Programs and Activities

The law school has two scholarly publications, edited and staffed entirely by students, that are an integral part of the law school experience: *The University of Memphis Law Review* and *Tennessee Journal of Practice and Procedure*. The Moot Court Board (MCB) is composed of 20 third-year students who are dedicated to the development of advocacy skills. Members of the MCB plan, organize, and oversee three intraschool competitions. The law school also fields several moot court teams in national moot court and mock trial competitions. The Student Bar Association (SBA) is the student government of the law school. The SBA coordinates a wide variety of extracurricular activities. Students can also choose from approximately 20 other organizations, ranging from legal fraternities to special interest organizations.

■ Admission

Some applicants are admitted based on a weighted combination of the LSAT score and the cumulative undergraduate GPA. Other applicants are selected by the Faculty Admission Committee through the nonquantifiable admission process. Other factors, such as quality of the applicant's undergraduate institution, level and rigor of coursework, letters of recommendation, graduate work, employment during and after college, extracurricular activities, educational diversity, and state of residence are considered in this process. In an attempt to attract a diverse student population, the School of Law has developed a selection process that provides a full review of qualified applicants but assures that admission is on the merits of each applicant.

■ Career Services

The Career Services Office actively assists students and alumni by developing their interest in specific areas of the law, enhancing their professional skills, and providing information about opportunities for part-time and full-time employment in their law careers. A comprehensive national Internet job bank as well as a network of alumni mentors is available to help students who are interested in law careers outside the Memphis area.

In addition to hosting a large number of firms, corporations, and public interest/governmental employers for fall and spring on-campus interviewing and seminars, the School of Law is a member of several organizations that conduct annual recruiting conferences that provide second- and third-year law students and judicial law clerks with the opportunity to interview with law firms, government agencies, and corporations throughout the nation.

Employment statistics for Memphis law graduates have remained consistently high during the last decade. According to the National Association for Law Placement, the 2005 class of Memphis graduates reported a 98.7 percent employment rate within nine months of graduation. Memphis has graduates practicing in all 50 states and in several foreign countries.

■ Tennessee Institute for Pre-Law

The Tennessee Institute for Pre-Law facilitates admission of Tennessee residents from underrepresented populations who apply to one or both of the state-supported law schools in Tennessee. This five-week summer program is housed at the University of Memphis School of Law. Participants who successfully complete the program and who meet specified requirements for admission will be guaranteed admission at the state-supported law school(s) to which they applied.

Applicant Profile

The University of Memphis—Cecil C. Humphreys School of Law
This grid includes only applicants who earned 120–180 LSAT scores under standard administrations.

LSAT Score	3.75+		3.50–3.74		3.25–3.49		3.00–3.24		2.75–2.99		2.50–2.74		2.25–2.49		2.00–2.24		Below 2.00		No GPA		Total	
	Apps	Adm	Apps	Adm	Apps	Adm	Apps	Adm	Apps	Adm	Apps	Adm	Apps	Adm	Apps	Adm	Apps	Adm	Apps	Adm	Apps	Adm
175–180	1	1	1	1	0	0	0	0	0	0	0	0	0	0	0	0	0	0	0	0	2	2
170–174	0	0	0	0	0	0	0	0	0	0	0	0	0	0	0	0	0	0	0	0	0	0
165–169	4	4	5	5	2	2	5	5	2	2	1	1	1	1	0	0	0	0	0	0	20	20
160–164	13	13	4	4	3	3	12	11	10	6	9	3	5	2	4	1	0	0	1	0	61	43
155–159	16	12	50	42	47	34	40	28	34	21	14	8	3	2	8	0	0	0	1	1	213	148
150–154	32	23	59	20	64	16	68	10	47	6	28	2	8	0	5	0	0	0	5	1	316	78
145–149	23	1	35	1	57	3	46	4	42	1	27	0	13	0	3	1	3	0	3	0	252	11
140–144	8	0	11	1	27	2	28	1	23	4	11	1	11	0	6	0	2	0	1	0	128	9
135–139	2	1	6	0	7	0	14	2	17	0	12	1	5	0	5	0	2	0	2	0	72	4
130–134	0	0	0	0	0	0	3	0	7	0	3	0	3	0	3	0	0	0	1	0	20	0
125–129	0	0	0	0	0	0	1	0	0	0	0	0	2	0	2	0	0	0	0	0	5	0
120–124	0	0	0	0	0	0	0	0	0	0	0	0	1	0	0	0	0	0	0	0	1	0
Total	99	55	171	74	207	60	217	61	182	40	105	16	52	5	36	2	7	0	14	2	1090	315

Apps = Number of Applicants
Adm = Number Admitted
Reflects 98% of the total applicant pool.

Mercer University—Walter F. George School of Law

1021 Georgia Avenue
Macon, GA 31207
Phone: 478.301.2605; Fax: 478.301.2989
E-mail: martin_sv@mercer.edu; Website: www.law.mercer.edu

The Basics

Type of school	Private
Term	Semester
Application deadline	3/15
Application fee	$50
Financial aid deadline	4/1
Can first year start other than fall?	No
Student to faculty ratio	11.7 to 1
Does the university offer:	
housing restricted to law students?	No
graduate housing for which law students are eligible?	Yes

Faculty and Administrators

	Total		Men		Women		Minorities	
	Fall	Spr	Fall	Spr	Fall	Spr	Fall	Spr
Full-time	28	28	20	20	8	8	2	2
Other Full-time	0	0	0	0	0	0	0	0
Deans, librarians, & others who teach	10	10	5	5	5	5	0	0
Part-time	13	26	9	20	4	6	1	0
Total	**51**	**64**	**34**	**45**	**17**	**19**	**3**	**2**

Curriculum

		Full-time	Part-time
Typical first-year section size		78	0
Is there typically a "small section" of the first-year class, other than Legal Writing, taught by full-time faculty		Yes	No
If yes, typical size offered last year		24	
# of classroom course titles beyond first-year curriculum		97	
# of upper division courses, excluding seminars with an enrollment:	Under 25	116	
	25–49	41	
	50–74	13	
	75–99	19	
	100+	0	
# of seminars		14	
# of seminar positions available		210	
# of seminar positions filled		135	0
# of positions available in simulation courses		799	
# of simulation positions filled		664	0
# of positions available in faculty supervised clinical courses		9	
# of faculty supervised clinical positions filled		8	0
# involved in field placements		62	0
# involved in law journals		47	0
# involved in interschool competitions		31	0
# of credit hours required to graduate		91	

JD Enrollment and Ethnicity

	Men		Women		Full-time		Part-time		1st-year		Total		JD Degs. Awd.
	#	%	#	%	#	%	#	%	#	%	#	%	
African Amer.	16	6.3	33	17.4	49	11.0	0	0.0	20	11.6	49	11.0	8
Amer. Indian	1	0.4	1	0.5	2	0.4	0	0.0	1	0.6	2	0.4	2
Asian Amer.	5	2.0	7	3.7	12	2.7	0	0.0	3	1.7	12	2.7	3
Mex. Amer.	1	0.4	0	0.0	1	0.2	0	0.0	0	0.0	1	0.2	0
Puerto Rican	2	0.8	0	0.0	2	0.4	0	0.0	2	1.2	2	0.4	1
Hispanic	4	1.6	3	1.6	7	1.6	0	0.0	5	2.9	7	1.6	0
Total Minority	29	11.3	44	23.2	73	16.4	0	0.0	31	18.0	73	16.4	14
For. Nation.	2	0.8	1	0.5	3	0.7	0	0.0	3	1.7	3	0.7	0
Caucasian	193	75.4	125	65.8	318	71.3	0	0.0	112	65.1	318	71.3	102
Unknown	32	12.5	20	10.5	52	11.7	0	0.0	26	15.1	52	11.7	11
Total	256	57.4	190	42.6	446	100.0	0	0.0	172	38.6	446		127

Transfers

Transfers in	0
Transfers out	10

Tuition and Fees

	Resident	Nonresident
Full-time	$30,146	$30,146
Part-time	$0	$0

Living Expenses

Estimated living expenses for singles

Living on campus	Living off campus	Living at home
$14,200	$14,200	$14,200

Mercer University—Walter F. George School of Law

ABA
Approved
Since
1925

GPA and LSAT Scores

	Total	Full-time	Part-time
# of apps	1,290	1,290	0
# of offers	457	457	0
# of matrics	176	176	0
75% GPA	3.67	3.67	0.00
Median GPA	3.45	3.45	0.00
25% GPA	3.03	3.03	0.00
75% LSAT	158	158	0
Median LSAT	156	156	0
25% LSAT	153	153	0

Grants and Scholarships (from prior year)

	Total		Full-time		Part-time	
	#	%	#	%	#	%
Total # of students	408		407		1	
Total # receiving grants	151	37.0	151	37.1	0	0.0
Less than 1/2 tuition	82	20.1	82	20.1	0	0.0
Half to full tuition	9	2.2	9	2.2	0	0.0
Full tuition	30	7.4	30	7.4	0	0.0
More than full tuition	30	7.4	30	7.4	0	0.0
Median grant amount			$12,000		$0	

Informational and Library Resources

# of volumes and volume equivalents	338,207
# of titles	75,032
# of active serial subscriptions	3,269
Study seating capacity inside the library	387
# of full-time professional librarians	6
Hours per week library is open	68
# of open, wired connections available to students	724
# of networked computers available for use by students	54
# of simultaneous wireless users	80
Require computer?	Yes

JD Attrition (from prior year)

	Academic	Other	Total	
	#	#	#	%
1st year	0	8	8	5.2
2nd year	0	2	2	1.6
3rd year	0	1	1	0.8
4th year	0	0	0	0.0

Employment (9 months after graduation)

	Total	Percentage
Employment status known	148	100.0
Employment status unknown	0	0.0
Employed	139	93.9
Pursuing graduate degrees	5	3.4
Unemployed seeking employment	4	2.7
Unemployed not seeking employment	0	0.0
Unemployed and studying for the bar	0	0.0
Type of Employment		
# employed in law firms	87	62.6
# employed in business and industry	16	11.5
# employed in government	11	7.9
# employed in public interest	10	7.2
# employed as judicial clerks	14	10.1
# employed in academia	1	0.7
Geographic Location		
# employed in state	112	80.6
# employed in foreign countries	0	0.0
# of states where employed		13

Bar Passage Rates

Jurisdiction	Georgia		
Exam	Sum 05	Win 06	Total
# from school taking bar for the first time	113	8	121
School's pass rate for all first-time takers	91%	75%	90%
State's pass rate for all first-time takers	86%	79%	84%

Mercer University—Walter F. George School of Law

Office of Admissions, 1021 Georgia Avenue
Macon, GA 31207
Phone: 478.301.2605; Fax: 478.301.2989
E-mail: martin_sv@mercer.edu; Website: www.law.mercer.edu

■ Introduction

The Walter F. George School of Law of Mercer University is located in Macon, Georgia, about 80 miles south of Atlanta. Founded in 1873, it is one of the oldest private law schools in the nation. Named for a distinguished alumnus who served as a United States senator for 36 years, the school became a member of AALS in 1923 and has been ABA-approved since 1925. In 1987, George Woodruff bequeathed the school 15 million dollars. Two major initiatives were pursued as a result of Mr. Woodruff's beneficence: Enrollment was reduced to approximately 400 students, and a new curriculum was put in place. The new curriculum emphasizes small classes, an innovative progression in the course of study, and a unique sixth semester designed to facilitate the transition from student to lawyer.

■ Admission

Mercer University's Walter F. George School of Law accepts applications between September 1 and March 15 from prospective students wishing to begin their studies in the fall semester. The requirements for application are straightforward. Applicants must have completed a bachelor's degree prior to law school enrollment. They must register with LSDAS and take the LSAT, preferably in the summer or fall before application is made. Applicants must submit two letters of recommendation, an application fee, and a personal statement candidly discussing their strengths and weaknesses as prospective law students.

LSAT performance and undergraduate grades are very important in determining admission to Mercer Law School, but other factors will be considered to arrive at a fair evaluation of an applicant's potential to become a competent and ethical attorney. Postgraduate work, employment, community and military service, leadership ability, personal circumstances, and other relevant background information will be evaluated.

■ Library Facilities

The Furman Smith Law Library is the primary resource center of the law school. The law library and computing facilities are accessible to students 24 hours a day. The library's over 335,000-volume collection is enhanced by a wide array of online services that supports the curricular and research needs of the law school community. Students are able to access network resources from any of the more than 54 computers and 724 network access points throughout the law school. In addition, each first-year student receives a laptop computer to use during his or her legal education at Mercer Law School. The law library staff of 15 includes seven professional law librarians who teach legal research courses and provide superior service to students and the legal community.

■ Curriculum

Mercer's Woodruff Curriculum and the atmosphere of the law school work together to provide students with the four Measures of Mercer: a thorough intellectual foundation, strong practical skills, professional relationships, and a commitment to ethical behavior. The combination of these measures offers the strongest possible foundation for success in the practice of law. Mercer is one of a few select schools in the country to receive the prestigious Gambrell Professionalism Award from the American Bar Association. The award cites the depth and excellence of the Woodruff Curriculum and its obvious commitment to professionalism.

Implemented in 1990, the practice-oriented Woodruff Curriculum helps ensure that Mercer graduates develop problem-solving, counseling, and trial and appellate advocacy skills, and acquire the legal knowledge to become exceptional practicing attorneys. Each year begins with an introductory week-long course exploring one role of the practicing lawyer.

One pervasive skill needed for law practice is the ability to write clearly and convincingly. All students take research and writing courses during at least four semesters of law study, and many take a research or writing course each term. Mercer is the first law school in the nation to offer a Certificate in Advanced Legal Writing, Research, and Drafting. Students are selected into the certificate program through a lottery system; those who complete the certificate program will have earned the equivalent of 17 credit hours in research and writing. This program is by far the most intense and thorough training in legal writing anywhere. In 2003, in recognition of Mercer's nationally known Legal Writing Program, the Legal Writing Institute selected Mercer as its host school. The Legal Writing Institute is the world's largest organization of lawyers, judges, and law professors devoted to improving legal writing.

The last semester of study is the most distinctive component of the Woodruff Curriculum as it offers students a unique opportunity to make the transition from law school to law practice. An intensive session features advanced courses in a variety of practical lawyering skills such as Advanced Counseling, Pretrial Practice, and Advanced Trial Practice.

■ Joint JD/MBA Program

Mercer's School of Law and Mercer's School of Business and Economics offer a joint program leading to both the Juris Doctor and Master of Business Administration degrees. An applicant to the program must indicate on the application to the law school his or her intent to also apply to the School of Business and Economics. Both units will share the information on the application, including required standardized test scores (LSAT and GMAT). The applicant must be admitted separately to each school.

■ Business Certificate Program

Students in good standing in the Walter F. George School of Law may choose to take up to three graduate courses in the School of Business and Economics without applying for admission to the MBA program. Currently, two specific combinations of courses can be taken for a Certificate in Practice Management or a Certificate in Corporate Finance.

■ Special Programs

The Woodruff Curriculum is one of the most innovative and exciting education programs available, and it is offered to

Mercer University—Walter F. George School of Law

every Mercer student. A more complete description of the program is listed under the Curriculum heading.

Since 1985, the National Criminal Defense College (NCDC) has held its Summer Trial Practice Institute every year on the Mercer Law School campus. NCDC conducts two 2-week trial skills sessions for nearly 200 public defenders and criminal defense attorneys from across the country.

■ Student Activities

At Mercer University's Walter F. George School of Law, excellence is measured by more than what happens inside the classroom. You will find a broad array of activities outside the classroom that have been designed to engage the members of our academic community and enable our students to stand out once they enter the professional world.

In Mercer's moot court program, students improve their written and oral advocacy, negotiation, and client counseling skills. The team members' commitment and superior preparation are evident in our moot court competition victories.

The Mercer Law Review (the oldest continually published law review in Georgia) has been edited and published quarterly by law students since 1949.

Students may also gain editorial experience in connection with the *Journal of Southern Legal History*, which is published by the law school.

In addition to moot court and *Law Review*, Mercer offers its students the opportunity to participate in over two dozen student organizations where they can gain valuable leadership and relationship building experiences.

■ Financial Aid

Mercer awards over 2 million dollars in scholarship aid every year to students whose academic records, LSAT scores, and personal achievements demonstrate the potential for outstanding performance in the study of law. Two of our most prestigious scholarships are the George W. Woodruff Scholarship (full tuition plus a $5,000 stipend) and the Walter F. George Foundation Public Service Scholarship (full tuition plus a $3,500 summer community service grant). In order to be considered for these scholarships, you must have your admission application and scholarship application completed and received in our office no later than February 1. A complete list of scholarships is available on our website at *www.law.mercer.edu* under Prospective Students. In addition to scholarship aid, students may qualify for student loans, and work-study is available after the first year of law school.

■ Career Services

Mercer Law School has an active career services office. Alumni and faculty members support students in their efforts to find satisfying employment. The office assists students in obtaining permanent, summer, and part-time employment.

Services of the office include arranging on-campus interviews with employers, career-planning seminars, and off-campus interviewing consortia. Individual career counseling and résumé and cover-letter writing workshops also comprise much of the work of the office. An extensive library of career resources is available for student use.

The Office of Career Services reports that 96.6 percent of the Class of 2005 was employed or pursuing LLM degrees within six to nine months after graduation.

Applicant Profile

Mercer University—Walter F. George School of Law
This grid includes only applicants who earned 120–180 LSAT scores under standard administrations.

LSAT Score	3.75 +		3.50–3.74		3.25–3.49		3.00–3.24		2.75–2.99		2.50–2.74		2.25–2.49		2.00–2.24		Below 2.00		No GPA		Total	
	Apps	Adm	Apps	Adm	Apps	Adm	Apps	Adm	Apps	Adm	Apps	Adm	Apps	Adm	Apps	Adm	Apps	Adm	Apps	Adm	Apps	Adm
175–180	0	0	0	0	0	0	0	0	0	0	0	0	0	0	0	0	0	0	0	0	0	0
170–174	0	0	2	2	0	0	0	0	0	0	1	1	0	0	0	0	0	0	0	0	3	3
165–169	6	5	0	0	3	2	0	0	0	0	3	1	1	1	0	0	0	0	0	0	13	9
160–164	4	4	17	17	17	14	20	15	17	16	7	6	2	2	0	0	0	0	0	0	84	74
155–159	25	23	61	54	58	50	50	41	46	29	27	11	11	7	4	1	1	0	0	0	283	216
150–154	45	33	63	33	104	30	103	14	57	5	21	3	13	3	2	0	1	0	0	0	409	121
145–149	29	9	44	7	62	6	59	2	41	2	22	0	11	0	7	0	2	0	3	0	189	3
140–144	10	1	28	1	35	1	34	0	36	0	23	0	15	0	4	0	1	0	4	0	277	26
135–139	1	0	4	0	5	0	13	0	10	0	10	0	5	0	3	0	1	0	4	0	56	0
130–134	1	0	1	0	2	0	4	0	5	0	4	0	2	0	0	0	2	0	2	0	23	0
125–129	0	0	2	0	0	0	0	0	0	0	2	0	0	0	2	0	0	0	1	0	7	0
120–124	0	0	0	0	0	0	1	0	0	0	0	0	1	0	0	0	0	0	1	0	3	0
Total	121	75	222	114	286	103	284	72	212	52	120	22	61	13	22	1	7	0	12	0	1347	452

Apps = Number of Applicants
Adm = Number Admitted
Reflects 99% of the total applicant pool.
This chart is to be used as a general guide only. Nonnumerical factors are strongly considered for all applicants.

University of Miami School of Law

PO Box 248087
Coral Gables, FL 33124-8087
Phone: 305.284.2523; Fax: 305.284.3084
E-mail: admissions@law.miami.edu; Website: www.law.miami.edu

ABA Approved Since 1941

The Basics

Type of school	Private
Term	Semester
Application deadline	7/31
Application fee	$60
Financial aid deadline	3/1
Can first year start other than fall?	No
Student to faculty ratio	18.2 to 1
Does the university offer:	
housing restricted to law students?	No
graduate housing for which law students are eligible?	Yes

Faculty and Administrators

	Total		Men		Women		Minorities	
	Fall	Spr	Fall	Spr	Fall	Spr	Fall	Spr
Full-time	51	53	37	39	14	14	8	6
Other Full-time	4	4	1	1	3	3	1	0
Deans, librarians, & others who teach	13	12	6	5	7	7	3	3
Part-time	113	141	80	101	33	40	18	25
Total	**181**	**210**	**124**	**146**	**57**	**64**	**30**	**34**

Curriculum

	Full-time	Part-time
Typical first-year section size	100	0
Is there typically a "small section" of the first-year class, other than Legal Writing, taught by full-time faculty	Yes	No
If yes, typical size offered last year	50	
# of classroom course titles beyond first-year curriculum	102	

# of upper division courses, excluding seminars with an enrollment:		
Under 25	43	
25–49	26	
50–74	13	
75–99	6	
100+	14	

# of seminars	40	
# of seminar positions available	600	
# of seminar positions filled	342	0
# of positions available in simulation courses	684	
# of simulation positions filled	502	0
# of positions available in faculty supervised clinical courses	83	
# of faculty supervised clinical positions filled	83	0
# involved in field placements	96	0
# involved in law journals	212	0
# involved in interschool competitions	70	0
# of credit hours required to graduate	88	

JD Enrollment and Ethnicity

	Men		Women		Full-time		Part-time		1st-year		Total		JD Degs. Awd.
	#	%	#	%	#	%	#	%	#	%	#	%	
African Amer.	34	5.0	50	9.5	82	7.1	2	4.4	31	7.5	84	7.0	19
Amer. Indian	0	0.0	3	0.6	3	0.3	0	0.0	0	0.0	3	0.2	2
Asian Amer.	33	4.8	18	3.4	50	4.3	1	2.2	19	4.6	51	4.2	7
Mex. Amer.	0	0.0	0	0.0	0	0.0	0	0.0	0	0.0	0	0.0	0
Puerto Rican	0	0.0	0	0.0	0	0.0	0	0.0	0	0.0	0	0.0	0
Hispanic	62	9.1	80	15.2	137	11.8	5	11.1	53	12.7	142	11.8	36
Total Minority	129	18.9	151	28.7	272	23.4	8	17.8	103	24.8	280	23.2	64
For. Nation.	25	3.7	26	4.9	48	4.1	3	6.7	21	5.0	51	4.2	34
Caucasian	473	69.4	315	59.9	756	65.0	32	71.1	262	63.0	788	65.2	215
Unknown	55	8.1	34	6.5	87	7.5	2	4.4	30	7.2	89	7.4	18
Total	682	56.5	526	43.5	1163	96.3	45	3.7	416	34.4	1208		331

Transfers

Transfers in	20
Transfers out	30

Tuition and Fees

	Resident	Nonresident
Full-time	$32,820	$32,820
Part-time	$24,316	$24,316

Living Expenses

Estimated living expenses for singles

Living on campus	Living off campus	Living at home
N/A	$16,820	$8,725

University of Miami School of Law

ABA Approved Since 1941

GPA and LSAT Scores

	Total	Full-time	Part-time
# of apps	4,777	4,688	89
# of offers	2,340	2,330	10
# of matrics	420	416	4
75% GPA	3.66	3.66	3.40
Median GPA	3.47	3.47	2.81
25% GPA	3.25	3.25	2.48
75% LSAT	160	160	162
Median LSAT	158	158	158
25% LSAT	156	156	155

Grants and Scholarships (from prior year)

	Total #	Total %	Full-time #	Full-time %	Part-time #	Part-time %
Total # of students	1,151		1,099		52	
Total # receiving grants	398	34.6	398	36.2	0	0.0
Less than 1/2 tuition	201	17.5	201	18.3	0	0.0
Half to full tuition	185	16.1	185	16.8	0	0.0
Full tuition	2	0.2	2	0.2	0	0.0
More than full tuition	10	0.9	10	0.9	0	0.0
Median grant amount			$15,000		$0	

Informational and Library Resources

# of volumes and volume equivalents	613,078
# of titles	95,445
# of active serial subscriptions	6,964
Study seating capacity inside the library	750
# of full-time professional librarians	13
Hours per week library is open	111
# of open, wired connections available to students	111
# of networked computers available for use by students	146
# of simultaneous wireless users	1,800
Require computer?	No

JD Attrition (from prior year)

	Academic #	Other #	Total #	Total %
1st year	3	38	41	10.1
2nd year	0	2	2	0.5
3rd year	0	1	1	0.3
4th year	0	0	0	0.0

Employment (9 months after graduation)

	Total	Percentage
Employment status known	380	94.5
Employment status unknown	22	5.5
Employed	352	92.6
Pursuing graduate degrees	12	3.2
Unemployed seeking employment	2	0.5
Unemployed not seeking employment	5	1.3
Unemployed and studying for the bar	9	2.4

Type of Employment

	Total	Percentage
# employed in law firms	227	64.5
# employed in business and industry	38	10.8
# employed in government	35	9.9
# employed in public interest	35	9.9
# employed as judicial clerks	14	4.0
# employed in academia	0	0.0

Geographic Location

	Total	Percentage
# employed in state	254	72.2
# employed in foreign countries	0	0.0
# of states where employed	21	

Bar Passage Rates

Jurisdiction	Florida Sum 05	Florida Win 06	Florida Total	New York Sum 05	New York Win 06	New York Total
# from school taking bar for the first time	267	26	293	32	11	43
School's pass rate for all first-time takers	79%	69%	78%	94%	73%	88%
State's pass rate for all first-time takers	71%	73%	71%	76%	61%	74%

University of Miami School of Law

PO Box 248087
Coral Gables, FL 33124-8087
Phone: 305.284.2523; Fax: 305.284.3084
E-mail: admissions@law.miami.edu; Website: www.law.miami.edu

■ Introduction

Established in 1926 in Coral Gables, Florida, the University of Miami School of Law is part of one of the largest private research universities in the United States. The school's location on the main campus enables students to attend law school in a tranquil subtropical setting while taking advantage of the opportunities available in one of the most dynamic and rapidly expanding legal communities in the country. Miami is accredited by the ABA, is a member of the AALS, and has a chapter of the prestigious scholastic society, the Order of the Coif.

■ Faculty

The faculty of the University of Miami have exceptional credentials—including education at the world's top universities and law schools; significant prior work experience in private practice, government, and prestigious judicial clerkships; and extensive research, writing, and pro bono activities. Their expertise is especially strong in international and foreign law (with half of them having written or taught in those fields); taxation and estate planning; the interaction of legal doctrine with contemporary social issues, such as immigration, crime, the Internet, and intellectual property; legal ethics; and other fields.

■ Library

With approximately 600,000 volumes in print and microform, the Law Library is one of the largest in the Southeast. The library has liberal hours, a superb service-oriented staff, computer labs, and ample seating for individual study and group study rooms. Carrels throughout the library contain computers or ports for easy access to electronic resources. The campus is wireless.

■ Curriculum

The school provides a solid foundation in all the traditional subjects basic to understanding and practicing the law throughout the nation. It also offers ambitious programs designed to teach students the craft as well as the theory of the law, to develop the research and writing skills critical to the legal profession, and to expose students to other skills necessary for effective professional service.

Choosing from more than 160 courses, workshops, and seminars, students ordinarily complete the JD degree in three academic years of full-time study. Summer sessions are available. Miami's course offerings in inter-American, international, and comparative law are outstanding. Miami regularly offers comparative law classes, taught in Spanish, allowing students to better understand the nuances of law in Spanish-speaking countries. Joint JD/Masters programs are offered in business administration, public health, and marine affairs, and a JD/LLM is offered in taxation.

Master of Laws (LLM) programs include inter-American law, international law, ocean and coastal law, taxation, estate planning, real property development, and comparative law. A JD degree (or equivalent degree from a foreign law school) is required for entrance into an LLM program.

■ Special Programs

The school offers one of the most comprehensive and sophisticated skills training programs in the nation, integrating trial, pretrial, and clinical experiences into one program. Directed by a full-time faculty member, distinguished trial attorneys and judges from both state and federal courts assist with the trial and pretrial courses and help supervise the clinical placements. Additional skills training is available in transactional skills, alternative dispute resolution, mediation, and domestic and international legal research.

The school has distinguished itself by winning state, regional, and national competitions in moot court, mock trial, negotiation, and client counseling.

The Center for Ethics and Public Service is an interdisciplinary project teaching the values of ethical judgment, professional responsibility, and public service.

The Children & Youth Law Clinic provides representation to abused and neglected children and youth in the foster care system.

The Community Health Rights Education Clinic is an interdisciplinary program providing legal advice and advocacy to vulnerable low-income populations in cooperation with the Schools of Nursing and Medicine.

HOPE (Helping Others Through Pro Bono Efforts) is the law school's community outreach and advocacy project, offering a myriad of service opportunities for the law school community.

The Center for the Study of Human Rights is an interdisciplinary program with a mission to increase knowledge and understanding of international human rights issues with three basic components—scholarship, community outreach, and curriculum.

The James Weldon Johnson/Robert H. Waters Summer Institute acquaints selected incoming students with the tools necessary to succeed in law school.

Study-abroad options consist of five summer integrated module programs that are held in England, Spain, and the Mediterranean.

■ Admission

Admission is competitive. LSAT scores and undergraduate averages are used in the selection process, and letters of recommendation are required. Also considered are the applicant's work and extracurricular history, special skills, and background. Entering students are admitted only in the fall semester. Applicants are urged to apply for admission as early as possible after September 1. Applications received after February 5 will be considered on a space-available basis.

■ The Student Body and Student Life

Miami's student body is highly talented and exceptionally diverse, enriching students' educational experience by exposing them to a wide variety of viewpoints and life experiences. The school is consistently among the leaders in numbers of Hispanic, African American, and foreign students graduated from its JD program.

The school's many student activities include an active Student Bar Association, Honor Council, and more than 30 diverse student organizations, including the Black, Hispanic, and Asian/Pacific American Law Student Organizations, OUTlaw, Christian Legal Society, Federalist Society, European Union Law Society, International Law Society, Entertainment and Sports Law Society, Society for Peace and Justice, the Student Animal Legal Defense Fund, and many more. Students regularly take part in a wide range of pro bono activities. Miami's law journals include the *University of Miami Law Review*; the *University of Miami Inter-American Law Review*; the *University of Miami International and Comparative Law Review*; the *Business Law Review*; and *Psychology, Public Policy, and Law*.

■ Expenses and Financial Aid

Scholarship aid available through the school normally does not exceed the cost of tuition. Most scholarships are merit-based, although need is sometimes considered. Admitted applicants are automatically considered for most scholarship awards. Applicants who wish to be considered for a merit scholarship should complete their files prior to January 5. Most scholarships are awarded on a rolling basis. Those admitted by February 1 are considered for the prestigious Harvey T. Reid

and Soia Mentschikoff scholarships. In addition, admitted students are eligible to apply for the public-interest-related Miami Scholars Program, which requires a separate application with a deadline of March 15. The law school assists students in applying for public and private loans.

Federal loans may be applied for by filing the FAFSA online at *www.fafsa.ed.gov*. Our Federal School Code is E00532. Private loans may also be applied for online, and this information is sent to students upon admission.

■ Career Services

The Career Planning Center provides individual career counseling to law students and alumni. The center offers a wide range of job-related programming and job fairs; networking opportunities with attorneys in varied practice areas; and access to a resource library and national job postings via the Internet. The On-Campus Interview Program attracts national and local employers, providing opportunities with law firms, government agencies, public service organizations, corporate counsel, and the judiciary.

Applicant Profile

University of Miami School of Law
This grid includes only applicants who earned 120–180 LSAT scores under standard administrations.

LSAT Score	GPA									
	3.75 +	3.50–3.74	3.25–3.49	3.00–3.24	2.75–2.99	2.50–2.74	2.25–2.49	2.00–2.24	Below 2.00	No GPA
175–180										
170–174										
165–169										
160–164										
155–159										
150–154										
145–149										
140–144										
135–139										
130–134										
125–129										
120–124										

■ Good Possibility   □ Possible   ▨ Unlikely

When reviewing the grid, it is important to note that admission to the school is based upon all aspects of an applicant's background, and not limited to the LSAT and undergraduate grade-point average.

The University of Michigan Law School

Hutchins Hall, 625 South State Street
Ann Arbor, MI 48109-1215
Phone: 734.764.1358
E-mail: law.jd.admissions@umich.edu; Website: www.law.umich.edu

*ABA
Approved
Since
1923*

The Basics

Type of school	Public
Term	Semester
Application deadline	11/15 2/15
Application fee	$60
Financial aid deadline	
Can first year start other than fall?	Yes
Student to faculty ratio	14.5 to 1
Does the university offer:	
housing restricted to law students?	Yes
graduate housing for which law students are eligible?	Yes

Curriculum

	Full-time	Part-time
Typical first-year section size	91	0
Is there typically a "small section" of the first-year class, other than Legal Writing, taught by full-time faculty	Yes	No
If yes, typical size offered last year	46	
# of classroom course titles beyond first-year curriculum	147	
# of upper division courses, excluding seminars with an enrollment: Under 25	56	
25–49	37	
50–74	12	
75–99	14	
100+	17	
# of seminars	62	
# of seminar positions available	1,071	
# of seminar positions filled	851	0
# of positions available in simulation courses	336	
# of simulation positions filled	280	0
# of positions available in faculty supervised clinical courses	210	
# of faculty supervised clinical positions filled	186	0
# involved in field placements	25	0
# involved in law journals	444	0
# involved in interschool competitions	60	0
# of credit hours required to graduate	82	

Faculty and Administrators

	Total		Men		Women		Minorities	
	Fall	Spr	Fall	Spr	Fall	Spr	Fall	Spr
Full-time	67	60	49	42	18	18	7	5
Other Full-time	8	8	4	4	4	4	1	1
Deans, librarians, & others who teach	3	3	2	2	1	1	0	0
Part-time	26	37	14	23	12	14	1	4
Total	104	108	69	71	35	37	9	10

JD Enrollment and Ethnicity

	Men		Women		Full-time		Part-time		1st-year		Total		JD Degs. Awd.
	#	%	#	%	#	%	#	%	#	%	#	%	
African Amer.	35	5.6	44	8.7	79	7.0	0	0.0	26	7.0	79	7.0	25
Amer. Indian	16	2.6	11	2.2	27	2.4	0	0.0	8	2.2	27	2.4	13
Asian Amer.	71	11.4	73	14.4	144	12.7	0	0.0	50	13.5	144	12.7	50
Mex. Amer.	0	0.0	0	0.0	0	0.0	0	0.0	0	0.0	0	0.0	0
Puerto Rican	0	0.0	0	0.0	0	0.0	0	0.0	0	0.0	0	0.0	0
Hispanic	36	5.8	28	5.5	64	5.7	0	0.0	19	5.1	64	5.7	31
Total Minority	158	25.4	156	30.8	314	27.8	0	0.0	103	27.8	314	27.8	119
For. Nation.	22	3.5	19	3.7	41	3.6	0	0.0	10	2.7	41	3.6	7
Caucasian	369	59.2	289	57.0	658	58.2	0	0.0	219	59.2	658	58.2	273
Unknown	74	11.9	43	8.5	117	10.4	0	0.0	38	10.3	117	10.4	32
Total	623	55.1	507	44.9	1130	100.0	0	0.0	370	32.7	1130		431

Transfers

Transfers in	37
Transfers out	8

Tuition and Fees

	Resident	Nonresident
Full-time	$35,502	$38,502
Part-time	$0	$0

Living Expenses

Estimated living expenses for singles

Living on campus	Living off campus	Living at home
$14,480	$14,480	$5,600

The University of Michigan Law School

*ABA
Approved
Since
1923*

GPA and LSAT Scores

	Total	Full-time	Part-time
# of apps	5,664	5,664	0
# of offers	1,165	1,165	0
# of matrics	369	369	0
75% GPA	3.80	3.80	0.00
Median GPA	3.67	3.67	0.00
25% GPA	3.53	3.53	0.00
75% LSAT	170	170	0
Median LSAT	168	168	0
25% LSAT	166	166	0

Grants and Scholarships (from prior year)

	Total		Full-time		Part-time	
	#	%	#	%	#	%
Total # of students	1,179		1,179		0	
Total # receiving grants	690	58.5	690	58.5	0	0.0
Less than 1/2 tuition	620	52.6	620	52.6	0	0.0
Half to full tuition	26	2.2	26	2.2	0	0.0
Full tuition	0	0.0	0	0.0	0	0.0
More than full tuition	44	3.7	44	3.7	0	0.0
Median grant amount			$9,431		$0	

Informational and Library Resources

# of volumes and volume equivalents	960,387
# of titles	318,089
# of active serial subscriptions	9,071
Study seating capacity inside the library	855
# of full-time professional librarians	11
Hours per week library is open	112
# of open, wired connections available to students	295
# of networked computers available for use by students	200
# of simultaneous wireless users	2,000
Require computer?	No

JD Attrition (from prior year)

	Academic	Other	Total	
	#	#	#	%
1st year	0	1	1	0.3
2nd year	0	8	8	2.0
3rd year	1	0	1	0.2
4th year	0	0	0	0.0

Employment (9 months after graduation)

	Total	Percentage
Employment status known	361	100.0
Employment status unknown	0	0.0
Employed	337	93.4
Pursuing graduate degrees	9	2.5
Unemployed seeking employment	1	0.3
Unemployed not seeking employment	14	3.9
Unemployed and studying for the bar	0	0.0
Type of Employment		
# employed in law firms	241	71.5
# employed in business and industry	6	1.8
# employed in government	11	3.3
# employed in public interest	30	8.9
# employed as judicial clerks	44	13.1
# employed in academia	4	1.2
Geographic Location		
# employed in state	46	13.6
# employed in foreign countries	9	2.7
# of states where employed	31	

Bar Passage Rates

Jurisdiction	New York			Illinois		
Exam	Sum 05	Win 06	Total	Sum 05	Win 06	Total
# from school taking bar for the first time	95	20	115	68	27	95
School's pass rate for all first-time takers	96%	100%	97%	99%	96%	98%
State's pass rate for all first-time takers	76%	61%	74%	86%	83%	85%

The University of Michigan Law School

Hutchins Hall, 625 South State Street
Ann Arbor, MI 48109-1215
Phone: 734.764.1358
E-mail: law.jd.admissions@umich.edu; Website: www.law.umich.edu

■ Introduction

The University of Michigan Law School, founded in 1859, is one of the nation's finest institutions of legal education. The school is home to a distinguished and diverse faculty, many of its scholars preeminent in their fields. Our students come from around the globe to contribute their remarkable talents and accomplishments to make the Law School a collegial community that exudes a sense of serious purpose, high academic achievement, and social commitment. Our graduates serve with distinction in all sectors of law, business, government, and the judiciary. Never restricted to the privileged, in 1870, Michigan—then the largest law school in the country—became the second American university to confer a law degree on an African American. That same year, Michigan became the first major law school to admit a woman, and in 1871, its graduate, Sarah Killgore, became the first woman with a law degree in the nation to be admitted to the bar.

■ Faculty

Michigan has over 75 full-time faculty members, with many distinguished visiting scholars and practitioners further enhancing course offerings. While maintaining a long tradition of eminence in constitutional, criminal, international, and comparative law, the interdisciplinary breadth of the faculty is reflected in an extraordinary range of expertise, including classics, economics, English, feminist theory, history, life sciences, philosophy, political theory, psychology, public policy, and sociology. The depth is reflected in a critical and distinctive fact: while many law schools have faculty members with interdisciplinary training, Michigan is unique in the number of law professors who are also governing faculty members of a world-class department in another discipline. Further, more than 40 percent of the faculty hold doctorates in nonlaw fields, while nine are Fellows of the American Academy of Arts and Sciences. The contributions of Michigan Law faculty to public policy and academic debates are well recognized.

■ Physical Facilities and Library

The location of residential and academic buildings within the strikingly beautiful Gothic architecture of the William W. Cook Law Quadrangle fosters the integration of activities for both students and faculty.

With over 960,000 volumes, the law library has one of the world's premier collections. Law students also have access to other university libraries. Wireless access technology allows law students network access throughout the Quadrangle and beyond.

■ Curriculum

Recognized as preeminent in interdisciplinary legal studies, the insights and methods of other fields are apparent throughout Michigan's broad curriculum. Formal joint programs are available in 13 disciplines, and students may count nine credits of other graduate-level work toward their JD.

A key component of the first year is the Legal Practice Program. A leader among top law schools, Michigan's program provides individualized instruction in legal writing, research, and oral advocacy taught by full-time faculty to first-year students, as well as upper-level corporate drafting instruction.

As one of the leaders in American legal education, Michigan's curriculum is strong across-the-board. Those with particular interest in business, corporate, and securities law; intellectual property; and public interest should, however, pay special attention to Michigan's extensive offerings in these areas.

Particularly renowned for international scholarship, Michigan has since 2001 required all students to complete Transnational Law. Externships such as the South African Program provide students with advanced training in their areas of interest. Internships are also available through such initiatives as the Program for Cambodian Law and Development.

■ Clinical Opportunities

For over 30 years, the Law School has provided a clinical practice program. As early as the first semester of their second year, students represent clients selected from a rich pool of cases, and the nature of local court dockets allows students to handle many cases from beginning to end. Offerings include a General Clinic, in which students may be involved in civil and/or criminal trial work; a Child Advocacy Law Clinic; a Criminal Appellate Practice Clinic; the transactional Urban Communities Clinic; a Mediation Clinic; and the medicolegal Pediatric Advocacy Clinic. Students can also enroll in a practicum in environmental law or asylum and refugee law, or participate in the Family Law Project, a student-run advocacy program for victims of domestic violence.

■ Admission and Student Body

The quality of the applicant's educational experience and LSAT scores are important in the admission process, but extracurricular and work experience, the personal statement, and letters of recommendation are also relied on heavily. Refer to Applicant Profile for more information.

■ Student Activities

Approximately 400 students participate in six journals: the *Michigan Law Review*, the *Journal of Law Reform*, the *Michigan Journal of International Law*, the *Michigan Journal of Gender and Law*, the *Michigan Telecommunications and Technology Law Review*, and the *Michigan Journal of Race and Law*. Students interested in honing oral advocacy and legal writing skills may choose to enter numerous available moot court competitions. The Law School Student Senate funds more than 50 student organizations, and students also participate in groups throughout the larger university community.

■ Expenses and Financial Aid

Our financial aid resources are substantial, and we distribute more than $3 million in grants annually to an entering class. Grants range in size from $5,000 to as much as full tuition plus a stipend; most grants are in the amount of $12,000 to $14,000 annually. The Law School's financial aid resources are divided evenly between grants made with reference to financial need, and merit awards made to outstanding candidates who are remarkable for their anticipated contribution to the Law School and the profession.

Michigan's Debt Management Program is the most progressive of its kind. It provides graduates with the flexibility to choose jobs from an unlimited range of law-related opportunities, including lower-paying public interest positions, while still maintaining a reasonable lifestyle and remaining current on outstanding loan obligations.

■ Career Services/Public Service

Michigan consistently places in the top echelon of law schools for career prospects. All of our attorney-counselors have both private and public sector experience, and can advise students about the full range of professional opportunities. Graduates enjoy a 99 percent employment rate. Our On-Campus Interview Program regularly brings in more than 750 employers from the most prestigious firms nationally and abroad; students choose interviews by lottery (employers are not permitted to prescreen), and 2Ls average more than 20 interviews. An additional 1,800 employers contact the Law School to solicit applications from students. The largest number of our graduates go to New York City and Chicago, followed closely by California; Washington, DC; and Detroit.

Reflecting our long-standing commitment, the Office of Public Service is dedicated to providing career counseling and connecting students with mentors, pro bono opportunities, and inspiring jobs. The staff acts as a link between our students and the hundreds of our graduates doing public service work throughout the world.

Career counselors and Law School faculty advise and support students seeking judicial clerkships. In recent years, an average of 18 percent of the graduating class has accepted prestigious clerkships with federal, state, and international courts. Michigan graduates are leaders in obtaining other prestigious legal positions as well. About 400 of our graduates teach, making Michigan one of a handful of feeder schools for this profession. Likewise, Michigan has graduated the third highest number of state and federal judges in the country.

■ Housing

Ann Arbor combines ease of living with superb cultural, athletic, and entertainment offerings. High-quality off-campus housing is available in a wide variety of choices and neighborhoods. Economical family housing is available to married students, domestic partners, and single parents with custody of their children. Approximately half of first-year students reside in the Lawyers Club, enjoying the easy access and camaraderie of life in the Quadrangle.

Applicant Profile

We choose not to provide an applicant profile because we do not believe a grid based on undergraduate GPA and LSAT scores can accurately reflect our comprehensive admission process, which focuses on many elements in an application in order to determine an applicant's particular intellectual strengths, nonacademic achievements, and unique personal circumstances. We view our student body as one of our greatest assets, and our goal is to admit a group of students who, individually and collectively, are among the best applying to American law schools in a given year. We seek a mix of

students with varying backgrounds and experiences who will respect and learn from each other. Our most general measures are an applicant's LSAT score and undergraduate GPA. As measured by those statistics, Michigan is among the handful of the most selective law schools in the country. However, each of these measures is far from perfect. Even the highest possible scores will not guarantee admission, and low scores will likewise not automatically result in a denial, as both circumstances may have significant offsetting considerations.

Michigan State University College of Law

230 Law College Building
East Lansing, MI 48824-1300
Phone: 800.844.9352, 517.432.0222; Fax: 517.432.0098
E-mail: law@law.msu.edu; Website: www.law.msu.edu

The Basics

Type of school	Private
Term	Semester
Application deadline	3/1
Application fee	$60
Financial aid deadline	4/1
Can first year start other than fall?	No
Student to faculty ratio	19.5 to 1
Does the university offer:	
housing restricted to law students?	No
graduate housing for which law students are eligible?	Yes

Faculty and Administrators

	Total		Men		Women		Minorities	
	Fall	Spr	Fall	Spr	Fall	Spr	Fall	Spr
Full-time	39	39	23	23	16	16	6	6
Other Full-time	2	2	2	2	0	0	0	0
Deans, librarians, & others who teach	14	14	6	6	8	8	1	1
Part-time	41	53	31	40	10	13	1	1
Total	**96**	**108**	**62**	**71**	**34**	**37**	**8**	**8**

Curriculum

	Full-time	Part-time
Typical first-year section size	68	80
Is there typically a "small section" of the first-year class, other than Legal Writing, taught by full-time faculty	No	No
If yes, typical size offered last year		
# of classroom course titles beyond first-year curriculum	180	
# of upper division courses, excluding seminars with an enrollment: Under 25	71	
25–49	54	
50–74	14	
75–99	13	
100+	4	
# of seminars	73	
# of seminar positions available	1,312	
# of seminar positions filled	849	142
# of positions available in simulation courses	858	
# of simulation positions filled	539	85
# of positions available in faculty supervised clinical courses	190	
# of faculty supervised clinical positions filled	68	15
# involved in field placements	269	35
# involved in law journals	153	8
# involved in interschool competitions	64	5
# of credit hours required to graduate	88	

JD Enrollment and Ethnicity

	Men		Women		Full-time		Part-time		1st-year		Total		JD Degs. Awd.
	#	%	#	%	#	%	#	%	#	%	#	%	
African Amer.	20	3.8	27	6.5	30	4.1	17	8.2	14	5.2	47	5.0	14
Amer. Indian	6	1.2	7	1.7	10	1.4	3	1.4	3	1.1	13	1.4	1
Asian Amer.	19	3.6	18	4.3	32	4.4	5	2.4	8	3.0	37	3.9	12
Mex. Amer.	0	0.0	0	0.0	0	0.0	0	0.0	0	0.0	0	0.0	0
Puerto Rican	0	0.0	0	0.0	0	0.0	0	0.0	0	0.0	0	0.0	0
Hispanic	19	3.6	5	1.2	16	2.2	8	3.9	7	2.6	24	2.6	1
Total Minority	64	12.3	57	13.7	88	12.1	33	15.9	32	11.9	121	12.9	28
For. Nation.	28	5.4	20	4.8	43	5.9	5	2.4	19	7.1	48	5.1	19
Caucasian	417	80.0	331	79.6	579	79.3	169	81.6	208	77.3	748	79.8	171
Unknown	12	2.3	8	1.9	20	2.7	0	0.0	10	3.7	20	2.1	176
Total	521	55.6	416	44.4	730	77.9	207	22.1	269	28.7	937		394

Transfers

Transfers in	45
Transfers out	17

Tuition and Fees

	Resident	Nonresident
Full-time	$28,182	$28,182
Part-time	$21,434	$21,434

Living Expenses

Estimated living expenses for singles

Living on campus	Living off campus	Living at home
$13,514	$13,514	$13,514

Michigan State Univ

ABA Approved Since 1941

GPA and LSAT Scores

	Total	Full-time	Part-time
# of apps	2,743	2,489	254
# of offers	1,140	1,001	139
# of matrics	267	188	79
75% GPA	3.61	3.67	3.52
Median GPA	3.37	3.40	3.32
25% GPA	3.06	3.05	3.07
75% LSAT	159	160	154
Median LSAT	155	157	152
25% LSAT	153	155	149

Grants and Scholarships (from prior year)

	Total		Full-time		Part-time	
	#	%	#	%	#	%
Total # of students	1,044		825		219	
Total # receiving grants	359	34.4	317	38.4	42	19.2
Less than 1/2 tuition	81	7.8	73	8.8	8	3.7
Half to full tuition	105	10.1	92	11.2	13	5.9
Full tuition	173	16.6	152	18.4	21	9.6
More than full tuition	0	0.0	0	0.0	0	0.0
Median grant amount			$15,627		$14,734	

Informational and Library Resources

# of volumes and volume equivalents	279,406
# of titles	143,148
# of active serial subscriptions	4,088
Study seating capacity inside the library	455
# of full-time professional librarians	7
Hours per week library is open	109
# of open, wired connections available to students	1,189
# of networked computers available for use by students	72
# of simultaneous wireless users	20,480
Require computer?	Yes

JD Attrition (from prior year)

	Academic #			
1st year	5	11	16	5.7
2nd year	1	20	21	5.8
3rd year	0	0	0	0.0
4th year	0	0	0	0.0

Employment (9 months after graduation)

	Total	Percentage
Employment status known	294	93.3
Employment status unknown	21	6.7
Employed	252	85.7
Pursuing graduate degrees	14	4.8
Unemployed seeking employment	12	4.1
Unemployed not seeking employment	1	0.3
Unemployed and studying for the bar	15	5.1
Type of Employment		
# employed in law firms	122	48.4
# employed in business and industry	39	15.5
# employed in government	36	14.3
# employed in public interest	13	5.2
# employed as judicial clerks	19	7.5
# employed in academia	7	2.8
Geographic Location		
# employed in state	159	63.1
# employed in foreign countries	5	2.0
# of states where employed	25	

Bar Passage Rates

Jurisdiction	Michigan		
Exam	Sum 05	Win 06	Total
# from school taking bar for the first time	143	27	170
School's pass rate for all first-time takers	80%	67%	78%
State's pass rate for all first-time takers	78%	65%	74%

...te University College of Law

...ns & Financial Aid, 230 Law College Building
...I 48824-1300
...844.9352, 517.432.0222; Fax: 517.432.0098
...aw@law.msu.edu; Website: www.law.msu.edu

■ Introduction

MSU College of Law is fully integrated with Michigan State University—a Big Ten school and one of the top research universities in the world. While we remain a private, financially independent law school, MSU Law is a constituent college within MSU and is located in a state-of-the-art facility in the center of MSU's East Lansing campus. Our association with a major university means that you will benefit from distinctive interdisciplinary programs. MSU Law is fully accredited by the ABA and is a member of the AALS.

■ Enrollment/Student Body

The students of MSU Law represent a diversity of educational backgrounds, experiences, and national origins. MSU College of Law students receive a legal education in the theory and purpose of the law, along with its practical application, thus equipping them to fulfill unique and complicated demands in legal and nonlegal careers.

■ Faculty

The faculty is composed of resident professors who are devoted to the teaching of law, legal research instructors, and a cadre of adjunct faculty members and practicing attorneys who are specialists with extensive experience in the field of law that they teach.

■ Library and Physical Facilities

This major research collection includes the statutes of the 50 states, the United States, and Canada, as well as collections of numerous decisions, legal periodicals, and treatises. The computer lab is equipped with 40 networked computers. Students have access to word processing, CALI tutorials, Westlaw, LexisNexis, individual e-mail accounts, and the Internet. Most classrooms, the library, and some study areas are fully wired, and students are encouraged to use their laptops during class. The law college also offers a complete wireless network throughout the building. In fall 2004, MSU Law completed $600,000 in renovations to its moot courtroom, making it one of the most technologically advanced teaching courtrooms in the nation.

■ Special Programs

One of the nation's most prominent practicing trial lawyers—MSU Law alumnus Geoffrey N. Fieger, 1979—has partnered with the law college to establish the first trial practice institute at a law school, designed specifically to train law students as successful trial lawyers. The institute offers:

- a rigorous, comprehensive, two-year certificate program designed in collaboration with practicing trial lawyers and judges
- a selective admission process that admits students based on their potential for successful trial advocacy
- a scholarship program
- an annual lecture series that showcases nationally known trial lawyers

- hands-on learning experiences through clinics, externships, field placements, and simulations
- the law college's moot courtroom, one of the most technologically advanced teaching courtrooms in the nation
- national and international trial advocacy and moot court competition teams
- interdisciplinary learning opportunities, which include collaborations with the MSU Department of Theatre to teach courtroom communication and the study of forensic science

MSU Law Concentrations include alternative dispute resolution, corporate law, criminal law, environmental and natural resource law, family law, health law, intellectual property and communications law, international and comparative law, public law and regulation, and taxation. The concentrations allow students to use a portion of their elective credits to develop expertise in a particular practice area.

Certificate Programs—In addition to the Trial Practice Certificate Program, MSU Law offers an Indigenous Law Certificate Program and a Child and Family Advocacy Certificate Program in cooperation with the MSU School of Social Work.

Dual Degrees—MSU Law's affiliation with MSU—and its relationship with Grand Valley State University in Grand Rapids—make it possible for law students to pursue both a JD and another advanced degree at the same time. You can choose from 15 dual-degree programs in the following areas: accounting; business; bioethics, humanities, and society; English; fisheries and wildlife; forestry; labor relations and human resources; park, recreation, and tourism resources; taxation; or urban and regional planning. It is possible to earn a law degree and a master's degree in just four years. A joint LLB/JD degree program is available in conjunction with the University of Ottawa Faculty of Law.

Study-abroad Programs—The MSU Law Canadian Summer Externship Program and Canadian Study Abroad Program provide students with the opportunity to study US-Canadian and international law and gain legal work experience in Ottawa. The Study Abroad in Mexico Program gives students international law experience during one-, two-, or three-week summer programs in Guadalajara.

Dean Charles H. King Scholarship Program is designed to enhance educational opportunities for high achievers by offering selected candidates a substantial scholarship to study law at MSU Law. King Scholars receive merit-based scholarships that cover 100 percent of tuition. First-year students must have a minimum 161 LSAT score and 3.5 undergraduate grade-point average to be considered for the King Scholarship.

A Master of Laws (LLM) program requiring one full year of study is offered for foreign lawyers. An LLM/MJ (Master of Jurisprudence) is offered in Intellectual Property and Communications Law for domestic and foreign students.

■ Admission

MSU Law is committed to a broad inquiry into the role and function of law in society and seeks a diverse student body as an integral part of its educational program. The primary considerations for admission are the applicant's undergraduate grade-point average and LSAT score.

■ Curricular Activities

MSU Law Clinics—MSU Law operates six law clinics to benefit low-income citizens and give law students an opportunity to put their legal knowledge into practice. Second- and third-year law students can provide legal counsel under the supervision of clinic faculty who are members of the State Bar of Michigan. The clinics include Rental Housing, Tax, Small Business and Nonprofit Law, Chance at Childhood Law and Social Work, Indigenous Law, and Midwest Student Press Clinic.

Externships—The MSU Law externship programs are classified under three broad categories: judicial, legal aid, and government attorney externships. There is a Washington, DC federal externship program in addition to an innovative environmental law externship. Students may propose externships as well.

The Law Review, Journal of International Law, and Moot Court and Trial Advocacy Board each provide students with opportunities to excel academically and practice their lawyering, legal research, and writing skills.

■ Student Activities

ABA/Law Student Division, ACLU of MSU Law, Amnesty International, Asian Pacific American Association, Association of Trial Lawyers of America, Business Law Society, Canadian Student Legal Association, Chinese Legal Society, Christian Legal Society, Delta Theta Phi, Entertainment and Sports Law Society, Environmental Law Society, Family Law Society, Federalist Society, Intellectual Property Law Society, International Law Society, Jewish Legal Organization of MSU Law, Jewish Legal Society, *Journal of International Law, Journal of Medicine and Law,* Labor and Employment Law Society, *Michigan State Intellectual Property Review, Michigan State Law Review,* Medical Legal Society, Military Law Society, Moot Court and Advocacy Board, MSU Law Basketball Association, MSU Law Ice Hockey Club, MSU Law Rugby, Phi Alpha Delta, Phi Delta Phi, Public Interest Law Society, St. Thomas More Society, Student Animal Legal Defense Fund, Student Bar Association, Tax and Estate Planning Society, Triangle Bar Association, Wolverine Student Bar Association, and Women's Law Caucus.

Applicant Profile

Michigan State University College of Law
This grid includes only applicants who earned 120–180 LSAT scores under standard administrations.

LSAT Score	3.75 +		3.50–3.74		3.25–3.49		3.00–3.24		2.75–2.99		2.50–2.74		2.25–2.49		2.00–2.24		Below 2.00		No GPA		Total	
	Apps	Adm	Apps	Adm	Apps	Adm	Apps	Adm	Apps	Adm	Apps	Adm	Apps	Adm	Apps	Adm	Apps	Adm	Apps	Adm	Apps	Adm
175–180	1	1	0	0	1	1	1	1	0	0	0	0	0	0	0	0	0	0	0	0	3	3
170–174	2	2	3	2	1	1	2	0	0	0	1	1	0	0	0	0	0	0	0	0	9	6
165–169	11	9	15	15	18	15	16	16	6	6	3	3	5	4	2	0	0	0	0	0	76	68
160–164	45	42	51	49	55	49	36	34	26	23	16	11	14	7	5	0	1	0	2	2	251	217
155–159	63	60	99	97	123	118	99	93	78	56	46	19	21	8	5	1	2	0	8	5	544	457
150–154	77	51	157	90	204	80	205	43	124	22	73	8	26	2	8	0	2	0	8	4	884	300
145–149	38	8	100	12	154	12	115	4	66	1	60	3	24	2	6	0	2	0	5	0	570	42
140–144	14	0	34	0	40	2	55	2	47	1	35	1	13	0	7	0	3	0	5	0	253	6
135–139	0	0	4	0	12	0	20	0	18	0	21	0	6	0	7	0	1	0	3	0	92	0
130–134	1	0	2	0	1	0	5	1	9	0	2	0	7	0	5	0	3	0	1	0	36	1
125–129	0	0	0	0	0	0	0	0	0	0	3	0	0	0	2	0	0	0	0	0	5	0
120–124	0	0	0	0	0	0	0	0	0	0	0	0	0	0	0	0	0	0	0	0	0	0
Total	252	173	465	265	609	278	554	194	374	109	260	46	116	23	47	1	14	0	32	11	2723	1100

Apps = Number of Applicants
Adm = Number Admitted
Reflects 99% of the total applicant pool.

University of Minnesota Law School

290 Walter F. Mondale Hall, 229 19th Avenue South
Minneapolis, MN 55455
Phone: 612.625.3487; Fax: 612.626.1874
E-mail: umnlsadm@umn.edu; Website: www.law.umn.edu

The Basics

Type of school	Public
Term	Semester
Application deadline	3/1
Application fee	$70
Financial aid deadline	5/15
Can first year start other than fall?	No
Student to faculty ratio	11.1 to 1
Does the university offer:	
housing restricted to law students?	No
graduate housing for which law students are eligible?	No

Faculty and Administrators

	Total		Men		Women		Minorities	
	Fall	Spr	Fall	Spr	Fall	Spr	Fall	Spr
Full-time	57	62	40	41	17	21	5	6
Other Full-time	3	4	0	1	3	3	0	1
Deans, librarians, & others who teach	9	10	4	5	5	5	3	4
Part-time	79	88	37	47	42	41	5	3
Total	148	164	81	94	67	70	13	14

Curriculum

	Full-time	Part-time
Typical first-year section size	108	0
Is there typically a "small section" of the first-year class, other than Legal Writing, taught by full-time faculty	Yes	No
If yes, typical size offered last year	54	
# of classroom course titles beyond first-year curriculum	196	

# of upper division courses, excluding seminars with an enrollment:		
Under 25	58	
25–49	46	
50–74	16	
75–99	10	
100+	2	

# of seminars	64	
# of seminar positions available	837	
# of seminar positions filled	817	0
# of positions available in simulation courses	351	
# of simulation positions filled	339	0
# of positions available in faculty supervised clinical courses	305	
# of faculty supervised clinical positions filled	293	0
# involved in field placements	130	0
# involved in law journals	223	0
# involved in interschool competitions	197	0
# of credit hours required to graduate	88	

JD Enrollment and Ethnicity

	Men		Women		Full-time		Part-time		1st-year		Total		JD Degs. Awd.
	#	%	#	%	#	%	#	%	#	%	#	%	
African Amer.	9	2.0	9	2.6	18	2.2	0	0.0	6	2.3	18	2.2	6
Amer. Indian	5	1.1	2	0.6	7	0.9	0	0.0	3	1.2	7	0.9	0
Asian Amer.	33	7.2	39	11.4	72	9.0	0	0.0	27	10.5	72	9.0	28
Mex. Amer.	0	0.0	0	0.0	0	0.0	0	0.0	0	0.0	0	0.0	0
Puerto Rican	0	0.0	0	0.0	0	0.0	0	0.0	0	0.0	0	0.0	0
Hispanic	18	3.9	16	4.7	34	4.2	0	0.0	9	3.5	34	4.2	7
Total Minority	65	14.2	66	19.2	131	16.4	0	0.0	45	17.5	131	16.4	41
For. Nation.	8	1.7	6	1.7	14	1.7	0	0.0	4	1.6	14	1.7	11
Caucasian	353	77.1	247	72.0	600	74.9	0	0.0	183	71.2	600	74.9	208
Unknown	32	7.0	24	7.0	56	7.0	0	0.0	25	9.7	56	7.0	10
Total	458	57.2	343	42.8	801	100.0	0	0.0	257	32.1	801		270

Transfers

Transfers in	15
Transfers out	11

Tuition and Fees

	Resident	Nonresident
Full-time	$21,984	$31,484
Part-time	$0	$0

Living Expenses

Estimated living expenses for singles

Living on campus	Living off campus	Living at home
$11,240	$13,392	$6,410

ABA
Approved
Since
1923

University of Minnesota Law School

GPA and LSAT Scores

	Total	Full-time	Part-time
# of apps	3,147	3,147	0
# of offers	757	757	0
# of matrics	257	257	0
75% GPA	3.74	3.74	0.00
Median GPA	3.53	3.53	0.00
25% GPA	3.25	3.25	0.00
75% LSAT	167	167	0
Median LSAT	165	165	0
25% LSAT	163	163	0

Grants and Scholarships (from prior year)

	Total #	Total %	Full-time #	Full-time %	Part-time #	Part-time %
Total # of students	808		808		0	
Total # receiving grants	426	52.7	426	52.7	0	0.0
Less than 1/2 tuition	265	32.8	265	32.8	0	0.0
Half to full tuition	114	14.1	114	14.1	0	0.0
Full tuition	9	1.1	9	1.1	0	0.0
More than full tuition	38	4.7	38	4.7	0	0.0
Median grant amount			$5,570		$0	

Informational and Library Resources

# of volumes and volume equivalents	1,034,054
# of titles	291,234
# of active serial subscriptions	10,610
Study seating capacity inside the library	774
# of full-time professional librarians	15
Hours per week library is open	81
# of open, wired connections available to students	0
# of networked computers available for use by students	894
# of simultaneous wireless users	1,024
Require computer?	No

JD Attrition (from prior year)

	Academic #	Other #	Total #	Total %
1st year	0	14	14	5.1
2nd year	1	2	3	1.1
3rd year	0	0	0	0.0
4th year	0	0	0	0.0

Employment (9 months after graduation)

	Total	Percentage
Employment status known	259	99.2
Employment status unknown	2	0.8
Employed	249	96.1
Pursuing graduate degrees	4	1.5
Unemployed seeking employment	1	0.4
Unemployed not seeking employment	4	1.5
Unemployed and studying for the bar	1	0.4

Type of Employment

# employed in law firms	130	52.2
# employed in business and industry	31	12.4
# employed in government	22	8.8
# employed in public interest	12	4.8
# employed as judicial clerks	47	18.9
# employed in academia	7	2.8

Geographic Location

# employed in state	148	59.4
# employed in foreign countries	4	1.6
# of states where employed		27

Bar Passage Rates

Jurisdiction	Minnesota		
Exam	Sum 05	Win 06	Total
# from school taking bar for the first time	152	15	167
School's pass rate for all first-time takers	99%	100%	99%
State's pass rate for all first-time takers	89%	88%	89%

University of Minnesota Law School

290 Walter F. Mondale Hall, 229 19th Avenue South
Minneapolis, MN 55455
Phone: 612.625.3487; Fax: 612.626.1874
E-mail: umnlsadm@umn.edu; Website: www.law.umn.edu

■ Introduction

The University of Minnesota Law School, founded in 1888, is one of the country's premier law schools. The quality of Minnesota's faculty, the academic credentials of its students, and the caliber of its library and physical facilities are the strongest in the history of the school. The school's century-old tradition of excellence and innovation in legal education has made it among the best in the nation. In keeping with its Midwestern traditions, the Law School provides a personal, collegial environment for the study of law. At the same time, the school's location in the midst of a thriving cosmopolitan area provides a variety of academic, employment, cultural, and recreational opportunities. Students have easy access to the resources of a world-class research university and to the Twin Cities of Minneapolis and St. Paul, one of the most progressive and livable metropolitan communities in the country.

■ Faculty

The faculty's wide-ranging expertise allows students to choose from an academically rich and innovative curriculum that integrates theory and doctrine with skills, ethics, and practice.

Faculty members are prolific and influential scholars, having published over 250 books and close to 2,500 articles. Thirty-six percent of the tenured faculty are invited members of the prestigious American Law Institute, and sixty-three percent of them have been honored with chair-level appointments. Members of the faculty include a recent chair of the United Nations Sub-Commission on the Promotion and Protection of Human Rights (the first US citizen to chair the commission since Eleanor Roosevelt), a member of the American Academy of Arts and Sciences, and a former counselor on international law for the US Department of State.

But while the faculty's scholarship has earned them national acclaim, their equally energetic passion for teaching and mentoring, along with a 13:1 student-faculty ratio, have earned them the respect and appreciation of their students.

■ Student Body/Admission

With 260 students in the entering class, the student body is large enough to enjoy the benefits of diverse backgrounds, perspectives, and interests, while remaining small enough to foster the kind of collegial and supportive community that is a hallmark of Minnesota life.

Although the atmosphere and camaraderie reflect distinctly Minnesotan values, 45 states, 9 countries, and 231 undergraduate institutions are represented in the current JD student body. The admissions committee looks beyond a simple evaluation of LSAT and undergraduate GPA to compose a class that will produce leaders in the legal profession. Many students have advanced degrees and prior work experience.

■ Library and Physical Facilities

The award-winning Walter F. Mondale Hall was substantially expanded in 2001. The building houses all faculty offices, 10 law school research institutes, model classrooms in varying sizes, a beautiful auditorium, the law clinics, a cafeteria, the law school bookstore, student lockers, offices for student organizations and publications, a variety of lounge areas, and a computer lab. All incoming JD students are issued laptops, and wireless access is available in all student areas of the building.

Mondale Hall also houses the law library, which is the eighth largest in the US with over one million volumes. The library offers students 24-hour access. The professional staff takes pride in the outstanding collection of materials and in the individualized service it provides to students and faculty.

■ Curriculum

Hallmarks of the Minnesota curriculum include an unusually strong public law selection, a distinguished tradition in constitutional law and scholarship, and a program of human rights and international law that is respected around the world. Minnesota is one of only a handful of schools with three years of writing requirements and enjoys one of the smallest first-year writing section sizes, with 12–14 students per section. The upper-level curriculum includes a remarkably diverse selection of clinical and simulation courses.

Drawing on the strength of our world-class university, qualified students may pursue dual or joint degrees with a myriad of nationally ranked graduate and professional schools. Especially noteworthy is Minnesota's unique joint-degree program in law, health, and the life sciences. Students also enjoy the opportunity to specialize in various subject areas. Currently, concentrations are available in health law and bioethics, human rights, and labor and employment law.

■ Clinical Programs

With 19 separate clinics, Minnesota has one of the country's largest and most active clinical programs. Through the clinics, students represent real clients under the close tutelage of the clinic faculty. Over 50 percent of the student body participates in a live-client clinic prior to graduation, providing more than 18,000 hours of pro bono legal work for the Twin Cities community each year.

■ Special Programs

Minnesota hosts international exchange programs in France, Germany, Ireland, the Netherlands, Spain, Sweden, and Uruguay. The University of Minnesota Law School also hosts a six-week Summer Study-Abroad Program in Beijing, China. These programs enable interested students to study abroad and allow our students to benefit from the international perspectives students from these countries bring to our classrooms.

Through the Law School Public Service Program, students are asked to perform 50 hours of pro bono legal service for low-income and disadvantaged Minnesotans. Those who complete at least 50 hours of service are recognized for their dedication with a notation on their transcript and at the graduation ceremony.

Ten major research institutes are housed in the law school: Human Rights Center; Institute on Race and Poverty; Kommerstad Center for Business Law and Entrepreneurship; Consortium on Law and Values in Health, Environment, and the Life Sciences; Institute on Crime and Public Policy; Institute on Intellectual Property; Institute on Law and Economics; Institute on Law and Politics; Institute on Law and Rationality; and Minnesota Center for Legal Studies. These institutes enrich the school's intellectual life, contribute to policy debate and formation, and provide research and employment opportunities for selected law students.

Student Activities

Minnesota hosts four student-edited journals: *Minnesota Law Review*; *Law and Inequality: A Journal of Theory and Practice*; *Minnesota Journal of International Law*; and *Minnesota Journal of Law, Science, and Technology*. Students receive academic credit for their journal work.

Students also receive credit for moot court participation. The breadth of Minnesota's moot court program is unusual, with eight programs spanning a wide variety of subject areas: Civil Rights Moot Court, Intellectual Property Moot Court, International Moot Court, Environmental Moot Court, Wagner Labor Law Moot Court, National Moot Court, ABA Moot Court, and Maynard Pirsig Moot Court.

Student extracurricular activities include 50 separate student organizations, spanning the full spectrum of political view points, social interests, and intellectual and recreational activities (not to mention a full-blown musical theatre production).

Expenses and Financial Aid

In recent years, approximately 85 percent of the student body has received financial aid, primarily loans, but also including a substantial number of scholarships. Second- and third-year students also may apply for research assistantships.

Career and Professional Development

With alumni in all 50 states and over 260 federal and state court judges nationwide, our graduates are leaders in the judiciary, government, law practice, business, and academics. Employers interview on campus, at regional interview programs sponsored by the Career and Professional Development Center, and at job fairs for nearly 700 offices, including law firms, corporations, and governmental agencies from around the US. Employers nationwide regularly solicit résumés from our students for job postings. Each year, 20-25 percent of our graduates accept prestigious judicial clerkships, and 99 percent are employed within six months of graduation.

Applicant Profile

University of Minnesota Law School

LSAT Score	3.75 +		3.50–3.74		3.25–3.49		3.00–3.24		2.75–2.99		2.50–2.74		2.25–2.49		2.00–2.24		Below 2.00		No GPA		Total	
	Apps	Adm	Apps	Adm	Apps	Adm	Apps	Adm	Apps	Adm	Apps	Adm	Apps	Adm	Apps	Adm	Apps	Adm	Apps	Adm	Apps	Adm
175–180	4	4	4	4	3	3	4	3	1	0	2	2	0	0	0	0	0	0	0	0	18	16
170–174	28	25	26	23	20	16	17	13	7	4	1	0	1	1	1	1	0	0	0	0	101	83
165–169	97	82	125	97	98	70	80	57	29	17	11	7	5	2	2	0	0	0	3	1	450	333
160–164	243	95	308	85	183	38	97	26	46	3	22	1	8	2	3	0	0	0	15	4	925	254
155–159	203	17	240	22	180	14	106	2	55	4	26	1	11	0	2	0	0	0	14	0	837	60
150–154	59	1	131	2	126	3	91	1	56	0	29	0	15	0	9	0	3	0	9	0	528	7
145–149	16	0	32	0	42	0	36	0	21	0	5	0	8	0	4	0	1	0	6	0	171	0
140–144	6	0	10	0	13	0	10	0	7	0	6	0	1	0	3	0	0	0	5	0	61	0
135–139	0	0	2	0	2	0	8	0	4	0	2	0	3	0	0	0	0	0	0	0	21	0
130–134	0	0	0	0	0	0	2	0	4	0	2	0	0	0	0	0	0	0	0	0	8	0
125–129	0	0	0	0	0	0	0	0	1	0	1	0	1	0	0	0	0	0	1	0	4	0
120–124	0	0	0	0	0	0	0	0	0	0	0	0	0	0	0	0	0	0	0	0	0	0
Total	656	224	878	233	667	144	451	102	231	28	107	11	53	5	24	1	4	0	53	5	3124	753

Apps = Number of Applicants
Adm = Number Admitted
Reflects 99% of the total applicant pool.

This grid includes all applicants who earned 120–180 LSAT scores.
This chart is to be used as a general guide only. Nonnumerical factors are strongly considered for all applicants.

The University of Mississippi School of Law

Lamar Law Center, PO Box 1848
University, MS 38677
Phone: Admission: 662.915.6910, Main: 662.915.7361; Fax: 662.915.1289
E-mail: bvinson@olemiss.edu; Website: www.law.olemiss.edu

ABA
Approved
Since
1930

The Basics

Type of school	Public
Term	Semester
Application deadline	3/1
Application fee	$40
Financial aid deadline	3/15
Can first year start other than fall?	Yes
Student to faculty ratio	14.4 to 1
Does the university offer:	
housing restricted to law students?	No
graduate housing for which law students are eligible?	Yes

Faculty and Administrators

	Total		Men		Women		Minorities	
	Fall	Spr	Fall	Spr	Fall	Spr	Fall	Spr
Full-time	30	30	20	20	10	10	4	4
Other Full-time	7	7	5	5	2	2	1	1
Deans, librarians, & others who teach	6	6	4	4	2	2	0	0
Part-time	10	9	8	7	2	2	0	0
Total	53	52	37	36	16	16	5	5

Curriculum

	Full-time	Part-time
Typical first-year section size	63	0
Is there typically a "small section" of the first-year class, other than Legal Writing, taught by full-time faculty	No	No
If yes, typical size offered last year		
# of classroom course titles beyond first-year curriculum	73	

# of upper division courses, excluding seminars with an enrollment:		
Under 25	27	
25–49	23	
50–74	10	
75–99	7	
100+	2	

# of seminars	22	
# of seminar positions available	488	
# of seminar positions filled	353	0
# of positions available in simulation courses	375	
# of simulation positions filled	370	0
# of positions available in faculty supervised clinical courses	66	
# of faculty supervised clinical positions filled	66	0
# involved in field placements	62	0
# involved in law journals	53	0
# involved in interschool competitions	24	0
# of credit hours required to graduate	90	

JD Enrollment and Ethnicity

	Men		Women		Full-time		Part-time		1st-year		Total		JD Degs. Awd.
	#	%	#	%	#	%	#	%	#	%	#	%	
African Amer.	13	4.7	36	15.8	49	9.7	0	0.0	16	9.1	49	9.7	22
Amer. Indian	2	0.7	1	0.4	3	0.6	0	0.0	0	0.0	3	0.6	1
Asian Amer.	1	0.4	7	3.1	8	1.6	0	0.0	3	1.7	8	1.6	0
Mex. Amer.	0	0.0	0	0.0	0	0.0	0	0.0	0	0.0	0	0.0	0
Puerto Rican	0	0.0	0	0.0	0	0.0	0	0.0	0	0.0	0	0.0	0
Hispanic	2	0.7	1	0.4	3	0.6	0	0.0	2	1.1	3	0.6	0
Total Minority	18	6.5	45	19.7	63	12.5	0	0.0	21	12.0	63	12.5	23
For. Nation.	0	0.0	0	0.0	0	0.0	0	0.0	0	0.0	0	0.0	0
Caucasian	258	93.1	179	78.5	437	86.5	0	0.0	151	86.3	437	86.5	185
Unknown	1	0.4	4	1.8	5	1.0	0	0.0	3	1.7	5	1.0	0
Total	277	54.9	228	45.1	505	100.0	0	0.0	175	34.7	505		208

Transfers

Transfers in	3
Transfers out	9

Tuition and Fees

	Resident	Nonresident
Full-time	$8,300	$16,180
Part-time	$0	$0

Living Expenses

Estimated living expenses for singles

Living on campus	Living off campus	Living at home
$14,858	$14,858	$14,858

The University of Mississippi School of Law

ABA
Approved
Since
1930

GPA and LSAT Scores

	Total	Full-time	Part-time
# of apps	1,550	1,550	0
# of offers	489	489	0
# of matrics	175	175	0
75% GPA	3.76	3.76	0.00
Median GPA	3.53	3.53	0.00
25% GPA	3.25	3.25	0.00
75% LSAT	158	158	0
Median LSAT	155	155	0
25% LSAT	152	152	0

Grants and Scholarships (from prior year)

	Total #	Total %	Full-time #	Full-time %	Part-time #	Part-time %
Total # of students	555		554		1	
Total # receiving grants	164	29.5	164	29.6	0	0.0
Less than 1/2 tuition	87	15.7	87	15.7	0	0.0
Half to full tuition	47	8.5	47	8.5	0	0.0
Full tuition	1	0.2	1	0.2	0	0.0
More than full tuition	29	5.2	29	5.2	0	0.0
Median grant amount			$6,318		$0	

Informational and Library Resources

# of volumes and volume equivalents	331,051
# of titles	75,717
# of active serial subscriptions	2,320
Study seating capacity inside the library	302
# of full-time professional librarians	7
Hours per week library is open	102
# of open, wired connections available to students	717
# of networked computers available for use by students	44
# of simultaneous wireless users	400
Require computer?	No

JD Attrition (from prior year)

	Academic #	Other #	Total #	Total %
1st year	3	16	19	10.1
2nd year	0	1	1	0.6
3rd year	0	0	0	0.0
4th year	0	0	0	0.0

Employment (9 months after graduation)

	Total	Percentage
Employment status known	191	96.0
Employment status unknown	8	4.0
Employed	175	91.6
Pursuing graduate degrees	3	1.6
Unemployed seeking employment	8	4.2
Unemployed not seeking employment	2	1.0
Unemployed and studying for the bar	3	1.6

Type of Employment

# employed in law firms	105	60.0
# employed in business and industry	13	7.4
# employed in government	23	13.1
# employed in public interest	6	3.4
# employed as judicial clerks	28	16.0
# employed in academia	0	0.0

Geographic Location

# employed in state	111	63.4
# employed in foreign countries	2	1.1
# of states where employed		18

Bar Passage Rates

Jurisdiction	Mississippi		
Exam	Sum 05	Win 06	Total
# from school taking bar for the first time	112	27	139
School's pass rate for all first-time takers	92%	93%	92%
State's pass rate for all first-time takers	88%	83%	87%

The University of Mississippi School of Law

Lamar Law Center, PO Box 1848
University, MS 38677
Phone: Admission: 662.915.6910, Main: 662.915.7361; Fax: 662.915.1289
E-mail: bvinson@olemiss.edu; Website: www.law.olemiss.edu

■ Introduction

Recognizing the need for formal law instruction in the state of Mississippi, the legislature, in 1854, established the Department of Law at the University of Mississippi. Over the years, the law department has evolved into today's modern law center. Located in Oxford, on the main campus of the University of Mississippi, the law center is housed in Lamar Hall, named in honor of the late Mississippian, L.Q.C. Lamar, former Associate Justice of the United States Supreme Court and one of the first law professors at the university. Oxford, a small town of approximately 12,000 people, lies nestled in the quiet hills of North Mississippi, just 75 miles southeast of bustling Memphis, Tennessee, and 180 miles north of the state capital of Jackson.

The University of Mississippi is the fourth-oldest state-supported law school in the nation. The School of Law is fully approved by the American Bar Association and is a long-standing member of the Association of American Law Schools.

■ Library and Physical Facilities

The library houses one of the most extensive federal, state, and international law collections in the Southeast. The library's experienced, service-oriented staff is available to assist patrons with these materials and to provide training in all aspects of traditional and computer-assisted legal research. Other library features include open stacks, an online catalog, two state-of-the-art computer labs, and private study rooms and carrels that may be reserved. The library has a strong commitment to new information technologies and has recently added additional multimedia support, along with enhanced wired and wireless network access for patrons.

■ Admission

Admission to law school is gained by committee approval based upon an applicant's credentials. These credentials include a satisfactory LSAT score and an acceptable academic record at the undergraduate level. A bachelor's degree from an accredited school is required before an applicant can register for law school.

There are no prelaw requisites. Every applicant must take the LSAT and register with LSDAS. An LSAT score obtained more than three years before application is not valid, and the applicant will be required to retake the test. Applications are available the September preceding admission, with the application completion deadline for both summer and fall enrollment being March 1. However, early application is encouraged. Applicants who file late risk being placed on a waiting list.

Although the LSAT and GPA are the most important factors in the admission process, other considerations are (1) grade patterns and progression; (2) quality of undergraduate institution; (3) difficulty of major field of study; (4) number of years since bachelor's degree was earned; (5) job experience; (6) social, personal, or economic circumstances that may have affected college grades or performance on the LSAT or

academic record; (7) nonacademic achievements; (8) letters of recommendation; and (9) residency.

■ Entrance Dates

Students are given the option to enter in the summer or fall of each admission year. Because summer and fall enrollees are considered as one class, the same standards are applied in the decision-making process.

■ Curriculum

First-year students complete a predetermined curriculum that focuses on the development of analytical skills and a foundation of substantive knowledge. Largely, second- and third-year students are free to select their own courses of study and emphasis, although a number of courses are recommended to ensure a broad-based substantive and procedural background. Students may select from a large number of elective courses, including seminars, clinical, and trial advocacy courses. The elective curriculum offers generous opportunities for students to pursue special interests such as constitutional and individual rights, business and commercial transactions, federal taxation, international law, and environmental law.

■ Clinical Programs

Civil Legal Clinic—Under the supervision of the director of the clinic, students provide legal counseling for low-income clients on civil matters. The program includes clinical units in Elder Law, Consumer Law, Child Advocacy, Legislation, and Domestic Violence.

Criminal Appeals Clinic—The Criminal Appeals Clinic was established by the National Center for Justice and the Rule of Law. The course of study is designed to give students practical experience representing clients in criminal appellate cases and includes direct student participation in the pro bono representation of indigent persons in their cases on appeal.

Prosecution Externship Program—The Prosecution Externship was established by the National Center for Justice and the Rule of Law. It is designed to prepare law students for careers in criminal law by combining academic training with placements as externs in local, state, and federal prosecutor offices.

■ Student Activities

The *Mississippi Law Journal,* edited and published by law students three times each year, includes articles by distinguished professors, judges, and practitioners.

The *Journal of Space Law* is the oldest journal dedicated to space law and is the only one of its kind in the United States. The National Center for Remote Sensing, Air and Space Law faculty regularly supervise an editorial team of 15–18 law student editors, staff, and authors on this journal.

The **Moot Court Board** oversees several moot court competitions, including the Steen, Reynolds, and Dalehite trial competition each fall and the McGlinchey Stafford oral-advocacy competition each spring.

Summer-abroad Programs

The School of Law offers an opportunity to earn up to six semester credit hours in its summer session held annually in England at Downing College, Cambridge University. Classes offered are for full academic credit and are subject to the same academic standards maintained in the domestic program.

Special Programs

One of the most active organizations is the **Public Interest Law Foundation**. The student-run organization focuses its efforts on community groups that need legal assistance—victims of domestic violence, children, and defendants who cannot afford an attorney. The organization raises money to support students working in public interest jobs.

The **National Center for Justice and the Rule of Law** is a component of the law center funded by a multimillion dollar grant from the Department of Justice. The center works cooperatively with agencies in sponsoring research, hosting international and national conferences, and presenting educational programs on issues related to criminal justice, such as international and domestic terrorism, drug-trafficking, and the role of the proposed International Criminal Court.

The **National Center for Remote Sensing, Air and Space Law** is funded by a grant from NASA. The only center of its kind in the United States, it serves as a research, advisory, and training resource for the emerging commercial geospatial industry, the international legal community, and related user groups.

Housing

The majority of law students live off campus in rental units. On-campus housing is available, and students who are interested in living on campus should make early application to the Housing Office.

Career Services

A full-time director of career services assists students in finding employment. Seventy-five to 100 law firms and other prospective employers interview at the law school each year. Approximately 60 percent of graduating seniors are employed prior to graduation, with the remaining number being placed within six months of graduation. The law school is an active member of the National Association for Law Placement (NALP) and annually participates in the Atlanta Legal Hiring Conference, the Equal Justice Works Public Interest Career Fair, the Patent Law Interview Program, and the Southeastern Minority Job Fair.

Applicant Profile

The University of Mississippi School of Law
This grid includes only applicants who earned 120–180 LSAT scores under standard administrations.

LSAT Score	3.75 +		3.50–3.74		3.25–3.49		3.00–3.24		2.75–2.99		2.50–2.74		2.25–2.49		2.00–2.24		Below 2.00		No GPA		Total	
	Apps	Adm	Apps	Adm	Apps	Adm	Apps	Adm	Apps	Adm	Apps	Adm	Apps	Adm	Apps	Adm	Apps	Adm	Apps	Adm	Apps	Adm
175–180	0	0	0	0	0	0	0	0	0	0	0	0	0	0	0	0	0	0	0	0	0	0
170–174	0	0	0	0	1	1	0	0	0	0	1	1	0	0	0	0	0	0	0	0	2	2
165–169	5	5	6	6	5	5	6	5	4	3	3	1	2	1	0	0	0	0	0	0	31	26
160–164	26	24	18	18	21	21	36	29	12	5	8	1	6	1	4	0	0	0	2	0	133	99
155–159	65	64	69	56	84	49	58	16	38	9	20	7	9	2	3	0	0	0	4	0	350	203
150–154	64	34	95	36	132	20	105	11	45	6	29	1	14	0	5	1	2	0	2	0	493	109
145–149	32	12	61	8	63	4	46	2	34	2	22	1	16	0	4	0	0	0	2	0	280	29
140–144	12	3	17	4	21	2	24	1	25	1	16	0	7	0	3	0	0	0	7	0	132	11
135–139	5	3	7	1	4	0	11	1	10	0	9	0	5	0	5	0	1	0	0	0	57	5
130–134	0	0	0	0	2	0	1	0	5	0	4	0	2	0	2	0	1	0	1	0	18	0
125–129	0	0	1	0	0	0	1	0	0	0	1	0	0	0	1	0	0	0	0	0	4	0
120–124	0	0	0	0	0	0	0	0	0	0	0	0	0	0	0	0	0	0	0	0	0	0
Total	209	145	274	129	333	102	288	65	173	26	113	12	61	4	27	1	4	0	18	0	1500	484

Apps = Number of Applicants
Adm = Number Admitted
Reflects 97% of the total applicant pool.

Mississippi College School of Law

151 E. Griffith Street
Jackson, MS 39201
Phone: 800.738.1236 or 601.925.7152
E-mail: nscriven@mc.edu; Website: law.mc.edu

ABA
Approved
Since
1980

The Basics

Type of school	Private
Term	Semester
Application deadline	6/1
Application fee	$50
Financial aid deadline	7/1
Can first year start other than fall?	No
Student to faculty ratio	23.2 to 1
Does the university offer:	
housing restricted to law students?	No
graduate housing for which law students are eligible?	No

Faculty and Administrators

	Total		Men		Women		Minorities	
	Fall	Spr	Fall	Spr	Fall	Spr	Fall	Spr
Full-time	18	18	12	12	6	6	2	2
Other Full-time	0	0	0	0	0	0	0	0
Deans, librarians, & others who teach	5	5	2	2	3	3	0	0
Part-time	33	24	21	20	12	4	3	0
Total	**56**	**47**	**35**	**34**	**21**	**13**	**5**	**2**

Curriculum

	Full-time	Part-time
Typical first-year section size	97	0
Is there typically a "small section" of the first-year class, other than Legal Writing, taught by full-time faculty	No	No
If yes, typical size offered last year		
# of classroom course titles beyond first-year curriculum		66
# of upper division courses, excluding seminars with an enrollment: Under 25		51
25–49		20
50–74		15
75–99		7
100+		1
# of seminars		8
# of seminar positions available		125
# of seminar positions filled	81	0
# of positions available in simulation courses		546
# of simulation positions filled	477	0
# of positions available in faculty supervised clinical courses		36
# of faculty supervised clinical positions filled	27	0
# involved in field placements	52	0
# involved in law journals	40	0
# involved in interschool competitions	30	0
# of credit hours required to graduate		90

JD Enrollment and Ethnicity

	Men #	Men %	Women #	Women %	Full-time #	Full-time %	Part-time #	Part-time %	1st-year #	1st-year %	Total #	Total %	JD Degs. Awd.
African Amer.	9	2.9	25	11.7	34	6.4	0	0.0	16	8.2	34	6.4	13
Amer. Indian	1	0.3	0	0.0	1	0.2	0	0.0	0	0.0	1	0.2	0
Asian Amer.	2	0.6	0	0.0	2	0.4	0	0.0	0	0.0	2	0.4	0
Mex. Amer.	0	0.0	0	0.0	0	0.0	0	0.0	0	0.0	0	0.0	0
Puerto Rican	0	0.0	1	0.5	1	0.2	0	0.0	1	0.5	1	0.2	0
Hispanic	1	0.3	3	1.4	4	0.8	0	0.0	2	1.0	4	0.8	0
Total Minority	13	4.1	29	13.6	42	8.0	0	0.0	19	9.8	42	8.0	13
For. Nation.	0	0.0	0	0.0	0	0.0	0	0.0	0	0.0	0	0.0	0
Caucasian	286	90.8	182	85.4	468	88.6	0	0.0	169	87.1	468	88.6	113
Unknown	16	5.1	2	0.9	18	3.4	0	0.0	6	3.1	18	3.4	0
Total	315	59.7	213	40.3	528	100.0	0	0.0	194	36.7	528		126

Transfers

Transfers in	0
Transfers out	15

Tuition and Fees

	Resident	Nonresident
Full-time	$20,140	$20,140
Part-time	$0	$0

Living Expenses

Estimated living expenses for singles

Living on campus	Living off campus	Living at home
N/A	$17,200	$17,200

ABA Approved Since 1980

GPA and LSAT Scores

	Total	Full-time	Part-time
# of apps	1,122	1,122	0
# of offers	507	507	0
# of matrics	195	195	0
75% GPA	3.54	3.54	0.00
Median GPA	3.32	3.32	0.00
25% GPA	3.00	3.00	0.00
75% LSAT	152	152	0
Median LSAT	150	150	0
25% LSAT	147	147	0

Grants and Scholarships (from prior year)

	Total #	Total %	Full-time #	Full-time %	Part-time #	Part-time %
Total # of students	490		490		0	
Total # receiving grants	144	29.4	144	29.4	0	0.0
Less than 1/2 tuition	88	18.0	88	18.0	0	0.0
Half to full tuition	17	3.5	17	3.5	0	0.0
Full tuition	18	3.7	18	3.7	0	0.0
More than full tuition	21	4.3	21	4.3	0	0.0
Median grant amount			$2,000		$0	

Informational and Library Resources

# of volumes and volume equivalents	336,226
# of titles	175,939
# of active serial subscriptions	3,484
Study seating capacity inside the library	396
# of full-time professional librarians	4
Hours per week library is open	103
# of open, wired connections available to students	72
# of networked computers available for use by students	23
# of simultaneous wireless users	650
Require computer?	No

JD Attrition (from prior year)

	Academic #	Other #	Total #	Total %
1st year	6	9	15	7.6
2nd year	0	15	15	9.4
3rd year	0	0	0	0.0
4th year	0	0	0	0.0

Employment (9 months after graduation)

	Total	Percentage
Employment status known	138	99.3
Employment status unknown	1	0.7
Employed	126	91.3
Pursuing graduate degrees	3	2.2
Unemployed seeking employment	4	2.9
Unemployed not seeking employment	0	0.0
Unemployed and studying for the bar	5	3.6

Type of Employment

	Total	Percentage
# employed in law firms	80	63.5
# employed in business and industry	10	7.9
# employed in government	10	7.9
# employed in public interest	3	2.4
# employed as judicial clerks	22	17.5
# employed in academia	1	0.8

Geographic Location

	Total	Percentage
# employed in state	96	76.2
# employed in foreign countries	0	0.0
# of states where employed		11

Bar Passage Rates

Jurisdiction	Mississippi			Louisiana		
Exam	Sum 05	Win 06	Total	Sum 05	Win 06	Total
# from school taking bar for the first time	79	15	94	10	1	11
School's pass rate for all first-time takers	85%	67%	82%	80%	0%	73%
State's pass rate for all first-time takers	88%	83%	87%	73%	48%	70%

Mississippi College School of Law

151 E. Griffith Street
Jackson, MS 39201
Phone: 800.738.1236 or 601.925.7152
E-mail: nscriven@mc.edu; Website: law.mc.edu

■ Introduction

Mississippi College School of Law (MCSOL) is a showplace in the center of downtown Jackson, the state's capital and largest city, and serves as a state-of-the-art legal center for the mid-South. Jackson, with a metropolitan population of nearly 400,000, is the legal, political, cultural, and commercial center of Mississippi.

MCSOL's innovative campus includes an administrative building; an 18,000-square-foot classroom building that houses high-tech classrooms, a multipurpose courtroom and lecture hall, seminar rooms, a jury room, judges' chambers, and teaching centers; a nationally recognized law library; and a newly constructed Student Center that contains a food court, campus bookstore, and a large conference center with an attractive outdoor plaza. An ample and convenient student parking lot located directly across from the law school guarantees quick and safe access. Within walking distance of the law school lies a vibrant, thriving legal community, as well as the legislature, federal, and state administrative agencies and courts.

Founded in 1826, Mississippi College is the oldest college in Mississippi. The law school was acquired by Mississippi College in 1975. The main campus is located in Clinton, a suburb 12 miles west of Jackson. The School of Law is fully accredited by the American Bar Association and is a member of the Association of American Law Schools. In addition, the law school is also a charter member of the International Association of Law Schools.

■ Admission

When admitting students, the Admissions Office uses a whole-person concept. The law school has rolling admission, and the admission standards are set annually by the faculty. The standards are based on the college undergraduate grade-point average, the LSAT score, and personal or academic achievements or honors. A degree from an accredited four-year college or university is a prerequisite to admission. Every applicant must take the LSAT and register for the LSDAS prior to being considered for admission. The school makes admission decisions without discrimination against any person on the basis of race, religion, sex, or national origin. The application deadline is May 1, and a $50 fee must accompany the application. When an applicant is accepted, a deposit of $250 is required to reserve a seat in the entering class. A second deposit of $250 must be received by June 1. Upon enrollment, these nonrefundable payments are credited to the applicant's tuition.

■ Learning Environment

Our students receive one-on-one attention and interaction with professors extends beyond the classroom. The school is dedicated to maintaining a collegial environment. Because of our small size and friendly atmosphere, students form lasting relationships with one another.

■ Curriculum

MCSOL is a foundational law school. Our course of study integrates the theoretical aspects of the law with practical, hands-on training. First-year law students are required to take fundamental courses that focus on the major doctrinal areas of law, as well as development of legal writing and research skills. The law school offers a diverse list of second- and third-year elective courses. Our curriculum emphasizes the following disciplines: Trial and Litigation Practice, Family Law, and Business and Commerce. MCSOL is one of the few law schools in the nation that provides a Louisiana Civil Law Certification program.

The law school's Child Advocacy Program is a premier training ground, equipping students and community volunteers with the skills required to shepherd children in need of an advocate through the court system. It gives second- and third-year students the opportunity to work under faculty supervision in handling numerous adoptions and other child-related cases.

The law school operates on a semester basis, and a beginning student must enter in the fall semester. A summer term is available to second- and third-year students who wish to accelerate or enrich their studies.

■ Externship Program

At MCSOL, classroom theory and practical application go hand-in-hand. In addition to courses in legal doctrine, a wide range of instruction in the skills of modern practice is offered. Student externs work alongside practicing attorneys in government offices and public interest organizations. Depending on the particular externship, students present cases in court, interview witnesses, prepare pleadings and other legal documents, take depositions, negotiate with opposing parties, research legal issues, and draft court opinions. This program allows students to practice in the real world what they have learned in more traditional law school classes.

■ Student Activities

The *Mississippi College Law Review* is a legal journal edited and published by law students who are selected on the basis of scholarship and the ability to do creative, scholarly research and writing. The students write comments and notes on legal developments and significant cases and edit lead articles and book reviews written by professors, lawyers, judges, legislators, and other scholars. Membership on the *Law Review* staff is recognized as both an honor and a unique educational experience. The law school also provides an appellate advocacy program administered by the Moot Court Board, composed of second- and third-year students. This required program provides students with instruction and practice in both brief writing and oral argument. The Law Student Bar Association is the organized student government of the law school. All students are members and are eligible to hold office in the association. Other student activities include three national legal fraternity chapters, Phi Alpha Delta, Delta Theta Phi, and Phi Delta Phi; a student chapter of the Mississippi Trial Lawyers Association; the Women's Student Bar; Christian

Legal Society; Black Law Students Association; Federalist Society; Mississippi Defense Lawyers Association; Sports and Entertainment Law; Technology Group; Young Democrats, Republican Lawyers Association; and the Environmental Law Club.

■ Career Services

The Career Services Office assists in placement activities. In addition to the traditional on-campus interviews, the law school participates in regional interviews and a clerkship interaction program to help students find employment prior to graduation. Graduates are locating employment with major law firms, corporations, and government agencies throughout the United States, with a primary focus in the Southeast. Students have received clerkships with the United States Circuit Court of Appeals, United States District Courts, and the Supreme Courts of various states.

■ Minority Program

The law school offers a variety of programs to assist minority students: dedicated scholarships/stipends and an Academic Support Program. Minority students are strongly encouraged to apply, and each applicant's entire record will be carefully considered.

■ Faculty

Teaching is our strength. Our esteemed faculty members have impeccable credentials and are leaders in their fields of study. From insurance to international law and from constitutional to sports law, our professors are regularly cited in courts, scholarly journals, and the media. MCSOL is renowned for the extraordinary level of interaction between faculty and students.

Because of our strategic location, federal and state judges and some of the best legal minds in the South teach as adjunct professors, giving our students valuable practical training and enviable networking opportunities.

■ Library

The law library has a collection of more than 300,000 volumes and is committed to acquiring materials for both the immediate and the long-term needs of the law school. Emphasis is placed on development of the collections of statutes, legal periodicals, federal and state legislative materials, reports of all federal and all state appellate courts, federal administrative agency materials, specialized loose-leaf services, and microforms and treatises that support our mission. The library is a government depository and is a member of the American Association of Law Libraries.

Applicant Profile

Mississippi College School of Law
This grid includes only applicants with 120–180 LSAT scores earned under standard administrations.

LSAT Score	3.75 +		3.50–3.74		3.25–3.49		3.00–3.24		2.75–2.99		2.50–2.74		2.25–2.49		2.00–2.24		Below 2.00		No GPA		Total	
	Apps	Adm	Apps	Adm	Apps	Adm	Apps	Adm	Apps	Adm	Apps	Adm	Apps	Adm	Apps	Adm	Apps	Adm	Apps	Adm	Apps	Adm
175–180	0	0	0	0	0	0	0	0	0	0	0	0	0	0	0	0	0	0	0	0	0	0
170–174	0	0	0	0	0	0	0	0	0	0	0	0	0	0	0	0	0	0	0	0	0	0
165–169	1	1	1	1	1	0	0	0	0	0	0	0	1	1	0	0	0	0	0	0	4	3
160–164	1	1	4	3	3	2	1	1	4	4	2	2	2	2	1	0	0	0	0	0	18	15
155–159	10	9	13	10	8	7	11	11	13	8	11	7	6	4	1	0	1	0	0	0	74	56
150–154	26	21	44	33	66	53	68	60	48	33	31	18	15	3	1	0	1	0	0	0	300	221
145–149	28	24	74	56	80	44	80	35	65	16	44	3	27	2	13	0	1	0	4	2	416	182
140–144	14	2	32	7	47	3	53	1	30	4	27	5	18	0	8	0	1	1	4	0	234	23
135–139	3	1	2	0	11	1	9	2	12	0	15	0	11	0	5	0	2	0	4	0	74	4
130–134	0	0	1	0	2	0	3	0	4	0	3	0	4	0	1	0	0	0	3	0	21	0
125–129	0	0	0	0	1	0	2	0	0	0	1	0	0	0	0	0	0	0	0	0	4	0
120–124	0	0	1	0	0	0	0	0	0	0	0	0	0	0	0	0	0	0	0	0	1	0
Total	83	59	172	110	219	110	227	110	176	65	134	35	84	12	30	0	6	1	15	2	1146	504

Apps = Number of Applicants
Adm = Number Admitted
Reflects 98% of the total applicant pool.

University of Missouri—Columbia School of Law

103 Hulston Hall
Columbia, MO 65211
Phone: 573.882.6042, toll-free: 888.MULaw4U; Fax: 573.882.9625
E-mail: umclawadmissions@missouri.edu; Website: www.law.missouri.edu

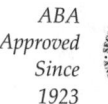

*ABA
Approved
Since
1923*

The Basics

Type of school	Public
Term	Semester
Application deadline	3/1
Application fee	$50
Financial aid deadline	3/1
Can first year start other than fall?	No
Student to faculty ratio	15.9 to 1
Does the university offer:	
housing restricted to law students?	No
graduate housing for which law students are eligible?	No

Faculty and Administrators

	Total		Men		Women		Minorities	
	Fall	Spr	Fall	Spr	Fall	Spr	Fall	Spr
Full-time	23	23	13	14	10	9	0	2
Other Full-time	0	0	0	0	0	0	0	0
Deans, librarians, & others who teach	13	12	11	10	2	2	2	2
Part-time	6	15	3	11	3	4	1	1
Total	42	50	27	35	15	15	3	5

Curriculum

	Full-time	Part-time
Typical first-year section size	76	0
Is there typically a "small section" of the first-year class, other than Legal Writing, taught by full-time faculty	Yes	No
If yes, typical size offered last year	29	
# of classroom course titles beyond first-year curriculum	124	

# of upper division courses, excluding seminars with an enrollment:		
Under 25	88	
25–49	21	
50–74	11	
75–99	3	
100+	1	

# of seminars	4	
# of seminar positions available	77	
# of seminar positions filled	60	0
# of positions available in simulation courses	365	
# of simulation positions filled	242	0
# of positions available in faculty supervised clinical courses	56	
# of faculty supervised clinical positions filled	49	0
# involved in field placements	41	0
# involved in law journals	87	0
# involved in interschool competitions	0	0
# of credit hours required to graduate	89	

JD Enrollment and Ethnicity

	Men #	Men %	Women #	Women %	Full-time #	Full-time %	Part-time #	Part-time %	1st-year #	1st-year %	Total #	Total %	JD Degs. Awd.
African Amer.	10	3.5	14	8.3	23	5.2	1	20.0	8	5.2	24	5.3	4
Amer. Indian	5	1.8	4	2.4	9	2.0	0	0.0	7	4.5	9	2.0	2
Asian Amer.	8	2.8	12	7.1	20	4.5	0	0.0	13	8.4	20	4.4	1
Mex. Amer.	0	0.0	0	0.0	0	0.0	0	0.0	0	0.0	0	0.0	0
Puerto Rican	0	0.0	0	0.0	0	0.0	0	0.0	0	0.0	0	0.0	0
Hispanic	6	2.1	6	3.6	12	2.7	0	0.0	8	5.2	12	2.7	1
Total Minority	29	10.3	36	21.3	64	14.3	1	20.0	36	23.2	65	14.4	8
For. Nation.	1	0.4	0	0.0	1	0.2	0	0.0	1	0.6	1	0.2	0
Caucasian	235	83.3	132	78.1	363	81.4	4	80.0	112	72.3	367	81.4	128
Unknown	17	6.0	1	0.6	18	4.0	0	0.0	6	3.9	18	4.0	6
Total	282	62.5	169	37.5	446	98.9	5	1.1	155	34.4	451		142

Transfers

Transfers in	9
Transfers out	9

Tuition and Fees

	Resident	Nonresident
Full-time	$14,752	$28,175
Part-time	$0	$0

Living Expenses

Estimated living expenses for singles

Living on campus	Living off campus	Living at home
$14,052	$14,052	$14,052

University of Missouri—Columbia School of Law

*ABA
Approved
Since
1923*

GPA and LSAT Scores

	Total	Full-time	Part-time
# of apps	875	875	0
# of offers	381	381	0
# of matrics	152	152	0
75% GPA	3.72	3.72	0.00
Median GPA	3.49	3.49	0.00
25% GPA	3.24	3.24	0.00
75% LSAT	160	160	0
Median LSAT	158	158	0
25% LSAT	156	156	0

Grants and Scholarships (from prior year)

	Total #	Total %	Full-time #	Full-time %	Part-time #	Part-time %
Total # of students	446		440		6	
Total # receiving grants	177	39.7	177	40.2	0	0.0
Less than 1/2 tuition	164	36.8	164	37.3	0	0.0
Half to full tuition	10	2.2	10	2.3	0	0.0
Full tuition	3	0.7	3	0.7	0	0.0
More than full tuition	0	0.0	0	0.0	0	0.0
Median grant amount			$3,000		$0	

Informational and Library Resources

# of volumes and volume equivalents	379,960
# of titles	196,797
# of active serial subscriptions	2,770
Study seating capacity inside the library	474
# of full-time professional librarians	8
Hours per week library is open	70
# of open, wired connections available to students	0
# of networked computers available for use by students	58
# of simultaneous wireless users	600
Require computer?	No

JD Attrition (from prior year)

	Academic #	Other #	Total #	Total %
1st year	7	9	16	10.5
2nd year	0	10	10	6.9
3rd year	0	0	0	0.0
4th year	0	0	0	0.0

Employment (9 months after graduation)

	Total	Percentage
Employment status known	136	98.6
Employment status unknown	2	1.4
Employed	125	91.9
Pursuing graduate degrees	7	5.1
Unemployed seeking employment	2	1.5
Unemployed not seeking employment	2	1.5
Unemployed and studying for the bar	0	0.0

Type of Employment

# employed in law firms	73	58.4
# employed in business and industry	10	8.0
# employed in government	13	10.4
# employed in public interest	8	6.4
# employed as judicial clerks	15	12.0
# employed in academia	3	2.4

Geographic Location

# employed in state	109	87.2
# employed in foreign countries	0	0.0
# of states where employed	12	

Bar Passage Rates

Jurisdiction	Missouri			Kansas		
Exam	Sum 05	Win 06	Total	Sum 05	Win 06	Total
# from school taking bar for the first time	117	11	128	0	4	4
School's pass rate for all first-time takers	90%	91%	90%		100%	100%
State's pass rate for all first-time takers	88%	90%	89%	78%	90%	82%

University of Missouri—Columbia School of Law

Office of Admissions, 103 Hulston Hall
Columbia, MO 65211
Phone: 573.882.6042, toll-free: 888.MULaw4U; Fax: 573.882.9625
E-mail: umclawadmissions@missouri.edu; Website: www.law.missouri.edu

■ Introduction

The University of Missouri—Columbia is a dynamic and collegial community. Founded in 1839, MU is the first state university west of the Mississippi. The School of Law was established in 1872 and has had an enviable history of service to the state and nation. Graduates include judges, governors, attorneys general, and legislators who serve nationwide. The law school is a charter member of the AALS and is fully accredited.

Located in Columbia, MU is 35 miles from Jefferson City, the state capital. Our location provides students with easy access to the legislature, the Supreme Court, and various offices of state. In addition to living and studying in one of America's most livable cities, students are within two hours of the cultural, athletic, and entertainment centers of St. Louis and Kansas City. Students and their families enjoy Columbia's Midwestern friendliness. It combines a small town feel with the diversity and opportunities often found only in large cities. Columbia truly offers something for everyone.

■ Enrollment/Student Body

The student body of the law school is composed of students from numerous states and several foreign countries. This diverse group provides a wealth of experiences and fosters a stimulating learning environment.

■ Faculty

The faculty at MU is strong and vibrant. MU is among the top 10 percent of law schools in American Law Institute membership. Four members of the faculty serve as commissioners to the National Conference of Commissioners on Uniform State Laws and two serve as reporters. The Executive Director of the National Conference is an emeritus professor. A recent president of the AALS is also on the faculty. The faculty focus is on teaching, research, and service. Faculty maintain an open-door policy for students.

■ Library and Physical Facilities

John K. Hulston Hall is dominated by open spaces, skylights, and windows. It is a magnificent, state-of-the-art laboratory in which to study law. The law school is part of the campus wireless network. Students can access the Internet and computer-assisted legal services anywhere on campus or in the law building. Exams are offered on laptop computers.

The law library houses an extensive collection of legal volumes and reference materials and a rare book collection. It employs a large staff of specialized librarians, researchers, and computer support personnel. Faculty and students have 24-hour access to the law library.

■ Curriculum

The academic program leading to the JD degree traditionally consists of six semesters of study. One seven-week semester is offered each summer. The first-year curriculum is proscribed, as is a portion of the second-year curriculum.

To graduate, students must complete 89 semester hours, including a writing requirement and a professional perspectives requirement. Students must have a minimum average of 70 on a scale of 55 to 100 to graduate.

■ Special Programs: Alternative Dispute Resolution

The Center for the Study of Dispute Resolution is a unique feature of the law school and provides national leadership in this rapidly developing area of the law. First-year students are exposed to an overview of dispute resolution processes. MU also offers a variety of dispute resolution courses and opportunities for second- and third-year students.

The center also houses a Master of Laws in Dispute Resolution degree program, one of the first programs of its kind in the country.

■ Dual-degree Programs

The School of Law offers several dual-degree programs, including: Business Administration (JD/MBA), Public Administration (JD/MPA), Health Administration (JD/MHA), Library Science (JD/MLS), and Journalism (JD/MA and JD/PhD). The law school will consider establishing other dual-degree programs to meet individual interests. Traditionally, dual-degree students spend their first year in the School of Law. (Students must fulfill the entrance requirements of both schools.)

■ Certificate Programs

The law school offers a certificate in Alternative Dispute Resolution. Students can complete this certificate by concentrating their elective hours in this area of the law.

In addition, a certificate in Journalism, the Digital Globe, or the European Union is available to law students through the Graduate School.

MU is one of 10 European Union (EU) centers in the United States. The EU Center is working to develop a better understanding of the transatlantic agenda between the EU and the United States.

■ Study Abroad

The School of Law offers two opportunities to study abroad. Since 2004, MU has offered a summer program in Capetown, South Africa. The program is available to all law students and consists of three two-credit courses in different areas of comparative law. Students reside in De Waterkant Village, one of Cape Town's trendiest neighborhoods, and are transported to their classes at the University of the Western Cape. Field trips to the Cape of Good Hope, the Stellenbosch wine region, Robben Island—the prison home of Nelson Mandela—and other scenic and historical locales are included in the itinerary. MU is also part of the London Law Consortium. The group of seven ABA-approved schools offers second- and third-year law students a culturally enriching spring semester in London.

■ Clinics and Externships

MU provides students with practical experience to enhance lawyering skills and to promote awareness of ethical issues. An active externship and judicial clerkship program and four clinical programs—the Criminal Prosecution Clinic, Family Violence Clinic, Legislative Clinic, and Mediation Clinic—have been developed to address these needs.

■ Student Activities

All students are eligible to participate in the writing competition for membership on the *Missouri Law Review*, the *Journal of Dispute Resolution*, or the *Missouri Environmental Law and Policy Review*. The Board of Advocates sponsors a wide variety of advocacy competitions. The school has chapters of the Order of the Coif, the Order of Barristers, Student Bar Association, and two legal fraternities. Other student organizations, encompassing almost every aspect of social and academic life, are offered.

■ Admission

A faculty committee reviews all applications. In many cases, factors other than the GPA or LSAT score have proven to be determinative. If the LSAT is repeated, the committee will consider all scores in its evaluation. Applications from disadvantaged students are especially encouraged.

Students are encouraged to apply early and to visit the law school. The admissions office can arrange for students to meet with an admission counselor, attend a class, and tour the facility.

■ Expenses and Financial Aid

Law school is a career investment. MU offers an outstanding value for the cost. In addition, the cost of housing, utilities, and related expenses in Columbia are low when compared to urban standards.

Financial assistance is available to students.

■ Career Services

The Career Development Office serves as a liaison between students or alumni and prospective employers. Students are taught to use their analytical and advocacy skills to achieve career goals. Workshops, seminars, and individual counseling are offered to help students employ their lawyering skills. Typically, over 90 percent of each graduating class accepts employment within nine months of graduation.

Applicant Profile

University of Missouri—Columbia School of Law
This grid includes only applicants who earned 120–180 LSAT scores under standard administrations.

LSAT Score	GPA								
	3.75 +	3.50–3.74	3.25–3.49	3.00–3.24	2.75–2.99	2.50–2.74	2.25–2.49	2.00–2.24	Below 2.00
175–180									
170–174									
165–169									
160–164									
155–159									
150–154									
145–149									
140–144									
135–139									
130–134									
125–129									
120–124									

Good Possibility   Possible   Unlikely

This chart is to be used as a general guide only. Nonnumerical factors are strongly considered for all applicants.

University of Missouri—Kansas City School of Law

5100 Rockhill Road
Kansas City, MO 64110
Phone: 816.235.1644; Fax: 816.235.5276
E-mail: law@umkc.edu; Website: www.law.umkc.edu

ABA
Approved
Since
1936

The Basics

Type of school	Public
Term	Semester
Application deadline	
Application fee	$50
Financial aid deadline	3/1
Can first year start other than fall?	No
Student to faculty ratio	14.4 to 1
Does the university offer:	
housing restricted to law students?	No
graduate housing for which law students are eligible?	No

Faculty and Administrators

	Total		Men		Women		Minorities	
	Fall	Spr	Fall	Spr	Fall	Spr	Fall	Spr
Full-time	30	23	20	17	10	6	4	3
Other Full-time	2	8	1	3	1	5	0	0
Deans, librarians, & others who teach	8	5	5	3	3	2	0	0
Part-time	17	29	13	25	4	4	0	0
Total	57	65	39	48	18	17	4	3

Curriculum

	Full-time	Part-time
Typical first-year section size	56	0
Is there typically a "small section" of the first-year class, other than Legal Writing, taught by full-time faculty	No	No
If yes, typical size offered last year		

# of classroom course titles beyond first-year curriculum		99
# of upper division courses, excluding seminars with an enrollment:	Under 25	83
	25–49	20
	50–74	17
	75–99	8
	100+	0
# of seminars		15
# of seminar positions available		270
# of seminar positions filled	192	0
# of positions available in simulation courses		418
# of simulation positions filled	329	0
# of positions available in faculty supervised clinical courses		83
# of faculty supervised clinical positions filled	63	0
# involved in field placements	68	0
# involved in law journals	112	0
# involved in interschool competitions	37	0
# of credit hours required to graduate		91

JD Enrollment and Ethnicity

	Men		Women		Full-time		Part-time		1st-year		Total		JD Degs. Awd.
	#	%	#	%	#	%	#	%	#	%	#	%	
African Amer.	8	2.8	8	3.9	15	3.1	1	9.1	7	4.2	16	3.3	4
Amer. Indian	1	0.4	3	1.5	3	0.6	1	9.1	3	1.8	4	0.8	3
Asian Amer.	4	1.4	10	4.9	14	2.9	0	0.0	5	3.0	14	2.9	6
Mex. Amer.	1	0.4	0	0.0	1	0.2	0	0.0	0	0.0	1	0.2	0
Puerto Rican	0	0.0	0	0.0	0	0.0	0	0.0	0	0.0	0	0.0	0
Hispanic	5	1.8	6	2.9	11	2.3	0	0.0	6	3.6	11	2.2	1
Total Minority	19	6.7	27	13.1	44	9.2	2	18.2	21	12.7	46	9.4	14
For. Nation.	1	0.4	1	0.5	2	0.4	0	0.0	1	0.6	2	0.4	3
Caucasian	239	84.5	167	81.1	397	83.1	9	81.8	136	81.9	406	83.0	134
Unknown	24	8.5	11	5.3	35	7.3	0	0.0	8	4.8	35	7.2	5
Total	283	57.9	206	42.1	478	97.8	11	2.2	166	33.9	489		156

Transfers

Transfers in	8
Transfers out	8

Tuition and Fees

	Resident	Nonresident
Full-time	$13,183	$25,234
Part-time	$9,486	$18,094

Living Expenses

Estimated living expenses for singles

Living on campus	Living off campus	Living at home
$23,458	$25,778	$16,678

University of Missouri—Kansas City School of Law

*ABA
Approved
Since
1936*

GPA and LSAT Scores

	Total	Full-time	Part-time
# of apps	1,170	1,141	29
# of offers	430	423	7
# of matrics	166	161	5
75% GPA	3.74	3.75	3.22
Median GPA	3.47	3.49	2.94
25% GPA	3.22	3.25	2.90
75% LSAT	156	156	163
Median LSAT	154	154	154
25% LSAT	152	152	153

Grants and Scholarships (from prior year)

	Total #	Total %	Full-time #	Full-time %	Part-time #	Part-time %
Total # of students	523		499		24	
Total # receiving grants	182	34.8	182	36.5	0	0.0
Less than 1/2 tuition	90	17.2	90	18.0	0	0.0
Half to full tuition	73	14.0	73	14.6	0	0.0
Full tuition	10	1.9	10	2.0	0	0.0
More than full tuition	9	1.7	9	1.8	0	0.0
Median grant amount			$8,600		$0	

Informational and Library Resources

# of volumes and volume equivalents	328,349
# of titles	102,305
# of active serial subscriptions	1,820
Study seating capacity inside the library	387
# of full-time professional librarians	10
Hours per week library is open	100
# of open, wired connections available to students	18
# of networked computers available for use by students	64
# of simultaneous wireless users	2,700
Require computer?	No

JD Attrition (from prior year)

	Academic #	Other #	Total #	Total %
1st year	15	11	26	14.3
2nd year	1	10	11	6.1
3rd year	0	0	0	0.0
4th year	0	0	0	0.0

Employment (9 months after graduation)

	Total	Percentage
Employment status known	154	100.0
Employment status unknown	0	0.0
Employed	148	96.1
Pursuing graduate degrees	0	0.0
Unemployed seeking employment	1	0.6
Unemployed not seeking employment	0	0.0
Unemployed and studying for the bar	5	3.2

Type of Employment

	Total	Percentage
# employed in law firms	98	66.2
# employed in business and industry	11	7.4
# employed in government	6	4.1
# employed in public interest	8	5.4
# employed as judicial clerks	20	13.5
# employed in academia	4	2.7

Geographic Location

	Total	Percentage
# employed in state	109	73.6
# employed in foreign countries	1	0.7
# of states where employed	8	

Bar Passage Rates

Jurisdiction	Missouri			Kansas		
Exam	Sum 05	Win 06	Total	Sum 05	Win 06	Total
# from school taking bar for the first time	125	13	138	21	25	46
School's pass rate for all first-time takers	88%	62%	86%	81%	92%	87%
State's pass rate for all first-time takers	88%	90%	89%	78%	90%	82%

University of Missouri—Kansas City School of Law

5100 Rockhill Road
Kansas City, MO 64110
Phone: 816.235.1644; Fax: 816.235.5276
E-mail: law@umkc.edu; Website: www.law.umkc.edu

The information on these pages was provided by the law school.

■ Introduction

Located in the midst of a beautiful college campus, UMKC takes pride in being the urban public law school with a small liberal arts feel. From this unique vantage point, UMKC serves and collaborates with the legal communities in two major metropolitan areas of the states of Missouri and Kansas. Students, faculty, and alumni actively lead and participate in professional activities with area bar associations, lawyers, and law firms, as well as government agencies and the judiciary. A variety of community-based projects benefit from this involvement.

UMKC law school graduates hold important positions in legal arenas across the country, distinguishing themselves in private practice, government service, academia, and corporate roles. Notable UMKC alumni include a president of the United States, a justice of the US Supreme Court, and a director of the FBI. Many other UMKC alumni currently serve as judges at the federal, state, and local levels—an unmistakable sign of community respect for the school and its graduates.

The law school enjoys support from its alumni, a number of whom participate in the Inns of UMKC, a program designed to help students achieve academic success, improve their preparation for the bar exam, and better prepare them for life as practicing attorneys. Modeled after the English Inns of Court system of training young lawyers, each Inn is led by prominent members of the local bar—attorneys and a judge—as well as law school faculty. Inns meet on a regular basis throughout the year. Each student meets with his or her faculty advisor for individual advising on a prescribed schedule.

Founded in 1895, the school is accredited by the ABA and is a member of the AALS.

■ Library and Physical Facilities

Office suites shared by faculty and students are designed to foster the exchange of ideas and to promote collegiality between faculty and students. The school has over 121,000 square feet of modern, usable space, which includes wireless computer access throughout the building, a comfortable student lounge with an attached outdoor courtyard, recently renovated lecture halls, student offices, and a newly remodeled courtroom with state-of-the-art technology and an innovative viewing theater.

The Leon E. Bloch Law Library is a modern facility that combines the traditions of print media with emerging electronic media in preparing the lawyer of the future and supporting the legal community.

■ Curriculum

UMKC School of Law is a community of learners bridging the gap between theory and practice. Courses are taught in a variety of formats, but all have high-quality teaching and student-faculty interaction. Many of the substantive courses include problem solving, service learning, and the development of skills components essential to the practice of law.

The first-year JD program is prescribed, with classes that average fewer than 60 students each. A year-long intensive course in Introduction to Law and Lawyering Processes provides instruction in legal analysis, research, writing, and advocacy. The upper-level program includes a combination of required courses, as well as a broad selection of elective courses, including approved nonlaw courses in other UMKC divisions. No class offered is larger than 80 students, and most are significantly smaller.

The school is committed to the success of its students. Academic enrichment opportunities in the form of supervised, structured study groups, lecture series, and weekly workshops are offered. Additional opportunities include a weeklong summer program available on a limited basis.

While the school's innovative new Solo and Small Firm Initiative prepares students for general practice, those seeking more focused study can pursue one of our four emphasis areas: Litigation; Business and Entrepreneurial Law; Urban, Land Use and Environmental Law; and Law in Service to Children and Families. These emphases build on our long-standing tradition of excellence in these areas and prepare students to enter the job market with specialized knowledge and skills.

A part-time day program is available for those students with family or career responsibilities who are unable to enroll on a full-time basis. Students may graduate in two and one-half years by attending two summer sessions.

■ JD/MBA and JD/MPA Programs

The School of Law has established dual-degree programs with the Henry W. Bloch School of Business and Public Administration. The program allows students to earn a JD degree and a Master of Business Administration or Master of Public Administration degree on an accelerated basis through cross-acceptance of some credit hours. Applicants must satisfy the admission requirements of each school.

■ JD/LLM and Combined-degree Programs

The School of Law has adopted combined-degree programs that allow qualified JD students to apply up to 12 credit hours (with the permission of the Graduate Studies Committee) of UMKC tax or estate planning courses approved for this purpose toward an LLM on an accelerated basis, generally requiring only one additional semester (or two summer sessions) beyond that required for the JD degree.

■ Student Activities

The law school's location in a metropolitan area provides many opportunities for students to engage in real-life representation of clients (under faculty supervision) in clinical programs that include UMKC's Child and Family Services Clinic, Tax Clinic, Entrepreneurial Law and Practice Clinic, and Wrongful Convictions (the school's "Innocence Project"). The school also offers a number of field placements, including judicial clerkships with federal and state judges, and internships with prosecutors, public defenders, Legal Aid, the Department of Labor, the EPA, and the US Attorney's Office.

Students write and edit a substantial portion of the *UMKC Law Review*, a scholarly legal journal, and also serve as assistant editors of the *Urban Lawyer*, published by the ABA Section of

Local Government Law, and the national and international *Journal of the American Academy of Matrimonial Lawyers*.

Students obtain advanced skills development in trial and appellate advocacy through sequenced upper-level courses and competition participation. Students also participate in client counseling and negotiation competitions. UMKC teams frequently win regional and national honors in these competitions.

UMKC benefits from an active Student Bar Association, which represents students at faculty and committee meetings and plays an important role in establishing school policy. Three national legal fraternities have chapters at the school, as do the following law student associations: Black Law Students, Hispanic Law Students, Jewish Law Students, Asian Pacific Islander Students, Women Law Students, and Non-traditional Law Students. Additional student organizations specialize in Environmental Law, Public Interest Law, Intellectual Property Law, International Law, and other areas of interest, comprising over 30 student organizations. Students also have the opportunity to participate in one of two annual study-abroad programs that visit China and Ireland.

■ Admission

While some students are admitted primarily on undergraduate GPA and LSAT scores, most applications are considered by a committee that examines applicants' complete files to ensure that the entering class contains persons of diverse backgrounds and interests whose achievements qualify them for law study.

Our admission process aims to identify those who demonstrate a likelihood of success in law school, who will be active contributors to our law school community, and who will become competent, ethical members of the legal profession and the larger community.

Students may be admitted with a bachelor's degree from an approved institution or, in appropriate cases, with 90 hours of acceptable academic work. A $200 seat deposit is payable by April 1 or within 20 days of admission, whichever comes later, and a second $200 seat deposit is due June 15. Applicants are strongly encouraged to visit the school. Arrangements can be made to meet with students and faculty, visit a class, or tour the law school.

■ Career Services

The Office of Career Services assists law students in exploring and defining career options. It also provides advice and assistance in résumé preparation and interviewing skills. The office sponsors a series of programs to introduce students to a variety of career opportunities, including large firms, small firms, government, corporate, and public interest law. Participants in the school's Judicial Clerkship Initiative have enjoyed a high placement rate in pursuing clerkships with state and federal judges.

Applicant Profile

University of Missouri—Kansas City School of Law

LSAT Score	GPA								
	3.75 +	3.50–3.74	3.25–3.49	3.00–3.24	2.75–2.99	2.50–2.74	2.25–2.49	2.00–2.24	Below 2.00
175–180									
170–174									
165–169									
160–164									
155–159									
150–154									
145–149									
140–144									
135–139									
130–134									
125–129									
120–124									

Good Possibility   Possible   Unlikely

University of Montana School of Law

32 Campus Drive
Missoula, MT 59812
Phone: 406.243.4311
E-mail: lawadmis@umontana.edu; Website: www.umt.edu/law

ABA Approved Since 1923

The Basics

Type of school	Public
Term	Semester
Application deadline	3/1
Application fee	$60
Financial aid deadline	3/1
Can first year start other than fall?	No
Student to faculty ratio	13.4 to 1
Does the university offer:	
housing restricted to law students?	Yes
graduate housing for which law students are eligible?	Yes

Faculty and Administrators

	Total Fall	Total Spr	Men Fall	Men Spr	Women Fall	Women Spr	Minorities Fall	Minorities Spr
Full-time	15	15	12	11	3	4	2	2
Other Full-time	3	3	1	1	2	2	1	1
Deans, librarians, & others who teach	1	1	0	0	1	1	0	0
Part-time	14	17	11	14	3	3	0	0
Total	**33**	**36**	**24**	**26**	**9**	**10**	**3**	**3**

Curriculum

	Full-time	Part-time
Typical first-year section size	43	0
Is there typically a "small section" of the first-year class, other than Legal Writing, taught by full-time faculty	No	No
If yes, typical size offered last year		
# of classroom course titles beyond first-year curriculum		70
# of upper division courses, excluding seminars with an enrollment: Under 25		17
25–49		9
50–74		1
75–99		0
100+		0
# of seminars		27
# of seminar positions available		243
# of seminar positions filled	243	0
# of positions available in simulation courses		122
# of simulation positions filled	122	0
# of positions available in faculty supervised clinical courses		22
# of faculty supervised clinical positions filled	16	0
# involved in field placements	48	0
# involved in law journals	30	0
# involved in interschool competitions	39	0
# of credit hours required to graduate		90

JD Enrollment and Ethnicity

	Men #	Men %	Women #	Women %	Full-time #	Full-time %	Part-time #	Part-time %	1st-year #	1st-year %	Total #	Total %	JD Degs. Awd.
African Amer.	1	0.8	0	0.0	1	0.4	0	0.0	0	0.0	1	0.4	0
Amer. Indian	9	7.4	11	9.2	20	8.3	0	0.0	7	8.4	20	8.3	0
Asian Amer.	2	1.6	3	2.5	5	2.1	0	0.0	2	2.4	5	2.1	1
Mex. Amer.	0	0.0	0	0.0	0	0.0	0	0.0	0	0.0	0	0.0	0
Puerto Rican	0	0.0	1	0.8	1	0.4	0	0.0	0	0.0	1	0.4	0
Hispanic	0	0.0	0	0.0	0	0.0	0	0.0	0	0.0	0	0.0	0
Total Minority	12	9.8	15	12.5	27	11.2	0	0.0	9	10.8	27	11.2	1
For. Nation.	0	0.0	0	0.0	0	0.0	0	0.0	0	0.0	0	0.0	0
Caucasian	110	90.2	105	87.5	215	88.8	0	0.0	74	89.2	215	88.8	82
Unknown	0	0.0	0	0.0	0	0.0	0	0.0	0	0.0	0	0.0	0
Total	122	50.4	120	49.6	242	100.0	0	0.0	83	34.3	242		83

Transfers

Transfers in	2
Transfers out	1

Tuition and Fees

	Resident	Nonresident
Full-time	$9,978	$20,354
Part-time	$0	$0

Living Expenses

Estimated living expenses for singles		
Living on campus	Living off campus	Living at home
$10,500	$10,500	$8,100

University of Montana School of Law

ABA
Approved
Since
1923

GPA and LSAT Scores

	Total	Full-time	Part-time
# of apps	479	479	0
# of offers	174	174	0
# of matrics	83	83	0
75% GPA	3.71	3.71	0.00
Median GPA	3.44	3.44	0.00
25% GPA	3.23	3.23	0.00
75% LSAT	156	156	0
Median LSAT	153	153	0
25% LSAT	150	150	0

Grants and Scholarships (from prior year)

	Total #	Total %	Full-time #	Full-time %	Part-time #	Part-time %
Total # of students	237		237		0	
Total # receiving grants	120	50.6	120	50.6	0	0.0
Less than 1/2 tuition	111	46.8	111	46.8	0	0.0
Half to full tuition	8	3.4	8	3.4	0	0.0
Full tuition	0	0.0	0	0.0	0	0.0
More than full tuition	1	0.4	1	0.4	0	0.0
Median grant amount			$1,500		$0	

Informational and Library Resources

# of volumes and volume equivalents	127,368
# of titles	23,319
# of active serial subscriptions	1,228
Study seating capacity inside the library	364
# of full-time professional librarians	2
Hours per week library is open	106
# of open, wired connections available to students	177
# of networked computers available for use by students	33
# of simultaneous wireless users	350
Require computer?	No

JD Attrition (from prior year)

	Academic #	Other #	Total #	Total %
1st year	0	0	0	0.0
2nd year	0	6	6	7.9
3rd year	0	0	0	0.0
4th year	0	0	0	0.0

Employment (9 months after graduation)

	Total	Percentage
Employment status known	76	96.2
Employment status unknown	3	3.8
Employed	70	92.1
Pursuing graduate degrees	3	3.9
Unemployed seeking employment	1	1.3
Unemployed not seeking employment	2	2.6
Unemployed and studying for the bar	0	0.0

Type of Employment

	Total	Percentage
# employed in law firms	35	50.0
# employed in business and industry	3	4.3
# employed in government	13	18.6
# employed in public interest	2	2.9
# employed as judicial clerks	17	24.3
# employed in academia	0	0.0

Geographic Location

	Total	Percentage
# employed in state	50	71.4
# employed in foreign countries	0	0.0
# of states where employed		12

Bar Passage Rates

Jurisdiction	Montana		
Exam	Sum 05	Win 06	Total
# from school taking bar for the first time	67	8	75
School's pass rate for all first-time takers	91%	100%	92%
State's pass rate for all first-time takers	89%	95%	91%

University of Montana School of Law

32 Campus Drive
Missoula, MT 59812
Phone: 406.243.4311
E-mail: lawadmis@umontana.edu; Website: www.umt.edu/law

■ Introduction

The University of Montana (UM) is located in Missoula on the west slopes of the Rocky Mountains. Missoula is situated halfway between Yellowstone and Glacier national parks and is surrounded by several of the largest designated wilderness areas in the continental United States. The city is known for its outdoor opportunities and quality of life.

The University of Montana School of Law was established in 1911 and serves as a legal center for the state. It has been accredited by the AALS since 1914 and by the ABA since 1923. As one of the smallest law schools in the nation, the University of Montana School of Law offers students a congenial academic, intellectual, and social environment.

■ UM's Program

The University of Montana School of Law integrates theory and practice throughout its curriculum to instill entry-level practice and competence in its graduates. The School of Law's curriculum, teaching methodology, and assessment techniques are designed to address the following components of a lawyer's work: (1) knowledge of the law, (2) ability to apply legal rules to solve problems, (3) ability to use lawyering skills (e.g., negotiation and client counseling), (4) perspective on the societal role and responsibility of lawyers, and (5) sensitivity to the dynamics of social and interpersonal interaction.

The school has created three distinctive programs to acquaint first-year students with the ways lawyers think and work: (1) the Introductory Program, (2) the Lawyer Skills Program, and (3) the Law Firm Program. In the Introductory Program, students are initiated into the legal culture by surveying legal history, the American legal system, the litigation process, legal writing, and legal analysis and jurisprudence. The School of Law is one of the few to introduce first-year students to the skills involved in dispute resolution, including client counseling, legal document drafting, and oral argument. UM's program encourages students to cooperate and collaborate rather than compete as they begin to think and work as lawyers. Entering students belong to "law firms": groups of six students (called associates) directed by upper-class students.

The school has long emphasized performance in its curriculum. The school's legal writing and dispute-resolution programs represent a coherent and comprehensive approach to lawyering skills. Students master specific transactional skills such as planning an estate, drafting a contract, and creating a small business.

The upper-division clinical training program provides students with a wide range of opportunities to earn required academic credit by working on actual cases under the supervision of faculty and practicing attorneys in Missoula. The clinical offerings include the Natural Resource Clinic, Indian Law Clinic, Montana Legal Services Association Clinic, Prosecutory clinics (federal, state, county, and municipal), University of Montana Legal Counsel Clinic, and the Disability Law Clinic.

■ Special Programs

Because of Montana's natural setting, many students enroll in the natural resource and environmental law courses. Montana offers a certificate program in environmental and natural resources law, natural resource clinics, and the opportunity to participate on the *Public Land and Resources Law Review.*

The School of Law also offers concentrations in the areas of trial advocacy and dispute resolution, Indian law, and business and tax law. Montana is home to seven Indian reservations. The School of Law's Indian Law courses, Indian Law Clinic, and Native American Law Student Association provide opportunities for students to learn about and participate in the administration of justice for Montana's Native Americans.

The School of Law offers three joint-degree programs. Students can combine their law degrees with a Master of Science in Environmental Studies, a Master of Business Administration, or a Master of Public Administration. These programs can lead to completion of joint degrees in as little as four years.

■ Admission

A committee of law faculty reviews applications. Candidates must be of good moral character, have intellectual promise, and have a baccalaureate degree from an approved college or university prior to matriculation. Applicants are considered in two distinct pools: resident and nonresident. The School of Law seeks a diverse student body and welcomes applications from members of groups historically underrepresented in the legal profession.

The School of Law recommends that you submit your application as soon as possible. We begin reviewing completed applications after January 1. Applications are not considered complete until all application materials, including the LSDAS report, are received. If your file is completed by February 15, you will be notified of a decision (admit, deny, or retain for further review) by March 15. If your file is completed by March 15, you will be notified of a decision by April 15. Files completed after March 15 may be considered on a space-available basis.

The most important admission criteria are the cumulative undergraduate GPA and the LSAT score. If the LSAT is repeated, all scores will be used in evaluating the applicant. The admission committee weighs such factors as writing ability; college attended; trend in grades; quality of work in difficult courses; experience prior to application to law school, including graduate study; ability to overcome economic or other disadvantages; and change in performance after an absence from school.

The school recognizes a commitment to provide full opportunities for the study of law and entry into the legal profession of qualified members of groups (notably racial and ethnic minorities) who have been victims of discrimination.

■ Student Activities

All students are members of the Student Bar Association. Its programs contribute to the professional development and the social life of the student body. Clayberg Inn of Phi Delta Phi national law fraternity encourages scholarship, promotes fellowship, and fosters the ideals of the profession. Other organizations include student chapters of the American Trial Lawyers Association—the Montana Trial Lawyers Association and the Montana Defense Trial Lawyers Association—the

University of Montana School of Law

Women's Law Caucus, the Environmental Law Group, the Native American Law Student Association, the Federalist Society, and the University of Montana Public Interest Law Coalition. The *Montana Law Review* and the *Public Land and Resources Law Review* afford supplementary training in analyzing legal problems precisely and presenting legal issues cogently.

The University of Montana School of Law is proud of its performance in interscholastic competitions. Nearly every year, the School of Law fields teams that compete at the national level. Most recently, UM won the 2000 National Moot Court Championship. UM won the ATLA trial competition national championship in 1992 and the national ABA client-counseling championship in 1990.

Applicant Profile

University of Montana School of Law
This grid includes only applicants who earned 120–180 LSAT scores under standard administrations.

LSAT Score	3.75 +		3.50–3.74		3.25–3.49		3.00–3.24		2.75–2.99		2.50–2.74		2.25–2.49		2.00–2.24		Below 2.00		No GPA		Total	
	Apps	Adm	Apps	Adm	Apps	Adm	Apps	Adm	Apps	Adm	Apps	Adm	Apps	Adm	Apps	Adm	Apps	Adm	Apps	Adm	Apps	Adm
175–180	0	0	0	0	0	0	0	0	0	0	0	0	0	0	0	0	0	0	0	0	0	0
170–174	0	0	1	1	0	0	0	0	0	0	0	0	0	0	0	0	0	0	0	0	1	1
165–169	3	3	2	0	1	0	1	1	2	2	1	0	0	0	0	0	0	0	0	0	10	6
160–164	6	5	8	6	6	4	2	2	3	2	2	1	0	0	1	1	0	0	0	0	28	21
155–159	14	14	14	13	18	12	22	11	11	1	4	0	3	0	0	0	0	0	1	0	86	51
150–154	24	16	36	21	36	13	34	9	19	5	13	0	5	0	3	0	0	0	2	0	171	64
145–149	9	5	19	8	28	5	29	4	23	2	5	0	4	0	2	0	0	0	2	0	121	24
140–144	2	0	7	1	7	0	9	0	14	0	7	0	5	1	4	1	0	0	2	0	57	3
135–139	1	0	2	0	1	0	5	0	4	0	0	0	2	0	1	0	0	0	2	0	18	0
130–134	0	0	0	0	2	0	0	0	0	0	0	0	1	0	0	0	0	0	0	0	3	0
125–129	0	0	0	0	0	0	0	0	0	0	1	0	0	0	0	0	0	0	0	0	1	0
120–124	0	0	0	0	0	0	0	0	0	0	0	0	0	0	0	0	0	0	1	0	1	0
Total	59	43	89	50	99	34	102	27	76	12	33	1	20	1	11	2	0	0	8	0	497	170

Apps = Number of Applicants
Adm = Number Admitted
Reflects 99% of the total applicant pool.

University of Nebraska College of Law

PO Box 830902
Lincoln, NE 68583-0902
Phone: 402.472.2161; Fax: 402.472.5185
E-mail: lawadm@unl.edu; Website: http://law.unl.edu/

ABA
Approved
Since
1923

The Basics

Type of school	Public
Term	Semester
Application deadline	3/1
Application fee	$25
Financial aid deadline	5/1
Can first year start other than fall?	No
Student to faculty ratio	12.4 to 1
Does the university offer:	
housing restricted to law students?	No
graduate housing for which law students are eligible?	Yes

Faculty and Administrators

	Total		Men		Women		Minorities	
	Fall	Spr	Fall	Spr	Fall	Spr	Fall	Spr
Full-time	26	27	19	19	7	8	2	2
Other Full-time	0	0	0	0	0	0	0	0
Deans, librarians, & others who teach	9	9	6	6	3	3	0	0
Part-time	22	28	14	18	8	10	0	0
Total	57	64	39	43	18	21	2	2

Curriculum

	Full-time	Part-time
Typical first-year section size	70	0
Is there typically a "small section" of the first-year class, other than Legal Writing, taught by full-time faculty	Yes	No
If yes, typical size offered last year	25	
# of classroom course titles beyond first-year curriculum		79
# of upper division courses, excluding seminars with an enrollment: Under 25		58
25–49		21
50–74		9
75–99		2
100+		0
# of seminars		11
# of seminar positions available		139
# of seminar positions filled	139	0
# of positions available in simulation courses		332
# of simulation positions filled	332	0
# of positions available in faculty supervised clinical courses		53
# of faculty supervised clinical positions filled	53	0
# involved in field placements	17	0
# involved in law journals	37	0
# involved in interschool competitions	57	0
# of credit hours required to graduate		93

JD Enrollment and Ethnicity

	Men		Women		Full-time		Part-time		1st-year		Total		JD Degs. Awd.
	#	%	#	%	#	%	#	%	#	%	#	%	
African Amer.	9	4.3	10	5.2	19	4.8	0	0.0	12	8.0	19	4.8	3
Amer. Indian	1	0.5	3	1.6	4	1.0	0	0.0	2	1.3	4	1.0	1
Asian Amer.	2	1.0	8	4.2	9	2.3	1	33.3	4	2.7	10	2.5	5
Mex. Amer.	6	2.9	9	4.7	14	3.5	1	33.3	8	5.3	15	3.8	3
Puerto Rican	0	0.0	0	0.0	0	0.0	0	0.0	0	0.0	0	0.0	0
Hispanic	1	0.5	3	1.6	4	1.0	0	0.0	4	2.7	4	1.0	0
Total Minority	19	9.1	33	17.3	50	12.6	2	66.7	30	20.0	52	13.0	12
For. Nation.	0	0.0	0	0.0	0	0.0	0	0.0	0	0.0	0	0.0	2
Caucasian	189	90.9	158	82.7	346	87.4	1	33.3	120	80.0	347	87.0	114
Unknown	0	0.0	0	0.0	0	0.0	0	0.0	0	0.0	0	0.0	0
Total	208	52.1	191	47.9	396	99.2	3	0.8	150	37.6	399		128

Transfers

Transfers in	3
Transfers out	0

Tuition and Fees

	Resident	Nonresident
Full-time	$9,213	$21,580
Part-time	$0	$0

Living Expenses

Estimated living expenses for singles		
Living on campus	Living off campus	Living at home
$11,436	$11,176	$6,926

University of Nebraska College of Law

*ABA
Approved
Since
1923*

GPA and LSAT Scores

	Total	Full-time	Part-time
# of apps	877	877	0
# of offers	366	366	0
# of matrics	144	144	0
75% GPA	3.84	3.84	0.00
Median GPA	3.64	3.64	0.00
25% GPA	3.27	3.27	0.00
75% LSAT	160	160	0
Median LSAT	156	156	0
25% LSAT	154	154	0

Grants and Scholarships (from prior year)

	Total		Full-time		Part-time	
	#	%	#	%	#	%
Total # of students	394		389		5	
Total # receiving grants	173	43.9	173	44.5	0	0.0
Less than 1/2 tuition	64	16.2	64	16.5	0	0.0
Half to full tuition	61	15.5	61	15.7	0	0.0
Full tuition	10	2.5	10	2.6	0	0.0
More than full tuition	38	9.6	38	9.8	0	0.0
Median grant amount			$7,000		$0	

Informational and Library Resources

# of volumes and volume equivalents	406,759
# of titles	61,408
# of active serial subscriptions	2,461
Study seating capacity inside the library	372
# of full-time professional librarians	5
Hours per week library is open	109
# of open, wired connections available to students	12
# of networked computers available for use by students	27
# of simultaneous wireless users	400
Require computer?	No

JD Attrition (from prior year)

	Academic	Other	Total	
	#	#	#	%
1st year	9	11	20	14.5
2nd year	0	4	4	3.2
3rd year	0	4	4	3.0
4th year	0	0	0	0.0

Employment (9 months after graduation)

	Total	Percentage
Employment status known	134	96.4
Employment status unknown	5	3.6
Employed	124	92.5
Pursuing graduate degrees	3	2.2
Unemployed seeking employment	3	2.2
Unemployed not seeking employment	1	0.7
Unemployed and studying for the bar	3	2.2
Type of Employment		
# employed in law firms	64	51.6
# employed in business and industry	22	17.7
# employed in government	17	13.7
# employed in public interest	11	8.9
# employed as judicial clerks	7	5.6
# employed in academia	3	2.4
Geographic Location		
# employed in state	74	59.7
# employed in foreign countries	1	0.8
# of states where employed	24	

Bar Passage Rates

Jurisdiction	Nebraska		
Exam	Sum 05	Win 06	Total
# from school taking bar for the first time	67	7	74
School's pass rate for all first-time takers	90%	86%	89%
State's pass rate for all first-time takers	88%	62%	86%

University of Nebraska College of Law

PO Box 830902
Lincoln, NE 68583-0902
Phone: 402.472.2161; Fax: 402.472.5185
E-mail: lawadm@unl.edu; Website: http://law.unl.edu/

■ Introduction

Founded in 1888, the University of Nebraska College of Law offers an excellent legal education at a reasonable cost. It is large enough to provide students with a diverse curriculum, yet small enough to ensure that students are not lost in a faceless crowd. The College of Law is a charter member of the AALS and is accredited by the ABA. The University of Nebraska College of Law is located on the East Campus of the University of Nebraska in Lincoln, a city of approximately 235,000 and the state capital.

■ Curriculum

The College of Law's academic year runs from late August to early May. A two-day orientation before the beginning of the fall semester introduces first-year students to the law school. Each incoming student is assigned a faculty advisor who can answer questions about law school, course selections, and career goals. The first-year curriculum is 15 hours the first semester and 18 hours the second semester and includes civil procedure, contracts, criminal law, legal writing, property, and torts. Courses in the second and third years are elective, with the exception of required courses in constitutional law, professional responsibility, a research seminar, and a professional skills course. The curriculum encompasses a broad range of areas. The curriculum offers particular depth in the areas of litigation, alternative dispute resolution, taxation, environmental, employment, international, and corporate and commercial law. Students who wish to focus on a particular area of the law may pursue the Litigation Skills or Business Transaction Concentration or develop an individualized program of concentrated study.

The College of Law provides an Academic Resource Program for first-year students to assist them in developing and improving fundamental skills such as note-taking, briefing cases, legal analysis, outlining, and writing examinations. The program provides weekly skills classes as well as a series of lectures and individual academic counseling.

Although completing the requirements for a JD degree normally takes three years, it is possible to graduate in two and one-half years by attending summer school. The college offers no night classes and rarely accepts part-time students. Students receiving the JD degree are qualified to practice in any state upon passage of that state's bar examination.

■ Skills and Clinical Education

The College of Law recognizes that becoming a lawyer involves more than learning legal theory. Students need to be able to develop practical skills to effectively represent clients and function as lawyers. The College of Law has offered courses that emphasize "learning by doing" since the early 1970s. The college offers professional skills courses in pretrial litigation, trial advocacy, appellate advocacy, mediation, negotiations, alternative dispute resolution, client interviewing and counseling, construction law, business planning, civil clinic, and criminal clinic. These classes allow second- and third-year students to develop lawyering skills in simulated settings or in the handling of real cases for actual clients. In civil clinic, third-year students represent clients in and out of court in matters such as bankruptcy, domestic relations, immigration, and landlord-tenant disputes. Students in criminal clinic prosecute misdemeanor cases in Lancaster County.

■ Joint-degree Programs

The college's interdisciplinary program in Law and Psychology is recognized as one of the finest in the nation. The college also participates in seven other joint-degree programs and will work with students to individually design programs in disciplines not covered by a formal program. In each program, students will earn two degrees with fewer credit hours and in less time than if the degrees were pursued separately. The formal joint-degree programs include JD/MBA (Business), JD/MPA (Accounting), JD/PhD (Psychology), JD/MA (Political Science), JD/MA or MS (Economics), JD/MCRP (Community and Regional Planning), JD/PhD (Educational Administration), and JD/MA (International Affairs, in cooperation with the University of Denver).

■ Library and Physical Facilities

The Schmid Law Library has a collection of about 395,000 volumes and a full complement of the latest developments in information technology. The library provides seating for 335 students and has 14 group study rooms, each with full access to power and fast data connections, both wired and wireless, for the best access to the Internet from any place in the library. The five professional librarians and their staff strive to create a service-oriented environment for legal research and scholarship. All these attributes combine to make the Schmid Law Library not only the largest, but the most effective, efficient, and friendliest law library in the region.

The College of Law's classrooms and Welpton Courtroom include attractive decor, adjustable chairs, laptop compatibility, and state-of-the-art technology.

■ Student Activities

The *Nebraska Law Review*, published by a student editorial board, publishes leading articles from well-known authorities in their fields, as well as student notes and comments. Other extracurricular academic programs include the National Moot Court Competition, Client Counseling Competition, and National Trial Competition.

Students can become involved in over 25 activities and organizations, including the Student Bar Association, Women's Law Caucus, Black Law Students Association, Entertainment and Sports Law Association, Equal Justice Society, Federalist Society, Multicultural Legal Society, and two national legal fraternities.

■ Career Services

The College of Law operates its own career services office for students seeking full-time employment or summer clerkships. The office provides students with a variety of placement-related services and also organizes on-campus interviews by private law firms, governmental agencies, corporations, and other potential employers. As of December 2005, approximately 96 percent of the members of the class of 2005 were employed or were enrolled in advanced-degree programs.

■ Admission

The College of Law starts reviewing applications in early January, and the application deadline is March 1. Admission decisions are made on a rolling basis. Students are required to have a bachelor's degree from an accredited institution, take the LSAT, and register for the LSDAS. In making its decisions, the Admissions Committee seeks to identify those individuals who have the ability to compete successfully in a rigorous academic environment. The major factors that the committee considers are the applicant's LSAT score and the applicant's undergraduate grade-point average. However, admission decisions are not simply a function of the numbers. The committee also takes into account any upward (or downward) trend in the applicant's academic performance over time, quality of the applicant's undergraduate institution, course of study, personal statement, work experience, graduate study, extracurricular activities, letters of recommendation, and other information supplied by the applicant.

The college takes special care in evaluating applications from members of minority groups that have been underrepresented in the legal profession.

The College of Law will waive the application fee upon demonstration of financial need. To visit a law class, meet with admission personnel, or tour the law college, contact the admission office.

Applicant Profile

University of Nebraska College of Law
This grid includes only applicants who earned 120–180 LSAT scores under standard administrations.

GPA

LSAT Score	3.75 +		3.50–3.74		3.25–3.49		3.00–3.24		2.75–2.99		2.50–2.74		2.25–2.49		2.00–2.24		Below 2.00		No GPA		Total	
	Apps	Adm	Apps	Adm	Apps	Adm	Apps	Adm	Apps	Adm	Apps	Adm	Apps	Adm	Apps	Adm	Apps	Adm	Apps	Adm	Apps	Adm
175–180	0	0	0	0	0	0	0	0	0	0	0	0	0	0	0	0	0	0	0	0	5	4
170–174	3	3	1	1	0	0	0	0	0	0	0	0	0	0	1	0	0	0	0	0	18	16
165–169	9	8	1	1	2	2	2	2	1	1	2	2	0	0	0	0	0	0	1	0	67	60
160–164	23	23	17	17	13	12	5	4	2	2	4	2	3	0	0	0	0	0	0	0	67	60
155–159	63	62	56	50	50	33	23	16	18	5	7	3	3	1	4	1	0	0	2	0	226	171
150–154	60	38	67	23	68	6	59	8	23	3	16	3	5	2	0	0	1	0	2	1	301	84
145–149	29	4	35	3	34	1	24	3	20	1	9	1	5	2	1	0	0	0	1	0	158	15
140–144	10	3	13	3	17	2	19	3	12	0	7	0	6	2	0	0	0	0	4	0	88	13
135–139	3	0	2	0	6	0	5	1	5	0	3	0	2	0	0	0	0	0	1	0	27	1
130–134	0	0	2	0	1	0	0	0	1	0	1	0	1	0	0	0	0	0	2	0	8	0
125–129	0	0	0	0	0	0	0	0	0	0	0	0	1	0	0	0	0	0	0	0	1	0
120–124	0	0	0	0	0	0	0	0	0	0	0	0	0	0	0	0	0	0	0	0	0	0
Total	200	141	194	98	191	56	137	37	82	12	49	11	26	7	6	1	1	0	13	1	899	364

Apps = Number of Applicants
Adm = Number Admitted
Reflects 99% of the total applicant pool.

University of Nevada, Las Vegas, William S. Boyd School of Law

4505 Maryland Parkway, Box 451003
Las Vegas, NV 89154-1003
Phone: 702.895.2440; Fax: 702.895.2414
E-mail: request@law.unlv.edu; Website: www.law.unlv.edu

*ABA
Approved
Since
2000*

The Basics

Type of school	Public
Term	Semester
Application deadline	3/15
Application fee	$50
Financial aid deadline	2/1
Can first year start other than fall?	No
Student to faculty ratio	15.6 to 1
Does the university offer:	
housing restricted to law students?	No
graduate housing for which law students are eligible?	No

Faculty and Administrators

	Total		Men		Women		Minorities	
	Fall	Spr	Fall	Spr	Fall	Spr	Fall	Spr
Full-time	21	23	11	14	10	9	7	7
Other Full-time	9	10	5	5	4	5	0	0
Deans, librarians, & others who teach	12	13	6	6	6	7	0	0
Part-time	11	12	10	8	1	4	1	1
Total	53	58	32	33	21	25	8	8

Curriculum

	Full-time	Part-time
Typical first-year section size	55	44
Is there typically a "small section" of the first-year class, other than Legal Writing, taught by full-time faculty	No	No
If yes, typical size offered last year		
# of classroom course titles beyond first-year curriculum		70

# of upper division courses, excluding seminars with an enrollment:		
	Under 25	88
	25–49	31
	50–74	7
	75–99	2
	100+	0

	Full-time	Part-time
# of seminars		10
# of seminar positions available		157
# of seminar positions filled	85	35
# of positions available in simulation courses		213
# of simulation positions filled	115	43
# of positions available in faculty supervised clinical courses		42
# of faculty supervised clinical positions filled	46	20
# involved in field placements	103	18
# involved in law journals	43	9
# involved in interschool competitions	21	7
# of credit hours required to graduate		89

JD Enrollment and Ethnicity

	Men		Women		Full-time		Part-time		1st-year		Total		JD Degs. Awd.
	#	%	#	%	#	%	#	%	#	%	#	%	
African Amer.	7	2.9	15	6.6	15	4.4	7	5.3	9	5.9	22	4.7	3
Amer. Indian	3	1.2	3	1.3	6	1.8	0	0.0	3	2.0	6	1.3	0
Asian Amer.	24	9.9	33	14.5	43	12.7	14	10.5	13	8.5	57	12.1	11
Mex. Amer.	11	4.5	13	5.7	15	4.4	9	6.8	8	5.2	24	5.1	6
Puerto Rican	3	1.2	2	0.9	4	1.2	1	0.8	3	2.0	5	1.1	0
Hispanic	9	3.7	4	1.8	6	1.8	7	5.3	5	3.3	13	2.8	4
Total Minority	57	23.5	70	30.7	89	26.3	38	28.6	41	26.8	127	27.0	24
For. Nation.	0	0.0	0	0.0	0	0.0	0	0.0	0	0.0	0	0.0	0
Caucasian	169	69.5	144	63.2	225	66.6	88	66.2	101	66.0	313	66.5	109
Unknown	17	7.0	14	6.1	24	7.1	7	5.3	11	7.2	31	6.6	9
Total	243	51.6	228	48.4	338	71.8	133	28.2	153	32.5	471		142

Transfers

Transfers in	5
Transfers out	4

Tuition and Fees

	Resident	Nonresident
Full-time	$9,568	$18,468
Part-time	$8,252	$15,860

Living Expenses

Estimated living expenses for singles

Living on campus	Living off campus	Living at home
$13,800	$13,350	$8,830

University of Nevada, Las Vegas, William S. Boyd School of Law

*ABA
Approved
Since
2000*

GPA and LSAT Scores

	Total	Full-time	Part-time
# of apps	2,206	1,892	314
# of offers	358	291	67
# of matrics	156	110	46
75% GPA	3.67	3.71	3.65
Median GPA	3.50	3.54	3.42
25% GPA	3.27	3.31	3.15
75% LSAT	160	161	158
Median LSAT	158	158	155
25% LSAT	155	156	151

Grants and Scholarships (from prior year)

	Total		Full-time		Part-time	
	#	%	#	%	#	%
Total # of students	479		322		157	
Total # receiving grants	195	40.7	181	56.2	14	8.9
Less than 1/2 tuition	110	23.0	105	32.6	5	3.2
Half to full tuition	54	11.3	48	14.9	6	3.8
Full tuition	31	6.5	28	8.7	3	1.9
More than full tuition	0	0.0	0	0.0	0	0.0
Median grant amount			$3,500		$5,000	

Informational and Library Resources

# of volumes and volume equivalents	300,997
# of titles	188,879
# of active serial subscriptions	4,134
Study seating capacity inside the library	323
# of full-time professional librarians	8
Hours per week library is open	101
# of open, wired connections available to students	1,004
# of networked computers available for use by students	80
# of simultaneous wireless users	600
Require computer?	No

JD Attrition (from prior year)

	Academic	Other	Total	
	#	#	#	%
1st year	4	13	17	11.5
2nd year	3	2	5	3.6
3rd year	0	0	0	0.0
4th year	1	0	1	2.1

Employment (9 months after graduation)

	Total	Percentage
Employment status known	119	92.2
Employment status unknown	10	7.8
Employed	104	87.4
Pursuing graduate degrees	3	2.5
Unemployed seeking employment	3	2.5
Unemployed not seeking employment	4	3.4
Unemployed and studying for the bar	5	4.2

Type of Employment

	Total	Percentage
# employed in law firms	49	47.1
# employed in business and industry	17	16.3
# employed in government	12	11.5
# employed in public interest	8	7.7
# employed as judicial clerks	18	17.3
# employed in academia	0	0.0

Geographic Location

	Total	Percentage
# employed in state	94	90.4
# employed in foreign countries	0	0.0
# of states where employed	8	

Bar Passage Rates

Jurisdiction	Nevada		
Exam	Sum 05	Win 06	Total
# from school taking bar for the first time	80	23	103
School's pass rate for all first-time takers	69%	70%	69%
State's pass rate for all first-time takers	64%	67%	65%

University of Nevada, Las Vegas, William S. Boyd School of Law

4505 Maryland Parkway, Box 451003
Las Vegas, NV 89154-1003
Phone: 702.895.2440; Fax: 702.895.2414
E-mail: request@law.unlv.edu; Website: www.law.unlv.edu

■ Introduction

The William S. Boyd School of Law is a relatively new, state-supported law school, the first in Nevada's history. Located at the University of Nevada, Las Vegas, in a desert mountain setting, and in one of the fastest-growing cities in the country, the law school commenced classes in August 1998. The Boyd School of Law is fully accredited by the American Bar Association and is a member of the Association of American Law Schools.

■ Faculty

The Boyd School of Law has assembled a faculty of more than 40 experienced, accomplished, and well-respected legal educators. All faculty have excellent credentials, experience, and reputations; all are people for whom teaching and mentoring of students is very important; and all are people who are eager to serve their community through scholarship or other community outreach programs.

■ Curriculum

The Boyd School of Law offers and encourages its students to undertake a generalist curriculum. Specific course offerings are constantly reviewed and revised as societal needs change. The curriculum generally emphasizes the responsibilities, skills, and values required of members of the legal profession. This emphasis comes to the fore in Lawyering Process, a three-semester required course that offers students the opportunity to examine the relationship between legal analysis and other legal skills such as research, writing, oral advocacy, and client interviewing and counseling, with significant emphasis on professionalism and ethics.

■ Programs of Study

The Boyd School of Law offers a traditional three-year, full-time JD program, as well as a four-year, part-time JD program during evening hours and a four-year, part-time JD program during day hours. Each part-time program requires the completion of summer coursework. The Boyd School of Law and the UNLV College of Business offer a dual Juris Doctor/Master of Business Administration degree program that allows students to pursue the two degrees concurrently. In addition, the Boyd School of Law and the UNLV School of Social Work offer a dual Juris Doctor/Master of Social Work degree program that allows students to pursue the two degrees concurrently.

■ Community Service

The law school requires first-year students to participate in a community service program. Working with Clark County Legal Services and Nevada Legal Services, teams of students prepare and conduct weekly workshops for unrepresented people on basic procedures in family or small claims court and on paternity, custody, guardianship, and bankruptcy matters. This program, by offering students the chance to educate groups of people in a general way without giving specific legal advice, reinforces students' commitment to community service and acquaints them with the large unmet need for legal services.

■ Hands-on Experience

The Thomas and Mack Legal Clinic houses the school's "law firm" and offers an integrated academic and practice-based educational experience that teaches students to be reflective practitioners and community-oriented professionals. The clinic currently focuses on five specific areas: child welfare, juvenile justice, capital defense, education, and immigration. Additionally, the law school has made a significant commitment to provide an extensive externship program. Working closely with the legal community, the externship director has established a year-round program to provide opportunities for approximately 100 students with the federal and state judiciary, government and public service agencies, and Nevada and US legislatures.

■ Saltman Center for Conflict Resolution

The Saltman Center for Conflict Resolution was established in 2003 to provide a venue for advanced study of the nature of conflict and the methods through which conflicts may be resolved. The work of the center encompasses conflicts arising out of regional, national, and international concerns, in both the public and private sectors. Recognizing that a sophisticated understanding of conflict necessarily requires insights derived from disciplines other than law, the center places particular emphasis on interdisciplinary approaches to understanding and resolving disputes.

■ Student Activities

The *Nevada Law Journal* is a publication devoted to scholarly research on the subject of national legal interest as well as on issues of particular interest to the Nevada legal community.

The Society of Advocates is the school's appellate and trial forensic program. The society consists of an executive board and team members who participate in interscholastic competitions. Teams compete in mock trial, client counseling, negotiation, mediation, and alternative dispute resolution competitions, as well as traditional appellate advocacy.

Among the student organizations established at the Boyd School of Law are the Student Bar Association, Environmental Law Society, Minority Law Students Association, Criminal Law Society, Gaming Law Student Association, Sports and Entertainment Law Association, Federalist Society, Black Law Student Association, Public Interest Law Association, Sexual and Gender Equality, American Constitution Society, Vegas Immigration Student Association, Asian Pacific American Law Students Association, and Phi Alpha Delta.

■ Career Services

The Department of Career Services offers personalized career counseling, employment workshops, a job opportunity board, on-campus interviewing programs, and a state-of-the-art online job search program to assist students.

Academic Success Program

The objective of the Boyd School of Law Academic Success Program is to provide a comprehensive network of presentations, activities, tutorials, and workshops designed to stimulate learning and to amplify the classroom experience. The program supplements the curriculum with opportunities to enhance learning skills and develop more efficient and effective methods of studying, comprehending, and writing. The Academic Success Program supervises a student-operated mentoring, advising, and tutoring program.

Facility

The Boyd School of Law facility, comprising William S. Boyd Hall and the James E. Rogers Center for Administration and Justice, was dedicated in September 2002. Classrooms include the technology necessary for presentations using PowerPoint, video, and document cameras. The largest classroom and trial courtroom are equipped to facilitate videoconferencing and distance learning. Lounge and study space offer students indoor and outdoor seating areas where they can make productive use of their time between classes.

Library

The Wiener-Rogers Law Library holds the most substantial collection of legal materials in the state of Nevada. The library is staffed by excellent, service-oriented librarians who have come from major libraries across the country. Patrons and students have access to a core collection of important material in printed and micro formats. The library houses two computer labs and provides numerous carrels for individual study, as well as group study rooms. The growing library collection now exceeds 300,000 volumes and microform volume equivalents.

Admission

The Boyd School of Law seeks to enroll an accomplished and diverse group of women and men who will enrich the educational program, the community, and the legal profession. The school seeks students who have demonstrated significant accomplishments in their lives by achieving distinguished academic records, by succeeding in important and challenging careers, by providing community service, or by meeting challenges associated with their race, ethnicity, gender, economic status, or disability. Students with diverse backgrounds, attitudes, and interests contribute to the breadth and quality of the classroom and out-of-classroom dialogue that is a critical element of legal education.

Applicant Profile

The Boyd School of Law has elected not to publish an admission profile based on LSAT score and undergraduate GPA. Those two factors, while certainly important, are not the only factors taken into consideration. The Boyd School of Law uses no form of indexing system in reaching its admission decisions. Each completed application file is reviewed in its entirety.

New England School of Law

154 Stuart Street
Boston, MA 02116
Phone: 617.422.7210; Fax: 617.457.3033
E-mail: admit@admin.nesl.edu; Website: http://www.nesl.edu

ABA
Approved
Since
1969

The Basics

Type of school	Private
Term	Semester
Application deadline	3/15
Application fee	$65
Financial aid deadline	4/20
Can first year start other than fall?	No
Student to faculty ratio	22.3 to 1
Does the university offer:	
housing restricted to law students?	No
graduate housing for which law students are eligible?	No

Faculty and Administrators

	Total		Men		Women		Minorities	
	Fall	Spr	Fall	Spr	Fall	Spr	Fall	Spr
Full-time	36	36	22	22	14	14	4	4
Other Full-time	0	0	0	0	0	0	0	0
Deans, librarians, & others who teach	7	7	5	5	2	2	1	1
Part-time	83	72	54	46	29	26	4	4
Total	126	115	81	73	45	42	9	9

Curriculum

	Full-time	Part-time
Typical first-year section size	135	130
Is there typically a "small section" of the first-year class, other than Legal Writing, taught by full-time faculty	No	No
If yes, typical size offered last year		
# of classroom course titles beyond first-year curriculum		115
# of upper division courses, excluding seminars with an enrollment: Under 25		59
25–49		36
50–74		13
75–99		9
100+		8
# of seminars		42
# of seminar positions available		853
# of seminar positions filled	318	305
# of positions available in simulation courses		900
# of simulation positions filled	509	183
# of positions available in faculty supervised clinical courses		66
# of faculty supervised clinical positions filled	43	3
# involved in field placements	229	24
# involved in law journals	113	21
# involved in interschool competitions	16	0
# of credit hours required to graduate		86

JD Enrollment and Ethnicity

	Men		Women		Full-time		Part-time		1st-year		Total		JD Degs. Awd.
	#	%	#	%	#	%	#	%	#	%	#	%	
African Amer.	6	1.2	14	2.4	13	1.8	7	1.8	11	2.8	20	1.8	11
Amer. Indian	1	0.2	1	0.2	2	0.3	0	0.0	1	0.3	2	0.2	0
Asian Amer.	29	5.7	42	7.1	59	8.2	12	3.1	40	10.2	71	6.5	22
Mex. Amer.	2	0.4	3	0.5	2	0.3	3	0.8	2	0.5	5	0.5	3
Puerto Rican	2	0.4	5	0.9	6	0.8	1	0.3	2	0.5	7	0.6	2
Hispanic	7	1.4	15	2.6	15	2.1	7	1.8	6	1.5	22	2.0	3
Total Minority	47	9.2	80	13.6	97	13.5	30	7.9	62	15.8	127	11.5	41
For. Nation.	0	0.0	0	0.0	0	0.0	0	0.0	0	0.0	0	0.0	0
Caucasian	403	78.7	458	77.9	554	77.1	307	80.6	282	71.9	861	78.3	261
Unknown	62	12.1	50	8.5	68	9.5	44	11.5	48	12.2	112	10.2	7
Total	512	46.5	588	53.5	719	65.4	381	34.6	392	35.6	1100		309

Transfers

Transfers in	3
Transfers out	33

Tuition and Fees

	Resident	Nonresident
Full-time	$25,865	$25,865
Part-time	$19,415	$19,415

Living Expenses

Estimated living expenses for singles		
Living on campus	Living off campus	Living at home
N/A	$15,405	$9,880

*ABA
Approved
Since
1969*

GPA and LSAT Scores

	Total	Full-time	Part-time
# of apps	3,500	2,762	738
# of offers	1,691	1,356	335
# of matrics	393	270	123
75% GPA	3.45	3.47	3.40
Median GPA	3.25	3.27	3.22
25% GPA	3.04	3.05	2.97
75% LSAT	154	154	152
Median LSAT	151	152	150
25% LSAT	150	150	148

Grants and Scholarships (from prior year)

	Total		Full-time		Part-time	
	#	%	#	%	#	%
Total # of students	1,095		699		396	
Total # receiving grants	433	39.5	319	45.6	114	28.8
Less than 1/2 tuition	324	29.6	249	35.6	75	18.9
Half to full tuition	27	2.5	15	2.1	12	3.0
Full tuition	82	7.5	55	7.9	27	6.8
More than full tuition	0	0.0	0	0.0	0	0.0
Median grant amount			$3,500		$4,000	

Informational and Library Resources

# of volumes and volume equivalents	350,109
# of titles	55,974
# of active serial subscriptions	3,175
Study seating capacity inside the library	419
# of full-time professional librarians	10
Hours per week library is open	104
# of open, wired connections available to students	426
# of networked computers available for use by students	49
# of simultaneous wireless users	200
Require computer?	No

JD Attrition (from prior year)

	Academic	Other	Total	
	#	#	#	%
1st year	22	48	70	18.2
2nd year	0	9	9	2.8
3rd year	0	0	0	0.0
4th year	0	1	1	1.3

Employment (9 months after graduation)

	Total	Percentage
Employment status known	297	94.3
Employment status unknown	18	5.7
Employed	216	72.7
Pursuing graduate degrees	8	2.7
Unemployed seeking employment	22	7.4
Unemployed not seeking employment	3	1.0
Unemployed and studying for the bar	48	16.2

Type of Employment

# employed in law firms	101	46.8
# employed in business and industry	31	14.4
# employed in government	39	18.1
# employed in public interest	4	1.9
# employed as judicial clerks	15	6.9
# employed in academia	6	2.8

Geographic Location

# employed in state	131	60.6
# employed in foreign countries	1	0.5
# of states where employed	16	

Bar Passage Rates

Jurisdiction	Massachusetts		
Exam	Sum 05	Win 06	Total
# from school taking bar for the first time	181	22	203
School's pass rate for all first-time takers	73%	73%	73%
State's pass rate for all first-time takers	84%	75%	82%

New England School of Law

154 Stuart Street
Boston, MA 02116
Phone: 617.422.7210; Fax: 617.457.3033
E-mail: admit@admin.nesl.edu; Website: http://www.nesl.edu

■ Introduction

New England School of Law was founded in 1908 as Portia Law School, the only law school in the nation exclusively for women. Coeducational since 1938, the law school is accredited by the American Bar Association and is a member of the Association of American Law Schools. It is an independent institution, not affiliated with a university, and, as a result, is able to make its own decisions on how to develop and improve its educational program.

■ Location

Situated in the heart of Boston's theater district and a block from the famous Public Garden, New England School of Law is within walking distance of prominent law firms, courthouses, and government agencies. This central location opens extensive possibilities for clinical placements, clerkships, and part-time employment.

Relying on a good public transportation system, residents can take advantage of the city's lively and varied neighborhoods, historic sights, fine cultural institutions, and professional sports teams. With nearly three dozen colleges, universities, and professional schools in the city, Boston has a large population of students and young professionals.

■ Curriculum and Academic Activities

The curriculum at New England School of Law prepares students to practice in any jurisdiction in the United States. In addition to required courses, students can choose from among approximately 150 electives. Courses and cocurricular activities can be combined to focus on areas such as tax, international, business, public interest, criminal, family, and environmental law. New England School of Law also has an extensive clinical program that allows students to combine fieldwork with classroom study in 16 subject areas. About 60 percent of the students take a clinical course while they are in law school.

The law school is a pioneer in incorporating relevant international law into domestic law courses throughout the curriculum. Students in Business Organizations, Contracts, Criminal Law, Family Law, Tax Law, and other classes learn about applicable international law, laws of other nations that have an impact on Americans, and American laws that affect foreign nationals.

The law school has three nationally distributed journals, the *New England Law Review*, the *New England Journal on Criminal and Civil Confinement*, and the *New England Journal of International and Comparative Law*. The *Journal on Criminal and Civil Confinement* is the only publication produced by law students that is devoted solely to prison and incarceration issues.

The required Legal Research and Writing Program includes a moot court component in the first semester of the second year. The law school also sponsors six cocurricular advocacy teams. Competition teams have reached advanced rounds and won brief or oralist awards in recent years. The Philip C. Jessup International Law Moot Court Team advanced to the international competition in 2001 and received the best brief award.

Three programs provide various types of judicial clerkship opportunities. The school's Academic Excellence Program offers optional academic support and supervised skills practice for first-year students.

■ Study Options

Students may enroll in the full-time day division, the part-time day or evening divisions, or the Special Part-time Program, a unique arrangement for parents with primary childrearing responsibilities.

New England School of Law accepts foreign lawyers in an advanced placement JD program or an LLM program in Advanced Legal Studies.

■ Academic Centers

New England School of Law is home to the Center for International Law and Policy, which sponsors an annual conference on a current issue in international law; other programs on international law; and several hands-on projects, including the Interstate Complicity Project/CIA Renditions in Europe, the Congo Project, and the International War Crimes Project.

The Center for Law and Social Responsibility, also located at the law school, sponsors symposia and supports a variety of projects through which faculty and students engage in legal work that focuses on social problems. The center includes the following programs: criminal justice, environmental advocacy, public service, and sexual and domestic violence.

The Center for Business Law builds on the law school's offerings in various areas of business law and serves as a forum for faculty and students to integrate coursework with policy research. Activities focus on the areas of intellectual property law, tax law, and corporate governance and ethics. The center sponsors an annual conference.

■ Study-abroad

Students may study in the law school's summer abroad programs in Galway, Ireland; London/Edinburgh; Malta; or Prague, or in semester-abroad programs in the Netherlands or Denmark and at the University of Paris X-Nanterre. A summer program in California, Mexico, and Canada focuses on NAFTA. An international criminal process clinic in The Hague enrolls students for the summer or semester.

■ Faculty

Full-time faculty members are dedicated teachers, accessible to students, and maintain a high level of scholarly publication. Nearly all have practiced in their fields of law. The full-time faculty is supplemented by an outstanding adjunct faculty of practicing attorneys and judges.

■ Technology

Wireless technology throughout the law school allows Internet access from anywhere in the building. All lecture halls and portions of the library are hardwired for Internet access. All large classrooms have multimedia presentation technology. The Computer and Media Center houses viewing equipment for audiovisual materials and reader/printers for microform materials. It maintains PC labs and provides laptops for checkout.

The law school's website includes a Web board that faculty use to post materials and answer student questions, student-run online discussions on class topics, and extensive links to legal research sites.

■ Financial Aid

Financial aid consists of a combination of federal loan programs, private loans, and institutional grants and scholarships. Most grants are need based; however, the law school awards several academic and merit scholarships. Federal work-study grants are also available.

■ Student Activities

New England School of Law has a Student Bar Association, which oversees more than two dozen student groups. Many of these organizations sponsor speakers, social events, and volunteer activities during the year. Student representatives sit on most faculty committees.

■ Career Services

The Career Services Office provides students with individual counseling, networking information, and programs on job-related issues. The office maintains an extensive resource library of directories of lawyers and legal organizations, books on practice areas, and periodicals. The Career Services website features more than 3,200 career-related links and a Web-based program that manages most Career Services functions. The online Recruitment and Programming Center offers a searchable job-posting database, online recruitment, an e-mail service that communicates job postings to students, an alumni networking and mentoring program, and postings of job-related programs sponsored by the Career Services Office and by outside law-related organizations. As a member of the Massachusetts Law School Consortium, New England School of Law participates in recruitment programs with the state's six other ABA-accredited law schools. The school is also a member of the Northeast Law School Consortium and participates in recruitment programs with eight ABA-accredited law schools in the region.

Most students take the Massachusetts bar exam, while many take exams in New York, the District of Columbia, Florida, New Hampshire, and New Jersey.

Applicant Profile

New England School of Law
This grid includes only applicants who earned 120–180 LSAT scores under standard administrations.

LSAT Score	3.75+ Apps	Adm	3.50–3.74 Apps	Adm	3.25–3.49 Apps	Adm	3.00–3.24 Apps	Adm	2.75–2.99 Apps	Adm	2.50–2.74 Apps	Adm	2.25–2.49 Apps	Adm	2.00–2.24 Apps	Adm	Below 2.00 Apps	Adm	No GPA Apps	Adm	Total Apps	Adm
175–180	0	0	0	0	0	0	0	0	0	0	0	0	0	0	0	0	0	0	0	0	0	0
170–174	0	0	0	0	0	0	0	0	0	0	1	0	0	0	0	0	0	0	0	0	1	0
165–169	1	1	2	2	1	1	5	5	7	7	5	4	1	1	0	0	0	0	0	0	22	21
160–164	8	8	14	14	20	18	23	22	13	8	15	10	7	3	6	5	2	0	2	0	110	88
155–159	42	40	66	64	97	94	92	91	67	58	44	35	10	5	12	8	3	0	4	1	437	396
150–154	63	62	205	192	267	246	231	210	174	102	101	48	38	16	10	2	0	0	5	1	1094	879
145–149	58	25	177	60	242	74	216	64	186	39	112	15	60	3	15	1	1	0	12	1	1079	282
140–144	17	0	50	0	92	2	102	3	71	0	59	0	36	0	3	0	3	0	10	0	443	5
135–139	0	0	12	0	21	0	23	0	35	0	19	0	11	0	3	0	3	0	8	0	135	0
130–134	1	0	4	0	5	0	8	0	13	0	5	0	4	0	6	0	3	0	1	0	50	0
125–129	1	0	0	0	0	0	0	0	1	0	1	0	3	0	3	0	1	0	1	0	11	0
120–124	0	0	0	0	0	0	0	0	0	0	0	0	1	0	0	0	1	0	0	0	2	0
Total	191	136	530	332	745	435	700	395	567	214	362	112	171	28	58	16	17	0	43	3	3384	1671

Apps = Number of Applicants
Adm = Number Admitted
Reflects 98% of the total applicant pool.

The University of New Mexico School of Law

MSC11-6070, 1 University of New Mexico
Albuquerque, NM 87131-0001
Phone: 505.277.2146; Fax: 505.277.9958
E-mail: admissions@law.unm.edu; Website: http://lawschool.unm.edu

ABA
Approved
Since
1948

The Basics

Type of school	Public
Term	Semester
Application deadline	2/15
Application fee	$50
Financial aid deadline	3/1
Can first year start other than fall?	No
Student to faculty ratio	10.0 to 1
Does the university offer:	
housing restricted to law students?	No
graduate housing for which law students are eligible?	No

Faculty and Administrators

	Total		Men		Women		Minorities	
	Fall	Spr	Fall	Spr	Fall	Spr	Fall	Spr
Full-time	25	32	12	18	13	14	11	14
Other Full-time	6	6	4	3	2	3	1	1
Deans, librarians, & others who teach	12	13	3	4	9	9	4	5
Part-time	11	16	5	9	6	6	2	4
Total	54	67	24	34	30	32	18	24

Curriculum

	Full-time	Part-time
Typical first-year section size	59	0
Is there typically a "small section" of the first-year class, other than Legal Writing, taught by full-time faculty	Yes	No
If yes, typical size offered last year	40	
# of classroom course titles beyond first-year curriculum	106	
# of upper division courses, excluding seminars with an enrollment: Under 25	58	
25–49	24	
50–74	3	
75–99	0	
100+	0	
# of seminars	44	
# of seminar positions available	550	
# of seminar positions filled	439	0
# of positions available in simulation courses	178	
# of simulation positions filled	185	0
# of positions available in faculty supervised clinical courses	124	
# of faculty supervised clinical positions filled	111	0
# involved in field placements	86	0
# involved in law journals	107	0
# involved in interschool competitions	33	0
# of credit hours required to graduate	86	

JD Enrollment and Ethnicity

	Men		Women		Full-time		Part-time		1st-year		Total		JD Degs. Awd.
	#	%	#	%	#	%	#	%	#	%	#	%	
African Amer.	5	2.9	7	4.1	12	3.5	0	0.0	5	4.5	12	3.5	6
Amer. Indian	17	9.9	23	13.5	40	11.7	0	0.0	12	10.7	40	11.7	9
Asian Amer.	3	1.7	6	3.5	9	2.6	0	0.0	4	3.6	9	2.6	1
Mex. Amer.	47	27.3	47	27.5	94	27.4	0	0.0	35	31.3	94	27.4	25
Puerto Rican	0	0.0	0	0.0	0	0.0	0	0.0	0	0.0	0	0.0	0
Hispanic	0	0.0	0	0.0	0	0.0	0	0.0	0	0.0	0	0.0	0
Total Minority	72	41.9	83	48.5	155	45.2	0	0.0	56	50.0	155	45.2	41
For. Nation.	0	0.0	0	0.0	0	0.0	0	0.0	0	0.0	0	0.0	0
Caucasian	82	47.7	75	43.9	157	45.8	0	0.0	52	46.4	157	45.8	71
Unknown	18	10.5	13	7.6	31	9.0	0	0.0	4	3.6	31	9.0	7
Total	172	50.1	171	49.9	343	100.0	0	0.0	112	32.7	343		119

Transfers

Transfers in	2
Transfers out	3

Tuition and Fees

	Resident	Nonresident
Full-time	$9,566	$23,213
Part-time	$0	$0

Living Expenses

Estimated living expenses for singles

Living on campus	Living off campus	Living at home
$12,164	$13,188	$8,168

The University of New Mexico School of Law

ABA Approved Since 1948

GPA and LSAT Scores

	Total	Full-time	Part-time
# of apps	1,405	1,405	0
# of offers	248	248	0
# of matrics	115	115	0
75% GPA	3.72	3.72	0.00
Median GPA	3.40	3.40	0.00
25% GPA	3.03	3.03	0.00
75% LSAT	158	158	0
Median LSAT	155	155	0
25% LSAT	152	152	0

Grants and Scholarships (from prior year)

	Total		Full-time		Part-time	
	#	%	#	%	#	%
Total # of students	357		357		0	
Total # receiving grants	89	24.9	89	24.9	0	0.0
Less than 1/2 tuition	23	6.4	23	6.4	0	0.0
Half to full tuition	28	7.8	28	7.8	0	0.0
Full tuition	28	7.8	28	7.8	0	0.0
More than full tuition	10	2.8	10	2.8	0	0.0
Median grant amount			$7,500		$0	

Informational and Library Resources

# of volumes and volume equivalents	429,740
# of titles	132,181
# of active serial subscriptions	3,296
Study seating capacity inside the library	351
# of full-time professional librarians	15
Hours per week library is open	90
# of open, wired connections available to students	326
# of networked computers available for use by students	105
# of simultaneous wireless users	300
Require computer?	Yes

JD Attrition (from prior year)

	Academic	Other	Total	
	#	#	#	%
1st year	0	0	0	0.0
2nd year	2	8	10	8.7
3rd year	0	1	1	0.8
4th year	0	0	0	0.0

Employment (9 months after graduation)

	Total	Percentage
Employment status known	99	100.0
Employment status unknown	0	0.0
Employed	91	91.9
Pursuing graduate degrees	1	1.0
Unemployed seeking employment	2	2.0
Unemployed not seeking employment	2	2.0
Unemployed and studying for the bar	3	3.0
Type of Employment		
# employed in law firms	40	44.0
# employed in business and industry	5	5.5
# employed in government	22	24.2
# employed in public interest	4	4.4
# employed as judicial clerks	14	15.4
# employed in academia	3	3.3
Geographic Location		
# employed in state	73	80.2
# employed in foreign countries	0	0.0
# of states where employed		10

Bar Passage Rates

Jurisdiction	New Mexico		
Exam	Sum 05	Win 06	Total
# from school taking bar for the first time	77	13	90
School's pass rate for all first-time takers	95%	100%	96%
State's pass rate for all first-time takers	90%	92%	90%

The University of New Mexico School of Law

MSC11-6070, 1 University of New Mexico
Albuquerque, NM 87131-0001
Phone: 505.277.2146; Fax: 505.277.9958
E-mail: admissions@law.unm.edu; Website: http://lawschool.unm.edu

■ Introduction

Located in Albuquerque, the School of Law is known for its small classes, easy student-faculty interaction, and special programs in clinical law, natural resources law, and Indian law. The 10:1 student-faculty ratio, one of the best in the country, facilitates a sense of community in the educational experience. It also allows the school to offer more courses with smaller enrollments. The school is a member of the AALS and is approved by the ABA. The University of New Mexico is the state's flagship institution with approximately 33,000 students on its main and branch campuses.

■ Curriculum

The Juris Doctor program is a full-time day curriculum. Students normally complete the required 86 hours of law credit for the JD degree in three academic years (six semesters). First-year students must take a full first-year curriculum, including basic courses in torts, contracts, civil procedure, property, criminal law, and constitutional law. Emphasis is also placed on the skills of advocacy: legal writing, oral argument, litigation, counseling, and negotiation. First-year classes range in size from approximately 13 to 58 students. Second- and third-year courses are elective except for Ethics and a clinical program. Typically, one-half of the electives have fewer than 15 students. Every student must complete the advanced writing requirement.

■ Special Programs

Clinical Law. UNM's program in Clinical Law is regarded as one of the finest practical-lawyering programs in the country and includes the Law Practice Clinic, the Children's Advocacy Clinic, the Economic Development and Tax Clinic, the Community Lawyering Clinic, and the Southwest Indian Law Clinic. Students may also participate in the extern placement program and elect assignment to a judge's office, the public defender's office, federal and state administrative offices, and private practitioners. The school also offers an innovative course in Criminal Law in Practice, in which students receive hands-on experience in either prosecution or defense of criminal cases at both the misdemeanor and felony levels. Unlike most other law schools, UNM requires six credit hours of clinical work for graduation. In 1970, the New Mexico Supreme Court adopted a rule permitting students to practice before state courts.

Indian Law. UNM has long been a leader in Indian law and has developed one of the most comprehensive programs in the country. The school offers students the Southwest Indian Law Clinic, the *Tribal Law Journal*, the Indian Law Certificate (ILC), scholarly research, guest lectures, seminars, and social activities. An ILC student completes the JD while enrolling in 21 hours of required and elective Indian law courses.

Natural Resources Law. The UNM School of Law is widely known for its strength in the areas of natural resources and environmental law and offers a number of electives in these subjects. Students who want to gain a more comprehensive understanding of resource problems may participate in the Natural Resources Certificate Program, which may include work on the *Natural Resources Journal*, an internationally recognized quarterly.

Business Law. UNM's Economic Development Program gives students the training they need to become well-prepared business lawyers. An enhanced curriculum includes the Economic Development and Tax Clinic, which offers services to small businesses, start-ups, nonprofit organizations, and economic development programs. Students learn how to advise entrepreneurs on a wide range of business issues.

International Law. The school has developed a variety of programs and courses that provide opportunities for students interested in international law. Students may expand their experience through coursework at the law school and through the study-abroad and exchange programs.

- Guanajuato Summer Law Institute. The School of Law, in conjunction with the Universidad de Guanajuato, Southwestern University, and Texas Tech University, offers six weeks of summer law study in Guanajuato, Mexico. The institute features an introduction to Mexican law and international law subjects related to Latin America. The institute is ABA approved.
- North American Exchange Program. Students can participate in a semester exchange with a Canadian or Mexican law school. Students may visit for a semester in the second or third years and receive up to 12 credits.
- Tasmania. Students have the opportunity to study for one semester at the University of Tasmania School of Law and receive up to 12 credits.
- Visiting Programs. Students may visit at other ABA-approved programs around the world.

■ Dual-degree Program

Four established dual JD and master's degree programs are offered: the JD and MA in Public Administration, the JD and MBA, the JD and MA in Water Resources, and the JD and MA in Latin American Studies. Students can also earn the JD degree and an MA, MS, or PhD in other academic fields. Students must satisfy the admission and academic requirements of both the School of Law and the graduate school.

■ Facilities

The School of Law, a state-of-the-art facility, is located on the northern edge of the UNM campus. The building is wireless and laptop friendly. The law school includes classroom and seminar rooms, all faculty offices, student organization and publication offices, two computer labs, the Clinical Program, and the law library. The law school is also home to the American Indian Law Center, Inc., and the Utton Transboundary Resources Center. The Utton Center uses multidisciplinary scholarship to address complex resource issues, focusing primarily on the Rio Bravo/Rio Grande and the Mexican–US border. Adjacent to the law school is the New Mexico Law Center in which the Institute of Public Law and the Albuquerque branch of the New Mexico Court of Appeals are located.

Law Library. The UNM Law Library is the largest legal research facility in New Mexico. The library offers a wide variety of electronic products, and its book and microform collection of 429,740 includes special collections in American Indian law, Mexican and Latin American law, land grant law, and natural resources law. The library's 32,443 square feet of space provides 240 seats, including 111 student carrels, plus numerous areas for study, lounging, and browsing. Wireless Internet broadcasters, group study rooms equipped with audiovisual equipment, photocopy facilities, the school's second computer lab for student use, and a classroom for legal research instruction are found in the library. The library is also home to the Governor Bruce King Archives and Reading Room, which serves as meeting space for special events.

Career and Student Services. The school's smaller size allows for individualized attention in all aspects of career development and job search methodology. Regular workshops are provided on résumé and cover letter writing, interviewing, and job search strategies. In addition, the law school sponsors on-campus interviews, a mock interview program, and presentations on various practice opportunities. Career counseling for students and graduates is provided by two full-time attorney counselors.

■ Student Activities

Extracurricular activities include the *Natural Resources Journal*, the *New Mexico Law Review*, the *Tribal Law Journal*, and several moot court and mock trial competitions. All law students are members of the university's Graduate/Professional Student Association and the Student Bar Association. Students may participate in nearly 30 law student organizations.

■ Admission and Financial Aid

Applicants must take the LSAT, register for the LSDAS, and have a bachelor's degree from an accredited university or college before registration in the fall. A five-member committee reviews applications. Substantial weight is given to the applicant's personal statement, prior work experience, extracurricular activities, letters of recommendation, and other information supplied by the applicant. Applications from New Mexico residents are given a preference. Students apply for financial aid by filing the FAFSA; no additional loan application is necessary. Types of financial aid include loans, grants, and work-study. The school awards grants to students based on the Access Group's Need Access application.

■ Albuquerque

The Albuquerque metropolitan area has a population of approximately 750,000. Located along the Rio Grande, the city is located at a high desert elevation of 5,000–7,000 feet and is surrounded by the Sandia Mountains.

From golf to skiing to hiking to fly-fishing, students have access to outdoor New Mexico. In addition, students have the opportunity to visit museums and art galleries and take in concerts and theater. The combination of multiple cultures reflected in food, music, art, architecture, and local customs heightens Albuquerque's appeal.

Applicant Profile

The University of New Mexico School of Law
This grid includes only applicants who earned 120–180 LSAT scores under standard administrations.

LSAT Score	3.75 + Apps	Adm	3.50–3.74 Apps	Adm	3.25–3.49 Apps	Adm	3.00–3.24 Apps	Adm	2.75–2.99 Apps	Adm	2.50–2.74 Apps	Adm	2.25–2.49 Apps	Adm	2.00–2.24 Apps	Adm	Below 2.00 Apps	Adm	No GPA Apps	Adm	Total Apps	Adm
175–180	1	1	0	0	0	0	0	0	0	0	0	0	0	0	0	0	0	0	0	0	1	1
170–174	1	1	1	1	3	3	2	1	0	0	0	0	0	0	0	0	0	0	1	1	8	7
165–169	9	8	5	3	5	3	4	1	2	2	2	1	0	0	0	0	0	0	0	0	27	18
160–164	17	14	20	18	18	8	17	3	10	3	10	5	3	0	2	0	0	0	0	0	97	51
155–159	38	17	66	23	79	15	60	15	43	7	8	0	8	2	0	0	1	0	3	0	411	61
150–154	46	14	70	10	86	7	104	17	58	7	23	3	14	1	6	2	1	0	3	0	281	24
145–149	26	5	44	4	74	7	52	5	36	1	24	2	15	0	3	0	0	0	5	0	170	5
140–144	12	0	24	1	36	0	36	1	20	1	21	1	13	1	3	0	0	0	2	0	66	0
135–139	1	0	7	0	14	0	16	0	14	0	5	0	5	0	2	0	0	0	2	0	21	0
130–134	0	0	0	0	3	0	6	0	2	0	4	0	3	0	1	0	0	0	1	0	4	0
125–129	1	0	0	0	0	0	0	0	1	0	1	0	0	0	0	0	0	0	1	0	4	0
120–124	0	0	0	0	0	0	0	0	0	0	0	0	0	0	0	0	0	0	0	0	0	0
Total	152	60	237	60	318	43	297	43	186	21	98	12	61	4	19	2	3	0	17	1	1388	246

Apps = Number of Applicants
Adm = Number Admitted
Reflects 99% of the total applicant pool.

New York Law School

57 Worth Street
New York, NY 10013
Phone: 212.431.2888; Fax: 212.966.1522
E-mail: admissions@nyls.edu; Website: www.nyls.edu

The Basics

Type of school	Private
Term	Semester
Application deadline	4/2
Application fee	$60
Financial aid deadline	4/2
Can first year start other than fall?	No
Student to faculty ratio	20.9 to 1
Does the university offer:	
housing restricted to law students?	Yes
graduate housing for which law students are eligible?	No

Faculty and Administrators

	Total		Men		Women		Minorities	
	Fall	Spr	Fall	Spr	Fall	Spr	Fall	Spr
Full-time	55	52	37	36	18	16	7	7
Other Full-time	6	6	2	2	4	4	0	0
Deans, librarians, & others who teach	11	11	6	6	5	5	0	0
Part-time	94	94	58	61	36	32	8	7
Total	166	163	103	105	63	57	15	14

Curriculum

	Full-time	Part-time
Typical first-year section size	134	134
Is there typically a "small section" of the first-year class, other than Legal Writing, taught by full-time faculty	Yes	Yes
If yes, typical size offered last year	44	44
# of classroom course titles beyond first-year curriculum	211	
# of upper division courses, excluding seminars with an enrollment: Under 25	110	
25–49	42	
50–74	12	
75–99	10	
100+	21	
# of seminars	76	
# of seminar positions available	1,282	
# of seminar positions filled	731	208
# of positions available in simulation courses	211	
# of simulation positions filled	136	25
# of positions available in faculty supervised clinical courses	147	
# of faculty supervised clinical positions filled	98	0
# involved in field placements	149	12
# involved in law journals	166	34
# involved in interschool competitions	113	8
# of credit hours required to graduate	86	

JD Enrollment and Ethnicity

	Men		Women		Full-time		Part-time		1st-year		Total		JD Degs. Awd.
	#	%	#	%	#	%	#	%	#	%	#	%	
African Amer.	26	3.7	62	7.7	54	4.7	34	9.4	26	4.8	88	5.8	20
Amer. Indian	0	0.0	3	0.4	3	0.3	0	0.0	1	0.2	3	0.2	4
Asian Amer.	66	9.3	74	9.2	97	8.4	43	11.9	55	10.1	140	9.3	28
Mex. Amer.	8	1.1	9	1.1	16	1.4	1	0.3	9	1.6	17	1.1	2
Puerto Rican	5	0.7	12	1.5	12	1.0	5	1.4	10	1.8	17	1.1	6
Hispanic	28	4.0	53	6.6	64	5.6	17	4.7	34	6.2	81	5.4	15
Total Minority	133	18.8	213	26.5	246	21.4	100	27.7	135	24.7	346	22.9	75
For. Nation.	3	0.4	6	0.7	9	0.8	0	0.0	0	0.0	9	0.6	5
Caucasian	407	57.5	391	48.7	604	52.5	194	53.7	338	61.8	798	52.8	299
Unknown	165	23.3	193	24.0	291	25.3	67	18.6	74	13.5	358	23.7	31
Total	708	46.9	803	53.1	1150	76.1	361	23.9	547	36.2	1511		410

Transfers

Transfers in	18
Transfers out	29

Tuition and Fees

	Resident	Nonresident
Full-time	$40,478	$40,478
Part-time	$31,124	$31,124

Living Expenses

Estimated living expenses for singles		
Living on campus	Living off campus	Living at home
$19,950	$19,950	$8,490

*ABA
Approved
Since
1954*

GPA and LSAT Scores

	Total	Full-time	Part-time
# of apps	5,557	4,660	897
# of offers	2,423	2,119	304
# of matrics	549	424	125
75% GPA	3.51	3.54	3.42
Median GPA	3.27	3.33	3.16
25% GPA	2.98	3.00	2.91
75% LSAT	156	157	156
Median LSAT	155	155	153
25% LSAT	152	152	151

Grants and Scholarships (from prior year)

	Total		Full-time		Part-time	
	#	%	#	%	#	%
Total # of students	1,480		1,106		374	
Total # receiving grants	508	34.3	425	38.4	83	22.2
Less than 1/2 tuition	465	31.4	386	34.9	79	21.1
Half to full tuition	43	2.9	39	3.5	4	1.1
Full tuition	0	0.0	0	0.0	0	0.0
More than full tuition	0	0.0	0	0.0	0	0.0
Median grant amount			$8,000		$4,875	

Informational and Library Resources

# of volumes and volume equivalents	518,496
# of titles	274,776
# of active serial subscriptions	5,528
Study seating capacity inside the library	525
# of full-time professional librarians	15
Hours per week library is open	98
# of open, wired connections available to students	50
# of networked computers available for use by students	142
# of simultaneous wireless users	1,000
Require computer?	No

JD Attrition (from prior year)

	Academic	Other	Total	
	#	#	#	%
1st year	30	52	82	15.0
2nd year	5	4	9	1.9
3rd year	0	1	1	0.3
4th year	0	0	0	0.0

Employment (9 months after graduation)

	Total	Percentage
Employment status known	508	93.0
Employment status unknown	38	7.0
Employed	469	92.3
Pursuing graduate degrees	5	1.0
Unemployed seeking employment	22	4.3
Unemployed not seeking employment	12	2.4
Unemployed and studying for the bar	0	0.0

Type of Employment

# employed in law firms	237	50.5
# employed in business and industry	81	17.3
# employed in government	45	9.6
# employed in public interest	14	3.0
# employed as judicial clerks	31	6.6
# employed in academia	3	0.6

Geographic Location

# employed in state	329	70.1
# employed in foreign countries	0	0.0
# of states where employed		18

Bar Passage Rates

Jurisdiction	New York		
Exam	Sum 05	Win 06	Total
# from school taking bar for the first time	438	37	475
School's pass rate for all first-time takers	72%	81%	73%
State's pass rate for all first-time takers	76%	61%	74%

New York Law School

57 Worth Street
New York, NY 10013
Phone: 212.431.2888; Fax: 212.966.1522
E-mail: admissions@nyls.edu; Website: www.nyls.edu

■ Introduction

New York Law School has developed a unique approach to legal education that it calls *The Right Program for Each Student*. At its core is an acknowledgment that different practice settings require different levels of training. For example, students working in larger organizations with extensive in-house training programs have less need for hands-on training than those who will open a solo practice. Those in larger organizations may need training in a specialized area, while those in general practice may need more breadth and less specialized expertise. The following components of *The Right Program for Each Student* are described on our website: Harlan Scholars Program, Individual Program, Comprehensive Curriculum, and the Professional Development Project.

Founded in 1891, New York Law School is one of the oldest independent law schools in the country. The school is fully accredited by the American Bar Association and is a member of the Association of American Law Schools.

■ Location/Physical Facilities/Library

New York Law School is located in Manhattan's historic district, TriBeCa, in Lower Manhattan. It is an extraordinary setting for the study of law and one of the city's most colorful and dynamic neighborhoods. Lower Manhattan is the site of New York's largest concentration of government agencies, courts, law firms, banks, corporate headquarters, and securities exchanges. Federal Courts, New York State Civil and Criminal Courts, Family Court, and the Court of International Trade are within a four-block radius of the Law School. The Law School's four connected buildings are located on a single block in the heart of TriBeCa, with easy access to major public transportation systems.

The Mendik Law Library, with its staff of 15 professional law librarians, includes nearly 500,000 volumes and a variety of computer-assisted research services. Its collection features concentrations in constitutional law, communications, labor law, and international and comparative law. The library also is a partial depository for state and federal documents.

■ Student Life

We are committed to giving students a first-rate law school experience—in and out of the classroom. In return, we demand of them the seriousness of purpose necessary to become ethical professionals—the kind of lawyers sought by clients, law firms, government agencies, advocacy groups, and corporations.

New York Law School has a long-standing and continuing interest in enrolling students from varied backgrounds, including older students, minority students, women, career-changers, and public servants. Students range in age from 21 to 65, with the average age being 26.

■ Faculty

The Law School's distinguished full-time faculty is composed of productive scholars who are dedicated educators and who share a strong commitment to the school's vision and philosophy embodied in its core values: embracing innovation, fostering integrity and professionalism, and advancing justice for a diverse society. A national survey of law faculty scholarship includes them among the 50 most prolific law faculties in the country and notes the significant number of their books that are published by university presses. Leading jurists and attorneys who work in nearby offices are members of the adjunct faculty.

■ Curriculum and Special Programs

The required curriculum, comprising the entire first year and part of the second year, provides a foundation in legal reasoning and in areas of law that are considered indispensable building blocks of a legal education. In the second year and thereafter, students may design their programs with elective courses chosen from an extraordinarily rich array.

Elements such as legal analysis and legal writing, counseling, interviewing, negotiating, advocacy, planning, and strategizing form the core subject areas of the school's Lawyering Skills Program. The Civil and Human Rights Clinic offers students the opportunity to represent real clients.

Externship and judicial internship programs permit students to do actual lawyering work in law offices.

■ Admission

In the admission process, a number of factors are taken into account, including the applicant's academic record and LSAT scores. The admission committee also looks for those applicants who have demonstrated leadership ability, motivation, and a sense of service and responsibility to society. Excellence in a particular field of study, progression of grades, strength of undergraduate curriculum, work and community service experience, graduate study in other disciplines, and extracurricular activities all are considered as well. Writing ability receives particular attention, and the admission committee strongly urges applicants to submit the optional writing sample.

The school seeks to enroll students who, through their diversity of backgrounds, experiences, perspectives, and ambitions, promise to enrich the law school community and, ultimately, the larger society.

Under a special admission option, the Wallace Stevens Scholars Program, a small group of professionals with postgraduate degrees and significant work experience will be admitted without having taken the LSAT but will be required to take the LSAT after admission to the Law School.

■ Academic Centers

The Institute for Information Law and Policy is the home for the study of technology, intellectual property, and information law. It includes our Media Law Center.

The Center for New York City Law focuses on governmental and legal processes in the urban setting.

The Center for International Law focuses on legal issues relating to international trade and finance.

The Justice Action Center seeks to develop students' expertise in civil rights and civil liberties law and international human rights.

The Center on Business Law and Policy focuses on business and corporate law.

The Center for Professional Values serves as a vehicle through which to examine the role of the legal profession and alternative approaches to the practice of law.

■ Moot Court/Law Journals/Student Organizations

New York Law School students exhibit well-honed courtroom skills, in recent years winning outright three national moot court competitions and earning awards in many others. The school's annual Robert F. Wagner Sr. Labor and Employment Law Competition is one of the nation's largest student-run moot court competitions.

The Law School currently has three scholarly publications, edited and staffed by students, that are an integral part of the Law School's program: *Law Review, Journal of International and Comparative Law,* and *Journal of Human Rights.*

Students have established some 32 interest organizations as well.

■ Expenses and Financial Aid

New York Law School has established a program of financial aid to assist students in meeting the costs of a legal education through grants, scholarships, work-study awards, and loans. Scholarships are awarded on the basis of academic merit and financial need.

■ Office of Professional Development

The Office of Professional Development brings together three key student services: Student Life, Career Services, and Public Interest and Community Service. This innovative structure allows us to offer students personal attention from their first day of study to help them pursue their professional goals. The Career Services Office offers a wide array of services, including individual career counseling, on-campus interview programs, career panels and workshops, alumni network and mentoring programs, online employer databases, and information on summer, full-time, and part-time positions and alternative career opportunities.

Applicant Profile

New York Law School
This grid includes only applicants who earned 120–180 LSAT scores under standard administrations.

LSAT Score	GPA 3.50 +		3.25–3.49		3.00–3.24		2.75–2.99		2.50–2.74		2.00–2.49		Below 2.00		No GPA		Total	
	Apps	Adm	Apps	Adm	Apps	Adm	Apps	Adm	Apps	Adm	Apps	Adm	Apps	Adm	Apps	Adm	Apps	Adm
165–180	37	36	15	15	16	16	13	13	6	6	2	2	0	0	1	0	90	88
155–164	503	494	370	358	326	303	222	199	99	65	67	17	4	1	21	13	1612	1450
145–154	676	337	648	221	636	159	442	110	271	24	168	9	4	0	37	8	2882	868
Below 145	138	2	154	0	176	2	177	0	127	0	112	0	17	1	38	0	939	5
Total	1354	869	1187	594	1154	480	854	322	503	95	349	28	25	2	97	21	5523	2411

Apps = Number of Applicants
Adm = Number Admitted
Reflects 98% of the total applicant pool.

New York University School of Law

40 Washington Square South
New York, NY 10012
Phone: 212.998.6060; Fax: 212.995.4527
E-mail: law.moreinfo@nyu.edu; Website: www.law.nyu.edu

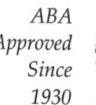

ABA
Approved
Since
1930

The Basics

Type of school	Private
Term	Semester
Application deadline	2/1
Application fee	$85
Financial aid deadline	4/15
Can first year start other than fall?	No
Student to faculty ratio	10.7 to 1
Does the university offer:	
housing restricted to law students?	Yes
graduate housing for which law students are eligible?	No

Faculty and Administrators

	Total		Men		Women		Minorities	
	Fall	Spr	Fall	Spr	Fall	Spr	Fall	Spr
Full-time	117	104	82	67	35	37	12	13
Other Full-time	18	20	6	8	12	12	7	6
Deans, librarians, & others who teach	4	4	3	3	1	1	0	0
Part-time	64	81	46	60	18	21	4	7
Total	203	209	137	138	66	71	23	26

Curriculum

	Full-time	Part-time
Typical first-year section size	112	0
Is there typically a "small section" of the first-year class, other than Legal Writing, taught by full-time faculty	Yes	No
If yes, typical size offered last year	56	
# of classroom course titles beyond first-year curriculum	258	

# of upper division courses, excluding seminars with an enrollment:		
	Under 25	77
	25–49	55
	50–74	37
	75–99	14
	100+	28

# of seminars	128	
# of seminar positions available	2,360	
# of seminar positions filled	1,881	0
# of positions available in simulation courses	48	
# of simulation positions filled	48	0
# of positions available in faculty supervised clinical courses	200	
# of faculty supervised clinical positions filled	199	0
# involved in field placements	104	0
# involved in law journals	623	0
# involved in interschool competitions	101	0
# of credit hours required to graduate	83	

JD Enrollment and Ethnicity

	Men		Women		Full-time		Part-time		1st-year		Total		JD Degs. Awd.
	#	%	#	%	#	%	#	%	#	%	#	%	
African Amer.	45	5.8	79	11.8	124	8.6	0	0.0	38	8.6	124	8.6	34
Amer. Indian	0	0.0	0	0.0	0	0.0	0	0.0	0	0.0	0	0.0	0
Asian Amer.	65	8.4	88	13.2	153	10.6	0	0.0	43	9.7	153	10.6	42
Mex. Amer.	5	0.6	3	0.4	8	0.6	0	0.0	2	0.5	8	0.6	3
Puerto Rican	2	0.3	4	0.6	6	0.4	0	0.0	1	0.2	6	0.4	3
Hispanic	29	3.7	25	3.7	54	3.7	0	0.0	14	3.2	54	3.7	22
Total Minority	146	18.8	199	29.8	345	23.9	0	0.0	98	22.1	345	23.9	104
For. Nation.	31	4.0	22	3.3	53	3.7	0	0.0	14	3.2	53	3.7	9
Caucasian	395	51.0	294	44.1	689	47.8	0	0.0	237	53.4	689	47.8	199
Unknown	203	26.2	152	22.8	355	24.6	0	0.0	95	21.4	355	24.6	153
Total	775	53.7	667	46.3	1442	100.0	0	0.0	444	30.8	1442		465

Transfers

Transfers in	51
Transfers out	0

Tuition and Fees

	Resident	Nonresident
Full-time	$40,385	$40,385
Part-time	$0	$0

Living Expenses

Estimated living expenses for singles

Living on campus	Living off campus	Living at home
$21,333	$21,333	$21,333

New York University School of Law

ABA
Approved
Since
1930

GPA and LSAT Scores

	Total	Full-time	Part-time
# of apps	7,571	7,571	0
# of offers	1,597	1,597	0
# of matrics	448	448	0
75% GPA	3.89	3.89	0.00
Median GPA	3.75	3.75	0.00
25% GPA	3.58	3.58	0.00
75% LSAT	172	172	0
Median LSAT	171	171	0
25% LSAT	168	168	0

Grants and Scholarships (from prior year)

	Total #	Total %	Full-time #	Full-time %	Part-time #	Part-time %
Total # of students	1,424		1,424		0	
Total # receiving grants	446	31.3	446	31.3	0	0.0
Less than 1/2 tuition	243	17.1	243	17.1	0	0.0
Half to full tuition	90	6.3	90	6.3	0	0.0
Full tuition	113	7.9	113	7.9	0	0.0
More than full tuition	0	0.0	0	0.0	0	0.0
Median grant amount			$17,500		$0	

Informational and Library Resources

# of volumes and volume equivalents	1,098,652
# of titles	293,950
# of active serial subscriptions	7,100
Study seating capacity inside the library	850
# of full-time professional librarians	13
Hours per week library is open	101
# of open, wired connections available to students	745
# of networked computers available for use by students	179
# of simultaneous wireless users	1,200
Require computer?	Yes

JD Attrition (from prior year)

	Academic #	Other #	Total #	Total %
1st year	0	5	5	1.1
2nd year	0	1	1	0.2
3rd year	0	0	0	0.0
4th year	0	0	0	0.0

Employment (9 months after graduation)

	Total	Percentage
Employment status known	451	100.0
Employment status unknown	0	0.0
Employed	431	95.6
Pursuing graduate degrees	7	1.6
Unemployed seeking employment	3	0.7
Unemployed not seeking employment	10	2.2
Unemployed and studying for the bar	0	0.0

Type of Employment

# employed in law firms	329	76.3
# employed in business and industry	3	0.7
# employed in government	16	3.7
# employed in public interest	29	6.7
# employed as judicial clerks	53	12.3
# employed in academia	0	0.0

Geographic Location

# employed in state	291	67.5
# employed in foreign countries	4	0.9
# of states where employed	28	

Bar Passage Rates

Jurisdiction	New York		
Exam	Sum 05	Win 06	Total
# from school taking bar for the first time	336	14	350
School's pass rate for all first-time takers	94%	79%	93%
State's pass rate for all first-time takers	76%	61%	74%

New York University School of Law

40 Washington Square South
New York, NY 10012
Phone: 212.998.6060; Fax: 212.995.4527
E-mail: law.moreinfo@nyu.edu; Website: www.law.nyu.edu

■ Introduction

Founded in 1835, New York University School of Law has a record of academic excellence and national scholarly influence extending back into the nineteenth century. More than 100 years ago, it became one of the first law schools to routinely admit women and those from groups discriminated against by many other institutions.

NYU School of Law has been a pioneer in such widely diverse programs as clinical education, law and business, public service, interdisciplinary colloquia, and global studies.

These traditions remain vibrant today as the School of Law, located on the university's campus in Greenwich Village, continues to use its position in New York City to create a twenty-first century legal education in global justice, grounded in solid sociological and jurisprudential training and reflected in sensitive professional service to the world's peoples.

■ Library and Physical Facilities

As one of the largest academic law libraries in the world, NYU School of Law's collection boasts widely recognized strengths in tax, legal history, intellectual property, constitutional law, and the law of democratic institutions. The extensive public law collection is complemented by primary law materials for over 20 non-US jurisdictions. The library's award-winning home page is a gateway to specialized legal research guides, e-journals, annotated foreign and international law sites, and commercial databases.

In 2004, the School of Law opened Furman Hall, its first new academic building in 50 years. Furman Hall is adjacent to the recently renovated Vanderbilt Hall and connects underground via the law library. The law school also owns two apartment buildings that provide housing for more than 800 law students, many with spouses, partners, and children.

■ Curriculum

NYU School of Law's curriculum is distinguished by its strength in traditional areas of legal study, interdisciplinary study, and clinical education, and has long been committed to educating lawyers who will use their degrees to serve the public. Students enjoy the intellectual and pedagogical diversity of the law school by mixing traditional courses with colloquia, global courses, clinics, independent research, journal work, study abroad, fellowships, and more.

The JD program is enriched by the graduate program, which offers advanced degrees in corporation law, general studies, international legal studies, international taxation, labor and employment law, taxation, and trade regulation.

■ Institutes and Centers

The curriculum is complemented by 19 institutes and centers, which represent the law school's extraordinary commitment of resources and energy to the collegial study of law at the most advanced level. These include the Brennan Center for Justice, the Hauser Global Law School Program, the Institute for International Law and Justice, the Center for Environmental and Land Use Law, and the Pollack Center for Law and Business.

■ Admission

The admission process is highly selective and seeks to enroll men and women of exceptional ability. The Committee on Admissions makes decisions after considering all the information in an application. It reviews the undergraduate transcript closely, with attention to factors such as trends in the applicant's grades, class rank, the ratio of pass/fail to graded courses, the diversity and depth of coursework, and the length of time since graduation. Factors other than undergraduate grades and LSAT scores may be particularly significant for applicants who have experienced educational or socioeconomic disadvantage. In all cases, however, other aspects of the application significantly influence the decision. The committee evaluates work experience and extracurricular and community activities for evidence of advancement, leadership, and capacity for assuming responsibility. A recommendation letter is particularly valuable when the writer provides substantive information about the applicant's abilities, activities, and personal qualities. The personal statement provides an opportunity for the applicant to supplement the information supplied in the application.

The committee seeks to enroll an entering class of students with diverse experience, backgrounds, and points of view. Applicants are encouraged to provide information to help the committee reach thoughtful, informed decisions on their applications.

■ Student Activities

Student-edited publications are *New York University Law Review, Annual Survey of American Law, Environmental Law Journal, Journal of International Law and Politics, Journal of Legislation and Public Policy, Review of Law and Social Change,* and *Tax Law Review.* The *Commentator* is the law school newspaper. There are more than 45 student organizations.

■ Financial Aid

NYU School of Law will award a number of Root-Tilden-Kern Scholarships to entering students chosen for their intellectual potential, capacity for, and demonstrated commitment to public service through law. A limited number of awards will also be made on the basis of outstanding intellectual potential or substantial records indicating that the student will enrich the educational experience at the law school. The AnBryce Scholarship will be awarded to a small number of outstanding students who are the first in their immediate families to pursue a graduate degree. The Furman Academic Scholarship will be awarded to a small number of students who show promise in becoming legal academics. Scholarships are also available in the areas of business law, criminal law, environmental law, housing and urban policy, intellectual property, international law, Latino human rights, and law and economics. Federal and private loans also provide funding. Graduates who pursue careers in public service may be eligible for postgraduation benefits through the Loan Repayment Assistance Program.

■ Career Services

NYU School of Law has an extensive career services program. Career planning for first-year students includes personal career counseling, workshops on all aspects of the job search, specialty panels featuring speakers from all areas of practice, and a videotape mock interview program. Each year, more than 500 private law firms, public interest organizations, government agencies, corporations, and public accounting firms visit the law school to interview students. Over 60 percent of these employers are from outside New York.

The focal point of the law school's public service activities is the Public Interest Law Center, which provides students interested in public service with comprehensive support, including advice on courses and career opportunities. The Public Interest Summer Scholarship Program guarantees funding to all first- and second-year students who want to work in public interest positions. The Public Interest Law Center, with area law schools, also annually sponsors a public interest legal career symposium.

Applicant Profile

NYU School of Law does not provide a profile chart because we believe that while an applicant's undergraduate record and LSAT are important, they are not the sole determinants for admission to the law school. No index or cutoff is used in reviewing applications. There is no combination of grades or scores, therefore, that assures admission or denial.

An applicant's transcripts are analyzed for breadth and depth of coursework, trend in grades, and rank; the competitiveness of the school and major are taken into consideration, as are special honors, awards, and activities. Other aspects of the application significantly influence the decision, such as letters of recommendation, activities, and work experience.

In making its decision, the committee aims to enroll an entering class of students with the strongest combination of qualifications and the greatest potential to contribute to NYU School of Law and to the legal profession.

University of North Carolina School of Law

Campus Box 3380, 5026 Van Hecke-Wettach Hall
Chapel Hill, NC 27599-3380
Phone: 919.962.5109; Fax: 919.843.7939
E-mail: law_admission@unc.edu; Website: www.law.unc.edu

ABA Approved Since 1923

The Basics

Type of school	Public
Term	Semester
Application deadline	2/1
Application fee	$70
Financial aid deadline	3/1
Can first year start other than fall?	No
Student to faculty ratio	20.1 to 1
Does the university offer:	
housing restricted to law students?	No
graduate housing for which law students are eligible?	No

Faculty and Administrators

	Total		Men		Women		Minorities	
	Fall	Spr	Fall	Spr	Fall	Spr	Fall	Spr
Full-time	28	31	19	22	9	9	3	5
Other Full-time	2	1	1	1	1	0	0	0
Deans, librarians, & others who teach	18	18	5	6	13	12	1	1
Part-time	34	45	24	29	10	16	1	9
Total	82	95	49	58	33	37	5	15

Curriculum

	Full-time	Part-time
Typical first-year section size	77	0
Is there typically a "small section" of the first-year class, other than Legal Writing, taught by full-time faculty	Yes	No
If yes, typical size offered last year	27	
# of classroom course titles beyond first-year curriculum	122	

# of upper division courses, excluding seminars with an enrollment:		
	Under 25	52
	25–49	22
	50–74	9
	75–99	6
	100+	5

# of seminars	44	
# of seminar positions available	707	
# of seminar positions filled	628	0
# of positions available in simulation courses	1,020	
# of simulation positions filled	982	0
# of positions available in faculty supervised clinical courses	64	
# of faculty supervised clinical positions filled	55	0
# involved in field placements	96	0
# involved in law journals	208	0
# involved in interschool competitions	51	0
# of credit hours required to graduate	86	

JD Enrollment and Ethnicity

	Men		Women		Full-time		Part-time		1st-year		Total		JD Degs. Awd.
	#	%	#	%	#	%	#	%	#	%	#	%	
African Amer.	23	6.2	28	8.3	51	7.2	0	0.0	13	5.7	51	7.2	37
Amer. Indian	6	1.6	8	2.4	14	2.0	0	0.0	4	1.7	14	2.0	2
Asian Amer.	18	4.8	27	8.0	45	6.3	0	0.0	24	10.5	45	6.3	12
Mex. Amer.	2	0.5	3	0.9	5	0.7	0	0.0	0	0.0	5	0.7	0
Puerto Rican	0	0.0	0	0.0	0	0.0	0	0.0	0	0.0	0	0.0	0
Hispanic	20	5.4	15	4.4	35	4.9	0	0.0	16	7.0	35	4.9	6
Total Minority	69	18.5	81	23.9	150	21.1	0	0.0	57	24.9	150	21.1	57
For. Nation.	0	0.0	0	0.0	0	0.0	0	0.0	0	0.0	0	0.0	0
Caucasian	288	77.2	243	71.7	531	74.6	0	0.0	159	69.4	531	74.6	178
Unknown	16	4.3	15	4.4	31	4.4	0	0.0	13	5.7	31	4.4	3
Total	373	52.4	339	47.6	712	100.0	0	0.0	229	32.2	712		238

Transfers

Transfers in	4
Transfers out	2

Tuition and Fees

	Resident	Nonresident
Full-time	$12,947	$25,365
Part-time	$0	$0

Living Expenses

Estimated living expenses for singles

Living on campus	Living off campus	Living at home
$16,848	$16,848	$7,034

University of North Carolina School of Law

*ABA
Approved
Since
1923*

GPA and LSAT Scores

	Total	Full-time	Part-time
# of apps	3,581	3,581	0
# of offers	543	543	0
# of matrics	229	229	0
75% GPA	3.77	3.77	0.00
Median GPA	3.57	3.57	0.00
25% GPA	3.39	3.39	0.00
75% LSAT	164	164	0
Median LSAT	162	162	0
25% LSAT	158	158	0

Grants and Scholarships (from prior year)

	Total #	Total %	Full-time #	Full-time %	Part-time #	Part-time %
Total # of students	715		715		0	
Total # receiving grants	558	78.0	558	78.0	0	0.0
Less than 1/2 tuition	516	72.2	516	72.2	0	0.0
Half to full tuition	33	4.6	33	4.6	0	0.0
Full tuition	0	0.0	0	0.0	0	0.0
More than full tuition	9	1.3	9	1.3	0	0.0
Median grant amount			$4,665		$0	

Informational and Library Resources

# of volumes and volume equivalents	523,733
# of titles	109,686
# of active serial subscriptions	6,917
Study seating capacity inside the library	481
# of full-time professional librarians	12
Hours per week library is open	109
# of open, wired connections available to students	563
# of networked computers available for use by students	128
# of simultaneous wireless users	700
Require computer?	No

JD Attrition (from prior year)

	Academic #	Other #	Total #	Total %
1st year	0	5	5	2.2
2nd year	0	0	0	0.0
3rd year	0	0	0	0.0
4th year	0	0	0	0.0

Employment (9 months after graduation)

	Total	Percentage
Employment status known	223	97.8
Employment status unknown	5	2.2
Employed	190	85.2
Pursuing graduate degrees	10	4.5
Unemployed seeking employment	2	0.9
Unemployed not seeking employment	5	2.2
Unemployed and studying for the bar	16	7.2

Type of Employment

# employed in law firms	112	58.9
# employed in business and industry	14	7.4
# employed in government	24	12.6
# employed in public interest	11	5.8
# employed as judicial clerks	25	13.2
# employed in academia	4	2.1

Geographic Location

# employed in state	108	56.8
# employed in foreign countries	2	1.1
# of states where employed	24	

Bar Passage Rates

Jurisdiction	North Carolina			New York		
Exam	Sum 05	Win 06	Total	Sum 05	Win 06	Total
# from school taking bar for the first time	126	19	145	15	2	17
School's pass rate for all first-time takers	87%	63%	83%	93%	100%	94%
State's pass rate for all first-time takers	72%	69%	71%	76%	61%	74%

University of North Carolina School of Law

Campus Box 3380, 5026 Van Hecke-Wettach Hall
Chapel Hill, NC 27599-3380
Phone: 919.962.5109; Fax: 919.843.7939
E-mail: law_admission@unc.edu; Website: www.law.unc.edu

■ Introduction

The University of North Carolina, the first state university chartered in the United States, has offered degrees in law since 1845. The School of Law has been a member of the American Association of Law Schools since 1920 and has been an approved school since the American Bar Association began its accreditation activities in 1923. The School of Law is one of the outstanding institutions in the United States, and the University of North Carolina is recognized as being among the nation's leaders in graduate and professional education. The programs at the School of Law reflect a powerful, active commitment to the goals of teaching, scholarship, and public service. The town of Chapel Hill, a university community, is close to the Research Triangle Park, the metropolitan and industrial centers of Greensboro and Durham, and the state capital, Raleigh. The immediate area offers an attractive blend of a strong academic atmosphere in a multicultural, cosmopolitan setting.

■ Library and Physical Facilities

Housed on five floors within the law school, the library provides critical support to the school's academic program and to lawyers and members of the public throughout the state. Its collection, which totals over 488,000 volumes, includes court reports for American and English appellate courts, current codes and session laws for all states, and other primary legal materials. Within the library, a university computer lab provides Internet access, electronic mail, and word processing capabilities and is easily accessible to law students. Additionally, students can bring their own laptop computers and connect to the university's network in many of the high technology classrooms, library study carrels, and other areas in the building.

The School of Law aims to provide a quality legal education that will prepare students to practice successfully in any jurisdiction. The three-year Juris Doctor program begins with a first-year core curriculum designed to provide a theoretical and analytical foundation for law students. The second-year curriculum provides an important bridge between the core instruction of the first year and the culminating electives, seminars, and skills-oriented instruction of the third year. Finally in the third year, the curriculum is designed to provide a capstone for students' legal education and begins the transition into practice.

■ Joint-degree Programs/Certificate Programs

Ten formal joint JD and master's degree programs are available: JD/MPP (in conjunction with Duke University), JD/MBA, JD/MPA, JD/MPH, JD/MRP, JD/MSW, JD/MASA, JD/MAMC, JD/MSLS, or MSIS.

The Nonprofit Leadership Certificate Program prepares graduate students for leadership roles in North Carolina's rapidly growing nonprofit sector. The program provides an in-depth examination of leadership issues within human services, education, the arts, and other nonprofit organizations.

■ International Study Opportunities

In addition to the regularly taught courses in international business and human rights and the *International Law Journal*, students interested in international law can enhance their legal experience further with foreign study during the spring semester in France, the Netherlands, Mexico, England, and Scotland. Additionally, after the first year, students may also participate in the school's Summer Law Programs in Sydney, Australia; Augsburg, Germany; or Nice, France.

■ Centers and Initiatives

Carolina boasts nationally recognized centers in banking and financial services law, civil rights, and our new Center on Poverty, Work, and Opportunity. All are key areas tied to our history and the unique opportunities unfolding in North Carolina and the South. These centers and initiatives expand and enliven our curriculum, push the frontiers of teaching and research, and open new channels of scholarship for students.

■ Student Activities

Out of the classroom, student organizations provide a forum for the enormous talent and energy characteristic of Carolina Law students. Students can write for five prominent student publications—the *North Carolina Law Review*, the *North Carolina Journal of International Law and Commercial Regulation*, the *North Carolina Banking Institute Journal*, the *First Amendment Law Review*, and the *North Carolina Journal of Law and Technology*. The Student Bar Association sponsors a full range of professional, athletic, and social events; a speakers program; minority recruitment events; a legal research service for practicing lawyers; and participation in school governance. The Moot Court Program is student operated and fields a number of successful teams in regional, national, and international competitions. Over 50 student organizations are active in the School of Law, including the Black Law Students Association, Child Action, the Federalist Society, the Hispanic/Latino Law Students Association, the Native American Law Students Association, Second Careers in Law, Women in Law, and our nationally recognized Pro Bono Program.

■ Expenses and Financial Aid

Full-time tuition and fees—North Carolina resident, $12,947.08; nonresident, $25,356.08. Estimated additional expenses—$16,032. Chancellors' Scholars Program scholarships are available, as well as other merit-based scholarships. Need-based assistance is awarded on the basis of FAFSA information. Students must submit parental information to FAFSA to be considered for need-based grants.

Admitted applicants are automatically considered for merit-based scholarships. Awards range from $1,000 to $12,500. Scholarship offers are made beginning in February.

■ Housing

There are graduate dormitories near the law school for single students. University student family housing and private apartments are available. Information may be obtained from the University Housing Office, Carr Building CB 5500, Chapel Hill, NC 27399-5580; 919.962.5401.

■ Career Services Office

The Career Services Office staff assists students and alumni with summer and permanent positions. Each year, approximately 200 employers from across the nation interview at the School of Law. Of those 2005 graduates reporting to the Career Services Office, 99 percent had accepted employment or were in graduate school within nine months of graduation. Of those 2005 graduates who entered into the practice arena, 59 percent entered private practice; 32 percent entered public sector work, including public interest; 13 percent accepted judicial clerkships; approximately 13 percent entered government practice (district attorneys'/public defenders' offices, government, and military); 6 percent entered legal services/nonprofit; 7 percent entered business/corporate related practice; and 2 percent entered academia.

Applicant Profile

University of North Carolina School of Law
This grid includes only applicants who earned 120–180 LSAT scores under standard administrations.

LSAT Score	3.75 +		3.50–3.74		3.25–3.49		3.00–3.24		2.75–2.99		2.50–2.74		2.25–2.49		2.00–2.24		Below 2.00		No GPA		Total	
	Apps	Adm	Apps	Adm	Apps	Adm	Apps	Adm	Apps	Adm	Apps	Adm	Apps	Adm	Apps	Adm	Apps	Adm	Apps	Adm	Apps	Adm
175–180	0	0	2	1	0	0	2	0	1	0	1	0	1	0	0	0	0	0	0	0	7	1
170–174	21	18	18	14	20	8	8	0	6	0	3	0	2	0	0	0	0	0	1	0	78	40
165–169	99	87	100	26	84	24	39	3	23	1	9	1	0	0	1	0	0	0	6	0	356	142
160–164	240	87	294	63	223	43	108	14	55	6	21	3	11	0	4	0	0	0	10	0	962	216
155–159	214	29	337	25	256	27	129	9	65	3	24	1	10	1	3	0	2	0	7	0	1040	93
150–154	82	13	134	10	156	15	101	2	57	1	24	0	13	1	3	0	0	0	5	0	240	5
145–149	19	0	50	2	48	1	50	1	28	0	24	0	13	0	4	0	1	0	1	0	131	0
140–144	12	0	18	0	23	0	26	0	19	0	19	0	8	0	1	0	2	0	3	0	59	0
135–139	2	0	5	0	12	0	13	0	10	0	6	0	5	0	1	0	2	0	1	0	21	0
130–134	0	0	2	0	3	0	4	0	4	0	4	0	1	0	0	0	0	0	0	0	3	0
125–129	0	0	0	0	0	0	1	0	0	0	2	0	0	0	0	0	0	0	0	0	0	0
120–124	0	0	0	0	0	0	0	0	0	0	0	0	0	0	0	0	0	0	0	0	0	0
Total	689	234	960	141	825	118	481	29	268	11	135	5	57	2	17	0	7	0	34	0	3473	540

Apps = Number of Applicants
Adm = Number Admitted
Reflects 99% of the total applicant pool.

North Carolina Central University School of Law

1512 South Alston Avenue
Durham, NC 27707
Phone: 919.530.6333; Fax: 919.530.6339
E-mail: sbrownb@nccu.edu; Website: www.nccu.edu/law

Official ABA Data

*ABA
Approved
Since
1950*

The Basics

Type of school	Public
Term	Semester
Application deadline	3/31
Application fee	$40
Financial aid deadline	7/1
Can first year start other than fall?	No
Student to faculty ratio	21.8 to 1
Does the university offer:	
housing restricted to law students?	No
graduate housing for which law students are eligible?	Yes

Faculty and Administrators

	Total		Men		Women		Minorities	
	Fall	Spr	Fall	Spr	Fall	Spr	Fall	Spr
Full-time	18	18	9	9	9	9	11	10
Other Full-time	2	1	1	0	1	1	1	1
Deans, librarians, & others who teach	14	14	3	3	11	11	10	10
Part-time	20	15	11	10	9	5	7	9
Total	**54**	**48**	**24**	**22**	**30**	**26**	**29**	**30**

Curriculum

	Full-time	Part-time
Typical first-year section size	90	62
Is there typically a "small section" of the first-year class, other than Legal Writing, taught by full-time faculty	No	No
If yes, typical size offered last year		
# of classroom course titles beyond first-year curriculum		60
# of upper division courses, excluding seminars with an enrollment: Under 25		46
25–49		17
50–74		8
75–99		3
100+		1
# of seminars		22
# of seminar positions available		440
# of seminar positions filled	176	25
# of positions available in simulation courses		304
# of simulation positions filled	146	83
# of positions available in faculty supervised clinical courses		170
# of faculty supervised clinical positions filled	123	0
# involved in field placements	54	7
# involved in law journals	43	5
# involved in interschool competitions	36	4
# of credit hours required to graduate		88

JD Enrollment and Ethnicity

	Men		Women		Full-time		Part-time		1st-year		Total		JD Degs. Awd.
	#	%	#	%	#	%	#	%	#	%	#	%	
African Amer.	74	32.6	168	54.2	228	53.5	14	12.6	99	44.0	242	45.1	40
Amer. Indian	3	1.3	2	0.6	2	0.5	3	2.7	2	0.9	5	0.9	2
Asian Amer.	10	4.4	8	2.6	13	3.1	5	4.5	7	3.1	18	3.4	6
Mex. Amer.	1	0.4	0	0.0	1	0.2	0	0.0	1	0.4	1	0.2	0
Puerto Rican	0	0.0	3	1.0	1	0.2	2	1.8	0	0.0	3	0.6	1
Hispanic	2	0.9	6	1.9	6	1.4	2	1.8	4	1.8	8	1.5	4
Total Minority	90	39.6	187	60.3	251	58.9	26	23.4	113	50.2	277	51.6	53
For. Nation.	0	0.0	0	0.0	0	0.0	0	0.0	0	0.0	0	0.0	0
Caucasian	127	55.9	108	34.8	154	36.2	81	73.0	103	45.8	235	43.8	66
Unknown	10	4.4	15	4.8	21	4.9	4	3.6	9	4.0	25	4.7	2
Total	227	42.3	310	57.7	426	79.3	111	20.7	225	41.9	537		121

Transfers

Transfers in	3
Transfers out	4

Tuition and Fees

	Resident	Nonresident
Full-time	$4,625	$16,485
Part-time	$4,625	$16,485

Living Expenses

Estimated living expenses for singles

Living on campus	Living off campus	Living at home
$6,950	$10,450	$3,150

North Carolina Central University School of Law

*ABA
Approved
Since
1950*

GPA and LSAT Scores

	Total	Full-time	Part-time
# of apps	2,439	1,752	687
# of offers	534	437	97
# of matrics	227	190	37
75% GPA	3.49	3.49	3.57
Median GPA	3.22	3.20	3.29
25% GPA	2.93	2.91	3.21
75% LSAT	153	152	158
Median LSAT	148	148	153
25% LSAT	144	144	150

Grants and Scholarships (from prior year)

	Total		Full-time		Part-time	
	#	%	#	%	#	%
Total # of students	476		372		104	
Total # receiving grants	130	27.3	130	34.9	0	0.0
Less than 1/2 tuition	38	8.0	38	10.2	0	0.0
Half to full tuition	49	10.3	49	13.2	0	0.0
Full tuition	23	4.8	23	6.2	0	0.0
More than full tuition	20	4.2	20	5.4	0	0.0
Median grant amount			$3,144		$0	

Informational and Library Resources

# of volumes and volume equivalents	352,022
# of titles	65,430
# of active serial subscriptions	4,250
Study seating capacity inside the library	294
# of full-time professional librarians	7
Hours per week library is open	100
# of open, wired connections available to students	54
# of networked computers available for use by students	49
# of simultaneous wireless users	500
Require computer?	No

JD Attrition (from prior year)

	Academic	Other	Total	
	#	#	#	%
1st year	31	13	44	22.1
2nd year	3	1	4	3.0
3rd year	0	3	3	2.4
4th year	0	0	0	0.0

Employment (9 months after graduation)

	Total	Percentage
Employment status known	98	90.7
Employment status unknown	10	9.3
Employed	88	89.8
Pursuing graduate degrees	4	4.1
Unemployed seeking employment	0	0.0
Unemployed not seeking employment	1	1.0
Unemployed and studying for the bar	5	5.1

Type of Employment

# employed in law firms	51	58.0
# employed in business and industry	16	18.2
# employed in government	8	9.1
# employed in public interest	9	10.2
# employed as judicial clerks	4	4.5
# employed in academia	0	0.0

Geographic Location

# employed in state	76	86.4
# employed in foreign countries	0	0.0
# of states where employed		11

Bar Passage Rates

Jurisdiction	North Carolina		
Exam	Sum 05	Win 06	Total
# from school taking bar for the first time	80	8	88
School's pass rate for all first-time takers	81%	75%	81%
State's pass rate for all first-time takers	72%	69%	71%

North Carolina Central University School of Law

1512 South Alston Avenue
Durham, NC 27707
Phone: 919.530.6333; Fax: 919.530.6339
E-mail: sbrownb@nccu.edu; Website: www.nccu.edu/law

■ Introduction

The North Carolina Central University School of Law was established in 1939. The School of Law is located in Durham, North Carolina. North Carolina Central University is one of the 16 constituent institutions of the University of North Carolina system.

The School of Law has been accredited by the North Carolina State Bar Council and the ABA since 1950. Today, NCCU School of Law is one of the most affordable and diverse in the country. The School of Law offers two programs leading to the Juris Doctor degree: a full-time day program and the only ABA accredited part-time evening program between Atlanta, Georgia, and Washington, DC. The School of Law participates in an inter-institutional agreement with Duke University and the University of North Carolina at Chapel Hill that permits students to enroll in electives at any member school with no increase in tuition.

■ Facilities, Library, and Technology

The School of Law recently completed an $11 million addition and renovation. The Albert L. Turner Law School is now a state-of-the-art facility that provides the law school community with an attractive, comfortable, and technology-friendly environment in which to work and study.

The School of Law provides a seamless integration of technology throughout the facility. The entire building is wireless and provides software for students who use laptops to take exams. There are two computer labs for student use. All classrooms are equipped with state-of-the-art multimedia resources, including smart boards, video and teleconferencing capabilities, and computers with Internet access.

The School of Law has several group study rooms, a moot courtroom, and a Great Hall. The Great Hall is used for receptions, meetings, conferences, and is equipped with the same multimedia resources found in the classrooms.

The law library, with more than 352,022 volumes and volume equivalents, provides the resources needed to support the Juris Doctor program, the JD/MLS and JD/MBA dual-degree programs, and the legal community. There are nine public access terminals in the law library that provide access to the library and electronic resources, the Internet, and e-mail. The law library is a selective North Carolina and United States government depository and has a special collection in civil rights law.

■ Special Academic Programs

- **Joint-degree Options**—There are two joint-degree programs available to Day Program students. The joint-degree JD/MBA Program allows students who are interested in a career in law and business to receive both degrees in four years. The joint-degree JD/MLS Program allows students who are interested in a career in law librarianship to simultaneously pursue both degrees. Students must apply and be accepted to each program separately.
- **Evening Program**—The Evening Program is a four-year, year-round program that offers a unique opportunity for motivated professionals to pursue a legal education while maintaining their current daytime work commitments.

- **Academic Support Program**—The Academic Support Program is available to assist students with the rigors of law school. The support program consists of a first-year, noncredit writing lab; tutorials; academic success workshops; and individual counseling and guidance sessions. In addition, a skills enhancement clinic is offered to second- and third-year students and workshops on bar preparation are offered to third-year students.
- **Faculty Advising Program**—Each student is assigned a faculty advisor who is available to discuss questions or problems related to the School of Law experience, career choices, and personal problems that might affect academic performance. They also advise students on taking appropriate classes and monitor their progress.
- **Clinical Program**—The award-winning Clinical Program operates year-round from a state-of-the-art model law office. The clinical experiences currently offered at the School of Law are Alternative Dispute Resolution, Civil Litigation, Criminal Litigation, Family Law, Small Business Planning and Development, Juvenile Justice, and a General Externship Program, making it the most comprehensive program of any law school in the state. Under the supervision of a licensed attorney, clinical students represent real clients with real legal issues.
- **Pro Bono Program**—The Pro Bono Program provides opportunities for law students to volunteer on supervised projects with nonprofit public interest law organizations, government agencies, and private attorneys representing clients on a free or reduced-fee basis. The program also features two in-house student-led projects, the NCCU Law Innocence Project and VITA (Volunteer Income Tax Assistance), as well as an opportunity to work with the Durham Public Schools through the Street Law program.

■ Admission

Admission to the School of Law is highly competitive. Approximately 2,000 applicants compete for approximately 150–180 seats in the Day Program, and 35–40 seats in the Evening Program. Students are admitted only for the fall semester. Since applicants are more than just numbers, selection for admission is based upon a thorough evaluation of all factors in an applicant's file: Law School Admission Test (LSAT) score, writing sample, undergraduate school grades, recommendations, and personal statement. Careful consideration is given to an applicant's professional experience, volunteer or community service, unusual achievements, special circumstances, honors, economic hardship, undergraduate degree, undergraduate college, graduate degree, graduate school, and grade trends. Because it is presumed that Evening Program students will have full-time employment, the Admissions Committee places greater weight on the quantifiable performance predictors for applicants to the Evening Program. Electronic applications for admission are accepted from October 1 through April 15 through our website at *www.nccu.edu/law* or the Law School Admission Council's website at *www.LSAC.org*. Please note that our application cycle will be changing to October 1, 2007 through March 31, 2008 for applications received for fall of 2008.

Please note: Prospective applicants should contact 919.530.7173 or *www.nccu.edu/law* for information. For applicant status, contact 919.530.5243 or *sbrownb@nccu.edu*.

Performance-based Admission Program (PBAP)

As part of its commitment to the school's mission, North Carolina Central offers prospective students opportunities to gain admission through its Performance-Based Admissions Program (PBAP). The PBAP enables applicants whose numerical predictors fall below the presumptively admissible range to demonstrate their ability through a rigorous two-week, noncredit program in the spring. The Office of Admissions selects PBAP participants based on a number of factors, including but not limited to: a history of below-average standardized test scores followed by academic achievement, work experience, a significant time lapse between the undergraduate degree and law school application, and students who come from socially disadvantaged backgrounds. Students who successfully complete PBAP are then offered admission to NCCU's Day Program. A number of students who entered the Day Program through PBAP have gone on to successfully matriculate through law school, and are now doing outstanding work as lawyers.

Student Organizations

The *North Carolina Central Law Journal* is devoted to a broad range of legal topics submitted by diverse authors, including legal scholars, attorneys, and law students. Students are selected for membership based upon GPA and performance in the annual Law Journal Writing Competition.

The Moot Court Board consists of upper-class students who have demonstrated exceptional ability in appellate skills through the Appellate Advocacy class and intraschool competition.

The Trial Advocacy Board consists of student teams who participate in mock jury trial competitions. The board has gained regional and national recognition for its excellence in trial advocacy.

Other student organizations include the Student Bar Association, ACLU, American Trial Lawyers Association, Black Law Students Association, Christian Legal Society, Environmental Law Society, Federalist Society, Hispanic Law Student Association, Innocence Project, Intellectual Property Society and Trademark Moot Court, Native American Law Student Association, Outlaw Alliance, Public Interest Law Organization, Sports and Entertainment Law Society, Women's Caucus, and chapters of the legal fraternities of Phi Alpha Delta and Phi Delta Phi.

Career Services

The Office of Career Services offers a range of career planning and placement services, including career counseling, interview preparation, résumé writing workshops, firm and résumé referral banks, and an on-campus interview program. Graduates find employment in law firms, corporations, state and federal government agencies, public interest organizations, the judiciary, and the military.

Financial Aid

For information about financial aid, please visit our website at *www.nccu.edu/law/admissions/financial.html* or contact the Office of Scholarships and Student Aid at 919.530.6180.

Tuition and Expenses

NCCU School of Law provides one of the most cost effective legal educations in the country.

For information on tuition, fees, and expenses, please visit our website at *www.nccu.edu/law/admissions/expenses.html* or contact Student Accounting at 919.530.5071.

Housing

Limited on-campus housing is available for single law students. Write the Department of Residential Life, North Carolina Central University, PO Box 19382, Durham, NC 27707, or call 919.530.6227.

Applicant Profile Not Available

University of North Dakota School of Law

215 Centennial Drive Stop 9003
Grand Forks, ND 58202
Phone: 701.777.2104; Fax: 701.777.6447
E-mail: hoffman@law.und.edu; Website: www.law.und.edu

ABA Approved Since 1923

The Basics

Type of school	Public
Term	Semester
Application deadline	4/1
Application fee	$35
Financial aid deadline	4/14
Can first year start other than fall?	No
Student to faculty ratio	21.2 to 1
Does the university offer:	
housing restricted to law students?	No
graduate housing for which law students are eligible?	Yes

Faculty and Administrators

	Total		Men		Women		Minorities	
	Fall	Spr	Fall	Spr	Fall	Spr	Fall	Spr
Full-time	10	8	6	4	4	4	0	2
Other Full-time	2	1	1	0	1	1	0	0
Deans, librarians, & others who teach	7	7	3	3	4	4	0	0
Part-time	8	13	7	10	1	3	0	0
Total	**27**	**29**	**17**	**17**	**10**	**12**	**0**	**2**

Curriculum

	Full-time	Part-time
Typical first-year section size	76	0
Is there typically a "small section" of the first-year class, other than Legal Writing, taught by full-time faculty	No	No
If yes, typical size offered last year		
# of classroom course titles beyond first-year curriculum	41	
# of upper division courses, excluding seminars with an enrollment: Under 25	20	
25–49	13	
50–74	8	
75–99	0	
100+	0	
# of seminars	1	
# of seminar positions available	10	
# of seminar positions filled	2	0
# of positions available in simulation courses	120	
# of simulation positions filled	110	0
# of positions available in faculty supervised clinical courses	36	
# of faculty supervised clinical positions filled	35	0
# involved in field placements	30	0
# involved in law journals	67	0
# involved in interschool competitions	59	0
# of credit hours required to graduate	90	

JD Enrollment and Ethnicity

	Men		Women		Full-time		Part-time		1st-year		Total		JD Degs. Awd.
	#	%	#	%	#	%	#	%	#	%	#	%	
African Amer.	2	1.6	0	0.0	2	0.8	0	0.0	0	0.0	2	0.8	1
Amer. Indian	5	3.9	1	0.9	6	2.5	0	0.0	1	1.3	6	2.5	1
Asian Amer.	4	3.1	5	4.6	9	3.8	0	0.0	3	3.8	9	3.8	2
Mex. Amer.	0	0.0	0	0.0	0	0.0	0	0.0	0	0.0	0	0.0	0
Puerto Rican	0	0.0	0	0.0	0	0.0	0	0.0	0	0.0	0	0.0	0
Hispanic	4	3.1	3	2.8	7	3.0	0	0.0	3	3.8	7	3.0	1
Total Minority	15	11.8	9	8.3	24	10.2	0	0.0	7	9.0	24	10.2	5
For. Nation.	5	3.9	8	7.3	13	5.5	0	0.0	5	6.4	13	5.5	0
Caucasian	92	72.4	81	74.3	173	73.3	0	0.0	56	71.8	173	73.3	53
Unknown	15	11.8	11	10.1	26	11.0	0	0.0	10	12.8	26	11.0	1
Total	127	53.8	109	46.2	236	100.0	0	0.0	78	33.1	236		59

Transfers

Transfers in	3
Transfers out	1

Tuition and Fees

	Resident	Nonresident
Full-time	$8,386	$18,038
Part-time	$0	$0

Living Expenses

Estimated living expenses for singles		
Living on campus	Living off campus	Living at home
$13,500	$13,500	$13,500

University of North Dakota School of Law

ABA
Approved
Since
1923

GPA and LSAT Scores

	Total	Full-time	Part-time
# of apps	632	632	0
# of offers	191	191	0
# of matrics	77	77	0
75% GPA	3.73	3.73	0.00
Median GPA	3.34	3.34	0.00
25% GPA	3.10	3.10	0.00
75% LSAT	155	155	0
Median LSAT	151	151	0
25% LSAT	149	149	0

Grants and Scholarships (from prior year)

	Total #	Total %	Full-time #	Full-time %	Part-time #	Part-time %
Total # of students	224		224		0	
Total # receiving grants	100	44.6	100	44.6	0	0.0
Less than 1/2 tuition	64	28.6	64	28.6	0	0.0
Half to full tuition	16	7.1	16	7.1	0	0.0
Full tuition	7	3.1	7	3.1	0	0.0
More than full tuition	13	5.8	13	5.8	0	0.0
Median grant amount			$1,325		$0	

Informational and Library Resources

# of volumes and volume equivalents	321,806
# of titles	119,535
# of active serial subscriptions	1,936
Study seating capacity inside the library	210
# of full-time professional librarians	7
Hours per week library is open	99
# of open, wired connections available to students	145
# of networked computers available for use by students	52
# of simultaneous wireless users	1,400
Require computer?	No

JD Attrition (from prior year)

	Academic #	Other #	Total #	Total %
1st year	1	2	3	3.3
2nd year	1	2	3	4.3
3rd year	0	0	0	0.0
4th year	0	0	0	0.0

Employment (9 months after graduation)

	Total	Percentage
Employment status known	62	96.9
Employment status unknown	2	3.1
Employed	54	87.1
Pursuing graduate degrees	2	3.2
Unemployed seeking employment	1	1.6
Unemployed not seeking employment	2	3.2
Unemployed and studying for the bar	3	4.8

Type of Employment

# employed in law firms	23	42.6
# employed in business and industry	3	5.6
# employed in government	6	11.1
# employed in public interest	7	13.0
# employed as judicial clerks	14	25.9
# employed in academia	1	1.9

Geographic Location

# employed in state	27	50.0
# employed in foreign countries	0	0.0
# of states where employed	11	

Bar Passage Rates

Jurisdiction	North Dakota Sum 05	North Dakota Win 06	North Dakota Total	Minnesota Sum 05	Minnesota Win 06	Minnesota Total
# from school taking bar for the first time	31	0	31	16	8	24
School's pass rate for all first-time takers	94%		94%	88%	88%	88%
State's pass rate for all first-time takers	90%	0%	90%	89%	88%	89%

University of North Dakota School of Law

Office of the Dean, 215 Centennial Drive Stop 9003
Grand Forks, ND 58202
Phone: 701.777.2104; Fax: 701.777.6447
E-mail: hoffman@law.und.edu; Website: www.law.und.edu

■ Introduction

Founded in 1899, the University of North Dakota (UND) School of Law blends quality, opportunity, and a sense of community in its education of approximately 230 students. The school is a fully accredited graduate professional school awarding the JD degree. It has been a member of the AALS since 1910 and was approved by the ABA in 1923. UND Law is part of a highly respected, nationally recognized university, located in Grand Forks, North Dakota. Grand Forks, a community of nearly 60,000, is in the heart of the Red River Valley on the North Dakota/Minnesota border. It offers a small-town feel with all the opportunities of an urban area and has a large legal community including county, state, and federal trial courts.

■ Library and Physical Facilities

The Thormodsgard Law Library manages a growing collection of comprehensive resources necessary for the study of law and provides a home for students. The school and library are linked everywhere with high-speed Ethernet and wireless access points. The Computer Services office supports the Web, e-mail, file sharing, database, group scheduling, servers, and the in-house video system as well as student laptops. The elegant, traditionally appointed Baker Courtroom provides facilities for trial and appellate arguments and is used by the North Dakota Supreme Court and occasionally by other federal and district courts.

■ Curriculum

The curriculum of the School of Law covers a period of three full academic years. All the work of the first year is prescribed. Courses in the second and third years are elective, except for the course in Professional Responsibility.

■ Special Programs

The size of the student body is ideally suited for close professional contact with faculty, the visiting courts, legal professionals, and alumni. Students are given ample opportunity to participate in the governance of the school. Elected members of the Student Bar Association attend regularly scheduled faculty meetings and are active voting participants in most law school committees.

In consultation with area tribes and Indian leaders, the UND School of Law has established the region's first Northern Plains Indian Law Center. The center is a clearinghouse for American Indian legal materials and provides a forum for discussing and resolving legal issues confronting Indian tribes, the states, and the federal government. It also supports tribal advocacy training programs. Among the center's programs are the Tribal Judicial Institute, the Institute for the Study of Tribal Gaming Law and Policy, the Native American Law Project, and the Tribal Environmental Law Project.

The Clinical Education Program of the UND School of Law provides students with the opportunity to integrate the theory and practice of law in a real law office setting. In the clinic, students assume the role of lawyers and, in doing so, move beyond the classroom into the world of law practice. In the course of representing their clients, students gain firsthand experience with substantive law, the many skills of lawyering, and the rules of professional ethics. Students reflect on their experiences during clinic class discussions, "case-rounds" sessions, one-on-one faculty supervision, and legal research and writing assignments.

A comprehensive Externship Program allows students an opportunity to earn academic credit while gaining practical experience in a variety of placements. Externship students receive local and state field placements throughout the academic year, as well as during the summer in the Federal Externship Program.

The school has an extensive Trial Advocacy Program in which students learn trial skills in a simulated advocacy setting under the close supervision of experienced trial lawyers. Each student in this course is responsible, with one student advocate cocounsel, for the trial of at least one full civil or criminal case during the semester.

During sessions of the state legislature, selected students serve as legislative interns at the North Dakota state capital in Bismarck.

Central Legal Research (CLR) provides select students with opportunities to work with attorneys and judges across North Dakota on the issues and problems faced in practice. Focusing primarily on criminal law and procedure issues, CLR students work closely with an experienced lawyer and with each other, honing their skills by writing, researching, analyzing, and discussing their individual projects. CLR students receive a full in-state tuition waiver and develop a broad writing portfolio.

UND offers a joint Juris Doctor/Master of Public Administration (JD/MPA) degree. Utilizing free summer time, the joint-degree program could be completed in four years or less.

The UND School of Law is one of approximately 80 law schools throughout the United States that have a chapter of the national legal honorary society, the Order of the Coif. The Order of the Coif was founded to encourage legal scholarship and advance the ethical standards of the legal profession.

UND law students may receive credit for summer law study at the University of Oslo Faculty of Law, Oslo, Norway. The program provides six weeks of instruction and offers students specialized instruction in such areas as the Norwegian legal system, comparative criminal justice, and European law. As part of this exchange program, up to 15 Norwegian law students also attend the UND School of Law during the spring semester.

■ Admission

The School of Law has no specific undergraduate course prerequisites and agrees with the observations in the introduction to this guide. The school admits students only in August and only for full-time study. Applications are available upon request. The policy of the faculty of the School of Law is to admit those applicants who, in the determination of the faculty, will be able to satisfactorily complete the law school program. The admission committee utilizes the following criteria to achieve this goal: (1) LSAT score; (2) undergraduate GPA; (3) past performance in an academic environment; (4) past performance in activities that would tend to predict the applicant's ability to complete successfully the law school program; and (5) other evidence relevant to predicted success and prospective professional responsibility. The total number of students admitted is, of course, limited by considerations involving space and faculty courseload.

The law school does not have a nonresident quota; however, preference is given to residents.

Students who have begun the study of law in other accredited law schools may be admitted in exceptional circumstances to advanced standing, provided they have fulfilled the requirements for admission to the University of North Dakota School of Law. Ordinarily, no transfer credit will be allowed for more than two semesters of work completed elsewhere, nor will transfer credit be given for any courses in which an unsatisfactory or failing grade has been received. Moreover, admission may be conditioned upon meeting such additional requirements as the faculty may prescribe. No student will be admitted as a transfer student with advanced standing who is not eligible to continue as a student at his or her present law school.

■ Student Activities

The *North Dakota Law Review* provides research and writing opportunities. Students participate in various moot court activities, with the North Dakota Supreme Court judging the moot court finals. Student organizations include the Environmental Law Society, Law Women's Caucus, Native American Law Students Association, Public Interest Law Students Association, Student Trial Lawyers Association, and an active Student Bar Association. One of the more popular activities during the year is the Malpractice Bowl, pitting law students against medical school students in an annual football game. The School of Law also has chapters of the Order of the Coif and legal fraternities.

■ Expenses and Financial Aid

Tuition and fees per semester for academic year 2006–2007 were $4,193 per resident, $5,638 per contiguous states, and $9,019 per nonresident. The semester fees include student activity and university fees totaling $446 per semester and an $800 per semester professional fee. The student activity and university fees cover payment for health services, the university center, campus publications, and drama and athletic events. The professional fee is assessed by the School of Law and is used to support and improve the law school program. Fees are subject to change without notice. Loan funds for all qualified students are available through the university Student Financial Aid Office, PO Box 8371, Grand Forks, ND 58202.

■ Housing

The university has a comprehensive housing system with options including family housing facilities, student apartment housing, and traditional residence halls for single students. For more detailed information, visit *www.housing.und.edu*.

■ Career Services

The Career Services Office serves students and alumni by assisting with the job-search process and employment information, and provides job seekers with knowledge about types of employment, specific employers, positions available, and wage and salary information. The office also assists in job-search strategies and skills such as résumé writing, interviewing techniques, and electronic job-search strategies. Over 90 percent of graduates find employment within six months of graduation. While a majority choose employment in North Dakota and Minnesota, graduates are employed nationally and internationally.

Applicant Profile

University of North Dakota School of Law
This grid includes only applicants who earned 120–180 LSAT scores under standard administrations.

LSAT Score	3.75 + Apps	3.75 + Adm	3.50–3.74 Apps	3.50–3.74 Adm	3.25–3.49 Apps	3.25–3.49 Adm	3.00–3.24 Apps	3.00–3.24 Adm	2.75–2.99 Apps	2.75–2.99 Adm	2.50–2.74 Apps	2.50–2.74 Adm	2.25–2.49 Apps	2.25–2.49 Adm	2.00–2.24 Apps	2.00–2.24 Adm	Below 2.00 Apps	Below 2.00 Adm	No GPA Apps	No GPA Adm	Total Apps	Total Adm
175–180	0	0	0	0	0	0	0	0	0	0	0	0	0	0	0	0	0	0	0	0	0	0
170–174	0	0	0	0	0	0	0	0	0	0	0	0	0	0	0	0	0	0	0	0	0	0
165–169	1	1	0	0	1	1	0	0	0	0	0	0	0	0	0	0	0	0	0	0	2	2
160–164	6	6	2	2	2	2	0	0	1	1	2	1	1	0	1	1	0	0	0	0	15	13
155–159	8	8	13	11	7	6	11	9	1	0	1	0	0	0	0	0	0	0	0	0	41	34
150–154	11	7	32	20	37	18	27	14	21	6	22	9	5	0	3	0	4	0	2	0	164	74
145–149	26	15	49	17	48	8	45	12	20	1	15	2	12	2	4	0	0	0	1	0	220	57
140–144	4	0	21	2	27	1	31	1	24	1	17	2	7	1	2	0	0	0	3	0	136	8
135–139	5	0	4	0	3	0	15	0	7	0	3	0	2	0	1	0	0	0	1	0	41	0
130–134	1	0	0	0	2	0	0	0	3	0	2	0	5	0	1	0	0	0	0	0	14	0
125–129	0	0	1	0	0	0	0	0	0	0	2	0	1	0	0	0	0	0	0	0	4	0
120–124	0	0	0	0	0	0	0	0	0	0	0	0	0	0	0	0	0	0	0	0	0	0
Total	62	37	122	52	127	36	129	36	77	9	64	14	33	3	12	1	4	0	7	0	637	188

Apps = Number of Applicants
Adm = Number Admitted
Reflects 99% of the total applicant pool.

Northeastern University School of Law

400 Huntington Avenue
Boston, MA 02115
Phone: 617.373.2395; Fax: 617.373.8865
E-mail: lawadmissions@neu.edu; Website: www.slaw.neu.edu

ABA
Approved
Since
1969

The Basics

Type of school	Private
Term	Quarter
Application deadline	3/1
Application fee	$75
Financial aid deadline	2/15
Can first year start other than fall?	No
Student to faculty ratio	17.3 to 1
Does the university offer:	
housing restricted to law students?	No
graduate housing for which law students are eligible?	Yes

Faculty and Administrators

	Total		Men		Women		Minorities	
	Fall	Spr	Fall	Spr	Fall	Spr	Fall	Spr
Full-time	28	32	13	15	15	17	7	8
Other Full-time	0	0	0	0	0	0	0	0
Deans, librarians, & others who teach	8	8	3	3	5	5	2	1
Part-time	45	27	20	14	25	13	5	1
Total	81	67	36	32	45	35	14	10

Curriculum

	Full-time	Part-time
Typical first-year section size	70	0
Is there typically a "small section" of the first-year class, other than Legal Writing, taught by full-time faculty	No	No
If yes, typical size offered last year		
# of classroom course titles beyond first-year curriculum	60	
# of upper division courses, excluding seminars with an enrollment: Under 25	40	
25–49	24	
50–74	11	
75–99	5	
100+	1	
# of seminars	16	
# of seminar positions available	256	
# of seminar positions filled	245	0
# of positions available in simulation courses	256	
# of simulation positions filled	230	0
# of positions available in faculty supervised clinical courses	114	
# of faculty supervised clinical positions filled	108	0
# involved in field placements	414	0
# involved in law journals	0	0
# involved in interschool competitions	15	0
# of credit hours required to graduate	103	

JD Enrollment and Ethnicity

	Men #	Men %	Women #	Women %	Full-time #	Full-time %	Part-time #	Part-time %	1st-year #	1st-year %	Total #	Total %	JD Degs. Awd.
African Amer.	7	2.7	31	8.4	38	6.1	0	0.0	11	5.1	38	6.1	16
Amer. Indian	3	1.2	3	0.8	6	1.0	0	0.0	1	0.5	6	1.0	3
Asian Amer.	22	8.5	49	13.3	71	11.3	0	0.0	18	8.4	71	11.3	17
Mex. Amer.	0	0.0	0	0.0	0	0.0	0	0.0	0	0.0	0	0.0	0
Puerto Rican	0	0.0	0	0.0	0	0.0	0	0.0	0	0.0	0	0.0	0
Hispanic	19	7.4	35	9.5	54	8.6	0	0.0	21	9.8	54	8.6	12
Total Minority	51	19.8	118	32.1	169	27.0	0	0.0	51	23.8	169	27.0	48
For. Nation.	0	0.0	1	0.3	1	0.2	0	0.0	1	0.5	1	0.2	1
Caucasian	157	60.9	203	55.2	360	57.5	0	0.0	120	56.1	360	57.5	134
Unknown	50	19.4	46	12.5	96	15.3	0	0.0	42	19.6	96	15.3	3
Total	258	41.2	368	58.8	626	100.0	0	0.0	214	34.2	626		186

Transfers

Transfers in	6
Transfers out	4

Tuition and Fees

	Resident	Nonresident
Full-time	$34,737	$34,737
Part-time	$0	$0

Living Expenses

Estimated living expenses for singles

Living on campus	Living off campus	Living at home
$17,400	$17,400	$9,420

Northeastern University School of Law

ABA Approved Since 1969

GPA and LSAT Scores

	Total	Full-time	Part-time
# of apps	3,355	3,355	0
# of offers	988	988	0
# of matrics	218	218	0
75% GPA	3.65	3.65	0.00
Median GPA	3.40	3.40	0.00
25% GPA	3.17	3.17	0.00
75% LSAT	162	162	0
Median LSAT	161	161	0
25% LSAT	156	156	0

Grants and Scholarships (from prior year)

	Total #	Total %	Full-time #	Full-time %	Part-time #	Part-time %
Total # of students	623		623		0	
Total # receiving grants	486	78.0	486	78.0	0	0.0
Less than 1/2 tuition	447	71.7	447	71.7	0	0.0
Half to full tuition	38	6.1	38	6.1	0	0.0
Full tuition	1	0.2	1	0.2	0	0.0
More than full tuition	0	0.0	0	0.0	0	0.0
Median grant amount			$8,500		$0	

Informational and Library Resources

# of volumes and volume equivalents	327,998
# of titles	132,515
# of active serial subscriptions	3,091
Study seating capacity inside the library	430
# of full-time professional librarians	9
Hours per week library is open	95
# of open, wired connections available to students	65
# of networked computers available for use by students	90
# of simultaneous wireless users	200
Require computer?	No

JD Attrition (from prior year)

	Academic #	Other #	Total #	Total %
1st year	0	9	9	4.3
2nd year	1	1	2	0.9
3rd year	0	0	0	0.0
4th year	0	0	0	0.0

Employment (9 months after graduation)

	Total	Percentage
Employment status known	190	98.4
Employment status unknown	3	1.6
Employed	173	91.1
Pursuing graduate degrees	0	0.0
Unemployed seeking employment	5	2.6
Unemployed not seeking employment	7	3.7
Unemployed and studying for the bar	5	2.6

Type of Employment

# employed in law firms	78	45.1
# employed in business and industry	27	15.6
# employed in government	17	9.8
# employed in public interest	28	16.2
# employed as judicial clerks	22	12.7
# employed in academia	1	0.6

Geographic Location

# employed in state	131	75.7
# employed in foreign countries	2	1.2
# of states where employed	21	

Bar Passage Rates

Jurisdiction	Massachusetts		
Exam	Sum 05	Win 06	Total
# from school taking bar for the first time	123	17	140
School's pass rate for all first-time takers	94%	88%	94%
State's pass rate for all first-time takers	84%	75%	82%

Northeastern University School of Law

400 Huntington Avenue
Boston, MA 02115
Phone: 617.373.2395; Fax: 617.373.8865
E-mail: lawadmissions@neu.edu; Website: www.slaw.neu.edu

■ Introduction

Northeastern University School of Law, located in Boston, offers the nation's premier Cooperative Legal Education Program. Combining classroom theory with practical work, Northeastern law students receive their JD degrees in the same three-year time period as students at other law schools, but graduate with one full year of hands-on legal employment gained in law offices around the world.

Northeastern provides a supportive, student-centered learning environment. The curriculum is rigorous, with students receiving detailed narrative evaluations of their work in each academic course in lieu of alphabetic or numeric grades. In addition, co-op employers submit written appraisals of each student's professional performance. These academic and professional evaluations comprise the student's permanent record, clearly indicating the quality of a student's performance. Without grades and class ranking, there is a culture of cooperation based on constructive relationships and mutual respect, avoiding the adversarial attitude that often characterizes legal education.

■ Cooperative Legal Education

Northeastern's Cooperative Legal Education Program alternates periods of academic study with equal periods of workplace experience during the second and third years of law school. During the first year of law school, students follow a traditional, full-time academic schedule. At the end of the first year, half of the class begins the first academic quarter of its second year during the summer, while the other half starts its first co-op. For the remaining two years, students alternate every three months between working full time as legal interns and attending classes. By participating in four, 11-week co-op placements with four different legal employers, students are provided with an extraordinary opportunity to experience the actual practice of law and to determine their career paths based on practical training.

More than 800 employers nationwide currently participate in the co-op program, representing virtually every practice area, including law firms of all sizes, trial and appellate judges in federal and state courts, public defender and legal services organizations, government agencies, corporate and union legal departments, and a variety of advocacy groups.

While many co-op placements are in the Greater Boston area, students work with employers in more than 40 states and countries in any given quarter. In recent years, students have increasingly developed their own co-ops both in the United States and abroad. All students are required to successfully complete four full-time legal internships in order to graduate.

While the co-op program is not intended as a financial aid program, earnings from co-op employment may somewhat reduce the net cost of attending law school during the second and third years. Salaries range from nominal amounts for public interest jobs to $2,500 per week in major law firms. To assist students in low-paying co-ops in the public interest area and the judiciary, the school provides approximately $500,000 in stipends each year.

■ Clinics and Institutes

Nationally recognized for its clinical education program, Northeastern offers students the opportunity to engage in advocacy on behalf of individuals and community organizations too often unacknowledged or underrepresented by the justice system. Students can participate with faculty and staff in the work of outstanding research and service centers: the Domestic Violence Institute, the Public Health Advocacy Institute, and the Program on Human Rights and the Global Economy. Together, the clinics and institutes reflect and fulfill a commitment to social and economic justice that distinguishes Northeastern as one of the nation's foremost public interest law schools.

Northeastern offers five clinics: Criminal Advocacy, Domestic Violence, Poverty Law and Practice, Prisoners' Rights, and Public Health. The clinics differ from one another by substantive legal focus, advocacy experience, and the primary skills each seeks to impart. Students engage in challenging legal practice, with the support of clinical faculty who provide the requisite training, close supervision, and opportunity for reflection.

■ Dual-degree Programs

Four dual-degree programs are offered. In cooperation with Tufts University School of Medicine, students may pursue both the JD and the Master of Public Health degrees. With a specialized curriculum, the two institutions enhance the training of law students who seek to understand the role advocacy and public action can play in reducing risk and ameliorating conditions that threaten community health. Completion of the dual-degree program takes three and one-half years, rather than the average five years if the degrees were obtained sequentially.

Concurrent degrees are also available from other schools and colleges at Northeastern University. A four-year program coordinates the academic and cooperative features of the School of Law and the Graduate School of Business Administration, enabling students to earn both the JD and the MBA degrees in 45 months rather than the 54 months required if undertaken sequentially.

Law students with nonaccounting undergraduate degrees are eligible for admission to a program leading to a concurrent JD/MS/MBA. The program enables students to earn these degrees in 45 months rather than the 48 months required if undertaken sequentially.

The Law, Policy, and Society JD/MS/PhD interdisciplinary graduate program is designed to offer students in the School of Law the opportunity to study policy, social issues, and the law in pursuit of an MS or PhD in Law, Policy, and Society. The program is based in the Graduate School of Arts and Sciences and is affiliated with graduate schools throughout the university.

■ Student Life

The student body is diverse and active. More than 60 percent of the students are women, and approximately 25 percent are people of color. Students are active participants in the law school community, serving on all of the school's standing committees, including the Admissions Committee. Students also run a wide variety of organizations.

■ Career Services

The Office of Career Services actively assists students and graduates in their pursuit of professionally rewarding careers. The school's placement rate is impressive: 97 percent of the class of 2005 obtained employment within six months of graduation. Students also generally find their postgraduate prospects to be substantially enhanced through the co-op program; on average, 40 percent accept postgraduate employment with one of their former co-op employers. Northeastern graduates are employed throughout the world in every practice area. They may be found teaching at distinguished law schools, sitting on the bench at both the state and federal levels, practicing as partners in prominent law firms, and serving as directors of legal aid and public defender programs throughout the nation. The school is also well known for its emphasis on public service. Graduates of Northeastern enter public service careers at a rate that is five times the national average. In addition, graduates have been consistently awarded prestigious postgraduate fellowships, including those granted by Equal Justice Works, Echoing Green, Georgetown, and Soros.

Applicant Profile

Northeastern University School of Law
This grid includes only applicants who earned 120–180 LSAT scores under standard administrations.

LSAT Score	3.75 +		3.50–3.74		3.25–3.49		3.00–3.24		2.75–2.99		2.50–2.74		2.25–2.49		2.00–2.24		Below 2.00		No GPA		Total	
	Apps	Adm	Apps	Adm	Apps	Adm	Apps	Adm	Apps	Adm	Apps	Adm	Apps	Adm	Apps	Adm	Apps	Adm	Apps	Adm	Apps	Adm
175–180	1	1	2	1	1	1	1	1	1	1	0	0	0	0	0	0	0	0	0	0	6	5
170–174	5	5	9	9	12	12	4	3	6	5	4	2	1	0	1	0	0	0	0	0	42	36
165–169	38	37	42	42	37	36	38	37	28	18	6	2	2	0	0	0	0	0	1	1	192	173
160–164	90	83	148	134	149	124	120	98	42	25	30	6	5	0	5	0	0	0	4	1	593	471
155–159	132	40	283	76	307	36	198	23	84	2	37	0	8	0	8	0	1	0	10	2	1068	179
150–154	77	9	184	29	185	15	152	19	84	3	45	0	19	0	2	0	1	0	3	1	752	76
145–149	28	2	66	4	84	8	83	4	52	1	33	0	13	0	6	0	0	0	7	0	372	19
140–144	10	0	25	1	50	3	43	1	26	0	13	0	3	0	1	0	3	0	6	0	180	5
135–139	1	0	3	0	12	0	11	0	14	0	11	0	2	0	3	0	0	0	0	0	57	0
130–134	1	0	3	0	2	0	4	0	3	0	2	0	1	0	1	0	0	0	2	0	19	0
125–129	0	0	1	0	0	0	1	0	1	0	0	0	0	0	3	0	0	0	1	0	7	0
120–124	0	0	0	0	0	0	0	0	1	0	0	0	1	0	0	0	0	0	0	0	2	0
Total	383	177	766	296	839	235	655	186	342	55	181	10	55	0	30	0	5	0	34	5	3290	964

Apps = Number of Applicants
Adm = Number Admitted
Reflects 99% of the total applicant pool.

Northern Illinois University College of Law

Swen Parson Hall, Room 151
DeKalb, IL 60115-2890
Phone: 800.892.3050 or 815.753.9485; Fax: 815.753.5680
E-mail: Lawadm@niu.edu; Website: http://law.niu.edu

ABA Approved Since 1978

The Basics

Type of school	Public
Term	Semester
Application deadline	5/15
Application fee	$50
Financial aid deadline	3/1
Can first year start other than fall?	No
Student to faculty ratio	16.9 to 1
Does the university offer:	
housing restricted to law students?	Yes
graduate housing for which law students are eligible?	Yes

Faculty and Administrators

	Total Fall	Total Spr	Men Fall	Men Spr	Women Fall	Women Spr	Minorities Fall	Minorities Spr
Full-time	16	15	9	8	7	7	6	6
Other Full-time	5	5	2	2	3	3	0	0
Deans, librarians, & others who teach	7	7	5	5	2	2	1	1
Part-time	8	7	7	7	1	0	1	0
Total	**36**	**34**	**23**	**22**	**13**	**12**	**8**	**7**

Curriculum

	Full-time	Part-time
Typical first-year section size	55	0
Is there typically a "small section" of the first-year class, other than Legal Writing, taught by full-time faculty	No	No
If yes, typical size offered last year		
# of classroom course titles beyond first-year curriculum	62	
# of upper division courses, excluding seminars with an enrollment: Under 25	48	
25–49	18	
50–74	28	
75–99	4	
100+	0	
# of seminars	7	
# of seminar positions available	96	
# of seminar positions filled	90	0
# of positions available in simulation courses	196	
# of simulation positions filled	153	0
# of positions available in faculty supervised clinical courses	24	
# of faculty supervised clinical positions filled	24	0
# involved in field placements	28	0
# involved in law journals	40	0
# involved in interschool competitions	26	0
# of credit hours required to graduate	90	

JD Enrollment and Ethnicity

	Men #	Men %	Women #	Women %	Full-time #	Full-time %	Part-time #	Part-time %	1st-year #	1st-year %	Total #	Total %	JD Degs. Awd.
African Amer.	10	6.5	17	10.8	25	8.4	2	12.5	11	9.9	27	8.6	12
Amer. Indian	0	0.0	1	0.6	0	0.0	1	6.3	0	0.0	1	0.3	1
Asian Amer.	7	4.5	9	5.7	16	5.4	0	0.0	2	1.8	16	5.1	9
Mex. Amer.	3	1.9	1	0.6	4	1.3	0	0.0	4	3.6	4	1.3	9
Puerto Rican	2	1.3	0	0.0	2	0.7	0	0.0	0	0.0	2	0.6	0
Hispanic	7	4.5	10	6.3	17	5.7	0	0.0	8	7.2	17	5.4	1
Total Minority	29	18.7	38	24.1	64	21.5	3	18.8	25	22.5	67	21.4	32
For. Nation.	0	0.0	1	0.6	1	0.3	0	0.0	1	0.9	1	0.3	0
Caucasian	119	76.8	113	71.5	220	74.1	12	75.0	76	68.5	232	74.1	77
Unknown	7	4.5	6	3.8	12	4.0	1	6.3	12	10.8	13	4.2	0
Total	155	49.5	158	50.5	297	94.9	16	5.1	111	35.5	313		109

Transfers

Transfers in	0
Transfers out	6

Tuition and Fees

	Resident	Nonresident
Full-time	$11,938	$21,490
Part-time	$0	$0

Living Expenses

Estimated living expenses for singles

Living on campus	Living off campus	Living at home
$12,966	$12,966	$12,966

Northern Illin

*ABA
Approved
Since
1978*

Northern Illinois Univ

Swen Parson Hall, Room 151
DeKalb, IL 60115-2890
Phone: 800.892.3050 or 8
E-mail: Lawadm@ni

GPA and LSAT Scores

	Total	Full-time	Part-time
# of apps	1,267	1,236	31
# of offers	379	369	10
# of matrics	111	106	5
75% GPA	3.66	3.68	3.63
Median GPA	3.38	3.38	3.41
25% GPA	3.06	3.04	3.36
75% LSAT	157	157	161
Median LSAT	155	155	158
25% LSAT	150	150	153

Grants and Scholarships (from prior year)

	Total		Full-time		Part-time	
	#	%	#	%	#	%
Total # of students	334		320		14	
Total # receiving grants	67	20.1	67	20.9	0	0.0
Less than 1/2 tuition	7	2.1	7	2.2	0	0.0
Half to full tuition	13	3.9	13	4.1	0	0.0
Full tuition	28	8.4	28	8.8	0	0.0
More than full tuition	19	5.7	19	5.9	0	0.0
Median grant amount			$8,910		$0	

Informational and Library Resources

# of volumes and volume equivalents	246,885
# of titles	40,471
# of active serial subscriptions	3,273
Study seating capacity inside the library	215
# of full-time professional librarians	6
Hours per week library is open	99
# of open, wired connections available to students	16
# of networked computers available for use by students	29
# of simultaneous wireless users	150
Require computer?	No

JD Attrition (from

	Aca
1st year	1
2nd year	
3rd year	
4th year	0	0	0	0.0

Employment (9 months after graduation)

	Total	Percentage
Employment status known	95	96.0
Employment status unknown	4	4.0
Employed	89	93.7
Pursuing graduate degrees	0	0.0
Unemployed seeking employment	1	1.1
Unemployed not seeking employment	0	0.0
Unemployed and studying for the bar	5	5.3

Type of Employment

	Total	Percentage
# employed in law firms	44	49.4
# employed in business and industry	16	18.0
# employed in government	17	19.1
# employed in public interest	8	9.0
# employed as judicial clerks	0	0.0
# employed in academia	4	4.5

Geographic Location

	Total	Percentage
# employed in state	79	88.8
# employed in foreign countries	0	0.0
# of states where employed	9	

Bar Passage Rates

Jurisdiction	Illinois		
Exam	Sum 05	Win 06	Total
# from school taking bar for the first time	90	7	97
School's pass rate for all first-time takers	84%	71%	84%
State's pass rate for all first-time takers	86%	83%	85%

...ersity College of Law

...15.753.9485; Fax: 815.753.5680
...edu; Website: http://law.niu.edu

...on

...Illinois University was founded in 1895, and the ...ge of Law was established in 1978. The College of Law ...s to prepare its graduates not only for the traditional role ...f lawyers, but also for the tasks we can assume will be performed in the future by lawyers. The school has a diverse and professionally distinguished faculty dedicated to teaching and scholarship.

■ Our Campus

The College of Law is located in DeKalb, a community conveniently located approximately 65 miles west of Chicago and 25 miles from the suburban area on the Ronald Reagan Memorial Tollway (I-88). DeKalb is close enough to the Chicago metropolitan area to draw on its many resources, yet retain its own college town flavor—a safe and affordable environment with a high quality of life.

Northern's main campus is set on 756 acres of rolling country land. The lush campus features two lagoons, museums, and a vast variety of cultural opportunities. It ultimately provides an excellent environment for the study of law.

Though on a relatively large campus with all of the associated activities and opportunities, the College of Law is a small oasis at its center. For an online tour go to our website at *http://law.niu.edu*.

■ Libraries

The David C. Shapiro Memorial Law Library provides one of the best ratios of library materials to students of any American law school. The law library offers in-depth research-level coverage of more than 32 areas of American law and study-level coverage of almost all other areas. Coverage of international, European Union, and British law is provided at study level. As a federally designated depository, the law library also receives selected government documents. In addition to its physical collection of over 246,885 volumes and volume equivalents, the library also offers access to Westlaw, LexisNexis, and a wide range of other Web-based legal resources. Laptop users enjoy convenient access to these electronic products anywhere in the law school through the College of Law's wireless network. Access to most of these resources is available off campus as well. The library also features a student computer lab that offers desktop high-speed Internet access and laser printing.

Further research support is provided through Founders Memorial Library, the university's main library, which is conveniently located adjacent to the College of Law. Founders Memorial Library contains roughly 2 million volumes and an additional 1.3 million federal, state, and international government documents. It also subscribes to diverse collections of nonlegal Web-based resources that may be accessed either on or off campus.

■ Enrollment/Student Body

Northern's student body represents universities from coast-to-coast and reflects a broad spectrum of ethnic, cultural, and geographic diversity. Our low student-faculty ratio, which is normally 15 to 1, facilitates a supportive environment with a lively exchange of ideas. The law school provides an atmosphere of shared goals and achievement and a genuine sense of community.

■ Curriculum and Clinical Experience Opportunities

The College of Law provides its students with a curriculum that will make them well-rounded legal professionals. The first-year program consists of the traditional ABA-required courses. After the first year, the only required courses are Constitutional Law II, Professional Responsibility, and a seminar; the remaining 90 hours are from a wide range of electives. Northern offers an Academic Support Program during the first year of classes. The ultimate goal is to help students succeed in law school.

During the summer, electives are offered on the main campus. Also during the summer, NIU offers an international law program in France. During this program, students receive six hours of credit in international and comparative law.

The clinical lawyering skills programs offer students the opportunity to acquire essential techniques needed in pretrial and trial work through structured simulations and experiences in an array of legal settings. The externship programs provide students with sound experience under the supervision of a highly qualified practicing attorney or the opportunity to be a law clerk for a state or federal judge. The Zeke Giorgi Legal Clinic in Rockford gives students the opportunity to apply legal theory by representing clients and resolving disputes in a real-world setting.

■ Admission

Considering Northern's small entering class size of between 110 and 120 out of an applicant pool ranging from 1,200 to 1,500, we are a relatively selective institution. The College of Law grants admission on a competitive basis through an evaluation of an applicant's aptitude and professional promise. Factors of most importance to the admission committee are the applicant's undergraduate record, LSAT score, reasons for seeking admission, school or community activities and accomplishments, employment background, and ability to add diversity to the law school community and the legal profession.

Applicants may submit their application either online at *http://law.niu.edu* or by paper form. In addition to the application, prospective students must submit a personal statement and application fee directly to the Office of Admission and Financial Aid. Northern requires applicants to use the LSDAS. International students who do not have a degree from a US institution must submit all foreign transcripts and TOEFL scores to LSAC's JD Credential Assembly Service. In order for Northern to receive LSAT scores, applicants need to submit official undergraduate and graduate transcripts as well as two letters of recommendation to LSAC. To be considered for the part-time option, an additional application, also available online, is required. Applicants are encouraged to submit their application early, even if the LSAT has not yet been taken, due to the limited number of seats in each entering class. Prospective students are encouraged to visit the College of Law.

Student Activities

Students are offered a wide variety of educational and professionally oriented activities. Among these are the *Law Review*, a forum for the expression of serious legal scholarship, and *The Advocate*, a newspaper published by law students. Students compete in a wide selection of moot court and alternative dispute resolution competitions. Organizations range from the Asian American Law Student Organization to the Women's Law Caucus.

Expenses and Financial Aid

Northern offers its students small class sizes and a quality legal education all at an affordable cost. For the 2006–2007 academic year, in-state tuition is $9,552 and out-of-state tuition is $19,104. Out-of-state residents can also qualify for in-state tuition in six months, which is why so few students after the first year are classified as out-of-state residents.

Scholarships and grants are available for students from a variety of sources. After the first year, students may qualify for research assistantships.

Scholarship, grant, and loan information is on our website at *http://law.niu.edu/go.cfm?do=Page.View&ID=3*. The priority deadline for the FAFSA form is March 1.

Career Opportunities

The Career Opportunities Office has a strong track record in assisting and preparing our graduates for rewarding careers through references to prospective employers and on-campus interviews. The office assists current students in obtaining enriching summer legal employment. Due to Northern's small class size, personalized counseling, normally not available at larger law schools, is offered.

Housing

Affordable housing is available both on and off campus. The new Northern View Community apartments for married and graduate students will offer one-, two-, and three-bedroom units. It includes a wireless community center which houses a computer lab and other facilities for residents. Tentative rental rates range between $699 to $749 per month. Handicap accessible housing is available. For information about on-campus housing you may telephone 815.753.5125, or visit our website at *www.shds.niu.edu*.

Many moderately priced apartments are available close to the university. The housing budget is $8,336. You may contact off-campus housing at 815.753.5105 or visit our website at *www.niu.edu/ComNonTrad/OCH.shtml*.

Correspondence

We encourage you to visit our campus and our website. Check our calendar on our website at *http://law.niu.edu* for activities, or call us toll free at 800.892.3050. Once you visit us, we are confident you will agree that Northern is the law school for you.

Applicant Profile

Northern Illinois University College of Law
This grid includes only applicants who earned 120–180 LSAT scores under standard administrations.

LSAT Score	3.75 + Apps	3.75 + Adm	3.50–3.74 Apps	3.50–3.74 Adm	3.25–3.49 Apps	3.25–3.49 Adm	3.00–3.24 Apps	3.00–3.24 Adm	2.75–2.99 Apps	2.75–2.99 Adm	2.50–2.74 Apps	2.50–2.74 Adm	2.25–2.49 Apps	2.25–2.49 Adm	2.00–2.24 Apps	2.00–2.24 Adm	Total Apps	Total Adm
175–180	0	0	0	0	0	0	0	0	0	0	0	0	0	0	0	0	0	0
170–174	0	0	0	0	0	0	0	0	0	0	0	0	0	0	0	0	0	0
165–169	1	1	2	2	0	0	2	2	1	1	0	0	0	0	0	0	6	6
160–164	8	8	11	11	7	7	10	10	10	10	8	8	2	1	2	1	58	56
155–159	27	26	33	30	36	36	33	28	31	22	23	11	7	2	2	1	192	156
150–154	37	21	54	29	98	34	80	16	67	9	26	5	14	0	3	0	379	114
145–149	25	4	54	6	69	11	77	4	48	4	35	5	20	2	4	0	332	36
140–144	7	0	18	0	33	6	50	2	33	0	27	0	14	0	3	0	185	8
Below 140	2	1	6	0	10	0	23	0	16	0	17	0	13	0	15	0	102	1
Total	107	61	178	78	253	94	275	62	206	46	136	29	70	5	29	2	1254	377

Apps = Number of Applicants
Adm = Number Admitted
Reflects 98% of the total applicant pool.

Northern Kentucky University—Salmon P. Chase College of Law

Nunn Hall, Nunn Drive
Highland Heights, KY 41099
Phone: 859.572.5490; Fax: 859.572.6081
E-mail: folger@nku.edu; Website: http://chaselaw.nku.edu/

ABA Approved Since 1954

The Basics

Type of school	Public
Term	Semester
Application deadline	3/1
Application fee	$40
Financial aid deadline	3/1 12/1
Can first year start other than fall?	No
Student to faculty ratio	15.1 to 1
Does the university offer:	
housing restricted to law students?	No
graduate housing for which law students are eligible?	No

Faculty and Administrators

	Total		Men		Women		Minorities	
	Fall	Spr	Fall	Spr	Fall	Spr	Fall	Spr
Full-time	25	25	18	18	7	7	3	3
Other Full-time	1	1	0	1	1	0	0	0
Deans, librarians, & others who teach	7	4	3	2	4	2	0	0
Part-time	15	13	8	9	7	4	2	0
Total	48	43	29	30	19	13	5	3

Curriculum

	Full-time	Part-time
Typical first-year section size	50	79
Is there typically a "small section" of the first-year class, other than Legal Writing, taught by full-time faculty	No	Yes
If yes, typical size offered last year		40
# of classroom course titles beyond first-year curriculum		65
# of upper division courses, excluding seminars with an enrollment: Under 25		27
25–49		13
50–74		10
75–99		9
100+		0
# of seminars		44
# of seminar positions available		785
# of seminar positions filled	335	277
# of positions available in simulation courses		217
# of simulation positions filled	95	122
# of positions available in faculty supervised clinical courses		8
# of faculty supervised clinical positions filled	0	0
# involved in field placements	47	13
# involved in law journals	19	11
# involved in interschool competitions	36	23
# of credit hours required to graduate		90

JD Enrollment and Ethnicity

	Men		Women		Full-time		Part-time		1st-year		Total		JD Degs. Awd.
	#	%	#	%	#	%	#	%	#	%	#	%	
African Amer.	6	2.1	13	5.6	9	3.2	10	4.3	6	4.3	19	3.7	6
Amer. Indian	3	1.1	0	0.0	2	0.7	1	0.4	0	0.0	3	0.6	2
Asian Amer.	4	1.4	1	0.4	2	0.7	3	1.3	2	1.4	5	1.0	1
Mex. Amer.	0	0.0	0	0.0	0	0.0	0	0.0	0	0.0	0	0.0	0
Puerto Rican	0	0.0	0	0.0	0	0.0	0	0.0	0	0.0	0	0.0	0
Hispanic	7	2.5	6	2.6	4	1.4	9	3.8	6	4.3	13	2.5	2
Total Minority	20	7.0	20	8.7	17	6.0	23	9.8	14	9.9	40	7.8	11
For. Nation.	0	0.0	0	0.0	0	0.0	0	0.0	0	0.0	0	0.0	0
Caucasian	265	93.0	211	91.3	265	94.0	211	90.2	127	90.1	476	92.2	131
Unknown	0	0.0	0	0.0	0	0.0	0	0.0	0	0.0	0	0.0	0
Total	285	55.2	231	44.8	282	54.7	234	45.3	141	27.3	516		142

Transfers

Transfers in	2
Transfers out	3

Tuition and Fees

	Resident	Nonresident
Full-time	$11,112	$24,240
Part-time	$8,334	$18,180

Living Expenses

Estimated living expenses for singles

Living on campus	Living off campus	Living at home
$9,278	$19,320	$7,070

Northern Kentucky University—Salmon P. Chase College of Law

*ABA
Approved
Since
1954*

GPA and LSAT Scores

	Total	Full-time	Part-time
# of apps	1,117	913	204
# of offers	345	264	81
# of matrics	146	87	59
75% GPA	3.58	3.59	3.54
Median GPA	3.32	3.35	3.24
25% GPA	3.08	3.16	2.96
75% LSAT	156	157	155
Median LSAT	154	155	152
25% LSAT	152	154	150

Grants and Scholarships (from prior year)

	Total		Full-time		Part-time	
	#	%	#	%	#	%
Total # of students	579		296		283	
Total # receiving grants	156	26.9	127	42.9	29	10.2
Less than 1/2 tuition	63	10.9	44	14.9	19	6.7
Half to full tuition	0	0.0	0	0.0	0	0.0
Full tuition	93	16.1	83	28.0	10	3.5
More than full tuition	0	0.0	0	0.0	0	0.0
Median grant amount			$10,128		$2,900	

Informational and Library Resources

# of volumes and volume equivalents	332,151
# of titles	69,295
# of active serial subscriptions	2,301
Study seating capacity inside the library	222
# of full-time professional librarians	6
Hours per week library is open	168
# of open, wired connections available to students	23
# of networked computers available for use by students	60
# of simultaneous wireless users	600
Require computer?	No

JD Attrition (from prior year)

	Academic	Other	Total	
	#	#	#	%
1st year	20	18	38	20.2
2nd year	10	9	19	10.1
3rd year	3	2	5	3.4
4th year	1	1	2	3.7

Employment (9 months after graduation)

	Total	Percentage
Employment status known	130	97.0
Employment status unknown	4	3.0
Employed	114	87.7
Pursuing graduate degrees	2	1.5
Unemployed seeking employment	6	4.6
Unemployed not seeking employment	1	0.8
Unemployed and studying for the bar	7	5.4

Type of Employment

	Total	Percentage
# employed in law firms	59	51.8
# employed in business and industry	24	21.1
# employed in government	10	8.8
# employed in public interest	11	9.6
# employed as judicial clerks	7	6.1
# employed in academia	3	2.6

Geographic Location

	Total	Percentage
# employed in state	53	46.5
# employed in foreign countries	0	0.0
# of states where employed	8	

Bar Passage Rates

Jurisdiction	Kentucky			Ohio		
Exam	Sum 05	Win 06	Total	Sum 05	Win 06	Total
# from school taking bar for the first time	59	22	81	57	17	74
School's pass rate for all first-time takers	80%	73%	78%	70%	65%	69%
State's pass rate for all first-time takers	81%	67%	77%	81%	76%	81%

Northern Kentucky University—Salmon P. Chase College of Law

Nunn Hall, Nunn Drive
Highland Heights, KY 41099
Phone: 859.572.5490; Fax: 859.572.6081
E-mail: folger@nku.edu; Website: http://chaselaw.nku.edu/

■ Introduction

The Salmon P. Chase College of Law, founded in 1893, is located in Nunn Hall on the main campus of Northern Kentucky University, a learner-centered metropolitan university in a thriving legal and business community just seven miles south of Cincinnati, Ohio. Chase offers both a full-time day division and a part-time evening division. Chase is accredited by the American Bar Association and is a member of the Association of American Law Schools.

■ Library and Learning Environment

Chase students have access to the law library 24 hours a day, 7 days a week. Students may access the library's electronic resources in the legal information technology lab or throughout the building via the library's wireless network. The library provides access to a wide range of online resources, including HeinOnline, LexisNexis, Westlaw, e-mail, CALI exercises, and many other Web-based products.

Nunn Hall's two courtrooms are equipped with state-of-the-art video and computer technology, as are a majority of the classrooms.

■ Curriculum

The curriculum consists of required courses, core courses, and elective courses. Ninety credit hours are required to graduate. Fifty-two hours are in required courses. Full-time students may complete the program in three years, while part-time students generally complete the program in four years. Chase offers a number of academic support and development programs designed to enhance the law school experience.

■ Joint-degree Program

Chase offers a Juris Doctor/Master of Business Administration (JD/MBA) degree program. This program is an attractive alternative for individuals who wish to practice law or business in an increasingly complex environment. Courses in the College of Law serve as electives for the MBA degree, and specific MBA courses serve as electives for the law degree. Thus, the number of hours required to obtain both degrees through the combined program is less than the number of hours required to complete each degree separately.

■ Special Programs

The **Clinical Extern Program** aids law students in the development of practical legal skills through work experience in supervised governmental and nonprofit-organization legal settings. Opportunities include placements with state and federal judges, prosecutors, public defenders, legal aid programs, and various governmental agencies.

Through the **Federal Trial Practice Seminar**, students serve as law clerks for a United States District Court judge or magistrate. Students conduct legal research and prepare bench memoranda on legal issues pending before the court.

The **IOLTA Public Interest Fellowships** enable a number of students each year to serve in paid fellowships with local public interest organizations, Northern Kentucky Legal Aid, and the Children's Law Center.

The **IRS Chief Counsel Externships** and **Chase Tax Clinic** are excellent opportunities for students interested in practicing in the area of taxation. The **Volunteer Income Tax Assistance Program** assists low-income, elderly, and disabled taxpayers in the northern Kentucky community in filing their federal and state returns.

Students participating in the **Kentucky Innocence Project** assist the Kentucky Department of Public Advocacy (DPA) by investigating and possibly litigating claims of innocence from state and federal prisoners. The clinic focuses on the discovery and analysis of new evidence, especially DNA evidence. Participants are placed in the field and work directly under the supervision of DPA attorneys.

The **Local Government Law Center** externships provide unique opportunities in which students assist city and county governments throughout Kentucky. Externships are individually tailored to meet each student's background, experience, and career interest.

■ Admission

Chase seeks to admit those applicants who have the best prospect of high-quality academic work; thus, the Admission Committee relies heavily on the applicant's undergraduate grades and performance on the LSAT during the application review process. Additional factors considered include upward trend of undergraduate grades; time between college graduation and application to Chase; college grading and course selection patterns; outside work while in college; letters of recommendation; graduate study; cultural, educational, or sociological deprivation; employment background; leadership ability; speaking or linguistic ability; and demonstrated competence in another profession or vocation. Chase seeks diversity in the student body by considering, in no particular order, sex, age, cultural or geographic background, and minority status. First-year students enter in the fall semester.

■ Student Activities

The Chase College of Law **Moot Court** program is available to those students with a demonstrated ability and interest in research, brief writing, and oral advocacy. The teams have competed successfully in national and regional competitions.

The *Northern Kentucky Law Review* is published by Chase students and includes scholarly legal writings by law professors, practitioners, jurists, and students.

Chase's **National Trial Advocacy Team** promotes excellence in trial advocacy through training, education, and development of trial advocacy skills with one-on-one attention from expert practitioners. The team has successfully competed in state and national mock trial competitions.

The **Student Bar Association** sponsors professional, social, and community service events, and selects students to participate on several faculty committees. Other student organizations include chapters of the **American Constitution Society**, the **American Trial Lawyers Association**, the **Black Law Students Association**, **Delta Theta Phi**, the **Federalist Society**, **Phi Alpha Delta**, the **Chase Public Interest Group**, the **Chase Intellectual Property Society**, the **Chase Christian Legal Society**, the **International Law Student Association**, and the **National Women's Law Student Association**.

■ Career Development

The Career Development Office assists students and alumni with career planning, networking, and developing job-search skills and strategies. The director of career development is an attorney with significant law firm and litigation experience.

The office schedules fall and spring on-campus interviews, posts job notices daily, and holds seminars and workshops to prepare students for the job market. Chase law students attend a variety of job fairs and recruiting programs, and many obtain legal work experience for pay while in law school. The Lunch With a Lawyer/Dinner With a Lawyer program series, sponsored by the Chase Alumni Association and the Career Development Office, enables students to network with alumni and learn about a wide variety of legal specialties and career options at frequent sessions held throughout the year.

Applicant Profile

Northern Kentucky University—Salmon P. Chase College of Law
This grid includes only applicants who earned 120–180 LSAT scores under standard administrations.

LSAT Score	3.75 +		3.50–3.74		3.25–3.49		3.00–3.24		2.75–2.99		2.50–2.74		2.25–2.49		2.00–2.24		Below 2.00		No GPA		Total	
	Apps	Adm	Apps	Adm	Apps	Adm	Apps	Adm	Apps	Adm	Apps	Adm	Apps	Adm	Apps	Adm	Apps	Adm	Apps	Adm	Apps	Adm
175–180	0	0	0	0	0	0	0	0	0	0	0	0	0	0	0	0	0	0	0	0	0	0
170–174	0	0	0	0	1	0	0	0	0	0	0	0	0	0	0	0	0	0	0	0	1	0
165–169	3	3	1	1	2	1	0	0	1	1	0	0	0	0	1	1	0	0	0	0	8	7
160–164	5	5	6	6	4	4	9	8	5	4	4	3	2	2	2	0	0	0	0	0	37	32
155–159	24	21	31	30	32	31	36	33	20	12	16	5	9	3	0	0	1	0	2	0	169	135
150–154	44	30	69	38	77	30	77	23	60	12	28	3	15	1	3	0	1	0	3	0	377	137
145–149	31	9	40	4	68	7	66	0	46	1	29	1	13	0	5	0	1	0	5	0	305	22
140–144	8	1	16	1	29	3	34	3	19	5	15	1	13	0	3	0	1	0	3	0	145	14
135–139	1	0	5	0	1	0	8	0	9	0	10	0	3	0	3	0	0	0	0	0	44	0
130–134	0	0	0	0	1	0	1	0	0	0	3	0	3	0	0	0	0	0	1	0	8	0
125–129	0	0	1	0	0	0	0	0	1	0	3	0	1	0	0	0	0	0	0	0	7	0
120–124	0	0	0	0	0	0	0	0	0	0	1	0	0	0	1	0	0	0	0	0	2	0
Total	116	69	169	80	215	76	231	67	161	35	109	13	65	6	18	1	5	0	14	0	1103	347

Apps = Number of Applicants
Adm = Number Admitted
Reflects 99% of the total applicant pool.

Northwestern University School of Law

357 East Chicago Avenue
Chicago, IL 60611-3069
Phone: 312.503.3100; Fax: 312.503.0178
E-mail: admissions@law.northwestern.edu; Website: www.law.northwestern.edu

ABA Approved Since 1923

The Basics

Type of school	Private
Term	Semester
Application deadline	2/15
Application fee	$80
Financial aid deadline	2/15
Can first year start other than fall?	No
Student to faculty ratio	10.6 to 1
Does the university offer:	
housing restricted to law students?	No
graduate housing for which law students are eligible?	Yes

Faculty and Administrators

	Total		Men		Women		Minorities	
	Fall	Spr	Fall	Spr	Fall	Spr	Fall	Spr
Full-time	65	56	42	37	23	19	9	8
Other Full-time	35	35	5	5	30	30	3	3
Deans, librarians, & others who teach	5	5	4	4	1	1	0	0
Part-time	63	54	54	37	9	17	2	4
Total	168	150	105	83	63	67	14	15

Curriculum

		Full-time	Part-time
Typical first-year section size		65	0
Is there typically a "small section" of the first-year class, other than Legal Writing, taught by full-time faculty		No	No
If yes, typical size offered last year			
# of classroom course titles beyond first-year curriculum		205	
# of upper division courses, excluding seminars with an enrollment:	Under 25	81	
	25–49	68	
	50–74	20	
	75–99	3	
	100+	1	
# of seminars		70	
# of seminar positions available		1,661	
# of seminar positions filled		1,148	0
# of positions available in simulation courses		678	
# of simulation positions filled		611	0
# of positions available in faculty supervised clinical courses		253	
# of faculty supervised clinical positions filled	235		0
# involved in field placements		151	0
# involved in law journals		252	0
# involved in interschool competitions		110	0
# of credit hours required to graduate		86	

JD Enrollment and Ethnicity

	Men #	Men %	Women #	Women %	Full-time #	Full-time %	Part-time #	Part-time %	1st-year #	1st-year %	Total #	Total %	JD Degs. Awd.
African Amer.	26	6.3	38	10.7	64	8.3	0	0.0	26	11.2	64	8.3	18
Amer. Indian	1	0.2	4	1.1	5	0.7	0	0.0	3	1.3	5	0.7	0
Asian Amer.	66	15.9	67	18.9	133	17.3	0	0.0	45	19.3	133	17.3	39
Mex. Amer.	7	1.7	2	0.6	9	1.2	0	0.0	7	3.0	9	1.2	1
Puerto Rican	6	1.4	3	0.8	9	1.2	0	0.0	5	2.1	9	1.2	1
Hispanic	23	5.6	23	6.5	46	6.0	0	0.0	11	4.7	46	6.0	24
Total Minority	129	31.2	137	38.7	266	34.6	0	0.0	97	41.6	266	34.6	83
For. Nation.	15	3.6	17	4.8	32	4.2	0	0.0	11	4.7	32	4.2	0
Caucasian	270	65.2	200	56.5	470	61.2	0	0.0	125	53.6	470	61.2	153
Unknown	0	0.0	0	0.0	0	0.0	0	0.0	0	0.0	0	0.0	29
Total	414	53.9	354	46.1	768	100.0	0	0.0	233	30.3	768		265

Transfers

Transfers in	40
Transfers out	10

Tuition and Fees

	Resident	Nonresident
Full-time	$40,680	$40,680
Part-time	$0	$0

Living Expenses

Estimated living expenses for singles

Living on campus	Living off campus	Living at home
$19,706	$19,706	$11,687

Northwestern University School of Law

*ABA
Approved
Since
1923*

GPA and LSAT Scores

	Total	Full-time	Part-time
# of apps	5,015	5,015	0
# of offers	869	869	0
# of matrics	233	233	0
75% GPA	3.80	3.80	0.00
Median GPA	3.70	3.70	0.00
25% GPA	3.40	3.40	0.00
75% LSAT	172	172	0
Median LSAT	170	170	0
25% LSAT	166	166	0

Grants and Scholarships (from prior year)

	Total		Full-time		Part-time	
	#	%	#	%	#	%
Total # of students	772		772		0	
Total # receiving grants	254	32.9	254	32.9	0	0.0
Less than 1/2 tuition	124	16.1	124	16.1	0	0.0
Half to full tuition	120	15.5	120	15.5	0	0.0
Full tuition	2	0.3	2	0.3	0	0.0
More than full tuition	8	1.0	8	1.0	0	0.0
Median grant amount			$20,000		$0	

Informational and Library Resources

# of volumes and volume equivalents	747,808
# of titles	337,543
# of active serial subscriptions	5,566
Study seating capacity inside the library	636
# of full-time professional librarians	11
Hours per week library is open	105
# of open, wired connections available to students	248
# of networked computers available for use by students	112
# of simultaneous wireless users	900
Require computer?	Yes

JD Attrition (from prior year)

	Academic	Other	Total	
	#	#	#	%
1st year	3	0	3	1.2
2nd year	0	10	10	3.8
3rd year	3	0	3	1.1
4th year	0	0	0	0.0

Employment (9 months after graduation)

	Total	Percentage
Employment status known	265	100.0
Employment status unknown	0	0.0
Employed	255	96.2
Pursuing graduate degrees	3	1.1
Unemployed seeking employment	0	0.0
Unemployed not seeking employment	6	2.3
Unemployed and studying for the bar	1	0.4

Type of Employment

# employed in law firms	182	71.4
# employed in business and industry	22	8.6
# employed in government	9	3.5
# employed in public interest	7	2.7
# employed as judicial clerks	35	13.7
# employed in academia	0	0.0

Geographic Location

# employed in state	113	44.3
# employed in foreign countries	3	1.2
# of states where employed		28

Bar Passage Rates

Jurisdiction	Illinois		
Exam	Sum 05	Win 06	Total
# from school taking bar for the first time	129	8	137
School's pass rate for all first-time takers	95%	100%	95%
State's pass rate for all first-time takers	86%	83%	85%

Northwestern University School of Law

357 East Chicago Avenue
Chicago, IL 60611-3069
Phone: 312.503.3100; Fax: 312.503.0178
E-mail: admissions@law.northwestern.edu; Website: www.law.northwestern.edu

■ Introduction

Northwestern University School of Law, founded in 1859, advances the understanding of law and produces graduates prepared to excel in a rapidly changing world. Northwestern uniquely blends a rigorous intellectual environment within a collegial and supportive community. With one of the lowest student-faculty ratios in the country, students have unusually close contact with full-time professors who are noted scholars.

The law school's lakefront location in the heart of downtown Chicago provides a wealth of part-time employment options for students while in school and a spectacular setting in which to study law. Northwestern's proximity to courts, commerce, and public interest activities enables students to experience the practice of law as well as its theory.

■ Enrollment and Admission

By limiting the total JD enrollment, the law school maintains a close-knit and supportive community that fosters friendships among students and faculty. Northwestern seeks students diverse in experience, background, and perspective. The Admissions Committee considers many factors beyond test scores and GPAs when evaluating applicants. More than 90 percent enter with at least one year of full-time work experience; 75 percent have two or more years of work experience. Through its unique interviewing program, Northwestern attracts not only students with strong academic credentials, but also those with the interpersonal skills and maturity needed to thrive in the law school community.

■ Faculty

The faculty is composed of nationally recognized scholars, diverse in background and perspective, whose research and writing make major contributions to important academic and public policy debates. Northwestern professors have a passion for teaching and for engaging students in theoretical and practical legal applications.

The faculty includes scholars with advanced degrees in economics, history, philosophy, and political science, as well as law. It includes a former chair of the Securities and Exchange Commission; a former US Ambassador-at-Large for War Crimes Issues; a leading expert on race, gender, and the law; an author of more than 50 books on tax law; the first American attorney to argue before the European Court of Human Rights; and the senior author of the most widely used casebook on American legal history. The full-time faculty is supplemented by a distinguished group of adjunct professors who teach a wide variety of specialized courses.

■ Curriculum

In the rigorous first year of study, Northwestern provides a superior foundation in legal reasoning, analysis, and writing, as well as a thorough understanding of the structures and policies of the law. Communication, teamwork, cross-training in business, and real-world experience are also hallmarks of Northwestern.

The law school's size enables students to have one-on-one relationships with professors. Required first-year courses are taught in sections of approximately 60 students. The JD program requires 86 semester hours of credit and can ordinarily be completed in three years, although permission can be given for a four-year program.

The broad and flexible curriculum gives upper-level students the opportunity to specialize in particular areas, to pursue advanced research in legal theory, or to pursue a range of hands-on simulation and live-client opportunities. The Owen L. Coon/James A. Rahl Senior Research Program enables third-year students to do individual research under the supervision of a professor, using library, field, and interdisciplinary research methods.

■ Special-degree Programs

A combined program in law and business is offered with Northwestern's Kellogg School of Management in which students earn both a JD from the law school and an MBA degree from Kellogg after only three years of study. Students may also enroll in a joint JD/PhD program with the law school and one of the social sciences departments. In a joint program with Northwestern's Medill School of Journalism, non-JD students interested in reporting about the law and legal institutions can earn both a Master of Science in Journalism (MSJ) degree and a Master of Studies in Law (MSL) degree.

Students who wish to specialize in the study of tax law can earn an LLM in Taxation. Students educated outside the United States can earn an LLM through a nine-month program of advanced study or an LLM degree and a certificate in business administration from Kellogg through a 12-month program in law and business. Legal and business professionals in Korea and Europe can earn an LLM degree from Northwestern through our Executive LLM Programs in Seoul, Korea, and in Madrid, Spain.

■ Legal Clinics

In Northwestern's comprehensive clinical program, students learn strong litigation and negotiation skills and gain direct experience with representing clients and reforming laws.

The innovative simulation-based curriculum, including the **Program on Advocacy and Professionalism** and the **Program on Negotiation and Mediation**, gives students the skills they need to negotiate and communicate effectively, solve problems, prepare briefs, examine witnesses, present evidence, and argue cases.

Students represent impoverished clients as well as challenge the fairness of our legal institutions and propose solutions for reform. Working in teams, they prepare cases in juvenile justice, immigration and asylum, and criminal matters. In addition to fine-tuning their skills as advocates, they often effect change in the law and legal institutions. **Bluhm Legal Clinic** centers—**Fred Bartlit Center for Trial Strategy, Children and Family Justice Center, Small Business Opportunity Center, Center for International Human Rights, Center on Wrongful Convictions, Investor Protection Center,** and **MacArthur Justice Center**—are nationally recognized for their direct involvement in legal reform.

■ Library and Physical Facilities

With more than a half million volumes and access to a wide range of electronic resources, the Pritzker Legal Research Center is one of the country's largest law libraries.

Wireless technology and Ethernet connections are available throughout the law school. Most large classrooms are equipped with smart podiums including video projection and Internet connections. The law school's three interconnected buildings along Chicago's lakefront also house the national headquarters of the American Bar Foundation.

■ Student Activities

Northwestern students take an intense and energetic interest in their community and education. Six scholarly journals are available for research, writing, and editing. Students automatically belong to the Student Bar Association, which gives them a voice in curriculum and administration, and they have an opportunity to participate in more than 30 student organizations. Students also enjoy the benefits of living, studying, and working in one of the most vibrant legal and business communities in the world.

■ Expenses and Financial Aid

The law school annually awards $5.5 million in grants and scholarships in addition to long-term, low-interest institutional loans. These resources enable the law school to cover 100 percent of a student's calculated financial need. Approximately 85 percent of the students currently enrolled are receiving financial aid.

■ Career Services

The Center for Career Strategy and Advancement staff aggressively cultivates relationships with potential employers while assisting students in focusing their goals and developing short- and long-term career strategies. In the fall of 2005, more than 700 national employers recruited our students. In recent years, approximately 75 percent of the recruiters were based in regions outside the Midwest. In 2005, about half of our students chose to remain in the Midwest.

Applicant Profile

At Northwestern, emphasis on teamwork, communication, and interpersonal skills begins during the admission process in which every applicant is urged to interview. Currently about 75 percent of applicants are interviewed, and college seniors must be interviewed. We also place a heavy emphasis on work experience, which contributes to an environment where students learn a great deal from not only faculty but also each other.

Notre Dame Law School

112 Law School
Notre Dame, IN 46556
Phone: 574.631.6626; Fax: 574.631.5474
E-mail: lawadmit@nd.edu; Website: www.lawadmissions.nd.edu

ABA Approved Since 1925

The Basics

Type of school	Private
Term	Semester
Application deadline	3/1
Application fee	$55
Financial aid deadline	2/15
Can first year start other than fall?	No
Student to faculty ratio	13.7 to 1
Does the university offer:	
housing restricted to law students?	No
graduate housing for which law students are eligible?	Yes

Faculty and Administrators

	Total Fall	Total Spr	Men Fall	Men Spr	Women Fall	Women Spr	Minorities Fall	Minorities Spr
Full-time	36	36	24	24	12	12	6	6
Other Full-time	2	2	0	0	2	2	0	0
Deans, librarians, & others who teach	17	17	11	11	6	6	1	1
Part-time	41	41	23	23	18	18	2	1
Total	96	96	58	58	38	38	9	8

Curriculum

	Full-time	Part-time
Typical first-year section size	88	0
Is there typically a "small section" of the first-year class, other than Legal Writing, taught by full-time faculty	No	No
If yes, typical size offered last year		
# of classroom course titles beyond first-year curriculum	109	

# of upper division courses, excluding seminars with an enrollment:		
Under 25	68	
25–49	36	
50–74	13	
75–99	5	
100+	2	

# of seminars	34	
# of seminar positions available	579	
# of seminar positions filled	476	0
# of positions available in simulation courses	217	
# of simulation positions filled	201	0
# of positions available in faculty supervised clinical courses	66	
# of faculty supervised clinical positions filled	65	0
# involved in field placements	42	0
# involved in law journals	157	0
# involved in interschool competitions	102	0
# of credit hours required to graduate	90	

JD Enrollment and Ethnicity

	Men #	Men %	Women #	Women %	Full-time #	Full-time %	Part-time #	Part-time %	1st-year #	1st-year %	Total #	Total %	JD Degs. Awd.
African Amer.	16	4.4	12	5.7	28	4.9	0	0.0	8	4.0	28	4.9	10
Amer. Indian	4	1.1	5	2.4	9	1.6	0	0.0	4	2.0	9	1.6	1
Asian Amer.	26	7.2	16	7.6	42	7.4	0	0.0	13	6.6	42	7.4	16
Mex. Amer.	8	2.2	2	0.9	10	1.8	0	0.0	6	3.0	10	1.8	4
Puerto Rican	2	0.6	1	0.5	3	0.5	0	0.0	0	0.0	3	0.5	3
Hispanic	17	4.7	19	9.0	36	6.3	0	0.0	16	8.1	36	6.3	6
Total Minority	73	20.3	55	26.1	128	22.5	0	0.0	47	23.7	128	22.4	40
For. Nation.	2	0.6	4	1.9	6	1.1	0	0.0	0	0.0	6	1.1	2
Caucasian	243	67.5	127	60.2	369	64.7	1	100.0	125	63.1	370	64.8	131
Unknown	42	11.7	25	11.8	67	11.8	0	0.0	26	13.1	67	11.7	0
Total	360	63.0	211	37.0	570	99.8	1	0.2	198	34.7	571		173

Transfers

Transfers in	16
Transfers out	5

Tuition and Fees

	Resident	Nonresident
Full-time	$34,120	$34,120
Part-time	$0	$0

Living Expenses

Estimated living expenses for singles

Living on campus	Living off campus	Living at home
$14,100	$14,100	$14,100

ABA
Approved
Since
1925

GPA and LSAT Scores

	Total	Full-time	Part-time
# of apps	3,502	3,502	0
# of offers	853	853	0
# of matrics	198	198	0
75% GPA	3.69	3.69	0.00
Median GPA	3.50	3.50	0.00
25% GPA	3.28	3.28	0.00
75% LSAT	167	167	0
Median LSAT	166	166	0
25% LSAT	164	164	0

Grants and Scholarships (from prior year)

	Total #	Total %	Full-time #	Full-time %	Part-time #	Part-time %
Total # of students	539		538		1	
Total # receiving grants	346	64.2	346	64.3	0	0.0
Less than 1/2 tuition	238	44.2	238	44.2	0	0.0
Half to full tuition	102	18.9	102	19.0	0	0.0
Full tuition	5	0.9	5	0.9	0	0.0
More than full tuition	1	0.2	1	0.2	0	0.0
Median grant amount			$12,500		$0	

Informational and Library Resources

# of volumes and volume equivalents	637,059
# of titles	206,333
# of active serial subscriptions	7,217
Study seating capacity inside the library	416
# of full-time professional librarians	13
Hours per week library is open	95
# of open, wired connections available to students	118
# of networked computers available for use by students	98
# of simultaneous wireless users	570
Require computer?	No

JD Attrition (from prior year)

	Academic #	Other #	Total #	Total %
1st year	1	5	6	3.4
2nd year	0	0	0	0.0
3rd year	0	0	0	0.0
4th year	0	0	0	0.0

Employment (9 months after graduation)

	Total	Percentage
Employment status known	197	98.5
Employment status unknown	3	1.5
Employed	185	93.9
Pursuing graduate degrees	3	1.5
Unemployed seeking employment	7	3.6
Unemployed not seeking employment	1	0.5
Unemployed and studying for the bar	1	0.5

Type of Employment

# employed in law firms	114	61.6
# employed in business and industry	16	8.6
# employed in government	21	11.4
# employed in public interest	4	2.2
# employed as judicial clerks	28	15.1
# employed in academia	2	1.1

Geographic Location

# employed in state	14	7.6
# employed in foreign countries	2	1.1
# of states where employed		33

Bar Passage Rates

Jurisdiction	Illinois			California		
Exam	Sum 05	Win 06	Total	Sum 05	Win 06	Total
# from school taking bar for the first time	43	12	55	24	3	27
School's pass rate for all first-time takers	91%	100%	93%	67%	67%	67%
State's pass rate for all first-time takers	86%	83%	85%	64%	54%	62%

Notre Dame Law School

Admissions Office, 112 Law School
Notre Dame, IN 46556
Phone: 574.631.6626; Fax: 574.631.5474
E-mail: lawadmit@nd.edu; Website: www.lawadmissions.nd.edu

■ Introduction

With a rich history that dates to its founding in 1869, Notre Dame Law School today enjoys a national and international reputation for preparing consummate professionals—men and women who are extraordinarily competent in their professional endeavors and who commit themselves to serve their clients and the profession effectively and honorably. Distinctive among nationally regarded law schools as a result of the school's and the university's Catholic heritage and tradition, faith and values, and community spirit, the Law School inspires students to examine their practice of law within the context of their responsibilities as members of the bar, as leaders within their respective fields, and as citizens of the world community.

■ Enrollment/Student Body

The student body represents the national stature and international nature of the programs of the Law School and the university. Our student body of approximately 570 students represents all states and a number of foreign countries. The small size of the student body fosters a sense of community and allows significant interaction between faculty and students.

■ Faculty

Faculty members come to the Notre Dame Law School with extensive experience in private practice and government service, and represent a wide range of undergraduate institutions, law schools, and state bars. Members of the faculty are well regarded for their commitment to teaching and their accessibility to students outside of the classroom. Notre Dame law faculty supports students' professional development through active counseling, mentoring, and advising.

■ Library and Physical Facilities

The Kresge Law Library is among the top tier of American law school research libraries. The library is considered a national leader in legal research techniques using automated technology. The Law School provides significant computing support for students and other members of the law school community. A staff of five full-time professionals offer assistance with both hardware and software, in addition to other computing and technology needs.

■ Curriculum

The JD curriculum provides a strong foundation in those areas that have proven to be fundamental to the actual practice of law in every American jurisdiction, while giving students the opportunity to tailor coursework to particular career aspirations. Required courses, those that are critical to a mastery of specialized areas of the law, total 42 of the 90 credit hours needed for graduation. In addition to the JD degree, the Law School confers three graduate law degrees: an LLM in International and Comparative Law, an LLM in International Human Rights, and a JSD (also in International Human Rights). The LLM in International and Comparative Law is offered exclusively at the Law School's London Law Centre.

■ London Programs

Notre Dame Law School recognizes that today's legal practice increasingly involves matters of international law. JD candidates may augment their legal education by participating in one of two programs offered by the Law School through its London Law Centre. Second-year students who wish to immerse themselves in comparative and international law, as well as in the traditions of the American and British common-law systems, can study in the only year-long overseas program offered by an American law school. Students who desire a shorter international-study experience and who have completed their first year of law school can spend six weeks in London during Notre Dame's summer program.

■ Admission

Notre Dame offers both an Early Decision and a Regular Decision Program. The Early Decision Program is designed for those candidates who have researched other law schools and who are committed to enrolling at Notre Dame if admitted. The application deadline for applying via Early Decision is November 1, and all supporting admission material must be on file in the Law School Admissions Office no later than November 10. Early decision applicants will be notified of an admission decision by December 15 and, if admitted, have until January 5 to accept or decline the offer of admission.

The Regular Decision Program follows a rolling admission process, with the first round of acceptances typically mailed on or about December 15. Regular decision applicants are encouraged to apply at the earliest possible date. Candidates who apply February 15 or earlier are charged a reduced application fee of $55. Candidates whose applications are postmarked February 16 or later must pay a $70 application fee. March 1 is the deadline for submitting an application.

■ Student Life

The sense of community and the quality of student life at Notre Dame have developed out of long-standing traditions that make the Notre Dame Law School experience different: admission policies that emphasize the importance of qualitative factors such as service to others; a mission that focuses on teaching, scholarship, and service in the legal and Judeo-Christian traditions; and an emphasis on forming and nurturing collegial relationships among and between students and faculty. The Law School is centrally located on the Notre Dame campus, and law students fully participate in athletic, cultural, religious, and social events on the campus. Law students also manage to find a comfortable balance between their studies and involvement in the Law School's four law journals and any of 25 organizations that reflect and respond to the professional and personal interests of the student body.

■ Expenses and Financial Aid

Notre Dame is committed to providing a legal education of the highest quality at a tuition structure that compares favorably to other nationally regarded private law schools. Additionally, law students benefit from the low cost of living in northern Indiana.

Fellowship assistance is provided annually to approximately 65 percent of the entering students on the basis of merit, commitment to the Law School's mission, and financial need. Fellowships range from $5,000 to $25,000 and are renewable for all three years of legal study.

■ Housing

Many single law students choose to live on campus in graduate-student housing. Married students with children can live in the unfurnished University Village apartments. Students who wish to live off-campus can find reasonably priced accommodations near the campus and can secure on-campus parking for a nominal additional charge.

■ Career Services

Graduates of Notre Dame Law School find success in identifying and obtaining a spectrum of rewarding and satisfying careers in all areas of the nation and abroad. For recent graduating classes, the employment rate has been 95 percent or better within six months of graduation. Each year, approximately 250 employers visit the campus to interview Notre Dame law students. These employers, and others, are interested in interviewing Notre Dame law students because of the law school's reputation for preparing extraordinarily competent lawyers. A national network of over 8,000 Law School alumni and friends assist students and graduates in finding employment opportunities across the country.

Graduates of Notre Dame Law School have been especially successful in terms of obtaining judicial clerkships, with 15 to 18 percent of recent graduating classes choosing this career option. These highly sought-after positions provide graduates with a unique opportunity to learn first-hand about the inner workings of the judicial system, while at the same time honing important legal skills and problem-solving abilities.

The Career Services Office (CSO) also coordinates a variety of initiatives to encourage students who wish to be employed in public-interest work following graduation. These include a variety of informational programs and services, including a public-interest reception that brings to campus public-interest attorneys from across the country. The CSO also coordinates participation in public-interest career fairs held in Washington, DC and Chicago, as well as a campus-wide, not-for-profit career fair. Additionally, in 2001, the Law School established an expanded Loan Repayment Assistance Program (LRAP) to assist eligible law school graduates who choose to work in public interest, public service, or other similar positions after graduation. By expanding LRAP, the Law School seeks to help alleviate an obstacle that prevents graduates from pursuing positions in public-interest and public-service employment.

■ Applicant Profile

The Law School Admissions Committee employs a whole-person review philosophy. Academic ability, as reflected in the LSAT score and academic performance in college, are important. However, the committee considers a broad array of elements in addition to the essential factors of LSAT score and GPA with a view toward assembling a diverse class while at the same time arriving at a fair appraisal of the individual applicant. Notre Dame Law School officials involved in the admission process are mindful of the school's objective to produce lawyers who are competent, compassionate, and committed to serving their clients with integrity. Admission decisions are inevitably the result of selecting a relatively small class from a large number of highly qualified applicants.

Applicant Profile

The Notre Dame Law School Admissions Committee has chosen not to publish a data grid, as every effort is made to consider a wide variety of factors as each application for admission is reviewed.

Nova Southeastern University—Shepard Broad Law Center

3305 College Avenue
Fort Lauderdale, FL 33314-7721
Phone: 954.262.6117; Fax: 954.262.3844
E-mail: admission@nsu.law.nova.edu; Website: www.nsulaw.nova.edu

*ABA
Approved
Since
1975*

The Basics

Type of school	Private
Term	Semester
Application deadline	3/1
Application fee	$50
Financial aid deadline	4/1
Can first year start other than fall?	No
Student to faculty ratio	13.9 to 1
Does the university offer:	
housing restricted to law students?	No
graduate housing for which law students are eligible?	No

Faculty and Administrators

	Total		Men		Women		Minorities	
	Fall	Spr	Fall	Spr	Fall	Spr	Fall	Spr
Full-time	47	54	22	26	25	28	9	11
Other Full-time	9	11	3	6	6	5	4	3
Deans, librarians, & others who teach	10	9	4	3	6	6	2	2
Part-time	53	40	36	26	17	14	6	8
Total	119	114	65	61	54	53	21	24

Curriculum

	Full-time	Part-time
Typical first-year section size	54	61
Is there typically a "small section" of the first-year class, other than Legal Writing, taught by full-time faculty	No	No
If yes, typical size offered last year		
# of classroom course titles beyond first-year curriculum		126

# of upper division courses, excluding seminars with an enrollment:		
	Under 25	187
	25–49	28
	50–74	22
	75–99	12
	100+	1

# of seminars		20
# of seminar positions available		400
# of seminar positions filled	243	34
# of positions available in simulation courses		1,636
# of simulation positions filled	926	196
# of positions available in faculty supervised clinical courses		216
# of faculty supervised clinical positions filled	80	13
# involved in field placements	138	4
# involved in law journals	104	14
# involved in interschool competitions	35	5
# of credit hours required to graduate		90

JD Enrollment and Ethnicity

	Men #	Men %	Women #	Women %	Full-time #	Full-time %	Part-time #	Part-time %	1st-year #	1st-year %	Total #	Total %	JD Degs. Awd.
African Amer.	12	2.6	30	6.4	25	3.4	17	9.3	7	2.1	42	4.5	15
Amer. Indian	1	0.2	2	0.4	2	0.3	1	0.5	1	0.3	3	0.3	0
Asian Amer.	10	2.2	15	3.2	23	3.1	2	1.1	7	2.1	25	2.7	6
Mex. Amer.	3	0.7	1	0.2	4	0.5	0	0.0	1	0.3	4	0.4	2
Puerto Rican	2	0.4	11	2.4	6	0.8	7	3.8	7	2.1	13	1.4	8
Hispanic	49	10.7	90	19.2	102	13.7	37	20.3	44	13.5	139	15.0	54
Total Minority	77	16.8	149	31.8	162	21.7	64	35.2	67	20.6	226	24.4	85
For. Nation.	10	2.2	11	2.4	20	2.7	1	0.5	7	2.1	21	2.3	5
Caucasian	338	73.6	276	59.0	512	68.7	102	56.0	212	65.0	614	66.2	170
Unknown	34	7.4	32	6.8	51	6.8	15	8.2	40	12.3	66	7.1	6
Total	459	49.5	468	50.5	745	80.4	182	19.6	326	35.2	927		266

Transfers

Transfers in	16
Transfers out	22

Tuition and Fees

	Resident	Nonresident
Full-time	$27,550	$27,550
Part-time	$20,788	$20,788

Living Expenses

Estimated living expenses for singles

Living on campus	Living off campus	Living at home
N/A	$18,796	$10,408

Nova Southeastern University—Shepard Broad Law Center

ABA Approved Since 1975

GPA and LSAT Scores

	Total	Full-time	Part-time
# of apps	2,821	2,456	365
# of offers	953	844	109
# of matrics	315	268	47
75% GPA	3.46	3.47	3.36
Median GPA	3.19	3.19	3.09
25% GPA	2.91	2.94	2.82
75% LSAT	153	153	152
Median LSAT	151	151	150
25% LSAT	148	149	148

Grants and Scholarships (from prior year)

	Total		Full-time		Part-time	
	#	%	#	%	#	%
Total # of students	943		744		199	
Total # receiving grants	58	6.2	49	6.6	9	4.5
Less than 1/2 tuition	12	1.3	9	1.2	3	1.5
Half to full tuition	2	0.2	1	0.1	1	0.5
Full tuition	42	4.5	37	5.0	5	2.5
More than full tuition	2	0.2	2	0.3	0	0.0
Median grant amount			$25,280		$18,496	

Informational and Library Resources

# of volumes and volume equivalents	364,376
# of titles	152,708
# of active serial subscriptions	5,475
Study seating capacity inside the library	532
# of full-time professional librarians	11
Hours per week library is open	104
# of open, wired connections available to students	0
# of networked computers available for use by students	30
# of simultaneous wireless users	1,500
Require computer?	Yes

JD Attrition (from prior year)

	Academic	Other	Total	
	#	#	#	%
1st year	41	31	72	21.8
2nd year	8	6	14	4.7
3rd year	2	1	3	1.1
4th year	0	0	0	0.0

Employment (9 months after graduation)

	Total	Percentage
Employment status known	271	97.1
Employment status unknown	8	2.9
Employed	219	80.8
Pursuing graduate degrees	10	3.7
Unemployed seeking employment	6	2.2
Unemployed not seeking employment	5	1.8
Unemployed and studying for the bar	31	11.4

Type of Employment

	Total	Percentage
# employed in law firms	134	61.2
# employed in business and industry	35	16.0
# employed in government	22	10.0
# employed in public interest	14	6.4
# employed as judicial clerks	7	3.2
# employed in academia	5	2.3

Geographic Location

	Total	Percentage
# employed in state	188	85.8
# employed in foreign countries	0	0.0
# of states where employed	11	

Bar Passage Rates

Jurisdiction	Florida		
Exam	Sum 05	Win 06	Total
# from school taking bar for the first time	209	39	248
School's pass rate for all first-time takers	65%	56%	64%
State's pass rate for all first-time takers	71%	73%	71%

Nova Southeastern University—Shepard Broad Law Center

3305 College Avenue
Fort Lauderdale, FL 33314-7721
Phone: 954.262.6117; Fax: 954.262.3844
E-mail: admission@nsu.law.nova.edu; Website: www.nsulaw.nova.edu

■ Introduction

NSU Law Center is one of 20 graduate and professional
schools of Nova Southeastern University, the largest private
independent university in Florida and the seventh largest in
the US. NSU Law is accredited by the ABA and is a member
of the AALS. The Law Center is located in the suburbs of
Fort Lauderdale, in the heart of South Florida's fast-growing
Broward, Miami-Dade, Palm Beach area. We encourage
applicants to tour the campus and speak with the staff of
the Admissions Office.

■ Two Admission Programs

The Law Center's Admissions Committee oversees two
separate programs. The Regular Admission Program combines
each applicant's undergraduate grades and LSAT score
according to a weighted formula based on the academic
success of NSU Law students. The committee also values the
applicant's personal statement, writing sample, work
experience, and letters of recommendation. While no single
factor is determinative, if the LSAT/UGPA combination does
not demonstrate the promise of academic achievement, an
applicant is unlikely to be offered regular admission.

Selected applicants who are denied regular admission will
be offered the opportunity to earn admission to the Law Center
by successful performance in NSU Law's unique Alternative
Admission Model Program for Legal Education (AAMPLE).
In 28 years of AAMPLE's operation, more than 1,000 students
have qualified for admission. AAMPLE students who enroll in
a six-week summer session and earn a C+ average in the two
courses are offered admission to the Law Center. AAMPLE is
presented in two formats, the traditional on-campus program
and a new and innovative online model.

Approximately one-third of our applicants are offered seats
through the Regular Admission Program. Another 15 percent
are invited to the AAMPLE Program. Applicants are
encouraged to review the charts that follow this narrative to
evaluate the likelihood of being admitted to the Law Center via
the Regular Admission or the AAMPLE Program. NSU Law's
two admission programs produce a diverse student body.
Recent classes are about evenly divided between men and
women, with approximately 25 percent of the class members of
minority groups. The average age of first-year day students is
24; of evening students, 30.

The Admissions Committee awards full-tuition scholarships
to approximately 6 percent of students admitted through the
Regular Admission Program on the basis of academic merit.

■ Faculty

NSU Law professors have a long tradition of teaching
excellence. The faculty's open-door policy is enhanced by our
sophisticated wireless communications system and pioneering
laptop program. Limits on the size of first-year sections result
in more individualized feedback. The faculty's expertise is
reflected in rich classroom discussion and a wide range of
scholarly publications and professional service activities.

■ Curriculum and Special Academic/Professional Programs

The Law Center offers a rigorous traditional academic program
in three-year day and four-year evening versions. NSU Law
prides itself on preparing graduates to make a smooth
transition from the classroom to the courtroom or boardroom.

Lawyering Skills and Values (LSV)—Every student
completes a four-semester LSV sequence that combines
traditional legal reasoning, writing, and research with an
introduction to lawyer interviewing, counseling, negotiating,
mediating, advocating, and other critical skills in a simulated
law firm experience.

Guaranteed Clinical Opportunity—NSU students are
guaranteed a clinical experience in their final year. In seven
clinical programs, students are introduced to a practice
specialty under the guidance of a seasoned mentor. Each
clinical semester begins with intensive classes that focus on
advanced substantive law and lawyering skills in the clinic
specialty plus interdisciplinary topics. For the rest of the term,
students are placed in practice settings where faculty supervise
their representation of clients. Students are placed in Law
Center Clinics or in public and private law offices throughout
Florida, across the country, or around the world.

Dual Law Degree Opportunities—NSU Law students can
earn a civil law degree from the University of Barcelona in
accelerated study programs. NSU students who complete the
University of Barcelona program can qualify to practice in the
US and Spain. Other opportunities are being planned.

Joint Degrees—NSU Law offers students opportunities to
earn a second graduate degree in a complementary discipline
and in a compressed time frame.

Internship—In addition to an award-winning pro
bono service program, the Law Center operates judicial
internship, mediation, street law, consumer protection, and
dependency workshop programs that provide valuable
real-world experiences.

■ Library and Physical Facilities

The Law Center's spacious, modern building includes
state-of-the-art information technology. The first law school
facility with a wireless technology system and an early
advocate of mandatory laptops for all students, NSU Law
leads the way in the use of computers in legal education. While
most classrooms have power at each desk, the latest long-life
batteries permit all students to connect with classmates,
professors, the library, and the Internet from any point in
the building.

The Law Library's extensive holdings include special
collections in tax, criminal law, law and popular culture,
admiralty, and international law. The library is a depository for
state, federal, and United Nations documents.

Goodwin Hall, the Law Center's building, has two
courtrooms used by students in our trial advocacy and moot
court program, by the National Institute for Trial Advocacy,
and by state appellate court judges.

■ Student Activities

The Law Center is home to three significant publications: the *Nova Law Review*, the *Journal of International and Comparative Law*, and the *International Citator and Research Project*.

The Moot Court Society sponsors intramural competitions. Members of the society compete in major national events. ATLA and other student advocacy groups field teams in competitions around the country.

Students shape the life of the Law Center by their involvement in a wide range of service organizations and social clubs. Groups such as the Asian Pacific American Law Students Association, Black Law Students Association, Jewish Law Students Association, Hispanic Law Student Association, Lambda, Student Bar Association, Florida Association for Women Lawyers, National Association for Public Interest Law, International Law Society, and a variety of practice specialty and sports clubs are extremely active. Students also guide chapters of national legal fraternities, participate with lawyers and judges in the Inns of Court, and serve on faculty committees.

■ Career Services

Our Career Development Office assists students and alumni with career counseling and the employment process. In addition to facilitating on-campus interviews and résumé distributions, the director coordinates career-option seminars and interviewing workshops. The office also sponsors skill courses and assists students in finding pro bono experiences with law firms and legal agencies throughout the country.

Applicant Profile

Nova Southeastern University—Shepard Broad Law Center

LSAT Score	GPA								
	3.75 +	3.50–3.74	3.25–3.49	3.00–3.24	2.75–2.99	2.50–2.74	2.25–2.49	2.00–2.24	Below 2.00
165–180									
160–164									
155–159									
150–154									
145–149									
140–144									
135–139									
130–134									
Below 130									

■ Good Possibility   □ Possible   ■ Unlikely

Please use this chart as a general guide in determining admission chances for the Regular Admission Program. Nonnumerical factors are also considered during the file-evaluation process.

AAMPLE®

Enrolled/Successful

LSAT Score	GPA								
	3.75 +	3.50–3.74	3.25–3.49	3.00–3.24	2.75–2.99	2.50–2.74	2.25–2.49	2.00–2.24	Below 2.00
150–159						3/0	1/0	2/2	
145–149	3/1	4/4	15/9	16/10	12/6	5/2	6/2		
140–144	3/3	6/3	12/6	7/1	8/4	7/0	1/0	2/0	
135–139			2/0	1/0	2/0		1/0	2/0	
130–134		1/0	1/0						

Please use this chart to determine the possibility of being admitted through AAMPLE® (Alternative Admission Model Program for Legal Education). The chart reflects admission data for the summer 2006 on-campus AAMPLE class and a portion of the online AAMPLE class. The traditional indicators (LSAT and GPA) are not identified for the online AAMPLE students who were referred to NSU Law by the LSAC. Overall, there were 76 students enrolled online and 17 were successful in 2006.

Ohio Northern University—Claude W. Pettit College of Law

525 South Main Street
Ada, OH 45810
Phone: 877.452.9668, 419.772.2211; Fax: 419.772.3042
E-mail: law-admissions@onu.edu; Website: www.law.onu.edu

ABA
Approved
Since
1948

The Basics

Type of school	Private
Term	Semester
Application deadline	
Application fee	$40
Financial aid deadline	6/1
Can first year start other than fall?	No
Student to faculty ratio	12.6 to 1
Does the university offer:	
housing restricted to law students?	Yes
graduate housing for which law students are eligible?	Yes

Faculty and Administrators

	Total		Men		Women		Minorities	
	Fall	Spr	Fall	Spr	Fall	Spr	Fall	Spr
Full-time	21	20	14	13	7	7	2	2
Other Full-time	0	0	0	0	0	0	0	0
Deans, librarians, & others who teach	6	6	4	4	2	2	0	0
Part-time	6	7	5	5	1	2	0	0
Total	**33**	**33**	**23**	**22**	**10**	**11**	**2**	**2**

Curriculum

	Full-time	Part-time
Typical first-year section size	65	0
Is there typically a "small section" of the first-year class, other than Legal Writing, taught by full-time faculty	No	No
If yes, typical size offered last year		
# of classroom course titles beyond first-year curriculum	58	
# of upper division courses, excluding seminars with an enrollment: Under 25	45	
25–49	17	
50–74	8	
75–99	3	
100+	0	
# of seminars	7	
# of seminar positions available	84	
# of seminar positions filled	83	0
# of positions available in simulation courses	88	
# of simulation positions filled	87	0
# of positions available in faculty supervised clinical courses	45	
# of faculty supervised clinical positions filled	31	0
# involved in field placements	75	0
# involved in law journals	38	0
# involved in interschool competitions	29	0
# of credit hours required to graduate	88	

JD Enrollment and Ethnicity

	Men		Women		Full-time		Part-time		1st-year		Total		JD Degs. Awd.
	#	%	#	%	#	%	#	%	#	%	#	%	
African Amer.	9	5.5	10	6.8	19	6.1	0	0.0	7	5.8	19	6.1	7
Amer. Indian	0	0.0	1	0.7	1	0.3	0	0.0	0	0.0	1	0.3	1
Asian Amer.	4	2.4	4	2.7	8	2.6	0	0.0	3	2.5	8	2.6	3
Mex. Amer.	0	0.0	0	0.0	0	0.0	0	0.0	0	0.0	0	0.0	0
Puerto Rican	0	0.0	0	0.0	0	0.0	0	0.0	0	0.0	0	0.0	0
Hispanic	2	1.2	1	0.7	3	1.0	0	0.0	2	1.7	3	1.0	3
Total Minority	15	9.1	16	11.0	31	10.0	0	0.0	12	10.0	31	10.0	14
For. Nation.	0	0.0	0	0.0	0	0.0	0	0.0	0	0.0	0	0.0	0
Caucasian	144	87.3	127	87.0	271	87.1	0	0.0	100	83.3	271	87.1	98
Unknown	6	3.6	3	2.1	9	2.9	0	0.0	8	6.7	9	2.9	0
Total	165	53.1	146	46.9	311	100.0	0	0.0	120	38.6	311		112

Transfers

Transfers in	0
Transfers out	14

Tuition and Fees

	Resident	Nonresident
Full-time	$25,050	$25,050
Part-time	$0	$0

Living Expenses

Estimated living expenses for singles

Living on campus	Living off campus	Living at home
$11,237	$12,137	$12,137

Ohio Northern University—Claude W. Pettit College of Law

ABA
Approved
Since
1948

GPA and LSAT Scores

	Total	Full-time	Part-time
# of apps	1,424	1,424	0
# of offers	472	472	0
# of matrics	120	120	0
75% GPA	3.65	3.65	0.00
Median GPA	3.35	3.35	0.00
25% GPA	3.09	3.09	0.00
75% LSAT	155	155	0
Median LSAT	152	152	0
25% LSAT	150	150	0

Grants and Scholarships (from prior year)

	Total		Full-time		Part-time	
	#	%	#	%	#	%
Total # of students	324		324		0	
Total # receiving grants	178	54.9	178	54.9	0	0.0
Less than 1/2 tuition	49	15.1	49	15.1	0	0.0
Half to full tuition	122	37.7	122	37.7	0	0.0
Full tuition	7	2.2	7	2.2	0	0.0
More than full tuition	0	0.0	0	0.0	0	0.0
Median grant amount			$15,000		$0	

Informational and Library Resources

# of volumes and volume equivalents	401,273
# of titles	130,929
# of active serial subscriptions	2,269
Study seating capacity inside the library	318
# of full-time professional librarians	4
Hours per week library is open	113
# of open, wired connections available to students	223
# of networked computers available for use by students	81
# of simultaneous wireless users	800
Require computer?	No

JD Attrition (from prior year)

	Academic	Other	Total	
	#	#	#	%
1st year	4	18	22	19.0
2nd year	1	1	2	2.1
3rd year	0	0	0	0.0
4th year	0	0	0	0.0

Employment (9 months after graduation)

	Total	Percentage
Employment status known	78	94.0
Employment status unknown	5	6.0
Employed	63	80.8
Pursuing graduate degrees	4	5.1
Unemployed seeking employment	1	1.3
Unemployed not seeking employment	0	0.0
Unemployed and studying for the bar	10	12.8

Type of Employment

# employed in law firms	29	46.0
# employed in business and industry	6	9.5
# employed in government	13	20.6
# employed in public interest	0	0.0
# employed as judicial clerks	5	7.9
# employed in academia	0	0.0

Geographic Location

# employed in state	21	33.3
# employed in foreign countries	0	0.0
# of states where employed		18

Bar Passage Rates

Jurisdiction	Ohio			Florida		
Exam	Sum 05	Win 06	Total	Sum 05	Win 06	Total
# from school taking bar for the first time	25	6	31	7	0	7
School's pass rate for all first-time takers	84%	83%	84%	86%		86%
State's pass rate for all first-time takers	81%	76%	81%	71%	73%	71%

Ohio Northern University—Claude W. Pettit College of Law

525 South Main Street
Ada, OH 45810
Phone: 877.452.9668, 419.772.2211; Fax: 419.772.3042
E-mail: law-admissions@onu.edu; Website: www.law.onu.edu

■ Introduction

Men and women have been studying law at Ohio Northern University for well over a century. Since 1885, generations of law students have found the Claude W. Pettit College of Law the ideal place to begin remarkable careers in private practice, public service, business, and industry.

Located in the heart of Ohio, the college sits on a beautiful campus with facilities that reflect well over a century of investment. The college offers its students opportunities to study law in small classes, seminars, clinical programs, law offices, and judges' chambers.

■ Faculty and Students

The faculty of the College of Law strives for excellence in both teaching and scholarship. All faculty members have practiced law, bringing a wealth of practical experience gained from law firms, corporate law departments, and government to the classroom. The faculty also maintains a high level of scholarly productivity and professional service.

Small classes and personalized attention are the hallmarks of the college. First-year classes are generally limited to 60 or fewer students. Enrollment in upper-division classes and seminars is often much smaller. The faculty prides itself on offering a student-centered education. Members of the faculty meet regularly with students outside the classroom.

The students of the college bring remarkably diverse backgrounds and interests to the study of law. The college draws students from across the nation and the world. Students from virtually every state in the union have entered the college. The law students currently enrolled in the college have degrees from more than 200 undergraduate colleges and universities.

■ The College and the University

The Claude W. Pettit College of Law is accredited by the American Bar Association and is a member of the Association of American Law Schools. The college is centered in newly renovated Tilton Hall, a modern building that houses all law classes and the Taggart Law Library. Recent additions to this building include a second trial courtroom, a state-of-the-art technology classroom, skylit student lounges, and a faculty office wing where students are always welcome.

The Taggart Law Library, a federal government depository, is devoted to the research needs of the students and faculty of the law college. The current collection numbers 401,273 volumes. The library has computer and communication facilities that are second to none and an extensive collection of books and periodicals acquired over decades. The reading rooms of the library offer ideal locations for both quiet and group study.

The College of Law lies at the center of the tree-lined campus. The university's facilities are readily available to all law students and are located only steps away from the law building. These facilities include hiking and biking trails, a sports center, and the Freed Center for the Performing Arts. Law students may bowl, swim, and play handball, racquet sports, and basketball all year-round in indoor and outdoor facilities. The sports center houses a wide variety of modern fitness machines and one of the best indoor tracks in the Midwest. The Freed Center brings the very best in the performing arts to the campus.

■ The Curriculum and Special Programs

Students may choose from more than 70 elective courses, including advanced courses and seminars. In addition, the College of Law offers many opportunities for experiential learning through its clinical education program. The clinical experiences available to Ohio Northern students include externships in environmental law, bankruptcy, and government. Students can also counsel nonprofit corporations in the transactional clinic. Legal aid clinics that focus on the concerns of the economically disadvantaged and elderly are offered at offices in nearby Lima and Findlay. Finally, students can also participate in criminal and judicial externships with judges, legal aid societies, public defenders' offices, and prosecutors' offices.

The College of Law shares a student exchange program with the law school at the University of Iceland. Participating students travel to Iceland to experience its culture and legal system.

The College of Law has an academic support program to assist all students in attaining their full academic potential.

Throughout the academic year, the college hosts speakers and symposia on contemporary legal issues. Topics treated recently include capital punishment, affirmative action, and the revolution in federal and state relations.

The College of Law offers a Summer Starter Program for a small number of selected students. These individuals begin taking first-year law courses the summer prior to the regular school year and receive academic support on a weekly basis. In the fall, summer starters take the remaining first-year courses not completed during the summer.

■ Student Activities

Students can choose from a variety of extracurricular activities. The College of Law publishes the *Ohio Northern University Law Review*, a student-edited commentary on legal issues whose excellence has been recognized by the Ohio Supreme Court.

Intraschool, regional, and national moot court competitions are open to all students. Ohio Northern students participate in at least 10 national and regional moot court competitions each year.

Through the Student Bar Association, students participate in a variety of extracurricular activities such as the environmental law and international law societies. Students volunteer their services through the Street Law and Volunteer Income Tax Assistance Programs.

■ Admission and Financial Aid

While Ohio Northern gives significant weight to the LSAT and undergraduate GPA, the Admissions Committee may consider other factors such as candidates' undergraduate programs, grade trends, completion of other graduate degrees, professional accomplishments, and socioeconomic or cultural barriers faced by the applicant. Although letters of recommendation are not required, letters from persons who

Ohio Northern University—Claude W. Pettit College of Law

have a basis to assess the candidate's intellectual ability and potential for success in law school, such as former professors or employers, are strongly recommended.

Ohio Northern University is committed to a culturally and socially diverse student body. Applications from women and minorities are strongly encouraged. In order to foster diversity in the student body and the legal profession, the university awards grants-in-aid to eligible students.

The College of Law also provides scholarship awards for students whose undergraduate records demonstrate academic excellence. The scholarship amounts range from $5,000 to $25,000 and are renewable provided the student remains in good academic standing. Additionally, substantial scholarships are awarded to students who excel in their first year of law school.

The facilities of the College of Law are accessible to students with physical disabilities.

■ Student Services and Housing

The staff of the College of Law takes pride in the quality of its student services. The size of the college permits these services to be tailored to the individual needs of each student. Through individualized counseling, students and graduates obtain valuable guidance in obtaining summer jobs and permanent positions. The Office of Career Strategies assists in the application and interviewing processes; provides current listings of positions in law firms, governmental agencies, and corporations; and hosts many on-campus interviews.

Housing is generally available to law students in the university's apartments. Most law students live off-campus. Listings of available apartments can be obtained from the admission office. Visit the Pettit College of Law website at *www.law.onu.edu*. Better still, call the admission office to arrange a campus tour at 877.452.9668.

Applicant Profile

Ohio Northern University—Claude W. Pettit College of Law
This grid includes only applicants who earned 120–180 LSAT scores under standard administrations.

LSAT Score	GPA								
	3.75 +	3.50–3.74	3.25–3.49	3.00–3.24	2.75–2.99	2.50–2.74	2.25–2.49	2.00–2.24	Below 2.00
175–180									
170–174									
165–169									
160–164									
155–159									
150–154									
145–149									
140–144									
135–139									
130–134									
125–129									
120–124									

■ Good Possibility   □ Possible   ▨ Unlikely

The Ohio State University Moritz College of Law

John Deaver Drinko Hall, 55 West 12th Avenue
Columbus, OH 43210-1391
Phone: 614.292.8810; Fax: 614.292.1492
E-mail: lawadmit@osu.edu; Website: www.moritzlaw.osu.edu

ABA
Approved
Since
1923

The Basics

Type of school	Public
Term	Semester
Application deadline	3/1
Application fee	$60
Financial aid deadline	3/1
Can first year start other than fall?	No
Student to faculty ratio	14.1 to 1
Does the university offer:	
housing restricted to law students?	No
graduate housing for which law students are eligible?	Yes

Faculty and Administrators

	Total		Men		Women		Minorities	
	Fall	Spr	Fall	Spr	Fall	Spr	Fall	Spr
Full-time	44	39	28	26	16	13	6	6
Other Full-time	2	1	2	1	0	0	0	0
Deans, librarians, & others who teach	14	15	7	6	7	9	5	6
Part-time	16	26	16	21	0	5	2	3
Total	**76**	**81**	**53**	**54**	**23**	**27**	**13**	**15**

Curriculum

	Full-time	Part-time
Typical first-year section size	70	0
Is there typically a "small section" of the first-year class, other than Legal Writing, taught by full-time faculty	Yes	No
If yes, typical size offered last year	40	
# of classroom course titles beyond first-year curriculum	109	

# of upper division courses, excluding seminars with an enrollment:		
	Under 25	47
	25–49	35
	50–74	25
	75–99	3
	100+	3

# of seminars	24	
# of seminar positions available	480	
# of seminar positions filled	300	0
# of positions available in simulation courses	112	
# of simulation positions filled	106	0
# of positions available in faculty supervised clinical courses	160	
# of faculty supervised clinical positions filled	145	0
# involved in field placements	42	0
# involved in law journals	206	0
# involved in interschool competitions	63	0
# of credit hours required to graduate	88	

JD Enrollment and Ethnicity

	Men		Women		Full-time		Part-time		1st-year		Total		JD Degs. Awd.
	#	%	#	%	#	%	#	%	#	%	#	%	
African Amer.	24	6.1	33	11.2	57	8.3	0	0.0	19	8.3	57	8.3	22
Amer. Indian	3	0.8	3	1.0	6	0.9	0	0.0	3	1.3	6	0.9	0
Asian Amer.	34	8.6	32	10.9	66	9.6	0	0.0	18	7.8	66	9.6	23
Mex. Amer.	6	1.5	5	1.7	11	1.6	0	0.0	5	2.2	11	1.6	0
Puerto Rican	1	0.3	1	0.3	2	0.3	0	0.0	1	0.4	2	0.3	2
Hispanic	9	2.3	9	3.1	18	2.6	0	0.0	7	3.0	18	2.6	5
Total Minority	77	19.5	83	28.2	160	23.3	0	0.0	53	23.0	160	23.3	52
For. Nation.	12	3.0	3	1.0	15	2.2	0	0.0	6	2.6	15	2.2	6
Caucasian	293	74.4	202	68.7	495	71.9	0	0.0	153	66.5	495	71.9	210
Unknown	12	3.0	6	2.0	18	2.6	0	0.0	18	7.8	18	2.6	0
Total	394	57.3	294	42.7	688	100.0	0	0.0	230	33.4	688		268

Transfers

Transfers in	7
Transfers out	9

Tuition and Fees

	Resident	Nonresident
Full-time	$17,551	$31,969
Part-time	$0	$0

Living Expenses

Estimated living expenses for singles

Living on campus	Living off campus	Living at home
$16,694	$16,694	$16,694

The Ohio State University Moritz College of Law

*ABA
Approved
Since
1923*

GPA and LSAT Scores

	Total	Full-time	Part-time
# of apps	2,289	2,289	0
# of offers	653	653	0
# of matrics	232	232	0
75% GPA	3.79	3.79	0.00
Median GPA	3.61	3.61	0.00
25% GPA	3.36	3.36	0.00
75% LSAT	163	163	0
Median LSAT	161	161	0
25% LSAT	158	158	0

Grants and Scholarships (from prior year)

	Total		Full-time		Part-time	
	#	%	#	%	#	%
Total # of students	723		723		0	
Total # receiving grants	564	78.0	564	78.0	0	0.0
Less than 1/2 tuition	485	67.1	485	67.1	0	0.0
Half to full tuition	49	6.8	49	6.8	0	0.0
Full tuition	1	0.1	1	0.1	0	0.0
More than full tuition	29	4.0	29	4.0	0	0.0
Median grant amount			$4,000		$0	

Informational and Library Resources

# of volumes and volume equivalents	802,748
# of titles	181,142
# of active serial subscriptions	7,750
Study seating capacity inside the library	689
# of full-time professional librarians	8
Hours per week library is open	107
# of open, wired connections available to students	0
# of networked computers available for use by students	93
# of simultaneous wireless users	512
Require computer?	No

JD Attrition (from prior year)

	Academic	Other	Total	
	#	#	#	%
1st year	0	0	0	0.0
2nd year	0	16	16	6.8
3rd year	0	0	0	0.0
4th year	0	0	0	0.0

Employment (9 months after graduation)

	Total	Percentage
Employment status known	225	99.1
Employment status unknown	2	0.9
Employed	215	95.6
Pursuing graduate degrees	6	2.7
Unemployed seeking employment	1	0.4
Unemployed not seeking employment	3	1.3
Unemployed and studying for the bar	0	0.0
Type of Employment		
# employed in law firms	106	49.3
# employed in business and industry	26	12.1
# employed in government	46	21.4
# employed in public interest	14	6.5
# employed as judicial clerks	11	5.1
# employed in academia	12	5.6
Geographic Location		
# employed in state	147	68.4
# employed in foreign countries	0	0.0
# of states where employed	21	

Bar Passage Rates

Jurisdiction	Ohio		
Exam	Sum 05	Win 06	Total
# from school taking bar for the first time	152	13	165
School's pass rate for all first-time takers	90%	85%	90%
State's pass rate for all first-time takers	81%	76%	81%

The Ohio State University Moritz College of Law

John Deaver Drinko Hall, 55 West 12th Avenue
Columbus, OH 43210-1391
Phone: 614.292.8810; Fax: 614.292.1492
E-mail: lawadmit@osu.edu; Website: www.moritzlaw.osu.edu

■ Introduction

Founded in 1891, the Ohio State University Moritz College of Law has played a leading role in the legal profession through countless contributions made by graduates and faculty. The administration of the College of Law is committed to advancing the quality and reputation of the college through ongoing improvements to the academic program and student services, thereby creating a learning environment second to none.

Ohio State's 9,100 law alumni are central to the college's national reputation. Graduates of the college include justices of the Ohio Supreme Court, current and former US senators and representatives, managing partners in law firms, chief executive officers, professors, and attorneys with nonprofit organizations and public interest law firms.

The comprehensive scope of the university and its location in the state capital provide law students with access to a wealth of educational, professional, cultural, and recreational resources and opportunities. Law students are able to pursue joint degrees with one of the university's more than 100 graduate programs and also may extern with federal and state judges or find employment with one of the more than 500 law firms located in central Ohio.

■ Academic Program

With approximately 135 classes offered annually, Ohio State students have a rich array of courses from which to choose. The curriculum is designed to provide a strong theoretical and analytical foundation, as well as multiple opportunities for developing and honing lawyering skills.

Alternative Dispute Resolution—The College of Law is widely regarded as having one of the nation's finest programs in the area of Alternative Dispute Resolution. The program emphasizes training in an array of dispute resolution methods beyond litigation, including negotiation, mediation, and arbitration. Students with an especially strong interest may want to serve as a member or editor of the *Ohio State Journal on Dispute Resolution* or pursue a certificate in Dispute Resolution.

Clinical Opportunities—The College of Law offers an extensive selection of clinics in civil, criminal, children's issues, housing, mediation, and legislation. Students enrolled in a clinic course receive the benefit of working with real clients, the court, or other parties while receiving intensive feedback and supervision from one of the college's 15 clinical faculty. The fieldwork component of each clinic course is augmented by a classroom component in which topics such as lawyering skills, legal doctrine, and ethical and strategic issues are addressed.

Judicial Externship Program—Ohio State law students have the opportunity to gain first-hand insight into the judicial system through the college's Judicial Externship Program. As externs, students earn academic credit for conducting legal research and drafting legal documents for justices of the Ohio Supreme Court and for judges at the federal and county levels.

A Global Perspective on the Law—Students with an interest in international law may select from a menu of approximately 16 courses that have an international law or comparative law focus, including a semester-long and summer study-abroad program in Oxford, England. The College of Law awards a Certificate in International Trade and Development to students who combine their law coursework with select courses in international economics, politics, history, culture, and foreign language.

■ Faculty

One of the most frequently cited strengths of the College of Law is the quality of the faculty. Faculty members consistently are recognized for the experiences they bring to the classroom, for the clarity of their teaching, and for their accessibility to students outside of the classroom. As a group, they are highly regarded for being committed teachers who care about students. Members of the Ohio State law faculty also have earned a reputation within the profession for their expertise in specific areas of the law. Faculty are regularly cited in court and in the national media; they serve on legal reform commissions, help draft model statutes, and provide testimony before Congress.

■ Moritz Law Library

The Moritz Law Library provides Ohio State law students with the 14th largest collection among law school libraries in the nation and access to a vast array of electronic databases. Law students with a laptop and network card can tap into online resources from virtually any point within the Moritz Law Library or the law building. All classrooms are wired for use of laptop computers.

■ Extracurricular Opportunities

Learning Outside of the Classroom—Recognizing that a student's legal education rests upon what occurs in the classroom as well as the intellectual interchange and professional development outside of the classroom, the College of Law strives to provide an environment that is rich with extracurricular and cocurricular opportunities. Each year, the college brings to campus more than 100 speakers to address students, law faculty, and members of the bar.

Ohio State law students have the opportunity to refine their legal writing skills through participation in one of the college's five highly regarded law journals: the *Ohio State Law Journal*, the *Ohio State Journal on Dispute Resolution*, the *Ohio State Journal of Criminal Law*, the *I/S: A Journal of Law and Policy for the Information Society*, and the *Entrepreneurial Business Law Journal*. Students are able to refine their skills in the areas of oral advocacy and legal writing through a variety of intramural and interscholastic competitions. In recent years, Ohio State law students have competed in the National Moot Court Competition, the Jessup International Law Moot Court Competition, the Frederick Douglass Moot Court Competition, the National Health Law Moot Court Competition, the National Environmental Law Moot Court Competition, and the National Tax Moot Court Competition.

Service to the Public—The College of Law enjoys a strong reputation for its commitment to public service as part of the educational mission of the college. Ohio State law students are encouraged to become involved in the Leadership Program or in one or more of the college's many public interest initiatives, such as the Pro Bono Research Group. To encourage Ohio State law students to accept low-paying or volunteer positions with public interest organizations during the summer, the college and the Public Interest Law Foundation annually offer several student-funded fellowships.

■ Placement Opportunities

Moritz College of Law students and graduates are provided with an array of career and professional development services by a staff of six full- and part-time professionals, one of whom has a JD. Students and alumni have access to an Internet-based online job posting system and a wide variety of programs, workshops, and events. All programming and counseling services are designed to teach skills and to provide a foundation for gaining legal and professional career experience. The on-campus recruiting program, which brings over 120 employers to campus to interview students annually, is conducted through a state-of-the-art web-based recruiting system that allows students access at all hours. Alumni and practitioners interact with students through many avenues, including a practice interview program and a mentoring database. Each year, students find employment across the country. Cutting edge technology, current resources, talented staff, and creative initiatives give College of Law students a sound professional development foundation.

■ Admission and Financial Aid

The Moritz College of Law is committed to enrolling highly motivated men and women who have excelled academically and who bring to the College of Law a diversity of personal and professional backgrounds. In selecting members of each entering class, the Admissions Committee seeks to enroll men and women who represent all segments of society, as well as those who, as attorneys, will respect the profession's public service obligations.

An Ohio State legal education is among the best values among nationally regarded law schools. The annual cost of tuition for residents of Ohio is below half the tuition charged by comparably ranked private law schools. Nonresidents of Ohio who relocate to the state may be reclassified as Ohio residents after residing in the state for 12 months. Each year, the College of Law awards more than $2.5 million in need-based and merit-based financial aid to members of the student body.

Applicant Profile

The Ohio State University Moritz College of Law
This grid includes only applicants who earned 120–180 LSAT scores under standard administrations.

LSAT Score	3.75 +		3.50–3.74		3.25–3.49		3.00–3.24		2.75–2.99		2.50–2.74		2.25–2.49		2.00–2.24		Below 2.00		No GPA		Total	
	Apps	Adm	Apps	Adm	Apps	Adm	Apps	Adm	Apps	Adm	Apps	Adm	Apps	Adm	Apps	Adm	Apps	Adm	Apps	Adm	Apps	Adm
175–180	0	0	2	2	2	2	0	0	1	1	0	0	0	0	0	0	0	0	0	0	5	5
170–174	9	9	6	6	4	4	2	2	1	0	1	0	0	0	0	0	0	0	0	0	23	21
165–169	48	47	52	50	30	28	23	19	8	6	8	3	1	0	1	0	0	0	3	3	174	156
160–164	116	104	113	90	89	54	72	29	23	0	12	1	5	0	2	0	0	0	3	1	435	279
155–159	154	45	205	46	183	8	101	3	45	2	18	0	12	0	0	0	0	0	6	1	724	105
150–154	92	11	134	16	139	16	82	5	49	2	19	0	8	0	1	0	1	0	7	1	532	51
145–149	26	3	49	3	53	6	51	4	23	0	10	0	2	0	3	0	0	0	2	0	219	16
140–144	11	3	23	2	32	3	27	1	12	0	15	0	4	0	0	0	0	0	3	0	127	9
135–139	1	0	1	0	2	0	6	0	4	0	3	0	3	0	2	0	0	0	1	0	23	0
130–134	2	0	1	0	1	0	3	0	2	0	2	0	1	0	0	0	0	0	0	0	12	0
125–129	0	0	0	0	0	0	1	0	0	0	1	0	0	0	1	0	1	0	0	0	4	0
120–124	0	0	0	0	0	0	0	0	0	0	0	0	0	0	0	0	0	0	0	0	0	0
Total	459	222	586	215	535	121	368	63	168	11	89	4	36	0	10	0	2	0	25	6	2278	642

Apps = Number of Applicants
Adm = Number Admitted
Reflects 99% of total applicant pool.

University of Oklahoma College of Law

Andrew M. Coats Hall, 300 Timberdell Road
Norman, OK 73019
Phone: 405.325.4726; Fax: 405.325.0502
E-mail: law-admissions@ou.edu; Website: www.law.ou.edu

ABA Approved Since 1923

The Basics

Type of school	Public
Term	Semester
Application deadline	3/15
Application fee	$50
Financial aid deadline	3/1
Can first year start other than fall?	No
Student to faculty ratio	11.8 to 1
Does the university offer:	
housing restricted to law students?	No
graduate housing for which law students are eligible?	Yes

Faculty and Administrators

	Total		Men		Women		Minorities	
	Fall	Spr	Fall	Spr	Fall	Spr	Fall	Spr
Full-time	36	37	21	22	15	15	6	5
Other Full-time	1	2	0	1	1	1	0	0
Deans, librarians, & others who teach	7	8	6	6	1	2	0	1
Part-time	11	17	9	11	2	6	0	0
Total	55	64	36	40	19	24	6	6

Curriculum

	Full-time	Part-time
Typical first-year section size	43	0
Is there typically a "small section" of the first-year class, other than Legal Writing, taught by full-time faculty	Yes	No
If yes, typical size offered last year	43	
# of classroom course titles beyond first-year curriculum		100

# of upper division courses, excluding seminars with an enrollment:		
	Under 25	48
	25–49	33
	50–74	16
	75–99	3
	100+	0

	Full-time	Part-time
# of seminars		15
# of seminar positions available		248
# of seminar positions filled	223	0
# of positions available in simulation courses		278
# of simulation positions filled	274	0
# of positions available in faculty supervised clinical courses		35
# of faculty supervised clinical positions filled	27	0
# involved in field placements	16	0
# involved in law journals	131	0
# involved in interschool competitions	78	0
# of credit hours required to graduate		90

JD Enrollment and Ethnicity

	Men		Women		Full-time		Part-time		1st-year		Total		JD Degs. Awd.
	#	%	#	%	#	%	#	%	#	%	#	%	
African Amer.	16	5.8	12	5.4	28	5.6	0	0.0	7	4.5	28	5.6	6
Amer. Indian	22	7.9	30	13.4	52	10.4	0	0.0	13	8.4	52	10.4	13
Asian Amer.	13	4.7	9	4.0	22	4.4	0	0.0	9	5.8	22	4.4	1
Mex. Amer.	8	2.9	11	4.9	19	3.8	0	0.0	6	3.9	19	3.8	4
Puerto Rican	0	0.0	0	0.0	0	0.0	0	0.0	0	0.0	0	0.0	0
Hispanic	1	0.4	0	0.0	1	0.2	0	0.0	0	0.0	1	0.2	0
Total Minority	60	21.7	62	27.7	122	24.4	0	0.0	35	22.6	122	24.4	24
For. Nation.	0	0.0	0	0.0	0	0.0	0	0.0	0	0.0	0	0.0	1
Caucasian	200	72.2	148	66.1	348	69.5	0	0.0	115	74.2	348	69.5	128
Unknown	17	6.1	14	6.3	31	6.2	0	0.0	5	3.2	31	6.2	11
Total	277	55.3	224	44.7	501	100.0	0	0.0	155	30.9	501		164

Transfers

Transfers in	6
Transfers out	5

Tuition and Fees

	Resident	Nonresident
Full-time	$13,564	$23,493
Part-time	$0	$0

Living Expenses

Estimated living expenses for singles

Living on campus	Living off campus	Living at home
$13,751	$15,185	$10,199

University of Oklahoma College of Law

*ABA
Approved
Since
1923*

GPA and LSAT Scores

	Total	Full-time	Part-time
# of apps	1,055	1,055	0
# of offers	341	341	0
# of matrics	164	164	0
75% GPA	3.76	3.76	0.00
Median GPA	3.57	3.57	0.00
25% GPA	3.36	3.36	0.00
75% LSAT	160	160	0
Median LSAT	157	157	0
25% LSAT	154	154	0

Grants and Scholarships (from prior year)

	Total #	Total %	Full-time #	Full-time %	Part-time #	Part-time %
Total # of students	516		516		0	
Total # receiving grants	326	63.2	326	63.2	0	0.0
Less than 1/2 tuition	238	46.1	238	46.1	0	0.0
Half to full tuition	80	15.5	80	15.5	0	0.0
Full tuition	0	0.0	0	0.0	0	0.0
More than full tuition	8	1.6	8	1.6	0	0.0
Median grant amount			$2,500		$0	

Informational and Library Resources

# of volumes and volume equivalents	350,540
# of titles	153,535
# of active serial subscriptions	5,121
Study seating capacity inside the library	409
# of full-time professional librarians	7
Hours per week library is open	96
# of open, wired connections available to students	107
# of networked computers available for use by students	111
# of simultaneous wireless users	600
Require computer?	No

JD Attrition (from prior year)

	Academic #	Other #	Total #	Total %
1st year	2	10	12	7.0
2nd year	0	2	2	1.1
3rd year	0	1	1	0.6
4th year	0	0	0	0.0

Employment (9 months after graduation)

	Total	Percentage
Employment status known	172	99.4
Employment status unknown	1	0.6
Employed	158	91.9
Pursuing graduate degrees	4	2.3
Unemployed seeking employment	0	0.0
Unemployed not seeking employment	3	1.7
Unemployed and studying for the bar	7	4.1
Type of Employment		
# employed in law firms	107	67.7
# employed in business and industry	12	7.6
# employed in government	30	19.0
# employed in public interest	4	2.5
# employed as judicial clerks	4	2.5
# employed in academia	1	0.6
Geographic Location		
# employed in state	111	70.3
# employed in foreign countries	1	0.6
# of states where employed	19	

Bar Passage Rates

Jurisdiction	Oklahoma		
Exam	Sum 05	Win 06	Total
# from school taking bar for the first time	126	15	141
School's pass rate for all first-time takers	97%	100%	97%
State's pass rate for all first-time takers	91%	88%	90%

University of Oklahoma College of Law

Andrew M. Coats Hall, 300 Timberdell Road
Norman, OK 73019
Phone: 405.325.4726; Fax: 405.325.0502
E-mail: law-admissions@ou.edu; Website: www.law.ou.edu

■ Introduction

The University of Oklahoma College of Law is located on the main campus of the university in Norman, a city of approximately 100,000 adjacent to the Oklahoma City metropolitan area. The college was founded in 1909 and joined the membership of the Association of American Law Schools in 1911. The law school has been accredited by the American Bar Association's Section on Legal Education since that list was first published in 1923.

The College of Law is housed in beautiful Andrew M. Coats Hall, located on the south part of the university campus. A substantial addition to the existing building was completed in 2002. It has the largest law library in Oklahoma and houses three courtrooms for training and enrichment purposes. The entering classes are limited to 175 students so that the first-year sections consist of not more than 45 students. Admission is very competitive. More than 90 percent of the students admitted will graduate. More than 90 percent will pass the bar exam on their first try, and more than 90 percent will have employment using their legal skills within three months of graduation.

The College of Law benefits from being part of a strong university community. The University of Oklahoma, the state's flagship university, is a major doctoral degree-granting research university. Founded in 1890, the university has 18 colleges.

■ Admission

The College of Law utilizes a rolling admission process. A faculty committee meets regularly throughout the academic year to review applications. Admission to the College of Law is highly competitive, and many factors are considered in the selection process. Although considerable weight is given to undergraduate grade-point average and performance on the LSAT, thoughtful attention is also given to an applicant's extracurricular activities, employment experience, graduate studies, military service, adjustments to personal difficulties, and other relevant factors.

In addition to the regular fall entering class, the College of Law conducts a special Early Admission Program each summer. Admission is offered to a select group of approximately 20 students whose statistical scores may not meet the current standards for regular admission, but who have demonstrated a probable capacity for success in the study and practice of law. Students in the program receive six hours of credit for the summer study and then join the fall class.

■ International Programs

For the 33rd year, the College of Law will conduct a summer program at Oxford University for American law students. The program affords students an opportunity to live and study in stimulating and beautiful surroundings under the guidance of American and English legal educators. Other opportunities exist for foreign study abroad in almost any country in which a student wishes to study.

■ Library and Physical Facilities

Andrew M. Coats Hall provides 170,000 square feet of instructional space for its programs. The modern facility provides wireless Internet access and multimedia technology in classrooms, the library, and student areas. The building features three courtrooms, one of which has seating for 250 persons and is equipped with the latest in technological innovations. The library offers access to electronic Web-based services and maintains over 350,000 volumes and equivalents and also contains one of the nation's largest Native People's collections.

■ Student Activities

The College of Law sponsors three major student-directed journals, the *Oklahoma Law Review*, the *American Indian Law Review*, and the newly created *Oklahoma Journal of Law and Technology*, which focuses on intellectual property law.

Since 1948, the *Oklahoma Law Review* has been published quarterly to give expression to legal scholarship nationally and to serve the profession and the public with timely discussion of important legal issues.

The *American Indian Law Review*, published biannually, serves as a nationwide scholarly forum for the presentation of important developments in Indian law and affairs. The *Review* offers in-depth articles written by nationally recognized experts on a wide range of issues in the rapidly expanding field of Indian law.

The *Oklahoma Journal of Law and Technology* is a Web-based collection of important articles on the various aspects of intellectual property. The student board of editors continually monitors and updates the articles and other material on the website.

The College of Law recently substantially expanded the opportunities for students to participate in a wide range of extracurricular interscholastic appellate moot court, counseling and interviewing, negotiation, and trial advocacy competitions. The student Board of Advocates works closely with the students to facilitate participation in these competitions and provide intramural competitions for 1L and upper-level students.

All students at the College of Law may join a wide variety of organizations and participate in many kinds of extracurricular activities. The law school has an active Student Bar Association, affiliated with the Law Student Division of the American Bar Association. The student-elected Board of Governors supervises student activities and works with the faculty and administration of the law school.

■ Career Services

The College of Law's Career Services Office provides comprehensive professional planning and placement services to all students. The director and the assistant dean for external affairs work personally with students on the entire range of career development services, including offering workshops on interviewing and résumé and cover letter writing, using Web-based resources, scheduling on-campus interviews, and providing individual counseling. The office works closely with law firms, government agencies, judges, and alumni around the country to expand employment opportunities for graduates.

Employment opportunities have continually expanded for University of Oklahoma law graduates, and the market placement has been very strong. In recent years, over 95 percent of graduates consistently are employed within nine months of graduation, placing the College of Law among the upper echelon of schools nationally. Approximately two-thirds of the college's graduates practice in Oklahoma. The other one-third are found in all 50 states and 14 foreign countries, with concentrations in Texas; Washington, DC; and California. In addition to traditional legal careers as attorneys, prosecutors, and judges, University of Oklahoma law graduates work in areas such as corporate management, banking, journalism, public service, government, entrepreneurial enterprises, teaching, and academia.

Applicant Profile

University of Oklahoma College of Law
This grid includes only applicants who earned 120–180 LSAT scores under standard administrations.

LSAT Score	3.75 +		3.50–3.74		3.25–3.49		3.00–3.24		2.75–2.99		2.50–2.74		2.25–2.49		2.00–2.24		Below 2.00		No GPA		Total	
	Apps	Adm	Apps	Adm	Apps	Adm	Apps	Adm	Apps	Adm	Apps	Adm	Apps	Adm	Apps	Adm	Apps	Adm	Apps	Adm	Apps	Adm
175–180	1	1	0	0	0	0	0	0	0	0	0	0	0	0	0	0	0	0	0	0	1	1
170–174	6	6	1	1	4	3	0	0	0	0	0	0	0	0	0	0	0	0	0	0	11	10
165–169	8	8	9	9	4	4	4	3	3	1	1	1	0	0	0	0	0	0	0	0	29	26
160–164	29	28	25	24	32	28	12	9	9	6	10	2	2	1	2	0	0	0	2	0	123	98
155–159	48	37	63	44	50	26	36	6	24	4	7	1	2	0	0	0	0	0	3	1	233	119
150–154	46	22	64	25	74	12	56	7	38	2	16	0	8	0	1	0	1	0	2	0	306	68
145–149	20	4	33	3	44	3	38	2	17	0	15	0	9	0	3	0	0	0	2	0	181	12
140–144	6	0	16	1	16	0	26	1	17	0	7	0	2	0	1	0	0	0	2	0	41	0
135–139	3	0	3	0	3	0	9	0	12	0	6	0	2	0	1	0	0	0	1	0	13	0
130–134	0	0	0	0	3	0	2	0	3	0	0	0	0	0	4	0	1	0	0	0	1	0
125–129	0	0	0	0	0	0	0	0	0	0	0	0	0	0	0	0	1	0	0	0	1	0
120–124	0	0	0	0	0	0	0	0	0	0	0	0	0	0	0	0	0	0	1	0	1	0
Total	167	106	214	107	230	76	183	28	123	13	62	4	32	1	11	0	2	0	16	1	1040	336

Apps = Number of Applicants
Adm = Number Admitted
Reflects 99% of the total applicant pool.

Oklahoma City University School of Law

2501 North Blackwelder Avenue
Oklahoma City, OK 73106-1493
Phone: 866.529.6281 or 405.208.5354
E-mail: lawadmit@okcu.edu; Website: www.okcu.edu/law

ABA
Approved
Since
1960

The Basics

Type of school	Private
Term	Semester
Application deadline	8/1
Application fee	$50
Financial aid deadline	3/1
Can first year start other than fall?	No
Student to faculty ratio	19.9 to 1
Does the university offer:	
housing restricted to law students?	No
graduate housing for which law students are eligible?	No

Faculty and Administrators

	Total Fall	Total Spr	Men Fall	Men Spr	Women Fall	Women Spr	Minorities Fall	Minorities Spr
Full-time	25	23	19	16	6	7	3	4
Other Full-time	4	5	0	0	4	5	1	1
Deans, librarians, & others who teach	7	6	4	3	3	3	1	1
Part-time	23	34	17	24	6	10	1	3
Total	**59**	**68**	**40**	**43**	**19**	**25**	**6**	**9**

Curriculum

	Full-time	Part-time
Typical first-year section size	59	57
Is there typically a "small section" of the first-year class, other than Legal Writing, taught by full-time faculty	Yes	No
If yes, typical size offered last year	55	
# of classroom course titles beyond first-year curriculum		87
# of upper division courses, excluding seminars with an enrollment: Under 25		76
25–49		27
50–74		14
75–99		13
100+		0
# of seminars		14
# of seminar positions available		224
# of seminar positions filled	125	42
# of positions available in simulation courses		284
# of simulation positions filled	192	63
# of positions available in faculty supervised clinical courses		0
# of faculty supervised clinical positions filled	0	0
# involved in field placements	38	8
# involved in law journals	21	6
# involved in interschool competitions	13	4
# of credit hours required to graduate		90

JD Enrollment and Ethnicity

	Men #	Men %	Women #	Women %	Full-time #	Full-time %	Part-time #	Part-time %	1st-year #	1st-year %	Total #	Total %	JD Degs. Awd.
African Amer.	5	1.4	12	4.8	11	2.2	6	5.7	3	1.5	17	2.8	7
Amer. Indian	25	7.0	16	6.5	29	5.8	12	11.4	14	7.0	41	6.8	15
Asian Amer.	14	3.9	7	2.8	20	4.0	1	1.0	6	3.0	21	3.5	9
Mex. Amer.	15	4.2	13	5.2	24	4.8	4	3.8	11	5.5	28	4.6	9
Puerto Rican	0	0.0	0	0.0	0	0.0	0	0.0	0	0.0	0	0.0	0
Hispanic	0	0.0	0	0.0	0	0.0	0	0.0	0	0.0	0	0.0	0
Total Minority	59	16.5	48	19.4	84	16.8	23	21.9	34	16.9	107	17.7	40
For. Nation.	4	1.1	2	0.8	6	1.2	0	0.0	1	0.5	6	1.0	1
Caucasian	288	80.7	193	77.8	399	79.8	82	78.1	163	81.1	481	79.5	170
Unknown	6	1.7	5	2.0	11	2.2	0	0.0	3	1.5	11	1.8	0
Total	357	59.0	248	41.0	500	82.6	105	17.4	201	33.2	605		211

Transfers

Transfers in	1
Transfers out	17

Tuition and Fees

	Resident	Nonresident
Full-time	$27,161	$27,161
Part-time	$18,416	$18,416

Living Expenses

Estimated living expenses for singles

Living on campus	Living off campus	Living at home
$13,740	$15,740	$15,740

Oklahoma City University School of Law

*ABA
Approved
Since
1960*

GPA and LSAT Scores

	Total	Full-time	Part-time
# of apps	1,351	1,245	106
# of offers	639	589	50
# of matrics	202	177	25
75% GPA	3.47	3.47	3.32
Median GPA	3.20	3.21	3.10
25% GPA	2.95	2.97	2.90
75% LSAT	153	153	155
Median LSAT	150	150	151
25% LSAT	149	148	149

Grants and Scholarships (from prior year)

	Total		Full-time		Part-time	
	#	%	#	%	#	%
Total # of students	684		546		138	
Total # receiving grants	169	24.7	134	24.5	35	25.4
Less than 1/2 tuition	110	16.1	78	14.3	32	23.2
Half to full tuition	45	6.6	42	7.7	3	2.2
Full tuition	1	0.1	1	0.2	0	0.0
More than full tuition	13	1.9	13	2.4	0	0.0
Median grant amount			$12,778		$6,000	

Informational and Library Resources

# of volumes and volume equivalents	317,134
# of titles	96,875
# of active serial subscriptions	5,444
Study seating capacity inside the library	364
# of full-time professional librarians	6
Hours per week library is open	102
# of open, wired connections available to students	147
# of networked computers available for use by students	73
# of simultaneous wireless users	3,000
Require computer?	No

JD Attrition (from prior year)

	Academic	Other	Total	
	#	#	#	%
1st year	15	32	47	21.0
2nd year	9	9	18	9.0
3rd year	0	0	0	0.0
4th year	0	0	0	0.0

Employment (9 months after graduation)

	Total	Percentage
Employment status known	168	95.5
Employment status unknown	8	4.5
Employed	141	83.9
Pursuing graduate degrees	3	1.8
Unemployed seeking employment	14	8.3
Unemployed not seeking employment	4	2.4
Unemployed and studying for the bar	6	3.6

Type of Employment

# employed in law firms	71	50.4
# employed in business and industry	35	24.8
# employed in government	26	18.4
# employed in public interest	1	0.7
# employed as judicial clerks	6	4.3
# employed in academia	1	0.7

Geographic Location

# employed in state	96	68.1
# employed in foreign countries	0	0.0
# of states where employed		19

Bar Passage Rates

Jurisdiction	Oklahoma		
Exam	Sum 05	Win 06	Total
# from school taking bar for the first time	84	41	125
School's pass rate for all first-time takers	88%	71%	82%
State's pass rate for all first-time takers	91%	88%	90%

Oklahoma City University School of Law

2501 North Blackwelder Avenue
Oklahoma City, OK 73106-1493
Phone: 866.529.6281 or 405.208.5354
E-mail: lawadmit@okcu.edu; Website: www.okcu.edu/law

■ Introduction

At Oklahoma City University School of Law (OCU LAW) we introduce students to an educational philosophy that purposefully and carefully blends the theory and practice of law in all of its forms. Located within minutes of some of Oklahoma's largest law firms, corporations, banks, city and state government agencies, the state capitol, and state and federal courts, our location enables our students to gain valuable experience before graduation.

Oklahoma City, the capital of Oklahoma, boasts a metropolitan population that numbers over one million and covers 625 square miles. In the past 10 years, Oklahoma City has undergone a revitalization resulting in a new AAA baseball stadium, the establishment of Bricktown as a premier historic entertainment district, a new public library, creation of a new riverfront recreation area, and increased investment in public schools. It is considered an easy, comfortable, and friendly place to live.

■ Faculty

The faculty at OCU LAW are committed to the intellectual and professional growth of every student. They hold law degrees from a variety of law schools, including the nation's most prestigious. Many faculty members also hold advanced degrees in law and other fields of study, and most have significant practice-based experience.

■ Library and Physical Facilities

Classes at OCU LAW are held in the Sarkeys Law Center. It houses two moot courtrooms and classrooms equipped with contemporary technology. The building features several common areas that foster interaction between students and faculty. The OCU LAW Library, located in the nearby historic Gold Star Memorial Building, houses a collection of over 304,000 volumes and volume equivalents and features computer labs with access to all online research databases. A wireless network is available in all law school facilities.

■ Scheduling Options

The School of Law offers a full-time JD program with either a traditional day or sunset (late afternoon/early evening) schedule. Our part-time program is available with day or evening classes. By attending summer sessions, full-time students may complete their degree requirements (90 semester hours) in as little as two and one-half years and part-time students in three and one-half years.

■ Special Programs

In Oklahoma, students who have completed just 50 course hours are eligible for a limited license, and those who qualify may appear in court under certain circumstances. As a companion to this state licensing policy, OCU LAW has created a range of externship opportunities where academic credit can be earned in a variety of practice placement sites with field supervisors, operating under the guidance of a full-time director of externship programs.

The School of Law operates three legal centers for its students and the legal community. The Center on Alternative Dispute Resolution provides students with practical training opportunities in mediation, arbitration, and negotiation. The Native American Legal Resource Center focuses on Native American law and provides legal services to tribes and tribal courts, frequently through federal grants. The Center for the Study of State Constitutional Law and Government promotes scholarship and discussion on important issues relating to state government.

OCU LAW cosponsors (with Stetson University) summer international programs in Buenos Aires, Argentina; Granada, Spain; Freiberg, Germany; The Hague, the Netherlands; and Tianjin, China.

■ Office of Admission

OCU LAW seeks serious, motivated students who value education and demonstrate a commitment to the values and ethics of the legal profession. Many factors are considered in the evaluation of applications. Reviewers look for evidence of analytical and critical thinking, and reading, research, and writing skills that suggest the applicant is prepared for law school. Additionally, the committee considers factors such as work and life experience, cultural and economic background, advanced degrees, and extracurricular and community activities.

The Alternate Summer Admission Program (ASAP) offers a limited number of applicants who do not meet traditional admission requirements an opportunity to demonstrate their capacity for law study and to earn admission for the fall by attending and passing two summer classes. Any applicant not offered direct admission will automatically be considered for admission through the summer program.

OCU LAW uses a rolling admission review process and will review applications until the class is filled. Applications received by February 15 with LSAT scores on record will receive priority consideration for admission and scholarship assistance. To be eligible for priority review, applicants should take the June, October, or December LSAT in the year prior to which they are applying.

■ Scholarships

Each year, new applicants are evaluated for merit scholarships including some full-tuition awards. Incoming students are also invited to apply for the Hatton W. Sumners Scholarship, a full-tuition award that includes a book and living expense stipend. The Sumners Scholarships are competitive and awarded based on academic and leadership potential demonstrated within the scholarship application and during an on-campus interview. Applications for the Sumners award are due February 1. Additional scholarship assistance is available to returning upper-division students based on academic performance.

Student Services

OCU LAW actively provides law students with opportunities to be engaged with the larger legal community. Numerous guest speakers, programs, and activities are sponsored to provide students with exposure to local, state, and national leaders, scholars, and legal professionals.

The entire staff at the law school is committed to assisting law students. The associate dean for students offers broad support to students and student organizations. An in-house financial aid advisor provides loan and debt management counseling, and a student technology coordinator assists students with their computing needs. A very accessible professional library staff, that includes five librarians with JD degrees, aids students in the development of important research skills.

Professional and Career Development Center

The Professional and Career Development Center (PCDC) hosts a wide range of workshops and guest speakers in addition to offering personal career counseling and employer cultivation efforts. The center seeks to expose law students to various areas of the law, to provide the resources needed to successfully conduct an employment search, and to guide them in developing the skills, ethics, and values of a legal professional. Details of services provided, contact information for career counselors, and a list of programs and workshops are available on the Professional and Career Development section of the OCU LAW website.

Curriculum

The School of Law offers a joint JD/MBA program and specialized certificate programs in alternative dispute resolution, public law, and business law (with concentrations in e-commerce or in financial services and commercial law). The core curriculum for every OCU LAW student includes a purposeful balance of legal theory and practical application. It provides a well-grounded foundation in the basic doctrines, functions, and ethical principles that underlie law and law practice, and is designed to produce graduates who have a breadth of understanding that enables them to become leaders in law, business, government, and civic life.

Applicant Profile

Oklahoma City University School of Law
This grid includes only applicants who earned 120–180 LSAT scores under standard administrations.

LSAT Score	3.75 +		3.50–3.74		3.25–3.49		3.00–3.24		2.75–2.99		2.50–2.74		2.25–2.49		2.00–2.24		Below 2.00		No GPA		Total	
	Apps	Adm	Apps	Adm	Apps	Adm	Apps	Adm	Apps	Adm	Apps	Adm	Apps	Adm	Apps	Adm	Apps	Adm	Apps	Adm	Apps	Adm
175–180	0	0	0	0	0	0	0	0	0	0	0	0	0	0	0	0	0	0	0	0	0	0
170–174	0	0	1	1	1	1	0	0	0	0	0	0	0	0	0	0	0	0	0	0	2	2
165–169	1	1	2	2	3	3	0	0	0	0	2	2	0	0	0	0	0	0	0	0	8	8
160–164	4	4	4	4	3	2	4	4	4	4	5	5	2	2	1	0	1	1	0	0	28	26
155–159	21	20	19	19	16	16	15	15	6	6	7	5	6	6	0	0	0	0	1	1	91	88
150–154	30	29	40	35	55	50	50	47	58	42	47	38	22	12	8	2	3	1	0	0	313	256
145–149	24	20	55	40	79	63	107	66	78	32	48	11	46	3	9	0	5	0	7	1	451	237
140–144	8	1	39	5	57	2	70	8	54	0	33	0	25	0	9	0	5	0	7	1	307	17
135–139	3	0	5	0	10	0	18	1	22	0	11	0	11	0	4	0	1	0	2	0	87	1
130–134	3	0	0	0	7	0	8	0	7	0	3	0	3	0	2	0	2	0	2	0	37	0
125–129	0	0	0	0	1	0	1	0	1	0	1	0	1	0	0	0	1	0	0	0	6	0
120–124	0	0	2	0	0	0	0	0	0	0	0	0	0	0	0	0	0	0	0	0	2	0
Total	94	75	167	106	232	137	273	141	230	84	157	61	116	23	33	2	16	3	14	3	1332	635

Apps = Number of Applicants
Adm = Number Admitted
Reflects 99% of the total applicant pool.

University of Oregon School of Law

1221 University of Oregon
Eugene, OR 97403-1221
Phone: 541.346.3846
E-mail: admissions@law.uoregon.edu; Website: www.law.uoregon.edu

*ABA
Approved
Since
1923*

The Basics

Type of school	Public
Term	Semester
Application deadline	3/1
Application fee	$50
Financial aid deadline	3/1
Can first year start other than fall?	No
Student to faculty ratio	21.3 to 1
Does the university offer:	
housing restricted to law students?	No
graduate housing for which law students are eligible?	Yes

Faculty and Administrators

	Total		Men		Women		Minorities	
	Fall	Spr	Fall	Spr	Fall	Spr	Fall	Spr
Full-time	22	19	14	14	8	5	3	5
Other Full-time	3	3	0	0	3	3	1	1
Deans, librarians, & others who teach	10	10	1	1	9	9	1	1
Part-time	23	23	15	17	8	6	2	0
Total	**58**	**55**	**30**	**32**	**28**	**23**	**7**	**7**

Curriculum

	Full-time	Part-time
Typical first-year section size	63	0
Is there typically a "small section" of the first-year class, other than Legal Writing, taught by full-time faculty	No	No
If yes, typical size offered last year		
# of classroom course titles beyond first-year curriculum	116	

# of upper division courses, excluding seminars with an enrollment:		
	Under 25	27
	25–49	23
	50–74	12
	75–99	6
	100+	0

# of seminars		24	
# of seminar positions available		519	
# of seminar positions filled	328		0
# of positions available in simulation courses		271	
# of simulation positions filled	199		0
# of positions available in faculty supervised clinical courses		169	
# of faculty supervised clinical positions filled	101		0
# involved in field placements	59		0
# involved in law journals	111		0
# involved in interschool competitions	53		0
# of credit hours required to graduate		85	

JD Enrollment and Ethnicity

	Men #	Men %	Women #	Women %	Full-time #	Full-time %	Part-time #	Part-time %	1st-year #	1st-year %	Total #	Total %	JD Degs. Awd.
African Amer.	11	3.6	9	3.9	20	3.7	0	0.0	6	3.4	20	3.7	1
Amer. Indian	2	0.7	5	2.2	7	1.3	0	0.0	3	1.7	7	1.3	3
Asian Amer.	23	7.5	19	8.2	42	7.8	0	0.0	14	7.9	42	7.8	11
Mex. Amer.	9	3.0	5	2.2	14	2.6	0	0.0	5	2.8	14	2.6	3
Puerto Rican	0	0.0	0	0.0	0	0.0	0	0.0	0	0.0	0	0.0	2
Hispanic	12	3.9	4	1.7	16	3.0	0	0.0	6	3.4	16	3.0	5
Total Minority	57	18.7	42	18.2	99	18.5	0	0.0	34	19.1	99	18.5	25
For. Nation.	2	0.7	4	1.7	6	1.1	0	0.0	1	0.6	6	1.1	3
Caucasian	246	80.7	185	80.1	431	80.4	0	0.0	143	80.3	431	80.4	149
Unknown	0	0.0	0	0.0	0	0.0	0	0.0	0	0.0	0	0.0	0
Total	305	56.9	231	43.1	536	100.0	0	0.0	178	33.2	536		177

Transfers

Transfers in	12
Transfers out	4

Tuition and Fees

	Resident	Nonresident
Full-time	$18,690	$23,262
Part-time	$0	$0

Living Expenses

Estimated living expenses for singles

Living on campus	Living off campus	Living at home
$11,130	$11,130	$6,189

University of Oregon School of Law

ABA
Approved
Since
1923

GPA and LSAT Scores

	Total	Full-time	Part-time
# of apps	2,015	2,015	0
# of offers	807	807	0
# of matrics	178	178	0
75% GPA	3.63	3.63	0.00
Median GPA	3.40	3.40	0.00
25% GPA	3.08	3.08	0.00
75% LSAT	161	161	0
Median LSAT	159	159	0
25% LSAT	157	157	0

Grants and Scholarships (from prior year)

	Total #	Total %	Full-time #	Full-time %	Part-time #	Part-time %
Total # of students	526		526		0	
Total # receiving grants	262	49.8	262	49.8	0	0.0
Less than 1/2 tuition	238	45.2	238	45.2	0	0.0
Half to full tuition	18	3.4	18	3.4	0	0.0
Full tuition	0	0.0	0	0.0	0	0.0
More than full tuition	6	1.1	6	1.1	0	0.0
Median grant amount			$3,300		$0	

Informational and Library Resources

# of volumes and volume equivalents	373,222
# of titles	73,861
# of active serial subscriptions	2,693
Study seating capacity inside the library	285
# of full-time professional librarians	6
Hours per week library is open	107
# of open, wired connections available to students	1,370
# of networked computers available for use by students	31
# of simultaneous wireless users	3,200
Require computer?	Yes

JD Attrition (from prior year)

	Academic #	Other #	Total #	Total %
1st year	0	0	0	0.0
2nd year	0	9	9	5.2
3rd year	0	0	0	0.0
4th year	0	0	0	0.0

Employment (9 months after graduation)

	Total	Percentage
Employment status known	166	98.2
Employment status unknown	3	1.8
Employed	151	91.0
Pursuing graduate degrees	4	2.4
Unemployed seeking employment	4	2.4
Unemployed not seeking employment	0	0.0
Unemployed and studying for the bar	7	4.2

Type of Employment

	Total	Percentage
# employed in law firms	64	42.4
# employed in business and industry	23	15.2
# employed in government	23	15.2
# employed in public interest	11	7.3
# employed as judicial clerks	26	17.2
# employed in academia	4	2.6

Geographic Location

	Total	Percentage
# employed in state	84	55.6
# employed in foreign countries	0	0.0
# of states where employed	22	

Bar Passage Rates

Jurisdiction	Oregon		
Exam	Sum 05	Win 06	Total
# from school taking bar for the first time	93	19	112
School's pass rate for all first-time takers	80%	84%	80%
State's pass rate for all first-time takers	76%	74%	76%

University of Oregon School of Law

1221 University of Oregon
Eugene, OR 97403-1221
Phone: 541.346.3846
E-mail: admissions@law.uoregon.edu; Website: www.law.uoregon.edu

■ Introduction

Founded in 1884, the University of Oregon School of Law is one of the oldest and smallest law schools in the West. It is a closely knit community that is characterized by informality, camaraderie, and a spirited commitment to public service. The School of Law is situated on the historic flagship campus of the University of Oregon in Eugene, the state's third largest city. About 20,000 students attend the University of Oregon, a state-supported institution, with 525 engaged in full-time study in the School of Law. The University of Oregon School of Law is the smallest public law school on the West Coast. Students enjoy a rigorous legal education led by a talented faculty of devoted scholar-teachers. It is the only law school in Oregon with membership in the Order of the Coif, an honor claimed by just 80 law schools in the United States that are distinguished for exemplary faculty scholarship. Students are drawn to the School of Law from throughout the United States. About 100 undergraduate schools are represented in its small first-year class. Historically, more than half of the graduating class chooses to work in Oregon upon graduation, many influenced to stay by the state's spectacular natural beauty and coveted quality of life.

■ Environs

Eugene, Oregon, is an ideal environment for legal training. An active legal community mentors and employs law students as clerks and externs. Eugene is the county seat and home to a new federal courthouse. The School of Law partners with local entities to offer students a range of clinical and pro bono opportunities. Eugene provides its 146,000 residents many urban amenities, but boasts small city friendliness and affordability. Within minutes of campus are the Hult Center for the Performing Arts, Saturday Market, Civic Stadium, galleries, bookstores, and restaurants. Residents value Eugene's many trails, bike paths, parks, and its setting at the confluence of the Willamette and McKenzie Rivers. In 2008, the city will host the Olympic Track and Field Trials. Within one hour of Eugene lie the Pacific Coast, Cascade Mountains, and Salem, the state capital. Many graduates practice in Portland, about two hours north. It is home to the law school's Portland Center, which coordinates the Portland Interview Program, externships, summer courses, and conferences.

Built in 1999 on the east edge of the university's 295-acre campus, the William W. Knight Law Center is an inspiring setting for legal education. The four-story, light-filled, neotraditional building offers classrooms, seminar and conference rooms, the Wayne Morse Commons, a gallery, and quiet places for study. Its technological infrastructure ensures its state-of-the-art status for the future. The building is wireless, though students also enjoy wired access from each seat in every classroom. The John E. Jaqua Law Library anchors the building's south end. Its 389,000 volume collection supports research in international law and several other interdisciplinary areas, and is also home to special ocean and coastal law resources. The collection is part of the 2.6 million volume collection of the university's libraries, and the Law Library is a member of the Orbis Cascade Alliance. The Knight Law Center also houses a computer lab (PCs/Macs), student offices and lockers, a café/bookstore, and a basketball court.

■ Curriculum

The curriculum offers students many choices. A broad base of common understanding is established in the first year of study. The core curriculum emphasizes traditional legal subjects. The elective curriculum allows students the option of concentrating their studies in areas for which the School of Law is nationally recognized: environmental and natural resources law; business, financial, and corporate law; public interest and public service law; and appropriate dispute resolution. The law school awards the JD, undertaken on a full-time basis, and offers four concurrent master's/JD programs and 10 specialized certificates of completion.

■ Centers and Programs

Special endowed academic centers and programs provide students with the opportunity to specialize or enrich their knowledge in particular areas of the law. Among them are the Appropriate Dispute Resolution Center, Environmental and Natural Resources Law Center, Center for Law and Entrepreneurship, Ocean and Coastal Law Center, the Portland Program, Public Interest-Public Service Program, and the Wayne Morse Center for Law and Politics. The Oregon Child Advocacy Project is also housed at the law school. In addition, the law school has received a substantial contribution to its Oregon Tribes Professorship, reflecting its long commitment to American Indian law and legal scholarship.

Appropriate Dispute Resolution: The Appropriate Dispute Resolution program has quickly achieved national recognition. The law school is keenly aware of the extent to which appropriate methods of dispute resolution (ADR) are now a staple of legal practice. The ADR program provides extensive integration of ADR into the traditional curriculum; specialized training in the skills of mediation, counseling, and negotiation; and opportunities to practice those skills. The innovative ADR master's degree is the only program of its kind to be housed in a law school. For more information, visit *www.law.uoregon.edu/org/adr/masters/*.

Concurrent Degrees: Law students also can concurrently pursue one of several master's degree options. A student in the JD program can achieve a specialized master's degree in one year, rather than two. The concurrent degree programs include business administration (JD/MBA), environmental studies (JD/MA or JD/MS), international studies (JD/MA), and conflict and dispute resolution (JD/MA or JD/MS). Students apply *separately* to the master's program of their choice.

Certificates of Completion: Certificates of completion enable students to concentrate their legal study in the second and third year. The certificates offered include business law, law and entrepreneurship, criminal practice, environmental and natural resources law, estate planning, tax law, intellectual property, public interest and public service law, international law, and ocean and coastal law.

Clinics and Skills Training: Valuable skills training and real-world experience are provided to students in a clinical setting. Clinics include business law, criminal prosecution, criminal defense, civil practice, environmental law, domestic violence, and mediation. In addition, legal writing and research skills are honed in an intensive, required, year-long research and writing program that is taught in small sections to enable more personalized instruction. The course culminates with students presenting final oral arguments in a courtroom setting.

International Exchange Program: Students may apply to the law school's semester-long international exchange program at the University of Adelaide School of Law, situated in South Australia's capital city. The University of Adelaide is one of Australia's oldest and most respected institutions. The coursework selected must meet academic standards established by the law school and the American Bar Association.

Oregon LLM Program: The master of laws program offers a concentration in environmental and natural resources law, preparing graduates for national and international leadership careers working with governments, companies, and civil society organizations. Applicants must possess a US or foreign law degree. For more information, visit *www.law.uoregon.edu/llm/*.

■ Admission and Financial Aid

For fall 2006, 2,015 students competed for 180 first-year seats. The admission committee uses a holistic approach to evaluate the full range of an applicant's accomplishments. Qualitative factors such as GPA and LSAT performance are important. The 75th, median, and 25th percentile cumulative undergraduate GPAs are 3.63, 3.40, and 3.08, respectively. The 75th, median, and 25th percentile LSAT scores are 161, 159, and 157, respectively. The mission of the law school affirms diversity as an important consideration. Women comprised 42 percent of the entering class and students of color comprised 20 percent. Oregon residents comprised 39 percent of the class and 100 universities and colleges were represented. Forty percent of the class were scholarship recipients. No additional application is needed for scholarship consideration. The FAFSA is required for federal and private loan evaluation. A loan repayment assistance program is available to alumni practicing public interest/public service law.

■ Student Activities

The School of Law enjoys the reputation of a committed and energetic community, attracting students with strong public interest, public service, and international experience. Since 2001, Oregon School of Law students have contributed the most pro bono hours of any law school in Oregon. There are 40 active and diverse student organizations, including Outlaws (LGBT), the Oregon Innocence Project, the Law and Entrepreneurship Student Association, the Pacific Wine Law Society, the Christian Legal Society, the Women's Law Forum, and six multicultural groups. Each March, students in Land Air Water host PIELC, the largest public interest environmental law conference in the world. There are three student-run law journals: *Oregon Law Review*, *Journal of Environmental Law and Litigation*, and *Oregon Review of International Law*. The Moot Court Board sponsors five in-house school competitions. The Student Bar Association sponsors activities that enrich the intellectual and professional experiences of students, as well as supports projects that serve the needs of the Eugene community. Students also serve on all faculty committees.

■ Career Services

The Career Services Office provides comprehensive and personalized career counseling, including assistance with job-search strategies, interviewing, and résumé development. It utilizes a network of 5,500 alumni and oversees a busy on-campus interview program, which brings law firms, government entities, and public service/public interest organizations to Eugene. A popular Portland Interview Program is offered, as is a Portland Mentor Program. More than half of the most recent graduating class chose to remain in Oregon, but alumni work on Wall Street, in Washington, DC, and throughout the West. Graduates have risen to prominent positions, particularly in Portland and Seattle, and in federal and state courts. For more information, visit *www.law.uoregon.edu/career/*.

Applicant Profile

University of Oregon School of Law

LSAT Score	GPA								
	3.75 +	3.50–3.74	3.25–3.49	3.00–3.24	2.75–2.99	2.50–2.74	2.25–2.49	2.00–2.24	Below 2.00
175–180									
170–174									
165–169									
160–164									
155–159									
150–154									
145–149									
140–144									
135–139									
130–134									
125–129									
120–124									

■ Good Possibility   □ Possible   ▢ Unlikely

Pace University School of Law

78 North Broadway
White Plains, NY 10603
Phone: 914.422.4210; Fax: 914.989.8714
E-mail: admissions@law.pace.edu; Website: www.law.pace.edu

The Basics

Type of school	Private
Term	Semester
Application deadline	11/1 3/1
Application fee	$65
Financial aid deadline	2/1
Can first year start other than fall?	No
Student to faculty ratio	15.3 to 1
Does the university offer:	
housing restricted to law students?	No
graduate housing for which law students are eligible?	Yes

Faculty and Administrators

	Total		Men		Women		Minorities	
	Fall	Spr	Fall	Spr	Fall	Spr	Fall	Spr
Full-time	35	35	21	20	14	15	3	4
Other Full-time	4	3	3	2	1	1	0	0
Deans, librarians, & others who teach	4	4	3	2	1	2	0	0
Part-time	42	49	21	27	21	22	2	2
Total	**85**	**91**	**48**	**51**	**37**	**40**	**5**	**6**

Curriculum

	Full-time	Part-time
Typical first-year section size	57	72
Is there typically a "small section" of the first-year class, other than Legal Writing, taught by full-time faculty	Yes	Yes
If yes, typical size offered last year	22	24
# of classroom course titles beyond first-year curriculum	142	
# of upper division courses, excluding seminars with an enrollment: Under 25	108	
25–49	36	
50–74	9	
75–99	6	
100+	0	
# of seminars	28	
# of seminar positions available	420	
# of seminar positions filled	256	114
# of positions available in simulation courses	178	
# of simulation positions filled	138	27
# of positions available in faculty supervised clinical courses	90	
# of faculty supervised clinical positions filled	63	13
# involved in field placements	81	11
# involved in law journals	91	22
# involved in interschool competitions	55	11
# of credit hours required to graduate	84	

JD Enrollment and Ethnicity

	Men		Women		Full-time		Part-time		1st-year		Total		JD Degs. Awd.
	#	%	#	%	#	%	#	%	#	%	#	%	
African Amer.	7	2.2	14	3.2	9	1.8	12	4.7	4	1.5	21	2.8	7
Amer. Indian	0	0.0	1	0.2	1	0.2	0	0.0	0	0.0	1	0.1	2
Asian Amer.	26	8.0	43	10.0	54	10.8	15	5.9	23	8.4	69	9.1	17
Mex. Amer.	1	0.3	1	0.2	1	0.2	1	0.4	1	0.4	2	0.3	1
Puerto Rican	4	1.2	2	0.5	3	0.6	3	1.2	2	0.7	6	0.8	1
Hispanic	11	3.4	20	4.6	15	3.0	16	6.3	9	3.3	31	4.1	2
Total Minority	49	15.2	81	18.8	83	16.6	47	18.4	39	14.3	130	17.2	30
For. Nation.	4	1.2	7	1.6	11	2.2	0	0.0	3	1.1	11	1.5	2
Caucasian	216	66.9	295	68.3	330	66.1	181	70.7	188	68.9	511	67.7	170
Unknown	54	16.7	49	11.3	75	15.0	28	10.9	43	15.8	103	13.6	22
Total	323	42.8	432	57.2	499	66.1	256	33.9	273	36.2	755		224

Transfers

Transfers in	10
Transfers out	11

Tuition and Fees

	Resident	Nonresident
Full-time	$35,904	$35,904
Part-time	$26,758	$26,758

Living Expenses

Estimated living expenses for singles

Living on campus	Living off campus	Living at home
$15,662	$17,240	$6,740

ABA Approved Since 1978

GPA and LSAT Scores

	Total	Full-time	Part-time
# of apps	2,935	2,467	468
# of offers	1,091	909	182
# of matrics	273	196	77
75% GPA	3.56	3.58	3.53
Median GPA	3.33	3.35	3.26
25% GPA	3.13	3.16	3.01
75% LSAT	156	157	154
Median LSAT	154	155	153
25% LSAT	152	153	151

Grants and Scholarships (from prior year)

	Total		Full-time		Part-time	
	#	%	#	%	#	%
Total # of students	743		495		248	
Total # receiving grants	359	48.3	277	56.0	82	33.1
Less than 1/2 tuition	291	39.2	218	44.0	73	29.4
Half to full tuition	67	9.0	58	11.7	9	3.6
Full tuition	1	0.1	1	0.2	0	0.0
More than full tuition	0	0.0	0	0.0	0	0.0
Median grant amount			$10,000		$4,000	

Informational and Library Resources

# of volumes and volume equivalents	386,258
# of titles	129,825
# of active serial subscriptions	3,844
Study seating capacity inside the library	474
# of full-time professional librarians	9
Hours per week library is open	102
# of open, wired connections available to students	229
# of networked computers available for use by students	71
# of simultaneous wireless users	750
Require computer?	No

JD Attrition (from prior year)

	Academic	Other	Total	
	#	#	#	%
1st year	13	29	42	16.7
2nd year	7	5	12	5.3
3rd year	0	1	1	0.5
4th year	0	0	0	0.0

Employment (9 months after graduation)

	Total	Percentage
Employment status known	220	94.4
Employment status unknown	13	5.6
Employed	201	91.4
Pursuing graduate degrees	4	1.8
Unemployed seeking employment	3	1.4
Unemployed not seeking employment	10	4.5
Unemployed and studying for the bar	2	0.9

Type of Employment

# employed in law firms	99	49.3
# employed in business and industry	47	23.4
# employed in government	24	11.9
# employed in public interest	11	5.5
# employed as judicial clerks	8	4.0
# employed in academia	10	5.0

Geographic Location

# employed in state	121	60.2
# employed in foreign countries	3	1.5
# of states where employed	8	

Bar Passage Rates

Jurisdiction	New York		
Exam	Sum 05	Win 06	Total
# from school taking bar for the first time	198	25	223
School's pass rate for all first-time takers	71%	76%	72%
State's pass rate for all first-time takers	76%	61%	74%

Pace University School of Law

78 North Broadway
White Plains, NY 10603
Phone: 914.422.4210; Fax: 914.989.8714
E-mail: admissions@law.pace.edu; Website: www.law.pace.edu

■ Introduction

Located on a sprawling 12-acre campus just 20 miles from New York City, Pace University School of Law combines the beauty of open spaces and classic buildings with the convenience of technology and the amenities of a small, vibrant urban community. Law firms are abundant in White Plains, the federal and district courthouses are close by, and the new City Center has just been built.

The law school is home to the New York State Judicial Institute, an innovative center for judicial education and the only center of its kind in the United States. Students working with the Institute through the Center for Judicial Studies will pursue a rigorous course of study leading to enhanced opportunities for judicial fellowships and clerkships.

Students are attracted nationally and from abroad to our congenial atmosphere, diverse population, and our award-winning centers. Extensive opportunities exist through our clinics, externships, and internships for students to learn practical lawyering skills and to become litigators.

Pace Law School has a history of student-centered growth and innovation built on a foundation of deep mutual respect between faculty and students. Students from diverse backgrounds come together to learn lawyering skills, gain vital professional experience, and contribute to the creation of a more just society.

■ Curriculum

The JD program provides students with the fundamental skills necessary for the practice of law nationally, and the flexibility to shape their elective coursework based on particular career goals. The curriculum is based on the concept that rigorous standards and high-quality teaching can coexist with an atmosphere congenial to learning and enjoyment. Students can obtain certificates in Environmental Law and in International Law by completing a sequence of courses with a specified GPA in the applicable area. Pace offers the opportunity to pursue joint degrees in the JD/MBA and JD/MPA with Pace University, as well as the JD/MEM with Yale University School of Forestry, JD/MS in Environmental Policy with Bard College, and the JD/MA in Women's History with Sarah Lawrence College. These programs can be completed on a full-time or part-time basis. Graduate law degrees, an LLM in Comparative Legal Studies or Environmental Law, and an SJD in Environmental Law attract attorneys from around the world.

The majority of classes have less than 25 students, which enables close faculty-student relationships. The range of scholarship reflects a faculty of diverse interests, and the curriculum offers courses in traditional areas of legal study, legal theory, and specialized studies. Curricular concentrations include constitutional law, commercial law, corporate law, criminal law and criminal procedure, evidence, family law, litigation, real estate, women's justice, and land use law. Faculty scholarship also covers such specialized areas as the Americans With Disabilities Act, children's legal representation, environmental and toxic torts, equal pay, hazardous waste, health care fraud, international commercial law, land use, legal and ethical issues in health care, nonprofit

organizations, prosecutorial and judicial ethics, racially motivated violence, securities fraud, and white-collar crime.

■ Advocacy and Skills Training

The Women's Justice Center is a training, resource, and direct legal services center that trains thousands of judges, attorneys, and others who work to eradicate injustice to women. Pace law students participate in all aspects of the program, including direct representation of clients in family court.

Pace Law School has one of the top environmental programs in the country. The program offers over 20 classes in environmental law; opportunities to conduct research in energy and land use law; externships in Washington, DC and New York; and international environmental law classes taught in Brazil.

The Land Use Law Center teaches students to understand how best to develop and conserve the land through research and publications, outreach and community service, and project management and technology.

The Federal Judicial Extern Honors Program allows students to hone their writing skills in a mentoring program with a faculty member, and as judicial externs in a United States district or circuit judge's chambers.

Direct representation clinics enable students to take their extensive classroom training and make the transition to representing clients or prosecuting charges. Students take full responsibility for their own caseloads under the close supervision of a full-time faculty member. In addition, externship programs are clinical courses in which fieldwork is conducted under the supervision of practicing attorneys who are not full-time members of the faculty. Simulation courses give students the opportunity to learn specific components of lawyering work such as written and oral advocacy, interviewing and counseling clients, negotiating, analyzing a trial record, developing strategy, opening and closing arguments, selecting a jury and drafting jury instructions, and preparing and examining witnesses.

■ Library and Physical Facilities

The Pace Law Library is housed in an airy, modern facility, the Gerber Glass Law Center. The law library contains an extensive collection of law and law-related publications, provides access to materials in other libraries in metropolitan New York and throughout the United States, and subscribes to national online research systems such as LexisNexis, Westlaw, and Dialog. Pace Law students have free access to these databases from computer terminals distributed throughout the law library, in the student lounge, and from their home computers. A wireless network is available in the law library, classroom buildings, and throughout the campus. The library was recently renovated, and features attractive, comfortable space in which students can study individually or in groups.

■ Financial Aid

A comprehensive aid program has been developed to include scholarships, need-based grants, employment, loans, and a loan forgiveness program for graduates who choose a public interest career. Over 1.8 million dollars have been allocated for first-year students in 2007. These funds may be available on the basis of financial need, academic merit, education costs, or credit considerations.

■ Career Services

The Center for Career Development offers a number of services to students and alumni, including one-to-one counseling and résumé review, panels and programs regarding the many areas of legal practice and specific job opportunities provided through our website, and on-campus interview and résumé collection programs. The center publishes and distributes to all first-year students a comprehensive Legal Employment Guidebook, which provides an overview of the legal employment market, descriptions of the various types of legal employers, and specific legal recruiting information. The staff actively solicits and identifies employment opportunities through targeted mailings and other outreach activities, as well as develops and maintains an extensive collection of resources for students and alumni to use in their job search. Respondents to the 2005 class survey reported 91.4 percent employment within the nine months following graduation.

■ Student Activities

Pace Law School publishes three law reviews, the *Pace Law Review*, the *Pace Environmental Law Review*, and the *Pace International Law Review*. Students compete in interscholastic moot court competitions and host the largest environmental moot court competition in the country. The school offers more than 26 organizations in which students can participate. Available activities include professional organizations, minority student groups, issue-centered organizations, political groups, social action groups, religious groups, a student bar association, and a student newspaper.

■ Interviews/Visits to Campus

Pace seeks students with demonstrated potential to contribute meaningfully to the diversity of the law school community and the legal profession. Pace offers a unique opportunity for candidates to participate in a formal interview as part of the application process.

The law school hosts several open house programs which include tours; discussions with faculty, administrators, and students; and information regarding the admission process, financial aid, placement, and life at Pace Law School. For a complete list of our on-campus events, visit our website at *www.law.pace.edu*.

Applicant Profile

Pace University School of Law
This grid includes only applicants who earned 120–180 LSAT scores under standard administrations.

LSAT Score	3.75 +		3.50–3.74		3.25–3.49		3.00–3.24		2.75–2.99		2.50–2.74		2.25–2.49		2.00–2.24		Below 2.00		No GPA		Total	
	Apps	Adm	Apps	Adm	Apps	Adm	Apps	Adm	Apps	Adm	Apps	Adm	Apps	Adm	Apps	Adm	Apps	Adm	Apps	Adm	Apps	Adm
175–180	0	0	0	0	0	0	0	0	0	0	1	0	0	0	0	0	0	0	0	0	1	0
170–174	1	1	4	4	1	1	2	1	0	0	0	0	0	0	0	0	0	0	2	2	10	9
165–169	3	3	10	10	2	2	5	5	1	1	1	1	1	0	0	0	0	0	1	1	24	23
160–164	22	20	22	22	24	22	29	27	18	18	12	5	5	2	3	0	2	0	2	1	139	117
155–159	62	57	102	94	147	134	109	89	62	42	33	21	16	0	6	0	2	0	8	6	547	443
150–154	88	61	192	112	227	123	206	88	122	24	84	9	25	2	13	0	1	0	8	5	966	424
145–149	36	7	112	13	154	12	164	3	106	2	62	3	39	0	9	0	1	0	15	0	698	40
140–144	20	0	40	2	71	0	71	1	78	0	44	1	28	0	6	0	4	0	8	0	370	4
135–139	3	0	12	0	21	0	21	0	24	0	29	0	17	0	7	0	3	0	7	0	144	0
130–134	2	0	5	0	4	0	8	0	14	0	11	0	4	0	4	0	3	0	5	0	60	0
125–129	0	0	0	0	0	0	2	0	1	0	2	0	0	0	3	0	1	0	1	0	10	0
120–124	0	0	0	0	0	0	0	0	0	0	0	0	0	0	0	0	0	0	0	0	0	0
Total	237	149	499	257	651	294	617	214	426	87	279	40	135	4	51	0	17	0	57	15	2969	1060

Apps = Number of Applicants
Adm = Number Admitted
Reflects 98% of the total applicant pool.

University of the Pacific, McGeorge School of Law

3200 Fifth Avenue
Sacramento, CA 95817
Phone: 916.739.7105; Fax: 916.739.7134
E-mail: admissionsmcgeorge@pacific.edu; Website: www.mcgeorge.edu

ABA
Approved
Since
1969

The Basics

Type of school	Private
Term	Semester
Application deadline	5/1
Application fee	$50
Financial aid deadline	
Can first year start other than fall?	No
Student to faculty ratio	13.4 to 1
Does the university offer:	
housing restricted to law students?	Yes
graduate housing for which law students are eligible?	Yes

Faculty and Administrators

	Total		Men		Women		Minorities	
	Fall	Spr	Fall	Spr	Fall	Spr	Fall	Spr
Full-time	50	58	29	37	21	21	9	9
Other Full-time	7	6	2	2	5	4	0	0
Deans, librarians, & others who teach	7	7	4	4	3	3	0	0
Part-time	25	39	17	29	8	10	2	3
Total	89	110	52	72	37	38	11	12

Curriculum

	Full-time	Part-time
Typical first-year section size	79	106
Is there typically a "small section" of the first-year class, other than Legal Writing, taught by full-time faculty	Yes	Yes
If yes, typical size offered last year	40	46
# of classroom course titles beyond first-year curriculum	122	
# of upper division courses, excluding seminars with an enrollment: Under 25	91	
25–49	49	
50–74	25	
75–99	19	
100+	5	
# of seminars	12	
# of seminar positions available	340	
# of seminar positions filled	154	79
# of positions available in simulation courses	1,264	
# of simulation positions filled	587	290
# of positions available in faculty supervised clinical courses	184	
# of faculty supervised clinical positions filled	72	43
# involved in field placements	149	58
# involved in law journals	95	11
# involved in interschool competitions	39	14
# of credit hours required to graduate	88	

JD Enrollment and Ethnicity

	Men #	Men %	Women #	Women %	Full-time #	Full-time %	Part-time #	Part-time %	1st-year #	1st-year %	Total #	Total %	JD Degs. Awd.
African Amer.	17	3.1	15	3.3	15	2.5	17	4.3	17	5.4	32	3.2	1
Amer. Indian	3	0.5	5	1.1	7	1.2	1	0.3	4	1.3	8	0.8	6
Asian Amer.	61	11.2	59	13.0	80	13.2	40	10.1	34	10.9	120	12.0	37
Mex. Amer.	22	4.0	20	4.4	22	3.6	20	5.1	18	5.8	42	4.2	10
Puerto Rican	1	0.2	0	0.0	0	0.0	1	0.3	0	0.0	1	0.1	2
Hispanic	13	2.4	11	2.4	12	2.0	12	3.0	9	2.9	24	2.4	3
Total Minority	117	21.4	110	24.2	136	22.5	91	23.0	82	26.2	227	22.7	59
For. Nation.	8	1.5	6	1.3	9	1.5	5	1.3	4	1.3	14	1.4	0
Caucasian	421	77.1	339	74.5	460	76.0	300	75.8	227	72.5	760	75.9	242
Unknown	0	0.0	0	0.0	0	0.0	0	0.0	0	0.0	0	0.0	0
Total	546	54.5	455	45.5	605	60.4	396	39.6	313	31.3	1001		301

Transfers

Transfers in	15
Transfers out	12

Tuition and Fees

	Resident	Nonresident
Full-time	$32,905	$32,905
Part-time	$21,901	$21,901

Living Expenses

Estimated living expenses for singles

Living on campus	Living off campus	Living at home
$19,371	$19,371	$19,371

University of the Pacific, McGeorge School of Law

ABA
Approved
Since
1969

GPA and LSAT Scores

	Total	Full-time	Part-time
# of apps	3,408	3,033	375
# of offers	1,168	1,006	162
# of matrics	309	216	93
75% GPA	3.55	3.59	3.33
Median GPA	3.32	3.42	3.10
25% GPA	3.01	3.15	2.89
75% LSAT	159	160	156
Median LSAT	156	158	154
25% LSAT	154	155	151

Grants and Scholarships (from prior year)

	Total		Full-time		Part-time	
	#	%	#	%	#	%
Total # of students	1,042		641		401	
Total # receiving grants	503	48.3	351	54.8	152	37.9
Less than 1/2 tuition	429	41.2	290	45.2	139	34.7
Half to full tuition	60	5.8	48	7.5	12	3.0
Full tuition	10	1.0	9	1.4	1	0.2
More than full tuition	4	0.4	4	0.6	0	0.0
Median grant amount			$10,950		$5,000	

Informational and Library Resources

# of volumes and volume equivalents	489,603
# of titles	117,820
# of active serial subscriptions	4,595
Study seating capacity inside the library	529
# of full-time professional librarians	17
Hours per week library is open	108
# of open, wired connections available to students	305
# of networked computers available for use by students	75
# of simultaneous wireless users	640
Require computer?	No

JD Attrition (from prior year)

	Academic	Other	Total	
	#	#	#	%
1st year	23	26	49	14.3
2nd year	2	17	19	6.3
3rd year	1	1	2	0.6
4th year	0	3	3	3.4

Employment (9 months after graduation)

	Total	Percentage
Employment status known	330	100.0
Employment status unknown	0	0.0
Employed	303	91.8
Pursuing graduate degrees	7	2.1
Unemployed seeking employment	7	2.1
Unemployed not seeking employment	6	1.8
Unemployed and studying for the bar	7	2.1

Type of Employment

	Total	Percentage
# employed in law firms	164	54.1
# employed in business and industry	39	12.9
# employed in government	44	14.5
# employed in public interest	16	5.3
# employed as judicial clerks	14	4.6
# employed in academia	24	7.9

Geographic Location

	Total	Percentage
# employed in state	271	89.4
# employed in foreign countries	0	0.0
# of states where employed	12	

Bar Passage Rates

Jurisdiction	California		
Exam	Sum 05	Win 06	Total
# from school taking bar for the first time	263	25	288
School's pass rate for all first-time takers	64%	76%	65%
State's pass rate for all first-time takers	64%	54%	62%

University of the Pacific, McGeorge School of Law

3200 Fifth Avenue
Sacramento, CA 95817
Phone: 916.739.7105; Fax: 916.739.7134
E-mail: admissionsmcgeorge@pacific.edu; Website: www.mcgeorge.edu

■ Overview

The University of the Pacific, McGeorge School of Law is in Sacramento, California, capital of the nation's most populous state with one of the world's leading economies. The school is a member of the AALS, is accredited by the ABA, and has a chapter of the Order of the Coif.

Day and evening division programs provide flexibility to earn a JD degree in three, four, or five years of study. More than 1,000 students pursue a JD, LLM, or JSD on Pacific McGeorge's unique 13-acre law-school-only campus. The school's reputation for educating well-prepared, practice-ready lawyers grows from the vitality of students and faculty working together. The diversity of the student body is reflected in the 150 or more colleges and universities students attended as undergraduates, the 50 or more major fields, the range in years of age from 20 to over 60, and the gender and ethnic diversity represented each year by the growing number of students from a wide range of ethnic and cultural heritages.

■ Library and Physical Facilities

Pacific McGeorge's students study on a campus designed exclusively for legal education that includes class and seminar rooms; a student center; a technologically equipped trial courtroom; a lecture hall; a clinical legal education center; a law library and computer center; administrative, faculty, and student services offices; recreational facilities; and student apartments.

The Gordon D. Schaber Law Library is a comprehensive legal research facility of nearly 500,000 volumes. The library includes a brand-new state-of-the-art student study area, computer lab, group study rooms, and wireless Internet capabilities. Pacific McGeorge librarians are experts in legal research methodology and assist students in using the library's electronic and traditional resources.

■ Curriculum

Pacific McGeorge offers more than 100 advanced elective offerings, ranging from comprehensive courses in traditional areas such as business, constitutional law, criminal justice, and family and juvenile law to a wide variety of courses in specialty areas such as environmental (both US and international), entertainment, labor, intellectual property, mass media, banking, and elder law. Certificate and concentration curricula are offered for those with specific career interests.

Clinical Experience—Pacific McGeorge believes that clinical education—working in a practice setting while guided by a faculty mentor—is a key part of the law school experience. On-campus clinics include Community Legal Services, Business and Community Development, Administrative Adjudication, Parole Representation, Bankruptcy, Immigration, and Legislative Process. Off-campus, the internship program makes available more than 125 placements.

■ Governmental Affairs Program

Pacific McGeorge's Governmental Affairs Program prepares students for private practice or public service and policymaking careers in governmental positions. Significant opportunities are offered for hands-on work and networking contacts with governmental entities. Graduates of the program are practicing in law firms whose clients are involved with governmental regulatory matters as consultants, lobbyists, or in-house counsel with business and nonprofit organizations, and in staff and policy positions with legislative branches, executive departments, or administrative agencies at all levels of government. A one- or two-year LLM program in Government and Public Policy is available.

■ International Legal Studies

Law and accounting firms, government agencies, and corporations require lawyers who better understand international law. Pacific McGeorge offers an International Law certificate and concentration programs. Students can also study in an international setting at the Center for International Legal Studies in Salzburg, Austria. The Summer Institute offers international and comparative law courses in Austria. Pacific McGeorge also offers LLMs in International Water Resources Law and Transnational Business Practice and a JSD in International Water Resources Law.

■ Trial and Appellate Advocacy

In its broadest sense, advocacy is an integral part of any legal career, whether representing clients in civil and criminal litigation or at administrative hearings, negotiating business agreements, resolving disputes through alternative dispute-resolution mechanisms, or advising on legal matters to avoid litigation. Pacific McGeorge's curriculum offers the opportunity for all students to gain advanced advocacy skills. For those especially attracted to courtroom advocacy, Pacific McGeorge's concentration equips future litigators for success.

■ Intellectual Property Law

Intellectual property is one of the fastest growing practice areas. Pacific McGeorge graduates are practicing in diverse settings and areas of intellectual property law that include the entertainment industry; music and theater law; intellectual property litigation; sports, trademark, and domain-name law; patent and biotechnology law; and the rapidly emerging areas of computer and Internet law.

■ Taxation

Pacific McGeorge has responded to the need for tax expertise in a booming economy by creating a tax concentration within its JD program that provides students with the needed foundation to enter business or estate-planning practice.

■ Criminal Justice

Pacific McGeorge's criminal justice curriculum includes advanced electives in a wide range of subjects, including sentencing and postconviction remedies, white-collar crime, capital punishment, criminal pretrial litigation, specialized evidence courses, juvenile law, family violence, and problems in criminal justice. Hands-on training is available through a rich program of internship opportunities. A concentration curriculum is structured for those who wish to specialize.

Student Activities

Over 40 professional, social, and academic student organizations at Pacific McGeorge represent the breadth of interests and diversity of the student community. Student staffs manage, edit, and write for the *McGeorge Law Review* and the *Pacific McGeorge Global Business and Development Law Journal.* Pacific McGeorge competition teams compete with notable success in a wide range of trial, appellate, counseling, and dispute-resolution competitions on the regional and national levels as well as at the Vis International Commercial Arbitration Moot Competition in Vienna, Austria.

Admission and Financial Aid

Admission is competitive. Prelegal education includes at least a bachelor's degree or senior standing from an accredited college or university. An applicant's undergraduate record and LSAT results are important factors in the decision process. When there are multiple LSAT scores, the highest may be accorded significant weight. Other factors considered are grade patterns or trends, employment and career accomplishments, graduate work, and extracurricular or community activities. Ethnic, cultural, and experiential backgrounds that contribute to student-body diversity are valued. Strong merit- and need-based financial aid programs provide scholarship awards and grants to entering and advanced students. A knowledgeable financial aid staff

provides counseling to assist students in minimizing student loan indebtedness.

Housing

Pacific McGeorge has 150 on-campus apartments, furnished and unfurnished, including one- and two-bedroom units, studios, and townhouses. Early application is advised. The school's full-time housing coordinator also assists in locating off-campus accommodations that are readily available in Sacramento.

Career Services

The Pacific McGeorge Career Development Office (CDO) provides comprehensive career search assistance for permanent, part-time, and summer employment. The CDO staff is available to help students identify their interests, introduce them to the vast array of career development and employment opportunity resources, and assist with career decision making. The CDO focuses on career counseling, individualized review and critique of résumés and cover letters, and job search strategy development.

Pacific McGeorge faculty and alumni play a major role in our programs, sharing their experience and offering advice to students seeking career opportunities in their fields of expertise. Alumni participate in a "Day in the Life" speaker's series, the Alumni Mentor Program, and mock interviews. In addition, the CDO hosts employer on-campus interviews for students and maintains up-to-date listings of specific employment opportunities, as well as an extensive library of resource materials.

Applicant Profile

University of the Pacific, McGeorge School of Law
This grid includes only applicants who earned 120–180 LSAT scores under standard administrations.

LSAT Score	3.75 +		3.50–3.74		3.25–3.49		3.00–3.24		2.75–2.99		2.50–2.74		2.25–2.49		2.00–2.24		Below 2.00		No GPA		Total	
	Apps	Adm	Apps	Adm	Apps	Adm	Apps	Adm	Apps	Adm	Apps	Adm	Apps	Adm	Apps	Adm	Apps	Adm	Apps	Adm	Apps	Adm
165–180	15	15	22	20	17	17	30	29	16	14	8	5	8	3	1	0	0	0	2	1	119	104
160–164	49	44	80	77	68	67	62	55	35	17	32	11	19	7	11	1	0	0	2	1	358	280
155–159	111	95	218	171	261	147	189	76	115	38	74	9	20	3	6	0	1	0	4	2	999	541
150–154	56	26	140	55	236	64	202	39	134	21	61	6	37	3	9	0	1	0	6	2	882	216
145–149	25	2	84	6	117	4	121	2	104	4	66	0	21	0	13	0	3	0	14	1	426	0
120–144	12	0	30	0	53	0	113	0	89	0	65	0	29	0	13	0	4	0	18	0	568	19
Total	268	182	574	329	752	299	717	201	493	94	306	31	134	16	53	1	9	0	46	7	3352	1160

Apps = Number of Applicants
Adm = Number Admitted
Reflects 98% of the total applicant pool.

Penn State University, The Dickinson School of Law

150 South College Street, Carlisle, PA 17013-2899, Phone: 800.840.1122; 717.240.5207; Fax: 717.241.3503
100 Beam Building, University Park, PA 16802-1589, Phone: 800.840.1122; 814.867.1251; Fax: 814.867.0405
E-mail: dsladmit@psu.edu; Website: www.dsl.psu.edu

ABA Approved Since 1931

The Basics

Type of school	Public
Term	Semester
Application deadline	3/1
Application fee	$60
Financial aid deadline	3/1
Can first year start other than fall?	No
Student to faculty ratio	11.9 to 1
Does the university offer:	
housing restricted to law students?	Yes
graduate housing for which law students are eligible?	Yes

Curriculum

	Full-time	Part-time
Typical first-year section size	65	65
Is there typically a "small section" of the first-year class, other than Legal Writing, taught by full-time faculty	No	No
If yes, typical size offered last year		
# of classroom course titles beyond first-year curriculum	126	
# of upper division courses, excluding seminars with an enrollment: Under 25	140	
25–49	33	
50–74	20	
75–99	9	
100+	0	
# of seminars	29	
# of seminar positions available	461	
# of seminar positions filled	309	0
# of positions available in simulation courses	552	
# of simulation positions filled	501	0
# of positions available in faculty supervised clinical courses	125	
# of faculty supervised clinical positions filled	52	0
# involved in field placements	100	0
# involved in law journals	145	0
# involved in interschool competitions	44	0
# of credit hours required to graduate	88	

Faculty and Administrators

	Total		Men		Women		Minorities	
	Fall	Spr	Fall	Spr	Fall	Spr	Fall	Spr
Full-time	45	36	27	23	18	13	4	4
Other Full-time	3	1	1	1	2	0	0	0
Deans, librarians, & others who teach	8	6	5	3	3	3	2	0
Part-time	39	17	30	15	9	2	5	0
Total	95	60	63	42	32	18	11	4

Transfers

Transfers in	19
Transfers out	16

JD Enrollment and Ethnicity

	Men		Women		Full-time		Part-time		1st-year		Total		JD Degs. Awd.
	#	%	#	%	#	%	#	%	#	%	#	%	
African Amer.	20	6.1	39	13.8	49	9.1	10	14.7	24	10.0	59	9.7	10
Amer. Indian	1	0.3	0	0.0	0	0.0	1	1.5	1	0.4	1	0.2	1
Asian Amer.	20	6.1	22	7.8	37	6.9	5	7.4	17	7.1	42	6.9	14
Mex. Amer.	0	0.0	0	0.0	0	0.0	0	0.0	0	0.0	0	0.0	0
Puerto Rican	5	1.5	7	2.5	12	2.2	0	0.0	4	1.7	12	2.0	1
Hispanic	10	3.1	14	5.0	22	4.1	2	2.9	7	2.9	24	3.9	11
Total Minority	56	17.2	82	29.1	120	22.2	18	26.5	53	22.1	138	22.7	37
For. Nation.	7	2.1	6	2.1	12	2.2	1	1.5	9	3.8	13	2.1	1
Caucasian	260	79.8	187	66.3	400	74.1	47	69.1	172	71.7	447	73.5	161
Unknown	3	0.9	7	2.5	8	1.5	2	2.9	6	2.5	10	1.6	1
Total	326	53.6	282	46.4	540	88.8	68	11.2	240	39.5	608		200

Tuition and Fees

	Resident	Nonresident
Full-time	$28,054	$28,054
Part-time	$24,604	$24,604

Living Expenses

Estimated living expenses for singles

Living on campus	Living off campus	Living at home
$16,284	$16,284	$16,284

Penn State University, The Dickinson School of Law

*ABA
Approved
Since
1931*

GPA and LSAT Scores

	Total	Full-time	Part-time
# of apps	3,350	3,350	0
# of offers	1,042	959	83
# of matrics	237	181	56
75% GPA	3.68	3.59	3.78
Median GPA	3.31	3.24	3.62
25% GPA	2.91	2.85	3.30
75% LSAT	159	159	156
Median LSAT	157	158	153
25% LSAT	154	157	150

Grants and Scholarships (from prior year)

	Total		Full-time		Part-time	
	#	%	#	%	#	%
Total # of students	580		580		0	
Total # receiving grants	217	37.4	217	37.4	0	0.0
Less than 1/2 tuition	180	31.0	180	31.0	0	0.0
Half to full tuition	5	0.9	5	0.9	0	0.0
Full tuition	32	5.5	32	5.5	0	0.0
More than full tuition	0	0.0	0	0.0	0	0.0
Median grant amount			$4,200		$0	

Informational and Library Resources

# of volumes and volume equivalents	515,035
# of titles	94,696
# of active serial subscriptions	6,829
Study seating capacity inside the library	246
# of full-time professional librarians	7
Hours per week library is open	87
# of open, wired connections available to students	24
# of networked computers available for use by students	113
# of simultaneous wireless users	2,688
Require computer?	No

JD Attrition (from prior year)

	Academic	Other	Total	
	#	#	#	%
1st year	2	16	18	8.9
2nd year	0	2	2	1.1
3rd year	1	2	3	1.5
4th year	0	0	0	0.0

Employment (9 months after graduation)

	Total	Percentage
Employment status known	231	97.1
Employment status unknown	7	2.9
Employed	206	89.2
Pursuing graduate degrees	7	3.0
Unemployed seeking employment	6	2.6
Unemployed not seeking employment	5	2.2
Unemployed and studying for the bar	7	3.0

Type of Employment

# employed in law firms	90	43.7
# employed in business and industry	26	12.6
# employed in government	29	14.1
# employed in public interest	7	3.4
# employed as judicial clerks	35	17.0
# employed in academia	4	1.9

Geographic Location

# employed in state	118	57.3
# employed in foreign countries	1	0.5
# of states where employed	21	

Bar Passage Rates

Jurisdiction	Pennsylvania		
Exam	Sum 05	Win 06	Total
# from school taking bar for the first time	165	9	174
School's pass rate for all first-time takers	81%	67%	80%
State's pass rate for all first-time takers	79%	75%	78%

Penn State University, The Dickinson School of Law

150 South College Street, Carlisle, PA 17013-2899, Phone: 800.840.1122; 717.240.5207; Fax: 717.241.3503
100 Beam Building, University Park, PA 16802-1589, Phone: 800.840.1122; 814.867.1251; Fax: 814.867.0405
E-mail: dsladmit@psu.edu; Website: www.dsl.psu.edu

■ Introduction

The merger of Penn State University and the Dickinson School of Law has been transformative for the law school. Since the merger, applications for admission have increased by more than 100 percent, student body diversity has tripled, student body academic credentials have improved significantly, our faculty has grown to include several of the world's top legal scholars, and the university is investing more than $110 million in new facilities for the law school.

■ Faculty

Our faculty is composed of outstanding teachers of unquestionably high scholarly standing. These scholars include former law clerks to Supreme Court Justices Harry Blackmun and Ruth Bader Ginsburg; the world's preeminent authority on the law of Russia; the first chief counsel to the African Union; internationally renowned scholars of antitrust law, arbitration, sports law, and gay rights; a leading financial institutions scholar who served recently as counsel to the presidency of the European Union; and many more faculty of similar caliber.

■ Curriculum

Our curriculum is designed to produce leaders and lawyers with high professional and ethical standards and the ability to contend with legal, policy, and social developments in all areas of human endeavor. The first-year curriculum, which includes an integrated legal writing program, is required and provides the building blocks for advanced study in the remaining two years, when students can choose additional elective courses in areas such as corporate and commercial law, criminal law, dispute resolution and trial advocacy, environmental and natural resources law, government and politics, international and comparative law, public interest, science and intellectual property, and sports law. Students have access to similar programs, courses, and organizations regardless of their campus location.

The law school also offers a daytime part-time program that enables a student to pursue a JD degree with a lower-than-ordinary credit-hour load during each semester.

■ Academic Programs and Activities

Students can pursue specialized research and training through the Penn State Institute of Arbitration Law and Practice (the law school's alternative dispute resolution program is recognized as one of the top 10 programs in the country); the Miller Center for Public Interest Advocacy; the Penn State Institute for Sports Law, Policy, and Research; the Vinogradoff Institute, devoted to the study of the legal systems of Russia and CIS nations; and the Agricultural Law Resource and Reference Center. The law school also offers a wide array of live client experiences, including a Refugee Clinic, Children's Advocacy Clinic, Disability Law Clinic, Elder Law and Consumer Protection Clinic, and Family Law Clinic.

Our field placement programs offer additional opportunities for real-world training. These include a Washington, DC Semester that enables third-year students to participate in externships with federal agencies and nonprofit organizations,

multiple academic-year externships with federal and state agencies and courts in Pennsylvania, and the possibility of externship placements with international agencies and tribunals.

Additionally, students can pursue joint-degree programs and other forms of study with Penn State's top graduate departments and professors.

■ International Programs

Many of our faculty have exceptional depth in international issues, thus enabling the law school to offer advanced coursework in comparative and international commercial law, constitutional law, corporate law, environmental law, and humanitarian law, among other areas. In addition, the law school facilitates study-abroad opportunities with law schools throughout the world.

Penn State Dickinson also offers one of the oldest and most prestigious master of laws programs for foreign-trained lawyers, whose presence at the law school enriches the diversity of our educational experience. The entire JD curriculum is available to LLM students.

■ Library and Technology

With holdings of more than a half million volumes and access to a wealth of electronic resources, the Law Library fully supports the research and study activities of students, faculty, and members of the bar. Additionally, legal and interdisciplinary research is greatly enhanced through access to the vast print and electronic collections held by other Penn State University libraries. Wireless networks provide laptop computer users with access to all electronic resources from virtually every point within our facilities.

■ $110 Million Investment in New Facilities

In June 2006, the Council of the ABA Section of Legal Education and Admissions to the Bar acquiesced in the law school's plan to commence operations on Penn State's flagship University Park campus in State College, Pennsylvania. Consequently, all credits earned by a student at our new University Park location count toward a Penn State Dickinson JD degree even while the law school completes the full approval process prescribed by the ABA. The law school now operates as a unified enterprise with facilities in both University Park and in our original home of Carlisle, Pennsylvania.

Currently, the university is investing $110 million in new facilities for the law school in Carlisle and University Park (occupancy 2009), which will be reciprocally designed and equipped with state-of-the-art audiovisual and telecommunications capacity to enable real-time delivery of classes and programs between facilities. Each facility will feature state-of-the-art courtrooms, classrooms, conferencing facilities, reading rooms, indoor and outdoor gathering spaces, and an auditorium designed for law school and public use. The law school's website *www.dsl.psu.edu* provides substantial information about our building projects, including pictures of the new designs. The university is also allocating an additional several million dollars to the law school on a recurring annual basis to support new faculty and programs. These initiatives represent the largest investment in an academic unit in the history of Penn State University.

■ Student Activities

Students edit and publish four journals: the *Penn State Law Review*, the *Penn State Environmental Law Review*, the *Penn State International Law Review*, and the *Journal of American Arbitration.* Second- and third-year students can also gain valuable trial experience by engaging in moot court team competitions at both the regional and national levels. Our vibrant student body supports approximately 40 active student groups.

■ Career Services

The Career Services Office (CSO) provides counseling, resources, and programming to assist students in identifying

and achieving their career goals. The CSO maintains contact with employers across the country, resulting in two formal, on-campus interview programs and the posting of more than 1,000 positions annually. Students can participate in 17 job fairs, including one in the District of Columbia, one exclusively devoted to public interest, several minority job fairs, and one exclusively devoted to patent law.

■ Admission and Financial Aid

You can apply online at *www.dsl.psu.edu/apply/.* Applicants may indicate a preference to attend first-year classes in University Park or Carlisle, Pennsylvania.

The Financial Aid Office works with accepted students to obtain the funding necessary to finance their education. All admitted students are considered for scholarship opportunities.

Applicant Profile

Penn State University, The Dickinson School of Law
This grid includes only applicants who earned 120–180 LSAT scores under standard administrations.

LSAT Score	3.75 +		3.50–3.74		3.25–3.49		3.00–3.24		2.75–2.99		2.50–2.74		2.25–2.49		2.00–2.24		Below 2.00		No GPA		Total	
	Apps	Adm	Apps	Adm	Apps	Adm	Apps	Adm	Apps	Adm	Apps	Adm	Apps	Adm	Apps	Adm	Apps	Adm	Apps	Adm	Apps	Adm
175–180	0	0	0	0	1	1	0	0	0	0	0	0	0	0	0	0	0	0	0	0	1	1
170–174	1	1	5	4	0	0	2	2	0	0	1	0	0	0	0	0	0	0	0	0	9	7
165–169	10	9	2	0	5	4	12	11	7	5	7	3	1	0	0	0	0	0	0	0	44	32
160–164	36	30	49	45	68	57	63	56	29	23	25	14	15	13	3	0	1	0	2	1	291	239
155–159	141	96	252	160	230	133	179	90	110	61	69	35	21	12	6	1	0	0	10	4	1018	592
150–154	120	15	243	25	247	23	198	13	142	7	45	5	24	2	5	0	3	0	3	0	631	90
145–149	48	5	106	7	151	10	148	7	93	5	48	5	23	1	5	0	0	0	9	0	233	11
140–144	8	1	38	4	45	1	74	1	32	2	23	1	10	1	1	0	1	0	1	0	59	0
135–139	0	0	7	0	9	0	16	0	9	0	6	0	4	0	4	0	1	0	3	0	20	0
130–134	0	0	1	0	3	0	5	0	4	0	3	0	1	0	0	0	0	0	3	0	2	0
125–129	0	0	0	0	0	0	0	0	0	0	1	0	0	0	1	0	0	0	0	0	0	0
120–124	0	0	0	0	0	0	0	0	0	0	0	0	0	0	0	0	0	0	0	0	0	0
Total	364	157	703	245	759	229	697	180	426	103	228	63	99	29	25	1	6	0	31	5	3338	1012

Apps = Number of Applicants
Adm = Number Admitted
Reflects 99% of the total applicant pool.

University of Pennsylvania Law School

3400 Chestnut Street
Philadelphia, PA 19104-6204
Phone: 215.898.7400; Fax: 215.898.9606
E-mail: admissions@law.upenn.edu; Website: www.law.upenn.edu

ABA
Approved
Since
1923

The Basics

Type of school	Private
Term	Semester
Application deadline	11/1 2/15
Application fee	$75
Financial aid deadline	3/1
Can first year start other than fall?	No
Student to faculty ratio	12.1 to 1
Does the university offer:	
housing restricted to law students?	No
graduate housing for which law students are eligible?	Yes

Faculty and Administrators

	Total		Men		Women		Minorities	
	Fall	Spr	Fall	Spr	Fall	Spr	Fall	Spr
Full-time	53	52	40	41	13	11	4	5
Other Full-time	3	2	0	1	3	1	1	1
Deans, librarians, & others who teach	5	5	4	4	1	1	0	0
Part-time	41	45	30	36	11	9	4	7
Total	102	104	74	82	28	22	9	13

Curriculum

	Full-time	Part-time
Typical first-year section size	80	0
Is there typically a "small section" of the first-year class, other than Legal Writing, taught by full-time faculty	No	No
If yes, typical size offered last year		
# of classroom course titles beyond first-year curriculum	142	
# of upper division courses, excluding seminars with an enrollment: Under 25	62	
25–49	38	
50–74	19	
75–99	4	
100+	4	
# of seminars	54	
# of seminar positions available	876	
# of seminar positions filled	746	0
# of positions available in simulation courses	250	
# of simulation positions filled	219	0
# of positions available in faculty supervised clinical courses	114	
# of faculty supervised clinical positions filled	114	0
# involved in field placements	18	0
# involved in law journals	298	0
# involved in interschool competitions	128	0
# of credit hours required to graduate	89	

JD Enrollment and Ethnicity

	Men		Women		Full-time		Part-time		1st-year		Total		JD Degs. Awd.
	#	%	#	%	#	%	#	%	#	%	#	%	
African Amer.	21	5.1	40	11.3	61	8.0	0	0.0	19	7.7	61	8.0	20
Amer. Indian	3	0.7	2	0.6	5	0.7	0	0.0	2	0.8	5	0.7	3
Asian Amer.	45	11.0	65	18.4	110	14.4	0	0.0	31	12.5	110	14.4	35
Mex. Amer.	5	1.2	4	1.1	9	1.2	0	0.0	3	1.2	9	1.2	2
Puerto Rican	5	1.2	3	0.8	8	1.0	0	0.0	3	1.2	8	1.0	3
Hispanic	21	5.1	17	4.8	38	5.0	0	0.0	14	5.6	38	5.0	12
Total Minority	100	24.4	131	37.1	231	30.3	0	0.0	72	29.0	231	30.3	75
For. Nation.	13	3.2	22	6.2	35	4.6	0	0.0	10	4.0	35	4.6	9
Caucasian	286	69.9	186	52.7	472	61.9	0	0.0	154	62.1	472	61.9	190
Unknown	10	2.4	14	4.0	24	3.1	0	0.0	12	4.8	24	3.1	0
Total	409	53.7	353	46.3	762	100.0	0	0.0	248	32.5	762		274

Transfers

Transfers in	25
Transfers out	9

Tuition and Fees

	Resident	Nonresident
Full-time	$39,330	$39,330
Part-time	$0	$0

Living Expenses

Estimated living expenses for singles

Living on campus	Living off campus	Living at home
$17,050	$17,050	$8,704

University of Pennsylvania Law School

ABA
Approved
Since
1923

GPA and LSAT Scores

	Total	Full-time	Part-time
# of apps	5,649	5,649	0
# of offers	879	879	0
# of matrics	249	249	0
75% GPA	3.84	3.84	0.00
Median GPA	3.72	3.72	0.00
25% GPA	3.47	3.47	0.00
75% LSAT	171	171	0
Median LSAT	170	170	0
25% LSAT	167	167	0

Grants and Scholarships (from prior year)

	Total		Full-time		Part-time	
	#	%	#	%	#	%
Total # of students	777		777		0	
Total # receiving grants	272	35.0	272	35.0	0	0.0
Less than 1/2 tuition	168	21.6	168	21.6	0	0.0
Half to full tuition	88	11.3	88	11.3	0	0.0
Full tuition	16	2.1	16	2.1	0	0.0
More than full tuition	0	0.0	0	0.0	0	0.0
Median grant amount			$14,520		$0	

Informational and Library Resources

# of volumes and volume equivalents	839,545
# of titles	371,122
# of active serial subscriptions	7,522
Study seating capacity inside the library	509
# of full-time professional librarians	14
Hours per week library is open	110
# of open, wired connections available to students	165
# of networked computers available for use by students	131
# of simultaneous wireless users	2,160
Require computer?	No

JD Attrition (from prior year)

	Academic	Other	Total	
	#	#	#	%
1st year	0	7	7	2.9
2nd year	0	7	7	2.7
3rd year	0	2	2	0.7
4th year	0	0	0	0.0

Employment (9 months after graduation)

	Total	Percentage
Employment status known	314	100.0
Employment status unknown	0	0.0
Employed	306	97.5
Pursuing graduate degrees	3	1.0
Unemployed seeking employment	2	0.6
Unemployed not seeking employment	2	0.6
Unemployed and studying for the bar	1	0.3

Type of Employment

	Total	Percentage
# employed in law firms	243	79.4
# employed in business and industry	6	2.0
# employed in government	10	3.3
# employed in public interest	6	2.0
# employed as judicial clerks	38	12.4
# employed in academia	3	1.0

Geographic Location

	Total	Percentage
# employed in state	55	18.0
# employed in foreign countries	3	1.0
# of states where employed	25	

Bar Passage Rates

Jurisdiction	New York			Pennsylvania		
Exam	Sum 05	Win 06	Total	Sum 05	Win 06	Total
# from school taking bar for the first time	169	8	177	66	10	76
School's pass rate for all first-time takers	96%	88%	95%	89%	70%	87%
State's pass rate for all first-time takers	76%	61%	74%	79%	75%	78%

University of Pennsylvania Law School

3400 Chestnut Street
Philadelphia, PA 19104-6204
Phone: 215.898.7400; Fax: 215.898.9606
E-mail: admissions@law.upenn.edu; Website: www.law.upenn.edu

■ Introduction

Penn Law, one of the nation's most distinguished law schools, offers talented students a first-rate education in an intellectually stimulating, cross-disciplinary environment. The Law School takes advantage of its role as a professional school at Penn, an Ivy League institution and one of the world's preeminent research universities. Our faculty collaborate with world-renowned scholars in other departments throughout the university. Our students enrich their legal education with study in other disciplines via courses, certificate programs (including one at the Wharton School for Business), or formal joint-degree programs, either those currently defined or those self-initiated by the motivated student.

The rich university community is complemented by a collegial environment. We pride ourselves on our well-known reputation as a supportive environment for students as they engage in the rigors of legal study. Students develop close relationships with their faculty and colleagues. Penn Law staff is committed to getting to know students as individuals and to working with them to support their law school experiences.

Minutes from downtown Philadelphia, Penn Law enjoys a university campus neighborhood and close proximity to one of the nation's most lively urban areas, providing an exciting, invigorating, and affordable world.

■ Faculty

Penn Law's outstanding faculty are national leaders in every major area of the law. More than 70 percent hold advanced degrees, and almost 50 percent hold secondary appointments or have an affiliation with other schools within the University of Pennsylvania.

Their scholarship is recognized worldwide. Students have opportunities to engage in research in the classroom, as research assistants, and in faculty presentations.

Faculty commitment to students and the Law School's low student-faculty ratio allow the development of close personal and professional relationships, which often develop into lifelong mentorships.

■ Libraries

Biddle Law Library is one of the world's premier law libraries. Our librarians help students make full use of the Biddle's and university's collections. They also teach legal research courses and provide research assistance to support students in their intellectual endeavors.

■ Curriculum

Penn Law's first-year curriculum includes the standard first-year law school courses and also allows students the choice of two first-year electives. Students receive small-group individualized legal writing and research instruction.

In the upper years, the work is elective, allowing an opportunity to concentrate in particular areas or to study more broadly. Penn Law students can take up to four courses at Penn's other graduate and professional schools.

Penn Law offers students a wide choice of clinical courses. And, Penn Law students enjoy participating in our ABA award-winning pro bono program; in fact, over 60 percent of this year's graduating class exceeded the mandatory 70 hours of pro bono service.

In addition to the JD, we offer the Master of Laws (LLM), Master of Comparative Law (LLCM), and Doctor of Juridical Science (SJD).

■ Special Programs

As noted, Penn Law is unique in its interrelatedness with the other graduate and professional programs on campus.

Students can engage these departments through individual courses; through certificate programs in Business and Public Policy (Wharton), Gender and Sexuality Studies (School of Arts and Sciences), Environmental Policy or Environmental Science (School of Arts and Sciences); or through formal joint- and dual-degree programs (JD/MBA, JD/MGA [Government], JD/MBioethics, JD/MCP [City Planning], JD/MSW, MA/MS programs in Criminology, Education, Environment, Philosophy, International Studies, and Public Health; and PhDs in American legal history and in philosophy); and other programs including Global Business (studying at the Panthéon-Sorbonne Law School and Institut d'Études Politiques). Students have also pursued JD/MD (Medicine), JD/MSHP (Historic Preservation), JD/EdD (Education), and PhDs in Communications and Near Eastern Languages and Civilization.

Students' opportunities at Penn are limited only by their imaginations—we work with students to create possibilities that meet their intellectual curiosity and professional goals.

■ Student Body

Students come from all over the country and from more than 196 undergraduate institutions, creating one of the nation's most diverse student bodies. About 15 percent hold advanced degrees and, on average, 65 percent do not enroll directly from undergraduate studies. Approximately 36 percent of our student body is composed of students of color. The diversity of our community creates a dynamic and engaging classroom environment and enriches every aspect of the school.

■ Student Activities

The nation's oldest law review, now the *University of Pennsylvania Law Review*, was founded in 1852. Penn Law also publishes the *Journal of Constitutional Law*, the *Journal of International Economic Law*, and the *Journal of Labor and Employment Law*. Students also self-publish three additional journals, the *Journal of Law and Social Change* (hybrid), the *Journal of International Law and Policy*, and the *Journal of Animal Law and Ethics*.

Students participate in numerous moot court and mock trial activities and in a chapter of the Inns of Court.

The student government is particularly active, and council representatives serve as voting members of many faculty/student committees.

There are more than 50 student organizations.

Admission

The demand for a Penn Law legal education has risen dramatically in recent years. In the 2005–2006 admission cycle, close to 5,700 applicants sought admission for the JD program. Fifteen percent of those applicants were accepted, with a median LSAT score in the 98th percentile.

While academic excellence is of primary importance for admission, we take all factors in each application into consideration and do not have numeric cutoff points for LSAT or GPA. Instead, we read each individual file, including letters of recommendation, personal statements, and the résumé, to get a full picture of the applicant.

We begin processing applications on October 1. Applications received by November 1, and completed by November 15, will be considered for our early notification program (nonbinding) or early decision (binding) program; these applicants receive a decision by the end of December. The regular admission deadline is February 15. Our program is limited to fall semester full-time students.

Current first-year JD students who have achieved excellent records at other law schools may apply as transfer students after completion of their first year only; we do not accept midsemester or second-year transfer students. All applicants must apply by July 15. Decisions are made on a rolling basis, beginning in mid-June.

Housing

Penn Law students select from the wide range of affordable living arrangements both on campus and in private housing.

Expenses and Financial Aid

The Law School maintains a substantial program of need-based grant and loan aid, with approximately 80 percent of the student body receiving financial assistance.

Penn Law extends merit-based scholarships to a select group of applicants. Every applicant is considered.

Penn Law invites students with a demonstrated previous involvement in public service, who are committed to public-sector employment following graduation, to apply for the Toll Public Interest Scholarship. Penn Law has a strong loan forgiveness program to assist graduates who choose public sector work.

Career Services

The Career Planning and Placement Office has a successful record of assisting law students in finding employment coast-to-coast and counseling students and alumni on employment opportunities. The office offers specialized counseling for public interest work, first-year job searches, judicial clerkships, and alternate careers.

About 65–80 percent of graduates start their careers in private practice, 15–22 percent take judicial clerkships, 4–8 percent work in government or public interest positions, 1–2 percent engage in university or law school teaching or study, and 2–4 percent accept opportunities in the business world.

Applicant Profile

Penn Law has chosen not to include an applicant profile because a grid that contains only LSAT scores and GPA would not capture the other qualities that make our students so dynamic. We value their diverse backgrounds, rich life experiences, leadership, community service, professional accomplishments, advanced degrees and coursework, motivation, initiative, and exemplary writing skills. While admission to Penn Law is highly selective, the admissions committee takes all of the factors mentioned above into consideration when reviewing applications.

Pepperdine University School of Law

24255 Pacific Coast Highway
Malibu, CA 90263
Phone: 310.506.4611; Fax: 310.506.7668
E-mail: soladmis@pepperdine.edu; Website: law.pepperdine.edu

ABA
Approved
Since
1972

The Basics

Type of school	Private
Term	Semester
Application deadline	2/1
Application fee	$50
Financial aid deadline	4/1
Can first year start other than fall?	No
Student to faculty ratio	17.8 to 1
Does the university offer:	
housing restricted to law students?	No
graduate housing for which law students are eligible?	Yes

Faculty and Administrators

	Total		Men		Women		Minorities	
	Fall	Spr	Fall	Spr	Fall	Spr	Fall	Spr
Full-time	31	30	24	23	7	7	6	4
Other Full-time	1	1	1	1	0	0	0	0
Deans, librarians, & others who teach	11	12	7	7	4	5	0	0
Part-time	35	47	25	33	10	14	1	1
Total	78	90	57	64	21	26	7	5

Curriculum

	Full-time	Part-time
Typical first-year section size	75	0
Is there typically a "small section" of the first-year class, other than Legal Writing, taught by full-time faculty	No	No
If yes, typical size offered last year		
# of classroom course titles beyond first-year curriculum	113	
# of upper division courses, excluding seminars with an enrollment: Under 25	104	
25–49	65	
50–74	6	
75–99	8	
100+	6	
# of seminars	33	
# of seminar positions available	561	
# of seminar positions filled	448	0
# of positions available in simulation courses	1,625	
# of simulation positions filled	1,405	0
# of positions available in faculty supervised clinical courses	183	
# of faculty supervised clinical positions filled	183	0
# involved in field placements	152	0
# involved in law journals	170	0
# involved in interschool competitions	66	0
# of credit hours required to graduate	88	

JD Enrollment and Ethnicity

	Men		Women		Full-time		Part-time		1st-year		Total		JD Degs. Awd.
	#	%	#	%	#	%	#	%	#	%	#	%	
African Amer.	11	3.5	14	4.3	25	3.9	0	0.0	7	3.3	25	3.9	7
Amer. Indian	1	0.3	2	0.6	3	0.5	0	0.0	1	0.5	3	0.5	0
Asian Amer.	19	6.0	33	10.2	52	8.1	0	0.0	12	5.6	52	8.1	28
Mex. Amer.	7	2.2	10	3.1	17	2.7	0	0.0	5	2.3	17	2.7	4
Puerto Rican	0	0.0	0	0.0	0	0.0	0	0.0	0	0.0	0	0.0	0
Hispanic	9	2.8	6	1.9	15	2.3	0	0.0	6	2.8	15	2.3	1
Total Minority	47	14.9	65	20.1	112	17.5	0	0.0	31	14.5	112	17.5	40
For. Nation.	0	0.0	0	0.0	0	0.0	0	0.0	0	0.0	0	0.0	0
Caucasian	190	60.1	187	57.9	377	59.0	0	0.0	136	63.6	377	59.0	151
Unknown	79	25.0	71	22.0	150	23.5	0	0.0	47	22.0	150	23.5	54
Total	316	49.5	323	50.5	639	100.0	0	0.0	214	33.5	639		245

Transfers

Transfers in	7
Transfers out	7

Tuition and Fees

	Resident	Nonresident
Full-time	$33,590	$33,590
Part-time	$0	$0

Living Expenses

Estimated living expenses for singles

Living on campus	Living off campus	Living at home
$20,090	$20,090	$20,090

Pepperdine University School of Law

ABA
Approved
Since
1972

GPA and LSAT Scores

	Total	Full-time	Part-time
# of apps	3,134	3,134	0
# of offers	917	917	0
# of matrics	213	213	0
75% GPA	3.72	3.72	0.00
Median GPA	3.54	3.54	0.00
25% GPA	3.34	3.34	0.00
75% LSAT	163	163	0
Median LSAT	160	160	0
25% LSAT	156	156	0

Grants and Scholarships (from prior year)

	Total		Full-time		Part-time	
	#	%	#	%	#	%
Total # of students	704		704		0	
Total # receiving grants	528	75.0	528	75.0	0	0.0
Less than 1/2 tuition	394	56.0	394	56.0	0	0.0
Half to full tuition	104	14.8	104	14.8	0	0.0
Full tuition	1	0.1	1	0.1	0	0.0
More than full tuition	29	4.1	29	4.1	0	0.0
Median grant amount			$4,000		$0	

Informational and Library Resources

# of volumes and volume equivalents	379,958
# of titles	124,375
# of active serial subscriptions	3,603
Study seating capacity inside the library	493
# of full-time professional librarians	6
Hours per week library is open	105
# of open, wired connections available to students	83
# of networked computers available for use by students	54
# of simultaneous wireless users	700
Require computer?	No

JD Attrition (from prior year)

	Academic	Other	Total	
	#	#	#	%
1st year	19	16	35	14.6
2nd year	0	0	0	0.0
3rd year	0	0	0	0.0
4th year	0	0	0	0.0

Employment (9 months after graduation)

	Total	Percentage
Employment status known	224	99.1
Employment status unknown	2	0.9
Employed	183	81.7
Pursuing graduate degrees	7	3.1
Unemployed seeking employment	4	1.8
Unemployed not seeking employment	30	13.4
Unemployed and studying for the bar	0	0.0
Type of Employment		
# employed in law firms	112	61.2
# employed in business and industry	34	18.6
# employed in government	15	8.2
# employed in public interest	3	1.6
# employed as judicial clerks	13	7.1
# employed in academia	2	1.1
Geographic Location		
# employed in state	130	71.0
# employed in foreign countries	0	0.0
# of states where employed	25	

Bar Passage Rates

Jurisdiction	California		
Exam	Sum 05	Win 06	Total
# from school taking bar for the first time	157	14	171
School's pass rate for all first-time takers	73%	86%	74%
State's pass rate for all first-time takers	64%	54%	62%

Pepperdine University School of Law

24255 Pacific Coast Highway
Malibu, CA 90263
Phone: 310.506.4611; Fax: 310.506.7668
E-mail: soladmis@pepperdine.edu; Website: law.pepperdine.edu

■ Introduction

Pepperdine School of Law is located in Malibu, California, just 30 miles from downtown Los Angeles, making it a conducive environment for the intense study of law. Malibu offers an almost rural setting, yet it is an integral part of greater Los Angeles, providing access to one of the largest legal communities in the world. Pepperdine is a Christian university committed to the highest standards of academic excellence and Christian values, where students are strengthened for lives of purpose, service, and leadership.

■ Student Body

Pepperdine students bring a broad spectrum of backgrounds. They share a strong desire to attain high levels of achievement, in academics, in their personal lives, and in their careers. Students come to Pepperdine from diverse socioeconomic, cultural, and religious backgrounds for the emphasis on integrity, service, and justice with a desire to become trusted leaders.

■ Faculty

Although the faculty have distinguished themselves through scholarly research and writing as well as leadership positions in prestigious legal organizations, the faculty's primary mission is to teach—to help students see the structure of legal thought and to be available as professional examples of a multifaceted profession. They demonstrate to their students that lawyers should be people-oriented individuals with strong moral character, capable of guiding their clients toward what is just and honorable as well as what is legally permissible.

■ Library and Physical Facilities

The School of Law occupies the Odell McDonnell Law Center, located on the university's 830-acre campus overlooking the Pacific Ocean. The Jerene Appleby Harnish Library is the focal point of the school, housing a collection of over 365,000 volumes and volume equivalents. Students enjoy access to online legal research services and the Internet via the law school's network in three computer resource centers and at 70 wired study carrels. Wireless network access is available throughout the Law Center. The facility contains a high-tech courtroom, as well as lecture halls, seminar rooms, a bookstore, student dining area, and lounges.

■ Curriculum

Pepperdine offers a three-year, full-time JD program; four-year, full-time JD/MBA and JD/MPP joint-degree programs; a five-year, full-time JD/MDiv joint-degree program; a concurrent JD/MDR degree program; and an LLM in Dispute Resolution. A student enrolled full-time in a summer session can accelerate graduation by one semester. The required core courses are complemented by an extensive selection of elective courses.

■ The Palmer Center for Entrepreneurship and the Law

Unique in the nation, the Palmer Center prepares students for the modern hybrid role of lawyer, business consultant, financial strategist, and venture capitalist, and equips them with credentials and options in the field of entrepreneurship. Through carefully tailored coursework, the Palmer Center integrates multifaceted law and business disciplines into a distinctive and dynamic certificate program that supplements and complements the traditional JD degree.

■ Straus Institute for Dispute Resolution

The Straus Institute is the most comprehensive program of its type in the nation. The institute's faculty involvement as mediators, continuing legal education educators, and consultants enriches the practical application of course materials. Students studying in the field of dispute resolution can complete a special certificate program as part of their Juris Doctor degree program or a Master of Dispute Resolution. The LLM in Dispute Resolution began January 2003.

■ London Program

Students have the opportunity to study law in London at Pepperdine's university-owned facility in the museum district of South Kensington. While in London, students may serve as externs in clinical placements.

■ Exchange Programs

Students have the opportunity to participate in exchange programs with the University of Copenhagen and the University of Augsburg.

■ Clinical Education

Clinical law programs provide students the opportunity to refine their skills under the supervision of faculty, lawyers, and judges. The majority of clinical law opportunities are with the district attorneys, public defenders, and state and federal court judges. There are a number of programs offering experience in corporate and securities law, tax law, juvenile law, family law, labor law, consumer protection, environmental law, and trade regulation. Placements are also available within the film, television, and music industries.

■ Public Interest Opportunities

Pepperdine has partnered with the Los Angeles Union Rescue Mission to develop the Pepperdine/Union Rescue Mission Legal Aid Clinic. Located in downtown Los Angeles, the mission provides emergency food and shelter, health services, recovery programs, education, job training, and counseling within a Christian context. Students volunteer at the mission, where they meet with residents regarding legal concerns. The Pepperdine/Union Rescue Mission Family Law Clinic helps clients resolve issues such as child custody and support. The Special Education Advocacy Clinic, housed at the School of Law, gives students an opportunity to gain valuable experience advocating for children with disabilities. Students work to help ensure that children with special needs receive proper accommodations in public schools.

Student Activities

Pepperdine has earned a national reputation for excellence in appellate advocacy and trial advocacy competitions. Editorial and staff positions are awarded with the *Pepperdine Law Review*, *Pepperdine Dispute Resolution Law Journal*, and the *National Association of Administrative Law Judges Journal*.

Admission

Admission is based on the applicant's academic record, LSAT score, a written personal statement as well as a response to the university's mission statement, and other information that reflects outstanding academic and professional promise. Applications are also evaluated on the basis of employment experience, extracurricular activities, community involvement, commitment to high standards of morality and ethics, maturity, initiative, and motivation. The admission process is guided by the view that a student body that reflects diversity provides a superior educational environment. Admission decisions may be based on consideration of factors that include racial and ethnic origin, unique work or service experience, a history of overcoming disadvantage, or unusual life experiences. First-year students are admitted only in the fall.

Housing

The George Page Residential Complex is located directly across the street from the Law Center. The 72-unit complex houses graduate students in two- and four-bedroom apartments. The Admission Office also provides an extensive housing referral service.

Expenses and Financial Aid

An active financial aid program provides over 85 percent of the student body with some type of assistance. Scholarship grants are available to students with outstanding academic credentials and to those with demonstrated financial need. The deadline for completed applications for financial aid is April 1 of the entering year.

Career Development Office

The Career Development Office is committed to helping every law student explore, define, and achieve their career goals through career-related workshops, guest speaker programs, and one-on-one counseling sessions. The office also sponsors a robust Alumni Mentoring Program. Annually, over 100 employers participate in Pepperdine recruiting programs.

Applicant Profile

Pepperdine University School of Law
This grid includes only applicants who earned 120–180 LSAT scores under standard administrations.

LSAT Score	GPA 3.75 +		3.50–3.74		3.25–3.49		3.00–3.24		2.75–2.99		2.50 -2.74		Below 2.50		No GPA		Total	
	Apps	Adm	Apps	Adm	Apps	Adm	Apps	Adm	Apps	Adm	Apps	Adm	Apps	Adm	Apps	Adm	Apps	Adm
175–180	0	0	2	2	0	0	1	1	0	0	0	0	0	0	0	0	3	3
170–174	16	15	11	11	6	4	1	1	3	0	0	0	1	0	0	0	38	31
165–169	30	27	49	43	22	21	24	20	13	6	7	1	5	1	0	0	150	119
160–164	100	89	127	117	106	93	93	65	47	12	25	13	11	4	2	0	511	393
155–159	167	100	271	119	285	70	174	14	93	11	54	5	14	1	6	0	1064	320
150–154	73	9	172	14	202	11	164	7	94	1	42	0	27	0	7	0	781	42
Below 150	41	0	104	1	150	1	160	0	120	0	62	0	42	0	12	0	691	2
Total	427	240	736	307	771	200	617	108	370	30	190	19	100	6	27	0	3238	910

Apps = Number of Applicants
Adm = Number Admitted
Reflects 99% of the total applicant pool.

University of Pittsburgh School of Law

3900 Forbes Avenue, Barco Law Building
Pittsburgh, PA 15260
Phone: 412.648.1413; Fax: 412.648.1318
E-mail: admissions@law.pitt.edu; Website: www.law.pitt.edu

ABA
Approved
Since
1923

The Basics

Type of school	Public
Term	Semester
Application deadline	3/1
Application fee	$55
Financial aid deadline	3/1
Can first year start other than fall?	No
Student to faculty ratio	14.2 to 1
Does the university offer:	
housing restricted to law students?	No
graduate housing for which law students are eligible?	No

Faculty and Administrators

	Total		Men		Women		Minorities	
	Fall	Spr	Fall	Spr	Fall	Spr	Fall	Spr
Full-time	44	38	29	23	15	15	7	4
Other Full-time	2	1	0	0	2	1	1	0
Deans, librarians, & others who teach	12	13	4	5	8	8	1	2
Part-time	46	51	34	38	12	13	2	2
Total	**104**	**103**	**67**	**66**	**37**	**37**	**11**	**8**

Curriculum

	Full-time	Part-time
Typical first-year section size	82	0
Is there typically a "small section" of the first-year class, other than Legal Writing, taught by full-time faculty	Yes	No
If yes, typical size offered last year	27	
# of classroom course titles beyond first-year curriculum	163	

# of upper division courses, excluding seminars with an enrollment:	Under 25	105
	25–49	29
	50–74	15
	75–99	8
	100+	3

# of seminars	20	
# of seminar positions available	251	
# of seminar positions filled	179	0
# of positions available in simulation courses	254	
# of simulation positions filled	209	0
# of positions available in faculty supervised clinical courses	173	
# of faculty supervised clinical positions filled	128	0
# involved in field placements	130	0
# involved in law journals	189	0
# involved in interschool competitions	132	0
# of credit hours required to graduate	88	

JD Enrollment and Ethnicity

	Men		Women		Full-time		Part-time		1st-year		Total		JD Degs. Awd.
	#	%	#	%	#	%	#	%	#	%	#	%	
African Amer.	13	3.1	30	9.8	43	5.9	0	0.0	13	5.4	43	5.9	15
Amer. Indian	0	0.0	1	0.3	1	0.1	0	0.0	0	0.0	1	0.1	7
Asian Amer.	17	4.0	23	7.5	40	5.5	0	0.0	19	7.9	40	5.5	6
Mex. Amer.	0	0.0	3	1.0	3	0.4	0	0.0	1	0.4	3	0.4	3
Puerto Rican	3	0.7	0	0.0	3	0.4	0	0.0	1	0.4	3	0.4	0
Hispanic	1	0.2	7	2.3	8	1.1	0	0.0	2	0.8	8	1.1	2
Total Minority	34	8.0	64	20.9	98	13.4	0	0.0	36	14.9	98	13.4	33
For. Nation.	0	0.0	0	0.0	0	0.0	0	0.0	0	0.0	0	0.0	0
Caucasian	285	67.1	173	56.5	458	62.7	0	0.0	147	60.7	458	62.7	135
Unknown	106	24.9	69	22.5	175	23.9	0	0.0	59	24.4	175	23.9	44
Total	425	58.1	306	41.9	731	100.0	0	0.0	242	33.1	731		212

Transfers

Transfers in	15
Transfers out	12

Tuition and Fees

	Resident	Nonresident
Full-time	$21,408	$29,706
Part-time	$0	$0

Living Expenses

Estimated living expenses for singles

Living on campus	Living off campus	Living at home
$14,710	$14,710	$14,710

University of Pittsburgh School of Law

ABA Approved Since 1923

GPA and LSAT Scores

	Total	Full-time	Part-time
# of apps	2,369	2,369	0
# of offers	736	736	0
# of matrics	243	243	0
75% GPA	3.63	3.63	0.00
Median GPA	3.40	3.40	0.00
25% GPA	3.11	3.11	0.00
75% LSAT	161	161	0
Median LSAT	159	159	0
25% LSAT	158	158	0

Grants and Scholarships (from prior year)

	Total #	Total %	Full-time #	Full-time %	Part-time #	Part-time %
Total # of students	714		691		23	
Total # receiving grants	375	52.5	375	54.3	0	0.0
Less than 1/2 tuition	223	31.2	223	32.3	0	0.0
Half to full tuition	143	20.0	143	20.7	0	0.0
Full tuition	6	0.8	6	0.9	0	0.0
More than full tuition	3	0.4	3	0.4	0	0.0
Median grant amount			$10,000		$0	

Informational and Library Resources

# of volumes and volume equivalents	447,986
# of titles	251,414
# of active serial subscriptions	2,619
Study seating capacity inside the library	438
# of full-time professional librarians	16
Hours per week library is open	103
# of open, wired connections available to students	304
# of networked computers available for use by students	35
# of simultaneous wireless users	740
Require computer?	No

JD Attrition (from prior year)

	Academic #	Other #	Total #	Total %
1st year	0	0	0	0.0
2nd year	0	14	14	6.2
3rd year	0	0	0	0.0
4th year	0	0	0	0.0

Employment (9 months after graduation)

	Total	Percentage
Employment status known	258	99.6
Employment status unknown	1	0.4
Employed	233	90.3
Pursuing graduate degrees	9	3.5
Unemployed seeking employment	2	0.8
Unemployed not seeking employment	10	3.9
Unemployed and studying for the bar	4	1.6

Type of Employment

# employed in law firms	132	56.7
# employed in business and industry	48	20.6
# employed in government	11	4.7
# employed in public interest	8	3.4
# employed as judicial clerks	27	11.6
# employed in academia	4	1.7

Geographic Location

# employed in state	171	73.4
# employed in foreign countries	2	0.9
# of states where employed		18

Bar Passage Rates

Jurisdiction	Pennsylvania		
Exam	Sum 05	Win 06	Total
# from school taking bar for the first time	192	12	204
School's pass rate for all first-time takers	84%	67%	83%
State's pass rate for all first-time takers	79%	75%	78%

University of Pittsburgh School of Law

3900 Forbes Avenue, Barco Law Building
Pittsburgh, PA 15260
Phone: 412.648.1413; Fax: 412.648.1318
E-mail: admissions@law.pitt.edu; Website: www.law.pitt.edu

■ Introduction

The University of Pittsburgh School of Law (Pitt), founded in 1895, is a leader in the world of legal education. It features a broad and varied curriculum, an internationally accomplished faculty, state-of-the-art physical facilities, and a talented and diverse student body hailing from all over the globe. The School of Law is located in its own modern six-story building on campus in Oakland, the cultural and educational center of Pittsburgh. State and federal courts, major corporate headquarters, and hundreds of law firms are located nearby in downtown Pittsburgh, only minutes from campus. The dynamic Oakland area is home to four colleges and universities, the world-renowned, multi-hospital University of Pittsburgh Medical Center, numerous scientific and high-tech offices and research centers, museums, art galleries, coffee houses, and libraries. The Pitt campus abuts a beautiful 429-acre city park. Desirable and affordable residential areas are situated nearby. Quality housing is readily available, and all mass transit in the city is free to Pitt students with ID cards.

■ Library and Physical Facilities

The newly renovated Barco Law Library is an attractive, 440,000-volume, open-stack research facility, housed on three floors of the School of Law building. Full of natural light, it contains several study rooms, a computer lab, and ample seating space. The Fawcett Student Commons in the library is a comfortable gathering spot for students, faculty, and staff, and contains the Sidebar Café, featuring Starbucks coffee products. Faculty offices ring the perimeter of the first and third floors of the library, encouraging ease of interaction between students and faculty. Classrooms with state-of-the-art technology are located on the first and ground floors of the School of Law building. A spacious and comfortable student lounge and the elegant Teplitz Memorial Courtroom are located on the ground floor. Student computing is supported through a wireless network and wired carrels and seating.

■ Special Programs

- *Clinical Programs*—Academics and reality meet head-on in our legal clinics. Pitt law students have the opportunity to obtain hands-on experience in several different clinical programs, which include a Tax Clinic; an Environmental Law Clinic; a Civil Practice Clinic that selects a focus on either Health Law, Elder Law, or Family Law and Related Matters; and a Community Economic Development Clinic. With a supervising attorney, students do it all: pretrial preparation, negotiation, litigation, and counseling real-life clients about real-life legal concerns.
- *Certificate Programs*—One way to practice proficiently in an interdependent world is to develop specialized expertise. Pitt law students may seize that advantage through participation in our certificate programs, a collection of sharply focused courses that culminate in certification to specialize in a high-demand area of practice. Certificate programs currently exist in the areas of civil litigation; environmental law, science, and policy; health law; international and comparative law; and intellectual property and technology law. These certificate programs can be completed within the regular 88 credits.
- *Joint-degree Programs*—Motivated by the growing management and social science needs of attorneys and the increasingly intricate legal needs of society, we offer several joint-degree programs that provide rigorous, integrated training, effectively merging law and a number of allied fields. They include the JD/MBA with both Pitt and Carnegie Mellon University; the JD/MPH with our Graduate School of Public Health; the JD/MPA, JD/MPIA, and JD/MID with our Graduate School of Public and International Affairs; the JD/MA(Bioethics); and the JD/MS with the Heinz School at Carnegie Mellon University.
- *Mellon Legal Writing Program*—The Mellon Program provides academic support to students at the law school who wish to improve their writing, exam-taking, and study skills. Exam preparation sessions include general discussion regarding the form and substance of law school exams as well as more specific guidance relating to particular topics and classes. All workshops are led by the Associate Dean for Student Affairs.

■ Center for International Legal Education (CILE)

In today's world, legal transactions inevitably involve many nations and many sets of laws. The successful lawyer—today's global lawyer—understands the political, cultural, and social influences on the legal systems of other countries and uses that knowledge for the benefit of his or her clients. CILE faculty prepare Pitt law students for successful futures in this modern world. Students study the workings of foreign legal systems and explore the wide array of issues facing practicing attorneys in the global marketplace. The center also coordinates international programs at Pitt with the University Center for International Studies and affiliated area studies programs, and it supervises a number of specialized language classes, for example, French for Lawyers, Spanish for Lawyers, German for Lawyers, Chinese for Lawyers, and Japanese for Lawyers.

■ Admission

Applicants are reviewed on a rolling basis. Pitt Law is highly competitive, and decisions are based upon several factors, with the GPA and LSAT being the most important. When evaluating an undergraduate degree, the committee pays careful attention to the strength of the major field of study, as evidenced by the courses listed on the undergraduate transcript. The school is looking for applicants who have demonstrated the discipline and ability to handle a rigorous and demanding program. The same assessment is made of graduate and professional work. A required personal statement gives the committee a view into the nonacademic world of the applicant. This is critical in our ability to enroll a diverse class. Letters of recommendation play an equally important role in this process, as they can reveal the strengths of the academic achievements of the applicant. Résumés are also recommended, to give the admissions committee a broader view of your achievements.

Scholarships

If you are accepted to Pitt Law, we make every effort to assist you in securing the financial resources you will need in order to cover the cost of your legal education. Approximately 43 percent of the student body receives merit- or need-based scholarship funds. The University of Pittsburgh School of Law also offers a Public Interest Scholarship and has several firm-sponsored scholarships available. Once a student is accepted to Pitt Law the file goes automatically to our Scholarship committee so if you are eligible for a Dean's Scholarship or Tuition Scholarship you will be notified usually within three weeks of your acceptance. Please visit our website for a complete list and description of all our scholarships.

Student Activities

The *Law Review*, the *Journal of Law and Commerce*, and the *Journal of Law and Technology* are legal periodicals published by upper-class law students. In addition, more than 30 law student organizations exist under the auspices of the Student Bar Association, reflecting the diverse social and intellectual interests and experiences of our students. They include the Asian Law Students Association, the Black Law Students Association, the Environmental Law Council, the Federalist Society, the Hispanic Law Society, the Jewish Law Students Association, the Lesbian-Gay Rights Organization (OUTLAW), the Pitt Law Women's Association, and the Pitt Legal Income Sharing Foundation, to name a few.

Career Services

The Career Service's Office provides year-round assistance to Pitt students and graduates. The office serves as a clearinghouse for information on summer, part-time, and permanent work with law firms, corporations, accounting firms, government agencies, judges, and other legal employers. It also helps students develop practical job-search strategies, helps demystify the dynamics of the legal job market, offers strategies for finding the perfect job in that market, and offers information and counseling regarding nontraditional careers utilizing professional skills gained in law school. The placement rate for the class of 2005 was 97 percent.

Applicant Profile

University of Pittsburgh School of Law
This grid includes only applicants who earned 120–180 LSAT scores under standard administrations.

LSAT Score	3.75 +		3.50–3.74		3.25–3.49		3.00–3.24		2.75–2.99		2.50–2.74		Below 2.50		No GPA		Total	
	Apps	Adm	Apps	Adm	Apps	Adm	Apps	Adm	Apps	Adm	Apps	Adm	Apps	Adm	Apps	Adm	Apps	Adm
165–180	43	31	42	35	35	24	17	9	17	12	10	2	6	1	1	0	171	114
160–164	86	70	134	101	118	74	95	56	60	32	23	9	10	2	2	0	528	344
155–159	118	42	207	64	216	69	150	28	72	18	28	3	13	0	9	1	813	225
150–154	68	8	105	7	126	13	97	7	53	4	20	0	15	0	6	0	490	39
145–149	18	2	26	2	43	1	49	2	21	0	15	2	12	0	2	0	186	9
Below 145	12	0	27	0	20	0	24	0	28	0	14	0	24	0	32	0	181	0
Total	345	153	541	209	558	181	432	102	251	66	110	16	80	3	52	1	2369	731

Apps = Number of Applicants
Adm = Number Admitted
Reflects 99% of the total applicant pool.

Pontifical Catholic University of Puerto Rico School of Law

2250 Avenida Las Americas
Ponce, PR 00732
Phone: 787.841.2000, exts. 1836, 1837; Fax: 787.841.4620
E-mail: derecho@pucpr.edu; Website: www.pucpr.edu/derecho

ABA Approved Since 1967

The Basics

Type of school	Private
Term	Semester
Application deadline	4/15 9/30
Application fee	$75
Financial aid deadline	
Can first year start other than fall?	Yes
Student to faculty ratio	16.3 to 1
Does the university offer:	
housing restricted to law students?	No
graduate housing for which law students are eligible?	No

Faculty and Administrators

	Total		Men		Women		Minorities	
	Fall	Spr	Fall	Spr	Fall	Spr	Fall	Spr
Full-time	24	24	18	18	6	6	24	24
Other Full-time	0	0	0	0	0	0	0	0
Deans, librarians, & others who teach	5	5	4	4	1	1	5	5
Part-time	14	18	12	14	2	4	14	18
Total	43	47	34	36	9	11	43	47

Curriculum

	Full-time	Part-time
Typical first-year section size	42	38
Is there typically a "small section" of the first-year class, other than Legal Writing, taught by full-time faculty	Yes	Yes
If yes, typical size offered last year	19	15
# of classroom course titles beyond first-year curriculum	85	
# of upper division courses, excluding seminars with an enrollment: Under 25	50	
25–49	47	
50–74	17	
75–99	2	
100+	0	
# of seminars	18	
# of seminar positions available	403	
# of seminar positions filled	156	181
# of positions available in simulation courses	170	
# of simulation positions filled	46	114
# of positions available in faculty supervised clinical courses	6	
# of faculty supervised clinical positions filled	6	0
# involved in field placements	0	0
# involved in law journals	113	2
# involved in interschool competitions	0	0
# of credit hours required to graduate	94	

JD Enrollment and Ethnicity

	Men		Women		Full-time		Part-time		1st-year		Total		JD Degs. Awd.
	#	%	#	%	#	%	#	%	#	%	#	%	
African Amer.	0	0.0	0	0.0	0	0.0	0	0.0	0	0.0	0	0.0	0
Amer. Indian	0	0.0	0	0.0	0	0.0	0	0.0	0	0.0	0	0.0	0
Asian Amer.	0	0.0	0	0.0	0	0.0	0	0.0	0	0.0	0	0.0	0
Mex. Amer.	1	0.4	0	0.0	1	0.3	0	0.0	1	0.6	1	0.2	0
Puerto Rican	245	99.2	262	100.0	349	99.4	158	100.0	161	99.4	507	99.6	141
Hispanic	1	0.4	0	0.0	1	0.3	0	0.0	0	0.0	1	0.2	0
Total Minority	247	100.0	262	100.0	351	100.0	158	100.0	162	100.0	509	100.0	141
For. Nation.	0	0.0	0	0.0	0	0.0	0	0.0	0	0.0	0	0.0	0
Caucasian	0	0.0	0	0.0	0	0.0	0	0.0	0	0.0	0	0.0	0
Unknown	0	0.0	0	0.0	0	0.0	0	0.0	0	0.0	0	0.0	0
Total	247	48.5	262	51.5	351	69.0	158	31.0	162	31.8	509		141

Transfers

Transfers in	1
Transfers out	23

Tuition and Fees

	Resident	Nonresident
Full-time	$13,141	$0
Part-time	$9,419	$0

Living Expenses

Estimated living expenses for singles

Living on campus	Living off campus	Living at home
$7,651	$9,482	$6,782

Pontifical Catholic University of Puerto Rico School of Law

*ABA
Approved
Since
1967*

GPA and LSAT Scores

	Total	Full-time	Part-time
# of apps	517	356	161
# of offers	218	146	72
# of matrics	169	109	60
75% GPA	3.57	3.57	3.55
Median GPA	3.21	3.22	3.23
25% GPA	2.95	2.76	2.93
75% LSAT	139	139	139
Median LSAT	136	136	136
25% LSAT	133	134	133

Grants and Scholarships (from prior year)

	Total		Full-time		Part-time	
	#	%	#	%	#	%
Total # of students	520		360		160	
Total # receiving grants	53	10.2	46	12.8	7	4.4
Less than 1/2 tuition	1	0.2	1	0.3	0	0.0
Half to full tuition	43	8.3	37	10.3	6	3.8
Full tuition	9	1.7	8	2.2	1	0.6
More than full tuition	0	0.0	0	0.0	0	0.0
Median grant amount			$4,810		$4,440	

Informational and Library Resources

# of volumes and volume equivalents	221,516
# of titles	28,325
# of active serial subscriptions	2,504
Study seating capacity inside the library	184
# of full-time professional librarians	4
Hours per week library is open	92
# of open, wired connections available to students	80
# of networked computers available for use by students	35
# of simultaneous wireless users	500
Require computer?	No

JD Attrition (from prior year)

	Academic	Other	Total	
	#	#	#	%
1st year	5	27	32	16.0
2nd year	1	7	8	5.1
3rd year	0	3	3	2.1
4th year	0	5	5	20.8

Employment (9 months after graduation)

	Total	Percentage
Employment status known	125	81.7
Employment status unknown	28	18.3
Employed	63	50.4
Pursuing graduate degrees	5	4.0
Unemployed seeking employment	43	34.4
Unemployed not seeking employment	0	0.0
Unemployed and studying for the bar	14	11.2

Type of Employment

# employed in law firms	23	36.5
# employed in business and industry	3	4.8
# employed in government	8	12.7
# employed in public interest	0	0.0
# employed as judicial clerks	2	3.2
# employed in academia	0	0.0

Geographic Location

# employed in state	62	98.4
# employed in foreign countries	0	0.0
# of states where employed		0

Bar Passage Rates

Jurisdiction	Puerto Rico		
Exam	Sum 05	Win 06	Total
# from school taking bar for the first time	110	44	154
School's pass rate for all first-time takers	31%	48%	36%
State's pass rate for all first-time takers	50%	33%	46%

Pontifical Catholic University of Puerto Rico School of Law

2250 Avenida Las Americas
Ponce, PR 00732
Phone: 787.841.2000, exts. 1836, 1837; Fax: 787.841.4620
E-mail: derecho@pucpr.edu; Website: www.pucpr.edu/derecho

■ Introduction

The School of Law of the Pontifical Catholic University of Puerto Rico was founded in 1961. It is located within the main campus of the Pontifical Catholic University of Puerto Rico, on the southern part of the island in the historical city of Ponce, one of the most beautiful places in Puerto Rico.

The primary objective of the Pontifical Catholic University School of Law is the formation of lawyers imbued with a deep love and concern for their Catholic faith and imbedded in the redeeming truths of Christian philosophy and ethics. The law school of the Pontifical Catholic University of Puerto Rico hopes to contribute to upholding the high ethical, cultural, and literary accomplishments of the Puerto Rican bar, which historically represents a tradition of moral austerity, intellectual achievement, and professional competence.

■ Library and Physical Facilities

The School of Law occupies the Spellman Building. Its location on the campus of Pontifical Catholic University of Puerto Rico enables students to study related academic disciplines, to participate in the intellectual life, and to enjoy many other facilities of the university.

Among the materials in the library is a comprehensive and growing collection of legal treatises, tests, monographs, and periodicals, including the most important and recent publications in civil, common, and comparative law. Modern audiovisual equipment and computerized services are also available. The library is an authorized depository for the United Nations documents as well as for United States government documents. In addition, it offers the services of the Westlaw and LexisNexis systems, which permit computer-assisted legal research.

■ Curriculum

The required subjects are Developments and Evolution of the Institutions of the Civil Law, Constitutional Law, Torts, Property Law, Legal Ethics and Professional Responsibility, Theology, Family Law, Successions and Donations, Penal Law, Criminal Procedure, Administrative Law, Obligations, Contracts, Notarial Law, Civil Procedure, Evidence, Mortgages, Trial Practice, Legal Aid Clinic, Corporations, Mercantile Law, Negotiable Instruments, Federal Jurisdiction, Analysis of Jurisprudence, Legal Document Workshop, and Legal Bibliography. The basic program covers three years in the day division or four years in the evening division.

The school curriculum includes a clinical program for third-year students. Pursuant to a rule approved by the Supreme Court of the Commonwealth of Puerto Rico in 1974, students practice trial advocacy under the supervision of law school professors in the Courts of First Instance and in administrative agencies.

The Pontifical Catholic University of Puerto Rico also offers a combined JD/MBA degree. For the combined degree, students are required to complete 85 credit hours at the School of Law (79 required credits and 6 elective credits), plus 9 credit hours in electives completed at the Graduate Program of the School of Business Administration, for a total of 94 credit hours. In addition, the students must complete 34 credit hours at the School of Business Administration (31 required credits and 3 electives) and an additional 9 approved elective credits in JD for a total of 43 credits, plus four hours of Theology.

■ Admission

Application for admission is open to men and women of good character who have received a bachelor's degree from a qualified institution and have obtained a 2.5 grade-point average.

The required forms for application for admission and all other information may be obtained from the registrar of the law school and should be filed with all supporting documents before April 15. The School of Law admits beginning students in August and January for both the full-time and part-time programs.

Applicants are required to take both the LSAT and the Examen de Admision a Estudios de Posgrado (EXADEP) (formerly PAEG).

Test scores are not the only factor considered. Besides the objective factors, there are many intangible and personal considerations, such as strong motivation, disadvantaged circumstances, evidence of improving performance, and relevant work experience. A personal interview of the applicant by a committee is essential before a decision is made. Applicants of both sexes and from all religious, racial, social, and ethnic backgrounds are encouraged to apply.

All courses are offered only in Spanish. Consequently, students are required to be proficient in Spanish.

■ Student Activities

The law review, *Revista de Derecho Puertorriqueño*, is devoted to scholarly analysis and discussion of development of the law. It publishes student notes, comments, and surveys, as well as articles of outstanding quality submitted by attorneys, judges, and other members of the legal profession. The school has a student council, a chapter of the National Association of Law Students of Puerto Rico, and an Association for Women's Rights. Local chapters of Phi Alpha Delta international law fraternity, the Delta Theta Phi law fraternity, and the Law Student Division of the ABA are also active and well organized in the law school.

■ Housing

Students live either in university residences or private housing. Inquiries concerning housing facilities should be addressed to the Housing Office, Pontifical Catholic University of Puerto Rico, Ponce, Puerto Rico 00732.

■ Expenses and Financial Aid

There is a deferred plan for students who have financial difficulties at the time of registration. The university has made available for law students several full-tuition scholarships to be awarded on the basis of scholastic excellence. The university also has an office for student loans and other types of financial services.

Applicant Profile Not Available

University of Puerto Rico School of Law

PO Box 23349, UPR Station
San Juan, PR 00931-3349
Phone: 787.999.9595; Fax: 787.999.9564
E-mail: arosario-lebron@law.upr.edu

*ABA
Approved
Since
1945*

The Basics

Type of school	Public
Term	Semester
Application deadline	2/15
Application fee	$20
Financial aid deadline	4/27
Can first year start other than fall?	No
Student to faculty ratio	13.9 to 1
Does the university offer:	
housing restricted to law students?	Yes
graduate housing for which law students are eligible?	No

Faculty and Administrators

	Total		Men		Women		Minorities	
	Fall	Spr	Fall	Spr	Fall	Spr	Fall	Spr
Full-time	40	37	23	22	17	15	38	35
Other Full-time	2	4	1	2	1	2	0	1
Deans, librarians, & others who teach	6	7	4	4	2	3	6	7
Part-time	31	26	20	17	11	9	28	24
Total	**79**	**74**	**48**	**45**	**31**	**29**	**72**	**67**

Curriculum

	Full-time	Part-time
Typical first-year section size	47	30
Is there typically a "small section" of the first-year class, other than Legal Writing, taught by full-time faculty	No	No
If yes, typical size offered last year		
# of classroom course titles beyond first-year curriculum	120	

# of upper division courses, excluding seminars with an enrollment:		
	Under 25	73
	25–49	47
	50–74	32
	75–99	9
	100+	1

# of seminars		46
# of seminar positions available		690
# of seminar positions filled	284	179
# of positions available in simulation courses	170	
# of simulation positions filled	71	35
# of positions available in faculty supervised clinical courses	390	
# of faculty supervised clinical positions filled	215	92
# involved in field placements	43	13
# involved in law journals	16	1
# involved in interschool competitions	4	0
# of credit hours required to graduate	92	

JD Enrollment and Ethnicity

	Men		Women		Full-time		Part-time		1st-year		Total		JD Degs. Awd.
	#	%	#	%	#	%	#	%	#	%	#	%	
African Amer.	0	0.0	0	0.0	0	0.0	0	0.0	0	0.0	0	0.0	0
Amer. Indian	0	0.0	0	0.0	0	0.0	0	0.0	0	0.0	0	0.0	0
Asian Amer.	0	0.0	0	0.0	0	0.0	0	0.0	0	0.0	0	0.0	0
Mex. Amer.	0	0.0	0	0.0	0	0.0	0	0.0	0	0.0	0	0.0	0
Puerto Rican	314	98.1	378	99.0	511	98.1	181	100.0	264	96.4	692	98.6	149
Hispanic	0	0.0	0	0.0	0	0.0	0	0.0	0	0.0	0	0.0	3
Total Minority	314	98.1	378	99.0	511	98.1	181	100.0	264	96.4	692	98.6	152
For. Nation.	5	1.6	3	0.8	8	1.5	0	0.0	8	2.9	8	1.1	0
Caucasian	1	0.3	1	0.3	2	0.4	0	0.0	2	0.7	2	0.3	0
Unknown	0	0.0	0	0.0	0	0.0	0	0.0	0	0.0	0	0.0	0
Total	320	45.6	382	54.4	521	74.2	181	25.8	274	39.0	702		152

Transfers

Transfers in	21
Transfers out	1

Tuition and Fees

	Resident	Nonresident
Full-time	$3,858	$5,413
Part-time	$2,958	$7,159

Living Expenses

Estimated living expenses for singles

Living on campus	Living off campus	Living at home
$8,845	$11,655	$8,405

University of Puerto Rico School of Law

ABA Approved Since 1945

GPA and LSAT Scores

	Total	Full-time	Part-time
# of apps	561	341	220
# of offers	215	145	70
# of matrics	197	131	66
75% GPA	3.78	3.79	3.76
Median GPA	3.56	3.61	3.48
25% GPA	3.32	3.39	3.14
75% LSAT	148	148	148
Median LSAT	144	144	145
25% LSAT	141	141	141

Grants and Scholarships (from prior year)

	Total		Full-time		Part-time	
	#	%	#	%	#	%
Total # of students	698		427		271	
Total # receiving grants	1	0.1	1	0.2	0	0.0
Less than 1/2 tuition	0	0.0	0	0.0	0	0.0
Half to full tuition	1	0.1	1	0.2	0	0.0
Full tuition	0	0.0	0	0.0	0	0.0
More than full tuition	0	0.0	0	0.0	0	0.0
Median grant amount			$2,395		$0	

Informational and Library Resources

# of volumes and volume equivalents	451,763
# of titles	81,381
# of active serial subscriptions	5,203
Study seating capacity inside the library	407
# of full-time professional librarians	12
Hours per week library is open	112
# of open, wired connections available to students	150
# of networked computers available for use by students	42
# of simultaneous wireless users	200
Require computer?	No

JD Attrition (from prior year)

	Academic	Other	Total	
	#	#	#	%
1st year	9	10	19	9.4
2nd year	4	3	7	2.8
3rd year	0	4	4	2.2
4th year	0	0	0	0.0

Employment (9 months after graduation)

	Total	Percentage
Employment status known	71	39.9
Employment status unknown	107	60.1
Employed	57	80.3
Pursuing graduate degrees	1	1.4
Unemployed seeking employment	11	15.5
Unemployed not seeking employment	2	2.8
Unemployed and studying for the bar	0	0.0

Type of Employment

	Total	Percentage
# employed in law firms	29	50.9
# employed in business and industry	10	17.5
# employed in government	7	12.3
# employed in public interest	0	0.0
# employed as judicial clerks	9	15.8
# employed in academia	2	3.5

Geographic Location

	Total	Percentage
# employed in state	0	0.0
# employed in foreign countries	0	0.0
# of states where employed	1	

Bar Passage Rates

Jurisdiction	Puerto Rico		
Exam	Sum 05	Win 06	Total
# from school taking bar for the first time	158	12	170
School's pass rate for all first-time takers	69%	33%	66%
State's pass rate for all first-time takers	50%	33%	46%

University of Puerto Rico School of Law

PO Box 23349, UPR Station
San Juan, PR 00931-3349
Phone: 787.999.9595; Fax: 787.999.9564
E-mail: arosario-lebron@law.upr.edu

■ Introduction

The University of Puerto Rico School of Law was founded in 1913 at its present site on the University Campus at Rio Piedras, within the metropolitan area of San Juan. The University of Puerto Rico is accredited by the Middle States Colleges Association. The School of Law has been accredited by the American Bar Association since 1945 and by the Association of American Law Schools since 1948. It is also accredited by the Council on Higher Education and the Puerto Rico Supreme Court.

■ Library and Physical Facilities

The School of Law's library is the largest law library in the Caribbean. Its collection encompasses both the Romano-Germanic civil law and Anglo-American common law traditions. The law library contains a comprehensive collection of legal materials from the Caribbean Basin, including resources from Mexico, Central America, Venezuela, and Colombia. In addition to containing hard copy and microform materials, the law library subscribes to a variety of computerized legal research services. The law library has been designated as a European Documentation Center by the European Union and is also a selective depository for US government documents.

■ Clinical Program

In March 1974, the Puerto Rico Supreme Court approved rules for the local courts to allow students to practice law and participate in judicial proceedings. The US District Court followed suit in 1991. The School of Law's curriculum requires that students in their last year of law school complete a clinical program. Its Legal Aid Clinic handles over 1,300 cases per year.

■ Special Programs

The School of Law has student exchange programs with the University of Arizona James E. Rogers College of Law, the University of Connecticut School of Law, the University of Palermo in Argentina, the University of Chile Law School, the University of Ottawa Faculty of Law in Canada, and the University of Amberes in Belgium. Under these programs, the students will register at their home institution but will take a full courseload at the host institution. The credits and grades earned during a single semester will be awarded by the home institution according to the standard procedure of the home law school.

Students also have a chance to attend two different law programs at the University of Barcelona, Spain. The first one is a summer law program. The other is a four-year program: three years of study at the University of Puerto Rico School of Law and one year abroad at the University of Barcelona. At the end of this program, the student will receive a Juris Doctor from the University of Puerto Rico and a law degree from the University of Barcelona, which will enable him or her to practice law in the European Union.

The law school also has three joint-degree programs: a JD/MBA program with the University of Puerto Rico Graduate School of Business Administration, a JD/MPP program with the Hubert H. Humphrey Institute of Public Policy of the University of Minnesota, and a JD/MD program with the University of Puerto Rico School of Medicine.

Also, the school has a winter exchange program with the University of Ottawa Faculty of Law in Canada in which the students can earn four credits studying Law and Technology for one week in Canada and two weeks in Puerto Rico.

The law school also offers an LLM Program for Latin American Lawyers.

■ Admission

In order to be admitted to the University of Puerto Rico School of Law, applicants must take the LSAT and the Examen de Admision a Estudios de Posgrado (EXADEP), administered by the Educational Testing Service, no later than the February or March, respectively, of the year of application. Applicants must complete their undergraduate degree before enrolling in the law school. The LSAT, the EXADEP, and the graduating index are converted into the student's admission index.

Cases of applicants with disabilities, who, by reason of their disability, cannot take the required aptitude tests, are considered individually by the Admissions Committee.

The University of Puerto Rico does not discriminate against students on the basis of race, color, religion, gender, age, marital status, national origin, or disability.

■ Expenses and Financial Aid

Resident law students pay tuition and fees amounting to $100 per credit each semester. Nonresident students who are American citizens pay the same amount that would be required from Puerto Rican students if they were to study in the state from which the nonresidents come, thus establishing a reciprocity principle.

Regular fees for basic medical services amount to $337 for the first semester and $473 for the second semester, which includes summer. The medical fee for the summer session is only $135.

Nonresident students—Nonresident students who are not American citizens pay additional tuition and fees amounting to $1,750 for eight or more credits for each semester.

Additional regular fees for basic medical services amount to $115 for the first semester and $161 for the second semester, which includes summer.

All financial aid for the University of Puerto Rico School of Law is administered by the school's Office of Financial Aid. Each student is considered on his or her own merit and need. Awards are made only after an applicant has been admitted.

■ Career Services

Since 1981, the school has had an Office of Student Affairs under an assistant dean that offers a variety of services, including placement. The placement officer, with the aid of the Puerto Rico Bar Association, the Department of Justice, and other government agencies, helps students obtain part-time jobs, full-time jobs, or scholarships.

The Office of Student Affairs has initiated a series of statistical studies on the school's alumni, which include a former governor of Puerto Rico, the secretary of justice, several Puerto Rico Supreme Court justices, and many cabinet members, judges, and legislators.

Applicant Profile

University of Puerto Rico School of Law
This grid includes only applicants who earned 120–180 LSAT scores under standard administrations.

LSAT Score	3.75+ Apps	Adm	3.50–3.74 Apps	Adm	3.25–3.49 Apps	Adm	3.00–3.24 Apps	Adm	2.75–2.99 Apps	Adm	2.50–2.74 Apps	Adm	2.25–2.49 Apps	Adm	2.00–2.24 Apps	Adm	Below 2.00 Apps	Adm	No GPA Apps	Adm	Total Apps	Adm
175–180	0	0	0	0	0	0	0	0	0	0	0	0	0	0	0	0	0	0	0	0	0	0
170–174	0	0	0	0	0	0	0	0	0	0	0	0	0	0	0	0	0	0	0	0	1	0
165–169	0	0	1	0	0	0	0	0	0	0	0	0	0	0	0	0	0	0	0	0	2	2
160–164	0	0	0	0	1	1	0	0	0	0	1	1	0	0	0	0	0	0	0	0	5	4
155–159	2	1	0	0	1	1	0	0	1	1	0	0	0	0	0	0	1	1	0	0	41	35
150–154	9	9	5	5	7	7	10	8	4	2	4	3	1	0	1	1	0	0	2	0	87	65
145–149	15	14	14	13	17	15	10	9	14	9	8	3	6	2	1	0	0	0	1	0	132	68
140–144	23	19	38	28	24	16	17	3	14	1	12	1	2	0	0	0	1	0	6	1	149	33
135–139	21	16	38	11	33	5	17	0	19	0	6	0	9	0	3	0	2	0	7	0	130	5
130–134	18	5	23	0	24	0	21	0	17	0	6	0	3	0	3	0	1	0	11	0	57	0
125–129	5	0	11	0	6	0	15	0	3	0	2	0	3	0	0	0	0	0	0	0	11	0
120–124	1	0	4	0	2	0	1	0	1	0	1	0	0	0	1	0	0	0	0	0	615	212
Total	94	64	134	57	115	45	91	20	73	13	44	8	24	2	7	1	6	1	27	1	615	212

Apps = Number of Applicants
Adm = Number Admitted
Reflects 99% of the total applicant pool.

Quinnipiac University School of Law

275 Mt. Carmel Avenue
Hamden, CT 06518
Phone: 203.582.3400; Fax: 203.582.3339
E-mail: ladm@quinnipiac.edu; Website: http://law.quinnipiac.edu

ABA Approved Since 1992

The Basics

Type of school	Private
Term	Semester
Application deadline	3/1
Application fee	$40
Financial aid deadline	4/15
Can first year start other than fall?	No
Student to faculty ratio	13.1 to 1
Does the university offer:	
housing restricted to law students?	No
graduate housing for which law students are eligible?	No

Faculty and Administrators

	Total		Men		Women		Minorities	
	Fall	Spr	Fall	Spr	Fall	Spr	Fall	Spr
Full-time	28	27	18	15	10	12	3	3
Other Full-time	4	4	2	2	2	2	1	0
Deans, librarians, & others who teach	2	2	2	2	0	0	0	0
Part-time	33	48	25	29	8	19	0	2
Total	67	81	47	48	20	33	4	5

Curriculum

	Full-time	Part-time
Typical first-year section size	31	67
Is there typically a "small section" of the first-year class, other than Legal Writing, taught by full-time faculty	No	No
If yes, typical size offered last year		
# of classroom course titles beyond first-year curriculum		146
# of upper division courses, excluding seminars with an enrollment: Under 25		87
25–49		30
50–74		9
75–99		5
100+		0
# of seminars		15
# of seminar positions available		257
# of seminar positions filled	113	94
# of positions available in simulation courses		468
# of simulation positions filled	169	217
# of positions available in faculty supervised clinical courses		189
# of faculty supervised clinical positions filled	101	22
# involved in field placements	99	0
# involved in law journals	60	22
# involved in interschool competitions	20	10
# of credit hours required to graduate		86

Transfers

Transfers in	4
Transfers out	9

Tuition and Fees

	Resident	Nonresident
Full-time	$33,840	$33,840
Part-time	$23,840	$23,840

Living Expenses

Estimated living expenses for singles

Living on campus	Living off campus	Living at home
N/A	$17,206	$11,922

JD Enrollment and Ethnicity

	Men		Women		Full-time		Part-time		1st-year		Total		JD Degs. Awd.
	#	%	#	%	#	%	#	%	#	%	#	%	
African Amer.	5	2.2	6	2.6	4	1.3	7	4.3	5	3.7	11	2.4	3
Amer. Indian	1	0.4	2	0.9	2	0.7	1	0.6	2	1.5	3	0.6	1
Asian Amer.	9	3.9	15	6.4	15	5.0	9	5.5	5	3.7	24	5.2	6
Mex. Amer.	0	0.0	0	0.0	0	0.0	0	0.0	0	0.0	0	0.0	0
Puerto Rican	0	0.0	0	0.0	0	0.0	0	0.0	0	0.0	0	0.0	0
Hispanic	3	1.3	10	4.3	11	3.7	2	1.2	4	3.0	13	2.8	3
Total Minority	18	7.8	33	14.1	32	10.7	19	11.6	16	11.9	51	11.0	13
For. Nation.	1	0.4	1	0.4	2	0.7	0	0.0	0	0.0	2	0.4	0
Caucasian	188	81.7	178	76.1	236	78.7	130	79.3	114	84.4	366	78.9	170
Unknown	23	10.0	22	9.4	30	10.0	15	9.1	5	3.7	45	9.7	12
Total	230	49.6	234	50.4	300	64.7	164	35.3	135	29.1	464		195

Quinnipiac University School of Law

*ABA
Approved
Since
1992*

GPA and LSAT Scores

	Total	Full-time	Part-time
# of apps	2,865	2,486	379
# of offers	811	648	163
# of matrics	127	61	66
75% GPA	3.54	3.66	3.39
Median GPA	3.22	3.36	3.19
25% GPA	2.97	3.00	2.96
75% LSAT	158	160	155
Median LSAT	156	158	154
25% LSAT	154	157	152

Grants and Scholarships (from prior year)

	Total		Full-time		Part-time	
	#	%	#	%	#	%
Total # of students	548		381		167	
Total # receiving grants	334	60.9	263	69.0	71	42.5
Less than 1/2 tuition	259	47.3	207	54.3	52	31.1
Half to full tuition	72	13.1	53	13.9	19	11.4
Full tuition	3	0.5	3	0.8	0	0.0
More than full tuition	0	0.0	0	0.0	0	0.0
Median grant amount			$12,000		$6,000	

Informational and Library Resources

# of volumes and volume equivalents	413,563
# of titles	157,819
# of active serial subscriptions	2,664
Study seating capacity inside the library	400
# of full-time professional librarians	7
Hours per week library is open	99
# of open, wired connections available to students	395
# of networked computers available for use by students	114
# of simultaneous wireless users	500
Require computer?	No

JD Attrition (from prior year)

	Academic	Other	Total	
	#	#	#	%
1st year	2	15	17	12.9
2nd year	0	3	3	1.7
3rd year	0	2	2	1.1
4th year	0	0	0	0.0

Employment (9 months after graduation)

	Total	Percentage
Employment status known	200	97.6
Employment status unknown	5	2.4
Employed	183	91.5
Pursuing graduate degrees	7	3.5
Unemployed seeking employment	3	1.5
Unemployed not seeking employment	3	1.5
Unemployed and studying for the bar	4	2.0
Type of Employment		
# employed in law firms	70	38.3
# employed in business and industry	40	21.9
# employed in government	26	14.2
# employed in public interest	4	2.2
# employed as judicial clerks	14	7.7
# employed in academia	19	10.4
Geographic Location		
# employed in state	126	68.9
# employed in foreign countries	0	0.0
# of states where employed		15

Bar Passage Rates

Jurisdiction	Connecticut		
Exam	Sum 05	Win 06	Total
# from school taking bar for the first time	147	28	175
School's pass rate for all first-time takers	80%	86%	81%
State's pass rate for all first-time takers	81%	83%	82%

Quinnipiac University School of Law

275 Mt. Carmel Avenue
Hamden, CT 06518
Phone: 203.582.3400; Fax: 203.582.3339
E-mail: ladm@quinnipiac.edu; Website: http://law.quinnipiac.edu

■ Introduction

Excellent law schools share many common traits—faculty renowned for their scholarship and commitment to teaching; academically rigorous courses; loyal, successful alumni; and motivated focused students. All of these are essential components of Quinnipiac Law's identity. However, what sets Quinnipiac apart is its personal, student-centered approach to the law school experience. Contributing to this identity is a favorable 13:1 student-faculty ratio, the extraordinary accessibility of the faculty, and an environment that both challenges and supports its students as they prepare for careers in law.

Nestled among the hills, woods, and waterways of Connecticut on one of the most beautiful campuses in New England, yet just 75 miles from New York City, Quinnipiac's setting and location are ideal. The beautiful, state-of-the-art law center opened in 1995. Wireless computer access throughout provides students with a modern, relaxed, and safe environment for study.

■ Faculty

Our faculty's academic credentials span the nation's leading law schools from Harvard, Yale, and Berkeley to Chicago, Michigan, and Columbia. They combine excellence in scholarship and teaching with exceptional accessibility. Indeed, the care with which faculty members demonstrate their interest in each student's progress and success is a distinguishing characteristic of Quinnipiac Law. Most faculty have an open-door policy and generously share their expertise, insight, and time. The low student-faculty ratio (13:1) allows students to work closely with faculty, and this translates into a different kind of law school experience.

■ Library and Physical Facilities

The 50,000-square-foot law library is at the center of the School of Law complex. With a collection of more than 420,000 volumes, it also provides comprehensive access to numerous electronic resources and databases such as LexisNexis, Westlaw/Dialog, JSTOR, and other Web-based services. Its interlibrary loan network makes it possible to obtain materials from any library in the world. The beautiful facility features spacious public areas and numerous reading rooms and individual study carrels, providing a comfortable and relaxing environment for research and study.

■ Curriculum

The law school is fully approved by the ABA and is a member of AALS. Full-time day and part-time evening programs are offered beginning each fall. The academic program is designed to prepare students to be generalists or specialists. The program provides a dynamic blend of traditional classroom instruction and extensive experiential learning opportunities. Students who wish to focus on a specific area of study may choose from six different concentrations—**Civil Advocacy and Dispute Resolution, Criminal Law and Advocacy, Family and Juvenile Law, Health Law, Intellectual Property,** and **Tax**. The

law school also offers a joint JD/MBA degree (with a health care management track) and a summer study-abroad program with Trinity College in Dublin, Ireland.

■ Special Programs

Quinnipiac is recognized as having one of the premier clinical and externship programs in the country, and students often cite their experiences in these programs as one of the highlights of their law school career. These experiential learning opportunities allow students to bridge the gap between theory and practice. A total of 16 clinical and externship programs are available to students.

The seven clinical programs include **Civil, Health Law, Tax, Advanced, Evening** (for part-time students), **Defense Appellate,** and **Prosecution Appellate**. The nine externship programs are **Corporate Counsel, Criminal Justice, Family and Juvenile Law, Judicial, Legal Services, Legislative, Mediation, Public Interest,** and **Field Placement II**.

Quinnipiac has established two centers in specialized fields of law—the **Center for Health Law and Policy** and the **Center on Dispute Resolution**—both of which draw on the considerable academic strengths and resources within the law school community.

■ Admission

Admission is competitive and based upon a variety of factors: undergraduate academic record, LSAT scores, personal statement, letters of recommendation, and other evidence such as advanced degrees, life and work experience, and extracurricular activities. Applications are welcomed from students of color, nontraditional students, and all students who add to the diversity of the student body. A rolling admission system is employed; however, the priority application deadline for admission and scholarship consideration is March 1. *Candidates for the full-tuition Dean's Fellows awards must apply by January 15.*

■ Student Activities

Quinnipiac students often comment about the strong sense of community that permeates the law school. That sense of community is enhanced by the numerous and varied opportunities for students to participate in cocurricular activities, including a dynamic Student Bar Association, more than 30 different student organizations, a thriving Moot Court Society, an active *Quinnipiac Law Review*, and two student journals—the *Health Law Journal* and the *Probate Law Journal*.

■ Expenses and Financial Aid

Approximately 90 percent of the student body receives some form of financial assistance. Every applicant is considered for merit-based scholarships that range from $3,000 to full tuition per year. March 1 is the admission deadline for most merit awards. However, candidates for the full-tuition Dean's Fellows scholarships must submit applications by January 15. Total institutional scholarships and grants for the 2006–2007 academic year exceeded $3.4 million.

■ Housing

Campus housing for graduate and professional students is not available. However, there is ample, affordable housing available near the campus and throughout New Haven county. The School of Law Admissions Office and the university Office of Residential Life assist students in securing off-campus accommodations.

■ Career Services

The Office of Career Services provides students and graduates with the expert guidance necessary to make informed career decisions. It offers substantial support through individual counseling and workshops on topics such as writing résumés and interviewing techniques.

The office coordinates on- and off-campus recruitment programs. Students interview with employers for a variety of summer internships and permanent jobs in the private and public sector.

Over the past five years, more than 90 percent of our graduates have been employed within nine months of graduation. The most recent class found employment as follows: 38 percent entered private practice, 22 percent took positions in business and industry, 14 percent chose government service work, 8 percent received judicial clerkships. The remainder went into public interest work or were studying for advanced degrees.

Applicant Profile

Quinnipiac University School of Law
This grid includes only applicants who earned 120–180 LSAT scores under standard administrations.

LSAT Score	3.75 +		3.50–3.74		3.25–3.49		3.00–3.24		2.75–2.99		2.50–2.74		2.25–2.49		2.00–2.24		Below 2.00		No GPA		Total	
	Apps	Adm	Apps	Adm	Apps	Adm	Apps	Adm	Apps	Adm	Apps	Adm	Apps	Adm	Apps	Adm	Apps	Adm	Apps	Adm	Apps	Adm
175–180	0	0	0	0	0	0	0	0	0	0	0	0	1	1	0	0	0	0	0	0	12	12
170–174	5	5	0	0	2	2	2	2	2	2	0	0	2	2	0	0	1	1	0	0	52	51
165–169	9	9	11	11	6	6	9	9	9	9	5	4	2	2	5	1	2	2	0	0	216	201
160–164	38	38	49	47	41	41	33	32	20	19	20	15	8	6	5	1	2	0	9	5	504	369
155–159	69	62	98	87	111	86	90	65	65	48	33	11	19	5	8	0	2	0	5	2	968	211
150–154	90	24	176	47	236	56	198	41	138	22	79	16	27	3	16	0	3	0	5	2	568	16
145–149	33	4	77	2	118	3	126	2	82	1	76	2	34	0	12	1	3	0	7	1	242	0
140–144	17	0	22	0	51	0	46	0	50	0	37	0	12	0	3	0	0	0	4	0	94	0
135–139	1	0	4	0	10	0	13	0	27	0	12	0	13	0	8	0	2	0	4	0	34	0
130–134	0	0	5	0	2	0	6	0	9	0	6	0	2	0	0	0	2	0	2	0	8	0
125–129	1	0	0	0	0	0	2	0	0	0	2	0	1	0	0	0	2	0	0	0	1	0
120–124	0	0	0	0	0	0	1	0	0	0	0	0	0	0	0	0	0	0	0	0	1	0
Total	263	142	442	194	577	194	526	151	402	101	270	48	119	17	52	2	17	3	31	8	2699	860

Apps = Number of Applicants
Adm = Number Admitted

This total number reflects dual applicants/accepts for the fall term (99% of the total applicant pool).

Regent University School of Law

1000 Regent University Drive, RH239
Virginia Beach, VA 23464
Phone: 757.226.4584; Fax: 757.226.4139
E-mail: lawschool@regent.edu; Website: www.regent.edu/law

ABA
Approved
Since
1989

The Basics

Type of school	Private
Term	Semester
Application deadline	6/1
Application fee	$40
Financial aid deadline	6/1
Can first year start other than fall?	No
Student to faculty ratio	20.3 to 1
Does the university offer:	
housing restricted to law students?	No
graduate housing for which law students are eligible?	Yes

Faculty and Administrators

	Total Fall	Total Spr	Men Fall	Men Spr	Women Fall	Women Spr	Minorities Fall	Minorities Spr
Full-time	22	22	16	16	6	6	5	5
Other Full-time	4	4	3	3	1	1	1	1
Deans, librarians, & others who teach	6	6	6	6	0	0	0	0
Part-time	19	23	13	18	6	5	1	0
Total	51	55	38	43	13	12	7	6

Curriculum

	Full-time	Part-time
Typical first-year section size	80	0
Is there typically a "small section" of the first-year class, other than Legal Writing, taught by full-time faculty	No	No
If yes, typical size offered last year		
# of classroom course titles beyond first-year curriculum	118	
# of upper division courses, excluding seminars with an enrollment: Under 25	81	
25–49	23	
50–74	13	
75–99	5	
100+	0	
# of seminars	6	
# of seminar positions available	139	
# of seminar positions filled	52	5
# of positions available in simulation courses	617	
# of simulation positions filled	432	34
# of positions available in faculty supervised clinical courses	25	
# of faculty supervised clinical positions filled	18	0
# involved in field placements	47	5
# involved in law journals	35	3
# involved in interschool competitions	44	0
# of credit hours required to graduate	90	

JD Enrollment and Ethnicity

	Men #	Men %	Women #	Women %	Full-time #	Full-time %	Part-time #	Part-time %	1st-year #	1st-year %	Total #	Total %	JD Degs. Awd.
African Amer.	2	0.8	23	9.2	21	4.6	4	12.9	6	3.7	25	5.1	10
Amer. Indian	3	1.2	0	0.0	3	0.7	0	0.0	2	1.2	3	0.6	2
Asian Amer.	5	2.1	13	5.2	17	3.7	1	3.2	5	3.1	18	3.7	4
Mex. Amer.	0	0.0	0	0.0	0	0.0	0	0.0	0	0.0	0	0.0	0
Puerto Rican	0	0.0	0	0.0	0	0.0	0	0.0	0	0.0	0	0.0	0
Hispanic	6	2.5	7	2.8	12	2.6	1	3.2	5	3.1	13	2.6	1
Total Minority	16	6.6	43	17.3	53	11.5	6	19.4	18	11.2	59	12.0	17
For. Nation.	0	0.0	3	1.2	3	0.7	0	0.0	3	1.9	3	0.6	0
Caucasian	217	89.7	201	80.7	394	85.7	24	77.4	136	84.5	418	85.1	121
Unknown	9	3.7	2	0.8	10	2.2	1	3.2	4	2.5	11	2.2	5
Total	242	49.3	249	50.7	460	93.7	31	6.3	161	32.8	491		143

Transfers

Transfers in	1
Transfers out	5

Tuition and Fees

	Resident	Nonresident
Full-time	$25,616	$25,616
Part-time	$19,056	$19,056

Living Expenses

Estimated living expenses for singles		
Living on campus	Living off campus	Living at home
$14,993	$14,993	$14,993

*ABA
Approved
Since
1989*

GPA and LSAT Scores

	Total	Full-time	Part-time
# of apps	560	537	23
# of offers	306	297	9
# of matrics	161	156	5
75% GPA	3.61	3.61	2.93
Median GPA	3.36	3.38	2.59
25% GPA	3.00	3.00	2.54
75% LSAT	156	156	155
Median LSAT	153	153	154
25% LSAT	151	151	151

Grants and Scholarships (from prior year)

	Total #	Total %	Full-time #	Full-time %	Part-time #	Part-time %
Total # of students	489		444		45	
Total # receiving grants	351	71.8	328	73.9	23	51.1
Less than 1/2 tuition	227	46.4	206	46.4	21	46.7
Half to full tuition	88	18.0	87	19.6	1	2.2
Full tuition	29	5.9	28	6.3	1	2.2
More than full tuition	7	1.4	7	1.6	0	0.0
Median grant amount			$4,900		$1,000	

Informational and Library Resources

# of volumes and volume equivalents	392,449
# of titles	67,658
# of active serial subscriptions	3,484
Study seating capacity inside the library	360
# of full-time professional librarians	7
Hours per week library is open	105
# of open, wired connections available to students	241
# of networked computers available for use by students	70
# of simultaneous wireless users	120
Require computer?	No

JD Attrition (from prior year)

	Academic #	Other #	Total #	Total %
1st year	7	8	15	9.1
2nd year	0	7	7	4.3
3rd year	0	0	0	0.0
4th year	0	0	0	0.0

Employment (9 months after graduation)

	Total	Percentage
Employment status known	150	96.8
Employment status unknown	5	3.2
Employed	124	82.7
Pursuing graduate degrees	2	1.3
Unemployed seeking employment	9	6.0
Unemployed not seeking employment	12	8.0
Unemployed and studying for the bar	3	2.0

Type of Employment

	Total	Percentage
# employed in law firms	43	34.7
# employed in business and industry	27	21.8
# employed in government	28	22.6
# employed in public interest	11	8.9
# employed as judicial clerks	6	4.8
# employed in academia	9	7.3

Geographic Location

	Total	Percentage
# employed in state	73	58.9
# employed in foreign countries	0	0.0
# of states where employed	20	

Bar Passage Rates

Jurisdiction / Exam	Virginia Sum 05	Virginia Win 06	Virginia Total	North Carolina Sum 05	North Carolina Win 06	North Carolina Total
# from school taking bar for the first time	68	12	80	8	5	13
School's pass rate for all first-time takers	71%	50%	68%	63%	80%	69%
State's pass rate for all first-time takers	76%	65%	74%	72%	69%	71%

Regent University School of Law

1000 Regent University Drive, RH239
Virginia Beach, VA 23464
Phone: 757.226.4584; Fax: 757.226.4139
E-mail: lawschool@regent.edu; Website: www.regent.edu/law

■ Introduction

Regent University is distinctive among ABA-approved law schools because of its integration of Christian principles into the curriculum. It is this balance of professional legal training and affirmation of biblical principles that enables Regent graduates to provide excellent legal counsel to their clients while carrying forth the mission of the university—Christian Leadership to Change the World. Approximately 3,300 men and women are pursuing graduate degrees at Regent University. The law school is composed of approximately 500 students. Regent University is situated on a stately, Georgian-style campus in Virginia Beach, minutes from the Atlantic Ocean, less than a two-hour drive from Richmond, and less than four hours from Washington, DC.

■ Christian Distinction

The foremost distinction of Regent University School of Law is its Christian perspective. The School of Law is unique in that its mission embraces a Christian world-view, and the school seeks to nurture students' faith. This mission provides a strong basis for teaching the highest ethical standards for lawyers. The mission also helps make Regent a great overall experience for students. Regent has received national recognition for its students' high quality of life and accessibility to faculty.

■ Academic Program/Legal Skills

Regent law school places great emphasis on developing practical lawyering skills. Courses have been designed to provide in-depth training and opportunities to develop these skills. Regent law students have enjoyed tremendous success in student competitions, winning national and regional awards in negotiations, moot court, trial practice, client counseling, and appellate advocacy. The practical lawyering skills and strong ethical values of Regent graduates have enabled them to successfully obtain employment with top law firms, federal and state courts, business and technology companies, and national public interest law firms.

■ Clinical Opportunities—Public Interest Law

Regent law students are noted for their commitment to public service and their determination to fight for equal justice for all. The School of Law provides opportunities for hands-on, student-client contact through Litigation and Family Mediation clinics. Additionally, the School of Law enjoys a special relationship with the American Center for Law and Justice (ACLJ), the nation's foremost public interest law firm defending religious liberties. Selected law students may obtain volunteer and paid positions to assist ACLJ staff attorneys involved in profamily and proliberty cases and may participate in a semester in DC program with ACLJ attorneys.

■ Full- and Part-time Programs

The School of Law offers full- and part-time, 90-semester-hour Juris Doctor programs, in-residence only. Students in the full-time program normally complete their degrees in three years; part-time students in four to five years.

■ Admission and the Bar

Applicants to the law school are required to submit a personal statement as part of the admission process. This personal statement, unique in style to Regent, is considered very carefully along with the applicant's LSAT score, undergraduate record, résumé, and letters of recommendation. The law school is committed to considering the entire application in the decision process, ultimately offering admission to prospective students who present a strong likelihood for success in law school. This commitment has resulted in a diverse student body. Applications from prospective students with LSAT scores of 150 and above and UGPAs above 3.0 are especially encouraged, as the law school has evidence that such students are very likely to succeed in law school and also very likely to pass the bar exam on their first attempt. Regent's overall bar passage rate for graduates with LSAT scores of 150 or above is 76 percent; with LSAT scores of 155 or above, 82 percent; and with LSAT scores of 160 and above, 89 percent.

■ Academic Assistance

Regent University School of Law is on the cutting edge in offering academic assistance to its students. The law school employs a full-time faculty member who serves as the director of academic success and who oversees the three components of the school's Academic Success Program. Under the first component, the school invites selected first-year students to attend a two-week preenrollment program as a condition for admission into the school. The preenrollment program helps students develop good law school study skills and introduces them to selected areas of the law in small sections taught by members of the full-time faculty. Under the second component, the director of academic assistance offers study skills workshops and one-on-one advising during the spring and fall semesters. These services are available to all students needing extra assistance in their studies. As the third component, the director teaches a for-credit course on advanced legal reasoning, analysis, and writing. The class, offered to third-year students, enables the students to fine-tune their analytical and writing skills in concrete ways that will benefit them in their future legal careers.

■ The Law Library

The Regent University Law Library occupies the entire third floor of the 150,000-square-foot university library building. Immediately adjacent to the School of Law, the Law Library contains approximately 382,000 volumes, substantial electronic resources, and an extensive microform collection.

■ International Law and Summer Abroad/Exchange Programs

The law school has established the *Regent Journal of International Law* and has a very active International Law Society. In addition, Regent offers many opportunities for students interested in international law and overseas study. The law school hosts a summer program in Strasbourg, France, focusing on international law and human rights. Regent faculty and other distinguished scholars and attorneys, such as Attorney General John Ashcroft, teach in the program. The law school also offers semester-abroad opportunities. Students may spend a semester studying international law at Handong International Law School in South Korea. The law school has created student-exchange programs with Spanish universities in Barcelona and Madrid. Students are able to spend a semester in Spain and take subjects such as civil law, European institutions, and international private law.

■ Housing

Regent Village is located three-quarters of a mile from campus. The apartment-style complex consists of 112 two-bedroom, one-bath units; 56 two-bedroom, two-bath units; and 56 three-bedroom, two-bath units. Rates are comparable to or less than similar apartment complexes in the nearby vicinity.

■ Financial Aid

The School of Law is committed to helping students finance their legal education. The Scholarship Committee annually awards approximately $2.5 million in scholarships and grants to law students, ranging in value from $500 to full tuition. In recent years, approximately 70 percent of law students received some type of scholarship or grant. Scholarships are awarded on the basis of academic promise, with attention given to the applicant's undergraduate academic performance, LSAT scores, leadership, public service, and other factors indicative of the applicant's potential for law school success. Regent law school also provides grant assistance for qualified students who are called to serve minority communities upon graduation. Students not awarded financial assistance the first year of law school may qualify for assistance in future years based on academic performance. Residents of Virginia attending a private Virginia university may qualify for the Virginia Tuition Assistance Grant. Regent law school provides a student loan repayment assistance program (LRAP) for qualified graduates practicing in the area of public interest law. Additionally, a variety of loan programs, including Stafford and Graduate PLUS, are available to meet the tuition and living expenses related to law school.

■ Campus Visitations

Campus visitations: *www.regent.edu/lawvisitation*.

To RSVP for campus visitations or to arrange a visit to the law school, please contact *lawschool@regent.edu* or telephone 757.226.4584.

Applicant Profile

Regent University School of Law
This grid includes only applicants who earned 120–180 LSAT scores under standard administrations.

LSAT Score	GPA								
	3.75 +	3.50–3.74	3.25–3.49	3.00–3.24	2.75–2.99	2.50–2.74	2.25–2.49	2.00–2.24	Below 2.00
160–180									
153–159									
152									
151									
150									
149									
147–148									
120–146									

☐ Strong Possibility   ▨ Possible   ■ Unlikely

This grid is intended to provide prospective applicants a general sense of our admission standards, as based upon competition for entry into recent classes entering the law school. This grid does not adequately describe the numerous nonquantifiable factors that are considered by our Admission Committee. Prospective applicants are encouraged to review our admission materials for a fuller understanding of the admission-review standards used by Regent University School of Law.

University of Richmond School of Law

28 Westhampton Way
University of Richmond, VA 23173
Phone: 804.289.8189; Fax: 804.287.6516
E-mail: lawadmissions@richmond.edu; Website: law.richmond.edu

ABA Approved Since 1928

The Basics

Type of school	Private
Term	Semester
Application deadline	1/15
Application fee	$35
Financial aid deadline	2/25
Can first year start other than fall?	Yes
Student to faculty ratio	16.0 to 1
Does the university offer:	
housing restricted to law students?	Yes
graduate housing for which law students are eligible?	Yes

Faculty and Administrators

	Total Fall	Total Spr	Men Fall	Men Spr	Women Fall	Women Spr	Minorities Fall	Minorities Spr
Full-time	28	23	19	16	9	7	4	4
Other Full-time	4	3	3	3	1	0	0	0
Deans, librarians, & others who teach	5	3	2	2	3	1	0	0
Part-time	47	52	35	32	12	19	2	1
Total	84	81	59	53	25	27	6	5

Curriculum

	Full-time	Part-time
Typical first-year section size	55	0
Is there typically a "small section" of the first-year class, other than Legal Writing, taught by full-time faculty	Yes	No
If yes, typical size offered last year	40	
# of classroom course titles beyond first-year curriculum		86
# of upper division courses, excluding seminars with an enrollment: Under 25		78
25–49		22
50–74		8
75–99		6
100+		0
# of seminars		16
# of seminar positions available		242
# of seminar positions filled	193	0
# of positions available in simulation courses		489
# of simulation positions filled	421	0
# of positions available in faculty supervised clinical courses		40
# of faculty supervised clinical positions filled	39	0
# involved in field placements	80	0
# involved in law journals	185	0
# involved in interschool competitions	24	0
# of credit hours required to graduate		86

JD Enrollment and Ethnicity

	Men #	Men %	Women #	Women %	Full-time #	Full-time %	Part-time #	Part-time %	1st-year #	1st-year %	Total #	Total %	JD Degs. Awd.
African Amer.	10	3.7	25	10.7	34	6.8	1	14.3	22	13.9	35	6.9	6
Amer. Indian	0	0.0	1	0.4	1	0.2	0	0.0	0	0.0	1	0.2	1
Asian Amer.	7	2.6	6	2.6	13	2.6	0	0.0	4	2.5	13	2.6	6
Mex. Amer.	0	0.0	0	0.0	0	0.0	0	0.0	0	0.0	0	0.0	0
Puerto Rican	0	0.0	0	0.0	0	0.0	0	0.0	0	0.0	0	0.0	0
Hispanic	1	0.4	0	0.0	1	0.2	0	0.0	1	0.6	1	0.2	2
Total Minority	18	6.6	32	13.7	49	9.8	1	14.3	27	17.1	50	9.9	15
For. Nation.	0	0.0	1	0.4	1	0.2	0	0.0	1	0.6	1	0.2	0
Caucasian	255	93.4	201	85.9	450	90.0	6	85.7	130	82.3	456	89.9	135
Unknown	0	0.0	0	0.0	0	0.0	0	0.0	0	0.0	0	0.0	0
Total	273	53.8	234	46.2	500	98.6	7	1.4	158	31.2	507		150

Transfers

Transfers in	29
Transfers out	22

Tuition and Fees

	Resident	Nonresident
Full-time	$28,390	$28,390
Part-time	$0	$0

Living Expenses

Estimated living expenses for singles

Living on campus	Living off campus	Living at home
$11,371	$14,040	$6,495

University of Richmond School of Law

ABA
Approved
Since
1928

GPA and LSAT Scores

	Total	Full-time	Part-time
# of apps	1,873	1,873	0
# of offers	626	626	0
# of matrics	158	158	0
75% GPA	3.58	3.58	0.00
Median GPA	3.36	3.36	0.00
25% GPA	3.07	3.07	0.00
75% LSAT	162	162	0
Median LSAT	161	161	0
25% LSAT	159	159	0

Grants and Scholarships (from prior year)

	Total #	Total %	Full-time #	Full-time %	Part-time #	Part-time %
Total # of students	485		483		2	
Total # receiving grants	269	55.5	269	55.7	0	0.0
Less than 1/2 tuition	244	50.3	244	50.5	0	0.0
Half to full tuition	24	4.9	24	5.0	0	0.0
Full tuition	0	0.0	0	0.0	0	0.0
More than full tuition	1	0.2	1	0.2	0	0.0
Median grant amount			$7,500		$0	

Informational and Library Resources

# of volumes and volume equivalents	384,400
# of titles	167,626
# of active serial subscriptions	4,627
Study seating capacity inside the library	640
# of full-time professional librarians	7
Hours per week library is open	106
# of open, wired connections available to students	890
# of networked computers available for use by students	68
# of simultaneous wireless users	700
Require computer?	Yes

JD Attrition (from prior year)

	Academic #	Other #	Total #	Total %
1st year	2	23	25	14.5
2nd year	1	2	3	1.8
3rd year	0	0	0	0.0
4th year	0	0	0	0.0

Employment (9 months after graduation)

	Total	Percentage
Employment status known	165	100.0
Employment status unknown	0	0.0
Employed	146	88.5
Pursuing graduate degrees	4	2.4
Unemployed seeking employment	5	3.0
Unemployed not seeking employment	10	6.1
Unemployed and studying for the bar	0	0.0

Type of Employment

	Total	Percentage
# employed in law firms	90	61.6
# employed in business and industry	8	5.5
# employed in government	18	12.3
# employed in public interest	2	1.4
# employed as judicial clerks	27	18.5
# employed in academia	1	0.7

Geographic Location

	Total	Percentage
# employed in state	116	79.5
# employed in foreign countries	0	0.0
# of states where employed	17	

Bar Passage Rates

Jurisdiction	Virginia		
Exam	Sum 05	Win 06	Total
# from school taking bar for the first time	121	17	138
School's pass rate for all first-time takers	86%	76%	85%
State's pass rate for all first-time takers	76%	65%	74%

University of Richmond School of Law

28 Westhampton Way
University of Richmond, VA 23173
Phone: 804.289.8189; Fax: 804.287.6516
E-mail: lawadmissions@richmond.edu; Website: law.richmond.edu

■ Introduction

The University of Richmond School of Law, founded in 1870, enjoys an established reputation for preparing its graduates for legal careers. Accredited by the ABA and a member of the AALS, its graduates are qualified to seek admission to the bar of all 50 states and the District of Columbia.

Situated on the university's gorgeous 350-acre suburban campus, the school is only a 20-minute drive from downtown Richmond and its thriving legal community. In addition to being home to a number of international law firms, Richmond is the capital of the Commonwealth of Virginia, with numerous state and federal offices, and is the seat of both the Supreme Court of Virginia and the US Court of Appeals for the Fourth Circuit.

■ Library and Physical Facilities

The law school is housed in a collegiate gothic-style building, which includes a magnificent moot courtroom that is the site of many classes, events, and mock trials, and where a panel of federal judges from the Fourth Circuit hears oral arguments once a year. The building is outfitted with state-of-the-art instructional technology, including wireless access. Every first-year student is assigned an individual study carrel bearing his/her name, which functions as an office in the law library. The library's holdings are comprehensive and include several special collections.

■ Curriculum

Courses in contracts, torts, criminal law, civil procedure, property, and constitutional law and a choice of one elective comprise the first-year curriculum. Required upper-level courses include professional responsibility and a third-year writing seminar. Elective courses in a variety of areas are available. In addition, all students complete a comprehensive, two-year program in legal reasoning, writing, research, and fundamental lawyering skills and values.

■ Academic Success Program and Bar Passage

Richmond Law has a comprehensive Academic Success Program geared toward assisting students to achieve at their highest possible academic level. The program also supports students in preparing for the bar exam, in whatever jurisdiction they choose to take it. In February 2004, Richmond Law graduates who took the Virginia bar exam for the first time achieved a 100 percent passage rate.

■ Special Programs

Several dual-degree programs allow students to earn the JD degree as well as a master's degree in a related discipline. Dual-degree programs are available in business administration, health administration, social work, urban studies and planning, and public administration as well as others.

The law school operates the Children's Law Center through which students may participate in the Delinquency Clinic, the Disabilities Clinic, or the Advanced Children's Clinic.

Exciting clinical placements are arranged for academic credit in courts, law offices, and corporations. Externships are available in civil, criminal, judicial, and business law.

The Intellectual Property Institute has developed a curriculum to enable students to obtain a certificate of concentration in Intellectual Property Law, and in collaboration with the Media Institute, we have launched the National CyberEducation Project, aimed at engaging undergraduate college students in legal issues arising in the context of intellectual property protection in the digital age.

■ International Programs

Richmond Law offers an extremely popular summer program at Emmanuel College in Cambridge, England, and an exchange program with the University of Paris as well as with more than 20 universities worldwide, nine of which have acclaimed law programs.

The Institute for Actual Innocence (IAI) works to identify, investigate, and exonerate wrongfully convicted individuals in the Commonwealth of Virginia. It joins a national community of innocence projects with similar goals. Students, with hands-on involvement by faculty and practicing lawyers, conduct reinvestigations of cases where credible evidence of actual innocence is present. Students learn the subtleties and pitfalls involved in interviewing witnesses, inmates, and other parties central to criminal cases. They learn to analyze a criminal trial or appellate record for new evidentiary perspectives. The IAI offers a lively, energetic environment for students to express their problem-solving, interpersonal, and analytical skills.

■ Student Activities

A student board publishes the *University of Richmond Law Review* on a quarterly basis. The *Richmond Journal of Law and Technology*, the first student-edited scholarly journal in the world to be published exclusively in electronic form, went online April 10, 1995. The *Richmond Journal of Law and the Public Interest* is a second online journal published by our students as an interdisciplinary journal dedicated to current and often controversial issues affecting the public. The *Richmond Journal of Global Law and Business* provides scholarly and practical insight into major legal and business issues affecting our global economy.

Richmond's moot court activities allow students to test their research, brief-writing, trial, and appellate advocacy skills. Students participate in intraschool tournaments that lead to membership on the Moot Court Board and on teams that represent the law school in regional and national competitions.

■ Admission

Applications are reviewed as they become complete. All decisions are released by May 15. The admission committee considers the UGPA and LSAT as two important items, although extracurricular and community service activities and employment experience are also of interest. The law school provides an equal educational opportunity without regard to race, color, national origin, sex, disability, or religion.

Admission conferences are available in December, January, and February. They are invaluable in providing information and answering questions. We encourage class visits, and in keeping with our very personal approach to admission, we also encourage you to take advantage of meeting with a law student. Law students are available to give tours Monday through Saturday and may be reached at *LSAR@richmond.edu*.

■ Expenses and Financial Aid

Institutional aid in the form of grants and scholarships is available on the basis of need and merit. To qualify for grants based on need, you must file a completed FAFSA form that the federal processor must receive no later than February 25. Parental income is not considered in determining financial aid for students who are considered to be independent by the law school.

John Marshall Scholars Program—The law school's most prestigious awards offer $10,000 annual stipends in addition to other merit aid, as well as other honors, and are renewable annually if criteria are met. The general application must be **completed** by February 1. If invited to compete for these awards, a separate application must be submitted in early March. Committee consideration for these scholarships is based solely on merit and personal attributes. Some applicants may be able to demonstrate the required attributes by having successfully overcome serious disadvantages or obstacles. John

Marshall Scholars will be awarded institutional grants and scholarships in addition to their JM Scholarship.

■ Housing

Limited on-campus housing is available on a first-come, first-served basis. Richmond offers an abundance of good, affordable housing in proximity to the law school. For information on housing, contact the Admissions Office.

■ Career Services

The role of the Career Services Office is to serve law students and alumni in obtaining employment by helping them develop the skills and the knowledge necessary to conduct successful job searches. The office organizes a comprehensive, on-campus interview program. It also participates in a number of regional and national job fairs.

Richmond has more types of courts than any city in the US outside of Washington, DC, or Boston, which provide a myriad of opportunities for part-time employment while students are in their second and third year of study, thereby giving our students the benefit of gaining crucial legal experience and producing income for educational purposes.

For the last several years, our graduates have reported between 98 and 100 percent employment within six months of graduation.

Applicant Profile

University of Richmond School of Law
This grid includes only applicants who earned 120–180 LSAT scores under standard administrations.

LSAT Score	3.75 +		3.50–3.74		3.25–3.49		3.00–3.24		2.75–2.99		2.50–2.74		2.25–2.49		2.00–2.24		Below 2.00		No GPA		Total	
	Apps	Adm	Apps	Adm	Apps	Adm	Apps	Adm	Apps	Adm	Apps	Adm	Apps	Adm	Apps	Adm	Apps	Adm	Apps	Adm	Apps	Adm
175–180	0	0	0	0	0	0	0	0	1	1	0	0	0	0	0	0	1	0	0	0	2	1
170–174	2	2	3	3	5	5	3	3	5	5	1	0	1	1	0	0	0	0	0	0	20	19
165–169	11	9	19	18	20	20	17	17	2	2	7	6	3	2	2	1	0	0	0	0	81	75
160–164	46	40	85	83	84	81	65	60	48	33	20	14	10	7	3	1	0	0	2	1	363	320
155–159	70	24	135	46	149	33	95	21	59	10	36	6	8	1	1	0	0	0	5	2	558	143
150–154	51	4	80	14	108	10	102	10	74	4	24	1	12	3	2	0	0	0	6	1	459	47
145–149	17	1	28	2	46	3	49	6	34	2	22	1	10	0	3	0	0	0	2	0	211	15
140–144	3	0	13	0	26	0	23	1	20	0	16	0	4	0	1	0	0	0	1	0	107	1
135–139	0	0	2	0	4	0	10	0	11	0	7	0	3	0	3	0	1	0	2	0	43	0
130–134	0	0	2	0	2	0	2	0	5	0	2	0	1	0	2	0	1	0	2	0	19	0
125–129	0	0	1	0	0	0	1	0	1	0	0	0	1	0	2	0	0	0	1	0	7	0
120–124	0	0	0	0	0	0	0	0	0	0	0	0	0	0	0	0	0	0	0	0	0	0
Total	200	80	368	166	444	152	367	118	260	57	135	28	53	14	19	2	3	0	21	4	1870	621

Apps = Number of Applicants
Adm = Number Admitted
Reflects 99% of the total applicant pool.

Roger Williams University, Ralph R. Papitto School of Law

Ten Metacom Avenue
Bristol, RI 02809-5171
Phone: 401.254.4555 or 800.633.2727; Fax: 401.254.4516
E-mail: admissions@law.rwu.edu; Website: law.rwu.edu

ABA
Approved
Since
1995

The Basics

Type of school	Private
Term	Semester
Application deadline	3/15
Application fee	$60
Financial aid deadline	3/15
Can first year start other than fall?	No
Student to faculty ratio	20.5 to 1
Does the university offer:	
housing restricted to law students?	No
graduate housing for which law students are eligible?	Yes

Faculty and Administrators

	Total		Men		Women		Minorities	
	Fall	Spr	Fall	Spr	Fall	Spr	Fall	Spr
Full-time	24	22	16	15	8	7	4	3
Other Full-time	6	5	1	1	5	4	0	0
Deans, librarians, & others who teach	9	9	3	3	6	6	0	0
Part-time	15	26	12	21	3	5	1	0
Total	**54**	**62**	**32**	**40**	**22**	**22**	**5**	**3**

Curriculum

	Full-time	Part-time
Typical first-year section size	89	0
Is there typically a "small section" of the first-year class, other than Legal Writing, taught by full-time faculty	No	No
If yes, typical size offered last year		

# of classroom course titles beyond first-year curriculum		103
# of upper division courses, excluding seminars with an enrollment:	Under 25	56
	25–49	22
	50–74	6
	75–99	5
	100+	0

	Full-time	Part-time
# of seminars		30
# of seminar positions available		662
# of seminar positions filled	490	74
# of positions available in simulation courses	296	
# of simulation positions filled	261	27
# of positions available in faculty supervised clinical courses	66	
# of faculty supervised clinical positions filled	51	7
# involved in field placements	47	4
# involved in law journals	31	4
# involved in interschool competitions	38	0
# of credit hours required to graduate	90	

JD Enrollment and Ethnicity

	Men		Women		Full-time		Part-time		1st-year		Total		JD Degs. Awd.
	#	%	#	%	#	%	#	%	#	%	#	%	
African Amer.	10	3.3	9	3.1	18	3.4	1	1.7	4	2.0	19	3.2	1
Amer. Indian	0	0.0	2	0.7	2	0.4	0	0.0	0	0.0	2	0.3	1
Asian Amer.	12	3.9	15	5.2	24	4.5	3	5.0	7	3.5	27	4.6	7
Mex. Amer.	2	0.7	0	0.0	2	0.4	0	0.0	2	1.0	2	0.3	0
Puerto Rican	0	0.0	3	1.0	3	0.6	0	0.0	0	0.0	3	0.5	0
Hispanic	9	2.9	7	2.4	14	2.6	2	3.3	4	2.0	16	2.7	2
Total Minority	33	10.7	36	12.6	63	11.8	6	10.0	17	8.5	69	11.6	11
For. Nation.	3	1.0	2	0.7	5	0.9	0	0.0	3	1.5	5	0.8	0
Caucasian	221	72.0	206	72.0	380	71.3	47	78.3	151	75.1	427	72.0	145
Unknown	50	16.3	42	14.7	85	15.9	7	11.7	29	14.4	92	15.5	21
Total	307	51.8	286	48.2	533	89.9	60	10.1	201	33.9	593		177

Transfers

Transfers in	10
Transfers out	17

Tuition and Fees

	Resident	Nonresident
Full-time	$29,670	$29,670
Part-time	$22,629	$22,629

Living Expenses

Estimated living expenses for singles

Living on campus	Living off campus	Living at home
$16,200	$16,200	$16,200

Roger Williams University, Ralph R. Papitto School of Law

*ABA
Approved
Since
1995*

GPA and LSAT Scores

	Total	Full-time	Part-time
# of apps	1,640	1,640	0
# of offers	838	838	0
# of matrics	204	204	0
75% GPA	3.46	3.46	0.00
Median GPA	3.21	3.21	0.00
25% GPA	2.97	2.97	0.00
75% LSAT	156	156	0
Median LSAT	152	152	0
25% LSAT	151	151	0

Grants and Scholarships (from prior year)

	Total #	Total %	Full-time #	Full-time %	Part-time #	Part-time %
Total # of students	608		511		97	
Total # receiving grants	298	49.0	268	52.4	30	30.9
Less than 1/2 tuition	166	27.3	152	29.7	14	14.4
Half to full tuition	76	12.5	68	13.3	8	8.2
Full tuition	53	8.7	45	8.8	8	8.2
More than full tuition	3	0.5	3	0.6	0	0.0
Median grant amount			$10,000		$7,735	

Informational and Library Resources

# of volumes and volume equivalents	293,351
# of titles	130,748
# of active serial subscriptions	3,617
Study seating capacity inside the library	403
# of full-time professional librarians	7
Hours per week library is open	110
# of open, wired connections available to students	196
# of networked computers available for use by students	88
# of simultaneous wireless users	300
Require computer?	No

JD Attrition (from prior year)

	Academic #	Other #	Total #	Total %
1st year	14	24	38	18.7
2nd year	1	1	2	1.0
3rd year	0	0	0	0.0
4th year	0	0	0	0.0

Employment (9 months after graduation)

	Total	Percentage
Employment status known	146	89.0
Employment status unknown	18	11.0
Employed	116	79.5
Pursuing graduate degrees	9	6.2
Unemployed seeking employment	10	6.8
Unemployed not seeking employment	1	0.7
Unemployed and studying for the bar	10	6.8
Type of Employment		
# employed in law firms	40	34.5
# employed in business and industry	31	26.7
# employed in government	19	16.4
# employed in public interest	6	5.2
# employed as judicial clerks	20	17.2
# employed in academia	0	0.0
Geographic Location		
# employed in state	56	48.3
# employed in foreign countries	0	0.0
# of states where employed	21	

Bar Passage Rates

Jurisdiction	Rhode Island Sum 05	Rhode Island Win 06	Rhode Island Total	Massachusetts Sum 05	Massachusetts Win 06	Massachusetts Total
Exam						
# from school taking bar for the first time	76	11	87	65	12	77
School's pass rate for all first-time takers	61%	55%	60%	77%	58%	74%
State's pass rate for all first-time takers	70%	73%	71%	84%	75%	82%

Roger Williams University, Ralph R. Papitto School of Law

Ten Metacom Avenue
Bristol, RI 02809-5171
Phone: 401.254.4555 or 800.633.2727; Fax: 401.254.4516
E-mail: admissions@law.rwu.edu; Website: law.rwu.edu

■ Introduction

Roger Williams University School of Law is located on a peninsula in the historic seacoast town of Bristol, Rhode Island. Providence, the state's capital and legal center, is 20 minutes away and offers extensive employment and externship opportunities. The resort town of Newport is located close by and is the hub of significant cultural, sporting, and recreational events. Boston is one hour to the north. The School of Law is the only law school in the state of Rhode Island. As a small school, the faculty is both accessible and approachable. While the academic environment is challenging, a collegial atmosphere exists.

■ Library and Physical Facilities

The School of Law is self-contained in a multimillion-dollar building designed exclusively for the study of law. The four-level facility contains class and seminar rooms and is equipped with state-of-the-art audiovisual and computer technology. The law library contains more than 280,000 volumes and equivalents, including wireless Internet access. The *WebCatalog* is available through the Internet, as are many library publications and resources. Access to the LexisNexis and Westlaw/Dialog services, Internet, and CD-ROM publications is provided in three separate computer labs. Word processing and research-related and instructional programs are available to students in the labs.

■ Curriculum

The curriculum integrates intellectual theory, case analysis, and practical lawyering skills. The fundamental building blocks of effective lawyering constitute the first- and second-year curriculum. Students learn the skills of traditional legal analysis and the ability to elicit and convey information that every lawyer must master. The Legal Methods program and other required courses prepare students to become problem solvers; to comprehend, analyze, and synthesize complex material; and to communicate their positions effectively. In the latter years of their education, students gain expertise in legal specialties through clustering elective courses in particular fields of interest.

The School of Law no longer enrolls a part-time extended division class.

■ Joint-degree Programs

Roger Williams University offers a JD/Master of Science in Criminal Justice. This program is designed to prepare graduates to formulate system policy and serve effectively as administrators to United States justice system agencies.

The School of Law also offers two joint-degree programs in conjunction with the University of Rhode Island. The JD/Master of Marine Affairs program is geared toward students interested in maritime, admiralty, and environmental law. The JD/Master of Science in Labor Relations and Human Resources program is designed for students interested in issues relating to employment and labor relations.

■ Special Programs

Marine Affairs Institute—The institute is recognized as a distinguished focal point for the exploration of legal, economic, and policy issues raised by the development of the oceans and coastal zone. Students take elective courses in traditional admiralty law and practice, pollution and environmental regulation, coastal zoning, fisheries, and the international law of the sea.

Feinstein Institute—The school believes that lawyers should serve the communities that support them. Introducing students to volunteerism and public service as part of their legal education, therefore, sets the stage for a lifetime of commitment. Thus, students are required to complete 20 hours of community service.

■ Honors Program

The Honors Program is a three-year program of seminars, clinics, and externships. Scholarships of half to full tuition are awarded to students selected for the Honors Program. The Admissions Committee selects students, evaluating them on their academic records, LSAT scores, and recommendations.

■ Practical Experience

The School of Law operates a Criminal Defense Clinic and a Community Justice and Legal Assistance Clinic in Providence. These clinics provide a service to the community by helping indigent clients and at the same time provide an excellent opportunity for students to represent clients before courts and agencies under the supervision of a faculty member. The School of Law also operates a Mediation Clinic in Bristol. Law student-mediators assist people or groups in conflict resolution in a wide range of disputes or other community-sourced problems. As the only law school in Rhode Island, externship opportunities abound. Students may engage in a semester-long supervised clerkship in a judge's chambers or in a public interest or governmental law office for academic credit.

■ Study Abroad

The London Comparative Advocacy Internships Program combines classroom learning at the Inner Temple (one of the four Inns of Court) with a unique and privileged opportunity for students to be trained in English common law trial techniques with a barrister. The Lisbon Program is the only legal study-abroad program in Portugal. The classes are taught in English by professors from the Catholic University of Portugal and Roger Williams University School of Law. Students enrolled in the Lisbon Program attend classes with students from around Europe.

■ Admission

Admission is competitive and is based on the undergraduate grade-point average (UGPA) and the Law School Admission Test (LSAT) score, as well as other indicators of probable success in the study of law, such as graduate degree, work experience, undergraduate extracurricular activities, and community service. Applicants must register with Law School Data Assembly Service (LSDAS). A personal statement and the $60 fee must accompany all applications. One letter of recommendation is required.

■ Financial Aid

Merit-based scholarships of up to full tuition are available; no separate application is required. Federal and state governmental agencies, as well as private lenders, offer students loans at comparative rates and flexible repayment terms. Students must file the Free Application for Federal Student Aid (FAFSA) to be considered for federal loans.

■ Student Activities

Law Review—Membership on the *Roger Williams University Law Review* is considered one of the most valuable and prestigious student activities available. The law review is staffed and primarily administered by students who are selected based upon superior academic achievement and writing ability.

Moot Court Board—The Moot Court Board is composed of students possessing superior appellate advocacy and writing

ability. This prestigious organization sponsors speakers and programs on appellate advocacy, organizes an intraschool competition, and sends moot court teams to interschool competitions.

Extracurricular Activities—Student organizations include, but are not limited to, *The Docket* (student newspaper), Multicultural Law Students Association, Women's Law Association, the Alliance (LGBT), Black Law Students Association, Latino Law Students Association, Asian Pacific American Law Students Association, Older Wiser Law Students, Maritime Law Society, Sports and Entertainment Law Society, International Law Society, Association for Public Interest Law, and Association of Trial Lawyers of America.

■ Career Services

The Office of Career Services is dedicated to serving the needs of law students, alumni, and the legal community. The office features a welcoming suite for career research, on-campus interviews, and mock interviews. All of these tools help to prepare students to take advantage of the versatility of the Juris Doctor degree.

Applicant Profile

Roger Williams University, Ralph R. Papitto School of Law

LSAT Score	GPA								
	3.75 +	3.50–3.74	3.25–3.49	3.00–3.24	2.75–2.99	2.50–2.74	2.25–2.49	2.00–2.24	Below 2.00
175–180									
170–174									
165–169									
160–164									
155–159									
150–154									
145–149									
140–144									
135–139									
130–134									
125–129									
120–124									

■ Good Possibility ▪ Possible □ Unlikely

This chart is to be used as a general guide only. Nonnumerical factors are strongly considered for all applicants.

Rutgers—The State University of New Jersey—School of Law—Camden

217 North Fifth Street
Camden, NJ 08102
Phone: 856.225.6102 or 800.466.7561; Fax: 856.969.7903
E-mail: admissions@camlaw.rutgers.edu; Website: www-camlaw.rutgers.edu/

ABA
Approved
Since
1950

The Basics

Type of school	Public
Term	Semester
Application deadline	3/1 4/1 6/1
Application fee	$60
Financial aid deadline	3/15
Can first year start other than fall?	Yes
Student to faculty ratio	14.5 to 1
Does the university offer:	
housing restricted to law students?	No
graduate housing for which law students are eligible?	Yes

Faculty and Administrators

	Total		Men		Women		Minorities	
	Fall	Spr	Fall	Spr	Fall	Spr	Fall	Spr
Full-time	50	50	30	30	20	20	3	3
Other Full-time	6	6	2	2	4	4	1	1
Deans, librarians, & others who teach	7	7	3	3	4	4	1	1
Part-time	40	40	28	27	12	13	4	6
Total	103	103	63	62	40	41	9	11

Curriculum

	Full-time	Part-time
Typical first-year section size	68	43
Is there typically a "small section" of the first-year class, other than Legal Writing, taught by full-time faculty	No	No
If yes, typical size offered last year		
# of classroom course titles beyond first-year curriculum	111	
# of upper division courses, excluding seminars with an enrollment: Under 25	99	
25–49	47	
50–74	12	
75–99	2	
100+	4	
# of seminars	19	
# of seminar positions available	293	
# of seminar positions filled	200	34
# of positions available in simulation courses	646	
# of simulation positions filled	496	67
# of positions available in faculty supervised clinical courses	115	
# of faculty supervised clinical positions filled	82	15
# involved in field placements	67	3
# involved in law journals	143	13
# involved in interschool competitions	42	7
# of credit hours required to graduate	84	

JD Enrollment and Ethnicity

	Men		Women		Full-time		Part-time		1st-year		Total		JD Degs. Awd.
	#	%	#	%	#	%	#	%	#	%	#	%	
African Amer.	17	3.7	24	7.8	34	6.1	7	3.3	6	2.7	41	5.4	12
Amer. Indian	1	0.2	0	0.0	0	0.0	1	0.5	0	0.0	1	0.1	0
Asian Amer.	34	7.4	31	10.1	50	9.0	15	7.1	19	8.7	65	8.5	20
Mex. Amer.	4	0.9	5	1.6	8	1.4	1	0.5	4	1.8	9	1.2	1
Puerto Rican	5	1.1	5	1.6	6	1.1	4	1.9	1	0.5	10	1.3	3
Hispanic	24	5.2	13	4.2	33	5.9	4	1.9	8	3.7	37	4.8	6
Total Minority	85	18.6	78	25.3	131	23.6	32	15.2	38	17.4	163	21.3	42
For. Nation.	1	0.2	1	0.3	0	0.0	2	1.0	0	0.0	2	0.3	3
Caucasian	372	81.2	229	74.4	425	76.4	176	83.8	181	82.6	601	78.5	203
Unknown	0	0.0	0	0.0	0	0.0	0	0.0	0	0.0	0	0.0	0
Total	458	59.8	308	40.2	556	72.6	210	27.4	219	28.6	766		248

Transfers

Transfers in	44
Transfers out	4

Tuition and Fees

	Resident	Nonresident
Full-time	$19,867	$28,220
Part-time	$15,851	$22,904

Living Expenses

Estimated living expenses for singles

Living on campus	Living off campus	Living at home
$13,864	$17,884	$6,748

Rutgers—The State University of New Jersey—School of Law—Camden

ABA
Approved
Since
1950

GPA and LSAT Scores

	Total	Full-time	Part-time
# of apps	2,152	2,152	N/A
# of offers	562	562	N/A
# of matrics	219	106	113
75% GPA	3.64	3.65	3.64
Median GPA	3.40	3.40	3.40
25% GPA	3.04	3.09	3.02
75% LSAT	162	162	160
Median LSAT	160	162	157
25% LSAT	156	160	154

Grants and Scholarships (from prior year)

	Total		Full-time		Part-time	
	#	%	#	%	#	%
Total # of students	787		571		216	
Total # receiving grants	302	38.4	278	48.7	24	11.1
Less than 1/2 tuition	272	34.6	248	43.4	24	11.1
Half to full tuition	22	2.8	22	3.9	0	0.0
Full tuition	2	0.3	2	0.4	0	0.0
More than full tuition	6	0.8	6	1.1	0	0.0
Median grant amount			$4,500		$1,350	

Informational and Library Resources

# of volumes and volume equivalents	443,623
# of titles	94,635
# of active serial subscriptions	4,639
Study seating capacity inside the library	403
# of full-time professional librarians	7
Hours per week library is open	103
# of open, wired connections available to students	170
# of networked computers available for use by students	74
# of simultaneous wireless users	1,000
Require computer?	Yes

JD Attrition (from prior year)

	Academic	Other	Total	
	#	#	#	%
1st year	3	13	16	6.1
2nd year	0	1	1	0.4
3rd year	0	2	2	0.8
4th year	0	0	0	0.0

Employment (9 months after graduation)

	Total	Percentage
Employment status known	247	95.0
Employment status unknown	13	5.0
Employed	225	91.1
Pursuing graduate degrees	6	2.4
Unemployed seeking employment	15	6.1
Unemployed not seeking employment	1	0.4
Unemployed and studying for the bar	0	0.0
Type of Employment		
# employed in law firms	83	36.9
# employed in business and industry	20	8.9
# employed in government	14	6.2
# employed in public interest	2	0.9
# employed as judicial clerks	90	40.0
# employed in academia	2	0.9
Geographic Location		
# employed in state	79	35.1
# employed in foreign countries	0	0.0
# of states where employed		12

Bar Passage Rates

Jurisdiction	New Jersey		
Exam	Sum 05	Win 06	Total
# from school taking bar for the first time	188	21	209
School's pass rate for all first-time takers	81%	81%	81%
State's pass rate for all first-time takers	78%	73%	77%

Rutgers—The State University of New Jersey—School of Law—Camden

217 North Fifth Street
Camden, NJ 08102
Phone: 856.225.6102 or 800.466.7561; Fax: 856.969.7903
E-mail: admissions@camlaw.rutgers.edu; Website: www-camlaw.rutgers.edu/

■ Introduction

Chartered in 1766 by George III of Great Britain as the Queen's College, Rutgers—the State University of New Jersey is one of the oldest and largest state higher educational systems in the nation. The law school at the Camden campus is proud to continue this national reputation of excellence. With more than 100 faculty and staff members, the law school is a leading center of legal education. Noted for excellence in scholarship and rigor in training of new lawyers, the law school faculty is internationally recognized in fields as diverse as international law, health law, family and women's rights law, state constitutional law, and legal history.

Located at the base of the Benjamin Franklin Bridge, just minutes from the Liberty Bell and Independence Hall in Philadelphia, the law school is in one of the nation's largest legal markets. Rutgers' thriving, 25-acre, tree-lined urban campus in Camden, New Jersey, is a handsome blend of converted Victorian buildings and newly constructed facilities. The Tweeter Center at the Waterfront, an indoor/outdoor concert venue; Adventure Aquarium; the USS Battleship New Jersey; the newly renovated, historic "Victor" building with its upscale apartments; the new RiverLINE rail system; and Campbell Field (the minor league baseball stadium), just a few blocks from the law school, are centerpieces for the ongoing development of Camden's waterfront. Camden, which is the county seat, has federal and local courts adjacent to the law school. A member of the Association of American Law Schools, the school is included on the list of approved schools of the American Bar Association.

■ Faculty

Faculty scholarship has been cited by numerous courts, including the United States Supreme Court, and faculty members have authored numerous casebooks and significant legal works. Faculty members testify regularly before Congress and serve as consultants and reporters for the American Bar Association, the American Law Institute, and several federal and state commissions, and act as counsel in important public interest litigation.

■ Library and Physical Facilities

The law school building houses research facilities, seminar and reading rooms, student lounges, a clinical suite, computer labs, study areas, a cafeteria, classrooms, and faculty offices. A new law school building is being constructed and annexed to the existing 93,860-square-foot structure. The new building design includes courtrooms, state-of-the-art classrooms, and enhanced student spaces. A selective federal repository, the law library, with more than 440,000 bibliographic units is one of the largest in the state. In addition to the traditional materials, students are trained on a number of computerized research systems, including a myriad of databases available on the Internet. The library consists of three floors of book stacks, a bridge that overlooks the campus and Philadelphia skyline, and a large computer lab for LexisNexis and Westlaw training. Over 400 individual working areas, carrels, and lounge seats are available.

■ Curriculum and Special Programs

The first-year curriculum includes the traditional core legal courses. Central to the curriculum is the lawyering program that engages students in simulated lawyering activities and practical applications of the law. Upper-class students can typically choose from more than 100 exciting elective courses each year, including cyberlaw, trial advocacy, sports law, children's law, and international business transactions.

An outstanding Externship Program offers third-year students the opportunity to work with federal and state judges, public agencies, and public interest organizations. Other students participate in the Civil Practice Clinic and pro bono programs at the law school. Live client experiences include the Domestic Violence Project, the Pro Bono Bankruptcy Project, the Immigration Project, the Mediation Project, and the Elder Law Clinic, or representing clients in connection with the LEAP Charter School. Each of these programs constitutes a comprehensive initiative that reflects the law school's commitment to public service.

Students may pursue their legal studies in the full-time day program as well as the part-time program, available day or evening. Both programs are subject to the same rigorous admission and academic standards.

■ Joint-degree Programs

Eight formal joint JD and master's or doctoral degree programs are available with the University of Medicine and Dentistry, Graduate School of Business, Bloustein School of Planning and Public Policy, School of Social Work, and Graduate School–Camden, including JD/MD, JD/DO, JD/MPA, JD/MBA, JD/MSW, and JD/MCRP. Upon approval of the faculty, students may also pursue self-designed joint-degree programs within Rutgers University or with other graduate institutions.

■ Admission

Although admission is highly competitive, the Committee on Admissions does consider each applicant's file individually, and special qualities may occasionally overcome lower numbers. Important factors to the committee include LSAT, undergraduate and graduate grade-point average, undergraduate and graduate institutions, work experience, and letters of recommendation. Typically, half of the full-time entering class scores in the top quartile on the LSAT (162 or higher) with an average GPA of 3.5 or higher. The entering class size each fall is about 165 full- and 80 part-time day and evening students. The law school draws from 34 states, the District of Columbia, and five foreign countries. More than 255 colleges and universities are represented in the student body. Decisions are made on a rolling basis beginning in early December. The law school has rolling admission and will consider candidates who take the February and June LSAT. However, early applicants have an enhanced opportunity for admission. Applicants may also apply for advanced standing as a transfer student but are only eligible upon completion of one year of law study. Students may request an application from the law school or apply online at *www.camlaw.rutgers.edu/*.

■ Housing

Air-conditioned and carpeted law school apartments are located on campus, and nearby the renovated historic "Victor" building, with its spectacular views of the Philadelphia skyline, provides upscale apartment living. There are also abundant housing opportunities in the nearby suburbs and excellent public transportation systems. First-year admitted students are invited to utilize the law school's housing webpage and to attend the Dean's Law and Housing Day in the spring.

■ Financial Aid

In the 2005-2006 academic year, over $18 million was distributed to law students through fellowships, grants, loans, and employment. The average financial aid package was approximately $25,250, with 90 percent of the student body receiving some form of assistance. The Federal Direct Loan Program, the largest financial aid program, provided more than $11.5 million to over 650 students in the last academic year. For fall consideration, the FAFSA should be submitted by March 1. Merit-based scholarships are also available for outstanding academic performance.

■ Career Services

As a direct result of the quality of legal education at Rutgers, typically more than 97 percent of each year's class obtains employment in the legal profession within nine months of graduation. All major Philadelphia, New Jersey, and Delaware firms recruit from Rutgers, as do prestigious firms from New York City, California, and Washington, DC. The school's more than 7,600 alumni are leading members of the judiciary, government, and bar throughout this nation. The average salary of an associate who joins a private law firm is in excess of $76,000, with top students typically making in excess of $100,000. The school's placement rate is one of the best in the country (40 percent of last year's class) for highly desirable state and federal clerkships.

■ Student Activities

Among the numerous student organizations are the Latino Law Students Association, Asian/Pacific American Law Students Association, Association for Public Interest Law, Black Law Students Association, Christian Legal Society, Community Outreach Group, Cyberlaw, Environmental Law Students Association, Francis Deak International Law Society, OUTLAW Student Bar Association, Health Law Society, Italian-American Law Students Organization, Jewish Law Students Association, Law Journal (publishes the *Rutgers Law Journal*), *Journal of Law and Urban Policy, Rutgers Journal of Law and Religion*, Phi Alpha Delta law fraternity, Pro Bono/Public Interest Steering Committee, and the Women's Law Caucus.

Applicant Profile

Rutgers—The State University of New Jersey—School of Law—Camden
This grid includes only applicants who earned 120–180 LSAT scores under standard administrations.

LSAT Score	GPA								
	3.75 +	3.50–3.74	3.25–3.49	3.00–3.24	2.75–2.99	2.50–2.74	2.25–2.49	2.00–2.24	Below 2.00
170–180									
165–169									
161–164									
158–160									
155–157									
150–154									
Below 150									

Very Likely   Likely   Possible   Unlikely*

*Special attributes may sometimes overcome lower scores/GPAs.
This chart is to be used as a general guide only. Nonnumerical factors are strongly considered for all applicants.

Rutgers University School of Law—Newark

Center for Law and Justice, 123 Washington Street
Newark, NJ 07102
Phone: 973.353.5554/7; Fax: 973.353.3459
E-mail: lawinfo@andromeda.rutgers.edu; Website: law.newark.rutgers.edu

ABA
Approved
Since
1941

The Basics

Type of school	Public
Term	Semester
Application deadline	3/15
Application fee	$60
Financial aid deadline	3/15
Can first year start other than fall?	No
Student to faculty ratio	15.4 to 1
Does the university offer:	
housing restricted to law students?	No
graduate housing for which law students are eligible?	Yes

Faculty and Administrators

	Total		Men		Women		Minorities	
	Fall	Spr	Fall	Spr	Fall	Spr	Fall	Spr
Full-time	37	42	22	23	15	19	11	11
Other Full-time	2	2	1	1	1	1	0	0
Deans, librarians, & others who teach	11	9	6	5	5	4	5	4
Part-time	36	43	26	29	10	14	4	4
Total	**86**	**96**	**55**	**58**	**31**	**38**	**20**	**19**

Curriculum

	Full-time	Part-time
Typical first-year section size	60	70
Is there typically a "small section" of the first-year class, other than Legal Writing, taught by full-time faculty	Yes	Yes
If yes, typical size offered last year	30	35
# of classroom course titles beyond first-year curriculum	112	
# of upper division courses, excluding seminars with an enrollment: Under 25	78	
25–49	31	
50–74	11	
75–99	5	
100+	2	
# of seminars	26	
# of seminar positions available	468	
# of seminar positions filled	242	49
# of positions available in simulation courses	420	
# of simulation positions filled	316	82
# of positions available in faculty supervised clinical courses	280	
# of faculty supervised clinical positions filled	182	29
# involved in field placements	86	7
# involved in law journals	191	15
# involved in interschool competitions	21	0
# of credit hours required to graduate	84	

JD Enrollment and Ethnicity

	Men #	Men %	Women #	Women %	Full-time #	Full-time %	Part-time #	Part-time %	1st-year #	1st-year %	Total #	Total %	JD Degs. Awd.
African Amer.	66	13.9	54	15.9	86	15.3	34	13.4	35	14.0	120	14.7	22
Amer. Indian	2	0.4	0	0.0	2	0.4	0	0.0	0	0.0	2	0.2	1
Asian Amer.	55	11.6	47	13.8	72	12.8	30	11.8	31	12.4	102	12.5	31
Mex. Amer.	5	1.1	4	1.2	8	1.4	1	0.4	2	0.8	9	1.1	2
Puerto Rican	11	2.3	19	5.6	22	3.9	8	3.1	5	2.0	30	3.7	11
Hispanic	26	5.5	23	6.8	33	5.9	16	6.3	15	6.0	49	6.0	10
Total Minority	165	34.7	147	43.2	223	39.8	89	35.0	88	35.2	312	38.3	77
For. Nation.	6	1.3	10	2.9	5	0.9	11	4.3	5	2.0	16	2.0	7
Caucasian	304	64.0	183	53.8	333	59.4	154	60.6	157	62.8	487	59.8	132
Unknown	0	0.0	0	0.0	0	0.0	0	0.0	0	0.0	0	0.0	0
Total	475	58.3	340	41.7	561	68.8	254	31.2	250	30.7	815		216

Transfers

Transfers in	17
Transfers out	15

Tuition and Fees

	Resident	Nonresident
Full-time	$19,623	$27,976
Part-time	$12,691	$18,337

Living Expenses

Estimated living expenses for singles

Living on campus	Living off campus	Living at home
$13,908	$18,108	$6,808

Rutgers University School of Law—Newark

ABA Approved Since 1941

GPA and LSAT Scores

	Total	Full-time	Part-time
# of apps	3,671	3,010	661
# of offers	825	702	123
# of matrics	251	182	69
75% GPA	3.57	3.57	3.57
Median GPA	3.34	3.34	3.34
25% GPA	3.04	3.10	2.98
75% LSAT	161	162	159
Median LSAT	158	159	157
25% LSAT	154	154	155

Grants and Scholarships (from prior year)

	Total #	Total %	Full-time #	Full-time %	Part-time #	Part-time %
Total # of students	804		564		240	
Total # receiving grants	304	37.8	255	45.2	49	20.4
Less than 1/2 tuition	245	30.5	207	36.7	38	15.8
Half to full tuition	27	3.4	23	4.1	4	1.7
Full tuition	18	2.2	12	2.1	6	2.5
More than full tuition	14	1.7	13	2.3	1	0.4
Median grant amount			$4,000		$4,000	

Informational and Library Resources

# of volumes and volume equivalents	528,600
# of titles	191,120
# of active serial subscriptions	3,060
Study seating capacity inside the library	522
# of full-time professional librarians	15
Hours per week library is open	95
# of open, wired connections available to students	540
# of networked computers available for use by students	178
# of simultaneous wireless users	600
Require computer?	

JD Attrition (from prior year)

	Academic #	Other #	Total #	Total %
1st year	0	22	22	8.8
2nd year	1	7	8	2.9
3rd year	0	1	1	0.4
4th year	0	0	0	0.0

Employment (9 months after graduation)

	Total	Percentage
Employment status known	225	96.6
Employment status unknown	8	3.4
Employed	210	93.3
Pursuing graduate degrees	1	0.4
Unemployed seeking employment	6	2.7
Unemployed not seeking employment	7	3.1
Unemployed and studying for the bar	1	0.4

Type of Employment

# employed in law firms	87	41.4
# employed in business and industry	26	12.4
# employed in government	22	10.5
# employed in public interest	8	3.8
# employed as judicial clerks	58	27.6
# employed in academia	7	3.3

Geographic Location

# employed in state	144	68.6
# employed in foreign countries	0	0.0
# of states where employed		11

Bar Passage Rates

Jurisdiction	New Jersey			New York		
Exam	Sum 05	Win 06	Total	Sum 05	Win 06	Total
# from school taking bar for the first time	202	25	227	142	11	153
School's pass rate for all first-time takers	78%	68%	77%	80%	64%	78%
State's pass rate for all first-time takers	78%	73%	77%	76%	61%	74%

Rutgers University School of Law—Newark

Center for Law and Justice, 123 Washington Street
Newark, NJ 07102
Phone: 973.353.5554/7; Fax: 973.353.3459
E-mail: lawinfo@andromeda.rutgers.edu; Website: law.newark.rutgers.edu

■ Introduction

Rutgers University School of Law—Newark is a leading center for the study of theory and practice of law, the advancement of law reform, and the application of law to promote equality and social justice. Four core principles shape the work of our faculty and students: academic excellence, scholarship, public service, and equal opportunity. Through a unique combination of traditional doctrinal courses and clinical education, we prepare our students to become highly skilled, ethical lawyers who will assume influential roles in the law and other disciplines. Our alumni have fulfilled that responsibility as practitioners, judges, legislators, public officials, and leaders in business. Our internationally recognized faculty regularly contributes to the development of legal theory and produces scholarship that addresses significant social issues from interdisciplinary perspectives. Through our clinical program and pro bono activities, faculty and students give the principles of justice and equality a practical significance. Rutgers—Newark is the home of the oldest chapter of the Order of the Coif in New Jersey.

■ The Center for Law and Justice

Located on the campus of Rutgers University—Newark, the Center for Law and Justice is one of the most technologically advanced law school buildings in the country. Highlights include a light-filled library housing over 500,000 volumes and five computer labs; lecture rooms with excellent acoustics, sightlines, and power lines at every seat; an attractive courtroom complex where the Appellate Division of the Superior Court regularly hears cases; and numerous lounge and study areas. Wireless Internet access is available throughout the building and in all classrooms. The center opens onto a pedestrian plaza and a garden terrace—favorite gathering spots for students and faculty.

■ Faculty

The faculty contributes to every aspect of the law school experience. Faculty members examine, shape, and resolve new and developing issues of law, such as gender and race studies, dispute resolution, international transactions, and new theories of the corporation. They engage students through teaching styles that range from traditional Socratic method to interactive problem-solving. The faculty is diverse, ensuring the kind of intellectual inquiry that provides a rich foundation for a career in law.

■ Curriculum

The rigorous curriculum ensures the development of professional skills and values within a theoretical framework that promotes intellectual growth and a commitment to justice.

First-year students learn the essential conceptual, analytical, and research methods to be effective lawyers in complex environments. Upper-level students build on those skills through our extensive curriculum of over 200 class, clinic, and seminar options. The faculty reviews the curriculum regularly to ensure that the offerings prepare students for a rapidly changing legal environment.

The Global Legal Studies Program offers students interested in public and private international law a rich array of academic courses, clinical programs, and experiential learning opportunities, focusing on the human condition in an interconnected world. An accredited semester of study abroad sends students to Leiden University in the Netherlands for an intensive program in international law, European Union law, comparative law, legal history, and law and international economics. The Rutgers Division of Global Affairs, located in our building, also serves as a nexus for students interested in the international dimension.

Joint-degree programs are available with the Rutgers Graduate Schools of Business, Urban Planning, and Social Work, as well as the University of Medicine and Dentistry of New Jersey. Students are encouraged to take advantage of the rich curriculum offerings throughout the university through cross-disciplinary registration. The Foreign Lawyer Program permits persons with foreign law degrees to earn a JD in two years.

■ Clinics and Public Service

With over 35 years of pacesetting experience and a historic commitment to public service, Rutgers—Newark offers students extensive opportunities for hands-on legal experience in real cases involving underrepresented clients, communities, or causes. Guided by talented and accomplished faculty with expertise in litigation, legislation, mediation, or transactional practice, our eight clinics are noted for their diversity, breadth, and comprehensiveness of experiences, and involvement in cases and projects of social and community impact. Clinical students work for underserved clients and causes, and provide corporate, transactional, and intellectual property legal services to nonprofit corporations, start-up for-profit businesses, and other entities. Other opportunities include pro bono work, internships, fellowships, and summer placements. The Loan Repayment Assistance Program, one of the largest in the country, assists graduates pursuing careers in public service.

■ Students and Student Life

Rutgers enrolls students of extraordinary academic and professional promise who enrich the community with their intellectual strength and significant life and work experience. Many students have earned advanced degrees while others provide a global perspective to the classroom.

Diversity of views enlivens the classroom and creates an inclusive environment. Our Minority Student Program reflects the faculty's long-standing commitment to preserve the diversity of the law school and to improve diversity in the legal profession. Student-run organizations reflect myriad interests, political positions, and backgrounds, from the Lawyers Guild to the Sports and Entertainment Law Society. Student publications include the *Rutgers Law Review*, *Rutgers Computer and Technology Journal*, the *Women's Rights Law Reporter*, the *Rutgers Race and the Law Review*, and the online student newspaper, the *Rutgers Law Record*.

■ Admission

The faculty believes that diverse perspectives and backgrounds are essential to a complete understanding of the law and its relation to contemporary society. The law school seeks and attracts a talented student body with a breadth of experience, and provides unparalleled opportunities for those who have been historically excluded from the legal profession.

The Admission Committee considers a broad range of factors, including but not limited to educational and employment experiences, community service, LSAT, UGPA, race, ethnicity, socioeconomic background, and extraordinary family circumstances. Every applicant can choose to compete for admission with primary emphasis placed on numerical indicators (LSAT and UGPA), or nonnumerical indicators (experiences and accomplishments).

In each entering class, 35–40 percent of our students are people of color. All regions of the country and more than two dozen foreign countries are represented.

■ Housing

On-campus graduate housing is located in close proximity to the law school. The addition of a new residence hall in 2006 has increased the availability of on-campus housing for law students. Nearby suburban communities offer a variety of housing options. Public transportation is widely available.

■ Career Services

The Office of Career Services provides traditional and innovative services and programs, helping students and graduates develop career goals and conduct successful job searches. Individual counseling, panels, workshops, networking events, and on- and off-campus interview programs that attract many of the nation's leading law firms are a few of a myriad of services offered.

Applicant Profile

Rutgers University School of Law—Newark

LSAT Score	GPA									
	3.75 +	3.50–3.74	3.25–3.49	3.00–3.24	2.75–2.99	2.50–2.74	2.25–2.49	2.00–2.24	Below 2.00	No GPA
175–180										
170–174										
165–169										
160–164										
157–159										
154–156										
150–153										
145–149										
140–144										
135–139										
130–134										
125–129										
120–124										

■ Highly Possible ■ Possible □ Unlikely

The information contained in this grid should be used as an approximate gauge as to the likelihood of admission. The Admissions Committee gives considerable weight to individual accomplishments and other nonnumerical factors in the admissions process. LSAT and UGPA are not the sole determinants for admission.

St. John's University School of Law

8000 Utopia Parkway
Queens, NY 11439
Phone: 718.990.6474; Fax: 718.990.2526
E-mail: lawinfo@stjohns.edu; Website: www.law.stjohns.edu

ABA
Approved
Since
1937

The Basics

Type of school	Private
Term	Semester
Application deadline	4/1
Application fee	$60
Financial aid deadline	3/1
Can first year start other than fall?	No
Student to faculty ratio	15.7 to 1
Does the university offer:	
housing restricted to law students?	Yes
graduate housing for which law students are eligible?	Yes

Faculty and Administrators

	Total		Men		Women		Minorities	
	Fall	Spr	Fall	Spr	Fall	Spr	Fall	Spr
Full-time	46	46	28	27	18	19	9	8
Other Full-time	3	0	1	0	2	0	1	0
Deans, librarians, & others who teach	8	7	4	4	4	3	1	1
Part-time	47	49	36	40	11	9	2	2
Total	**104**	**102**	**69**	**71**	**35**	**31**	**13**	**11**

Curriculum

	Full-time	Part-time
Typical first-year section size	80	65
Is there typically a "small section" of the first-year class, other than Legal Writing, taught by full-time faculty	Yes	No
If yes, typical size offered last year	26	
# of classroom course titles beyond first-year curriculum	157	
# of upper division courses, excluding seminars with an enrollment: Under 25	117	
25–49	46	
50–74	30	
75–99	16	
100+	2	
# of seminars	17	
# of seminar positions available	354	
# of seminar positions filled	177	9
# of positions available in simulation courses	384	
# of simulation positions filled	249	53
# of positions available in faculty supervised clinical courses	125	
# of faculty supervised clinical positions filled	119	5
# involved in field placements	193	14
# involved in law journals	99	4
# involved in interschool competitions	47	3
# of credit hours required to graduate	86	

JD Enrollment and Ethnicity

	Men #	Men %	Women #	Women %	Full-time #	Full-time %	Part-time #	Part-time %	1st-year #	1st-year %	Total #	Total %	JD Degs. Awd.
African Amer.	19	4.0	35	7.8	35	4.8	19	9.6	9	3.0	54	5.9	18
Amer. Indian	1	0.2	1	0.2	0	0.0	2	1.0	1	0.3	2	0.2	0
Asian Amer.	37	7.8	52	11.7	67	9.3	22	11.2	23	7.6	89	9.7	22
Mex. Amer.	2	0.4	3	0.7	3	0.4	2	1.0	0	0.0	5	0.5	3
Puerto Rican	3	0.6	5	1.1	6	0.8	2	1.0	2	0.7	8	0.9	2
Hispanic	33	6.9	19	4.3	37	5.1	15	7.6	13	4.3	52	5.6	11
Total Minority	95	20.0	115	25.8	148	20.4	62	31.5	48	15.8	210	22.8	56
For. Nation.	18	3.8	17	3.8	29	4.0	6	3.0	4	1.3	35	3.8	5
Caucasian	293	61.7	251	56.3	439	60.6	105	53.3	201	66.3	544	59.1	242
Unknown	69	14.5	63	14.1	108	14.9	24	12.2	50	16.5	132	14.3	16
Total	475	51.6	446	48.4	724	78.6	197	21.4	303	32.9	921		319

Transfers

Transfers in	16
Transfers out	5

Tuition and Fees

	Resident	Nonresident
Full-time	$32,700	$32,700
Part-time	$24,525	$24,525

Living Expenses

Estimated living expenses for singles

Living on campus	Living off campus	Living at home
$18,110	$18,110	$8,740

St. John's University School of Law

*ABA
Approved
Since
1937*

GPA and LSAT Scores

	Total	Full-time	Part-time
# of apps	3,677	2,843	834
# of offers	1,294	1,000	294
# of matrics	307	215	92
75% GPA	3.68	3.72	3.51
Median GPA	3.48	3.53	3.35
25% GPA	3.24	3.28	3.18
75% LSAT	161	162	156
Median LSAT	158	160	155
25% LSAT	155	157	152

Grants and Scholarships (from prior year)

	Total		Full-time		Part-time	
	#	%	#	%	#	%
Total # of students	952		756		196	
Total # receiving grants	399	41.9	362	47.9	37	18.9
Less than 1/2 tuition	198	20.8	172	22.8	26	13.3
Half to full tuition	70	7.4	67	8.9	3	1.5
Full tuition	117	12.3	110	14.6	7	3.6
More than full tuition	14	1.5	13	1.7	1	0.5
Median grant amount			$17,500		$7,000	

Informational and Library Resources

# of volumes and volume equivalents	495,349
# of titles	165,853
# of active serial subscriptions	4,809
Study seating capacity inside the library	507
# of full-time professional librarians	10
Hours per week library is open	99
# of open, wired connections available to students	141
# of networked computers available for use by students	118
# of simultaneous wireless users	750
Require computer?	No

JD Attrition (from prior year)

	Academic	Other	Total	
	#	#	#	%
1st year	4	10	14	4.6
2nd year	4	15	19	6.8
3rd year	0	0	0	0.0
4th year	0	0	0	0.0

Employment (9 months after graduation)

	Total	Percentage
Employment status known	294	99.7
Employment status unknown	1	0.3
Employed	259	88.1
Pursuing graduate degrees	6	2.0
Unemployed seeking employment	9	3.1
Unemployed not seeking employment	20	6.8
Unemployed and studying for the bar	0	0.0
Type of Employment		
# employed in law firms	132	51.0
# employed in business and industry	55	21.2
# employed in government	48	18.5
# employed in public interest	5	1.9
# employed as judicial clerks	10	3.9
# employed in academia	8	3.1
Geographic Location		
# employed in state	236	91.1
# employed in foreign countries	0	0.0
# of states where employed		15

Bar Passage Rates

Jurisdiction	New York		
Exam	Sum 05	Win 06	Total
# from school taking bar for the first time	268	8	276
School's pass rate for all first-time takers	89%	88%	89%
State's pass rate for all first-time takers	76%	61%	74%

St. John's University School of Law

8000 Utopia Parkway
Queens, NY 11439
Phone: 718.990.6474; Fax: 718.990.2526
E-mail: lawinfo@stjohns.edu; Website: www.law.stjohns.edu

■ Introduction

St. John's University School of Law is a forceful presence and an integral part of the New York metropolitan area. It imparts to its students training and competency in the basic skills and techniques of the legal profession, a grasp of the history and the system of common law, and a familiarity with important statutes and decisions in federal and state jurisdictions, including the state of New York.

The law school is a state-of-the-art facility with a gross total square footage of 179,400, one of the highest space-per-student ratios in the country. Some highlights of the facility include new student activities areas, alumni function areas, a student lounge, faculty offices, classrooms for teaching clinical and lawyering skills, and a state-of-the-art moot courtroom.

The School of Law is located on the Queens Campus of St. John's University. Situated on almost 100 rolling acres in a residential area, the campus boasts a spectacular view of the Manhattan skyline. St. John's School of Law is approved by the ABA and is a member of the AALS.

■ Library and Physical Facilities

The showpiece of the law school building is its beautiful law library, which incorporates the most recent advances in law library science and technology. It contains a computer classroom, a computer laboratory, and eight study rooms for student conferences. The library occupies approximately 50,000 square feet on five of the eight building levels. It has been designated a depository library for US government and UN documents.

The School of Law has recently completed a major renovation of its moot court, producing a beautiful, state-of-the-art facility that incorporates technologies that further the teaching and research missions of St. John's. In addition, the School of Law has completed renovations of first-year classrooms and clinic offices.

■ Special Programs and LLM in Bankruptcy

Elective clinical programs and externships are available to second- and third-year full-time students.

In the Civil Externship Program, students work in (1) a legal services office assisting lawyers who provide legal representation to the poor; or (2) a public service or governmental agency such as the United States Attorney's Office, the Securities and Exchange Commission, or the New York Legal Aid Society. In the Criminal Justice Externship Program, students work in a district attorney's office, a legal aid office, or the law department of the supreme court or criminal court. In the Judicial Externship Program, students work in the federal, state, or city court system.

In the Elder Law Clinic, students represent elderly clients with legal problems that involve the danger of losing their homes, denial of disability benefits, unlawful collection practices, and illegal lending schemes. The Securities Arbitration Clinic positions students to work with small investors who are in securities disputes with broker-dealers. The Child Advocacy Clinic provides students the opportunity to represent children who have been abused or neglected.

Students in the Domestic Violence Clinic represent women who are victims of spousal abuse. The students perform services that include client interviews, negotiating settlements, and making court appearances. The Prosecution Clinic allows students to witness the criminal justice system at work—not just by observing, but by prosecuting real cases. The Refugee and Immigration Rights Clinic is coordinated in partnership with Catholic Charities and exposes students to the legal problems faced by immigrants, refugees, and asylees.

St. John's has the nation's first master's program in bankruptcy. It is designed to meet an important and special educational need in the field of bankruptcy law. Matriculating students will be required to complete 30 credits, including the preparation and defense of a major thesis on a current significant bankruptcy topic. Students may matriculate on a full- or part-time basis.

■ Special Diversity Admission Program

The School of Law sponsors a program for individuals who have suffered the effects of discrimination, chronic financial hardship, or other social, educational, or physical disadvantages to such an extent that their undergraduate performance or LSAT score would not otherwise warrant unconditional acceptance into the entering class. This Summer Institute program, which is available at no additional charge to the participants, consists of a substantive course taught and graded according to the same qualitative standard applied to all first-year courses, as well as a legal writing course. The program enables individuals whose LSAT scores and GPAs are not reliable predictors of their success to demonstrate their ability to succeed in the study of law.

■ Vincentian Scholarship Program

The mission statement of St. John's University School of Law calls for the law school "to provide a superior legal education for a diverse population of students with special awareness for economic fairness and equal opportunity, consistent with and in fulfillment of the Vincentian tradition and mission." In furtherance of this Vincentian tradition and mission, the School of Law provides five full-tuition Vincentian scholarships each year in its ongoing effort to achieve a diverse student body. These are in addition to the extensive financial scholarship aid provided to law students annually. Applicants seeking a Vincentian scholarship are encouraged to so indicate on their applications for admission and to discuss their qualifications in an addendum to their applications.

■ Student Activities

Publications—*St. John's Law Review/St. Thomas More Institute for Research*, the *Journal of Catholic Legal Studies*, *Journal of Legal Commentary*, *New York International Law Review*, *American Bankruptcy Institute Law Review*, and *N.Y. Litigator*.

Mock Trial and Appellate Activities—Moot Court, Polestino Trial Advocacy Institute.

Specialized Legal Activities—The Student Bar Association, Admiralty Law Society, Women's Law Association, Bankruptcy Law Society, Environmental Law Club, Entertainment and

Sports Club, International Law Society, Intellectual Property, Labor and Employment Club, Real Property Club, the Black Law Students Association, the Asian American Law Students Association, the Latino American Law Students Association, and Client Counseling Competition. The school also maintains chapters in two legal societies, Phi Delta Phi and Phi Alpha Delta.

■ Expenses and Financial Aid

The School of Law provides extensive financial scholarship aid to students annually. There are new campus housing facilities, and many students find other suitable living accommodations in the vicinity of the university. In addition, the Admission Office coordinates a housing network for students. Students with housing needs are invited to contact the Admission Office for assistance and information.

■ Career Services

Career Services provides an array of services, including résumé and cover letter critiquing, mock interview coaching, job and judicial clerkship postings, newsletters, lists of prospective employers, interview programs, and career education panels.

Recent graduates have obtained employment in many areas of the legal profession. Approximately 5 percent accept federal and state judicial clerkships. For the class of 2005, the employment rate (nine months after graduation) was 97 percent.

Alumni of the law school are currently practicing throughout the United States and its territories. Many have achieved positions of prominence in executive and legislative branches of the government, as members of the judiciary, and in both private and corporate practice. Two recent governors of New York, a congressman for New York, a recent governor of the US Virgin Islands, and a former governor of California were graduates of St. John's School of Law.

■ Bar Passage Rate

St. John's University School of Law bar passage rate for first-time test takers rose to 91 percent on the 2006 bar examination, ranking 4th among the 15 New York law schools, behind only Cornell, NYU, and Columbia. St. John's has consistently placed among the top New York law schools in percentage of first-time test takers passing the bar exam and the School of Law's 91 percent passing rate far exceeds the average state passing rate of 79 percent.

Applicant Profile

St. John's University School of Law

LSAT Score	GPA								
	3.75 +	3.50–3.74	3.25–3.49	3.00–3.24	2.75–2.99	2.50–2.74	2.25–2.49	2.00–2.24	Below 2.00
175–180									
170–174									
165–169									
160–164									
155–159									
150–154									
145–149									
140–144									
135–139									
130–134									
125–129									
120–124									

Good Possibility   Possible   Unlikely

Saint Louis University School of Law

3700 Lindell Boulevard
St. Louis, MO 63108
Phone: 314.977.2800; Fax: 314.977.1464
E-mail: admissions@law.slu.edu; Website: law.slu.edu

ABA
Approved
Since
1924

The Basics

Type of school	Private
Term	Semester
Application deadline	3/1
Application fee	$50
Financial aid deadline	3/1
Can first year start other than fall?	No
Student to faculty ratio	17.4 to 1
Does the university offer:	
housing restricted to law students?	No
graduate housing for which law students are eligible?	No

Faculty and Administrators

	Total		Men		Women		Minorities	
	Fall	Spr	Fall	Spr	Fall	Spr	Fall	Spr
Full-time	40	40	26	26	14	14	3	3
Other Full-time	7	7	1	1	6	6	1	1
Deans, librarians, & others who teach	4	4	3	3	1	1	0	0
Part-time	28	39	17	27	11	12	0	0
Total	79	90	47	57	32	33	4	4

Curriculum

	Full-time	Part-time
Typical first-year section size	0	75
Is there typically a "small section" of the first-year class, other than Legal Writing, taught by full-time faculty	Yes	No
If yes, typical size offered last year	30	
# of classroom course titles beyond first-year curriculum	111	
# of upper division courses, excluding seminars with an enrollment: Under 25	89	
25–49	41	
50–74	11	
75–99	7	
100+	11	
# of seminars	31	
# of seminar positions available	372	
# of seminar positions filled	277	58
# of positions available in simulation courses	363	
# of simulation positions filled	311	52
# of positions available in faculty supervised clinical courses	84	
# of faculty supervised clinical positions filled	74	10
# involved in field placements	113	4
# involved in law journals	76	8
# involved in interschool competitions	44	6
# of credit hours required to graduate	91	

JD Enrollment and Ethnicity

	Men		Women		Full-time		Part-time		1st-year		Total		JD Degs. Awd.
	#	%	#	%	#	%	#	%	#	%	#	%	
African Amer.	18	3.7	28	6.1	30	4.2	16	6.9	18	5.4	46	4.9	6
Amer. Indian	3	0.6	2	0.4	4	0.6	1	0.4	1	0.3	5	0.5	0
Asian Amer.	14	2.9	18	3.9	28	3.9	4	1.7	13	3.9	32	3.4	0
Mex. Amer.	0	0.0	0	0.0	0	0.0	0	0.0	0	0.0	0	0.0	0
Puerto Rican	0	0.0	0	0.0	0	0.0	0	0.0	0	0.0	0	0.0	0
Hispanic	5	1.0	12	2.6	15	2.1	2	0.9	6	1.8	17	1.8	9
Total Minority	40	8.3	60	13.0	77	10.8	23	9.9	38	11.4	100	10.6	15
For. Nation.	2	0.4	2	0.4	4	0.6	0	0.0	0	0.0	4	0.4	0
Caucasian	404	83.5	373	80.9	587	82.4	190	81.5	275	82.6	777	82.2	224
Unknown	38	7.9	26	5.6	44	6.2	20	8.6	20	6.0	64	6.8	3
Total	484	51.2	461	48.8	712	75.3	233	24.7	333	35.2	945		242

Transfers

Transfers in	5
Transfers out	6

Tuition and Fees

	Resident	Nonresident
Full-time	$30,190	$30,190
Part-time	$21,995	$21,995

Living Expenses

Estimated living expenses for singles

Living on campus	Living off campus	Living at home
$21,980	$21,980	$21,980

ABA
Approved
Since
1924

GPA and LSAT Scores

	Total	Full-time	Part-time
# of apps	2,508	2,007	501
# of offers	1,068	910	158
# of matrics	340	244	96
75% GPA	3.72	3.75	3.67
Median GPA	3.52	3.56	3.45
25% GPA	3.27	3.29	3.20
75% LSAT	159	159	154
Median LSAT	156	157	152
25% LSAT	153	155	151

Grants and Scholarships (from prior year)

	Total		Full-time		Part-time	
	#	%	#	%	#	%
Total # of students	880		664		216	
Total # receiving grants	376	42.7	332	50.0	44	20.4
Less than 1/2 tuition	224	25.5	184	27.7	40	18.5
Half to full tuition	104	11.8	100	15.1	4	1.9
Full tuition	42	4.8	42	6.3	0	0.0
More than full tuition	6	0.7	6	0.9	0	0.0
Median grant amount			$13,000		$3,000	

Informational and Library Resources

# of volumes and volume equivalents	647,772
# of titles	302,777
# of active serial subscriptions	3,571
Study seating capacity inside the library	410
# of full-time professional librarians	8
Hours per week library is open	101
# of open, wired connections available to students	700
# of networked computers available for use by students	58
# of simultaneous wireless users	900
Require computer?	No

Saint Louis University School of L

3700 Lindell Boulevard
St. Louis, MO 63108
Phone: 314.977.2800; Fax: 314.977.1464
E-mail: admissions@law.slu.edu; Website

■ Introduction

The mission of Saint Louis
advance the understandi
prepare students to ac
satisfaction through
school is guided b
freedom of inqu
Located in
School of
unparal
impr
go

Employment status unknown	0	0.0
Employed	224	91.8
Pursuing graduate degrees	5	2.0
Unemployed seeking employment	3	1.2
Unemployed not seeking employment	1	0.4
Unemployed and studying for the bar	11	4.5

Type of Employment

# employed in law firms	152	67.9
# employed in business and industry	32	14.3
# employed in government	20	8.9
# employed in public interest	8	3.6
# employed as judicial clerks	5	2.2
# employed in academia	6	2.7

Geographic Location

# employed in state	160	71.4
# employed in foreign countries	1	0.4
# of states where employed	18	

Bar Passage Rates

Jurisdiction	Missouri			Illinois		
Exam	Sum 05	Win 06	Total	Sum 05	Win 06	Total
# from school taking bar for the first time	149	37	186	65	63	128
School's pass rate for all first-time takers	88%	84%	87%	86%	92%	89%
State's pass rate for all first-time takers	88%	90%	89%	86%	83%	85%

aw

law.slu.edu

University School of Law is to
...ng and the development of law, and
...ieve professional success and personal
...leadership and service to others. The
...y the Jesuit tradition of academic excellence,
...iry, and respect for individual differences.
...scenic midtown St. Louis, Saint Louis University
...Law is perfectly positioned to provide students with
...eled exposure to the legal world. St. Louis boasts an
...ssive array of law firms, corporate offices, and
...ernmental agencies; there are local, state, and federal
...ourthouses throughout the city and surrounding counties,
including the largest federal courthouse in the United States.

With an accomplished, accessible faculty and a diverse
curriculum, the School of Law provides a challenging yet
collegial environment designed to foster success for dedicated
students. Whatever the interest—corporate and finance,
criminal, health, international, intellectual property, tax,
securities, real estate, labor and employment, litigation, or
sports and entertainment law—the school can help students
achieve their desired career goals.

First-year, full-time law students benefit from the school's
unique small section program, where two of five classes
contain less than 35 students. This allows for individualized
instruction and focused student interaction, and, most
importantly, builds a sense of community among classmates.
The remaining classes are formed by combining different small
sections to allow students to get to know others in their class.

For those who work full time and are unable to attend
classes during the day, the school offers a challenging part-time
Evening Program—the only program of its kind in the state of
Missouri. Through this program, students can earn their law
degree in four years with summer attendance or five years
without summer attendance.

■ Special Academic Programs

Centers for Excellence—The school features one of the
premier health law studies programs in the nation along
with specialized centers in employment law and international
and comparative law.

- The **Center for Health Law Studies** boasts a nationally
  recognized faculty, an unparalleled curriculum, and some
  of the country's finest health law publications.
  Visit: *law.slu.edu/healthlaw*.
- The **Wefel Center for Employment Law** specializes in
  issues of labor disputes, benefits, hiring and discharging,
  and arbitration. Visit: *law.slu.edu/emplaw*.
- The **Center for International and Comparative Law** offers
  a specialized program of study in areas such as public
  international law, international criminal law, and
  international corporate law. Students receive instruction
  from faculty who have experienced and studied foreign
  legal systems. Visit: *law.slu.edu/cicl*.

Concentrations—In addition to our three certificate
programs through our Centers for Excellence, the School of
Law offers concentrations in the following areas: Business
Transactional Law, Civil Litigation Skills, Criminal Litigation
Skills, Taxation, and Urban Development, Land Use, and
Environmental Law.

Study Abroad—Through the Center for International and
Comparative Law, students can study law at Saint Louis
University's campus in Madrid, Spain, earning up to six credit
hours of comparative law with foreign and American
professors who have extensive experience in the fields of
foreign and American criminal law, civil law, and global
human rights. Pending ABA final approval, there will also be a
summer study-abroad program in Berlin, Germany. The school
also maintains cooperative agreements with the University
College in Cork, Ireland; Université d'Orléans and Université
de Paris-Dauphine in France; University of Georgia in Brussels,
Belgium; and the Ruhr University in Bochum, Germany.

Dual-degree Programs—The School of Law offers intensive
dual-degree programs in cooperation with other university
schools. Students must meet the admission requirements of
both schools, including each school's entrance examination.
Candidates in a dual-degree program must complete the
first-year law curriculum before beginning the dual program.
Candidates must complete both degrees within the same
semester. The dual-degree programs available are JD/MBA,
JD/MHA, JD/MA in Public Administration, JD/MA in Urban
Affairs, JD/MPH, and JD/PhD in Health Care Ethics.

■ Public Service

Throughout the year, the School of Law sponsors and
participates in numerous public service events and projects.
Some of the programs include Make a Difference
Day-Homeward Bound, Habitat for Humanity, Court
Appointed Special Advocates, Stand Down for Homeless
Veterans, and the Tax Assistance Project.

■ Practical Skills Training

Students are presented with a variety of opportunities to
practice law throughout their education. **Legal Clinics** provide
immediate exposure to the legal world through a variety of
service-oriented programs. Students represent clients in court,
clerk for judges, and participate in externships at law firms,
corporations, and government agencies. Visit:
law.slu.edu/clinics. The **Trial Advocacy** program helps students
develop skills in all aspects of trial preparation. Through the
Client Counseling program, students learn to communicate
with clients, learning how to ask the right questions, listen
effectively, and encourage clients to talk. In the **Negotiation**
program, students experience firsthand the practice of
negotiation through a variety of simulation activities.

■ Cocurricular Activities

The school allows students to perfect their writing and
editing skills by working on one of three law journals—*Saint
Louis University Law Journal, Saint Louis University Public Law
Review*, and the *Journal of Health Law*. Qualifying students are
invited to write and edit the collections of scholarly work
submitted from lawyers and law professors across the world.
The **Moot Court Competitions** hone a student's litigation skills
in research, analysis, writing, and oral argument. Students

interested in international law may participate in the **Jessup Moot Court Competition**. In addition, there is a **Health Law Moot Court** and an **Intellectual Property Moot Court**. The school also offers **Trial Advocacy Competitions** and **Client Counseling Competitions**.

■ Financial Aid/Scholarships

Saint Louis University School of Law awards a substantial number of merit-based scholarships to a select group of highly qualified admitted students, including 10 full-tuition scholarships through the 1843 Scholars program. The school has a variety of ways to help students meet their financial goals. Contact the School of Law's Financial Aid Coordinator at *fin_aid@law.slu.edu*.

■ Library

The Omer Poos Law Library serves as the center for legal research. It provides a state-of-the-art research environment with access to hundreds of databases as well as a collection of over 600,000 volumes. The law library is among the top 20 law schools in the nation in the number of titles held. A staff of 20, including five JD/MLS reference librarians, takes pride in providing personal attention and service to our students. Visit: *law.slu.edu/library*.

■ Career Services

The Career Services Office, staffed by two licensed attorneys and a licensed professional counselor, assists students in identifying their career goals. Through a litany of career resources, students are able to pursue employment opportunities that meet their goals and suit their needs. The graduating classes within the past five years have averaged over a 90 percent employment rate within six months of graduation. Visit: *law.slu.edu/careersvcs*.

Applicant Profile

Saint Louis University School of Law

This grid includes only applicants who earned 120–180 LSAT scores under standard administrations.

LSAT Score	3.75+ Apps	3.75+ Adm	3.50–3.74 Apps	3.50–3.74 Adm	3.25–3.49 Apps	3.25–3.49 Adm	3.00–3.24 Apps	3.00–3.24 Adm	2.75–2.99 Apps	2.75–2.99 Adm	2.50–2.74 Apps	2.50–2.74 Adm	2.25–2.49 Apps	2.25–2.49 Adm	2.00–2.24 Apps	2.00–2.24 Adm	Below 2.00 Apps	Below 2.00 Adm	No GPA Apps	No GPA Adm	Total Apps	Total Adm
175–180	1	1	0	0	0	0	0	0	0	0	0	0	0	0	0	0	0	0	0	0	1	1
170–174	7	7	1	1	0	0	1	1	0	0	0	0	1	0	0	0	0	0	0	0	10	9
165–169	17	17	19	19	14	13	10	10	5	5	2	1	0	0	1	0	1	0	1	1	70	66
160–164	68	64	73	70	48	44	35	34	21	14	10	4	7	2	4	1	1	0	3	0	270	233
155–159	118	109	160	141	141	109	97	68	50	24	23	4	11	1	1	1	0	0	3	0	604	457
150–154	99	51	175	71	161	49	100	29	76	11	27	3	19	1	5	0	0	0	3	0	665	215
145–149	43	12	56	11	89	12	59	6	47	4	23	1	20	1	2	1	0	0	1	0	340	48
140–144	15	1	29	4	29	1	39	4	18	2	18	1	13	1	1	0	2	0	6	1	170	15
135–139	2	0	5	0	6	0	17	1	17	1	7	0	10	0	5	0	2	0	2	0	73	2
130–134	1	0	0	0	1	0	1	0	3	0	4	0	4	0	1	0	1	0	1	0	17	0
125–129	0	0	1	0	0	0	0	0	2	0	2	0	2	0	2	0	0	0	0	0	9	0
120–124	0	0	0	0	0	0	0	0	0	0	0	0	0	0	0	0	0	0	0	0	0	0
Total	371	262	519	317	489	228	359	153	239	61	116	14	87	6	22	3	7	0	20	2	2229	1046

Apps = Number of Applicants
Adm = Number Admitted
Reflects 99% of the total applicant pool.

St. Mary's University School of Law

One Camino Santa Maria
San Antonio, TX 78228-8601
Phone: 210.436.3523; Toll-free: 866.639.5831; Fax: 210.431.4202
E-mail: lawadmissions@stmarytx.edu; Website: law.stmarytx.edu

ABA
Approved
Since
1948

The Basics

Type of school	Private
Term	Semester
Application deadline	3/1
Application fee	$55
Financial aid deadline	3/24
Can first year start other than fall?	No
Student to faculty ratio	21.9 to 1
Does the university offer:	
housing restricted to law students?	No
graduate housing for which law students are eligible?	Yes

Faculty and Administrators

	Total		Men		Women		Minorities	
	Fall	Spr	Fall	Spr	Fall	Spr	Fall	Spr
Full-time	29	27	22	20	7	7	6	5
Other Full-time	8	10	4	5	4	5	2	2
Deans, librarians, & others who teach	8	7	6	6	2	1	4	5
Part-time	32	42	21	22	11	20	7	6
Total	77	86	53	53	24	33	19	18

Curriculum

	Full-time	Part-time
Typical first-year section size	65	0
Is there typically a "small section" of the first-year class, other than Legal Writing, taught by full-time faculty	No	No
If yes, typical size offered last year		
# of classroom course titles beyond first-year curriculum	104	

# of upper division courses, excluding seminars with an enrollment:	Under 25	48
	25–49	25
	50–74	13
	75–99	18
	100+	0

# of seminars	5	
# of seminar positions available	60	
# of seminar positions filled	39	0
# of positions available in simulation courses	237	
# of simulation positions filled	225	0
# of positions available in faculty supervised clinical courses	57	
# of faculty supervised clinical positions filled	57	0
# involved in field placements	25	0
# involved in law journals	88	0
# involved in interschool competitions	81	0
# of credit hours required to graduate	90	

JD Enrollment and Ethnicity

	Men		Women		Full-time		Part-time		1st-year		Total		JD Degs. Awd.
	#	%	#	%	#	%	#	%	#	%	#	%	
African Amer.	6	1.4	10	3.2	16	2.2	0	0.0	6	2.4	16	2.2	9
Amer. Indian	6	1.4	6	1.9	12	1.6	0	0.0	4	1.6	12	1.6	4
Asian Amer.	16	3.7	18	5.7	34	4.6	0	0.0	11	4.3	34	4.6	7
Mex. Amer.	50	11.7	48	15.3	98	13.2	0	0.0	41	16.1	98	13.2	47
Puerto Rican	0	0.0	4	1.3	4	0.5	0	0.0	3	1.2	4	0.5	1
Hispanic	35	8.2	26	8.3	61	8.2	0	0.0	25	9.8	61	8.2	2
Total Minority	113	26.4	112	35.7	225	30.3	0	0.0	90	35.4	225	30.3	70
For. Nation.	0	0.0	0	0.0	0	0.0	0	0.0	0	0.0	0	0.0	0
Caucasian	315	73.6	202	64.3	517	69.7	0	0.0	164	64.6	517	69.7	167
Unknown	0	0.0	0	0.0	0	0.0	0	0.0	0	0.0	0	0.0	0
Total	428	57.7	314	42.3	742	100.0	0	0.0	254	34.2	742		237

Transfers

Transfers in	4
Transfers out	6

Tuition and Fees

	Resident	Nonresident
Full-time	$22,040	$22,040
Part-time	$0	$0

Living Expenses

Estimated living expenses for singles		
Living on campus	Living off campus	Living at home
$13,426	$13,426	$13,426

St. Mary's University School of Law

ABA
Approved
Since
1948

GPA and LSAT Scores

	Total	Full-time	Part-time
# of apps	1,902	1,902	0
# of offers	764	764	0
# of matrics	257	257	0
75% GPA	3.39	3.39	0.00
Median GPA	3.11	3.11	0.00
25% GPA	2.76	2.76	0.00
75% LSAT	156	156	0
Median LSAT	154	154	0
25% LSAT	151	151	0

Grants and Scholarships (from prior year)

	Total		Full-time		Part-time	
	#	%	#	%	#	%
Total # of students	762		762		0	
Total # receiving grants	344	45.1	344	45.1	0	0.0
Less than 1/2 tuition	319	41.9	319	41.9	0	0.0
Half to full tuition	13	1.7	13	1.7	0	0.0
Full tuition	10	1.3	10	1.3	0	0.0
More than full tuition	2	0.3	2	0.3	0	0.0
Median grant amount			$2,600		$0	

Informational and Library Resources

# of volumes and volume equivalents	416,721
# of titles	77,853
# of active serial subscriptions	4,540
Study seating capacity inside the library	390
# of full-time professional librarians	9
Hours per week library is open	104
# of open, wired connections available to students	619
# of networked computers available for use by students	37
# of simultaneous wireless users	750
Require computer?	No

JD Attrition (from prior year)

	Academic	Other	Total	
	#	#	#	%
1st year	15	6	21	8.0
2nd year	3	12	15	6.0
3rd year	0	1	1	0.4
4th year	0	0	0	0.0

Employment (9 months after graduation)

	Total	Percentage
Employment status known	218	91.2
Employment status unknown	21	8.8
Employed	200	91.7
Pursuing graduate degrees	8	3.7
Unemployed seeking employment	3	1.4
Unemployed not seeking employment	5	2.3
Unemployed and studying for the bar	2	0.9

Type of Employment

	Total	Percentage
# employed in law firms	114	57.0
# employed in business and industry	19	9.5
# employed in government	36	18.0
# employed in public interest	9	4.5
# employed as judicial clerks	14	7.0
# employed in academia	3	1.5

Geographic Location

	Total	Percentage
# employed in state	183	91.5
# employed in foreign countries	1	0.5
# of states where employed	10	

Bar Passage Rates

Jurisdiction	Texas		
Exam	Sum 05	Win 06	Total
# from school taking bar for the first time	206	26	232
School's pass rate for all first-time takers	72%	81%	73%
State's pass rate for all first-time takers	81%	77%	80%

St. Mary's University School of Law

One Camino Santa Maria
San Antonio, TX 78228-8601
Phone: 210.436.3523; Toll-free: 866.639.5831; Fax: 210.431.4202
E-mail: lawadmissions@stmarytx.edu; Website: law.stmarytx.edu

■ Introduction

St. Mary's University School of Law was founded in 1927 as part of the oldest and largest Catholic university in the Southwest. St. Mary's is located in the beautiful, unique, and legendary city of San Antonio. San Antonio combines a diverse blend of historic sites, natural beauty, charming vistas, and urban amenities. With its culturally rich population and environment, San Antonio is the perfect backdrop for the mission and goals of the School of Law. Enriched by the spirit of the Society of Mary (Marianists), the school imparts to its students the knowledge and attributes of mind and character essential to public service. St. Mary's is vigilant of the need to preserve a tradition of excellence in legal education, with development of new programs and methodologies for the changing world, and St. Mary's now offers a **part-time evening program** in addition to its traditional full-time day program.

■ Library and Physical Facilities

The Sarita Kenedy East Law Library is the largest legal information center in San Antonio and the surrounding area. A federal depository library, the collection consists of print, microfilm, and multimedia items totaling over 400,000 volumes (or equivalent), which cover a wide range of subjects—US federal and state laws, and foreign, comparative, and international law. The collection and resources are cataloged and searchable through an automated library information system. The library subscribes to LexisNexis, Westlaw, Loislaw, HeinOnline, LLMC-Digital, the Center for Computer-Assisted Legal Instruction (CALI), Index to Legal Periodicals Full Text, Lexis Congressional, AccessUN, United Nations Treaty Series, and other information databases. Computers and Internet access, both wire and wireless, are available and supported throughout the library facilities.

The Law Classroom Building contains four amphitheater-style classrooms with electronically retractable walls and a newly renovated and technologically advanced modern courtroom as its center. Electrical outlets and data ports are at each student's seat, and the public lounges provide wireless access.

The law school's four primary buildings are located around an oak-shaded quadrangle, forming a central gathering spot. The recently completed Alumni Athletic and Convocation Center provides 135,000 square feet of wellness and fitness options. The center provides for ceremonial facilities as well as athletic endeavors.

■ Curriculum

Required first-year courses are Constitutional Law, Contracts, Criminal Law, Legal Research and Writing, Civil Procedure, Property, and Torts. All students must also take the following required courses: Professional Responsibility, Evidence, and Texas Civil Procedure (only required of those planning to take the Texas bar examination), and a specified number of courses from a menu-style core curriculum. Students must also complete a research paper. The size of first-year sections provides personalized attention and instruction from faculty.

■ Clinical Legal Education

The Clinical Program at St. Mary's offers three classes: Civil Justice, Criminal Justice, and Immigration/Human Rights. The clinics teach lawyering skills and responsibilities through supervised representation of low-income clients and through development of community-based projects. Civil Justice offers three components: community development, homeless issues, and representation; crime victim issues and representation; and housing, including landlord-tenant. Students engage in office practice, family law, wills and probate, and housing law. Criminal Justice students defend low-income individuals of any age in misdemeanor and low-felony cases. Immigration/Human Rights students represent indigent foreign nationals and refugees. Students appear in Immigration Court and assist clients with applications for residence, asylum, and benefits under the Violence Against Women Act.

■ International Law

The St. Mary's Institute on World Legal Problems is conducted at the University of Innsbruck in Austria during July and August. The program is designed to provide law students with a broader understanding of global issues and the role that law can play in their peaceful resolution.

Five justices of the United States Supreme Court have participated in the program as distinguished visiting jurists (former Chief Justice William H. Rehnquist, Justice Antonin Scalia, Justice John Paul Stevens, Justice Ruth Bader Ginsburg, and former Justice Sandra Day O'Connor). The program draws students and faculty from all parts of the United States and abroad. It has included students from at least 100 American law schools, as well as from Austria, Hungary, China, and Russia. More than 40 visiting professors from law schools in the United States and several foreign countries have participated in the institute.

The Innsbruck Institute is part of the law school's program in international and comparative law, which also includes an LLM in international and comparative law and cooperation with Mexican law schools.

St. Mary's now houses a new **Center for Terrorism Law**, a nonpartisan, nonprofit institution dedicated to the study of legal issues associated with terrorism, with particular emphasis on cyberspace and information assurance technologies.

■ Judicial Internships

St. Mary's students participate in a wide range of pregraduation judicial internships with outstanding state and federal courts. Students work under the supervision of a judge or staff attorney performing legal research and writing projects, which often include the drafting of orders that will be used to decide pending cases, composing jury instructions, researching evidentiary questions, or attending settlement conferences.

■ Admission Standards

St. Mary's goal is to create an intellectually stimulating student body composed of persons with diverse backgrounds who share a desire for academic excellence and accomplishment in the practice of law. In addition to academic ability, St. Mary's seeks evidence of qualities such as leadership ability, maturity, community organization skills, knowledge of other languages and cultures, a history of overcoming disadvantage, public interest accomplishments, or success in a previous career. A faculty committee reviews all applications. No one is automatically rejected. All files are read.

■ Student Activities

St. Mary's has over 30 active student organizations. Student organizations are a key part of the collegial environment of the law school.

St. Mary's has two law reviews—the *St. Mary's Law Journal* and *The Scholar: St. Mary's Law Review on Minority Issues*. The reviews offer students excellent opportunities to develop advanced legal research and writing skills. The *Law Journal* has been cited as a persuasive authority in hundreds of court decisions.

St. Mary's students are active in moot court and mock trial competitions. During the spring semester, first-year students participate in a school-wide moot court competition. Second- and third-year students can compete in on-campus tournaments and in St. Mary's External Advocacy Program (EAP). St. Mary's EAP students travel throughout the US to attend the ABA National Moot Court, National Mock Trial, ATLA Mock Trial, and negotiation competitions.

■ Career Services

The role of the Office of Career Services is to assist law students and graduates with their self-directed career searches by informing them of career options and job-search strategies and connecting them with potential employers. Career Services does so by sponsoring programs designed to educate, facilitate, and connect students with potential employers during and after law school.

One-on-one confidential strategy sessions with the director provide a unique opportunity for students to develop a personal plan to assess and meet their career goals. The office maintains a job bank and a résumé bank. The office also publishes *Professional Pathways*, a weekly e-newsletter with job information and career advice. A Student Resource Center offers an extensive and up-to-date library of career resources and directories of attorneys, as well as computer terminals with employer databases to help students direct and begin their careers in legal and nontraditional positions. Students have extensive opportunities to interact with alumni, who assist with career programming throughout the year.

For the students in the class of 2005 who reported employment status, 92 percent are employed, with almost all of them in the legal field.

Applicant Profile

St. Mary's University School of Law
This grid includes only applicants who earned 120–180 LSAT scores under standard administrations.

LSAT Score	3.75+ Apps	3.75+ Adm	3.50–3.74 Apps	3.50–3.74 Adm	3.25–3.49 Apps	3.25–3.49 Adm	3.00–3.24 Apps	3.00–3.24 Adm	2.75–2.99 Apps	2.75–2.99 Adm	2.50–2.74 Apps	2.50–2.74 Adm	2.25–2.49 Apps	2.25–2.49 Adm	2.00–2.24 Apps	2.00–2.24 Adm	Below 2.00 Apps	Below 2.00 Adm	No GPA Apps	No GPA Adm	Total Apps	Total Adm
175–180	0	0	0	0	0	0	0	0	0	0	0	0	0	0	0	0	0	0	0	0	0	0
170–174	0	0	0	0	0	0	0	0	0	0	0	0	0	0	0	0	0	0	0	0	13	13
165–169	1	1	3	3	3	3	0	0	0	0	3	3	3	3	0	0	1	1	0	0	98	98
160–164	11	11	13	13	17	17	23	23	14	14	13	13	6	6	0	0	1	1	0	0	232	226
155–159	18	18	42	42	53	53	42	41	33	31	23	23	14	12	6	5	2	0	5	2	542	366
150–154	41	38	70	67	111	94	126	78	80	40	65	29	32	15	10	3	2	0	8	0	491	49
145–149	29	3	67	11	90	14	114	7	83	6	55	6	33	2	10	2	3	0	4	0	328	5
140–144	11	0	33	1	51	0	76	0	61	1	48	0	29	2	12	1	2	0	6	0	129	0
135–139	5	0	8	0	14	0	31	0	28	0	20	0	7	0	8	0	2	0	5	0	41	0
130–134	3	0	2	0	3	0	7	0	8	0	4	0	4	0	3	0	1	0	1	0	7	0
125–129	0	0	0	0	0	0	1	0	0	0	1	0	1	0	2	0	0	0	0	0	0	0
120–124	0	0	0	0	0	0	0	0	0	0	0	0	0	0	0	0	0	0	0	0	1881	757
Total	119	71	238	137	342	181	420	149	307	92	232	74	129	40	51	9	14	2	29	2		

Apps = Number of Applicants
Adm = Number Admitted
Reflects 99% of the total applicant pool.

University of St. Thomas School of Law—Minneapolis

1000 LaSalle Avenue
Minneapolis, MN 55403
Phone: 651.962.4895
E-mail: lawschool@stthomas.edu; Website: www.stthomas.edu/law

ABA
Approved
Since
2003

The Basics

Type of school	Private
Term	Semester
Application deadline	7/1
Application fee	$50
Financial aid deadline	6/1
Can first year start other than fall?	No
Student to faculty ratio	17.5 to 1
Does the university offer:	
housing restricted to law students?	No
graduate housing for which law students are eligible?	No

Faculty and Administrators

	Total		Men		Women		Minorities	
	Fall	Spr	Fall	Spr	Fall	Spr	Fall	Spr
Full-time	24	24	14	14	10	10	5	5
Other Full-time	3	3	0	0	3	3	0	0
Deans, librarians, & others who teach	7	7	6	6	1	1	0	0
Part-time	40	49	25	33	15	16	4	4
Total	74	83	45	53	29	30	9	9

Curriculum

	Full-time	Part-time
Typical first-year section size	74	0
Is there typically a "small section" of the first-year class, other than Legal Writing, taught by full-time faculty	No	No
If yes, typical size offered last year		
# of classroom course titles beyond first-year curriculum	68	
# of upper division courses, excluding seminars with an enrollment: Under 25	95	
25–49	17	
50–74	7	
75–99	5	
100+	0	
# of seminars	23	
# of seminar positions available	464	
# of seminar positions filled	314	0
# of positions available in simulation courses	370	
# of simulation positions filled	326	0
# of positions available in faculty supervised clinical courses	48	
# of faculty supervised clinical positions filled	47	0
# involved in field placements	560	0
# involved in law journals	38	0
# involved in interschool competitions	26	0
# of credit hours required to graduate	88	

Transfers

Transfers in	3
Transfers out	3

Tuition and Fees

	Resident	Nonresident
Full-time	$27,200	$0
Part-time	$0	$0

Living Expenses

Estimated living expenses for singles

Living on campus	Living off campus	Living at home
N/A	$15,900	$15,900

JD Enrollment and Ethnicity

	Men		Women		Full-time		Part-time		1st-year		Total		JD Degs. Awd.
	#	%	#	%	#	%	#	%	#	%	#	%	
African Amer.	10	4.4	9	4.2	19	4.3	0	0.0	8	5.2	19	4.3	5
Amer. Indian	1	0.4	3	1.4	4	0.9	0	0.0	1	0.7	4	0.9	1
Asian Amer.	5	2.2	19	8.9	24	5.4	0	0.0	5	3.3	24	5.4	7
Mex. Amer.	2	0.9	3	1.4	5	1.1	0	0.0	3	2.0	5	1.1	0
Puerto Rican	1	0.4	0	0.0	1	0.2	0	0.0	0	0.0	1	0.2	0
Hispanic	5	2.2	6	2.8	11	2.5	0	0.0	3	2.0	11	2.5	3
Total Minority	24	10.5	40	18.7	64	14.4	0	0.0	20	13.1	64	14.4	16
For. Nation.	0	0.0	0	0.0	0	0.0	0	0.0	0	0.0	0	0.0	1
Caucasian	169	73.8	139	65.0	308	69.5	0	0.0	113	73.9	308	69.5	95
Unknown	36	15.7	35	16.4	71	16.0	0	0.0	20	13.1	71	16.0	7
Total	229	51.7	214	48.3	443	100.0	0	0.0	153	34.5	443		119

University of St. Thomas School of Law—Minneapolis

ABA Approved Since 2003

GPA and LSAT Scores

	Total	Full-time	Part-time
# of apps	1,135	1,135	0
# of offers	517	517	0
# of matrics	155	155	0
75% GPA	3.71	3.71	0.00
Median GPA	3.42	3.42	0.00
25% GPA	2.91	2.91	0.00
75% LSAT	159	159	0
Median LSAT	156	156	0
25% LSAT	153	153	0

Grants and Scholarships (from prior year)

	Total #	Total %	Full-time #	Full-time %	Part-time #	Part-time %
Total # of students	418		418		0	
Total # receiving grants	332	79.4	332	79.4	0	0.0
Less than 1/2 tuition	181	43.3	181	43.3	0	0.0
Half to full tuition	58	13.9	58	13.9	0	0.0
Full tuition	93	22.2	93	22.2	0	0.0
More than full tuition	0	0.0	0	0.0	0	0.0
Median grant amount			$12,000		$0	

Informational and Library Resources

# of volumes and volume equivalents	182,331
# of titles	132,518
# of active serial subscriptions	1,380
Study seating capacity inside the library	373
# of full-time professional librarians	6
Hours per week library is open	83
# of open, wired connections available to students	595
# of networked computers available for use by students	96
# of simultaneous wireless users	750
Require computer?	No

JD Attrition (from prior year)

	Academic #	Other #	Total #	Total %
1st year	1	9	10	6.8
2nd year	0	4	4	2.7
3rd year	0	0	0	0.0
4th year	0	0	0	0.0

Employment (9 months after graduation)

	Total	Percentage
Employment status known	88	100.0
Employment status unknown	0	0.0
Employed	82	93.2
Pursuing graduate degrees	1	1.1
Unemployed seeking employment	3	3.4
Unemployed not seeking employment	0	0.0
Unemployed and studying for the bar	2	2.3

Type of Employment

# employed in law firms	27	32.9
# employed in business and industry	20	24.4
# employed in government	6	7.3
# employed in public interest	10	12.2
# employed as judicial clerks	19	23.2
# employed in academia	0	0.0

Geographic Location

# employed in state	72	87.8
# employed in foreign countries	0	0.0
# of states where employed	9	

Bar Passage Rates

Jurisdiction	Minnesota			Wisconsin		
Exam	Sum 05	Win 06	Total	Sum 05	Win 06	Total
# from school taking bar for the first time	71	7	78	3	0	3
School's pass rate for all first-time takers	86%	71%	85%	100%		100%
State's pass rate for all first-time takers	89%	88%	89%	79%	74%	77%

University of St. Thomas School of Law—Minneapolis

1000 LaSalle Avenue
Minneapolis, MN 55403
Phone: 651.962.4895
E-mail: lawschool@stthomas.edu; Website: www.stthomas.edu/law

■ Introduction

The University of St. Thomas integrates faith and reason in the search for truth through a focus on morality and social justice. The close-knit community, drawn together by this unique mission, shares a distinctive vision of what law and the legal profession can be. The University of St. Thomas attracts students from across the country who want to be servant leaders and who understand their responsibility to serve their clients, the community, and those who are most in need of, and least able to pay for, legal assistance.

■ Curriculum

The School of Law offers more than 80 advanced, elective courses in addition to 16 required courses.

The University of St. Thomas offers a unique, nationally recognized, structured mentor externship integrated into the curriculum that matches each student with an experienced lawyer or judge for each year of law school. Mentors introduce students to a range of lawyering tasks. In addition to gaining practical knowledge, students talk with their mentors about the intellectual, ethical, and moral challenges facing attorneys.

At the Interprofessional Center for Counseling and Legal Services, law students work side by side with students from graduate programs in social work and professional psychology. The center allows students to work with actual clients on active cases and provides experience with the sum total of a client's legal problems.

Students can also pursue one of five joint-degree programs, including the College of Business (JD/MBA), Catholic Studies (JD/MA), Public Policy (JD/MA), Professional Psychology (JD/MA), and Social Work (JD/MSW).

■ Special Programs

All students are required to perform 50 hours of community service work. The School of Law expects all students to explore a variety of ways in which their interests, skills, and talents can best serve the public.

■ The Area

The University of St. Thomas School of Law is located in downtown Minneapolis, the regional center for business and culture. Minneapolis and the nearby capital city of St. Paul make up the core of the Twin Cities metropolitan area— a metro area of more than 3.5 million residents. The Twin Cities are home to a vibrant business community that features 12 of Fortune 500's largest corporations. The Twin Cities are also home to a lively legal community that has embraced the School of Law through the mentor program and summer employment opportunities.

The seemingly limitless recreational opportunities and distinctive beauty of the region add immeasurably to the quality of life. The Twin Cities boast 949 lakes in the metropolitan area. Outdoor enthusiasts have plenty of options from which to choose.

■ Admission

The School of Law seeks to identify students who show the potential to distinguish themselves academically and to integrate the fundamental characteristics of faith and values into their professional character and identity.

The Admission Committee reviews applications with the goal of understanding the strengths, skills, and unique perspectives of each applicant. While the committee examines quantitative criteria such as LSAT scores and undergraduate transcripts, it also focuses on evidence of writing skills, leadership experience and potential, motivation, and commitment to our mission.

The committee carefully examines all materials submitted to determine whether the university and the student are a good fit. A student's personal statement, letters of recommendation, and other subjective information play an important role in assisting the committee with its goal.

■ Faculty

The faculty are a distinguished group of scholars with an impressive mixture of skills, expertise, and experience. Faculty members are nationally recognized for their professional and scholarly proficiency; all have experience as teachers and as practicing lawyers or expert witnesses, and 12 have advanced degrees in other disciplines.

Of equal importance, faculty members have demonstrated a commitment to service and leadership. All have developed reputations as caring, accessible mentors for students, and each has an inspiring record of service to the community. Faculty members share a strong commitment to our mission and a dedication to assisting each student in his or her formation as an accomplished servant leader.

Each academic year, the full-time faculty is supplemented by over 60 practicing attorneys and judges who serve as adjunct professors.

■ Enrollment/Student Body

The student body is diverse. In the fall 2006 entering class, students represented 20 states and 71 undergraduate institutions. While many students come to the School of Law directly from undergraduate institutions, others have earned postgraduate degrees or have work experience.

■ Library and Physical Facilities

In July 2003, the School of Law moved into a new 114,334-square-foot building in downtown Minneapolis. The building combines a state-of-the-art education center with the unique character of the School of Law.

Modern technology enhances the classrooms, library, group study areas, moot courtroom, and private offices. A computer lab and training center accommodate student research needs. Twelve group study rooms are available in the library as are a number of individual study spaces.

The 39,289-square-foot library includes shelving for up to 210,000 books and storage space for 250,000 microform volume equivalents. New technologies and alternative information formats supplement the collection. Students have access to major legal-related databases.

■ Financial Aid

St. Thomas is committed to making high-quality legal education available to students by offering scholarships, grants, employment, and loans. The School of Law administers two scholarship programs that acknowledge applicants who have outstanding academic records, who contribute to our dedicated diversity effort, or who are particularly likely to contribute to the school's mission. All incoming students are automatically considered for scholarship awards.

The Loan Repayment Assistance Program (LRAP) will provide up to $6,000 in annual assistance for up to 10 years for qualifying applicants. In general, graduates who undertake public service jobs benefiting the poor and underserved will be eligible to receive assistance.

■ Career Services

Alumni and students work with federal and state judges; international, national, and local public interest organizations; corporations; banks; and law firms of all sizes.

The Office of Career and Professional Development supports students wherever they are in their career paths and encourages them to consider how their career choices complement their spiritual and ethical beliefs. Available resources include résumé and cover letter writing workshops and individual review, interviewing skills seminars, mock interviews, an online job center, a resource center, practice area panel discussions with local attorneys, networking events, career fairs, and on-campus interviewing.

■ Student Activities

Students are encouraged to form and join student organizations that help them integrate their faith or passion for social justice with their image of themselves as lawyers. Students have created several unique student organizations dedicated to integrating faith and reason in the search for truth with an emphasis on social justice.

The *University of St. Thomas Law Journal* gives students the opportunity to contribute to the development of legal scholarship and further hone their research, analytical, and writing abilities. The Board of Advocates oversees interscholastic competitions in moot court, trial advocacy, client counseling, and negotiation.

Applicant Profile

University of St. Thomas School of Law—Minneapolis
This grid includes only applicants who earned 120–180 LSAT scores under standard administrations.

LSAT Score	3.75 +		3.50–3.74		3.25–3.49		3.00–3.24		2.75–2.99		2.50–2.74		2.25–2.49		2.00–2.24		Below 2.00		No GPA		Total	
	Apps	Adm	Apps	Adm	Apps	Adm	Apps	Adm	Apps	Adm	Apps	Adm	Apps	Adm	Apps	Adm	Apps	Adm	Apps	Adm	Apps	Adm
175–180	1	1	1	1	0	0	0	0	0	0	0	0	0	0	0	0	0	0	0	0	2	2
170–174	2	2	0	0	2	2	0	0	0	0	0	0	0	0	0	0	0	0	0	0	4	4
165–169	4	3	11	11	3	3	2	2	1	1	2	2	0	0	0	0	0	0	1	1	24	23
160–164	23	23	20	20	19	19	7	7	8	8	5	5	1	1	2	2	0	0	0	0	85	85
155–159	51	51	53	53	48	45	35	31	18	17	16	15	8	7	2	1	1	1	2	1	234	222
150–154	33	29	71	48	76	36	66	22	37	12	20	6	13	4	7	3	1	0	3	0	325	160
145–149	18	2	49	6	50	3	52	1	31	2	16	0	12	0	3	0	0	0	6	0	240	16
140–144	5	1	20	1	17	0	31	0	24	0	15	0	9	0	1	0	2	0	1	0	133	3
135–139	3	0	6	0	8	0	12	0	9	0	3	0	2	0	0	0	0	0	1	0	57	0
130–134	0	0	1	1	0	0	3	0	6	0	3	0	1	0	0	0	1	0	3	0	16	1
125–129	0	0	0	0	0	0	0	0	1	0	3	0	1	0	0	0	0	0	0	0	9	0
120–124	0	0	0	0	0	0	0	0	0	0	0	0	0	0	0	0	0	0	18	2	0	0
Total	140	112	232	141	223	108	208	64	135	40	86	28	62	14	20	6	5	1	18	2	1129	516

Apps = Number of Applicants
Adm = Number Admitted
Reflects 100% of the total applicant pool.

St. Thomas University School of Law

16401 NW 37th Avenue
Miami Gardens, FL 33054
Phone: 800.245.4569, 305.623.2310; Fax: 305.623.2357
E-mail: admitme@stu.edu; Website: www.stu.edu/lawschool

ABA
Approved
Since
1988

The Basics

Type of school	Private
Term	Semester
Application deadline	5/2
Application fee	$45
Financial aid deadline	5/1
Can first year start other than fall?	No
Student to faculty ratio	18.8 to 1
Does the university offer:	
housing restricted to law students?	Yes
graduate housing for which law students are eligible?	No

Curriculum

	Full-time	Part-time
Typical first-year section size	70	0
Is there typically a "small section" of the first-year class, other than Legal Writing, taught by full-time faculty	No	No
If yes, typical size offered last year		
# of classroom course titles beyond first-year curriculum	107	
# of upper division courses, excluding seminars with an enrollment: Under 25	152	
25–49	44	
50–74	24	
75–99	8	
100+	0	
# of seminars	17	
# of seminar positions available	144	
# of seminar positions filled	191	0
# of positions available in simulation courses	274	
# of simulation positions filled	225	0
# of positions available in faculty supervised clinical courses	26	
# of faculty supervised clinical positions filled	26	0
# involved in field placements	165	0
# involved in law journals	77	0
# involved in interschool competitions	18	0
# of credit hours required to graduate	90	

Faculty and Administrators

	Total		Men		Women		Minorities	
	Fall	Spr	Fall	Spr	Fall	Spr	Fall	Spr
Full-time	31	32	16	18	15	14	5	6
Other Full-time	3	2	2	1	1	1	0	0
Deans, librarians, & others who teach	7	7	6	6	1	1	3	3
Part-time	39	46	26	30	13	16	9	15
Total	80	87	50	55	30	32	17	24

JD Enrollment and Ethnicity

	Men #	Men %	Women #	Women %	Full-time #	Full-time %	Part-time #	Part-time %	1st-year #	1st-year %	Total #	Total %	JD Degs. Awd.
African Amer.	26	7.1	34	11.4	60	9.0	0	0.0	17	7.5	60	9.0	14
Amer. Indian	0	0.0	1	0.3	1	0.2	0	0.0	0	0.0	1	0.2	1
Asian Amer.	15	4.1	16	5.4	31	4.7	0	0.0	8	3.5	31	4.7	11
Mex. Amer.	2	0.5	5	1.7	7	1.1	0	0.0	1	0.4	7	1.1	2
Puerto Rican	4	1.1	5	1.7	9	1.4	0	0.0	2	0.9	9	1.4	4
Hispanic	63	17.2	102	34.1	165	24.8	0	0.0	63	27.6	165	24.8	81
Total Minority	110	30.1	163	54.5	273	41.1	0	0.0	91	39.9	273	41.1	113
For. Nation.	7	1.9	8	2.7	15	2.3	0	0.0	7	3.1	15	2.3	7
Caucasian	235	64.2	116	38.8	351	52.8	0	0.0	123	53.9	351	52.8	128
Unknown	14	3.8	12	4.0	26	3.9	0	0.0	7	3.1	26	3.9	10
Total	366	55.0	299	45.0	665	100.0	0	0.0	228	34.3	665		258

Transfers

Transfers in	1
Transfers out	42

Tuition and Fees

	Resident	Nonresident
Full-time	$26,580	$26,580
Part-time	$0	$0

Living Expenses

Estimated living expenses for singles		
Living on campus	Living off campus	Living at home
$17,146	$17,578	N/A

ABA
Approved
Since
1988

GPA and LSAT Scores

	Total	Full-time	Part-time
# of apps	2,765	2,765	0
# of offers	1,166	1,166	0
# of matrics	235	235	0
75% GPA	3.38	3.38	0.00
Median GPA	3.04	3.04	0.00
25% GPA	2.70	2.70	0.00
75% LSAT	152	152	0
Median LSAT	150	150	0
25% LSAT	147	147	0

Grants and Scholarships (from prior year)

	Total #	Total %	Full-time #	Full-time %	Part-time #	Part-time %
Total # of students	806		806		0	
Total # receiving grants	232	28.8	232	28.8	0	0.0
Less than 1/2 tuition	144	17.9	144	17.9	0	0.0
Half to full tuition	88	10.9	88	10.9	0	0.0
Full tuition	0	0.0	0	0.0	0	0.0
More than full tuition	0	0.0	0	0.0	0	0.0
Median grant amount			$12,000		$0	

Informational and Library Resources

# of volumes and volume equivalents	328,842
# of titles	117,124
# of active serial subscriptions	2,269
Study seating capacity inside the library	472
# of full-time professional librarians	6
Hours per week library is open	106
# of open, wired connections available to students	60
# of networked computers available for use by students	53
# of simultaneous wireless users	2,000
Require computer?	No

JD Attrition (from prior year)

	Academic #	Other #	Total #	Total %
1st year	51	42	93	28.5
2nd year	6	0	6	2.6
3rd year	2	0	2	0.8
4th year	0	0	0	0.0

Employment (9 months after graduation)

	Total	Percentage
Employment status known	165	100.0
Employment status unknown	0	0.0
Employed	111	67.3
Pursuing graduate degrees	11	6.7
Unemployed seeking employment	7	4.2
Unemployed not seeking employment	2	1.2
Unemployed and studying for the bar	34	20.6
Type of Employment		
# employed in law firms	71	64.0
# employed in business and industry	11	9.9
# employed in government	15	13.5
# employed in public interest	9	8.1
# employed as judicial clerks	3	2.7
# employed in academia	2	1.8
Geographic Location		
# employed in state	106	95.5
# employed in foreign countries	0	0.0
# of states where employed	5	

Bar Passage Rates

Jurisdiction	Florida		
Exam	Sum 05	Win 06	Total
# from school taking bar for the first time	121	31	152
School's pass rate for all first-time takers	58%	35%	53%
State's pass rate for all first-time takers	71%	73%	71%

The information on these pages was provided by the law school.

St. Thomas University School of Law

16401 NW 37th Avenue
Miami Gardens, FL 33054
Phone: 800.245.4569, 305.623.2310; Fax: 305.623.2357
E-mail: admitme@stu.edu; Website: www.stu.edu/lawschool

■ Introduction

St. Thomas University School of Law, a fully accredited law school by the American Bar Association and the prestigious Association of American Law Schools, was founded in 1984 and is one of the most culturally diverse and technologically advanced law schools in the country. St. Thomas emphasizes professional ethics throughout its programs, provides intensive academic support on an individual and small-group basis, and offers a broad curriculum, including an array of clinical experiences.

St. Thomas University is located on a 140-acre campus several miles northwest of Miami. Fifteen miles southeast, in downtown Miami, stands the federal courthouse, the location of the United States District Court for the Southern District of Florida. State trial and appellate courts are several blocks away. Approximately 20 miles to the north of the law school is the city of Ft. Lauderdale, another venue for state and appellate courts.

■ Library and Physical Facilities

The St. Thomas University Law Library furnishes students with an online catalog to assist them in locating both digital content and traditional materials. The library meets the needs of students in the twenty-first century by providing them with a wide array of online databases to assist with their research and allow them to pursue their interests in scholarship. Moreover, the library has a large microform collection to provide added collection depth. A wireless network enables students, through their laptops or one of 30 library workstations, to access digital information resources from anywhere on campus. Students may also access most of the databases from home through the school's proxy server. A professional reference staff provides instruction in performing online and traditional research. Reference services are also available to assist students in the evenings and on weekends.

■ Clinical Legal Education Programs

St. Thomas University School of Law requires six credits of professional skills courses to graduate. Students are eligible to participate in any of the law school's 10 clinical offerings in an effort to meet that requirement.

Bankruptcy Clinic—The Bankruptcy Clinic offers a comprehensive set of legal services focused on assisting and empowering low-income individuals in their interaction with the bankruptcy system.

Family Court Clinic—This clinic allows third-year students an opportunity to represent clients in both Family Court and the Domestic Violence Court. The Family Court Clinic is a two-semester, two-track, four-credits-per-semester course. The family division track allows students to learn about family law matters, including the dissolution of marriage, paternity, custody, and adoption cases. In the domestic violence division, students are given the opportunity to provide in-court representation to victims of domestic violence in civil permanent injunction hearings.

Appellate Litigation Clinic—This is a year-long clinical program open to third-year students that provides experience in handling criminal cases in state appellate courts. Each student will have primary responsibility for at least two cases from inception through record preparation, all relevant motions, and the writing of briefs and oral arguments. The program also features a weekly seminar in the appellate process.

Immigration Clinic—Third-year law students will represent asylum seekers, battered spouses and children who have fled their native country, and other noncitizens seeking immigration relief in Immigration Court before the Board of Immigration Appeals and the Department of Homeland Security (formerly the INS).

Judicial Internship—Judicial internships provide an opportunity for students to hear arguments, discuss cases with judges, and apply research and writing skills to real facts. Interns will work closely with supervising staff attorneys and judges.

Tax Clinic—The Tax Clinic, offered to second- and third-year students, is one of the components of the law school's skills training program. The student represents clients before the Internal Revenue Service (IRS), the District Counsel, and the United States Tax Court. In addition, the student is expected to attend conferences with the IRS, job fairs in the community, and Tax Court sessions.

Civil Practice Clinic—This course can be taken full-time or part-time in one semester and is available to second- and third-year students. Those students whose placement requires they be a Certified Legal Intern must be in their third year. Typical placements include Legal Aid, City Attorney, County Attorney, Attorney General, Human Rights Institute, School Board, or other public sector agencies handling civil matters.

Criminal Practice Clinic—This course can be taken full-time or part-time in one semester and is only available to incoming third-year students. Typical placements include the offices of the State Attorney, US Attorney, and Public Defender. The externship also contains a classroom component in which students discuss their cases and review relevant law.

Students learn through a combination of actual trial practice and classroom work. Under the supervision of an assistant state attorney, the students engage in plea bargain negotiations and try cases.

Placement in the Public Defender's office provides students with the opportunity to defend indigent adults and minors charged with felonies and misdemeanor crimes such as assault, theft, or drug and weapons possession.

Elder Law Clinic—This course covers the growing legal needs of the elderly. Students will work with the Probate Division of the Circuit Court and members of the Elder Law Bar on case management issues and strategies to deal with a continually aging population.

Florida Supreme Court—For one semester, the intern will function as a law clerk to an individual justice or as a central staff law clerk working for all of the justices.

■ Graduate-degree Programs

The **LLM/MA in Intercultural Human Rights** offers in-depth instruction on a critical issue of our time: the protection of human dignity across political, cultural, and religious lines. The faculty of global distinction includes top-level United Nations experts, outstanding scholars, judges, and practitioners in the field.

The **JSD Program in Intercultural Human Rights** provides a premier opportunity for budding human rights scholars to make a lasting contribution to this dynamic and action-oriented field.

Special Programs

- **Summer-in-Spain Program**—Law students have the opportunity to take six credits at the Royal College University Escorial Maria Cristina, a part of the University of Madrid. The program is designed to prepare participants for practicing law in the globalized twenty-first century, broadening their understanding of foreign legal systems.
- **Summer Conditional Program**—Applicants who may not have strong academic credentials, but nonetheless possess the abilities necessary to succeed in a rigorous program of legal study, may be invited to participate in a summer conditional program. Students who successfully complete the Summer Conditional Program are offered admission to the fall entering class. This program is usually offered each year, but, under special circumstances, may not be available.
- **Joint-degree Programs**—The law school offers four joint-degree programs in cooperation with other graduate divisions of the university. A JD/MBA in Accounting couples lawyering skills with those traditionally in great demand in the corporate, tax, and accounting worlds. The joint JD/MBA in International Business opens the burgeoning field of international transactional law to the new attorney. The JD/MS in Marriage and Family Counseling, one of the only programs of its kind in the country, fills a serious need in the family lawyer's repertory of skills. A joint JD/MS in Sports Administration prepares participants for a diverse set of positions in the world of sports. The undergraduate sports program was started in 1973 and today offers one of the most esteemed curriculums in the country.
- **Academic Support Program**—The law school is committed to the success of its students, and offers a comprehensive support system including Dean's Fellows, tutors, practice examinations, lectures, a director for academic support, and a program to assist graduates with the bar examination.

Career Services

The Office of Career Services is dedicated to assisting students in identifying and attaining their professional goals. It offers a range of traditional and innovative services, including a career services resource center; on-campus interviews with major law firms, corporations, and government agencies; interviewing and résumé-writing workshops; networking opportunities; and speakers drawn from various areas of legal practice.

Student Activities

The *St. Thomas Law Review* is a student-operated scholarly journal, publishing articles submitted by law faculty and members of the bench and bar nationwide. Membership is determined on the basis of academic excellence and demonstrated writing ability.

The Student Bar Association sponsors various social and educational programs for the student body and otherwise represents student interests. In the student-run Moot Court Program, teams of student advocates compete in interscholastic tournaments across the country, preparing written briefs and presenting oral arguments in simulated appellate cases presided over by members of the bench and bar. Numerous student organizations are active on campus.

Housing

Law students can reserve on-campus housing at the University Inn, which offers private rooms with private baths and a choice of meal plans.

For law students desiring to live off campus, numerous apartment complexes are located within minutes of the law school.

Applicant Profile

St. Thomas University School of Law
This grid includes only applicants who earned 120–180 LSAT scores under standard administrations.

LSAT Score	3.75 +		3.50–3.74		3.25–3.49		3.00–3.24		2.75–2.99		2.50–2.74		2.25–2.49		2.00–2.24		Below 2.00		No GPA		Total	
	Apps	Adm	Apps	Adm	Apps	Adm	Apps	Adm	Apps	Adm	Apps	Adm	Apps	Adm	Apps	Adm	Apps	Adm	Apps	Adm	Apps	Adm
175–180	0	0	0	0	0	0	0	0	0	0	0	0	0	0	0	0	0	0	0	0	0	0
170–174	0	0	0	0	0	0	0	0	0	0	0	0	0	0	0	0	0	0	0	0	0	0
165–169	2	2	1	1	0	0	2	2	0	0	1	1	4	4	0	0	0	0	0	0	10	10
160–164	2	2	4	3	3	3	4	3	4	4	6	6	1	1	1	1	0	0	1	0	26	24
155–159	8	7	20	20	20	20	35	33	27	26	17	17	17	17	8	7	5	3	2	2	153	147
150–154	19	17	59	57	97	93	114	105	102	98	81	78	36	32	27	21	3	0	14	8	542	506
145–149	49	32	119	70	184	110	205	100	193	47	125	40	66	7	34	2	5	0	18	3	992	417
140–144	25	6	69	15	123	20	132	10	128	2	109	0	64	2	32	0	2	0	10	1	705	58
135–139	6	0	11	1	41	1	45	0	45	0	43	1	31	0	9	0	1	0	8	0	250	5
130–134	2	0	7	0	7	0	16	0	17	0	14	0	13	0	9	0	1	0	3	0	94	0
125–129	1	0	2	0	0	0	2	0	1	0	2	0	3	0	6	0	0	0	0	0	21	0
120–124	0	0	0	0	0	0	1	0	0	0	0	0	0	0	0	0	0	0	0	0	1	0
Total	114	66	292	167	475	247	556	253	517	177	398	143	235	63	133	33	17	3	57	15	2794	1167

Apps = Number of Applicants   Adm = Number Admitted

Reflects 98% of the total applicant pool.

Samford University, Cumberland School of Law

800 Lakeshore Drive
Birmingham, AL 35229
Phone: 800.888.7213, 205.726.2702; Fax: 205.726.2057
E-mail: law.admissions@samford.edu; Website: www.cumberland.samford.edu

ABA
Approved
Since
1949

The Basics

Type of school	Private
Term	Semester
Application deadline	2/28 5/1
Application fee	$50
Financial aid deadline	3/1
Can first year start other than fall?	No
Student to faculty ratio	18.1 to 1
Does the university offer:	
housing restricted to law students?	No
graduate housing for which law students are eligible?	No

Faculty and Administrators

	Total		Men		Women		Minorities	
	Fall	Spr	Fall	Spr	Fall	Spr	Fall	Spr
Full-time	22	24	18	18	4	6	1	2
Other Full-time	1	1	0	0	1	1	0	0
Deans, librarians, & others who teach	5	4	2	2	3	2	2	1
Part-time	24	26	16	20	8	6	3	1
Total	52	55	36	40	16	15	6	4

Curriculum

	Full-time	Part-time
Typical first-year section size	58	0
Is there typically a "small section" of the first-year class, other than Legal Writing, taught by full-time faculty	No	No
If yes, typical size offered last year		
# of classroom course titles beyond first-year curriculum	94	

# of upper division courses, excluding seminars with an enrollment:		
	Under 25	42
	25–49	46
	50–74	21
	75–99	3
	100+	0

	Full-time	Part-time
# of seminars	15	
# of seminar positions available	215	
# of seminar positions filled	162	0
# of positions available in simulation courses	408	
# of simulation positions filled	370	0
# of positions available in faculty supervised clinical courses	0	
# of faculty supervised clinical positions filled	0	0
# involved in field placements	76	0
# involved in law journals	109	0
# involved in interschool competitions	37	0
# of credit hours required to graduate	90	

JD Enrollment and Ethnicity

	Men		Women		Full-time		Part-time		1st-year		Total		JD Degs. Awd.
	#	%	#	%	#	%	#	%	#	%	#	%	
African Amer.	11	3.8	31	14.8	42	8.4	0	0.0	11	6.7	42	8.4	6
Amer. Indian	3	1.0	1	0.5	4	0.8	0	0.0	1	0.6	4	0.8	3
Asian Amer.	2	0.7	4	1.9	6	1.2	0	0.0	2	1.2	6	1.2	1
Mex. Amer.	0	0.0	1	0.5	1	0.2	0	0.0	0	0.0	1	0.2	0
Puerto Rican	0	0.0	0	0.0	0	0.0	0	0.0	0	0.0	0	0.0	0
Hispanic	4	1.4	2	1.0	6	1.2	0	0.0	0	0.0	6	1.2	0
Total Minority	20	6.9	39	18.6	59	11.8	0	0.0	14	8.5	59	11.8	14
For. Nation.	1	0.3	3	1.4	4	0.8	0	0.0	0	0.0	4	0.8	0
Caucasian	236	81.9	142	67.6	378	75.9	0	0.0	113	68.5	378	75.9	169
Unknown	31	10.8	26	12.4	57	11.4	0	0.0	38	23.0	57	11.4	10
Total	288	57.8	210	42.2	498	100.0	0	0.0	165	33.1	498		193

Transfers

Transfers in	10
Transfers out	11

Tuition and Fees

	Resident	Nonresident
Full-time	$26,190	$26,190
Part-time	$15,426	$15,426

Living Expenses

Estimated living expenses for singles

Living on campus	Living off campus	Living at home
N/A	$19,310	$19,310

Samford University, Cumberland School of Law

ABA
Approved
Since
1949

GPA and LSAT Scores

	Total	Full-time	Part-time
# of apps	1,267	1,267	0
# of offers	458	458	0
# of matrics	167	167	0
75% GPA	3.59	3.59	0.00
Median GPA	3.28	3.28	0.00
25% GPA	2.96	2.96	0.00
75% LSAT	159	159	0
Median LSAT	156	156	0
25% LSAT	154	154	0

Grants and Scholarships (from prior year)

	Total #	Total %	Full-time #	Full-time %	Part-time #	Part-time %
Total # of students	532		527		5	
Total # receiving grants	157	29.5	157	29.8	0	0.0
Less than 1/2 tuition	44	8.3	44	8.3	0	0.0
Half to full tuition	31	5.8	31	5.9	0	0.0
Full tuition	60	11.3	60	11.4	0	0.0
More than full tuition	22	4.1	22	4.2	0	0.0
Median grant amount			$12,000		$0	

Informational and Library Resources

# of volumes and volume equivalents	296,933
# of titles	37,637
# of active serial subscriptions	1,997
Study seating capacity inside the library	474
# of full-time professional librarians	6
Hours per week library is open	107
# of open, wired connections available to students	200
# of networked computers available for use by students	43
# of simultaneous wireless users	405
Require computer?	No

JD Attrition (from prior year)

	Academic #	Other #	Total #	Total %
1st year	0	4	4	2.3
2nd year	0	12	12	7.4
3rd year	0	0	0	0.0
4th year	0	0	0	0.0

Employment (9 months after graduation)

	Total	Percentage
Employment status known	170	98.3
Employment status unknown	3	1.7
Employed	155	91.2
Pursuing graduate degrees	8	4.7
Unemployed seeking employment	4	2.4
Unemployed not seeking employment	3	1.8
Unemployed and studying for the bar	0	0.0
Type of Employment		
# employed in law firms	105	67.7
# employed in business and industry	20	12.9
# employed in government	14	9.0
# employed in public interest	2	1.3
# employed as judicial clerks	11	7.1
# employed in academia	0	0.0
Geographic Location		
# employed in state	101	65.2
# employed in foreign countries	0	0.0
# of states where employed	11	

Bar Passage Rates

Jurisdiction	Alabama		
Exam	Sum 05	Win 06	Total
# from school taking bar for the first time	103	14	117
School's pass rate for all first-time takers	93%	79%	91%
State's pass rate for all first-time takers	84%	68%	79%

The information on these pages was provided by the law school.

Samford University, Cumberland School of Law

800 Lakeshore Drive
Birmingham, AL 35229
Phone: 800.888.7213, 205.726.2702; Fax: 205.726.2057
E-mail: law.admissions@samford.edu; Website: www.cumberland.samford.edu

■ Introduction

The Cumberland School of Law, established in 1847 as a part of Cumberland University in Lebanon, Tennessee, is one of the oldest law schools in the country. The law school was acquired by Samford University in 1961. Today, Samford University is the largest privately supported and fully accredited institution of higher learning in Alabama. The beautiful campus is located in a suburban area of Birmingham, Alabama's largest city. Birmingham is the state's industrial, business, and cultural center. The Cumberland School of Law has been a member of the Association of American Law Schools (AALS) since 1952 and has been accredited by the American Bar Association (ABA) since 1949.

■ Library and Physical Facilities

The Lucille Stewart Beeson Law Library, an $8.4 million, freestanding, Georgian structure, is visually stunning, as well as superbly functional. This 61,000-square-foot, three-and-one-half-story building is connected to the law school by a second-story breezeway. The building's design is intended to make all facilities easily accessible to students with disabilities.

Complete training on Westlaw, LexisNexis, and LegalTrac is part of the first-year curriculum through the Lawyering and Legal Reasoning course. All study carrels and conference rooms are wired for data transmission. In addition, law students have full access to the university's four campus libraries, as well as six computer labs. Wireless Internet access is available in many areas around campus.

■ Joint-degree Programs

To broaden their thinking or help them prepare for careers in special fields, Cumberland students may opt to pursue seven different joint degrees: JD/MAcc, JD/MBA, JD/MPH, JD/MPA, JD/MDivinity, JD/MTheological Studies, and JD/MS in Environmental Management.

■ Center for Biotechnology, Law, and Ethics

Dedicated to furthering practical training in the legal disciplines critical to biotechnology, Cumberland's unique program builds on a base of intellectual property, health care, environmental, tort, and natural resources law. The center's specific focus on biotechnology includes issues related to the medical, pharmaceutical, and agricultural sectors and offers students research opportunities.

■ International Law

Cumberland conducts two ABA-approved international summer programs that are offered at Sidney Sussex College, Cambridge, England, and Federal University of Ceara, Fortaleza, Brazil. The graduate degree of Master of Comparative Law (MCL) is offered to international law school graduates.

■ Advocacy and Skills Training

Cumberland's emphasis on teaching students the art and science of courtroom advocacy begins in the first-year curriculum, where a six-credit, two-semester course titled Lawyering and Legal Reasoning provides students with hands-on, practical instruction in prelitigation skills, such as client interviewing, counseling, memorandum preparation, and negotiation; pretrial litigation skills, including summary judgment motions and making compelling oral arguments; and appellate litigation skills. This intensive course prepares students to work effectively in their first summer clerkships, where they may be expected to research cases and write briefs in their first week.

The new state-of-the-art Advanced Trial Advocacy Courtroom provides students with access to modern technology found in courtrooms across the country. In Cumberland's Advanced Trial Advocacy course, students can access databases and the Internet at each counsel table and learn how to reproduce evidence with three-dimensional digital presenters, video, and DVD reenactments. By mastering this technology and completing the hands-on training in the Advanced Trial Advocacy course, students will be equipped for success in any courtroom.

Cumberland has an exceptional record of recent trial-advocacy competition victories, winning both the ABA and Association of Trial Lawyers of America national championships (including several national second- and third-place awards); winning 33 regional championships; and winning the coveted American College of Trial Lawyers' Emil Gumpert Award for Excellence in Teaching Trial Advocacy. The law school also offers a Certificate in Trial Advocacy to recognize students' achievements. Cumberland students have the chance to get class credit and a professional leg up working for Birmingham's major law firms, judges' offices, and corporate legal departments. The clinical curriculum offers second- and third-year students judicial and corporate externships, as well as externships in the offices of the IRS, US Attorney, and organizations that serve underrepresented or economically disadvantaged groups. In addition, the Alabama Third-Year Practice Rule gives third-year students a chance to practice law under the supervision of a licensed attorney.

■ Flex Program

Cumberland's flex program allows students a maximum of five years to complete their studies. A limited number of students will be enrolled in the flex program, which requires students to take a minimum of eight credit hours each semester. Flex students attend classes during the day and pay the hourly tuition rate.

■ Admission

Cumberland School of Law does not use a number index system or formula when choosing who will be admitted. Every applicant's file is thoroughly reviewed by the Faculty Admissions Committee. In addition to the Law School Admission Test score and undergraduate grade-point average, other important factors considered are undergraduate school;

grade trend and difficulty of major; extracurricular activities and/or employment while in undergraduate school; whether economic, physical, or other challenges have been overcome; graduate work; scholarly achievements; employment experience; personal statement; and letters of recommendation. Applicants who because of their backgrounds will bring to the School of Law different and enlightening perspectives will be recognized by the committee. The law school seeks a diverse student body that will make a contribution to the law school and to the legal profession.

Admitted applicants are required to pay a nonrefundable $650 seat deposit that is credited toward tuition. The first installment of $150 is due April 1; the second installment of $500 is due June 15.

■ Student Activities

The Student Bar Association (SBA) functions as the first professional organization of a law student's career. Since many students in the entering class come from other states, student bar chapters keep students in touch with job opportunities and bar requirements.

In addition to many outstanding organizations, students may also be invited to join one of three national legal fraternities and be inducted into two honorary societies, Order of the Barrister and Curia Honoris. Student-run publications include *Cumberland Law Review*, *American Journal of Trial Advocacy*, and *Pro Confesso*.

■ Scholarships

All admitted applicants are automatically considered for merit- and recruiting-scholarship awards. Various other scholarships are available to outstanding students who distinguish themselves academically, make outstanding contributions through leadership in the law school's program, or demonstrate financial need.

■ Career Services

Through the Career Services Office, the law school assists all law students in locating summer clerkships and part-time and permanent employment upon graduation. Students also receive individual counseling and take part in workshops. The office schedules on-campus interview programs during the fall and spring semesters. Cumberland students and graduates are encouraged to attend well-known recruiting conferences in Chicago, Atlanta, Nashville, and Washington, DC. The Career Services Office surveys each graduating class nine months after graduation; based on data collected from the most recent graduates (Class of 2005), 96 percent had successfully obtained employment or were attending graduate school.

Applicant Profile

Samford University, Cumberland School of Law

LSAT Score	GPA								
	3.75 +	3.50–3.74	3.25–3.49	3.00–3.24	2.75–2.99	2.50–2.74	2.25–2.49	2.00–2.24	Below 2.00
175–180									
170–174									
165–169									
160–164									
155–159									
150–154									
145–149									
140–144									
135–139									
130–134									
125–129									
120–124									

■ Good Possibility   □ Possible   ▨ Unlikely

University of San Diego—School of Law

Warren Hall—Room 203, 5998 Alcalá Park
San Diego, CA 92110-2492
Phone: 619.260.4528; Fax: 619.260.2218
E-mail: jdinfo@sandiego.edu; Website: www.law.sandiego.edu

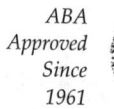

ABA
Approved
Since
1961

The Basics

Type of school	Private
Term	Semester
Application deadline	2/1
Application fee	$50
Financial aid deadline	3/1
Can first year start other than fall?	No
Student to faculty ratio	14.3 to 1
Does the university offer:	
housing restricted to law students?	No
graduate housing for which law students are eligible?	No

Faculty and Administrators

	Total		Men		Women		Minorities	
	Fall	Spr	Fall	Spr	Fall	Spr	Fall	Spr
Full-time	49	57	37	43	12	14	5	6
Other Full-time	6	6	1	1	5	5	1	1
Deans, librarians, & others who teach	10	10	4	4	6	6	1	1
Part-time	35	32	25	23	8	9	8	7
Total	**100**	**105**	**67**	**71**	**31**	**34**	**15**	**15**

Curriculum

	Full-time	Part-time
Typical first-year section size	85	85
Is there typically a "small section" of the first-year class, other than Legal Writing, taught by full-time faculty	Yes	Yes
If yes, typical size offered last year	43	43
# of classroom course titles beyond first-year curriculum	114	
# of upper division courses, excluding seminars with an enrollment: Under 25	145	
25–49	40	
50–74	16	
75–99	22	
100+	1	
# of seminars	30	
# of seminar positions available	640	
# of seminar positions filled	405	51
# of positions available in simulation courses	505	
# of simulation positions filled	395	80
# of positions available in faculty supervised clinical courses	244	
# of faculty supervised clinical positions filled	204	21
# involved in field placements	116	15
# involved in law journals	131	20
# involved in interschool competitions	83	5
# of credit hours required to graduate	85	

JD Enrollment and Ethnicity

	Men		Women		Full-time		Part-time		1st-year		Total		JD Degs. Awd.
	#	%	#	%	#	%	#	%	#	%	#	%	
African Amer.	15	2.6	17	3.7	23	3.1	9	3.0	10	3.0	32	3.1	6
Amer. Indian	6	1.0	5	1.1	9	1.2	2	0.7	5	1.5	11	1.1	1
Asian Amer.	81	14.2	78	16.8	113	15.3	46	15.5	60	18.0	159	15.4	42
Mex. Amer.	25	4.4	29	6.3	39	5.3	15	5.1	19	5.7	54	5.2	12
Puerto Rican	2	0.3	5	1.1	5	0.7	2	0.7	2	0.6	7	0.7	2
Hispanic	14	2.4	25	5.4	26	3.5	13	4.4	10	3.0	39	3.8	11
Total Minority	143	25.0	159	34.3	215	29.1	87	29.3	106	31.8	302	29.2	74
For. Nation.	0	0.0	2	0.4	2	0.3	0	0.0	0	0.0	2	0.2	0
Caucasian	429	75.0	302	65.2	521	70.6	210	70.7	227	68.2	731	70.6	239
Unknown	0	0.0	0	0.0	0	0.0	0	0.0	0	0.0	0	0.0	0
Total	572	55.3	463	44.7	738	71.3	297	28.7	333	32.2	1035		313

Transfers

Transfers in	21
Transfers out	15

Tuition and Fees

	Resident	Nonresident
Full-time	$35,896	$35,896
Part-time	$25,516	$25,516

Living Expenses

Estimated living expenses for singles

Living on campus	Living off campus	Living at home
$17,884	$17,884	$8,882

University of San Diego—School of Law

ABA
Approved
Since
1961

GPA and LSAT Scores

	Total	Full-time	Part-time
# of apps	4,893	4,436	457
# of offers	1,518	1,322	196
# of matrics	342	252	90
75% GPA	3.54	3.56	3.46
Median GPA	3.31	3.33	3.24
25% GPA	3.04	3.06	3.00
75% LSAT	163	164	159
Median LSAT	160	161	158
25% LSAT	158	159	156

Grants and Scholarships (from prior year)

	Total		Full-time		Part-time	
	#	%	#	%	#	%
Total # of students	1,066		763		303	
Total # receiving grants	363	34.1	289	37.9	74	24.4
Less than 1/2 tuition	167	15.7	141	18.5	26	8.6
Half to full tuition	134	12.6	94	12.3	40	13.2
Full tuition	51	4.8	43	5.6	8	2.6
More than full tuition	11	1.0	11	1.4	0	0.0
Median grant amount			$17,000		$12,000	

Informational and Library Resources

# of volumes and volume equivalents	523,397
# of titles	297,399
# of active serial subscriptions	4,760
Study seating capacity inside the library	588
# of full-time professional librarians	9
Hours per week library is open	112
# of open, wired connections available to students	240
# of networked computers available for use by students	66
# of simultaneous wireless users	2,432
Require computer?	No

JD Attrition (from prior year)

	Academic	Other	Total	
	#	#	#	%
1st year	7	31	38	10.6
2nd year	0	5	5	1.6
3rd year	0	4	4	1.1
4th year	0	0	0	0.0

Employment (9 months after graduation)

	Total	Percentage
Employment status known	282	91.3
Employment status unknown	27	8.7
Employed	234	83.0
Pursuing graduate degrees	18	6.4
Unemployed seeking employment	9	3.2
Unemployed not seeking employment	8	2.8
Unemployed and studying for the bar	13	4.6

Type of Employment

# employed in law firms	142	60.7
# employed in business and industry	38	16.2
# employed in government	32	13.7
# employed in public interest	9	3.8
# employed as judicial clerks	6	2.6
# employed in academia	1	0.4

Geographic Location

# employed in state	187	79.9
# employed in foreign countries	2	0.9
# of states where employed		19

Bar Passage Rates

Jurisdiction	California			Nevada		
Exam	Sum 05	Win 06	Total	Sum 05	Win 06	Total
# from school taking bar for the first time	234	30	264	12	1	13
School's pass rate for all first-time takers	80%	77%	80%	75%	100%	77%
State's pass rate for all first-time takers	64%	54%	62%	64%	67%	65%

University of San Diego—School of Law

Warren Hall—Room 203, 5998 Alcalá Park
San Diego, CA 92110-2492
Phone: 619.260.4528; Fax: 619.260.2218
E-mail: jdinfo@sandiego.edu; Website: www.law.sandiego.edu

■ Introduction

The University of San Diego—School of Law is an outstanding center of legal education with a distinguished faculty, a talented student body, and a dedication to innovation. It is a leader in creating programs and courses to prepare future lawyers to practice in a rapidly changing world marked by globalization and dramatic advancements in technology. Founded in 1954, the School of Law is part of the University of San Diego, a private, nonprofit, independent Roman Catholic university. The university is located on a spectacular 182-acre campus overlooking Mission Bay and the Pacific Ocean, featuring magnificent Spanish Renaissance architecture and beautiful grounds. The San Diego area, with a population of three million, is renowned for its ideal climate, unique cultural heritage, and unsurpassed recreational resources.

■ Admission

The educational mission of the School of Law embraces a commitment to academic excellence, individual dignity, and the need to develop the knowledge, values, and skills of its students to prepare them for service to their professional, global, civic, and faith communities. The law school strives to draw talented students from all regions of the country and from different ethnic and social backgrounds. The University of San Diego is committed to advancing academic excellence, expanding liberal and professional knowledge, creating a diverse and inclusive community, and preparing leaders dedicated to ethical conduct and compassionate service.

■ Accreditation and Membership

Accredited: ABA, Committee of Bar Examiners—State of California. Membership: AALS, Order of the Coif.

■ Legal Research Center

The Pardee Legal Research Center offers a full range of traditional and state-of-the-art electronic services. Computer legal research systems include LexisNexis, Westlaw, Dialog, and LegalTrac. The LRC offers an instructional computer lab with networked computers replicating lawyers' workstations. Laptop access to the Internet is provided at more than 100 library carrels and through a wireless network. Among all law libraries at ABA-accredited schools, USD is in the top one-third based on collection size and is number 15 in the nation based on title count.

■ Special Programs

Institute on International and Comparative Law—The institute conducts summer law programs in England, France, Ireland, Italy, Russia, Spain, and Mexico. The programs introduce American law students to foreign law and legal institutions and provide intensive study.

Clinical Education Program—The Clinical Education Program is recognized as one of the most extensive and successful in the nation. The law school received the Emil Gumpert Award from the American College of Trial Lawyers for excellence in trial advocacy training. Students interview, counsel, and represent clients under the supervision of a clinical professor.

Research and Advocacy Institutes—The Center for Public Interest Law and Children's Advocacy Institute offer unique research and clinical opportunities.

Concurrent Degrees—Students desiring to concentrate in business or international relations may concurrently pursue the JD/MBA, JD/International MBA, or JD/MA in International Relations.

Lawyering Skills—Students receive extensive training in a variety of legal skills, including first-year legal writing and research, interviewing, counseling, discovery, trial advocacy, and alternative dispute resolution. In addition, the law school provides an outstanding Academic Support Program.

Oral Advocacy—The National Mock Trial Team is evidence of USD's commitment to trial advocacy. Trial teams consistently rank among the finest teams in the nation. The trial team has taken first place in the prestigious American Inns of Court's National Tournament of Champions. The trial team has won the Western Regional Championship of the Association of Trial Lawyers of America nine times and has been selected as the best team in the Ninth Circuit for seven of the last nine years. The USD Mock Trial Team competes in the ABA's National Trial competitions and has placed first in the Western Regional for many years. The USD Moot Court hosts several prestigious oral advocacy tournaments throughout the year, including the McLennon Honors competition, which has featured justices of the United States Supreme Court as presiding judges.

■ Campus Highlights

The University of San Diego's Joan B. Kroc Institute for Peace and Justice joined the ranks of the world's most important centers for promoting global peace and social justice. The institute hosts international conferences and workshops, as well as service-learning programs and conflict resolution and mediation services. The institute offers an interdisciplinary master's degree in peace studies. A gift from the estate of Joan B. Kroc will soon lead to the establishment of a School of Peace Studies on campus.

The Jenny Craig Pavilion showcases Division 1 athletics and hosts special events. The Donald P. Shiley Center for Science and Technology and the Degheri Alumni Center are two recent additions to the campus.

■ Distinguished Visitors and Speakers

The School of Law hosts annual conferences, symposia, and speakers series to enhance the classroom experience, provide an environment in which legal scholars can work on cutting-edge and interdisciplinary issues, and promote the exchange of ideas. Among these are the annual US-Mexico International Tax Update, the Nathaniel L. Nathanson Memorial Lecture Series, the Joan E. Bowes-James Madison Distinguished Speaker Series, and the Jane Ellen Bergman Lecture on Women, Children, and Human Rights. Such events have brought many eminent speakers, including US Supreme Court justices, to campus to discuss issues of national significance. The Law, Economics, and Politics Workshop Series is presented in conjunction with the University of California at San Diego.

Student Activities

Approximately 38 organizations serve the student body by developing a sense of community, and activities range from writing for a legal journal and doing scholarly research to participating in the student/faculty intramural sports activities. The *San Diego Law Review* is a student-run law journal addressing major issues and topics in law.

Students also submit to the *San Diego International Law Journal* articles, comments, book reviews, and case notes concerning important international law topics.

Financial Aid

The School of Law is committed to providing all possible financial assistance to eligible students whose personal resources are insufficient to meet their educational expenses. Sources of financial aid include approximately 380 need/merit, merit, and diversity-based scholarships; federal plans, such as work-study programs; the Perkins, Stafford, and Graduate PLUS federal loan programs; and institutional loans. Private loan programs are also available to assist law students with supplemental financing.

Career Services

University of San Diego law students have diverse career goals, and Career Services at the School of Law is committed to supporting all students in achieving their career objectives. Throughout their law school years, students are offered opportunities to explore career options with private law firms, government agencies, and public interest organizations, and to obtain internships, fellowships, and clerkships with federal and state courts nationwide. Each fall, more than 225 interviewers, some of whom are named in the *National Law Journal*'s and the *American Lawyer*'s lists of the top 250 law firms in the country, contact USD students as part of an extensive recruiting process.

USD's law graduates practice in 50 states, the District of Columbia, and 14 foreign countries. For the graduating class of 2005, within nine months of graduation, approximately 90 percent were employed or enrolled in a full-time degree program. For the Class of 2005, approximately 61 percent accepted positions with law firms and 20 percent began their careers in public service, including local, state, and federal government; federal courts; and public interest agencies. Others pursued careers in a range of business and corporate positions. Those in private practice had an average salary of $79,000. Those working in government had an average salary of $54,000.

Housing

The USD Housing Office and the School of Law Admission Office assist in providing information and resources in locating on- and off-campus accommodations.

Applicant Profile

University of San Diego—School of Law
(Note: This chart is to be used as a general guide only. Nonnumerical factors are also considered.)

LSAT Score	GPA								
	3.75 +	3.50–3.74	3.25–3.49	3.00–3.24	2.75–2.99	2.50–2.74	2.25–2.49	2.00–2.24	Below 2.00
175–180									
170–174									
165–169									
160–164									
155–159									
150–154									
145–149									
140–144									
135–139									
130–134									
125–129									
120–124									

■ Very Likely   ▨ Possible   ☐ Unlikely

University of San Francisco School of Law

USF School of Law, 2130 Fulton Street
San Francisco, CA 94117-1080
Phone: 415.422.6586; Fax: 415.422.5442
E-mail: lawadmissions@usfca.edu; Website: www.usfca.edu/law

ABA
Approved
Since
1935

The Basics

Type of school	Private
Term	Semester
Application deadline	2/1 4/2
Application fee	$60
Financial aid deadline	2/15
Can first year start other than fall?	No
Student to faculty ratio	17.3 to 1
Does the university offer:	
housing restricted to law students?	No
graduate housing for which law students are eligible?	Yes

Faculty and Administrators

	Total Fall	Total Spr	Men Fall	Men Spr	Women Fall	Women Spr	Minorities Fall	Minorities Spr
Full-time	32	32	23	22	9	10	10	9
Other Full-time	1	1	0	0	1	1	0	0
Deans, librarians, & others who teach	5	5	2	2	3	3	1	1
Part-time	46	53	28	32	18	21	13	13
Total	**84**	**91**	**53**	**56**	**31**	**35**	**24**	**23**

Curriculum

	Full-time	Part-time
Typical first-year section size	96	51
Is there typically a "small section" of the first-year class, other than Legal Writing, taught by full-time faculty	Yes	No
If yes, typical size offered last year	48	
# of classroom course titles beyond first-year curriculum		90
# of upper division courses, excluding seminars with an enrollment: Under 25		68
25–49		33
50–74		12
75–99		7
100+		1
# of seminars		12
# of seminar positions available		235
# of seminar positions filled	187	19
# of positions available in simulation courses		160
# of simulation positions filled	135	13
# of positions available in faculty supervised clinical courses		100
# of faculty supervised clinical positions filled	92	5
# involved in field placements	216	11
# involved in law journals	82	7
# involved in interschool competitions	99	9
# of credit hours required to graduate		86

JD Enrollment and Ethnicity

	Men #	Men %	Women #	Women %	Full-time #	Full-time %	Part-time #	Part-time %	1st-year #	1st-year %	Total #	Total %	JD Degs. Awd.
African Amer.	12	3.5	26	7.3	22	3.9	16	11.4	17	7.3	38	5.4	11
Amer. Indian	2	0.6	2	0.6	2	0.4	2	1.4	1	0.4	4	0.6	1
Asian Amer.	57	16.5	82	23.0	115	20.5	24	17.1	44	19.0	139	19.8	33
Mex. Amer.	18	5.2	18	5.0	29	5.2	7	5.0	17	7.3	36	5.1	8
Puerto Rican	1	0.3	2	0.6	3	0.5	0	0.0	1	0.4	3	0.4	1
Hispanic	17	4.9	15	4.2	21	3.7	11	7.9	7	3.0	32	4.6	6
Total Minority	107	31.0	145	40.6	192	34.2	60	42.9	87	37.5	252	35.9	60
For. Nation.	2	0.6	3	0.8	4	0.7	1	0.7	1	0.4	5	0.7	0
Caucasian	169	49.0	168	47.1	275	48.9	62	44.3	108	46.6	337	48.0	135
Unknown	67	19.4	41	11.5	91	16.2	17	12.1	36	15.5	108	15.4	36
Total	345	49.1	357	50.9	562	80.1	140	19.9	232	33.0	702		231

Transfers

Transfers in	3
Transfers out	10

Tuition and Fees

	Resident	Nonresident
Full-time	$32,190	$0
Part-time	$23,045	$0

Living Expenses

Estimated living expenses for singles

Living on campus	Living off campus	Living at home
$15,804	$19,060	$7,970

University of San Francisco School of Law

ABA Approved Since 1935

GPA and LSAT Scores

	Total	Full-time	Part-time
# of apps	3,468	3,090	378
# of offers	1,124	1,031	93
# of matrics	235	178	57
75% GPA	3.54	3.55	3.49
Median GPA	3.28	3.32	3.03
25% GPA	3.00	3.08	2.79
75% LSAT	161	161	159
Median LSAT	159	159	158
25% LSAT	156	157	155

Grants and Scholarships (from prior year)

	Total #	Total %	Full-time #	Full-time %	Part-time #	Part-time %
Total # of students	729		599		130	
Total # receiving grants	210	28.8	169	28.2	41	31.5
Less than 1/2 tuition	156	21.4	129	21.5	27	20.8
Half to full tuition	42	5.8	39	6.5	3	2.3
Full tuition	12	1.6	1	0.2	11	8.5
More than full tuition	0	0.0	0	0.0	0	0.0
Median grant amount			$9,171		$3,500	

Informational and Library Resources

# of volumes and volume equivalents	350,499
# of titles	185,979
# of active serial subscriptions	3,453
Study seating capacity inside the library	428
# of full-time professional librarians	7
Hours per week library is open	98
# of open, wired connections available to students	981
# of networked computers available for use by students	96
# of simultaneous wireless users	480
Require computer?	No

JD Attrition (from prior year)

	Academic #	Other #	Total #	Total %
1st year	21	20	41	16.2
2nd year	2	1	3	1.4
3rd year	2	0	2	0.9
4th year	0	0	0	0.0

Employment (9 months after graduation)

	Total	Percentage
Employment status known	189	95.9
Employment status unknown	8	4.1
Employed	184	97.4
Pursuing graduate degrees	2	1.1
Unemployed seeking employment	2	1.1
Unemployed not seeking employment	1	0.5
Unemployed and studying for the bar	0	0.0

Type of Employment

	Total	Percentage
# employed in law firms	119	64.7
# employed in business and industry	21	11.4
# employed in government	13	7.1
# employed in public interest	16	8.7
# employed as judicial clerks	3	1.6
# employed in academia	3	1.6

Geographic Location

	Total	Percentage
# employed in state	171	92.9
# employed in foreign countries	3	1.6
# of states where employed	5	

Bar Passage Rates

Jurisdiction	California		
Exam	Sum 05	Win 06	Total
# from school taking bar for the first time	176	15	191
School's pass rate for all first-time takers	74%	60%	73%
State's pass rate for all first-time takers	64%	54%	62%

University of San Francisco School of Law

USF School of Law, 2130 Fulton Street
San Francisco, CA 94117-1080
Phone: 415.422.6586; Fax: 415.422.5442
E-mail: lawadmissions@usfca.edu; Website: www.usfca.edu/law

■ Introduction

Founded in 1912, the School of Law is located on the University of San Francisco's 55-acre hilltop campus in a quiet residential part of San Francisco. It overlooks Golden Gate Park, the Pacific Ocean, and downtown San Francisco. The campus is only minutes by public transportation from the many educational, cultural, social, and recreational choices the San Francisco Bay Area offers.

The city and surrounding communities extend the classroom, providing an extraordinary laboratory for the study of law. The law school is in close proximity to San Francisco's civic center and financial district, where numerous private law practices have offices; where federal, state, and local governmental agencies are located; and where both federal and state trial and appellate courts, including the California Supreme Court, are in session. All of this provides exceptional learning, practice, internship, and service opportunities.

The law school is fully accredited by the American Bar Association and is a member of the Association of American Law Schools.

■ A School With a Mission

USF's law school has a tradition of excellence in educating skilled and effective lawyers with high ethical standards, a global perspective, and a social conscience. We train professionals who care about the well-being of others. We believe that law is a noble profession and that lawyers are capable of doing enormous good. Consistent with our mission, the law school has developed an array of programs dedicated to serving communities throughout the United States and around the globe. The law school has also developed a unique curriculum for ethics and professional responsibility that helps put into practice what we teach.

■ Degree Programs

The law school offers both full-time and part-time instructional programs leading to the JD degree. Students entering through the traditional four-year, part-time program may accelerate their studies and complete the degree in seven semesters or they may convert to the full-time program after the first year and complete their degree in three years. Either option requires attendance at one or more summer session. In conjunction with the university's School of Business and Management, the law school offers a four-year, full-time concurrent JD and MBA degree program. The law school also offers a Master of Laws (LLM) in International Transactions and Comparative Law for foreign lawyers who have earned first degrees in law from a non-American university, as well as a Master of Laws (LLM) in Intellectual Property and Technology Law.

■ Facilities

The University of San Francisco School of Law's Koret Law Center includes Kendrick Hall and the Dorraine Zief Law Library. Kendrick Hall, built in the 1960s, has been thoroughly renovated, while retaining its original architectural integrity. The building's rotunda skylight, spiral stairways, and circular configurations enhance the use of natural light and offer informal gathering space. In addition to expanding the student services and programming areas, the renovation ensures a twenty-first century infrastructure for classroom technology. The wireless network is accessible throughout the building, and all the major classrooms include power and data connections at every seat. The new 70-seat moot courtroom prepares students for contemporary trial advocacy.

Adjacent to Kendrick Hall is the Dorraine Zief Law Library, which opened in 2000. The modern technologically equipped library provides both wired and wireless network access in a comfortable, flexible, fully accessible research and study environment. Students will find tables, carrels, lounge seating, and study rooms available for their use, as well as computer classrooms, laboratories, and specially designed training and research rooms.

Because the law school is located on USF's campus, students have available to them all the amenities and facilities one expects to find at a major urban university, including the outstanding recreational and fitness facilities at USF's Health and Recreation Center.

■ The Curriculum

The core curriculum, concentrated in the first year of the full-time program and the first and second years of the part-time program, includes courses essential to a solid understanding of dominant legal concepts. It orients students to central areas of the law and ensures mastery of basic doctrine and the fundamental analytical and communication skills demanded in the practice of law. It is also designed to make students aware of basic social interests and the role of law in ordering them. The core curriculum is complemented by a rich offering of specialized courses and programs providing almost unlimited opportunities for specialized study and practical experience. Elective courses are constantly updated to reflect changes in the law and legal practice, to meet the relentless pace of technological change, and to match student interest.

There are JD certificate programs and curricular concentrations in several areas of law. Notable among these are courses in International and Comparative Law, Public Interest Law, Advocacy and Alternative Dispute Resolution, and Intellectual Property and Cyberspace Law. There are also opportunities for participation in unique clinical programs, including a Mediation Clinic, an Investor Justice Clinic, a Family Law Clinic, and an International Human Rights Clinic.

■ International Programs

USF has a unique International Human Rights clinic that affords many of its students an opportunity, in the spring semester, to personally present their research and policy proposals to the United Nations Commission on Human Rights on Geneva or the Commission on Women's Rights in New York. USF offers traditional summer study-abroad programs in Budapest, Dublin, and Prague, as well as a clinical program in Bilbao. Our Center for Law and Global Justice administers a range of programs, both abroad and on campus. It sponsors legal assistance projects in China and East Timor and offers a summer class for USF students in Cambodia. Summer interns have worked in the Dominican Republic, the Philippines, India, and El Salvador. Students at home may participate in a "virtual internship" summer program providing research and advocacy in support of justice in Haiti. The law school also has faculty exchange programs with sister schools in Ireland, the Czech Republic, China, and Hungary. These programs bring law school faculty from around the globe to teach international law subjects in areas in which they have unique expertise.

Student Activities

The law school has a wide array of academic and extracurricular activities for students. Student representatives participate in faculty meetings and on many law school committees. Students serve as editors and publish the *USF Law Review*, the *USF Maritime Law Journal*, and the *USF Intellectual Property Law Bulletin*. A student board of directors organizes the Moot Court Program and the advanced intraschool competitions. The Director of Advanced Moot Court Competitions coaches teams in regional and national competitions. Frequent panels, guest speakers, and special programs provide students with repeated opportunities for informal interchange with faculty, alumni, members of the bench and bar, and visiting dignitaries. Some examples of symposia topics include the death penalty, employment law, alternative dispute resolution, complex litigation, water law, human trafficking, and current events including elections and political issues. The Student Bar Association funds and oversees 38 student organizations, which reflect the diversity and varied interests of USF law students. Opportunities for service and giving back to the community are available through the Pro Bono Program and the Law in Motion Service Program.

Faculty

The law school's faculty members are accomplished scholars as well as dedicated teachers committed to quality education and to developing each student's full potential. Faculty members are especially accessible outside the classroom, welcoming interaction with students. They create an intellectually challenging but supportive atmosphere in which each student may grow as a professional and as an individual. Full-time faculty members have achieved numerous scholastic accomplishments, graduating from the most elite law schools, earning honors, and serving as editors of prestigious law journals. Almost all have had substantial practical experience and continue to be involved in service to the community and the profession. Collectively, they have authored hundreds of treatises, casebooks, practice guides, law review articles, and book reviews. Yet, they remain passionate about teaching, which is each faculty member's highest priority.

The full-time faculty is augmented by approximately 60 adjunct professors, including federal and state court judges, attorneys from many public agencies, and other distinguished members of the bar who are in private practice or serving as counsel for leading business ventures. The availability in the San Francisco Bay Area legal community of so many talented and experienced people allows the law school to expand its curriculum with specialized courses and provide students access to a wealth of practical expertise.

Applicant Profile

University of San Francisco School of Law
This grid includes only applicants who earned 120–180 LSAT scores under standard administrations.

LSAT Score	3.75 +		3.50–3.74		3.25–3.49		3.00–3.24		2.75–2.99		2.50–2.74		2.25–2.49		2.00–2.24		Below 2.00		No GPA		Total	
	Apps	Adm	Apps	Adm	Apps	Adm	Apps	Adm	Apps	Adm	Apps	Adm	Apps	Adm	Apps	Adm	Apps	Adm	Apps	Adm	Apps	Adm
175–180	1	1	0	0	0	0	0	0	2	2	0	0	0	0	0	0	0	0	0	0	3	3
170–174	3	3	4	4	9	7	2	2	6	4	1	0	1	0	0	0	0	0	0	0	26	20
165–169	12	12	19	19	31	29	22	21	22	16	9	6	2	2	1	0	0	0	1	1	119	106
160–164	48	48	100	99	122	119	98	89	47	37	35	20	22	10	12	3	0	0	4	3	488	428
155–159	114	90	235	155	278	124	181	62	118	26	60	10	20	2	4	0	1	0	11	7	1022	476
150–154	54	6	144	14	233	21	218	13	135	8	46	2	25	0	10	0	3	0	8	2	876	66
145–149	28	5	82	2	119	5	126	1	89	4	51	0	20	0	5	0	0	0	13	0	533	17
140–144	12	0	20	0	52	0	58	0	47	0	29	0	21	0	7	0	2	0	3	0	251	0
135–139	1	0	5	0	12	0	19	0	21	0	16	0	3	0	1	0	1	0	2	0	81	0
130–134	1	0	3	0	0	0	6	0	5	0	4	0	1	0	1	0	1	0	2	0	24	0
125–129	0	0	2	0	0	0	1	0	0	0	1	0	1	0	1	0	0	0	0	0	6	0
120–124	0	0	0	0	0	0	0	0	0	0	0	0	0	0	0	0	0	0	0	0	0	0
Total	274	165	614	293	856	305	731	188	492	97	252	38	116	14	42	3	8	0	44	13	3429	1116

Apps = Number of Applicants
Adm = Number Admitted
Reflects 99% of the total applicant pool.

Santa Clara University School of Law

500 El Camino Real
Santa Clara, CA 95053
Phone: 408.554.5048; Fax: 408.554.7897
E-mail: lawadmissions@scu.edu; Website: www.scu.edu/law

*ABA
Approved
Since
1937*

The Basics

Type of school	Private
Term	Semester
Application deadline	2/1
Application fee	$75
Financial aid deadline	3/1
Can first year start other than fall?	No
Student to faculty ratio	20.3 to 1
Does the university offer:	
housing restricted to law students?	Yes
graduate housing for which law students are eligible?	No

Faculty and Administrators

	Total		Men		Women		Minorities	
	Fall	Spr	Fall	Spr	Fall	Spr	Fall	Spr
Full-time	35	35	20	20	15	15	9	9
Other Full-time	16	16	6	6	10	10	1	1
Deans, librarians, & others who teach	9	9	3	3	6	6	1	1
Part-time	35	40	19	23	16	17	4	3
Total	95	100	48	52	47	48	15	14

Curriculum

	Full-time	Part-time
Typical first-year section size	80	61
Is there typically a "small section" of the first-year class, other than Legal Writing, taught by full-time faculty	Yes	No
If yes, typical size offered last year	40	
# of classroom course titles beyond first-year curriculum	230	
# of upper division courses, excluding seminars with an enrollment: Under 25	167	
25–49	35	
50–74	19	
75–99	16	
100+	1	
# of seminars	36	
# of seminar positions available	795	
# of seminar positions filled	521	0
# of positions available in simulation courses	226	
# of simulation positions filled	188	0
# of positions available in faculty supervised clinical courses	200	
# of faculty supervised clinical positions filled	154	0
# involved in field placements	250	0
# involved in law journals	96	0
# involved in interschool competitions	20	0
# of credit hours required to graduate	86	

JD Enrollment and Ethnicity

	Men #	Men %	Women #	Women %	Full-time #	Full-time %	Part-time #	Part-time %	1st-year #	1st-year %	Total #	Total %	JD Degs. Awd.
African Amer.	17	3.6	29	6.2	37	5.0	9	4.8	20	6.7	46	4.9	8
Amer. Indian	1	0.2	3	0.6	2	0.3	2	1.1	0	0.0	4	0.4	1
Asian Amer.	112	24.0	131	28.2	190	25.6	53	28.0	83	27.9	243	26.1	92
Mex. Amer.	0	0.0	0	0.0	0	0.0	0	0.0	0	0.0	0	0.0	0
Puerto Rican	0	0.0	0	0.0	0	0.0	0	0.0	0	0.0	0	0.0	0
Hispanic	36	7.7	49	10.5	73	9.8	12	6.3	19	6.4	85	9.1	32
Total Minority	166	35.5	212	45.6	302	40.6	76	40.2	122	40.9	378	40.6	133
For. Nation.	0	0.0	0	0.0	0	0.0	0	0.0	0	0.0	0	0.0	0
Caucasian	287	61.5	237	51.0	418	56.3	106	56.1	151	50.7	524	56.2	152
Unknown	14	3.0	16	3.4	23	3.1	7	3.7	25	8.4	30	3.2	0
Total	467	50.1	465	49.9	743	79.7	189	20.3	298	32.0	932		285

Transfers

Transfers in	27
Transfers out	14

Tuition and Fees

	Resident	Nonresident
Full-time	$33,600	$33,600
Part-time	$23,520	$23,520

Living Expenses

Estimated living expenses for singles

Living on campus	Living off campus	Living at home
$18,792	$18,792	$18,792

Santa Clara University School of Law

*ABA
Approved
Since
1937*

GPA and LSAT Scores

	Total	Full-time	Part-time
# of apps	3,639	3,313	326
# of offers	1,498	1,392	106
# of matrics	301	243	58
75% GPA	3.55	3.57	3.46
Median GPA	3.32	3.34	3.25
25% GPA	3.09	3.12	2.98
75% LSAT	161	161	161
Median LSAT	158	158	158
25% LSAT	156	156	156

Grants and Scholarships (from prior year)

	Total		Full-time		Part-time	
	#	%	#	%	#	%
Total # of students	955		721		234	
Total # receiving grants	285	29.8	238	33.0	47	20.1
Less than 1/2 tuition	217	22.7	192	26.6	25	10.7
Half to full tuition	63	6.6	44	6.1	19	8.1
Full tuition	5	0.5	2	0.3	3	1.3
More than full tuition	0	0.0	0	0.0	0	0.0
Median grant amount			$11,000		$10,500	

Informational and Library Resources

# of volumes and volume equivalents	360,901
# of titles	147,867
# of active serial subscriptions	4,352
Study seating capacity inside the library	446
# of full-time professional librarians	9
Hours per week library is open	106
# of open, wired connections available to students	694
# of networked computers available for use by students	41
# of simultaneous wireless users	450
Require computer?	No

JD Attrition (from prior year)

	Academic	Other	Total	
	#	#	#	%
1st year	24	29	53	16.9
2nd year	0	5	5	1.8
3rd year	0	0	0	0.0
4th year	0	1	1	1.9

Employment (9 months after graduation)

	Total	Percentage
Employment status known	298	99.0
Employment status unknown	3	1.0
Employed	256	85.9
Pursuing graduate degrees	5	1.7
Unemployed seeking employment	10	3.4
Unemployed not seeking employment	27	9.1
Unemployed and studying for the bar	0	0.0
Type of Employment		
# employed in law firms	159	62.1
# employed in business and industry	40	15.6
# employed in government	34	13.3
# employed in public interest	10	3.9
# employed as judicial clerks	3	1.2
# employed in academia	4	1.6
Geographic Location		
# employed in state	208	81.2
# employed in foreign countries	6	2.3
# of states where employed		13

Bar Passage Rates

Jurisdiction	California		
Exam	Sum 05	Win 06	Total
# from school taking bar for the first time	251	29	280
School's pass rate for all first-time takers	65%	72%	66%
State's pass rate for all first-time takers	64%	54%	62%

Santa Clara University School of Law

500 El Camino Real
Santa Clara, CA 95053
Phone: 408.554.5048; Fax: 408.554.7897
E-mail: lawadmissions@scu.edu; Website: www.scu.edu/law

■ Introduction

Santa Clara University School of Law is located 46 miles from San Francisco, near the southern tip of San Francisco Bay. It is situated on the university campus, which was founded by the Jesuit fathers in 1851 and which surrounds the Mission of Santa Clara de Asis, the eighth of California's original 21 missions. The School of Law was added to the Santa Clara College in 1912 when the college became a university. The school is approved by the ABA and is a member of the AALS.

For 150 years, Santa Clara has fostered an exceptional academic program based on the Jesuit tradition. Located adjacent to San Jose and situated in the midst of one of the nation's greatest concentrations of high technology industry, internationally known as Silicon Valley, the law school has established a curriculum that addresses the fundamental demands of law practice and the evolving needs of society.

■ Enrollment/Student Body

Over 37 percent of the applicants were from outside California including applicants from all 50 states and 55 foreign countries. Santa Clara is consistently among the top 10 law schools nationwide in terms of ethnic diversity. The entering class for 2006 was 46 percent minorities and 48 percent women.

■ Library and Physical Facilities

The School of Law is on the 105-acre university campus. Towering palm trees, spacious lawns, and extensive flower gardens surround the Heafey Law Library. A traditional moot courtroom provides the setting for advocacy training and activities of the Edwin A. Heafey Jr. Center for Trial and Appellate Advocacy. Other facilities include Bergin Hall faculty office building, Bannan Hall with its technologically equipped classrooms, and Loyola Hall, where our law career services, Academic Success Program, and many other programs are located. Students also have access to other campus facilities, including computer laboratories, Cowell Student Health Center, Benson Memorial Center, and Pat Malley Fitness Center with its pool; basketball, volleyball, and racquetball courts; and steam room and sauna.

■ Curriculum

Full-time and part-time programs, Academic Success Program, 86 semester units required to graduate, over 200 courses available. Degrees available: JD, JD/MBA, LLM in International Law, LLM in US Law for Foreign Attorneys, and LLM in Intellectual Property. An academic orientation introduces first-year students to the study of law. The first-year curriculum is prescribed.

JD/MBA Combined-degree program is a powerful union of Santa Clara's nationally recognized School of Law and Leavey School of Business. This is an opportunity to earn both degrees in a full-time program lasting three and one-half to four years.

■ International Law Certificate

A specialized curriculum allows students to earn a Certificate in International Law. The Institute of International and Comparative Law sponsors summer law study programs in Munich, Germany; Strasbourg, France; Geneva, Switzerland; Oxford, England; Hong Kong; Singapore; Seoul, South Korea; Bangkok, Thailand; Ho Chi Minh City, Socialist Republic of Vietnam; Beijing, People's Republic of China; Kuala Lumpur, Malaysia; Tokyo, Japan; and Sydney, Australia. The institute is exploring opportunities for additional programs in Latin America and Eastern Europe. All of the programs, with the exception of Oxford, offer internships with law offices, corporations, or groups particularly suited to give students on-site observation and participation in areas of international law.

■ Computer and High Technology Law Certificate

Santa Clara has capitalized on its Silicon Valley location by establishing a specialized curriculum that emphasizes computer and high technology law. Students seeking an emphasis on high technology issues can enroll in courses such as patent law, copyright, biotechnology law, and technology licensing. They may also intern with a leading high tech firm and may earn a certificate in High Technology Law.

■ Public Interest and Social Justice Law Certificate

Students concerned with social issues, social justice, and public service can earn a Certificate in Public Interest. Santa Clara's Center for Social Justice and Public Service offers an impressive array of resources for students who want to focus on social justice and public interest work during their legal education and in practice. Santa Clara University is distinctive in making explicit its intention to evoke from students "a commitment to fashioning a more humane and just world."

■ Clinical Programs

The Santa Clara University Law Clinic allows students to practice law under the supervision of an experienced attorney. Students participate in all phases of a case from the initial client interview through the trial. Students have the opportunity to earn credit for work as law clerks with public agencies such as the district attorney or public defender, with legal aid offices, or with private law offices. Students may also work as judges' clerks in appellate courts, including the California Supreme Court; or trial courts, including the United States District Court and local superior court. Northern California Innocence Project (NCIP) is a clinical program developed by the Santa Clara University Criminal Defense Clinic. NCIP identifies prisoners with innocence claims and provides direct services to them. NCIP serves as a resource center for the legal community in innocence cases. Law students in the NCIP program investigate, evaluate, and where possible, pursue relief for claims of wrongful conviction.

Student Activities

The school's quarterly, *Santa Clara Law Review*, is published by a student editorial board. The *Computer and High Technology Law Journal* provides a practical resource for the high technology industry and the corresponding legal community. The new *Journal of International Law* is an Internet-based publication. Through the Student Bar Association and student-faculty committees, students participate in the decision processes of the law school.

Admission

A faculty committee reviews all applications. No one is automatically accepted or rejected. When the LSAT is repeated, the highest score received is used.

Recognizing the critical need for persons from underrepresented groups to gain access to the legal profession, the School of Law has adopted a policy for special admission. Applicants may request a special consideration because of race, disadvantaged background, or other factors. Over 46 percent of the entering class is composed of students of color and 48 percent are women.

Applicants are encouraged to visit the School of Law. Arrangements can be made through the Admissions Office to attend a law class, meet with an admission counselor, or tour the campus.

Career Services

The Career Services Office serves as a liaison between students and prospective employers. Firms, businesses, and government agencies interview on campus each year. Graduates find employment in the legal profession throughout the 50 states. Office services include individual career counseling and a series of workshops in job-search strategies. Strong alumni support assists students in all stages of their career exploration and development. Current employment statistics are on the school's website: *www.scu.edu/law*.

Applicant Profile

Santa Clara University School of Law
This grid includes only applicants who earned 120–180 LSAT scores under standard administrations.

LSAT Score	3.75 +		3.50–3.74		3.25–3.49		3.00–3.24		2.75–2.99		2.50–2.74		2.25–2.49		2.00–2.24		Below 2.00		No GPA		Total	
	Apps	Adm	Apps	Adm	Apps	Adm	Apps	Adm	Apps	Adm	Apps	Adm	Apps	Adm	Apps	Adm	Apps	Adm	Apps	Adm	Apps	Adm
175–180	2	2	0	0	1	1	1	1	0	0	0	0	0	0	0	0	0	0	1	1	4	4
170–174	18	18	6	5	9	7	4	3	6	5	1	1	1	0	0	0	0	0	3	2	46	40
165–169	46	45	43	43	38	38	34	33	21	14	13	5	7	4	1	1	1	1	11	10	206	185
160–164	110	108	149	147	130	129	89	84	55	29	31	14	18	2	9	1	1	1	11	10	603	525
155–159	118	106	267	205	275	178	205	96	113	21	55	10	18	0	6	2	2	0	20	7	1079	625
150–154	69	12	164	29	258	35	211	27	115	8	48	2	22	0	7	0	2	0	16	3	912	116
145–149	21	0	80	0	114	2	104	0	80	0	32	0	17	0	0	0	0	0	12	0	460	2
140–144	12	0	22	0	36	0	57	0	41	0	27	0	14	0	5	0	1	0	1	0	61	0
135–139	0	0	4	0	9	0	14	0	16	0	11	0	3	0	2	0	0	0	1	0	16	0
130–134	1	0	1	0	1	0	2	0	3	0	5	0	0	0	1	0	0	0	0	0	3	0
125–129	0	0	1	0	0	0	0	0	0	0	1	0	0	0	0	0	0	0	0	0	1	0
120–124	0	0	0	0	0	0	0	0	0	0	0	0	1	0	0	0	0	0	0	0	1	0
Total	397	291	737	429	871	390	721	244	450	77	224	32	101	6	33	4	6	1	68	23	3608	1497

Apps = Number of Applicants
Adm = Number Admitted
Reflects 99% of the total applicant pool.

Seattle University School of Law

901 12th Avenue, Sullivan Hall
Seattle, WA 98122-1090
Phone: 206.398.4200; Fax: 206.398.4058
E-mail: lawadmis@seattleu.edu; Website: www.law.seattleu.edu

ABA
Approved
Since
1994

The Basics

Type of school	Private
Term	Semester
Application deadline	4/1
Application fee	$50
Financial aid deadline	
Can first year start other than fall?	Yes
Student to faculty ratio	15.6 to 1
Does the university offer:	
housing restricted to law students?	No
graduate housing for which law students are eligible?	Yes

Faculty and Administrators

	Total		Men		Women		Minorities	
	Fall	Spr	Fall	Spr	Fall	Spr	Fall	Spr
Full-time	53	54	28	29	25	25	15	12
Other Full-time	3	1	3	1	0	0	0	0
Deans, librarians, & others who teach	14	14	6	6	8	8	2	3
Part-time	40	51	31	28	9	23	4	5
Total	110	120	68	64	42	56	21	20

Curriculum

	Full-time	Part-time
Typical first-year section size	90	71
Is there typically a "small section" of the first-year class, other than Legal Writing, taught by full-time faculty	No	No
If yes, typical size offered last year		
# of classroom course titles beyond first-year curriculum	149	

# of upper division courses, excluding seminars with an enrollment:		
Under 25	112	
25–49	54	
50–74	18	
75–99	18	
100+	1	

# of seminars	42	
# of seminar positions available	842	
# of seminar positions filled	493	47
# of positions available in simulation courses	810	
# of simulation positions filled	364	209
# of positions available in faculty supervised clinical courses	196	
# of faculty supervised clinical positions filled	141	12
# involved in field placements	138	4
# involved in law journals	98	6
# involved in interschool competitions	38	1
# of credit hours required to graduate	90	

JD Enrollment and Ethnicity

	Men		Women		Full-time		Part-time		1st-year		Total		JD Degs. Awd.
	#	%	#	%	#	%	#	%	#	%	#	%	
African Amer.	24	4.7	23	4.0	33	3.8	14	6.2	17	5.0	47	4.3	14
Amer. Indian	7	1.4	9	1.6	11	1.3	5	2.2	6	1.7	16	1.5	1
Asian Amer.	53	10.3	89	15.5	122	14.1	20	8.8	44	12.8	142	13.0	44
Mex. Amer.	18	3.5	14	2.4	28	3.2	4	1.8	11	3.2	32	2.9	9
Puerto Rican	6	1.2	3	0.5	7	0.8	2	0.9	3	0.9	9	0.8	2
Hispanic	6	1.2	13	2.3	14	1.6	5	2.2	5	1.5	19	1.7	5
Total Minority	114	22.1	151	26.3	215	24.9	50	22.0	86	25.1	265	24.3	75
For. Nation.	5	1.0	4	0.7	9	1.0	0	0.0	3	0.9	9	0.8	6
Caucasian	366	71.1	400	69.6	601	69.6	165	72.7	240	70.0	766	70.3	246
Unknown	30	5.8	20	3.5	38	4.4	12	5.3	13	3.8	50	4.6	16
Total	515	47.2	575	52.8	863	79.2	227	20.8	343	31.5	1090		343

Transfers

Transfers in	12
Transfers out	9

Tuition and Fees

	Resident	Nonresident
Full-time	$27,826	$27,826
Part-time	$18,552	$18,552

Living Expenses

Estimated living expenses for singles

Living on campus	Living off campus	Living at home
$15,797	$15,797	$8,705

Seattle University School of Law

ABA Approved Since 1994

GPA and LSAT Scores

	Total	Full-time	Part-time
# of apps	3,151	2,880	271
# of offers	928	834	94
# of matrics	352	289	63
75% GPA	3.63	3.64	3.58
Median GPA	3.38	3.40	3.20
25% GPA	3.19	3.20	2.91
75% LSAT	160	160	161
Median LSAT	157	158	156
25% LSAT	155	155	153

Grants and Scholarships (from prior year)

	Total		Full-time		Part-time	
	#	%	#	%	#	%
Total # of students	1,109		874		235	
Total # receiving grants	479	43.2	407	46.6	72	30.6
Less than 1/2 tuition	465	41.9	404	46.2	61	26.0
Half to full tuition	14	1.3	3	0.3	11	4.7
Full tuition	0	0.0	0	0.0	0	0.0
More than full tuition	0	0.0	0	0.0	0	0.0
Median grant amount			$7,000		$5,500	

Informational and Library Resources

# of volumes and volume equivalents	359,282
# of titles	81,874
# of active serial subscriptions	2,930
Study seating capacity inside the library	410
# of full-time professional librarians	16
Hours per week library is open	119
# of open, wired connections available to students	2,116
# of networked computers available for use by students	17
# of simultaneous wireless users	9,999
Require computer?	Yes

JD Attrition (from prior year)

	Academic	Other	Total	
	#	#	#	%
1st year	3	14	17	4.8
2nd year	0	2	2	0.6
3rd year	1	0	1	0.3
4th year	0	0	0	0.0

Employment (9 months after graduation)

	Total	Percentage
Employment status known	348	100.0
Employment status unknown	0	0.0
Employed	336	96.6
Pursuing graduate degrees	7	2.0
Unemployed seeking employment	0	0.0
Unemployed not seeking employment	2	0.6
Unemployed and studying for the bar	3	0.9

Type of Employment

# employed in law firms	151	44.9
# employed in business and industry	94	28.0
# employed in government	41	12.2
# employed in public interest	29	8.6
# employed as judicial clerks	17	5.1
# employed in academia	4	1.2

Geographic Location

# employed in state	289	86.0
# employed in foreign countries	3	0.9
# of states where employed		16

Bar Passage Rates

Jurisdiction	Washington		
Exam	Sum 05	Win 06	Total
# from school taking bar for the first time	229	69	298
School's pass rate for all first-time takers	78%	77%	78%
State's pass rate for all first-time takers	75%	74%	75%

Seattle University School of Law

901 12th Avenue, Sullivan Hall
Seattle, WA 98122-1090
Phone: 206.398.4200; Fax: 206.398.4058
E-mail: lawadmis@seattleu.edu; Website: www.law.seattleu.edu

■ Introduction

Seattle University School of Law is a vital part of Seattle University, the Northwest's largest independent university. Here students are trained to lead and serve others with integrity and compassion by faculty dedicated to their growth in the law. In our community, curriculum, and programs, the School of Law as a Jesuit institution seeks to reflect a tradition of academic distinction and open inquiry.

The School of Law serves an impressive body of students, whose diversity encompasses age, life experience, and cultural heritage. Fittingly, the law school has been recognized nationally for its diverse faculty and welcoming environment for older students. Home to the only part-time legal education program in the state of Washington, Seattle University School of Law educates lawyers who distinguish themselves through their outstanding legal skills and their dedication to law in the service of justice.

The law school is fully accredited by the ABA and holds full membership in AALS. Students may pursue a Juris Doctor or an LLM in American Legal Studies (limited to students with law degrees from non-US institutions).

Sullivan Hall, home to the School of Law, lies on the eastern boundary of Seattle University's 42-acre campus. The five-floor, handsomely appointed structure features a street-front law clinic, media-equipped classrooms, a modern and impressive law library, a spacious courtroom, and comfortable activity areas. Wireless connectivity is available throughout the entire building, allowing students to use laptops to connect to classes, the SU law community, and the Internet. Together, these amenities provide an attractive and accommodating setting in which students learn and thrive.

■ Location

Seattle University School of Law sits in a landscaped, urban setting in the First Hill neighborhood of Seattle, less than a mile from downtown. A sophisticated city, Seattle is also one of the most livable cities in the United States, offering a rich mix of business, culture, adventure, and industry that provides a natural extension of our classrooms.

Being minutes from a vibrant downtown only enhances prospects for students seeking career-building opportunities. We are part of a strong legal community that welcomes new talent, and our students pursue summer and school-year employment with multinational and regional law firms, public agencies, private corporations, and boutique partnerships whose legal specialties reflect the special interests of Northwest natives.

■ Focus Area Curriculum

After completion of rigorous first-year studies that emphasize sound legal analytical skills, the law school curriculum allows students to select a primary area of interest and support that interest with enrollment in a prescribed range of courses. Students may focus their upper-division legal studies in one of 14 substantive areas, including Civil Advocacy, Criminal Practice, Environmental Law, Health Law, Labor and Employment, and Real Estate Law.

■ Faculty

Seattle University law faculty always places teaching first. This means instruction uses numerous pedagogical styles, from Socratic classroom dialogue to drafting laboratories and seminar discussion.

While emphasizing the importance of teaching, faculty also recognize the critical role that scholarship plays in academic excellence. Since 1997, law school faculty members have published more than 20 books, 25 book chapters, and 100 articles that have appeared in law reviews—including several of the most frequently cited publications—and specialized journals.

We do not choose among teaching, scholarship, and service. Our faculty engages in cutting-edge scholarship while at the same time engaging with our students and challenging them to not only learn but to live the law, through clinical programs and externship. We value innovation and creativity that enrich the classroom experience and deepen understanding.

■ Academic Enrichment Programs

Access to Justice Institute (AtJI)—The Access to Justice Institute is an outgrowth of the law school's dedication to social justice and the need to deliver legal services to underrepresented communities. Through the institute and under the supervision of an attorney, students can work at one of AtJI's Community Justice Centers directly serving low-income persons. The institute also sponsors in-house projects, including the Immigration Court Project, the Language Bank, and the Unemployment Insurance for Battered Women Project. Over 300 law students volunteer with AtJI each year.

Center on Corporations, Law, and Society—The Center on Corporations, Law, and Society serves as a platform for enhanced scholarly inquiry while providing a forum for sustained discussion among academics, legal practitioners, business leaders, activists, policymakers, and citizens on the complex and important relationships between business enterprises and their many stakeholders.

International Initiatives—Seattle University School of Law is fast becoming a leader in global legal education by expanding its international reach to offer students and faculty a greater world view. The law school is creating new partnerships with outside faculty and institutions, both in the United States and abroad. The School of Law aims to promote the understanding that in order to be a competent professional in today's legal world, lawyers must be conversant in both global and national legal developments. Among the many compelling programs in this area are the International and Comparative Law Program and the Center for Global Mexico/Latin American Initiatives. In keeping with our mission, programs emphasize issues of social justice on a global level.

■ Admission and Financial Aid

In admission decisions, the law school places equal emphasis on three factors: (1) LSAT performance; (2) the undergraduate academic record; and (3) personal achievements, especially talents or factors that contribute to our law school community in special and significant ways.

We also admit a limited group of applicants annually through a wholly discretionary process. The law school's **Alternative Admission Program** addresses those cases where traditional admission criteria are inadequate predictors of success in law school and in the practice of law. Members of historically disadvantaged, underrepresented, or physically challenged groups are among those individuals considered for this program (limited to no more than 10 percent of the entering class).

The law school's **Scholarship Program** is among the most ambitious in the region, awarding over $3 million per year to approximately 350 students. Its objectives are twofold: to offer to all students—regardless of economic or social background—the advantages of a private legal education; and to recognize and reward—regardless of financial need—the achievements and outstanding potential of the most highly qualified students in the applicant pool. Upon admission to the School of Law, all entering students are automatically considered for scholarships.

Consistent with preparing students who are committed to contributing to the common good by shaping an equitable legal system, the **Loan Repayment Assistance Program** and the three-year, full-tuition **Scholars for Justice Award** support students and graduates who choose full-time public interest legal careers as licensed attorneys doing law-related, public interest work in both content and spirit.

Applicant Profile

Seattle University School of Law

LSAT Score	GPA									
	3.75 +	3.50–3.74	3.25–3.49	3.00–3.24	2.75–2.99	2.50–2.74	2.25–2.49	2.00–2.24	Below 2.00	No GPA
175–180	■	■	■	■	■	▨				■
170–174	■	■	■	■	■	▨				■
165–169	■	■	■	■	■	■				■
160–164	■	■	■	■	■	■				■
155–159	■	■	■	■	▨					▨
150–154	▨	▨	▨	▨						
145–149										
140–144										
135–139										
130–134										
125–129										
120–124										

■ Likely   ▨ Possible   (blank) Unlikely

Of applicants in the Unlikely category, about one in 20 candidates was admitted to the Alternative Admission Program.

Seton Hall University School of Law

One Newark Center
Newark, NJ 07102-5210
Phone: 888.415.7271, 973.642.8747; Fax: 973.642.8876
E-mail: admitme@shu.edu; Website: http://law.shu.edu

The Basics

Type of school	Private
Term	Semester
Application deadline	4/1
Application fee	$65
Financial aid deadline	4/1
Can first year start other than fall?	No
Student to faculty ratio	15.2 to 1
Does the university offer:	
housing restricted to law students?	No
graduate housing for which law students are eligible?	No

Faculty and Administrators

	Total		Men		Women		Minorities	
	Fall	Spr	Fall	Spr	Fall	Spr	Fall	Spr
Full-time	53	54	35	35	18	19	10	9
Other Full-time	1	1	1	1	0	0	0	0
Deans, librarians, & others who teach	8	9	2	2	6	7	3	3
Part-time	80	83	56	57	24	26	10	9
Total	142	147	94	95	48	52	23	21

Curriculum

	Full-time	Part-time
Typical first-year section size	80	110
Is there typically a "small section" of the first-year class, other than Legal Writing, taught by full-time faculty	No	No
If yes, typical size offered last year		
# of classroom course titles beyond first-year curriculum	145	
# of upper division courses, excluding seminars with an enrollment: Under 25	76	
25–49	54	
50–74	25	
75–99	13	
100+	0	
# of seminars	70	
# of seminar positions available	1,176	
# of seminar positions filled	615	423
# of positions available in simulation courses	1,083	
# of simulation positions filled	554	338
# of positions available in faculty supervised clinical courses	108	
# of faculty supervised clinical positions filled	98	6
# involved in field placements	137	14
# involved in law journals	112	6
# involved in interschool competitions	37	4
# of credit hours required to graduate	85	

JD Enrollment and Ethnicity

	Men		Women		Full-time		Part-time		1st-year		Total		JD Degs. Awd.
	#	%	#	%	#	%	#	%	#	%	#	%	
African Amer.	15	2.5	22	4.6	20	2.8	17	4.6	12	3.3	37	3.4	13
Amer. Indian	1	0.2	1	0.2	0	0.0	2	0.5	0	0.0	2	0.2	1
Asian Amer.	41	6.7	52	10.8	54	7.4	39	10.7	24	6.6	93	8.5	26
Mex. Amer.	0	0.0	4	0.8	1	0.1	3	0.8	2	0.6	4	0.4	0
Puerto Rican	10	1.6	3	0.6	8	1.1	5	1.4	1	0.3	13	1.2	5
Hispanic	11	1.8	24	5.0	16	2.2	19	5.2	10	2.8	35	3.2	23
Total Minority	78	12.8	106	21.9	99	13.6	85	23.2	49	13.5	184	16.8	68
For. Nation.	7	1.1	9	1.9	7	1.0	9	2.5	5	1.4	16	1.5	6
Caucasian	524	85.9	367	76.0	619	85.1	272	74.3	307	84.6	891	81.5	296
Unknown	1	0.2	1	0.2	2	0.3	0	0.0	2	0.6	2	0.2	0
Total	610	55.8	483	44.2	727	66.5	366	33.5	363	33.2	1093		370

Transfers

Transfers in	11
Transfers out	10

Tuition and Fees

	Resident	Nonresident
Full-time	$35,400	$35,400
Part-time	$26,054	$26,054

Living Expenses

Estimated living expenses for singles

Living on campus	Living off campus	Living at home
N/A	$17,345	$10,070

Seton Hall University School of Law

ABA Approved Since 1951

GPA and LSAT Scores

	Total	Full-time	Part-time
# of apps	3,005	2,400	605
# of offers	1,090	714	376
# of matrics	359	192	167
75% GPA	3.58	3.66	3.48
Median GPA	3.33	3.40	3.25
25% GPA	3.08	3.17	2.98
75% LSAT	160	163	156
Median LSAT	157	160	154
25% LSAT	154	158	151

Grants and Scholarships (from prior year)

	Total		Full-time		Part-time	
	#	%	#	%	#	%
Total # of students	1,142		766		376	
Total # receiving grants	374	32.7	344	44.9	30	8.0
Less than 1/2 tuition	237	20.8	207	27.0	30	8.0
Half to full tuition	79	6.9	79	10.3	0	0.0
Full tuition	58	5.1	58	7.6	0	0.0
More than full tuition	0	0.0	0	0.0	0	0.0
Median grant amount			$16,000		$3,000	

Informational and Library Resources

# of volumes and volume equivalents	453,919
# of titles	183,283
# of active serial subscriptions	9,900
Study seating capacity inside the library	544
# of full-time professional librarians	8
Hours per week library is open	88
# of open, wired connections available to students	126
# of networked computers available for use by students	167
# of simultaneous wireless users	2,000
Require computer?	Yes

JD Attrition (from prior year)

	Academic	Other	Total	
	#	#	#	%
1st year	19	18	37	9.8
2nd year	5	3	8	2.6
3rd year	0	1	1	0.3
4th year	1	0	1	1.6

Employment (9 months after graduation)

	Total	Percentage
Employment status known	401	96.9
Employment status unknown	13	3.1
Employed	386	96.3
Pursuing graduate degrees	1	0.2
Unemployed seeking employment	4	1.0
Unemployed not seeking employment	4	1.0
Unemployed and studying for the bar	6	1.5

Type of Employment

# employed in law firms	150	38.9
# employed in business and industry	43	11.1
# employed in government	22	5.7
# employed in public interest	7	1.8
# employed as judicial clerks	150	38.9
# employed in academia	1	0.3

Geographic Location

# employed in state	264	68.4
# employed in foreign countries	3	0.8
# of states where employed	18	

Bar Passage Rates

Jurisdiction	New Jersey			New York		
Exam	Sum 05	Win 06	Total	Sum 05	Win 06	Total
# from school taking bar for the first time	342	34	376	258	14	272
School's pass rate for all first-time takers	85%	65%	84%	89%	43%	86%
State's pass rate for all first-time takers	78%	73%	77%	76%	61%	74%

Seton Hall University School of Law

Office of Admissions, One Newark Center
Newark, NJ 07102-5210
Phone: 888.415.7271, 973.642.8747; Fax: 973.642.8876
E-mail: admitme@shu.edu; Website: http://law.shu.edu

■ Introduction

Founded in 1951, Seton Hall University School of Law is the only private law school in the state of New Jersey. While it values its Catholic identity, the law school is a pluralistic community representing a diversity of racial, cultural, religious, and socioeconomic backgrounds. The school is consistently recognized for its outstanding teaching and high level of student satisfaction.

■ One Newark Center, Our Home

Rich in history and culture, Newark is a city to explore. Whatever your interest, you'll find it here—the performing and visual arts, sports, great food, and captivating architecture are within easy reach. The law school is a block from Newark's Penn Station, from which a 20-minute train ride takes students to Manhattan and the world's largest law firms. Students can walk to Newark's major law firms, government agencies, and the federal and state courthouses. Housing options are extensive. Students enjoy living in nearby historic buildings and with its expansive network of train lines, Newark is within easy reach of New York City, Hoboken, Jersey City, and many suburban communities. The law school's open, welcoming design is a reflection of the faculty and administration's commitment to students. Offices, classrooms, moot courtrooms, and the library are interconnected by balconies overlooking a striking five-story, glass-encased atrium. The entire law school complex is saturated with Wi-Fi Internet connectivity, including access to wireless printing. The building has unusually large student space, including newly renovated student journal and organization offices, lounges, meeting rooms, a chapel, and a cafeteria. The Peter W. Rodino Jr. Law Library is located on three floors and accommodates 600 students and 100 terminals for student use. The Law Library's collection contains more than 425,000 volumes covering a wide array of law and law-related subjects. Health and Intellectual Property law are areas of particular strength. The Rodino Library is a depository for US government documents and for New Jersey state documents.

■ Curriculum

The JD requires 85 credits to graduate and may be completed as a full-time or a part-time program. The school offers both a day and an evening program following a semester calendar. The program emphasizes humanistic principles and encourages their synthesis with knowledge of the law and professional responsibility. The law school is committed to in-depth training in legal writing and research.

In addition to the core required courses, more than 200 courses are offered in a wide range of areas grouped as follows: Commercial Law, Corporate Law, Criminal Law and Procedure, Environmental Law, Health and Drug Law, History and Philosophy of Law, Intellectual Property and Entertainment Law, International Legal Studies, Labor and Employment Law, Personal and Family Law, Property and Estates Law, Public Interest, and Taxation. Externships, journals, pro bono, and moot court programs are also included in the school's offerings.

Master of Laws (LLM) and a Master of Science in Jurisprudence (MSJ) are also offered in the areas of health, science, and technology law.

■ Public Interest

Seton Hall School of Law is committed to public interest and clinical education. Through the Seton Hall Law Center for Social Justice, students are provided with one of the most comprehensive clinical and pro bono programs offered by any New York area law school. The school's clinics presently represent more than 3,000 disadvantaged and underrepresented clients each year in a wide range of litigation such as civil litigation, family law, impact litigation, immigration and human rights, and juvenile justice. Clinical projects include International Human Rights/Rule of Law and Urban Revitalization. The Center for Social Justice provides services in the public's interest while training and mentoring future attorneys whose careers will be dedicated in whole or in part to public interest work. Students can take part in various programs geared towards public interest beginning as early as their first year, including clinical programs, externships, and pro bono assignments. Scholarship and other financial assistance are available through the Distinguished Public Interest Scholarship, Summer Public Interest Law Fellowship, and Public Interest Loan Repayment Assistance Program.

■ Special Programs

Internships—The law school offers judicial internships with justices of the New Jersey Supreme Court, judges of the New Jersey Appellate Division, Chancery and Law Courts, the Third Circuit Court of Appeals, the US District Courts, and the US Bankruptcy Courts. There are myriad internship programs with nonprofit and government agencies.

Externships—Externship offerings include environmental law, health law, entertainment law, international organizations, the European Court of Justice or Court of First Instance, the Federal Public Defender, Securities and Exchange Commission, New York Stock Exchange, Internal Revenue Service, National Labor Relations Board, and US Attorney.

Concentrations—The law school offers concentrations in Health Law and Intellectual Property Law that allow students to study a specialized curriculum developed by faculty in consultation with attorneys and government officials working in the field. The breadth and depth of both curricula is unparalleled. In addition to coursework, students have the opportunity to participate in externships and take part in frequent symposia and colloquia.

Joint-degree Programs—JD/MBA—A four-year program with Seton Hall University Stillman School of Business, **JD/MADIR**—A four-year program with Seton Hall University School of Diplomacy and International Relations, **JD/MD**—A six-year program with the Robert Wood Johnson Medical School of the University of Medicine and Dentistry of New Jersey, **MSJ/MD**—A five-year program with the Robert Wood Johnson Medical School of the University of Medicine and Dentistry of New Jersey.

Journals—The law school offers students an opportunity to advance legal scholarship through four student journals—the

Seton Hall University School of Law

Seton Hall Law Review, Seton Hall Legislative Journal, Seton Hall Sports and Entertainment Law Journal, and the *Circuit Review.*

International Study—Each summer the law school cosponsors, with the University of Parma, a course of international studies for American law students in Parma, Italy. The law school also offers a summer program for the study of law in the Middle East at the American University of Cairo in Egypt and a program at Galway University in Ireland focusing on intellectual property.

LLM and MSJ Degrees—Seton Hall offers an LLM degree in health law, which provides attorneys the opportunity to broadly explore health law and policy or focus more narrowly on courses designed for the lawyer planning to represent the health provider, payer, or regulator; the pharmaceutical company; or the biotechnology company.

Seton Hall also offers a Master of Science in Jurisprudence (MSJ) degree in Health Law, Science, and Technology, which provides professionals with a solid foundation in legal aspects of health care and intellectual property regulation. Such a concentrated exposure to health law issues can be vital to medical directors, regulatory and contract compliance officers, risk and case managers, employee benefits personnel, lobbyists, and pharmaceutical employees. Full- and part-time programs are available for both the LLM and MSJ degrees.

Moot Court Program—Students represent the law school in the National Moot Court competition as well as in 10 interschool competitions focusing on specific areas of law.

LEO Institute—The Monsignor Thomas Fahy Legal Education Opportunities Institute provides an intense, summer-long classroom experience for educationally disadvantaged students. Applicants from disadvantaged groups, regardless of race, religion, age, sex, sexual orientation, or national origin, may wish to inquire about this program.

■ Student Activities

There are over 35 student organizations at Seton Hall Law, representing various personal and professional interests. The Student Bar Association (SBA) and other student organizations sponsor a variety of practical, social, and educational events. The SBA plays a major role in orientation, and sponsors a holiday party each November in Newark and a Barristers' Ball in the spring. Organizations sponsor career seminars focused on different areas of the law, host symposiums and panel discussions that focus on current legal and societal issues, and plan annual banquets and networking receptions during the year.

■ Committed to Your Success

At Seton Hall you will find a school committed to your success. Our first-time bar passage rates are among the highest both in New York and New Jersey. The majority of our students participate in hands-on clinical training or externships, and 95 percent of our students are employed within 9 months of graduation. Seton Hall Law maintains a proactive Career Services Office staffed by full-time counselors who assist students in defining their career objectives and goals and establishing contact with employers. Each fall and spring, law firms, accounting firms, and public interest and governmental employers conduct interviews through the school's On-Campus Interview Program. Alumni are practicing nationwide.

Applicant Profile

Seton Hall University School of Law
This grid includes only applicants who earned 120–180 LSAT scores under standard administrations.

LSAT Score	3.75+		3.50–3.74		3.25–3.49		3.00–3.24		2.75–2.99		2.50–2.74		2.25–2.49		2.00–2.24		Below 2.00		No GPA		Total	
	Apps	Adm	Apps	Adm	Apps	Adm	Apps	Adm	Apps	Adm	Apps	Adm	Apps	Adm	Apps	Adm	Apps	Adm	Apps	Adm	Apps	Adm
175–180	0	0	0	0	0	0	0	0	0	0	0	0	0	0	0	0	0	0	0	0	19	18
170–174	4	4	3	2	1	1	7	7	3	3	1	1	0	0	0	0	0	0	0	0	79	76
165–169	14	14	16	16	16	15	13	11	11	11	5	5	2	2	1	1	1	1	0	0	338	312
160–164	41	39	62	59	97	91	56	52	37	34	22	18	15	13	5	4	1	1	2	1	722	474
155–159	85	72	137	111	176	130	149	90	93	43	39	10	21	5	11	7	2	1	9	5	849	174
150–154	61	24	156	37	207	51	185	36	124	15	62	4	26	2	14	0	1	0	13	5	529	31
145–149	38	2	84	8	92	8	116	9	98	2	54	1	29	1	7	0	1	0	10	0	313	16
140–144	15	2	39	2	43	4	58	3	61	4	43	1	29	0	11	0	3	0	11	0	133	1
135–139	5	0	9	0	18	0	26	0	26	1	16	0	16	0	8	0	2	0	7	0	49	0
130–134	1	0	5	0	2	0	7	0	10	0	7	0	5	0	7	0	3	0	2	0	10	0
125–129	0	0	0	0	1	0	1	0	1	0	3	0	2	0	0	0	1	0	1	0	4	0
120–124	0	0	1	0	0	0	0	0	0	0	0	0	1	0	1	0	0	0	1	0	3045	1102
Total	264	157	512	235	653	300	618	208	464	113	252	40	146	23	65	12	15	3	56	11	3045	1102

Apps = Number of Applicants
Adm = Number Admitted
Reflects 99% of the total applicant pool.

SMU Dedman School of Law

PO Box 750110
Dallas, TX 75275-0110
Phone: 214.768.2550, 888.768.5291; Fax: 214.768.2549
E-mail: lawadmit@smu.edu; Website: www.law.smu.edu

*ABA
Approved
Since
1927*

The Basics

Type of school	Private
Term	Semester
Application deadline	12/1 2/15 4/1
Application fee	$60
Financial aid deadline	4/1
Can first year start other than fall?	No
Student to faculty ratio	14.5 to 1
Does the university offer:	
housing restricted to law students?	No
graduate housing for which law students are eligible?	No

Faculty and Administrators

	Total		Men		Women		Minorities	
	Fall	Spr	Fall	Spr	Fall	Spr	Fall	Spr
Full-time	46	44	29	26	17	18	8	8
Other Full-time	4	4	3	3	1	1	0	0
Deans, librarians, & others who teach	2	2	1	1	1	1	0	0
Part-time	23	39	18	33	5	6	0	0
Total	75	89	51	63	24	26	8	8

Curriculum

	Full-time	Part-time
Typical first-year section size	95	90
Is there typically a "small section" of the first-year class, other than Legal Writing, taught by full-time faculty	No	No
If yes, typical size offered last year		
# of classroom course titles beyond first-year curriculum	134	

# of upper division courses, excluding seminars with an enrollment:		
Under 25	77	
25–49	35	
50–74	15	
75–99	12	
100+	2	

# of seminars	17	
# of seminar positions available	320	
# of seminar positions filled	297	12
# of positions available in simulation courses	344	
# of simulation positions filled	274	19
# of positions available in faculty supervised clinical courses	161	
# of faculty supervised clinical positions filled	161	0
# involved in field placements	64	0
# involved in law journals	193	18
# involved in interschool competitions	66	5
# of credit hours required to graduate	87	

JD Enrollment and Ethnicity

	Men		Women		Full-time		Part-time		1st-year		Total		JD Degs. Awd.
	#	%	#	%	#	%	#	%	#	%	#	%	
African Amer.	12	2.5	26	6.4	24	4.3	14	4.3	8	2.7	38	4.3	8
Amer. Indian	5	1.1	3	0.7	5	0.9	3	0.9	2	0.7	8	0.9	1
Asian Amer.	49	10.3	36	8.8	59	10.6	26	7.9	34	11.6	85	9.6	20
Mex. Amer.	7	1.5	5	1.2	9	1.6	3	0.9	3	1.0	12	1.4	16
Puerto Rican	0	0.0	1	0.2	1	0.2	0	0.0	1	0.3	1	0.1	0
Hispanic	19	4.0	36	8.8	36	6.5	19	5.8	19	6.5	55	6.2	0
Total Minority	92	19.4	107	26.2	134	24.2	65	19.8	67	22.9	199	22.6	45
For. Nation.	1	0.2	2	0.5	2	0.4	1	0.3	1	0.3	3	0.3	0
Caucasian	352	74.3	279	68.4	389	70.2	242	73.8	225	76.8	631	71.5	215
Unknown	29	6.1	20	4.9	29	5.2	20	6.1	0	0.0	49	5.6	4
Total	474	53.7	408	46.3	554	62.8	328	37.2	293	33.2	882		264

Transfers

Transfers in	30
Transfers out	2

Tuition and Fees

	Resident	Nonresident
Full-time	$32,844	$32,844
Part-time	$24,633	$24,633

Living Expenses

Estimated living expenses for singles

Living on campus	Living off campus	Living at home
$15,700	$15,700	$15,700

SMU Dedman School of Law

ABA
Approved
Since
1927

GPA and LSAT Scores

	Total	Full-time	Part-time
# of apps	2,608	2,066	542
# of offers	630	455	175
# of matrics	293	180	113
75% GPA	3.80	3.83	3.67
Median GPA	3.54	3.70	3.46
25% GPA	3.23	3.33	3.01
75% LSAT	163	164	160
Median LSAT	161	163	157
25% LSAT	154	158	151

Grants and Scholarships (from prior year)

	Total #	Total %	Full-time #	Full-time %	Part-time #	Part-time %
Total # of students	829		618		211	
Total # receiving grants	465	56.1	434	70.2	31	14.7
Less than 1/2 tuition	345	41.6	314	50.8	31	14.7
Half to full tuition	87	10.5	87	14.1	0	0.0
Full tuition	27	3.3	27	4.4	0	0.0
More than full tuition	6	0.7	6	1.0	0	0.0
Median grant amount			$14,000		$3,000	

Informational and Library Resources

# of volumes and volume equivalents	614,677
# of titles	224,059
# of active serial subscriptions	4,699
Study seating capacity inside the library	732
# of full-time professional librarians	6
Hours per week library is open	104
# of open, wired connections available to students	0
# of networked computers available for use by students	113
# of simultaneous wireless users	1,048
Require computer?	No

JD Attrition (from prior year)

	Academic #	Other #	Total #	Total %
1st year	2	5	7	2.4
2nd year	1	5	6	2.2
3rd year	1	2	3	1.1
4th year	0	0	0	0.0

Employment (9 months after graduation)

	Total	Percentage
Employment status known	265	99.6
Employment status unknown	1	0.4
Employed	248	93.6
Pursuing graduate degrees	4	1.5
Unemployed seeking employment	3	1.1
Unemployed not seeking employment	8	3.0
Unemployed and studying for the bar	2	0.8

Type of Employment

# employed in law firms	159	64.1
# employed in business and industry	25	10.1
# employed in government	40	16.1
# employed in public interest	5	2.0
# employed as judicial clerks	14	5.6
# employed in academia	5	2.0

Geographic Location

# employed in state	216	87.1
# employed in foreign countries	0	0.0
# of states where employed	15	

Bar Passage Rates

Jurisdiction	Texas		
Exam	Sum 05	Win 06	Total
# from school taking bar for the first time	224	18	242
School's pass rate for all first-time takers	88%	89%	88%
State's pass rate for all first-time takers	81%	77%	80%

SMU Dedman School of Law

The information on these pages was provided by the law school.

Office of Admissions, PO Box 750110
Dallas, TX 75275-0110
Phone: 214.768.2550, 888.768.5291; Fax: 214.768.2549
E-mail: lawadmit@smu.edu; Website: www.law.smu.edu

■ Introduction

Founded in 1925, SMU Dedman School of Law is located on a magnificent tree-lined campus in a beautiful residential neighborhood just five miles north of downtown Dallas. SMU offers an intimate learning community within a vibrant urban center.

With a relatively small entering class size, an outstanding teaching faculty, and distinguished guest lecturers, SMU offers a scholarly community with fantastic opportunities both inside and outside the classroom. SMU also has a well-rounded, diverse student body from approximately 200 colleges and universities, 30 states, and 20 countries.

■ Law School Campus

SMU offers a beautiful setting in which to pursue legal studies. The Law School Quadrangle, a six-acre self-contained corner of the campus, offers students convenient access to all law school facilities. The larger SMU campus offers students a variety of housing options, a childcare facility, a health center, and a new fitness/wellness center.

SMU recently completed a multimillion-dollar renovation to all of the law school classrooms. A four-story parking garage with 500 spaces is available exclusively for law student parking, and a new dining hall opened in 2005.

■ Curriculum

SMU offers seven degree programs: JD (full-time day or part-time evening), JD/MBA, JD/MA in Economics, LLM (General), LLM (Taxation), LLM (International and Comparative Law—for foreign attorneys only), and SJD.

Students find a sophisticated curriculum that complements SMU's wide breadth of class offerings with extensive depth of focus. The JD curriculum is designed to achieve the goal of producing lawyers who are capable and responsible professionals through its emphasis on providing substantive knowledge, ethical and moral training, and practical skills to serve their clients in local, national, and global communities.

Each JD student must complete 87 credit hours. Thirty-one of these hours comprise the mandatory first-year curriculum. After the first year, students must complete a course in professional responsibility and two upper-level writing courses (including an edited writing seminar in which an extensive scholarly, expository writing project is reviewed and critiqued by the professor).

SMU offers many small classes in which students will get to know their classmates and professors. Each entering class is divided into three sections (two full-time day and one part-time evening) of approximately 90 students each. Each semester, first-year students are assigned to a legal research, writing, and advocacy class of approximately 25 students. Over one-half of SMU's upper-division courses have fewer than 25 students, and approximately three-fourths have fewer than 50 students.

SMU's rich upper-division curricular offerings, with over 150 upper-division courses per year, offer students a wide range of courses and the freedom to tailor a program of study that furthers their professional and personal goals. With traditional strengths in business, litigation, tax, and international law, the curriculum extends to many areas, including intellectual property, health care, environmental, and family law.

SMU's tax, international, and general LLM programs are intended to enhance careers in the private practice of law, teaching, and public service by providing the opportunity for students who already have their basic law degree to increase their understanding of legal theory and policies. The LLM program in Comparative and International Law is the largest graduate program, enrolling approximately 40 students from about 20 countries each year. SMU has over 1,300 international alumni from over 70 countries, including many who hold significant positions in major international corporations, in the highest courts of their nations, and in other key government and private entities.

■ Student Activities and Law Reviews

Students are able to enhance their legal education by participating in numerous programs and conferences sponsored by various faculty and student groups and centers. Selected law students serve on five major journals for which they receive academic credit. Law students are able to expand their legal education experience through participating in over 20 moot court, trial advocacy, client counseling, and negotiation competitions held at the local, regional, national, and international level, and by becoming active members in over 30 student organizations.

■ Externships and Clinics

Externships offer students the opportunity to work at a government agency for up to two hours of course credit. Popular externships include those with the US Attorney, the SEC, and the EPA.

Clinics offer students an opportunity to engage in the practice of law for up to six hours of course credit. Currently SMU has eight clinical programs: civil litigation, criminal defense, criminal prosecution, tax, small business, consumer advocacy, mediation, and child advocacy.

■ Public Service

All students are required to perform 30 hours of public service prior to graduation. This model public service program not only allows the student to learn in a hands-on setting, but also provides an early exposure to pro bono practice, which is integral to the US legal system. SMU professors voluntarily hold themselves to this same requirement.

■ Overseas Study

SMU offers students an opportunity to study law for six weeks at University College at Oxford University in England.

■ Career Services and Bar Passage

SMU provides students with job placement assistance throughout their legal careers. The Career Services Office helps students develop their job search and career development skills, and partners with students in locating summer and permanent job opportunities.

SMU graduates fare very well in the legal market. Within nine months of graduation, 98 percent of the class of 2005 was employed. They had a median starting salary of $90,000 in the private sector and a median starting salary of $70,000 overall.

In July 2006, over 90 percent of SMU first-time test takers passed the Texas bar exam, while the average bar passage rate in Texas was less than 78 percent.

■ Admission

SMU looks for excellent, well-rounded students with strong academic backgrounds, life experiences, and perspectives that will enrich its educational community. Each application is considered in its entirety: LSAT score, undergraduate performance, graduate studies, work experience, activities, personal statement, and letters of recommendation are all read and evaluated. Applications can be downloaded from the Web.

■ Scholarships

SMU provides approximately 50 percent of its entering class with scholarship assistance. SMU law scholarships, including several full-tuition Hutchison scholarships, are awarded on the basis of the admission application, including the applicant's answer to an optional question (question 15 on the application). In addition, two private foundations, the Hatton W. Sumners Foundation and the Dallas Bar Foundation, fund and select five to nine additional full-tuition scholarships per entering class. Both foundations require a separate scholarship application, available from the SMU Admissions Office. The Sarah T. Hughes Scholarships, sponsored by the Dallas Bar Association, are awarded to outstanding minority applicants. The Sumners Scholars are selected from a competitive pool of applicants with strong academics and extracurricular activities. Both foundations require that the SMU application, the respective scholarship application, and all supporting documents be submitted no later than February 15. The law firm of Haynes and Boone, LLP, also awards scholarships to two exceptional minority students. A separate scholarship application is due by August 1, 2007.

Applicant Profile

SMU Dedman School of Law
This grid includes only applicants who earned 120–180 LSAT scores under standard administrations.

LSAT Score	3.75 +		3.50–3.74		3.25–3.49		3.00–3.24		2.75–2.99		2.50–2.74		2.25–2.49		2.00–2.24		Below 2.00		No GPA		Total	
	Apps	Adm	Apps	Adm	Apps	Adm	Apps	Adm	Apps	Adm	Apps	Adm	Apps	Adm	Apps	Adm	Apps	Adm	Apps	Adm	Apps	Adm
175–180	1	1	0	0	0	0	0	0	0	0	0	0	0	0	0	0	0	0	0	0	1	1
170–174	12	12	8	8	2	2	0	0	5	3	0	0	1	0	0	0	0	0	0	0	28	25
165–169	36	35	31	30	37	34	21	20	13	11	5	4	1	1	0	0	0	0	0	0	144	135
160–164	87	59	97	61	78	49	64	38	31	19	19	10	11	5	3	3	1	1	3	1	394	246
155–159	111	44	156	23	142	10	105	9	49	6	34	2	11	0	8	0	3	0	6	1	617	95
150–154	61	34	115	25	125	14	102	3	50	2	38	1	15	0	8	0	3	0	6	1	523	80
145–149	24	12	61	17	59	5	76	1	34	0	25	1	15	0	5	0	1	0	7	0	307	36
140–144	10	1	15	0	34	1	40	1	24	0	24	0	17	0	6	0	2	0	10	0	180	3
135–139	4	0	2	0	7	0	15	0	13	0	10	0	9	0	3	0	2	0	5	0	69	0
130–134	1	0	2	0	0	0	2	0	0	0	8	0	3	0	1	0	2	0	5	0	24	0
125–129	0	0	0	0	0	0	0	0	2	0	3	0	0	0	1	0	1	0	2	0	9	0
120–124	0	0	0	0	0	0	0	0	0	0	0	0	0	0	0	0	0	0	0	0	0	0
Total	347	198	487	164	484	115	425	72	221	41	166	18	83	6	28	3	10	1	45	3	2296	621

Apps = Number of Applicants
Adm = Number Admitted
Reflects 98% of the total applicant pool.

University of South Carolina School of Law

701 South Main Street
Columbia, SC 29208
Phone: 803.777.2771; Fax: 803.777.7751
E-mail: usclaw@law.sc.edu; Website: www.law.sc.edu

ABA Approved Since 1925

The Basics

Type of school	Public
Term	Semester
Application deadline	3/30
Application fee	$60
Financial aid deadline	3/15
Can first year start other than fall?	No
Student to faculty ratio	17.5 to 1
Does the university offer:	
housing restricted to law students?	No
graduate housing for which law students are eligible?	Yes

Faculty and Administrators

	Total		Men		Women		Minorities	
	Fall	Spr	Fall	Spr	Fall	Spr	Fall	Spr
Full-time	35	33	26	25	9	8	4	2
Other Full-time	1	0	1	0	0	0	0	0
Deans, librarians, & others who teach	9	10	4	5	5	5	0	0
Part-time	28	41	21	24	7	17	1	2
Total	**73**	**84**	**52**	**54**	**21**	**30**	**5**	**4**

Curriculum

	Full-time	Part-time
Typical first-year section size	77	0
Is there typically a "small section" of the first-year class, other than Legal Writing, taught by full-time faculty	No	No
If yes, typical size offered last year		
# of classroom course titles beyond first-year curriculum	111	

# of upper division courses, excluding seminars with an enrollment:		
	Under 25	57
	25–49	27
	50–74	12
	75–99	22
	100+	2

# of seminars	13	
# of seminar positions available	231	
# of seminar positions filled	178	0
# of positions available in simulation courses	320	
# of simulation positions filled	299	0
# of positions available in faculty supervised clinical courses	55	
# of faculty supervised clinical positions filled	53	0
# involved in field placements	7	0
# involved in law journals	236	0
# involved in interschool competitions	19	0
# of credit hours required to graduate	90	

JD Enrollment and Ethnicity

	Men		Women		Full-time		Part-time		1st-year		Total		JD Degs. Awd.
	#	%	#	%	#	%	#	%	#	%	#	%	
African Amer.	21	5.2	26	8.6	47	6.7	0	0.0	18	8.1	47	6.6	16
Amer. Indian	1	0.2	1	0.3	2	0.3	0	0.0	1	0.5	2	0.3	0
Asian Amer.	5	1.2	7	2.3	12	1.7	0	0.0	3	1.4	12	1.7	3
Mex. Amer.	0	0.0	0	0.0	0	0.0	0	0.0	0	0.0	0	0.0	0
Puerto Rican	0	0.0	0	0.0	0	0.0	0	0.0	0	0.0	0	0.0	0
Hispanic	9	2.2	6	2.0	15	2.1	0	0.0	7	3.2	15	2.1	4
Total Minority	36	8.9	40	13.2	76	10.8	0	0.0	29	13.1	76	10.7	23
For. Nation.	4	1.0	4	1.3	8	1.1	0	0.0	2	0.9	8	1.1	2
Caucasian	363	89.9	259	85.5	621	88.0	1	100.0	191	86.0	622	88.0	219
Unknown	1	0.2	0	0.0	1	0.1	0	0.0	0	0.0	1	0.1	0
Total	404	57.1	303	42.9	706	99.9	1	0.1	222	31.4	707		244

Transfers

Transfers in	12
Transfers out	5

Tuition and Fees

	Resident	Nonresident
Full-time	$16,156	$32,048
Part-time	$0	$0

Living Expenses

Estimated living expenses for singles

Living on campus	Living off campus	Living at home
$15,092	$15,092	$8,023

University of South Carolina School of Law

ABA
Approved
Since
1925

GPA and LSAT Scores

	Total	Full-time	Part-time
# of apps	1,609	1,609	0
# of offers	535	535	0
# of matrics	220	220	0
75% GPA	3.69	3.69	0.00
Median GPA	3.43	3.43	0.00
25% GPA	3.19	3.19	0.00
75% LSAT	161	161	0
Median LSAT	159	159	0
25% LSAT	156	156	0

Grants and Scholarships (from prior year)

	Total #	Total %	Full-time #	Full-time %	Part-time #	Part-time %
Total # of students	740		739		1	
Total # receiving grants	121	16.4	121	16.4	0	0.0
Less than 1/2 tuition	85	11.5	85	11.5	0	0.0
Half to full tuition	30	4.1	30	4.1	0	0.0
Full tuition	6	0.8	6	0.8	0	0.0
More than full tuition	0	0.0	0	0.0	0	0.0
Median grant amount			$6,773		$0	

Informational and Library Resources

# of volumes and volume equivalents	526,550
# of titles	77,927
# of active serial subscriptions	3,349
Study seating capacity inside the library	497
# of full-time professional librarians	8
Hours per week library is open	107
# of open, wired connections available to students	71
# of networked computers available for use by students	71
# of simultaneous wireless users	700
Require computer?	Yes

JD Attrition (from prior year)

	Academic #	Other #	Total #	Total %
1st year	2	1	3	1.3
2nd year	1	6	7	2.7
3rd year	0	0	0	0.0
4th year	0	0	0	0.0

Employment (9 months after graduation)

	Total	Percentage
Employment status known	238	97.5
Employment status unknown	6	2.5
Employed	216	90.8
Pursuing graduate degrees	8	3.4
Unemployed seeking employment	7	2.9
Unemployed not seeking employment	5	2.1
Unemployed and studying for the bar	2	0.8

Type of Employment

	Total	Percentage
# employed in law firms	114	52.8
# employed in business and industry	19	8.8
# employed in government	27	12.5
# employed in public interest	8	3.7
# employed as judicial clerks	47	21.8
# employed in academia	1	0.5

Geographic Location

	Total	Percentage
# employed in state	178	82.4
# employed in foreign countries	1	0.5
# of states where employed	13	

Bar Passage Rates

Jurisdiction	South Carolina		
Exam	Sum 05	Win 06	Total
# from school taking bar for the first time	205	19	224
School's pass rate for all first-time takers	89%	84%	88%
State's pass rate for all first-time takers	85%	76%	82%

University of South Carolina School of Law

701 South Main Street
Columbia, SC 29208
Phone: 803.777.2771; Fax: 803.777.7751
E-mail: usclaw@law.sc.edu; Website: www.law.sc.edu

■ Introduction

The University of South Carolina School of Law, established in 1867, is located in Columbia, South Carolina. With a metropolitan population approaching 700,000, Columbia combines the advantages of a progressive, growing area with the pace of a smaller city. The School of Law is located two blocks from the state capitol building. As the seat of state government, the South Carolina Supreme Court, Court of Appeals, federal district court, and criminal, civil, and special jurisdiction courts meet in Columbia. There are also numerous law firms in proximity to the law school. Situated in the center of the state, there is easy access to the mountains and the coast. The School of Law is accredited by the American Bar Association. The School of Law has been a member of the Association of American Law Schools since 1924.

■ Library and Physical Facilities

Since its founding, the School of Law has provided excellent preparation for law students. The curriculum combines traditional teaching methods and courses with modern, state-of-the-art instruction. The School of Law houses a major research library with a collection of about 450,000 volumes and extensive computer-assisted research capabilities, including LexisNexis, Westlaw, Loislaw, Dialog, RLIN, OCLC, and USCAN, the online card catalog. The library also includes the South Carolina Legal History Collection. A highly skilled staff of librarians provides assistance and instruction in research and reference techniques. The library is open more than 100 hours per week and for extended hours during the examination period. The computer lab and two electronic resource learning centers are also located within the library. Individual closed study carrels are available for assignment to students, and larger study rooms and open carrels are also available for students.

The School of Law offers a full-time-only day program leading to the Juris Doctor degree. In order to earn the JD, a student must successfully complete 90 semester hours of coursework. In each semester, a student must register for a minimum of 12 credit hours. The School of Law offers one seven-week summer session each year.

In addition to all first-year courses, students are required to take Constitutional Law II, Criminal Procedure, Professional Responsibility, and a perspective course, and satisfy an upper-level writing requirement. The School of Law offers advanced courses that allow detailed study in corporate and commercial law, tax and estate planning, and litigation. The peer-assistance tutoring program provides academic support to first-year students, and a mentoring program pairs a first-year student with an upper-class student. Numerous resources are available to assist students in succeeding academically.

■ Dual-degree Programs

The School of Law, in cooperation with other graduate programs at USC, currently offers dual JD and master's degrees in the following: international master of business administration (IMBA), human resource management, accounting, economics, public administration, criminal justice, social work, earth and environmental resource management, and health administration.

The USC School of Law and Vermont Law School offer a dual degree in environmental law. Students may earn a JD from USC and a Master of Studies in Environmental Law (MSEL) degree from Vermont Law School in only three years.

■ Special Programs

The School of Law recognizes that experiential learning in the area of professional skills is essential to a well-rounded legal education. Under special court rule, third-year law students in South Carolina may represent clients and appear in court when enrolled in a clinical legal education course. The clinical education program offers courses designed to develop critical lawyering skills. The program offers training in trial advocacy, interviewing, counseling, negotiation, alternative dispute resolution, and legal drafting. Clinics include environmental law, criminal practice, juvenile justice, veterans' rights, domestic practice, bankruptcy, and federal litigation. Judicial internships place students with trial and appellate court judges.

The Pro Bono Program, one of the longest operating programs of its type, has an outstanding national and local reputation. Under the leadership of a full-time director and a student board, the program offers students an opportunity to be involved in activities such as income tax assistance, Habitat for Humanity, and legal research.

The National Advocacy Center and the National College of District Attorneys are located on the USC campus. The Advocacy Center, operated by the US Department of Justice, provides intensive training to approximately 15,000 federal prosecutors and attorneys from across the country. The National College of District Attorneys provides training to nearly 2,000 prosecutors.

■ Admission

The School of Law seeks to enroll qualified students who will enhance and embrace the school's rigorous educational environment and, as graduates, make positive societal contributions to South Carolina, the region, and the nation. In making decisions, the Faculty Committee on Admissions employs a holistic approach, taking into account all information available about each candidate. No single factor is conclusive. While undergraduate GPA and the Law School Admission Test (LSAT) are emphasized, the committee's decision is also influenced by other factors, including the applicant's personal statement, employment or other life experience, residency, letters of recommendation, and diversity.

■ Student Activities

The School of Law publishes the *South Carolina Law Review;* the *ABA Real Property, Probate, and Trust Journal;* the *Southeastern Environmental Law Journal;* the *Journal of Law and Education;* and the *South Carolina Journal of International Law and Business.* Moot court teams are sponsored in the national, international, ABA, and various other competitions. Students who have obtained high academic achievement are eligible for membership in the

Order of the Coif, a national legal honorary society, and the Order of the Wig and Robe, a local scholastic organization founded in 1935. Student organizations include the Student Bar Association, Black Law Students Association, Women in Law, Hispanic Law Students Association, Asian Law Students Association, Christian Legal Society, Environmental Law Society, Children's Advocacy Law Society, Criminal Law Society, Federalist Society, Health Law Society, Healing Species, Intellectual Property Law Society, James L. Petigru Public Interest Law Society, Just Democracy, International Law Society, Sports and Entertainment Law Society, Law School Democrats, and Law School Republicans, among others.

■ Expenses and Financial Aid

While most students depend primarily on federal and private student loans to finance their legal education, the School of Law does offer both merit-based and need-based scholarships. Merit-based scholarships cover up to the full cost of tuition. Awards are made on a rolling basis. Candidates who want priority consideration for merit-based scholarships should make sure that the completed application and all supporting materials are received in the Office of Admissions as soon as possible after October 1 but not later than February 1. There is no separate application for merit-based scholarships.

The application for need-based scholarships is available on the Web at *www.law.sc.edu/admissions/financial.shtml*. The deadline for applying for need-based scholarships is June 1, 2007. Applicants for need-based scholarships will be notified of a decision by early July.

■ Office of Career Services

The Office of Career Services serves as liaison between students and legal employers and offers services to equip students with the skills and information necessary for a successful employment search. The Office of Career Services uses eAttorney and OCI+. Services available include individual counseling, résumé writing and interviewing seminars, on-campus interviews, and participation in job fairs. The School of Law regularly participates in the Southeastern Law Placement Consortium in Atlanta; the Mid-Atlantic Legal Recruiting Conference in Washington, DC; the Southeastern Minority Job Fair; the Patent Law Interview Program in Chicago; the Atlanta Legal Hiring Conference; and the National Public Interest Career Fair.

Applicant Profile

University of South Carolina School of Law
This grid includes only applicants who earned 120–180 LSAT scores under standard administrations.

LSAT Score	3.75 +		3.50–3.74		3.25–3.49		3.00–3.24		2.75–2.99		2.50–2.74		2.25–2.49		2.00–2.24		Below 2.00		No GPA		Total	
	Apps	Adm	Apps	Adm	Apps	Adm	Apps	Adm	Apps	Adm	Apps	Adm	Apps	Adm	Apps	Adm	Apps	Adm	Apps	Adm	Apps	Adm
175–180	0	0	0	0	0	0	1	1	0	0	0	0	0	0	0	0	0	0	0	0	1	1
170–174	3	3	0	0	1	1	2	1	0	0	1	1	0	0	0	0	0	0	0	0	7	6
165–169	12	10	9	8	10	9	7	6	0	0	2	2	0	0	0	0	0	0	0	0	40	35
160–164	30	27	44	42	42	38	41	37	28	27	14	13	7	7	1	1	0	0	1	0	208	192
155–159	71	49	114	60	109	54	89	26	42	11	22	5	12	3	2	0	0	0	0	0	461	208
150–154	46	11	96	20	118	15	98	13	53	8	20	3	16	2	4	0	0	0	3	0	454	72
145–149	23	4	55	3	45	4	38	1	35	2	24	1	10	0	3	0	1	0	2	0	236	15
140–144	8	1	20	2	23	1	21	0	23	1	13	0	11	0	3	0	1	0	2	0	125	5
135–139	2	0	4	0	8	0	13	0	11	0	5	0	2	0	2	0	1	0	2	0	50	0
130–134	0	0	1	0	0	0	4	0	3	0	2	0	2	0	0	0	0	0	1	0	13	0
125–129	0	0	0	0	1	0	1	0	0	0	1	0	1	0	1	0	1	0	1	0	7	0
120–124	0	0	0	0	0	0	0	0	0	0	0	0	1	0	0	0	0	0	0	0	1	0
Total	195	105	343	135	357	122	315	85	195	49	104	25	62	12	16	1	4	0	12	0	1603	534

Apps = Number of Applicants
Adm = Number Admitted
Reflects 99% of the total applicant pool.

The University of South Dakota School of Law

414 E. Clark
Vermillion, SD 57069-2390
Phone: 605.677.5443; Fax: 605.677.5417
E-mail: Law.School@usd.edu; Website: www.usd.edu/law

*ABA
Approved
Since
1923*

The Basics

Type of school	Public
Term	Semester
Application deadline	3/1
Application fee	$35
Financial aid deadline	3/1
Can first year start other than fall?	No
Student to faculty ratio	18.1 to 1
Does the university offer:	
housing restricted to law students?	No
graduate housing for which law students are eligible?	Yes

Faculty and Administrators

	Total		Men		Women		Minorities	
	Fall	Spr	Fall	Spr	Fall	Spr	Fall	Spr
Full-time	11	11	8	9	3	2	1	1
Other Full-time	3	3	2	2	1	1	0	0
Deans, librarians, & others who teach	2	2	2	2	0	0	0	0
Part-time	3	4	3	3	0	1	0	0
Total	**19**	**20**	**15**	**16**	**4**	**4**	**1**	**1**

Curriculum

	Full-time	Part-time
Typical first-year section size	88	0
Is there typically a "small section" of the first-year class, other than Legal Writing, taught by full-time faculty	Yes	No
If yes, typical size offered last year	44	

# of classroom course titles beyond first-year curriculum		44
# of upper division courses, excluding seminars with an enrollment:	Under 25	28
	25–49	10
	50–74	9
	75–99	2
	100+	0
# of seminars		0
# of seminar positions available		0
# of seminar positions filled	0	0
# of positions available in simulation courses		187
# of simulation positions filled	185	0
# of positions available in faculty supervised clinical courses		0
# of faculty supervised clinical positions filled	0	0
# involved in field placements	23	0
# involved in law journals	42	0
# involved in interschool competitions	33	0
# of credit hours required to graduate		90

JD Enrollment and Ethnicity

	Men		Women		Full-time		Part-time		1st-year		Total		JD Degs. Awd.
	#	%	#	%	#	%	#	%	#	%	#	%	
African Amer.	1	0.7	0	0.0	1	0.4	0	0.0	0	0.0	1	0.4	0
Amer. Indian	3	2.2	1	1.0	4	1.7	0	0.0	1	1.4	4	1.7	2
Asian Amer.	0	0.0	1	1.0	1	0.4	0	0.0	0	0.0	1	0.4	1
Mex. Amer.	0	0.0	0	0.0	0	0.0	0	0.0	0	0.0	0	0.0	0
Puerto Rican	1	0.7	0	0.0	1	0.4	0	0.0	0	0.0	1	0.4	0
Hispanic	1	0.7	2	2.0	3	1.3	0	0.0	0	0.0	3	1.3	1
Total Minority	6	4.4	4	4.0	10	4.3	0	0.0	1	1.4	10	4.3	4
For. Nation.	0	0.0	0	0.0	0	0.0	0	0.0	0	0.0	0	0.0	1
Caucasian	130	95.6	95	96.0	221	95.7	4	100.0	70	95.9	225	95.7	81
Unknown	0	0.0	0	0.0	0	0.0	0	0.0	0	0.0	0	0.0	0
Total	136	57.9	99	42.1	231	98.3	4	1.7	73	31.1	235		86

Transfers

Transfers in	1
Transfers out	0

Tuition and Fees

	Resident	Nonresident
Full-time	$8,326	$16,609
Part-time	$4,163	$8,304

Living Expenses

Estimated living expenses for singles

Living on campus	Living off campus	Living at home
$9,132	$12,007	$12,007

The University of South Dakota School of Law

*ABA
Approved
Since
1923*

GPA and LSAT Scores

	Total	Full-time	Part-time
# of apps	448	445	3
# of offers	166	164	2
# of matrics	72	71	1
75% GPA	3.72	3.72	0.00
Median GPA	3.49	3.48	0.00
25% GPA	3.07	3.06	0.00
75% LSAT	155	155	0
Median LSAT	152	152	0
25% LSAT	151	151	0

Grants and Scholarships (from prior year)

	Total #	Total %	Full-time #	Full-time %	Part-time #	Part-time %
Total # of students	250		247		3	
Total # receiving grants	66	26.4	66	26.7	0	0.0
Less than 1/2 tuition	59	23.6	59	23.9	0	0.0
Half to full tuition	3	1.2	3	1.2	0	0.0
Full tuition	2	0.8	2	0.8	0	0.0
More than full tuition	2	0.8	2	0.8	0	0.0
Median grant amount			$1,356		$0	

Informational and Library Resources

# of volumes and volume equivalents	207,871
# of titles	41,541
# of active serial subscriptions	1,872
Study seating capacity inside the library	227
# of full-time professional librarians	6
Hours per week library is open	168
# of open, wired connections available to students	227
# of networked computers available for use by students	37
# of simultaneous wireless users	180
Require computer?	No

JD Attrition (from prior year)

	Academic #	Other #	Total #	Total %
1st year	0	0	0	0.0
2nd year	0	0	0	0.0
3rd year	0	0	0	0.0
4th year	0	0	0	0.0

Employment (9 months after graduation)

	Total	Percentage
Employment status known	83	100.0
Employment status unknown	0	0.0
Employed	58	69.9
Pursuing graduate degrees	2	2.4
Unemployed seeking employment	21	25.3
Unemployed not seeking employment	0	0.0
Unemployed and studying for the bar	2	2.4

Type of Employment

# employed in law firms	26	44.8
# employed in business and industry	5	8.6
# employed in government	7	12.1
# employed in public interest	2	3.4
# employed as judicial clerks	15	25.9
# employed in academia	1	1.7

Geographic Location

# employed in state	36	62.1
# employed in foreign countries	0	0.0
# of states where employed		8

Bar Passage Rates

Jurisdiction	South Dakota		
Exam	Sum 05	Win 06	Total
# from school taking bar for the first time	47	8	55
School's pass rate for all first-time takers	89%	63%	85%
State's pass rate for all first-time takers	85%	82%	84%

The University of South Dakota School of Law

414 E. Clark
Vermillion, SD 57069-2390
Phone: 605.677.5443; Fax: 605.677.5417
E-mail: Law.School@usd.edu; Website: www.usd.edu/law

■ Introduction

The School of Law, located on the university campus in Vermillion, is noted for its contributions in training distinguished leaders for the bench, the bar, and the lawmaking bodies of the state and region. Founded in 1901, the school is accredited by the ABA and is an AALS member. The city of Vermillion, with a population of approximately 10,000, provides a small-town atmosphere for students, faculty, and staff.

■ Library and Physical Facilities

The three-story McKusick Law Library is equipped to meet the research needs of students, faculty, and members of the bar. Students, staff, and faculty have access to the law school facility 7 days a week, 24 hours a day through swipe-card access. It is South Dakota's largest and most complete law library, providing essential research services to the courts, legislature, government agencies, lawyers, private citizens, and students conducting interdisciplinary research. The book and microform collections include court reports, statutes, and other legal authorities.

The School of Law building, completed in 1981, has received national recognition for its design. The law school's balconied courtroom, situated in the middle of the building, is the architectural focal point. The courtroom is fully equipped with state-of-the-art videoconferencing technologies and has an adjoining audiovisual control room and judges' chambers. The building also contains two large classrooms, two smaller classrooms, a seminar room, a computer laboratory, a student lounge and locker area, and suites of offices for faculty, administration, and student organizations. The law school building is equipped for wireless network connectivity. The student organization suites contain study carrels for member use. The law library has 227 study seats, including 166 carrels assigned to members of the student body.

■ Curriculum

Ninety semester credits are required for the JD degree. The first-year curriculum is required of all students. In the second and third years, electives are available in addition to required courses. During the summer, an externship program is offered for six credit hours. Externs learn by doing under the close supervision of an attorney and the externship director. Skills training is also available to second- and third-year students in the trial techniques course, negotiations, and other courses, each of which utilizes to the fullest extent the technological capabilities of the law school.

■ Special Programs

- Joint-degree Programs—There are nine programs with other graduate departments, with master's degrees available in professional accountancy, business administration, history, English, psychology, education administration, political science, public administration, and administrative studies. Students may transfer nine hours of approved interdisciplinary coursework for JD credit and must complete both programs in three years to receive maximum credit.

- Interdisciplinary Study—For upper-division students not in a joint-degree program, up to six graduate credits in other university divisions may be taken and applied toward the hours required for the JD degree. This allows a law student to broaden his or her education by the pursuit of new disciplines.
- Curricular Emphases—Two areas of emphasis are identified. Instruction in these areas is informally structured and encompasses curricular, cocurricular, and extracurricular opportunities for enhancement. Emphasis is offered in environmental and natural resources law, as well as Indian law.
- Flex-time Program—This program permits certain well-qualified students to take less than the normal load of credits each semester and obtain a JD in five years instead of three. The program admits a limited number of students who could not attend law school on a full-time basis. The law school does not offer evening or weekend courses.
- Accelerated Admission—An applicant may apply for accelerated admission, and be admitted to and enroll in law school without final completion of the requirements for the applicant's undergraduate degree. The undergraduate degree must be attained by the applicant prior to graduation from law school.
- Law Honors Scholars Program—High school seniors who are accepted as USD undergraduate Honors Scholars may apply for and receive provisional (automatic) admission to the law school upon successful completion of their undergraduate degree in four years with a 3.5 GPA, fulfillment of Honors Program requirements, and completion of the LSAT for statistical purposes only.
- Law Screening Program—Applicants who are not regularly admitted may be invited to participate in the Law Screening Program. The summer program consists of two courses offered in five weeks of lectures and finals during the sixth week. Participants are admitted or denied admission on the basis of their performance on final exams, which are graded anonymously.
- The USD School of Law and Vermont Law School offer a dual degree in environmental law. Students earn a JD from USD and a Master of Science in Environmental Law (MSEL) from Vermont Law School.

■ Student Activities

The *South Dakota Law Review* publishes articles by legal scholars, lawyers, jurists, and students three times a year. The *Great Plains Natural Resources Journal* publishes articles on environmental law and natural resources law topics. Other cocurricular activities include a Moot Court Board, Client Counseling and Negotiations Board, and Trial Advocacy teams. Boards successfully compete at the intramural, regional, and national levels. The school is active in the Law Student Division of the ABA. Other organizations include Student Bar Association, Women in Law, Native American Law Students Association, Black Law Students Association, Christian Legal Society, Environmental Law Society, International Law Students Association, Law School Democrats, Federalist Society, American Constitution Society, Delta Theta Phi, Phi Alpha Delta, Phi Delta Phi, R.D. Hurd Pro Bono Society (pro bono legal work under the supervision of legal services attorneys in surrounding communities and reservations), Trial Advocacy Group, Military and Veterans Law Society, regular participation in the Volunteer Income Tax Assistance (VITA) program, and the South Dakota Innocence Project. Each spring, USD School of Law hosts the three-day March term of the Supreme Court of South Dakota, which provides an extraordinary opportunity for law and undergraduate students, faculty, and the public to observe oral arguments before the state's highest appeals court. The law school also works closely with Access to Justice, the pro bono office of the State Bar of South Dakota.

■ Career Services

The placement opportunities for third-year law students are excellent in South Dakota, the surrounding areas, and throughout the United States. Approximately 27 percent of the graduates are placed in judicial clerkships, and one-third are employed outside South Dakota. The law school has an active program to place first- and second-year students in summer internship programs with law firms.

Applicant Profile

The University of South Dakota School of Law

LSAT Score	GPA								
	3.75 +	3.50–3.74	3.25–3.49	3.00–3.24	2.75–2.99	2.50–2.74	2.25–2.49	2.00–2.24	– 2.00
165 +									
160–164									
155–159									
150–154									
145–149									
140–144									
– 140									

Good Possibility   Possible   Unlikely

USD School of Law considers many factors beyond LSAT score and GPA. This chart should be used only as a general rule.

For fall 2006:

Applicants:	458	
Completed applications:	448	
Standard full-time admits:	151	
Standard flex-time admits:	2	
Accepted from Law Screening or PLSI:	13	
Total admitted:	166	
Matriculated full-time:	71	
Matriculated flex-time:	1	

Stats for the 151 standard admits:	LSAT	GPA
75th:	157	3.76
Median:	154	3.51
25th:	152	3.17

South Texas College of Law

1303 San Jacinto Street
Houston, TX 77002-7000
Phone: 713.659.8040; Fax: 713.646.2906
E-mail: admissions@stcl.edu; Website: www.stcl.edu

ABA
Approved
Since
1959

The Basics

Type of school	Private
Term	Semester
Application deadline	2/15 10/1
Application fee	$50
Financial aid deadline	5/1 10/1
Can first year start other than fall?	Yes
Student to faculty ratio	21.8 to 1
Does the university offer:	
housing restricted to law students?	No
graduate housing for which law students are eligible?	No

Faculty and Administrators

	Total		Men		Women		Minorities	
	Fall	Spr	Fall	Spr	Fall	Spr	Fall	Spr
Full-time	44	42	27	27	17	15	5	3
Other Full-time	2	1	1	0	1	1	0	0
Deans, librarians, & others who teach	7	7	5	5	2	2	1	1
Part-time	45	42	32	30	13	12	8	4
Total	98	92	65	62	33	30	14	8

Curriculum

	Full-time	Part-time
Typical first-year section size	95	60
Is there typically a "small section" of the first-year class, other than Legal Writing, taught by full-time faculty	No	No
If yes, typical size offered last year		
# of classroom course titles beyond first-year curriculum	114	
# of upper division courses, excluding seminars with an enrollment: Under 25	96	
25–49	43	
50–74	24	
75–99	42	
100+	0	
# of seminars	22	
# of seminar positions available	440	
# of seminar positions filled	89	240
# of positions available in simulation courses	894	
# of simulation positions filled	484	410
# of positions available in faculty supervised clinical courses	53	
# of faculty supervised clinical positions filled	39	14
# involved in field placements	84	30
# involved in law journals	212	75
# involved in interschool competitions	47	17
# of credit hours required to graduate	90	

JD Enrollment and Ethnicity

	Men		Women		Full-time		Part-time		1st-year		Total		JD Degs. Awd.
	#	%	#	%	#	%	#	%	#	%	#	%	
African Amer.	20	2.9	24	4.4	14	1.5	30	9.3	26	3.8	44	3.6	15
Amer. Indian	8	1.2	2	0.4	5	0.5	5	1.5	6	0.9	10	0.8	4
Asian Amer.	58	8.4	64	11.7	91	10.0	31	9.6	75	10.9	122	9.9	39
Mex. Amer.	23	3.3	25	4.6	34	3.7	14	4.3	31	4.5	48	3.9	12
Puerto Rican	2	0.3	2	0.4	2	0.2	2	0.6	2	0.3	4	0.3	1
Hispanic	24	3.5	27	4.9	35	3.8	16	4.9	30	4.4	51	4.1	16
Total Minority	135	19.6	144	26.3	181	19.8	98	30.2	170	24.7	279	22.6	87
For. Nation.	2	0.3	1	0.2	3	0.3	0	0.0	3	0.4	3	0.2	1
Caucasian	552	80.1	403	73.5	729	79.8	226	69.8	516	74.9	955	77.2	304
Unknown	0	0.0	0	0.0	0	0.0	0	0.0	0	0.0	0	0.0	0
Total	689	55.7	548	44.3	913	73.8	324	26.2	689	55.7	1237		392

Transfers

Transfers in	4
Transfers out	14

Tuition and Fees

	Resident	Nonresident
Full-time	$22,440	$22,440
Part-time	$15,160	$15,160

Living Expenses

Estimated living expenses for singles

Living on campus	Living off campus	Living at home
N/A	$15,422	$11,122

South Texas College of Law

ABA
Approved
Since
1959

GPA and LSAT Scores

	Total	Full-time	Part-time
# of apps	2,633	2,256	377
# of offers	1,145	971	174
# of matrics	454	344	110
75% GPA	3.46	3.40	3.50
Median GPA	3.20	3.25	3.13
25% GPA	2.95	2.98	2.82
75% LSAT	156	156	154
Median LSAT	153	153	151
25% LSAT	150	151	149

Grants and Scholarships (from prior year)

	Total		Full-time		Part-time	
	#	%	#	%	#	%
Total # of students	1,262		959		303	
Total # receiving grants	395	31.3	322	33.6	73	24.1
Less than 1/2 tuition	365	28.9	300	31.3	65	21.5
Half to full tuition	22	1.7	15	1.6	7	2.3
Full tuition	5	0.4	5	0.5	0	0.0
More than full tuition	3	0.2	2	0.2	1	0.3
Median grant amount			$1,380		$1,061	

Informational and Library Resources

# of volumes and volume equivalents	511,900
# of titles	87,026
# of active serial subscriptions	4,331
Study seating capacity inside the library	877
# of full-time professional librarians	11
Hours per week library is open	103
# of open, wired connections available to students	1,023
# of networked computers available for use by students	102
# of simultaneous wireless users	500
Require computer?	No

JD Attrition (from prior year)

	Academic	Other	Total	
	#	#	#	%
1st year	9	35	44	6.6
2nd year	4	6	10	3.2
3rd year	1	0	1	0.4
4th year	0	0	0	0.0

Employment (9 months after graduation)

	Total	Percentage
Employment status known	345	94.3
Employment status unknown	21	5.7
Employed	276	80.0
Pursuing graduate degrees	9	2.6
Unemployed seeking employment	17	4.9
Unemployed not seeking employment	4	1.2
Unemployed and studying for the bar	39	11.3

Type of Employment

	Total	Percentage
# employed in law firms	188	68.1
# employed in business and industry	33	12.0
# employed in government	34	12.3
# employed in public interest	2	0.7
# employed as judicial clerks	7	2.5
# employed in academia	2	0.7

Geographic Location

	Total	Percentage
# employed in state	256	92.8
# employed in foreign countries	0	0.0
# of states where employed		10

Bar Passage Rates

Jurisdiction	Texas		
Exam	Sum 05	Win 06	Total
# from school taking bar for the first time	268	83	351
School's pass rate for all first-time takers	77%	78%	77%
State's pass rate for all first-time takers	81%	77%	80%

South Texas College of Law

1303 San Jacinto Street
Houston, TX 77002-7000
Phone: 713.659.8040; Fax: 713.646.2906
E-mail: admissions@stcl.edu; Website: www.stcl.edu

■ Introduction

South Texas College of Law, situated at the very core of Houston's vibrant downtown legal and financial centers, is a private, nonprofit, independent law school founded in 1923. South Texas is the oldest law school in Houston and one of the largest in the nation, and is accredited by the American Bar Association and a member of the AALS. The college offers full- and part-time programs leading to the Doctor of Jurisprudence degree.

■ Admission

Students are admitted to South Texas both in the fall and spring semesters. Admission application deadlines are February 15 for fall consideration and October 1 for spring. Early application is encouraged. A bachelor's degree is required as well as taking the LSAT and registering with LSDAS.

Students are admitted primarily on the basis of their LSAT score and undergraduate GPA. However, a significant percentage of each incoming class is selected on the basis of additional factors. Every attempt is made to evaluate each applicant as an individual, a prospective student, and a future professional.

■ Curriculum

The curriculum at South Texas combines traditional classroom instruction with a broad range of innovative simulated and clinical courses. The college offers a class scheduling system whereby students may select convenient class times rather than having to choose between day and evening divisions. To accommodate part-time working students, a complete curriculum of classes is scheduled after 5:30 PM, with a few classes also scheduled on Saturdays.

For students interested in the increased globalization of law, South Texas offers a variety of foreign programs throughout the year. Two ABA-approved cooperative exchange programs allow students to study for a semester in the Netherlands and Denmark. Summer programs are offered in Malta, Turkey, Ireland, England, Czech Republic, and Mexico.

■ JD/MBA Cooperative Program

Through a special cooperative program, students in the JD program at South Texas College of Law are eligible to apply for admission to the MBA program at Mays Business School, Texas A&M University. Upon acceptance into the MBA program, students are granted a leave of absence after their second year of law studies to attain their MBA and then return to South Texas to complete their JD degree.

■ Special Programs

Development of strong legal and advocacy skills is important at South Texas, as evidenced by its five Centers of Excellence and its skills and clinical programs.

Since 1980, the **Advocacy Program** has outperformed all other law school teams in the nation by winning an array of state, regional, and national championship victories. The **Frank Evans Center for Conflict Resolution** allows students to learn from and interact with practicing attorneys who specialize in

mediation and arbitration. The **Law Institute for Medical Studies** focuses on legal issues facing the medical profession and provides students with the opportunity to work with those in the field. The **Corporate Compliance Center** involves students who are interested in working as in-house counsel, corporate counsel, outside counsel, and business lawyers. The center explores issues such as how companies promote policies and procedures that ensure legal and ethical behavior and how companies detect and deter wrongdoing. The **Transactional Practice Center** is designed to teach students the fundamental elements of completing a business transaction such as a real estate purchase or development, buying or selling a corporation, or creating a partnership.

South Texas offers off-site clinics that place students in the real world of lawyering, including state and federal trial and appellate court chambers, prosecutors' and defenders' offices, public interest legal service providers, and state and federal government agencies. In the **International Criminal Process Clinic**, students work with defenders involved with the United Nations' ad hoc International Criminal Tribunal for the former Yugoslavia. In the **General Civil Clinic**, students work in an on-site clinic while providing direct representation for clients in a variety of administrative and state court settings.

Academic Assistance and Counseling. Students are encouraged to participate in the varied programs and services offered, which are designed to help them reach their full academic potential.

The **Langdell Scholar Program**, conducted by course-proficient upperclassmen, continues to benefit eligible students in mastering the framework of legal analysis, while garnering a proficiency in effective outlining, study skills, and exam-taking techniques. Students are selected into the program based on their LSAT performance, undergraduate GPA, and academic assistance diagnostic test.

■ Student Activities

Students at South Texas have the opportunity to become members of numerous active student organizations representing a wide range of interests.

■ Scholarly Publications

South Texas College of Law students participate in journals on the basis of outstanding scholarship or writing ability. Our students edit and publish a variety of scholarly publications, including the *South Texas Law Review, Currents: International Trade Law Journal,* and the *Corporate Counsel Review,* and coedit the *Construction Law Journal* and *Texas Business Journal* in conjunction with each journal's respective state bar section.

■ Library and Physical Facilities

Recent additions to the South Texas campus ensure that students have access to and are trained with state-of-the-art tools now used in the legal profession. The T. Gerald Treece Courtroom houses a nine-seat judges' bench and boasts the very latest courtroom technology available to trial attorneys. The courtroom is heavily used by the school's nationally recognized advocacy program for practice and competition. It is also available to the members of Houston's legal community, including the judiciary.

The Fred Parks Law Library encompasses more than 72,000 square feet. Each of the 780 seats in the six-story facility is wired for data and power. The building is crowned with a conference center and rooftop terrace that is perfect for congregating students and campus events.

The college is also the home of the First and Fourteenth Texas Courts of Appeals, distinguishing South Texas as only one of two American law schools housing appellate courts on a permanent basis.

■ Financial Assistance

South Texas offers an extensive financial aid program, in terms of both scholarships and outside funding options. Depending on their qualifications, Texas residents are eligible for state and federal tuition assistance grants, which have amounted to as much as several thousand dollars in prior years. In addition, the Office of Scholarships and Financial Aid administers financial assistance through the Federal Work-study Program, federal and private loans, and a variety of scholarship offerings. Incoming students are considered for merit scholarships based on UGPA and LSAT achievement.

Continuing students are eligible for both merit- and need-based scholarships. Contact the Office of Scholarships and Financial Aid for eligibility and documentation requirements (713.646.1820).

■ Career Services

In light of today's competitive job market, the Career Resources Center (CRC) continues to provide South Texas students and graduates with a full range of services to assist in their employment search, while at the same time being responsive to the changes in hiring trends and patterns. The office serves as a counseling and resource center for students seeking employment on either a full- or part-time basis and assists graduates pursuing permanent employment. In addition to on-campus recruiting, the CRC also offers workshops on résumé preparation and courses on developing skills that will help during the interviewing process. The objective of the CRC staff is to aid students in exploring career options, while helping them build valuable job search skills utilizing their strengths and abilities. By taking advantage of the many programs and services offered by the CRC, students are better equipped to maximize their career-planning opportunities.

Applicant Profile

South Texas College of Law
This grid includes only applicants who earned 120–180 LSAT scores under standard administrations.

LSAT Score	GPA																				
	3.75 +		3.50–3.74		3.25–3.49		3.00–3.24		2.75–2.99		2.50–2.74		2.25–2.49		2.00–2.24		Below 2.00		No GPA		Total	
	Apps	Adm	Apps	Adm	Apps	Adm	Apps	Adm	Apps	Adm	Apps	Adm	Apps	Adm	Apps	Adm	Apps	Adm	Apps	Adm	Apps	Adm
170–180	2	2	0	0	0	0	0	0	0	0	1	0	0	0	0	0	0	0	0	0	3	2
165–169	3	3	3	3	0	0	1	1	4	3	4	3	1	0	0	0	0	0	1	1	17	14
160–164	10	10	16	14	21	19	32	32	21	21	16	13	10	6	0	0	0	0	0	0	126	115
155–159	45	45	68	67	90	84	60	58	47	45	25	13	18	5	4	2	2	0	4	0	363	319
150–154	37	35	104	90	124	108	124	93	85	56	61	17	27	3	15	0	3	0	3	1	583	403
145–149	27	12	75	20	113	22	126	14	88	8	55	2	26	0	15	0	4	0	9	3	529	81
140–144	5	0	31	0	55	0	78	0	59	0	48	0	30	1	15	0	4	0	8	0	335	1
Below 140	4	0	7	0	19	0	31	0	33	0	40	0	20	0	12	0	6	0	8	0	180	0
Total	133	107	304	194	422	233	452	198	337	133	250	48	132	15	54	2	17	0	35	5	2136	935

Apps = Number of Applicants
Adm = Number Admitted
Reflects 99% of the total applicant pool.

University of Southern California, Gould School of Law

Los Angeles, CA 90089-0074
Phone: 213.740.2523; Fax: 213.740.4570
E-mail: admissions@law.usc.edu; Website: www.law.usc.edu

The Basics

Type of school	Private
Term	Semester
Application deadline	2/1
Application fee	$70
Financial aid deadline	2/15
Can first year start other than fall?	No
Student to faculty ratio	13.1 to 1
Does the university offer:	
housing restricted to law students?	No
graduate housing for which law students are eligible?	Yes

Faculty and Administrators

	Total		Men		Women		Minorities	
	Fall	Spr	Fall	Spr	Fall	Spr	Fall	Spr
Full-time	41	36	30	26	11	10	5	5
Other Full-time	1	1	0	0	1	1	0	0
Deans, librarians, & others who teach	15	16	6	6	9	10	2	2
Part-time	53	60	33	38	20	21	15	15
Total	110	113	69	70	41	42	22	22

Curriculum

	Full-time	Part-time
Typical first-year section size	70	0
Is there typically a "small section" of the first-year class, other than Legal Writing, taught by full-time faculty	No	No
If yes, typical size offered last year		
# of classroom course titles beyond first-year curriculum	92	
# of upper division courses, excluding seminars with an enrollment: Under 25	61	
25–49	27	
50–74	7	
75–99	4	
100+	8	
# of seminars	17	
# of seminar positions available	318	
# of seminar positions filled	192	0
# of positions available in simulation courses	360	
# of simulation positions filled	290	0
# of positions available in faculty supervised clinical courses	87	
# of faculty supervised clinical positions filled	77	0
# involved in field placements	108	0
# involved in law journals	159	0
# involved in interschool competitions	17	0
# of credit hours required to graduate	88	

JD Enrollment and Ethnicity

	Men		Women		Full-time		Part-time		1st-year		Total		JD Degs. Awd.
	#	%	#	%	#	%	#	%	#	%	#	%	
African Amer.	14	4.5	38	13.1	52	8.6	0	0.0	13	6.1	52	8.6	15
Amer. Indian	1	0.3	1	0.3	2	0.3	0	0.0	1	0.5	2	0.3	1
Asian Amer.	49	15.6	69	23.7	118	19.5	0	0.0	42	19.6	118	19.5	40
Mex. Amer.	32	10.2	18	6.2	50	8.3	0	0.0	23	10.7	50	8.3	10
Puerto Rican	1	0.3	1	0.3	2	0.3	0	0.0	2	0.9	2	0.3	2
Hispanic	5	1.6	9	3.1	14	2.3	0	0.0	7	3.3	14	2.3	6
Total Minority	102	32.5	136	46.7	238	39.3	0	0.0	88	41.1	238	39.3	74
For. Nation.	3	1.0	5	1.7	8	1.3	0	0.0	4	1.9	8	1.3	1
Caucasian	177	56.4	124	42.6	301	49.8	0	0.0	105	49.1	301	49.8	121
Unknown	32	10.2	26	8.9	58	9.6	0	0.0	17	7.9	58	9.6	19
Total	314	51.9	291	48.1	605	100.0	0	0.0	214	35.4	605		215

Transfers

Transfers in	9
Transfers out	5

Tuition and Fees

	Resident	Nonresident
Full-time	$40,262	$40,262
Part-time	$0	$0

Living Expenses

Estimated living expenses for singles

Living on campus	Living off campus	Living at home
$17,364	$17,364	$6,808

University of Southern California, Gould School of Law

ABA Approved Since 1924

GPA and LSAT Scores

	Total	Full-time	Part-time
# of apps	5,670	5,670	0
# of offers	1,084	1,084	0
# of matrics	217	217	0
75% GPA	3.75	3.75	0.00
Median GPA	3.63	3.63	0.00
25% GPA	3.47	3.47	0.00
75% LSAT	167	167	0
Median LSAT	166	166	0
25% LSAT	165	165	0

Grants and Scholarships (from prior year)

	Total		Full-time		Part-time	
	#	%	#	%	#	%
Total # of students	628		628		0	
Total # receiving grants	329	52.4	329	52.4	0	0.0
Less than 1/2 tuition	288	45.9	288	45.9	0	0.0
Half to full tuition	25	4.0	25	4.0	0	0.0
Full tuition	9	1.4	9	1.4	0	0.0
More than full tuition	7	1.1	7	1.1	0	0.0
Median grant amount			$10,000		$0	

Informational and Library Resources

# of volumes and volume equivalents	420,547
# of titles	171,873
# of active serial subscriptions	4,983
Study seating capacity inside the library	230
# of full-time professional librarians	8
Hours per week library is open	100
# of open, wired connections available to students	60
# of networked computers available for use by students	115
# of simultaneous wireless users	650
Require computer?	No

JD Attrition (from prior year)

	Academic	Other	Total	
	#	#	#	%
1st year	2	6	8	3.9
2nd year	0	2	2	1.0
3rd year	0	0	0	0.0
4th year	0	0	0	0.0

Employment (9 months after graduation)

	Total	Percentage
Employment status known	198	99.0
Employment status unknown	2	1.0
Employed	184	92.9
Pursuing graduate degrees	2	1.0
Unemployed seeking employment	2	1.0
Unemployed not seeking employment	10	5.1
Unemployed and studying for the bar	0	0.0

Type of Employment

	Total	Percentage
# employed in law firms	118	64.1
# employed in business and industry	23	12.5
# employed in government	12	6.5
# employed in public interest	9	4.9
# employed as judicial clerks	18	9.8
# employed in academia	3	1.6

Geographic Location

	Total	Percentage
# employed in state	161	87.5
# employed in foreign countries	0	0.0
# of states where employed	12	

Bar Passage Rates

Jurisdiction	California		
Exam	Sum 05	Win 06	Total
# from school taking bar for the first time	186	1	187
School's pass rate for all first-time takers	82%	0%	81%
State's pass rate for all first-time takers	64%	54%	62%

University of Southern California, Gould School of Law

Los Angeles, CA 90089-0074
Phone: 213.740.2523; Fax: 213.740.4570
E-mail: admissions@law.usc.edu; Website: www.law.usc.edu

■ Introduction

The University of Southern California Gould School of Law is a private, highly selective national law school with a 100-year history and a reputation for academic excellence. Under the leadership of a stellar, energetic faculty, the school's rigorous, interdisciplinary program focuses on the law as an expression of social values and an instrument for implementing social goals. USC is known for its diverse student body, its leadership in clinical education, and its tight-knit alumni network composed of national leaders in the legal profession, business, and the public sector. With 200 students in each class, the school is small, informal, and collegial.

The School of Law is located on the beautiful main campus of the University of Southern California, just south of downtown Los Angeles and in the heart of the city's exciting "Arts and Education Corridor." A dynamic laboratory for legal training, Los Angeles is a center of state, national, and international commerce and government, and the city's legal market is among the most extensive in the world. The law school is housed in a five-level, technologically advanced facility that provides a superb setting for professional training and sophisticated legal research.

■ Curriculum

USC's curriculum is comprehensive, uniquely interdisciplinary, and designed to challenge. Courses provide a solid foundation in all substantive areas of law as well as extensive opportunities to explore specializations in traditional and emerging fields. Many faculty members have expertise in both law and other disciplines, such as economics, communication, public policy, medicine, history, psychology, and philosophy. The first-year curriculum consists of courses that examine the foundation of the legal system. The second and third years of study allow students to pursue individual interests in such areas as international law, intellectual property, corporations and business-government relationships, taxation, bioethics, civil rights and liberties, and judicial administration.

■ Special Programs

Dual Degrees: The law school offers 16 dual-degree programs in coordination with USC graduate and professional schools and the California Institute of Technology. These programs enable qualified students to earn a law degree and a master's degree in the following fields: Business Administration, Business Taxation, Economics, Communications Management, Gerontology, International Relations, Philosophy, Political Science, Public Administration, Public Policy, Real Estate Development, and Social Work. A JD/PhD program in Political Science, a JD/PharmD program, and a JD/PhD program in Social Science with the California Institute of Technology are also offered.

Legal Clinics: The nationally recognized Post-Conviction Justice Project, the Children's Legal Issues Clinic, the Employer Legal Advice Clinic, and the Immigration Law Clinic enable students to gain valuable advocacy and lawyering skills by representing real clients under faculty supervision. Students in the Intellectual Property Clinic review technology contracts,

engage in patent evaluation and application, assist with litigation, and perform film clearance work.

Public Service Programs: The Office of Public Service provides comprehensive opportunities and coordination for all external service learning and community service. These opportunities include more than 60 clinical field placements, allowing students to earn academic credit while engaging in service learning at government and public interest agencies and with federal and state judges, as well as pro bono and community service in the surrounding Los Angeles neighborhoods.

International Programs: USC offers students several opportunities to study abroad. Students can participate in the law school's semester abroad exchange program with the University of Hong Kong, which is designed for individuals interested in international business or comparative law. And the law school offers a dual-degree program (JD/LLM) with the London School of Economics. Moreover, students may participate in programs offered around the world by other ABA-approved law schools.

Research Centers: Law students participate in the scholarly activities of several interdisciplinary research centers: the Center for Communications Law and Policy; the Pacific Center for Health Policy and Ethics; the Center for Law, Economics, and Organization; the USC-Caltech Center for the Study of Law and Politics; the Center for Law, History, and Culture; and the Center for Law and Philosophy.

Continuing Legal Education: Students help coordinate the law school's practice-oriented programs and serve as research assistants for the Entertainment Law Institute and the Intellectual Property Institute.

■ Student Activities and Cocurricular Programs

Academic life is exciting and fast-paced, and students are often engaged in numerous scholarly pursuits and cocurricular programs. The *Southern California Law Review* has one of the largest circulations in the country. Students also publish the *Southern California Interdisciplinary Law Journal* and the *Southern California Review of Law and Social Justice*. The Moot Court Honors Program sends participants to national and state competitions.

Public service activities abound. The Public Interest Law Foundation is one of the largest in the country, providing summer grants for public service employment as well as the Irmas Fellowship for Public Interest Law, which awards a year's salary to a third-year student committed to postgraduate work in public interest.

The School of Law has a long tradition of student participation in governance, and elected student members serve on most committees and attend and vote at faculty meetings. The Student Bar Association allocates funds to support voluntary student organizations. Asian, African American, and Latino law students are represented by associations. Other student organizations include international and entertainment law societies, Women's Law Association, Middle Eastern and South Asian Law Association, Gay and Lesbian Law Union, Christian Legal Society, Jewish Law Students, and chapters of the ACLU and the Federalist Society.

■ Professional Careers

USC graduates accept job offers in all regions of the country, with New York and Washington, DC, the most popular placement locations outside the West Coast. A significant percentage of graduates begin their professional careers as judicial law clerks to federal and state judges. Each year, several hundred private firms, government agencies, public interest organizations, and corporations from throughout the country come to USC to recruit students for summer and permanent employment. An off-campus recruiting program helps coordinate interviews with East Coast employers. The school's enthusiastic network of alumni is a valuable tool in the job-search process. The Law Alumni Mentor Program pairs first-year students with a graduate who practices in the student's field of interest, and other programs bring alumni from a range of fields to campus to discuss career opportunities. Overall placement statistics are consistently strong; historically, more than 95 percent of each graduating class finds employment. Average starting salaries are among the highest in the nation.

■ Housing

Housing is available in an apartment-style residence located within easy walking distance of the law school for a limited number of incoming students. The apartments are fully furnished and equipped with high-speed Ethernet lines. A roommate referral service is available to help incoming students arrange shared housing in various LA neighborhoods.

■ Admission and Financial Aid

Admission decisions are made on the basis of the student's academic record, LSAT score, personal statement, letters of recommendation, and other information in the file. The Admissions Committee gives primary consideration to outstanding academic and professional promise and to qualities that will enhance the diversity of the student body or enrich the law school educational environment. Two letters of recommendation are required; applicants are strongly urged to submit at least one academic recommendation letter. The law school operates on a semester basis and admits only full-time students. USC is committed to helping students successfully finance their legal education. In addition to various loan programs, the School of Law offers substantial scholarship awards to a large percentage of the incoming class. Most scholarships are based on merit and need, although a number of scholarships are awarded based solely on the applicant's potential as indicated by the admission file. In addition, the Loan Repayment Assistance Program assists graduates who accept employment with low-paying public interest organizations. Prospective applicants should not allow financial concerns to deter their interest in USC.

Applicant Profile

University of Southern California, Gould School of Law
This grid includes only applicants who earned 120–180 LSAT scores under standard administrations.

LSAT Score	GPA 3.75 +		3.50–3.74		3.25–3.49		3.00–3.24		2.75–2.99		Below 2.75		No GPA		Total	
	Apps	Adm	Apps	Adm	Apps	Adm	Apps	Adm	Apps	Adm	Apps	Adm	Apps	Adm	Apps	Adm
175–180	14	13	12	12	12	9	5	1	7	0	4	0	0	0	54	35
170–174	93	89	96	91	68	38	27	3	15	0	6	0	1	0	306	221
165–169	265	231	385	311	233	92	134	9	33	1	19	0	10	1	1079	645
160–164	384	28	511	56	346	29	143	12	63	0	41	0	23	2	1511	127
155–159	239	6	356	17	303	18	146	6	72	2	46	0	16	0	1178	49
150–154	80	0	173	1	220	0	122	0	69	1	58	0	13	0	735	2
Below 150	44	0	116	0	158	0	153	0	121	1	114	0	39	0	745	1
Total	1119	367	1649	488	1340	186	730	31	380	5	288	0	102	3	5608	1080

Apps = Number of Applicants
Adm = Number Admitted
Reflects 99% of the total applicant pool.

Southern Illinois University School of Law

School of Law Welcome Center, 1209 W. Chautauqua, Mailcode 6811
Carbondale, IL 62901
Phone: 800.739.9187 or 618.453.8858; Fax: 618.453.8921
E-mail: lawadmit@siu.edu; Website: www.law.siu.edu

ABA Approved Since 1974

The Basics

Type of school	Public
Term	Semester
Application deadline	3/1
Application fee	$50
Financial aid deadline	4/1
Can first year start other than fall?	No
Student to faculty ratio	12.2 to 1
Does the university offer:	
housing restricted to law students?	No
graduate housing for which law students are eligible?	Yes

Faculty and Administrators

	Total		Men		Women		Minorities	
	Fall	Spr	Fall	Spr	Fall	Spr	Fall	Spr
Full-time	26	23	14	12	12	11	1	0
Other Full-time	3	3	1	1	2	2	1	1
Deans, librarians, & others who teach	7	9	4	4	3	5	2	2
Part-time	7	5	4	4	3	1	0	0
Total	43	40	23	21	20	19	4	3

Curriculum

	Full-time	Part-time
Typical first-year section size	65	0
Is there typically a "small section" of the first-year class, other than Legal Writing, taught by full-time faculty	No	No
If yes, typical size offered last year		
# of classroom course titles beyond first-year curriculum	74	

# of upper division courses, excluding seminars with an enrollment:		
Under 25	60	
25–49	20	
50–74	16	
75–99	2	
100+	0	

# of seminars	9	
# of seminar positions available	108	
# of seminar positions filled	88	0
# of positions available in simulation courses	413	
# of simulation positions filled	265	0
# of positions available in faculty supervised clinical courses	72	
# of faculty supervised clinical positions filled	36	0
# involved in field placements	38	0
# involved in law journals	60	0
# involved in interschool competitions	26	0
# of credit hours required to graduate	90	

JD Enrollment and Ethnicity

	Men		Women		Full-time		Part-time		1st-year		Total		JD Degs. Awd.
	#	%	#	%	#	%	#	%	#	%	#	%	
African Amer.	6	2.9	7	4.8	13	3.7	0	0.0	7	5.8	13	3.7	1
Amer. Indian	1	0.5	0	0.0	1	0.3	0	0.0	1	0.8	1	0.3	0
Asian Amer.	7	3.3	4	2.7	11	3.1	0	0.0	2	1.7	11	3.1	4
Mex. Amer.	1	0.5	0	0.0	1	0.3	0	0.0	0	0.0	1	0.3	0
Puerto Rican	1	0.5	1	0.7	2	0.6	0	0.0	1	0.8	2	0.6	0
Hispanic	1	0.5	1	0.7	2	0.6	0	0.0	1	0.8	2	0.6	3
Total Minority	17	8.1	13	8.9	30	8.5	0	0.0	12	10.0	30	8.5	8
For. Nation.	0	0.0	0	0.0	0	0.0	0	0.0	0	0.0	0	0.0	0
Caucasian	173	82.8	123	84.2	294	83.3	2	100.0	101	84.2	296	83.4	106
Unknown	19	9.1	10	6.8	29	8.2	0	0.0	7	5.8	29	8.2	16
Total	209	58.9	146	41.1	353	99.4	2	0.6	120	33.8	355		130

Transfers

Transfers in	6
Transfers out	6

Tuition and Fees

	Resident	Nonresident
Full-time	$10,861	$28,621
Part-time	$0	$0

Living Expenses

Estimated living expenses for singles

Living on campus	Living off campus	Living at home
$11,674	$11,674	$5,068

Southern Illinois University School of Law

*ABA
Approved
Since
1974*

GPA and LSAT Scores

	Total	Full-time	Part-time
# of apps	709	709	0
# of offers	330	330	0
# of matrics	123	123	0
75% GPA	3.70	3.70	0.00
Median GPA	3.50	3.50	0.00
25% GPA	3.00	3.00	0.00
75% LSAT	156	156	0
Median LSAT	153	153	0
25% LSAT	149	149	0

Grants and Scholarships (from prior year)

	Total		Full-time		Part-time	
	#	%	#	%	#	%
Total # of students	378		377		1	
Total # receiving grants	226	59.8	226	59.9	0	0.0
Less than 1/2 tuition	146	38.6	146	38.7	0	0.0
Half to full tuition	73	19.3	73	19.4	0	0.0
Full tuition	6	1.6	6	1.6	0	0.0
More than full tuition	1	0.3	1	0.3	0	0.0
Median grant amount			$4,000		$0	

Informational and Library Resources

# of volumes and volume equivalents	400,596
# of titles	75,148
# of active serial subscriptions	3,766
Study seating capacity inside the library	348
# of full-time professional librarians	7
Hours per week library is open	78
# of open, wired connections available to students	14
# of networked computers available for use by students	52
# of simultaneous wireless users	600
Require computer?	No

JD Attrition (from prior year)

	Academic	Other	Total	
	#	#	#	%
1st year	5	8	13	10.7
2nd year	0	3	3	2.4
3rd year	0	0	0	0.0
4th year	0	0	0	0.0

Employment (9 months after graduation)

	Total	Percentage
Employment status known	119	98.3
Employment status unknown	2	1.7
Employed	95	79.8
Pursuing graduate degrees	2	1.7
Unemployed seeking employment	10	8.4
Unemployed not seeking employment	0	0.0
Unemployed and studying for the bar	12	10.1
Type of Employment		
# employed in law firms	61	64.2
# employed in business and industry	7	7.4
# employed in government	19	20.0
# employed in public interest	1	1.1
# employed as judicial clerks	2	2.1
# employed in academia	4	4.2
Geographic Location		
# employed in state	59	62.1
# employed in foreign countries	0	0.0
# of states where employed	13	

Bar Passage Rates

Jurisdiction	Illinois		
Exam	Sum 05	Win 06	Total
# from school taking bar for the first time	68	19	87
School's pass rate for all first-time takers	87%	100%	90%
State's pass rate for all first-time takers	86%	83%	85%

Southern Illinois University School of Law

Office of Admissions, School of Law Welcome Center, 1209 W. Chautauqua, Mailcode 6811
Carbondale, IL 62901
Phone: 800.739.9187 or 618.453.8858; Fax: 618.453.8921
E-mail: lawadmit@siu.edu; Website: www.law.siu.edu

■ Introduction

Southern Illinois University School of Law is located in a community of 27,000 people in one of the most scenic areas of Illinois. National forests, state parks, historic sites, campgrounds, theaters, festivals, and cultural events make Carbondale's quality of life among the highest in small cities in Illinois. The School of Law is one of many colleges of Southern Illinois University Carbondale, a 130-year-old university with a tradition of excellence as well as a diverse, multicultural student body of 23,000. The 12.2:1 student to faculty ratio at the School of Law is among the best in the nation. The School of Law is fully accredited by the ABA and the AALS.

■ Library and Physical Facilities

Students enjoy a completely renovated library, courtroom, and classrooms. Technological improvements include 24-hour keypad access to the law building and library, a wireless network allowing Internet access anywhere in or near the building, and distance-learning capabilities allowing live correspondence with national law schools. The new courtroom and classrooms are stocked with the latest computers, televisions, video cameras, and digital projectors to enhance learning. The vast collection of legal authorities the law library houses meets the demanding research needs of the prospective lawyer. All facilities are accessible to individuals with disabilities.

■ Curriculum

All students have a uniform first-year curriculum. A broad range of courses and seminars are offered in the second and third years. Throughout the curriculum, the faculty emphasizes professional skills such as writing, oral argumentation, drafting documents, interviewing, negotiating, and counseling.

An innovative and nationally recognized first-year Lawyering Skills Program gives students a strong foundation in basic lawyering skills, including legal research and writing, oral advocacy, client interviewing and counseling, and negotiation.

The school has a very strong health law curriculum and is the site for the National Health Law Moot Court Competition as well as a Center for Health Law and Policy. The school also has groups of courses in trial/litigation skills, intellectual property, and criminal, labor, corporate, family, international, and environmental law.

■ Special Programs

Clinical programs enable senior law students to represent clients under the supervision of licensed attorneys. The Elderly Clinic provides direct legal assistance to persons 60 years of age and older in the 13 southernmost counties of Illinois. Students may participate in the Externship Program and obtain academic credit while working at nonprofit, local, state, or federal legal offices. The Alternative Dispute Resolution Clinic allows students to develop mediation skills and use them through community, peer, and in-court mediation services. The Domestic Violence Clinic provides legal assistance to victims of domestic violence. Students can also gain valuable experience through work in the Illinois Agriculture Mediation Program and the award-winning Self Help Legal Center.

The school provides a comprehensive trial and appellate moot court program with teams that have competed in the National Moot Court, ABA Moot Court, all-Illinois Moot Court, and Philip C. Jessup International Law Moot Court competitions. The school also provides an annual intraschool Client Interviewing and Counseling Competition and a Negotiation Competition.

All entering law students are assigned a study group and a senior law student tutor as part of the Academic Success Program.

The School of Law sponsors two annual lecture series: the Hiram H. Lesar Distinguished Lecture Series and the Dr. Arthur Grayson Distinguished Lecture Series. Past speakers include Morris Dees, Dr. David Kessler, Nadine Strossen, Governor Douglas Wilder, and Kerry Kennedy Cuomo. In addition, the school cosponsors an annual health law symposium, the Health Policy Institute, which brings experts in health law policy from across the country to Carbondale.

Students participate in the Professional Development Workshop Series, which received the 2004 E. Smythe Gambrell Professionalism Award from the American Bar Association.

■ Joint-degree Programs

Concurrent JD/master's degree programs in education, social work, public administration, accounting, and business administration are offered in conjunction with the graduate school. A concurrent PhD program is available in political science. A six-year program offered in cooperation with the School of Medicine permits students to concurrently obtain JD and MD degrees.

■ Career Services

Employment opportunities are notable. Our graduates find employment nationwide, with alumni in 47 states, and internationally. Our graduates continue to exceed with bar passage rates at or above the state and national averages. The Office of Career Services provides services for both enrolled students and alumni, including individual career counseling, on-campus interviews, career workshops, subscriptions to a variety of job newsletters, a job-vacancy bulletin updated daily, and job-bulletin exchanges with other law schools. Special presentations that cover a variety of career and employment topics are offered throughout the year, and students have the opportunity to participate in a variety of regional and national job fairs and career conferences. The Career Library contains diverse career materials, including national and international directories, judicial clerkship information, and government and public interest job information. Students can contact the Office of Career Services at 618.453.8707 or by e-mail at *lawjobs@siu.edu*.

■ Expenses, Scholarships, and Financial Aid

Due to a generous program of scholarships for both current and existing students, graduates of the SIU School of Law enjoy an average debt load that is more than 30 percent below the national law school average. Students can qualify for the in-state resident tuition rate after they have been an Illinois resident for six consecutive months. Student loans, work-study opportunities, and most other forms of financial aid are administered by the university's Financial Aid Office. Information concerning loans and financial aid procedures may be obtained from the Financial Aid Office at 618.453.4334 or by e-mail at *fao@siu.edu.*

■ Admission

Admission decisions are based on a number of factors, the LSAT score and undergraduate GPA being the most important. The highest LSAT score is used for repeat test takers. Other factors considered by the Admission Committee include trends in academic performance, writing ability, leadership and maturity, letters of recommendation, work experience, community and public service, and obstacles imposed by religious, ethnic, gender, or disability discrimination.

■ Student Activities

The school publishes the *SIU Law Journal*, which provides editorial and writing experience for a number of upper-class students. Students with a particular interest in health law can also publish articles in the *Journal of Legal Medicine.*

All students belong to the Student Bar Association. The SBA schedules lectures and social affairs, provides services to its members, and serves as a channel of communication between students and faculty. Students play an active role in law school governance, serving on most faculty committees. Past and current student organizations include Equal Justice Works, Phi Alpha Delta, International Law Society, Women's Law Forum, Environmental Law Society, Parents as Law Students, Animal Legal Defense Fund, Business Law Society, Black Law Student Association, Federalist Society, Law School Democrats, Law School Republicans, Media Law Society, Lesbian and Gay Law Students, Sports Law Society, Phi Delta Phi, Law and Medicine Society, Christian Legal Society, Hispanic Law Student Association, Asian Pacific Law Student Association, and law student divisions of the Illinois State Bar Association and the American Bar Association.

Applicant Profile

Southern Illinois University School of Law
This grid includes only applicants who earned 120–180 LSAT scores under standard administrations.

LSAT Score	GPA							
	3.75 or Above	3.50–3.74	3.25–3.49	3.00–3.24	2.75–2.99	2.50–2.74	2.25–2.49	2.24 or Below
165 or Above								
160–164								
158–159								
156–157								
155								
154								
153								
152								
Below 152								

Probable   Competitive   Unlikely

This grid reflects the highest LSAT score of the applicant.

Southern University Law Center

PO Box 9294
Baton Rouge, LA 70813
Phone: 225.771.5340 or 800.537.1135; Fax: 225.771.2121
E-mail: admission@sulc.edu; Website: www.sulc.edu

ABA Approved Since 1953

The Basics

Type of school	Public
Term	Semester
Application deadline	2/28 5/1
Application fee	$25
Financial aid deadline	4/15
Can first year start other than fall?	No
Student to faculty ratio	12.8 to 1
Does the university offer:	
housing restricted to law students?	No
graduate housing for which law students are eligible?	Yes

Faculty and Administrators

	Total		Men		Women		Minorities	
	Fall	Spr	Fall	Spr	Fall	Spr	Fall	Spr
Full-time	29	29	16	16	13	13	18	18
Other Full-time	0	0	0	0	0	0	0	0
Deans, librarians, & others who teach	5	5	4	4	1	1	4	4
Part-time	15	15	11	11	4	4	12	12
Total	49	49	31	31	18	18	34	34

Curriculum

	Full-time	Part-time
Typical first-year section size	44	45
Is there typically a "small section" of the first-year class, other than Legal Writing, taught by full-time faculty	No	No
If yes, typical size offered last year		

# of classroom course titles beyond first-year curriculum		41
# of upper division courses, excluding seminars with an enrollment:	Under 25	35
	25–49	26
	50–74	6
	75–99	0
	100+	0
# of seminars		6
# of seminar positions available		130
# of seminar positions filled	89	0
# of positions available in simulation courses		219
# of simulation positions filled	179	14
# of positions available in faculty supervised clinical courses		135
# of faculty supervised clinical positions filled	81	0
# involved in field placements	7	0
# involved in law journals	21	0
# involved in interschool competitions	15	0
# of credit hours required to graduate		96

JD Enrollment and Ethnicity

	Men		Women		Full-time		Part-time		1st-year		Total		JD Degs. Awd.
	#	%	#	%	#	%	#	%	#	%	#	%	
African Amer.	97	44.3	170	65.1	232	58.9	35	40.7	101	56.1	267	55.6	96
Amer. Indian	0	0.0	0	0.0	0	0.0	0	0.0	0	0.0	0	0.0	0
Asian Amer.	0	0.0	5	1.9	2	0.5	3	3.5	5	2.8	5	1.0	2
Mex. Amer.	0	0.0	0	0.0	0	0.0	0	0.0	0	0.0	0	0.0	0
Puerto Rican	0	0.0	0	0.0	0	0.0	0	0.0	0	0.0	0	0.0	0
Hispanic	4	1.8	0	0.0	4	1.0	0	0.0	2	1.1	4	0.8	0
Total Minority	101	46.1	175	67.0	238	60.4	38	44.2	108	60.0	276	57.5	98
For. Nation.	0	0.0	0	0.0	0	0.0	0	0.0	0	0.0	0	0.0	0
Caucasian	117	53.4	83	31.8	152	38.6	48	55.8	72	40.0	200	41.7	40
Unknown	1	0.5	3	1.1	4	1.0	0	0.0	0	0.0	4	0.8	0
Total	219	45.6	261	54.4	394	82.1	86	17.9	180	37.5	480		138

Transfers

Transfers in	1
Transfers out	2

Tuition and Fees

	Resident	Nonresident
Full-time	$6,610	$11,210
Part-time	$5,496	$10,096

Living Expenses

Estimated living expenses for singles

Living on campus	Living off campus	Living at home
$14,309	$14,309	$14,309

Southern University Law Center

*ABA
Approved
Since
1953*

GPA and LSAT Scores

	Total	Full-time	Part-time
# of apps	994	798	196
# of offers	312	243	69
# of matrics	180	126	54
75% GPA	3.34	3.42	3.19
Median GPA	3.15	2.99	2.89
25% GPA	2.55	2.60	2.41
75% LSAT	149	149	149
Median LSAT	147	147	146
25% LSAT	143	144	143

Grants and Scholarships (from prior year)

	Total #	Total %	Full-time #	Full-time %	Part-time #	Part-time %
Total # of students	487		418		69	
Total # receiving grants	142	29.2	142	34.0	0	0.0
Less than 1/2 tuition	83	17.0	83	19.9	0	0.0
Half to full tuition	55	11.3	55	13.2	0	0.0
Full tuition	0	0.0	0	0.0	0	0.0
More than full tuition	4	0.8	4	1.0	0	0.0
Median grant amount			$1,442		$0	

Informational and Library Resources

# of volumes and volume equivalents	475,081
# of titles	91,924
# of active serial subscriptions	4,599
Study seating capacity inside the library	284
# of full-time professional librarians	6
Hours per week library is open	99
# of open, wired connections available to students	55
# of networked computers available for use by students	36
# of simultaneous wireless users	420
Require computer?	No

JD Attrition (from prior year)

	Academic #	Other #	Total #	Total %
1st year	16	8	24	14.0
2nd year	2	1	3	1.8
3rd year	0	0	0	0.0
4th year	0	0	0	0.0

Employment (9 months after graduation)

	Total	Percentage
Employment status known	111	95.7
Employment status unknown	5	4.3
Employed	82	73.9
Pursuing graduate degrees	4	3.6
Unemployed seeking employment	22	19.8
Unemployed not seeking employment	3	2.7
Unemployed and studying for the bar	0	0.0

Type of Employment

# employed in law firms	43	52.4
# employed in business and industry	6	7.3
# employed in government	17	20.7
# employed in public interest	7	8.5
# employed as judicial clerks	8	9.8
# employed in academia	1	1.2

Geographic Location

# employed in state	65	79.3
# employed in foreign countries	0	0.0
# of states where employed	10	

Bar Passage Rates

Jurisdiction	Louisiana		
Exam	Sum 05	Win 06	Total
# from school taking bar for the first time	80	10	90
School's pass rate for all first-time takers	39%	30%	38%
State's pass rate for all first-time takers	73%	48%	70%

Southern University Law Center

Admission Office, PO Box 9294
Baton Rouge, LA 70813
Phone: 225.771.5340 or 800.537.1135; Fax: 225.771.2121
E-mail: admission@sulc.edu; Website: www.sulc.edu

■ Introduction

In September 1947, the Southern University school of law was officially opened, and it was redesignated as a law center in 1985. Accredited by the American Bar Association, the Supreme Court of Louisiana, and the Southern Association of Colleges and Secondary Schools, the Law Center maintains a high standard of professional education. It is fully approved by the Veterans Administration for the training of eligible veterans. The Southern University Law Center adheres to the principle of equal opportunity without regard to race, sex, color, creed, national origin, age, disability, or marital status.

The Law Center is located in Baton Rouge, the capital of Louisiana. With a population of over 500,000, this seat of state government includes state agencies and courts. As a hub of legal activity, Baton Rouge offers law students many opportunities to participate in state government through interaction with the legislature, state agencies, and private law firms.

■ Library

The law library contains more than 450,000 volumes; 1,000,000 microfiche; 40,000 rolls of microfilm; and 800 law reviews. The library offers research assistance and reference services to students, faculty, and the public. Its collection adequately supports the curriculum and conforms to the standards of the American Bar Association. Both federal and Louisiana state governments have designated Southern University Law Center Library as an official depository for government documents. A complete collection of Louisiana legal materials, including continuing legal education materials of the Louisiana Bar Association, is provided in the library. Although library acquisitions reflect the civil law tradition of Louisiana, sufficient materials for research in the common law and a substantial number of basic legal reference works are available. Media equipment in the library includes copying machines for printed materials and microform.

The library occupies a 30,000-square-foot area, which includes computer and multimedia law learning labs. Cooperative arrangements with the Louisiana State University Law Center Library provide access to one of the largest Anglo-American and civil law resource collections in the southern region. Interlibrary loans from other libraries can be made through the Southern University Law Library.

■ Curriculum

The program of study is designed to give students a comprehensive knowledge of both the civil law and the common law. While emphasis is given to the substantive and procedural law of Louisiana with its French and Spanish origins, Anglo-American law is strongly integrated into the curriculum. Fundamental differences in method and approach, and the results reached in the two systems, are analyzed.

The civil law system of Louisiana offers the law student a unique educational opportunity. The program of instruction examines the historical background of the Anglo-American setting. Students are trained in the art of advocacy, legal research, and the sources and social purposes of legal principles. Techniques to discipline the students' minds in legal reasoning are an integral part of the educational objectives of the Law Center. Students are instructed in the ethics of the legal profession and the professional responsibility of the lawyer to society.

The Juris Doctor (JD) degree is offered at the Southern University Law Center through a full-time and a part-time day/evening program. The JD program has a three-year curriculum requiring 96 hours of academic credits. The part-time program requires enrollment in at least eight credit hours a semester. A JD and Master of Public Administration (JD/MPA) joint degree is also offered by the Law Center and the Southern University Nelson Mandela School of Public Policy and Urban Affairs. The JD/MPA joint-degree program requires 123 hours of academic credit and can be completed in four years.

■ Admission

The Law Center does not prescribe any prelegal courses but strongly recommends a foundation in such courses as English, speech, political science, history, economics, psychology, logic, mathematics and analytical courses, and science.

Students beginning the study of law are admitted only in the fall semester. Applicants are advised to take the LSAT prior to the February test date of the expected year of enrollment. Under no circumstances will a score received on a test administered more than three years prior to the anticipated date of acceptance be considered. All applications for admission are reviewed by a special committee. Many variables are taken into consideration for admission, including, but not limited to, the undergraduate grade-point average and the LSAT. Work experience and past pursuits are also reviewed.

Completed application forms, in addition to two letters of recommendation and one copy of an official transcript, should be filed with the admission office during the fall semester prior to the year in which admission is sought.

■ Student Activities

Students with advanced standing are eligible to enroll in the Clinical Education Program, which allows students to handle cases under the direct supervision of a full-time faculty member of the Law Center.

The *Southern University Law Review* is a scholarly periodical published under the auspices of the Southern University Law Center. Editorial administration and managerial responsibilities are handled by the student members of the *Law Review* staff with guidance from a faculty advisor. Membership is conditional on the submission of a manuscript deemed by the editorial board to be publishable. *Law Review* membership provides eligible students with a wealth of experience in legal research and writing.

The purpose of the Student Bar Association is to promote the general welfare of the Law Center, encourage among its members high scholarship, and cultivate rapport and cooperation among the students, faculty, and members of the legal profession.

■ Housing

Limited dormitory accommodations are available for law students. All students desiring to live in campus housing are required to submit an application to the Housing Office, in addition to a security deposit of $50. Applications should be made to the Director of Housing, Southern University, as early as possible.

■ Other Student Organizations

Other student organizations include the Moot Court Board; Law Student Division, ABA; Black Law Students Association; Delta Theta Phi Law Fraternity International; Phi Alpha Delta Law Fraternity, International; Women in Law; Environmental Law Society; Sports and Entertainment Legal Association; Louisiana Trial Lawyers Association; Christians at Law Society; International Law Students Association; Southern Student Association of Criminal Defense Lawyers; Public Interest Law Society; and Phi Delta Phi International Legal Fraternity.

■ Career Services

The Office of Career Counseling and Development assists students and alumni in obtaining meaningful employment opportunities. Information on part-time employment before graduation is available through this office. Assistance is also given in job-seeking skills and interviewing techniques. The Law Center is a member of the National Association for Law Placement and subscribes to its standards for promoting career planning and development activities.

Applicant Profile Not Available

Southwestern Law School

3050 Wilshire Boulevard
Los Angeles, CA 90010-1106
Phone: 213.738.6717; Fax: 213.383.1688
E-mail: admissions@swlaw.edu; Website: www.swlaw.edu

ABA
Approved
Since
1970

The Basics

Type of school	Private
Term	Semester
Application deadline	4/1
Application fee	$50
Financial aid deadline	6/1
Can first year start other than fall?	No
Student to faculty ratio	15.8 to 1
Does the university offer:	
housing restricted to law students?	No
graduate housing for which law students are eligible?	No

Faculty and Administrators

	Total		Men		Women		Minorities	
	Fall	Spr	Fall	Spr	Fall	Spr	Fall	Spr
Full-time	46	45	28	27	18	18	9	9
Other Full-time	3	2	3	2	0	0	0	0
Deans, librarians, & others who teach	9	8	5	5	4	3	1	1
Part-time	23	26	14	20	9	6	5	3
Total	81	81	50	54	31	27	15	13

Curriculum

	Full-time	Part-time
Typical first-year section size	74	88
Is there typically a "small section" of the first-year class, other than Legal Writing, taught by full-time faculty	No	No
If yes, typical size offered last year		
# of classroom course titles beyond first-year curriculum	145	
# of upper division courses, excluding seminars with an enrollment: Under 25	101	
25–49	47	
50–74	27	
75–99	8	
100+	0	
# of seminars	20	
# of seminar positions available	404	
# of seminar positions filled	228	59
# of positions available in simulation courses	795	
# of simulation positions filled	506	130
# of positions available in faculty supervised clinical courses	0	
# of faculty supervised clinical positions filled	0	0
# involved in field placements	220	34
# involved in law journals	66	11
# involved in interschool competitions	73	10
# of credit hours required to graduate	87	

JD Enrollment and Ethnicity

	Men		Women		Full-time		Part-time		1st-year		Total		JD Degs. Awd.
	#	%	#	%	#	%	#	%	#	%	#	%	
African Amer.	13	2.8	37	7.4	24	3.6	26	9.0	23	6.7	50	5.2	7
Amer. Indian	0	0.0	7	1.4	5	0.7	2	0.7	1	0.3	7	0.7	2
Asian Amer.	70	15.2	105	20.9	120	17.8	55	19.1	66	19.2	175	18.2	63
Mex. Amer.	31	6.7	37	7.4	45	6.7	23	8.0	21	6.1	68	7.1	13
Puerto Rican	3	0.7	2	0.4	3	0.4	2	0.7	2	0.6	5	0.5	1
Hispanic	12	2.6	26	5.2	33	4.9	5	1.7	13	3.8	38	3.9	9
Total Minority	129	28.0	214	42.5	230	34.0	113	39.2	126	36.6	343	35.6	95
For. Nation.	6	1.3	6	1.2	9	1.3	3	1.0	1	0.3	12	1.2	4
Caucasian	264	57.3	219	43.5	348	51.5	135	46.9	187	54.4	483	50.1	161
Unknown	62	13.4	64	12.7	89	13.2	37	12.8	30	8.7	126	13.1	6
Total	461	47.8	503	52.2	676	70.1	288	29.9	344	35.7	964		266

Transfers

Transfers in	13
Transfers out	19

Tuition and Fees

	Resident	Nonresident
Full-time	$31,700	$31,700
Part-time	$19,100	$19,100

Living Expenses

Estimated living expenses for singles		
Living on campus	Living off campus	Living at home
N/A	$14,400	$8,550

*ABA
Approved
Since
1970*

GPA and LSAT Scores

	Total	Full-time	Part-time
# of apps	3,555	3,011	544
# of offers	1,087	922	165
# of matrics	348	245	103
75% GPA	3.55	3.59	3.33
Median GPA	3.29	3.39	3.13
25% GPA	3.04	3.12	2.90
75% LSAT	157	157	156
Median LSAT	155	155	153
25% LSAT	152	153	151

Grants and Scholarships (from prior year)

	Total		Full-time		Part-time	
	#	%	#	%	#	%
Total # of students	931		658		273	
Total # receiving grants	232	24.9	201	30.5	31	11.4
Less than 1/2 tuition	158	17.0	138	21.0	20	7.3
Half to full tuition	69	7.4	60	9.1	9	3.3
Full tuition	5	0.5	3	0.5	2	0.7
More than full tuition	0	0.0	0	0.0	0	0.0
Median grant amount			$10,000		$5,000	

Informational and Library Resources

# of volumes and volume equivalents	475,147
# of titles	133,894
# of active serial subscriptions	4,507
Study seating capacity inside the library	610
# of full-time professional librarians	9
Hours per week library is open	103
# of open, wired connections available to students	442
# of networked computers available for use by students	116
# of simultaneous wireless users	4,500
Require computer?	No

JD Attrition (from prior year)

	Academic	Other	Total	
	#	#	#	%
1st year	17	18	35	10.5
2nd year	5	18	23	7.8
3rd year	0	1	1	0.4
4th year	0	0	0	0.0

Employment (9 months after graduation)

	Total	Percentage
Employment status known	285	94.4
Employment status unknown	17	5.6
Employed	254	89.1
Pursuing graduate degrees	0	0.0
Unemployed seeking employment	7	2.5
Unemployed not seeking employment	13	4.6
Unemployed and studying for the bar	11	3.9

Type of Employment

# employed in law firms	152	59.8
# employed in business and industry	50	19.7
# employed in government	24	9.4
# employed in public interest	7	2.8
# employed as judicial clerks	4	1.6
# employed in academia	4	1.6

Geographic Location

# employed in state	226	89.0
# employed in foreign countries	0	0.0
# of states where employed		13

Bar Passage Rates

Jurisdiction	California		
Exam	Sum 05	Win 06	Total
# from school taking bar for the first time	244	40	284
School's pass rate for all first-time takers	66%	75%	68%
State's pass rate for all first-time takers	64%	54%	62%

Southwestern Law School

3050 Wilshire Boulevard
Los Angeles, CA 90010-1106
Phone: 213.738.6717; Fax: 213.383.1688
E-mail: admissions@swlaw.edu; Website: www.swlaw.edu

■ Introduction

With a long-standing emphasis on diversity, public service, and innovative programs, and a midcity campus featuring a world-renowned Art Deco landmark, Southwestern reflects the vibrancy of Los Angeles and provides an ideal setting for law study. Founded in 1911 as an independent, nonprofit, nonsectarian institution, Southwestern is fully approved by the ABA and is a member of the AALS. It is the only law school to offer four JD courses of study that differ in scheduling and instructional approach, including traditional full- and part-time programs as well as a unique two-year alternative curriculum. Southwestern's 10,000 alumni include prominent public officials—from members of Congress to mayors, and over 200 judges—as well as founders of major law firms and general counsels of multinational corporations. The law school has strong ties to the legal, business, and civic sectors, and its Biederman Entertainment and Media Law Institute is closely linked to the entertainment industry in Hollywood and internationally.

■ Diverse and Talented Student Body

Students come to Southwestern from virtually every state and a dozen foreign countries, and represent over 250 undergraduate institutions. About two-thirds have prior work experience or have already completed advanced degrees in diverse disciplines from accounting to urban planning. The most recent entering class is equally divided between women and men, while minorities make up 38 percent, and students report fluency in over 35 foreign languages. The average age is 26, with a range from 20 to 52.

■ Distinguished Faculty

Southwestern's faculty focus on enhancing the quality of both the classroom experience and the attention provided to students as individuals. The full-time faculty includes nationally recognized experts in antitrust, civil rights, criminal justice, entertainment and media, environmental, human rights, intellectual property, international, and urban development, among other areas of the law. The adjunct faculty of distinguished judges and attorneys are known for their expertise in specialized practices and enjoy sharing their real-world knowledge with students.

■ Award-winning Campus Facilities

Encompassing nearly two city blocks, Southwestern's campus includes the extraordinary Bullocks Wilshire building that is listed on the National Register of Historic Places. In 2004, the law school completed a $29 million campus expansion and enhancement effort. The award-winning facilities feature state-of-the-art multimedia technology in the classrooms, wireless Internet access, spacious dining facilities and student lounges in restored historic areas, large terraces with panoramic city views, and tranquil student commons and promenade plazas, as well as a 10,000-square-foot spa-quality fitness center. Southwestern's Leigh H. Taylor Law Library is the second largest academic law library facility in California.

The law school's new Julian C. Dixon Courtroom and Advocacy Center is the most technologically sophisticated center of its kind in the country.

■ Two-, Three-, and Four-year JD Programs

Four JD programs are offered: a three-year, full-time day program; a four-year, part-time evening program; PLEAS—a four-year, part-time day program for students with child-care responsibilities; and SCALE®—an accelerated two-year, full-time program featuring small classes, practical skills training, and real-world experience.

■ Comprehensive Curriculum

The required traditional curriculum includes 17 courses. A new cutting-edge first-year curriculum provides more time for students to digest class material, learn about the realities of legal practice, and take an elective as early as their second semester. Over 150 elective courses and more than 100 externship placement settings allow students to design a broad-based legal education or emphasize an area of law. As a result of Southwestern's location, faculty expertise, alumni presence in the profession, and history, the law school has developed a reputation for leading innovation and excellence, particularly in entertainment and media law, international law, criminal law, and trial advocacy/litigation. Southwestern sponsors summer law programs in Argentina, Canada, England, and Mexico. Academic Support Programs are offered in the summer and during the academic year.

■ Entertainment and Media Law Institute

Taking advantage of its position in the heart of the Entertainment Capital of the World and the Digital Coast, Southwestern established the Biederman Entertainment and Media Law Institute. The law school has the largest contingent of full-time entertainment and media law faculty of any law school, and benefits from an extensive network of alumni and adjunct faculty who hold prominent positions in these industries. The institute sponsors over 40 courses, 50 externships, a special law firm practicum, a scholarly journal, and summer programs in Los Angeles and London, and presents lectures and symposia with industry leaders. Southwestern also established the first LLM program in Entertainment and Media Law.

■ Student Activities

Southwestern's interscholastic Moot Court Honors Program, which sends teams to 15 competitions each year, is considered to be among the largest and best in the country. Members of the Interscholastic Trial Advocacy Program as well as the client counseling and negotiation teams also consistently earn top awards in regional and national competitions. Students demonstrate their outstanding research, writing, and editing skills through service on the law school's three scholarly journals, the *Southwestern University Law Review* and the *Southwestern Journal of Law and Trade in the Americas*, as well as the new *Journal of International Media and Entertainment Law* that was recently established in conjunction with the ABA Forum on Communications Law. The Student Bar Association sponsors award-winning student welfare programs and community outreach projects. There are also over 35 on-campus student organizations, including three legal fraternities; minority, cultural, political, and religious groups; and societies concerned with specific areas of law.

■ Public Interest Involvement

Southwestern encourages students to pursue public interest service through special scholarship funds, a loan forgiveness program, the Silbert Public Interest Fellowship Program, and extensive summer grant opportunities for students working with public service agencies, extensive student volunteer work with local schools and community organizations, and a variety of externships. During the annual Public Interest Law Week, the entire law school community rallies to raise awareness and funds supporting public interest activities.

■ Career Services

The Career Services Office coordinates career planning, counseling, workshops, networking events, and panel presentations as well as the Alumni Resource Network to help students prepare for and secure legal employment. The office sponsors intensive on- and off-campus interview programs and

provides online access to extensive job listings and on-campus interview opportunities through Symplicity and LawCrossing. Although the majority of Southwestern graduates choose to practice in California, alumni can be found in 47 states and 17 foreign countries.

■ Admission Criteria

Admission to Southwestern is highly selective, with an average acceptance rate over the past four years of 25 percent. While emphasis is placed on undergraduate GPA and LSAT scores earned within the past three years, community involvement, work experience, motivation, recommendations, and diversity are also major factors. Transfer applications are considered from students who have successfully completed at least one year at another ABA-approved law school.

■ Financial Aid/Scholarships

About 90 percent of Southwestern's students receive some form of financial aid that may include scholarships, grants, loans, and work-study funds. Among the more than 50 institutional scholarship funds are the Paul W. Wildman Scholarship and the John J. Schumacher Minority Leadership Scholarship programs, which provide up to full-tuition renewable scholarships to members of the entering class who demonstrate exceptional academic and leadership potential.

Applicant Profile

Southwestern Law School

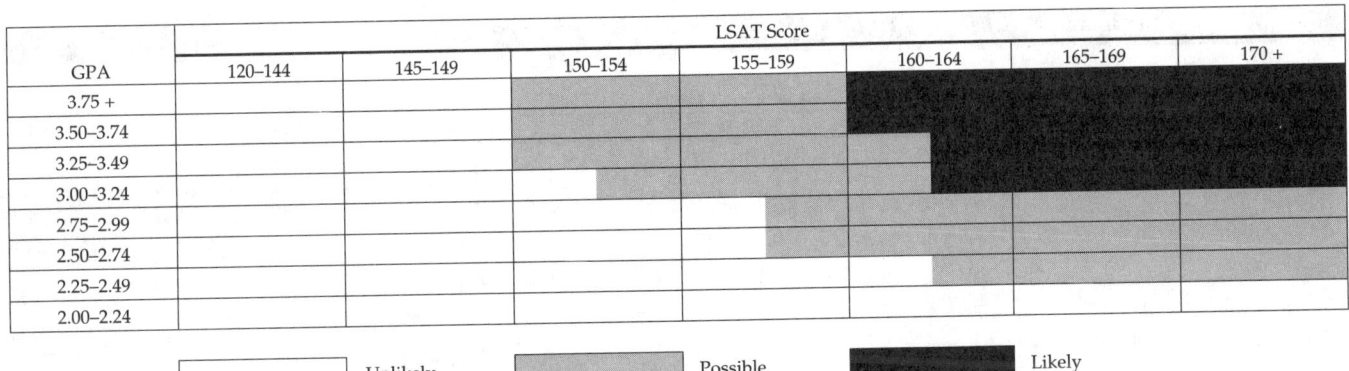

GPA	LSAT Score						
	120–144	145–149	150–154	155–159	160–164	165–169	170 +
3.75 +							
3.50–3.74							
3.25–3.49							
3.00–3.24							
2.75–2.99							
2.50–2.74							
2.25–2.49							
2.00–2.24							

Unlikely   Possible   Likely

Note: This chart is to be used as a general guide only in determining chances for admittance. Nonnumerical factors are seriously considered for all applicants.

Stanford University Law School

559 Nathan Abbott Way
Stanford, CA 94305-8610
Phone: 650.723.4985; Fax: 650.723.0838
E-mail: Admissions@law.stanford.edu; Website: www.law.stanford.edu

ABA Approved Since 1923

The Basics

Type of school	Private
Term	Semester
Application deadline	2/1
Application fee	$70
Financial aid deadline	3/15
Can first year start other than fall?	No
Student to faculty ratio	8.6 to 1
Does the university offer:	
housing restricted to law students?	No
graduate housing for which law students are eligible?	Yes

Faculty and Administrators

	Total		Men		Women		Minorities	
	Fall	Spr	Fall	Spr	Fall	Spr	Fall	Spr
Full-time	52	51	32	32	20	19	9	7
Other Full-time	18	19	6	9	12	10	4	4
Deans, librarians, & others who teach	14	14	6	6	8	8	4	4
Part-time	26	32	16	22	10	10	0	4
Total	110	116	60	69	50	47	17	19

Curriculum

	Full-time	Part-time
Typical first-year section size	60	0
Is there typically a "small section" of the first-year class, other than Legal Writing, taught by full-time faculty	Yes	No
If yes, typical size offered last year	28	
# of classroom course titles beyond first-year curriculum	148	
# of upper division courses, excluding seminars with an enrollment: Under 25	83	
25–49	26	
50–74	5	
75–99	3	
100+	2	
# of seminars	57	
# of seminar positions available	902	
# of seminar positions filled	691	0
# of positions available in simulation courses	358	
# of simulation positions filled	341	0
# of positions available in faculty supervised clinical courses	179	
# of faculty supervised clinical positions filled	173	0
# involved in field placements	23	0
# involved in law journals	386	0
# involved in interschool competitions	40	0
# of credit hours required to graduate	86	

JD Enrollment and Ethnicity

	Men #	Men %	Women #	Women %	Full-time #	Full-time %	Part-time #	Part-time %	1st-year #	1st-year %	Total #	Total %	JD Degs. Awd.
African Amer.	20	6.6	17	7.3	37	6.9	0	0.0	13	7.6	37	6.9	18
Amer. Indian	3	1.0	3	1.3	6	1.1	0	0.0	4	2.3	6	1.1	3
Asian Amer.	25	8.3	41	17.7	66	12.4	0	0.0	20	11.7	66	12.4	16
Mex. Amer.	31	10.3	21	9.1	52	9.7	0	0.0	15	8.8	52	9.7	22
Puerto Rican	0	0.0	4	1.7	4	0.7	0	0.0	2	1.2	4	0.7	2
Hispanic	1	0.3	2	0.9	3	0.6	0	0.0	2	1.2	3	0.6	1
Total Minority	80	26.5	88	37.9	168	31.5	0	0.0	56	32.7	168	31.5	62
For. Nation.	9	3.0	6	2.6	15	2.8	0	0.0	3	1.8	15	2.8	3
Caucasian	172	57.0	123	53.0	295	55.2	0	0.0	92	53.8	295	55.2	91
Unknown	41	13.6	15	6.5	56	10.5	0	0.0	20	11.7	56	10.5	19
Total	302	56.6	232	43.4	534	100.0	0	0.0	171	32.0	534		175

Transfers

Transfers in	12
Transfers out	0

Tuition and Fees

	Resident	Nonresident
Full-time	$37,836	$0
Part-time	$0	$0

Living Expenses

Estimated living expenses for singles

Living on campus	Living off campus	Living at home
$19,872	$23,122	N/A

*ABA
Approved
Since
1923*

Stanford University Law School

GPA and LSAT Scores

	Total	Full-time	Part-time
# of apps	4,567	4,567	0
# of offers	398	398	0
# of matrics	171	171	0
75% GPA	3.96	3.96	0.00
Median GPA	3.87	3.87	0.00
25% GPA	3.77	3.77	0.00
75% LSAT	172	172	0
Median LSAT	170	170	0
25% LSAT	167	167	0

Grants and Scholarships (from prior year)

	Total #	Total %	Full-time #	Full-time %	Part-time #	Part-time %
Total # of students	527		527		0	
Total # receiving grants	204	38.7	204	38.7	0	0.0
Less than 1/2 tuition	129	24.5	129	24.5	0	0.0
Half to full tuition	70	13.3	70	13.3	0	0.0
Full tuition	4	0.8	4	0.8	0	0.0
More than full tuition	1	0.2	1	0.2	0	0.0
Median grant amount			$15,149		$0	

Informational and Library Resources

# of volumes and volume equivalents	543,405
# of titles	215,648
# of active serial subscriptions	7,301
Study seating capacity inside the library	507
# of full-time professional librarians	9
Hours per week library is open	103
# of open, wired connections available to students	165
# of networked computers available for use by students	321
# of simultaneous wireless users	1,000
Require computer?	Yes

JD Attrition (from prior year)

	Academic #	Other #	Total #	Total %
1st year	0	0	0	0.0
2nd year	0	0	0	0.0
3rd year	0	0	0	0.0
4th year	0	0	0	0.0

Employment (9 months after graduation)

	Total	Percentage
Employment status known	162	100.0
Employment status unknown	0	0.0
Employed	159	98.1
Pursuing graduate degrees	0	0.0
Unemployed seeking employment	2	1.2
Unemployed not seeking employment	0	0.0
Unemployed and studying for the bar	1	0.6

Type of Employment

# employed in law firms	103	64.8
# employed in business and industry	6	3.8
# employed in government	2	1.3
# employed in public interest	6	3.8
# employed as judicial clerks	41	25.8
# employed in academia	1	0.6

Geographic Location

# employed in state	72	45.3
# employed in foreign countries	3	1.9
# of states where employed	25	

Bar Passage Rates

Jurisdiction	California			New York		
Exam	Sum 05	Win 06	Total	Sum 05	Win 06	Total
# from school taking bar for the first time	83	14	97	41	0	41
School's pass rate for all first-time takers	88%	79%	87%	95%		95%
State's pass rate for all first-time takers	64%	54%	62%	76%	61%	74%

Stanford University Law School

Office of Admissions, 559 Nathan Abbott Way
Stanford, CA 94305-8610
Phone: 650.723.4985; Fax: 650.723.0838
E-mail: Admissions@law.stanford.edu; Website: www.law.stanford.edu

■ Introduction

Stanford Law School is part of one of the world's leading research institutions, providing plentiful opportunities for interdisciplinary cooperation. Stanford University is a private university located in the heart of Silicon Valley, just 35 miles south of San Francisco. The university's 8,180 acres stretch between the foothills of the Santa Cruz Mountains and the cities of Palo Alto and Menlo Park, in a part of the country that offers an ideal, Mediterranean climate of dry, warm summers and wet, but temperate winters.

Current enrollment at the university is approximately 16,000 students, of whom about 8,200 are graduate students. The Law School is small, with about 530 JD students, 40 LLM and JSM students, and a faculty of 40-plus permanent members. The school has teaching and research ties with schools and departments across campus. Law School courses are taught in 16 beautiful, recently renovated multimedia classrooms with full wireless Internet connectivity.

Stanford Law School offers a unique combination of the classic and cutting edge in legal education. The school is preparing its students for a rich and varied professional life in an era of great excitement and rapid change—much of it generated by the remarkable innovations in information technology pioneered in Silicon Valley—and for careers in an increasingly global community.

■ Faculty

Stanford Law School has an exceptional faculty, distinguished not only for its scholarship, but also for its commitment to teaching and curricular innovation. The school's unusually low student/faculty ratio creates an intimate, collegial environment that fosters students' intellectual and professional development both in and out of the classroom. Students have many opportunities to work closely with faculty members as research assistants on scholarly projects; indeed, the faculty actively encourage interested students to develop their own scholarship for future academic careers. The relationships formed between Stanford faculty and students often last a lifetime.

Instruction at Stanford takes place primarily in small classes and seminars and through individually directed research. It also takes innovative forms: Stanford is a leader in the development of clinical teaching through simulation and individualized feedback via a diverse range of legal clinics.

The faculty is continually engaged in developing new teaching methods to complement curricular innovations. Case studies, similar to those of business schools, challenge students to consider the interaction of legal and nonlegal factors involved in a given situation. Interdisciplinary research projects allow faculty and students from the law school and other parts of the university, joined by practitioners and policymakers, to engage in applied research in fields such as technology policy and international law.

■ Library and Physical Facilities

Housed within Crown Quadrangle is the Robert Crown Law Library, which holds an excellent collection of print materials and an even richer and growing collection of online resources.

The library and school are configured for wireless access. Popular with the law students are the library's reading rooms, which are flooded with natural light from floor-to-ceiling windows and feature technology-enabled conference rooms, modern decor, and even loaner bicycles. The 28 friendly and service-minded staff members at the Robert Crown Law Library are dedicated to helping students, faculty, and staff with all their research needs.

■ Special Programs

Joint-degree Programs—Stanford Law School is actively expanding its joint-degree programs, leveraging the highly rated graduate schools and academic programs throughout Stanford University. For students with specialized career aspirations, opportunities to customize a joint degree are limitless; the law school reaches out to virtually every Stanford school or department where there's an opportunity for students to work across disciplines. To facilitate interdisciplinary study and scholarship with the wider university and simplify the pursuit of joint degrees, we are adapting the law school calendar to be compatible with those of other Stanford schools and departments.

Established joint-study programs with several other Stanford departments include a JD/MBA with the Graduate School of Business, a JD/PhD with the Department of Economics, a JD/MS with the Interdisciplinary Graduate Program in Environment and Resources, and a JD/PhD with the Department of Sociology. Joint-degree programs are also offered with Princeton's Woodrow Wilson School of Public and International Affairs and the School of Advanced International Studies at Johns Hopkins University. In addition, the school will consider requests for joint programs on an individually designed basis.

Programs and Centers—Stanford Law School's scholarly programs and innovative centers offer a sophisticated array of options and give students the opportunity for concentrated study and close interaction with faculty. Students may engage in graduate-level research and policy-oriented study through centers and programs such as Stanford Constitutional Law Center; Stanford Criminal Justice Center; Stanford Program in International Law, including the Gould Negotiation and Mediation Teaching Program; Stanford Center on Conflict Negotiation; the Programs in Law, Economics, and Business, including the Arthur and Toni Rembe Rock Center for Corporate Governance; Law, Science and Technology, including the Center for Internet and Society, Center for Law and BioSciences, and Center for Computers and the Law; and International Law, Business and Policy.

Team-taught Courses and Concentration—Embarking on a new educational concept, Stanford Law now offers team-oriented, problem-solving courses, many of which are cotaught by law school faculty and faculty from Stanford's other top-rated schools and departments. Classes are open to students from a variety of disciplines.

Students interested in a particular area of law can specialize by taking a customized selection of law school courses.

Clinical Program—Stanford is a leader in the development of clinical teaching and, through its expanded clinical program, offers students the opportunity to undertake, under the close supervision of experienced practitioners, the roles and responsibilities of practicing lawyers. Students engage in witness examination, depositions, discovery, negotiations, drafting pleadings and memos, oral arguments, and analysis of tactical and ethical problems. Supervised work with clients may take place in any of Stanford's nine clinics, including our Community Law Clinic, Criminal Prosecution Clinic, Immigrants' Rights Clinic, or Supreme Court Litigation Clinic.

■ Housing

Stanford provides a variety of subsidized on-campus housing options. Housing is guaranteed to all new, matriculated students who apply for housing by the early-May deadline and are willing to live in any graduate residence. The university maintains listings of off-campus housing opportunities. More information about housing is available at the Housing Assignment Services website *www.stanford.edu/dept/hds/has/*.

■ Student Activities

Fifty-one student organizations enrich the law school experience. Opportunities for scholarly work are provided through the *Stanford Law Review; Stanford Journal of Civil Rights and Civil Liberties; Stanford Journal of International Law; Stanford Journal of Law, Business and Finance; Stanford Law and Policy Review; Stanford Technology Law Review;* and *Stanford Environmental Law Journal.* Advocacy skills are developed in moot court and mock trial.

Students who are female, Asian, African American, Latino, Native American, Christian, Jewish, bisexual, gay, or lesbian will all find groups with their particular concerns. Other organizations focus on environmental law, international law, law and technology, and public interest law. Local affiliates of the Federalist Society, the American Constitution Society, and the National Lawyers Guild are present.

■ Expenses and Financial Aid

Estimated expenses are as follows: For 2006–2007, full-time tuition was $37,440, with additional expenses including housing estimated at $20,268 for single students living on campus and $23,518 for single students living off campus. Scholarships are awarded on the basis of financial need. The purpose of financial aid is to assist students who would otherwise be unable to pursue a legal education at Stanford. Approximately 80 percent of the student body receives tuition fellowship or loan assistance.

Stanford law students planning public service careers may apply for Public Service Fellowships for their second and third years of school. The school also offers funding to students who dedicate a law school summer to qualified public service work. And for graduates who take low-paying public interest jobs and have substantial educational debt, the school has an excellent Loan Repayment Assistance Program.

■ Career Services

The Office of Career Services helps students find employment. More than 300 employers representing 600 offices worldwide participate in the spring and fall on-campus interview programs. The office also offers counseling and information on traditional and nontraditional careers and employers. The school encourages students to consider public interest and public-sector employment and assists students to secure such positions.

A survey of students graduating in the class of 2005 shows the following employment patterns: law firm associates, 65 percent; judicial clerks, 26 percent; and business (legal and nonlegal), public interest, government, or law teaching, 9 percent.

Applicant Profile

Our admission process takes into consideration many factors besides the undergraduate GPA and LSAT score. A statistical grid, as is typically provided here, only takes into consideration these two factors. We have chosen not to provide applicants with such a grid because our admission process would not be accurately portrayed.

Stetson University College of Law

1401 61st Street South
Gulfport, FL 33707
Phone: 727.562.7802; Fax: 727.343.0136
E-mail: lawadmit@law.stetson.edu; Website: www.law.stetson.edu

ABA
Approved
Since
1930

The Basics

Type of school	Private
Term	Semester
Application deadline	3/15 9/15
Application fee	$55
Financial aid deadline	
Can first year start other than fall?	Yes
Student to faculty ratio	17.0 to 1
Does the university offer:	
housing restricted to law students?	Yes
graduate housing for which law students are eligible?	No

Faculty and Administrators

	Total		Men		Women		Minorities	
	Fall	Spr	Fall	Spr	Fall	Spr	Fall	Spr
Full-time	46	44	27	25	19	18	5	6
Other Full-time	1	5	1	3	0	2	1	0
Deans, librarians, & others who teach	6	6	1	1	5	5	0	0
Part-time	37	38	24	26	13	12	4	4
Total	**90**	**93**	**53**	**55**	**37**	**37**	**10**	**10**

Curriculum

	Full-time	Part-time
Typical first-year section size	69	74
Is there typically a "small section" of the first-year class, other than Legal Writing, taught by full-time faculty	No	No
If yes, typical size offered last year		
# of classroom course titles beyond first-year curriculum	119	
# of upper division courses, excluding seminars with an enrollment: Under 25	62	
25–49	28	
50–74	9	
75–99	0	
100+	0	
# of seminars	18	
# of seminar positions available	313	
# of seminar positions filled	207	52
# of positions available in simulation courses	790	
# of simulation positions filled	439	283
# of positions available in faculty supervised clinical courses	151	
# of faculty supervised clinical positions filled	123	10
# involved in field placements	187	10
# involved in law journals	51	4
# involved in interschool competitions	73	7
# of credit hours required to graduate	88	

Transfers

Transfers in	2
Transfers out	10

Tuition and Fees

	Resident	Nonresident
Full-time	$27,860	$27,860
Part-time	$19,300	$19,300

Living Expenses

Estimated living expenses for singles

Living on campus	Living off campus	Living at home
$13,837	$17,021	$7,840

JD Enrollment and Ethnicity

	Men		Women		Full-time		Part-time		1st-year		Total		JD Degs. Awd.
	#	%	#	%	#	%	#	%	#	%	#	%	
African Amer.	25	5.2	35	6.4	34	4.2	26	11.5	25	7.0	60	5.8	17
Amer. Indian	2	0.4	4	0.7	5	0.6	1	0.4	2	0.6	6	0.6	1
Asian Amer.	13	2.7	14	2.6	21	2.6	6	2.6	10	2.8	27	2.6	5
Mex. Amer.	2	0.4	2	0.4	4	0.5	0	0.0	2	0.6	4	0.4	1
Puerto Rican	8	1.7	8	1.5	11	1.4	5	2.2	6	1.7	16	1.5	6
Hispanic	39	8.1	49	8.9	78	9.7	10	4.4	20	5.6	88	8.5	28
Total Minority	89	18.4	112	20.4	153	19.0	48	21.1	65	18.2	201	19.5	58
For. Nation.	1	0.2	5	0.9	6	0.7	0	0.0	4	1.1	6	0.6	1
Caucasian	383	79.1	420	76.5	626	77.7	177	78.0	282	78.8	803	77.7	221
Unknown	11	2.3	12	2.2	21	2.6	2	0.9	7	2.0	23	2.2	7
Total	484	46.9	549	53.1	806	78.0	227	22.0	358	34.7	1033		287

Stetson University College of Law

*ABA
Approved
Since
1930*

GPA and LSAT Scores

	Total	Full-time	Part-time
# of apps	3,182	2,684	498
# of offers	929	768	161
# of matrics	355	274	81
75% GPA	3.60	3.62	3.46
Median GPA	3.38	3.44	3.18
25% GPA	3.13	3.19	3.01
75% LSAT	157	157	155
Median LSAT	154	155	153
25% LSAT	152	152	150

Grants and Scholarships (from prior year)

	Total		Full-time		Part-time	
	#	%	#	%	#	%
Total # of students	987		757		230	
Total # receiving grants	152	15.4	138	18.2	14	6.1
Less than 1/2 tuition	28	2.8	28	3.7	0	0.0
Half to full tuition	38	3.9	27	3.6	11	4.8
Full tuition	36	3.6	33	4.4	3	1.3
More than full tuition	50	5.1	50	6.6	0	0.0
Median grant amount			$16,525		$9,010	

Informational and Library Resources

# of volumes and volume equivalents	413,166
# of titles	124,957
# of active serial subscriptions	3,813
Study seating capacity inside the library	619
# of full-time professional librarians	7
Hours per week library is open	105
# of open, wired connections available to students	1,255
# of networked computers available for use by students	113
# of simultaneous wireless users	2,600
Require computer?	Yes

JD Attrition (from prior year)

	Academic	Other	Total	
	#	#	#	%
1st year	0	14	14	4.1
2nd year	2	14	16	5.0
3rd year	1	2	3	1.0
4th year	0	0	0	0.0

Employment (9 months after graduation)

	Total	Percentage
Employment status known	235	99.2
Employment status unknown	2	0.8
Employed	219	93.2
Pursuing graduate degrees	5	2.1
Unemployed seeking employment	6	2.6
Unemployed not seeking employment	3	1.3
Unemployed and studying for the bar	2	0.9

Type of Employment

	Total	Percentage
# employed in law firms	128	58.4
# employed in business and industry	20	9.1
# employed in government	43	19.6
# employed in public interest	12	5.5
# employed as judicial clerks	13	5.9
# employed in academia	2	0.9

Geographic Location

	Total	Percentage
# employed in state	199	90.9
# employed in foreign countries	0	0.0
# of states where employed	12	

Bar Passage Rates

Jurisdiction	Florida		
Exam	Sum 05	Win 06	Total
# from school taking bar for the first time	136	101	237
School's pass rate for all first-time takers	74%	80%	77%
State's pass rate for all first-time takers	71%	73%	71%

Stetson University College of Law

1401 61st Street South
Gulfport, FL 33707
Phone: 727.562.7802; Fax: 727.343.0136
E-mail: lawadmit@law.stetson.edu; Website: www.law.stetson.edu

■ Introduction

Founded in 1900, Stetson University College of Law is Florida's first law school. The college's main campus is in Gulfport, which is a suburb of St. Petersburg. Located in a former resort hotel, the campus provides an outstanding environment in which to study law. A satellite campus in downtown Tampa hosts some classes in our part-time and full-time JD programs and houses judges on Florida's Second District Court of Appeal. Stetson is fully accredited by the American Bar Association and has been an Association of American Law Schools member since 1931. The college is an equal opportunity education institution. For additional information, visit *www.law.stetson.edu.*

■ Library and Physical Facilities

Modern in every educational aspect, the facilities include six courtrooms. The Law Library and Legal Information Center is one of the most advanced research and communications technology centers in the Southeast. It contains more than 415,000 volumes, a wireless network, and 43 group study rooms. The Tampa Law Center includes a satellite library to support students, alumni, and judges. There is a laptop requirement for all admitted students.

■ Admission

Stetson received 3,228 applications, offered admission to 929 applicants, and enrolled 355 first-year students: 274 full time and 81 part time. The 2006 entering class included 19 percent minority students and 50 percent women. There are 132 undergraduate institutions and 32 states/territories represented. These numbers represent the spring and fall full-time and part-time 2006 entering classes. The student body consists of approximately 800 full-time and 230 part-time JD students, as well as 15 LLM students (from eight countries). Our students, faculty, and staff work together toward one common goal: preparing our students to be the best lawyers and leaders possible.

■ Faculty

The intellectual exchange among students and faculty is continuous, both inside and outside the classroom. The 53 full-time professors are engaged in projects that bring them regional, national, and international prominence, but make teaching and working with students their top priority. Each semester, full-time faculty is supplemented by approximately 50 practicing attorneys and judges who serve as adjunct professors in specialized areas.

■ Curriculum

Academic Success Programs: Stetson offers many programs, including academic advising, an academic orientation, a semester-long academic skills workshop, and a Writing Clinic, designed to assist all students in achieving their academic potential.

Lawyering Skills: Stetson's academic program focuses on the lawyering process. Stetson is a pioneer and national leader in advocacy and clinical training.

Additional Academic Offerings: Stetson offers a part-time JD program that allows a student to earn a law degree in four years by taking classes in the evenings. Classes must be taken at both the Gulfport campus and Tampa Law Center. Stetson also offers a joint JD/MBA program that prepares students for careers in law and business. The Master of Laws (LLM) program in International Law has included lawyers from 35 different countries. A new, online LLM in Elder Law will be offered in fall 2007. Stetson offers summer-abroad opportunities in Argentina, Germany, The Hague, China, and Spain. Stetson has Centers for Excellence in Advocacy, Elder Law, Higher Education Law and Policy, and International Law. Stetson also hosts the National Clearinghouse for Science, Technology and the Law, and the Institute for Biodiversity Law and Policy.

■ Expenses and Financial Aid

Full-time tuition for 2006–2007 (fall/spring) is $27,660, and part-time tuition for 2006–2007 (fall/spring/summer) is $23,900. Partial and full merit and diversity scholarships are offered on a competitive basis. Need and endowed scholarships are offered for continuing students. There is no financial aid deadline and a completed FAFSA is the only required form.

■ Special Programs

Trial Advocacy: Stetson is recognized as one of the best law schools for advocacy. Stetson's teams routinely win national, regional, and state mock trial, moot court, and client skills competitions. Stetson was the first law school to win all five major national mock trial competitions in a single academic year. And Stetson was the first American law school since 1996 to win the Willem C. Vis International Commercial Arbitration Moot in Vienna, Austria, in 2005; the team won the silver medal in 2006.

Clinics and Internships: Stetson offers upper-level students a wide variety of opportunities to work closely with attorneys and judges, and, in some cases, actually represent clients and try cases. Clinical opportunities include Civil Poverty Law, Elder Law, Employment Discrimination, Immigration, Local Government, Prosecution, and Public Defender. Internships include Bankruptcy Judicial Internship, Caribbean Law Internship, Elder Law Internship, Environmental Law Internship, EEOC Internship, In-House Counsel Internship, Intellectual Property Internship, Federal and State Judicial Internships, Labor Law Internship, State and Federal Litigation Internships, and US Court of Appeals for Veterans Claims Internship.

Certificates of Concentration: Students can apply to a certificate program in which they focus their elective credits on advocacy, elder law, or international law.

Law Review: The *Stetson Law Review* publishes three issues each year. Students are selected based on grades and writing ability. Stetson serves as headquarters for the National Conference of Law Reviews. Stetson also publishes the *Journal of International Aging Law and Policy* in cooperation with the AARP, and the *Journal of International Wildlife Law and Policy.*

Honors Program: Students with a 3.5 GPA after their first or second semester are invited to join the Honors Program, which features a special colloquium and seminar. Honors students also are invited to attend a wide variety of faculty colloquia and other special events.

Continuing Legal Education: Students are encouraged to attend the numerous seminars and conferences sponsored by the college for practicing attorneys, judges, and other professionals.

■ Residential Life

Stetson has limited on-campus dormitories, as well as approximately 50 single-family homes and a 32-unit apartment complex located within a few blocks of the campus. A wait list is maintained for placement in all of these spaces. For more information, contact the Office of Residential Life by e-mail at *housing@law.stetson.edu* or visit *www.law.stetson.edu/housing/*.

■ Career Development

Stetson's commitment to helping students achieve their goals is reflected in its strong career services program. The Office of Career Development assists students and alumni in securing all types of legal and law-related employment and provides group seminars and individual counseling on subjects ranging from interviewing techniques to résumé writing. More than 96 percent of the 2005 graduating class reported that they found employment within nine months of graduation. Approximately 91 percent of recent Stetson graduates practice within Florida; however, alumni are located in 48 states and 22 countries.

■ Office of Student Life

The Office of Student Life offers student activities that support Stetson's academic mission and enrich the law school experience, such as cultural programs, experiential education trips, community service opportunities, and monthly leadership luncheons. Stetson has nearly 40 diverse and active student organizations. The Student Bar Association is the umbrella organization under which all others are coordinated. The Stetson Chapter of the American Bar Association Law Student Division has been recognized regionally and nationally as one of the best, and the Student Leadership Development Program was recently awarded the ABA's prestigious E. Smythe Gambrell Award for excellence in professionalism programming. A strong Office of Student Life presence on campus allows students many opportunities to hone their leadership and communication skills, network socially with their peers and legal professionals, and grow interpersonally as strong future members of the legal profession.

Applicant Profile

Stetson University College of Law
This grid includes only applicants who earned 120–180 LSAT scores under standard administrations.

LSAT Score	3.75 +		3.50–3.74		3.25–3.49		3.00–3.24		2.75–2.99		2.50–2.74		2.25–2.49		2.00–2.24		Below 2.00		No GPA		Total	
	Apps	Adm	Apps	Adm	Apps	Adm	Apps	Adm	Apps	Adm	Apps	Adm	Apps	Adm	Apps	Adm	Apps	Adm	Apps	Adm	Apps	Adm
175–180	0	0	1	1	1	1	0	0	1	1	0	0	0	0	0	0	0	0	0	0	3	3
170–174	3	3	0	0	1	0	0	0	0	0	1	1	0	0	0	0	0	0	0	0	5	4
165–169	6	5	4	4	3	2	4	3	3	3	2	1	3	0	0	0	0	0	0	0	25	18
160–164	16	16	26	24	28	22	23	20	15	6	9	2	7	2	2	0	0	0	3	2	128	94
155–159	60	53	90	74	115	79	99	59	62	21	34	3	13	2	9	1	1	1	3	2	486	295
150–154	88	64	150	81	206	70	165	39	117	12	47	6	22	0	7	0	2	0	3	1	807	273
145–149	67	12	119	13	147	10	141	13	98	5	53	3	28	2	12	0	2	0	7	0	674	58
140–144	21	1	56	5	67	1	72	5	57	1	43	1	17	0	11	0	2	0	6	1	352	15
135–139	5	0	13	0	11	0	24	0	17	0	11	0	12	0	11	0	2	0	2	0	109	0
130–134	2	0	3	0	4	0	6	0	5	0	4	0	8	0	3	0	0	0	2	0	37	0
125–129	1	0	1	0	0	0	1	0	0	0	0	0	1	0	3	0	0	0	0	0	7	0
120–124	0	0	0	0	0	0	1	0	0	0	0	0	1	0	0	0	0	0	0	0	2	0
Total	269	154	463	202	583	185	536	139	375	49	204	17	112	6	58	1	9	1	26	6	2635	760

Apps = Number of Applicants
Adm = Number Admitted
Reflects 99% of the total applicant pool.

Suffolk University Law School

David J. Sargent Hall, 120 Tremont Street
Boston, MA 02108-4977
Phone: 617.573.8144; Fax: 617.523.1367
E-mail: lawadm@suffolk.edu; Website: www.law.suffolk.edu

ABA
Approved
Since
1953

The Basics

Type of school	Private
Term	Semester
Application deadline	3/1
Application fee	$60
Financial aid deadline	3/1
Can first year start other than fall?	No
Student to faculty ratio	17.8 to 1
Does the university offer:	
housing restricted to law students?	No
graduate housing for which law students are eligible?	No

Faculty and Administrators

	Total		Men		Women		Minorities	
	Fall	Spr	Fall	Spr	Fall	Spr	Fall	Spr
Full-time	68	66	47	46	21	20	9	8
Other Full-time	9	6	4	1	5	5	2	2
Deans, librarians, & others who teach	8	9	6	7	2	2	1	1
Part-time	66	77	53	53	13	24	3	4
Total	**151**	**158**	**110**	**107**	**41**	**51**	**15**	**15**

Curriculum

	Full-time	Part-time
Typical first-year section size	89	92
Is there typically a "small section" of the first-year class, other than Legal Writing, taught by full-time faculty	Yes	Yes
If yes, typical size offered last year	45	46
# of classroom course titles beyond first-year curriculum	284	
# of upper division courses, excluding seminars with an enrollment: Under 25	119	
25–49	66	
50–74	24	
75–99	10	
100+	13	
# of seminars	52	
# of seminar positions available	960	
# of seminar positions filled	456	296
# of positions available in simulation courses	1,314	
# of simulation positions filled	623	491
# of positions available in faculty supervised clinical courses	93	
# of faculty supervised clinical positions filled	80	13
# involved in field placements	99	6
# involved in law journals	163	22
# involved in interschool competitions	87	17
# of credit hours required to graduate	84	

JD Enrollment and Ethnicity

	Men #	Men %	Women #	Women %	Full-time #	Full-time %	Part-time #	Part-time %	1st-year #	1st-year %	Total #	Total %	JD Degs. Awd.
African Amer.	21	2.5	26	3.2	27	2.6	20	3.3	15	2.8	47	2.9	7
Amer. Indian	5	0.6	3	0.4	6	0.6	2	0.3	4	0.8	8	0.5	1
Asian Amer.	47	5.6	58	7.2	69	6.7	36	5.9	37	7.0	105	6.4	22
Mex. Amer.	0	0.0	0	0.0	0	0.0	0	0.0	0	0.0	0	0.0	0
Puerto Rican	0	0.0	0	0.0	0	0.0	0	0.0	0	0.0	0	0.0	0
Hispanic	21	2.5	30	3.7	33	3.2	18	2.9	22	4.2	51	3.1	11
Total Minority	94	11.2	117	14.5	135	13.1	76	12.4	78	14.8	211	12.8	41
For. Nation.	13	1.5	10	1.2	11	1.1	12	2.0	13	2.5	23	1.4	11
Caucasian	648	77.2	617	76.6	786	76.2	479	78.3	384	72.7	1265	76.9	416
Unknown	84	10.0	61	7.6	100	9.7	45	7.4	53	10.0	145	8.8	27
Total	839	51.0	805	49.0	1032	62.8	612	37.2	528	32.1	1644		495

Transfers

Transfers in	15
Transfers out	20

Tuition and Fees

	Resident	Nonresident
Full-time	$33,874	$33,874
Part-time	$25,406	$25,406

Living Expenses

Estimated living expenses for singles

Living on campus	Living off campus	Living at home
N/A	$18,069	$8,939

Suffolk University Law School

ABA Approved Since 1953

GPA and LSAT Scores

	Total	Full-time	Part-time
# of apps	3,040	2,429	611
# of offers	1,469	1,136	333
# of matrics	530	331	199
75% GPA	3.51	3.53	3.49
Median GPA	3.24	3.28	3.15
25% GPA	2.96	3.01	2.88
75% LSAT	158	159	157
Median LSAT	155	156	154
25% LSAT	153	154	152

Grants and Scholarships (from prior year)

	Total		Full-time		Part-time	
	#	%	#	%	#	%
Total # of students	1,671		1,058		613	
Total # receiving grants	653	39.1	528	49.9	125	20.4
Less than 1/2 tuition	591	35.4	483	45.7	108	17.6
Half to full tuition	59	3.5	43	4.1	16	2.6
Full tuition	2	0.1	2	0.2	0	0.0
More than full tuition	1	0.1	0	0.0	1	0.2
Median grant amount			$5,000		$4,000	

Informational and Library Resources

# of volumes and volume equivalents	367,096
# of titles	183,408
# of active serial subscriptions	6,630
Study seating capacity inside the library	880
# of full-time professional librarians	10
Hours per week library is open	103
# of open, wired connections available to students	3,650
# of networked computers available for use by students	278
# of simultaneous wireless users	900
Require computer?	No

JD Attrition (from prior year)

	Academic	Other	Total	
	#	#	#	%
1st year	27	18	45	8.2
2nd year	3	7	10	2.0
3rd year	1	4	5	1.0
4th year	0	1	1	0.7

Employment (9 months after graduation)

	Total	Percentage
Employment status known	479	98.6
Employment status unknown	7	1.4
Employed	417	87.1
Pursuing graduate degrees	11	2.3
Unemployed seeking employment	31	6.5
Unemployed not seeking employment	6	1.3
Unemployed and studying for the bar	14	2.9

Type of Employment

# employed in law firms	192	46.0
# employed in business and industry	86	20.6
# employed in government	71	17.0
# employed in public interest	17	4.1
# employed as judicial clerks	39	9.4
# employed in academia	6	1.4

Geographic Location

# employed in state	325	77.9
# employed in foreign countries	1	0.2
# of states where employed		25

Bar Passage Rates

Jurisdiction	Massachusetts		
Exam	Sum 05	Win 06	Total
# from school taking bar for the first time	366	46	412
School's pass rate for all first-time takers	81%	65%	80%
State's pass rate for all first-time takers	84%	75%	82%

Suffolk University Law School

David J. Sargent Hall, 120 Tremont Street
Boston, MA 02108-4977
Phone: 617.573.8144; Fax: 617.523.1367
E-mail: lawadm@suffolk.edu; Website: www.law.suffolk.edu

■ Introduction

Suffolk University Law School was founded by Gleason Archer in 1906. His mission was to make Suffolk University Law School a welcoming portal for all who wished to study the law, regardless of ethnicity, economic status, education, or place of birth. In a city where the cobblestones and gas lamps of Beacon Hill coexist with cutting-edge organizations that include education, medicine, high technology, and finance, Suffolk University Law School is woven into Boston's rich past and bright future. Boston offers the authenticity of what was, with the very best of what is—and Sargent Hall is a grand and visible extension of the city's two faces. Our students are steps away from city, state, and federal courthouses, governmental agencies, and the legal community, where they obtain valuable training through one of our many internship or clinical placements.

This year Suffolk University Law School celebrates its 100th anniversary. Although the Law School has evolved in many ways in the past 100 years, we remain committed to the original mission of Gleason Archer, which is to be a welcoming community where everyone shares a commitment to diversity in legal education and the legal profession. The 2006 incoming class consisted of students from approximately 200 different colleges and universities, 31 states, and 18 foreign countries.

■ Technology and Physical Facilities

In 1999, we opened a new, state-of-the-art law school building, Sargent Hall, which is one of the most technologically advanced law schools in the country. The technology includes a high-speed data network with over 3,000 data nodes. Every seat in each classroom, the library, and the common area has direct access to the high-speed network. Most areas of the building have wireless connections.

All classrooms contain multimedia capabilities, including electric screens, LCD projectors, automated lighting controls, wireless microphones, hearing assistance, advanced speaker systems, and auxiliary computer connections for laptop computer presentations. An additional classroom is equipped for teleconferencing/distance learning.

■ Concentrations and Joint-degree Programs

Students may enroll in one of five area concentrations in Intellectual Property Law, Civil Litigation, Health and Biomedical Law, Business Law and Financial Services, or International Law. In addition, there are five joint-degree programs that combine a Juris Doctor with a Master of Business Administration, Public Administration, International Economics, Finance, or Criminal Justice.

■ Clinical and Internship Programs

Students are encouraged to enroll in one of our clinical programs. Suffolk Law's clinics include the Disability Advocacy, Evening Landlord and Tenant, Family Advocacy, Housing and Consumer Protection, Juvenile Justice, and Suffolk Defenders clinics, as well as the Battered Women's Advocacy and Suffolk Prosecutors programs. Additionally, students may participate in the Civil and Judicial Internship Program, in which students may intern in a variety of legal settings including state and federal courts; federal, state, and local government agencies; legal aid organizations; public defenders' offices; and private law firms and companies.

■ Foreign and Graduate Programs

Suffolk University Law School, in conjunction with the University of Lund, offers a summer study-abroad program held in June and July in Lund, Sweden. The program combines the strengths of the international law curriculum of Suffolk University Law School with the international expertise offered by members of the University of Lund law faculty and the Swedish Bar and Judiciary.

Suffolk University Law School has an exclusive agreement with the Center for International Legal Studies (CILS) to offer internships to US law students and externships to graduates with law degrees. International internships are available to JD students for credit in conformity with the American Bar Association guidelines, and international externships are for LLM students and other post-graduates with law degrees. Internships are available in law firms and businesses in almost every country of the world.

Suffolk University Law School offers two LLM degree programs. One is in Global Law and Technology, which offers concentrations in Intellectual Property, Biomedicine and Biotechnology, International Law and Business, and Information Technology, and is held in Boston, MA. The second offers an LLM in US Law for International Business Lawyers exclusively to lawyers from international jurisdictions and is held at law schools abroad only.

■ Academic Support Programs

The goal of the Academic Support Program (ASP) is for students to make the most out of their abilities. To accomplish this goal, the faculty conducts weekly classes on such diverse topics as: Legal Analysis and Writing, Course Outlining, and Time Management. The faculty are always available for individual student meetings to address specific questions. The ASP also has a lending library containing material on substantive legal topics, study aids, and legal writing. Additionally, the ASP library contains exercises on grammar, legal writing, and analysis. All students are encouraged to stop by and take advantage of these resources.

■ Student Activities, Publications, and Opportunities

Students have a number of opportunities to develop legal skills outside of the classroom through participation in the *Suffolk University Law Review*, the *Suffolk Transnational Law Review*, the *Suffolk Journal of Trial and Appellate Advocacy*, the *Journal of High Technology Law* (*www.law.suffolk.edu/highlights/stuorgs/jhtl*), and the *Suffolk Journal of Health and Biomedical Law*. Students may also participate in moot court competitions such as the National Trial Competition, ATLA Trial Team, Constitutional Law Team, Information Technology and Privacy Law Team, Intellectual Property Law Team, Jessup International Law Team, National Invitational Trial Tournament of Champions, National Moot Court Team, Securities Law Team, Sports Law Team, and Tax Law Team. Students may also join one of our more than 30 student organizations or participate in our Student Bar Association.

■ Scholarships and Loans

Suffolk University Law School participates in a number of student financial aid programs in order to assist students in financing the cost of their legal education. Both need-based and merit-based aid is available. Financial aid awards (scholarships, grants, loans, and employment awards) are made to assist students in financing educational costs when their personal and family resources may not be sufficient. Merit-based scholarships are awarded by the Law School's Admissions Committee at the time a candidate is admitted to the Law School. These awards are made to students based on outstanding academic achievement.

Suffolk University Law School also has a loan repayment assistance program for students who, upon graduation, pursue low-income, public service, law-related employment. A minimum of five recent graduates are selected into the program each year.

■ Office of Career Development

Suffolk University Law School is committed to preparing students for the increasingly complex and rapidly changing world in which they will serve their clients and communities. Suffolk's balanced curriculum provides a solid foundation essential for a successful practitioner, and offers ample opportunities for individual concentration in specialized areas of the law. We are very proud of the school's rich diversity. Almost 30 percent of our students speak a foreign language. Our 19,000 graduates practice law throughout the United States, as well as in 20 foreign countries. They can be found in private practice, corporations, public interest organizations, the military, and the executive, judicial, and legislative branches of government.

The Office of Career Development coordinates the fall recruiting program, résumé collection, and webpage links to job postings and national employment information. The office arranges on- and off-campus interview programs and hosts, in conjunction with other law schools, several placement programs that serve students with special interests or special needs.

■ Peer Mentoring Program

This program helps nontraditional students adjust to the rigors of law school and achieve their full potential as law students. Suffolk defines nontraditional students as those who have been historically excluded or marginalized from the law school community based on any of the following factors: (1) race; (2) ethnicity; (3) socio-economic disadvantage; or (4) history of low performance on standardized tests.

The program starts with a two-week summer session that begins two weeks before orientation. During this session, participating students attend classes on criminal law and contracts and receive extensive training in case briefing, legal analysis, outlining, exam preparation, and exam writing. Students also receive feedback on both case briefs and two practice exams, and at the end of each class, an upper-class student mentor will lead a small group discussion regarding the class material.

Building on the summer session, the program holds weekly seminars during the academic year to help students master the skills necessary to perform well on both multiple-choice and essay exams. Participating students also have the opportunity to meet individually on an ongoing basis with both an upper-class student mentor and the faculty director. The purpose of both the weekly seminars and individual meetings is to help students develop and adhere to sound time management practices, effective study habits, and critical thinking skills.

Applicant Profile

Suffolk University Law School

LSAT Score	GPA								
	3.75 +	3.50–3.74	3.25–3.49	3.00–3.24	2.75–2.99	2.50–2.74	2.25–2.49	2.00–2.24	Below 2.00
175–180									
170–174									
165–169									
160–164									
155–159									
150–154									
145–149									
140–144									
135–139									
130–134									
125–129									
120–124									

■ Very Likely   □ Possible   ▨ Unlikely

Syracuse University College of Law

Syracuse, NY 13244-1030
Phone: 315.443.1962; Fax: 315.443.9568
E-mail: admissions@law.syr.edu; Website: www.law.syr.edu

The Basics

Type of school	Private
Term	Semester
Application deadline	4/1
Application fee	$70
Financial aid deadline	2/15
Can first year start other than fall?	No
Student to faculty ratio	15.5 to 1
Does the university offer:	
housing restricted to law students?	No
graduate housing for which law students are eligible?	Yes

Curriculum

	Full-time	Part-time
Typical first-year section size	68	0
Is there typically a "small section" of the first-year class, other than Legal Writing, taught by full-time faculty	Yes	No
If yes, typical size offered last year	40	
# of classroom course titles beyond first-year curriculum	140	
# of upper division courses, excluding seminars with an enrollment: Under 25	123	
25–49	44	
50–74	10	
75–99	16	
100+	2	
# of seminars	16	
# of seminar positions available	256	
# of seminar positions filled	159	0
# of positions available in simulation courses	688	
# of simulation positions filled	592	0
# of positions available in faculty supervised clinical courses	100	
# of faculty supervised clinical positions filled	90	0
# involved in field placements	146	0
# involved in law journals	85	0
# involved in interschool competitions	0	0
# of credit hours required to graduate	87	

Faculty and Administrators

	Total		Men		Women		Minorities	
	Fall	Spr	Fall	Spr	Fall	Spr	Fall	Spr
Full-time	37	40	21	26	16	14	6	6
Other Full-time	16	17	6	6	10	11	2	2
Deans, librarians, & others who teach	9	9	5	5	4	4	1	1
Part-time	18	39	15	31	3	8	3	5
Total	80	105	47	68	33	37	12	14

JD Enrollment and Ethnicity

	Men		Women		Full-time		Part-time		1st-year		Total		JD Degs. Awd.
	#	%	#	%	#	%	#	%	#	%	#	%	
African Amer.	12	3.1	20	6.6	30	4.4	2	33.3	13	5.0	32	4.6	13
Amer. Indian	4	1.0	5	1.6	9	1.3	0	0.0	2	0.8	9	1.3	1
Asian Amer.	31	8.1	39	12.8	70	10.2	0	0.0	32	12.3	70	10.2	15
Mex. Amer.	0	0.0	0	0.0	0	0.0	0	0.0	0	0.0	0	0.0	0
Puerto Rican	0	0.0	0	0.0	0	0.0	0	0.0	0	0.0	0	0.0	0
Hispanic	15	3.9	12	3.9	27	4.0	0	0.0	9	3.5	27	3.9	14
Total Minority	62	16.1	76	24.9	136	19.9	2	33.3	56	21.5	138	20.0	43
For. Nation.	3	0.8	8	2.6	11	1.6	0	0.0	3	1.2	11	1.6	5
Caucasian	224	58.3	170	55.7	390	57.1	4	66.7	144	55.4	394	57.2	198
Unknown	95	24.7	51	16.7	146	21.4	0	0.0	57	21.9	146	21.2	32
Total	384	55.7	305	44.3	683	99.1	6	0.9	260	37.7	689		278

Transfers

Transfers in	4
Transfers out	30

Tuition and Fees

	Resident	Nonresident
Full-time	$35,790	$35,790
Part-time	$30,909	$30,909

Living Expenses

Estimated living expenses for singles

Living on campus	Living off campus	Living at home
$15,988	$15,988	$15,988

Syracuse University College of Law

*ABA
Approved
Since
1923*

GPA and LSAT Scores

	Total	Full-time	Part-time
# of apps	2,798	2,768	30
# of offers	1,052	1,047	5
# of matrics	262	258	4
75% GPA	3.55	3.56	3.29
Median GPA	3.35	3.37	3.24
25% GPA	3.15	3.15	3.19
75% LSAT	157	157	152
Median LSAT	155	155	151
25% LSAT	153	153	147

Grants and Scholarships (from prior year)

	Total		Full-time		Part-time	
	#	%	#	%	#	%
Total # of students	756		749		7	
Total # receiving grants	619	81.9	619	82.6	0	0.0
Less than 1/2 tuition	579	76.6	579	77.3	0	0.0
Half to full tuition	39	5.2	39	5.2	0	0.0
Full tuition	1	0.1	1	0.1	0	0.0
More than full tuition	0	0.0	0	0.0	0	0.0
Median grant amount			$8,000		$0	

Informational and Library Resources

# of volumes and volume equivalents	463,300
# of titles	89,038
# of active serial subscriptions	3,354
Study seating capacity inside the library	405
# of full-time professional librarians	10
Hours per week library is open	104
# of open, wired connections available to students	19
# of networked computers available for use by students	79
# of simultaneous wireless users	250
Require computer?	Yes

JD Attrition (from prior year)

	Academic	Other	Total	
	#	#	#	%
1st year	5	30	35	13.2
2nd year	0	4	4	2.0
3rd year	0	1	1	0.4
4th year	0	0	0	0.0

Employment (9 months after graduation)

	Total	Percentage
Employment status known	249	98.0
Employment status unknown	5	2.0
Employed	226	90.8
Pursuing graduate degrees	3	1.2
Unemployed seeking employment	3	1.2
Unemployed not seeking employment	12	4.8
Unemployed and studying for the bar	5	2.0

Type of Employment

# employed in law firms	97	42.9
# employed in business and industry	43	19.0
# employed in government	36	15.9
# employed in public interest	11	4.9
# employed as judicial clerks	29	12.8
# employed in academia	8	3.5

Geographic Location

# employed in state	99	43.8
# employed in foreign countries	6	2.7
# of states where employed		32

Bar Passage Rates

Jurisdiction	New York		
Exam	Sum 05	Win 06	Total
# from school taking bar for the first time	137	10	147
School's pass rate for all first-time takers	71%	40%	69%
State's pass rate for all first-time takers	76%	61%	74%

Syracuse University College of Law

Office of Admissions and Financial Aid, Suite 340
Syracuse, NY 13244-1030
Phone: 315.443.1962; Fax: 315.443.9568
E-mail: admissions@law.syr.edu; Website: www.law.syr.edu

■ Introduction

Syracuse University College of Law was established in 1895. The college is a charter member of the AALS and is fully approved by the ABA. It is one of the oldest of the 12 schools and colleges comprising Syracuse University, a major teaching and research institution. The College of Law complex is located on the 200-acre Syracuse University campus overlooking scenic Central New York and the city of Syracuse.

■ Curriculum

Syracuse University College of Law's mission is guided by the philosophy that the best way to educate lawyers to practice in today's world is to engage them in a process of interdisciplinary learning while teaching them to apply what they learn in the classroom to real legal issues, problems, and clients. Beginning in the first year and continuing throughout the curriculum, students are exposed to educational settings that integrate opportunities to acquire a better understanding of legal theory and doctrine, develop professional skills, and gain exposure to the values and ethics of the legal profession. As a result, Syracuse students are better prepared for the practice of law.

■ Interdisciplinary Learning Opportunities

- **Center on Property, Citizenship, and Social Entrepreneurism**—Students explore issues related to modern real estate transactions and finance, community development and housing, global property law systems, and access to ownership for inclusion of the elderly, the poor, and persons with disabilities. The curriculum prepares students for a variety of opportunities in law firms, government agencies, financial institutions, development organizations, and business. The center engages students in coursework, team projects, and research opportunities in all areas of property law and theory, including real, personal, intangible, intellectual, and cultural property.
- **Family Law and Social Policy Center**—The center prepares students for a career in family law by engaging them in interdisciplinary research, providing them with applied learning experiences, and connecting them with the community to provide services that benefit families and children. The curriculum includes a variety of courses including bioethics, children and the law, estate planning, mediation, and domestic violence.
- **Center for Global Law and Practice**—The center provides a broad variety of opportunities, both in and out of the classroom, for students interested in global law. Course offerings are broad, and cocurricular activities include moot court competitions, the International Law Society, and the *Syracuse Journal of International Law and Commerce*. A summer abroad program is offered in London.
- **Technology Commercialization Law Program**—The program emphasizes interdisciplinary and applied learning approaches to commercial development of new technology. Students are immersed in a business curriculum that includes business planning, finance, intellectual property licensing, venture capital, and tax issues. Students

work in cross-disciplinary teams on real-world developments arranged through SU's Technology Commercialization Research Center with companies and research organizations.

- **Institute for National Security and Counterterrorism**—The institute, a joint enterprise of the College of Law and the Maxwell School of Citizenship and Public Affairs, is dedicated to the interdisciplinary study of important questions of law and policy related to national and international security and counterterrorism. Responding to the growing interest in terrorism and other security threats, the institute and its sponsoring schools have developed an extensive security studies curriculum and offer students two certificates in security and counterterrorism studies. The institute also sponsors conferences and lectures that are designed to further a research agenda in security or terrorism and bring together scholars, current and former government officials, and media representatives.
- **Center for Indigenous Law, Governance, and Citizenship**—The center focuses on programmatic activities that include conducting research relating to the citizenship, rights, and responsibilities of indigenous peoples and the governance of indigenous nations in the United States and Canada; providing technical assistance to indigenous nations seeking to reform their governing institutions and administrative laws, and to federal, state, local, and provincial governments seeking to reform their Indian affairs laws; and promoting a greater understanding of the law, governance, and history of the Haudenosaunee ("People of the Longhouse").
- **Disability Law and Policy Center**—The first such certificate program of its kind in the United States, it offers law students the opportunity to gain legal research and practice experience in disability law and advocacy. Students may earn a joint degree in law and disability studies, as well as a joint degree in law and social work.

■ Other Opportunities for Specialization

- **Clinical Programs**—Legal concepts learned in the classroom come to life for students who participate in the in-house clinics and externship program. Students work with lawyers in law offices, becoming immersed in the actual practice of law through their work on real cases affecting real clients. Students provide much-needed legal services to our community, as many of our clients are unable to afford private counsel. Diverse clinical opportunities at the College of Law include the Criminal Defense Law Clinic, the Community Development Law Clinic, the Children's Rights and Family Law Clinic, the Disability Rights Clinic, the Low Income Taxpayer Law Clinic, and the Securities Arbitration Clinic/Consumer Law Clinic. The college also offers several externship courses.
- **Joint-degree Programs**—Interdisciplinary study is an integral part of academic life in the college. Students who desire a greater degree of specialization may select from a number of joint-degree opportunities. Formal joint-degree programs exist in public administration, international relations, business administration or accounting, communications, environmental law, education (disability

studies), and engineering. Joint degrees may also be designed to fit special career objectives.

- **Advocacy Skills**—Syracuse Law is recognized for its exceptional advocacy programs. Students are actively involved and have been highly successful in national and regional moot court competitions. Syracuse students participate in intraschool programs throughout the year in trial and appellate competitions covering a wide variety of areas.

Library

The library spans four spacious levels within the College of Law complex. On the main floor, the circulation and reference desks offer conveniently located services and research support in close proximity to the Electronic Research Center. The library adds approximately 2,500 new titles to its catalog each year, including a growing number of licensed electronic databases. All holdings—print, microform, audio, video, and CD-ROM—are accessible through the university-wide online public catalog.

Admission

History reveals that undergraduate grades and LSAT scores are reliable measures, in most cases, for predicting probable success in law study. Thus, an index combining grades and test scores becomes a factor in most admission decisions. However, recognizing that numerical indicators are not always the best predictors of success in law school—even when considered in combination with other factors—the college admits a limited number of students each year through its Legal Education

Opportunity (LEO) Program. The program's dual objectives are to recruit and admit persons who may have been deprived of equal education opportunities for reasons of race, gender, poverty, or other factors beyond their control and persons with unusual accomplishments, backgrounds, and experiences that suggest traditional admissions criteria may be inadequate predictors of likely success in law study.

Financial Aid

The college makes available awards from a variety of sources, including merit-based scholarships, need-based tuition grants, university fellowships, and federal sources, such as the work-study program and the Perkins and Stafford Loan Programs and the Graduate PLUS Loan Program. Private loan programs are available to assist law students with supplemental financing for legal education expenses.

Career Services

Syracuse graduates are employed throughout the United States and around the world. The Office of Career Services is dedicated to assisting current students and alumni with their individual job searches. Career Services staff administer a comprehensive program that utilizes the most current resources available to assist students in developing a career plan and employment search strategy. The office provides a full range of services to students, including a broad mix of innovative and traditional support, empowering students with the confidence and skills necessary to conduct an effective job search.

Applicant Profile

Syracuse University College of Law
This grid includes only applicants who earned 120–180 LSAT scores under standard administrations.

LSAT Score	3.75 +		3.50–3.74		3.25–3.49		3.00–3.24		2.75–2.99		2.50–2.74		2.25–2.49		2.00–2.24		Below 2.00		No GPA		Total	
	Apps	Adm	Apps	Adm	Apps	Adm	Apps	Adm	Apps	Adm	Apps	Adm	Apps	Adm	Apps	Adm	Apps	Adm	Apps	Adm	Apps	Adm
170–180	1	1	1	1	0	0	0	0	0	0	0	0	0	0	0	0	0	0	0	0	2	2
165–169	6	6	8	8	1	1	8	8	2	2	3	2	2	1	0	0	0	0	0	0	30	28
160–164	11	11	30	27	39	38	24	20	17	16	14	9	3	2	4	0	1	0	1	0	144	123
155–159	53	52	121	114	151	140	120	113	58	32	36	12	16	4	4	0	0	0	2	2	561	469
150–154	97	57	238	103	250	93	218	52	127	20	51	2	20	1	6	0	2	0	6	1	1015	329
145–149	59	10	121	21	165	18	136	12	79	6	49	0	19	0	5	0	1	0	13	0	647	67
120–144	21	0	44	2	66	1	91	2	62	0	44	0	26	0	16	0	5	0	16	0	391	5
Total	248	137	563	276	672	291	597	207	345	76	197	25	86	8	35	0	9	0	38	3	2790	1023

Apps = Number of Applicants
Adm = Number Admitted
Reflects 99% of the total applicant pool.

This chart is provided as a general guide in assessing an applicant's possibility of admission based solely on quantitative factors. It should be noted that nonquantitative factors are also considered in all admission decisions.

Temple University—James E. Beasley School of Law

1719 North Broad Street
Philadelphia, PA 19122
Phone: 800.560.1428; Fax: 215.204.9319
E-mail: lawadmis@temple.edu; Website: www.law.temple.edu

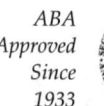

ABA
Approved
Since
1933

The Basics

Type of school	Public
Term	Semester
Application deadline	3/1
Application fee	$60
Financial aid deadline	3/1
Can first year start other than fall?	No
Student to faculty ratio	14.6 to 1
Does the university offer:	
housing restricted to law students?	No
graduate housing for which law students are eligible?	Yes

Faculty and Administrators

	Total		Men		Women		Minorities	
	Fall	Spr	Fall	Spr	Fall	Spr	Fall	Spr
Full-time	54	51	33	32	21	19	13	13
Other Full-time	0	0	0	0	0	0	0	0
Deans, librarians, & others who teach	14	14	7	7	7	7	2	2
Part-time	101	130	66	93	35	37	12	17
Total	**169**	**195**	**106**	**132**	**63**	**63**	**27**	**32**

Curriculum

	Full-time	Part-time
Typical first-year section size	60	60
Is there typically a "small section" of the first-year class, other than Legal Writing, taught by full-time faculty	No	No
If yes, typical size offered last year		
# of classroom course titles beyond first-year curriculum		171
# of upper division courses, excluding seminars with an enrollment: Under 25		188
25–49		53
50–74		22
75–99		14
100+		1
# of seminars		58
# of seminar positions available		773
# of seminar positions filled	593	159
# of positions available in simulation courses		1,090
# of simulation positions filled	669	162
# of positions available in faculty supervised clinical courses		56
# of faculty supervised clinical positions filled	52	1
# involved in field placements	201	10
# involved in law journals	158	13
# involved in interschool competitions	25	2
# of credit hours required to graduate		87

JD Enrollment and Ethnicity

	Men		Women		Full-time		Part-time		1st-year		Total		JD Degs. Awd.
	#	%	#	%	#	%	#	%	#	%	#	%	
African Amer.	31	5.8	50	10.7	66	8.5	15	6.6	25	8.3	81	8.1	23
Amer. Indian	2	0.4	4	0.9	6	0.8	0	0.0	3	1.0	6	0.6	1
Asian Amer.	54	10.1	54	11.5	86	11.1	22	9.6	25	8.3	108	10.8	35
Mex. Amer.	4	0.7	4	0.9	7	0.9	1	0.4	3	1.0	8	0.8	2
Puerto Rican	5	0.9	4	0.9	7	0.9	2	0.9	4	1.3	9	0.9	5
Hispanic	16	3.0	8	1.7	19	2.5	5	2.2	6	2.0	24	2.4	7
Total Minority	112	20.9	124	26.4	191	24.6	45	19.7	66	21.9	236	23.5	73
For. Nation.	6	1.1	4	0.9	7	0.9	3	1.3	3	1.0	10	1.0	1
Caucasian	402	75.1	336	71.6	559	72.1	179	78.2	227	75.2	738	73.5	257
Unknown	15	2.8	5	1.1	18	2.3	2	0.9	6	2.0	20	2.0	0
Total	535	53.3	469	46.7	775	77.2	229	22.8	302	30.1	1004		331

Transfers

Transfers in	16
Transfers out	5

Tuition and Fees

	Resident	Nonresident
Full-time	$14,902	$25,552
Part-time	$12,028	$20,548

Living Expenses

Estimated living expenses for singles

Living on campus	Living off campus	Living at home
$19,254	$19,254	$14,220

Temple University—James E. Beasley School of Law

ABA
Approved
Since
1933

GPA and LSAT Scores

	Total	Full-time	Part-time
# of apps	4,648	4,310	338
# of offers	1,719	1,605	114
# of matrics	300	240	60
75% GPA	3.60	3.60	3.55
Median GPA	3.38	3.39	3.31
25% GPA	3.18	3.23	3.01
75% LSAT	163	163	160
Median LSAT	161	161	158
25% LSAT	158	159	157

Grants and Scholarships (from prior year)

	Total		Full-time		Part-time	
	#	%	#	%	#	%
Total # of students	1,044		796		248	
Total # receiving grants	376	36.0	338	42.5	38	15.3
Less than 1/2 tuition	260	24.9	244	30.7	16	6.5
Half to full tuition	100	9.6	80	10.1	20	8.1
Full tuition	16	1.5	14	1.8	2	0.8
More than full tuition	0	0.0	0	0.0	0	0.0
Median grant amount			$6,000		$5,428	

Informational and Library Resources

# of volumes and volume equivalents	585,351
# of titles	113,055
# of active serial subscriptions	3,087
Study seating capacity inside the library	704
# of full-time professional librarians	12
Hours per week library is open	96
# of open, wired connections available to students	425
# of networked computers available for use by students	139
# of simultaneous wireless users	1,024
Require computer?	No

JD Attrition (from prior year)

	Academic	Other	Total	
	#	#	#	%
1st year	0	10	10	3.1
2nd year	2	6	8	2.5
3rd year	0	0	0	0.0
4th year	0	0	0	0.0

Employment (9 months after graduation)

	Total	Percentage
Employment status known	318	99.1
Employment status unknown	3	0.9
Employed	292	91.8
Pursuing graduate degrees	4	1.3
Unemployed seeking employment	11	3.5
Unemployed not seeking employment	11	3.5
Unemployed and studying for the bar	0	0.0
Type of Employment		
# employed in law firms	136	46.6
# employed in business and industry	48	16.4
# employed in government	32	11.0
# employed in public interest	22	7.5
# employed as judicial clerks	38	13.0
# employed in academia	8	2.7
Geographic Location		
# employed in state	209	71.6
# employed in foreign countries	1	0.3
# of states where employed	18	

Bar Passage Rates

Jurisdiction	Pennsylvania		
Exam	Sum 05	Win 06	Total
# from school taking bar for the first time	241	22	263
School's pass rate for all first-time takers	85%	77%	85%
State's pass rate for all first-time takers	79%	75%	78%

Temple University—James E. Beasley School of Law

1719 North Broad Street
Philadelphia, PA 19122
Phone: 800.560.1428; Fax: 215.204.9319
E-mail: lawadmis@temple.edu; Website: www.law.temple.edu

■ Introduction

Temple Law School is recognized both nationally and internationally as a leader in legal education. Our unique student-centered curriculum integrates both critical thinking and practical legal skills. We offer both day and evening programs, and students may enroll on either a full- or part-time basis. Students at Temple build lawyering skills both in the classroom and in the law firms, courts, public service agencies, and financial institutions of Philadelphia, the fifth largest city in the nation. Our students, faculty, and alumni share the qualities of intelligence, academic excellence, and professional responsibility that characterize the Temple lawyer.

■ Student Body and Faculty

Temple students are bright, dynamic, and diverse. They come from a variety of backgrounds and disciplines. Many have traveled and lived in other countries, and their real-life experiences vitalize classroom discussion. A recent entering class hailed from 131 colleges and universities, and from 40 states and foreign countries. Twelve percent had earned advanced degrees, and over 70 percent had at least one year of work experience before entering law school. Twenty-two percent were minority students, and 42 percent were women. The faculty is composed of a distinguished group of experienced attorneys who are continually recognized throughout the world as legal experts. While their accomplishments are many, it is their commitment to teaching that many students note as their greatest achievement.

■ Curriculum

Temple is consistently recognized for its prize-winning **trial advocacy** programs, including the distinction of being the only two-time winner of the American College of Trial Lawyers Emil Gumpert Award for Excellence in Teaching Trial Advocacy. Temple's record in law school trial competitions is unparalleled. Temple is the only school to win nine national open and invitational tournaments and has had the highest scoring team in national competitions for the last 10 years. Temple's successful trial advocacy curriculum is anchored by the innovative "Integrated Program," which combines the teaching of trial advocacy, evidence, and civil procedure.

Temple students have access to an extensive array of programs to prepare them to practice law in an increasingly global society. Temple's strength in **international law** includes opportunities for summer study in Rome, Italy, and semester-abroad programs in Tokyo, Japan; Beijing, China; Cork, Ireland; and Tel Aviv, Israel; a Master of Laws program for international students holding foreign law degrees; and active student organizations, such as an international law journal and the International Law Society. Temple's strong reputation in international law has been enhanced by the JD/LLM in Transnational Law for American law students; an LLM program in Beijing, China, in which Chinese lawyers study American law; and the creation of the Institute for International Law and Public Policy. Students may also design individualized study-abroad options at law schools around the world.

Temple is a pioneer in the uncharted territory of **intellectual property and technology law**, preparing students to learn and succeed in the virtual world. Temple has expanded the boundaries of traditional intellectual property law by integrating bodies of law that bear on the rapid expansion of the Internet, electronic commerce, biotechnologies, and other newly emerging legal issues. Through hands-on activities outside the classroom, and faculty members who are experts in the field, students learn how to meet the challenges of practicing law in a world without borders.

Temple offers superior training in **business and tax law**, including a creative program that combines the teaching of professional responsibility, substantive law courses, and business skills, such as interviewing, negotiating, and drafting. Prospective business lawyers can also pursue the JD/MBA dual-degree program, which is offered in conjunction with the Fox School of Business and Management, or the JD/LLM in Taxation.

Public service is a Temple tradition. Students provide legal services in the Philadelphia area through the extensive clinical program, the Temple Legal Aid Office, and various volunteer and community outreach programs. Public interest careers are supported by the Student Public Interest Network, which provides grants for summer internships; the Public Interest Scholars Program, which provides scholarships to entering students with a demonstrated commitment to public service; and the Barrack Public Interest Fellowships, a loan repayment assistance program for graduates in public interest jobs.

■ Technology and Facilities

The law school complex consists of three recently renovated buildings designed to provide students with a state-of-the-art educational environment. "Smart" classrooms equipped with cutting-edge technology, including video, audio, and Internet access, allow faculty to use technology in all of the classrooms. The law school's "anytime, anywhere" computer access program includes a combination of wired and wireless network access, wired study carrels, and state-of-the-art computer labs. The faculty and administration regularly communicate with students via e-mail, and the law school uses a sophisticated course management system that allows the faculty to post assignments, syllabi, announcements, and links to a variety of additional resources for each class.

■ Student Activities

Students are an integral part of policymaking and governance at the law school. The Student Bar Association is the governing organization that oversees the more than 30 student organizations that flourish at Temple, including the Black Law Students Association, the Latino Law Students Association, the Asian/Pacific Islander American Law Student Association, the Women's Law Caucus, and OUTLaw. Student publications include the *Temple Law Review*, the *Temple Journal of Science, Technology, and Environmental Law*, the *Temple International and Comparative Law Journal*, and the *Temple Political and Civil Rights Law Review*. Students who excel in advocacy may participate in the National Trial Team or the Moot Court Honor Society.

■ Career Planning

The Career Planning Office assists students with the development of strategies for securing employment and provides the resources necessary to supplement each student's individualized job search. Through the school's online career planning manager, students can search job postings, participate in various recruiting programs, and apply for jobs. In addition, one-on-one career counseling is available, and workshops and programs are offered to assist students in sharpening their job-search skills, including résumé writing, networking, and interviewing. Temple alumni are working in all 50 states and around the world. The 2005 graduating class had a placement rate of 92 percent.

■ Admission and Financial Aid

Temple has a highly competitive admission process, which is designed to look at the whole person. In keeping with Temple's commitment to diversity and its mission of offering opportunities to students who might otherwise be foreclosed from pursuing a high quality legal education, the faculty Admissions Committee may consider an application under its discretionary admission process, the Sp.A.C.E. program. Under this program, the faculty carefully selects applicants who have outstanding performance records and exceptional aptitudes for the study and practice of law that are not necessarily reflected by grades and LSAT scores alone.

Our financial aid program supports the admission process with loans and both need- and merit-based scholarships, including the Beasley Scholars program, Conwell Law Scholarships, Law Faculty Scholarships, the Public Interest Scholars program, and First Year Scholar Awards.

Applicant Profile

Temple University—James E. Beasley School of Law
This grid includes only applicants who earned 120–180 LSAT scores under standard administrations.

LSAT Score	3.75 +		3.50–3.74		3.25–3.49		3.00–3.24		2.75–2.99		2.50–2.74		2.25–2.49		2.00–2.24		Below 2.00		No GPA		Total	
	Apps	Adm	Apps	Adm	Apps	Adm	Apps	Adm	Apps	Adm	Apps	Adm	Apps	Adm	Apps	Adm	Apps	Adm	Apps	Adm	Apps	Adm
170–180	20	20	25	25	14	14	18	17	2	2	3	3	0	0	0	0	0	0	0	0	82	81
165–169	82	82	107	107	88	88	84	75	22	17	9	4	3	2	1	1	0	0	1	1	397	377
160–164	211	203	307	267	349	250	227	122	80	51	28	14	6	1	3	0	1	0	4	1	1216	909
155–159	148	43	298	78	327	90	225	53	108	31	43	4	20	4	4	0	0	0	9	2	1182	305
150–154	77	4	161	12	193	12	154	7	124	4	45	2	24	1	4	0	0	0	10	0	792	42
145–149	31	1	72	2	90	1	113	0	79	0	36	0	25	0	5	0	3	0	8	0	462	4
140–144	16	0	49	0	50	0	66	0	61	0	33	0	16	0	5	0	0	0	6	0	302	0
Below 140	6	0	16	0	33	0	43	0	34	0	15	0	14	0	12	0	3	0	8	0	184	0
Total	591	353	1035	491	1144	455	930	274	510	105	212	27	108	8	34	1	7	0	46	4	4617	1718

Apps = Number of Applicants
Adm = Number Admitted
Reflects 99% of the total applicant pool.

University of Tennessee College of Law

1505 W. Cumberland Avenue, Suite 161
Knoxville, TN 37996-1810
Phone: 865.974.4131; Fax: 865.974.1572
E-mail: lawadmit@utk.edu; Website: www.law.utk.edu

ABA
Approved
Since
1925

The Basics

Type of school	Public
Term	Semester
Application deadline	3/1
Application fee	$15
Financial aid deadline	3/1
Can first year start other than fall?	No
Student to faculty ratio	10.9 to 1
Does the university offer:	
housing restricted to law students?	No
graduate housing for which law students are eligible?	No

Faculty and Administrators

	Total Fall	Total Spr	Men Fall	Men Spr	Women Fall	Women Spr	Minorities Fall	Minorities Spr
Full-time	35	34	18	18	11	10	8	7
Other Full-time	4	2	3	1	1	1	1	0
Deans, librarians, & others who teach	18	18	8	8	9	9	0	0
Part-time	38	40	24	25	14	15	0	0
Total	95	94	53	52	35	35	9	7

Curriculum

	Full-time	Part-time
Typical first-year section size	55	0
Is there typically a "small section" of the first-year class, other than Legal Writing, taught by full-time faculty	No	No
If yes, typical size offered last year		
# of classroom course titles beyond first-year curriculum	105	

# of upper division courses, excluding seminars with an enrollment:		
	Under 25	90
	25–49	24
	50–74	10
	75–99	1
	100+	0

# of seminars	22	
# of seminar positions available	388	
# of seminar positions filled	325	0
# of positions available in simulation courses	712	
# of simulation positions filled	592	0
# of positions available in faculty supervised clinical courses	128	
# of faculty supervised clinical positions filled	110	0
# involved in field placements	19	0
# involved in law journals	116	0
# involved in interschool competitions	34	0
# of credit hours required to graduate	89	

JD Enrollment and Ethnicity

	Men #	Men %	Women #	Women %	Full-time #	Full-time %	Part-time #	Part-time %	1st-year #	1st-year %	Total #	Total %	JD Degs. Awd.
African Amer.	19	8.5	42	18.6	61	13.6	0	0.0	19	12.6	61	13.6	17
Amer. Indian	1	0.4	1	0.4	2	0.4	0	0.0	1	0.7	2	0.4	1
Asian Amer.	1	0.4	2	0.9	3	0.7	0	0.0	1	0.7	3	0.7	2
Mex. Amer.	0	0.0	0	0.0	0	0.0	0	0.0	0	0.0	0	0.0	0
Puerto Rican	0	0.0	0	0.0	0	0.0	0	0.0	0	0.0	0	0.0	0
Hispanic	3	1.3	2	0.9	5	1.1	0	0.0	1	0.7	5	1.1	3
Total Minority	24	10.8	47	20.8	71	15.8	0	0.0	22	14.6	71	15.8	23
For. Nation.	0	0.0	0	0.0	0	0.0	0	0.0	0	0.0	0	0.0	0
Caucasian	195	87.4	174	77.0	369	82.2	0	0.0	125	82.8	369	82.2	126
Unknown	4	1.8	5	2.2	9	2.0	0	0.0	4	2.6	9	2.0	1
Total	223	49.7	226	50.3	449	100.0	0	0.0	151	33.6	449		150

Transfers

Transfers in	4
Transfers out	6

Tuition and Fees

	Resident	Nonresident
Full-time	$9,934	$25,290
Part-time	$0	$0

Living Expenses

Estimated living expenses for singles

Living on campus	Living off campus	Living at home
$15,160	$15,160	$10,738

University of Tennessee College of Law

*ABA
Approved
Since
1925*

GPA and LSAT Scores

	Total	Full-time	Part-time
# of apps	1,390	1,390	0
# of offers	384	384	0
# of matrics	151	151	0
75% GPA	3.78	3.78	0.00
Median GPA	3.58	3.58	0.00
25% GPA	3.37	3.37	0.00
75% LSAT	161	161	0
Median LSAT	159	159	0
25% LSAT	155	155	0

Grants and Scholarships (from prior year)

	Total		Full-time		Part-time	
	#	%	#	%	#	%
Total # of students	457		457		0	
Total # receiving grants	202	44.2	202	44.2	0	0.0
Less than 1/2 tuition	91	19.9	91	19.9	0	0.0
Half to full tuition	76	16.6	76	16.6	0	0.0
Full tuition	1	0.2	1	0.2	0	0.0
More than full tuition	34	7.4	34	7.4	0	0.0
Median grant amount			$7,000		$0	

Informational and Library Resources

# of volumes and volume equivalents	571,108
# of titles	116,828
# of active serial subscriptions	6,733
Study seating capacity inside the library	437
# of full-time professional librarians	8
Hours per week library is open	112
# of open, wired connections available to students	205
# of networked computers available for use by students	103
# of simultaneous wireless users	900
Require computer?	No

JD Attrition (from prior year)

	Academic	Other	Total	
	#	#	#	%
1st year	2	7	9	5.8
2nd year	0	7	7	4.7
3rd year	0	1	1	0.6
4th year	0	0	0	0.0

Employment (9 months after graduation)

	Total	Percentage
Employment status known	133	97.8
Employment status unknown	3	2.2
Employed	118	88.7
Pursuing graduate degrees	4	3.0
Unemployed seeking employment	4	3.0
Unemployed not seeking employment	6	4.5
Unemployed and studying for the bar	1	0.8

Type of Employment

# employed in law firms	67	56.8
# employed in business and industry	11	9.3
# employed in government	21	17.8
# employed in public interest	5	4.2
# employed as judicial clerks	14	11.9
# employed in academia	0	0.0

Geographic Location

# employed in state	90	76.3
# employed in foreign countries	0	0.0
# of states where employed		15

Bar Passage Rates

Jurisdiction	Tennessee		
Exam	Sum 05	Win 06	Total
# from school taking bar for the first time	96	18	114
School's pass rate for all first-time takers	92%	72%	89%
State's pass rate for all first-time takers	81%	76%	80%

University of Tennessee College of Law

Admissions Office, 1505 W. Cumberland Avenue, Suite 161
Knoxville, TN 37996-1810
Phone: 865.974.4131; Fax: 865.974.1572
E-mail: lawadmit@utk.edu; Website: www.law.utk.edu

■ Introduction

For more than a century, the University of Tennessee College of Law has offered a strong combination of practical and theoretical legal training. Established in 1890, the College of Law is a charter member of the AALS and is ABA approved.

■ Enrollment/Student Body

The College of Law enrolls a small, selective, and diverse class each August. The 2006 entering class was composed of 151 students, of which 46 percent were women, 54 percent were men, and 17 percent were students of color. Entering students were graduates of 74 colleges and universities across the nation and the world and are residents of 14 states. Although many members of each entering class are pursuing a law degree directly from undergraduate school, a number of law students have advanced degrees and have had careers in fields as diverse as engineering, teaching, medicine, journalism, and business.

■ Faculty

The quality of our faculty is evidenced by their legal training at some of the finest law schools in the US, the significance of their scholarly writings, their activity in professional associations, and their involvement with public service. Current students at UT tell potential candidates for admission that they find the faculty to be excellent teachers, accessible, and caring.

■ College of Law, Library, and Physical Facilities

The law center at the University of Tennessee—a melding of the old with the new—is an exceptional setting for education in the twenty-first century. The 110,000-square-foot facility was completed in 1997 and is located on Cumberland Avenue, just across from the University Center, in the heart of the campus. The law center includes the Joel A. Katz Law Library, dedicated to a distinguished corporate and entertainment lawyer and alumnus.

■ Location

The College of Law is located on the main campus of the University of Tennessee at Knoxville, the largest city in eastern Tennessee and the third largest in the state. More than 28,000 students attend UTK. Knoxville has the natural advantage of being located in the foothills of the Great Smoky Mountains, making hiking, biking, golf, and fishing popular and accessible activities. Knoxville is close to major legal markets in the Southeast, including Atlanta, Nashville, and Charlotte.

■ Curriculum

First-year students begin law school with a week-long introductory period; a series of minicourses introduce students to the study of law. Second- and third-year students may choose from over 70 elective courses. Two dual-degree programs are offered—the JD/MBA and the JD/MPA (Master of Public Administration).

The College of Law offers two optional concentrations for students. The **Center for Entrepreneurial Law** allows second- and third-year students to focus on the legal aspects of the conduct of public and private enterprise, emphasizing the needs of small- and intermediate-sized business concerns. A **Business Clinic** is offered for students seeking practical experience working with business clients.

The **Center for Advocacy and Dispute Resolution** allows interested students to focus their second- and third-year experience toward a career in advocacy, commonly thought of as litigation or trial practice. UT was recognized by the American College of Trial Lawyers for the 1996 Emil Gumpert Award for Excellence in Teaching Trial Advocacy.

The **Charles H. Miller Legal Clinic** is the site for our clinical programs in advocacy and mediation. Established in 1947, this is one of the oldest continually operating clinical programs in the US. UT also offers a **Mediation Clinic**, in which students work in teams to mediate real civil and misdemeanor cases in the lower courts.

The **Prosecutorial Externship Program** enables students to prosecute real cases on behalf of the state under the supervision of experienced district attorneys in Knox County.

■ Student Activities and Programs

Students can choose from a variety of student programs, activities, publications, and organizations. A complete listing is available on our website.

UT moot court teams have distinguished themselves in competitions. Tennessee has won three Jerome Prince Evidence Moot Court national championships and was the first team in the history of that competition to win back-to-back titles in 2000 and 2001.

The *Tennessee Law Review* offers participants an excellent opportunity to conduct legal research and produce writings of a scholarly and practical nature. The *Transactions Business Journal* provides an opportunity for students to write about topical issues and legal developments of interest to the business bar. Students participating in the *Tennessee Journal of Law and Policy* analyze the latest developments in law and public decision making. The Student Bar Association and various other student organizations offer numerous programs, services, and special events. The national honor society, Order of the Coif, and two leading professional fraternities, Phi Delta Phi and Phi Alpha Delta, have local chapters here.

UT Pro Bono is a student-directed, community service organization. Working with local attorneys and legal aid organizations, UT Pro Bono serves as a resource by providing law students for research, educational, and investigatory assistance. UT Pro Bono currently operates the Tennessee Innocence Project, programs working with the homeless population, and family justice, immigrant assistance, animal law, and volunteer income tax assistance projects. Through an Equal Justice Works grant, the college also operates a Children's Advocacy Network-Lawyer's Education Advocacy Resource Network (CAN-LEARN), which provides education and support to attorneys working on children's educational law issues.

■ Admission

Admission to the College of Law is competitive. The Admissions Committee places substantial emphasis on traditional indicators of performance—UGPA and LSAT score. The committee also considers factors such as improvement in undergraduate grades and graduate school performance, strength of undergraduate institution and major course of study, extracurricular activities, community service, and employment and professional experience. Also considered are circumstances that may have affected an applicant's grades or LSAT score; economic, social, or cultural background; and success in overcoming social or economic disadvantage. Applicants are required to submit two letters of recommendation and write a personal statement and an essay.

The College of Law recognizes its obligation to assure legal education to qualified applicants who are members of historically underrepresented groups in the legal profession. The College of Law encourages applications from such students.

Successful completion of the CLEO Summer Institute and the Tennessee Institute for Pre-Law may also be considered by the Admissions Committee.

■ Expenses, Financial Aid, and Housing

The College of Law offers a number of scholarships for entering students. Scholarships may be based on academic credentials (LSAT score and UGPA), records of leadership and community service, or other factors as established by the scholarship donor. Several scholarships may be awarded for which financial need, as established by the university after the FAFSA process is complete, is a primary criteria. Candidates for admission should complete the FAFSA process as soon as possible after the first of the year to be considered for scholarships in which financial need is a factor. Candidates for admission will automatically be considered for all scholarships for which they are eligible, with the exception of the William M. Leech Jr. Memorial Scholarship, the Graduate Research Assistantships, and the Clarence and Augusta Kolwyck Memorial Achievement Scholarship, for which specific application is required. Please check our website or our Applicant Guide for more information and application guidelines. Campus apartment housing is open to law students. Knoxville also offers ample private apartment housing at a reasonable cost. Knoxville Place, a new campus living community, is adjacent to the law school.

■ Career Services

Recruiting and hiring practices in the legal job market require that making career decisions be an ongoing, developmental process that begins in the first year of law school and continues through and after graduation. Our students acquire the skills and knowledge necessary to research, select, and seek the right career path for them and gain necessary information about the professional areas in which a law degree can be used.

The staff of the Bettye B. Lewis Career Center offer a comprehensive menu of services for employers who seek to recruit Tennessee students through formal and informal recruitment methods, off-campus job fairs, and recruiting consortia. First-year students are introduced to career development and job search strategies through individual counseling and small group resource training sessions. Students are coached in the development of individual job search strategy plans throughout their law school careers.

These efforts have contributed to a consistently high employment rate for UT graduates that is well above the national average. Most graduates choose to stay in the southeastern US, but graduates accept positions across the country. For detailed information, please see the College of Law website at *www.law.utk.edu*.

Applicant Profile

University of Tennessee College of Law
This grid includes only applicants who earned 120–180 LSAT scores under standard administrations.

LSAT Score	3.75 +		3.50–3.74		3.25–3.49		3.00–3.24		2.75–2.99		2.50–2.74		2.25–2.49		2.00–2.24		Below 2.00		No GPA		Total	
	Apps	Adm	Apps	Adm	Apps	Adm	Apps	Adm	Apps	Adm	Apps	Adm	Apps	Adm	Apps	Adm	Apps	Adm	Apps	Adm	Apps	Adm
175–180	0	0	0	0	0	0	0	0	0	0	0	0	0	0	0	0	0	0	0	0	0	0
170–174	4	4	1	1	1	1	2	2	1	1	0	0	2	1	0	0	0	0	0	0	11	10
165–169	16	16	8	7	11	11	6	5	6	5	1	1	1	0	0	0	0	0	0	0	49	45
160–164	38	32	40	36	41	32	44	21	13	5	8	2	5	1	3	0	0	0	1	0	190	129
155–159	82	41	124	54	110	24	58	14	44	3	12	0	7	1	3	0	0	0	7	0	447	137
150–154	58	17	67	9	65	4	52	1	45	4	8	1	3	0	3	0	0	0	3	0	304	36
145–149	35	4	33	4	50	7	36	4	23	0	15	0	10	0	1	0	1	0	3	0	207	19
140–144	10	1	17	0	23	0	19	0	15	0	11	0	3	0	0	0	0	0	3	0	101	1
135–139	3	0	3	0	6	0	8	0	9	0	8	0	2	0	2	0	2	0	1	0	44	0
130–134	1	0	0	0	0	0	4	0	3	0	0	0	1	0	5	0	0	0	1	0	15	0
125–129	1	0	0	0	0	0	1	0	0	0	1	0	0	0	0	0	0	0	1	0	4	0
120–124	0	0	0	0	0	0	0	0	0	0	0	0	0	0	1	0	0	0	0	0	1	0
Total	248	115	293	111	307	79	230	47	159	18	64	4	34	3	15	0	3	0	20	0	1373	377

Apps = Number of Applicants   Adm = Number Admitted   Reflects 98% of the total applicant pool.

The University of Texas School of Law

727 East Dean Keeton
Austin, TX 78705
Phone: 512.232.1200; Fax: 512.471.2765
E-mail: admissions@mail.law.utexas.edu; Website: www.utexas.edu/law/

ABA Approved Since 1923

The Basics

Type of school	Public
Term	Semester
Application deadline	11/1 2/1
Application fee	$70
Financial aid deadline	3/31
Can first year start other than fall?	No
Student to faculty ratio	14.0 to 1
Does the university offer:	
housing restricted to law students?	No
graduate housing for which law students are eligible?	No

Faculty and Administrators

	Total		Men		Women		Minorities	
	Fall	Spr	Fall	Spr	Fall	Spr	Fall	Spr
Full-time	72	82	46	60	26	22	6	8
Other Full-time	2	2	0	0	2	2	1	1
Deans, librarians, & others who teach	7	8	3	4	4	4	2	2
Part-time	58	76	40	55	18	21	6	7
Total	**139**	**168**	**89**	**119**	**50**	**49**	**15**	**18**

Curriculum

	Full-time	Part-time
Typical first-year section size	112	0
Is there typically a "small section" of the first-year class, other than Legal Writing, taught by full-time faculty	Yes	No
If yes, typical size offered last year	28	
# of classroom course titles beyond first-year curriculum	161	
# of upper division courses, excluding seminars with an enrollment: Under 25	180	
25–49	55	
50–74	15	
75–99	11	
100+	18	
# of seminars	60	
# of seminar positions available	799	
# of seminar positions filled	683	0
# of positions available in simulation courses	478	
# of simulation positions filled	416	0
# of positions available in faculty supervised clinical courses	272	
# of faculty supervised clinical positions filled	226	0
# involved in field placements	160	0
# involved in law journals	0	0
# involved in interschool competitions	240	0
# of credit hours required to graduate	86	

JD Enrollment and Ethnicity

	Men #	Men %	Women #	Women %	Full-time #	Full-time %	Part-time #	Part-time %	1st-year #	1st-year %	Total #	Total %	JD Degs. Awd.
African Amer.	28	3.6	49	9.2	77	5.9	0	0.0	29	6.6	77	5.9	28
Amer. Indian	5	0.6	3	0.6	8	0.6	0	0.0	1	0.2	8	0.6	1
Asian Amer.	38	4.9	35	6.6	73	5.6	0	0.0	22	5.0	73	5.6	34
Mex. Amer.	117	15.0	79	14.9	196	14.9	0	0.0	67	15.2	196	14.9	63
Puerto Rican	0	0.0	0	0.0	0	0.0	0	0.0	0	0.0	0	0.0	0
Hispanic	38	4.9	24	4.5	62	4.7	0	0.0	17	3.9	62	4.7	22
Total Minority	226	28.9	190	35.8	416	31.7	0	0.0	136	30.9	416	31.7	148
For. Nation.	0	0.0	0	0.0	0	0.0	0	0.0	0	0.0	0	0.0	0
Caucasian	446	57.0	305	57.4	751	57.2	0	0.0	273	62.0	751	57.2	313
Unknown	110	14.1	36	6.8	146	11.1	0	0.0	31	7.0	146	11.1	41
Total	782	59.6	531	40.4	1313	100.0	0	0.0	440	33.5	1313		502

Transfers

Transfers in	14
Transfers out	10

Tuition and Fees

	Resident	Nonresident
Full-time	$18,208	$31,648
Part-time	$0	$0

Living Expenses

Estimated living expenses for singles

Living on campus	Living off campus	Living at home
$15,442	$15,623	$12,623

The University of Texas School of Law

ABA
Approved
Since
1923

GPA and LSAT Scores

	Total	Full-time	Part-time
# of apps	4,999	4,999	0
# of offers	1,085	1,085	0
# of matrics	433	433	0
75% GPA	3.80	3.80	0.00
Median GPA	3.60	3.60	0.00
25% GPA	3.33	3.33	0.00
75% LSAT	168	168	0
Median LSAT	166	166	0
25% LSAT	162	162	0

Grants and Scholarships (from prior year)

	Total		Full-time		Part-time	
	#	%	#	%	#	%
Total # of students	1,387		1,387		0	
Total # receiving grants	1086	78.3	1086	78.3	0	0.0
Less than 1/2 tuition	957	69.0	957	69.0	0	0.0
Half to full tuition	116	8.4	116	8.4	0	0.0
Full tuition	1	0.1	1	0.1	0	0.0
More than full tuition	12	0.9	12	0.9	0	0.0
Median grant amount			$4,500		$0	

Informational and Library Resources

# of volumes and volume equivalents	1,039,731
# of titles	385,981
# of active serial subscriptions	7,490
Study seating capacity inside the library	1,319
# of full-time professional librarians	14
Hours per week library is open	99
# of open, wired connections available to students	310
# of networked computers available for use by students	229
# of simultaneous wireless users	35,000
Require computer?	No

JD Attrition (from prior year)

	Academic	Other	Total	
	#	#	#	%
1st year	0	9	9	2.0
2nd year	0	13	13	3.1
3rd year	0	6	6	1.2
4th year	0	0	0	0.0

Employment (9 months after graduation)

	Total	Percentage
Employment status known	546	99.8
Employment status unknown	1	0.2
Employed	510	93.4
Pursuing graduate degrees	5	0.9
Unemployed seeking employment	5	0.9
Unemployed not seeking employment	7	1.3
Unemployed and studying for the bar	19	3.5

Type of Employment

# employed in law firms	328	64.3
# employed in business and industry	41	8.0
# employed in government	47	9.2
# employed in public interest	18	3.5
# employed as judicial clerks	53	10.4
# employed in academia	5	1.0

Geographic Location

# employed in state	378	74.1
# employed in foreign countries	4	0.8
# of states where employed	31	

Bar Passage Rates

Jurisdiction	Texas		
Exam	Sum 05	Win 06	Total
# from school taking bar for the first time	385	37	422
School's pass rate for all first-time takers	89%	92%	90%
State's pass rate for all first-time takers	81%	77%	80%

The University of Texas School of Law

727 East Dean Keeton
Austin, TX 78705
Phone: 512.232.1200; Fax: 512.471.2765
E-mail: admissions@mail.law.utexas.edu; Website: www.utexas.edu/law/

■ Introduction

The School of Law is located at the University of Texas at Austin. This location in the heart of the capital city provides ready access to the state legislature, the Supreme Court of Texas, the federal trial and appellate court, the offices of state and federal agencies, and the libraries and other main campus facilities. Recognized for its distinguished faculty and rich academic program, the law school has been a member of AALS since 1907, was approved by the ABA in 1923, and is fully accredited.

Situated on the banks of the Colorado River, Austin is an eclectic town noted for its politics, scholars, rolling hills, film industry, and live music and restaurant scene. The University of Texas plays an important role in this metropolitan area of over one million people, and many entertainment and cultural activities cater to the student population.

■ Library and Physical Facilities

The Tarlton Law Library of the Joseph D. Jamail Center for Legal Research, with over one million volumes, is the seventh largest academic law library in the United States and the finest legal research center in the Southwest. It houses working collections from many other countries, with special strength in primary legal materials from Latin America and Western European nations, as well as a full depository for European Union documents. A suite of rooms in the law library houses rare books, manuscripts, law school archives, and special collections of materials ranging from a fifteenth century Roman law codex to the papers of former Supreme Court Justice Tom C. Clark. The Hyder Collection, a 4,000-item collection of law-related artifacts, makes the library an unusually welcoming place for study.

■ Faculty

The University of Texas School of Law has long had one of the most outstanding faculties in the nation, both in terms of scholarly distinction of the faculty members and their success in the classroom. More than one-third of the faculty is elected to the American Law Institute, one of the highest percentage memberships in the nation. Texas is also one of nine schools with four faculty elected to the American Academy of Arts and Sciences, the nation's most prestigious learned society. The law school has consistently hired the best and brightest younger scholars, including eight former clerks for justices of the United States Supreme Court.

Texas enjoys a leadership position in many areas of legal study. The breadth and depth of offerings in several areas—constitutional law, environmental law, wills and estates, admiralty and maritime law, torts and product liability, labor law, jurisprudence and philosophy—is matched by few schools in the country. With one of the largest faculties in the country, Texas is able to offer students coverage of all fields of law and exposure to truly diverse scholarly perspectives on legal questions.

■ Enrollment/Student Body

As a Texas public institution, the Texas legislature limits nonresident enrollment to 35 percent of the population. We currently have over 147 undergraduate institutions and 29 states represented in our student body. Please refer to the statistical information for details as to the strength of the student body and the competition for admission.

■ Special Programs

The school offers clinical education courses for credit in such fields as capital punishment, children's rights, criminal defense, domestic violence, housing, immigration, juvenile justice, mediation, and mental health. Internships are available to qualified students with the Texas Supreme Court, the Texas Court of Criminal Appeals, and the Third Court of Appeals. A limited number of externships are available for credit in the public service area. The law school also has an extensive trial-advocacy program boasting several national championships. There are a number of joint-degree programs: JD/MPAff; JD/MBA; JD/Master of Arts in Latin American Studies; JD/Master of Science in Community and Regional Planning; JD/Master of Arts in Russian, East European, and Eurasian Studies; and JD/Master of Arts in Middle Eastern Studies, in addition to several combined programs with a PhD.

■ Curriculum

All first-year students are required to take a full courseload, averaging 15 hours per week, in contracts, property, torts, civil procedure, criminal law, constitutional law, brief writing and oral advocacy, and legal research and writing. After the first year, the only required courses are professional responsibility, advanced constitutional law, and a writing and research seminar. A student may design his or her course of study from an array of course offerings in many fields of law. These offerings include interdisciplinary and advanced public and private law courses.

■ Student-edited Journals

The School of Law offers many student-administered, cocurricular activities that enhance the law students' regular studies. Student-edited journals include *American Journal of Criminal Law; Texas Environmental Law Journal; Texas Journal on Civil Liberties and Civil Rights; Texas Hispanic Journal of Law and Policy; Texas Intellectual Property Law Journal; Texas International Law Journal; Texas Journal of Oil, Gas, and Energy Law; Texas Journal of Women and the Law; Texas Law Review; Texas Review of Entertainment and Sports Law; Texas Review of Law and Politics;* and the *Review of Litigation.*

■ Admission

Admission to the JD program at UT Law is competitive. For the entering class of 2006, approximately 5,000 applicants competed for the 450 seats in the entering class. As a general rule, there are no presumptive numbers. Every application completed and submitted is reviewed in its entirety. Each applicant must take the LSAT and have earned a baccalaureate degree from an accredited college or university with a minimum grade-point average of 2.2 as calculated by the

Law School Admission Council (LSAC), or have completed the equivalent of six semesters and expect to graduate during the current academic year. Each candidate must complete all application forms and fulfill all mandatory attachments as described in the application.

■ Financial Aid

A limited number of scholarships are available for first-year students on the basis of merit and financial need. The prestigious Townes-Rice Scholarship is offered to eight outstanding law students with full-tuition and fees plus stipends for all three years of law school. The law school also offers an Equal Justice scholarship for an entering student interested in a career in public interest. Scholarships and research assistantships are available for second- and third-year students. The law school administers several short-term and long-term loan funds for students with financial need, and the university offers substantial federally funded loan programs.

■ Housing

Approximately 95 percent of all law students live off-campus. The Division of Housing and Food Services (PO Box 7666, University Station, Austin, TX 78713; telephone 512.471.3136) has information regarding on-campus living. Other sources of information are classified ads in the student newspaper, the *Daily Texan*, apartment management services, rental agencies, and current students.

■ Career Services

Each year, nearly 500 employers participate in career services programs and recruit our students for summer and full-time positions through on-campus interviews, recruit-by-mail opportunities, and off-campus job fairs. Over 50 percent of on-campus employers are from outside the state of Texas. For the past three years, more than 99 percent of graduates who were actively seeking employment have secured it within nine months of graduation.

Applicant Profile

The University of Texas School of Law
This grid includes only applicants who earned 120–180 LSAT scores under standard administrations.

LSAT Score	3.75 +		3.50–3.74		3.25–3.49		3.00–3.24		2.75–2.99		2.50–2.74		2.25–2.49		2.00–2.24		Below 2.00		No GPA		Total	
	Apps	Adm	Apps	Adm	Apps	Adm	Apps	Adm	Apps	Adm	Apps	Adm	Apps	Adm	Apps	Adm	Apps	Adm	Apps	Adm	Apps	Adm
175–180	21	21	13	10	6	2	5	1	7	3	3	0	0	0	0	0	0	0	0	0	55	37
170–174	115	113	76	65	68	45	24	14	17	5	5	0	3	1	0	0	0	0	2	0	310	243
165–169	291	253	289	182	190	78	95	14	37	6	16	2	4	1	1	0	0	0	7	3	930	539
160–164	374	62	412	35	303	21	162	21	56	7	29	0	10	1	2	0	0	0	18	1	1366	148
155–159	224	18	309	24	250	19	133	11	68	3	21	1	7	0	5	0	0	0	10	0	1027	76
150–154	89	7	162	6	160	8	93	3	63	1	24	0	16	1	3	0	1	0	13	0	624	26
145–149	34	0	68	2	68	1	75	3	44	1	31	1	13	0	3	0	1	0	4	0	341	8
140–144	13	0	31	0	38	0	44	1	33	2	30	0	12	0	5	0	1	0	4	0	211	3
135–139	3	0	7	0	10	0	20	0	14	0	13	1	3	0	3	0	2	0	2	0	77	1
130–134	1	0	1	0	3	0	2	0	0	0	8	0	2	0	2	0	1	0	3	0	23	0
125–129	0	0	0	0	0	0	0	0	0	0	1	0	0	0	0	0	1	0	0	0	2	0
120–124	0	0	0	0	0	0	0	0	0	0	0	0	0	0	0	0	0	0	0	0	0	0
Total	1165	474	1368	324	1096	174	653	68	339	28	181	5	70	4	24	0	7	0	63	4	4966	1081

Apps = Number of Applicants
Adm = Number Admitted
Reflects 99% of the total applicant pool.

Texas Southern University—Thurgood Marshall School of Law

3100 Cleburne
Houston, TX 77004
Phone: 713.313.7114 or 713.313.7115; Fax: 713.313.7297
E-mail: erene@tsulaw.edu; Website: www.tsu.edu/academics/law

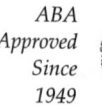

ABA Approved Since 1949

The Basics

Type of school	Public
Term	Semester
Application deadline	4/1
Application fee	$55
Financial aid deadline	4/1
Can first year start other than fall?	No
Student to faculty ratio	15.6 to 1
Does the university offer:	
housing restricted to law students?	No
graduate housing for which law students are eligible?	No

Faculty and Administrators

	Total		Men		Women		Minorities	
	Fall	Spr	Fall	Spr	Fall	Spr	Fall	Spr
Full-time	35	35	16	16	19	19	28	28
Other Full-time	2	4	0	1	2	3	2	4
Deans, librarians, & others who teach	15	14	6	5	9	9	14	13
Part-time	8	19	7	15	1	4	7	18
Total	**60**	**72**	**29**	**37**	**31**	**35**	**51**	**63**

Curriculum

	Full-time	Part-time
Typical first-year section size	65	0
Is there typically a "small section" of the first-year class, other than Legal Writing, taught by full-time faculty	No	No
If yes, typical size offered last year		
# of classroom course titles beyond first-year curriculum	115	
# of upper division courses, excluding seminars with an enrollment: Under 25	62	
25–49	23	
50–74	20	
75–99	8	
100+	0	
# of seminars	27	
# of seminar positions available	20	
# of seminar positions filled	282	0
# of positions available in simulation courses	252	
# of simulation positions filled	217	0
# of positions available in faculty supervised clinical courses	72	
# of faculty supervised clinical positions filled	53	0
# involved in field placements	30	0
# involved in law journals	39	0
# involved in interschool competitions	30	0
# of credit hours required to graduate	90	

JD Enrollment and Ethnicity

	Men #	Men %	Women #	Women %	Full-time #	Full-time %	Part-time #	Part-time %	1st-year #	1st-year %	Total #	Total %	JD Degs. Awd.
African Amer.	128	40.9	199	57.7	327	49.7	0	0.0	113	44.5	327	49.7	90
Amer. Indian	2	0.6	4	1.2	6	0.9	0	0.0	4	1.6	6	0.9	0
Asian Amer.	24	7.7	19	5.5	43	6.5	0	0.0	13	5.1	43	6.5	11
Mex. Amer.	80	25.6	68	19.7	148	22.5	0	0.0	64	25.2	148	22.5	45
Puerto Rican	0	0.0	0	0.0	0	0.0	0	0.0	0	0.0	0	0.0	0
Hispanic	13	4.2	8	2.3	21	3.2	0	0.0	9	3.5	21	3.2	2
Total Minority	247	78.9	298	86.4	545	82.8	0	0.0	203	79.9	545	82.8	148
For. Nation.	0	0.0	0	0.0	0	0.0	0	0.0	0	0.0	0	0.0	0
Caucasian	64	20.4	47	13.6	111	16.9	0	0.0	49	19.3	111	16.9	52
Unknown	2	0.6	0	0.0	2	0.3	0	0.0	2	0.8	2	0.3	0
Total	313	47.6	345	52.4	658	100.0	0	0.0	254	38.6	658		200

Transfers

Transfers in	2
Transfers out	10

Tuition and Fees

	Resident	Nonresident
Full-time	$11,228	$14,978
Part-time	$0	$0

Living Expenses

Estimated living expenses for singles

Living on campus	Living off campus	Living at home
$12,005	$12,005	$12,005

Texas Southern University—Thurgood Marshall School of Law

ABA
Approved
Since
1949

GPA and LSAT Scores

	Total	Full-time	Part-time
# of apps	2,429	2,429	0
# of offers	692	692	0
# of matrics	252	252	0
75% GPA	3.19	3.19	0.00
Median GPA	2.91	2.91	0.00
25% GPA	2.65	2.65	0.00
75% LSAT	150	150	0
Median LSAT	147	147	0
25% LSAT	145	145	0

Grants and Scholarships (from prior year)

	Total #	Total %	Full-time #	Full-time %	Part-time #	Part-time %
Total # of students	657		657		0	
Total # receiving grants	261	39.7	261	39.7	0	0.0
Less than 1/2 tuition	231	35.2	231	35.2	0	0.0
Half to full tuition	20	3.0	20	3.0	0	0.0
Full tuition	10	1.5	10	1.5	0	0.0
More than full tuition	0	0.0	0	0.0	0	0.0
Median grant amount			$3,000		$0	

Informational and Library Resources

# of volumes and volume equivalents	659,551
# of titles	152,805
# of active serial subscriptions	2,777
Study seating capacity inside the library	372
# of full-time professional librarians	8
Hours per week library is open	108
# of open, wired connections available to students	945
# of networked computers available for use by students	85
# of simultaneous wireless users	300
Require computer?	No

JD Attrition (from prior year)

	Academic #	Other #	Total #	Total %
1st year	22	20	42	17.9
2nd year	4	0	4	1.8
3rd year	0	0	0	0.0
4th year	0	0	0	0.0

Employment (9 months after graduation)

	Total	Percentage
Employment status known	148	93.7
Employment status unknown	10	6.3
Employed	104	70.3
Pursuing graduate degrees	5	3.4
Unemployed seeking employment	6	4.1
Unemployed not seeking employment	0	0.0
Unemployed and studying for the bar	33	22.3

Type of Employment

# employed in law firms	72	69.2
# employed in business and industry	14	13.5
# employed in government	7	6.7
# employed in public interest	7	6.7
# employed as judicial clerks	1	1.0
# employed in academia	1	1.0

Geographic Location

# employed in state	81	77.9
# employed in foreign countries	1	1.0
# of states where employed	14	

Bar Passage Rates

Jurisdiction	Texas		
Exam	Sum 05	Win 06	Total
# from school taking bar for the first time	96	26	122
School's pass rate for all first-time takers	59%	77%	63%
State's pass rate for all first-time takers	81%	77%	80%

Texas Southern University—Thurgood Marshall School of Law

Office of Admissions, 3100 Cleburne
Houston, TX 77004
Phone: 713.313.7114 or 713.313.7115; Fax: 713.313.7297
E-mail: erene@tsulaw.edu; Website: www.tsu.edu/academics/law

■ Introduction

The Thurgood Marshall School of Law, a state institution founded in 1947, seeks to provide a legal education and an opportunity to excel to students from a wide range of backgrounds, including those who otherwise would not have an opportunity for legal training. The law school is accredited by the ABA. The student body is truly multiethnic and multicultural. The law school is housed in a tri-level structure that is located just outside of downtown Houston. Near-campus housing is available in the form of modern apartments for single and married students. The school makes extensive use of legal facilities in Houston through its clinical programs.

■ Enrollment/Student Body

A majority of the students are from Texas, but all parts of the country are represented. Approximately 49 percent of the students are black, 23 percent Chicano, 17 percent Caucasian, and 6 percent Asian and Native American. The median age range is about 26 to 36 years.

■ Library and Physical Facilities

Students receive individual or group orientation and intensive training in the use of the library. The law school has undergone approximately $16 million in renovations, expanding the available space from 103,000 to 108,000 square feet.

■ Curriculum

Upon entry to the School of Law, all students in the first-year class are required to attend a week-long orientation program. Attention is given to examinations, briefing cases, outlining, and an overview of law school life and expectations.

The law school offers a three-year, full-time JD program. The minimum courseload is 12 hours. Required courses for the first year are Lawyering Process I and II, Civil Procedure, Property, Contracts, Torts, and Criminal Law. Second-year students must take Constitutional Law, Evidence, Criminal Procedure, Trial Simulation, Business Associations, Commercial Law, Professional Responsibility, and Wills and Trusts. Second- or third-year students are required to take Federal Jurisdiction and Procedure, a seminar/independent research project, and Basic Federal Taxation. Third-year students are required to take Consumer Rights and Texas Practice. The remaining hours required to complete the degree may be selected from a number of areas of interest.

The law school operates a full-time, in-house clinic in which students work under the supervision of faculty and adjunct faculty members. Internships are available with the Harris County District Attorney's Office, the Federal Magistrates, Gulf Coast Legal Foundation, the Federal Bankruptcy Court, the Harris County Attorney's Office, the Internal Revenue Service, and the US District Court. The school operates a number of clinics, including advanced skills, basic skills, civil and criminal externships, environmental justice, family law, and housing law. A judicial externship with state and federal judges is available to academically outstanding third-year students.

■ Admission

The admission decision is based primarily on the applicant's motivation and intellectual capacity as demonstrated by his or her undergraduate records, and on his or her aptitude for the study of law as measured by the LSAT. Leadership ability, prior community service, work experience, the student's background, extracurricular activities, and graduate study in another discipline are all considered.

No particular undergraduate major is preferred, but the school looks for applicants with broad backgrounds in the social sciences, natural sciences, humanities, and business sciences. Newly admitted students must send two seat deposits ($150 upon acceptance and $100 in June), which are refundable upon matriculation. The law school's student body represents one of the most culturally and ethnically diverse student bodies in the country. Transfer applications are accepted; students must submit a transcript and letter from the Dean of his/her former law school stating that they are in good standing. All newly admitted students must submit an official transcript from the baccalaureate degree-granting institution as well as all law schools attended. No application will be evaluated by the Admissions Committee until the LSDAS report has been received.

In order to ensure complete review, applications must be received by the Office of Admissions no later than April 1, although earlier submission is encouraged. Entering students are admitted only in August (fall semester). Students are notified of acceptance after the Admissions Committee has reviewed the complete file. Admission decisions are made on a rolling basis.

■ Student Activities

Numerous law school organizations are active on campus. A student board edits the *Thurgood Marshall Law Review*. Moot court competitions are held in trial and appellate work, labor law, and client counseling.

■ Expenses and Financial Aid

About 90 percent of the students receive some form of aid. The law school administers its own scholarship program, which is competitive. Scholarships are awarded on the basis of both need and merit, and may range up to full tuition. The university also offers additional scholarship aid, and the law school and the university offer loan assistance. Ten to 15 percent of the students hold assistantships. The aid application deadline is April 1.

The scholarship program makes several awards (approximately 60) each year. The awards have enabled out-of-state residents to qualify for resident-tuition rates. In addition, a number of law students each year qualify for the federal work-study and loan programs. Additional limited scholarship aid is available to students after they have completed a year of law study. An applicant in need of other financial assistance should make arrangements for financial aid through the Law School Financial Aid Counselor by either calling 713.313.7243 or e-mailing *kepercival@tsulaw.edu*.

Texas Southern University—Thurgood Marshall School of Law

■ Career Development

The law school employs a full-time career development officer. Graduates are placed primarily with law firms, federal and state agencies, legal services, judges, and businesses. The Career Development Office also conducts a major national effort to encourage legal employers in every major city in the United States to recruit Texas Southern University—Thurgood Marshall School of Law graduates.

Applicant Profile

Texas Southern University—Thurgood Marshall School of Law
This grid includes only applicants who earned 120–180 LSAT scores under standard administrations.

LSAT Score	GPA 3.75 +		3.50–3.74		3.25–3.49		3.00–3.24		2.75–2.99		2.50–2.74		2.25–2.49		2.00–2.24		Below 2.00		No GPA		Total	
	Apps	Adm	Apps	Adm	Apps	Adm	Apps	Adm	Apps	Adm	Apps	Adm	Apps	Adm	Apps	Adm	Apps	Adm	Apps	Adm	Apps	Adm
175–180	0	0	0	0	0	0	0	0	0	0	0	0	0	0	0	0	0	0	0	0	0	0
170–174	0	0	0	0	0	0	0	0	0	0	0	0	0	0	0	0	0	0	0	0	0	0
165–169	0	0	1	0	0	0	0	0	0	0	0	0	0	0	0	0	0	0	0	0	1	0
160–164	1	1	3	2	2	1	3	1	1	1	5	5	2	2	0	0	0	0	0	0	17	13
155–159	5	5	8	7	6	3	11	9	11	8	15	10	5	4	2	1	0	0	2	1	65	48
150–154	14	12	35	29	34	25	50	43	36	24	35	22	18	10	10	6	2	0	1	1	235	172
145–149	23	18	83	50	93	55	109	60	122	60	98	47	52	11	31	8	6	0	8	1	625	310
140–144	14	5	68	17	118	16	172	34	169	28	147	18	102	6	37	0	11	0	16	3	854	127
135–139	7	0	19	0	51	0	86	0	88	0	76	1	52	0	28	0	6	0	8	0	421	1
130–134	3	0	6	0	11	0	21	0	19	0	23	1	23	0	16	0	3	0	10	0	135	1
125–129	0	0	1	0	1	0	1	0	5	0	8	0	3	0	5	0	3	0	1	0	28	0
120–124	1	0	0	0	0	0	1	0	0	0	1	0	1	0	1	0	0	0	0	0	5	0
Total	68	41	224	105	316	100	454	147	451	121	408	104	258	33	130	15	31	0	46	6	2386	672

Apps = Number of Applicants
Adm = Number Admitted
Reflects 99% of the total applicant pool.

Texas Tech University School of Law

1802 Hartford Avenue
Lubbock, TX 79409
Phone: 806.742.3791; Fax: 806.742.4617
E-mail: admissions.law@ttu.edu; Website: www.law.ttu.edu

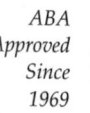

ABA Approved Since 1969

The Basics

Type of school	Public
Term	Semester
Application deadline	11/1 2/1
Application fee	$50
Financial aid deadline	4/15
Can first year start other than fall?	Yes
Student to faculty ratio	15.3 to 1
Does the university offer:	
housing restricted to law students?	No
graduate housing for which law students are eligible?	No

Faculty and Administrators

	Total		Men		Women		Minorities	
	Fall	Spr	Fall	Spr	Fall	Spr	Fall	Spr
Full-time	39	38	25	27	14	11	7	6
Other Full-time	0	1	0	1	0	0	0	0
Deans, librarians, & others who teach	8	8	5	5	3	3	2	2
Part-time	16	17	14	13	2	4	3	2
Total	63	64	44	46	19	18	12	10

Curriculum

	Full-time	Part-time
Typical first-year section size	60	0
Is there typically a "small section" of the first-year class, other than Legal Writing, taught by full-time faculty	No	No
If yes, typical size offered last year		
# of classroom course titles beyond first-year curriculum		91
# of upper division courses, excluding seminars with an enrollment: Under 25		55
25–49		26
50–74		20
75–99		3
100+		5
# of seminars		22
# of seminar positions available		370
# of seminar positions filled	288	0
# of positions available in simulation courses		356
# of simulation positions filled	296	0
# of positions available in faculty supervised clinical courses		112
# of faculty supervised clinical positions filled	104	0
# involved in field placements	74	0
# involved in law journals	116	0
# involved in interschool competitions	45	0
# of credit hours required to graduate		90

JD Enrollment and Ethnicity

	Men		Women		Full-time		Part-time		1st-year		Total		JD Degs. Awd.
	#	%	#	%	#	%	#	%	#	%	#	%	
African Amer.	11	2.8	17	5.4	28	4.0	0	0.0	12	5.3	28	4.0	3
Amer. Indian	3	0.8	2	0.6	5	0.7	0	0.0	1	0.4	5	0.7	0
Asian Amer.	18	4.6	12	3.8	30	4.3	0	0.0	8	3.5	30	4.3	2
Mex. Amer.	33	8.5	38	12.1	71	10.1	0	0.0	25	11.0	71	10.1	25
Puerto Rican	3	0.8	0	0.0	3	0.4	0	0.0	2	0.9	3	0.4	0
Hispanic	0	0.0	0	0.0	0	0.0	0	0.0	0	0.0	0	0.0	0
Total Minority	68	17.5	69	22.0	137	19.5	0	0.0	48	21.1	137	19.5	30
For. Nation.	1	0.3	1	0.3	2	0.3	0	0.0	1	0.4	2	0.3	0
Caucasian	311	80.2	232	73.9	543	77.4	0	0.0	172	75.8	543	77.4	172
Unknown	8	2.1	12	3.8	20	2.8	0	0.0	6	2.6	20	2.8	1
Total	388	55.3	314	44.7	702	100.0	0	0.0	227	32.3	702		203

Transfers

Transfers in	2
Transfers out	3

Tuition and Fees

	Resident	Nonresident
Full-time	$12,615	$19,720
Part-time	$0	$0

Living Expenses

Estimated living expenses for singles

Living on campus	Living off campus	Living at home
$12,196	$12,196	N/A

Texas Tech University School of Law

*ABA
Approved
Since
1969*

GPA and LSAT Scores

	Total	Full-time	Part-time
# of apps	1,790	1,790	0
# of offers	585	585	0
# of matrics	226	226	0
75% GPA	3.76	3.76	0.00
Median GPA	3.61	3.61	0.00
25% GPA	3.41	3.41	0.00
75% LSAT	157	157	0
Median LSAT	155	155	0
25% LSAT	151	151	0

Grants and Scholarships (from prior year)

	Total		Full-time		Part-time	
	#	%	#	%	#	%
Total # of students	701		701		0	
Total # receiving grants	526	75.0	526	75.0	0	0.0
Less than 1/2 tuition	377	53.8	377	53.8	0	0.0
Half to full tuition	31	4.4	31	4.4	0	0.0
Full tuition	61	8.7	61	8.7	0	0.0
More than full tuition	57	8.1	57	8.1	0	0.0
Median grant amount			$3,500		$0	

Informational and Library Resources

# of volumes and volume equivalents	307,959
# of titles	69,979
# of active serial subscriptions	3,157
Study seating capacity inside the library	587
# of full-time professional librarians	8
Hours per week library is open	168
# of open, wired connections available to students	848
# of networked computers available for use by students	238
# of simultaneous wireless users	420
Require computer?	No

JD Attrition (from prior year)

	Academic	Other	Total	
	#	#	#	%
1st year	9	9	18	6.4
2nd year	2	1	3	1.2
3rd year	0	0	0	0.0
4th year	0	0	0	0.0

Employment (9 months after graduation)

	Total	Percentage
Employment status known	227	97.0
Employment status unknown	7	3.0
Employed	222	97.8
Pursuing graduate degrees	0	0.0
Unemployed seeking employment	5	2.2
Unemployed not seeking employment	0	0.0
Unemployed and studying for the bar	0	0.0

Type of Employment

# employed in law firms	196	88.3
# employed in business and industry	0	0.0
# employed in government	14	6.3
# employed in public interest	5	2.3
# employed as judicial clerks	6	2.7
# employed in academia	0	0.0

Geographic Location

# employed in state	214	96.4
# employed in foreign countries	0	0.0
# of states where employed	4	

Bar Passage Rates

Jurisdiction	Texas		
Exam	Sum 05	Win 06	Total
# from school taking bar for the first time	178	23	201
School's pass rate for all first-time takers	91%	74%	89%
State's pass rate for all first-time takers	81%	77%	80%

Texas Tech University School of Law

1802 Hartford Avenue
Lubbock, TX 79409
Phone: 806.742.3791; Fax: 806.742.4617
E-mail: admissions.law@ttu.edu; Website: www.law.ttu.edu

■ Introduction

The school, which accepted its first class in 1967, is located on the main campus of Texas Tech University in Lubbock. It is fully accredited with the Supreme Court of Texas and the ABA and is a member of the AALS. Its graduates are eligible to take the bar examination in any state in the nation. In 1974, a chapter of the Order of the Coif was established, a distinction accorded to only one-third of American law schools. The faculty embraces an open-door policy, enabling students to engage in continuing dialogue beyond formal class hours.

■ Library and Physical Facilities

The school is designed to meet the needs of a contemporary legal education. The law library supports the research and academic needs of the students and faculty as evinced by superb computer resources and wireless Internet access, complementing a substantial collection of printed materials. All students have 24/7 access to the library and assigned library carrels that serve as small office-like workspaces. All classrooms are equipped with state-of-the-art technology. Also, a new $13.5 million Professional Development Center to support advocacy training is being constructed.

■ Curriculum

The program of study equips students to practice law as advocates, counselors, judges, or law teachers, and the school recognizes that legal education is also a stepping-stone to careers in government, politics, or business. The required curriculum provides a broad-based legal education. Elective courses afford students the opportunity to create an area of concentration, ranging from business law to emerging areas such as health law, natural resources law, and national security law. The School of Law offers an Academic Success Program to assist students in developing the skills to succeed in the study and practice of law.

■ Programs of Study

The school offers several joint-degree programs: the JD/MBA; the JD/MPA; the JD/MS in Agriculture and Applied Economics; the JD/MS in Accounting (Taxation); the JD/Master of Environmental Toxicology; the JD/Master of Biotechnology; the JD/MS in Crop and Soil Sciences; and the JD/MS in Personal Financial Planning, which qualifies students to sit for the Certified Financial Planning exam. Also, a Law and Science Certificate Program allows for specialization in areas including environmental law, health law, intellectual property law, and biodefense law.

■ Admission

The school uses a rolling admission policy. The Admissions Committee admits applicants from a wide range of backgrounds and experiences. While an applicant's LSAT and GPA figure significantly in the admission process, the committee also considers other factors, including extracurricular activities, public interest service, previous employment, and leadership qualities. A bachelor's degree from an accredited college or university is required.

The school offers a binding Early Decision Program with an application deadline of November 1 and an LSDAS report deadline of November 10. The deadline for regular decision applicants is February 1. Some students may be admitted through a Summer Entry Program.

Written recommendations are required. Anyone filing an application after February 1 will be at a disadvantage. Those applicants accepted in the Early Decision Program will be required to pay a nonrefundable deposit of $750, and those accepted in the regular admission process must pay a deposit of $300 to hold their places.

■ Legal Publication and Research Opportunities

Texas Tech has several publications that allow students to hone their research and writing skills. The *Texas Tech Law Review* publishes articles written by students and leading jurists, practitioners, and academics.

The State Bar of Texas selected the school to publish the *Texas Tech Administrative Law Journal*. The *Texas Bank Lawyer* publishes articles about banking and commercial law.

The school is home to the Center for Water Law and Policy, the Center for Military Law and Policy, and the Center for Biodefense Law and Policy, which all provide research and scholarship opportunities.

Students take the lead in writing and producing the school's alumni magazine, the *Texas Tech Lawyer*.

■ Clinical Program

The school boasts a newly remodeled clinic facility that includes a state-of-the-art multimedia teleconference room. Students have the opportunity to represent clients and participate in real cases through several clinical courses taught by full-time tenure-track faculty. Students enrolled in the Civil Litigation Clinic represent clients in a wide range of civil matters. The Criminal Justice Clinic provides a unique opportunity for third-year law students to represent actual clients in state and federal criminal courts. In the Tax Clinic, students represent taxpayers in disputes with the IRS. The Alternative Dispute Resolution Clinic and Health Care and Bioethics Mediation Clinic focus on resolving legal issues without litigation. The Innocence Project Clinic considers claims by prisoners of actual innocence. The school also offers a wide array of externship opportunities.

■ Advocacy Program

Students gain advocacy experience in simulated practice settings and through intraschool and interscholastic competitions. The school has an excellent reputation in various competitions. The school boasts 15 national and global titles and numerous top finishes in competitions, including the school's first World Championship in International Negotiation in Dublin, Ireland, in 2005, and the 2003 John Marshall Moot Court National Championship. The school is also in the process of constructing a state-of-the-art courtroom for advocacy training.

■ Student Activities

The Student Bar Association is the focal point for many student activities. The school has approximately 40 student organizations and three legal fraternities. Transitional groups are designed to assist students in their adjustment to law school.

■ Study-abroad Programs

Texas Tech is a consortium partner in the Summer Law Institute, a cooperative teaching program with the historic University of Guanajuato, Mexico. The Summer Law Institute offers an introduction to Mexican law, international law, and legal subjects of interest to both US and Mexican lawyers, such as the NAFTA. See *www.law.ttu.edu* for additional information.

French- or Spanish-fluent students are offered legal study for credit through cooperative programs with the Universidad de Pablo Olavide in Seville, Spain, and the University of Lyon in France. The law school has a third cooperative exchange program with La Trobe University in Melbourne, Australia.

■ Expenses and Financial Aid

The School of Law offers numerous scholarships to entering students. In-state Tuition Scholarships are awarded to many nonresident applicants. Additional scholarships are available for second- and third-year students.

Long-term educational loan funds are available through the Office of Student Financial Aid, and short-term loans are available through the Law School Foundation.

■ Housing

Information about campus housing may be obtained from the Housing Office at *www.housing.ttu.edu*.

■ Career Services

The school is a member of NALP. The school participates in on- and off-campus interviewing programs. Ninety-eight percent of 2005 graduates were employed within six months of graduation.

Please contact *www.law.ttu.edu*, or 806.742.3990, extension 273, for additional information.

Applicant Profile

Texas Tech University School of Law
This grid includes only applicants who earned 120–180 LSAT scores under standard administrations.

LSAT Score	3.75 +		3.50–3.74		3.25–3.49		3.00–3.24		2.75–2.99		2.50–2.74		2.25–2.49		2.00–2.24		Below 2.00		No GPA		Total	
	Apps	Adm	Apps	Adm	Apps	Adm	Apps	Adm	Apps	Adm	Apps	Adm	Apps	Adm	Apps	Adm	Apps	Adm	Apps	Adm	Apps	Adm
175–180	0	0	0	0	0	0	0	0	0	0	0	0	0	0	0	0	0	0	0	0	1	1
170–174	1	1	0	0	0	0	0	0	0	0	0	0	0	0	0	0	0	0	0	0	14	12
165–169	4	3	5	5	2	2	2	2	0	0	1	0	0	0	0	0	0	0	1	0	150	109
160–164	26	26	26	25	29	26	29	20	19	8	12	3	5	1	3	0	0	0	2	1	365	212
155–159	54	51	76	71	99	63	69	15	39	8	20	3	5	0	1	0	0	0	1	1	545	183
150–154	70	60	125	71	141	32	104	13	53	3	35	3	12	0	3	0	1	0	2	0	424	47
145–149	38	9	91	24	93	10	90	4	57	0	30	0	18	0	4	0	1	0	3	1	218	14
140–144	12	2	38	9	39	1	52	1	29	0	23	0	13	0	9	0	0	0	3	0	82	0
135–139	3	0	5	0	10	0	20	0	21	0	7	0	8	0	4	0	1	0	1	0	11	0
130–134	1	0	1	0	0	0	0	0	2	0	1	0	2	0	1	0	1	0	0	0	3	0
125–129	0	0	0	0	0	0	1	0	1	0	0	0	0	0	0	0	0	0	0	0	0	0
120–124	0	0	0	0	0	0	0	0	0	0	0	0	0	0	0	0	0	0	0	0	0	0
Total	209	152	367	205	413	134	367	55	221	19	129	9	63	1	25	0	6	0	13	3	1813	578

Apps = Number of Applicants
Adm = Number Admitted
Reflects 99% of the total applicant pool.

Texas Wesleyan University School of Law

1515 Commerce Street
Fort Worth, TX 76102
Phone: 800.733.9529; 817.212.4000; Fax: 817.212.4141
E-mail: lawadmissions@law.txwes.edu; Website: www.law.txwes.edu

ABA Approved Since 1994

The Basics

Type of school	Private
Term	Semester
Application deadline	3/31
Application fee	$55
Financial aid deadline	3/15
Can first year start other than fall?	No
Student to faculty ratio	17.0 to 1
Does the university offer:	
housing restricted to law students?	No
graduate housing for which law students are eligible?	No

Faculty and Administrators

	Total Fall	Total Spr	Men Fall	Men Spr	Women Fall	Women Spr	Minorities Fall	Minorities Spr
Full-time	27	28	19	19	8	9	3	4
Other Full-time	0	0	0	0	0	0	0	0
Deans, librarians, & others who teach	5	4	1	1	4	3	0	0
Part-time	28	25	18	20	10	5	2	3
Total	**60**	**57**	**38**	**40**	**22**	**17**	**5**	**7**

Curriculum

	Full-time	Part-time
Typical first-year section size	85	89
Is there typically a "small section" of the first-year class, other than Legal Writing, taught by full-time faculty	No	No
If yes, typical size offered last year		
# of classroom course titles beyond first-year curriculum		91
# of upper division courses, excluding seminars with an enrollment: Under 25		61
25–49		22
50–74		17
75–99		14
100+		1
# of seminars		14
# of seminar positions available		224
# of seminar positions filled	123	61
# of positions available in simulation courses		294
# of simulation positions filled	154	94
# of positions available in faculty supervised clinical courses		60
# of faculty supervised clinical positions filled	37	20
# involved in field placements	23	16
# involved in law journals	52	15
# involved in interschool competitions	23	6
# of credit hours required to graduate		90

JD Enrollment and Ethnicity

	Men #	Men %	Women #	Women %	Full-time #	Full-time %	Part-time #	Part-time %	1st-year #	1st-year %	Total #	Total %	JD Degs. Awd.
African Amer.	7	2.1	22	6.6	14	3.3	15	6.3	11	4.5	29	4.4	8
Amer. Indian	5	1.5	5	1.5	8	1.9	2	0.8	6	2.4	10	1.5	1
Asian Amer.	15	4.6	23	6.9	28	6.6	10	4.2	16	6.5	38	5.8	13
Mex. Amer.	0	0.0	0	0.0	0	0.0	0	0.0	0	0.0	0	0.0	0
Puerto Rican	0	0.0	0	0.0	0	0.0	0	0.0	0	0.0	0	0.0	0
Hispanic	23	7.0	28	8.4	32	7.6	19	8.0	19	7.8	51	7.7	17
Total Minority	50	15.2	78	23.5	82	19.4	46	19.3	52	21.2	128	19.4	39
For. Nation.	0	0.0	0	0.0	0	0.0	0	0.0	0	0.0	0	0.0	0
Caucasian	264	80.5	246	74.1	326	77.3	184	77.3	189	77.1	510	77.3	143
Unknown	14	4.3	8	2.4	14	3.3	8	3.4	4	1.6	22	3.3	11
Total	328	49.7	332	50.3	422	63.9	238	36.1	245	37.1	660		193

Transfers

Transfers in	9
Transfers out	10

Tuition and Fees

	Resident	Nonresident
Full-time	$21,660	$21,660
Part-time	$15,630	$15,630

Living Expenses

Estimated living expenses for singles

Living on campus	Living off campus	Living at home
$10,088	$14,840	$8,251

Texas Wesleyan University School of Law

ABA
Approved
Since
1994

GPA and LSAT Scores

	Total	Full-time	Part-time
# of apps	2,027	1,585	442
# of offers	815	600	215
# of matrics	242	139	103
75% GPA	3.40	3.45	3.31
Median GPA	3.15	3.17	3.07
25% GPA	2.84	2.94	2.75
75% LSAT	156	157	154
Median LSAT	154	155	151
25% LSAT	151	153	150

Grants and Scholarships (from prior year)

	Total		Full-time		Part-time	
	#	%	#	%	#	%
Total # of students	670		432		238	
Total # receiving grants	209	31.2	156	36.1	53	22.3
Less than 1/2 tuition	171	25.5	128	29.6	43	18.1
Half to full tuition	32	4.8	23	5.3	9	3.8
Full tuition	6	0.9	5	1.2	1	0.4
More than full tuition	0	0.0	0	0.0	0	0.0
Median grant amount			$3,000		$2,500	

Informational and Library Resources

# of volumes and volume equivalents	248,233
# of titles	153,373
# of active serial subscriptions	4,895
Study seating capacity inside the library	383
# of full-time professional librarians	8
Hours per week library is open	112
# of open, wired connections available to students	0
# of networked computers available for use by students	60
# of simultaneous wireless users	180
Require computer?	No

JD Attrition (from prior year)

	Academic	Other	Total	
	#	#	#	%
1st year	8	20	28	10.5
2nd year	4	2	6	2.8
3rd year	0	33	33	18.6
4th year	0	0	0	0.0

Employment (9 months after graduation)

	Total	Percentage
Employment status known	163	90.1
Employment status unknown	18	9.9
Employed	147	90.2
Pursuing graduate degrees	0	0.0
Unemployed seeking employment	9	5.5
Unemployed not seeking employment	0	0.0
Unemployed and studying for the bar	7	4.3

Type of Employment

# employed in law firms	66	44.9
# employed in business and industry	26	17.7
# employed in government	31	21.1
# employed in public interest	4	2.7
# employed as judicial clerks	2	1.4
# employed in academia	1	0.7

Geographic Location

# employed in state	127	86.4
# employed in foreign countries	1	0.7
# of states where employed	10	

Bar Passage Rates

Jurisdiction	Texas		
Exam	Sum 05	Win 06	Total
# from school taking bar for the first time	123	40	163
School's pass rate for all first-time takers	83%	83%	83%
State's pass rate for all first-time takers	81%	77%	80%

Texas Wesleyan University School of Law

1515 Commerce Street
Fort Worth, TX 76102
Phone: 800.733.9529; 817.212.4000; Fax: 817.212.4141
E-mail: lawadmissions@law.txwes.edu; Website: www.law.txwes.edu

■ Introduction

Established in 1989, the law school became part of Texas Wesleyan University in 1992. A comprehensive university, Texas Wesleyan was founded in 1890 and offers degrees in business, education, fine arts, humanities, sciences, and law. The law school is fully approved by the ABA and offers both full-time and part-time studies in day and evening programs leading to the Juris Doctor degree. The law school is located in downtown Fort Worth, Texas, in close proximity to the legal and judicial communities. The Fort Worth/Dallas Metroplex, with approximately 5.8 million residents, has rapidly grown to be one of the largest and most diverse metropolitan areas in the country, offering a relatively low cost of living, a growing economy, and extensive opportunities for professional advancement.

■ Student Body

Texas Wesleyan is committed to educating students of diverse backgrounds, varied life experiences, and educational perspectives. In its short 17-year history, Texas Wesleyan School of Law has provided excellence in legal education to traditional full-time students as well as accomplished nontraditional part-time students. The increasing rise in the quality of students is a reflection of our continued emphasis on service to a diverse student body, the profession, and the community. Students in the fall 2006 class ranged in age from 19 to 59. The median age for the day class was 24, evening class was 28, and overall was 25. In the past five years, applications have doubled, median LSAT scores have risen to 155, and median undergraduate GPAs have risen from 3.00 to 3.20. Last year alone, over 2,000 applicants applied for one of the 240 open seats, a true testament to the increasing quality of education at Texas Wesleyan law school.

■ Faculty

Texas Wesleyan has a highly qualified, energetic, accessible faculty. The 29 members of the faculty hold degrees from the top law schools across the country and have diverse professional backgrounds and experience. They have served in a variety of high-level governmental positions, in the judiciary and state legislatures, and in law firms. Faculty members are talented and active scholars and have published numerous books and articles. The student-to-faculty ratio of approximately 16:1 ensures that students have the attention they need, both inside and outside of the classroom.

■ Library and Physical Facilities

The law school boasts first-rate facilities, including spacious classrooms, well-designed courtrooms, an in-house law clinic, and an impressive library. The Wesleyan law library contains over 250,000 volumes and equivalents. The law library's mission is to support the educational, instructional, curricular, and research needs of the faculty, students, and staff. In addition to its law book collection, the law library subscribes to major online electronic legal information services, including LexisNexis, Westlaw, legal research Internet sites, and several CD-ROM legal research tools.

Complementing book and electronic sources, an extensive collection of US Congressional documents, including full transcripts of all congressional hearings since 1970, are available on microfiche. The law library has 8 full-time librarians and a staff of 14 and is open 112 hours per week, 89 of which reference services are available.

■ Curriculum

Ninety hours of academic course credit are required for completion of the Juris Doctor degree. Students may choose between full-time day, part-time day, or part-time evening courseloads. The part-time program and Wesleyan's flexible scheduling make it possible for those with continuing business and family responsibilities to meet their obligations while obtaining a legal education. The law school offers over 115 courses divided among traditional law courses and advanced courses that provide training in a variety of specialized law areas. Students are required to complete 30 hours of pro bono activities before graduation.

■ Skills Training

To help students develop necessary practical lawyering skills, Texas Wesleyan has developed a series of courses in its Juris Doctor curriculum, each termed a *practicum*, in discrete substantive areas and in particular skills areas. The term *practicum* identifies courses involving the supervised practical application of previously studied theory.

The law school offers a variety of externships with trial and appellate courts, government agencies, nonprofit organizations, and law firms. For academic credit, students perform legal tasks and apply their academic studies to real client cases, gaining valuable insight into the operation of legal institutions. Wesleyan also has an in-house legal clinic that functions as an actual law office where students represent indigent clients in court under the direction of a faculty supervisor. All skills programs are coordinated by a full-time professor, ensuring significant legal experience in interviewing, negotiating, counseling clients, or alternative dispute resolutions.

The law school also prides itself on its ability to help students apply lessons learned in the classroom to real-world legal problems through the Equal Justice Program, a mandatory 30-hour community-related pro bono requirement that must be completed by every student before graduation. Texas Wesleyan School of Law is proud to be one of only 31 ABA-accredited schools that have such a requirement. Students can fulfill this requirement in many ways, such as by volunteering with a public service agency or a private attorney doing pro bono work. In addition, the school is committed to serving the community through a variety of programs such as National Adoption Day, Street Law, and High School Law Day, in which students can receive legal experience while helping to address community legal needs.

■ Student Life

Texas Wesleyan student organizations provide a broad spectrum of opportunities for student involvement. Our enthusiastic law students engage in competitions and leadership activities at the state, regional, and national levels. Students have won numerous competitions in negotiations, mock trial, and recently, the national moot court championships in entertainment law and information technology and privacy law. Through membership in law student organizations, participants reap the benefits of professional contacts, social activities, and exposure to legal specialties. Thirty-four student organizations provide opportunities for students to engage in professional bar associations, legal specialties, networking opportunities, and public service projects. In addition, the *Texas Wesleyan Law Review* encourages legal scholarships on issues of interest to academicians, practitioners, and law students. The *Law Review* is published by student editors with a faculty advisor. Participation is limited to those who meet academic requirements and those who are selected through a writing competition.

■ Career Services

The Wesleyan law school Career Services Office assists students, graduates, and employers in their mutual efforts to link those seeking legal positions with those providing legal employment opportunities. Career Services also supports students securing part-time or temporary employment while attending law school. A range of services, such as one-on-one career counseling, résumé and cover letter review, career seminars, on-campus interviews, off-campus job fairs, and an online job bank are available to students and graduates. The Career Services Office also provides numerous online and hard copy career resources in the career planning library. The school is a member of NALP, the association for legal career professionals.

■ Expenses and Financial Aid

Texas Wesleyan offers a relatively low private tuition. Tuition and general costs vary by courseload. For 2006–2007, annual tuition for full-time students was $21,060; for part-time students, $15,030; and for summer, $715 per credit hour. Fees are an additional $300 per semester. The university works with individual students to provide the best financial aid package the student is eligible to receive. The financial aid package may include several types of assistance for financing a law school education, including scholarships, grants, employment opportunities, and loan programs. A majority of law students receive some form of financial assistance.

■ Admission

To be considered for admission, an applicant to Texas Wesleyan School of Law must hold a baccalaureate degree from a regionally accredited college or university prior to enrollment. A Law School Admission Test score is also required.

The law school offers full-time, part-time, and evening programs. Students are admitted only in the fall. March 31 of each year is the suggested application deadline; however, the School of Law uses a rolling admission process and will continue to accept applications until the entering class is full.

The admission committee will endeavor to determine the academic and professional promise of each applicant. Accordingly, the admission committee evaluates all factors relevant to an applicant's potential to be successful in meeting the academic standards of the Juris Doctor program, as well as his or her potential for success on the bar examination and in other professional endeavors.

Traditional criteria, such as undergraduate academic achievement, LSAT performance, graduate studies, work experience, life experience, activities, honors, personal statement, recommendation letters, and other experiences, are used in the admission evaluation process.

Applicant Profile

Texas Wesleyan University School of Law
This grid includes only applicants who earned 120–180 LSAT scores under standard administrations.

LSAT Score	3.75 + Apps	3.75 + Adm	3.50–3.74 Apps	3.50–3.74 Adm	3.25–3.49 Apps	3.25–3.49 Adm	3.00–3.24 Apps	3.00–3.24 Adm	2.75–2.99 Apps	2.75–2.99 Adm	2.50–2.74 Apps	2.50–2.74 Adm	2.25–2.49 Apps	2.25–2.49 Adm	2.00–2.24 Apps	2.00–2.24 Adm	Below 2.00 Apps	Below 2.00 Adm	No GPA Apps	No GPA Adm	Total Apps	Total Adm
175–180	1	1	0	0	0	0	0	0	0	0	0	0	0	0	0	0	0	0	0	0	1	1
170–174	0	0	0	0	0	0	0	0	1	1	0	0	0	0	0	0	0	0	0	0	1	1
165–169	0	0	1	1	5	5	5	5	2	2	1	1	2	2	0	0	0	0	0	0	16	16
160–164	0	0	1	1	5	5	5	5	2	2	1	1	2	2	0	0	0	0	0	0	82	77
155–159	12	12	13	13	13	12	17	16	5	5	12	11	7	6	3	2	0	0	1	1	274	248
150–154	30	28	45	42	59	54	57	54	37	33	24	22	18	11	2	2	1	1	3	0	542	355
145–149	47	38	76	67	119	90	111	77	78	42	68	29	26	10	13	2	1	0	3	0	547	97
140–144	40	20	82	24	103	17	120	19	96	11	45	1	37	4	13	0	2	0	9	1	349	3
135–139	5	0	25	0	59	2	72	1	69	0	58	0	37	0	16	0	1	0	7	0	140	0
130–134	2	0	9	0	22	0	29	0	23	0	27	0	13	0	8	0	3	0	4	0	44	0
125–129	2	0	3	0	5	0	5	0	5	0	5	0	8	0	2	0	3	0	6	0	21	0
120–124	0	0	1	0	0	0	2	0	2	0	3	0	2	0	3	0	2	0	6	0	3	0
120–124	0	0	0	0	0	0	0	0	0	0	1	0	1	0	1	0	0	0	0	0	2020	798
Total	139	99	255	147	385	180	418	172	318	94	244	64	151	33	61	6	13	1	36	2	2020	798

Apps = Number of Applicants   Adm = Number Admitted   Reflects 98% of the total applicant pool.

The Thomas M. Cooley Law School

PO Box 13038, 300 S. Capitol Avenue
Lansing, MI 48901
Phone: 517.371.5140, ext. 2244; Fax: 517.334.5718
E-mail: admissions@cooley.edu; Website: www.cooley.edu

ABA Approved Since 1975

The Basics

Type of school	Private
Term	Semester
Application deadline	9/1 1/1 5/1
Application fee	$0
Financial aid deadline	9/5 1/5 5/7
Can first year start other than fall?	Yes
Student to faculty ratio	23.7 to 1
Does the university offer:	
housing restricted to law students?	No
graduate housing for which law students are eligible?	Yes

Faculty and Administrators

	Total		Men		Women		Minorities	
	Fall	Spr	Fall	Spr	Fall	Spr	Fall	Spr
Full-time	87	82	52	51	35	31	11	11
Other Full-time	1	1	0	0	1	1	0	0
Deans, librarians, & others who teach	16	16	8	8	8	8	3	3
Part-time	154	145	101	90	53	55	10	10
Total	258	244	161	149	97	95	24	24

Curriculum

	Full-time	Part-time
Typical first-year section size	57	57
Is there typically a "small section" of the first-year class, other than Legal Writing, taught by full-time faculty	No	No
If yes, typical size offered last year		
# of classroom course titles beyond first-year curriculum	193	
# of upper division courses, excluding seminars with an enrollment: Under 25	283	
25–49	81	
50–74	68	
75–99	56	
100+	28	
# of seminars	248	
# of seminar positions available	5,479	
# of seminar positions filled	698	3,774
# of positions available in simulation courses	2,745	
# of simulation positions filled	386	2,090
# of positions available in faculty supervised clinical courses	219	
# of faculty supervised clinical positions filled	34	185
# involved in field placements	83	450
# involved in law journals	32	172
# involved in interschool competitions	12	63
# of credit hours required to graduate	90	

JD Enrollment and Ethnicity

	Men		Women		Full-time		Part-time		1st-year		Total		JD Degs. Awd.
	#	%	#	%	#	%	#	%	#	%	#	%	
African Amer.	101	5.3	288	16.9	33	5.9	356	11.7	217	10.6	389	10.8	96
Amer. Indian	9	0.5	5	0.3	4	0.7	10	0.3	11	0.5	14	0.4	3
Asian Amer.	111	5.9	108	6.3	42	7.5	177	5.8	139	6.8	219	6.1	45
Mex. Amer.	34	1.8	19	1.1	7	1.3	46	1.5	32	1.6	53	1.5	15
Puerto Rican	8	0.4	10	0.6	2	0.4	16	0.5	8	0.4	18	0.5	5
Hispanic	52	2.7	60	3.5	22	3.9	90	3.0	71	3.5	112	3.1	27
Total Minority	315	16.6	490	28.7	110	19.6	695	22.8	478	23.4	805	22.3	191
For. Nation.	60	3.2	75	4.4	27	4.8	108	3.5	86	4.2	135	3.7	25
Caucasian	1470	77.5	1102	64.5	405	72.3	2167	71.1	1424	69.7	2572	71.3	434
Unknown	52	2.7	42	2.5	18	3.2	76	2.5	54	2.6	94	2.6	15
Total	1897	52.6	1709	47.4	560	15.5	3046	84.5	2042	56.6	3606		665

Transfers

Transfers in	7
Transfers out	185

Tuition and Fees

	Resident	Nonresident
Full-time	$24,260	$24,260
Part-time	$17,340	$17,340

Living Expenses

Estimated living expenses for singles

Living on campus	Living off campus	Living at home
N/A	$11,160	$11,160

Th

The Thomas M. Cooley L

PO Box 13038, 300 S. Capitol Avenue
Lansing, MI 48901
Phone: 517.371.5140, ext. 224
E-mail: admissions@cooley

■ **Introduction**

The Thomas
students in
successf
offerin
curri

GPA and LSAT Scores

	Total	Full-time	Part-time
# of apps	5,718	4,958	760
# of offers	3,802	3,304	498
# of matrics	1,691	342	1,349
75% GPA	3.32	3.37	3.30
Median GPA	3.05	3.05	3.05
25% GPA	2.73	2.79	2.71
75% LSAT	149	152	149
Median LSAT	146	148	146
25% LSAT	144	146	143

Grants and Scholarships (from prior year)

	Total		Full-time		Part-time	
	#	%	#	%	#	%
Total # of students	3,252		503		2,749	
Total # receiving grants	1699	52.2	436	86.7	1263	45.9
Less than 1/2 tuition	1279	39.3	269	53.5	1010	36.7
Half to full tuition	337	10.4	143	28.4	194	7.1
Full tuition	83	2.6	24	4.8	59	2.1
More than full tuition	0	0.0	0	0.0	0	0.0
Median grant amount			$7,507		$4,950	

Informational and Library Resources

# of volumes and volume equivalents	559,792
# of titles	190,267
# of active serial subscriptions	6,723
Study seating capacity inside the library	1,008
# of full-time professional librarians	21
Hours per week library is open	124
# of open, wired connections available to students	48
# of networked computers available for use by students	181
# of simultaneous wireless users	1,750
Require computer?	No

JD Attrition

1st year	
2nd year	
3rd year	
4th year	

Employment (9 months after graduation)

	Total	Percentage
Employment status known	342	68.0
Employment status unknown	161	32.0
Employed	279	81.6
Pursuing graduate degrees	11	3.2
Unemployed seeking employment	32	9.4
Unemployed not seeking employment	2	0.6
Unemployed and studying for the bar	18	5.3

Type of Employment

# employed in law firms	138	49.5
# employed in business and industry	47	16.8
# employed in government	41	14.7
# employed in public interest	15	5.4
# employed as judicial clerks	27	9.7
# employed in academia	5	1.8

Geographic Location

# employed in state	124	44.4
# employed in foreign countries	3	1.1
# of states where employed		30

Bar Passage Rates

Jurisdiction	Michigan		
Exam	Sum 05	Win 06	Total
# from school taking bar for the first time	101	121	222
School's pass rate for all first-time takers	66%	74%	71%
State's pass rate for all first-time takers	78%	65%	74%

...aw School

..., Fax: 517.334.5718
...edu; Website: www.cooley.edu

...... Cooley Law School's mission is to educate law ... the knowledge, skills, and ethics needed for ... practice. The school carries out this mission by ... a rigorous and practical education. The Juris Doctor ...iculum is offered at each of Cooley's three campuses in ...ichigan; in downtown Grand Rapids, in downtown Lansing, and on the campus of Oakland University in Rochester, a northern suburb of Detroit. Students can choose to take classes during the day, the evening, and/or on the weekends. Cooley has been accredited by the American Bar Association since 1978, and the Higher Learning Commission since 2001.

■ Admission and Scholarships

Cooley Law School operates a rolling admission process offering the option of beginning enrollment in January, May, or September. Cooley uses a straightforward, objective formula to determine eligibility (UGPA x 15 + Highest LSAT = Admission Index). Cooley reserves the right to deny eligible candidates based on negative character and fitness factors. No application fee is required.

Scholarships—Incoming students may earn up to 100 percent of tuition in two ways:
1. Admission Index levels:

Index	Honors Scholarship
215+	100%
210–214	75%
205–209	50%
195–204	25%

2. Student's highest LSAT score:

LSAT	Honors Scholarship
163+	100%
158–162	75%
153–157	50%
149–152	25%

Transfer students are eligible for scholarships similar to new entering students or based upon their class rank at the school from which their transfer occurs. **Michigan residents** who qualify for an entering LSAT Honors Scholarship are eligible for an additional 10 percent scholarship. The **Lester Bowles Pearson Canadian Bursary Program** allows qualified Canadian students to attend Cooley at a reduced cost. Please refer to the Cooley website at *www.cooley.edu* for the most current information.

■ Expenses

Tuition—$865 per credit hour in 2006–2007; fees—$20 per term; estimated additional expenses—$11,160 (room and board, books, personal, transportation, and health insurance); scholarships and financial aid available.

■ Facilities and Technology

Cooley provides three distinct campus environments, each with a full complement of faculty, staff, libraries, and services. At each site, facilities and technology are designed to meet the academic and research needs of today's legal community. Classrooms, mock courtrooms, and distance learning classrooms are fully equipped with the latest computing and technological equipment to enhance the educational experience. Wireless computing capability is available in every facility on each of Cooley's three campuses.

Cooley's law libraries employ 40 full-time staff including 21 professional librarians. The libraries are open 125 hours per week and feature state-of-the-art facilities and wireless technology. The 550,000 volume collection includes research materials from all 50 states as well as federal and international materials. The reference desks are staffed 100 hours per week and offer in-person, chat, e-mail, and toll-free phone reference services.

■ Flexible Scheduling

Cooley offers more scheduling options than most other law schools in the country, including the first and largest ABA-approved weekend program. Students may choose to enroll in either a full- or part-time program, ranging from two to five years. Students also have the option of day, evening, and weekend class schedules. New students are admitted three times a year: January, May, and September.

■ Practical Curriculum

Cooley's 90 credit-hour curriculum provides all students with the substantive knowledge, legal skills, and ethics to enter law practice. **Skills and Clinics**—Students build legal skills through practical simulation courses. Competitions in pretrial, trial, and appellate skills allow students to compete against law students from across the country. Cooley's expansive clinical programs immerse students in hands-on learning. Students can choose from the award winning Sixty Plus Inc., Elderlaw Clinic, the weekend or evening Estate Planning Clinic, the Innocence Project, the Public Defender Clinic, or the Domestic Violence Clinic. Students may also choose from more than 1,000 externship sites across the nation. **Leader in Plain English Writing**—Recognized as a world leader in training students in the use of plain language, Cooley has a strong legal writing curriculum. The required six-credit writing sequence provides training and experience in traditional and computer-assisted research. **Concentrations**—Students may focus their electives in Transactional Law; General Practice, Solo, and Small Firm; Litigation; or Public and International Law, which includes tracks in Administrative Law, Constitutional Law and Civil Rights, Environmental Law, and International Law.

■ Scholarly Community

More than 100 full-time faculty, and as many adjunct professors, teach Cooley students. **Scholarly publications**—Cooley's premier scholarly journal, the *Thomas M. Cooley Law Review*, provides students with the opportunities to edit and publish traditional in-depth scholarship. The student editors of the *Journal of Practical and Clinical Law* work with lawyers and academicians to address more practice-oriented issues. Cooley's newest publications include the *Art and Museum Law Journal*.

Symposia bring together scholars from around the world to discuss timely topics. Recent speakers include the president of the American Bar Association; the former US Secretary of Education; distinguished federal judges and state supreme court justices; high-level officials of the Justice Department; and internationally recognized academicians. **Centers** in Ethics and Responsibility, Forensic Science and the Law, and Indian Law foster discussion and research. **Collaborations** with major research institutions open opportunities for dual-degree programs, including a Juris Doctor/Master of Public Administration program with Western Michigan University and Oakland University, and a Juris Doctor/Master of Business Administration program with Oakland University.

■ Graduate and International Studies

LLM—Cooley offers graduate law degrees in Taxation and Intellectual Property. Graduate programs are based at the Oakland University campus, but are available through distance education to students at each campus site. Dual JD/LLM degree programs are available. **International Studies**—Cooley students study law around the world. Beginning each January, Cooley's 13-week program in Australia and New Zealand beckons students "down under." And in the summer, Cooley invites students to Toronto, Canada. Cooley cooperates with other law schools to provide students with many other options extending around the world, including Europe and Asia.

■ Academic Success

Before matriculating, Cooley students may begin their road to academic success by taking advantage of two programs: Cooley's online prelaw program (*www.introlaw.cooley.edu*) and *JumpStart*, our free, one-day on-campus program. These programs introduce students to the concepts of law and explore how to brief law cases, how to take effective notes, and how to analyze. All Cooley students take the Academic

Resource Center's free Introduction to Law course during their first semester. The center also offers free seminars, individual skills advising, and test-taking sessions. The staff, composed of lawyers and learning specialists, also meets with individuals and small groups.

■ Student Life

Of the over 3,600 total students enrolled at Cooley Law School, 25 percent are from historically underrepresented populations, 47 percent are women, 68 percent come from outside the state of Michigan, and 5 percent of these are international students. Students range in age from 20 to 66. All students are members of the Student Bar Association, and there are more than 40 clubs and organizations in which students can become involved. Students publish a newspaper, *The Pillar*, supervise the Student Tutorial Service, edit and publish the *Thomas M. Cooley Law Review* and the *Thomas M. Cooley Journal of Practical and Clinical Law*, and conduct active volunteer and intramural sports programs.

■ Professional Development

Professional development at Cooley entails a combination of classroom experience, volunteering, public service, pro bono work, clinical experience, employment, and mentoring. Faculty and Professional Development staff assist students in developing personalized professional development plans that prepare them for their chosen career path. Through the Career & Professional Development Office, students can also take advantage of résumé review services, mock interview programs, online job bulletins, and numerous workshops geared toward aiding them in their employment search.

Applicant Profile

The Thomas M. Cooley Law School

LSAT	Academic Success
*163+	100%
*158–162	98%
*153–157	91%
*149–152	83%
143–148	77%

LSAT Score and Corresponding Academic Success Rates January 1996–September 2005

The Law School Admission Test and undergraduate grades are good overall predictors of first-year law school performance, although they do not predict individual results. Mainly, these factors predict relative first-year class rank for large groups of first-year students. Students are urged to assess their own potential before making the commitment to law school.

*Law School Admission Test scores of 149 and above may qualify for an honors scholarship from 25 to 100 percent of tuition based on LSAT score only.

Thomas Jefferson School of Law

2121 San Diego Avenue
San Diego, CA 92110
Phone: 619.297.9700; 800.956.5070; Fax: 619.294.4713
E-mail: info@tjsl.edu; Website: www.tjsl.edu

ABA Approved Since 1996

The Basics

Type of school	Private
Term	Semester
Application deadline	12/1 10/1
Application fee	$35
Financial aid deadline	4/30
Can first year start other than fall?	Yes
Student to faculty ratio	15.2 to 1
Does the university offer:	
housing restricted to law students?	No
graduate housing for which law students are eligible?	No

Faculty and Administrators

	Total		Men		Women		Minorities	
	Fall	Spr	Fall	Spr	Fall	Spr	Fall	Spr
Full-time	38	38	18	17	20	21	7	7
Other Full-time	2	2	1	1	1	1	0	0
Deans, librarians, & others who teach	3	3	2	2	1	1	0	0
Part-time	35	25	25	19	10	6	3	1
Total	**78**	**68**	**46**	**39**	**32**	**29**	**10**	**8**

Curriculum

	Full-time	Part-time
Typical first-year section size	80	40
Is there typically a "small section" of the first-year class, other than Legal Writing, taught by full-time faculty	No	No
If yes, typical size offered last year		
# of classroom course titles beyond first-year curriculum	107	
# of upper division courses, excluding seminars with an enrollment: Under 25	42	
25–49	33	
50–74	15	
75–99	12	
100+	0	
# of seminars	28	
# of seminar positions available	605	
# of seminar positions filled	327	173
# of positions available in simulation courses	323	
# of simulation positions filled	180	91
# of positions available in faculty supervised clinical courses	32	
# of faculty supervised clinical positions filled	15	8
# involved in field placements	161	28
# involved in law journals	63	15
# involved in interschool competitions	81	15
# of credit hours required to graduate	88	

JD Enrollment and Ethnicity

	Men		Women		Full-time		Part-time		1st-year		Total		JD Degs. Awd.
	#	%	#	%	#	%	#	%	#	%	#	%	
African Amer.	12	2.8	24	7.1	32	5.5	4	2.1	30	6.4	36	4.7	3
Amer. Indian	3	0.7	1	0.3	2	0.3	2	1.1	4	0.9	4	0.5	1
Asian Amer.	22	5.1	34	10.0	46	7.9	10	5.3	38	8.1	56	7.3	27
Mex. Amer.	18	4.2	15	4.4	19	3.3	14	7.4	18	3.8	33	4.3	12
Puerto Rican	4	0.9	4	1.2	4	0.7	4	2.1	6	1.3	8	1.0	0
Hispanic	11	2.6	10	2.9	20	3.4	1	0.5	21	4.5	21	2.7	6
Total Minority	70	16.3	88	25.9	123	21.2	35	18.4	117	25.0	158	20.5	49
For. Nation.	0	0.0	0	0.0	0	0.0	0	0.0	0	0.0	0	0.0	0
Caucasian	333	77.4	225	66.2	418	72.1	140	73.7	298	63.7	558	72.5	230
Unknown	27	6.3	27	7.9	39	6.7	15	7.9	53	11.3	54	7.0	0
Total	430	55.8	340	44.2	580	75.3	190	24.7	468	60.8	770		279

Transfers

Transfers in	2
Transfers out	16

Tuition and Fees

	Resident	Nonresident
Full-time	$30,250	$30,250
Part-time	$19,050	$19,050

Living Expenses

Estimated living expenses for singles

Living on campus	Living off campus	Living at home
N/A	$23,898	$23,898

Thomas Jefferson School of Law

*ABA
Approved
Since
1996*

GPA and LSAT Scores

	Total	Full-time	Part-time
# of apps	3,285	3,032	253
# of offers	1,539	1,432	107
# of matrics	294	254	40
75% GPA	3.29	3.29	3.41
Median GPA	2.99	2.96	3.15
25% GPA	2.75	2.74	2.80
75% LSAT	154	154	154
Median LSAT	151	151	151
25% LSAT	149	149	148

Grants and Scholarships (from prior year)

	Total		Full-time		Part-time	
	#	%	#	%	#	%
Total # of students	803		609		194	
Total # receiving grants	457	56.9	338	55.5	119	61.3
Less than 1/2 tuition	279	34.7	207	34.0	72	37.1
Half to full tuition	104	13.0	73	12.0	31	16.0
Full tuition	74	9.2	58	9.5	16	8.2
More than full tuition	0	0.0	0	0.0	0	0.0
Median grant amount			$7,000		$4,000	

Informational and Library Resources

# of volumes and volume equivalents	253,565
# of titles	122,128
# of active serial subscriptions	3,457
Study seating capacity inside the library	266
# of full-time professional librarians	8
Hours per week library is open	115
# of open, wired connections available to students	48
# of networked computers available for use by students	39
# of simultaneous wireless users	1,000
Require computer?	Yes

JD Attrition (from prior year)

	Academic	Other	Total	
	#	#	#	%
1st year	13	28	41	11.4
2nd year	2	7	9	4.4
3rd year	1	1	2	0.9
4th year	1	1	2	7.4

Employment (9 months after graduation)

	Total	Percentage
Employment status known	196	85.2
Employment status unknown	34	14.8
Employed	163	83.2
Pursuing graduate degrees	7	3.6
Unemployed seeking employment	8	4.1
Unemployed not seeking employment	3	1.5
Unemployed and studying for the bar	15	7.7

Type of Employment

	Total	Percentage
# employed in law firms	74	45.4
# employed in business and industry	42	25.8
# employed in government	21	12.9
# employed in public interest	16	9.8
# employed as judicial clerks	6	3.7
# employed in academia	3	1.8

Geographic Location

	Total	Percentage
# employed in state	103	63.2
# employed in foreign countries	3	1.8
# of states where employed	24	

Bar Passage Rates

Jurisdiction	California		
Exam	Sum 05	Win 06	Total
# from school taking bar for the first time	112	57	169
School's pass rate for all first-time takers	38%	47%	41%
State's pass rate for all first-time takers	64%	54%	62%

Thomas Jefferson School of Law

2121 San Diego Avenue
San Diego, CA 92110
Phone: 619.297.9700; 800.956.5070; Fax: 619.294.4713
E-mail: info@tjsl.edu; Website: www.tjsl.edu

■ Introduction

The Thomas Jefferson School of Law is a private, nonprofit, independent law school that emphasizes an individualized approach to legal education. This approach features small classes, written feedback on student performance during the semester, close student/faculty interaction in a supportive environment, and a flexible curriculum that allows students to attend full or part time and accelerate graduation by attending classes in the summer.

The mission of the School of Law is to provide an outstanding legal education for a nationally based student body in a collegial and supportive environment with attention to newly emerging areas of law, particularly those related to technological development, globalization, and the quest for social justice.

San Diego boasts what many consider to be the finest climate in the continental United States. The seventh largest city in the nation offers all of the professional, social, and cultural opportunities of a major metropolitan area.

■ Faculty

The Thomas Jefferson faculty is distinguished by three features: its qualifications, youth, and commitment to teaching. Members of the faculty were educated at many of the finest law schools in the nation and all practiced law before turning to academic careers.

The youth and vitality of the faculty are suggested by the fact that more than 85 percent of the faculty have joined Thomas Jefferson since 1990. All contribute to creating the student-centered environment that is a defining characteristic of Thomas Jefferson.

The full-time faculty is very unusual in that nearly half of its members are women.

■ Library and Physical Facilities

The law school is housed in two modern buildings situated in the beautiful and historic Old Town section of San Diego. The library includes the law school's two computer labs and numerous private study rooms that students may reserve for group or individual study. Our classrooms utilize natural and artificial light and are wired for laptop use. The campus has wireless access to its network throughout.

■ Curriculum

Students may commence their studies at Thomas Jefferson in either August or January. The law school offers a three-year full-time program and a four-year part-time program that students may attend.

All programs have the same admission standards and graduation requirements. Students who take additional classes during the summer may accelerate graduation by one semester. The full-time faculty teaches more than two-thirds of the coursework in both the day and evening divisions.

The curriculum is highly interactive and collaborative between the faculty and the students. During their first semester, entering students have the opportunity, in all their courses, to receive feedback from the faculty on their written legal analytical skills in order to enhance their understanding of the course material and hone their performance prior to final exams. First-year students are assigned faculty advisors, but all members of the faculty emphasize being available to students outside of class. The law school has an extensive Academic Support Program that permits students in all three years of law school to meet individually with special tutors who can help them excel as law students.

■ Special Programs

The law school has acquired special strength in the areas of law that most reflect our changing world. To provide an institutional framework for the study of technological change and globalization and their effects on both traditional areas of practice and emerging new fields, the law school has established three academic centers. In addition to a broad program of course offerings, each center represents substantial engagement by faculty in scholarly research, speaker programs, and opportunities for student participation beyond the classroom.

The Center for Law, Technology, and Communications prepares students for careers in fields of law related to high technology and communications. Course offerings include traditional intellectual property law, emerging new specialties such as cyberspace law, biotechnology law and bioethics, media and telecommunications law, and sports and entertainment law.

The Center for Global Legal Studies prepares students for the transborder aspects of contemporary legal practice and offers a wide variety of courses in international law, including international business law, international environmental law, international criminal law, and international human rights.

The Center for Law and Social Justice prepares students for a law practice geared toward the preservation of the values of liberty and equality in a changing working world. Recent activity has focused on issues related to gender and the law, especially the problems of women, gays, lesbians, intersexuals, and transgender.

Each year the law school also offers a large number of courses that train students in professional skills, supplemented by a variety of field placement programs. The judicial internship program allows students to work for a semester with local federal and state judges, gaining experience in drafting opinions and observing courtroom proceedings. Students also may work for credit at a variety of public agencies and private law firms. California law allows students who have completed certain coursework to obtain certification to appear in court.

■ Admission

Applicants are reviewed on a rolling basis. The fall application deadline is March 1. The spring application deadline is October 1. Thomas Jefferson conducts a rolling admission process under which applicants are considered when their applications are complete. Because the law school admits two entering classes each year, the admission committee meets continuously throughout the year, and there are no formal application deadlines. Early applications are encouraged, however, and those who apply early increase their chance of a favorable decision.

The admission committee gives each applicant careful, thorough, and personalized consideration. In addition to the LSAT score, the committee considers the applicant's undergraduate record, extracurricular activities, work experience, and history of overcoming adversity.

The law school accepts applications from transfer students in both the fall and spring semesters. Transfer students must be in good academic standing.

■ Expenses and Financial Aid

Thomas Jefferson offers a variety of need- and merit-based aid, and uses its funds for both recruitment as well as retention. Because of the broad array of scholarship funds and criteria, applicants need not submit a separate scholarship application. Awards are based on data already accessible to the law school in your application. Should you have significant financial need that you would like us to consider, you have an opportunity to submit a detailed written statement outlining your circumstances during the financial aid application process. Scholarship offers are made on a rolling basis as quickly after admission as possible. All scholarship recipients receive a detailed offer letter containing the terms of the award and any criteria for renewal.

Student loans and work-study funds also are available. Students interested in these programs should apply as early as possible and should not wait for an admission decision before applying for financial assistance.

■ Student Activities

The most prestigious cocurricular activity is the *Thomas Jefferson Law Review*, a journal of legal scholarship edited and managed by students.

Cocurricular programs include the moot court and mock trial competitions. Extracurricular activities serve a variety of student interests and needs. Some student organizations are formed as a result of heightened student interest in substantive areas of law practice, such as the International Law Society, the Entertainment and Sports Law Societies, the Law and Medicine Society, and the Public Interest Law Foundation. Many student organizations provide a source of mutual support for various groups of students, including the Black Students Association, La Raza, and the Pan Asian Law Students Association.

■ Career Services

The Career Services Office assists students and alumni in finding temporary and permanent law-related employment. The office maintains listings of employment opportunities and schedules on-campus interviewing. It also assists students in obtaining placement with state and federal judges and with various public agencies, where they can work during the year for academic credit.

The Career Services Office has developed an alumni mentoring program, through which Thomas Jefferson students can obtain advice and assistance from some of the law school's more than 4,000 alumni.

Applicant Profile Not Available

The University of Toledo College of Law

2801 West Bancroft Street
Toledo, OH 43606-3390
Phone: 419.530.4131; Fax: 419.530.4345
E-mail: law.admissions@utoledo.edu; Website: www.utlaw.edu

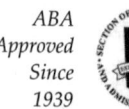

*ABA
Approved
Since
1939*

The Basics

Type of school	Public
Term	Semester
Application deadline	7/1
Application fee	$40
Financial aid deadline	8/1
Can first year start other than fall?	No
Student to faculty ratio	14.1 to 1
Does the university offer:	
housing restricted to law students?	No
graduate housing for which law students are eligible?	No

Faculty and Administrators

	Total		Men		Women		Minorities	
	Fall	Spr	Fall	Spr	Fall	Spr	Fall	Spr
Full-time	29	27	16	17	13	10	2	2
Other Full-time	0	2	0	2	0	0	0	1
Deans, librarians, & others who teach	2	2	2	1	0	1	0	0
Part-time	14	21	9	16	5	5	0	0
Total	**45**	**52**	**27**	**36**	**18**	**16**	**2**	**3**

Curriculum

		Full-time	Part-time
Typical first-year section size		64	37
Is there typically a "small section" of the first-year class, other than Legal Writing, taught by full-time faculty		No	No
If yes, typical size offered last year			
# of classroom course titles beyond first-year curriculum		96	
# of upper division courses, excluding seminars with an enrollment:	Under 25	106	
	25–49	22	
	50–74	12	
	75–99	3	
	100+	0	
# of seminars		2	
# of seminar positions available		27	
# of seminar positions filled		9	2
# of positions available in simulation courses		461	
# of simulation positions filled		239	40
# of positions available in faculty supervised clinical courses		119	
# of faculty supervised clinical positions filled	63		2
# involved in field placements		114	2
# involved in law journals		42	3
# involved in interschool competitions		29	1
# of credit hours required to graduate		89	

JD Enrollment and Ethnicity

	Men		Women		Full-time		Part-time		1st-year		Total		JD Degs. Awd.
	#	%	#	%	#	%	#	%	#	%	#	%	
African Amer.	8	2.6	6	2.8	6	1.7	8	4.4	8	3.6	14	2.7	6
Amer. Indian	2	0.6	0	0.0	2	0.6	0	0.0	1	0.4	2	0.4	0
Asian Amer.	6	1.9	4	1.9	7	2.0	3	1.7	2	0.9	10	1.9	4
Mex. Amer.	0	0.0	0	0.0	0	0.0	0	0.0	0	0.0	0	0.0	0
Puerto Rican	0	0.0	0	0.0	0	0.0	0	0.0	0	0.0	0	0.0	0
Hispanic	7	2.2	6	2.8	4	1.2	9	5.0	11	4.9	13	2.5	4
Total Minority	23	7.3	16	7.6	19	5.5	20	11.1	22	9.8	39	7.4	14
For. Nation.	0	0.0	0	0.0	0	0.0	0	0.0	0	0.0	0	0.0	2
Caucasian	195	62.3	140	66.4	214	62.2	121	67.2	136	60.7	335	63.9	93
Unknown	95	30.4	55	26.1	111	32.3	39	21.7	66	29.5	150	28.6	28
Total	313	59.7	211	40.3	344	65.6	180	34.4	224	42.7	524		137

Transfers

Transfers in	2
Transfers out	11

Tuition and Fees

	Resident	Nonresident
Full-time	$14,839	$25,082
Part-time	$11,750	$19,860

Living Expenses

Estimated living expenses for singles

Living on campus	Living off campus	Living at home
N/A	$13,166	$6,877

The University of Toledo College of Law

ABA Approved Since 1939

GPA and LSAT Scores

	Total	Full-time	Part-time
# of apps	1,216	937	279
# of offers	340	201	139
# of matrics	190	74	116
75% GPA	3.69	3.82	3.51
Median GPA	3.39	3.68	3.24
25% GPA	2.97	3.02	2.94
75% LSAT	157	160	155
Median LSAT	155	158	153
25% LSAT	153	155	151

Grants and Scholarships (from prior year)

	Total		Full-time		Part-time	
	#	%	#	%	#	%
Total # of students	510		351		159	
Total # receiving grants	252	49.4	231	65.8	21	13.2
Less than 1/2 tuition	77	15.1	67	19.1	10	6.3
Half to full tuition	26	5.1	25	7.1	1	0.6
Full tuition	77	15.1	77	21.9	0	0.0
More than full tuition	72	14.1	62	17.7	10	6.3
Median grant amount			$12,432		$1,707	

Informational and Library Resources

# of volumes and volume equivalents	347,567
# of titles	53,769
# of active serial subscriptions	3,357
Study seating capacity inside the library	418
# of full-time professional librarians	5
Hours per week library is open	113
# of open, wired connections available to students	23
# of networked computers available for use by students	11
# of simultaneous wireless users	200
Require computer?	No

JD Attrition (from prior year)

	Academic	Other	Total	
	#	#	#	%
1st year	12	19	31	14.4
2nd year	1	2	3	2.1
3rd year	0	2	2	1.6
4th year	0	0	0	0.0

Employment (9 months after graduation)

	Total	Percentage
Employment status known	145	98.0
Employment status unknown	3	2.0
Employed	139	95.9
Pursuing graduate degrees	2	1.4
Unemployed seeking employment	2	1.4
Unemployed not seeking employment	1	0.7
Unemployed and studying for the bar	1	0.7

Type of Employment

	Total	Percentage
# employed in law firms	68	48.9
# employed in business and industry	22	15.8
# employed in government	28	20.1
# employed in public interest	4	2.9
# employed as judicial clerks	3	2.2
# employed in academia	4	2.9

Geographic Location

	Total	Percentage
# employed in state	87	62.6
# employed in foreign countries	1	0.7
# of states where employed	18	

Bar Passage Rates

Jurisdiction	Ohio			Michigan		
Exam	Sum 05	Win 06	Total	Sum 05	Win 06	Total
# from school taking bar for the first time	75	21	96	20	7	27
School's pass rate for all first-time takers	81%	67%	78%	75%	100%	81%
State's pass rate for all first-time takers	81%	76%	81%	78%	65%	74%

The University of Toledo College of Law

2801 West Bancroft Street
Toledo, OH 43606-3390
Phone: 419.530.4131; Fax: 419.530.4345
E-mail: law.admissions@utoledo.edu; Website: www.utlaw.edu

■ Introduction

The University of Toledo is a state university of more than 19,000 students, conveniently located on the western edge of Toledo, Ohio, in one of the city's nicest residential areas.

The College of Law, located on the main campus of The University of Toledo, is accredited by the ABA and is a member of the AALS and the League of Ohio Law Schools. It has been training lawyers since 1906 and, in 1984, was awarded a chapter of the Order of the Coif. The college provides a quality legal education with a personal touch at an affordable price. The nationally recognized faculty emphasizes classroom teaching and student accessibility as its primary function. The College of Law is committed to its open-door policy that provides total student support.

■ Student Body

The college seeks a diverse student body. Nearly two-thirds of the students hail from outside the local area. More than 200 undergraduate institutions are represented. This diversity exposes students to an interesting, stimulating, and creative atmosphere where insights and ideas flourish. Diversity is reflected in student groups and activities, representing a broad spectrum of social, political, ethnic, and religious perspectives.

■ Faculty

The full-time faculty earned law degrees from some of the most outstanding universities in the country. Many have advanced law degrees.

While legal scholarship is important and many faculty members have national reputations for scholarship, the faculty places a high priority on effective teaching and accessibility to students.

■ Library and Physical Facilities

The spacious, newly renovated Law Center includes tiered classrooms, a striking student lounge, a state-of-the-art moot courtroom, and an amphitheater-style auditorium. The entire building supports wireless web technology.

Occupying four levels within the Law Center, the library contains group-study rooms, videotaping facilities, and a modern computer lab available for use by law students. Students are trained in the use of two vast electronic law libraries—LexisNexis and Westlaw.

■ Curriculum

The College of Law requires the successful completion of 89 semester hours for graduation. The curriculum in the first year of the full-time program and the first two years of the part-time program consists of required courses. An extensive and ever-growing curriculum covers traditional subjects as well as cutting edge environmental law, international law, and cyberlaw subjects, and incorporates the development of professional legal skills and values.

Our academic success program provides teaching assistants for students in all basic required courses and offers tutors for

any student who requests academic support. Students can graduate with certificates in environmental, homeland security, intellectual property, international, and labor/employment law.

The College of Law has joint-degree programs with the Colleges of Engineering, Business, and Arts and Sciences, leading to a Master of Science in Engineering, PhD in Engineering, Master of Business Administration, Master of Public Administration, or Master of Criminal Justice. Students may also design individual joint-degree programs.

■ Special Programs

Cybersecurities Law Institute—The institute focuses on the impact of Internet technology on securities and investment law. The institute sponsors conferences, research, lectures, symposia, and the development of courses and online resources.

Legal Clinics—A pioneer in clinical legal education, the college provides an atmosphere for learning basic lawyering techniques and allows students the opportunity to further sharpen their skills in live client settings. Advanced students, under close supervision, appear in court in both civil and criminal cases.

Through the Dispute Resolution Clinic, mediation experience is available in a variety of matters, including unruly child complaints and custody and visitation issues in parentage cases in juvenile court. Students in the Public Service Externship Clinic are assigned to public service legal entities, such as the judiciary, legal services offices, pro bono programs, public defender offices, legislative bodies, government agencies, and public interest organizations.

Legal Institute of the Great Lakes—The institute supports research, publishes a scholarly journal, and sponsors conferences on the legal, economic, and social issues of importance to the Great Lakes region of the United States and Canada. The highlight of these discussions is an annual symposium on the national and international water crisis and the need for fresh water.

■ Admission

A bachelor's degree from an accredited institution is required. Grades and LSAT scores are the most important determinants of admission. However, the Admission Committee carefully considers each application on its own merits. Letters of recommendation are important.

Prospective students are encouraged to visit the law school, talk to our students and faculty, and sit in on a class. Appointments can be made through the Admission Office.

■ Student Activities

The *University of Toledo Law Review* is published four times a year by students selected on the basis of scholarship. Students may also qualify by submitting a publishable article. Training and practice in brief writing and oral argument beyond the required appellate advocacy course are obtained through the Moot Court Program, in the Charles Fornoff Intramural Moot Court Competition, and in several national and regional competitions.

The Student Bar Association, American Civil Liberties Union, Black Law Students Association, Business Law Society, Christian Legal Society, Criminal Justice Society, Environmental Law Society, Federalist Society, Health Law Association, Hispanic Law Students Association, International Law Society, Jewish Law Students Association, Labor and Employment Law Association, OUTLAW, Sports Law Association, and Women Law Students Association are among many active organizations.

■ Financial Aid

The College of Law strives to provide an affordable legal education without sacrificing quality. Every effort is made to ensure that students graduate without large financial obligations that may take years to repay. The College of Law awards scholarships totaling in excess of $1,500,000 each year. Residents of the following Michigan counties are treated as in-state residents for tuition purposes: Hillsdale, Lenawee, Monroe, Oakland, Washtenaw, and Wayne. The goal of the financial aid program is to ensure that graduates become the lawyers they want to be and not the lawyers they have to be to repay financial obligations.

■ Career Services

The college places top priority on providing comprehensive career planning and placement for its students and graduates. The Law Career Services Office assists students through workshops, videotapes, and counseling, and provides guest speakers on legal career options.

As a result of both on- and off-campus interviews, second- and third-year students accept summer or attorney positions in all major cities of Ohio and Michigan, as well as locations throughout the US.

The college's Judicial Clerkship Program places graduates as clerks with federal and state courts around the country. Graduates are successfully practicing in major law firms, government offices, the judiciary, and in public interest positions in nearly every state. Graduates also can be found in Asia, Europe, and Africa.

Graduates are a valuable resource for current students as they pursue employment opportunities nationwide.

Applicant Profile

The University of Toledo College of Law

GPA	\multicolumn{9}{c}{LSAT (10) Percentile Intervals}
	0-20	21-30	31-40	41-50	51-60	61-70	71-80	81-90	91-99
3.75 Above									
3.74 3.50									
3.49 3.25									
3.24 3.00									
2.99 2.75									
2.74 2.50									
2.49 2.25									
2.24 2.00									
Below 2.00									

■ Highly Likely   □ Possible   □ Unlikely

Touro College—Jacob D. Fuchsberg Law Center

225 Eastview Drive
Central Islip, NY 11722
Phone: 631.761.7010; Fax: 631.421.9708
E-mail: admissions@tourolaw.edu; Website: www.tourolaw.edu

The Basics

Type of school	Private
Term	Semester
Application deadline	8/1
Application fee	$60
Financial aid deadline	4/15
Can first year start other than fall?	No
Student to faculty ratio	17.1 to 1
Does the university offer:	
housing restricted to law students?	Yes
graduate housing for which law students are eligible?	No

Faculty and Administrators

	Total		Men		Women		Minorities	
	Fall	Spr	Fall	Spr	Fall	Spr	Fall	Spr
Full-time	33	30	20	19	13	11	4	3
Other Full-time	2	2	1	2	1	0	0	0
Deans, librarians, & others who teach	7	7	3	3	4	4	0	0
Part-time	26	25	17	18	9	7	2	2
Total	68	64	41	42	27	22	6	5

Curriculum

	Full-time	Part-time
Typical first-year section size	71	64
Is there typically a "small section" of the first-year class, other than Legal Writing, taught by full-time faculty	No	No
If yes, typical size offered last year		
# of classroom course titles beyond first-year curriculum		68
# of upper division courses, excluding seminars with an enrollment: Under 25		64
25–49		26
50–74		25
75–99		2
100+		3
# of seminars		19
# of seminar positions available		342
# of seminar positions filled	207	69
# of positions available in simulation courses		380
# of simulation positions filled	170	158
# of positions available in faculty supervised clinical courses		100
# of faculty supervised clinical positions filled	37	28
# involved in field placements	104	9
# involved in law journals	20	9
# involved in interschool competitions	24	7
# of credit hours required to graduate		88

JD Enrollment and Ethnicity

	Men		Women		Full-time		Part-time		1st-year		Total		JD Degs. Awd.
	#	%	#	%	#	%	#	%	#	%	#	%	
African Amer.	27	6.8	49	14.8	40	8.0	36	15.6	28	10.8	76	10.4	17
Amer. Indian	3	0.8	1	0.3	1	0.2	3	1.3	0	0.0	4	0.5	0
Asian Amer.	32	8.0	27	8.1	43	8.6	16	6.9	11	4.2	59	8.1	15
Mex. Amer.	0	0.0	0	0.0	0	0.0	0	0.0	0	0.0	0	0.0	0
Puerto Rican	0	0.0	0	0.0	0	0.0	0	0.0	0	0.0	0	0.0	0
Hispanic	13	3.3	15	4.5	17	3.4	11	4.8	8	3.1	28	3.8	16
Total Minority	75	18.8	92	27.7	101	20.2	66	28.6	47	18.1	167	22.8	48
For. Nation.	4	1.0	8	2.4	12	2.4	0	0.0	10	3.9	12	1.6	1
Caucasian	311	77.8	221	66.6	377	75.2	155	67.1	187	72.2	532	72.7	154
Unknown	10	2.5	11	3.3	11	2.2	10	4.3	14	5.4	21	2.9	1
Total	400	54.6	332	45.4	501	68.4	231	31.6	259	35.4	732		204

Transfers

Transfers in	19
Transfers out	43

Tuition and Fees

	Resident	Nonresident
Full-time	$32,300	$32,300
Part-time	$24,300	$24,300

Living Expenses

Estimated living expenses for singles

Living on campus	Living off campus	Living at home
$22,271	$22,271	$10,502

Touro College—Jacob D. Fuchsberg Law Center

*ABA
Approved
Since
1983*

GPA and LSAT Scores

	Total	Full-time	Part-time
# of apps	2,403	1,903	500
# of offers	923	758	165
# of matrics	265	197	68
75% GPA	3.40	3.41	3.37
Median GPA	3.10	3.34	3.09
25% GPA	2.83	2.86	2.77
75% LSAT	153	153	152
Median LSAT	151	151	151
25% LSAT	150	150	150

Grants and Scholarships (from prior year)

	Total		Full-time		Part-time	
	#	%	#	%	#	%
Total # of students	761		521		240	
Total # receiving grants	374	49.1	276	53.0	98	40.8
Less than 1/2 tuition	347	45.6	259	49.7	88	36.7
Half to full tuition	20	2.6	14	2.7	6	2.5
Full tuition	5	0.7	1	0.2	4	1.7
More than full tuition	2	0.3	2	0.4	0	0.0
Median grant amount			$4,500		$3,400	

Informational and Library Resources

# of volumes and volume equivalents	431,651
# of titles	70,429
# of active serial subscriptions	4,073
Study seating capacity inside the library	380
# of full-time professional librarians	10
Hours per week library is open	86
# of open, wired connections available to students	0
# of networked computers available for use by students	51
# of simultaneous wireless users	1,100
Require computer?	No

JD Attrition (from prior year)

	Academic	Other	Total	
	#	#	#	%
1st year	31	74	105	37.4
2nd year	7	1	8	3.8
3rd year	0	0	0	0.0
4th year	0	0	0	0.0

Employment (9 months after graduation)

	Total	Percentage
Employment status known	144	76.2
Employment status unknown	45	23.8
Employed	124	86.1
Pursuing graduate degrees	2	1.4
Unemployed seeking employment	9	6.2
Unemployed not seeking employment	1	0.7
Unemployed and studying for the bar	8	5.6

Type of Employment

# employed in law firms	68	54.8
# employed in business and industry	26	21.0
# employed in government	15	12.1
# employed in public interest	6	4.8
# employed as judicial clerks	4	3.2
# employed in academia	5	4.0

Geographic Location

# employed in state	114	91.9
# employed in foreign countries	0	0.0
# of states where employed	7	

Bar Passage Rates

Jurisdiction	New York		
Exam	Sum 05	Win 06	Total
# from school taking bar for the first time	145	19	164
School's pass rate for all first-time takers	65%	74%	66%
State's pass rate for all first-time takers	76%	61%	74%

Touro College—Jacob D. Fuchsberg Law Center

225 Eastview Drive
Central Islip, NY 11722
Phone: 631.761.7010; Fax: 631.421.9708
E-mail: admissions@tourolaw.edu; Website: www.tourolaw.edu

■ New Building and New Location

Established in 1980, Touro Law Center is fully accredited by the American Bar Association and is a member of the Association of American Law Schools. The Law Center occupies a new 180,000-square-foot state-of-the-art building in Central Islip on the south shore of Long Island, at the center of what is arguably the nation's first integrated "law campus," comprising a United States courthouse and federal building and a New York State court center, with supreme, family, and district courts. More than mere physical proximity, Touro students interact with legal professionals on a daily basis through classroom instruction, court visits, clinics, externships, and other academic and social forums.

Located about one hour by car or train from New York City, Central Islip boasts a wide variety of affordable housing options. Students may also use the Office of Admissions' Housing Information Network, which provides current listings of accommodations, as well as information regarding car pools and shared living arrangements. On-campus parking is plentiful and free of charge.

■ New Curriculum: Courtrooms as Classrooms

Touro is a leader in bridging the gap between law school and law practice, between the classroom and the courtroom. Beginning in the first week, students are exposed to the challenges of law practice through simulations in both litigation and nonlitigation settings and through faculty-supervised small-group visits to courts in session, court-related agencies, and court administration. In an effort to facilitate experiential learning, students not only observe live proceedings, but also discuss with the participants (judges, attorneys, and sometimes the parties themselves) their perspectives on law in action.

Practice modules: A central feature of the upper-level curriculum is the linkage of substantive law with practice modules in Business Organizations, Criminal Procedure, Family Law, and Trusts and Estates. Using the rules they have learned in the classroom, students solve practical problems, such as helping investors select an appropriate business entity, drawing up a criminal indictment, structuring a separation agreement, or drafting a will that satisfies an individual's personal and financial interests.

Clinics: Touro offers five in-house clinics, where clients bring real cases to on-campus offices: Civil Rights Litigation, Elder Law, Family Law, International Human Rights/Asylum Litigation, and Not-for-Profit Corporation Law, with the last two set up to accommodate the scheduling needs of part-time evening students. There are four field-placement clinics, in which students work off campus: Business, Law, and Technology (Internet and high-tech companies, corporate law departments, and law firms); Civil Practice (law firms, corporations, and private and public agencies); Criminal Law (District Attorneys' and Legal Aid/Public Defenders' offices); and Judicial Clerkship (state and federal judges' chambers).

In addition, Touro offers two "rotations," mirroring the medical school model, where students work intensively in practice groups at the US Attorney's Office for the Eastern District of New York or in Nassau/Suffolk Law Services (a regional legal services agency). To take full advantage of the synergies of its location within a court complex, the Law Center is also developing a Federal Practice Clinic and a Bankruptcy Clinic.

Externships: Touro provides an unlimited selection of externship placements in private law firms, corporate law departments, government agencies, the courts, and public interest organizations.

Public Service Projects: Students may earn academic credit by performing legal work on campus in the Law Center's Domestic Violence and Volunteer Income Tax Assistance projects.

Institutes: Touro hosts the Institute for Business, Law, and Technology, the Local and Suburban Law Institute, the Jewish Law Institute, and the Institute for Human Rights and the Holocaust.

Summer Programs: In addition to the Law Center's on-site summer program, which features special programs on New York law, there are opportunities for work and study abroad in Russia, India, China, Germany, and Israel. Touro also offers summer internships in law firms, courts, and government offices in Europe and Israel.

■ Students and Faculty

The Law Center's students, coming from diverse backgrounds and experiences, represent over 125 undergraduate institutions and a broad mix of majors. Women make up 44 percent of the total enrollment; minorities, 26 percent.

Students play an active role in governing the entire institution through the Student Bar Association and service on faculty committees, where they enjoy voting rights. There are two honor societies: the *Touro Law Review* and the Moot Court Board. There are also 30 student organizations devoted to specialized professional and social concerns.

Of Touro's 43 full-time faculty members, many have advanced degrees in other disciplines, including medicine, philosophy, business, and finance. Almost all have extensive practice backgrounds, ranging from the bench, major law firms, criminal prosecution and defense, government agencies, and public interest organizations.

While they embody a unique mix of talents and achievements, the faculty shares one common characteristic: accessibility to students. Every entering student is assigned a faculty advisor, matched by background or interest area, for discussions on any aspect of the law school experience: study strategy, course selection, career goals, and so on. With an open-door policy and a student faculty ratio of 15:1, everyone reaps the benefits of a personal and dynamic educational experience.

■ Academic Programs

Juris Doctor (JD): Touro offers the JD degree full time and part time in the day (Monday–Friday) and part time in the evening (Monday–Thursday). Students wishing to accelerate may graduate within two and one-half years (full time) and three and one-half years (part time), by attending summer sessions.

Dual Degrees: The JD may be combined with a Master of Business Administration (MBA), a Master of Public

Administration (MPA) in Health Care, or a Master of Social Work (MSW), allowing students to complete the two degrees with significant time and cost savings.

Master of Laws (LLM): The Law Center also offers a 24-credit general LLM, full time or part time, and a 27-credit LLM in US Legal Studies (for foreign law graduates), full time or part time.

■ Academic Support and Enrichment

The Law Center provides a unique program of outside-the-classroom assistance. Teaching assistants (TAs) review material covered in class and conduct small-group sessions on effective study methods and test-taking techniques. The Writing Resources Center offers workshops and tutorials to assist students in producing a professional work product. In addition, the Legal Education Access Program (LEAP) enhances the experience of students of color, through a four-week summer program for new students and mentoring during the academic year.

The Honors Program, beginning in the second year, allows outstanding students to become Faculty Fellows, where they receive additional scholarship assistance and access to academic enrichment initiatives.

■ Career Services

The Career Services Office finds students and graduates part-time, full-time, and summer employment. In addition to placing students in national, regional, and local law firms, there are opportunities in federal, state, and local courts and government agencies, and in the legal departments of corporations and municipalities.

■ Admission and Financial Aid

Touro Law Center does not provide an Applicant Profile Grid for its entering class because such data fail to reflect the complexity of the selection process.

At no point on a purely objective scale is an applicant assured of a particular decision. Among the most important criteria are the LSAT score and UGPA, but evaluation is based on a variety of factors that may be indicative of potential for success—college major and course selection, graduate study, work experience, community involvement, and character.

In order to finance law school, Touro provides access to federal loans and work study, New York State loan and assistance programs, and need-based Touro Grants. Most students receive some form of financial aid, and over 50 percent of entering students receive scholarships.

■ Scholarships

Institutional aid is available to entering students (based on LSAT/UGPA) and to continuing students (based on academic performance). Assistance includes dean's fellowships (full-tuition remission), merit scholarships (up to 75 percent tuition remission), and incentive awards (up to $8,000 per year). In addition, the Law Center offers stipends for Public Interest Law Fellowships, judicial clerkships, and federal work-study placements during the summer.

Applicant Profile Not Available

Tulane University Law School

John Giffen Weinmann Hall, 6329 Freret Street
New Orleans, LA 70118
Phone: 504.865.5930; Fax: 504.865.6710
E-mail: admissions@law.tulane.edu; Website: www.law.tulane.edu

ABA
Approved
Since
1925

The Basics

Type of school	Private
Term	Semester
Application deadline	
Application fee	$60
Financial aid deadline	2/15
Can first year start other than fall?	No
Student to faculty ratio	15.3 to 1
Does the university offer:	
housing restricted to law students?	No
graduate housing for which law students are eligible?	Yes

Faculty and Administrators

	Total		Men		Women		Minorities	
	Fall	Spr	Fall	Spr	Fall	Spr	Fall	Spr
Full-time	47	41	37	33	10	8	4	4
Other Full-time	11	11	1	1	10	10	2	2
Deans, librarians, & others who teach	4	4	1	1	3	3	1	1
Part-time	24	35	22	33	2	2	0	1
Total	86	91	61	68	25	23	7	8

Curriculum

	Full-time	Part-time
Typical first-year section size	44	0
Is there typically a "small section" of the first-year class, other than Legal Writing, taught by full-time faculty	No	No
If yes, typical size offered last year		
# of classroom course titles beyond first-year curriculum	143	

# of upper division courses, excluding seminars with an enrollment:		
Under 25	78	
25–49	42	
50–74	15	
75–99	5	
100+	0	

# of seminars	12	
# of seminar positions available	208	
# of seminar positions filled	177	0
# of positions available in simulation courses	119	
# of simulation positions filled	116	0
# of positions available in faculty supervised clinical courses	94	
# of faculty supervised clinical positions filled	80	0
# involved in field placements	23	0
# involved in law journals	243	0
# involved in interschool competitions	96	0
# of credit hours required to graduate	88	

JD Enrollment and Ethnicity

	Men		Women		Full-time		Part-time		1st-year		Total		JD Degs. Awd.
	#	%	#	%	#	%	#	%	#	%	#	%	
African Amer.	20	4.6	31	9.2	51	6.6	0	0.0	23	8.4	51	6.6	22
Amer. Indian	0	0.0	1	0.3	1	0.1	0	0.0	0	0.0	1	0.1	4
Asian Amer.	16	3.7	23	6.8	39	5.1	0	0.0	12	4.4	39	5.1	16
Mex. Amer.	3	0.7	2	0.6	5	0.7	0	0.0	1	0.4	5	0.7	0
Puerto Rican	3	0.7	3	0.9	6	0.8	0	0.0	5	1.8	6	0.8	3
Hispanic	11	2.6	10	3.0	21	2.7	0	0.0	9	3.3	21	2.7	6
Total Minority	53	12.3	70	20.7	123	16.0	0	0.0	50	18.2	123	16.0	51
For. Nation.	8	1.9	7	2.1	15	2.0	0	0.0	1	0.4	15	2.0	12
Caucasian	356	82.6	253	74.9	608	79.2	1	100.0	213	77.7	609	79.2	235
Unknown	14	3.2	8	2.4	22	2.9	0	0.0	10	3.6	22	2.9	18
Total	431	56.0	338	44.0	768	99.9	1	0.1	274	35.6	769		316

Transfers

Transfers in	13
Transfers out	13

Tuition and Fees

	Resident	Nonresident
Full-time	$34,696	$34,696
Part-time	$0	$0

Living Expenses

Estimated living expenses for singles

Living on campus	Living off campus	Living at home
$17,300	$17,300	$9,082

Tulane University Law School

*ABA
Approved
Since
1925*

GPA and LSAT Scores

	Total	Full-time	Part-time
# of apps	2,445	2,445	0
# of offers	818	818	0
# of matrics	274	274	0
75% GPA	3.70	3.70	0.00
Median GPA	3.57	3.57	0.00
25% GPA	3.35	3.35	0.00
75% LSAT	163	163	0
Median LSAT	161	161	0
25% LSAT	159	159	0

Grants and Scholarships (from prior year)

	Total #	Total %	Full-time #	Full-time %	Part-time #	Part-time %
Total # of students	814		813		1	
Total # receiving grants	539	66.2	539	66.3	0	0.0
Less than 1/2 tuition	470	57.7	470	57.8	0	0.0
Half to full tuition	61	7.5	61	7.5	0	0.0
Full tuition	8	1.0	8	1.0	0	0.0
More than full tuition	0	0.0	0	0.0	0	0.0
Median grant amount			$9,375		$0	

Informational and Library Resources

# of volumes and volume equivalents	639,419
# of titles	354,873
# of active serial subscriptions	4,939
Study seating capacity inside the library	557
# of full-time professional librarians	7
Hours per week library is open	114
# of open, wired connections available to students	310
# of networked computers available for use by students	129
# of simultaneous wireless users	500
Require computer?	No

JD Attrition (from prior year)

	Academic #	Other #	Total #	Total %
1st year	2	17	19	8.2
2nd year	4	2	6	2.2
3rd year	2	1	3	1.0
4th year	0	0	0	0.0

Employment (9 months after graduation)

	Total	Percentage
Employment status known	334	98.5
Employment status unknown	5	1.5
Employed	305	91.3
Pursuing graduate degrees	11	3.3
Unemployed seeking employment	10	3.0
Unemployed not seeking employment	8	2.4
Unemployed and studying for the bar	0	0.0

Type of Employment

	Total	Percentage
# employed in law firms	180	59.0
# employed in business and industry	33	10.8
# employed in government	37	12.1
# employed in public interest	13	4.3
# employed as judicial clerks	18	5.9
# employed in academia	1	0.3

Geographic Location

	Total	Percentage
# employed in state	78	25.6
# employed in foreign countries	2	0.7
# of states where employed		33

Bar Passage Rates

Jurisdiction	Louisiana Sum 05	Louisiana Win 06	Louisiana Total	New York Sum 05	New York Win 06	New York Total
Exam						
# from school taking bar for the first time	99	6	105	60	5	65
School's pass rate for all first-time takers	84%	33%	81%	67%	40%	65%
State's pass rate for all first-time takers	73%	48%	70%	76%	61%	74%

Tulane University Law School

John Giffen Weinmann Hall, 6329 Freret Street
New Orleans, LA 70118
Phone: 504.865.5930; Fax: 504.865.6710
E-mail: admissions@law.tulane.edu; Website: www.law.tulane.edu

■ Introduction

Tulane Law School, established in 1847, is the 12th oldest law school in the United States. The Law School is centrally located on the main university campus in uptown New Orleans, in a picturesque neighborhood of residences, both large and small, as well as restaurants, bookstores, and other commercial establishments. The campus itself and most surrounding neighborhoods have recovered from Hurricane Katrina. Not surprisingly, however, unparalleled opportunities abound to become involved in the rebuilding and renewal of virtually all aspects of the city.

New Orleans itself offers a surprising number of legal resources, including the US Court of Appeals for the Fifth Circuit, Federal District Court, the Louisiana Supreme Court, and lower state civil, criminal, and specialized courts. In addition to numerous events at Tulane University, students enjoy the advantages of city life and the richness of New Orleans culture. Most students live in a variety of off-campus neighborhoods throughout the New Orleans metropolitan area, although some on-campus housing is available for law students.

The Law School curriculum offers a complete selection of common law and federal subjects. In addition, Tulane offers electives in the civil law, with the result that students have the opportunity to pursue comparative education in the world's two major legal systems. The breadth and depth of the curriculum permit students to survey a broad range of subject areas or to concentrate in one or more. In addition, our students participate in the rebuilding of post-Katrina New Orleans through our mandatory community service program or in numerous other ways.

■ Facilities

The Law School's 160,000-square-foot building, John Giffen Weinmann Hall, was completed in 1995. Designed to integrate classrooms, other student spaces, excellent computer facilities, faculty offices, and a state-of-the-art library that contains both national and international collections, the building is centrally located on Tulane University's campus.

Immediately adjacent to Weinmann Hall is the Law School's Career Development Office. Within minutes of the Law School building are the university's Howard-Tilton Library, housing over one million volumes; the brand-new Lavin-Bernick Center for University Life; various university dining facilities; the university bookstore; the Reily Student Recreation Center; the Freeman School of Business; the Newcomb Art Gallery; and various auditoriums and performance venues.

■ The Academic Program

Six semesters in residence, completion of 88 credits with at least a C average, and fulfillment of an upper-level writing requirement and a 30-hour community service obligation are required for graduation from the JD degree program. The first-year curriculum comprises eight required courses and one elective. The first-year Legal Research and Writing Program is taught by instructors with significant experience as lawyers and writers, each assisted by senior fellows.

After the first year, all courses are elective, except for a required Legal Profession course. All first-year and many upper-class courses are taught in multiple sections to allow for smaller classes. The upper-class curriculum includes introductory as well as advanced courses in a broad range of subject areas, including international and comparative law, business and corporate law, environmental law, maritime law, criminal law, intellectual property, taxation, and litigation and procedure, among others.

At the graduate level, the Law School offers a general LLM program and an SJD program, as well as specialized LLM programs in Admiralty, Energy and Environmental Law, American Business Law, and International and Comparative Law.

■ Special Programs

The school offers five optional concentration programs that allow JD students to receive one certificate of completion of successful studies in (a) European Legal Studies, (b) Environmental Law, (c) Maritime Law, (d) Sports Law, or (e) Civil Law. Tulane's Eason-Weinmann Center for Comparative Law, its Maritime Law Center, and its Institute for Water Policy & Law add depth to the curriculum. Tulane also offers strong curricula in intellectual property law, constitutional law, and business, corporate, and commercial law.

Tulane conducts an annual summer school in New Orleans and offers summer-study programs abroad in England, the Netherlands, France, Italy, Germany, and Greece. It offers semester-long exchange programs with select law schools in a number of countries throughout the world.

■ Clinical Programs

The school offers six live-client clinical programs: civil litigation, criminal defense, juvenile litigation, domestic violence, environmental law, and legislative and administrative advocacy. In addition, there is a Trial Advocacy program, and third-year students may engage in externships with federal and state judges, with a local death penalty project, or with certain administrative agencies. The school was the first in the country to institute a pro bono program requiring that each student complete community service work prior to graduation. We anticipate that for the next few years, students will engage in community service work related to the rebuilding of New Orleans subsequent to Hurricane Katrina.

■ Joint-degree Programs

Joint-degree programs are offered in conjunction with Tulane's Freeman School of Business (JD/MBA and JD/MACCT), School of Public Health and Tropical Medicine (JD/MHA and JD/MPH), School of Social Work (JD/MSW), and several of the academic departments of the university. The JD/MS in International Development is offered in cooperation with Tulane's Payson Center for International Development and Technology Transfer, and the JD/MA in Latin American Studies is offered in cooperation with the Stone Center for Latin American Studies. Proposals for additional programs are considered on an ad hoc basis.

■ Admission

Our admission process is based on a complete review of all of the information in each candidate's file. This naturally includes the LSAT score and the undergraduate academic record. In the case of multiple LSAT scores, the school sees all scores but will give more weight to the higher score based on the candidate's explanation. Tulane looks closely at subjective factors such as grade trends, courseload, undergraduate school, nonacademic activities, the student's background and experience, barriers overcome, and the personal statement. The Law School processes applications for admission beginning October 1 and starts to announce decisions after December 1.

■ Student Activities

Journals published or edited at Tulane Law School include the *Tulane Law Review, Tulane Maritime Law Journal, Tulane Environmental Law Journal, Journal of Law and Sexuality, Tulane European and Civil Law Forum, Tulane Journal of International and Comparative Law, Journal of Technology and Intellectual Property,* and *Sports Lawyers Journal,* published by the national Sports Lawyers Association. An active moot court program holds trial and appellate competitions within the school and fields teams for a variety of interschool competitions. The Law School has a chapter of the Order of the Coif.

The Student Bar Association functions as the student government and recommends students for appointment to faculty committees. Over 40 student organizations are active at Tulane, including Tulane Law Women, Black Law Students Association, La Alianza, Asian Pacific American Law Students Association, Environmental Law Society, and several legal fraternities. The Tulane Public Interest Law Foundation raises funds, matched by the Law School, to support as many as 30 students each summer in public interest fellowships with a variety of organizations.

■ Career Services

The Law School Career Development Office assists both students and alumni in their job searches. Each student is assigned a career counselor as a first-year student and thereafter has access to a full range of career counseling services from the entire staff as well as to programs on job-search skills and practice areas. A large career-services library is available, including extensive online resources. Tulane organizes both on- and off-campus interview programs for its students. Career Development staff members also engage in employer development activities on a national basis. The office takes a proactive stance in assisting students with their job searches, with the result that Tulane graduates find law-related employment throughout the United States.

Applicant Profile

Tulane University Law School

LSAT Score	GPA									
	3.75 +	3.50–3.74	3.25–3.49	3.00–3.24	2.75–2.99	2.50–2.74	2.25–2.49	2.00–2.24	Below 2.00	No GPA
175–180										
170–174										
165–169										
160–164										
155–159										
150–154										
145–149										
140–144										
135–139										
130–134										
125–129										
120–124										

■ Excellent   ■ Good   ■ Possible   □ Unlikely

The University of Tulsa College of Law

3120 East Fourth Place
Tulsa, OK 74104-3189
Phone: 918.631.2406; Fax: 918.631.3630
E-mail: martha-cordell@utulsa.edu; april-fox@utulsa.edu; Website: www.law.utulsa.edu/tulaw

ABA Approved Since 1950

The Basics

Type of school	Private
Term	Semester
Application deadline	
Application fee	$30
Financial aid deadline	
Can first year start other than fall?	No
Student to faculty ratio	14.8 to 1
Does the university offer:	
housing restricted to law students?	No
graduate housing for which law students are eligible?	Yes

Faculty and Administrators

	Total		Men		Women		Minorities	
	Fall	Spr	Fall	Spr	Fall	Spr	Fall	Spr
Full-time	37	37	19	19	18	18	5	5
Other Full-time	0	0	0	0	0	0	0	0
Deans, librarians, & others who teach	10	10	5	5	5	5	2	2
Part-time	27	26	20	19	7	7	1	1
Total	**74**	**73**	**44**	**43**	**30**	**30**	**8**	**8**

Curriculum

	Full-time	Part-time
Typical first-year section size	50	0
Is there typically a "small section" of the first-year class, other than Legal Writing, taught by full-time faculty	Yes	No
If yes, typical size offered last year	65	
# of classroom course titles beyond first-year curriculum		92

# of upper division courses, excluding seminars with an enrollment:		
Under 25	84	
25–49	36	
50–74	15	
75–99	2	
100+	0	

# of seminars		9
# of seminar positions available		135
# of seminar positions filled	127	0
# of positions available in simulation courses		578
# of simulation positions filled	497	0
# of positions available in faculty supervised clinical courses		72
# of faculty supervised clinical positions filled	72	0
# involved in field placements	74	0
# involved in law journals	111	0
# involved in interschool competitions	33	0
# of credit hours required to graduate		88

JD Enrollment and Ethnicity

	Men		Women		Full-time		Part-time		1st-year		Total		JD Degs. Awd.
	#	%	#	%	#	%	#	%	#	%	#	%	
African Amer.	9	2.5	8	4.3	14	3.0	3	3.8	4	2.2	17	3.1	6
Amer. Indian	9	2.5	15	8.1	18	3.9	6	7.5	8	4.4	24	4.4	13
Asian Amer.	3	0.8	3	1.6	6	1.3	0	0.0	1	0.5	6	1.1	5
Mex. Amer.	6	1.7	4	2.2	7	1.5	3	3.8	3	1.6	10	1.9	8
Puerto Rican	0	0.0	0	0.0	0	0.0	0	0.0	0	0.0	0	0.0	0
Hispanic	0	0.0	0	0.0	0	0.0	0	0.0	0	0.0	0	0.0	0
Total Minority	27	7.6	30	16.1	45	9.8	12	15.0	16	8.8	57	10.6	32
For. Nation.	3	0.8	0	0.0	3	0.7	0	0.0	0	0.0	3	0.6	1
Caucasian	266	75.1	132	71.0	342	74.3	56	70.0	145	79.7	398	73.7	152
Unknown	58	16.4	24	12.9	70	15.2	12	15.0	23	12.6	82	15.2	21
Total	354	65.6	186	34.4	460	85.2	80	14.8	182	33.7	540		206

Transfers

Transfers in	3
Transfers out	14

Tuition and Fees

	Resident	Nonresident
Full-time	$25,331	$25,331
Part-time	$17,755	$17,755

Living Expenses

Estimated living expenses for singles

Living on campus	Living off campus	Living at home
$12,788	$16,070	$8,960

The University of Tulsa College of Law

ABA Approved Since 1950

GPA and LSAT Scores

	Total	Full-time	Part-time
# of apps	1,455	1,401	54
# of offers	612	588	24
# of matrics	197	179	18
75% GPA	3.53	3.55	3.66
Median GPA	3.22	3.24	3.05
25% GPA	2.93	2.93	2.91
75% LSAT	154	154	157
Median LSAT	152	152	152
25% LSAT	150	150	150

Grants and Scholarships (from prior year)

	Total		Full-time		Part-time	
	#	%	#	%	#	%
Total # of students	591		506		85	
Total # receiving grants	225	38.1	194	38.3	31	36.5
Less than 1/2 tuition	169	28.6	143	28.3	26	30.6
Half to full tuition	39	6.6	36	7.1	3	3.5
Full tuition	16	2.7	14	2.8	2	2.4
More than full tuition	1	0.2	1	0.2	0	0.0
Median grant amount			$6,220		$5,000	

Informational and Library Resources

# of volumes and volume equivalents	394,643
# of titles	186,487
# of active serial subscriptions	3,330
Study seating capacity inside the library	715
# of full-time professional librarians	9
Hours per week library is open	114
# of open, wired connections available to students	379
# of networked computers available for use by students	98
# of simultaneous wireless users	2,000
Require computer?	No

JD Attrition (from prior year)

	Academic	Other	Total	
	#	#	#	%
1st year	13	4	17	9.4
2nd year	1	17	18	9.6
3rd year	0	1	1	0.5
4th year	0	0	0	0.0

Employment (9 months after graduation)

	Total	Percentage
Employment status known	163	98.2
Employment status unknown	3	1.8
Employed	128	78.5
Pursuing graduate degrees	11	6.7
Unemployed seeking employment	15	9.2
Unemployed not seeking employment	0	0.0
Unemployed and studying for the bar	9	5.5

Type of Employment

	Total	Percentage
# employed in law firms	85	66.4
# employed in business and industry	22	17.2
# employed in government	13	10.2
# employed in public interest	3	2.3
# employed as judicial clerks	2	1.6
# employed in academia	3	2.3

Geographic Location

	Total	Percentage
# employed in state	94	73.4
# employed in foreign countries	1	0.8
# of states where employed	17	

Bar Passage Rates

Jurisdiction	Oklahoma			Texas		
Exam	Sum 05	Win 06	Total	Sum 05	Win 06	Total
# from school taking bar for the first time	73	33	106	12	7	19
School's pass rate for all first-time takers	88%	97%	91%	67%	57%	63%
State's pass rate for all first-time takers	91%	88%	90%	81%	77%	80%

The University of Tulsa College of Law

3120 East Fourth Place
Tulsa, OK 74104-3189
Phone: 918.631.2406; Fax: 918.631.3630
E-mail: martha-cordell@utulsa.edu; april-fox@utulsa.edu; Website: www.law.utulsa.edu/tulaw

■ Introduction

Expect an exceptional legal education from the University of Tulsa. The faculty and staff at TU prove daily that it is possible for friendliness, challenge, respect, and excellence to coexist in law school. Housed in technologically enhanced John Rogers Hall on the University of Tulsa campus, and fully accredited by the ABA, the law school presents a forum for study and exploration of legal issues enhanced impressively by professors with exemplary credentials. A true open-door policy and faculty mentoring program invites students to expand their legal education from the classroom to one-on-one accessibility and interaction. We also honor student talent with scholarships ranging up to full tuition. Approximately 36 percent of an entering class receives merit or need-based assistance. With most students coming to Tulsa from states other than Oklahoma, a rich fabric of diversity expands the learning experience of every student. Located in the beautiful, culturally diverse, and extraordinarily friendly city of Tulsa, law students can enjoy award-winning theater, national touring concerts, world-class museums, gorgeous parks, and vibrant neighborhood shopping areas. The city also boasts an internationally recognized burgeoning environment for high-tech industry and commerce.

■ Library and Physical Facilities

The new-century award-winning Mabee Legal Information Center (MLIC) is much more than a library. The center was designed for students. Enter the center and you will feel the warmth of Southwestern colors used throughout the MLIC, such as burnished mahogany, bayberry, and sienna. It would be very difficult to find a more attractive, pleasant place to spend your hours of study, research, and, yes, even relaxation. While the MLIC is proud of its technological innovations and numerous electronic resources, the center also pays homage to the traditional uses and print publications many students appreciate in a library. Yes, the center is just the latest proof that meeting the varied needs and uses of our students is our highest priority at Tulsa.

For students, the MLIC is their vibrant hub of activity, and an ideal locale for collaborative work preparing for class or exams, working on journal scholarship, discussing Student Bar Association issues, or preparing for a moot court competition. Due to student demand, a rededication of space in 2006 dramatically doubled the number of popular group collaborative study rooms available throughout the MLIC. Student staffing offices for the Board of Advocates, the *Tulsa Law Review*, the *Energy Law Journal*, and the *Tulsa Journal of Comparative and International Law* provide generous working space for these important enterprises at the College of Law. The Student Bar Association office in the center is host to lively discussions about student issues. Jobs are secured for summer or permanent employment in the comfortable interview rooms in the center. Specialized classrooms include a laptop lab and the Alternative Dispute Resolution Center, where negotiation exercises are possible within a variety of simulation configurations. The Native American Law Center and the International/Comparative Law Center offer inviting forums for study, research, and the exchange of ideas, with impressive

artwork contributing to the rich heritage represented by these two exceptional programs. Two computer labs offer 26 workstations with impressive credentials. Another 49 PCs are available for use throughout the information center, including 19 laptops available for checkout.

If quiet study is for you, the two grand main reading rooms reflect quiet, inviting, wide-open spaces with natural lighting. With over 700 seats available and seven miles of shelving space, there is plenty of space for students, alumni, and books. Nearly 300 carrels, many of which can be reserved a semester at a time, provide private work space.

Ten professional librarians, six with law degrees, are ready to help with legal research in the 400,000-volume collection. Numerous electronic resources are accessible to students on-site or from home.

The College of Law has wireless access throughout the building. Classrooms provide access for instruction from a variety of computerized configurations, including smart podiums, large-screen projection, and Internet feeds. Faculty are readily accessible for consultation with the students, since most of their offices are across the hallway from the classrooms. Both faculty and students appreciate the original Native American artwork throughout the school. The newly constructed legal clinic and the modern moot courtroom bring the same state-of-the-art capacities to the study and training for trial and appellate advocacy. They are outstanding laboratories in which the best in preparation may ensue for Tulsa law students as they prepare for both future legal practice as well as training for many regional and national moot court competitions. Successes in competition include the 2005 Health Law Moot Court National Championship.

■ Curriculum and Specialization

Full-time and part-time programs are available, as well as summer classes. Students may choose either general legal study, covering a broad expanse of expertise, or specialization. Eight areas of concentrated study include the Native American Law Certificate, the Health Law Certificate, the Public Policy and Regulation Certificate, the Lawyering Skills Certificate, the Comparative and International Law Certificate, the Alternative Dispute Resolution Certificate, the Entrepreneurial Law Certificate, and the Resources, Energy, and Environmental Law Certificate.

Summer- and semester-abroad programs ensure that Tulsa students will have the opportunity to become immersed in the excitement of broadening international horizons for legal training and personal exploration. The University of Tulsa International Law Program is augmented by exciting summer programs in Dublin (Ireland), Geneva (Switzerland), and Buenos Aires (Argentina), plus a semester of study in London.

Students at Tulsa have a great variety of career choices available to them, including interdisciplinary study. The following joint-degree programs are available: JD/MBA, JD/MA in Anthropology, JD/MA in History, JD/MA in Industrial/Organizational Psychology, JD/MA in English, JD/Master of Accountancy, JD/MS in Computer Science, JD/MS in Biological Sciences, JD/MA in Clinical Psychology, JD/MS in Geosciences, and JD/MS in Taxation.

■ Professors

Knowledge and experience, matched by the passion for teaching, typifies the character of the professors at the University of Tulsa. Recognized nationally and internationally for their expertise, Tulsa professors are always accessible to their students. Specializations and strong experiential expertise in areas as diverse as international trade, energy regulation, family and juvenile law, sports law, Native American tribal jurisdiction, trial advocacy, and bioethics confirm the rich learning available to Tulsa law students. The ability to develop strong relationships with professors will strengthen Tulsa students' law school experience and their future legal practice in remarkable ways.

■ Housing

Law students at Tulsa may choose to live on or off campus. On-campus housing includes apartments that are less than five years old. Each apartment unit includes computer connections and large, spacious floor plans. With a very attractive low cost of living, the city of Tulsa offers a great variety of affordable housing opportunities. Information about housing may be obtained by calling 918.631.5249 or by contacting the Office of Law Admissions at 918.631.2406.

■ Career Services

Students at Tulsa gain significant personalized assistance in career counseling. On-campus interview coordination, résumé/dossier preparation services, informative seminar offerings, and summer and permanent job placement make the Office of Career Services an invaluable resource for future success. Tulsa graduates practicing in all 50 states and internationally make networking a vital resource in the enhancement of employment potential for students and alumni.

■ Practical Experience

Tulsa law students gain firsthand training beyond the classroom. The Boesche Legal Clinic is housed conveniently in a beautiful, spacious new facility across the street from John Rogers Hall. The Legal Clinic offers programs such as the Health Law Project, the Muscogee (Creek) Nation Legal Program, and the Immigrant Rights Project. Federal and state judicial internships are available, as well as the Legal Internship Program, which enables a student to represent clients in criminal and civil cases, subject to rules authorized by the Oklahoma Supreme Court. The new Pro Bono Program allows students to assist with cases going to trial, assist with civil legal matters, participate in interviewing clients and witnesses, and perform research.

Applicant Profile

The University of Tulsa College of Law

GPA	LSAT Score						
	120–147	147–151	151–153	153–157	157–163	163–170	170–180
3.75 + Above	Unlikely	Possible	Likely	Likely	Likely	Likely	Likely
3.74–3.50	Unlikely	Possible	Likely	Likely	Likely	Likely	Likely
3.49–3.25	Unlikely	Possible	Likely	Likely	Likely	Likely	Likely
3.24–3.00	Unlikely	Possible	Likely	Likely	Likely	Likely	Likely
2.99–2.75	Unlikely	Unlikely	Possible	Likely	Likely	Likely	Likely
2.74–2.50	Unlikely	Unlikely	Possible	Possible	Likely	Likely	Likely
2.49–2.25	Unlikely	Unlikely	Possible	Possible	Possible	Likely	Likely
2.24–2.00	Unlikely	Unlikely	Possible	Possible	Possible	Possible	Likely

Unlikely*   Possible   Likely

*Individual accomplishments crucial

This chart is to be used as a general guide in determining the chances for admittance.

University of Utah S.J. Quinney College of Law

332 South 1400 East, Room 101
Salt Lake City, UT 84112-0730
Phone: 801.581.6833; Fax: 801.581.6897
E-mail: admissions@law.utah.edu; Website: www.law.utah.edu

ABA
Approved
Since
1927

The Basics

Type of school	Public
Term	Semester
Application deadline	3/10
Application fee	$60
Financial aid deadline	3/15
Can first year start other than fall?	No
Student to faculty ratio	11.6 to 1
Does the university offer:	
housing restricted to law students?	Yes
graduate housing for which law students are eligible?	Yes

Faculty and Administrators

	Total		Men		Women		Minorities	
	Fall	Spr	Fall	Spr	Fall	Spr	Fall	Spr
Full-time	27	29	17	17	10	12	5	5
Other Full-time	1	1	1	1	0	0	0	0
Deans, librarians, & others who teach	10	9	6	5	4	4	0	0
Part-time	27	21	20	15	7	6	1	0
Total	65	60	44	38	21	22	6	5

Curriculum

	Full-time	Part-time
Typical first-year section size	40	0
Is there typically a "small section" of the first-year class, other than Legal Writing, taught by full-time faculty	Yes	No
If yes, typical size offered last year	21	
# of classroom course titles beyond first-year curriculum		94
# of upper division courses, excluding seminars with an enrollment: Under 25		43
25–49		26
50–74		9
75–99		2
100+		0
# of seminars		14
# of seminar positions available		168
# of seminar positions filled	153	0
# of positions available in simulation courses	0	
# of simulation positions filled	388	0
# of positions available in faculty supervised clinical courses	0	
# of faculty supervised clinical positions filled	0	0
# involved in field placements	192	0
# involved in law journals	97	0
# involved in interschool competitions	21	0
# of credit hours required to graduate		88

JD Enrollment and Ethnicity

	Men		Women		Full-time		Part-time		1st-year		Total		JD Degs. Awd.
	#	%	#	%	#	%	#	%	#	%	#	%	
African Amer.	2	0.8	0	0.0	2	0.5	0	0.0	0	0.0	2	0.5	1
Amer. Indian	2	0.8	0	0.0	2	0.5	0	0.0	0	0.0	2	0.5	1
Asian Amer.	11	4.5	10	6.8	21	5.4	0	0.0	10	8.4	21	5.4	5
Mex. Amer.	0	0.0	2	1.4	2	0.5	0	0.0	0	0.0	2	0.5	0
Puerto Rican	1	0.4	0	0.0	1	0.3	0	0.0	0	0.0	1	0.3	0
Hispanic	8	3.3	4	2.7	12	3.1	0	0.0	2	1.7	12	3.1	5
Total Minority	24	9.9	16	10.8	40	10.2	0	0.0	12	10.1	40	10.2	12
For. Nation.	1	0.4	1	0.7	2	0.5	0	0.0	0	0.0	2	0.5	1
Caucasian	180	74.1	112	75.7	292	74.7	0	0.0	80	67.2	292	74.7	104
Unknown	38	15.6	19	12.8	57	14.6	0	0.0	27	22.7	57	14.6	12
Total	243	62.1	148	37.9	391	100.0	0	0.0	119	30.4	391		129

Transfers

Transfers in	15
Transfers out	4

Tuition and Fees

	Resident	Nonresident
Full-time	$11,758	$25,116
Part-time	$0	$0

Living Expenses

Estimated living expenses for singles

Living on campus	Living off campus	Living at home
$16,150	$16,150	$9,050

University of Utah S.J. Quinney College of Law

*ABA
Approved
Since
1927*

GPA and LSAT Scores

	Total	Full-time	Part-time
# of apps	1,130	1,130	0
# of offers	360	360	0
# of matrics	122	122	0
75% GPA	3.81	3.81	0.00
Median GPA	3.58	3.58	0.00
25% GPA	3.36	3.36	0.00
75% LSAT	162	162	0
Median LSAT	160	160	0
25% LSAT	157	157	0

Grants and Scholarships (from prior year)

	Total		Full-time		Part-time	
	#	%	#	%	#	%
Total # of students	398		398		0	
Total # receiving grants	168	42.2	168	42.2	0	0.0
Less than 1/2 tuition	131	32.9	131	32.9	0	0.0
Half to full tuition	34	8.5	34	8.5	0	0.0
Full tuition	0	0.0	0	0.0	0	0.0
More than full tuition	3	0.8	3	0.8	0	0.0
Median grant amount			$1,800		$0	

Informational and Library Resources

# of volumes and volume equivalents	338,683
# of titles	134,537
# of active serial subscriptions	4,805
Study seating capacity inside the library	356
# of full-time professional librarians	8
Hours per week library is open	100
# of open, wired connections available to students	634
# of networked computers available for use by students	45
# of simultaneous wireless users	1,040
Require computer?	No

JD Attrition (from prior year)

	Academic	Other	Total	
	#	#	#	%
1st year	0	4	4	3.2
2nd year	0	0	0	0.0
3rd year	0	0	0	0.0
4th year	0	0	0	0.0

Employment (9 months after graduation)

	Total	Percentage
Employment status known	137	97.9
Employment status unknown	3	2.1
Employed	126	92.0
Pursuing graduate degrees	0	0.0
Unemployed seeking employment	3	2.2
Unemployed not seeking employment	3	2.2
Unemployed and studying for the bar	5	3.6

Type of Employment

# employed in law firms	73	57.9
# employed in business and industry	14	11.1
# employed in government	18	14.3
# employed in public interest	2	1.6
# employed as judicial clerks	15	11.9
# employed in academia	2	1.6

Geographic Location

# employed in state	92	73.0
# employed in foreign countries	0	0.0
# of states where employed	17	

Bar Passage Rates

Jurisdiction	Utah		
Exam	Sum 05	Win 06	Total
# from school taking bar for the first time	93	22	115
School's pass rate for all first-time takers	91%	82%	90%
State's pass rate for all first-time takers	90%	92%	90%

University of Utah S.J. Quinney College of Law

332 South 1400 East, Room 101
Salt Lake City, UT 84112-0730
Phone: 801.581.6833; Fax: 801.581.6897
E-mail: admissions@law.utah.edu; Website: www.law.utah.edu

■ Introduction

Established in 1913, the University of Utah S.J. Quinney College of Law is nationally recognized for its academic reputation, innovative curriculum, and excellent faculty/student ratio. Among the students, there is a prevailing sense of community fostered by a faculty and administration that is friendly, open, and service-oriented.

The Quinney College of Law is situated in the foothills of the picturesque Wasatch Range of the Rocky Mountains. The law school is less than a 10-minute drive or light rail ride from downtown Salt Lake City—the seat of federal, state, and local governmental bodies. Salt Lake City is regularly voted one of America's most livable cities. This location provides ample professional opportunities for our students, as well as superb outdoor recreational access and a strong cultural scene.

■ Library and Physical Facilities

The S.J. Quinney Law Library and the law building provide first-year students with their own study hall and personal carrels. The building is set up for wired and wireless laptop computer access. Advanced students are provided a personal study carrel, which also has laptop access in the adjacent Quinney Law Library—a modern, spacious facility with the latest technological equipment and library research services.

The library contains more than 335,000 volumes of law and law-related material and serves as a depository for US government documents. CD-ROM and Web-based databases provide access to primary legal materials, journal indexes, directories, and other law-related information.

In the law building and library, there is a student computing lab, a computer support help desk, classrooms, and a moot courtroom auditorium with state-of-the-art video-computer projection equipment.

■ Curriculum

The Quinney law school's innovative academic programs blend theory and practice skills that prepare graduates to practice law in any jurisdiction. The curriculum is designed to allow more efficient and rational sequencing of legal education that responds to the evolving legal, social, and ethical needs of our society.

The entering students are first offered an intensive four-day Introduction to Law course before they begin the required first-year curriculum. The first-year doctrinal courses include a small section in which enrollment is limited to no more than 25 students, as well as a spring semester elective. Second-year students select from a variety of foundational courses. In the third year, students may take year-long intensive courses that provide the opportunity for in-depth study, research, and a practicum in a focused area of law.

Additionally, students may select from more than 50 advanced courses and seminars, a variety of clinical and skills courses, and numerous cocurricular opportunities.

■ Special Programs

The Wallace Stegner Center for Land, Resources, and the Environment provides opportunities for JD candidates to engage in academic courses and related law activities focusing on public lands, environmental and natural resources law, and energy law. A Certificate in Environmental and Natural Resources Law is awarded to candidates who complete a sequence of approved courses with a specified GPA. Courses regularly offered include Natural Resources Law, Oil and Gas, Mining and Minerals, Water Law, Public Land Use, and Environmental Law. The law school also offers a specialized LLM degree in natural resources and environmental law.

The Utah Criminal Justice Center is an interdisciplinary partnership between the University of Utah and state government. The center supports collaborative work among academic units at the university in partnership with the Utah Commission on Criminal and Juvenile Justice. The interdisciplinary character and the potential benefits for policymaking and employment make the Utah Criminal Justice Center unique in American higher education and a model for productive collaboration between academia and government.

The clinical programs offer both live and simulated opportunities for students to assume the lawyering role. In the Civil Clinic and the Criminal Clinic, students represent clients, investigate cases, and appear in court. In the Judicial Clinic, students act as clerks to judges, researching issues and drafting opinions in pending cases. The Judicial Extern Program allows students to spend a semester away from school working as full-time clerks for certain courts. Other clinical opportunities are available in our Environmental, Health Law, Legislative, and Mediation clinics.

The Pro Bono Initiative is a voluntary program offered to emphasize the centrality of public service to the legal profession. The initiative is founded on ABA Rule 6.1 of the Model Rules of Conduct. Under Rule 6.1, attorneys have a professional obligation to devote a portion of their time to the provision of legal services, at no charge or a reduced fee, to public service, charitable, not-for-profit organizations, or individuals of limited means. The Quinney College of Law encourages students to perform at least 50 hours of law-related volunteer work during their time in law school. The Pro Bono Initiative facilitates this opportunity by providing students with a broad spectrum of developed volunteer placements.

Through the London Law Consortium, students may engage in the law school's study-abroad program during their spring semester. This academic program consists of courses taught by visiting consortium faculty members residing in London and courses on the English legal system and law of the European Union taught by law lecturers from British universities.

The College of Law maintains two formal joint-degree programs. Students may earn joint degrees in the areas of business (JD/MBA) or public administration (JD/MPA).

The college's Academic Support Program provides assistance to students whose backgrounds and experiences before law school indicate a need for such assistance. Students apply to participate in the program after admission to the College of Law.

University of Utah S.J. Quinney College of Law

Admission Standards

No applicant is accepted or rejected without members of the Admission Committee having first fully considered the entire application. The personal statement should expand on the applicant's biographic and academic background and motivations for seeking a legal education. The College of Law makes a special effort to attract students from diverse cultural, educational, economic, ethnic, racial, and nontraditional backgrounds. Each applicant is evaluated for the contribution that person can make to the student body or the legal profession, in addition to evidence of demonstrated high academic ability.

Student Activities

The *Utah Law Review*, the *Journal of Law and Family Studies*, and the *Journal of Land, Resources, and Environmental Law* are professional journals edited and published by students. The *Utah Law Review* selects staff members on the basis of academic achievement and a writing competition. The journals select staff members based on a writing competition.

Student organizations include the Student Bar Association, the Women's Law Caucus, Natural Resources Law Forum, the Moot Court Society, the Minority Law Caucus, the International Law Society, Health Law Coalition, American Constitution Society, Intramural Sports, the Federalist Society, the Gay and Lesbian Law Student Alliance, Native American Law Student Association, the Public Interest Law Organization, and the Student Intellectual Property Law Association.

Expenses and Financial Aid

Tuition reported on the official ABA data page represents a three-year average. Students interested in need-based scholarships or long-term loans such as Perkins, Stafford, Graduate PLUS or private educational loans must submit a FAFSA and should contact the University of Utah, Office of Financial Aid, 201 S. 1460 E, Room 105, Salt Lake City, Utah 84112-9055, 801.581.6211. The FAFSA deadline to begin the financial aid process is March 15. Merit scholarships are awarded to selected candidates based on information contained in their application materials. The law school also has a Loan Forgiveness Program for qualified graduates who practice in the public sector or the public interest field.

Career Services

The College of Law and its graduates have access to one of the most technologically advanced Legal Career Services (LCS) programs in the country. The LCS office transmits information to prospective employers, both on and off campus. The LCS office also offers personal counseling, maintains a resource library, and sponsors numerous seminars throughout the year.

Applicant Profile

University of Utah S.J. Quinney College of Law
This grid includes only applicants who earned 120–180 LSAT scores under standard administrations.

LSAT Score	3.75 +		3.50–3.74		3.25–3.49		3.00–3.24		2.75–2.99		2.50–2.74		2.25–2.49		2.00–2.24		Below 2.00		No GPA		Total	
	Apps	Adm	Apps	Adm	Apps	Adm	Apps	Adm	Apps	Adm	Apps	Adm	Apps	Adm	Apps	Adm	Apps	Adm	Apps	Adm	Apps	Adm
175–180	1	1	0	0	0	0	0	0	0	0	1	1	0	0	0	0	0	0	0	0	2	2
170–174	8	8	4	4	5	4	2	1	4	2	1	0	0	0	0	0	0	0	0	0	24	19
165–169	19	19	28	28	12	9	7	5	4	3	2	0	1	0	1	0	0	0	1	0	224	132
160–164	46	43	71	46	48	22	34	13	8	3	12	4	3	1	1	0	0	0	1	1	335	102
155–159	77	53	82	31	81	12	58	4	24	1	10	0	2	0	0	0	0	0	2	1	262	31
150–154	36	12	70	10	59	3	56	2	22	3	8	0	9	0	0	0	0	0	2	1	262	31
145–149	9	2	19	1	41	2	23	1	20	0	8	0	2	0	3	0	1	0	3	0	129	6
140–144	4	1	8	1	7	0	15	0	9	0	4	0	4	0	1	0	1	0	0	0	53	2
135–139	0	0	2	0	4	0	3	0	1	0	2	0	0	0	2	0	0	0	2	0	16	0
130–134	1	0	0	0	2	0	1	0	1	0	1	0	0	0	2	0	0	0	0	0	8	0
125–129	0	0	0	0	0	0	0	0	0	0	0	0	0	0	0	0	0	0	0	0	0	0
120–124	0	0	0	0	0	0	0	0	0	0	1	0	0	0	0	0	0	0	0	0	1	0
Total	201	139	284	121	259	52	199	26	93	12	50	5	21	1	10	0	2	0	9	2	1128	358

Apps = Number of Applicants
Adm = Number Admitted
Reflects 99% of the total applicant pool.

Note: This chart is to be used as a general guide only. Nonnumerical factors are strongly considered for all applicants.

Valparaiso University School of Law

656 S. Greenwich—Wesemann Hall
Valparaiso, IN 46383-6493
Phone: 888.ValpoLaw, 219.465.7829; Fax: 219.465.7808
E-mail: valpolaw@valpo.edu; Website: www.valpo.edu/law/

ABA
Approved
Since
1929

The Basics

Type of school	Private
Term	Semester
Application deadline	4/1
Application fee	$50
Financial aid deadline	3/1
Can first year start other than fall?	No
Student to faculty ratio	16.5 to 1
Does the university offer:	
housing restricted to law students?	No
graduate housing for which law students are eligible?	No

Faculty and Administrators

	Total		Men		Women		Minorities	
	Fall	Spr	Fall	Spr	Fall	Spr	Fall	Spr
Full-time	25	25	14	14	11	11	2	2
Other Full-time	1	1	1	1	0	0	0	0
Deans, librarians, & others who teach	11	11	6	6	5	5	1	1
Part-time	24	27	13	18	11	9	0	1
Total	**61**	**64**	**34**	**39**	**27**	**25**	**3**	**4**

Curriculum

	Full-time	Part-time
Typical first-year section size	65	0
Is there typically a "small section" of the first-year class, other than Legal Writing, taught by full-time faculty	No	No
If yes, typical size offered last year		
# of classroom course titles beyond first-year curriculum	109	
# of upper division courses, excluding seminars with an enrollment: Under 25	92	
25–49	26	
50–74	8	
75–99	5	
100+	1	
# of seminars	12	
# of seminar positions available	204	
# of seminar positions filled	137	5
# of positions available in simulation courses	717	
# of simulation positions filled	339	15
# of positions available in faculty supervised clinical courses	60	
# of faculty supervised clinical positions filled	57	3
# involved in field placements	175	7
# involved in law journals	48	0
# involved in interschool competitions	47	1
# of credit hours required to graduate	90	

JD Enrollment and Ethnicity

	Men #	Men %	Women #	Women %	Full-time #	Full-time %	Part-time #	Part-time %	1st-year #	1st-year %	Total #	Total %	JD Degs. Awd.
African Amer.	13	4.6	11	4.8	17	3.7	7	13.7	12	5.8	24	4.7	8
Amer. Indian	1	0.4	0	0.0	0	0.0	1	2.0	1	0.5	1	0.2	1
Asian Amer.	8	2.8	3	1.3	10	2.2	1	2.0	6	2.9	11	2.1	3
Mex. Amer.	4	1.4	4	1.7	8	1.7	0	0.0	2	1.0	8	1.6	1
Puerto Rican	1	0.4	0	0.0	0	0.0	1	2.0	0	0.0	1	0.2	0
Hispanic	11	3.9	4	1.7	13	2.8	2	3.9	9	4.3	15	2.9	2
Total Minority	38	13.4	22	9.6	48	10.4	12	23.5	30	14.4	60	11.7	15
For. Nation.	3	1.1	2	0.9	5	1.1	0	0.0	3	1.4	5	1.0	1
Caucasian	226	79.9	199	86.5	387	83.8	38	74.5	154	74.0	425	82.8	143
Unknown	16	5.7	7	3.0	22	4.8	1	2.0	21	10.1	23	4.5	1
Total	283	55.2	230	44.8	462	90.1	51	9.9	208	40.5	513		160

Transfers

Transfers in	0
Transfers out	29

Tuition and Fees

	Resident	Nonresident
Full-time	$28,940	$28,940
Part-time	$18,088	$18,088

Living Expenses

Estimated living expenses for singles

Living on campus	Living off campus	Living at home
N/A	$10,650	$4,900

Valparai

GPA and LSAT Scores

	Total	Full-time	Part-time
# of apps	2,736	2,583	153
# of offers	828	769	59
# of matrics	200	174	26
75% GPA	3.57	3.59	3.50
Median GPA	3.31	3.33	3.14
25% GPA	3.09	3.12	2.74
75% LSAT	153	153	148
Median LSAT	151	151	147
25% LSAT	150	150	144

Grants and Scholarships (from prior year)

	Total		Full-time		Part-time	
	#	%	#	%	#	%
Total # of students	526		479		47	
Total # receiving grants	174	33.1	174	36.3	0	0.0
Less than 1/2 tuition	81	15.4	81	16.9	0	0.0
Half to full tuition	30	5.7	30	6.3	0	0.0
Full tuition	31	5.9	31	6.5	0	0.0
More than full tuition	32	6.1	32	6.7	0	0.0
Median grant amount			$13,200		$0	

Informational and Library Resources

# of volumes and volume equivalents	325,971
# of titles	136,347
# of active serial subscriptions	2,523
Study seating capacity inside the library	356
# of full-time professional librarians	6
Hours per week library is open	113
# of open, wired connections available to students	58
# of networked computers available for use by students	59
# of simultaneous wireless users	2,500
Require computer?	No

JD Attrition (from pr...

	Acade...			
	#			
1st year	9			
2nd year	2			
3rd year	0		0	0.0
4th year	0	0	0	0.0

Employment (9 months after graduation)

	Total	Percentage
Employment status known	189	99.5
Employment status unknown	1	0.5
Employed	163	86.2
Pursuing graduate degrees	2	1.1
Unemployed seeking employment	12	6.3
Unemployed not seeking employment	1	0.5
Unemployed and studying for the bar	11	5.8

Type of Employment

# employed in law firms	92	56.4
# employed in business and industry	23	14.1
# employed in government	26	16.0
# employed in public interest	6	3.7
# employed as judicial clerks	11	6.7
# employed in academia	2	1.2

Geographic Location

# employed in state	78	47.9
# employed in foreign countries	0	0.0
# of states where employed		20

Bar Passage Rates

Jurisdiction	Indiana			Illinois		
Exam	Sum 05	Win 06	Total	Sum 05	Win 06	Total
# from school taking bar for the first time	84	15	99	50	8	58
School's pass rate for all first-time takers	87%	93%	88%	80%	100%	83%
State's pass rate for all first-time takers	84%	77%	82%	86%	83%	85%

Valparaiso University
656 S. Greenwich—Weseman...
Valparaiso, IN 46383-6493
Phone: 888.ValpoLaw...
E-mail: valpolaw@...

School of Law

Hall

219.465.7829; Fax: 219.465.7808
alpo.edu; Website: www.valpo.edu/law/

tion

aiso University School of Law was founded in 1879.
oughout its 127-year history, and even more so today,
alpo Law is renowned for the following four traits:

Exceptional Legal Research and Writing: According to a survey by the American Bar Foundation, hiring partners at law firms ranked research and writing skills as the most important skill set a new lawyer can bring to the job. It is common for law schools to have one year of legal writing as part of the first-year curriculum. We have three years of research **and** writing.

Enduring Core Competencies: No matter how much the world and laws change, no matter how often attorneys change their practice, there are certain constants: the ability to engage in critical, analytical, and creative thinking, and the ability to communicate clearly and concisely. These core competencies comprise the cornerstone of your Valpo Law education. Visit *www.valpo.edu/law/academics/*.

Truly Personal Manner of Teaching and Learning: The teaching and learning style of Valpo Law is highly collaborative and integrated. You interact with faculty both in and out of the classroom. We know who you are and strive to provide a legal education that is tailored to you and your aspirations. Every pedagogical component, including the smaller student body, is designed to help you, as an individual, succeed in your professional endeavors. Visit *www.valpo.edu/law/academics/faculty/program/*.

Law as a Calling: We are a community dedicated to imparting not just skills and knowledge, but also values, a sense of self, and a commitment to service. Our graduates are not just solid lawyers, but great people; not just successful men and women, but noble men and women; not just influential leaders, but ones who use their influence for the highest service and the profoundest good.

■ Curriculum

Valpo provides a comprehensive and intensive study of the foundations of law, an introduction to the substantive areas of law, and an opportunity for advanced study in specific areas. The curriculum provides a grounding in legal analysis, legal writing and research, practical skills training, perspectives on the law, and ethics.

The Valpo Law curriculum may be segmented into six areas: **general practice, business law, public interest representation, property, litigation,** and **taxation.** To learn more, visit *www.valpo.edu/law/academics/courses/* and *www.valpo.edu/law/bulletin/*.

Students may participate in externships and enhance their skills in one of our six legal clinics. No matter how you choose to apply your education, you will have the tools and foundation to succeed.

Upon completing the required first-year curriculum, students are given the opportunity to explore various avenues of study. During the second year, students begin to take electives. By the third year, almost all required courses will be completed and students select courses for general legal competency or focus on areas of interest.

The School of Law is committed to the highest standards of professional ethics and to an inquiry into values, and is concerned that students not view the legal system as unchangeable and untouched by their own ethical and intellectual analysis. A 20-hour commitment of pro bono legal service is required of all students. Valpo Law is one of a few select law schools that require pro bono work.

■ Degree Programs

We offer full-time, part-time day, and two-and-one-half year options for our JD program. In addition, we offer dual-degree programs such as: JD/MA Psychology; JD/MA Clinical Mental Health; JD/MA Liberal Studies in either Gerontology, English, Ethics and Values, History, Human Behavior and Society, or Theology; JD/MBA; JD/MSSA Sports Administration; and JD/MSICP International Commerce and Policy. Valpo Law also has a one to one-and-one-half years full-time LLM program for international students who already have a law degree.

■ Special Programs

Clinical Law Program—Students enrolled in the live-client law clinic represent indigent clients and participate in all stages of representation. The six clinics based on practice areas are criminal, civil, mediation, juvenile, tax, and sports.

Current Representation—Faculty members often invite students to work on cases in which they are providing legal representation.

Externships—The School of Law currently sponsors over 70 externships throughout the US, including semester-away externships. To learn more, visit *www.valpo.edu/law/academics/externships/*.

Summer Study Abroad—Valparaiso's interest in international and comparative law is enhanced with its Summer Study Abroad program in Cambridge, England, and its new summer course in International Human Rights in Chile and Argentina.

Honors Program—The Honors Program offers an academic challenge to talented students. First-year students are selected after either the first or second semester based on academic credentials and demonstrated leadership skills. Personal interviews are required.

Summer Public Interest Scholarships—Each summer we award students who work in a public interest capacity a Summer Public Interest Scholarship. Visit *www.valpo.edu/law/admissions/financialaid/summerpublicinterestscholarship/*. Furthermore, Valpo Law has a Loan Repayment Assistance program. This program is designed to offer financial assistance to graduates who have chosen to go into public service employment, and who have accumulated substantial debt from educational loans. Grants range from $1,000 to $6,000 each year. This program is available to alumni who have graduated within three years from the law school.

Academic Success Program—The Academic Success Program is available to students who seek assistance with the transition from college or the work-force to law school.

■ Career Planning

Our service mission is to assist all students and graduates in planning career paths, preparing for the job market, and identifying or creating professional opportunities, and to work closely with employers in developing career-related networks for all our law students. Eighty-seven percent of our graduates are employed within nine months of graduation, and our bar passage rate averages 88 percent.

Our programs help you identify, define, and verbalize your goals; build the confidence to overcome obstacles; and articulate your skills and accomplishments.

■ Faculty

Our professors have been Fulbright scholars, clerks to federal appellate and state supreme court judges, and have served in government. They bring to their teaching practical experience in public and private sectors. Their scholarship interests span a broad range. Professors practice an open-door policy and each student is paired with a faculty advisor in the first year. Visit *www.valpo.edu/law/academics/faculty/program/*.

■ Library and Physical Facilities

The law library is the largest legal research facility in northwest Indiana. Individual and group study carrels are available for student use. A computer lab provides facilities for word processing and Web access, and offers access to LexisNexis, Westlaw, CALI, FolioViews, LOIS, and Dialog. Wired and wireless network ports are available for students' use throughout the campus. Wireless printing is also available. The School of Law occupies two buildings that house classrooms, the law library, a state-of-the-art courtroom and a jury room, the law clinic, and administration and faculty offices.

■ Student Activities

The *Valparaiso University Law Review* is a scholarly journal published three times a year. Because of Valpo's emphasis on legal writing, membership on the *Law Review* is based upon academic achievement as well as a writing submission.

Students interested in enhancing their advocacy skills may try out for the client counseling, mock trial, negotiation teams, and Moot Court Society (a program that provides the opportunity for study in persuasive writing and oral arguments at the appellate level).

Valpo Law has over 25 student organizations. Just as the students represent a wide cross section of society, so too do the organizations on campus. Visit *www.valpo.edu/law/studentlife/studentorganizations/*.

■ Student Body Profile

Our first-year student body is ethnically and religiously diverse, averaging a composition of students from 130 different colleges and universities, 35 states, and 5 foreign countries. The average age is 25, with an age range from 21 to 54.

■ Expenses and Financial Aid

Approximately 65 percent of the student body received merit scholarships or need-based grants. The School of Law awards approximately $3 million annually in financial aid. In addition, 90 percent of all law students received assistance through loan programs. Valparaiso also offers a Public Interest Loan Repayment Assistance Program and a Summer Public Interest Scholarship.

Applicant Profile

We seek highly motivated and talented individuals, therefore, LSAT scores and GPAs alone do not guarantee admission or denial.

Vanderbilt University Law School

131 21st Avenue South
Nashville, TN 37203
Phone: 615.322.6452; Fax: 615.322.1531
E-mail: admissions@law.vanderbilt.edu; Website: www.law.vanderbilt.edu

The Basics

Type of school	Private
Term	Semester
Application deadline	3/15
Application fee	$50
Financial aid deadline	2/15
Can first year start other than fall?	No
Student to faculty ratio	15.0 to 1
Does the university offer:	
housing restricted to law students?	Yes
graduate housing for which law students are eligible?	Yes

Faculty and Administrators

	Total Fall	Total Spr	Men Fall	Men Spr	Women Fall	Women Spr	Minorities Fall	Minorities Spr
Full-time	36	34	23	24	13	10	8	5
Other Full-time	2	2	2	1	0	1	0	1
Deans, librarians, & others who teach	10	10	7	7	3	3	0	0
Part-time	31	43	15	26	16	17	6	6
Total	**79**	**89**	**47**	**58**	**32**	**31**	**14**	**12**

Curriculum

	Full-time	Part-time
Typical first-year section size	95	0
Is there typically a "small section" of the first-year class, other than Legal Writing, taught by full-time faculty	Yes	No
If yes, typical size offered last year	50	
# of classroom course titles beyond first-year curriculum	122	
# of upper division courses, excluding seminars with an enrollment: Under 25	71	
25–49	34	
50–74	18	
75–99	4	
100+	4	
# of seminars	18	
# of seminar positions available	288	
# of seminar positions filled	240	0
# of positions available in simulation courses	162	
# of simulation positions filled	162	0
# of positions available in faculty supervised clinical courses	79	
# of faculty supervised clinical positions filled	79	0
# involved in field placements	108	0
# involved in law journals	194	0
# involved in interschool competitions	210	0
# of credit hours required to graduate	88	

JD Enrollment and Ethnicity

	Men #	Men %	Women #	Women %	Full-time #	Full-time %	Part-time #	Part-time %	1st-year #	1st-year %	Total #	Total %	JD Degs. Awd.
African Amer.	15	4.4	36	12.5	51	8.1	0	0.0	16	8.4	51	8.1	27
Amer. Indian	3	0.9	2	0.7	5	0.8	0	0.0	1	0.5	5	0.8	0
Asian Amer.	21	6.1	20	6.9	41	6.5	0	0.0	8	4.2	41	6.5	5
Mex. Amer.	0	0.0	0	0.0	0	0.0	0	0.0	0	0.0	0	0.0	0
Puerto Rican	0	0.0	0	0.0	0	0.0	0	0.0	0	0.0	0	0.0	0
Hispanic	12	3.5	6	2.1	18	2.9	0	0.0	5	2.6	18	2.9	9
Total Minority	51	14.9	64	22.2	115	18.3	0	0.0	30	15.8	115	18.2	41
For. Nation.	11	3.2	6	2.1	17	2.7	0	0.0	4	2.1	17	2.7	5
Caucasian	229	66.8	194	67.4	422	67.0	1	100.0	120	63.2	423	67.0	154
Unknown	52	15.2	24	8.3	76	12.1	0	0.0	36	18.9	76	12.0	2
Total	343	54.4	288	45.6	630	99.8	1	0.2	190	30.1	631		202

Transfers

Transfers in	24
Transfers out	6

Tuition and Fees

	Resident	Nonresident
Full-time	$36,322	$36,322
Part-time	$0	$0

Living Expenses

Estimated living expenses for singles

Living on campus	Living off campus	Living at home
$20,350	$20,350	$20,350

Vanderbilt University Law School

ABA
Approved
Since
1925

GPA and LSAT Scores

	Total	Full-time	Part-time
# of apps	3,640	3,640	0
# of offers	921	921	0
# of matrics	190	190	0
75% GPA	3.88	3.88	0.00
Median GPA	3.70	3.70	0.00
25% GPA	3.49	3.49	0.00
75% LSAT	167	167	0
Median LSAT	166	166	0
25% LSAT	164	164	0

Grants and Scholarships (from prior year)

	Total		Full-time		Part-time	
	#	%	#	%	#	%
Total # of students	627		626		1	
Total # receiving grants	395	63.0	395	63.1	0	0.0
Less than 1/2 tuition	239	38.1	239	38.2	0	0.0
Half to full tuition	143	22.8	143	22.8	0	0.0
Full tuition	2	0.3	2	0.3	0	0.0
More than full tuition	11	1.8	11	1.8	0	0.0
Median grant amount			$15,000		$0	

Informational and Library Resources

# of volumes and volume equivalents	600,865
# of titles	155,517
# of active serial subscriptions	6,956
Study seating capacity inside the library	301
# of full-time professional librarians	6
Hours per week library is open	111
# of open, wired connections available to students	405
# of networked computers available for use by students	61
# of simultaneous wireless users	1,000
Require computer?	No

JD Attrition (from prior year)

	Academic	Other	Total	
	#	#	#	%
1st year	0	7	7	3.5
2nd year	0	5	5	2.2
3rd year	0	0	0	0.0
4th year	0	0	0	0.0

Employment (9 months after graduation)

	Total	Percentage
Employment status known	200	100.0
Employment status unknown	0	0.0
Employed	183	91.5
Pursuing graduate degrees	8	4.0
Unemployed seeking employment	2	1.0
Unemployed not seeking employment	7	3.5
Unemployed and studying for the bar	0	0.0

Type of Employment

# employed in law firms	140	76.5
# employed in business and industry	11	6.0
# employed in government	8	4.4
# employed in public interest	2	1.1
# employed as judicial clerks	20	10.9
# employed in academia	1	0.5

Geographic Location

# employed in state	48	26.2
# employed in foreign countries	0	0.0
# of states where employed	31	

Bar Passage Rates

Jurisdiction		Tennessee			Georgia		
Exam		Sum 05	Win 06	Total	Sum 05	Win 06	Total
# from school taking bar for the first time		42	0	42	27	3	30
School's pass rate for all first-time takers		88%		88%	78%	100%	80%
State's pass rate for all first-time takers		81%	76%	80%	86%	79%	84%

Vanderbilt University Law School

131 21st Avenue South
Nashville, TN 37203
Phone: 615.322.6452; Fax: 615.322.1531
E-mail: admissions@law.vanderbilt.edu; Website: www.law.vanderbilt.edu

■ Welcome to a New Way of Thinking

Vanderbilt is recognized among the nation's leading law schools for its faculty of renowned scholars, its talented students drawn from across the nation and around the world, and its rigorous curriculum with an array of joint-degree, specialized, and interdisciplinary programs. Building on this tradition of excellence, Vanderbilt has established itself as a leader in designing innovative programs that connect outstanding theoretical training to real-world information and experiences relevant to twenty-first century law practice. A legal education that translates the best scholarly research into effective lawyering provides immediate advantages to Vanderbilt graduates.

With about 200 students in each entering class, Vanderbilt fosters a tradition of challenging intellectual inquiry in an atmosphere of mutual respect. This small-school sense of collegiality combined with an accessible and distinguished faculty creates an exceptional environment for law studies and professional development. With state-of-the-art facilities situated on a beautiful and vibrant university campus in a sophisticated, friendly, and livable city, Vanderbilt offers a first-rate legal education in a setting that promotes a great quality of life.

■ Faculty

Widely respected for the quality of both their scholarship and their teaching, Vanderbilt professors have open doors for students. The faculty includes leading experts in an array of fields, including corporate and business law, constitutional law, litigation, torts, criminal law, international law, law and human behavior, dispute resolution, and intellectual property. Professors draw on their cutting-edge research to create engaging and valuable classroom experiences and extend their availability to students well beyond class times.

■ Curriculum

An outstanding foundational curriculum reinforced by innovative and interdisciplinary approaches to advanced training are the hallmarks of a Vanderbilt legal education. First-year requirements provide the intellectual foundation on which to build a legal education tailored to individual needs and interests in the second and third years. Upper-level courses are almost entirely electives, allowing students to choose what they wish from a broad curriculum, combining courses, clinics, externships, independent studies, and courses outside the law school to meet their individual goals.

Vanderbilt is a leader in designing innovative programs that connect rigorous intellectual training to practice-based information and experiences. The Law and Business Program is designed to produce lawyers who understand how complex corporate finance and regulatory environments affect businesses and their managers. The Cecil D. Branstetter Litigation and Dispute Resolution Program is directed at translating scholarly research on litigation and court systems to practice-based skills and strategies that litigators use to settle disputes. The International Legal Studies Program offers advanced coursework in international law and a unique

International Law Practice Lab in which students undertake specific projects for real-world clients such as the Iraqi Special Tribunal and the International Criminal Court. The faculty takes similar approaches to designing programs in constitutional law and theory, law and human behavior, environmental law, regulatory law, technology and entertainment law, and social justice.

■ Special Programs, Clinics, Study Abroad, and Joint Degrees

The law and economics movement has been the most important innovation in legal scholarship over the past quarter century, and Vanderbilt's PhD in Law and Economics provides the next generation of training in this field: a combination of professional and academic degrees that will train scholars for academic positions, law practice, policymaking, and public interest work. Students will either have a JD upon entry to the PhD program, or will work on the requirements for both the PhD and the JD concurrently.

Other special programs include the First Amendment Center, where journalists and legal scholars promote understanding of First Amendment values, and the Vanderbilt Institute for Public Policy Studies, which offers faculty and students throughout the university a place to collaborate on issues ranging from health care policy to international trade.

The Law School's clinical programs provide opportunities to earn academic credit while serving the public in real practice settings. Clinical offerings include civil law, criminal law, intellectual property, domestic violence, juvenile justice, community and economic development, small business, and international law practice. Students also gain experience and earn academic credit as externs in nonprofits and government agencies in Nashville and around the nation through the Law School's Legal Aid Society and Public Interest Stipend Fund.

Vanderbilt in Venice allows students to study abroad in the rich cultural center of Venice, Italy. Taught by Vanderbilt Law and University of Venice faculty, the academic program covers topics in international law with intensive classwork augmented by outside resources and experiences.

Joint-degree programs make it possible to combine the JD with an MBA, MD, MDiv, MTS, MPP, MA, or PhD in conjunction with the university's various graduate and professional schools. The law school also offers an LLM program for international lawyers and the LLM/MA in Latin American Studies.

■ Law School Building and Library

Recently renovated and expanded, the Law School facilities are among the best designed in the nation. Situated on a park-like campus that is designated a national arboretum, the building is designed for twenty-first century legal studies and research with wireless connectivity, state-of-the-art classrooms and a trial courtroom, and on-site and remote access to a host of electronic resources. The law library provides a variety of comfortable study spaces, including two reading rooms and nearly 200 carrels. The service-oriented library staff oversees a collection of over 565,000 volumes and more than 250 electronic databases; and all other Vanderbilt libraries, containing more than 2.3 million volumes, are also available to law students.

■ Student Life and Law School Environs

One of the reasons that students choose Vanderbilt is the congenial, collaborative atmosphere on campus. Spirited competition in an atmosphere of mutual respect creates an intellectual vibrancy and a sense of community that are rare. The activities of more than 40 student organizations are enhanced by Hyatt Fund financial support for student-initiated events including speakers, symposia, and conferences. Three journals—the *Vanderbilt Law Review*, the *Vanderbilt Journal of Entertainment and Technology Law*, and the *Vanderbilt Journal of Transnational Law*—provide opportunities to strengthen legal research and writing skills.

In the natural beauty of Tennessee, Vanderbilt's hometown has emerged as a vibrant and progressive city that offers numerous professional opportunities, wide-ranging cultural and recreational options, and a great quality of life. Among the nation's most livable cities, Nashville is the state capital with a metropolitan-area population of 1.3 million, and Vanderbilt is ideally situated in this major center for legal activity, allowing law students an array of opportunities in law firms, state and federal courts and government, public agencies, nonprofits, and corporations.

■ Career Services

Vanderbilt Law graduates are in high demand throughout the US and abroad for their outstanding legal training. Each fall, employers representing approximately 550 law offices in 40 states, the District of Columbia, and cities like London, Beijing, Shanghai, and Tokyo come to the law school to interview students, and more than 800 employers solicit students' résumés throughout the year. A growing number of public service and government employers recruit on campus, and about 5 to 7 percent of recent graduates have chosen work in this sector. The faculty takes an active role with students interested in judicial clerkships, and recent graduates have accepted clerkships in each of the US Courts of Appeal and the Supreme Court of the United States. About 80 percent of recent graduates chose employment out-of-state, with the most popular destinations including Georgia, New York, DC, Texas, California, and Illinois. In all, Vanderbilt Law's 7,500 living alumni cover 49 states, DC, 3 US territories, and 27 foreign nations.

■ Financial Aid and Loan Repayment Assistance

Vanderbilt provides generous financial assistance through need- and merit-based scholarships and educational loans. All admitted applicants are considered for merit scholarships, and several Law Scholar Merit Awards of full tuition plus stipend are given each year through a supplemental application process. Vanderbilt's Loan Repayment Assistance Program provides financial support to graduates who choose to practice law in low-paying public service organizations upon graduation.

Applicant Profile

Admission to Vanderbilt is competitive, and our selection process reflects our belief that the quality of the educational environment at the law school benefits from considering a range of information about each prospective student that is far broader than GPA and LSAT. Each file is reviewed in its entirety for indicators of academic excellence, intellectual curiosity, hard work, interest in others' welfare, obstacles overcome, professionalism, and other characteristics of successful law students. We believe that talented students with a mix of backgrounds, perspectives, and aspirations promote a vibrant and civil teaching and learning environment and that full file review in the admission process is central to that objective. Vanderbilt does not provide a two-factor profile grid to describe its multifactored selection process in which admission decisions are based on experienced judgment applied to individual cases.

Vermont Law School

Chelsea Street, PO Box 96
South Royalton, VT 05068
Phone: 888.277.5985 (toll-free) or 802.831.1239; Fax: 802.763.7071
E-mail: admiss@vermontlaw.edu; Website: www.vermontlaw.edu

ABA
Approved
Since
1975

The Basics

Type of school	Private
Term	Semester
Application deadline	3/1
Application fee	$60
Financial aid deadline	3/1
Can first year start other than fall?	No
Student to faculty ratio	12.8 to 1
Does the university offer:	
housing restricted to law students?	No
graduate housing for which law students are eligible?	No

Faculty and Administrators

	Total Fall	Total Spr	Men Fall	Men Spr	Women Fall	Women Spr	Minorities Fall	Minorities Spr
Full-time	40	36	24	20	16	16	5	4
Other Full-time	4	3	4	3	0	0	0	0
Deans, librarians, & others who teach	9	9	2	2	7	7	1	1
Part-time	12	26	7	19	5	7	0	1
Total	**65**	**74**	**37**	**44**	**28**	**30**	**6**	**6**

Curriculum

	Full-time	Part-time
Typical first-year section size	65	0
Is there typically a "small section" of the first-year class, other than Legal Writing, taught by full-time faculty	Yes	No
If yes, typical size offered last year	35	
# of classroom course titles beyond first-year curriculum	118	
# of upper division courses, excluding seminars with an enrollment: Under 25	88	
25–49	30	
50–74	14	
75–99	2	
100+	0	
# of seminars	19	
# of seminar positions available	324	
# of seminar positions filled	253	0
# of positions available in simulation courses	262	
# of simulation positions filled	225	0
# of positions available in faculty supervised clinical courses	52	
# of faculty supervised clinical positions filled	39	0
# involved in field placements	167	0
# involved in law journals	89	0
# involved in interschool competitions	31	0
# of credit hours required to graduate	87	

JD Enrollment and Ethnicity

	Men #	Men %	Women #	Women %	Full-time #	Full-time %	Part-time #	Part-time %	1st-year #	1st-year %	Total #	Total %	JD Degs. Awd.
African Amer.	18	6.8	21	7.3	39	7.1	0	0.0	20	10.0	39	7.1	16
Amer. Indian	4	1.5	4	1.4	8	1.4	0	0.0	4	2.0	8	1.4	2
Asian Amer.	6	2.3	9	3.1	15	2.7	0	0.0	5	2.5	15	2.7	3
Mex. Amer.	0	0.0	1	0.3	1	0.2	0	0.0	1	0.5	1	0.2	1
Puerto Rican	1	0.4	0	0.0	1	0.2	0	0.0	1	0.5	1	0.2	0
Hispanic	6	2.3	9	3.1	15	2.7	0	0.0	2	1.0	15	2.7	8
Total Minority	35	13.3	44	15.3	79	14.3	0	0.0	33	16.5	79	14.3	30
For. Nation.	2	0.8	2	0.7	4	0.7	0	0.0	3	1.5	4	0.7	0
Caucasian	202	76.5	220	76.4	422	76.4	0	0.0	146	73.0	422	76.4	137
Unknown	25	9.5	22	7.6	47	8.5	0	0.0	18	9.0	47	8.5	8
Total	264	47.8	288	52.2	552	100.0	0	0.0	200	36.2	552		175

Transfers

Transfers in	4
Transfers out	17

Tuition and Fees

	Resident	Nonresident
Full-time	$29,955	$29,955
Part-time	$0	$0

Living Expenses

Estimated living expenses for singles		
Living on campus	Living off campus	Living at home
N/A	$16,792	N/A

Vermont Law School

GPA and LSAT Scores

	Total	Full-time	Part-time
# of apps	1,119	1,119	0
# of offers	632	632	0
# of matrics	202	202	0
75% GPA	3.51	3.51	0.00
Median GPA	3.27	3.27	0.00
25% GPA	2.97	2.97	0.00
75% LSAT	157	157	0
Median LSAT	154	154	0
25% LSAT	149	149	0

Grants and Scholarships (from prior year)

	Total		Full-time		Part-time	
	#	%	#	%	#	%
Total # of students	564		562		2	
Total # receiving grants	331	58.7	331	58.9	0	0.0
Less than 1/2 tuition	301	53.4	301	53.6	0	0.0
Half to full tuition	29	5.1	29	5.2	0	0.0
Full tuition	1	0.2	1	0.2	0	0.0
More than full tuition	0	0.0	0	0.0	0	0.0
Median grant amount			$6,000		$0	

Informational and Library Resources

# of volumes and volume equivalents	245,105
# of titles	47,573
# of active serial subscriptions	1,856
Study seating capacity inside the library	382
# of full-time professional librarians	6
Hours per week library is open	110
# of open, wired connections available to students	110
# of networked computers available for use by students	108
# of simultaneous wireless users	400
Require computer?	No

JD Attrition (from prior year)

	Academic	Other	Total	
	#	#	#	%
1st year	0	23	23	11.9
2nd year	2	0	2	1.0
3rd year	0	0	0	0.0
4th year	0	0	0	0.0

Employment (9 months after graduation)

	Total	Percentage
Employment status known	168	100.0
Employment status unknown	0	0.0
Employed	135	80.4
Pursuing graduate degrees	17	10.1
Unemployed seeking employment	3	1.8
Unemployed not seeking employment	13	7.7
Unemployed and studying for the bar	0	0.0

Type of Employment

# employed in law firms	47	34.8
# employed in business and industry	35	25.9
# employed in government	19	14.1
# employed in public interest	13	9.6
# employed as judicial clerks	17	12.6
# employed in academia	2	1.5

Geographic Location

# employed in state	30	22.2
# employed in foreign countries	2	1.5
# of states where employed		38

Bar Passage Rates

Jurisdiction	Vermont		
Exam	Sum 05	Win 06	Total
# from school taking bar for the first time	35	3	38
School's pass rate for all first-time takers	66%	67%	66%
State's pass rate for all first-time takers	75%	76%	75%

Vermont Law School

Chelsea Street, PO Box 96
South Royalton, VT 05068
Phone: 888.277.5985 (toll-free) or 802.831.1239; Fax: 802.763.7071
E-mail: admiss@vermontlaw.edu; Website: www.vermontlaw.edu

■ Introduction

Five features distinguish legal education at Vermont Law School—a core JD curriculum that emphasizes the broader social context of the law in addition to focusing on legal doctrine and analysis; clinical/experiential programs that complement traditional classroom instruction; the internationally recognized Environmental Law programs; the informal atmosphere of a beautiful rural setting; and a real sense of community and commitment to public service.

Situated in a National Register Historic District along Vermont's scenic White River, the school's 13-acre campus is an integrated complex of renovated turn-of-the-century buildings, a new computer center, and a modern library and community center. A 25,000-square-foot classroom building was completed in summer 1998. Nearby Dartmouth College complements the Law School's social and cultural offerings. Ample housing is available in the area, and the Law School maintains an extensive landlord list.

■ Enrollment/Student Body

Vermont Law School is one of the most geographically diverse law schools in the country. Students bring a remarkable range of experience and backgrounds. Their ages range from 20 to over 50 years, with the average being 27.

Organizations that further support Vermont Law School's commitment to diversity include the Lesbian, Gay, Bisexual, Transgender, and Straight Alliance; Asian Pacific American Law Students Association; Black Law Students Association; Jewish Students Group; National Latino Law Students Association; Native American Law Society; and Women's Law Group.

■ Library and Technology

Opened in 1991, the 33,000-square-foot Cornell Library houses all primary sources needed for student research and features an exceptionally fine environmental law collection. It also serves as a selective depository for United States government documents. The library catalog is online and accessible from all computers on the network. Vermont Law School has a fully networked computer environment with Web-accessed e-mail. Six classrooms contain electronic teaching stations. All classrooms have easily accessible power outlets and the entire campus has wireless Internet access.

■ Curriculum

The curriculum prepares graduates to practice law in all 50 states. A wide variety of clinical programs, electives, seminars, and opportunities for supervised independent research are important adjuncts to a strong core curriculum.

Environmental Law Center—Vermont Law School's Environmental Law Center is recognized internationally as a preeminent center for the study of environmental law and policy. The Environmental Law Center offers one-year programs leading to either the Master of Studies (MSEL) or Master of Laws (LLM) in Environmental Law degree based upon a multidisciplinary curriculum of law, science, policy, and economics. The center offers over 50 environmental courses and an **Environmental Semester in Washington, DC**, and sponsors conferences and research. Through the **Environmental and Natural Resources Law Clinic**, students work on significant environmental law and policy issues and learn from some of the best environmental lawyers in the country and around the world. The **Environmental Tax Policy Institute** analyzes the ways in which the tax system can be used to address environmental concerns. The **Vermont Institute for Energy and the Environment** offers an advanced curriculum on energy and regulatory law, and provides forums and conferences for professional education and issue development. The **Land Use Institute** systematically addresses the legal and planning aspects of current land use issues.

Experiential Programs—The **Semester in Practice Program** allows students to participate in a full-credit, supervised clinical program in a legal environment outside the law school. Students currently work throughout the country, including New York, Boston, and Washington, DC. In the **Legislation Clinic**, students work under the direction of a legislative committee chair on research and draft projects directly related to legislation pending before the Vermont General Assembly. Students working with the **South Royalton Legal Clinic** develop legal skills while providing legal assistance to low-income clients. **Mediation Field Work** introduces students to nonlitigious approaches to dispute resolution, such as arbitration, mediation, and negotiation. **Judicial Externships** provide field-based experience in a judge's chambers for an entire semester. Through the **Law School Exchange Program**, students may spend a semester at one of eight participating law schools across the US, McGill University (Canada), Trento University (Italy), and University of Paris 13 (France). The **General Practice Program** has classes structured to operate as a law firm with professors in the role of senior partners.

Joint- and Dual-degree Programs—The joint **JD/MSEL** program can be completed in three years. The joint **JD/MEM** program, in collaboration with the Yale University School of Forestry and Environmental Studies, is a four-year program. The **JD/French Masters II** dual-degree program allows participants to earn in four years both a JD degree from Vermont Law School and an advanced level Master's Degree in Business Organization Law from the University of Cergy-Pontoise. Graduates may sit for the bar examination in each country, according to each country's requirements. Because of European Union reciprocity rules, successful bar candidates in France may practice in all member states of the European Union.

Summer Session—The Summer Session creates a unique atmosphere for learning that reflects the values of Vermont Law School and its Environmental Law Center. Faculty and staff are accessible and the atmosphere is informal. Most summer classes have an enrollment of fewer than 30 students, encouraging discussion and participation. Participants acquire a working knowledge of the law and science on which environmental policy is based, and explore cutting-edge environmental issues with leading national experts in a collaborative environment. Students attending the summer session include Vermont Law School JD, LLM, and MSEL students, JD students from other law schools, nonlaw graduate students, teachers, citizen advocates, practicing attorneys, planners, and state and federal agency personnel. The program offers intensive two-week, three-week, and eight-week courses. Both two-credit and three-credit courses are offered.

■ Admission

The school seeks candidates who will bring diverse perspectives and talents to the Law School community and the community at large. Successful applicants demonstrate substantial ability, motivation, life experience, and unique personal attributes. Two of the more important admission criteria are the academic record and application personal statements. Multiple LSAT scores are averaged. The school responds favorably to community and college involvement and work experience, and is committed to attracting people traditionally underrepresented in the legal profession.

■ Student Activities

A community-oriented and active student body supports more than 30 official organizations, including *Vermont Law Review* and *Vermont Journal of Environmental Law*. Student organizations and the Law School sponsor a full range of social, cultural, and academic events. Students also field several athletic teams.

■ Expenses and Financial Aid

Combinations of merit scholarships, loans, tuition grants, and work-study employment are used to meet demonstrated financial need. About 90 percent of the student body receives some form of assistance, and about 40–45 percent receive VLS grant aid. The Vermont Law School Loan Repayment Assistance Program aids graduates entering lower-paying public interest positions to repay educational debts.

■ Career Services

The Career Services office is directed by an attorney and provides a broad range of counseling and placement services. The school aggressively pursues employment opportunities nationwide, and graduates work in a full range of legal and nonlegal positions throughout the US. A Cooperative Legal Education program facilitates the transition from academics to legal practice.

Graduates work in all regions of the country, sitting for bar exams in over 30 states. Each year, over 90 percent either hold full-time positions or are enrolled in academic programs within six months of graduation.

Applicant Profile

Vermont Law School
This grid includes only applicants who earned 120–180 LSAT scores under standard administrations.

LSAT Score	3.75 +		3.50–3.74		3.25–3.49		3.00–3.24		2.75–2.99		2.50–2.74		Below 2.50		No GPA		Total	
	Apps	Adm	Apps	Adm	Apps	Adm	Apps	Adm	Apps	Adm	Apps	Adm	Apps	Adm	Apps	Adm	Apps	Adm
170–180	1	1	4	4	2	2	1	1	0	0	0	0	0	0	1	1	9	9
165–169	4	4	12	10	3	2	4	4	0	0	1	1	1	1	0	0	25	22
160–164	16	14	19	19	20	19	11	8	14	14	4	3	5	4	2	1	223	204
155–159	16	13	51	47	64	62	39	37	25	22	17	16	11	7	3	1	317	177
150–154	27	23	52	38	74	48	66	39	48	13	22	8	25	7	4	1	266	67
145–149	18	5	48	20	53	16	55	14	41	5	20	5	27	1	0	0	121	25
140–144	4	1	13	4	16	4	30	7	29	1	17	5	12	3	7	1	68	9
Below 140	1	0	4	1	7	1	11	1	14	3	13	1	11	1				
Total	87	61	203	143	239	154	217	111	171	58	94	39	92	24	17	5	1120	595

Apps = Number of Applicants
Adm = Number Admitted
Reflects 99% of the total applicant pool.

Vermont Law School does not use cutoff LSAT scores or GPAs.

Villanova University School of Law

299 North Spring Mill Road
Villanova, PA 19085
Phone: 610.519.7010; Fax: 610.519.6291
E-mail: admissions@law.villanova.edu; Website: www.law.villanova.edu

ABA
Approved
Since
1954

The Basics

Type of school	Private
Term	Semester
Application deadline	3/1
Application fee	$75
Financial aid deadline	
Can first year start other than fall?	No
Student to faculty ratio	17.5 to 1
Does the university offer:	
housing restricted to law students?	No
graduate housing for which law students are eligible?	No

Faculty and Administrators

	Total		Men		Women		Minorities	
	Fall	Spr	Fall	Spr	Fall	Spr	Fall	Spr
Full-time	35	35	22	23	13	12	4	3
Other Full-time	9	12	2	3	7	9	1	1
Deans, librarians, & others who teach	8	9	3	2	5	7	2	3
Part-time	43	53	30	37	13	16	4	3
Total	**95**	**109**	**57**	**65**	**38**	**44**	**11**	**10**

Curriculum

	Full-time	Part-time
Typical first-year section size	89	0
Is there typically a "small section" of the first-year class, other than Legal Writing, taught by full-time faculty	Yes	No
If yes, typical size offered last year	40	
# of classroom course titles beyond first-year curriculum		117
# of upper division courses, excluding seminars with an enrollment: Under 25		81
25–49		34
50–74		12
75–99		8
100+		8
# of seminars		17
# of seminar positions available		257
# of seminar positions filled	194	1
# of positions available in simulation courses		693
# of simulation positions filled	661	2
# of positions available in faculty supervised clinical courses		95
# of faculty supervised clinical positions filled	94	0
# involved in field placements	121	1
# involved in law journals	168	0
# involved in interschool competitions	50	0
# of credit hours required to graduate		88

JD Enrollment and Ethnicity

	Men		Women		Full-time		Part-time		1st-year		Total		JD Degs. Awd.
	#	%	#	%	#	%	#	%	#	%	#	%	
African Amer.	7	1.9	32	9.1	37	5.1	2	22.2	13	5.2	39	5.3	9
Amer. Indian	3	0.8	0	0.0	3	0.4	0	0.0	1	0.4	3	0.4	1
Asian Amer.	23	6.1	32	9.1	54	7.5	1	11.1	21	8.5	55	7.5	17
Mex. Amer.	0	0.0	0	0.0	0	0.0	0	0.0	0	0.0	0	0.0	0
Puerto Rican	0	0.0	0	0.0	0	0.0	0	0.0	0	0.0	0	0.0	0
Hispanic	14	3.7	15	4.3	29	4.0	0	0.0	11	4.4	29	4.0	16
Total Minority	47	12.5	79	22.4	123	17.1	3	33.3	46	18.5	126	17.3	43
For. Nation.	3	0.8	2	0.6	5	0.7	0	0.0	1	0.4	5	0.7	2
Caucasian	279	74.0	241	68.5	514	71.4	6	66.7	139	56.0	520	71.3	219
Unknown	48	12.7	30	8.5	78	10.8	0	0.0	62	25.0	78	10.7	0
Total	377	51.7	352	48.3	720	98.8	9	1.2	248	34.0	729		264

Transfers

Transfers in	11
Transfers out	17

Tuition and Fees

	Resident	Nonresident
Full-time	$29,340	$29,340
Part-time	$0	$0

Living Expenses

Estimated living expenses for singles

Living on campus	Living off campus	Living at home
N/A	$16,775	$6,910

Villanova University School of Law

*ABA
Approved
Since
1954*

GPA and LSAT Scores

	Total	Full-time	Part-time
# of apps	2,834	2,834	0
# of offers	1,022	1,022	0
# of matrics	248	248	0
75% GPA	3.62	3.62	0.00
Median GPA	3.44	3.44	0.00
25% GPA	3.27	3.27	0.00
75% LSAT	163	163	0
Median LSAT	162	162	0
25% LSAT	160	160	0

Grants and Scholarships (from prior year)

	Total		Full-time		Part-time	
	#	%	#	%	#	%
Total # of students	748		748		0	
Total # receiving grants	145	19.4	145	19.4	0	0.0
Less than 1/2 tuition	106	14.2	106	14.2	0	0.0
Half to full tuition	34	4.5	34	4.5	0	0.0
Full tuition	5	0.7	5	0.7	0	0.0
More than full tuition	0	0.0	0	0.0	0	0.0
Median grant amount			$6,705		$0	

Informational and Library Resources

# of volumes and volume equivalents	525,648
# of titles	146,622
# of active serial subscriptions	3,311
Study seating capacity inside the library	368
# of full-time professional librarians	10
Hours per week library is open	168
# of open, wired connections available to students	200
# of networked computers available for use by students	210
# of simultaneous wireless users	740
Require computer?	No

JD Attrition (from prior year)

	Academic	Other	Total	
	#	#	#	%
1st year	1	20	21	8.8
2nd year	1	0	1	0.4
3rd year	1	1	2	0.8
4th year	0	0	0	0.0

Employment (9 months after graduation)

	Total	Percentage
Employment status known	251	100.0
Employment status unknown	0	0.0
Employed	229	91.2
Pursuing graduate degrees	9	3.6
Unemployed seeking employment	8	3.2
Unemployed not seeking employment	5	2.0
Unemployed and studying for the bar	0	0.0

Type of Employment

	Total	Percentage
# employed in law firms	135	59.0
# employed in business and industry	31	13.5
# employed in government	20	8.7
# employed in public interest	2	0.9
# employed as judicial clerks	37	16.2
# employed in academia	2	0.9

Geographic Location

	Total	Percentage
# employed in state	152	66.4
# employed in foreign countries	0	0.0
# of states where employed		15

Bar Passage Rates

Jurisdiction	Pennsylvania		
Exam	Sum 05	Win 06	Total
# from school taking bar for the first time	176	12	188
School's pass rate for all first-time takers	83%	83%	83%
State's pass rate for all first-time takers	79%	75%	78%

Villanova University School of Law

299 North Spring Mill Road
Villanova, PA 19085
Phone: 610.519.7010; Fax: 610.519.6291
E-mail: admissions@law.villanova.edu; Website: www.law.villanova.edu

■ Introduction

Today, as never before, there is a need for law schools to teach far more than the letter of the law. They must give future lawyers a sense of the importance of their role in the larger society, and they must prepare lawyers to work in an environment of burgeoning technology with issues of global importance.

With its Catholic roots, Villanova offers a legal education designed to teach the rules of law and their application; to demonstrate how lawyers analyze legal issues and express arguments and conclusions; to inculcate the skills of the counselor, advocate, and decision maker; and to explore the ethical and moral dimensions of law practice and professional conduct. The school is also providing leadership in information technology, law and psychology, taxation, and international law, among other fields.

Few law schools are located in a more beautiful and tranquil environment. Adjacent to the university campus is Philadelphia's Main Line. The school is at the approximate midpoint of east coast legal centers in New York and Washington, and only 20 minutes by commuter rail from the center of Philadelphia.

Opened in 1953, the school is approved by the American Bar Association and is a member of the Association of American Law Schools. Students are graduates of well over 100 colleges and universities; many have significant work experience outside of the law. The atmosphere of the school is noted for its collegiality.

■ Faculty

While Villanova faculty members are recognized nationally and internationally for their legal scholarship and for their contributions to the study and practice of law, they are also deeply committed to teaching. The student-faculty ratio is 17 to 1.

■ Library and Physical Facilities

In the law library, students have access to approximately 130 computer workstations located in a state-of-the-art computer lab and throughout the library's stacks. Approximately 40 other computers are dedicated to student usage throughout the remainder of the law school. In addition, all students with laptops can access Villanova University's high-speed Internet connection and all of the technology resources throughout the law school via wired and wireless connections. Finally, the law library contains more than 525,000 volume-equivalents in books and microforms, along with subscriptions to numerous legal databases to which students have ready access.

The law school is currently constructing a new building and parking garage. The new building, approximately 174,000 square feet, will double the number of available classrooms and meet the sophisticated technology and design requirements of the law school community. The new structures are being built next to the current law school facility, so that students will continue to have easy access to all of the resources available on the Villanova University campus. The school expects construction to be completed by fall 2009.

■ Joint JD/MBA Program

The Villanova University School of Law and the Villanova School of Business offer a joint-degree program permitting simultaneous study for the Juris Doctor and the Master of Business Administration degrees. The Villanova School of Business is among a small group of business schools in the nation whose Master of Business Administration and Department of Accountancy program have been approved by the Association to Advance Collegiate Schools of Business.

In the program, credit is given for certain courses by both the School of Law and the School of Business. Through this program, degrees may be completed in less time than it would take to obtain them separately.

■ LLM in Taxation and JD/LLM

The interdisciplinary LLM program is conducted under the auspices of the School of Law and the Villanova School of Business. The program enriches the tax curriculum available to JD candidates, who are able to enroll in LLM courses. By participating in the joint JD/LLM program a law student can earn both a JD and an LLM in three and one-half years instead of the four years normally required for both degrees.

■ Special Programs

Beyond the skills of written and oral expression developed in the first-year writing program and the required upper-level moot court program, drafting, and seminar courses, Villanova students acquire the fundamental skills of the practicing lawyer—including counseling, negotiation, advocacy, mediation, dispute resolution, conciliation, and mature judgment. Hands-on clinical opportunities allow students to apply classroom experiences to real-world client representation, often while performing public service. Clinical programs include Federal Tax; Civil Justice; Asylum, Refugee, and Emigrant Services; and Farmworkers Legal Aid.

■ Student Activities

The *Villanova Law Review* is a scholarly journal prepared and edited by law students. Members are selected on the basis of academic rank or through an open writing competition.

The *Villanova Environmental Law Journal* publishes both student and outside articles dealing with environmental issues. Students are selected for membership by an open writing competition.

The *Villanova Sports and Entertainment Law Journal* contains articles prepared by practitioners and professors in sports and entertainment law as well as by students. Membership is earned by selection through an open writing competition.

Each year, second- and third-year students have the opportunity to practice lawyering skills through the Client Interviewing and Counseling Competition, the Reimel Moot Court Competition, and several outside moot court competitions.

Student organizations include Asian Pacific American Law Students, Black Law Students Association, Corporate Law Society, Criminal Law Society, Environmental and Energy Law Society, Gay/Straight Alliance, Health Law Society, Intellectual Property Society, International Law Society, Islamic Law

Forum, Jewish Law Students Association, Latin American Law Student Association, Justinian Society, Phi Delta Phi, Pro Bono Society, St. Thomas More Society, Sports and Entertainment Law Society, Student Animal Defense League, Tax Law Society, and Women's Caucus.

■ Career Strategy and Advancement

The mission of the Career Strategy and Advancement Office is to provide career planning education, recruitment programs, and individual counseling as the foundation for future career development and satisfaction of our students. Distinctive features and programs include three attorney-advisors, including a public service/pro bono specialist; an open-door policy, including a daily "on call" advisor for walk-ins and "quick questions"; small group workshops for 1Ls; dozens of career workshops and panel programs on topics ranging from interviews, résumés, and networking, to public interest careers, judicial clerkships, and a multitude of practice specialty areas; "Day in the Law," a program designed to expose 1Ls to the practice of law by matching them with a graduate for a day over winter break; recruitment programs throughout the year, including a diverse array of employers in private practice (large and small firms), government, nonprofits, the judiciary, and corporations; special recruitment programs designed to enhance diversity in the profession; job fairs targeting unique geographic or practice preferences; and job-search coaching for new graduates on the job market. Pro bono programs, such as "Lawyering Together" and other projects, provide students with the opportunity to serve the disadvantaged while developing skills and positive relationships with practicing attorneys.

Applicant Profile

Villanova has chosen not to provide prospective students with an admission profile based on individual undergraduate GPAs and LSAT scores. The Admissions Committee seeks to create a diverse community by adhering to a comprehensive evaluation of a candidate's file that includes academic performance as well as professional promise. Each candidate's background, interests, accomplishments, and goals are considered before a decision is made.

University of Virginia School of Law

580 Massie Road
Charlottesville, VA 22903-1789
Phone: 434.924.7351; Fax: 434.982.2128
E-mail: lawadmit@virginia.edu; Website: www.law.virginia.edu

ABA Approved Since 1923

The Basics

Type of school	Public
Term	Semester
Application deadline	3/1
Application fee	$70
Financial aid deadline	3/1
Can first year start other than fall?	No
Student to faculty ratio	13.9 to 1
Does the university offer:	
housing restricted to law students?	No
graduate housing for which law students are eligible?	Yes

Faculty and Administrators

	Total		Men		Women		Minorities	
	Fall	Spr	Fall	Spr	Fall	Spr	Fall	Spr
Full-time	70	66	51	50	19	16	7	5
Other Full-time	0	0	0	0	0	0	0	0
Deans, librarians, & others who teach	6	6	2	3	4	3	1	1
Part-time	74	88	65	76	9	12	0	2
Total	150	160	118	129	32	31	8	8

Curriculum

	Full-time	Part-time
Typical first-year section size	76	0
Is there typically a "small section" of the first-year class, other than Legal Writing, taught by full-time faculty	Yes	No
If yes, typical size offered last year	31	
# of classroom course titles beyond first-year curriculum	205	
# of upper division courses, excluding seminars with an enrollment: Under 25	86	
25–49	35	
50–74	27	
75–99	16	
100+	13	
# of seminars	85	
# of seminar positions available	1,335	
# of seminar positions filled	1,101	0
# of positions available in simulation courses	757	
# of simulation positions filled	679	0
# of positions available in faculty supervised clinical courses	48	
# of faculty supervised clinical positions filled	46	0
# involved in field placements	144	0
# involved in law journals	548	0
# involved in interschool competitions	118	0
# of credit hours required to graduate	86	

JD Enrollment and Ethnicity

	Men #	Men %	Women #	Women %	Full-time #	Full-time %	Part-time #	Part-time %	1st-year #	1st-year %	Total #	Total %	JD Degs. Awd.
African Amer.	33	4.7	65	14.4	98	8.6	0	0.0	38	10.2	98	8.6	24
Amer. Indian	3	0.4	5	1.1	8	0.7	0	0.0	5	1.3	8	0.7	3
Asian Amer.	42	6.0	30	6.7	72	6.3	0	0.0	24	6.4	72	6.3	36
Mex. Amer.	0	0.0	0	0.0	0	0.0	0	0.0	0	0.0	0	0.0	0
Puerto Rican	0	0.0	0	0.0	0	0.0	0	0.0	0	0.0	0	0.0	0
Hispanic	12	1.7	9	2.0	21	1.8	0	0.0	7	1.9	21	1.8	5
Total Minority	90	12.9	109	24.2	199	17.4	0	0.0	74	19.8	199	17.4	68
For. Nation.	6	0.9	0	0.0	6	0.5	0	0.0	4	1.1	6	0.5	0
Caucasian	439	63.2	270	59.9	709	61.9	0	0.0	212	56.8	709	61.9	238
Unknown	160	23.0	72	16.0	232	20.2	0	0.0	83	22.3	232	20.2	69
Total	695	60.6	451	39.4	1146	100.0	0	0.0	373	32.5	1146		375

Transfers

Transfers in	34
Transfers out	5

Tuition and Fees

	Resident	Nonresident
Full-time	$30,700	$35,700
Part-time	$0	$0

Living Expenses

Estimated living expenses for singles		
Living on campus	Living off campus	Living at home
$15,600	$15,600	$15,600

University of Virginia School of Law

ABA
Approved
Since
1923

GPA and LSAT Scores

	Total	Full-time	Part-time
# of apps	4,869	4,869	0
# of offers	1,225	1,225	0
# of matrics	375	375	0
75% GPA	3.82	3.82	0.00
Median GPA	3.68	3.68	0.00
25% GPA	3.49	3.49	0.00
75% LSAT	171	171	0
Median LSAT	169	169	0
25% LSAT	167	167	0

Grants and Scholarships (from prior year)

	Total		Full-time		Part-time	
	#	%	#	%	#	%
Total # of students	1,118		1,118		0	
Total # receiving grants	680	60.8	680	60.8	0	0.0
Less than 1/2 tuition	555	49.6	555	49.6	0	0.0
Half to full tuition	112	10.0	112	10.0	0	0.0
Full tuition	1	0.1	1	0.1	0	0.0
More than full tuition	12	1.1	12	1.1	0	0.0
Median grant amount			$12,000		$0	

Informational and Library Resources

# of volumes and volume equivalents	894,870
# of titles	279,834
# of active serial subscriptions	11,293
Study seating capacity inside the library	813
# of full-time professional librarians	12
Hours per week library is open	112
# of open, wired connections available to students	84
# of networked computers available for use by students	61
# of simultaneous wireless users	1,424
Require computer?	Yes

JD Attrition (from prior year)

	Academic	Other	Total	
	#	#	#	%
1st year	0	4	4	1.1
2nd year	0	10	10	2.7
3rd year	0	1	1	0.3
4th year	0	0	0	0.0

Employment (9 months after graduation)

	Total	Percentage
Employment status known	354	98.9
Employment status unknown	4	1.1
Employed	341	96.3
Pursuing graduate degrees	5	1.4
Unemployed seeking employment	0	0.0
Unemployed not seeking employment	8	2.3
Unemployed and studying for the bar	0	0.0
Type of Employment		
# employed in law firms	251	73.6
# employed in business and industry	5	1.5
# employed in government	17	5.0
# employed in public interest	10	2.9
# employed as judicial clerks	55	16.1
# employed in academia	0	0.0
Geographic Location		
# employed in state	40	11.7
# employed in foreign countries	8	2.3
# of states where employed	33	

Bar Passage Rates

Jurisdiction	New York			Virginia		
Exam	Sum 05	Win 06	Total	Sum 05	Win 06	Total
# from school taking bar for the first time	107	6	113	96	9	105
School's pass rate for all first-time takers	97%	83%	96%	93%	78%	91%
State's pass rate for all first-time takers	76%	61%	74%	76%	65%	74%

University of Virginia School of Law

Admissions Office, 580 Massie Road
Charlottesville, VA 22903-1789
Phone: 434.924.7351; Fax: 434.982.2128
E-mail: lawadmit@virginia.edu; Website: www.law.virginia.edu

■ Introduction

Founded in 1819, the University of Virginia School of Law is a world-renowned training ground for distinguished lawyers and public servants. As identified by *American Lawyer* magazine, Virginia is one of only two law schools in the country with graduates practicing in each of the nation's top 100 law firms. But the law school also is dedicated to upholding Thomas Jefferson's conviction that lawyers must serve the public interest and provides special career counseling and placement assistance, operates pro bono programs, and administers a loan assistance and forgiveness program.

At Virginia, law in its origins, impact, and implications is analyzed and debated in classes, workshops, lecture programs, student organizations, and faculty-student informal exchanges. Students are challenged to determine how and why the law developed in a certain way, whether it accomplishes its purpose, and how changes might affect social behavior. Faculty are fully committed to teaching, scholarship, and public service. They meet with and mentor students, explore ideas, and foster understanding. A third of the faculty hold advanced degrees in fields such as psychology, economics, philosophy, and history.

■ Curriculum and Degrees

Intellectual rigor, dynamic teaching, and rich diversity distinguish the Virginia curriculum. Each first-year student takes a first-semester class in a small section of 30 students. Other first-year classes range from 60 to 90 students. During the second semester, students choose five to seven hours of electives. In addition, the law school offers annually more than 200 different courses and seminars beyond the first-year curriculum.

The law school has strength in corporate and commercial law, rooted in exceptional faculty and enhanced by close relationships with the Darden Graduate Business School. The Law and Business program uniquely integrates business and legal analysis throughout a range of courses. Virginia's prominence in international law is built on a long tradition, with notable faculty in areas of immigration, human rights, environment, and constitutional law in other countries, as well as private and commercial law in a global community. Its reputation in legal and constitutional history stems from highly visible and influential faculty, many of whom hold doctorates in history. Environmental endeavors draw strength from the Center for Environmental Studies, the *Virginia Environmental Law Journal*, and opportunities for joint study and practice with others within and outside the university.

Students may enroll in several joint-degree programs. The JD-MBA program is a four-year program in conjunction with the Darden Graduate Business School. Other combined-degree programs include a JD-MA in bioethics, economics, English, government and foreign affairs, history, philosophy, or sociology; a JD-MS in accounting; a JD-MP in planning; and a JD-MPH in public health. In addition, students may combine a law degree from Virginia with the MPA from Princeton, MALD from the Fletcher School at Tufts, or the MA in International Relations and International Economics from Johns Hopkins.

■ Facilities

The Law Grounds, a complex of integrated buildings, offers an expansive and attractive setting reflecting Jefferson's position that an intellectual community in a beautiful environment fosters learning and personal growth. The library, with more than 882,000 volumes, is one of the largest law libraries in the country. But, more than a repository of books, the library is the law school's central research facility. Professional librarians provide research support for faculty, and assistance and training for students. The library is committed to a dynamic concept of information in which the traditional printed text is merely one of many learning tools. It is fully computerized and offers full LAN access, both wired and wireless, throughout the facility.

■ Admission

The Admission Committee believes that absolute standards based on a combination of LSAT score and GPA cannot be the only criteria for selection. Recognizing that the real meaning of GPA will vary with such factors as quality of the institution attended, rigor of courses selected, and degree of grade inflation, the committee considers an array of elements in addition to the essential LSAT and GPA, with a view toward assembling a diverse class while arriving at a fair appraisal of the individual applicant.

While the LSAT and GPA remain the primary determinants for admission, the committee takes other elements into account, including the maturing effect of some years away from formal education, trends in academic performance, employment history, significant personal achievement or unusual prior training, background, or ethnicity, which promises a contribution to the law school community. Successfully overcoming economic, social, or educational obstacles is viewed favorably.

The law school seeks to maintain a diverse student body in which the free exchange of ideas and viewpoints can flourish, creating a rich learning experience for all law school students. Therefore, the active recruitment of minority students is important to our admission process.

While individual interviews are not a part of the admission process, prospective students are encouraged to visit the School of Law. When classes are in session, student-led tours are available and classes are open to visitors. On most Friday afternoons throughout the summer and during the fall semester, the School of Law holds admission information sessions. Check our website at *www.law.virginia.edu/admissions* for details.

■ Financial Aid

The University of Virginia School of Law assists its students in financing their legal education through a variety of resources, including scholarship assistance; Title IV federally sponsored programs such as Stafford Student Loans, Perkins Loans, and College Work-study Funding; and private sector educational loans. Most scholarship assistance is awarded on a combined basis of academic merit and financial need. Some scholarships are awarded solely on merit. The Financial Aid Office works individually with students to develop realistic budgets that meet the costs of obtaining a legal education and to identify sources of financial support that will enable students to achieve their educational and professional goals.

Students who choose less financially lucrative positions in the public sector can benefit from a variety of financial assistance programs offered by Virginia. Summer fellowships are available for students who accept unpaid or low-paid summer internships with public sector employers. The Mortimer Caplin and Linda Fairstein Public Service Fellowships provide tuition assistance for the third year of law school as well as a living stipend for the first two years of a graduate's public sector legal practice. The Powell Fellowship in Legal Services awards $35,000 to a graduating student or judicial clerk to enable him or her to work under the sponsorship of a public interest organization to enhance the delivery of civil legal services to the poor. The law school also has a generous Loan Forgiveness Program available to graduates who choose qualifying employment.

■ Career Services

The law school boasts one of the most successful career services programs in legal education. An online job-search system gives students 24-hour, Web-based access to employment opportunities and employer information and provides the vehicle for interview sign-up and scheduling. Over 900 public and private sector law offices, from every region of the United States, annually conduct over 9,000 interviews with second- and third-year students. University of Virginia School of Law graduates are employed in all 50 states, the District of Columbia, and many foreign countries. In the 2006 graduating class, 60 students accepted a judicial clerkship with federal or state courts, and seven Virginia graduates earned clerkships with the Supreme Court of the United States during the 2005–2006 and 2006–2007 terms.

■ Student Life

The law school is continually enriched and diversified by student organizations, extracurricular activities, and community spirit. Intellectual challenges are complemented by cooperation and camaraderie, all integrated under Virginia's 164-year-old, student-run honor system. The array of opportunity includes nine academic journals, 65 interest-centered organizations, student governance, and social and athletic activities. The university and local community are large enough to offer something to meet anyone's interests and small enough to make active participation compatible with the rigors of an academic schedule.

Applicant Profile

The University of Virginia School of Law has elected not to provide an applicant profile based only on GPA and LSAT, as these numbers cannot be the sole criteria for selecting an entering class. Each applicant is assessed as an individual, taking into account not only LSAT scores and undergraduate grades, but also the strength of an applicant's undergraduate or graduate curriculum, trends in grades, the maturing effect of experiences since college, the nature and quality of any work experience, significant achievement in extracurricular activities, service in the military, contributions to campus or community through service and leadership, and personal qualities displayed.

Wake Forest University School of Law

PO Box 7206
Winston-Salem, NC 27109
Phone: 336.758.5437; Fax: 336.758.3930
E-mail: admissions@law.wfu.edu; Website: www.law.wfu.edu

ABA
Approved
Since
1936

The Basics

Type of school	Private
Term	Semester
Application deadline	3/1
Application fee	$60
Financial aid deadline	5/1
Can first year start other than fall?	No
Student to faculty ratio	10.5 to 1
Does the university offer:	
housing restricted to law students?	No
graduate housing for which law students are eligible?	No

Faculty and Administrators

	Total		Men		Women		Minorities	
	Fall	Spr	Fall	Spr	Fall	Spr	Fall	Spr
Full-time	38	39	23	24	15	15	5	2
Other Full-time	1	1	0	0	1	1	1	1
Deans, librarians, & others who teach	5	5	2	2	3	3	0	0
Part-time	17	13	14	10	3	3	0	0
Total	**61**	**58**	**39**	**36**	**22**	**22**	**6**	**3**

Curriculum

	Full-time	Part-time
Typical first-year section size	40	0
Is there typically a "small section" of the first-year class, other than Legal Writing, taught by full-time faculty	Yes	No
If yes, typical size offered last year	40	
# of classroom course titles beyond first-year curriculum		96
# of upper division courses, excluding seminars with an enrollment: Under 25		50
25–49		44
50–74		14
75–99		0
100+		0
# of seminars		26
# of seminar positions available		470
# of seminar positions filled	383	0
# of positions available in simulation courses		689
# of simulation positions filled	600	0
# of positions available in faculty supervised clinical courses		76
# of faculty supervised clinical positions filled	76	0
# involved in field placements	11	0
# involved in law journals	70	0
# involved in interschool competitions	36	0
# of credit hours required to graduate		89

JD Enrollment and Ethnicity

	Men		Women		Full-time		Part-time		1st-year		Total		JD Degs. Awd.
	#	%	#	%	#	%	#	%	#	%	#	%	
African Amer.	8	3.0	19	9.8	27	5.9	0	0.0	7	4.6	27	5.8	9
Amer. Indian	0	0.0	0	0.0	0	0.0	0	0.0	0	0.0	0	0.0	0
Asian Amer.	7	2.6	11	5.7	18	4.0	0	0.0	8	5.2	18	3.9	5
Mex. Amer.	0	0.0	0	0.0	0	0.0	0	0.0	0	0.0	0	0.0	0
Puerto Rican	0	0.0	0	0.0	0	0.0	0	0.0	0	0.0	0	0.0	0
Hispanic	12	4.4	6	3.1	18	4.0	0	0.0	5	3.3	18	3.9	9
Total Minority	27	10.0	36	18.7	63	13.9	0	0.0	20	13.1	63	13.6	23
For. Nation.	1	0.4	0	0.0	1	0.2	0	0.0	0	0.0	1	0.2	4
Caucasian	223	82.3	152	78.8	365	80.4	10	100.0	110	71.9	375	80.8	144
Unknown	20	7.4	5	2.6	25	5.5	0	0.0	23	15.0	25	5.4	0
Total	271	58.4	193	41.6	454	97.8	10	2.2	153	33.0	464		171

Transfers

Transfers in	13
Transfers out	5

Tuition and Fees

	Resident	Nonresident
Full-time	$29,500	$0
Part-time	$0	$0

Living Expenses

Estimated living expenses for singles

Living on campus	Living off campus	Living at home
N/A	$16,050	N/A

Wake Forest University School of Law

ABA
Approved
Since
1936

GPA and LSAT Scores

	Total	Full-time	Part-time
# of apps	2,142	2,142	0
# of offers	642	642	0
# of matrics	152	152	0
75% GPA	3.71	3.71	0.00
Median GPA	3.44	3.44	0.00
25% GPA	3.19	3.19	0.00
75% LSAT	165	165	0
Median LSAT	163	163	0
25% LSAT	161	161	0

Grants and Scholarships (from prior year)

	Total		Full-time		Part-time	
	#	%	#	%	#	%
Total # of students	488		468		20	
Total # receiving grants	207	42.4	207	44.2	0	0.0
Less than 1/2 tuition	73	15.0	73	15.6	0	0.0
Half to full tuition	51	10.5	51	10.9	0	0.0
Full tuition	67	13.7	67	14.3	0	0.0
More than full tuition	16	3.3	16	3.4	0	0.0
Median grant amount			$20,925		$0	

Informational and Library Resources

# of volumes and volume equivalents	436,139
# of titles	257,963
# of active serial subscriptions	5,230
Study seating capacity inside the library	593
# of full-time professional librarians	7
Hours per week library is open	108
# of open, wired connections available to students	110
# of networked computers available for use by students	59
# of simultaneous wireless users	1,600
Require computer?	Yes

JD Attrition (from prior year)

	Academic	Other	Total	
	#	#	#	%
1st year	0	4	4	2.6
2nd year	2	8	10	6.1
3rd year	0	2	2	1.2
4th year	0	0	0	0.0

Employment (9 months after graduation)

	Total	Percentage
Employment status known	149	98.0
Employment status unknown	3	2.0
Employed	142	95.3
Pursuing graduate degrees	3	2.0
Unemployed seeking employment	2	1.3
Unemployed not seeking employment	0	0.0
Unemployed and studying for the bar	2	1.3
Type of Employment		
# employed in law firms	92	64.8
# employed in business and industry	11	7.7
# employed in government	12	8.5
# employed in public interest	7	4.9
# employed as judicial clerks	18	12.7
# employed in academia	1	0.7
Geographic Location		
# employed in state	61	43.0
# employed in foreign countries	0	0.0
# of states where employed	27	

Bar Passage Rates

Jurisdiction	North Carolina		
Exam	Sum 05	Win 06	Total
# from school taking bar for the first time	74	7	81
School's pass rate for all first-time takers	93%	86%	93%
State's pass rate for all first-time takers	72%	69%	71%

The information on these pages was provided by the law school.

Wake Forest University School of Law

PO Box 7206
Winston-Salem, NC 27109
Phone: 336.758.5437; Fax: 336.758.3930
E-mail: admissions@law.wfu.edu; Website: www.law.wfu.edu

■ Introduction

Wake Forest University School of Law, established in 1894, is located in Winston-Salem, North Carolina. It is a member of the AALS and is ABA-approved. In 1998, the law school was awarded a chapter of the Order of the Coif, a national honorary society.

Wake Forest offers students a solid and personalized legal education. Class sizes are smaller than in virtually any other law school in the nation, with approximately 40 students in each first-year section and about 20 students in first-year legal writing sections.

Faculty members are nationally renowned teachers and scholars. The director of trial advocacy was awarded the Roscoe Pound Foundation's Richard S. Jacobson Award for Excellence in Teaching Trial Advocacy, and recently Wake Forest received the prestigious Emil Gumpert Award from the American College of Trial Lawyers for its outstanding trial advocacy program. Faculty chairs are held by six of the nation's most respected authorities in the areas of administrative law, commercial law, sports and entertainment law, constitutional law, torts and product liability, and health care law and policy.

Wake Forest law school embraces seven principal commitments: (1) to maintain a school of the right size that begins with a first-year class of approximately 160 students composed of four sections of about 40 students each; (2) to develop and retain a faculty strong in teaching, experience, and current scholarly writing; (3) to assure that students are taught substantive law and how to research through the maximum use of leading-edge technology; (4) to continue the school's emphasis on dispute resolution and litigation skills through instruction, competition, and clinical practice; (5) to build a bridge between law and management communities by an enhanced curriculum, the sharing of resources, and collaborative instruction; (6) to seek to provide career opportunities for our students and graduates that match their potential; and (7) to teach the transcendence of ethics and to inculcate in graduates the importance of doing good while doing well throughout their professional lives.

■ Admission

Requirements: Bachelor's degree from accredited college or university, application with dean's certification and academic recommendation, LSAT and LSDAS, application fee—$60, application deadline—March 1.

First-year students are admitted only in the fall semester for full-time study. The law school has a rolling admission policy. Completed files are individually reviewed to select a diverse group of students who are likely to succeed in law school and contribute to the legal profession. The LSAT and undergraduate GPA, as well as a number of subjective factors—including personal talents, work experience, community service, leadership potential, graduate study, and a history of overcoming social or economic hardship—indicating intellectual capacity, character, motivation, and maturity are considered. For multiple LSAT scores, the higher test score will be used.

A $300 nonrefundable deposit is due by April 15, and a tuition deposit must be paid by June 15. (Both fees are applicable toward tuition.) Personal interviews are not required; however, we encourage all applicants to visit the law school.

Transfer students meeting the admission requirements are accepted on a space-available basis after the successful completion of one year at an AALS or ABA-approved law school.

■ Expenses and Financial Aid

Tuition/fees—$29,500; estimated living expenses—$10,000-$15,000.

Merit, need-based, and diversity scholarships are available. The FAFSA is due April 1.

■ Clinical Programs

Two exceptional clinical programs allow students to gain hands-on legal experience. In the Litigation Clinic, students are placed in offices such as the US attorney's office, the district attorney's office, the public defender's office, legal aid, the National Labor Relations Board, private law firms, and corporate counsel. While receiving classroom instruction and skills training in interviewing, counseling, negotiation, and discovery, students represent clients under the supervision of an experienced attorney.

The Elder Law Clinic is an in-house clinic representing low- to moderate-income clients over the age of 60. Located at the Wake Forest University Baptist Medical Center, the clinic features a classroom component that is jointly taught by members of the law and medical school faculties. Students draft essential documents, such as wills, and handle administrative representation and state court litigation with a clinic professor/attorney.

■ Technology

Wake Forest prepares students to embrace the rapidly changing technological environment of the legal profession. Classrooms have been upgraded to multimedia theaters allowing technology to augment classroom teaching. Many professors routinely use webpages to distribute essential course information and provide online discussion forums outside of the classroom.

Each student is required to have a laptop. The law school wireless network gives students instant access to e-mail, essential legal research systems, the Internet, and a variety of other resources. A university-wide network allows students to register for courses, receive grades, obtain transcripts, and interact with university offices.

■ Joint-degree Programs

The law school offers a joint JD/MBA program with the Babcock Graduate School of Management. Admission and scholarship decisions are made independently at each school. The law school also offers an LLM in American Law for graduates of foreign law schools. A separate (LLM) application is required and may be obtained at *llm-admissions@law.wfu.edu* or by writing the director of the LLM program.

■ Foreign Study

Students in good standing may participate in a four-week program offered each summer at the Worrell House, the university's residential center near Regent's Park in London, England; at Casa Artom on the Grand Canal in Venice, Italy; and at the University of Vienna in Vienna, Austria. Students participating in this program can earn up to six hours of academic credit.

■ Career Services

The Career Services Office aggressively seeks opportunities for students in both summer and permanent legal positions. Knowledgeable staff members personally counsel students to assist them in developing solid career portfolios. The office also conducts workshops in résumé preparation, interviewing, and career planning. Faculty and staff expand career opportunities by visiting law firms, corporations, and agencies throughout the country to acquaint them with the exceptional Wake Forest program. A large number of employers interview students on campus each year or request that résumés be forwarded by the Career Services Office. Wake Forest law graduates are located throughout the country.

Applicant Profile

Wake Forest University School of Law
This grid includes only applicants who earned 120–180 LSAT scores under standard administrations.

LSAT Score	3.75 +		3.50–3.74		3.25–3.49		3.00–3.24		2.75–2.99		2.50–2.74		2.25–2.49		2.00–2.24		Below 2.00		No GPA		Total	
	Apps	Adm	Apps	Adm	Apps	Adm	Apps	Adm	Apps	Adm	Apps	Adm	Apps	Adm	Apps	Adm	Apps	Adm	Apps	Adm	Apps	Adm
175–180	0	0	1	0	0	0	0	0	0	0	1	0	0	0	0	0	0	0	0	0	2	0
170–174	11	11	5	4	4	4	10	8	3	3	5	0	4	1	0	0	0	0	0	0	42	31
165–169	35	33	37	35	43	39	28	25	24	14	13	1	2	0	0	0	0	0	1	0	183	147
160–164	143	82	198	117	181	105	127	58	51	12	25	2	7	0	2	0	0	0	1	0	735	376
155–159	97	11	164	15	141	10	88	8	34	4	13	0	8	1	2	0	0	0	2	0	549	49
150–154	47	4	68	6	87	7	79	3	27	4	19	0	7	0	3	0	0	0	0	0	337	24
145–149	10	1	32	2	36	2	31	2	24	1	8	1	8	1	2	0	1	0	1	0	153	10
140–144	7	0	17	0	16	0	19	0	17	0	12	0	5	0	3	0	1	0	1	0	98	0
135–139	1	0	2	0	7	0	10	0	5	0	5	0	3	0	3	0	3	0	1	0	40	0
130–134	0	0	1	0	1	0	2	0	3	0	2	0	0	0	1	0	0	0	0	0	10	0
125–129	0	0	1	0	0	0	1	0	0	0	0	0	1	0	0	0	1	0	0	0	4	0
120–124	0	0	0	0	0	0	0	0	0	0	0	0	0	0	0	0	0	0	0	0	0	0
Total	351	142	526	179	516	167	395	104	188	38	103	4	45	3	16	0	6	0	7	0	2153	637

Apps = Number of Applicants
Adm = Number Admitted
Reflects 99% of the total applicant pool.

Washburn University School of Law

1700 SW College Avenue
Topeka, KS 66621-1140
Phone: 800.WASHLAW or 800.927.4529; Fax: 785.670.1120
E-mail: admissions@washburnlaw.edu; Website: washburnlaw.edu

ABA
Approved
Since
1923

The Basics

Type of school	Public
Term	Semester
Application deadline	4/1
Application fee	$40
Financial aid deadline	6/1
Can first year start other than fall?	No
Student to faculty ratio	14.0 to 1
Does the university offer:	
housing restricted to law students?	No
graduate housing for which law students are eligible?	No

Faculty and Administrators

	Total		Men		Women		Minorities	
	Fall	Spr	Fall	Spr	Fall	Spr	Fall	Spr
Full-time	27	26	17	17	10	9	6	4
Other Full-time	2	3	1	2	1	1	0	0
Deans, librarians, & others who teach	5	6	4	5	1	1	1	1
Part-time	30	20	23	16	7	4	0	1
Total	64	55	45	40	19	15	7	6

Curriculum

	Full-time	Part-time
Typical first-year section size	75	0
Is there typically a "small section" of the first-year class, other than Legal Writing, taught by full-time faculty	Yes	No
If yes, typical size offered last year	32	
# of classroom course titles beyond first-year curriculum		84

# of upper division courses, excluding seminars with an enrollment:		
Under 25	52	
25–49	27	
50–74	10	
75–99	6	
100+	0	

# of seminars		16
# of seminar positions available		328
# of seminar positions filled	250	0
# of positions available in simulation courses	299	
# of simulation positions filled	197	0
# of positions available in faculty supervised clinical courses		103
# of faculty supervised clinical positions filled	101	0
# involved in field placements	53	0
# involved in law journals	56	0
# involved in interschool competitions	32	0
# of credit hours required to graduate		90

JD Enrollment and Ethnicity

	Men		Women		Full-time		Part-time		1st-year		Total		JD Degs. Awd.
	#	%	#	%	#	%	#	%	#	%	#	%	
African Amer.	7	2.6	12	6.6	19	4.2	0	0.0	3	1.9	19	4.2	3
Amer. Indian	4	1.5	4	2.2	8	1.8	0	0.0	5	3.2	8	1.8	2
Asian Amer.	10	3.7	5	2.7	15	3.3	0	0.0	3	1.9	15	3.3	4
Mex. Amer.	1	0.4	4	2.2	5	1.1	0	0.0	3	1.9	5	1.1	6
Puerto Rican	1	0.4	1	0.5	2	0.4	0	0.0	1	0.6	2	0.4	0
Hispanic	7	2.6	5	2.7	12	2.7	0	0.0	1	0.6	12	2.7	1
Total Minority	30	11.2	31	17.0	61	13.6	0	0.0	16	10.1	61	13.6	16
For. Nation.	1	0.4	1	0.5	2	0.4	0	0.0	0	0.0	2	0.4	1
Caucasian	233	87.3	147	80.8	380	84.6	0	0.0	139	88.0	380	84.6	129
Unknown	3	1.1	3	1.6	6	1.3	0	0.0	3	1.9	6	1.3	0
Total	267	59.5	182	40.5	449	100.0	0	0.0	158	35.2	449		146

Transfers

Transfers in	11
Transfers out	11

Tuition and Fees

	Resident	Nonresident
Full-time	$12,698	$20,846
Part-time	$0	$0

Living Expenses

Estimated living expenses for singles

Living on campus	Living off campus	Living at home
$13,805	$13,805	$13,805

Washburn University School of Law

ABA
Approved
Since
1923

GPA and LSAT Scores

	Total	Full-time	Part-time
# of apps	1,049	1,049	0
# of offers	447	447	0
# of matrics	158	158	0
75% GPA	3.71	3.71	0.00
Median GPA	3.37	3.37	0.00
25% GPA	3.04	3.04	0.00
75% LSAT	157	157	0
Median LSAT	154	154	0
25% LSAT	152	152	0

Grants and Scholarships (from prior year)

	Total		Full-time		Part-time	
	#	%	#	%	#	%
Total # of students	451		451		0	
Total # receiving grants	189	41.9	189	41.9	0	0.0
Less than 1/2 tuition	110	24.4	110	24.4	0	0.0
Half to full tuition	20	4.4	20	4.4	0	0.0
Full tuition	42	9.3	42	9.3	0	0.0
More than full tuition	17	3.8	17	3.8	0	0.0
Median grant amount			$5,000		$0	

Informational and Library Resources

# of volumes and volume equivalents	383,639
# of titles	260,308
# of active serial subscriptions	4,079
Study seating capacity inside the library	360
# of full-time professional librarians	17
Hours per week library is open	111
# of open, wired connections available to students	27
# of networked computers available for use by students	96
# of simultaneous wireless users	3,060
Require computer?	No

JD Attrition (from prior year)

	Academic	Other	Total	
	#	#	#	%
1st year	6	20	26	16.6
2nd year	0	0	0	0.0
3rd year	0	1	1	0.7
4th year	0	0	0	0.0

Employment (9 months after graduation)

	Total	Percentage
Employment status known	161	98.2
Employment status unknown	3	1.8
Employed	144	89.4
Pursuing graduate degrees	7	4.3
Unemployed seeking employment	3	1.9
Unemployed not seeking employment	3	1.9
Unemployed and studying for the bar	4	2.5

Type of Employment

# employed in law firms	76	52.8
# employed in business and industry	28	19.4
# employed in government	22	15.3
# employed in public interest	8	5.6
# employed as judicial clerks	6	4.2
# employed in academia	4	2.8

Geographic Location

# employed in state	76	52.8
# employed in foreign countries	0	0.0
# of states where employed		19

Bar Passage Rates

Jurisdiction	Kansas			Missouri		
Exam	Sum 05	Win 06	Total	Sum 05	Win 06	Total
# from school taking bar for the first time	79	23	102	15	12	27
School's pass rate for all first-time takers	75%	91%	78%	73%	92%	81%
State's pass rate for all first-time takers	78%	90%	82%	88%	90%	89%

Washburn University School of Law

1700 SW College Avenue
Topeka, KS 66621-1140
Phone: 800.WASHLAW or 800.927.4529; Fax: 785.670.1120
E-mail: admissions@washburnlaw.edu; Website: washburnlaw.edu

■ Introduction

Washburn University School of Law was founded in 1903, became a member of the AALS in 1905, and appeared on the initial list of ABA-approved schools in 1923. The essence of Washburn Law is the commitment of the law school community at every level—from the dean's office to facilities staff—to the success of our students. In addition, the law school endeavors to impart to its students the value of treating others with respect, dignity, and a sense of caring. For more than a century, the school's student-centered approach has produced well-prepared law professionals ready to engage in successful careers. Its network of more than 6,300 alumni located in all 50 states and many foreign countries includes nationally recognized lawyers, state and federal judges, politicians, journalists, and senior executives of Fortune 500 companies.

■ Curriculum

All entering students participate in the law school's Ex-L program, an elaborate and rigorous First-Week Program designed to teach students the learning strategies they need to succeed in law school. It includes a structured study-group program in which groups of 4–6 students meet twice per week to apply cooperative learning strategies to their law school learning under the supervision of carefully trained and supervised upper-division students. Second- and third-year students satisfy advanced writing and oral presentation requirements and take one or more classes from a group of perspectives on law courses.

■ Centers for Excellence

The Business and Transactional Law Center, the Center for Excellence in Advocacy, and the Children and Family Law Center complement Washburn's tradition of excellence in teaching. Students may add an element of concentration by participating in one of the school's six certificate programs, most of which are administered through the centers.

Business and Transactional Law Center—The center provides students with additional educational opportunities to expand their knowledge in business law while developing the essential skills of transactional lawyers. The hands-on involvement of alumni actively engaged in business and transactional law also allows the center to accomplish a major subsidiary goal: making the law school experience more realistic, and relevant, by providing additional opportunities to bridge the gap between theory and practice. The ultimate outcome from these efforts will be graduates who possess the knowledge and professional skills required to represent their clients effectively.

Center for Excellence in Advocacy—The center trains law students in the persuasive and skilled use of advocacy techniques. The center also supports research in trial behavior, trial process, and effective advocacy. Students hone their advocacy skills in Washburn's live-client law clinic and in a variety of advocacy skills courses. The center coordinates student participation in trial advocacy, negotiation, and client

counseling. The center also sponsors national and regional advocacy conferences and hosts a jurist in residence each year.

Children and Family Law Center—The center supports education, interdisciplinary research, advocacy, and training services focused on children and families involved in the legal system. Washburn houses the American Bar Association's *Family Law Quarterly*. Students working in the center have the opportunity to take a range of courses related to children and families and to participate in the Washburn Law Clinic representing clients in divorce, children in need of care, and other family law cases.

■ Certificate Programs

Washburn Law offers certificates of specialization in Advocacy, Business and Transactional Law, Estate Planning, Family Law, Natural Resources Law, and Tax Law. The certificate programs allow students to fully develop their legal interests in these fields. Students who earn certificates graduate with a highly developed working knowledge of the practice area.

■ Law Clinic

In 1970, Washburn Law Clinic was one of the nation's first in-house clinics. From its inception, faculty members teaching in the clinic have been on tenure track, placing our clinic at the forefront of legal education. Faculty-supervised students provide a full range of legal services to live clients, including programs in Native American law and transactional law.

■ International Programs

As early as 1968, Washburn recognized that the practice of law was becoming increasingly global and responded with a summer study-abroad program. Currently, Washburn expands students' understanding of different legal systems through its summer program at Utrecht University and its semester-long program at Maastrich University, both in the Netherlands.

■ Externships

Washburn's externship program allows students to earn course credit through placement in legal settings outside the law school. Students can experience the practice of law in a wide variety of settings tailored to their specific interests and needs. Students are closely supervised by an attorney and by the externship director.

■ Accelerated Degree Program

This program allows students to complete law school in two-and-one-half years by taking courses during both summers.

■ Facilities and Technology

For 20 years, the Washburn Law Library has ranked in the top quarter of all law school libraries for new titles added. It has been consistently ranked high among law school libraries because of its extensive collection and innovative use of technology. WashLaw has been a premier legal research portal since its creation in the early 1990s, and it is nationally acclaimed as a comprehensive source for legal information on the Internet. Students have wireless access throughout the building. Classrooms include enhanced audio, video, and computer technologies. The state-of-the-art Robinson Courtroom/Bianchino Technology Center offers students the opportunity to practice their skills in a high-tech environment.

■ Admission

While an applicant's LSAT score and GPA are significant factors, there is no bright-line cutoff. The Admissions Committee carefully considers other factors, including a determination of whether the individual would be an asset for the class as a whole based on gender, ethnicity, geographic diversity, international experience, and undergraduate institution.

■ Student Activities

More than 30 active student organizations, including Black, Hispanic, Asian, and Native American law student associations, accommodate the wide and diverse interests students bring to the law school and add to the cultural and intellectual life of the law school community.

Students have the opportunity to participate in two journals. They may be selected to serve on the board of editors of the *Washburn Law Journal* or the student editorial board of the

ABA's peer-reviewed *Family Law Quarterly*, which has been located at Washburn since 1992, enhancing the Children and Family Law Center.

■ Expenses and Financial Aid

Scholarships are awarded based upon a combination of academic performance and need. Contribution to diversity is considered in making scholarship awards. Resident status for tuition purposes can be established with a primary Kansas residence after six months. The Financial Aid Office assists law students in procuring federal loans and financial aid. Housing costs are reasonable. Most students live in the residential areas surrounding the campus.

■ Professional Development

The Office of Professional Development offers programs that emphasize assessment of career goals, exploration of varied applications of a legal education, and support for the transition into the professional marketplace. The office makes available extensive resources regarding local, regional, national, and international legal employment in the public and private sectors, graduate and foreign study, and judicial clerkships.

Washburn graduates enjoy great success in seeking employment. Washburn law school alumni reside in every state in the nation, the District of Columbia, and many foreign countries.

Applicant Profile

Washburn University School of Law
This chart is to be used for general purpose information only. Nonnumerical factors are weighed heavily in all admission decisions.

LSAT Score	3.75 +		3.50–3.74		3.25–3.49		3.00–3.24		2.75–2.99		2.50–2.74		2.25–2.49		Below 2.25		Total	
	Apps	Adm	Apps	Adm	Apps	Adm	Apps	Adm	Apps	Adm	Apps	Adm	Apps	Adm	Apps	Adm	Apps	Adm
175–180	0	0	0	0	0	0	0	0	0	0	0	0	0	0	0	0	0	0
170–174	0	0	0	0	1	1	0	0	0	0	0	0	0	0	0	0	1	1
165–169	3	3	1	1	1	1	1	1	2	2	1	1	1	0	0	0	44	44
160–164	10	10	5	5	11	11	6	6	7	7	3	3	2	2	3	1	127	123
155–159	23	22	23	23	35	35	19	19	16	15	4	4	4	4	3	1	274	187
150–154	37	35	51	41	64	45	54	37	33	19	20	7	11	2	4	1	248	29
145–149	26	8	41	5	55	10	49	5	44	0	16	1	13	0	4	0	156	12
140–144	7	0	24	2	27	3	34	3	27	2	15	2	14	0	8	0	80	1
Below 140	6	0	7	0	17	0	11	0	19	1	9	0	8	0	3	0		
Total	112	78	152	77	211	106	174	71	148	46	68	18	53	8	22	2	940	406

Apps = Number of Applicants
Adm = Number Admitted
Reflects 99% of the total applicant pool.

Note: The admissions in the grid above include individuals who gained admission through the fall 2006 class, not the spring 2006 class.

University of Washington School of Law

William H. Gates Hall, Box 35-3020
Seattle, WA 98195-3020
Phone: 206.543.4078
E-mail: lawadm@u.washington.edu; Website: www.law.washington.edu

ABA Approved Since 1924

The Basics

Type of school	Public
Term	Quarter
Application deadline	1/15
Application fee	$50
Financial aid deadline	2/28
Can first year start other than fall?	No
Student to faculty ratio	10.8 to 1
Does the university offer:	
housing restricted to law students?	No
graduate housing for which law students are eligible?	Yes

Faculty and Administrators

	Total		Men		Women		Minorities	
	Fall	Spr	Fall	Spr	Fall	Spr	Fall	Spr
Full-time	43	40	24	23	19	17	5	4
Other Full-time	8	8	6	7	2	1	3	3
Deans, librarians, & others who teach	3	4	3	3	0	1	2	2
Part-time	51	70	33	49	18	21	5	12
Total	105	122	66	82	39	40	15	21

Curriculum

	Full-time	Part-time
Typical first-year section size	90	0
Is there typically a "small section" of the first-year class, other than Legal Writing, taught by full-time faculty	Yes	No
If yes, typical size offered last year	30	
# of classroom course titles beyond first-year curriculum	126	

# of upper division courses, excluding seminars with an enrollment:		
	Under 25	86
	25–49	28
	50–74	10
	75–99	9
	100+	0

# of seminars	18	
# of seminar positions available	264	
# of seminar positions filled	235	0
# of positions available in simulation courses	160	
# of simulation positions filled	152	0
# of positions available in faculty supervised clinical courses	88	
# of faculty supervised clinical positions filled	75	0
# involved in field placements	202	0
# involved in law journals	120	0
# involved in interschool competitions	98	0
# of credit hours required to graduate	135	

JD Enrollment and Ethnicity

	Men		Women		Full-time		Part-time		1st-year		Total		JD Degs. Awd.
	#	%	#	%	#	%	#	%	#	%	#	%	
African Amer.	2	0.9	9	2.9	11	2.0	0	0.0	5	2.8	11	2.0	3
Amer. Indian	0	0.0	10	3.2	10	1.8	0	0.0	4	2.2	10	1.8	5
Asian Amer.	24	10.2	40	12.9	64	11.8	0	0.0	22	12.3	64	11.8	13
Mex. Amer.	1	0.4	5	1.6	6	1.1	0	0.0	1	0.6	6	1.1	0
Puerto Rican	0	0.0	1	0.3	1	0.2	0	0.0	1	0.6	1	0.2	0
Hispanic	9	3.8	6	1.9	15	2.8	0	0.0	5	2.8	15	2.8	2
Total Minority	36	15.3	71	23.0	107	19.7	0	0.0	38	21.2	107	19.7	23
For. Nation.	5	2.1	16	5.2	21	3.9	0	0.0	7	3.9	21	3.9	9
Caucasian	184	78.3	215	69.6	399	73.3	0	0.0	128	71.5	399	73.3	139
Unknown	10	4.3	7	2.3	17	3.1	0	0.0	6	3.4	17	3.1	7
Total	235	43.2	309	56.8	544	100.0	0	0.0	179	32.9	544		178

Transfers

Transfers in	8
Transfers out	7

Tuition and Fees

	Resident	Nonresident
Full-time	$16,255	$23,878
Part-time	$0	$0

Living Expenses

Estimated living expenses for singles

Living on campus	Living off campus	Living at home
$14,913	$14,913	$7,188

University of Washington School of Law

ABA
Approved
Since
1924

GPA and LSAT Scores

	Total	Full-time	Part-time
# of apps	2,545	2,545	0
# of offers	537	537	0
# of matrics	179	179	0
75% GPA	3.84	3.84	0.00
Median GPA	3.69	3.69	0.00
25% GPA	3.50	3.50	0.00
75% LSAT	166	166	0
Median LSAT	162	162	0
25% LSAT	159	159	0

Grants and Scholarships (from prior year)

	Total		Full-time		Part-time	
	#	%	#	%	#	%
Total # of students	561		561		0	
Total # receiving grants	237	42.2	237	42.2	0	0.0
Less than 1/2 tuition	138	24.6	138	24.6	0	0.0
Half to full tuition	91	16.2	91	16.2	0	0.0
Full tuition	0	0.0	0	0.0	0	0.0
More than full tuition	8	1.4	8	1.4	0	0.0
Median grant amount			$7,000		$0	

Informational and Library Resources

# of volumes and volume equivalents	605,991
# of titles	168,412
# of active serial subscriptions	5,581
Study seating capacity inside the library	398
# of full-time professional librarians	13
Hours per week library is open	89
# of open, wired connections available to students	0
# of networked computers available for use by students	75
# of simultaneous wireless users	500
Require computer?	No

JD Attrition (from prior year)

	Academic	Other	Total	
	#	#	#	%
1st year	0	5	5	2.8
2nd year	0	0	0	0.0
3rd year	0	2	2	1.0
4th year	0	0	0	0.0

Employment (9 months after graduation)

	Total	Percentage
Employment status known	163	100.0
Employment status unknown	0	0.0
Employed	147	90.2
Pursuing graduate degrees	7	4.3
Unemployed seeking employment	1	0.6
Unemployed not seeking employment	8	4.9
Unemployed and studying for the bar	0	0.0
Type of Employment		
# employed in law firms	58	39.5
# employed in business and industry	16	10.9
# employed in government	24	16.3
# employed in public interest	16	10.9
# employed as judicial clerks	24	16.3
# employed in academia	7	4.8
Geographic Location		
# employed in state	106	72.1
# employed in foreign countries	0	0.0
# of states where employed	15	

Bar Passage Rates

Jurisdiction	Washington			California		
Exam	Sum 05	Win 06	Total	Sum 05	Win 06	Total
# from school taking bar for the first time	127	13	140	9	1	10
School's pass rate for all first-time takers	87%	62%	84%	78%	100%	80%
State's pass rate for all first-time takers	75%	74%	75%	64%	54%	62%

University of Washington School of Law

William H. Gates Hall, Box 35-3020
Seattle, WA 98195-3020
Phone: 206.543.4078
E-mail: lawadm@u.washington.edu; Website: www.law.washington.edu

■ Introduction

Established in 1899, the School of Law is part of the main campus of the University of Washington, approximately four miles from downtown Seattle. The university, the largest single campus institution in the western United States, with an enrollment of 33,500 students, offers nearly every discipline for study. The School of Law has 46 full-time faculty members and about 500 JD students. Because of the favorable student-to-faculty ratio, classes are generally small, with frequent opportunities for student-teacher contacts. Each first-year student is usually in at least one class of 30 or fewer students, in addition to the Basic Legal Skills course. The school is a member of the AALS, is approved by the ABA, and has a chapter of the Order of the Coif.

■ Curriculum

The first-year curriculum is prescribed. After that, except for an advanced writing requirement and a class in professional responsibility, all courses in the second and third years are elective. In addition to traditional courses and seminars, advanced students may participate in one of nine clinics: Innocence Project Northwest, Berman Environmental Law, Mediation, Child Advocacy, Unemployment Compensation, Tribal Court Criminal Defense, Refugee and Immigrant Advocacy, Technology Law and Public Policy, Entrepreneurial Law, or Low-income Taxpayer; or in courses in trial advocacy. Judicial, legislative, agency, and public-interest externships are available. Students must also perform 60 hours of public service legal work.

Students are encouraged to rely on their initiative and to develop their own powers of perception. Classroom discussion, in which students participate fully, is one means used to assist this development. Independent research projects, either in the context of a seminar or through individualized study under faculty supervision, are also emphasized. Although it is a state law school, Washington state law is not emphasized unduly. Graduates of the school are prepared to practice law anywhere in the United States or in other common law countries.

■ Special Programs

Concentration tracks are available in Asian law, dispute resolution, environmental law, health law, intellectual property, and international and comparative law.

There are centers for Advanced Study and Research on Intellectual Property (CASRIP), Indian Law, and Law, Commerce, and Technology.

Students studying for the JD program may take courses in any of the LLM programs during the second and third years. The UW also offers a master's degree in Law Librarianship.

■ Admission Standards

In selecting the entering class, the law school does not make all of its admission decisions solely on the basis of predicted academic performance. Important academic objectives are furthered by classes composed of students having talents and skills derived from diverse backgrounds believed to be relevant to a rich and effective study of law.

About 23 percent of the incoming class are students of color, for whom the school provides student, faculty, and professional mentoring programs.

■ Gates Public Service Law Scholarship

The University of Washington School of Law is delighted to announce the inauguration of the Gates Public Service Law Scholarship Program. Five scholarships will be awarded on an annual basis to first-year students entering the UW School of Law JD program for the next 80 years. Each Gates PSL scholarship award will cover tuition, books, other normal fees imposed for university and UW School of Law enrollment, costs of room and board, and incidental expenses. Acceptance of a Gates PSL scholarship represents a commitment on the part of each recipient to work in public service for five years following graduation. You can find more information about the program at *www.law.washington.edu/GatesScholar/*.

■ Student Activities

The *Washington Law Review, Pacific Rim Law and Policy Journal,* and *Shidler Journal of Law, Commerce and Technology* are edited and published by students. The University of Washington is consistently among the top scoring moot court teams in the nation.

Through the Student Bar Association and student/faculty committees, students participate in the decision processes of the law school. Student organizations include the American Bar Association/Law Student Division; American Constitution Society; American Civil Liberties Union; Asian/Pacific American Law Student Association; Black Law Students Association; Center for Human Rights and Justice; Center for Labor and Employment Justice; Christian Legal Society; Federalist Society; GreenLaw; Student Health Law Organization; Immigrant Families Advocacy Project; Innocence Project Northwest; International Law Society; J. Reuben Clark Legal Society; Jewish Legal Society; Korean American Law Student Association; Latino/Latina Law Students Association; Law and Alternative Dispute Resolution; Law Students for Choice; Law Women's Caucus; Military Law Students' Association; Minority Law Students' Association; Moot Court Honor Board; National Lawyers Guild; Native American Law Student Association; Outlaws; PALS: Parents Attending Law School; Phi Delta Phi; Public Interest Law Association; Society for Small Business Development; Sports and Entertainment Law Club; Street Youth Legal Advocates of Washington; Student Animal Legal Defense Fund; Student Bar Association; Technology Law Society; and Title 29.

■ Career Services

The Career Services Office serves as a liaison between students and prospective employers. Firms, agencies, and other potential employers are invited to interview at the school and to list job openings in the regularly published placement bulletin. About 72 percent of the graduates choose to remain in Washington state.

■ William H. Gates Hall

The law school moved into its $80 million new facility in September 2003. The new building, named for one of its most distinguished graduates, features the latest technology, including wireless access, to educate lawyers for the twenty-first century.

■ Visitation

The law school invites prospective students to visit a large section first-year class. The schedule can be found at *www.law.washington.edu/Admissions/Visit.html*.

Applicant Profile

University of Washington School of Law
This grid includes only applicants who earned 120–180 LSAT scores under standard administrations.

									LSAT Score									
	120–153		154–156		157–159		160–162		163–165		166–168		169–180		Total	
GPA	Apps	Adm	Apps	Adm	Apps	Adm	Apps	Adm	Apps	Adm	Apps	Adm	Apps	Adm	Apps	Adm
3.75 +	69	5	69	11	93	17	109	38	82	54	64	60	43	43	529	228
3.50–3.74	120	8	103	11	146	18	137	24	126	36	85	45	53	51	770	193
3.25–3.49	136	4	80	6	107	8	103	11	71	5	42	15	34	22	573	71
3.00–3.24	110	1	49	2	43	1	59	1	51	5	34	9	17	5	363	24
2.75–2.99	47	0	17	2	14	1	23	2	12	0	10	0	7	3	130	8
2.50–2.74	28	0	12	0	6	0	12	1	7	0	7	1	6	2	78	4
0.10–2.49	25	0	4	0	4	0	2	0	2	0	0	0	2	0	39	0
LSAT only	20	0	6	2	8	0	9	4	4	2	2	0	2	1	51	9
Total	555	18	340	34	421	45	454	81	355	102	244	130	164	127	2533	537

Apps = Number of Applicants
Adm = Number Admitted

Washington and Lee University School of Law

Sydney Lewis Hall
Lexington, VA 24450
Phone: 540.458.8503; Fax: 540.458.8586
E-mail: lawadm@wlu.edu; Website: www.law.wlu.edu

ABA
Approved
Since
1923

The Basics

Type of school	Private
Term	Semester
Application deadline	2/1
Application fee	$50
Financial aid deadline	2/15
Can first year start other than fall?	No
Student to faculty ratio	9.8 to 1
Does the university offer:	
housing restricted to law students?	Yes
graduate housing for which law students are eligible?	Yes

Faculty and Administrators

	Total		Men		Women		Minorities	
	Fall	Spr	Fall	Spr	Fall	Spr	Fall	Spr
Full-time	33	37	23	25	10	12	4	5
Other Full-time	0	1	0	1	0	0	0	1
Deans, librarians, & others who teach	3	3	2	2	1	1	1	1
Part-time	6	20	4	15	2	5	0	1
Total	**42**	**61**	**29**	**43**	**13**	**18**	**5**	**8**

Curriculum

	Full-time	Part-time
Typical first-year section size	56	0
Is there typically a "small section" of the first-year class, other than Legal Writing, taught by full-time faculty	Yes	No
If yes, typical size offered last year	21	
# of classroom course titles beyond first-year curriculum		76
# of upper division courses, excluding seminars with an enrollment: Under 25		52
25–49		22
50–74		7
75–99		3
100+		0
# of seminars		14
# of seminar positions available		196
# of seminar positions filled	171	0
# of positions available in simulation courses		184
# of simulation positions filled	174	0
# of positions available in faculty supervised clinical courses		43
# of faculty supervised clinical positions filled	43	0
# involved in field placements	23	0
# involved in law journals	87	0
# involved in interschool competitions	116	0
# of credit hours required to graduate		85

JD Enrollment and Ethnicity

	Men		Women		Full-time		Part-time		1st-year		Total		JD Degs. Awd.
	#	%	#	%	#	%	#	%	#	%	#	%	
African Amer.	11	4.8	7	4.4	18	4.6	0	0.0	4	3.2	18	4.6	5
Amer. Indian	2	0.9	5	3.1	7	1.8	0	0.0	2	1.6	7	1.8	0
Asian Amer.	9	3.9	22	13.8	31	7.9	0	0.0	14	11.2	31	7.9	10
Mex. Amer.	0	0.0	2	1.3	2	0.5	0	0.0	1	0.8	2	0.5	0
Puerto Rican	0	0.0	0	0.0	0	0.0	0	0.0	0	0.0	0	0.0	0
Hispanic	4	1.7	0	0.0	4	1.0	0	0.0	1	0.8	4	1.0	0
Total Minority	26	11.3	36	22.6	62	15.9	0	0.0	22	17.6	62	15.9	15
For. Nation.	3	1.3	7	4.4	10	2.6	0	0.0	1	0.8	10	2.6	4
Caucasian	202	87.4	116	73.0	318	81.5	0	0.0	102	81.6	318	81.5	110
Unknown	0	0.0	0	0.0	0	0.0	0	0.0	0	0.0	0	0.0	0
Total	231	59.2	159	40.8	390	100.0	0	0.0	125	32.1	390		129

Transfers

Transfers in	18
Transfers out	7

Tuition and Fees

	Resident	Nonresident
Full-time	$31,300	$31,300
Part-time	$0	$0

Living Expenses

Estimated living expenses for singles

Living on campus	Living off campus	Living at home
$15,695	$15,695	$2,000

Washington and Lee University School of Law

*ABA
Approved
Since
1923*

GPA and LSAT Scores

	Total	Full-time	Part-time
# of apps	2,764	2,764	0
# of offers	867	867	0
# of matrics	126	126	0
75% GPA	3.73	3.73	0.00
Median GPA	3.61	3.61	0.00
25% GPA	3.28	3.28	0.00
75% LSAT	167	167	0
Median LSAT	166	166	0
25% LSAT	162	162	0

Grants and Scholarships (from prior year)

	Total		Full-time		Part-time	
	#	%	#	%	#	%
Total # of students	387		387		0	
Total # receiving grants	261	67.4	261	67.4	0	0.0
Less than 1/2 tuition	199	51.4	199	51.4	0	0.0
Half to full tuition	57	14.7	57	14.7	0	0.0
Full tuition	5	1.3	5	1.3	0	0.0
More than full tuition	0	0.0	0	0.0	0	0.0
Median grant amount			$10,000		$0	

Informational and Library Resources

# of volumes and volume equivalents	436,064
# of titles	163,233
# of active serial subscriptions	4,067
Study seating capacity inside the library	540
# of full-time professional librarians	6
Hours per week library is open	168
# of open, wired connections available to students	340
# of networked computers available for use by students	82
# of simultaneous wireless users	2,000
Require computer?	No

JD Attrition (from prior year)

	Academic	Other	Total	
	#	#	#	%
1st year	0	2	2	1.5
2nd year	0	10	10	8.1
3rd year	0	0	0	0.0
4th year	0	0	0	0.0

Employment (9 months after graduation)

	Total	Percentage
Employment status known	133	93.7
Employment status unknown	9	6.3
Employed	119	89.5
Pursuing graduate degrees	4	3.0
Unemployed seeking employment	2	1.5
Unemployed not seeking employment	0	0.0
Unemployed and studying for the bar	8	6.0

Type of Employment

	Total	Percentage
# employed in law firms	63	52.9
# employed in business and industry	10	8.4
# employed in government	14	11.8
# employed in public interest	3	2.5
# employed as judicial clerks	24	20.2
# employed in academia	1	0.8

Geographic Location

	Total	Percentage
# employed in state	32	26.9
# employed in foreign countries	0	0.0
# of states where employed	27	

Bar Passage Rates

Jurisdiction	Virginia		
Exam	Sum 05	Win 06	Total
# from school taking bar for the first time	41	4	45
School's pass rate for all first-time takers	93%	100%	93%
State's pass rate for all first-time takers	76%	65%	74%

The information on these pages was provided by the law school.

Washington and Lee University School of Law

Office of Admissions, Sydney Lewis Hall
Lexington, VA 24450
Phone: 540.458.8503; Fax: 540.458.8586
E-mail: lawadm@wlu.edu; Website: www.law.wlu.edu

■ Introduction

Washington and Lee University School of Law, founded in 1849, is located in Lexington, Virginia, approximately three hours southwest of Washington, DC, in the Blue Ridge Mountains. The School of Law is fully accredited by the ABA and is a member of the AALS. Washington and Lee is known for providing its students with an academically rigorous and professionally challenging legal education in an environment characterized by a commitment to students, small classes, a generous student-to-faculty ratio, and a collegial community.

■ The Honor System

The W&L community is governed by an Honor System that is the foundation for academic and student life at the university. The Honor System is an integral part of a professional education that fosters a sensitivity to the ethical imperatives of the legal profession. The Honor System means that the library is always open, exams are unproctored, the exam schedule for upper-class students is flexible, and professors are free to give take-home examinations. The Honor System contributes significantly to a law school environment characterized by mutual respect, trust, and collegiality.

■ Curriculum and Clinical Programs

All first-year classes are required. The second- and third-year curriculum is almost entirely elective, and students choose from over 120 upper-class courses. Offerings in corporate and business law, international law, health law, public policy and regulatory reform, and civil and criminal litigation are particularly strong. A wide variety of public interest clinical programs and externships provide students with opportunities for hands-on client contact experience as part of the academic program. Clinics include the Virginia Capital Case Clearinghouse, established to assist attorneys representing clients charged with or convicted of capital crimes; the Black Lung Administrative Law Clinic, in which students represent coal miners seeking disability benefits under federal law; the Community Legal Practice Center, which provides a range of legal services to qualified area residents; the Legal Aid Society, which provides legal services to indigent clients in a range of civil matters; the Public Prosecutors Program, in which students assist federal and state prosecutors with investigations, trial preparation, pretrial and trial practice, and appeals; and the Judicial Clerkship Program, through which students act as law clerks to trial, appellate, juvenile and domestic relations, and federal bankruptcy judges.

■ Special Programs

JD/MHA. With Virginia Commonwealth University in Richmond, W&L Law offers a program through which students can receive a JD and a master's in Health Administration on an accelerated basis. Dual-degree candidates must be accepted for the program by both VCU and W&L; a portion of the degree requirements are taken on the campus of each university.

LLM in United States Law. W&L Law offers a one-year program in United States law to attorneys who hold a foreign law degree.

■ Student Activities

Students have three journal opportunities: the *Washington and Lee Law Review*, a quarterly journal for scholarly discussion of legal issues; the *Journal of Civil Rights and Social Justice*, focusing on legal issues with an impact on racial and ethnic minorities; and the *Environmental Law Digest*, a practitioner-oriented newsletter covering environmental case law and legislation in Virginia and the Fourth Circuit. A variety of moot court and advocacy competitions allow upper-level students to hone advocacy, counseling, negotiation, and trial skills.

W&L Law students have established numerous groups such as the Black Law Students Association, Asian Pacific American Law Students Association, Women Law Students Organization, OUTLaw, Jewish Law Students Association, Christian Legal Society, Rationalist Society, Law Families, Federalist Society, American Constitution Society, National Lawyers Guild, and chapters of three national professional fraternities. Practice-oriented groups include the Environmental Law Society, International Law Society, Tax Law Society, Sports and Entertainment Law Society, Public Interest Law Students Association, Students for an Innocence Project, and Intellectual Property and Tech Law Society. Student groups foster a rich intellectual environment at the School of Law by presenting programs that address issues of special concern to their members.

■ Admission and Financial Aid

W&L Law actively seeks a diverse student body whose members are of different religious, racial, ethnic, economic, and geographic backgrounds. The admission process is highly individualized. Students are not ranked by any numerical index, nor is there an assigned weight given to any objective or subjective factor presented in the application. The Admissions Committee considers not only the cumulative undergraduate grade-point average, but also trends in grades, the rigor of an applicant's academic program and the quality of the school attended, the LSAT score, extracurricular activities, community service, evidence of leadership, graduate study, work experience, assessments of recommenders, and any information presented in the applicant's personal statement. An applicant may request an interview with a member of the admission office staff. Applicants are encouraged to visit the school to sit in on classes, tour the facility, and talk with students and faculty. A generous scholarship endowment allows W&L Law to assist a large percentage of its students with merit-based grant funds.

■ Career Planning and Professional Development

W&L Law graduates practice in every state and throughout the world. More than 70 percent of recent graduates practice outside Virginia. The two counseling professionals in the Office of Career Planning and Professional Development hold JD degrees and work with each student individually to develop a unique career plan. OCP&PD provides instruction in résumé and cover letter writing, networking, and other career development skills. It also provides programming on a wide variety of practice specialities and settings, and acts as a liaison between students and legal employers. Law students interview with prospective employers on campus, at a satellite location in Charlottesville, and at programs throughout the United States. An active alumni network assists students with contacts in every state.

■ Law Library and Physical Facilities

Sydney Lewis Hall, home of the School of Law, was built in 1976 and expanded in 1991 with the addition of the Lewis F. Powell Jr. Archives, which house the Supreme Court and professional papers of retired Supreme Court Justice Powell, a graduate of the university's college and law school. Wireless Internet access is available throughout the building. Every classroom has been renovated within the past five years and is equipped with state-of-the-art technology; the moot courtroom was completely renovated in 2006. The building, including the law library, is open 24 hours a day, 365 days a year. Students have access to the library collection on an open-stack basis.

Applicant Profile

Washington and Lee University School of Law
This grid includes only applicants who earned 120–180 LSAT scores under standard administrations.

LSAT Score	GPA																					
	3.75 +		3.50–3.74		3.25–3.49		3.00–3.24		2.75–2.99		2.50–2.74		2.25–2.49		2.00–2.24		Below 2.00		No GPA		Total	
	Apps	Adm	Apps	Adm	Apps	Adm	Apps	Adm	Apps	Adm	Apps	Adm	Apps	Adm	Apps	Adm	Apps	Adm	Apps	Adm	Apps	Adm
175–180	3	3	2	2	2	2	2	2	1	1	0	0	0	0	0	0	0	0	0	0	10	10
170–174	48	47	31	30	26	24	23	23	6	6	4	1	2	0	2	2	0	0	4	2	140	131
165–169	148	148	153	143	129	99	75	33	31	13	11	2	2	0	2	0	0	0	4	0	555	442
160–164	272	128	334	82	253	14	135	5	39	4	19	2	5	1	2	0	0	0	4	0	1063	236
155–159	83	6	122	14	107	4	63	3	32	2	13	0	6	1	1	0	0	0	3	0	430	30
150–154	45	7	78	4	60	4	51	0	31	0	18	0	1	0	0	0	0	0	2	0	286	15
145–149	15	0	31	1	35	1	35	0	15	0	7	0	6	0	3	0	0	0	4	0	151	2
140–144	5	0	8	0	13	0	21	0	11	0	5	0	5	0	1	0	0	0	3	0	72	0
135–139	0	0	4	0	4	0	8	0	6	0	4	0	2	0	2	0	0	0	0	0	30	0
130–134	1	0	2	0	0	0	3	0	1	0	1	0	0	0	0	0	0	0	2	0	10	0
125–129	0	0	0	0	0	0	0	0	0	0	1	0	0	0	0	0	0	0	1	0	2	0
120–124	0	0	0	0	0	0	0	0	0	0	0	0	0	0	0	0	0	0	0	0	0	0
Total	620	339	765	276	629	148	416	66	173	26	83	5	29	2	11	2	0	0	23	2	2749	866

Apps = Number of Applicants
Adm = Number Admitted
Reflects 99% of the total applicant pool.

Washington University School of Law

Box 1120, One Brookings Drive
St. Louis, MO 63130-4899
Phone: 314.935.4525; Fax: 314.935.8778
E-mail: admiss@wulaw.wustl.edu; Website: http://law.wustl.edu

ABA
Approved
Since
1923

The Basics

Type of school	Private
Term	Semester
Application deadline	3/1
Application fee	$70
Financial aid deadline	3/1
Can first year start other than fall?	No
Student to faculty ratio	11.5 to 1
Does the university offer:	
housing restricted to law students?	Yes
graduate housing for which law students are eligible?	Yes

Faculty and Administrators

	Total		Men		Women		Minorities	
	Fall	Spr	Fall	Spr	Fall	Spr	Fall	Spr
Full-time	56	54	29	25	27	29	5	5
Other Full-time	0	0	0	0	0	0	0	0
Deans, librarians, & others who teach	10	10	6	6	4	4	1	1
Part-time	56	70	42	60	14	10	8	4
Total	**122**	**134**	**77**	**91**	**45**	**43**	**14**	**10**

Curriculum

	Full-time	Part-time
Typical first-year section size	82	0
Is there typically a "small section" of the first-year class, other than Legal Writing, taught by full-time faculty	Yes	No
If yes, typical size offered last year	39	
# of classroom course titles beyond first-year curriculum		139
# of upper division courses, excluding seminars with an enrollment: Under 25		101
25–49		34
50–74		13
75–99		5
100+		6
# of seminars		24
# of seminar positions available		400
# of seminar positions filled	356	0
# of positions available in simulation courses	1,146	
# of simulation positions filled	879	0
# of positions available in faculty supervised clinical courses	91	
# of faculty supervised clinical positions filled	90	0
# involved in field placements	89	0
# involved in law journals	248	0
# involved in interschool competitions	43	0
# of credit hours required to graduate	85	

JD Enrollment and Ethnicity

	Men		Women		Full-time		Part-time		1st-year		Total		JD Degs. Awd.
	#	%	#	%	#	%	#	%	#	%	#	%	
African Amer.	19	4.1	24	7.1	42	5.3	1	8.3	14	5.8	43	5.4	14
Amer. Indian	4	0.9	2	0.6	5	0.6	1	8.3	2	0.8	6	0.8	2
Asian Amer.	40	8.6	24	7.1	64	8.1	0	0.0	13	5.4	64	8.0	23
Mex. Amer.	0	0.0	3	0.9	3	0.4	0	0.0	1	0.4	3	0.4	1
Puerto Rican	1	0.2	0	0.0	1	0.1	0	0.0	0	0.0	1	0.1	0
Hispanic	6	1.3	1	0.3	7	0.9	0	0.0	2	0.8	7	0.9	2
Total Minority	70	15.1	54	16.1	122	15.5	2	16.7	32	13.3	124	15.5	42
For. Nation.	19	4.1	20	6.0	38	4.8	1	8.3	5	2.1	39	4.9	17
Caucasian	239	51.5	194	57.7	426	54.1	7	58.3	133	55.2	433	54.1	159
Unknown	136	29.3	68	20.2	202	25.6	2	16.7	71	29.5	204	25.5	32
Total	464	58.0	336	42.0	788	98.5	12	1.5	241	30.1	800		250

Transfers

Transfers in	51
Transfers out	7

Tuition and Fees

	Resident	Nonresident
Full-time	$36,380	$36,380
Part-time	$0	$0

Living Expenses

Estimated living expenses for singles

Living on campus	Living off campus	Living at home
N/A	$19,600	$16,110

Washington University School of Law

ABA
Approved
Since
1923

GPA and LSAT Scores

	Total	Full-time	Part-time
# of apps	3,325	3,325	0
# of offers	933	933	0
# of matrics	241	241	0
75% GPA	3.70	3.70	0.00
Median GPA	3.60	3.60	0.00
25% GPA	3.20	3.20	0.00
75% LSAT	167	167	0
Median LSAT	166	166	0
25% LSAT	162	162	0

Grants and Scholarships (from prior year)

	Total #	Total %	Full-time #	Full-time %	Part-time #	Part-time %
Total # of students	745		743		2	
Total # receiving grants	438	58.8	438	59.0	0	0.0
Less than 1/2 tuition	287	38.5	287	38.6	0	0.0
Half to full tuition	114	15.3	114	15.3	0	0.0
Full tuition	5	0.7	5	0.7	0	0.0
More than full tuition	32	4.3	32	4.3	0	0.0
Median grant amount			$12,000		$0	

Informational and Library Resources

# of volumes and volume equivalents	689,882
# of titles	152,428
# of active serial subscriptions	6,071
Study seating capacity inside the library	485
# of full-time professional librarians	9
Hours per week library is open	120
# of open, wired connections available to students	760
# of networked computers available for use by students	103
# of simultaneous wireless users	800
Require computer?	No

JD Attrition (from prior year)

	Academic #	Other #	Total #	Total %
1st year	0	11	11	5.0
2nd year	0	3	3	1.1
3rd year	1	0	1	0.4
4th year	0	0	0	0.0

Employment (9 months after graduation)

	Total	Percentage
Employment status known	226	99.6
Employment status unknown	1	0.4
Employed	218	96.5
Pursuing graduate degrees	5	2.2
Unemployed seeking employment	1	0.4
Unemployed not seeking employment	2	0.9
Unemployed and studying for the bar	0	0.0

Type of Employment

	Total	Percentage
# employed in law firms	152	69.7
# employed in business and industry	13	6.0
# employed in government	22	10.1
# employed in public interest	7	3.2
# employed as judicial clerks	17	7.8
# employed in academia	0	0.0

Geographic Location

	Total	Percentage
# employed in state	79	36.2
# employed in foreign countries	2	0.9
# of states where employed	33	

Bar Passage Rates

Jurisdiction	Missouri			Illinois		
Exam	Sum 05	Win 06	Total	Sum 05	Win 06	Total
# from school taking bar for the first time	82	14	96	59	36	95
School's pass rate for all first-time takers	89%	100%	91%	90%	89%	89%
State's pass rate for all first-time takers	88%	90%	89%	86%	83%	85%

Washington University School of Law

Box 1120, One Brookings Drive
St. Louis, MO 63130-4899
Phone: 314.935.4525; Fax: 314.935.8778
E-mail: admiss@wulaw.wustl.edu; Website: http://law.wustl.edu

■ Introduction

Washington University School of Law offers its students an outstanding legal education in an intellectually challenging and collegial environment. Our faculty members are recognized for their excellent teaching and scholarship, and they are highly accessible to our students. The School of Law curriculum blends traditional theory with opportunities to participate in a wide variety of clinical programs and cocurricular activities that encourage the development of practical skills and interdisciplinary learning.

■ Library and Physical Facilities

The law school moved into its state-of-the-art facility, Anheuser-Busch Hall, in 1997. While Anheuser-Busch Hall itself appears to be traditional, the latest computing and multimedia technologies are incorporated in its design. Cutting-edge information technology provides students with quick access to the Internet where they can register for courses, view grades, order transcripts, view a photo directory of classmates, access their e-mail, and enhance their legal research capabilities. Wireless connections are available throughout the law school. The law library is the focal point for much of the intellectual activity in the law school. It has a collection of over 600,000 volumes with particularly strong collections in the areas of international law, environmental law, land use planning, urban law, tax law, and Chinese law.

■ Curriculum

Washington University law school offers a broad-based curriculum that highlights applied lawyering skills. A three-year, full-time course of study leads to the JD degree. All first-year students have half their courses in small sections of approximately 40 students or less. These small classes increase the opportunities for participation in class discussions and individualized teacher-student contact. Second- and third-year students choose their own classes and can tailor them to fit their own particular interests. Students may also opt to enroll in a course from another graduate program at the university and apply the credit toward the JD requirements. In addition, our Center for Interdisciplinary Studies, the Whitney R. Harris Institute for Global Legal Studies, and other school-sponsored conferences and symposia expose our students to a wide range of nationally and internationally renowned legal scholars.

■ Clinical Opportunities

The School of Law's exceptional Clinical Education Program provides law students with opportunities to learn professional skills and values by working with clients, attorneys, judges, and legislators under the close supervision of experienced and expert faculty. Every interested student is guaranteed at least one clinical course during his or her second or third year of law school. The School of Law offers a wide variety of clinical courses including Civil Justice, Interdisciplinary Environmental, Civil Rights and Community Justice, Government Lawyering, Criminal Justice, Appellate, Judicial Clerkship, and Intellectual Property and Business Formation Legal Clinics. In addition, the Congressional and Administrative Law Clinic, founded in 1977, offers students the opportunity to spend their final semester working in Washington, DC, for a member of the United States Congress, a congressional committee, or a federal administrative agency.

■ Special-degree Programs

Washington University complements its outstanding JD program with many different joint-degree opportunities. In addition to our formal joint-degree programs, students may design their own joint degrees, combining law and another course of study that leads to a master's degree. Joint degrees offered include a JD/MBA, JD/MSW, JD/MHA, and JD/PhD-Political Science. We are one of only a very few joint-degree programs in the nation combining law with an MA in East Asian Studies. The School of Law also offers LLM programs in Intellectual Property and Technology Law, Taxation, and US Law for International Students.

■ Study-abroad Opportunities

The School of Law offers students the opportunity to study abroad for a semester and for international law students to study at our law school. Our students take regular courses in leading international institutions, studying under the legal scholars of the country. Washington University has exchange or study-abroad agreements in place with each of the following law schools: Utrecht University, Utrecht, the Netherlands; Inns of Court School of Law, London, UK; the Gerd Bucerius Law School, Hamburg, Germany; National University of Singapore; and the University of KwaZulu-Natal, Durban, South Africa.

■ Student Activities

The School of Law publishes three student-edited law review periodicals, the *Washington University Law Review*, the *Washington University Journal of Law and Policy*, and the *Washington University Global Studies Law Review*. The Trial and Advocacy Program includes a very active moot court program, mock trial competitions, and competitions in negotiation and client counseling. Students are actively involved in over 40 student organizations, including the Women's Law Caucus, Student Bar Association, Black Law Students Association, Latin American Law Students Association, Asian American Law Students Association, Native American Law Students Association, and OUTLAW (gay and lesbian alliance). Students also participate in a number of volunteer public service projects through student organizations or the school's Public Service Project Program.

■ Public Interest

The School of Law has a longstanding commitment to public service and lawyering in the public interest. In addition to its nine clinics, public interest law is supported in a number of different ways: the Webster Society provides full-tuition public interest scholarships; guaranteed public interest summer stipends provide funding for students engaged in public interest work; a loan repayment assistance program helps graduates beginning their careers in public service positions; a public service director coordinates the Public Service Project; a Director of Public Service Advising is part of the Career Services Office professional staff; and the popular Public Interest Law Speakers Series is offered.

■ Housing

Students find that the cost of living in St. Louis is much less than in other large metropolitan areas. There is a wide range of affordable housing available near the School of Law. For university-owned housing information, students should contact Quadrangle Housing at 800.874.4330. For privately owned housing, contact Apartment Referral Service at 314.935.5092.

■ Scholarship and Financial Aid

The school offers merit- and need-based scholarships. Most student aid is in the form of government and privately

sponsored loans. Over half the students receive some scholarship assistance; two-thirds receive loans. (Virtually all of those receiving scholarships also receive loans.) The school also offers loan repayment assistance for students who choose qualifying public interest law jobs upon graduation.

■ Career Services

With individual counseling a high priority, each student is assigned to one of six attorneys in the Career Services Office as his or her primary contact. The CSO professionals help students investigate and strategize career paths and goals. In addition to providing both on-campus and off-campus interviewing programs, the CSO offers programs on networking and skill development, clerkships, fellowships, researching employers, and a variety of informational sessions on different practice areas. Within six months of graduation, 99 percent of the class of 2005 were employed in 33 different states and two foreign countries.

Applicant Profile

Washington University School of Law
This grid includes only applicants who earned 120–180 LSAT scores under standard administrations.

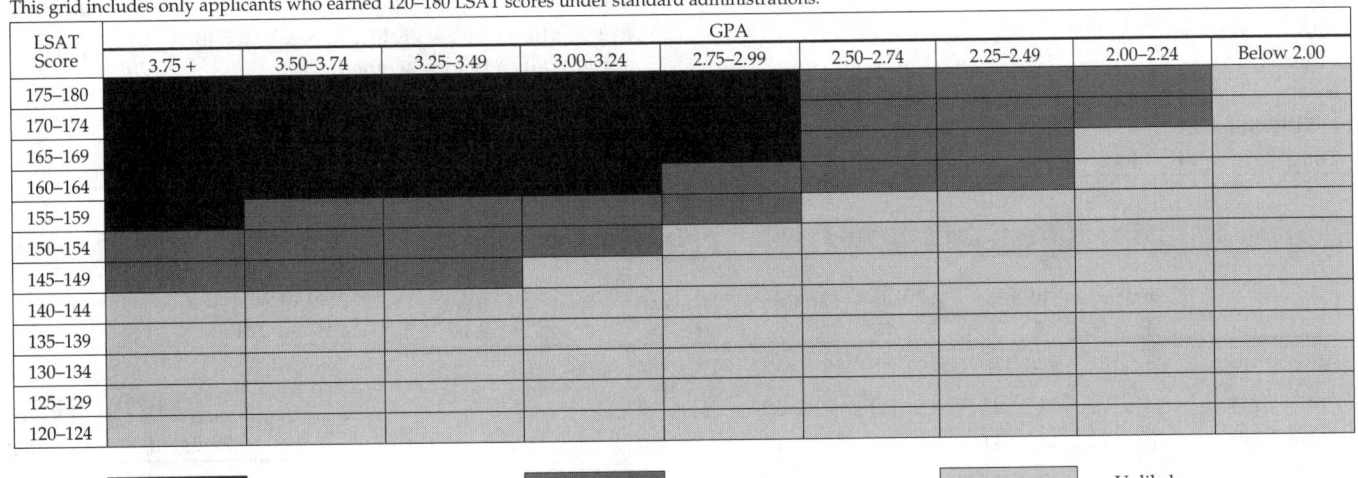

LSAT Score	GPA								
	3.75 +	3.50–3.74	3.25–3.49	3.00–3.24	2.75–2.99	2.50–2.74	2.25–2.49	2.00–2.24	Below 2.00
175–180									
170–174									
165–169									
160–164									
155–159									
150–154									
145–149									
140–144									
135–139									
130–134									
125–129									
120–124									

Good Possibility   Possible   Unlikely

Reflects 98% of the total applicant pool.

Wayne State University Law School

471 W. Palmer
Detroit, MI 48202
Phone: 313.577.3937; Fax: 313.993.8129
E-mail: lawinquire@wayne.edu; Website: www.law.wayne.edu

ABA Approved Since 1937

The Basics

Type of school	Public
Term	Semester
Application deadline	3/15
Application fee	$50
Financial aid deadline	3/30
Can first year start other than fall?	No
Student to faculty ratio	18.8 to 1
Does the university offer:	
housing restricted to law students?	Yes
graduate housing for which law students are eligible?	Yes

Faculty and Administrators

	Total		Men		Women		Minorities	
	Fall	Spr	Fall	Spr	Fall	Spr	Fall	Spr
Full-time	39	39	25	25	14	14	5	5
Other Full-time	7	7	2	2	5	5	1	1
Deans, librarians, & others who teach	7	7	4	4	3	3	2	2
Part-time	21	27	18	22	3	5	0	1
Total	**74**	**80**	**49**	**53**	**25**	**27**	**8**	**9**

Curriculum

	Full-time	Part-time
Typical first-year section size	93	38
Is there typically a "small section" of the first-year class, other than Legal Writing, taught by full-time faculty	No	No
If yes, typical size offered last year		
# of classroom course titles beyond first-year curriculum	75	
# of upper division courses, excluding seminars with an enrollment: Under 25	47	
25–49	21	
50–74	18	
75–99	7	
100+	1	
# of seminars	11	
# of seminar positions available	230	
# of seminar positions filled	138	33
# of positions available in simulation courses	387	
# of simulation positions filled	262	64
# of positions available in faculty supervised clinical courses	56	
# of faculty supervised clinical positions filled	41	5
# involved in field placements	120	8
# involved in law journals	70	7
# involved in interschool competitions	119	4
# of credit hours required to graduate	86	

JD Enrollment and Ethnicity

	Men		Women		Full-time		Part-time		1st-year		Total		JD Degs. Awd.
	#	%	#	%	#	%	#	%	#	%	#	%	
African Amer.	23	6.6	43	13.4	50	9.0	16	13.7	19	9.0	66	9.9	21
Amer. Indian	2	0.6	3	0.9	5	0.9	0	0.0	1	0.5	5	0.7	4
Asian Amer.	13	3.7	18	5.6	23	4.2	8	6.8	9	4.3	31	4.6	14
Mex. Amer.	2	0.6	2	0.6	4	0.7	0	0.0	0	0.0	4	0.6	4
Puerto Rican	0	0.0	0	0.0	0	0.0	0	0.0	0	0.0	0	0.0	0
Hispanic	13	3.7	8	2.5	19	3.4	2	1.7	7	3.3	21	3.1	4
Total Minority	53	15.2	74	23.1	101	18.3	26	22.2	36	17.1	127	19.0	47
For. Nation.	0	0.0	0	0.0	0	0.0	0	0.0	0	0.0	0	0.0	0
Caucasian	266	76.2	217	67.6	400	72.3	83	70.9	144	68.2	483	72.1	159
Unknown	30	8.6	30	9.3	52	9.4	8	6.8	31	14.7	60	9.0	20
Total	349	52.1	321	47.9	553	82.5	117	17.5	211	31.5	670		226

Transfers

Transfers in	1
Transfers out	10

Tuition and Fees

	Resident	Nonresident
Full-time	$17,358	$32,231
Part-time	$10,046	$18,545

Living Expenses

Estimated living expenses for singles

Living on campus	Living off campus	Living at home
$21,536	$21,536	$11,730

Wayne State University Law School

*ABA
Approved
Since
1937*

GPA and LSAT Scores

	Total	Full-time	Part-time
# of apps	1,216	1,079	137
# of offers	507	465	42
# of matrics	214	187	27
75% GPA	3.68	3.69	3.65
Median GPA	3.48	3.51	3.40
25% GPA	3.24	3.29	3.24
75% LSAT	159	160	159
Median LSAT	156	156	155
25% LSAT	153	154	152

Grants and Scholarships (from prior year)

	Total #	Total %	Full-time #	Full-time %	Part-time #	Part-time %
Total # of students	711		549		162	
Total # receiving grants	452	63.6	422	76.9	30	18.5
Less than 1/2 tuition	347	48.8	320	58.3	27	16.7
Half to full tuition	66	9.3	63	11.5	3	1.9
Full tuition	0	0.0	0	0.0	0	0.0
More than full tuition	39	5.5	39	7.1	0	0.0
Median grant amount			$3,500		$1,000	

Informational and Library Resources

# of volumes and volume equivalents	617,139
# of titles	255,865
# of active serial subscriptions	4,861
Study seating capacity inside the library	461
# of full-time professional librarians	5
Hours per week library is open	97
# of open, wired connections available to students	173
# of networked computers available for use by students	88
# of simultaneous wireless users	750
Require computer?	No

*Wayne State University Law School does not collect Grants and Scholarship information by full-time or part-time programs.

JD Attrition (from prior year)

	Academic #	Other #	Total #	Total %
1st year	2	18	20	8.5
2nd year	0	3	3	1.6
3rd year	0	4	4	1.7
4th year	0	2	2	3.5

Employment (9 months after graduation)

	Total	Percentage
Employment status known	184	77.3
Employment status unknown	54	22.7
Employed	131	71.2
Pursuing graduate degrees	0	0.0
Unemployed seeking employment	53	28.8
Unemployed not seeking employment	0	0.0
Unemployed and studying for the bar	0	0.0

Type of Employment

# employed in law firms	94	71.8
# employed in business and industry	15	11.5
# employed in government	10	7.6
# employed in public interest	1	0.8
# employed as judicial clerks	8	6.1
# employed in academia	1	0.8

Geographic Location

# employed in state	122	93.1
# employed in foreign countries	0	0.0
# of states where employed	7	

Bar Passage Rates

Jurisdiction	Michigan		
Exam	Sum 05	Win 06	Total
# from school taking bar for the first time	167	26	193
School's pass rate for all first-time takers	82%	69%	80%
State's pass rate for all first-time takers	78%	65%	74%

Wayne State University Law School

Admissions Office, 471 W. Palmer
Detroit, MI 48202
Phone: 313.577.3937; Fax: 313.993.8129
E-mail: lawinquire@wayne.edu; Website: www.law.wayne.edu

The information on these pages was provided by the law school.

■ Introduction

Wayne State University Law School in Detroit is the only public law school in the nation's eighth largest metropolitan area. Located on a beautiful 185-acre campus in the heart of Michigan's legal, economic, and cultural capital, the Law School blends cutting-edge legal theory with real-world practice skills, all at an affordable cost.

Wayne State law graduates serve at the highest levels of law and government. Fully one quarter of Michigan's judges earned their law degrees from Wayne State, as did the managing partners of many of the state's leading law firms and the directors of many of its nonprofit and community organizations. The Wayne State law faculty is made up of dedicated teachers and distinguished scholars known nationally and internationally for their contributions to legal study; they have published articles in the nation's top law journals, authored leading casebooks and treatises, litigated cases in the Supreme Court, and served with distinction in state and federal government. Established in 1927, Wayne State University Law School is accredited by the ABA, is a member of the AALS, and has a chapter of the Order of the Coif, the national honor society of the legal profession.

■ The Law School's Setting and Facilities

The Law School is a flagship unit of Wayne State University, a major metropolitan research university located in the Cultural Center district about four miles from downtown Detroit. Within blocks of the Law School are the Detroit Public Library, the Detroit Institute of Arts, the Charles H. Wright Museum of African-American History, the Detroit Science Center, and other cultural attractions. State and federal courts are concentrated nearby in the downtown area. The Law School complex sits at the north end of the university's main campus, a leafy urban oasis featuring several famous Yamasaki-designed buildings.

■ The Arthur Neef Law Library

The Arthur Neef Law Library is the second largest academic law library in Michigan and the twenty-third largest in the United States. With over 550,000 volumes, it serves as a major center of legal research in the Detroit and Michigan legal communities and is a designated federal government depository.

The majority of the study space in the recently renovated law library makes use of natural light. Comfortable reading tables and wired carrels are available throughout the building. The law library has recently installed a wireless network that can accommodate up to 340 simultaneous computer users; in addition, many study spaces are equipped with communication ports and electrical outlets for the convenient use of notebook computers.

A significant feature of the law library is the new 24-station computer laboratory, featuring personal computers available for the exclusive use of Wayne State law students. Mobile laptop carts are available for use by law students.

■ Clinical and Internship Programs

Wayne State University Law School offers its students a broad range of opportunities for practical legal training through its live-client clinics and its internship programs. The Law School operates five clinics: a Civil Rights Litigation Clinic, a Criminal Appellate Practice Clinic, a Disability Law Clinic, a Free Legal Aid Clinic, and a Nonprofit Corporations and Urban Development Law Clinic. These clinical offerings give students a chance to take first-chair responsibility in a choice of settings while serving the needs of Detroit's urban community. Students also have the chance to serve as interns for state and federal judges, public prosecutors, the State Appellate Defender's Office, and many nonprofit organizations.

■ Joint-degree Programs

Students may pursue joint-degree programs in one of five different areas: business administration, dispute resolution, history, political science, and economics. Joint-degree students must be admitted separately to the Law School and to the appropriate master's degree program at the university. Each joint-degree program requires a student to spend his or her first year taking exclusively law courses, followed by two and one-half to three years of concurrent studies.

■ Intellectual Property Law Institute

Intellectual property (IP) law and related fields, such as the emerging area of electronic commerce, are among the strengths of the Wayne State law faculty. The Law School offers a tremendous variety of courses and seminars on IP-related subjects. Wayne State law students may take courses at the University of Detroit Mercy and the University of Windsor, just across the river in Canada, through the Intellectual Property Law Institute (IPLI). IPLI, which was created in 1987 as a cooperative effort of these three law schools, offers a rich curriculum for IP-focused students, including courses and seminars in patent, copyright, trademark, computer and related technology, communications and media, and entertainment law.

■ International Law and Foreign Study Programs

International and comparative law is another area of curricular strength at Wayne State. The Law School offers a wide variety of courses in these fields, taught by faculty with global reputations. In addition, Wayne State law students have the opportunities to enroll in international and comparative law courses at the University of Windsor in Canada; to participate in one of the Law School's two international student exchange programs, at the University of Utrecht in the Netherlands or at the University of Warwick in England; and to apply for a summer study fellowship at The Hague.

■ Student Activities

Student-edited Law Journals—Wayne State University Law School publishes two student-edited law journals. *The Wayne Law Review*, a scholarly legal journal with a nationwide circulation, has been published since 1954 by upper-class law students selected on the basis of superior academic achievement and writing ability. The *Journal of Law in Society* publishes articles drawn from an annual spring symposium on topics such as affirmative action, environmental justice, reparations for slavery, school vouchers, and gentrification. Both journals offer an opportunity for students to enhance their research and writing skills and further their knowledge of the law while earning law school course credit.

Moot Court—Founded in 1949, Wayne State University's Moot Court program, which helps students hone their written and oral advocacy skills, has evolved into one of the most competitive appellate advocacy programs in the country. In 2003, a student team from Wayne State won first place in the 53rd annual National Moot Court Competition, beating out 188 teams from law schools across the nation.

Student Trial Advocacy Program—The Student Trial Advocacy Program (STAP) complements Wayne State's extensive offering of skills courses by providing students with instruction and experience in the techniques of trial litigation. Wayne State STAP members have successfully competed in trial advocacy competitions across the country.

■ Scholarships

Wayne State University Law School is committed to attracting and retaining highly credentialed students while maintaining economic accessibility to legal education and the legal profession. To further these goals, the Law School gave approximately $2.75 million in WSU and privately endowed scholarships and grants to students in the 2005–2006 academic year. Scholarships are based on the applicant's academic record. In almost all cases, no scholarship application is required.

■ Housing

The Towers Residential Suites offer students on-campus living in a high-rise tower. The top floors are reserved for graduate students. The majority of the rooms are suite style. There are also studio rooms available. Within the building are a cafe-style dining hall, a mini bookstore, and multiple fitness rooms. The Towers feature free internet access, cable connections, multiple social and study lounges, laundry rooms, and a 24-hour staffed reception area.

Applicant Profile

Wayne State University Law School
This grid includes only applicants who earned 120–180 LSAT scores under standard administrations.

LSAT Score	3.75 +		3.50–3.74		3.25–3.49		3.00–3.24		2.75–2.99		2.50–2.74		2.25–2.49		2.00–2.24		Below 2.00		No GPA		Total	
	Apps	Adm	Apps	Adm	Apps	Adm	Apps	Adm	Apps	Adm	Apps	Adm	Apps	Adm	Apps	Adm	Apps	Adm	Apps	Adm	Apps	Adm
175–180	1	1	0	0	0	0	0	0	0	0	0	0	0	0	0	0	0	0	0	0	1	1
170–174	0	0	1	1	0	0	3	1	0	0	1	0	2	1	0	0	0	0	0	0	7	3
165–169	6	5	8	7	7	7	5	5	1	1	1	1	0	0	0	0	0	0	0	0	28	26
160–164	22	20	22	22	30	29	21	21	12	10	7	4	8	1	1	0	0	0	1	0	124	107
155–159	36	35	64	64	54	48	58	33	18	8	21	2	9	1	3	0	0	0	2	1	265	192
150–154	35	32	69	42	74	38	77	16	37	8	31	3	5	1	5	0	3	0	3	2	339	142
145–149	16	3	45	6	63	8	59	7	30	4	31	2	12	0	4	0	1	0	3	0	264	30
140–144	8	0	13	1	24	0	30	0	30	0	17	0	9	0	3	0	2	0	1	0	137	1
135–139	1	0	1	0	7	0	14	0	7	0	10	0	5	0	6	0	0	0	3	0	54	0
130–134	0	0	1	0	2	0	5	0	4	0	5	0	3	0	3	0	0	0	2	0	25	0
125–129	0	0	2	0	1	0	0	0	2	0	1	0	0	0	1	0	0	0	0	0	7	0
120–124	0	0	0	0	0	0	0	0	1	0	0	0	0	0	0	0	0	0	0	0	1	0
Total	125	96	226	143	262	130	272	83	142	31	125	12	53	4	26	0	6	0	15	3	1252	502

Apps = Number of Applicants
Adm = Number Admitted
Reflects 98% of the total applicant pool.

West Virginia University College of Law

PO Box 6130
Morgantown, WV 26506-6130
Phone: 304.293.5301; Fax: 304.293.8102
E-mail: wvulaw.admissions@mail.wvu.edu; Website: www.wvu.edu/~law

ABA
Approved
Since
1923

The Basics

Type of school	Public
Term	Semester
Application deadline	2/1
Application fee	$50
Financial aid deadline	4/1
Can first year start other than fall?	No
Student to faculty ratio	15.1 to 1
Does the university offer:	
housing restricted to law students?	No
graduate housing for which law students are eligible?	Yes

Faculty and Administrators

	Total		Men		Women		Minorities	
	Fall	Spr	Fall	Spr	Fall	Spr	Fall	Spr
Full-time	26	26	18	18	8	8	4	4
Other Full-time	0	0	0	0	0	0	0	0
Deans, librarians, & others who teach	4	4	2	3	2	1	0	0
Part-time	26	17	17	12	9	5	0	0
Total	**56**	**47**	**37**	**33**	**19**	**14**	**4**	**4**

Curriculum

		Full-time	Part-time
Typical first-year section size		80	0
Is there typically a "small section" of the first-year class, other than Legal Writing, taught by full-time faculty		No	No
If yes, typical size offered last year			
# of classroom course titles beyond first-year curriculum		64	
# of upper division courses, excluding seminars with an enrollment:	Under 25	33	
	25–49	25	
	50–74	15	
	75–99	4	
	100+	3	
# of seminars		15	
# of seminar positions available		240	
# of seminar positions filled		192	0
# of positions available in simulation courses		386	
# of simulation positions filled		353	0
# of positions available in faculty supervised clinical courses		34	
# of faculty supervised clinical positions filled	34	0	
# involved in field placements		5	0
# involved in law journals		41	0
# involved in interschool competitions		42	0
# of credit hours required to graduate		91	

JD Enrollment and Ethnicity

	Men		Women		Full-time		Part-time		1st-year		Total		JD Degs. Awd.
	#	%	#	%	#	%	#	%	#	%	#	%	
African Amer.	14	5.3	20	9.4	34	7.2	0	0.0	15	9.2	34	7.1	6
Amer. Indian	1	0.4	0	0.0	1	0.2	0	0.0	0	0.0	1	0.2	1
Asian Amer.	4	1.5	6	2.8	10	2.1	0	0.0	4	2.5	10	2.1	1
Mex. Amer.	0	0.0	1	0.5	1	0.2	0	0.0	0	0.0	1	0.2	0
Puerto Rican	0	0.0	0	0.0	0	0.0	0	0.0	0	0.0	0	0.0	0
Hispanic	1	0.4	2	0.9	3	0.6	0	0.0	1	0.6	3	0.6	2
Total Minority	20	7.6	29	13.6	49	10.3	0	0.0	20	12.3	49	10.3	10
For. Nation.	0	0.0	1	0.5	1	0.2	0	0.0	0	0.0	1	0.2	0
Caucasian	243	92.4	183	85.9	424	89.5	2	100.0	143	87.7	426	89.5	132
Unknown	0	0.0	0	0.0	0	0.0	0	0.0	0	0.0	0	0.0	0
Total	263	55.3	213	44.7	474	99.6	2	0.4	163	34.2	476		142

Transfers

Transfers in	7
Transfers out	9

Tuition and Fees

	Resident	Nonresident
Full-time	$9,342	$21,710
Part-time	$0	$0

Living Expenses

Estimated living expenses for singles

Living on campus	Living off campus	Living at home
$12,481	$12,481	$12,481

West Virginia University College of Law

ABA
Approved
Since
1923

GPA and LSAT Scores

	Total	Full-time	Part-time
# of apps	903	903	0
# of offers	354	354	0
# of matrics	166	166	0
75% GPA	3.72	3.72	0.00
Median GPA	3.51	3.51	0.00
25% GPA	3.16	3.16	0.00
75% LSAT	155	155	0
Median LSAT	153	153	0
25% LSAT	149	149	0

Grants and Scholarships (from prior year)

	Total #	Total %	Full-time #	Full-time %	Part-time #	Part-time %
Total # of students	467		463		4	
Total # receiving grants	158	33.8	158	34.1	0	0.0
Less than 1/2 tuition	126	27.0	126	27.2	0	0.0
Half to full tuition	12	2.6	12	2.6	0	0.0
Full tuition	6	1.3	6	1.3	0	0.0
More than full tuition	14	3.0	14	3.0	0	0.0
Median grant amount			$1,600		$0	

Informational and Library Resources

# of volumes and volume equivalents	353,358
# of titles	60,167
# of active serial subscriptions	3,227
Study seating capacity inside the library	274
# of full-time professional librarians	3
Hours per week library is open	106
# of open, wired connections available to students	170
# of networked computers available for use by students	42
# of simultaneous wireless users	300
Require computer?	No

JD Attrition (from prior year)

	Academic #	Other #	Total #	Total %
1st year	3	12	15	9.9
2nd year	1	1	2	1.2
3rd year	0	1	1	0.7
4th year	0	0	0	0.0

Employment (9 months after graduation)

	Total	Percentage
Employment status known	136	97.8
Employment status unknown	3	2.2
Employed	126	92.6
Pursuing graduate degrees	3	2.2
Unemployed seeking employment	5	3.7
Unemployed not seeking employment	0	0.0
Unemployed and studying for the bar	2	1.5

Type of Employment

	Total	%
# employed in law firms	75	59.5
# employed in business and industry	11	8.7
# employed in government	6	4.8
# employed in public interest	2	1.6
# employed as judicial clerks	26	20.6
# employed in academia	1	0.8

Geographic Location

	Total	%
# employed in state	88	69.8
# employed in foreign countries	0	0.0
# of states where employed	15	

Bar Passage Rates

Jurisdiction	West Virginia		
Exam	Sum 05	Win 06	Total
# from school taking bar for the first time	93	7	100
School's pass rate for all first-time takers	73%	57%	72%
State's pass rate for all first-time takers	71%	41%	68%

West Virginia University College of Law

PO Box 6130
Morgantown, WV 26506-6130
Phone: 304.293.5301; Fax: 304.293.8102
E-mail: wvulaw.admissions@mail.wvu.edu; Website: www.wvu.edu/~law

■ Introduction

The College of Law, established in 1878, is the oldest professional school in West Virginia. The university is located in Morgantown, WV. Within a 500-mile radius of Morgantown is half of the population of the US and one third of the population of Canada. The College of Law has been a member of the AALS since 1914 and was fully accredited by the ABA in 1923. The college has had a chapter of the Order of the Coif since 1925.

■ Library and Physical Facilities

The College of Law facility measures 131,966 square feet and provides a spacious learning community for law students. The law center is home to six classrooms, two courtrooms, a distance learning center, financial aid, career services, and a law bookstore. Ample parking at the law center is available by permit for all law students.

The George R. Farmer Jr. Law Library, a three-story, 32,476-square-foot facility with 40,386 feet of shelving space, is home to the largest law library in the state of West Virginia. The law library is comprehensive in scope with a collection of over 300,000 volumes and equivalents. The library provides access to 42 networked computers, including the Carlin Computer Lab, a 16-computer teaching lab.

The Student Recreation Center is a $34 million, 177,000-square-foot facility complete with two swimming pools and a massive 50-foot climbing wall that stretches up through the center of the three-story building. The center also houses a wellness center, a resource library, a study area, a food-service operation, a small classroom, a meeting/conference room, and socialization areas.

■ Curriculum

Subject to modification, 91 hours are required for graduation. The 31-hour first-year curriculum is specified. The second- and third-year programs offer a number of course options and possibilities for concentration.

Students have the option, after being admitted, to request enrollment in the part-time program that offers daytime courses congruently with the full-time program. There is not a separate nighttime track.

■ Student Activities

West Virginia University College of Law has various student organizations. The Student Bar Association is the student government of the school. The *West Virginia Law Review*, the fourth oldest law review in the nation, selects members on the basis of performance during their first year in law school and a writing competition. An active Moot Court Program is conducted at the law school.

■ Opportunities for Minority Students

The College of Law is committed to maintaining a diverse student body by welcoming students who are members of groups traditionally underrepresented in the legal profession.

The Meredith Career Services Center assists minority students with securing summer employment through a Minority Clerkship Program. The College of Law also participates in the Southeast Minority Job Fair in Atlanta, a regional job fair that brings together employers and minority students. Student organizations, such as Black Law Students Association, provide additional opportunities for minority students.

■ Placement

Our graduates are employed at the major law firms in West Virginia, are members of the judiciary, and hold important positions in government. They are also in major law firms from New York City to Hong Kong, Rome to Pittsburgh, and San Diego to Richmond. Many graduates also run their own offices and work tirelessly for those who have little or no money but desperately need legal representation. Please visit the Meredith Career Services Center on our website for more information.

■ Admission

The College of Law admits first-year students only in the first (fall) semester. No specific prelaw curriculum is required for admission. The college subscribes to the suggestions on prelaw study in this book and stresses the value of college courses that require extensive analytic skills and writing assignments.

Persons are admitted to the College of Law on the basis of previous academic performance, scores on the Law School Admission Test, personal statements, letters of recommendation, and such other factors that bear upon the potential professional qualifications of the applicant as are determined by the College of Law.

Applications are accepted beginning in September of each year for the class to be admitted in the following August. Those accepted are required to make a deposit of $100 against tuition and fees within a designated period, but not before April 1.

■ Expenses and Financial Aid

Although WVU's reasonable tuition and fees are an excellent value, the College of Law recognizes that many students may not be able to afford the full cost of a legal education without financial assistance. Limited funds in the form of tuition waivers, scholarships, and college work-study are available each year through the university. Even if the student has not been accepted to the College of Law, he or she should apply for financial aid by March 1. The Free Application for Federal Student Aid (FAFSA) must be completed in order to receive any financial assistance, including all need-based scholarships. Students must complete the FAFSA each year in order to be considered for financial aid.

More information may be obtained by contacting Joanna Hastings, Financial Aid Counselor, PO Box 6130, Morgantown, WV 26506-6130; phone: 304.293.5302; joanna.hastings@mail.wvu.edu.

■ Housing

WVU Law students select from a wide range of living arrangements both on campus and in private housing. Contact the University Housing Office, located in Bennett Tower, Evansdale Residential Complex at 304.293.3621, for information concerning university-owned dormitories and apartments. Information concerning off-campus, privately owned housing may be obtained by calling the Office of Student Affairs in E. Moore Hall at 304.293.5613.

Applicant Profile

West Virginia University College of Law
This grid includes only applicants who earned 120–180 LSAT scores under standard administrations.

LSAT Score	GPA 3.75 +		3.50–3.74		3.25–3.49		3.00–3.24		2.75–2.99		2.50–2.74		2.25–2.49		2.00–2.24		Below 2.00		No GPA		Total	
	Apps	Adm	Apps	Adm	Apps	Adm	Apps	Adm	Apps	Adm	Apps	Adm	Apps	Adm	Apps	Adm	Apps	Adm	Apps	Adm	Apps	Adm
175–180	0	0	0	0	0	0	0	0	0	0	0	0	0	0	0	0	0	0	0	0	0	0
170–174	0	0	0	0	0	0	0	0	0	0	0	0	0	0	0	0	0	0	0	0	0	0
165–169	0	0	2	2	1	1	2	2	0	0	0	0	1	1	0	0	0	0	0	0	6	6
160–164	10	10	8	8	1	1	7	6	3	2	4	2	2	2	0	0	0	0	0	0	35	31
155–159	13	12	29	26	18	15	18	13	18	12	7	5	2	1	3	0	0	0	1	1	109	85
150–154	41	36	53	38	63	28	55	27	40	11	18	6	10	2	4	0	3	1	1	0	288	149
145–149	27	13	62	20	64	12	49	3	38	3	17	0	14	2	4	1	0	0	2	1	277	55
140–144	12	4	21	1	28	3	27	1	24	5	14	3	7	0	1	0	0	0	0	0	134	17
135–139	2	0	7	1	6	2	8	1	7	0	2	0	4	0	4	0	0	0	2	0	42	4
130–134	0	0	2	0	1	0	0	0	0	0	0	0	1	0	0	0	0	0	0	0	4	0
125–129	0	0	1	0	0	0	0	0	0	0	0	0	0	0	0	0	0	0	0	0	1	0
120–124	0	0	0	0	0	0	0	0	0	0	0	0	0	0	0	0	0	0	0	0	0	0
Total	105	75	185	96	182	62	166	53	130	33	62	16	41	8	16	1	3	1	6	2	896	347

Apps = Number of Applicants
Adm = Number Admitted
Reflects 98% of the total applicant pool.

Western New England College School of Law

1215 Wilbraham Road
Springfield, MA 01119-2684
Phone: 800.782.6665, 413.782.1406; Fax: 413.796.2067
E-mail: admissions@law.wnec.edu; Website: www.law.wnec.edu

ABA
Approved
Since
1974

The Basics

Type of school	Private
Term	Semester
Application deadline	3/15
Application fee	$50
Financial aid deadline	
Can first year start other than fall?	No
Student to faculty ratio	15.7 to 1
Does the university offer:	
housing restricted to law students?	Yes
graduate housing for which law students are eligible?	No

Faculty and Administrators

	Total		Men		Women		Minorities	
	Fall	Spr	Fall	Spr	Fall	Spr	Fall	Spr
Full-time	29	24	14	12	15	12	2	0
Other Full-time	5	5	2	2	3	3	1	1
Deans, librarians, & others who teach	4	4	3	3	1	1	0	0
Part-time	18	19	13	12	5	7	1	0
Total	56	52	32	29	24	23	4	1

Curriculum

		Full-time	Part-time
Typical first-year section size		49	51
Is there typically a "small section" of the first-year class, other than Legal Writing, taught by full-time faculty		No	No
If yes, typical size offered last year			
# of classroom course titles beyond first-year curriculum		93	
# of upper division courses, excluding seminars with an enrollment:	Under 25	57	
	25–49	50	
	50–74	5	
	75–99	4	
	100+	0	
# of seminars		9	
# of seminar positions available		149	
# of seminar positions filled		104	13
# of positions available in simulation courses		549	
# of simulation positions filled		270	46
# of positions available in faculty supervised clinical courses		128	
# of faculty supervised clinical positions filled	98	5
# involved in field placements		25	1
# involved in law journals		35	10
# involved in interschool competitions		16	0
# of credit hours required to graduate		88	

JD Enrollment and Ethnicity

	Men		Women		Full-time		Part-time		1st-year		Total		JD Degs. Awd.
	#	%	#	%	#	%	#	%	#	%	#	%	
African Amer.	8	2.6	9	3.6	11	2.9	6	3.6	11	5.4	17	3.1	7
Amer. Indian	0	0.0	0	0.0	0	0.0	0	0.0	0	0.0	0	0.0	0
Asian Amer.	6	2.0	7	2.8	11	2.9	2	1.2	4	2.0	13	2.4	6
Mex. Amer.	0	0.0	0	0.0	0	0.0	0	0.0	0	0.0	0	0.0	0
Puerto Rican	0	0.0	0	0.0	0	0.0	0	0.0	0	0.0	0	0.0	0
Hispanic	10	3.3	11	4.4	18	4.7	3	1.8	10	5.0	21	3.8	2
Total Minority	24	7.9	27	10.9	40	10.4	11	6.5	25	12.4	51	9.2	15
For. Nation.	9	3.0	12	4.8	18	4.7	3	1.8	3	1.5	21	3.8	8
Caucasian	206	67.5	156	62.9	253	65.9	109	64.5	140	69.3	362	65.5	127
Unknown	66	21.6	53	21.4	73	19.0	46	27.2	34	16.8	119	21.5	40
Total	305	55.2	248	44.8	384	69.4	169	30.6	202	36.5	553		190

Transfers

Transfers in	2
Transfers out	19

Tuition and Fees

	Resident	Nonresident
Full-time	$30,522	$30,522
Part-time	$22,566	$22,566

Living Expenses

Estimated living expenses for singles		
Living on campus	Living off campus	Living at home
N/A	$15,896	$7,260

Western New England College School of Law

ABA
Approved
Since
1974

GPA and LSAT Scores

	Total	Full-time	Part-time
# of apps	1,860	1,606	254
# of offers	919	822	97
# of matrics	201	147	54
75% GPA	3.37	3.39	3.29
Median GPA	3.08	3.09	3.03
25% GPA	2.67	2.66	2.70
75% LSAT	155	157	151
Median LSAT	152	154	150
25% LSAT	150	151	149

Grants and Scholarships (from prior year)

	Total		Full-time		Part-time	
	#	%	#	%	#	%
Total # of students	576		416		160	
Total # receiving grants	294	51.0	241	57.9	53	33.1
Less than 1/2 tuition	158	27.4	119	28.6	39	24.4
Half to full tuition	126	21.9	114	27.4	12	7.5
Full tuition	10	1.7	8	1.9	2	1.3
More than full tuition	0	0.0	0	0.0	0	0.0
Median grant amount			$14,000		$5,833	

Informational and Library Resources

# of volumes and volume equivalents	413,708
# of titles	167,151
# of active serial subscriptions	5,153
Study seating capacity inside the library	300
# of full-time professional librarians	7
Hours per week library is open	103
# of open, wired connections available to students	17
# of networked computers available for use by students	43
# of simultaneous wireless users	1,152
Require computer?	No

JD Attrition (from prior year)

	Academic	Other	Total	
	#	#	#	%
1st year	5	35	40	20.7
2nd year	0	4	4	2.4
3rd year	0	1	1	0.5
4th year	0	1	1	3.1

Employment (9 months after graduation)

	Total	Percentage
Employment status known	139	86.9
Employment status unknown	21	13.1
Employed	119	85.6
Pursuing graduate degrees	3	2.2
Unemployed seeking employment	9	6.5
Unemployed not seeking employment	1	0.7
Unemployed and studying for the bar	7	5.0
Type of Employment		
# employed in law firms	46	38.7
# employed in business and industry	32	26.9
# employed in government	27	22.7
# employed in public interest	4	3.4
# employed as judicial clerks	5	4.2
# employed in academia	3	2.5
Geographic Location		
# employed in state	46	38.7
# employed in foreign countries	2	1.7
# of states where employed	16	

Bar Passage Rates

Jurisdiction	Connecticut			Massachusetts		
Exam	Sum 05	Win 06	Total	Sum 05	Win 06	Total
# from school taking bar for the first time	50	21	71	43	15	58
School's pass rate for all first-time takers	62%	76%	66%	79%	67%	76%
State's pass rate for all first-time takers	81%	83%	82%	84%	75%	82%

The information on these pages was provided by the law school.

Western New England College School of Law

Office of Admissions, 1215 Wilbraham Road
Springfield, MA 01119-2684
Phone: 800.782.6665, 413.782.1406; Fax: 413.796.2067
E-mail: admissions@law.wnec.edu; Website: www.law.wnec.edu

■ Introduction

For more than three-quarters of a century, Western New England College School of Law has been preparing men and women to enter the legal profession. We are fully accredited by the ABA and are a member of the AALS. Our 6,000 alumni live in nearly all 50 states and several foreign countries and include judges, private practice attorneys, corporate lawyers, and armed services personnel. We offer both full- and part-time programs and are conveniently located 90 miles west of Boston and 150 miles north of New York City. Western New England College School of Law offers a full, well-rounded curriculum taught by experts and scholars in their respective fields—faculty who are interested in helping students learn and understand the law to their fullest ability. Our first-year section size is purposely among the smallest in the country in order to promote collegiality and effective learning. During the first year, day students are in sections of 50 students, and the evening section features a section of 40 students. These small sections encourage greater class participation and allow the students to interact more with each other and with their professors.

■ Admission and Scholarships

Every application is read by members of the Admissions Committee. All facets of the application are carefully considered, including race, gender, language, and educational, social, and economic obstacles overcome in the applicant's pursuit of higher education. We seek candidates with well-developed writing ability and analytical skills who will contribute to classroom discussions and the law school community.

Each year partial- and full-tuition scholarships are awarded to applicants whose credentials and backgrounds suggest they are likely to enrich the life of the School of Law. Several students are awarded full-tuition Oliver Wendell Holmes Jr. Scholarships. The Holmes Scholars usually score in the top 20 percent of the LSAT nationally and finish very near the top of their undergraduate classes.

Partial-tuition scholarships are also awarded on the basis of academic merit. Partial scholarships are available for applicants who demonstrate potential for success and who have overcome cultural, economic, societal, physical, or educational obstacles. All admitted applicants receive automatic scholarship consideration. Typically, 40 percent of the entering class receives scholarships of some type.

Western New England College School of Law will strengthen its commitment to public interest lawyering by offering six Public Interest Scholarships to full-time students. These yearly scholarships will range from $15,000 to full tuition, with an additional one-time $3,500 stipend awarded to each recipient. Students will take special public interest courses, have regular meetings with public interest practitioners to discuss cutting-edge issues in public interest practice, and will be mentored in their public interest careers by faculty and members of the Public Interest Advisory Board. Recipients will receive the $3,500 stipend to support the required public interest summer internship. The scholarship, the stipend, the curriculum, the special programming, and the mentoring provide an exceptional opportunity to offset the cost of law school while preparing for a career in public interest lawyering.

■ Faculty

The School of Law's 37 full-time faculty members have been educated at many of the nation's most prestigious law schools. All have practiced law prior to joining our faculty, with most having practiced in the fields of law that they now teach. They all share a love of teaching and take pride in their ability to engage students in rigorous law study in a collaborative, collegial environment. They are productive scholars who are consistently praised by our students for their accessibility.

■ Curriculum

All required courses, both day and evening, are taught by full-time faculty members. Some upper-level courses are taught through classroom discussions of judicial decisions and statutes. Others are taught through simulations in which students perform the roles of lawyers in lifelike situations and through clinics in which students represent actual clients. Part-time day and evening programs are also available.

Our broad-based curriculum allows students the opportunity to focus their legal studies in many different areas of the law, including tax, public interest, and corporate law. For a full list, please reference our website or bulletin.

We also offer three joint-degree programs:
- JD/MBA (Master of Business Administration) with Western New England College
- JD/MSW (Master of Social Work) with Springfield College
- JD/MRP (Master of Regional Planning) with the University of Massachusetts at Amherst

Western New England College School of Law offers a Master of Laws (LLM) degree in Estate Planning and Elder Law. The part-time evening program will prepare both new and established attorneys to meet the growing demand for estate planning and taxation counseling resulting from the aging baby boomer generation.

■ Experiential Learning: Clinics, Simulations, Externships

Clinics and simulation courses are integral components of the curriculum at Western New England College School of Law. Each type of course offers an opportunity to put theory into practice, thereby enhancing advocacy skills and enriching the understanding of core course materials. Students also apply their legal skills through externships.

Clinics provide an opportunity for upper-class students to represent clients with actual legal problems. Currently, the School of Law offers five different clinics in which students can gain valuable lawyering skills, such as legal writing, interviewing, and negotiating. The following clinical opportunities are offered:
- Criminal Law Clinic—students prosecute cases for the Hampden County District Attorney's Office;
- Legal Services Clinic—students work in the office of Western Massachusetts Legal Services, Inc.;
- Consumer Law Clinic—students work in the City of Springfield's Consumer Protection Program;
- Real Property Practicum—students work with practitioners in the real estate area; and

- Small Business Clinic—students help start-up businesses at the Springfield Enterprise Center's business incubator.

Simulation courses allow students to represent hypothetical clients with challenging legal problems drawn from the experiences of practicing lawyers. Students perform research, prepare legal documents, and negotiate with and argue against role-playing students and faculty.

Externships enable students to work with judges or alongside attorneys in public interest organizations or government agencies. Externs are called upon to perform research and prepare legal documents. Externships allow students to refine their lawyering skills and provide interaction with professionals who can offer advice and career insights. Students receive two or three hours of academic credit for one nonpaying externship.

Moot court competitions give our students the opportunity to hone their research, writing, and oral advocacy skills. Western New England College School of Law participates in many national trial, negotiation, and moot court competitions each year. In the past several years, our students have been strong competitors and have earned many honors, including national champions in 2004 at the First Amendment Moot Court Competition in Nashville, Tennessee; national champions in 2001 at the ABA Negotiation Moot Court Competition; and national finalists in 2002, 2003, and 2004 at the ABA Law Student Division Negotiation Competition.

■ Library, Facilities, and the Area

Our spacious law library, with its 416,000-volume collection, is enhanced by participation in the New England Law Library Consortium. This arrangement allows students to access 20 academic, 1 private, and 4 government law libraries.

The law school building is located on Western New England College's 215-acre campus in a residential section of Springfield. Ample, on-campus, free parking is available to all students.

Springfield is a small city that offers a wide array of recreational, social, and cultural attractions. The Pioneer Valley provides our students with a range of affordable housing options in a variety of settings. Attending the only law school in Western Massachusetts, Western New England College School of Law students have accessibility to a host of externship and clinical opportunities throughout the region.

The School of Law's location places students within reach of a rich and diverse legal community. State and federal courthouses; offices of the Attorney General, District Attorney, and Public Defender; and many small- and medium-sized law firms in Springfield, Northampton, and nearby Hartford, Connecticut, represent opportunities for externships and full- and part-time employment in traditional legal careers.

■ Student Activities

The Student Bar Association (SBA) is the student government of the School of Law. Officers are elected by the student body and representatives are elected by class from both the full-time and part-time divisions. The SBA plays a significant role in the administration of the School of Law with representation at the Faculty Meeting and on the Faculty/Student Committees.

The Multi-Cultural Law Students Association, the Women's Law Association, and OUTLaw are some of the student groups created around the common experience and interests of our students. They are important in assisting new students in becoming part of our community, and are active in bringing to the entire student body the experiences and views of their individual communities.

Applicant Profile

Western New England College School of Law
This grid includes only applicants who earned 120–180 LSAT scores under standard administrations.

LSAT Score	3.75 +		3.50–3.74		3.25–3.49		3.00–3.24		2.75–2.99		2.50–2.74		2.25–2.49		2.00–2.24		Below 2.00		No GPA		Total	
	Apps	Adm	Apps	Adm	Apps	Adm	Apps	Adm	Apps	Adm	Apps	Adm	Apps	Adm	Apps	Adm	Apps	Adm	Apps	Adm	Apps	Adm
175–180	0	0	0	0	0	0	0	0	0	0	0	0	0	0	0	0	0	0	0	0	0	0
170–174	0	0	0	0	0	0	0	0	0	0	2	2	0	0	0	0	0	0	0	0	2	2
165–169	2	2	2	2	2	2	3	3	1	1	4	3	2	2	1	1	0	0	0	0	17	16
160–164	12	12	11	11	18	18	15	15	10	10	12	10	2	2	5	4	0	0	1	0	86	82
155–159	22	21	39	39	43	42	34	32	44	43	25	25	9	9	10	10	0	0	2	0	228	221
150–154	40	40	73	71	111	103	118	106	108	93	71	49	25	14	16	7	3	0	6	2	571	485
145–149	25	7	75	20	93	27	125	29	85	14	59	9	39	4	6	1	0	0	3	2	510	113
140–144	9	0	33	1	55	0	51	1	52	0	44	1	17	0	8	0	1	0	4	0	274	3
135–139	3	0	12	0	11	0	24	0	22	0	15	0	10	0	6	0	1	0	4	0	108	0
130–134	0	0	4	0	2	0	8	0	5	0	3	0	3	0	2	0	2	0	1	0	30	0
125–129	0	0	1	0	0	0	0	0	1	0	2	0	0	0	4	0	2	0	2	0	12	0
120–124	0	0	0	0	0	0	0	0	0	0	0	0	1	0	0	0	0	0	0	0	1	0
Total	113	82	250	144	335	192	378	186	328	161	237	99	108	31	58	23	9	0	23	4	1839	922

Apps = Number of Applicants
Adm = Number Admitted
Reflects 99% of the total applicant pool.

Western State University—College of Law

1111 North State College Boulevard
Fullerton, CA 92831
Phone: 800.WSU.4LAW, 714.459.1101; Fax: 714.441.1748
E-mail: adm@wsulaw.edu; Website: www.wsulaw.edu

Provisional

ABA
Approved
Since
2006

The Basics

Type of school	Private
Term	Semester
Application deadline	5/1 10/1
Application fee	$50
Financial aid deadline	3/2 9/15
Can first year start other than fall?	Yes
Student to faculty ratio	22.5 to 1
Does the university offer:	
housing restricted to law students?	No
graduate housing for which law students are eligible?	No

Faculty and Administrators

	Total		Men		Women		Minorities	
	Fall	Spr	Fall	Spr	Fall	Spr	Fall	Spr
Full-time	15	15	10	10	5	5	5	5
Other Full-time	2	2	0	0	2	2	0	0
Deans, librarians, & others who teach	6	6	3	3	3	3	0	0
Part-time	28	37	19	20	9	17	3	4
Total	51	60	32	33	19	27	8	9

Curriculum

	Full-time	Part-time
Typical first-year section size	66	42
Is there typically a "small section" of the first-year class, other than Legal Writing, taught by full-time faculty	No	No
If yes, typical size offered last year		
# of classroom course titles beyond first-year curriculum	60	
# of upper division courses, excluding seminars with an enrollment: Under 25	51	
25–49	30	
50–74	8	
75–99	3	
100+	0	
# of seminars	5	
# of seminar positions available	125	
# of seminar positions filled	71	17
# of positions available in simulation courses	603	
# of simulation positions filled	315	173
# of positions available in faculty supervised clinical courses	45	
# of faculty supervised clinical positions filled	26	16
# involved in field placements	73	19
# involved in law journals	27	12
# involved in interschool competitions	7	5
# of credit hours required to graduate	88	

JD Enrollment and Ethnicity

	Men		Women		Full-time		Part-time		1st-year		Total		JD Degs. Awd.
	#	%	#	%	#	%	#	%	#	%	#	%	
African Amer.	8	3.7	10	4.3	15	4.9	3	2.1	9	5.2	18	4.0	13
Amer. Indian	3	1.4	2	0.9	4	1.3	1	0.7	4	2.3	5	1.1	1
Asian Amer.	31	14.5	51	21.7	59	19.2	23	16.3	30	17.3	82	18.3	36
Mex. Amer.	11	5.1	12	5.1	15	4.9	8	5.7	8	4.6	23	5.1	7
Puerto Rican	0	0.0	1	0.4	1	0.3	0	0.0	0	0.0	1	0.2	0
Hispanic	14	6.5	12	5.1	19	6.2	7	5.0	9	5.2	26	5.8	11
Total Minority	67	31.3	88	37.4	113	36.7	42	29.8	60	34.7	155	34.5	68
For. Nation.	0	0.0	0	0.0	0	0.0	0	0.0	0	0.0	0	0.0	0
Caucasian	131	61.2	129	54.9	177	57.5	83	58.9	104	60.1	260	57.9	77
Unknown	16	7.5	18	7.7	18	5.8	16	11.3	9	5.2	34	7.6	21
Total	214	47.7	235	52.3	308	68.6	141	31.4	173	38.5	449		166

Transfers

Transfers in	6
Transfers out	12

Tuition and Fees

	Resident	Nonresident
Full-time	$27,503	$27,503
Part-time	$18,603	$18,603

Living Expenses

Estimated living expenses for singles

Living on campus	Living off campus	Living at home
N/A	$16,574	$9,962

Western State University—College of Law

ABA
Approved
Since
2006

GPA and LSAT Scores

	Total	Full-time	Part-time
# of apps	1,713	1,356	357
# of offers	679	574	105
# of matrics	179	127	52
75% GPA	3.44	3.43	3.47
Median GPA	3.13	3.17	3.11
25% GPA	2.83	2.87	2.75
75% LSAT	154	154	153
Median LSAT	151	151	150
25% LSAT	149	149	149

Grants and Scholarships (from prior year)

	Total		Full-time		Part-time	
	#	%	#	%	#	%
Total # of students	489		323		166	
Total # receiving grants	185	37.8	114	35.3	71	42.8
Less than 1/2 tuition	126	25.8	85	26.3	41	24.7
Half to full tuition	51	10.4	26	8.0	25	15.1
Full tuition	8	1.6	3	0.9	5	3.0
More than full tuition	0	0.0	0	0.0	0	0.0
Median grant amount			$9,800		$6,000	

Informational and Library Resources

# of volumes and volume equivalents	200,536
# of titles	38,130
# of active serial subscriptions	2,948
Study seating capacity inside the library	336
# of full-time professional librarians	7
Hours per week library is open	109
# of open, wired connections available to students	241
# of networked computers available for use by students	60
# of simultaneous wireless users	960
Require computer?	No

JD Attrition (from prior year)

	Academic #	Other #	Total #	Total %
1st year	14	43	57	32.6
2nd year	0	5	5	5.1
3rd year	0	2	2	1.3
4th year	0	0	0	0.0

Employment (9 months after graduation)

	Total	Percentage
Employment status known	78	83.0
Employment status unknown	16	17.0
Employed	71	91.0
Pursuing graduate degrees	1	1.3
Unemployed seeking employment	3	3.8
Unemployed not seeking employment	3	3.8
Unemployed and studying for the bar	0	0.0

Type of Employment

	Total	Percentage
# employed in law firms	47	66.2
# employed in business and industry	7	9.9
# employed in government	9	12.7
# employed in public interest	3	4.2
# employed as judicial clerks	2	2.8
# employed in academia	3	4.2

Geographic Location

	Total	Percentage
# employed in state	69	97.2
# employed in foreign countries	0	0.0
# of states where employed	4	

Bar Passage Rates

Jurisdiction	California		
Exam	Sum 05	Win 06	Total
# from school taking bar for the first time	69	29	98
School's pass rate for all first-time takers	25%	31%	27%
State's pass rate for all first-time takers	64%	54%	62%

Western State University—College of Law

1111 North State College Boulevard
Fullerton, CA 92831
Phone: 800.WSU.4LAW, 714.459.1101; Fax: 714.441.1748
E-mail: adm@wsulaw.edu; Website: www.wsulaw.edu

■ Introduction

Western State University (WSU) College of Law, founded in 1966, is the oldest law school in Orange County, Southern California. Our 10,000 graduates have distinguished themselves as jurists, lawmakers, district attorneys, public defenders, and civil practitioners; they constitute a strong alumni network that mentors and enables an enviable job placement record for WSU graduates.

Located in the college town of Fullerton, in the heart of the vibrant economy and healthy legal market of Orange County, the WSU campus is about 30 miles south of Los Angeles and 100 miles north of San Diego, commuting distance from the metropolitan area, the fast-growing Inland Empire, and the Southland's beach cities and high technology, finance, and business centers.

A private law school fewer than 500 students, WSU offers small class sizes, personal interaction with faculty, and an extraordinary supportive learning environment. Repeatedly cited as one of the most ethnically diverse law school student bodies in the country, WSU is also known for giving students practical hands-on lawyering experience as well as a strong academic foundation.

■ Faculty

WSU prides itself on a faculty of excellent professors whose first priority is teaching and student success. Most bring extensive real-world legal experience to the classroom in addition to their strong academic and teaching credentials. The full-time faculty is supplemented by an outstanding adjunct faculty of practicing attorneys and judges. With a student faculty ratio of 22 to 1, and a highly accessible faculty, students benefit from individualized attention and mentoring.

■ Curriculum and Special Programs

WSU offers a full-time program that is normally completed in three years and part-time day or evening programs that take four years. Students may start in any of the programs in the fall. WSU also offers a January-start part-time evening program; students in good standing may transition to full time in the fall.

The Business Law Center and Criminal Law Practice Center programs give students the option to focus their electives to earn a Certificate in Business Law or Criminal Law and notation on their transcript indicating their special study emphasis. About one-third of students choose to earn a certificate in Business Law or Criminal Law. In addition to required and elective coursework, the centers also bring distinguished speakers to campus, arrange student visits to criminal justice facilities or business venues, and provide connections to practitioners, including internship and externship opportunities and career networking.

The On-site Legal Clinic functions as a small family and civil law practice, where student attorneys under supervision of the clinic director represent clients in the community, managing the cases from start to finish, including all court proceedings.

In the externship program, students receive placements in the courts, offices of district attorneys, public defenders, practicing attorneys and corporate legal departments, and public interest organizations where they gain hands-on experience and academic credit.

■ Student Body and Organizations

WSU's total student body is around 500 students, with the entering class about 150 students. Minority enrollment constitutes over a third of the total, with approximately even enrollment of men and women. The fall 2006 class entered from over 80 different undergraduate institutions; 25 percent came from 15 different states outside California.

More than 15 active student-led organizations enrich and complement the academic program with their cocurricular educational, networking, philanthropic, and social activities for students. These include the Student Bar Association, Asian Pacific American Law Student Association, Black Law Student Association, Latino Student Bar, Christian Legal Society, Business Law Association, Entertainment Sports Law Society, Animal Rights Association, and Phi Alpha Delta. Students who qualify for the law review and moot court team gain high visibility legal writing and advocacy experience.

■ Library and Physical Facilities

The library has over 200,000 volumes housed on three levels as well as access to electronic resources on campus and remotely. Students may use the library's 50 computers, including 25 located in a large computer classroom, or the wireless network. The library has 17 study rooms that may be used by students for group or individual study. The library maintains long hours to service the needs of our students. Our librarians provide extensive reference services and training in legal research, online research, and software.

WSU's campus is located in the heart of Fullerton's university district and consists of a main building and the library, with on-site parking. Most areas of both buildings are covered by wireless Wi-Fi. The main building contains 11 classrooms, the state-of-the-art Frank and Marleen Darras Moot Courtroom, an administrative suite, faculty offices, and a student lounge and café.

■ Admission

All applicants are assigned to an admission advisor who assists in the admission process, may conduct a personal or telephone informational interview, and arranges for visits to the campus and contact with professors, students, or alumni. Each applicant's entire file is reviewed; admission decisions are made by a faculty committee. A bachelor's degree or senior standing from an accredited college or university is required. A personal statement and two letters of recommendation are required, and a résumé is encouraged. Details of the applicant's undergraduate record and LSAT score, writing ability, and maturing life and work experiences are key indicators of potential for success in law school. When there are multiple LSAT scores, the highest, most recent score may be accorded significant weight. Admission is on a rolling basis, but application by April 1 for fall and October 1 for spring is highly encouraged.

■ Scholarships and Financial Aid

WSU offers generous merit-based scholarships; in the 2006 entering class about 50 percent of new students received scholarships. No separate application is required; admitted students are automatically considered for merit scholarships based on academic predictors. After the first year, law students are eligible to compete for merit scholarships provided they rank within the top 30 percent. A full range of loan programs is available to complement students' financial needs, including Stafford loans, Perkins loans, and private loans. All students receiving scholarship funds and or loans should plan to file the FAFSA and a preliminary financial aid application.

■ Career Services and Placement

With a 40-year history in Southern California and a strong alumni network of over 10,000 graduates, WSU has an enviable placement track record and the connections to assist students in their job search. Consistently in recent years, better than 90 percent of our graduates have been employed within six months of graduation. The most recent class found employment as follows: 66 percent private practice, 10 percent business and industry, 13 percent government, 4 percent public service, 4 percent academia, and 3 percent judicial clerkships.

The active Career Services Offices arranges on-campus interviews, career-related workshops, speaker panels, networking events, and individual counseling to help educate students about the many possible areas of practice and how to secure employment. The office serves as a liaison with legal employers, both public and private; it solicits job listings from alumni and local practitioners and assists students with permanent and summer employment.

The Career Resource Center provides students with hard-bound and electronic reference materials on résumé writing, job-search techniques, and study-abroad programs. Online job and résumé posting is provided by WSU to facilitate employment searches by students and alumni from the convenience of their home or office.

The Alumni Association sponsors a robust mentoring program for students and recent graduates. In addition, the Alumni Association assists with on-campus career fairs and networking events.

■ Contact Us

We encourage you to visit our website, speak to an admission advisor, and arrange to visit WSU in person, so you can sit in on a class and meet with students, alumni, and professors. Experience first hand the personal attention, supportive environment, and dedication to student success which set WSU apart.

Applicant Profile

Western State University—College of Law
This grid includes only applicants who earned 120–180 LSAT scores under standard administrations.

LSAT Score	3.75 +		3.50–3.74		3.25–3.49		3.00–3.24		2.75–2.99		2.50–2.74		2.25–2.49		2.00–2.24		Below 2.00		No GPA		Total	
	Apps	Adm	Apps	Adm	Apps	Adm	Apps	Adm	Apps	Adm	Apps	Adm	Apps	Adm	Apps	Adm	Apps	Adm	Apps	Adm	Apps	Adm
175–180	0	0	0	0	0	0	0	0	0	0	0	0	0	0	0	0	0	0	0	0	0	0
170–174	0	0	0	0	0	0	0	0	0	0	0	0	0	0	0	0	0	0	0	0	0	0
165–169	0	0	0	0	0	0	0	0	0	0	0	0	0	0	0	0	0	0	0	0	0	0
160–164	1	1	3	2	5	5	4	4	4	4	6	6	1	1	2	0	0	0	0	0	26	23
155–159	6	6	10	10	16	14	20	19	31	28	25	21	4	3	2	0	1	0	0	0	115	101
150–154	13	12	42	38	68	63	74	72	63	55	56	34	31	7	8	2	2	0	4	4	361	287
145–149	20	16	65	39	115	74	144	62	111	18	64	3	37	1	10	0	2	0	7	0	575	213
140–144	7	0	36	0	60	0	73	1	65	1	51	0	20	0	13	0	1	0	6	0	332	2
135–139	3	0	5	0	10	0	30	0	22	0	18	0	15	0	3	0	4	0	2	0	112	0
130–134	3	0	2	0	1	0	5	0	6	0	5	0	3	0	0	0	0	0	2	0	27	0
125–129	0	0	1	0	1	0	1	0	1	0	4	0	0	0	2	0	1	0	2	0	13	0
120–124	0	0	0	0	0	0	0	0	0	0	0	0	0	0	0	0	0	0	0	0	0	0
Total	53	35	164	89	276	156	351	158	303	106	229	64	111	12	40	2	11	0	23	4	1561	626

Apps = Number of Applicants
Adm = Number Admitted
Reflects 99% of the total applicant pool.

Whittier Law School

3333 Harbor Boulevard
Costa Mesa, CA 92626
Phone: 714.444.4141; Fax: 714.444.0250
E-mail: info@law.whittier.edu; Website: www.law.whittier.edu

Probation

ABA Approved Since 1978

The Basics

Type of school	Private
Term	Semester
Application deadline	3/15
Application fee	$50
Financial aid deadline	5/1 10/15
Can first year start other than fall?	No
Student to faculty ratio	16.9 to 1
Does the university offer:	
housing restricted to law students?	No
graduate housing for which law students are eligible?	No

Faculty and Administrators

	Total		Men		Women		Minorities	
	Fall	Spr	Fall	Spr	Fall	Spr	Fall	Spr
Full-time	30	29	18	17	12	12	1	1
Other Full-time	2	2	0	0	2	2	0	0
Deans, librarians, & others who teach	5	5	4	4	1	1	1	1
Part-time	24	23	15	13	9	10	6	4
Total	61	59	37	34	24	25	8	6

Curriculum

	Full-time	Part-time
Typical first-year section size	49	45
Is there typically a "small section" of the first-year class, other than Legal Writing, taught by full-time faculty	No	No
If yes, typical size offered last year		
# of classroom course titles beyond first-year curriculum	122	
# of upper division courses, excluding seminars with an enrollment: Under 25	184	
25–49	46	
50–74	31	
75–99	9	
100+	1	
# of seminars	19	
# of seminar positions available	360	
# of seminar positions filled	173	95
# of positions available in simulation courses	280	
# of simulation positions filled	105	94
# of positions available in faculty supervised clinical courses	79	
# of faculty supervised clinical positions filled	33	24
# involved in field placements	33	24
# involved in law journals	169	74
# involved in interschool competitions	48	23
# of credit hours required to graduate	87	

JD Enrollment and Ethnicity

	Men		Women		Full-time		Part-time		1st-year		Total		JD Degs. Awd.
	#	%	#	%	#	%	#	%	#	%	#	%	
African Amer.	5	1.5	14	4.1	9	2.0	10	4.5	3	1.6	19	2.8	16
Amer. Indian	3	0.9	1	0.3	0	0.0	4	1.8	0	0.0	4	0.6	1
Asian Amer.	60	18.0	65	19.2	91	20.3	34	15.2	34	18.5	125	18.6	60
Mex. Amer.	23	6.9	19	5.6	27	6.0	15	6.7	13	7.1	42	6.2	13
Puerto Rican	0	0.0	0	0.0	0	0.0	0	0.0	0	0.0	0	0.0	0
Hispanic	13	3.9	14	4.1	19	4.2	8	3.6	7	3.8	27	4.0	23
Total Minority	104	31.1	113	33.3	146	32.5	71	31.7	57	31.0	217	32.2	113
For. Nation.	2	0.6	3	0.9	4	0.9	1	0.4	0	0.0	5	0.7	1
Caucasian	168	50.3	162	47.8	212	47.2	118	52.7	91	49.5	330	49.0	115
Unknown	60	18.0	61	18.0	87	19.4	34	15.2	36	19.6	121	18.0	53
Total	334	49.6	339	50.4	449	66.7	224	33.3	184	27.3	673		282

Transfers

Transfers in	4
Transfers out	52

Tuition and Fees

	Resident	Nonresident
Full-time	$30,870	$30,870
Part-time	$20,620	$20,620

Living Expenses

Estimated living expenses for singles

Living on campus	Living off campus	Living at home
N/A	$17,056	$17,056

Whittier Law School

*ABA
Approved
Since
1978*

GPA and LSAT Scores

	Total	Full-time	Part-time
# of apps	2,568	2,201	367
# of offers	994	911	83
# of matrics	206	175	31
75% GPA	3.33	3.34	3.08
Median GPA	3.12	3.15	2.60
25% GPA	2.82	2.91	2.38
75% LSAT	155	155	155
Median LSAT	153	153	152
25% LSAT	151	151	151

Grants and Scholarships (from prior year)

	Total		Full-time		Part-time	
	#	%	#	%	#	%
Total # of students	871		499		372	
Total # receiving grants	342	39.3	231	46.3	111	29.8
Less than 1/2 tuition	177	20.3	113	22.6	64	17.2
Half to full tuition	93	10.7	76	15.2	17	4.6
Full tuition	30	3.4	20	4.0	10	2.7
More than full tuition	42	4.8	22	4.4	20	5.4
Median grant amount			$14,595		$6,000	

Informational and Library Resources

# of volumes and volume equivalents	428,386
# of titles	182,999
# of active serial subscriptions	3,202
Study seating capacity inside the library	386
# of full-time professional librarians	5
Hours per week library is open	102
# of open, wired connections available to students	223
# of networked computers available for use by students	109
# of simultaneous wireless users	0
Require computer?	No

JD Attrition (from prior year)

	Academic	Other	Total	
	#	#	#	%
1st year	76	58	134	51.5
2nd year	19	58	77	29.2
3rd year	3	19	22	8.0
4th year	2	4	6	8.3

Employment (9 months after graduation)

	Total	Percentage
Employment status known	222	96.5
Employment status unknown	8	3.5
Employed	202	91.0
Pursuing graduate degrees	4	1.8
Unemployed seeking employment	3	1.4
Unemployed not seeking employment	6	2.7
Unemployed and studying for the bar	7	3.2

Type of Employment

	Total	Percentage
# employed in law firms	97	48.0
# employed in business and industry	72	35.6
# employed in government	14	6.9
# employed in public interest	10	5.0
# employed as judicial clerks	2	1.0
# employed in academia	7	3.5

Geographic Location

	Total	Percentage
# employed in state	170	84.2
# employed in foreign countries	1	0.5
# of states where employed		15

Bar Passage Rates

Jurisdiction	California		
Exam	Sum 05	Win 06	Total
# from school taking bar for the first time	174	45	219
School's pass rate for all first-time takers	40%	38%	39%
State's pass rate for all first-time takers	64%	54%	62%

Whittier Law School

3333 Harbor Boulevard
Costa Mesa, CA 92626
Phone: 714.444.4141; Fax: 714.444.0250
E-mail: info@law.whittier.edu; Website: www.law.whittier.edu

■ Introduction

Whittier Law School was founded in 1966 as Beverly Law School. In 1975, the Law School became part of Whittier College, established by Quakers in 1887. The Law School is located in Costa Mesa, Orange County. Orange County, ranked among the top business centers in the United States, is home to over 10,000 lawyers, more lawyers than half the states in the nation. The Law School is 30 miles south of downtown Los Angeles, 100 miles north of San Diego, and minutes away from the local beach cities such as Huntington Beach and Newport Beach. Ideally situated, the Law School enjoys the vibrant economies produced within each area as well as within Orange County. The Whittier tradition stresses concern for individual student's intellectual and ethical development. This tradition is reflected in admission practices stressing diversity, a small student-to-faculty ratio, small elective classes, and individual student counseling and placement services.

■ Part-time Programs

In addition to the traditional three-year full-time program, the JD can also be completed in four years, including two summer sessions, in the flexible day or evening programs. First- and second-year part-time students generally attend classes three days a week. Standards for admission and retention are identical for all students, and the full-time faculty serves both programs.

■ Admission and Scholarships

In addition to the LSAT score and undergraduate GPA, subjective factors such as undergraduate school, major, graduate work, ethnic and economic background, work experience, and personal accomplishments are considered. Applicants are encouraged to discuss these factors in their written personal statements. The admission office automatically considers all applicants for merit-based scholarships.

■ Special Programs

Center for Children's Rights—The center enrolls up to 20 students yearly who receive fellowships and summer stipends to prepare for careers in children's rights advocacy. Fellows participate in special classes, symposia, and externships. The center also sponsors the National Juvenile Law Moot Court Competition.

Center for Intellectual Property Law—The center provides students and practitioners with academic instruction in intellectual property law. The cornerstones of the center are the Certificate Program, the Summer Institute, and the Distinguished Speaker Series. The center also awards IP Fellowships.

Center for International and Comparative Law—The center allows students to participate in a specialized legal writing course, attend the International Law Symposium and Colloquia series, and receive a certificate by enrolling in courses offered through the center. The center also awards CICL Fellowships.

Clinics—Whittier Law School boasts four clinics: the Children's Advocacy Clinic, the Special Education Clinic, the Family Violence Clinic, and the "clientless" Legal Policy Clinic.

Exchange Programs in France and Spain—Students with some knowledge of French or Spanish can spend one semester at the University of Paris X in Nanterre, France; the University of Cantabria in Santander, Spain; or the University of Seville, Spain.

Summer-abroad Programs—The Law School offers five summer study-abroad programs approved by the ABA. Students from around the country can choose to study at the prestigious Bar-Ilan University in Tel Aviv, Israel; the University of Cantabria in Santander, Spain; the University of Toulouse in Toulouse, France; the University of Nanjing in China; or at the Universiteit van Amsterdam in Amsterdam, the Netherlands.

Institute of Student and Graduate Academic Support—The institute, administered by five full-time professors, allows students to participate in workshops, small seminars, and individual sessions, all designed to teach students the skills essential for law school success. The first-year program is mandatory and students may take part in a first-year summer program to enhance basic study skills and a 13-week Bar Exam Preparation Program.

Institute of Legal Writing and Professional Skills—The staff, composed of eight full-time professors and 12 part-time professors, teaches students how to write and conduct themselves well as lawyers. With this institute, our students have proven to be more prepared to perform at summer jobs, as well as to enter practice generally, than students from many schools throughout the state. The institute also offers three specialized writing courses in the first-year curriculum for the Center for Children's Rights, Center for Intellectual Property Law, and the Center for International and Comparative Law. Concentrations in business and criminal law are offered.

■ Library and Physical Facilities

Whittier Law School is located in the city of Costa Mesa on a beautiful 15-acre campus with exceptional facilities, including one of the largest academic law research libraries in the region. The Law School is composed of four buildings that are completely accessible to people with disabilities, totaling 130,000 square feet, and offers plentiful on-site parking. With over 380,000 volumes, the library has a rapidly growing legal research collection and serves as a state and federal depository. Three student computer labs support a variety of software to aid students with computer-assisted instruction, online legal research, and Internet access. Numerous conference rooms are available for group study. The entire facility is equipped with Internet access for individual study.

■ Student Activities

The *Whittier Law Review* is open to students on the basis of grades and a writing competition and publishes the annual Health Law and International Law Symposia.

The *Whittier Journal of Child and Family Advocacy*, a student-run scholarly publication focusing on topics related to juvenile and family law, is one of the few journals of its kind in the nation.

Externships and Career Services

Whittier Law School provides assistance to students and alumni in obtaining clerkships, externships, and attorney positions. The Law School offers a variety of externships with trial and appellate judges, governmental agencies, and public interest organizations. The Career Services Office assists in résumé building exercises, career goal identification, and career planning strategies. Additional services include on-campus interviews, a mentor program, panels and symposia on career-related topics, a comprehensive library of career resources, and a mock interview program.

Members of the Moot Court Honors Board and the Trial Advocacy Honors Board utilize written and oral advocacy skills to represent the Law School in regional and national trial and appellate advocacy competitions.

The Student Bar Association's activities include support of various social functions and participation in student-faculty committees for school governance. Numerous other student organizations represent various ethnic groups and legal specialties.

Applicant Profile

Whittier Law School
This grid includes only applicants who earned 120–180 LSAT scores under standard administrations.

LSAT Score	3.75 +		3.50–3.74		3.25–3.49		3.00–3.24		2.75–2.99		2.50–2.74		2.25–2.49		2.00–2.24		Below 2.00		No GPA		Total	
	Apps	Adm	Apps	Adm	Apps	Adm	Apps	Adm	Apps	Adm	Apps	Adm	Apps	Adm	Apps	Adm	Apps	Adm	Apps	Adm	Apps	Adm
175–180	0	0	0	0	0	0	0	0	2	2	0	0	1	1	0	0	0	0	0	0	3	3
170–174	0	0	0	0	0	0	0	0	7	6	1	1	1	0	0	0	0	0	0	0	10	8
165–169	1	1	0	0	0	0	0	0	12	11	8	7	6	5	2	1	0	0	1	1	71	45
160–164	8	2	8	5	17	9	9	4	12	11	8	7	6	5	2	0	2	0	4	2	308	273
155–159	19	17	43	41	72	67	54	49	57	52	38	31	13	10	11	3	2	0	6	6	725	599
150–154	36	34	76	72	168	156	172	156	133	106	87	45	34	21	11	3	2	0	13	0	692	35
145–149	26	2	82	5	142	5	158	8	129	6	80	7	45	2	13	0	4	0	8	0	365	1
140–144	9	0	30	0	64	0	83	1	78	0	49	0	30	0	11	0	3	0	5	0	124	0
135–139	2	0	6	0	10	0	25	0	23	0	29	0	14	0	7	0	3	0	5	0	35	0
130–134	1	0	0	0	3	0	6	0	5	0	8	0	5	0	4	0	2	0	1	0	8	0
125–129	0	0	1	0	1	0	1	0	1	0	3	0	0	0	0	0	1	0	0	0	1	0
120–124	0	0	0	0	0	0	0	0	0	0	0	0	0	0	0	0	0	0	1	0	1	0
Total	102	56	246	123	477	237	508	218	447	183	303	91	149	39	54	8	17	0	39	9	2342	964

Apps = Number of Applicants
Adm = Number Admitted
Reflects 99% of the total applicant pool.

Widener University School of Law—Delaware

4601 Concord Pike, PO Box 7474
Wilmington, DE 19803-0474
Phone: 302.477.2162, Fax: 302.477.2224
E-mail: lawadmissions@mail.widener.edu; Website: www.law.widener.edu

ABA
Approved
Since
1975

The Basics

Type of school	Private
Term	Semester
Application deadline	5/15
Application fee	$60
Financial aid deadline	4/1
Can first year start other than fall?	No
Student to faculty ratio	15.9 to 1
Does the university offer:	
housing restricted to law students?	Yes
graduate housing for which law students are eligible?	Yes

Faculty and Administrators

	Total Fall	Total Spr	Men Fall	Men Spr	Women Fall	Women Spr	Minorities Fall	Minorities Spr
Full-time	46	45	26	27	20	18	3	3
Other Full-time	1	1	0	0	1	1	0	0
Deans, librarians, & others who teach	12	12	3	3	9	9	3	3
Part-time	48	74	32	51	16	23	3	8
Total	**107**	**132**	**61**	**81**	**46**	**51**	**9**	**14**

Curriculum

	Full-time	Part-time
Typical first-year section size	83	57
Is there typically a "small section" of the first-year class, other than Legal Writing, taught by full-time faculty	Yes	No
If yes, typical size offered last year	48	
# of classroom course titles beyond first-year curriculum	144	
# of upper division courses, excluding seminars with an enrollment: Under 25	136	
25–49	49	
50–74	22	
75–99	6	
100+	1	
# of seminars	36	
# of seminar positions available	720	
# of seminar positions filled	184	156
# of positions available in simulation courses	1,094	
# of simulation positions filled	427	352
# of positions available in faculty supervised clinical courses	110	
# of faculty supervised clinical positions filled	43	24
# involved in field placements	78	91
# involved in law journals	121	69
# involved in interschool competitions	112	75
# of credit hours required to graduate	88	

JD Enrollment and Ethnicity

	Men #	Men %	Women #	Women %	Full-time #	Full-time %	Part-time #	Part-time %	1st-year #	1st-year %	Total #	Total %	JD Degs. Awd.
African Amer.	26	4.7	32	7.5	20	3.3	38	9.9	21	6.1	58	5.9	13
Amer. Indian	2	0.4	1	0.2	1	0.2	2	0.5	1	0.3	3	0.3	0
Asian Amer.	36	6.5	35	8.2	49	8.1	22	5.7	22	6.4	71	7.2	11
Mex. Amer.	0	0.0	0	0.0	0	0.0	0	0.0	0	0.0	0	0.0	0
Puerto Rican	0	0.0	0	0.0	0	0.0	0	0.0	0	0.0	0	0.0	0
Hispanic	7	1.3	15	3.5	13	2.2	9	2.3	10	2.9	22	2.2	2
Total Minority	71	12.7	83	19.4	83	13.8	71	18.5	54	15.7	154	15.6	26
For. Nation.	4	0.7	1	0.2	4	0.7	1	0.3	1	0.3	5	0.5	1
Caucasian	389	69.8	277	64.7	413	68.6	253	66.1	223	65.0	666	67.6	238
Unknown	93	16.7	67	15.7	102	16.9	58	15.1	65	19.0	160	16.2	47
Total	557	56.5	428	43.5	602	61.1	383	38.9	343	34.8	985		312

Transfers

Transfers in	8
Transfers out	44

Tuition and Fees

	Resident	Nonresident
Full-time	$29,430	$29,430
Part-time	$22,050	$22,050

Living Expenses

Estimated living expenses for singles

Living on campus	Living off campus	Living at home
$13,494	$13,494	$8,994

Widener University School of Law—Delaware

ABA
Approved
Since
1975

GPA and LSAT Scores

	Total	Full-time	Part-time
# of apps	2,471	1,940	531
# of offers	1,123	863	260
# of matrics	337	216	121
75% GPA	3.39	3.48	3.25
Median GPA	3.08	3.12	2.93
25% GPA	2.78	2.85	2.60
75% LSAT	155	155	154
Median LSAT	152	153	151
25% LSAT	150	151	150

Grants and Scholarships (from prior year)

	Total		Full-time		Part-time	
	#	%	#	%	#	%
Total # of students	1,072		659		413	
Total # receiving grants	225	21.0	171	25.9	54	13.1
Less than 1/2 tuition	188	17.5	142	21.5	46	11.1
Half to full tuition	23	2.1	16	2.4	7	1.7
Full tuition	14	1.3	13	2.0	1	0.2
More than full tuition	0	0.0	0	0.0	0	0.0
Median grant amount			$4,000		$2,000	

Informational and Library Resources

# of volumes and volume equivalents	401,128
# of titles	69,784
# of active serial subscriptions	4,013
Study seating capacity inside the library	435
# of full-time professional librarians	9
Hours per week library is open	107
# of open, wired connections available to students	75
# of networked computers available for use by students	112
# of simultaneous wireless users	375
Require computer?	No

JD Attrition (from prior year)

	Academic	Other	Total	
	#	#	#	%
1st year	46	46	92	25.7
2nd year	10	11	21	6.5
3rd year	0	1	1	0.3
4th year	0	0	0	0.0

Employment (9 months after graduation)

	Total	Percentage
Employment status known	307	91.1
Employment status unknown	30	8.9
Employed	252	82.1
Pursuing graduate degrees	10	3.3
Unemployed seeking employment	19	6.2
Unemployed not seeking employment	5	1.6
Unemployed and studying for the bar	21	6.8

Type of Employment

# employed in law firms	103	40.9
# employed in business and industry	61	24.2
# employed in government	33	13.1
# employed in public interest	5	2.0
# employed as judicial clerks	44	17.5
# employed in academia	2	0.8

Geographic Location

# employed in state	58	23.0
# employed in foreign countries	0	0.0
# of states where employed		12

Bar Passage Rates

Jurisdiction	Pennsylvania		
Exam	Sum 05	Win 06	Total
# from school taking bar for the first time	188	64	252
School's pass rate for all first-time takers	67%	81%	71%
State's pass rate for all first-time takers	79%	75%	78%

Widener University School of Law—Harrisburg

3800 Vartan Way, PO Box 69381
Harrisburg, PA 17106-9381
Phone: 717.541.3903; Fax: 717.541.3999
E-mail: lawadmissions@mail.widener.edu; Website: www.law.widener.edu

ABA
Approved
Since
1994

The Basics

Type of school	Private
Term	Semester
Application deadline	5/15
Application fee	$60
Financial aid deadline	4/1
Can first year start other than fall?	No
Student to faculty ratio	16.1 to 1
Does the university offer:	
housing restricted to law students?	No
graduate housing for which law students are eligible?	No

Faculty and Administrators

	Total		Men		Women		Minorities	
	Fall	Spr	Fall	Spr	Fall	Spr	Fall	Spr
Full-time	21	20	13	13	8	7	0	0
Other Full-time	5	5	1	1	4	4	1	1
Deans, librarians, & others who teach	6	6	2	2	4	4	0	0
Part-time	24	29	18	20	6	9	1	1
Total	56	60	34	36	22	24	2	2

Curriculum

		Full-time	Part-time
Typical first-year section size		85	50
Is there typically a "small section" of the first-year class, other than Legal Writing, taught by full-time faculty		No	No
If yes, typical size offered last year			
# of classroom course titles beyond first-year curriculum		67	
# of upper division courses, excluding seminars with an enrollment:	Under 25	55	
	25–49	23	
	50–74	8	
	75–99	3	
	100+	0	
# of seminars		8	
# of seminar positions available		160	
# of seminar positions filled		46	50
# of positions available in simulation courses		504	
# of simulation positions filled		109	173
# of positions available in faculty supervised clinical courses		80	
# of faculty supervised clinical positions filled		13	28
# involved in field placements		31	29
# involved in law journals		61	31
# involved in interschool competitions		20	16
# of credit hours required to graduate		88	

JD Enrollment and Ethnicity

	Men #	Men %	Women #	Women %	Full-time #	Full-time %	Part-time #	Part-time %	1st-year #	1st-year %	Total #	Total %	JD Degs. Awd.
African Amer.	3	1.2	4	2.0	4	1.4	3	2.0	2	1.2	7	1.6	4
Amer. Indian	0	0.0	1	0.5	0	0.0	1	0.7	1	0.6	1	0.2	0
Asian Amer.	5	2.0	12	6.0	13	4.4	4	2.6	8	4.7	17	3.8	5
Mex. Amer.	0	0.0	0	0.0	0	0.0	0	0.0	0	0.0	0	0.0	0
Puerto Rican	0	0.0	0	0.0	0	0.0	0	0.0	0	0.0	0	0.0	0
Hispanic	4	1.6	4	2.0	5	1.7	3	2.0	2	1.2	8	1.8	0
Total Minority	12	4.8	21	10.6	22	7.4	11	7.2	13	7.6	33	7.3	9
For. Nation.	2	0.8	0	0.0	0	0.0	2	1.3	0	0.0	2	0.4	0
Caucasian	193	77.2	145	72.9	225	76.0	113	73.9	125	73.5	338	75.3	108
Unknown	43	17.2	33	16.6	49	16.6	27	17.6	32	18.8	76	16.9	29
Total	250	55.7	199	44.3	296	65.9	153	34.1	170	37.9	449		146

Transfers

Transfers in	2
Transfers out	13

Tuition and Fees

	Resident	Nonresident
Full-time	$29,430	$29,430
Part-time	$22,050	$22,050

Living Expenses

Estimated living expenses for singles

Living on campus	Living off campus	Living at home
$13,494	$13,494	$8,994

Widener University School of Law—Harrisburg

*ABA
Approved
Since
1994*

GPA and LSAT Scores

	Total	Full-time	Part-time
# of apps	1,036	827	209
# of offers	463	363	100
# of matrics	173	126	47
75% GPA	3.50	3.53	3.32
Median GPA	3.18	3.21	3.01
25% GPA	2.86	2.97	2.79
75% LSAT	153	153	154
Median LSAT	151	151	150
25% LSAT	149	150	149

Grants and Scholarships (from prior year)

	Total		Full-time		Part-time	
	#	%	#	%	#	%
Total # of students	499		338		161	
Total # receiving grants	118	23.6	88	26.0	30	18.6
Less than 1/2 tuition	109	21.8	79	23.4	30	18.6
Half to full tuition	6	1.2	6	1.8	0	0.0
Full tuition	3	0.6	3	0.9	0	0.0
More than full tuition	0	0.0	0	0.0	0	0.0
Median grant amount			$3,000		$1,350	

Informational and Library Resources

# of volumes and volume equivalents	207,250
# of titles	26,667
# of active serial subscriptions	3,100
Study seating capacity inside the library	335
# of full-time professional librarians	5
Hours per week library is open	105
# of open, wired connections available to students	10
# of networked computers available for use by students	58
# of simultaneous wireless users	200
Require computer?	No

JD Attrition (from prior year)

	Academic	Other	Total	
	#	#	#	%
1st year	34	23	57	30.5
2nd year	7	5	12	8.7
3rd year	0	2	2	1.6
4th year	0	0	0	0.0

Employment (9 months after graduation)

	Total	Percentage
Employment status known	146	98.0
Employment status unknown	3	2.0
Employed	126	86.3
Pursuing graduate degrees	6	4.1
Unemployed seeking employment	6	4.1
Unemployed not seeking employment	4	2.7
Unemployed and studying for the bar	4	2.7
Type of Employment		
# employed in law firms	52	41.3
# employed in business and industry	26	20.6
# employed in government	27	21.4
# employed in public interest	5	4.0
# employed as judicial clerks	11	8.7
# employed in academia	3	2.4
Geographic Location		
# employed in state	101	80.2
# employed in foreign countries	0	0.0
# of states where employed	10	

Bar Passage Rates

Jurisdiction	Pennsylvania		
Exam	Sum 05	Win 06	Total
# from school taking bar for the first time	101	24	125
School's pass rate for all first-time takers	59%	50%	58%
State's pass rate for all first-time takers	79%	75%	78%

Widener University School of Law

4601 Concord Pike, PO Box 7474, Wilmington, DE 19803-0474; Phone: 302.477.2162; Fax: 302.477.2224
3800 Vartan Way, PO Box 69381, Harrisburg, PA 17106-9381; Phone: 717.541.3903; Fax: 717.541.3999
E-mail: lawadmissions@mail.widener.edu; Website: www.law.widener.edu

■ Introduction

Widener University School of Law is unique among American law schools. Widener has two campuses—one in Wilmington, Delaware, the corporate and banking center of the United States; and the other in Harrisburg, Pennsylvania, the state capital and a major center of government and commerce. Each campus offers a comprehensive curriculum of basic and advanced courses complemented by one of the most extensive clinical and skills programs in the country. The Harrisburg campus features a unique admission and academic cooperative program with the Pennsylvania State System of Higher Education.

The rich curriculum is taught by a faculty committed to personal attention and individual counseling so that all students will be encouraged to fulfill their potential. The full-time faculty is supplemented by a distinguished group of adjuncts, including two justices of the Delaware Supreme Court, US Senator Joseph Biden, and numerous lower court judges from Pennsylvania, Delaware, and New Jersey. The school is a member of the AALS and is accredited by the ABA.

■ Library and Physical Facilities

The Legal Information Center houses one of the most significant legal collections in the region. The combined collections of the Delaware and Harrisburg campuses exceed 600,000 volumes. The library is a selective depository for United States government documents.

The attractive 34-acre Delaware campus is located in the heart of the beautiful Brandywine River Valley. The law building houses the Legal Information Center, state-of-the-art computer facilities, faculty offices, clinics, traditional and technologically enhanced classrooms, and two moot courtrooms. The scenic 19-acre Harrisburg campus is located in a contemporary complex within minutes of the state capital.

■ Special Programs and Institutes

Widener is a leader in developing a coordinated lawyering skills program. The program includes clinical practice, externship placements, and comprehensive simulations.

Clinics are designed to permit students to represent actual clients under the supervision of the clinic director before courts and administrative boards. Widener operates Environmental Law, Criminal Defense, Delaware Civil, Pennsylvania Civil, Harrisburg Civil, and Veterans Affairs Clinics. A large number of supervised externships permit students to work as lawyers-in-training with state and county government agencies and nonprofit corporations. An extensive judicial externship program places students with state and federal courts at both the trial and appellate levels in DC, Delaware, Maryland, New Jersey, Pennsylvania, and Virginia. Additional public interest service opportunities are also available.

The Public Interest Resource Center on the Delaware campus and the Public Interest Initiative on the Harrisburg campus cultivates pro bono volunteer opportunities for students in public interest agencies and government offices throughout Delaware, Pennsylvania, and New Jersey; offers counseling and guidance to students who seek careers in public interest law; and recognizes students and faculty for exceptional contributions to public service.

Widener offers certificate programs for specialized study in health law, law and government, business organizations law, and trial advocacy.

The Health Law Institute on the Delaware campus provides research, policy analysis, and specialty education for those seeking expertise in the area of health law. The Law and Government Institute on the Harrisburg campus provides hands-on experience with the operation and structure of government and practice before government agencies. The Institute of Delaware Corporate Law on the Delaware campus provides a fundamental knowledge of business law through participation in the Business Organizations Law concentration that serves as a predicate to advanced practice in business and corporate law. The Trial Advocacy Institute on the Delaware campus provides extensive litigation skills essential to being a competent, professionally responsible trial advocate. Additionally, both campuses offer a seven-day Intensive Trial Advocacy Program supervised by outstanding local trial lawyers and judges.

Widener offers four joint-degree programs. The JD/MBA is offered in conjunction with the university's School of Business Administration. The JD/PsyD is offered in conjunction with the university's Institute for Graduate Clinical Psychology. The JD/MSLS is offered in conjunction with Clarion University of Pennsylvania. The JD/MMP is offered in conjunction with The University of Delaware.

■ International Law Programs

Widener students have the opportunity to study international and comparative law while living abroad. Widener offers summer-abroad programs in Nairobi, Kenya; Geneva, Switzerland; Sydney, Australia; and Venice, Italy.

■ Student Activities

Selected Delaware students publish the *Delaware Journal of Corporate Law* and the *Widener Law Review*. Selected Harrisburg students publish the *Widener Law Journal*. Students at both campuses compete in regional and national interschool moot court and trial competitions.

Student organizations provide opportunities for intrascholastic and interscholastic competitions, public service, and association with others who share the same interests.

■ Admission

While there are no fixed admission criteria, great weight is given to the applicant's LSAT score and undergraduate grade-point average. The Admissions Committee carefully considers an applicant's personal statement. Graduate degrees, writing samples, extracurricular activities, and community and professional service may enhance the application. The law school encourages those with diverse backgrounds to apply.

Applications for admission must be received by May 15. Admission decisions are made on a rolling basis, and applicants are encouraged to apply early.

Each summer, Widener conducts the Trial Admissions Program (TAP) for a small number of carefully selected applicants who show potential for success in law school despite a relatively low score on the LSAT or a lower undergraduate grade-point average. TAP is a conditional admittance program. Participants who successfully complete the six-week program are offered admission to the fall entering class.

■ Financial Aid

The Office of Financial Aid works with any student wishing assistance in finding appropriate sources of funding. Additionally, all applicants are considered for Widener's merit- and need-based scholarships.

■ Career Development

The Career Development Office is strongly committed to helping students obtain the positions that best suit their individual needs and ambitions.

Widener's placement statistics evidence its success in helping graduates find a niche in the contemporary job market. Widener alumni have become judges in Delaware, New Jersey, New York, and Pennsylvania; members of the legislature; partners in major regional law firms; hospital administrators; legal educators; and broadcast journalists.

Applicant Profile

Widener University School of Law
This grid includes only applicants who earned 120–180 LSAT scores under standard administrations.

LSAT Score	3.75 +		3.50–3.74		3.25–3.49		3.00–3.24		2.75–2.99		2.50–2.74		2.25–2.49		2.00–2.24		Below 2.00		No GPA		Total	
	Apps	Adm	Apps	Adm	Apps	Adm	Apps	Adm	Apps	Adm	Apps	Adm	Apps	Adm	Apps	Adm	Apps	Adm	Apps	Adm	Apps	Adm
175–180	0	0	0	0	0	0	0	0	0	0	0	0	0	0	0	0	0	0	0	0	0	0
170–174	0	0	2	2	2	2	1	1	0	0	1	1	0	0	0	0	0	0	0	0	6	6
165–169	3	3	3	3	5	5	4	3	1	1	2	1	1	1	0	0	0	0	0	0	19	17
160–164	10	10	10	9	25	24	16	15	11	11	14	12	3	3	4	4	1	1	2	1	96	90
155–159	41	40	83	81	91	87	79	77	62	59	28	28	14	13	11	10	0	0	7	1	416	396
150–154	74	58	148	118	172	137	200	157	184	145	101	79	50	34	23	16	8	5	19	7	979	756
145–149	69	21	153	30	207	55	247	72	200	53	112	31	74	17	26	3	5	0	20	3	1113	285
140–144	20	0	77	0	112	0	135	1	114	0	91	0	49	0	20	0	7	0	25	0	650	1
135–139	6	0	18	0	34	0	54	0	41	0	42	1	35	0	22	0	3	0	20	0	275	1
130–134	2	0	3	0	7	0	17	0	24	0	15	0	12	0	12	0	4	0	10	0	106	0
125–129	0	0	2	0	2	0	2	0	3	0	1	0	1	0	1	0	2	0	4	0	18	0
120–124	0	0	0	0	0	0	2	0	0	0	0	0	0	0	1	0	0	0	1	0	4	0
Total	225	132	499	243	657	310	757	326	640	269	407	153	239	68	120	33	30	6	108	12	3682	1552

Apps = Number of Applicants
Adm = Number Admitted
Reflects 98% of the total applicant pool.

The grid includes applicants admitted based upon successful completion of our Trial Admissions Program, rather than upon their LSAT score and undergraduate grade-point average. Additionally, nonnumerical factors are strongly considered for all applicants.

Willamette University College of Law

Truman Wesley Collins Legal Center, 245 Winter Street SE
Salem, OR 97301
Phone: 503.370.6282; Fax: 503.370.6087
E-mail: law-admission@willamette.edu; Website: www.willamette.edu/wucl

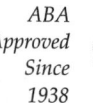

ABA Approved Since 1938

The Basics

Type of school	Private
Term	Semester
Application deadline	4/1
Application fee	$50
Financial aid deadline	
Can first year start other than fall?	No
Student to faculty ratio	13.8 to 1
Does the university offer:	
housing restricted to law students?	No
graduate housing for which law students are eligible?	No

Faculty and Administrators

	Total		Men		Women		Minorities	
	Fall	Spr	Fall	Spr	Fall	Spr	Fall	Spr
Full-time	25	26	17	19	8	7	3	4
Other Full-time	6	7	3	4	3	3	0	0
Deans, librarians, & others who teach	2	2	1	1	1	1	0	0
Part-time	12	10	10	7	2	3	0	1
Total	45	45	31	31	14	14	3	5

Curriculum

	Full-time	Part-time
Typical first-year section size	74	0
Is there typically a "small section" of the first-year class, other than Legal Writing, taught by full-time faculty	Yes	No
If yes, typical size offered last year	31	
# of classroom course titles beyond first-year curriculum	99	
# of upper division courses, excluding seminars with an enrollment: Under 25	56	
25–49	15	
50–74	13	
75–99	5	
100+	1	
# of seminars	14	
# of seminar positions available	218	
# of seminar positions filled	163	0
# of positions available in simulation courses	204	
# of simulation positions filled	186	0
# of positions available in faculty supervised clinical courses	39	
# of faculty supervised clinical positions filled	37	0
# involved in field placements	31	0
# involved in law journals	57	0
# involved in interschool competitions	125	0
# of credit hours required to graduate	90	

JD Enrollment and Ethnicity

	Men		Women		Full-time		Part-time		1st-year		Total		JD Degs. Awd.
	#	%	#	%	#	%	#	%	#	%	#	%	
African Amer.	2	0.8	1	0.6	3	0.7	0	0.0	0	0.0	3	0.7	2
Amer. Indian	3	1.2	4	2.3	7	1.7	0	0.0	2	1.3	7	1.7	3
Asian Amer.	9	3.6	9	5.1	18	4.3	0	0.0	9	5.7	18	4.2	4
Mex. Amer.	3	1.2	3	1.7	6	1.4	0	0.0	3	1.9	6	1.4	3
Puerto Rican	0	0.0	0	0.0	0	0.0	0	0.0	0	0.0	0	0.0	0
Hispanic	1	0.4	1	0.6	2	0.5	0	0.0	2	1.3	2	0.5	4
Total Minority	18	7.3	18	10.2	36	8.5	0	0.0	16	10.1	36	8.5	16
For. Nation.	3	1.2	0	0.0	3	0.7	0	0.0	0	0.0	3	0.7	0
Caucasian	195	78.9	134	75.7	327	77.5	2	100.0	122	76.7	329	77.6	106
Unknown	31	12.6	25	14.1	56	13.3	0	0.0	21	13.2	56	13.2	15
Total	247	58.3	177	41.7	422	99.5	2	0.5	159	37.5	424		137

Transfers

Transfers in	1
Transfers out	15

Tuition and Fees

	Resident	Nonresident
Full-time	$26,410	$0
Part-time	$0	$0

Living Expenses

Estimated living expenses for singles

Living on campus	Living off campus	Living at home
$15,480	$15,480	$15,480

Willamette University College of Law

ABA
Approved
Since
1938

GPA and LSAT Scores

	Total	Full-time	Part-time
# of apps	1,329	1,329	0
# of offers	501	501	0
# of matrics	159	159	0
75% GPA	3.54	3.54	0.00
Median GPA	3.23	3.23	0.00
25% GPA	2.99	2.99	0.00
75% LSAT	160	160	0
Median LSAT	157	157	0
25% LSAT	155	155	0

Grants and Scholarships (from prior year)

	Total		Full-time		Part-time	
	#	%	#	%	#	%
Total # of students	443		438		5	
Total # receiving grants	197	44.5	197	45.0	0	0.0
Less than 1/2 tuition	150	33.9	150	34.2	0	0.0
Half to full tuition	47	10.6	47	10.7	0	0.0
Full tuition	0	0.0	0	0.0	0	0.0
More than full tuition	0	0.0	0	0.0	0	0.0
Median grant amount			$10,000		$0	

Informational and Library Resources

# of volumes and volume equivalents	292,135
# of titles	40,462
# of active serial subscriptions	2,947
Study seating capacity inside the library	492
# of full-time professional librarians	2
Hours per week library is open	168
# of open, wired connections available to students	122
# of networked computers available for use by students	51
# of simultaneous wireless users	700
Require computer?	No

JD Attrition (from prior year)

	Academic	Other	Total	
	#	#	#	%
1st year	8	22	30	21.0
2nd year	4	2	6	3.8
3rd year	2	4	6	4.2
4th year	0	0	0	0.0

Employment (9 months after graduation)

	Total	Percentage
Employment status known	127	96.9
Employment status unknown	4	3.1
Employed	99	78.0
Pursuing graduate degrees	3	2.4
Unemployed seeking employment	10	7.9
Unemployed not seeking employment	3	2.4
Unemployed and studying for the bar	12	9.4

Type of Employment

	Total	Percentage
# employed in law firms	59	59.6
# employed in business and industry	10	10.1
# employed in government	12	12.1
# employed in public interest	4	4.0
# employed as judicial clerks	11	11.1
# employed in academia	2	2.0

Geographic Location

	Total	Percentage
# employed in state	61	61.6
# employed in foreign countries	1	1.0
# of states where employed	15	

Bar Passage Rates

Jurisdiction	Oregon			Washington		
Exam	Sum 05	Win 06	Total	Sum 05	Win 06	Total
# from school taking bar for the first time	70	8	78	22	6	28
School's pass rate for all first-time takers	76%	50%	73%	86%	83%	86%
State's pass rate for all first-time takers	76%	74%	76%	75%	74%	75%

Willamette University College of Law

Truman Wesley Collins Legal Center, 245 Winter Street SE
Salem, OR 97301
Phone: 503.370.6282; Fax: 503.370.6087
E-mail: law-admission@willamette.edu; Website: www.willamette.edu/wucl

■ Introduction

From the time the first student entered the classroom in 1883, Willamette University College of Law has been a pioneer of legal education in the western United States. Located across the street from the state capitol complex, the College of Law is situated in the epicenter of Oregon law, government, and business.

Willamette University is one of the nation's oldest academic institutions. It is situated in the historic riverfront capital city of Salem, Oregon. The university is an independent institution historically related to the United Methodist Church. College of Law students are members of a distinguished university community of 2,500 students enrolled in the undergraduate College of Liberal Arts and in graduate programs offered by the School of Education and the Atkinson Graduate School of Management.

Like its parent, the College of Law is an intimate, highly selective and intellectually challenging school and a widely recognized leader in legal education. The college is committed to the pursuit of academic and professional excellence in a supportive environment that maximizes each student's unique potential. Our small enrollment of approximately 450 full-time students creates an intellectual intimacy unmatched by most law schools in the United States.

For more than 120 years, Willamette has trained talented, skilled lawyers who stand on equal footing with the very best legal practitioners in the country. Among the College of Law's distinguished alumni are numerous heads of Fortune 500 companies and more than a dozen Supreme Court justices and members of the US Senate and House of Representatives.

■ Faculty

A law school faculty serves as both the brain and heart of the institution. Willamette's law faculty includes some of the most respected legal minds in the country. Together, they have more than 250 years of legal practice experience and more than 500 years of legal education experience. Yet it is their authentic, deep dedication—both as educators and as mentors—that distinguishes them from others.

These scholars and master teachers are nationally recognized for their research, publications, and contributions to the law, particularly in the areas of constitutional law, commercial and business law, international and comparative law, environmental law, and dispute resolution.

■ Academic Programs

The Doctor of Jurisprudence program (JD) requires three years of full-time study. After successfully completing the first year, in which all courses are prescribed, students may choose to create an individual program, electing courses from Willamette's broad-based curriculum.

The College of Law also offers a four-year joint-degree program that leads to the JD and MBA for Business, Government, and Not-for-Profit Management. Managed in concert with Willamette's Atkinson Graduate School of Management, the joint-degree program saves students one additional year of study. Students must apply separately for admission to each degree program and may begin the program either in the College of Law

or in the Atkinson School. Students may apply prior to matriculating to Willamette or while in their first year of either the JD or MBA program.

Willamette's nationally recognized certificate programs further solidify the strong educational foundation provided at the College of Law. These specialized programs prepare students for an exceptional legal career and further distinguish them from other law school graduates. The four certificate programs include International and Comparative Law, Business Law, Law and Government, and Dispute Resolution. Note that a separate application is required after the first year of law school to gain admission to the certificate programs.

Willamette's College of Law also offers the LLM in Transnational Law, an advanced degree available to those who have completed the JD at an ABA-accredited American law school or its equivalent from a foreign law school. For more information, visit *www.willamette.edu/wucl/llm.*

■ Facility

The College of Law is housed in the award-winning Truman Wesley Collins Legal Center on the beautifully landscaped 65-acre campus of the university. The school offers all the cutting-edge amenities a student would expect from a top law school. Bright, modern classrooms provide comfortable, professional environments for learning and include a state-of-the-art wireless network.

The J.W. Long Law Library anchors the north end of the Collins Legal Center. Its 296,000 volumes and microform equivalents include state and federal primary law sources, as well as the leading treatises, periodicals, and other secondary sources. Through a library consortium, an online shared catalog gives Willamette students access to a remarkably vast array of resources. The library, a selective federal government repository, houses special collections in public international law, tax law, and labor law.

Both the Collins Legal Center and the law library are accessible to law students 24 hours a day, 7 days a week.

■ International Study Programs

Willamette's College of Law students also have the opportunity to deepen their international experience by participating in study-abroad programs in Germany, Ecuador, and China. The summer China Program acquaints students with Chinese law and Pacific Rim legal issues. It is based in Shanghai at the East China University of Politics and Law. The Ecuador Program provides students with an intensive semester immersion in the fundamentals of a civil law system and Latin American legal institutions. Students take courses at the Pontifical Catholic University of Ecuador in Quito. Proficiency in Spanish is required. The semester-long Germany Program is held at the Bucerius Law School in Hamburg, the first private institution for legal study in Germany.

■ Academic Centers and Other Resources

The Clinical Law Program at Willamette University provides opportunities for students to participate in the Civil Practice Clinic, where they represent clients in actual cases and transactions under the close supervision of faculty, and the Externship Program, which immerses students in the fast-paced work of the practicing lawyer. In addition to a general civil clinic, Civil Practice Clinic course offerings include several specialized clinics that cover business law, trusts and estates, tribal law, family law, and general civil practice (which includes consumer fraud).

The nationally recognized Center for Dispute Resolution produces research on conflict theory and problem solving, serving various constituencies ranging from the federal government to the local school district. The center teaches the theory and practice of negotiation, mediation, arbitration, and other methods of resolving disputes. It also administers the Certificate Program in Dispute Resolution.

The Willamette Center for Law and Government provides an impartial forum for the study, discussion, and improvement of government and public policy. It also administers the Certificate Program in Law and Government.

The Oregon Law Commission, which is housed at Willamette's College of Law, was established by legislative statute to provide academic and practical support for ongoing law revision, reform, and improvement. The commission is led by an executive director who is also an associate dean of the College of Law.

■ Admission

Applicants are urged to apply in the fall prior to the year they intend to enter the law school. Willamette enrolls a first-year law class with a wide range of goals and backgrounds distinguished by academic achievements. Applications are reviewed closely and in their entirety to ensure an informed and fair decision. Although April 1 is the deadline for applications, students begin receiving admission decisions from Willamette in January.

■ Scholarships

The fiscal stability of Willamette University enables the College of Law to offer a strong program of financial aid to its students. Generous merit-based scholarships reward applicants whose accomplishments suggest continuing success in law school. Scholarships are renewable with a 2.90 cumulative law GPA. Every student is automatically considered for a scholarship when the application for admission is initially reviewed. All applicants to the College of Law should also complete and submit the Free Application for Federal Student Aid (FAFSA) prior to March 1. Federal and private loan monies also may be available.

■ Employment and Career Services

The College of Law maintains an active Office of Career Services, which provides comprehensive career counseling services to current Willamette law students and law alumni. Career Services oversees a busy on-campus interview program, bringing legal employers directly to the College of Law. A wide range of workshops, panels, and speakers also are made available to students throughout the academic year. In addition, the Career Services Library contains numerous resources to assist with career planning and job searches.

Historically, most Willamette graduates choose careers in private practice. Graduates in government-related practice, including judicial clerkships, compose the next largest group. Business and industry attract the third-largest group. Most graduates remain in the Pacific Northwest because of the region's unique lifestyle and natural environment. While the Willamette alumni network is strongest in Oregon and Washington, Career Services provides a comprehensive national job-search service. Thus, Willamette graduates practice nationwide, from Hawaii to Washington, DC, from Alaska to Florida, and internationally, as well.

■ Location

Willamette University is situated in the heart of Salem, Oregon's capital. Salem is home to a large, active legal community that readily employs and actively mentors Willamette law students. With 150,000 residents, Salem is neither a small college town nor a big city. This historic riverfront city offers all the amenities of a larger city, but has successfully maintained its hometown charm. A welcoming and affordable city, Salem boasts a vibrant downtown area, beautiful city parks, an innovative children's museum and popular community theater, great pubs and cafés, fine dining, numerous coffeehouses and microbreweries, and a wide range of small boutiques and department stores.

Salem is surrounded by award-winning vineyards and orchards that support countless wine and food festivals. The city is only a short drive from numerous beautiful state parks that provide wilderness hiking, fishing, camping, and winter sports. The desert is a little farther east, and Oregon's spectacular beaches are an hour's drive to the west. Metropolitan Portland is just 45 minutes to the north, offering easy access to national sporting events and premier music and art venues.

Applicant Profile Not Available

William & Mary Law School

613 South Henry Street
Williamsburg, VA 23185
Phone: 757.221.3785; Fax: 757.221.3261
E-mail: lawadm@wm.edu; Website: www.wm.edu/law/

The Basics

Type of school	Public
Term	Semester
Application deadline	3/1
Application fee	$50
Financial aid deadline	2/15
Can first year start other than fall?	No
Student to faculty ratio	15.6 to 1
Does the university offer:	
housing restricted to law students?	No
graduate housing for which law students are eligible?	No

Faculty and Administrators

	Total Fall	Total Spr	Men Fall	Men Spr	Women Fall	Women Spr	Minorities Fall	Minorities Spr
Full-time	35	35	25	25	10	10	3	3
Other Full-time	3	3	2	2	1	1	0	0
Deans, librarians, & others who teach	8	8	5	5	3	3	0	0
Part-time	37	48	24	32	13	16	2	1
Total	**83**	**94**	**56**	**64**	**27**	**30**	**5**	**4**

Curriculum

	Full-time	Part-time
Typical first-year section size	70	0
Is there typically a "small section" of the first-year class, other than Legal Writing, taught by full-time faculty	Yes	No
If yes, typical size offered last year	18	
# of classroom course titles beyond first-year curriculum	113	
# of upper division courses, excluding seminars with an enrollment: Under 25	116	
25–49	30	
50–74	14	
75–99	3	
100+	2	
# of seminars	25	
# of seminar positions available	378	
# of seminar positions filled	329	0
# of positions available in simulation courses	948	
# of simulation positions filled	933	0
# of positions available in faculty supervised clinical courses	30	
# of faculty supervised clinical positions filled	7	0
# involved in field placements	136	0
# involved in law journals	256	0
# involved in interschool competitions	80	0
# of credit hours required to graduate	86	

JD Enrollment and Ethnicity

	Men #	Men %	Women #	Women %	Full-time #	Full-time %	Part-time #	Part-time %	1st-year #	1st-year %	Total #	Total %	JD Degs. Awd.
African Amer.	18	5.6	42	14.8	60	9.9	0	0.0	22	10.2	60	9.9	11
Amer. Indian	2	0.6	0	0.0	2	0.3	0	0.0	2	0.9	2	0.3	2
Asian Amer.	15	4.6	14	4.9	29	4.8	0	0.0	10	4.7	29	4.8	8
Mex. Amer.	0	0.0	0	0.0	0	0.0	0	0.0	0	0.0	0	0.0	0
Puerto Rican	0	0.0	0	0.0	0	0.0	0	0.0	0	0.0	0	0.0	0
Hispanic	3	0.9	3	1.1	6	1.0	0	0.0	1	0.5	6	1.0	4
Total Minority	38	11.7	59	20.8	97	16.0	0	0.0	35	16.3	97	16.0	25
For. Nation.	2	0.6	4	1.4	6	1.0	0	0.0	3	1.4	6	1.0	0
Caucasian	238	73.5	193	68.2	431	71.0	0	0.0	138	64.2	431	71.0	151
Unknown	46	14.2	27	9.5	73	12.0	0	0.0	39	18.1	73	12.0	31
Total	324	53.4	283	46.6	607	100.0	0	0.0	215	35.4	607		207

Transfers

Transfers in	13
Transfers out	7

Tuition and Fees

	Resident	Nonresident
Full-time	$16,600	$26,800
Part-time	$0	$0

Living Expenses

Estimated living expenses for singles

Living on campus	Living off campus	Living at home
$13,600	$13,600	$13,600

ABA Approved Since 1932

GPA and LSAT Scores

	Total	Full-time	Part-time
# of apps	4,209	4,209	0
# of offers	1,014	1,014	0
# of matrics	204	204	0
75% GPA	3.84	3.84	0.00
Median GPA	3.64	3.64	0.00
25% GPA	3.33	3.33	0.00
75% LSAT	166	166	0
Median LSAT	165	165	0
25% LSAT	162	162	0

Grants and Scholarships (from prior year)

	Total		Full-time		Part-time	
	#	%	#	%	#	%
Total # of students	607		607		0	
Total # receiving grants	169	27.8	169	27.8	0	0.0
Less than 1/2 tuition	152	25.0	152	25.0	0	0.0
Half to full tuition	17	2.8	17	2.8	0	0.0
Full tuition	0	0.0	0	0.0	0	0.0
More than full tuition	0	0.0	0	0.0	0	0.0
Median grant amount			$5,000		$0	

Informational and Library Resources

# of volumes and volume equivalents	380,742
# of titles	170,836
# of active serial subscriptions	4,286
Study seating capacity inside the library	427
# of full-time professional librarians	16
Hours per week library is open	168
# of open, wired connections available to students	120
# of networked computers available for use by students	35
# of simultaneous wireless users	2,000
Require computer?	No

JD Attrition (from prior year)

	Academic	Other	Total	
	#	#	#	%
1st year	0	3	3	1.5
2nd year	0	8	8	4.0
3rd year	0	1	1	0.5
4th year	0	0	0	0.0

Employment (9 months after graduation)

	Total	Percentage
Employment status known	181	98.9
Employment status unknown	2	1.1
Employed	163	90.1
Pursuing graduate degrees	4	2.2
Unemployed seeking employment	3	1.7
Unemployed not seeking employment	7	3.9
Unemployed and studying for the bar	4	2.2

Type of Employment

	Total	Percentage
# employed in law firms	76	46.6
# employed in business and industry	13	8.0
# employed in government	32	19.6
# employed in public interest	9	5.5
# employed as judicial clerks	32	19.6
# employed in academia	1	0.6

Geographic Location

	Total	Percentage
# employed in state	58	35.6
# employed in foreign countries	2	1.2
# of states where employed		27

Bar Passage Rates

Jurisdiction	Virginia			New York		
Exam	Sum 05	Win 06	Total	Sum 05	Win 06	Total
# from school taking bar for the first time	93	3	96	15	2	17
School's pass rate for all first-time takers	88%	100%	89%	100%	100%	100%
State's pass rate for all first-time takers	76%	65%	74%	76%	61%	74%

William & Mary Law School

613 South Henry Street
Williamsburg, VA 23185
Phone: 757.221.3785; Fax: 757.221.3261
E-mail: lawadm@wm.edu; Website: www.wm.edu/law/

■ Introduction

Established in 1779 at the request of Thomas Jefferson, William & Mary Law School is the nation's oldest law school. At William & Mary, concern for students' intellectual development is accompanied by concern that they develop the character and values of constructive citizens who will do their part in society. The Law School is small enough for people to know one another by name and large enough to form a critical mass for learning and scholarship. Many assume it is a private school—it is not. William & Mary combines wonderful historic roots, a strong national reputation, and a wealth of programs with a cost that is a "very good buy." Members of the 2006–2007 student body earned undergraduate degrees from 225 colleges and universities and represent 47 states, DC, and nine other countries. The Law School is located a few blocks from Colonial Williamsburg and within short driving distance of the metropolitan areas of Washington, DC; Richmond; and Norfolk. Visits and student tours are encouraged.

■ Library and Physical Facilities

The library's collection of nearly 400,000 volumes and its service-oriented staff provide an excellent setting for study and research. Legal materials are available in all formats, including an extensive treatise collection covering all areas of law. A major library expansion and renovation project will be completed during spring 2007, resulting in a new modern facility with cutting-edge technology. Features of the new Law Library include two reading rooms and a large study area offering ample views of the outdoors, abundant seating with Internet access, group-study spaces, computer labs, and a rare book room. The Law School employs wireless technology for e-mail and Web access throughout the building.

The McGlothlin Courtroom at the Law School is the nation's most technologically advanced trial and appellate chamber. The courtroom is designed to permit trials with multiple remote appearances and Web-based evidence and offers students hands-on training in the use of state-of-the-art courtroom technology. It has a wide variety of features, including all available major court record systems, evidence presentation technologies, assistive and foreign language interpretation technologies, and critical infrastructure technologies.

The Law School is located between the National Center for State Courts and William & Mary's graduate apartment complex, where 20 percent of law students live. A wide variety of off-campus housing options are available in the Williamsburg area.

■ Curriculum

The required first-year curriculum includes constitutional law, contracts, torts, civil procedure, property, criminal law, and legal skills. The two-year Legal Skills Program, which begins with a week-long concentrated introduction to the legal system and law study before classes begin, allows students to experience and refine lawyering skills such as interviewing, negotiating, trial techniques, and oral advocacy. This innovative program utilizes simulated law offices, client representation, and mock trials to teach the skills necessary for

the practice of law as well as legal research, writing, and professional responsibility. To earn a Juris Doctor degree, students must successfully complete 86 credit hours through full-time study, all required courses, and a significant paper of publishable quality. Students may choose yearly from more than 100 upper-level courses covering a broad range of contemporary and traditional areas of law. The Law School offers four clinical programs (legal aid clinic, domestic violence clinic, federal tax clinic, and therapeutic jurisprudence) and a wide variety of externships, including externships at the Attorney General's Office, the Department of Employment Dispute Resolution, the Supreme Court of Virginia, the Virginia Court of Appeals, and the Virginia General Assembly. Students can also gain practical experience through the Judicial Clerk Externship, the Non-Profit Organization Externship, the Therapeutic Courts Practice Externship, and the General Practice Externship. In addition, second- and third-year students are encouraged to gain legal experience working in private firms and public law offices.

■ Joint-degree Programs

There are three joint-degree programs: JD/MBA, JD/MPP, and JD/MA in American Studies. The JD/MBA and the JD/MPP combine traditional five-year programs into four years of study. Students may complete the JD/MA in either three or four years.

■ International Programs

A summer session in Madrid, Spain, offers a five-week program in which students can earn up to six credits. William & Mary professors and prominent Spanish professors and practitioners teach the courses in English. In addition, students fluent in Spanish can complete a one-week externship in a Spanish law firm. JD students may also study abroad in Vienna, Austria; Madrid, Spain; Auckland, New Zealand; and Tokyo, Japan, during the academic year.

The Law School also offers an LLM in the American Legal System for students from outside the US who take courses with the JD students and bring the richness of their legal traditions to the classroom.

■ Special Programs

Through the Institute of Bill of Rights Law, the Law School has become one of the preeminent institutions studying the US Constitution's Bill of Rights. The institute sponsors lectures, symposia, and publications that entice scholars from around the country to examine important constitutional issues. The programs and initiatives of the Law School's Center for Legal and Court Technology seek to improve the administration of justice through the use of technology. The Center puts the latest technology to the test each year in a laboratory trial conducted by students in the McGlothlin Courtroom.

Exciting new cocurricular programs at the Law School include the Human Rights and National Security Law Program, which offers students the opportunity to learn about interplay between national defense and the protection of civil rights and has at its heart the objective of creating citizen lawyers who possess a deep appreciation for national security issues; the Therapeutic Jurisprudence Program, which is devoted to the study of law as a therapeutic agent and focuses on improving the administration of justice so that it has a positive effect on individuals, their families, and the community; the Property Rights Project, which encourages legal scholarship on the role that property rights play in society and also facilitates the exchange of ideas between scholars and practitioners; the Election Law Program, which seeks to provide practical assistance to state court judges who are called upon to resolve difficult election law disputes; and the George Wythe Society of Citizen Lawyers, a program that focuses on constructive citizenship.

The Loan Repayment Assistance Program provides up to $5,000 in loan forgiveness annually for a maximum of three years to selected graduates working full-time for private nonprofit organizations or government employers.

■ Student Activities

Legal scholars and practitioners frequently cite articles from our student-managed academic journals. These publications include *William & Mary Law Review, William & Mary Bill of Rights Journal, William & Mary Environmental Law and Policy Review,* and *Journal of Women and the Law.* The Law School also has a highly competitive Moot Court Program and National Trial Team. Two William & Mary students netted major honors in 2006. A member of the Moot Court team won the National Best Advocate award at the National Appellate Advocacy Competition sponsored by the ABA's Law Student Division.

A *Bill of Rights Journal* staff member was one of 14 students nationwide to receive a Burton Award for Legal Achievement for excellence in writing.

More than 30 student organizations reflect the broad and diverse interests of the student body. For more information about William & Mary's student organizations, visit the prospective students' section of the website.

■ Career Services

Career Services provides students and alumni with comprehensive professional services, including personal counseling, job-search strategies and networking, and speakers and workshops. Employers from 30 states, the District of Columbia, and three countries conducted on-campus interviews during 2005. Our video technology is also used for employment interviews. The Office of Career Services posted notices from more than 3,000 nonvisiting employers from 49 states, the District of Columbia, and several countries. In 2006, William & Mary students also had the opportunity to participate in 30 off-campus job fairs with a national employer base, including events in Atlanta, Boston, Chicago, Dallas, Los Angeles, and New York and specialized programs for intellectual property law, public interest and governmental positions, and small regional firms. The Law School awarded 93 fellowships to assist students working in low-paying or nonpaying public service positions during the summer of 2006. Ninety-eight percent of the class of 2005 were employed throughout the US and abroad or pursuing advanced degrees.

Applicant Profile

William & Mary Law School
This grid includes only applicants who earned 120–180 LSAT scores under standard administrations, and represents 99% of the total applicant pool.

LSAT Score	GPA 3.75 +		3.50–3.74		3.25–3.49		3.00–3.24		2.75–2.99		2.50–2.74		2.25–2.49		2.00–2.24		Below 2.00		No GPA		Total	
	Apps	Adm	Apps	Adm	Apps	Adm	Apps	Adm	Apps	Adm	Apps	Adm	Apps	Adm	Apps	Adm	Apps	Adm	Apps	Adm	Apps	Adm
175–180	11	11	7	5	6	5	3	3	4	1	1	0	0	0	0	0	0	0	0	0	32	25
170–174	72	69	53	47	48	26	30	14	15	4	8	1	2	0	1	0	0	0	0	0	229	161
165–169	249	229	257	190	213	79	129	22	54	6	22	2	6	1	3	0	0	0	6	3	939	532
160–164	287	115	378	63	263	19	142	7	64	4	29	3	6	0	4	0	0	0	7	0	1180	211
155–159	195	14	249	4	210	4	125	6	57	3	16	1	12	1	3	0	0	0	9	0	876	33
150–154	89	5	118	8	113	8	67	2	56	2	26	1	12	0	3	0	1	0	5	0	490	26
145–149	24	4	41	2	57	1	42	0	33	2	14	0	10	0	3	0	0	0	7	0	231	9
140–144	9	0	18	1	29	1	33	0	17	1	12	0	10	0	0	0	0	0	3	0	131	3
135–139	1	0	8	0	5	0	10	0	7	0	6	0	4	0	3	0	1	0	1	0	46	0
130–134	0	0	2	0	1	0	4	0	2	0	1	0	2	0	1	0	1	0	3	0	17	0
125–129	0	0	0	0	0	0	0	0	0	0	2	0	0	0	2	0	1	0	0	0	5	0
120–124	0	0	0	0	0	0	0	0	1	0	0	0	0	0	0	0	0	0	0	0	1	0
Total	937	447	1131	320	945	143	585	54	310	23	137	8	64	2	23	0	4	0	41	3	4177	1000

Apps = Number of Applicants
Adm = Number Admitted

William Mitchell College of Law

875 Summit Avenue
St. Paul, MN 55105
Phone: 651.290.6476; toll-free: 888.WMCL.LAW; Fax: 651.290.7535
E-mail: admissions@wmitchell.edu; Website: www.wmitchell.edu

ABA
Approved
Since
1938

The Basics

Type of school	Private
Term	Semester
Application deadline	5/1
Application fee	$50
Financial aid deadline	3/15
Can first year start other than fall?	No
Student to faculty ratio	24.4 to 1
Does the university offer:	
housing restricted to law students?	No
graduate housing for which law students are eligible?	No

Faculty and Administrators

	Total		Men		Women		Minorities	
	Fall	Spr	Fall	Spr	Fall	Spr	Fall	Spr
Full-time	38	38	22	22	16	16	6	6
Other Full-time	1	1	0	0	1	1	0	0
Deans, librarians, & others who teach	5	5	3	3	2	2	2	2
Part-time	212	214	125	124	87	90	54	43
Total	256	258	150	149	106	109	62	51

Curriculum

	Full-time	Part-time
Typical first-year section size	80	60
Is there typically a "small section" of the first-year class, other than Legal Writing, taught by full-time faculty	No	No
If yes, typical size offered last year		
# of classroom course titles beyond first-year curriculum	124	
# of upper division courses, excluding seminars with an enrollment: Under 25	99	
25–49	73	
50–74	24	
75–99	5	
100+	1	
# of seminars	54	
# of seminar positions available	1,247	
# of seminar positions filled	795	394
# of positions available in simulation courses	1,378	
# of simulation positions filled	811	394
# of positions available in faculty supervised clinical courses	271	
# of faculty supervised clinical positions filled	169	67
# involved in field placements	63	25
# involved in law journals	54	19
# involved in interschool competitions	65	12
# of credit hours required to graduate	86	

JD Enrollment and Ethnicity

	Men		Women		Full-time		Part-time		1st-year		Total		JD Degs. Awd.
	#	%	#	%	#	%	#	%	#	%	#	%	
African Amer.	13	2.5	20	3.4	14	1.9	19	5.2	13	3.7	33	3.0	13
Amer. Indian	0	0.0	5	0.9	5	0.7	0	0.0	1	0.3	5	0.5	1
Asian Amer.	28	5.4	29	4.9	39	5.3	18	4.9	22	6.2	57	5.2	10
Mex. Amer.	1	0.2	6	1.0	6	0.8	1	0.3	1	0.3	7	0.6	3
Puerto Rican	1	0.2	1	0.2	2	0.3	0	0.0	0	0.0	2	0.2	1
Hispanic	6	1.2	11	1.9	9	1.2	8	2.2	8	2.3	17	1.5	4
Total Minority	49	9.5	72	12.3	75	10.2	46	12.6	45	12.7	121	11.0	32
For. Nation.	2	0.4	5	0.9	6	0.8	1	0.3	4	1.1	7	0.6	3
Caucasian	372	72.1	440	75.0	546	74.0	266	72.9	252	71.2	812	73.6	264
Unknown	93	18.0	70	11.9	111	15.0	52	14.2	53	15.0	163	14.8	23
Total	516	46.8	587	53.2	738	66.9	365	33.1	354	32.1	1103		322

Transfers

Transfers in	9
Transfers out	3

Tuition and Fees

	Resident	Nonresident
Full-time	$27,530	$27,530
Part-time	$19,938	$19,938

Living Expenses

Estimated living expenses for singles

Living on campus	Living off campus	Living at home
N/A	$14,300	N/A

*ABA
Approved
Since
1938*

GPA and LSAT Scores

	Total	Full-time	Part-time
# of apps	1,758	1,323	435
# of offers	817	631	186
# of matrics	352	237	115
75% GPA	3.60	3.66	3.47
Median GPA	3.35	3.43	3.19
25% GPA	3.03	3.15	2.87
75% LSAT	158	158	157
Median LSAT	154	155	151
25% LSAT	150	152	147

Grants and Scholarships (from prior year)

	Total		Full-time		Part-time	
	#	%	#	%	#	%
Total # of students	1,114		732		382	
Total # receiving grants	413	37.1	366	50.0	47	12.3
Less than 1/2 tuition	304	27.3	268	36.6	36	9.4
Half to full tuition	98	8.8	89	12.2	9	2.4
Full tuition	11	1.0	9	1.2	2	0.5
More than full tuition	0	0.0	0	0.0	0	0.0
Median grant amount			$2,000		$3,500	

Informational and Library Resources

# of volumes and volume equivalents	338,756
# of titles	195,844
# of active serial subscriptions	3,867
Study seating capacity inside the library	671
# of full-time professional librarians	8
Hours per week library is open	109
# of open, wired connections available to students	240
# of networked computers available for use by students	89
# of simultaneous wireless users	1,048
Require computer?	Yes

°JD Attrition (from prior year)

	Academic	Other	Total	
	#	#	#	%
1st year	17	24	41	11.1
2nd year	1	0	1	0.3
3rd year	0	0	0	0.0
4th year	0	0	0	0.0

Employment (9 months after graduation)

	Total	Percentage
Employment status known	306	98.1
Employment status unknown	6	1.9
Employed	277	90.5
Pursuing graduate degrees	2	0.7
Unemployed seeking employment	9	2.9
Unemployed not seeking employment	6	2.0
Unemployed and studying for the bar	12	3.9

Type of Employment

	Total	Percentage
# employed in law firms	128	46.2
# employed in business and industry	75	27.1
# employed in government	16	5.8
# employed in public interest	15	5.4
# employed as judicial clerks	35	12.6
# employed in academia	3	1.1

Geographic Location

	Total	Percentage
# employed in state	250	90.3
# employed in foreign countries	0	0.0
# of states where employed		17

Bar Passage Rates

Jurisdiction	Minnesota		
Exam	Sum 05	Win 06	Total
# from school taking bar for the first time	236	56	292
School's pass rate for all first-time takers	85%	88%	85%
State's pass rate for all first-time takers	89%	88%	89%

William Mitchell College of Law

Office of Admissions, 875 Summit Avenue
St. Paul, MN 55105
Phone: 651.290.6476; toll-free: 888.WMCL.LAW; Fax: 651.290.7535
E-mail: admissions@wmitchell.edu; Website: www.wmitchell.edu

■ Introduction

William Mitchell College of Law, an independent, private law school in St. Paul, Minnesota, was founded in 1900 and named for one of the state's most respected judges. Our original purpose was to make legal education available to working people of modest means, many of them immigrants with families to support. To this day, William Mitchell is known for cultivating practical wisdom and for creating an environment that welcomes both traditional and nontraditional law students from all walks of life. The rigorous William Mitchell legal education stands apart in building both theoretical knowledge and real-life insights and skills at every step. This gives our graduates an enduring advantage as they meet the challenges of an increasingly complex world. William Mitchell College of Law's clinical, legal writing, and trial advocacy programs are nationally recognized, contributing to our reputation as "the lawyer's law school." The college has produced many distinguished leaders at the bench and bar and in the business and civic arenas, among them the 15th Chief Justice of the United States, Warren E. Burger, Class of '31, and the first woman to serve on the Minnesota Supreme Court, Rosalie E. Wahl, Class of '67. The largest law school in Minnesota, William Mitchell has just over 1,000 students, 42 full-time faculty members, and over 10,000 alumni.

The college is accredited by the ABA, is a member of the AALS, and is approved by the US Veterans Administration.

■ Faculty

In contrast with traditional law schools, this college was founded by practicing lawyers, who knew their professional experience would strengthen the learning process. William Mitchell continues to build on that legacy by nurturing a faculty that serves the legal community as active participants and critical observers. Our professors have a commitment to translating scholarly jurisprudence into the practice of law and using the practice of law to deepen their scholarship. They are rooted in the real world and the wide world of legal, judicial, and legislative practice. Some professors are deeply engaged in advising emerging democracies about establishing their legal systems. Others are pioneers in areas such as elder law and family law. Faculty members have led innovations in the practice of intellectual property law and are experts on how it's practiced in other nations. They've served on the bench as well as the bar, and had careers in public service, government, and corporations. They have spoken out on, published, or handled controversial legal issues or cases. We deliberately cultivate a strong adjunct faculty, in addition to our core faculty, knowing their contributions strengthen the educational process.

■ Academics

What distinguishes a William Mitchell education is our professors' engagement with legal practice and law reform. They are genuinely excited about serving the law, sharing their experiences, and using their knowledge to enrich the curriculum. As a result, students go through a learning process that balances scholarship and practice, emphasizes a strong connection with the profession, is intellectually rigorous, and instills an ethic of service to clients and community. On a micro level, this means

that many of our courses combine legal theory with developing legal skills. On the macro level, we train our students to understand, with breadth and depth, not just where the law is now, but where it's going. This blend of know-how, scholarly reflection, and ability to adapt over time is the essence of practical wisdom. William Mitchell graduates are prepared to put the law to work in the world.

We also strengthen our academics by deliberately cultivating a stimulating cross section of students and professors: the Mitchell Mix. Students who find themselves in a constitutional law class with a recent immigrant, a health law class with a nurse practitioner, or a family law class with someone sharing custody of a child, enter a different realm of legal education. They also learn from a professor who may have written the statute or argued the case they're studying. This sets the stage for a richer learning experience. As William Mitchell continues to pioneer a demanding, professionally engaged, legal education, we are launching new academic programs and processes. These include the Fellows Program, which pairs professors with the most exceptional students, who will assist with research and receive specialized training and opportunities. Our new pathways approach to the educational process will give students the resources and tools they need to be completely intentional about their legal education. Students nearing graduation will crystallize their cumulative learning through the Keystone Program, sparking the transition from law student into lawyer.

■ Flexible Scheduling

Over the past century, many William Mitchell students have enhanced their education, careers, and quality of life by taking advantage of our part-time and full-time enrollment options. Your first year, you enroll either as a part-time or full-time student. After your first year is completed, you can choose to carry either a part- or full-time courseload. You can change your enrollment status as frequently as each semester. Your commitment here is not to a part-time or full-time program; it's to your chosen pathway through the curriculum and to achieving your JD. Regardless of which enrollment status you choose, you get the same high-quality education. Advanced and elective classes are typically offered in the evening, so part-time and full-time students take classes together and have equal access to full-time and adjunct faculty. Although classes meet at set times, William Mitchell offers you enough flexibility to build your law school schedule around a clerkship, continue in your current career track or day job, or take care of other responsibilities.

■ Library and Physical Facilities

William Mitchell's handsome, accessibly designed Warren E. Burger Library has a reputation as the "go to" law library of the Twin Cities. Ten members of the library staff have library science degrees, six have law degrees, and several have substantial law practice experience, giving them a quick, intuitive grasp of legal research problems. The reference desk is open 76 hours a week, substantially more than many law libraries. These long reference desk hours reflect our commitment to the needs of our students, faculty, and alumni. William Mitchell's librarians play an active part in your educational process and are deeply engaged in expanding the library's electronic potential, in addition to its strong core collection.

The physical design of the campus as a whole mirrors the William Mitchell philosophy that practical skills are inseparable from legal doctrine. Our Rosalie Wahl Legal Practice Center, home to our top-rated clinical and skills programs, is located in the same building as classrooms and faculty offices. The campus is also equipped with technologically advanced moot courtrooms, computer labs, seminar rooms, a new student lounge and cafeteria, and offices for student organizations. William Mitchell's campus is located in St. Paul, the state capital, and faces elegant Summit Avenue. The campus is a short walk to the lively Grand and Selby Avenue shopping districts, and a substantial number of students find housing nearby. The Twin Cities is home to a vital law community and numerous Fortune 500 firms and is frequently cited as one of the top 10 places to live in the United States.

■ Public Service Opportunities

William Mitchell students provide more than 6,000 hours of supervised pro bono service each year to our partner, the Minnesota Justice Foundation. Students also perform approximately 14,000 hours of pro bono service annually through our for-credit legal clinic program.

■ Special Programs

William Mitchell's Law in Edinburgh and London program gives students the opportunity to study English and European Union law and practice for up to five weeks during the summer. We're also a member of the Consortium for Innovative Legal Education, providing students with the opportunity to enroll in 10 summer and semester study-abroad programs. Our Summer

Excellence Program is an intensive orientation to law school for a limited number of entering students.

■ Student Body

William Mitchell's student population ranges from age 20 to 59, with our recent entering class representing 30 states and 13 foreign countries. Many students come directly from undergraduate institutions, while others come from professional careers, parenting, or a combination. Our Mitchell Mix of students brings depth and breadth to the classroom that is rare in legal education. Students can participate in more than 25 on-campus student organizations, including the Student Bar Association and the *William Mitchell Law Review*.

■ Career Development

Because William Mitchell's curriculum emphasizes legal doctrine and skills training, students enter the marketplace knowing how to put the law to work. Employers clearly value our graduates, since 96.9 percent of the class of 2005 was employed within nine months of graduation. Career development is woven into each year of a student's legal education, and our career development office helps students polish presentation, networking, and personal marketing skills. Our powerful alumni network and well-connected faculty are also resources students can tap.

■ Scholarships/Financial Aid

Financial aid is available from William Mitchell in the form of both merit- and need-based scholarships, federal and alternative loans, and federal work-study. Approximately 90 percent of all William Mitchell students receive some type of financial aid.

Applicant Profile

William Mitchell College of Law
This grid includes only applicants who earned 120–180 LSAT scores under standard administrations.

LSAT Score	GPA																				
	3.75 +		3.50–3.74		3.25–3.49		3.00–3.24		2.75–2.99		2.50–2.74		2.25–2.49		2.00–2.24		Below 2.00		No GPA		Total
	Apps	Adm	Apps	Adm	Apps	Adm	Apps	Adm	Apps	Adm	Apps	Adm	Apps	Adm	Apps	Adm	Apps	Adm	Apps	Adm	Apps	Adm
175–180	0	0	1	1	1	0	0	0	0	0	0	0	0	0	0	0	0	0	0	0	2	1
170–174	0	0	2	2	1	1	1	1	0	0	0	0	0	0	0	0	0	0	0	0	4	4
165–169	3	3	11	11	4	3	11	11	4	4	0	0	2	2	0	0	0	0	1	1	36	35
160–164	30	29	31	30	23	22	17	15	13	12	14	13	3	3	2	1	0	0	1	1	134	126
155–159	45	44	65	62	59	51	49	42	24	20	18	16	10	8	3	0	2	1	1	1	276	245
150–154	39	35	90	59	93	53	71	32	53	22	21	7	14	7	10	4	1	1	7	4	399	224
145–149	23	11	65	26	79	25	78	17	44	7	30	5	18	4	12	1	1	0	6	4	356	100
140–144	8	4	16	4	22	5	43	14	38	5	27	5	7	0	5	0	1	0	5	1	172	38
135–139	0	0	3	2	5	1	15	1	9	0	12	0	5	0	1	0	1	0	6	0	57	4
130–134	0	0	1	0	1	0	2	1	4	0	4	0	2	0	1	0	1	0	1	0	17	1
125–129	0	0	0	0	0	0	0	0	1	0	3	0	0	0	1	0	1	0	2	0	8	0
120–124	0	0	0	0	0	0	0	0	0	0	1	0	0	0	0	0	0	0	0	0	1	0
Total	148	126	285	197	288	161	287	134	190	70	130	46	61	24	35	6	8	2	30	12	1462	778

Apps = Number of Applicants   Adm = Number Admitted   Reflects 99% of the total applicant pool.

University of Wisconsin Law School

975 Bascom Mall
Madison, WI 53706
Phone: 608.262.5914; Fax: 608.263.3190
E-mail: admissions@law.wisc.edu; Website: www.law.wisc.edu

ABA Approved Since 1923

The Basics

Type of school	Public
Term	Semester
Application deadline	2/1
Application fee	$45
Financial aid deadline	3/1
Can first year start other than fall?	No
Student to faculty ratio	12.9 to 1
Does the university offer:	
housing restricted to law students?	No
graduate housing for which law students are eligible?	Yes

Faculty and Administrators

	Total		Men		Women		Minorities	
	Fall	Spr	Fall	Spr	Fall	Spr	Fall	Spr
Full-time	54	50	33	32	21	18	12	7
Other Full-time	3	2	1	0	2	2	0	0
Deans, librarians, & others who teach	6	5	5	4	1	1	0	0
Part-time	57	55	25	29	32	26	5	3
Total	120	112	64	65	56	47	17	10

Curriculum

	Full-time	Part-time
Typical first-year section size	77	0
Is there typically a "small section" of the first-year class, other than Legal Writing, taught by full-time faculty	Yes	No
If yes, typical size offered last year	18	
# of classroom course titles beyond first-year curriculum	171	
# of upper division courses, excluding seminars with an enrollment: Under 25	106	
25–49	56	
50–74	15	
75–99	6	
100+	2	
# of seminars	70	
# of seminar positions available	1,460	
# of seminar positions filled	836	0
# of positions available in simulation courses	498	
# of simulation positions filled	382	0
# of positions available in faculty supervised clinical courses	520	
# of faculty supervised clinical positions filled	373	0
# involved in field placements	210	0
# involved in law journals	164	0
# involved in interschool competitions	126	0
# of credit hours required to graduate	90	

JD Enrollment and Ethnicity

	Men #	Men %	Women #	Women %	Full-time #	Full-time %	Part-time #	Part-time %	1st-year #	1st-year %	Total #	Total %	JD Degs. Awd.
African Amer.	31	6.9	37	8.9	62	7.6	6	12.5	25	8.2	68	7.9	25
Amer. Indian	8	1.8	16	3.9	23	2.8	1	2.1	10	3.3	24	2.8	4
Asian Amer.	21	4.7	38	9.2	58	7.1	1	2.1	20	6.5	59	6.8	15
Mex. Amer.	25	5.6	17	4.1	40	4.9	2	4.2	14	4.6	42	4.9	10
Puerto Rican	3	0.7	8	1.9	11	1.3	0	0.0	5	1.6	11	1.3	3
Hispanic	8	1.8	13	3.1	19	2.3	2	4.2	12	3.9	21	2.4	9
Total Minority	96	21.3	129	31.1	213	26.1	12	25.0	86	28.1	225	26.0	66
For. Nation.	8	1.8	9	2.2	12	1.5	5	10.4	8	2.6	17	2.0	7
Caucasian	328	72.9	257	61.9	559	68.4	26	54.2	193	63.1	585	67.6	192
Unknown	18	4.0	20	4.8	33	4.0	5	10.4	19	6.2	38	4.4	2
Total	450	52.0	415	48.0	817	94.5	48	5.5	306	35.4	865		267

Transfers

Transfers in	11
Transfers out	2

Tuition and Fees

	Resident	Nonresident
Full-time	$12,653	$30,816
Part-time	$1,058	$2,572

Living Expenses

Estimated living expenses for singles

Living on campus	Living off campus	Living at home
$13,650	$13,650	$8,090

*Part-time tuition and fees per credit.

University of Wisconsin Law School

*ABA
Approved
Since
1923*

GPA and LSAT Scores

	Total	Full-time	Part-time
# of apps	3,005	3,005	0
# of offers	774	774	0
# of matrics	283	283	0
75% GPA	3.72	3.72	0.00
Median GPA	3.53	3.53	0.00
25% GPA	3.23	3.23	0.00
75% LSAT	163	163	0
Median LSAT	161	161	0
25% LSAT	156	156	0

Grants and Scholarships (from prior year)

	Total		Full-time		Part-time	
	#	%	#	%	#	%
Total # of students	839		801		38	
Total # receiving grants	216	25.7	216	27.0	0	0.0
Less than 1/2 tuition	86	10.3	86	10.7	0	0.0
Half to full tuition	69	8.2	69	8.6	0	0.0
Full tuition	4	0.5	4	0.5	0	0.0
More than full tuition	57	6.8	57	7.1	0	0.0
Median grant amount			$11,700		$0	

Informational and Library Resources

# of volumes and volume equivalents	560,045
# of titles	292,035
# of active serial subscriptions	6,122
Study seating capacity inside the library	613
# of full-time professional librarians	9
Hours per week library is open	104
# of open, wired connections available to students	526
# of networked computers available for use by students	73
# of simultaneous wireless users	2,040
Require computer?	Yes

JD Attrition (from prior year)

	Academic	Other	Total	
	#	#	#	%
1st year	0	8	8	2.8
2nd year	0	0	0	0.0
3rd year	0	0	0	0.0
4th year	0	0	0	0.0

Employment (9 months after graduation)

	Total	Percentage
Employment status known	241	99.2
Employment status unknown	2	0.8
Employed	231	95.9
Pursuing graduate degrees	5	2.1
Unemployed seeking employment	1	0.4
Unemployed not seeking employment	1	0.4
Unemployed and studying for the bar	3	1.2

Type of Employment

# employed in law firms	129	55.8
# employed in business and industry	16	6.9
# employed in government	39	16.9
# employed in public interest	19	8.2
# employed as judicial clerks	17	7.4
# employed in academia	7	3.0

Geographic Location

# employed in state	128	55.4
# employed in foreign countries	3	1.3
# of states where employed		21

Bar Passage Rates

Jurisdiction	Wisconsin		
Exam	Sum 05	Win 06	Total
# from school taking bar for the first time	208	40	248
School's pass rate for all first-time takers	N/A	N/A	N/A
State's pass rate for all first-time takers	79%	74%	77%

All graduates were admitted to the Wisconsin bar via the diploma privilege.

University of Wisconsin Law School

975 Bascom Mall
Madison, WI 53706
Phone: 608.262.5914; Fax: 608.263.3190
E-mail: admissions@law.wisc.edu; Website: www.law.wisc.edu

■ A Preeminent Law School, A World-class University, A Beautiful City

The UW Law School is one of the most intellectually exciting law schools in the country, attracting students from around the world. Students represent a variety of backgrounds, ages, interests, races, nationalities, and life experiences which encourage a robust exchange of ideas.

Top students are drawn to the UW Law School because of its tradition of excellence, its beautiful setting in the heart of one of the world's leading research universities, and its *law-in-action* philosophy, an approach that differentiates it from other law schools.

The UW Law School is located in Madison, an affordable city strategically and conveniently situated in the middle of a triangle formed by Chicago, Minneapolis, and Milwaukee. As the state capital, Madison is home to many courts and state and federal government agencies—all within walking distance of the Law School.

■ A Commitment to Diversity and Community

A major indicator of the strength of any law school is its student body. The fall 2006 entering class of 283 students represents 25 states and 119 undergraduate institutions. Forty percent of our students are from outside of Wisconsin; 47 percent are women; and 34 percent are students of color. The UW Law School's admission policies enhance the diversity, vigor, social concern, and academic ability of the student community. There is a special feeling of community in the school and an informal, supportive atmosphere, reflecting a strong commitment by faculty and administrators to student learning, morale, and well-being.

■ The Faculty: Leading Scholars and Outstanding Teachers

The UW Law School's nationally recognized faculty come from a wide range of backgrounds and offer students strong role models and a variety of experiences. They are leading scholars who are also actively involved in the law. They advise on stem cell issues, represent clients on death row, work with congressional staffers to draft legislation, provide legal advice to poor farmers in the South, and work with the European Union on monetary policy. They are interesting lawyers doing interesting things, but first and foremost, they are excellent teachers who are committed to their students. A superb clinical faculty and an experienced adjunct faculty provide additional teaching resources.

■ The Curriculum: Law in Action

Students at the UW Law School have many opportunities to experience *law-in-action*. An extensive curriculum places an emphasis on the dynamics of the law (how the law relates to social change and to society as a whole) while at the same time emphasizing skill development, particularly legal analysis and writing. The first-year small-section program teaches the fundamentals of legal analysis and reasoning in a supportive setting. In the first semester, two of a student's five classes—

a substantive law class and a legal research and writing class—are small sections. Students receive individual feedback, and it is easy to form study groups and friendships because students from these small sections take all of their other classes together.

In the second and third years of law school, students have time both to explore the curriculum and to develop the lawyering skills they need. The UW Law School is a national law school that prepares students to practice wherever they choose. Students choose courses from an extraordinary breadth and depth of offerings, affording them the opportunity to explore cutting edge legal issues in the classroom and to apply their knowledge in one of the many clinical programs.

■ Dual-degree Programs

Renowned for its interdisciplinary approach, the UW Law School offers many opportunities for students to combine the study of law with a graduate degree in another subject. There are many existing dual-degree programs. If one of the existing programs does not meet a student's academic needs, the Law School will help create an individualized curriculum.

■ Clinicals and Skills Training: Hands-on Learning

The UW Law School is committed to practical experience as a part of legal education. With one of the largest clinical programs in the country, the UW Law School offers a wide variety of hands-on lawyering experiences with real clients and excellent supervision. From representing low-income clients to teaming up with medical students as advocates for newly diagnosed cancer patients or assisting inmates in state and federal prisons, these experiences are invaluable opportunities. Judicial internships, externships, and our innovative lawyering skills program provide additional hands-on learning experiences.

■ Going Global: International Law and Study Abroad

Ten professors devote their scholarship and teaching primarily to international or comparative law, and many others integrate analysis of foreign legal developments into their domestic law courses. The Law School hosts international students and professors, bringing diverse international perspectives to the classroom, and the university has one of the largest groups of international students in the country. Students can also study with one of the eight foreign law faculties with which the Law School has exchange agreements or participate in foreign study programs of other US law schools. Additional international opportunities are available through the Law School's East Asian Legal Studies Center, established to formalize and increase the Law School's interaction in East and Southeast Asia.

■ Student Activities

More than 30 organizations provide outstanding opportunities for students to pursue their talents and interests. Several moot court competitions at the UW Law School enable students to gain experience with brief writing and oral advocacy, and several student journals—*Wisconsin Law Review, Wisconsin International Law Journal,* and *Wisconsin Women's Law Journal*—give students an opportunity to contribute to the Law School's scholarly publications and gain invaluable training in legal research and writing.

■ Career Opportunities

Leading law firms, government agencies, businesses, and public interest organizations seek to hire UW Law School graduates. A broad range of legal employers from many major cities participate in the on-campus interview program. The Law School also participates in nine off-campus job fairs each year in New York; Washington, DC; Los Angeles; Chicago; and Minneapolis. Our students receive assistance from many of our more than 12,000 alumni throughout the country, and our graduates typically accept jobs in more than 20 different states from New York to California.

Applicant Profile

Admission to the University of Wisconsin Law School is competitive. The most recent entering class had a median LSAT score of 161 and a median GPA of 3.53. The Law School does not provide a profile chart because its admission decisions involve many factors that are not represented by undergraduate GPA and LSAT scores. The UW Law School Admissions Committee looks at an applicant's credentials taken as a whole. While candidates with higher grades and scores tend to be admitted at higher rates, GPA and LSAT scores alone are not necessarily good predictors of admission decisions on individual applications.

University of Wyoming College of Law

Dept. 3035, 1000 E. University Avenue
Laramie, WY 82071
Phone: 307.766.6416; Fax: 307.766.6417
E-mail: lawadmis@uwyo.edu; Website: www.uwyo.edu/law

ABA
Approved
Since
1923

The Basics

Type of school	Public
Term	Semester
Application deadline	3/1
Application fee	$50
Financial aid deadline	3/1
Can first year start other than fall?	No
Student to faculty ratio	12.2 to 1
Does the university offer:	
housing restricted to law students?	No
graduate housing for which law students are eligible?	Yes

Curriculum

	Full-time	Part-time
Typical first-year section size	85	0
Is there typically a "small section" of the first-year class, other than Legal Writing, taught by full-time faculty	No	No
If yes, typical size offered last year		
# of classroom course titles beyond first-year curriculum		61
# of upper division courses, excluding seminars with an enrollment: Under 25		43
25–49		11
50–74		8
75–99		0
100+		0
# of seminars		3
# of seminar positions available		30
# of seminar positions filled	22	0
# of positions available in simulation courses		102
# of simulation positions filled	75	0
# of positions available in faculty supervised clinical courses		70
# of faculty supervised clinical positions filled	63	0
# involved in field placements	27	0
# involved in law journals	24	0
# involved in interschool competitions	14	0
# of credit hours required to graduate		88

Faculty and Administrators

	Total		Men		Women		Minorities	
	Fall	Spr	Fall	Spr	Fall	Spr	Fall	Spr
Full-time	16	15	11	10	5	5	3	3
Other Full-time	1	2	1	2	0	0	1	1
Deans, librarians, & others who teach	6	6	2	2	4	4	0	0
Part-time	2	14	1	7	1	7	0	0
Total	**25**	**37**	**15**	**21**	**10**	**16**	**4**	**4**

JD Enrollment and Ethnicity

	Men #	Men %	Women #	Women %	Full-time #	Full-time %	Part-time #	Part-time %	1st-year #	1st-year %	Total #	Total %	JD Degs. Awd.
African Amer.	2	1.6	1	1.0	3	1.3	0	0.0	2	2.4	3	1.3	1
Amer. Indian	0	0.0	1	1.0	1	0.4	0	0.0	0	0.0	1	0.4	1
Asian Amer.	1	0.8	4	3.9	5	2.2	0	0.0	3	3.5	5	2.2	1
Mex. Amer.	5	3.9	4	3.9	9	3.9	0	0.0	4	4.7	9	3.9	3
Puerto Rican	0	0.0	0	0.0	0	0.0	0	0.0	0	0.0	0	0.0	1
Hispanic	0	0.0	0	0.0	0	0.0	0	0.0	0	0.0	0	0.0	0
Total Minority	8	6.3	10	9.7	18	7.8	0	0.0	9	10.6	18	7.8	7
For. Nation.	4	3.1	1	1.0	5	2.2	0	0.0	1	1.2	5	2.2	0
Caucasian	102	79.7	87	84.5	189	81.8	0	0.0	68	80.0	189	81.8	57
Unknown	14	10.9	5	4.9	19	8.2	0	0.0	7	8.2	19	8.2	10
Total	128	55.4	103	44.6	231	100.0	0	0.0	85	36.8	231		74

Transfers

Transfers in	3
Transfers out	1

Tuition and Fees

	Resident	Nonresident
Full-time	$7,635	$16,155
Part-time	$0	$0

Living Expenses

Estimated living expenses for singles

Living on campus	Living off campus	Living at home
$11,789	$11,789	$5,554

University of Wyoming College of Law

ABA
Approved
Since
1923

GPA and LSAT Scores

	Total	Full-time	Part-time
# of apps	809	809	0
# of offers	212	212	0
# of matrics	85	85	0
75% GPA	3.61	3.61	0.00
Median GPA	3.42	3.42	0.00
25% GPA	3.13	3.13	0.00
75% LSAT	154	154	0
Median LSAT	151	151	0
25% LSAT	150	150	0

Grants and Scholarships (from prior year)

	Total		Full-time		Part-time	
	#	%	#	%	#	%
Total # of students	227		227		0	
Total # receiving grants	185	81.5	185	81.5	0	0.0
Less than 1/2 tuition	172	75.8	172	75.8	0	0.0
Half to full tuition	8	3.5	8	3.5	0	0.0
Full tuition	3	1.3	3	1.3	0	0.0
More than full tuition	2	0.9	2	0.9	0	0.0
Median grant amount			$1,200		$0	

Informational and Library Resources

# of volumes and volume equivalents	288,557
# of titles	28,759
# of active serial subscriptions	1,703
Study seating capacity inside the library	258
# of full-time professional librarians	3
Hours per week library is open	107
# of open, wired connections available to students	262
# of networked computers available for use by students	25
# of simultaneous wireless users	200
Require computer?	No

JD Attrition (from prior year)

	Academic	Other	Total	
	#	#	#	%
1st year	1	2	3	3.8
2nd year	0	4	4	5.4
3rd year	1	0	1	1.3
4th year	0	0	0	0.0

Employment (9 months after graduation)

	Total	Percentage
Employment status known	75	96.2
Employment status unknown	3	3.8
Employed	62	82.7
Pursuing graduate degrees	3	4.0
Unemployed seeking employment	6	8.0
Unemployed not seeking employment	4	5.3
Unemployed and studying for the bar	0	0.0

Type of Employment

# employed in law firms	28	45.2
# employed in business and industry	7	11.3
# employed in government	7	11.3
# employed in public interest	4	6.5
# employed as judicial clerks	16	25.8
# employed in academia	0	0.0

Geographic Location

# employed in state	32	51.6
# employed in foreign countries	0	0.0
# of states where employed	14	

Bar Passage Rates

Jurisdiction	Wyoming		
Exam	Sum 05	Win 06	Total
# from school taking bar for the first time	40	17	57
School's pass rate for all first-time takers	75%	71%	74%
State's pass rate for all first-time takers	82%	71%	80%

University of Wyoming College of Law

Dept. 3035, 1000 E. University Avenue
Laramie, WY 82071
Phone: 307.766.6416; Fax: 307.766.6417
E-mail: lawadmis@uwyo.edu; Website: www.uwyo.edu/law

■ Introduction

The University of Wyoming College of Law is located on the campus of the University of Wyoming in Laramie. The university, the only four-year institution of higher learning in Wyoming, comprises seven colleges, a graduate school, and several organized research units. The university has a student body of 13,000.

The College of Law, founded in 1920, is a member of the AALS and is accredited by the ABA. An excellent faculty of 20 full-time professors and several lecturers instructs a student body of about 225. The limited size of the student body and the favorable student-faculty ratio create an atmosphere of friendliness and informality, and students enjoy a degree of access to faculty that students would rarely find at a larger institution.

Laramie is a town of 30,000 located in the southeastern part of Wyoming at an altitude of 7,200 feet on the high plains between two mountain ranges. Laramie's proximity to the mountains provides a variety of recreational activities, including skiing, backpacking, rock climbing, hiking, mountain biking, camping, fishing, and hunting. Denver is two hours to the south.

■ Faculty

The faculty has a proven record of excellence in teaching and research. Particular areas of strength include environmental and natural resource law, water law, constitutional law, and transactional law. Faculty members are actively engaged in public service and university functions. Because of our small student body, the University of Wyoming College of Law faculty has instructional and research opportunities that are often not available in larger institutions. Students regularly converse with their professors both inside and outside the classroom.

■ Curriculum

The first year consists entirely of required courses. During the second year, students must take additional required courses, including Evidence, Professional Responsibility, and a second semester of Constitutional Law and Civil Procedure. Students must also complete an advanced writing requirement prior to graduation. As a condition of graduation from the College of Law, all students must successfully complete at least two of the following three courses—Administrative Law, Business Organizations, and Trusts and Estates. In addition, all students must successfully complete at least one of the following three courses—Creditors' Rights, Income Taxation, or Secured Transactions.

In both the second and third years, practical legal training is available through courses in legal research, legal skills and problems, trial practice, and clinical work. The college has only limited non-classroom offerings in its summer session; however, graduation may be accelerated one semester by attending two summer sessions at other accredited law schools.

■ Special Programs

The College of Law has a strong program of elective courses in natural resources law. Courses are regularly offered in environmental law, hazardous waste and water pollution, oil and gas, mining law, public land resources, and water rights. Other electives include coverage of trial and appellate practice, business planning, estate planning, corporate and commercial law, administrative law, consumer law, and Indian law.

Students may obtain practical experience and receive academic credit for work in five clinical programs: (1) a defender aid program in which students brief and argue criminal appeals on behalf of indigent persons and assist penitentiary inmates in post-conviction cases; (2) a prosecution assistance program in which students work directly with prosecuting attorneys in criminal cases; (3) a legal services program in which students provide legal assistance to economically disadvantaged persons; (4) a clinic dealing with victims of domestic violence; and (5) a clinic providing legal services in civil matters to University of Wyoming students. All clinical programs operate under faculty supervision. Under a special state rule, students working in the clinics frequently brief and argue cases before the Wyoming Supreme Court, an opportunity that is rare—if not unique—among law schools.

■ Admission Standards

The College of Law generally restricts the entering class to 75–80 students. The school does not discriminate on the basis of race, color, religion, sex, national origin, disability, age, veteran status, sexual orientation, or political belief in making admission decisions.

Students are admitted only for the fall semester. The college begins to accept applications in October for the class entering the following August. The entering class is selected from applications completed and on file by March 1. To meet the March 1 deadline, applicants should take the LSAT no later than February and should register for the LSDAS and arrange for forwarding of official transcripts no later than mid-January.

As a general rule, applicants must have received an undergraduate degree prior to registration. Applicants may submit up to three letters of recommendation. Selection of the entering class is based on consideration of applicants' undergraduate records, LSAT scores, and other criteria relevant to success in the study and practice of law.

■ Student Activities

The College of Law publishes the *Wyoming Law Review,* a student-edited journal. Other student organizations include Potter Law Club, which provides student government and social activities with the Law Student Division of the ABA, three legal fraternities, Christian Legal Society, Intellectual Property Club, International Law Students Association, Minority Law Student Association, Natural Resources Law Forum, Women's Law Forum, and the Wyoming Trial Lawyers Association. Students represent the college each year in the National Moot Court Competition, National Environmental Law Moot Court Competition, National Client Counseling Competition, and the ATLA National Student Trial Advocacy Competition. Student organizations also include two law school honorary societies, the Order of the Coif and the Order of Barristers.

■ Career Services

About 75 percent of graduates remain in the Rocky Mountain region, but the College of Law has alumni around the globe. The curriculum is broad in scope, providing a core foundation of legal knowledge to prepare graduates to practice in a wide range of legal and geographic areas.

Graduates of the UW College of Law practice in primarily small private firms or are employed by state, local, tribal, and national governments. They also find work in public service, public interest organizations, and many alternative careers related to law. Twenty-five percent of graduates consistently work in state and federal judicial clerkships following law school. This is an extraordinary achievement, since national placement statistics in judicial clerkships are around 11 percent according to the National Association of Law Placement.

As with other aspects of the college's operation, the small size of the student body permits the Career Services Office to provide students with a level of personal attention that may not be feasible at larger institutions. Students receive one-on-one career counseling and job searching for permanent or summer employment. Career Services also works with students and alumni to develop insightful career panels and résumé/cover letter workshops. A network of loyal alumni hires often exclusively at the University of Wyoming College of Law. Fall and spring on-campus interviews also provide many firms and students with a chance to interview one another. An online posting system allows national and local organizations to post legal positions for UW students across the country.

■ Financial Aid

State and privately funded scholarships are available. Scholarship awards are based upon merit, need, and diversity. Students should file the FAFSA prior to March 1. Scholarship applications are submitted directly to the College of Law.

Applicant Profile

University of Wyoming College of Law
This grid includes only applicants who earned 120–180 LSAT scores under standard administrations.

LSAT Score	3.75 + Apps	Adm	3.50–3.74 Apps	Adm	3.25–3.49 Apps	Adm	3.00–3.24 Apps	Adm	2.75–2.99 Apps	Adm	2.50–2.74 Apps	Adm	2.25–2.49 Apps	Adm	2.00–2.24 Apps	Adm	Below 2.00 Apps	Adm	No GPA Apps	Adm	Total Apps	Adm
175–180	0	0	0	0	0	0	0	0	0	0	0	0	0	0	0	0	0	0	0	0	0	0
170–174	0	0	0	0	1	1	0	0	0	0	0	0	0	0	0	0	0	0	0	0	1	1
165–169	0	0	1	0	0	0	3	2	1	1	0	0	0	0	1	1	0	0	0	0	6	4
160–164	2	2	3	3	6	4	6	5	2	1	4	1	0	0	3	1	0	0	0	0	26	17
155–159	16	13	20	15	26	15	29	13	12	5	8	3	6	2	1	0	0	0	0	0	118	66
150–154	32	21	50	22	57	29	62	10	33	6	18	2	14	1	4	1	0	0	0	0	270	92
145–149	13	3	35	6	52	6	56	3	29	1	22	3	12	0	2	0	0	0	2	1	223	23
140–144	6	0	18	3	16	0	31	3	22	0	13	0	13	0	2	0	1	0	1	0	123	6
135–139	4	0	1	0	5	0	7	0	3	0	5	1	2	0	1	0	0	0	1	0	29	1
130–134	0	0	0	0	1	0	1	0	3	0	1	0	2	0	0	0	0	0	0	0	8	0
125–129	0	0	0	0	0	0	0	0	0	0	3	0	0	0	0	0	0	0	0	0	3	0
120–124	0	0	0	0	0	0	0	0	0	0	0	0	0	0	0	0	0	0	0	0	0	0
Total	73	39	128	49	164	55	195	36	105	14	74	10	49	3	14	3	1	0	4	1	807	210

Apps = Number of Applicants
Adm = Number Admitted
Reflects 100% of the total applicant pool.

Yale Law School

PO Box 208329
New Haven, CT 06520-8329
Phone: 203.432.4995
E-mail: admissions.law@yale.edu; Website: www.law.yale.edu

ABA
Approved
Since
1923

The Basics

Type of school	Private
Term	Semester
Application deadline	2/1
Application fee	$70
Financial aid deadline	3/15 4/15
Can first year start other than fall?	No
Student to faculty ratio	7.3 to 1
Does the university offer:	
housing restricted to law students?	Yes
graduate housing for which law students are eligible?	Yes

Faculty and Administrators

	Total		Men		Women		Minorities	
	Fall	Spr	Fall	Spr	Fall	Spr	Fall	Spr
Full-time	71	63	57	51	14	12	6	8
Other Full-time	6	6	2	1	4	5	1	1
Deans, librarians, & others who teach	10	11	9	10	1	1	2	2
Part-time	29	48	21	33	8	15	1	8
Total	**116**	**128**	**89**	**95**	**27**	**33**	**10**	**19**

Curriculum

	Full-time	Part-time
Typical first-year section size	62	0
Is there typically a "small section" of the first-year class, other than Legal Writing, taught by full-time faculty	Yes	No
If yes, typical size offered last year	17	
# of classroom course titles beyond first-year curriculum		146

# of upper division courses, excluding seminars with an enrollment:		
	Under 25	27
	25–49	27
	50–74	9
	75–99	8
	100+	3

# of seminars		72
# of seminar positions available		1,008
# of seminar positions filled	816	0
# of positions available in simulation courses		144
# of simulation positions filled	61	0
# of positions available in faculty supervised clinical courses		540
# of faculty supervised clinical positions filled	520	0
# involved in field placements	31	0
# involved in law journals	505	0
# involved in interschool competitions	191	0
# of credit hours required to graduate		83

JD Enrollment and Ethnicity

	Men #	Men %	Women #	Women %	Full-time #	Full-time %	Part-time #	Part-time %	1st-year #	1st-year %	Total #	Total %	JD Degs. Awd.
African Amer.	21	7.0	23	8.2	44	7.6	0	0.0	12	6.3	44	7.6	17
Amer. Indian	0	0.0	1	0.4	1	0.2	0	0.0	1	0.5	1	0.2	0
Asian Amer.	29	9.7	51	18.1	80	13.9	0	0.0	27	14.1	80	13.8	26
Mex. Amer.	4	1.3	6	2.1	10	1.7	0	0.0	0	0.0	10	1.7	6
Puerto Rican	2	0.7	1	0.4	3	0.5	0	0.0	0	0.0	3	0.5	2
Hispanic	17	5.7	16	5.7	32	5.6	1	33.3	8	4.2	33	5.7	12
Total Minority	73	24.5	98	34.9	170	29.5	1	33.3	48	25.1	171	29.5	63
For. Nation.	11	3.7	11	3.9	22	3.8	0	0.0	7	3.7	22	3.8	5
Caucasian	199	66.8	158	56.2	355	61.6	2	66.7	123	64.4	357	61.7	138
Unknown	15	5.0	14	5.0	29	5.0	0	0.0	13	6.8	29	5.0	6
Total	298	51.5	281	48.5	576	99.5	3	0.5	191	33.0	579		212

Transfers

Transfers in	9
Transfers out	0

Tuition and Fees

	Resident	Nonresident
Full-time	$40,900	$40,900
Part-time	$0	$0

Living Expenses

Estimated living expenses for singles

Living on campus	Living off campus	Living at home
$15,700	$15,700	$15,700

ABA
Approved
Since
1923

GPA and LSAT Scores

	Total	Full-time	Part-time
# of apps	3,677	3,677	0
# of offers	249	249	0
# of matrics	189	189	0
75% GPA	3.97	3.97	0.00
Median GPA	3.91	3.91	0.00
25% GPA	3.83	3.83	0.00
75% LSAT	176	176	0
Median LSAT	173	173	0
25% LSAT	170	170	0

Grants and Scholarships (from prior year)

	Total		Full-time		Part-time	
	#	%	#	%	#	%
Total # of students	586		585		1	
Total # receiving grants	267	45.6	267	45.6	0	0.0
Less than 1/2 tuition	146	24.9	146	25.0	0	0.0
Half to full tuition	119	20.3	119	20.3	0	0.0
Full tuition	2	0.3	2	0.3	0	0.0
More than full tuition	0	0.0	0	0.0	0	0.0
Median grant amount			$17,500		$0	

Informational and Library Resources

# of volumes and volume equivalents	1,150,867
# of titles	337,601
# of active serial subscriptions	11,267
Study seating capacity inside the library	414
# of full-time professional librarians	19
Hours per week library is open	133
# of open, wired connections available to students	1,009
# of networked computers available for use by students	111
# of simultaneous wireless users	650
Require computer?	No

JD Attrition (from prior year)

	Academic	Other	Total	
	#	#	#	%
1st year	0	0	0	0.0
2nd year	0	1	1	0.5
3rd year	0	0	0	0.0
4th year	0	0	0	0.0

Employment (9 months after graduation)

	Total	Percentage
Employment status known	200	99.5
Employment status unknown	1	0.5
Employed	194	97.0
Pursuing graduate degrees	5	2.5
Unemployed seeking employment	0	0.0
Unemployed not seeking employment	1	0.5
Unemployed and studying for the bar	0	0.0
Type of Employment		
# employed in law firms	71	36.6
# employed in business and industry	5	2.6
# employed in government	5	2.6
# employed in public interest	11	5.7
# employed as judicial clerks	99	51.0
# employed in academia	3	1.5
Geographic Location		
# employed in state	11	5.7
# employed in foreign countries	6	3.1
# of states where employed		24

Bar Passage Rates

Jurisdiction	New York		
Exam	Sum 05	Win 06	Total
# from school taking bar for the first time	82	4	86
School's pass rate for all first-time takers	96%	50%	94%
State's pass rate for all first-time takers	76%	61%	74%

Yale Law School

PO Box 208329
New Haven, CT 06520-8329
Phone: 203.432.4995
E-mail: admissions.law@yale.edu; Website: www.law.yale.edu

■ Introduction

Yale Law School is an extraordinary community in which to study law. Standing at the intersection of the worlds of thought and action, Yale seeks not only to promote an intellectual understanding of the law, but also to sustain the moral commitments that justice requires.

Extensive student-faculty interactions and institutional flexibility are hallmarks of the Yale Law School experience. Students enjoy countless opportunities for research and writing with professors. Our unmatched faculty-to-student ratio allows us to offer a wide range of courses and small classes, with an average class size of under 20 students.

The school is also part of one of the world's great research universities. Yale University is home to an abundance of intellectual, cultural, social, and athletic activities, all of which are accessible to Yale law students.

■ Students

The vitality of Yale Law School depends as much on the knowledge, experience, and interests of the students as it does on the faculty, the library, or the alumni. The school selects its entering class from applicants with the highest academic qualifications. Within this exceptional group, Yale seeks a diversity of backgrounds, experiences, and interests. This diversity is reflected in the many thriving student organizations and student-run journals found at the school.

■ Faculty

The faculty at Yale Law School is as broad-ranging in its interests and expertise as it is distinguished. It includes prominent scholars of economics, philosophy, and the social sciences as well as leading specialists in every area of law. Sixty-eight full-time professors are joined each year by visiting lecturers, adjunct professors from other parts of the university, and practicing lawyers. Additionally, dozens of guest lecturers from around the world—ranging from Madeleine Albright to Al Franken—help to make Yale Law School a vibrant intellectual community.

■ Facilities and Housing

The Sterling Law Building occupies one city block in the heart of Yale University and downtown New Haven. The recently renovated building was modeled on the English Inns of Court, with classrooms, a dining hall, faculty offices, and the law library surrounding three pleasant courtyards. All classrooms are Internet accessible, and a wireless network is available throughout the Law School. A day care center is located on site.

Yale campus housing is available, but most students live off campus, close to the Law School. Within a 10-minute walk of the school students can find housing options ranging from high-rise apartments downtown to Victorian houses in quiet residential neighborhoods.

■ Curriculum and Grading

The Yale Law School curriculum is very flexible. Students are able to shape their own course of study to satisfy their unique intellectual interests and goals. In the fall semester, all first-year students take classes in constitutional law, contracts, procedure, and torts. One of these classes is a small group of about 16 students, which includes instruction in legal research and writing. After the first term, students may select any classes they wish, including independent studies, clinics, and courses outside the Law School. Two major writing projects and courses in criminal law and professional responsibility are required for graduation.

In order to allow students to concentrate on learning, rather than on GPAs, Yale Law School does not use grades in the traditional sense. During the fall of the first year, all classes are credit/fail. In subsequent terms, grades are honors, pass, low pass, and fail, with credit/fail options available. Yale Law School does not calculate class rankings.

■ Joint Degrees, Special Programs, and Clinical Opportunities

Yale Law School sees the study of law as interrelated with other intellectual disciplines and with practical experience. The Law School offers a number of joint degrees with other schools and departments at Yale, including JD/MBAs, JD/PhDs, and JD/MDs. Joint degrees with other universities and opportunities for intensive semester experiences outside the Law School are available.

Yale Law School also offers a number of clinical opportunities to all students beginning in the first year. For example, students gain real-world experience participating in the Lowenstein International Human Rights Clinic, Supreme Court Advocacy Clinic, Environmental Law Clinic, and the Community Development Financial Institutions Clinic. Other clinics, including advocacy for prisoners, people with disabilities, children, and immigrants, provide opportunities for Yale law students to work on behalf of clients who cannot afford private attorneys.

■ Transfer Students and Advanced Degrees

Students who have completed two semesters of study at another ABA-approved law school may apply to transfer to Yale Law School. Transfer students must complete at least two years of work at Yale Law School.

In addition to the JD, Yale Law School offers an LLM degree for foreign lawyers who are interested in teaching law. The Master of Studies in Law (MSL) is a one-year program designed for professionals in other fields who desire an intensive introduction to the law. Yale also offers a JSD program for the school's LLM students.

■ Financial Aid and Loan Forgiveness

Financial aid is awarded solely on the basis of need, and admission decisions are made independently of financial aid decisions. Approximately 80 percent of the student body receives some form of financial aid. A financial aid award may consist of a portion in grant and a portion in loan; typically, the higher the total financial need, the higher the proportion of grant.

In addition to financial aid during law school, Yale has one of the most generous loan forgiveness programs in the country:

the Career Options Assistance Program (COAP). COAP provides grants to help repay the educational loans of graduates who take relatively low-paying jobs. Unlike many loan forgiveness programs, Yale's COAP includes not only law school loans, but some undergraduate loans as well. Last year, COAP covered over $2.3 million worth of loan payments for almost 300 graduates.

■ Career Development

Yale Law School graduates occupy leadership positions in a tremendous range of endeavors. The Law School's Career Development Office helps students explore the unparalleled diversity of opportunities available to them. Most students work for public interest organizations, private firms, or government entities during summer breaks. After graduation, a large number of students obtain judicial clerkships. Others work for law firms or corporations, while still others take advantage of public service fellowships available to Yale Law School graduates. In addition, many graduates pursue careers in academia.

■ The Admission Process

Yale Law School considers every application for admission in its entirety and no index or numerical cutoffs are used in the admission process. No single element in an application is decisive; the totality of available information about the applicant is taken into account. A personal statement and a 250-word essay on a subject of the applicant's choice are required. Applicants are encouraged to bring aspects of their personal background or other special characteristics to the attention of the admission committee. Two letters of recommendation are required; additional letters are also welcome.

Each application file is first read by the dean or the director of admissions. A group of the most highly rated files is then considered by faculty. Each faculty member rates applications on the basis of the faculty member's unique criteria; the weight given to various factors is within each reader's discretion.

The Law School issues most of its decisions by the beginning of April, but decisions continue to be made throughout the spring. Use of the wait list varies from year to year, and the list is not ranked until offers are made.

Applicant Profile

Yale Law School

Undergraduate GPA	Below 155		155–159		160–164		165–169		170–174		175–180		Total	
	Apps	Adm	Apps	Adm	Apps	Adm	Apps	Adm	Apps	Adm	Apps	Adm	Apps	Adm
3.75 +	90	0	116	1	219	11	506	44	469	102	209	94	1609	252
3.50–3.74	128	0	102	0	185	1	306	15	251	13	84	6	1056	35
3.25–3.49	105	0	69	0	84	0	126	0	90	0	31	0	505	0
3.00–3.24	69	0	24	0	35	0	45	0	15	0	8	1	196	1
Below 3.00	106	0	26	0	22	0	21	0	9	0	11	0	195	0
No GPA	33	0	10	0	16	0	14	2	9	4	1	0	83	6
Total	531	0	347	1	561	12	1018	61	843	119	344	101	3644	294

Average LSAT Score on the 120–180 Scale

Totals reflect 99% of applicant pool.
Apps = Number of Applicants
Adm = Number Admitted

Appendix A: Legal Education Statistics

Law School Attendance Figures, Fall 2006

		Full-time	Part-time	Total
First Year	Total	40,267	8,670	48,937
	Women	18,507	4,108	22,615
Second Year	Total	39,550	5,352	44,902
	Women	18,525	2,511	21,036
Third Year	Total	38,661	4,999	43,660
	Women	18,468	2,307	20,775
Fourth Year	Total	0	3,532	3,532
	Women	0	1,659	1,659
JD Total	Total	118,478	22,553	141,031
	Women	55,500	10,585	66,085
Post-JD	Total	4,378	2,058	6,436
	Women	2,009	986	2,995
Other	Total	696	15,670	1,231
	Women	351	322	673
Grand Total	Total	123,552	25,146	148,698
	Women	57,860	11,893	69,753

Professional Degrees Conferred, 2006

		Full-time	Part-time	Total
JD/LLB	Total	38,917	5,003	43,920
	Women	18,689	2,397	21,086
LLM	Total	3,522	617	4,139
	Women	1,557	276	1,833
MCL/MCJ	Total	66	0	66
	Women	14	0	14
SJD/JSD	Total	93	4	97
	Women	39	0	39
Other	Total	191	142	333
	Women	191	142	333
Total	Total	42,789	5,766	48,555
	Women	20,490	2,815	23,305

Teachers in Law Schools, 2006–2007

	Women	Minorities	Total
Full-time	2,694	1,206	7,474
Part-time	2,179	719	7,109
Deans & Administrators	2,548	873	4,053
Librarians	1,174	295	1,803

Total Minority Enrollment

Academic Year	Number of Schools Reporting*	First Year	Second Year	Third Year	Fourth Year	Total
2006–07	191	10,898	9,539	9,371	749	30,557
2005–06	190	10,462	9,644	9,061	818	29,985
2004–05	188	10,694	9,280	8,766	749	29,489
2003–04	187	10,468	9,144	8,062	721	28,318
2002–03	187	10,224	8,326	7,898	721	27,169
2001–02	184	9,557	8,172	7,785	743	26,257
2000–01	183	9,335	8,052	7,690	676	25,753
1999–00	182	9,079	7,876	7,547	751	25,253
1998–99	181	9,076	7,635	7,761	794	25,266
1997–98	178	8,493	7,740	7,705	747	24,685
1996–97	179	8,722	8,009	7,869	679	25,279
1995–96	178	9,119	8,402	7,411	622	25,554
1994–95	177	9,249	7,633	7,124	605	24,611
1993–94	176	8,595	7,244	6,409	551	22,799
1992–93	176	8,070	6,682	6,032	482	21,266
1991–92	176	7,575	6,155	5,255	425	19,410
1990–91	175	6,933	5,325	4,676	396	17,330
1989–90	175	6,172	4,890	4,264	394	15,720
1988–89	174	5,565	4,408	3,911	411	14,295
1987–88	175	5,130	3,994	3,717	409	13,250
1986–87	175	4,738	3,839	3,648	325	12,550

*Please note that the minority enrollment charts on pages 22 through 30 do not include students from the three Puerto Rico schools. JD enrollment for the law schools in Puerto Rico was 2,044 for fall 2006.

American Indian or Alaskan Native Enrollment

Academic Year	Number of Schools Reporting	First Year	Second Year	Third Year	Fourth Year	Total
2006–07	191	418	365	358	27	1,158
2005–06	190	399	369	360	33	1,161
2004–05	188	387	366	325	28	1,106
2003–04	187	396	341	291	20	1,048
2002–03	187	375	318	317	11	1,021
2001–02	184	365	323	275	27	990
2000–01	183	348	293	290	21	952
1999–00	182	342	294	312	30	978
1998–99	181	361	307	351	45	1,064
1997–98	178	355	348	355	27	1,085
1996–97	179	391	397	310	18	1,116
1995–96	178	436	338	294	17	1,085
1994–95	177	377	283	290	12	962
1993–94	176	336	280	243	14	873
1992–93	176	313	243	206	14	776
1991–92	176	286	219	176	11	692
1990–91	175	224	185	129	16	554
1989–90	175	220	147	143	17	527
1988–89	174	177	165	149	8	499
1987–88	175	189	144	148	11	492
1986–87	175	176	155	148	9	488

Asian or Pacific Islander Enrollment

Academic Year	Number of Schools Reporting	First Year	Second Year	Third Year	Fourth Year	Total
2006–07	191	3,839	3,635	3,577	255	11,306
2005–06	190	3,941	3,650	3,432	278	11,301
2004–05	188	3,982	3,440	3,217	217	10,856
2003–04	187	3,881	3,279	2,685	195	10,040
2002–03	187	3,602	2,819	2,578	182	9,181
2001–02	184	3,052	2,646	2,541	182	8,421
2000–01	183	2,924	2,570	2,510	169	8,173
1999–00	182	2,772	2,519	2,401	191	7,883
1998–99	181	2,762	2,403	2,497	215	7,877
1997–98	178	2,562	2,463	2,394	180	7,599
1996–97	179	2,695	2,451	2,380	180	7,706
1995–96	178	2,773	2,572	2,225	149	7,719
1994–95	177	2,740	2,247	2,087	122	7,196
1993–94	176	2,432	2,101	1,789	136	6,458
1992–93	176	2,235	1,873	1,618	97	5,823
1991–92	176	2,019	1,621	1,306	82	5,028
1990–91	175	1,753	1,343	1,134	76	4,306
1989–90	175	1,501	1,151	946	78	3,676
1988–89	174	1,282	954	825	72	3,133
1987–88	175	1,064	804	724	64	2,656
1986–87	175	929	685	650	39	2,303

African American Enrollment

Academic Year	Number of Schools Reporting	First Year	Second Year	Third Year	Fourth Year	Total
2006–07	191	3,516	2,836	2,927	250	9,529
2005–06	190	3,132	3,040	2,735	288	9,195
2004–05	188	3,457	2,873	2,845	313	9,488
2003–04	187	3,300	3,007	2,786	342	9,435
2002–03	187	3,491	2,875	2,773	297	9,436
2001–02	184	3,474	2,867	2,737	334	9,412
2000–01	183	3,402	2,890	2,757	305	9,354
1999–00	182	3,353	2,903	2,700	316	9,272
1998–99	181	3,478	2,728	2,754	311	9,271
1997–98	178	3,126	2,752	2,887	367	9,132
1996–97	179	3,223	3,013	2,991	315	9,542
1995–96	178	3,474	3,161	2,855	289	9,542
1994–95	177	3,600	3,000	2,771	310	9,681
1993–94	176	3,455	2,846	2,573	282	9,156
1992–93	176	3,303	2,603	2,465	267	8,638
1991–92	176	3,169	2,556	2,196	228	8,149
1990–91	175	2,982	2,222	2,023	205	7,432
1989–90	175	2,628	2,128	1,816	219	6,791
1988–89	174	2,463	1,913	1,728	217	6,321
1987–88	175	2,339	1,761	1,690	238	6,028
1986–87	175	2,159	1,800	1,735	200	5,894

Mexican American Enrollment

Academic Year	Number of Schools Reporting	First Year	Second Year	Third Year	Fourth Year	Total
2006–07	191	915	782	746	56	2,499
2005–06	190	866	757	787	47	2,457
2004–05	188	938	855	819	53	2,665
2003–04	187	923	831	738	47	2,539
2002–03	187	906	771	680	55	2,412
2001–02	184	896	705	686	47	2,334
2000–01	183	883	757	734	43	2,417
1999–00	182	901	772	750	60	2,483
1998–99	181	885	734	764	68	2,451
1997–98	178	859	766	777	50	2,452
1996–97	179	861	768	751	49	2,429
1995–96	178	896	820	743	36	2,495
1994–95	177	902	739	719	42	2,402
1993–94	176	838	698	639	28	2,203
1992–93	176	807	744	683	24	2,258
1991–92	176	770	644	584	29	2,027
1990–91	175	768	624	527	31	1,950
1989–90	175	640	531	469	23	1,663
1988–89	174	656	510	458	33	1,657
1987–88	175	610	528	472	34	1,644
1986–87	176	564	486	431	31	1,512

Puerto Rican Enrollment

Academic Year	Number of Schools Reporting	First Year	Second Year	Third Year	Fourth Year	Total
2006–07	191	207	179	149	16	551
2005–06	190	203	154	175	16	548
2004–05	188	181	206	182	25	594
2003–04	187	228	204	194	29	655
2002–03	187	208	198	204	29	639
2001–02	184	221	216	222	30	689
2000–01	183	249	213	191	27	680
1999–00	182	243	188	192	23	646
1998–99	181	206	205	196	25	632
1997–98	178	224	198	188	26	636
1996–97	179	206	213	238	29	686
1995–96	178	236	238	214	17	705
1994–95	177	263	244	186	25	718
1993–94	176	275	195	177	17	664
1992–93	176	202	193	177	15	587
1991–92	176	208	177	140	14	539
1990–91	175	183	153	158	12	506
1989–90	175	171	150	156	6	483
1988–89	174	168	156	141	13	478
1987–88	175	178	134	140	7	459
1986–87	175	183	152	130	6	471

Other Hispanic American Enrollment

Academic Year	Number of Schools Reporting	First Year	Second Year	Third Year	Fourth Year	Total
2006–07	191	2,003	1,742	1,624	145	5,514
2005–06	190	203	154	175	16	548
2004–05	188	1,749	1,540	1,378	113	4,780
2003–04	187	1,724	1,430	1,328	135	4,617
2002–03	187	1,642	1,345	1,346	147	4,480
2001–02	184	1,549	1,415	1,324	123	4,411
2000–01	183	1,529	1,329	1,208	111	4,177
1999–00	182	1,468	1,200	1,192	131	3,991
1998–99	181	1,384	1,258	1,199	130	3,971
1997–98	178	1,367	1,213	1,104	97	3,781
1996–97	179	1,346	1,167	1,199	88	3,880
1995–96	178	1,304	1,273	1,079	114	3,770
1994–95	177	1,367	1,120	1,071	94	3,652
1993–94	176	1,259	1,124	988	74	3,445
1992–93	176	1,210	966	883	65	3,124
1991–92	176	1,123	938	853	61	2,975
1990–91	175	1,023	798	705	56	2,582
1989–90	175	1,019	783	734	51	2,587
1988–89	174	819	710	610	68	2,207
1987–88	175	750	623	543	55	1,971
1986–87	175	727	561	554	40	1,882

Legal Education Statistics, 1983–2006

Academic Year	Number of Schools	Total LSAT Administrations	Applicants	First-year Enrollment	Total JD Enrollment	Total[1] Overall Enrollment	JD or LLB Awarded
2006–07	194	140,048	88,662	48,937	141,031	148,698	43,920
2005–06	191	137,444	95,760	48,241	140,472	148,532	42,673
2004–05	188	145,258	100,604	48,239	140,376	148,169	40,023
2003–04	187	147,617	100,604	48,867	137,676	145,088	38,314
2002–03	186	148,014	90,853	48,433	132,901	139,366	38,605
2001–02	184	134,251	77,235	45,070	127,610	135,091	37,687
2000–01	183	109,030	74,550	43,518	125,173	132,464	38,157
1999–00	182	107,153	74,380	43,152	125,184	132,276	39,071
1998–99	181	104,236	71,726	42,804	125,627	131,833	39,455
1997–98	178[2]	103,991	72,340	42,186	125,886	131,801	40,114
1996–97	179	105,315	76,715	43,245	125,623	134,949	39,920
1995–96	178	114,756	84,305	43,676	129,397	135,595	39,271
1994–95	177	128,553	89,633	44,298	128,989	134,784	39,710
1993–94	176	132,028	91,892	43,644	127,802	133,339	40,213
1992–93	176	140,054	97,720	42,793	128,212	133,783	39,425
1991–92	176	145,567	99,327	44,050	129,580	135,157	38,800
1990–91	175	152,685	92,958	44,104	127,261	132,433	36,385
1989–90	175	138,865	87,288	43,826	124,471	129,698	35,520
1988–89	174	137,088	78,930	42,860	120,694	125,870	35,701
1987–88	175	115,988	68,804	41,055	117,997	123,198	35,478
1986–87	175	101,235	65,168	40,195	117,813	132,277	36,121
1985–86	175	91,848	60,338	40,796	118,700	124,092	36,829
1984–85	174	95,563	63,801	40,747	119,847	125,698	36,687
1983–84	173	105,076	71,755	41,159	121,201	127,195	36,389

Note: Enrollment is in American Bar Association-approved law schools as of October 1, 2006. The LSAT year begins in June and ends in February of the following year. JD or LLB degrees are those awarded by approved schools for the academic year ending in the first year stated. Total new admissions to the bar include those admitted by office study, diploma privilege, and examination and study at an unapproved law school. The great bulk of those admitted graduated from approved schools.

[1] Total overall enrollment includes post-JD and other.

[2] The District of Columbia School of Law is not included in this figure.

Appendix B: Post-JD Programs

Standard 308 of the ABA's *Standards: Rules of Procedure for Approval of Law Schools* states that an ABA-approved law school may not establish a degree program in addition to its JD degree program unless the school is fully approved and the quality of its JD degree program meets the requirements of the *Standards*; the additional degree program may not detract from a law school's ability to maintain a sound JD degree program; and finally, the school must obtain the Council's acquiescence.

For additional information about post-JD programs, you should visit the Section of Legal Education and Admissions to the Bar's website at *www.abanet.org/legaled*. However, for specific information about post-JD programs, you should contact the school(s) directly. In addition, if you have not obtained a JD from an ABA-approved law school, you may wish to contact the bar admission authorities in the state(s) in which you intend to practice for more information on whether graduation from a post-JD program will qualify you to take the bar examination in that state. Please note, however, that it is the ABA Section of Legal Education and Admissions to the Bar Council's position that no graduate degree in law is or should be a substitute for the first professional degree in law (JD) and should not serve as the same basis for bar admission purposes as the JD degree.

For updates or corrections to the following list, please visit the Section's website: *www.abanet.org/legaled*.

■ Graduate Degrees Defined

While an individual law school's degree may differ slightly by name to similar programs elsewhere, most degrees offered through law schools fall into three general categories:

1) Academic master's degrees for nonlawyers, such as:
   MS   Master of Science or Master of Studies
   MPS   Master of Professional Studies

2) Post-JD law degrees for practicing lawyers and/or foreign lawyers seeking to practice in the US, such as:
   LLM   Master of Laws
   JM   Juris Master

   MCL   Master of Comparative Law
   MJ   Master of Jurisprudence
   MLS   Master of Legal Studies

3) Research and academic-based doctorate level degrees, such as:
   JSD   Doctor of Jurisprudence
   SJD   Doctor of Juridical Science
   DCL   Doctor of Comparative Law

For questions regarding specific degree descriptions, contact the school directly.

■ Post-JD Programs By School

Akron, University of
Intellectual Property, LLM

Alabama, University of
Taxation, LLM
General, LLM
Master of Laws (for foreign lawyers), LLM

Albany Law School
Advanced Legal Studies, LLM/MS
Government Administration and Regulations, LLM
Health Law, LLM
Intellectual Property, LLM
International Law, LLM

American University
International Legal Studies, LLM
Government and Public Policy, LLM
General, SJD

Arizona, University of
International Trade Law, LLM
Indigenous Peoples Law and Policy, LLM

Arizona State University
Biotechnology and Genomics, LLM
Tribal Policy, Law, and Government, LLM
Legal Studies, MLS

Arkansas (Fayetteville), University of
Agricultural Law, LLM

Baltimore, University of
Taxation, LLM
Laws of the US, LLM

Boston University
Taxation, LLM
Banking and Financial Law, LLM
American Law (for foreign lawyers), LLM
Intellectual Property, LLM

Brigham Young University
Comparative Law (for foreign lawyers), LLM

Buffalo State University of New York, University at
Criminal Law, LLM
General, LLM

California—Berkeley, University of
General, LLM; JSD

California—Davis, University of
General, LLM
US Law (for foreign lawyers), LLM

California—Hastings, University of
US Law (for foreign lawyers), LLM

California at Los Angeles, University of
As Approved (for foreign lawyers), LLM
General, SJD

California Western
Comparative Law (for foreign lawyers), LLM; MCL

Capital University
Taxation, LLM; MT
Taxation and Business, LLM

Cardozo School of Law
Intellectual Property Law, LLM
General, LLM

Case Western Reserve University
Taxation, LLM
US Legal Studies (for foreign lawyers), LLM

Catholic University of America
As Approved, LLM

Chapman University
Taxation, LLM

Chicago, University of
General, LLM; MCL; DCL; JSD

Chicago-Kent—Illinois Institute of Technology
Family Law, LLM
Taxation, LLM
International and Comparative Law, LLM
Financial Services Law, LLM
International Intellectual Property, LLM

Cleveland State University
General, LLM

Columbia University
General, LLM; JSD

Connecticut, University of
Insurance Law, LLM
US Legal Studies (for foreign lawyers), LLM

Cornell Law School
General, LLM; JSD
International and Comparative Law, LLM

Denver, University of
Natural Resources, LLM
American and Comparative Law (for foreign lawyers), LLM
Taxation, LLM

DePaul, University of
Taxation, LLM
Health Law, LLM
Intellectual Property, LLM

Duke University
Research, SJD

Duquesne University
US Legal Studies (for foreign lawyers), LLM

Emory University
General, LLM
Taxation, LLM
Litigation, LLM
International Tax, LLM

Florida, University of
Taxation, LLM; SJD
Comparative Law, LLM

Florida State University
American Law (for foreign lawyers), LLM

Fordham University
Banking, Corporate, and Finance Law, LLM
International Business and Trade Law, LLM
Intellectual Property, LLM

Franklin Pierce Law Center
Intellectual Property, Commerce and Technology, LLM; MIP
Education Law, MEL

George Mason University
General Studies, JM
Intellectual Property, LLM
Law and Economics, LLM

George Washington University
General, LLM
Environmental Law, LLM
Intellectual Property Law, LLM
Government Procurement Law, LLM
International and Comparative Law, LLM
Various, SJD
Litigation and Dispute Resolution, LLM

Georgetown University
General (for foreign lawyers), LLM
Taxation, LLM
International and Comparative Law, LLM
Securities and Financial Regulation, LLM
Advocacy, LLM
International Legal Studies (or general studies), LLM
As Approved (for foreign lawyers), SJD
Labor and Employment, LLM

Georgia, University of
General, LLM

Golden Gate University
Taxation, LLM
International Legal Studies, LLM; SJD
US Legal Studies (for foreign lawyers), LLM
Environmental Law, LLM
Intellectual Property, LLM

Hamline University
Foreign Lawyers, LLM

Harvard Law School
General, LLM; SJD

Hawai'i, University of
Foreign Lawyers, LLM

Hofstra University
American Legal Studies (for foreign lawyers), LLM
Family Law, LLM
International Law, LLM

Houston, University of
International Law, LLM
Energy, Environment and Natural Resources, LLM
Tax Law, LLM
Foreign Scholars Program, LLM
Health Law, LLM
Intellectual Property and Information Law, LLM

Howard University
International Law, LLM

Illinois, University of
General, JSD; LLM

Indiana University—Bloomington
As Approved, LLM; SJD
Comparative Law, MCL
Research, SJD

Indiana University—Indianapolis
American Law (for foreign lawyers), LLM

Iowa, University of
International and Comparative Law, LLM

John Marshall Law School
Taxation, LLM
Intellectual Property, LLM
Comparative Legal Studies, LLM
Real Estate, LLM
Information Technology, LLM; MS
International Business and Trade Law, LLM
Employee Benefits, LLM

Judge Advocate General's School
Military Law, LLM

Kansas
Elder Law, LLM

Lewis & Clark Law School
Environmental/Natural Resources, LLM

Louisiana State University
As Approved, BCL; LLM; MCL

Loyola Law School (Los Angeles)
Taxation, LLM
American and International Legal Practice, LLM

Loyola University—Chicago
Health Law, LLM; MJ
Child Law, LLM; MJ
Corporate Law, MJ
Business Law, LLM
Taxation, LLM
Health Law and Policy, DL; SJD

Miami, University of
Taxation, LLM
Estate Planning, LLM
Ocean and Coastal Law, LLM
International Law, LLM
Inter-American Law, LLM
Real Property, Land Development, and Finance Law, LLM
Comparative Law, LLM

Michigan State University
American Legal System (for foreign lawyers), LLM
Intellectual Property, LLM

Michigan, University of
As Approved, LLM; MCL; SJD

Minnesota, University of
American Law (for foreign lawyers), LLM

Missouri—Columbia, University of
Dispute Resolution, LLM

Missouri—Kansas City, University of
General, LLM
Taxation, LLM
Urban Affairs, LLM
Estate Planning, LLM

Nebraska, University of
Law/Psychology, MLS

New England School of Law
US Law (for foreign lawyers), LLM

New York Law School
Taxation, LLM

New York University
As Approved, JSD
Corporate Law, LLM
International Legal Studies, LLM
Taxation, LLM
Trade Regulation, LLM
General Studies, LLM
International Taxation, LLM
Comparative Jurisprudence, MCJ
Labor and Employment Law, LLM
International Public Interest, LLM

Northern Kentucky University
Law/Business, JD

Northwestern University
Research, SJD
As Approved, LLM

Notre Dame Law School
International and Comparative Law, LLM
International Human Rights, JSD; LLM

Ohio State University
General, MSL

Oregon, University of
Environmental and Natural Resources, LLM

Pace University
Environmental Law, LLM; SJD
Comparative Legal Studies, LLM

Pacific, McGeorge, University of
Taxation, LLM
Business and Taxation, LLM
Transnational Business Practice, LLM
Government and Public Policy, LLM
International Water Resources Law, JSD; LLM

Penn State University
Comparative Law, LLM

Pennsylvania, University of
As Approved, LLCM; LLM; SJD

Pepperdine University
Dispute Resolution, MDR; LLM

Pittsburgh, University of
International and Comparative Law, LLM
Advanced Studies, JSD

Puerto Rico, University of
General (for foreign lawyers), LLM

Quinnipiac University
Health Law, LLM

Regent University
International Tax, LLM

St. John's University
Bankruptcy, LLM

Saint Louis University
Health Law, LLM
American Law (for foreign lawyers), LLM

St. Mary's University
International and Comparative Law, LLM
American Legal Studies (for foreign lawyers), LLM

St. Thomas University
International Taxation, LLM
Intercultural Human Rights, JSD; LLM
Taxation, LLM

Samford University
Comparative Law, MCL
General, SJD
Law, Religion, Culture, LLM; SJD

San Diego, University of
Taxation, LLM
Comparative Law, LLM
General, LLM
International Law, LLM
Business and Corporate Law, LLM

San Francisco, University of
International Transactions and Comparative Law, LLM
Intellectual Property and Technology Law, LLM

Santa Clara University
Comparative Law (for foreign lawyers), LLM
Intellectual Property Law, LLM
Comparative and International Law, LLM

Seattle University
Foreign Lawyers, LLM

Seton Hall University
Health Law, LLM

SMU Dedman
General, LLM; SJD
Comparative and International Law, LLM
Taxation, LLM
Doctor of Science of Law, SJD

Southern California, University of
General (for foreign lawyers), LLM
Comparative Law, MCL

Southern Illinois
General, LLM
Health Law, LLM

Southwestern University
Entertainment/Media Law, LLM

Stanford University
As Approved, JSD; JSM
Corporate Governance, LLM
Law, Science, and Technology, LLM

Stetson University
International Law and Business, LLM

Suffolk University
International Intellectual Property, Comparative Biomedicine
    and Healthcare, Global Information Technology, LLM
US Law for International Business Lawyers, LLM

Temple University
General, LLM
Taxation, LLM
American Common Law Legal System, LLM
International and Comparative Law (for foreign lawyers), LLM
Law and Humanities, LLM
Clinical Legal Education, LLM
Trial Advocacy, LLM
General (in China), LLM

Texas, University of
General, LLM

Thomas M. Cooley Law School
Taxation, LLM
Intellectual Property, LLM

Touro College
American Legal Studies (for foreign lawyers), LLM
General, LLM
Professional Studies in Law, MPSL

Tulane University
General, LLM; SJD
Admiralty, LLM
Energy and Environment, LLM
Comparative Law, MCL
Comparative Law and Latin American Studies, MCL-MA
International and Comparative Law, LLM
American Business Law, LLM

Tulsa, University of
Comparative and International Law (for foreign lawyers), LLM
American Indian and Indigenous Law, LLM

Utah, University of
Environmental and Natural Resources Law, LLM

Valparaiso University
General, LLM

Vanderbilt University
General (for foreign lawyers), LLM

Vermont Law School
Environmental Law and Policy, LLM; MSEL
American Legal Studies, LLM

Villanova University
Taxation, LLM

Virginia, University of
General, LLM; SJD
Judicial Process, LLM

Wake Forest University
American Law (for foreign lawyers), LLM

Washington & Lee University
United States Law, LLM

Washington, University of
Asian and Comparative Law, LLM; PhD
Law and Marine Affairs, LLM
International Environmental Law, LLM
Sustainable International Development, LLM
Taxation, LLM
Intellectual Property and Technology Law, LLM

Washington University
Taxation, LLM
Research, JSD
Urban Studies, LLM
US Law, LLM
Intellectual Property and Technology Law, LLM

Wayne State University
General, LLM
Corporate and Finance Law, LLM
Labor Law, LLM
Taxation, LLM

Western New England
Estate Planning and Elder Law, LLM

Whittier Law School
US Legal Studies (for foreign lawyers), LLM

Widener University
Corporate Law and Finance, LLM
Health Law, DL; LLM; MJ; SJD

Willamette University
International and Comparative Law, LLM

William & Mary Law School
American Legal System (for foreign lawyers), LLM

Wisconsin, University of
Research, LLM; MLI; SJD

Yale Law School
General, LLM; JSD

■ Post-JD Programs by Category

Admiralty/Marine Affairs
Tulane University, LLM
Washington, University of, LLM

Advanced Studies
Pittsburgh, University of, JSD

Agricultural Law
Arkansas (Fayetteville), University of, LLM

American Business Law
Tulane University, LLM

American Legal Studies
Vermont Law School, LLM

Asian and Comparative Law
Washington, University of, LLM; PhD

Banking, Corporate, and Finance Law/Financial Services/Securities
Boston University, LLM
Chicago-Kent—Illinois Institute of Technology, LLM
Fordham University, LLM
Loyola University—Chicago, MJ
New York University, LLM
Stanford University, LLM
Wayne State University, LLM
Widener University, LLM

Bankruptcy Law
St. John's University, LLM

Biotechnology and Genomics
Arizona State University, LLM

Business and Taxation
Capital University, LLM
Pacific, McGeorge, University of, LLM

Business Law
Capital University, JD/LLM; LLM
Loyola University—Chicago, LLM
Northern Kentucky University, LLM
San Diego, University of, LLM

Child and Family Law
Loyola University—Chicago, LLM; MJ
Chicago Kent—Illinois Institute of Technology, LLM

Clinical Legal Education
Temple University, LLM

Comparative Biomedicine and Healthcare
Suffolk University, LLM

Comparative Law and Latin American Studies
Tulane University, MCL-MA

Comparative Law/Comparative Legal Studies/Comparative Jurisprudence
Florida, University of, LLM
Indiana University—Bloomington, MCL
John Marshall Law School, LLM
Miami, University of, LLM
New York University, MCJ
Pace University, LLM
Penn State University, LLM
Samford University, MCL
San Diego, University of, LLM
Southern California, University of, MCL
Tulane University, MCL

Criminal Law
Buffalo, State University of New York, University at, LLM

Dispute Resolution
Missouri—Columbia, University of, LLM
Pepperdine University, MDR

Education Law
Franklin Pierce Law Center, MEL

Elder Law
Kansas, University of, LLM
Western New England College, LLM

Employee Benefits
John Marshall Law School, LLM

Energy, Environment/Natural Resources
Denver, University of, LLM
George Washington University, LLM
Golden Gate University, LLM
Houston, University of, LLM
Lewis & Clark Law School, LLM
Oregon, University of, LLM
Pace University, LLM; SJD
Pacific, McGeorge, University of, JSD; LLM
Tulane University Law School, LLM
Utah, University of, LLM
Vermont Law School, LLM; MSEL

Entertainment/Media Law
Southwestern University, LLM

Estate Planning
Miami, University of, LLM
Missouri—Kansas City, University of, LLM
Western New England College, LLM

Family Law
Hofstra University, LLM

General or As Approved

Alabama, University of, LLM
Albany Law School, University of, LLM; MLS
American University, SJD
Buffalo, State University of New York, University at, LLM
California—Berkeley (Boalt Hall), University of, LLM; JSD
California—Davis, University of, LLM
Cardozo School of Law, LLM
Catholic University of America—School of Law, LLM
Chicago, University of, LLM; MCL; DCL; JSD
Cleveland State University, LLM
Columbia University, LLM; JSD
Cornell Law School, LLM; JSD
Emory University, LLM
George Mason University, JM
George Washington University, LLM; SJD
Georgetown University, LLM
Georgia, University of, LLM
Harvard Law School, LLM; SJD
Illinois, University of, JSD; LLM
Indiana University—Bloomington, LLM; SJD
Louisiana State University, BCL; LLM; MCL
Michigan, University of, LLM; MCL; SJD
Missouri—Kansas City, University of, LLM
New York University, LLM; JSD
Northwestern University, LLM
Ohio State University, LLM
Pennsylvania, University of, LLCM; LLM; SJD
Samford University, SJD
San Diego, University of, LLM
SMU Dedman, LLM; SJD
Southern Illinois University, LLM
Stanford University, JSD; JSM
Temple University, LLM
Texas, University of, LLM
Touro College, LLM
Tulane University, LLM; SJD
Valparaiso University, LLM
Virginia, University of, LLM; SJD
Wayne State University, LLM
Yale Law School, LLM; JSD

Global Technology

Suffolk University, LLM

Government and Public Policy

Albany Law School, LLM
American University, LLM
George Mason University, JM
George Washington University, LLM
Pacific, McGeorge, University of, LLM

Health Law

Albany Law School, LLM
DePaul University, LLM
Houston, University of, LLM
Loyola University—Chicago, LLM; MJ; DL; SJD
Quinnipiac University, LLM
Saint Louis University, LLM
Seton Hall University, LLM

Southern Illinois University, LLM
Suffolk University, LLM
Widener University, DL; LLM; MJ; SJD

Indigenous Law

Arizona, University of, LLM
Tulsa, University of, LLM

Insurance Law

Connecticut, University of, LLM

Intellectual Property/Technology/Information Technology Law

Albany Law School, LLM
Akron, University of, LLM
Boston University, LLM
Cardozo School of Law, LLM
DePaul University, LLM
Fordham University, LLM
Franklin Pierce Law Center, LLM; MIP
George Mason University, LLM
George Washington University, LLM
Golden Gate University, LLM
Houston, University of, LLM
John Marshall Law School, LLM; MS
Michigan State University, LLM
San Francisco, University of, LLM
Santa Clara University, LLM
Suffolk University, LLM
Washington, University of, LLM
Washington University, LLM

Inter-American Law

Miami, University of, LLM

Intercultural/International Human Rights/International Public Interest

New York University, LLM
Notre Dame Law School, JSD; LLM
St. Thomas University, LLM; JSD

International Business and Trade Law/Transnational Business Practice

Arizona, University of, LLM
Fordham University, LLM
John Marshall Law School, LLM
New York University, LLM
Pacific, McGeorge, University of, LLM
San Francisco, University of, LLM
Stetson University, LLM
Suffolk University, LLM

International Environmental Law

Washington, University of, LLM

International Taxation

Emory University, LLM
New York University, LLM
Regent University, LLM
St. Thomas University, LLM

International/International and Comparative Law/ Comparative and International Law/International Legal Studies
Albany Law School, LLM
American University, LLM
Chicago-Kent—Illinois Institute of Technology, LLM
Cornell Law School, LLM
George Washington University, LLM
Georgetown University, LLM
Golden Gate University, LLM; SJD
Hofstra University, LLM
Houston, University of, LLM
Howard University, LLM
Iowa, University of, LLM
Loyola Law School (Los Angeles), LLM
Miami, University of, LLM
New York University, LLM
Notre Dame Law School, LLM
Pittsburgh, University of, LLM
St. Mary's University, LLM
San Diego, University of, LLM
Santa Clara University, LLM
SMU Dedman, LLM
Tulane University, LLM
Willamette University, LLM

Judicial Process
Virginia, University of, LLM

Labor Law/Employment Law
Georgetown University, LLM
New York University, LLM
Wayne State University, LLM

Law and Economics
George Mason University, LLM

Law, Religion, and Culture
Samford University, LLM; SJD

Law, Science, and Technology
Stanford University, LLM

Law/Psychology
Nebraska, University of, MLS

Laws of the US
Baltimore, University of, LLM

Litigation/Trial Advocacy/Advocacy
California Western, LLM
Emory University, LLM
George Washington University, LLM
Georgetown University, LLM
Temple University, LLM

Military Law
Judge Advocate General's School, LLM

Ocean and Coastal Law
Miami, University of, LLM

Policy Analysis
George Mason University, LLM

Real Estate/Land Development
John Marshall Law School, LLM
Miami, University of, LLM

Research
Duke University, SJD
Indiana University—Bloomington, SJD
Northwestern University, SJD
Vanderbilt University, LLM
Washington University, JSD
Wisconsin, University of, LLM; MLI; SJD

Securities and Financial Regulation
Georgetown University, LLM

Sustainable International Development
Washington, University of, LLM

Taxation
Alabama, University of, LLM
Baltimore, University of, LLM
Boston University, LLM
Capital University, JD/LLM; LLM; MT
Case Western Reserve University, LLM
Chapman University, LLM
Chicago-Kent—Illinois Institute of Technology, LLM
Denver, University of, LLM
DePaul University, LLM
Emory University, LLM
Florida, University of, LLM; SJD
Georgetown University, LLM
Golden Gate University, LLM
Houston, University of, LLM
John Marshall Law School, LLM
Loyola Law School (Los Angeles), LLM
Loyola University—Chicago, LLM
Miami, University of, LLM
Missouri—Kansas City, University of, LLM
New York Law School, LLM
New York University, LLM
Pacific, McGeorge, University of, LLM
San Diego, University of, LLM
SMU Dedman, LLM
St. Thomas University, LLM
Temple University, LLM
Thomas M. Cooley, LLM
Villanova University, LLM
Washington, University of, LLM
Washington University, LLM
Wayne State University, LLM

Tribal Policy, Law, and Government
Arizona State University, LLM

Urban Affairs
Missouri—Kansas City, University of, LLM
Washington University, LLM

Programs for Foreign Lawyers or International Students
Boston University, LLM
Brigham Young University, LLM
California—Davis, University of, LLM
California—Hastings, University of, LLM
California at Los Angeles, University of, LLM
California Western, LLM; MCL
Case Western Reserve University, LLM
Connecticut, University of, LLM
Denver, University of, LLM
Duke University, LLM
Duquesne University, LLM
Florida State University, LLM
Georgetown University, SJD
Golden Gate University, LLM
Hamline University, LLM

Hawai'i, University of, LLM
Hofstra University, LLM
Houston, University of, LLM
Indiana University—Indianapolis, LLM
Minnesota, University of, LLM
New England School of Law, LLM
Puerto Rico, University of, LLM
Saint Louis University, LLM
St. Mary's University, LLM
Santa Clara University, LLM
Seattle University, LLM
Southern California, University of, LLM
Temple University, LLM
Touro College, LLM
Tulsa, University of, LLM
Wake Forest University, LLM
Washington University, LLM
Whittier Law School, LLM
William & Mary Law School, LLM

■ A Note to Graduates of Law Schools Located Outside the United States:

Degrees Other Than a JD and Bar Admission

In order to obtain a license to practice law in the United States, all candidates must apply for bar admission through a state board of bar examiners. Although this board is ordinarily an agency of the highest court in the jurisdiction, occasionally the board is connected to the state's bar association. The criteria for eligibility to take the bar examination or to otherwise qualify for bar admission are set by each state, not by the ABA or the Council of the Section of Legal Education and Admissions to the Bar.

In order to sit for the bar examination, most states require an applicant to hold a Juris Doctor (JD) degree from a law school that meets established educational standards. A JD earned at an ABA-approved law school meets the educational requirements in every jurisdiction in the United States. For those individuals who have not earned a JD degree from an ABA-approved law school, bar admission authorities have developed varying requirements and criteria to ascertain if such individuals meet the minimum educational requirements for bar admission. In most jurisdictions, individuals who lack such a JD will find that they do not satisfy the minimum educational requirements for bar admission and are ineligible to take the bar exam. In some of the remaining states, graduates of foreign law schools will find that additional schooling such as an LLM is required, and a few others recognize with regularity the sufficiency of a specific foreign legal education. A number offer an alternative licensure mechanism known as a Foreign Legal Consultant, which is a limited license to practice. And finally, some jurisdictions will allow individuals to be eligible for admission without examination under certain conditions if they have been admitted to the bar in another US jurisdiction.

In the past few years, there has been a large increase in the number of graduates from schools located outside the United States enrolled in advanced degree programs (such as the LLM). In fact, roughly half of all the individuals currently enrolled in LLM programs are graduates of foreign law schools. Upon graduating, many of these individuals return to their home country without seeking or obtaining bar licensure in the United States. However, an increasing number of these individuals seek to be admitted to a state bar.

Unlike the JD degree bestowed by an ABA-approved law school, which carries the indicia that the holder of that degree has completed a course of study imparting standards entitling him or her to engage in the practice of law, advanced degree programs at ABA-approved law schools are not regulated, and thus, not "approved." As a result, such degrees vary in content and rigor. In other words, the American Bar Association does NOT accredit degrees of any kind other than the JD.

It is the position of the Council of the Section of Legal Education and Admissions to the Bar of the American Bar Association that no graduate degree in law (LLM, MCL, SJD, etc.) is or should be a substitute for the first professional degree in law (JD), and that no graduate degree should substitute for the JD in order to meet the legal education requirements for admission to the bar.

As a result of the variance in state bar admission rules, the ABA strongly encourages individuals to contact the state board of bar examiners in the state(s) in which they are interested in being admitted to ascertain its requirements to sit for the bar examination. Contact information for all the state board of bar examiners is available at *www.abanet.org/legaled* and in the *Comprehensive Guide to Bar Admission Requirements*, which is available at the website above or through the ABA Service Center at 800.285.2221, Product Code: 5290087 (05ED).

Appendix C: Other Organizations

You may have questions concerning a variety of issues while you are applying to law school, once you are in law school, and even after you have your degree.

The following organizations may provide you with the answers you need.

American Association of Law Libraries (AALL)

The American Association of Law Libraries exists to provide leadership in the field of legal information, to foster the professional growth of law librarians, to develop the profession of law librarianship, and to enhance the value of law libraries to the legal community and to the public. AALL members come from all sizes and types of libraries: the Library of Congress, legislative libraries, academic law libraries, law firm libraries, bar association libraries, county law libraries, court libraries, and law libraries in business and industry. The association publishes a quarterly journal (*Law Library Journal*), a monthly magazine (*AALL Spectrum*), and an annual directory and handbook (which includes a minority law librarians directory).

For more information, contact:

American Association of Law Libraries
53 W. Jackson Boulevard, Suite 940
Chicago, IL 60604
Phone: 312.939.4764
URL: *www.aallnet.org*

American Bar Association (ABA)

The American Bar Association is the national organization of the legal profession. It is composed principally of practicing lawyers, judges, court administrators, law teachers, public service attorneys, many nonpracticing lawyers (such as business executives, government officials, etc.), and law students. Although the ABA does not have the power to discipline attorneys or enforce rules, the association leads by serving as the national voice of the profession.

The ABA, with over 413,108 members and 52,599 law student members, is the world's largest voluntary professional association. It serves a dual role as advocate for the profession and for the public. During the past decade, the association has initiated hundreds of programs addressing a wide range of public concerns. Response to these concerns is made possible by thousands of volunteers who contribute both time and money.

The Council of the Section of Legal Education and Admissions to the Bar of the ABA is identified by the US Department of Education as the "nationally recognized accrediting agency for professional schools of law." The role that the American Bar Association plays as a central accrediting body has allowed accreditation to become national in scope rather than fragmented among the 50 states, District of Columbia, the Commonwealth of Puerto Rico, and other territories. Most admitting jurisdictions require applicants for admission to be graduates of law schools approved by the American Bar Association.

The ABA may be contacted for information on the accreditation of law schools and the role of lawyers in the legal profession:

Office of the Consultant on Legal Education
American Bar Association
321 North Clark Street
Chicago, IL 60610
Phone: 312.988.6738
URL: *www.abanet.org/legaled*

Association of American Law Schools (AALS)

The Association of American Law Schools was founded for "the improvement of the legal profession through legal education." It is an association of law schools that serves as the law teachers' learned society. The association requires quality teaching and scholarship of its 168 member schools.

The organization provides a range of services to law schools. Among them are professional development workshops and conferences for law faculty, facilitation of law faculty recruitment, publication of the *AALS Directory of Law Teachers*, and interpretation of the mission and needs of legal education as the principal representative to other national higher education organizations, the federal government, and learned societies.

The AALS may be contacted for specific information about the role of legal education in the profession:

Association of American Law Schools
1201 Connecticut Avenue, NW
Suite 800
Washington, DC 20036-2605
Phone: 202.296.8851
URL: *www.aals.org*

HEATH Resource Center

The George Washington University operates the HEATH Resource Center, the national clearinghouse on postsecondary education for individuals with disabilities. HEATH provides information about disability-related accommodations, physical and programmatic access available at institutions of higher education, and issues related to choosing and applying to the most appropriate programs. Publications from the George Washington University HEATH Resource Center are available at no charge online at *www.heath.gwu.edu*.

For more information:

The HEATH Resource Center
The George Washington University
2134 G Street, NW
Washington, DC 20052
Phone (Voice/TTY): 800.544.3284 and 202.994.0904
URL: *www.heath.gwu.edu*

Law School Admission Council

The Law School Admission Council (LSAC) is a nonprofit corporation whose members are more than 200 law schools in the United States and Canada. It was founded in 1947 to coordinate, facilitate, and enhance the law school admission process. The organization also provides programs and services related to legal education. All law schools approved by the American Bar Association (ABA) are LSAC members. Canadian law schools recognized by a provincial or territorial law society or government agency are also included in the voting membership of the Council.

The services provided by LSAC include the Law School Admission Test (LSAT), the Law School Data Assembly Service (LSDAS), the Candidate Referral Service (CRS), and various publications and LSAT preparation tools. The LSAT, the LSDAS, and the CRS are provided to assist law schools in serving and evaluating applicants. LSAC does not engage in assessing an applicant's chances for admission to any law school; all admission decisions are made by individual law schools.

LSAC exists to serve both the law schools and their candidates for admission. Last year, LSAC administered 137,444 tests, and processed 181,500 transcripts, 582,681 law school report requests, 852,235 law school reports, and 221,429 letters of recommendation.

For more information on the LSAT, the LSDAS, and law school admission, contact:

Law School Admission Council
662 Penn Street
Box 2000
Newtown, PA 18940-0998
Phone: 215.968.1001
URL: *www.LSAC.org*

For information on minority opportunities in law, contact:

Law School Admission Council
Minority Opportunities in Law
662 Penn Street
Box 40
Newtown, PA 18940-0040
Phone: 215.968.1338
URL: *www.LSAC.org*

NALP—The Association for Legal Career Professionals™

NALP is a professional association of law schools and legal employers dedicated to facilitating legal career counseling and planning, recruitment and retention, and the professional development of law students and lawyers. NALP's core objectives include providing vision and expertise in research and education for legal career counseling and planning, recruitment, employment, and professional development; cultivating ethical practices and fairness in legal career counseling and planning, recruitment, employment, and professional development; promoting the full range of legal career opportunities and fostering access to legal public interest and public sector employment; and advocating for diversity in the legal profession and within NALP's membership.

NALP offers information and resources related to law careers through its website and online bookstore at *www.nalp.org*. In addition, NALP publishes an online directory of legal employers and their hiring criteria at *www.nalpdirectory.com* and offers an extensive database of public opportunities for law students and lawyers through *www.pslawnet.org* (NALP's Public Service Law Network Worldwide).

NALP is not an employment agency and does not offer placement or career counseling services. NALP believes that each law school offers unique programs and opportunities and, like the American Bar Association and the Law School Admission Council, does not rank law schools or career services offices.

For further information, contact:

NALP
1025 Connecticut Avenue, NW
Suite 1110
Washington, DC 20036-5413
Phone: 202.835.1001
URL: *www.nalp.org*

The following list of prelaw readings offers prospective law students an overview of selected classics and current titles in certain subjects: law school and legal education, the legal profession, biography, jurisprudence and legal issues, and financing a law school education. Some of these publications list sources for financial aid, but students will need to call or write the individual organizations for the most up-to-date information.

This list should not be construed as the official bibliography of Law School Admission Council or ABA; it is beyond the scope of those organizations to provide any sort of definitive catalog of prelaw readings.

Some of these books have already withstood the test of time and are as relevant today as when they were first written and published generations ago. Examples are Richard Kluger's *Simple Justice*—a rare glimpse into the private workings and deliberations of the Supreme Court; and Karl Llewellyn's *The Bramble Bush*—a classic study of how legal education shapes our legal institutions.

Some titles simply reflect the most current writing on the subjects listed above and are not necessarily recommended simply because they appear on this list. It will be up to you to search out the titles that pique your interest and make your own determination of their worth. The aim of our list is merely to give you a head start. We hope that those interested in pursuing legal studies will find the issues raised and the ideas discussed in these works helpful in making the decision to choose law as a career.

■ Law School and Legal Education

Barber, David H. *Winning in Law School: Stress Reduction.* 2nd ed. Dillon, CO: Spectra, 1986.

Bell, Susan J. *Full Disclosure: Do You Really Want to Be a Lawyer?* 2nd ed. Lawrenceville, NJ: Peterson's Guides, 1992.

Bodine, Paul. *Great Personal Statements for Law School.* New York: McGraw-Hill, 2006.

Boyer, Paul. *College Rankings Exposed.* Lawrenceville, NJ: Peterson's, 2003.

Briggs, Amy Thompson. *Degrees of Difference: A How-to Guide to Choosing a Law School.* Washington, DC: NALP, 1998.

Carey, Christen Civiletto, and **Kristen David Adams**. *The Practice of Law School: Getting In and Making the Most of Your Legal Education.* New York: ALM Publishing, 2003.

Carter, Lief H., and **Thomas F. Burke.** *Reason in Law.* 7th ed. New York: Longman, 2006.

Chase, William C. *The American Law School and the Rise of Administrative Government.* Madison, WI: University of Wisconsin Press, 1982.

Curry, Boykin, and **Emily Angel Baer,** eds. *Essays That Worked for Law Schools: 40 Essays from Successful Applications to the Nation's Top Law Schools.* rev. ed. New York: Ballantine Books, 2003.

Deaver, Jeff. *The Complete Law School Companion: How to Excel at America's Most Demanding Post-Graduate Curriculum.* 2nd ed. New York: Wiley, 1992.

Estrich, Susan. *How to Get Into Law School.* New York: Riverhead Books, 2004.

Falcon, Atticus. *Planet Law School II: What You Need to Know (Before You Go), But Didn't Know to Ask… and No One Else Will Tell You.* rev. ed. Honolulu: Fine Print Press, 2003.

Farnsworth, E. Allan. *An Introduction to the Legal System of the United States.* 3rd ed. Dobbs Ferry, NY: Oceana Publications, Inc., 1996.

Gillers, Stephen. *Looking at Law School.* 4th rev. ed. New York: Plume Books, 1997.

Goldfarb, Sally F., and **Carol-June Cassidy,** eds. *Inside the Law Schools: A Guide by Students for Students.* 7th ed. New York: Plume, 1998.

Goodrich, Chris. *Anarchy and Elegance: Confessions of a Journalist at Yale Law School.* Lincoln, NE: iUniverse, 2003.

Hirshman, Linda. *The Woman's Guide to Law School.* New York: Penguin, 1999.

Ivey, Anna. *The Ivey Guide to Law School Admissions: Straight Advice on Essays, Resumes, Interviews, and More.* New York: Harvest Books, 2005.

JD Jungle, (eds.). *The JD Jungle Law School Survival Guide.* New York: Perseus Books Group, 2003.

Kaplin, William A. *The Concepts and Methods of Constitutional Law.* Durham, NC: Carolina Academic Press, 1992.

Kaufman, Dan, and **Chris Dowhan.** *Essays That Will Get You Into Law School.* 2nd ed. Hauppage, NY: Barron's Educational Series, 2003.

Lammert-Reeves, Ruth. *Get into Law School: A Strategic Approach.* 2nd ed. New York: Kaplan, 2004.

Lermack, Paul. *How to Get Into the Right Law School.* 2nd ed. New York: McGraw Hill, 1996.

Llewellyn, Karl N. *Bramble Bush: On Our Law and Its Study.* 8th ed. Dobbs Ferry, NY: Oceana Publications, Inc., 1981. (First published in 1930.)

Martinson, Thomas H., David P. Waldherr, and **Arco Publishing.** *Getting Into Law School Today.* 3rd ed. New York: Macmillan, 1998.

McClurg, Andrew J. *The Law School Trip (The Insider's Guide to Law School).* Victoria, British Columbia: Trafford Publishing, 2001.

Miller, Robert H. *Law School Confidential—A Complete Guide to the Law School Experience: By Students, for Students.* rev. ed. New York: St. Martin's Griffin, 2004.

Moliterno, James E., and **Frederic I. Lederer.** *An Introduction to Law, Law Study, and the Lawyer's Role.* Durham, NC: Carolina Academic Press, 2004.

Munneke, Gary A. *How to Succeed in Law School.* 3rd ed. Hauppage, NY: Barron's Educational Series, 2001.

Owens, Eric. *Law School Essays That Made a Difference.* New York: Princeton Review, 2003.

Roth, George. *Slaying the Law School Dragon.* 2nd ed. New York: Wiley, 1991.

Schlag, Pierre, and **David Skover.** *Tactics of Legal Reasoning.* Durham, NC: Carolina Academic Press, 1986.

Schneider, Deborah, and **Gary Belsky.** *Should You Really Be a Lawyer? The Guide to Smart Career Choices Before, During, & After Law School.* Seattle: DecisionBooks, 2004.

Sells, Benjamin. *Soul of the Law.* London: Vega Books, 2002.

Shapo, Helene S., and **Marshall Shapo.** *Law School Without Fear: Strategies for Success.* 2nd ed. New York: Foundation Press, 2002.

Simenhoff, Mark, ed. *My First Year as a Lawyer: Real-World Stories from American Lawyers.* New York: Signet, 1996.

Stevens, Robert. *Law School: Legal Education in America from the 1850s to the 1980s.* Chapel Hill, NC: University of North Carolina Press, 1987.

Stover, Robert V., and **Howard S. Erlanger**, ed. *Making It and Breaking It: The Fate of Public Interest Commitment During Law School.* Urbana, IL: University of Illinois Press, 1989.

Swygert, Michael I., and **Robert Batey**, eds. *Maximizing the Law School Experience: A Collection of Essays.* St. Petersburg, FL: Stetson University College of Law, 1983.

Turow, Scott. *One L: The Turbulent True Story of a First Year at Harvard Law School.* New York: Warner Books, 1997.

Vanderbilt, Arthur T. *Law School: Briefing for a Legal Education.* New York: Penguin Books, 1981.

Versteeg, Russ. *Essential Latin for Lawyers.* Durham, NC: Carolina Academic Press, 1990.

Weaver, William G. *Peterson's Game Plan for Getting Into Law School.* Lawrenceville: NJ: Peterson's, 2000.

Williams, Glanville, and **A. T. H. Smith.** *Learning the Law.* 12th ed. London: Sweet & Maxwell, Ltd., 2002.

Wright, Carol L. *The Ultimate Guide to Law School Admission.* Center Valley, PA: Marriwell Publishing, 2003.

Wydick, Richard C. *Plain English for Lawyers.* 5th ed. Durham, NC: Carolina Academic Press, 2005.

■ Legal Profession

American Bar Association Center for Pro Bono. *Law School Public Interest Law Support Programs: A Directory.* Chicago: American Bar Association, 2000.

Abel, Richard L. *American Lawyers.* New York: Oxford University Press, 1989.

Abrams, Lisa L. *The Official Guide to Legal Specialties: An Insider's Guide to Every Major Practice Area.* Chicago: The BarBri Group, 2000.

Arron, Deborah. *Running from the Law: Why Good Lawyers Are Getting Out of the Legal Profession.* 3rd ed. Berkeley, CA: DecisionBooks, 2003.

Arron, Deborah. *What Can You Do With a Law Degree? A Lawyer's Guide to Career Alternatives Inside, Outside & Around the Law.* Seattle: DecisionBooks, 2003.

Bailey, F. Lee. *To Be a Trial Lawyer.* 2nd ed. New York: Wiley, 1994.

Bay, Monica. *Careers in Civil Litigation.* Chicago: American Bar Association, Law Student Division, 1990.

Bellow, Gary, and **Martha Minow**, eds. *Law Stories.* Ann Arbor: University of Michigan Press, 1998.

Bradley, Heather, and **Miriam Bamberger Grogan.** *Judge for Yourself: Clarity, Choice, and Action in Your Legal Career.* Chicago: American Bar Association, produced in cooperation with the Minority Corporate Counsel of America, 2006.

Caplan, Lincoln. *Skadden: Power, Money, and the Rise of a Legal Empire.* New York: Farrar, Straus & Giroux, 1994.

Carey, Christen Civiletto. *Full Disclosure: The New Lawyer's Must-Read Career Guide.* 2nd ed. New York: ALM Publishing, 2001.

Couric, Emily. *The Trial Lawyers: The Nation's Top Litigators Tell How They Win.* New York: St. Martin's Press, 1990.

Epstein, Cynthia Fuchs. *Women in Law.* 2nd ed. Urbana, IL: University of Illinois Press, 1993.

Epstein, Phyllis Horn. *Women-at-Law: Lessons Learned Along the Pathways to Success.* Chicago: American Bar Association, 2005.

Fontaine, Valerie A. *The Right Moves: Job Search and Career Development Strategies for Lawyers.* Washington, DC: NALP, 2006.

Foonberg, Jay G. *How to Start and Build a Law Practice.* 3rd ed. Chicago: American Bar Association, Law Student Division, 1991.

Fox, Ronald W. *Lawful Pursuit: Careers in Public Interest Law.* Career Series. Chicago: American Bar Association, 1995.

Galanter, Marc, and **Thomas Palay.** *Tournament of Lawyers: The Transformation of the Big Law Firm.* Chicago: University of Chicago Press, 1994.

Gerson, Donna. *Choosing Small, Choosing Smart: Job Search Strategies for Lawyers in the Small Firm Market.* 2nd ed. Washington, DC: NALP, 2005.

Greene, Robert Michael. *Making Partner: A Guide for Law Firm Associates.* Chicago: American Bar Association, Section of Law Practice Management, 1992.

Harrington, Mona. *Women Lawyers: Rewriting the Rules.* New York: Plume, 1995.

Henslee, William D. *Careers in Entertainment Law.* Chicago: American Bar Association, Law Student Division, 1990.

Hoffman, Richard E., Wilfredo Lopez, Gene W. Matthews, and **Karen L. Foster.** Edited by **Richard A. Goodman**, and **Mark A. Rothstein.** *Law in Public Health.* New York: Oxford University Press, 2002.

Horn, Carl, III. *Lawyer Life: Finding a Life and Higher Calling in the Practice of Law.* Chicago: American Bar Association, 2003.

Kauffman, George W. *Lawyer's Guide to Balancing Life and Work: Taking the Stress out of Success.* Chicago: American Bar Association, 1999.

Kelly, Michael J. *Lives of Lawyers: Journeys in the Organizations of Practice.* Ann Arbor: University of Michigan Press, 1994.

Killoughey, Donna M., ed. *Breaking Traditions: Work Alternatives for Lawyers.* Chicago: American Bar Association, Section of Law Practice Management, 1993.

Kronman, Anthony T. *The Lost Lawyer: Failing Ideals of the Legal Profession.* Cambridge, MA: The Belknap Press of Harvard University Press, 1995.

Linowitz, Sol M., with **Martin Mayer.** *The Betrayed Profession: Lawyering at the End of the Twentieth Century.* New York: Scribner, 1994.

López, Gerald P. *Rebellious Lawyering: One Chicano's Vision of Progressive Law Practice.* Boulder, CO: Westview Press, 1992.

Luney, Percy R., Jr. *Careers in Natural Resources and Environmental Law.* Chicago: American Bar Association, Law Student Division, 1987.

Mayer, Martin. *The Lawyers.* Westport, CT: Greenwood Press, 1980.

Miller, Henry G. *On Trial: Lessons from a Lifetime in the Courtroom.* New York: ALM Publishing, 2001.

Moll, Richard W. *The Lure of the Law: Why People Become Lawyers, and What the Profession Does to Them.* New York: Penguin Books, 1991.

Munneke, Gary A. *Careers in Law.* 3rd ed. New York: McGraw-Hill, 2004.

———. *The Legal Career Guide: From Law Student to Lawyer.* 4th ed. Career Series. Chicago: American Bar Association Career Series, 2003.

———. *Opportunities in Law Careers.* New York: McGraw-Hill, 2001.

Munneke, Gary A., and **William D. Henslee.** 4th ed. *Nonlegal Careers for Lawyers*. Chicago: American Bar Association, 2003.

O'Neill, Suzanne B., and **Catherine Gerhauser Sparkman.** *From Law School to Law Practice: The New Associate's Guide*. 2nd ed. Philadelphia: American Law Institute/American Bar Association Committee on Continuing Professional Education, 1998.

Peppers, Todd C. *Courtiers of the Marble Palace: The Rise and Influence of the Supreme Court Law Clerk*. Stanford, CA: Stanford University Press, 2006.

Shaffer, Thomas L., and **Mary M. Shaffer.** *American Lawyers and Their Communities: Ethics in the Legal Profession*. Notre Dame, IN: University of Notre Dame Press, 1991.

Shropshire, Kenneth. *Careers in Sports Law*. Chicago: American Bar Association, Law Student Division, 1990.

Smith, J. Clay, Jr., ed. *Rebels in Law: Voices in History of Black Women Lawyers*. Ann Arbor: The University of Michigan Press, 2000.

Smith, Janet. *Beyond L.A. Law: Break the Traditional "Lawyer" Mold*. Chicago: Harcourt Brace Legal and Professional Publications, 1998.

Stewart, James B. *The Partners*. New York: Simon & Schuster, 1983.

Strauss, Debra M. *Behind the Bench: The Guide to Judicial Clerkships*. Chicago: The BarBri Group, 2002.

Swartz, Salli A., and **Mark W. Janis.** *Careers in International Law*. 2nd ed. Chicago: American Bar Association, 2001.

Thorner, Abbie Willard, ed. *Now Hiring: Government Jobs for Lawyers*. (1990-1991 edition). Chicago: American Bar Association, Law Student Division, 1990.

Vlajcic, Sara. *Family Law Careers*. Chicago: American Bar Association, 1998.

Wayne, Ellen. *Careers in Labor Law*. Chicago: American Bar Association, Law Student Division, 1985.

■ Biography

Auchincloss, Louis. *Life, Law and Letters: Essays and Sketches*. Boston: Houghton Mifflin Co., 1979.

Baker, Leonard. *John Marshall: A Life in Law*. New York: Macmillan, 1974.

Cray, Ed. *Chief Justice: A Biography of Earl Warren*. New York: Simon & Schuster, 1997.

Darrow, Clarence. *The Story of My Life*. Cambridge: DeCapo Press, 1996. (First published in 1932.)

Davis, Deane C. *Justice in the Mountains: Stories & Tales by a Vermont Country Lawyer*. Shelburne, VT: New England Press, 1980.

Davis, Lenwood G. *I Have a Dream: The Life and Times of Martin Luther King*. Westport, CT: Greenwood Press, 1973.

Douglas, William O. *Go East Young Man: The Early Years*. New York: Random House, 1974.

———. *Court Years, 1939–1975: The Autobiography of William O. Douglas*. New York: Random House, 1980.

Dunne, Gerald T. *Hugo Black and the Judicial Revolution*. New York: Pocket, 1978.

Frankfurter, Felix. *Felix Frankfurter Reminisces*. New York: Reynal & Co., 1960.

Goldman, Roger, with **David Gallen.** *Justice William J. Brennan, Jr.: Freedom First*. New York: Carroll & Graf Publishers, Inc., 1994.

Griswold, Erwin N. *Ould Fields, New Corne: The Personal Memoirs of a Twentieth Century Lawyer*. St. Paul, MN: West Publishing, 1992.

Gunther, Gerald. *Learned Hand: The Man and the Judge*. New York: Alfred A. Knopf, 1994.

Holmes, Oliver Wendell, and **Richard A. Posner.** *The Essential Holmes: Selections from the Letters, Speeches, Judicial Opinions, and Other Writings of Oliver Wendell Holmes*. (reissue edition.) Chicago: University of Chicago Press, 1997.

Howe, Mark deWolfe. *Justice Oliver Wendell Holmes*. 2 vols. Cambridge, MA: Harvard University Press, 1957, 1963.

Jeffries, John, Jr. *Justice Lewis F. Powell*. New York: Scribner, 1994.

Kahlenberg, Richard D. *Broken Contract: A Memoir of Harvard Law School*. Amherst, MA: University of Massachusetts Press, 1999. (First published in 1992.)

Keates, William R. *Proceed With Caution: A Diary of the First Year at One of America's Largest, Most Prestigious Law Firms*. New York: Harcourt Brace Legal and Professional Publications, 1997.

Lynn, Conrad J. *There Is a Fountain: The Autobiography of a Civil Rights Lawyer*. 2nd ed. Chicago: Lawrence Hill Books, 1993.

Marke, Julius J. *The Holmes Reader*. 2nd ed. Dobbs Ferry, NY: Oceana Publications, Inc., 1964.

Miller, Henry G. *On Trial: Lessons from a Lifetime in the Courtroom*. New York: ALM Publishing, 2001.

Newton, Jim. *Justice for All: Earl Warren and the Nation He Made*. New York: Riverhead Books (Penguin), 2006.

Nizer, Louis. *Reflections Without Mirrors: An Autobiography of the Mind*. New York: Doubleday, 1978.

Noonan, John T., Jr. *Persons and Masks of the Law: Cardozo, Holmes, Jefferson, and Wythe as Makers of the Masks*. Berkeley, CA: University of California Press, 2002.

Pound, Roscoe, and **Karl Llewellyn.** *Searching for an American Jurisprudence*. Chicago: University of Chicago Press, 1998.

Rosenkranz, E. Joshua, and **Bernard Schwartz.** *Reason and Passion: Justice Brennan's Enduring Influence*. New York: Norton, 1997.

Rowan, Carl T. *Dream Makers, Dream Breakers. The World of Justice Thurgood Marshall*. Boston: Little Brown & Company, 1994.

Schwartz, Bernard. *Super Chief, Earl Warren and His Supreme Court—A Judicial Biography*. New York: New York University Press, 1983.

Simon, James F. *Independent Journey: The Life of William O. Douglas*. New York: Harper & Row, 1980.

Strum, Phillippa. *Brandeis: Beyond Progressivism*. Lawrence, KS: University Press of Kansas, 1993.

———. *Justice for the People*. New York: Schocken, 1989.

Thomas, Evan. *The Man to See*. New York: Simon & Schuster, 1991.

Walsh, Lawrence E. *The Gift of Insecurity: A Lawyers Life*. Chicago: American Bar Association, 2003.

Westin, Alan F. *Autobiography of the Supreme Court: Off-the-Bench Commentary by the Justices*. Westport, CT: Greenwood Press, 1978.

White, G. Edward. *Earl Warren: A Public Life*. New York: Oxford University Press, 1987.

Wigdor, David. *Roscoe Pound: Philosopher of Law*. Westport, CT: Greenwood Press, 1974.

Williams, Juan. *Thurgood Marshall: American Revolutionary*. New York: Three Rivers Press, 2000.

■ Jurisprudence and Legal Issues

Bodenhamer, David J., and James E. Ely, Jr., eds. *The Bill of Rights in Modern America*. Bloomington, IN: Indiana University Press, 1993.

Cahn, Edmond. *The Moral Decision: Right and Wrong in the Light of American Law*. Littleton, CO: Fred S. Rothman and Co, 1993. (First published in 1955.)

Cardozo, Benjamin N. *The Nature of the Judicial Process*. New Haven: Yale University Press, 1960. (First published in 1921.)

Fine, Toni M. *American Legal Systems: A Resource and Reference Guide*. Cincinnati, OH: Anderson Publishing, 1997.

Finkel, Norman J. *Insanity on Trial*. New York: Springer, 1988.

Friedrichs, David R. *Law In Our Lives: An Introduction*. 2nd edition. Los Angeles: Roxbury Publishing, 2005.

Friedman, Lawrence M. *Law in America: A Short History*. New York: Modern Library, 2004.

Friedman, Lawrence M., and Harry N. Scheiber, eds. *Legal Culture and the Legal Profession*. Boulder, CO: Westview Press, 1996.

Greenberg, Jack. *Crusaders in the Courts: How a Dedicated Band of Lawyers Fought for the Civil Rights Revolution*. New York: Twelve Tables Press, 1994.

Guinier, Lani. *The Tyranny of the Majority: Fundamental Fairness in Representative Democracy*. New York: Free Press, 1995.

Harr, Jonathan. *A Civil Action*. New York: Vintage, 1996.

Heilbroner, David. *Rough Justice*. New York: Pantheon, 1990.

Hoban, Thomas More, and Richard Oliver Brooks. *Green Justice: The Environment and the Courts*. Boulder, CO: Westview Press, 1996.

Irons, Peter. *A People's History of the Supreme Court*. New York: Penguin, 2000.

Irons, Peter, and Stephanie Guitton, eds. *May It Please the Court: The Most Significant Oral Arguments Made Before the Supreme Court Since 1955*. Audiocassette. New York: New Press, 1993.

Kennedy, Caroline, and Ellen Aldeman. *The Right to Privacy*. New York: Knopf, 1995.

Kluger, Richard. *Simple Justice: The History of Brown vs. Board of Education and Black America's Struggle for Equality*. New York: Vintage, 2004. (First published in 1976.)

Lewis, Anthony. *Gideon's Trumpet*. New York: Random House, 1964.

———. *Make No Law: The Sullivan Case and the First Amendment*. New York: Random House, 1991.

Pound, Roscoe. *Law and Morals*. South Hackensack, NJ: Rothman Reprints, 1969. (First published in 1926.)

Rehnquist, William H. *The Supreme Court: How It Was, How It Is*. rev. ed. New York: Vintage, 2002.

Rosen, Jeffrey. *The Supreme Court: The Personalities and Rivalries That Defined America*. New York: Times Books, 2007.

Savage, G. David. *Turning Right: The Making of the Rehnquist Supreme Court*. New York: Wiley, 1993.

Schwartz, Bernard. *A History of the Supreme Court*. New York: Oxford University Press, 1995.

Shapiro, Fred R. *The Oxford Dictionary of American Legal Quotations*. New York: Oxford University Press, 1993.

Shapiro, Joseph P. *No Pity: People With Disabilities Forging a New Civil Rights Movement*. New York: Three Rivers Press, 1994.

Simon, James F. *The Antagonists: Hugo Black, Felix Frankfurter and Civil Liberties in Modern America*. New York: Simon & Schuster, 1989.

Spence, Gerry. *With Justice for None*. New York: Penguin, 1990.

Stone, Geoffrey R., Richard Epstein, and Cass R. Sunstein, eds. *The Bill of Rights in the Modern State*. Chicago: University of Chicago Press, 1992.

Sunstein, Cass R. *Democracy and the Problem of Free Speech*. New York: Free Press, 1995.

Treanor, Richard Bryant. *We Overcame: The Story of Civil Rights for Disabled People*. Falls Church, VA: Regal Direct Publishing, 1993.

Tribe, Laurence H. *God Save This Honorable Court: How the Choice of Supreme Court Justices Shapes Our History*. New York: New American Library, 1986.

Tushnet, Mark V. *Making Civil Rights Law: Thurgood Marshall and the Supreme Court, 1936-1961*. New York: Oxford University Press, 1994.

Tushnet, Mark, ed. *The Warren Court in Historical and Political Perspective*. Charlottesville, VA: University Press of Virginia, 1993.

Vandevelde, Kenneth J. *Thinking Like a Lawyer: An Introduction to Legal Reasoning*. Boulder, CO: Westview Press, 1996.

Walker, Samuel. *Hate Speech: The History of an American Controversy*. Lincoln, NE: University of Nebraska Press, 1994.

———. *In Defense of American Liberties: A History of the ACLU*. New York: Oxford University Press, 1990.

Ward, Artemis, and David L. Weiden. *Sorcerers' Apprentices: 100 Years of Law Clerks at the United States Supreme Court*. New York: New York University Press, 2006.

Williams, Patricia J. *The Alchemy of Race and Rights*. Cambridge, MA: Harvard University Press, 1991.

Wishman, Seymour. *Anatomy of a Jury*. New York: Penguin, 1987.

■ Financing Law School

Schlachter, Gail Ann. *Financial Aid for Women, 2005–2007*. El Dorado Hills, CA: Reference Service Press, 2005.

———. *How to Pay for Your Law Degree, 2006–2008*. El Dorado Hills, CA: Reference Service Press, 2004.

Schlachter, Gail Ann, and R. David Weber. *Financial Aid for African Americans, 2005–2007*. El Dorado Hills, CA: Reference Service Press, 2006.

———. *Financial Aid for Asian Americans, 2005–2007*. El Dorado Hills, CA: Reference Service Press, 2006.

———. *Financial Aid for Hispanic Americans, 2005–2007*. El Dorado Hills, CA: Reference Service Press, 2006.

———. *Financial Aid for Native Americans, 2005–2007*. El Dorado Hills, CA: Reference Service Press, 2006.

———. *Financial Aid for the Disabled and Their Families, 2004–2006*. El Dorado Hills, CA: Reference Service Press, 2004.

———. *Financial Aid for Veterans, Military Personnel, and Their Dependents, 2004–2006*. El Dorado Hills, CA: Reference Service Press, 2004.

Quick, Amanda C., ed. *Scholarships, Fellowships, and Loans*. Farmington Hills, MI: Gale Group, 2003.

Appendix E: Canadian LSAC-Member Law Schools

University of Alberta Faculty of Law
Room 480, Admissions Office
Edmonton, Alberta
CANADA T6G 2H5

University of British Columbia Faculty of Law
1822 East Mall
Vancouver, British Columbia
CANADA V6T 1Z1

University of Calgary Faculty of Law
Murray Fraser Hall
Calgary, Alberta
CANADA T2N 1N4

Dalhousie Law School
6061 University Avenue
Halifax, Nova Scotia
CANADA B3H 4H9

University of Manitoba Faculty of Law
Robson Hall
Winnipeg, Manitoba
CANADA R3T 2N2

Faculty of Law McGill University
3644 Peel Street
Montreal, Quebec
CANADA H3A 1W9

Faculté de droit de l'Université de Moncton
Centre universitaire de Moncton
Service de l'admission, Faculté de droit
Moncton, Nouveau-Brunswick
CANADA E1A 3E9

University of New Brunswick Law School
PO Box 44271
Fredericton, New Brunswick
CANADA E3B 6C2

University of Ottawa Faculty of Law
57 Louis Pasteur Street
Ottawa, Ontario
CANADA K1N 6N5

Queen's University Faculty of Law
Director of Admissions, MacDonald Hall
Kingston, Ontario
CANADA K7L 3N6

University of Saskatchewan College of Law
Admissions Committee
15 Campus Drive
Saskatoon, Saskatchewan
CANADA S7N 5A6

University of Toronto Faculty of Law
78 Queen's Park
Toronto, Ontario
CANADA M5S 2C5

University of Victoria Faculty of Law
PO Box 2400, STN CSC
Victoria, British Columbia
CANADA V8W 3H7

The University of Western Ontario Faculty of Law
London, Ontario
CANADA N6A 3K7

University of Windsor Faculty of Law
401 Sunset Avenue
Windsor, Ontario
CANADA N9B 3P4

Osgoode Hall Law School, York University
4700 Keele Street
North York, Ontario
CANADA M3J 1P3

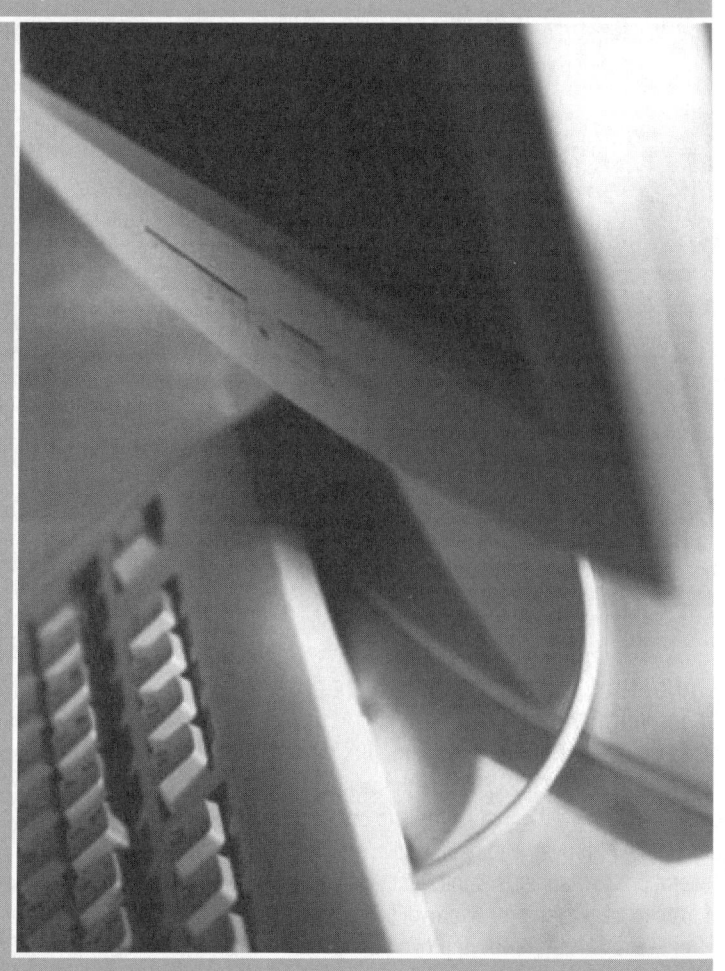

...blications Available from the ABA's Section

The Section publishes a number of books, reports, newsletters, and brochures to inform and educate its members and the public. All of the following publications are available by calling the ABA Service Center at 1.800.285.2221 or through the Section website: www.abanet.org/legaled.

THE OFFICIAL GUIDE TO ABA-APPROVED LAW SCHOOLS, 2008 EDITION

The Official Guide is published in cooperation with the Law School Admission Council and pursuant to the Section's Standard 509, modeled after Department of Education regulations requiring law schools to "publish basic consumer information in a fair and accurate manner reflective of actual practice." Admission data, tuition, fees, living costs, financial aid, enrollment data, graduation rates, composition and number of faculty and administrators, curricular offerings, library resources, physical facilities, placement rates, bar passage data, and post-JD programs are only some of the many categories covered in this comprehensive guide. Also available at major bookstores.

Product Code: 5290085 (08ED), Price: $24.00

STANDARDS: RULES OF PROCEDURE FOR APPROVAL OF LAW SCHOOLS

ABA Standards: Rules of Procedure for Approval of Law Schools sets forth the standards that a law school must meet to obtain or retain ABA Approval. The book is divided into several parts: Standards & Interpretations; Rules of Procedure; Criteria for Approval of Summer Foreign Programs of ABA Approved Schools; Criteria for Student Study at a Foreign Institution; Criteria for Approval of Semester Abroad Programs for Credit Granting Foreign Segment of Approved JD Program; Statement of Ethical Practices in the Process of Law School Accreditation; Internal Operating Practices; Council Statements.

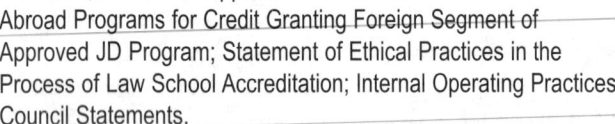

Product Code: 5290084 (05ED), Price: $15.00

OCCASIONAL PAPER #9:

OPPORTUNITIES AND CHALLENGES FOR LAWYERS AND LEGAL EDUCATORS IN A WORLD WITHOUT BORDERS

A transcript of a 1997 discussion during the ABA Annual Meeting organized by the Section of Legal Education & Admissions to the Bar, International Law Section, and the Young Lawyers Division.

Product Code: 5290092 (0009), Price: $4.00

COMPREHENSIVE GUIDE TO BAR ADMISSION REQUIREMENTS, 2006 EDITION

The Comprehensive Guide to Bar Admission Requirements is published each year by the Section and the National Conference of Bar Examiners. It sets out the rules and practices of all US jurisdictions for admission to the bar by examination and on motion; that is, legal education, character and fitness, bar examinations, and special licenses. Supplemental information follows each chart.

Product Code: 5290087 (06ED), Price: $12.50

TEACHING AND LEARNING PROFESSIONALISM

This is a 1996 report by the ABA Section of Legal Education and Admissions to the Bar Professionalism Committee. It examines the recent decline in professionalism and makes a number of recommendations designed to increase the level of professionalism among American law students, practicing lawyers, and judges.

Product Code: 5290083, Price: $3.75

TEACHING AND LEARNING PROFESSIONALISM: SYMPOSIUM PROCEEDINGS

The publication of this monograph brings to a conclusion the professionalism projects of the Section and the ABA Professionalism Committee. The initial Committee report entitled "Teaching and Learning Professionalism" and this publication, which reproduces the papers presented at and summarizes the discussion from a national invitational Symposium on Teaching and Learning Professionalism in October 1996 contains a broad range of ideas and recommendations for enhancing the level of professionalism among American law students and lawyers. Serious discussion and implementation of these ideas and recommendations by law faculties, judges, practitioners, and bar association officials will be the true test of this project's success.

Product Code: 5290086, Price: $3.75

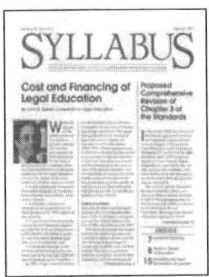

SYLLABUS

Syllabus is the news publication of the Section of Legal Education and Admissions to the Bar. Three times a year readers learn about Section conferences and workshops, as well as contemporary legal education topics. Statistical information pertaining to legal education is also included.

Product Code: 5290002, Price: $15.00 per year

ANNUAL REPORT OF THE CONSULTANT ON LEGAL EDUCATION TO THE ABA

The Consultant's Office Annual Report is a brief overview of the events and activities of the Section and the Consultant's Office for the year. The current year edition is now available as are limited quantities of editions from previous years. 56 pages.

Product Code: 5290089 (0405), Price $2.00

THE ABA'S FIRST SECTION: ASSURING A QUALIFIED BAR

This book was created by Susan Boyd as part of the Centennial Celebration of the Section in 1993. It is 148 pages in length and provides a history of the Section of Legal Education and Admissions to the Bar for the American Bar Association.

Product Code: 5290058, Price: $10.00

A MODEL FOR DIALOGUE: BAR EXAMINERS AND LAW SCHOOLS

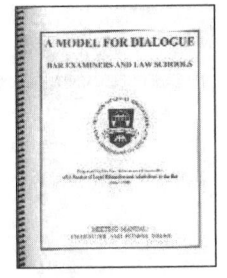

In the Spring of 2002 the Bar Admissions Committee updated this manual to be used as a tool to inform as well as encourage and facilitate dialogue between bar examiners, law schools, and supreme courts. The 70 page publication contains several provocative and realistic hypotheticals to facilitate discussion among these entities.

Product Code: 5290093 (02ED), Price: $4.00

LEGAL EDUCATION AND PROFESSIONAL DEVELOPMENT - AN EDUCATIONAL CONTINUUM ("MACCRATE REPORT")

In August 1992, the Council received the "Report of the Task Force on Law Schools and the Profession: Narrowing the Gap" chaired by Robert MacCrate. The report was distributed to deans and members of law school faculties, chief justices, bar presidents, and members of the Section. All were asked to discuss the recommendations of the Task Force. During the upcoming year we expect to revisit the MacCrate report by requesting schools, states, and individuals to report on the impact of MacCrate on legal education and the profession.

Product Code: 5290052, Price: $10.00

SOURCEBOOK ON LEGAL WRITING PROGRAMS

The aim of this newly revised edition is to establish the parameters and common features that define successful programs for teaching legal writing skills in law school and to help improve the quality of legal writing programs across the country. The Sourcebook is the primary reference source for those designing, directing, and teaching in legal writing programs.

Product Code: 529009106ED, Price: $19.00

CHAIRPERSONS' REFLECTIONS

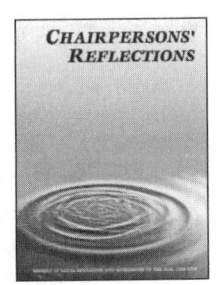

Chairpersons' Reflections contains thoughtful articles by former Section chairpersons from 1969 to 1993, including ABA President Phillip S. Anderson, Norman Redlich, Jose Garcia-Pedrosa, Judge Henry Ramsey, Jr., and Dean Nina S. Appel. It is a wonderful historic publication that shows the progress of legal education and the role of the Section and its Council from 1969 to 1993. The short essays of reflection by former Section Chairpersons give insights and perspectives on the work of the Section and the changing nature of legal education and the legal profession.

Product Code: 5290088, Price: $10.00

Call the ABA Service Center at 1.800.285.2221 to order Section Publications. Or visit the Section's website at www.abanet.org/legaled.

Serious Tools for . . .

Law School Guides

■ **ABA-LSAC Official Guide to ABA-Approved Law Schools™ (2008 Edition)**

This is the only *official* guide to all the American Bar Association (ABA)-approved law schools in the United States, and it's the only one that contains up-to-date admission criteria and other essential admission information provided by the schools themselves. The *Official Guide* is the one book in which each school tells its story so that you can compare and decide which schools are best for you. Each school submits data required from the ABA for accreditation, and most schools include applicant profile grids reflecting their admission decisions for the previous year. Tuition and living expenses, grants and scholarships, curriculum, class size, employment and bar-passage rates, special programs, and facilities are only some of the many categories covered in this handy guide.
$24

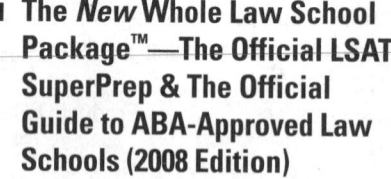

■ **The *New* Whole Law School Package™—The Official LSAT SuperPrep & The Official Guide to ABA-Approved Law Schools (2008 Edition)**

With this one package you can prepare for the LSAT and find the most accurate and up-to-date information about all ABA-approved law schools. Save money by buying the two books together.
$38 ($34.95 online)

LSAT® Preparation

■ **The Official LSAT SuperPrep®**

Three new *PrepTests* with a guide to LSAT logic *and* explanations for each item in all three tests. (LSATs previously administered in February 1996, February 1999, and February 2000.)
$28 ($19.95 online)

■ **10 Actual, Official LSAT PrepTests Series**

Each of these books contains actual, previously administered LSATs. For pure practice at an unbelievable price, you can't beat 10 *PrepTests* for $30—purchased individually, 10 practice tests would cost $80. Each test includes an answer key, writing sample, and score-conversion table.

■ **10 Actual, Official LSAT PrepTests™**

(contains PrepTests 7, 9, 10, 11, 12, 13, 14, 15, 16, 18)
$30 ($19.95 online)

■ **10 More Actual, Official LSAT PrepTests™**

(contains PrepTests 19 through 28)
$30 ($19.95 online)

■ **The Next 10 Actual, Official LSAT PrepTests™**

(contains PrepTests 29 through 38)
$30 ($19.95 online)

To order, go to www.LSAC.org or call 215.968.1001
Note: *Availability of all LSAC products is subject to change.*